T0181013

Lecture Notes in Computer Science 10232

Commenced Publication in 1973
Founding and Former Series Editors:
Gerhard Goos, Juris Hartmanis, and Jan van Leeuwen

More information about this series at http://www.springer.com/series/7407

Man Ho Allen Au · Arcangelo Castiglione
Kim-Kwang Raymond Choo · Francesco Palmieri
Kuan-Ching Li (Eds.)

Green, Pervasive, and Cloud Computing

12th International Conference, GPC 2017
Cetara, Italy, May 11–14, 2017
Proceedings

 Springer

Editors
Man Ho Allen Au
Hong Kong Polytechnic University
Hong Kong
Hong Kong

Arcangelo Castiglione
University of Salerno
Fisciano
Italy

Kim-Kwang Raymond Choo
University of Texas at San Antonio
San Antonio, TX
USA

Francesco Palmieri
University of Salerno
Fisciano
Italy

Kuan-Ching Li
Providence University
Taichung City
Taiwan

ISSN 0302-9743   ISSN 1611-3349 (electronic)
Lecture Notes in Computer Science
ISBN 978-3-319-57185-0   ISBN 978-3-319-57186-7   (eBook)
DOI 10.1007/978-3-319-57186-7

Library of Congress Control Number: 2017937283

LNCS Sublibrary: SL1 – Theoretical Computer Science and General Issues

Printed on acid-free paper

This Springer imprint is published by Springer Nature
The registered company is Springer International Publishing AG
The registered company address is: Gewerbestrasse 11, 6330 Cham, Switzerland

Preface

On behalf of the Organizing Committee, it is our pleasure to welcome you to the proceedings of the 12th International Conference on Green, Pervasive and Cloud Computing (GPC 2017), held in Cetara, Italy, during May 11–14, 2017. The papers included in the proceedings present novel ideas or state-of-the-art perspectives regarding the topics of interest of the conference.

GPC aims at bringing together international researchers and practitioners from both academia and industry who are working in the areas of green computing, pervasive computing, and cloud computing.

GPC 2017 was part of a series of highly successful events focusing on pervasive and environmentally sustainable computing. In the past 11 years, the GPC conference has been successfully held and organized all over the world: Taichung, Taiwan (2006), Paris, France (2007), Kunming, China (2008), Geneva, Switzerland (2009), Hualien, Taiwan (2010), Oulu, Finland (2011), Hong Kong (2012), Seoul, Korea (2013),Wuhan, China (2014), Plantation Island, Fiji (2015), and Xian, China (2016).

In this edition the value, overall quality, and scientific and technical depth of the GPC conference continued to strengthen and grow in importance for both the academic and industrial communities. Such strength was evidenced this year by having a significant number of high-quality submissions resulting in a highly selective program. All submissions received at least two reviews according to a high-quality peer review process involving about 140 Program Committee members and several additional reviewers. On the basis of the review results, 58 papers were selected for presentation at the conference, with an acceptance rate lower than 35%. In addition, the conference also featured four invited talks, a tutorial, and two satellite workshops.

The support and help of many people are needed in order to organize an international event. We would like to thank all authors for submitting and presenting their papers. We also greatly appreciated the support of the Program Committee members and the reviewers, who carried out the most difficult work of carefully evaluating the submitted papers.

We sincerely thank all the chairs and Steering Committee members. Without their hard work, the success of GPC 2017 would not have been possible.

Last but certainly not least, our thanks go to all the attendees who contributed to the success of the conference. Finally, we are sure that the beautiful location and the relaxing atmosphere of the venue were the perfect ingredients for a successful international event, and provided a unique opportunity for both researchers and technologists to present, share, and discuss leading research topics, developments, and future directions in their area of interest.

We hope you enjoy the conference proceedings.

May 2017

Man Ho Allen Au
Arcangelo Castiglione
Kim-Kwang Raymond Choo
Francesco Palmieri
Kuan-Ching Li

Organization

Main Conference

Honorary Chairs

A.B.M. Shawkat Ali   The University of Fiji, Fiji
Alfredo De Santis   University of Salerno, Italy
Moti Yung   Snapchat and Columbia University, USA
Wanlei Zhou   Deakin University, Australia

General Chairs

Elisa Bertino   Purdue University, USA
Francesco Palmieri   University of Salerno, Italy
Yang Xiang   Deakin University, Australia

Program Chairs

Man Ho Allen Au   The Hong Kong Polytechnic University, SAR China
Aniello Castiglione   University of Salerno, Italy
Kim-Kwang   University of Texas San Antonio, USA
  Raymond Choo

Program Vice-Chairs

Francesco Colace   University of Salerno, Italy
Joseph K. Liu   Monash University, Australia
Florin Pop   University Politehnica of Bucharest, Romania
Arcangelo Castiglione   University of Salerno, Italy

Steering Committee

Hai Jin   Huazhong University of Science and Technology,
                            China (Chair)
Nabil Abdennadher   University of Applied Sciences, Switzerland
Christophe Cerin   University of Paris XIII, France
Sajal K. Das   Missouri University of Science and Technology, USA
Jean-Luc Gaudiot   University of California – Irvine, USA
Kuan-Ching Li   Providence University, Taiwan, China
Cho-Li Wang   The University of Hong Kong, SAR China

Chao-Tung Yang   Tunghai University, Taiwan, China
Laurence T. Yang   St. Francis Xavier University, Canada

International Advisory Committee

Nik Bessis   Edge Hill University, UK
Jiannong Cao   The Hong Kong Polytechnic University, SAR China
Jinjun Chen   University of Technology Sydney, Australia
Athula Ginige   Western University of Sydney, Australia
Fred Glover   University of Colorado, Boulder, Colorado, USA
Lucas Chi Kwong Hui   The University of Hong Kong, SAR China
Hai Jiang   Arkansas State University, USA
Chris Mitchell   Royal Holloway, University of London, UK
Witold Pedrycz   University of Alberta, Canada
Willy Susilo   University of Wollongong, Australia
A Min Tjoa   Vienna University of Technology, Austria
Genoveffa Tortora   University of Salerno, Italy (Chair)
Xun Yi   Royal Melbourne Institute of Technology (RMIT),
                              Australia
Albert Zomaya   University of Sydney, Australia

Publicity Chairs

Christian Esposito   University of Salerno, Italy
Jin Li   Guangzhou University, China
Zhe Liu   University of Waterloo, Canada

Publication Chairs

Xinyi Huang   Fujian Normal University, China
Guojun Wang   Guangzhou University, China
Michele Nappi   University of Salerno, Italy

Workshop Chairs

Md Zakirul Alam Bhuiyan   Fordham University, USA
Alessandra De Benedictis   University of Naples Federico II, Italy
Fang-Yie Leu   Tunghai University, Taiwan

Industry Forum Committee

Nicolae Bogdan   Huawei German Research Center, Germany
Gerardo Costabile   British Telecom Italy, Italy
Leonardo Impagliazzo   Ansaldo STS and Hitachi Rail, Italy
Shinsaku Kiyomoto   KDDI Research Inc., Japan
Giovanni Motta   Google Inc., USA

Malek Ben Salem   Accenture Technology Labs, USA
Yang Yanjiang   Huawei Singapore Research Centre, Singapore

Local Organizing Committee

Andrea Bruno   University of Salerno, Italy
Arcangelo Castiglione   University of Salerno, Italy
Luigi Catuogno   University of Salerno, Italy
Raffaele Pizzolante   University of Salerno, Italy (Chair)

Technical Program Committee

Cristina Alcaraz   Universidad de Malaga, Spain
Saadat Mehmood Alhashmi   University of Sharjah – Abu Dhabi,
                                 United Arab Emirates
Flora Amato   University of Naples Federico II, Italy
Karl Andersson   Lulca University of Technology, Sweden
Jorge Barbosa   University of Porto, Portugal
Lynn Batten   Deakin University, Australia
Sebastiano Battiato   University of Catania, Italy
Giampaolo Bella   University of Catania, Italy
Paolo Bellavista   University of Bologna, Italy
Ion Bica   Military Technical Academy, Romania
Chiara Boldrini   National Research Council, Institute of Informatics
                                 and Telematics, Italy
Eleonora Borgia   National Research Council, Institute of Informatics
                                 and Telematics, Italy
Raffaele Bruno   National Research Council, Institute of Informatics
                                 and Telematics, Italy
Fulvio Bruno   Ericsson, Italy
Giuseppe Bruno   University of Naples Federico II, Italy
Massimo Cafaro   University of Salento, Italy
Bruno Carpentieri   University of Salerno, Italy
Giuliana Carullo   Coritel – University of Salerno, Italy
William Casey   Carnegie Mellon University and CERT, USA
Mario Casillo   University of Naples Federico II, Italy
Giuseppe Cattaneo   University of Salerno, Italy
Raffele Cerulli   University of Salerno, Italy
Rohitash Chandra   The University of South Pacific, Fiji
Xiaofeng Chen   Xidian University, China
Chin-Ling Chen   Chaoyang University of Technology, Taiwan
Yu Chen   Huazhong University of Science and Technology,
                                 China
Ray Chak-Chung Cheung   City University of Hong Kong, SAR China
Seong-je Cho   Dankook University, South Korea
Chang Choi   Chosun University, South Korea

Kaitai Liang	Manchester Metropolitan University, UK
Chu-Hsing Lin	Tunghai University, Taiwan
Jung-Chun Liu	Tunghai University, Taiwan
Marco Lombardi	University of Salerno, Italy
Javier Lopez	University of Malaga, Spain
Rongxing Lu	University of New Brunswick, Canada
Daniel Xiapu Luo	The Hong Kong Polytechnic University, SAR China
Victor Malyshkin	Russian Academy of Sciences, Russia
Daniele Manini	Università degli Studi di Torino, Italy
Stefano Marrone	University of Naples Federico II, Italy
Ben Martini	University of South Australia, Australia
Barbara Masucci	University of Salerno, Italy
Jaime Lloret Mauri	Universidad Politecnica de Valencia, Spain
Gianluigi Me	LUISS Guido Carli University, Italy
Weizhi Meng	Institute for Infocomm Research, Singapore
Fabio Mercorio	Università degli Studi di Milano Bicocca, Italy
Alessio Merlo	University of Genoa, Italy
Mario Mezzanzanica	Università degli Studi di Milano Bicocca, Italy
Mauro Migliardi	University of Padua, Italy
Tommi Mikkonen	Tampere University of Technology, Finland
Philip T. Moore	Lanzhou University, China
Jose A. Morales	Carnegie Mellon University and CERT, USA
Vincenzo Moscato	University of Naples Federico II, Italy
Yi Mu	University of Wollongong, Australia
Paolo Napoletano	Università degli Studi di Milano Bicocca, Italy
Surya Nepal	Data61 CSIRO, Australia
Marek R. Ogiela	AGH University of Science and Technology, Poland
Lidia Ogiela	AGH University of Science and Technology, Poland
Dana Petcu	West University of Timisoara, Romania
Antonio Picariello	University of Naples Federico II, Italy
Antonio Piccinno	University of Bari, Aldo Moro, Italy
Josef Pieprzyk	Queensland University of Technology, Australia
Raffaele Pizzolante	University of Salerno, Italy
Christian W. Probst	Technical University of Denmark, Denmark
Reza Reyhanitabar	NEC Laboratories Europe, Germany
Laura Ricci	University of Pisa, Italy
Sergio Ricciardi	Universitat Politecnica de Catalunya, BarcelonaTech, Spain
Eric Rondeau	Universitat de Lorraine, France
Stefano Russo	University of Naples Federico II, Italy
Ioan Salomie	Technical University of Cluj Napoca, Romania
Carlo Sansone	University of Naples Federico II, Italy
Kewei Sha	University of Houston – Clear Lake, USA
Siamak Fayyaz Shahandashti	Newcastle University, UK
Roopak Sinha	Auckland University of Technology, New Zealand

Fei Song	Beijing Jiao Tong University, China
Stelios Sotiriadis	University of Toronto, Canada
Giancarlo Sperlà	University of Naples Federico II, Italy
Mariarosaria Taddeo	University of Oxford, UK
Marco Tambasco	Coritel – University of Salerno, Italy
Pierguilio Tempesta	Universidad Complutense, Spain
Ruppa K. Thulasiram	University of Manitoba, Canada
Simon Tjoa	St. Pölten University of Applied Sciences, Austria
Mahesh Tripunitara	University of Waterloo, Canada
Marcello Trovati	Edge Hill University, UK
Allan Tucker	Brunel University London, UK
Giuliana Vitiello	University of Salerno, Italy
Cong Wang	City University of Hong Kong, SAR China
Yu Wang	Deakin University, Australia
Wei Wang	The University of Texas at San Antonio, USA
Lizhe Wang	Chinese Academy of Sciences, China
Sheng Wen	Deakin University, Australia
Tao Xiang	Chongqing University, China
Xiaofei Xing	Guangzhou University, China
Shouhuai Xu	University of Texas San Antonio, USA
Guomin Yang	University of Wollongong, Australia
Kangbin Yim	Soon Chun Hyang University, South Korea
Siu Ming Yiu	The University of Hong Kong, SAR China
Ilsun You	Soonchunhyang University, South Korea
Meng Yu	The University of Texas at San Antonio, USA
Yong Yu	Shaanxi Normal University, China
Tsz Hon Yuen	Huawei Singapore, Singapore
Daniela Zaharie	West University of Timisoara, Romania
Baokang Zhao	National University of Defense Technology, China
Tianqing Zhu	Deakin University, Australia
Xiaomin Zhu	National University of Defense Technology, China

First International Workshop on Digital Knowledge Ecosystems

Chairs

Athula Ginige	Western Sydney University, Australia
Giuliana Vitiello	University of Salerno, Italy

Technical Program Committee

Giovanni Acampora	Università di Napoli, Federico II, Italy
Ignacio Aedo	Universidad Carlos III de Madrid, Spain
Lasanthi De Silva	University of Colombo, Sri Lanka

Paloma Díaz	Universidad Carlos III de Madrid, Spain
Tamara Ginige	Australian Catholic University, Australia
Jeevani S. Goonatillake	University of Colombo, Sri Lanka
Walisadeera Anusha Indika	University of Ruhuna, Sri Lanka
Maria De Marsico	Università di Roma Sapienza, Italy
Ramesh Jain	University of California, Irvine, USA
David Lindley	justASK: Australians Sharing Knowledge Pty Ltd, Australia
Heinrich C. Mayr	Universität Klagenfurt, Austria
Deborah Richards	Macquarie University, Australia
Monica Sebillo	University of Salerno, Italy
Uma Srinivasan	Capital Markets Cooperative Research Centre (CMCRC), Australia
Genoveffa Tortora	University of Salerno, Italy
Gihan Wikramanayake	University of Colombo, Sri Lanka

First Workshop on Cloud Security Modeling, Monitoring and Management (CS3M 2017)

Chairs

Alessandra De Benedictis	University of Naples Federico II, Italy
Valentina Casola	University of Naples Federico II, Italy

Technical Program Committee

Massimiliano Albanese	George Mason University, USA
Flora Amato	University of Naples Federico II, Italy
Behdad Baniani	Patternlogix, USA
Wissam Mallouli	Montimage, France
Jolanda Modic	XLAB, Slovenia
Parnian Najafi	George Mason University, USA
Roberto Nardone	University of Naples Federico II, Italy
Massimiliano Rak	Second University of Naples, Italy
Umberto Villano	University of Sannio, Italy

Contents

XVI   Contents

Mobile and Pervasive Computing

Cybersecurity

Parallel and Distributed Computing

Ontologies and Smart Applications

Healthcare Support Systems

Cryptography, Security and Biometric Techniques

Reducing Costs in HSM-Based Data Centers

R. De Prisco[1,2(✉)], A. De Santis[1,2], and M. Mannetta[1]

[1] Dipartimento di Informatica, Università di Salerno, 84084 Fisciano, SA, Italy
robdep@unisa.it
[2] eTuitus s.r.l., c/o Dipartimento di Informatica, Università di Salerno,
84084 Fisciano, SA, Italy

Abstract. Hardware Security Modules (HSM) are special purpose devices designed for cryptographic operations, mostly used for cryptographic keys management. To achieve high security standard, an HSM stores keys internally and never exposes them in plaintext; operations involving the keys are performed internally and only the result is given outside the HSM. Thus an HSM must have storage space to store all the keys that have to be managed. In real-world application this might require a huge amount of space (e.g. millions of keys) resulting in large data centers needed to host many HSMs. Related costs, such as cost of the hardware, energy consumption, hosting, management, etc. are directly proportional to the number of HSMs used. In this paper we present a technique that allows to save space for storing keys in an HSM, thus reducing the number of needed HSMs. While saving space allows to reduce direct costs, it comes at the expense of computation time. We provide a preliminary experimental evaluation of the extra time needed.

1 Introduction

An hardware security module (HSM for short) is a device designed for implementing cryptographic operations. HSMs are used for crucial infrastructures needed, for example, for online banking applications or Certification Authorities (CAs). In the context of banking applications an HSM can be used to secure PIN processing (e.g. [6]). In a PKI context, a typical example of the use of an HSM, is the management (generation, storage and usage) of public and private keys. HSMs are designed to achieve high-security levels. There are several types of HSM with varying levels of security and different characteristic. An HSM can either be a plug-in card or an external stand alone device. See [8], for example, for a discussion about HSM.

Due to the crucial role of the HSM, security concerns have to be addressed. HSM are usually equipped with tamper-revealing seals, tamper-resistant chips or other mechanisms that help in prevent tampering. Normally, it is possible to interact with an HSM only through the Application Programming Interface (API) made available through the physical connection (either directly on the bus for plug-in cards or over communication channels, such as a wired connection for stand alone devices). This means that beside the hardware, the HSM comes

© Springer International Publishing AG 2017
M.H.A. Au et al. (Eds.): GPC 2017, LNCS 10232, pp. 3–14, 2017.
DOI: 10.1007/978-3-319-57186-7_1

equipped with software/firmware that implements the services offered by the device.

The level of security of an HSM can be assessed by the vendor who provides a certification of compliance with international standards (such as Common Criteria or FIPS 140). See [5] for a discussion about audit and backup procedures.

One of the main functions available on an HSM is the generation and management (storing and retrieval) of cryptographic keys that need to be protected with high-security standards. Normally, the keys generated and managed with an HSM never leave the device itself and they are used within the device itself. The HSM might offer also other functions, such as complete cryptographic functions like encryption, digital signature, etc. Some HSMs have also dedicated hardware for accelerated cryptographic operations.

As a real-world application we will consider, throughout the paper, the case of a CA that uses a cluster of HSMs to manage the cryptographic keys of its users. Moreover, as an example of service offered to the customers of the CA, we will consider the digital signing of documents. The CA uses HSMs to generate and store the pair of public and private keys for each user and, subsequently, uses the private key for signing the documents. This approach provides an high-security level because the keys are used only inside an HSM and the user simply gets the signed document. We remark that, this is just an example to help explaining the technique presented in the paper, which has a broad applicability.

The management of the keys in an HSM involves a database for storing the keys. Thus the space needed to store the keys is proportional to the number of keys. Many HSMs might be needed to handle all the keys, resulting in large data centers of HSMs. This result in huge costs since the total expense is proportional to the number of HSM needed, as with the increase of their number we have an increase of hardware costs, energy consumption, hosting costs, management costs, etc. As an example, assume that, for simplicity, a single HSM can host 1 million keys, and that the CA has 30 million users. Then the CA has to manage a data center of 30 HSMs, or perhaps at least 60 if we want to consider a minimum of one backup per HSM. Thus the total cost increases by a factor of 30 or 60 (compared with a solution that would use only one HSM, as the one we are proposing).

In this paper we focus the attention on the space usage in an HSM. More specifically we consider as a "cost" the stable storage space needed to store the keys managed by the HSM. We propose a technique that allows to save storage space. The technique exploits basic properties of pseudo-random number generators. Pushing it to the limits, it allows to manage all the keys with $O(1)$ space regardless of the number of keys that have to be managed. However this advantage comes at the cost of using time which, for the solution that only stores a fixed amount of information, can become a bottleneck. We also propose some trade-offs so that the extra computation time is reduced, but the space needed depends on the number of keys.

Paper organization. This paper is organized as follows. In Sect. 2 we recall the notion of pseudo-random number generator. In Sect. 3 we summarize the functioning of an HSM. In Sect. 4 we describe the technique that allows to save space for the key storage in an HSM; we call the resulting HSM an Enhanced HSM or EHSM for short. The technique will be instantiated with 3 variants, each one trading space with time in a different way. In Sect. 5 we report the result of some preliminary experimental evaluations and finally in Sect. 6 we draw some conclusions.

2 Pseudo-random Number Generators

Random numbers are fundamental for the implementation of cryptographic primitives. A True Random Number Generator (TRNG) is a device capable of generating numbers that are truly random. A TRNG uses physical inputs from which it extracts random bits and is typically based on microscopic phenomena, such as thermal noise, photoelectric effect or macroscopic ones, such as user keyboard typing, network traffic, and others. These phenomena are, at least in theory, completely unpredictable and thus extrapolating bits from them produces truly random values. In order to do so it is necessary to somehow transform the physical phenomenon into an electrical signal, then measure the signal and thus produce a bit value. By repeating the process over the randomly varying physical phenomenon it is possible to produce a sequence of random bits. However the above described process requires time for each single bit. The consequence is that a TRNG cannot produce random bits at a very high speed and thus the amount of random bits that it generates is limited. Usually TRNG are used to produce a limited number of truly random bits which are then used as a *seed* to produce a sequence of *pseudo-random* numbers with a Pseudo-Random Number Generator (PRNG).

A PRNG is a deterministic algorithm but the numbers that it generates have the property of being indistinguishable from truly random ones. Thus, pseudo-random numbers can be used in lieu of truly random ones.

The initial state of a PRNG is determined by the seed. The PRNG, at each iteration, generates a new value from the previous one (the very first one is generated from the seed).

A fundamental property of a pseudo-random number generator is the following: the sequence of numbers given in output is deterministically determined by the seed. That is, starting from the same seed s we get the same sequence of numbers $Seq(s) = r_1, r_2, \ldots$. At some point the sequence will repeat itself, that is there will be an index p such that $r_{jp+1} = r_1, r_{jp+2} = r_2$ for $j = 1, 2, \ldots$. The value of p is the period. The period cannot be more that 2^n, where n is the length in bits of the seed. The period depends on the specific implementation of the PRNG and in some cases can be explicited without actually producing all the values until the repetition starts.

We summarize below the basic properties of PRNGs:

1. The probability distribution of the generated numbers must be uniform over the entire possible interval;

2. Each element of the sequence must be independent from the other (that is all the values must be non-correlated).

Moreover for cryptographic applications some stronger properties must be satisfied in order to consider the PRNG cryptographically secure (CSPRNG):

1. The sequence of produced numbers must be indistinguishable from a truly random sequence (for the notion of indistinguishability see for example [7]).
2. It must be computationally infeasible for any attacker, to derive from a given subsequence of the numbers, previous or subsequent values.
3. It must be computationally infeasible for any attacker to derive, from a given internal state of the CSPRNG, past or future values.

We refer the reader to well-known standards, such as [1], or textbooks on cryptography, such as [7], for more details about PRNGs. There are several standard tests to certify that a PRNG is cryptographically secure. We refer the reader to [2] for more details about such tests.

As an example of pseudo-random generator we cite the well-known Blum-Blum-Shub generator [3]: the sequence is given by $x_{n+1} = x_n^2 \mod F$, where $F = p \times q$ is obtained by multiplying two large primes p and q. This generator is usually used to extract one pseudo-random bit, which is the parity of x_{n+1}; the seed should be a number not divisible for p and q. Other well-known pseudo-random number generators are the Blum-Micali [4] and the Park-Miller [10] ones.

3   HSM Description

An Hardware Security Module (HSM) is a device equipped with appropriate firmware/software that from the user perspective works as a "black box". The main purpose of an HSM is that of managing in a secure way cryptographic keys: it can generate new keys, store them, use the keys to encrypt or sign documents, etc.

The keys are protected in the sense that they are never directly accessible to the applications that have to use them. Instead, the keys can be used only through the application programming interface exposed by the HSM. The HSM can offer both fundamental cryptographic services, such as digital signatures, and the possibility of executing complex cryptographic manipulation on dedicated hardware.

Fig. 1. Stand-alone HSM and HSM on a PCI card

An HSM can take several forms: smart cards, PCI cards, USB tokens, embedded systems or stand alone devices that can communicate through various channels (USB, Ethernet, RS-232, etc.). Each single device has its own functionalities and is designed for specific goals. For this reason different devices are called in different ways: PCSM (Personal Computer Security Module), SAM (Secure Application Module), SCD (Secure Cryptographic Device), SSCD (Secure Signature Creation Device), TRSM (Tamper Resistant Security Module), etc. Figure 3 shows a stand alone HSM device and an HSM device on a PCI card.

Throughout this paper we will simply use HSM to identify all these devices. Indeed, regardless of the specific device and the specific functionalities offered, we can identify, for all of them, some main general objectives which are:

- Better performances for cryptographic operations.
- Efficient key management.
- Avoid data leakage or loss.

So we will use the generic term HSM to identify any device designed to meet the above general goals. To achieve these goals an HSM might offer functionalities such as hardware acceleration for cryptographic operations, private and public encryption, hashing, pseudo-random or true-random number generation. Moreover an HSM can be protected with tampering indicating seals, special screws, sensors for temperature, light and movement, data erasing upon un-authorized intrusion, etc.

There exist international standards and an HSM should come equipped with a certification of the standard compliance accomplished. Most of the HSMs are compliant with the FIPS 140-2 international standard approved by the U.S.A. government.

Most of the HSMs commercially available offer various types of APIs, such as the standards OASIS PKCS#11, MS CAPI/CNG, Java JCA/JCE, etc. Within these APIs it is possible to use most of the common cryptographic tools and objects, such as RSA keys, X.509 certificates, DES/Triple DES keys, etc. Through these API an HSM can be used to

- Create and securely store (in the HSM) cryptographic keys;
- Managing the keys
- Use the keys (to sign, encrypt and decrypt)

Figure 3 show a typical key generation process in an HSM. Let U be the user. Through the API the HSM receives a request for key generation from a (legitimate) user. In order to generate random values the true random number generator provides a random seed for the CSPRNG. Then the CSPRNG generates a random value r. This random value is used to derive a pair of keys (K_{pub}^U, K_{priv}^U). The private key K_{priv}^U will be stored in the stable storage of the HSM. Depending on the level of security that the HSM has to guarantee the key can be encrypted before being stored. The public key K_{pub}^U, instead, is passed to the module for the generation of the certificate which, in turn, is given back to the user, through the API. Notice that the private keys stays in the HSM and is

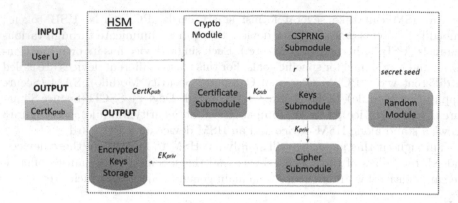

Fig. 2. Key generation process

not given back to the user. The user can use the key only through the operations allowed by the API of the HSM.

Figure 3 show the process for signing a document through the HSM. A legitimate user U requests the signature of a document D through the API. The HSM has to retrieve the private key K_{priv}^U of user U by means of a search in the embedded database. If the keys are encrypted the HSM needs to decrypt it. Then document D can be signed and the signed document is provided back to the user. Notice that the private K_{priv}^U is never exposed outside the HSM.

4   On-the-Fly Key Generation

To help the reader, we will consider an example of a real-world application of an HSM used by a certification authority (CA) to manage the cryptographic keys

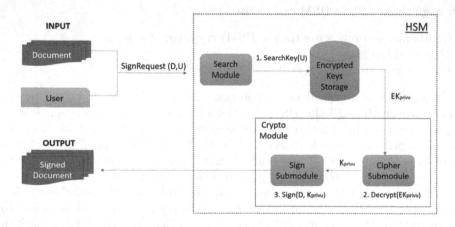

Fig. 3. Signature process

of the user and the documents signing process on behalf of the users. In such a situation one can identify two crucial points:

- There are potentially many keys to manage (e.g. millions): it is necessary to store them and have backup copies.
- The storage space can become a bottleneck: once all the available memory of the HSM has been used it is not possible to generate new keys.

The solution proposed in this paper aims at avoiding these problems. Without loss of generality we assume that for each user U we need to store a pair of keys (K_{pub}^U, K_{priv}^U). Other types of keys (e.g. keys for symmetric cryptography) can be handled in similar ways.

The basic idea is to save space by recomputing the keys when they are needed. This can be done exploiting the fundamental property of a CSPRNG: the sequence of pseudo-random numbers generated is a deterministic function of the seed. So we can store only one seed, that we call *master secret seed* (mss), and from this seed generate every time the same sequence of pseudo-random numbers. Let $Seq(mss) = r_1, r_2, \ldots r_p$ where p is the period. We use this sequence to generate the needed keys on-the-fly. Of course we have to make sure that (i) the keys dynamically generated for user U are always the same, and (ii) the security warranties are the same as for the case when the keys are stored in the HSM.

To achieve property (i), we associate to each user U of the system an index $i_U \in [1, p]$. That is, we associate to each user U the pseudo-random value r_{i_U}. When generating the pair of keys for user U we first retrieve r_{i_U} from the CSPRNG; r_{i_U} is uniquely determined by the user U, then we use it to generate (K_{pub}^U, K_{priv}^U). Thus for user U we always generate the same pair of public/private key.

Property (ii) is achieved because we don't store the keys; thus information leakage can happen only if an attacker gets the master secret seed. The master secret seed is stored internally in the HSM in lieu of the keys, so it is subject to the same protection as the keys in an HSM.

Normally the HSM stores for each user U its pair of private/public keys. Upon a user U request, the HSM retrieves (K_{pub}^U, K_{priv}^U) and use them for the requested operation. This requires the HSM to store all the keys. So on one extreme we have an HSM that stores all the keys, on the other extreme we have an EHSM that does not store any key but only the master secret seed (and each time a key is needed it gets generated). So the price we have to pay for not storing keys is the time needed to recompute the keys. Between these two extremes it is possible to have approaches that store only some keys.

Figure 4 shows the on-the-fly generation of the keys for an EHSM, and the generation of the certificate exposed through the API. The differences with the process described in Fig. 3 are the use of the database and the on-the-fly key generation process. The database contains only the master secret seed mss. Let U be the user that requests the generation of the keys. If this is the first request, i.e., no mss, has been generated yet, then the Random Module (TRNG) is used to generated the mss. The Index module associates to each user U a unique index i_U. Such a mapping can be done in several ways and the specific method

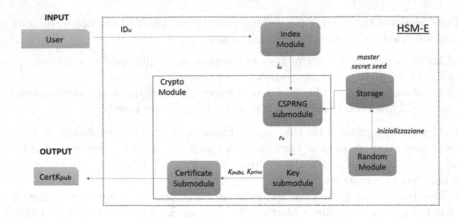

Fig. 4. On-the-fly key generation

chosen is irrelevant: what it is needed is simply that each user gets a unique index (if a user is allowed to have multiple keys then an index is required for each key; in other words this means that the user needs to have a pseudonym for each key). So the Index module simple has to implement the mapping $U \rightarrow i_U$. At this point the CSPRNG is used to generate the pseudo-random sequence of numbers starting from the master secret seed and generating *exactly* i_U numbers of the sequence. The last generated number r_{i_U} is then used to generate the pair of keys (K_{pub}^U, K_{priv}^U). At this point the HSM proceeds with the response to the user to pass back the certificate containing the public key. Notice that the private key is deleted.

Figure 4 shows the process of signing a document with an EHSM. The user U provides the document D in the request. As for the key generation request, the HSM uses the Index module to retrieve the index i_U associated to user U and basically repeats the key generation phase describe before (obviously if the user has not yet generated the key an error must be raised; in the setting of EHSM a user does not really need to have a key generation phase but an enrollment phase which correspond to the fact that the user is given a unique index). Once the private key K_{priv}^U has been regenerated, the HSM can sign the document D and give back the signed document through the API. The private K_{priv}^U (as well as the public key K_{pub}^U) gets deleted.

The key point in the approach used for an EHSM is the generation of r_{i_U}. In the following we discuss three approaches: in the first one we simply iterate on the sequence of pseudo-random numbers generated by the CSPRNG starting from the master secret seed for r_{i_U} times. We describe also two alternative approach that store some of the values of the sequence of pseudo-random values to speed up key generation (Fig. 5).

Let $\mathcal{U} = \{U_1, U_2, \ldots, U_n\}$ be the set of users. The indexing used to denote this set is immaterial in the sense that we cannot use $i_U = i$. The index i_U is assigned upon a registration process. Consider for example the case of CA: U_i are

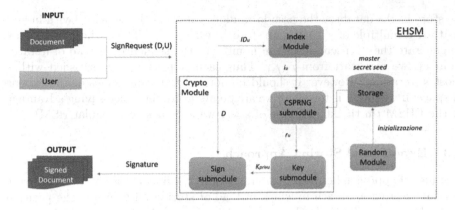

Fig. 5. On-the-fly document signature

the clients that register to the service; the index i_U is an index assigned when the person physically register to the service, for example, showing an official identification document. Let $\mathcal{I} = \{1, 2, \ldots Z\} \subseteq \mathbb{N}$ be the set of possible indexes. As we have already said there might be several ways in which the mapping $\mathcal{U} \to \mathcal{I}$ is constructed. For example one could use a pre-determined mapping, like a social security numbers or similar identification numbers. It is convenient to keep Z as small as possible; clearly Z needs also to be large enough to deal with all possible users. In fact we can set $\mathcal{I} = \mathbb{N}$, and indicate with Z the biggest index used. This index will affect the performance of the system and it is convenient to keep it as small as possible. This suggests that an efficient way to assign indexes is simply to use for a new user the smallest not yet used index. Notice that Z is tied to the period of the CSPRNG. More precisely we must ensure that $p > Z$.

Having set the mapping $\mathcal{U} \to \mathcal{I}$ we now concentrate on the mapping $\mathcal{I} \to \mathcal{R}$, where $\mathcal{R}$ is the set of pseudo-random numbers, that is on the mapping $i \to r_i$.

4.1 Iterative Approach

The iterative approach is the most obvious one. To generate the ith pseudo-random number of the sequence, we simply iterate on the sequence $r_1, r_2, \ldots$ starting from the first element r_1 up to the ith one r_i. This approach is very simple. It requires a exactly i iterations. This can be a problem if i is very large. This situation is actually what we expect since the main motivation for the use of an EHSM is the handling of a large number of keys, so large that we are worrying about space usage.

4.2 Linear Storing Approach

A simple improvement over the iterative approach is a "linear storing" technique. In order to diminish the time needed for the iterative approach we can store some keys in the database. Let s be a parameter (e.g., $s = 1000$). Upon first generation, we store in the database the pseudo-random values of the sequence with indexes that are a multiple of s, that is we store $r_s, r_{2s}, r_{3s}, \ldots$. Thus, when we will have to generate the ith pseudo-random number of the sequence, instead of iterating from r_1, we can start from $r_{\lfloor i/s \rfloor}$. Thus each request can be satisfied with at most s iterations. However it should be noticed that this comes at the expense of space: if we pick s is too small we are giving away the space-saving advantages of the EHSM (in th extreme case of $s = 1$ we are back to a regular HSM).

4.3 Exponential Storing Approach

A trade-off approach between the iterative and the linear storing one is an "exponential" storing approach in which instead of storing all values in the positions multiple of a constant s in the sequence, we store only the elements that are in the positions that are an exponent of a constant c. Take for example $c = 2$, then we would store the values $r_1, r_2, r_4, r_8, r_{16}, \ldots r_{1024}, \ldots$ and so on. This approach needs space that is logarithmic, thus still a substantial improvement over the linear space of a regular HSM. The time required to retrieve a pseudo-random value depends on the index: the smaller the index the fastest will be the retrieval. This is similar to what happens for the iterative approach but in this case we don't need to start form the first element but only from the biggest power of c that is smaller than the index.

5 Experimental Evaluation

In order to assess the advantages and the disadvantages of the proposed technique we have conducted some preliminary tests to evaluate the extra time needed by an EHSM. We have implemented the three proposed on-the-fly key generation techniques and measured the overall time needed to satisfy user request. More specifically we have conducted the following tests: for each test we assume a fixed number of users N, and a sequence of R user request. The sequence of requests is randomly generated. For each test we have measured the time needed to satisfy the request using a standard HSM and using an EHSM with each of the three proposed variants. The tests have been repeated for several values of N and R. To simplify the tests, we have assumed that an HSM database look-up takes 0.001 ms; thus in a standard HSM a sequence of R user requests will take $R \cdot 0.001$ ms to be satisfied. Table 1 reports the overall time consumption.

Not surprisingly the first variant is the one that takes more time since is the one that saves more space. Similarly the third variant takes more time than the second because it uses less space. We remark that these are only preliminary tests which have been performed by simulating all the operations involved. We leave as future work a deeper experimental analysis.

Table 1. Time analysis

N	R	HSM standard	EHSM iter.	EHSM linear	EHSM exp.
$N = 500$	$R = 50$	0.05 ms	0.126254 ms	0.066719 ms	0.092381 ms
$N = 500$	$R = 250$	0.25 ms	0.694908 ms	0.351560 ms	0.478326 ms
$N = 500$	$R = 500$	0.5 ms	1.437032 ms	0.728267 ms	0.987446 ms
$N = 500$	$R = 1000$	1 ms	2.914609 ms	1.484762 ms	2.334151 ms
$N = 500$	$R = 5000$	5000 ms	14.754216 ms	8.469253 ms	10.793652 ms
$N = 1000$	$R = 100$	0.1 ms	0.424951 ms	0.151915 ms	0.234031 ms
$N = 1000$	$R = 500$	0.5 ms	6.379910 ms	0.797040	1.249705 ms
$N = 1000$	$R = 1000$	1 ms	4.817138 ms	1.724952 ms	2.730875 ms
$N = 1000$	$R = 2000$	2 ms	9.500837 ms	3.130678 ms	6.526180 ms
$N = 1000$	$R = 10000$	10 ms	48.213974 ms	16.323661 ms	26.234565 ms
$N = 2000$	$R = 200$	0.2 ms	5.659341 ms	0.378247 ms	0.614331 ms
$N = 2000$	$R = 1000$	1 ms	10.501627 ms	2.045205	3.468380 ms
$N = 2000$	$R = 2000$	2 ms	16.015212 ms	4.520493 ms	9.032261 ms
$N = 2000$	$R = 4000$	4 ms	31.075311 ms	8.287571 ms	13.449596 ms
$N = 2000$	$R = 20000$	20 ms	146.675323 ms	43.090954 ms	69.572380 ms

6   Conclusions

In this paper we have investigated a technique that allows to save space in the key management of an Hardware Security Module. The technique is based on the use of pseudo-random number generator for the key generation and it trades storage space with computing time. Three variants of the technique have been proposed, each one achieving different tradeoffs between space and time. We have provided a preliminary experimental evaluation to measure the benefits and the drawbacks of the proposed technique. Future work include a more extensive experimental evaluation and the study of improvements of the on-the-fly key generation techniques aimed at reducing the cost in time of the keys re-generation. We are currently investigating the use of random function [9] to improve the time needed for the re-generation of the keys.

Acknowledgements. We thank the eTuitus staff, in particular Oliviero Trivellato, Pompeo Faruolo, Fabio Petagna and Maurizio Cembalo, for useful technical discussions.

References

1. National Institute of Standards and Technologies. Recommendation for Random Number Generation Using Deterministic Random Bit Generators. Technical report SP 800-90A Rev 1 (2015)
2. National Institute of Standards and Technologies. A Statistical Test Suite for Random and Pseudorandom Number Generators for Cryptographic Applications. Technical report SP 800-22 (2010)

14   R. De Prisco et al.

3. Blum, L., Blum, M., Shub, M.: A simple unpredictable pseudo-random number generator. SIAM J. Comput. **15**(2), 364–383 (1986)
4. Blum, M., Micali, S.: How to generate cryptographically strong sequences of pseudorandom bits. SIAM J. Comput. **13**(4), 850–864 (1984)
5. Salvaro, T.C., Martina, J.E., Custodio, R.F.: Audit and backup procedures for hardware security modules. In proceedings of the 7th Symposium on Identity and Trust on the Internet. ACM press, pp. 89–97 (2008)
6. Focardi, R., Luccio, F.L.: Secure upgrade of hardware security modules in bank networks. In: Armando, A., Lowe, G. (eds.) ARSPA-WITS 2010. LNCS, vol. 6186, pp. 95–110. Springer, Heidelberg (2010). doi:10.1007/978-3-642-16074-5_7
7. Katz, J., Lindell, Y.: Introduction to Modern Cryptography (Second Edition). CRC Press (2015). ISBN-13: 978-1466570269
8. Mavrovouniotis, S., Ganley, M.: Hardware security modules. In: Markantonakis, K., Mayes, K. (eds.) Secure Smart Embedded Devices, Platforms and Applications, pp. 383–405. Springer, New York (2014). doi:10.1007/978-1-4614-7915-4_17. ISBN 978-1-4614-7914-7. Chap. 17
9. Goldrech, O., Goldwasser, S., Micali, S.: How to construct random functions. J. Assoc. Comput. Mach. **33**(4), 792–807 (1986)
10. Park, S.K., Miller, K.W.: Random number generators: good ones are hard to find. Commun. ACM **31**(10), 1192–1201 (1988)

Secure User Authentication on Smartphones via Sensor and Face Recognition on Short Video Clips

Chiara Galdi[1,2](✉), Michele Nappi[1,2], and Jean-Luc Dugelay[1,2]

[1] EURECOM, Sophia Antipolis, France
{chiara.galdi,jean-luc.dugelay}@eurecom.fr
[2] Università degli Studi di Salerno, Fisciano, SA, Italy
nappi@unisa.it

Abstract. Smartphones play a key role in our daily life, they can replace our watch, calendar, and mail box but also our credit card, house keys and in the near future our identity documents. Their increasing use in storing sensitive information, has raised the need to protect users and their data through secure authentication protocols. The main achievement of this work is to make the smartphone not only the cause of the problem but also part of the solution. Here, the Sensor Pattern Noise of the smartphone embedded camera and the HOG features of the user's face are combined for a double check of user identity.

Keywords: SOCRatES · Video · SPN · PRNU · Face recognition · HOG features · Smartphone

1 Introduction

An innovative authentication procedure is presented in this paper. On the wake of a previous work, presented by Galdi et al. in [1,2], that proposes the combination of iris recognition and source camera identification from still images, here the authors present a feasibility study of a system performing face and sensor recognition from a single short video clip. The main objective of this study is to address the need of secure, fast, and easy-to-use authentication systems.

The ever increasing demand of automatic user identification and the exponential spreading of more and more sophisticated smartphones, have led to a natural migration of biometric recognition on mobile devices. However, once that the recognition process is moved to the "end-user side", on one hand it offers the advantage of ubiquitous authentication (the user can potentially get authenticated from any place and at any time) but on the other the anti-spoofing techniques have to be reviewed and revamped in the light of changes in technology. This work proposes an authentication system based on something the user is, namely the face, and something that the user has, that is the personal smartphone. By observing Fig. 1 it can be noticed that the combination "(5) something the user has + something the user is" assures a higher security level compared to the use of biometrics only (4).

© Springer International Publishing AG 2017
M.H.A. Au et al. (Eds.): GPC 2017, LNCS 10232, pp. 15–22, 2017.
DOI: 10.1007/978-3-319-57186-7_2

In addition, the increase in security is obtained without making the acquisition procedure too complex. Many works propose multi-modal systems in order to improve recognition performance and robustness to attacks [3], however they often require the user to collect several biometric traits separately. In the latter case, acquisition can take a long time and several sensors can be required for acquiring different biometric traits.

The proposed system, at authentication time, only requires the user to record a short video clip. From that single clip, both face and sensor recognition are performed. This acquisition modality gives room to improve the system by adding for example a liveness detector or by adding a speaker recognition module since during the recording the user could also utter a sentence.

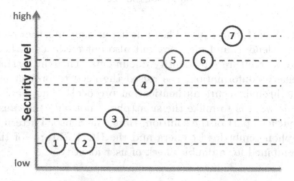

Fig. 1. Authentication systems security levels: (1) Something the user knows; (2) Something the user has; (3) Something the user knows + something the user has; (4) Something the user is or does; (5) Something the user has + something the user is or does; (6) Something the user knows + something the user is or does; (7) Something the user knows + something the user has + something the user is or does.

2   Related Works

As mentioned before, the presented work has been proposed on the wake of a research on the subject of the combination of biometry and "hardwaremetry". With the latter we refer to source digital camera identification. The first step in this direction is represented by the work presented by the authors in [1,2], where iris recognition is combined with sensor recognition, and the input data is a picture portraying the user's eye.

In this paper the input data is a short video clip. It is known that videos are strongly compressed, in particular the ones recorded with smartphones. Thus, in this case the face has been preferred to the iris, since better performance can be obtained even with low resolution or noisy images. However, the main point that has been investigated is the use of sensor recognition in this context. In particular it has been studied if small video clips, of about 2–5 s, are sufficient for the computation of the sensor "fingerprint". Otherwise the enrolment and acquisition processes would be too complex and/or time-consuming and the system would not meet the requirements of speed and ease-of-use.

Concerning sensor recognition, the Sensor Pattern Noise (hereinafter SPN) technique proposed by Lukas et al. [4, 5] and improved by Li [6] has been adopted. The latter achieves optimal performances on still images but sensor identification from videos is much more challenging. The SPN is strongly impacted by video compression, and it is demonstrated that the identification rate can be improved by selecting only I-frames, or a combination on I-frames and first P-frames, for the SPN computation. In [8], Chen et al. propose a technique for determining whatever two video clips came from the same camcorder by mean of the Maximum Likelihood Estimator for estimating the SPN, and of normalized cross-correlation for SPN comparison. In more recent articles, this issue is addressed by selecting only I-frames, or a weighted combination of I-frames and P-frames [7]. Other factors can affect the SPN, for example video stabilization [10] and the additional video compression operated by some website when uploading a video [9].

3   Proposed System

The input of the system consists in a short video clip depicting the user's face. From the recorded video, one single frame would be necessary for the following recognition processes. However, the presence of different images portraying the face could be exploited for performing best template selection. Concerning the sensor recognition module, only the I-frames are suitable, thus two possible strategies could be applied: (i) selecting one I-frame that portrays a good face image; (ii) selecting two images, the best for each module. Each module, namely the Face and the Sensor recognition modules, process independently the input image. The resulting scores are normalized and combined via weighted sum. In Fig. 2 an overview of the presented system is given.

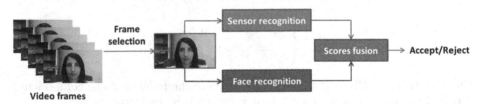

Fig. 2. System architecture.

3.1   Face Recognition

The adopted method for face recognition is based on the Histogram of Oriented Gradients (HOG) features [11]. The idea behind this technique is that object appearance and shape can be represented by the distribution of local intensity gradients or edge directions, even without precise knowledge of the corresponding gradient or edge positions. The method consists in dividing the image into small spatial regions, namely "cells". For each cell, a local 1D histogram of gradient directions or edge orientations is computed over the pixels of the cell. The extracted features correspond to the combined histogram entries. For better invariance to illumination and shadowing, contrast-normalization is recommended. This can be done by accumulating a measure of local histogram "energy" over larger spatial regions, namely "blocks", and using the results to normalize all the cells in the block [11]. The resulting HOG descriptors are then used as input of a conventional Super Vector Machine (SVM) based classifier.

3.2 Sensor Recognition

Each sensor has a noise pattern due to imperfections during the sensor manufacturing process and different sensitivity of pixels to light due to the inhomogeneity of silicon wafers [6]. This pattern is also referred as the sensor "fingerprint". Even sensors of the same model can be distinguished by analysing the Sensor Pattern Noise (SPN). This technique has been first presented by Lukáš et al. in [4] and further improved by Li in [6]. The SPN of a sensor is obtained by applying a de-noising filter in the wavelet domain:

$$n = DWT(I) - F(DWT(I))$$

where $DWT()$ is the discrete wavelet transform to be applied on image I and $F()$ is a de-noising function applied in the DWT domain. For $F()$ we used the filter proposed in Appendix A of [4].

Since both noise and scene details are located in high frequencies, it is observed that the SPN can be affected by the image content [6]. Li's approach, namely the Enhanced Sensor Pattern Noise (ESPN), is based on the idea that strong SPN components are more likely to have originated from the scene details and thus have to be suppressed, while weak components should be enhanced. The ESPN is computed according to the following formula:

$$n_e(i,j) = \begin{cases} e^{\frac{-0.5n^2(i,j)}{a^2}}, & \text{if } 0 \le n(i,j) \\ -e^{\frac{-0.5n^2(i,j)}{a^2}}, & \text{otherwise} \end{cases}$$

where n_e is the ESPN, n is the SPN, i and j are the indexes of the components of n and n_e, and α is a parameter that is set to 7, as indicated in [6].

Reference Sensor Pattern Noise. For each sensor, the RSPN has been estimated by selecting the I-frames from 9 videos. The videos have a duration that ranges between 2 and 5 s. Up to 4 I-frames per video have been extracted - the clips employed for the experiments are very short and thus contain only few I-frames. To extract the RSPN n_r of a sensor, the average SPN over N I-frames is computed:

$$n_r = \frac{1}{N} \times \sum_{k=1}^{N} n_k$$

4   Experimental Results

This section describes the dataset employed for the presented experiments and the final results obtained. Performances are assessed in terms of Equal Error Rate (EER), Recognition Rate (RR), Cumulative Match Score curve (CMS), Receiver Operating Characteristic curve (ROC), and Area under ROC curve (AUC).

4.1   Data Acquisition and Preprocessing

The experiments could be carried out thanks to the publicly available database for SOurce Camera REcognition on Smartphones, namely the SOCRatES database. SOCRatES is currently made up of about 6.200 images and 670 videos captured with 67 different smartphones of 13 different brands and about 40 different models. While images are all of JPEG format, videos are mostly of MP4 file format, with the exception of a few MOV files and one 3gp video.

Videos are treated with simple image processing operations. Video frames are extracted using the *VideoReader* MATLAB function. For the sensor recognition module, I-frames are selected and only a window centered in the image and of size 1024×1024 pixels is employed for the SPN estimation. The images to be given as input to the face feature extractor are first submitted to a face detector module using the *Cascade Object Detector* from MATLAB that implements the Viola-Jones [12] algorithm to detect people's faces. Cropped faces are then resized to 256×256 pixels and converted from RGB to gray level format.

4.2   Sensor Recognition Performance Evaluation

Before presenting the performance of the two modules and of the score fusion, an analysis of the sensor recognition from videos is presented in this section. In particular it has been investigated which I-frame yields to best performances. As mentioned before, SOCRatES contains short videos of about 2–5 s. In these short clips only few I-frames are present. The RSPN has been computed over N frames ($N = 36$ if the videos are long enough to have 4 I-frames each) extracted from 9 out of 10 clips. The 10th video has been used as test sample and its ESPN has been extracted using Li's technique on its I-frames. In the graphs illustrated in Fig. 3, a comparative performance evaluation shows that using the first I-frame of the test clip, leads to better recognition performances compared to the use of the second or third I-frame. Performances have been assessed on a pool of 630 videos recorded by 63 different sensors.

The performance values are summarized in the following:

– **First I-frame:** EER = 0.3013; RR = 0.3492; AUC = 0.7717.
– **Second I-frame:** EER = 0.3322; RR = 0.2857; AUC = 0.7339.
– **Third I-frame:** EER = 0.3360; RR = 0.2903; AUC = 0.7330.

Compared to the performances reported in [13] obtained on the same dataset but without I-frame selection, an improvement of around 7% of the rate of correct classification has been obtained.

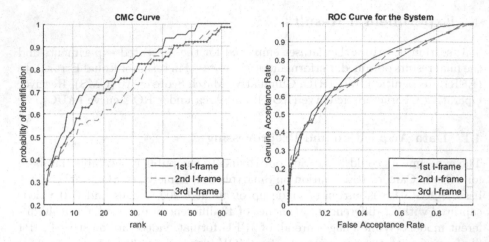

Fig. 3. Sensor recognition performances comparison when using the 1st, 2nd, or 3rd I-frame for SPN extraction.

4.3 System Performance Evaluation

The videos collected in the SOCRatES database do not portray face images, the system behavior is thus simulated by using the videos as input for the sensor recognition module and pictures of faces for the face recognition. The pictures have been collected with the same devices that recorded the videos. A total of 59 pairs device-face have been then defined. A sample is thus genuine if the combination device-person is enrolled in the system.

The details of the sensor recognition module performances assessment have been already discussed in Sect. 4.2. For what concerns face recognition, 10 face pictures for each user have been collected with the same sensors used to record the videos. The face image are characterized by different pose and illumination. Eight out of 10 images have been used to train a SVM on the extracted HOG features. One picture, randomly selected from the 2 remaining ones, has been used as test sample.

The performances obtained by the sensor recognition module are: EER = 0.3; RR = 0.35; AUC = 0.77. While the performances obtained by the face recognition module are: EER = 0.07; RR = 0.80; AUC = 0.97. Fusion is performed at score level. The modules contribute equally to the final score since they represent two different entities, i.e. the smartphone and the user, and have the same importance in the computation of the final score. Alternatively, a voting procedure could be used for the final accept/reject decision. The system performances after fusion are: EER = 0.06; RR = 0.83; AUC = 0.97. Figure 4 reports the performances graph for the aforementioned experiments.

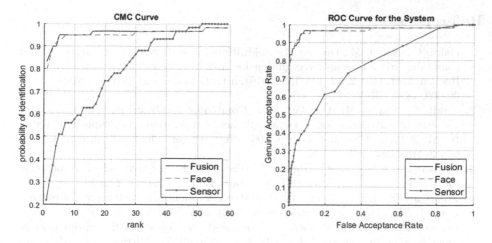

Fig. 4. Single features and fusion performance comparison.

5 Conclusions

An innovative authentication system has been presented. At the best of our knowledge, this is the first work proposing the combination of sensor and face recognition from videos for real-time user authentication. The authors have previously presented a system combining iris and sensor recognition from still images in [1,2]. Here, the use of videos as input data presents a considerable challenge. In fact, the performances of the sensor recognition module drastically drop when using videos in place of still images (of about the 20% [7,13]). The SPN is significantly affected by strong video compression. However, by simply selecting I-frames from a set of short video clips, a rate of correct classification equal to 77% is obtained by the sensor recognition module and a rate of 97% is achieved by the combination with the face module.

The objective is to obtain a more secure authentication system by combining different authentication items, namely the user's face and smartphone, while keeping simple and fast the acquisition process. In addition, the proposed acquisition, i.e. a short recording of the user's face, opens the way to further combination with other biometric traits, such us voice, or anti-spoofing or liveness detectors.

The method is tested on a large database of videos collected with 63 different smartphones, namely the SOCRatES database.

References

1. Galdi, C., Nappi, M., Dugelay, J.-L.: Multimodal authentication on smartphones: combining iris and sensor recognition for a double check of user identity. Patt. Recogn. Lett. Part 2, **82**, 144–153 (2016). http://dx.doi.org/10.1016/j.patrec.2015.09.009. ISSN: 0167-8655
2. Galdi, C., Nappi, M., Dugelay, J.-L.: Combining hardwaremetry and biometry for human authentication via smartphones. In: Murino, V., Puppo, E. (eds.) ICIAP 2015. LNCS, vol. 9280, pp. 406–416. Springer, Cham (2015). doi:10.1007/978-3-319-23234-8_38
3. De Marsico, M., Galdi, C., Nappi, M., Riccio, D.: Firme: face and iris recognition for mobile engagement. Image Vis. Comput. **32**(12), 1161–1172 (2014)
4. Lukáš, J., Fridrich, J., Goljan, M.: Digital camera identification from sensor pattern noise. IEEE Trans. Inf. Forensics Secur. **1**(2), 205–214 (2006)
5. Goljan, M., Fridrich, J., Filler, T.: Large scale test of sensor fingerprint camera identification. In: Memon, N.D., Delp, E.J., Wong, P.W., Dittmann, J. (eds.) Proceedings of SPIE. Electronic Imaging, Media Forensics and Security XI, vol. 7254, pp. 0I-01–0I-12, January 2009
6. Li, C.T.: Source camera identification using enhanced sensor pattern noise. IEEE Trans. Inf. Forensics Secur. **5**(2), 280–287 (2010)
7. Chuang, W.H., Su, H., Wu, M.: Exploring compression effects for improved source camera identification using strongly compressed video. In: 2011 18th IEEE International Conference on Image Processing, Brussels, pp. 1953–1956 (2011). doi:10.1109/ICIP.2011.6115855
8. Chen, M., Fridrich, J., Goljan, M., Lukáš, J.: Source digital camcorder identification using sensor photo response non-uniformity. In: Electronic Imaging, p. 65051G. International Society for Optics and Photonics (2007)
9. Van Houten, W., Geradts, Z.: Using sensor noise to identify low resolution compressed videos from Youtube. In: Geradts, Z.J.M.H., Franke, K.Y., Veenman, C.J. (eds.) IWCF 2009. LNCS, vol. 5718, pp. 104–115. Springer, Heidelberg (2009). doi:10.1007/978-3-642-03521-0_10
10. Taspinar, S., Mohanty, M., Memon, N.: Source camera attribution using stabilized video. In: 2016 IEEE International Workshop on Information Forensics and Security (WIFS), Abu Dhabi, pp. 1–6 (2016). doi:10.1109/WIFS.2016.7823918
11. Dalal, N., Triggs, B.: Histograms of oriented gradients for human detection. In: IEEE Computer Society Conference on Computer Vision and Pattern Recognition, vol. 1, pp. 886–893, June 2005
12. Viola, P., Michael, J.J.: Rapid object detection using a boosted cascade of simple features. In: Proceedings of the 2001 IEEE Computer Society Conference on Computer Vision and Pattern Recognition, vol. 1, pp. 511–518 (2001)
13. Galdi, C., Hartung, F., Dugelay, J.-L.: Videos versus still images: asymmetric sensor pattern noise comparison on mobile phones. In: Electronic Imaging (2017)

A Hybrid Approach for Private Data Protection in the Cloud

Amal Ghorbel[1]([✉]), Mahmoud Ghorbel[1]([✉]), and Mohamed Jmaiel[1,2]([✉])

[1] ReDCAD Laboratory, National School of Engineers of Sfax, University of Sfax,
B.P. 1173, 3038 Sfax, Tunisia
{amal.ghorbel,mahmoud.ghorbel,mohamed.jmaiel}@redcad.org
[2] Digital Research Center of Sfax, B.P. 275, Sakiet Ezzit, 3021 Sfax, Tunisia

Abstract. With the emergence of the cloud computing paradigm, the personal data usage has raised several privacy concerns like the lack of user control, the non-compliance with the user's preferences and/or regulations, the difficulty of the data flow tracking, etc. In particular, one unsolved problem is to ensure that customers data usage policies are enforced, regardless of who accesses the data, how they are processed, where are the data stored, transferred and duplicated. This issue calls for two requirements to be satisfied. First, data should be handled in accordance with both owners' preferences and regulations policies whenever it exists in the cloud and throughout its lifetime. Second, a consistent data flow tracking should be maintained to follow up the data derivation. Toward addressing these issues, we propose in this paper a hybrid approach to protect private data in the cloud. We propose the PriArmor data content for self-defending data when stored or transferred in the cloud and the PriArmor agent that acts as an armor for its privacy protection when processed by the cloud-based services. To facilitate the policy specification, we propose a novel privacy ontology model that drives the data owner to express his privacy requirements and to consider the regulations policies. Finally, we present the implementation details as well as a demonstration that shows flexibility and efficiency of our approach.

Keywords: Privacy · Cloud · Privacy policies · Ontology · Policy enforcement

1 Introduction

There is no doubt that cloud computing presents a real evolution in the IT world that offers many advantages for both particular and professional customers. In fact, reduction of IT costs and improvement of business agility are identified as the greatest assets for the cloud adoption. Nevertheless, the lack of trust and transparency about data handling, is at present, a key inhibitor in moving to the public cloud [1]. For cloud customers, there are many ambiguities regarding the data outsourcing in such remote hosting paradigm where data are stored and processed in remote machines not owned or controlled by the data owners [2].

© Springer International Publishing AG 2017
M.H.A. Au et al. (Eds.): GPC 2017, LNCS 10232, pp. 23–37, 2017.
DOI: 10.1007/978-3-319-57186-7_3

Therefore, the data owners don't have a clear idea about how and by whom their data are accessed, stored and used. Even worse, due to replication and backup cloud mechanisms, many copies of data may be created and stored on servers in different geographical locations where local laws can bring more privacy risks.

One major privacy concern in the public cloud is the data access and usage policy enforcement. This concern can cover the overall privacy issues as all aforementioned problems can be regulated by expressing well-defined privacy policies and enforcing them. Nevertheless, the majority of the current customers are unaware of the risks that threaten their private data in the public cloud environment, and thus, they are not able to define the appropriate policies that assure the protection of their data. Furthermore, the privacy policies are various and complex since they encode different access and usage restrictions including customer's business and regulatory requirements. A well-known regulatory requirement for data privacy is the physical location of the data (e.g., European regulation prohibits to store or transfer medical information out of the European fence [3]). Thus, it is not trivial for the cloud customer to express policies that exactly meets privacy requirements (customer's and regulation requirement) and at the same time considers all risk of data usage in the cloud. Second, ensuring that these policies are respected, is at present an important challenge. A commonly adopted approach is to associate policies with data while moving across the cloud system. Hence, data usage is permitted unless the attached policies are respected. To do this, some research works propose to emerge high-level mechanism to ensure that privacy policies are enforced before accessing the data. The main shortcoming of such solutions is the loss of control over the data once the usage request is checked and the data is released to the data actor. In fact, these approaches assume that the authorized users are trusted not to illegally leak or disseminate the data. Hence, they cannot prevent intentionally or inadvertently data misuse of the authorized users like keeping copies of data, sending data to unauthorized third parties, etc. Another policy enforcement concern involves the fact that outsourced data are always moving across the cloud ecosystem due to its dynamic feature. They can be stored, transferred and duplicated in forbidden locations specified by the data owner policy or regulation policies. Such actions are performed by the cloud service provider (CSP) using cloud infrastructure means (e.g., cloud manager, cloud balancer, etc.) and generally do not require permission to be performed on the data. Hence, privacy policy concerning data location can be easily and implicitly violated. The challenge here is that the integration of enforcement mechanisms in the cloud infrastructures in not a viable option.

In this paper, we propose an integrated approach for private data protection that enables cloud customer and regulation policy specification and that introduces new privacy structures and mechanisms for ensuring policy enforcement. We introduce the PriArmor (Privacy Armor) agent that enforces privacy policy on detected explicit data handle by cloud-based services (e.g., copy, share, collection, etc.). We introduce the new structure of data content named PriArmor data for self-location checking to deal with CSP implicit handling of data that cannot be detected by the enforcement mechanisms (e.g., transfer, storage, duplication). To enable policy specification, we propose a novel privacy ontology model as a semantic way to express access and usage control constraints. Based on this model, we introduce the Privacy Ontology-based Framework (POF) to be used by the data owner for automating the privacy policy specification. The POF integrates predefined domain specific ontologies that enable to consider regulatory policies. After the policies specification, the POF builds the PriArmor Data. The PriArmor data can be only used by a PriArmor agent VM which is integrated into the cloud infrastructure. This agent acts as an armor for data when it is processed by untrusted cloud-based services (application launched on the PriArmor agent VM). The PriArmor agent contributes by tackling the related problems: (1) providing appropriate guarantees to enforce policies contained in the PriArmor data, (2) tracking the protected data flows across the cloud environment and making clones of PriArmor data to include the derived data.

Problem statement. This paper address the problem of privacy requirement including customer's preferences and regulation policies regarding data access and usage in the cloud environment. The data access and usage control must be enforced on implicit and explicit actions done in the cloud. To this end, we study the three main problems below:

1. The data owner is unaware of data usage in the cloud and thus, he is not able to define the appropriate policies that assure his data protection. Moreover, it is not trivial for a data owner to explore regulation laws and to specify them as machine readable policies.
2. Actual enforcement mechanisms do not consider all cloud aspects in the enforcement process (dynamic data management, data duplication and transferring, etc.). Moreover, they do not consider implicit CSP data handling which leads generally to location-related policy breaches.
3. An enforcement mechanism must ensure a low-level usage control enforcement. Such mechanism requires knowing data flow to protect the derived data.

Contribution. We propose a hybrid approach that banks on several privacy solutions and contributes by tackling the three related sub-problems:

1. Enabling data owner preferences definition and legal policies consideration.
2. Providing appropriate guarantees to enforce location-related policy for the CSP implicit data usage without impacting cloud infrastructures.
3. Ensuring system call level policy enforcement for cloud-based services for explicit data handling and enabling data flows tracking across the system to protect the derived data.

The rest of this paper is structured as follows. In Sect. 2, we introduce a motivating use case. In Sect. 3, we present and detail the proposed approach. Section 4 introduces the data encryption and the key management solution. Section 5 includes some implementation details and a demonstration of the proposed approach. In Sect. 6, we analyze some related works. Section 7 concludes the paper.

2   Motivating Use Case

In order to have a clear view of the issues previously described, we have identified one critical scenario of privacy threats in cloud environments that will be used as a reference example in this paper.

We consider an insurance company serving both private customers and companies. In order to improve its business and to increase elasticity, the insurance decides to adopt cloud-based services for email, customer data storage, collaboration, and website. Consider a customer, that resides in Europe, who want to ask for health insurance offers using the insurance website. To have a personalized offer, the insurance asks the customer to provide some private information such as name, address, age, sex, job, an overview of his history of diseases and his Electronic Health Record (EHR), etc. Before releasing such information, the customer must have a way to define his privacy settings by specifying which entity can access his data, for what purposes, where it can be stored, what are the obligations that must be satisfied before or after the access to the data (e.g. notification, retention). He must also have a way to consider regulation policies and to integrate them with his privacy preferences. The insurance also must ensure that the used cloud-based services integrate an enforcement mechanism that enables compliance with data owner preferences and the corresponding regulation policies.

To allay customer' concerns, it is essential to provide an effective mechanism for users to specify their privacy preferences and to ensure their protection in the cloud. In our model attack, we try to protect the data when it is processed or stored in the cloud. Hence, the following threats are out of the scope of this paper: (1) taking a photo of the screen, (2) human memory, (3) peeking in the VM that deploys the cloud-based service when running and making copies of it.

3   The Proposed Approach

The main contribution of this paper is to provide an integrated approach to protect private data in the cloud throughout its lifetime (at rest, in use and in-transit). To enable this, we propose the privacy policy ontology (Sect. 3.1) and the Privacy Ontology-based Framework (Sect. 3.2) for privacy requirements specification. We introduce the PriArmor data container (Sect. 3.3) and the PriArmor agent (Sect. 3.4) to ensure the policy enforcement in the cloud ecosystem. We refer to the next subsections for an in-depth description.

3.1   Privacy Ontology Model

Policy specification is a very important step to ensure the data protection in the cloud. The data owner must specify a set of policies to express his preferences concerning the data access and usage. One major issue here is that most of the cloud customers don't have a clear idea about practices that data actors can perform with their private data. An unstudied specification of policies may create vulnerabilities which can be exploited to data misuse or leakage (for example a customer who is not aware of data collection and sharing in the cloud may not specify policies to regulate these practices). Further, the diversity and the complexity of the privacy policies, expressed either by legal requirement or by the data owner preferences, explain the need for a semantic modeling of the privacy policies to abstract its complexity and facilitate its automation and enforcement. To this end, we propose the privacy ontology model that catches and gathers various concepts related to the data access and usage in the cloud. Our privacy ontology model is split into two ontologies: the policy ontology and the data usage ontology. The two ontologies are represented respectively by Figs. 1 and 2. A description of their ontological concepts and relations are provided as follows.

Policy Ontology. The policy ontology represents the privacy policy and all its properties.

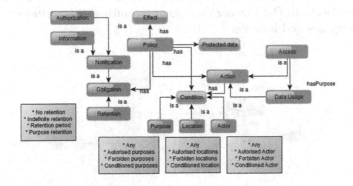

Fig. 1. Ontological concepts of privacy policy

- Protected data: a policy is defined for a target private data.
- Action: data action can be an access or a data usage. An action has an actor which is the data requester. The data owner can specify authorized, forbidden, or conditioned (that demand notification of data owner for information or for authorization) actors. Data usage presents the access purpose (collection, share, copy, display, etc.). The data owner can identify authorized, forbidden, or conditioned access purposes.
- Obligation: the obligation concept concerns retention and notification. For data retention, the data owner can specify indefinite retention when the period of retention is undefined, period retention to identify time period of retention of the collected data or purpose retention when data are retained only during the time period necessary to complete the purposes. A notification can be informational (to inform the data owner about an event) or seeking for authorization actions.
- Condition: each action has a condition that is defined by a set of context variables such as actor, the purpose of use, usage location, recipient of private data, the location of the recipient. If the condition evaluates to true based

on the values of the context variables, then the action is permitted or denied according to the policy effect.
- Effect: can be either allow or deny.

Data action ontology. In the data action ontology, we enumerate the possible data processing in the cloud and the corresponding conditions and obligations.

- Collection and Share: each of these concepts have a purpose and a recipient that has a location and (e.g., maintenance, marketing, statistical, personalization, profiling, etc.). The data owner must identify authorized, forbidden, or conditioned recipients, location recipient, and purposes.
- Transfer, Storage, and Duplication: these actions are generally performed implicitly by the CSP. We require that such actions must be done only on encrypted data.
- Read, Modification, Copy, and Deletion: each of these actions has a purpose and usage location. Data owner must identify authorized, forbidden or conditioned purposes and location.

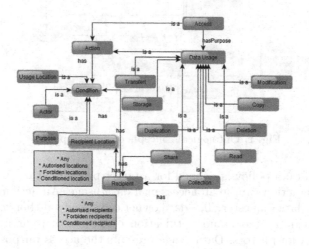

Fig. 2. Ontological concepts of data usage

3.2   Privacy Ontology-based Framework

We propose the Privacy Ontology-based Framework (POF) that implements the proposed ontology model to facilitate the policy generation. Our framework provides a graphical tool that hides the complexity of the ontology representation from the users. An ontology transformer, a consistency auditor and an efficiency tester are integrated to generate readable and coherent policies. The overall process of the policy generation is depicted in the Fig. 3.

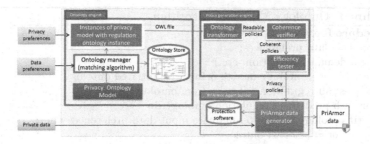

Fig. 3. Privacy Ontology-based Framework

At first, it is necessary for the data owner to identify the domain of the data (e.g., medical data, financial data, personal data, etc.), his location and many others preferences. An ontology matching algorithm is defined for the selection and the instantiation of the appropriate regulatory policy based on the specified preferences (see Algorithm 1) to be associated with our privacy ontology model. The data preferences (d: domain, l: location) are the inputs of the algorithm, *or* is the selected regulation ontology according to the data preferences and *orIns* is the instantiation of the selected ontology which is the output of the algorithm. Now, the data owner can express his privacy preferences concerning the data access, the data usage and the associated obligations to complete the ontology model specification using the provided graphical editor. The output from the graphical tool is an OWL file that contains all needed features (privacy regulatory and data owner preferences) to generate the policies. From the resulted OWL file, the ontology transformer automatically generates readable policies in a specific language (e.g., XACML [4], PPL [5], KAoS [6], etc.). Thereafter, the consistency auditor verifies the coherence of the policies and then the efficiency tester checks whether the generated policies gratify the data owner expectations or not. This last module avoids the user to have a syntactically correct policy but with unexpected effect. Finally, the POF encapsulates data with the policies and associates them with the protection software to build the PriArmor data. The integrated protection software is used to enforce the location-related policy using self-location checking and self-destruction algorithms. The PriArmor data also integrates a self-integrity checking software to enables it to protect itself. Now, the produced data content is ready to be uploaded to the cloud.

3.3   PriArmor Data

The PriArmor data is a movable container that encapsulates sensitive data and privacy policy and assures its location-related policy enforcement through the provision of effective software packages as shown in Fig. 4. These packages are signed and sealed by a known Trust Authority (TA). Based on a self-destruction mechanism, the introduced software packages enable:

Self-integrity checking. The PriArmor data checks the integrity of its contents at any random time. It computes the hash value for the sensitive data, the

Algorithm 1. Ontology Matching Algorithm

procedure REGONTOINS
    Input = data preferences;
    \\(d: domain, l: location, etc.)
    Variable or : ontology model; orIns : instantiated ontology;
    Request all regulation ontology from ontology store;
    for each predefined regulation ontology **do**
        if ontology regulation matches input data preferences **then**
            or = selected ontology
            orIns = instantiate (or)
            Return orIns
        else
            Return "Data has no regulation law";
        end if
    end for
end procedure

policies, and the protection software. Then, it verifies the signed hash value by comparing it to the computed hash value. If the verification fails, the PriArmor data performs the self-destruction mechanism to prevent compromises.

Self-location checking. The data cloud actor, such as the CSP, may simply store, transfer, or duplicate the PriArmor data without trying to access the data and to verify the associated policy. Such actions can be not permitted if the destination does not match the location requirements. Hence, the PriArmor data performs self-location checking at any random time and before being handled by any PriArmor agent. The PriArmor data performs a self-destruction if its physical location is prohibited by the defined policies.

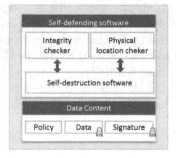

Fig. 4. PriArmor data content

3.4   PriArmor Agent

The PriArmor data structure can be only decrypted and handled in a PriArmor agent VM that is integrated into the cloud infrastructure. The PriArmor agent enables low level enforcement of the privacy policies using a System Call Interception (SCI) technique. By using such technique, the PriArmor agent is able to detect and prevent the intention for the policies breaching. Again, the PriArmor agent incorporates a data flow model that tracks private data and reflects the existence of the derived data through the system Fig. 5. The main functionalities of the PriArmor agent are:

Authentication. The PriArmor agent includes a claim-based authentication that requires a security token issued by the Trusted Authority (TA). TA authenticated the user at an early stage through a set of claims that specify the user identity, roles, assigned permissions, location etc. The authentication is done through the PriArmor agent interface whenever a user or an application (cloud actor) requires the usage of the protected data.

Active control. The PriArmor agent implements a data flow model that allow to monitor all actions performed on the data and detects the derived data (copies of data, modified data, appended data, etc.) from the data usage.

Policy enforcement. After authentication of authorized users, the PriArmor agent intercepts all requests for data usage, checks for their compliance with the defined policy and decides whether to allow or to deny the access to the protected data. The PriArmor agent is an instantiation of a generic representation of the policy management components which implement a system call interception solution. It consists of three components: the request analyzer, in charge of intercepting system calls and enforcing the corresponding privacy policy and obligations; the evaluation engine, responsible for deciding about the admission of the intercepted system call; and the metadata store, implements a data flow model and maintains a connection between data and its derivation within the system.

PriArmor engine. The PriArmor engine enables the PriArmor data generation whenever a data or its derivation must leave the active PriArmor VM. This engine clones the original PriArmor data to include the derived data.

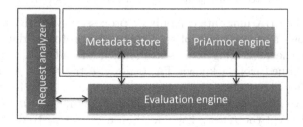

Fig. 5. PriArmor agent architecture

4   Data Encryption and Key Management

The PriArmor solution includes a symmetric-key cryptographic scheme to protect the larger-size content (protected data) and an asymmetric cryptographic
scheme for protecting the smaller-size items (the symmetric encryption key
Ku_{sym}).

Creation and encryption: we describe the implementation of the key management in our solution. The format of the protected data generated from the
POF is shown in Fig. 6. To create the PriArmor data, the owner first generates
a new symmetric key (Ku_{sym}), and uses it to encrypt the data. (Ku_{sym}) is
then encrypted using the PriArmor agent public key (Ka_{pub}). The POF associates the protection software to builds the PriArmor data. Then, it calculates
a cryptographic hash over the encrypted Ku_{sym}, the encrypted data, the policy
and the included software. The hash is signed by the TA using its private key
(Kta_{pri}) to ensure the data content control.

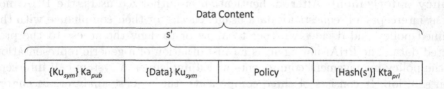

Fig. 6. Format of the protected data content

Transfer to the cloud: once the PriArmor data is created, it can be moved to
the cloud. The PriArmor data is a self-location checking content, hence it can
be stored and processed anywhere in the system.

Self-integrity checking: at any time, the PriArmor data checks for his
integrity. It calculates the hash of the encrypted Ku_{sym}, the encrypted data,
the policy and the protection software. Then, it compares it with the decrypted
hash in the signature to ensure that they have not tampered.

Decryption: the PriArmor data can only be processed by a PriArmor agentVM.
The latter follows a secure protocol to decrypt the protected data. First of all,
it ensures that the requesting user is authenticated and that the user owns a
security token issued from a known TA, otherwise the access is denied. Then,
the PriArmor agent retrieves the policy and compares it with the request. If
the decision is to grant access to the data, the PriArmor agent uses its private
key Ka_{pri} to decrypt the Ku_{sym} key and then uses Ku_{sym} to decrypt the data.
The Ka_{pri} key is stored in a TPM (Trusted Platform Module) tamper-resistant
hardware component that provides a shielded location to protect secret keys [8].

Re-encryption: if an authorized data processing requires the data to leave
the active PriArmor agent VM (send, share, etc.), then the PriArmor engine
searches for the originator PriArmor data in the metadata store. It encrypts the

data using Ku_{sym}. Then, if the data will be sent to another Ku_{sym} agent VM, it encrypts the Ku_{sym} using the destination public key. Otherwise, the Ku_{sym} is encrypted using Ka_{pub}. The PriArmor engine integrates a signed hash over the encrypted Ku_{sym}, the encrypted data, the policy and the protection software in the data content and builds the PriArmor data.

5   Implementation Details

5.1   Prototype

Our approach introduces the POF that enables cloud customer's and regulation policy specification. It also includes a protection mechanism that is based on the PriArmor solution. The principle of our mechanism is as follows: the PriArmor data can be only processed in a PriArmor agent VM that we assume its existence before the PriArmor data generation.

The POF facilitate the data owner mission for the policy specification by introducing a graphical tool and based on the proposed privacy ontology model. We carry on exploiting OWL [9] description language to implement privacy ontology model. First of all, the POF requires the data preferences that are the inputs of the regulation ontology instantiation algorithm. Next, an instance of the privacy ontology model is loaded including the selected regulation ontology instance. Thereafter, the POF guides the data owner to fill in the rest of the ontological concepts of our model by providing him a set of interfaces for specifying each data action. Second, the POF transforms the instantiated ontology into privacy policy (the current implementation of the POF supports the XACML policy). At present, the implementation of the POF does not support the consistency auditor and the efficiency tester. We aim to integrate it in the future work. Once the policies are generated, the POF bounds the data to the policies as described in Sect. 4 and associates them with the protection software packages to build the PriArmor data.

The software packages of the PriArmor data implementation banks on Vanish[1] core system [10]. The central security goal of Vanish software is to ensure the destruction of data regardless of whether it is copied, transmitted, or stored in a distributed system. Hence, the data becomes unreadable after a predefined period. We modify the Vanish data destruction software in a way that it will be triggered by the self-integrity checking and self-location checking software.

We implement a PriArmor agent prototype on an OpenBSD VM. Systrace framework [11], which is integrated by default in the OpenBSD, has been used to implement the request analyzer and the evaluation engine components. Using Systrace, no modifications to the operating system itself are needed. The meta-data store is implemented as a software layer on the top of the systrace device /dev/systrace. This software keeps track of protected data using the generic data flow model introduced in [7]. This model allows fine-grained data flow tracking at the system call level. The PriArmor engine software is launched whenever data

---

[1] https://vanish.cs.washington.edu/index.html.

are allowed to leave the actual PriArmor agent VM. Hence, PriArmor engine communicates with the metadata store to identify the original PriArmor data and clone it for the derived data.

5.2   Demonstration

To show the usefulness of our approach, we present a demonstration of the proposed mechanisms. We rely on additional assumptions in our demonstration that are: (i) the attacker does not have administrator privileges; (ii) the underlying OpenBSD operating system is free of vulnerabilities. Considering the use case presented in Sect. 2, we suppose that the insurance company has launched her services on a PriArmor agent VM located in Italy and has used cloud-based storage services located in Germany (see Fig. 7). Since Bob (the cloud customer) lives in France and that he will deliver his EHR then the POF will select and instantiate the predefined ontology of the European regulation for health data. The European directive requires that EHR must never leave the European fence. Hence, a policy that inhibits data transfer out on the European fence is defined. Now, the PriArmor data is uploaded to the PriArmor agent VM. The company's employee is authenticated and is permitted to view the sensitive data but not to disseminate it. Assume that the employee tries to share data with another unauthorized party. These practices are inhibited based on the PriArmor agent enforcement mechanism. Assume that Bob accepts the offer proposed by the company. His EHR is re-packaged in PriArmor data container (using the PriArmor engine) and is stored in the storage server S1 (Germany). Suppose that the S1 cloud manager performs duplication of Bob's PriArmor data and transfer it to be stored in the storage server S2 (US) to ensure the data availability. At any random time and before being used, the PriArmor data performs self-location checking and note that his location in forbidden by the specified policy. Hence, it runs the self-destruction algorithm.

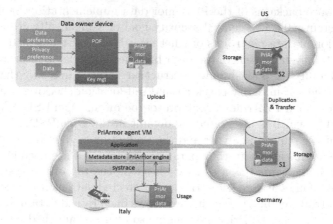

Fig. 7. Scenario of the proposed approach

6   Related Works

Various technologies have been introduced to deal with privacy compliance issues in the cloud. In the following, we give an overview of some related works. The first category of approaches focuses on how to protect data from the user side. The user is involved either in the expression of his preferences or in the consideration of legal texts. Rahmouni proposes in [12] to semantically model privacy obligations of legal, ethical or cultural nature. She aims to formalize privacy policies intercepted from the EU directive through the use of ontology modeling (OWL) and semantic web rule language (SWRL). These policies are then mapped to the XACML language in order to be enforced in the cloud. Nevertheless, this approach considers only legal policies (does not consider data owner preferences) and only the EU directive ones. Similarly, Papanikolaou et al. come up with a toolkit for automating compliance in cloud computing services [13]. This toolkit allows the semantic annotation and natural-language processing of policy texts (regulation text and/or data owner preferences text) to generate machine-readable rules. However, these user-centric approaches remain incomplete since they are not able to ensure enforcement of generated policies in the cloud.

Other solutions introduce data-centric approaches that emphasize mechanisms and techniques to automate sensitive data protection anywhere in the cloud. Squicciarini et al. introduce the Self-Controlling Objects (SCO) [14]. This object that encapsulates sensitive data along with their policies and assures their protection by means of object-oriented programming techniques. Each time, the access to the SCO protected content is attempted, its policy is evaluated according to the requester's credential and location. The SCO manages copies of data synchronizes and updates it if there was a change. Angin et al. introduce an entity-centric approach for identity management in the cloud [15]. This entity incorporates the data, the policy and a VM that manages the policy enforcement. This entity can perform a set of protection mechanisms to protect themselves such as integrity checks, apoptosis, evaporation and decoy. However, these approaches can only enforce access policy and loss the control over the data once access is granted.

The approach presented in [16,17] proposes to introduce a data protection module named CDPM (Client Data Protection Module) deployed in the user side to allow policies generation. To ensure policies enforcement in the cloud, authors propose to integrate the File Data Protection Module(FDPM) within the VM system file. FDPM will intercept, control and trace all operations done by applications on sensitive files. Castiglione et al. [18] propose an engine for lossless dynamic and adaptive compression of 3D medical images, which also allows the embedding of security watermarks within them. Gosman et al. [19] illustrate a security model for Intelligent Transportation Systems (ITS) where participants can specify how data sharing captured by an ITS application will behave in regards to their own privacy requirements. The proposed solution is able to maps the differences between ITS applications requirements regarding data usage and the user privacy constraints related to the location and timestamp of his shared data.

All the works outlined above are interesting. However, each of them has one of these drawbacks. First, we can remark that the majority of these approaches do not consider privacy policy specification or assume that data owner is able to express his policy. Second, part of the presented approaches consider only access control enforcement and loss the control once data are delivered. Besides, the majority of works cannot track the flow of data to maintain the same level of enforcement. Moreover, they do not consider the dynamic feature of cloud that probably leads to location-related policies violation.

7   Conclusion

In this paper, we propose a new policy based technology for privacy preservation in the cloud. We believe that the privacy protection in public cloud is a complex process that requires the implication of all involved entities to ensure the data protection throughout its lifetime. Thereby, in our solution, we have adopted a hybrid approach that involves the data, the data owner and the data actors in the data protection process. In fact, we propose a novel privacy ontology model that catches various concepts related to the data access and the usage in the cloud and considers multiple aspects of this environment. We propose the Privacy Ontology-based Framework (POF) that drives the data owner for speci-fying his privacy preferences based on the proposed privacy ontology model. Our framework includes predefined regulatory policy ontologies to consider privacy laws. The POF generates a new data content structure named PriArmor data that bundles the sensitive data, the defined policy and a set of self-defending soft-ware. These software include self-integrity and self-location checking algorithms that are able to launch a self-destruction k whenever there was a location-related policy or PriArmor data content violation. PriArmor data can be processed in PriArmor agent VM that ensures the policy enforcement and the data flow track-ing at system call level. We present the data encryption and key management used to generate the PriArmor Data and provide implementation details about the prototype architecture. We demonstrate the effectiveness of our approach and that is a viable option in real-life examples.

References

1. Hashem, I.A.T., Yaqoob, I., Anuar, N.B., Mokhtar, S., Gani, A., Khan, S.U.: The rise of "big data" on cloud computing: review and open research issues. Inf. Syst. **47**, 98–115 (2015)
2. Ghorbel, A., Ghorbel, M., Jmaiel, M.: Privacy in cloud computing environments: a survey and research challenges. J. Supercomput. 1–38 (2017)
3. EU Directive: 95/46/EC of the European Parliament and of the Council of 24 October 1995 on the protection of individuals with regard to the processing of personal data and on the free movement of such data. Offcial J. EC **23**(6) (1995)
4. Moses, T.: Extensible access control markup language (XACML) version 2.0. Oasis Standard, 200502 (2005)

5. Trabelsi, S., Njeh, A., Bussard, L., Neven, G.: PPL engine: a symmetric architecture for privacy policy handling. In: W3C Workshop on Privacy and data usage control, vol. 4, no. 5, October 2010

6. Uszok, A., Bradshaw, J., Jeffers, R., Suri, N., Hayes, P., Breedy, M., Bunch, L., Johnson, M., Kulkarni, S., Lott, J.: KAoS policy and domain services: toward a description-logic approach to policy representation, deconfliction, and enforcement. In: Proceedings of the IEEE 4th International Workshop on Policies for Distributed Systems and Networks, POLICY 2003, pp. 93–96. IEEE, June 2003

7. Harvan, M., Pretschner, A.: State-based usage control enforcement with data flow tracking using system call interposition. In: Third International Conference on Network and System Security, NSS 2009, pp. 373–380. IEEE, October 2009

8. Chen, L., Mitchell, C.J., Martin, A. (eds.): Trust 2009. LNCS, vol. 5471. Springer, Heidelberg (2009)

9. McGuinness, D.L., Van Harmelen, F.: OWL web ontology language overview. W3C recommendation, vol. 10, 10 February 2004

10. Geambasu, R., Kohno, T., Levy, A.A., Levy, H.M.: Vanish: increasing data privacy with self-destructing data. In: USENIX Security Symposium, pp. 299–316, August 2009

11. Provos, N.: Improving host security with system call policies. In: Usenix Security, vol. 3, p. 19, August 2003

12. Rahmouni, H.B.: Ontology based privacy compliance for health data disclosure in Europe. Doctoral dissertation, University of the West of England, Bristol (2011)

13. Papanikolaou, N., Pearson, S., Mont, M.C., Ko, R.K.: A toolkit for automating compliance in cloud computing services. Int. J. Cloud Comput. 2 3(1), 45–68 (2014)

14. Squicciarini, A.C., Petracca, G., Bertino, E.: Adaptive data protection in distributed systems. In: Proceedings of the Third ACM Conference on Data and Application security and privacy pp. 365–376. ACM, February 2013

15. Angin, P., Bhargava, B., Ranchal, R., Singh, N., Linderman, M., Othmane, L.B., Lilien, L.: An entity-centric approach for privacy and identity management in cloud computing. In: 2010 29th IEEE Symposium on Reliable Distributed Systems, pp. 177–183. IEEE, October 2010

16. Betgé-Brezetz, S., Kamga, G.B., Dupont, M.P., Guesmi, A.: Privacy control in cloud VM file systems. In: 2013 IEEE 5th International Conference on Cloud Computing Technology and Science (CloudCom), vol. 2, pp. 276–280. IEEE, December 2013

17. Betgé-Brezetz, S., Kamga, G.B., Ghorbel, M., Dupont, M.P.: Privacy control in the cloud based on multilevel policy enforcement. In: 2012 IEEE 1st International Conference on Cloud Networking (CLOUDNET), pp. 167–169. IEEE, November 2012

18. Castiglione, A., Pizzolante, R., De Santis, A., Carpentieri, B., Castiglione, A., Palmieri, F.: Cloud-based adaptive compression and secure management services for 3D healthcare data. Future Gener. Comput. Syst. **43**, 120–134 (2015)

19. Gosman, C., Cornea, T., Dobre, C., Pop, F., Castiglione, A.: Controlling and filtering users data in intelligent transportation system. Future Gener. Comput. Syst. (2016)

An Efficient and Secure Design of Redactable Signature Scheme with Redaction Condition Control

Jinhua Ma[1], Jianghua Liu[2], Min Wang[1], and Wei Wu[1(✉)]

[1] Fujian Provincial Key Laboratory of Network Security and Cryptology,
School of Mathematics and Computer Science,
Fujian Normal University, Fuzhou, China
jinhuama55@hotmail.com, wangmin919191@outlook.com, weiwu@fjnu.edu.cn
[2] School of Information Technology, Deakin University, Geelong, Australia
jianghualiu88@outlook.com

Abstract. Digital signatures, with the properties of data integrity and authenticity authentication, protect a signed message from any alteration. However, appropriate alteration of signed message should be allowed for the purposes of privacy protection or bandwidth saving in some scenarios, such as medical record or official information disclosure. Redactable signatures, a branch of homomorphic signatures for editing, allow any redactor to remove some submessage blocks from an originally signed message and generate a valid signature on the modified message without any help of the original signer. In this paper, we present a new design of redactable signature scheme with submessage redaction control structure. This scheme has the security properties of unforgeability, privacy, and transparency, which are formally defined and proved. Compared with state-of-the-art redactable signature schemes, our scheme is more efficient in communication and computation cost.

Keywords: Digital signature · Medical record · Homomorphic signature · Redactable signature · Redaction control structure

1 Introduction

Digital signature is a mathematical scheme for demonstrating the authenticity of a digital document [1]. It is a standard cryptographic primitive of most cryptographic protocols, and is widely used for contract management protocols, financial transactions, distributing software updates, and many other important fields.

The standard security definition of general digital signature schemes is "existentially unforgeable under adaptive chosen-message attacks (EUF-CMA)" [2] which prevents the forging of a signature for any 'new' message that has never been signed by the original signer. This also indicates that a general digital signature does not allow any alteration of the signed digital document matching to it.

© Springer International Publishing AG 2017
M.H.A. Au et al. (Eds.): GPC 2017, LNCS 10232, pp. 38–52, 2017.
DOI: 10.1007/978-3-319-57186-7_4

While the traditional digital signatures protect documents from modification by malicious users or attackers, they also prevent the signed documents from being processed which hinders the flexible and efficient use of digital documents. There exist some reality requirement of the privacy protection or bandwidth saving of a signed document. For example, privacy security is crucial for medical records. A personal medical record contains a patient's personal information. For individual privacy, the patient may not wish to reveal his/her critical diseases therapies to a surgeon, such as cancer. However, if the entire medical record is signed with a general digital signature, patients must disclose their entire privacy records to the surgeon for verification. Therefore, the privacy of personal medical record is incompatible with its integrity. This is called the "digital document sanitizing problem" [3]. Thus, the traditional digital signatures cannot assure both the integrity and confidentiality of a document.

Inspired by the group homomorphism of the RSA signature scheme, which satisfies $m_1{}^d \cdot m_2{}^d = (m_1 \cdot m_2)^d$, Rivest first investigated two novel homomorphic signature schemes in his series of talks [4]. They are prefix aggregation scheme and transitive signature scheme respectively. This type of homomorphic signature allows computation operations to be carried out on several signatures, and generates a new valid signature. For example, $\odot$ and $\otimes$ are binary operations, y, y' are the signatures on messages x and x' under signer's private key k', and they satisfy that $y \otimes_{k'} y' = Sig_{k'}(x \odot x')$. This type of homomorphism property has a broad reality applications, including medical application, multiparty computation, and public information disclosure.

Based on the works of Rivest [4], many research works about homomorphic signature are proposed. Johnson et al. [5] first formally defined the notion and security of homomorphic signatures. By comprehensively combining Merkle hash trees [6] with GGM tree construction [7], a particular homomorphic signature concept called "redactable signature scheme" (RSS) for binary operations was provided in [5]. Redactable signatures allow any redactor to modify the original signed message and generate a valid signature on the modified message without any help from the original signer. Thus, a patient can modify his personal medical record for privacy security by using RSS, such as Fig. 1.

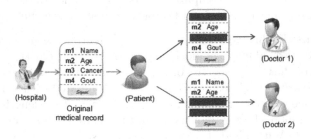

Fig. 1. A real-life application for redactable signatures.

With the underlying properties of accumulator technique [8], a set-homomorphic signature scheme was also proposed in [5]. This scheme simultaneously supports the union and subset operations on sets. However, the two homomorphic signature schemes in [5] have no redactable control structure, thus the signer can not prevent malicious removal operations of the redactors. This is called the "additional sanitizing attacks" [11].

Steinfeld et al. [9] proposed "Content Extraction Signature" (CES), a special homomorphic signature for editing, with "Content Extraction Access Structure" (CEAS), which prohibits the "additional sanitizing attacks". CEAS is an encoding of subsets of submessage indexes in the original document. CEAS belongs to fine-grained access control structure, and it specifies which subdocuments can be extracted by redactors legally. However, the encoding length of CEAS is exponential in n and without specific CEAS encoding mechanism given in this work. Later, Ateniese et al. [10] proposed the first "sanitizable signature scheme" (SSS) based on chameleon hash functions. Sanitizable signatures allow authorized semi-trusted censors to modify specified parts of a signed document, and come up with a valid signature without interacting with the signer. Only the sanitizer who has the secret key of the chameleon hash function can modify the signed message. Those SSSs can incontestably prove whether the signed document has been sanitized, with the property of accountability. State-of-the-art redactable signature constructions are mainly focus on documents represented by one specific data-structure, e.g., sets [11,12], lists [13,14], trees [15,16] or graphs [17,18] with different security models. Meer et al. [19] summarized the formal definitions of all the security properties about redactable and sanitizable signature schemes, and analyzed their relationships. Demirel et al. [20] investigated the state-of-the-art of specific variants of digital signature schemes, including homomorphic and sanitizable signature schemes.

Miyazaki et al. [11] proposed the first redactable scheme with disclosure condition control. In this scheme, a sanitizer can specify which parts of the signed document can be sanitized by subsequent sanitizers. However, the signature length of this scheme is relatively long, and reveals the number of sanitized portions. In order to solve above problems, Miyazaki et al. [12] proposed another digital signature sanitizing scheme with disclosure condition control based on bilinear maps. However, the computation cost of scheme [12] is relatively high. The goal of this paper is to optimal the performance of schemes [11,12].

Contributions: In this paper, we design an efficient and secure redactable signature scheme with submessage blocks redaction control structure (SRCS). The proposed scheme has the properties of correctness, privacy, unforgeability, transparency, which are formally defined and proved. Compared with schemes [11,12], the performance evaluate results show that the signature length of this new scheme is much more shorter than them, and the computation overhead is lower than scheme [12]. With a higher performance, this scheme can successfully guarantee the privacy and unforgeability of the signed messages and the transparency of redactable signature in a more efficient and flexible way.

The rest of this paper is organized as follows. Section 2 is devoted to the preliminaries required by this paper. The definition of redactable signature schemes is described in Sect. 3. Section 4 describes our proposed construction. Section 5 gives the security and performance analysis of proposed scheme. Section 6 concludes this paper.

2 Preliminaries

2.1 General Notations

The exp: $IR \rightarrow IR$ denotes the natural exponentiation function. Let $s \xleftarrow{R} S$ denote the assignment of a uniformly and independently distributed random element from the set S to the variable s. We use the notation $Pr[\textbf{Event}]_{\text{exp}}$ to denote the probability of event **Event** in experiment exp. The symbol '$\|$' denotes a concatenation of elements, which is uniquely reversible. The symbol $\perp \notin \{0,1\}^*$ denotes an error or an exception.

Integer $\lambda \in \mathbb{N}$ is the security parameter, which allows to control the security of schemes by controlling the length of secret keys. We say that a scheme achieves the security notion if the success probability for all efficient PPT (probabilistic polynomial time) attackers break the scheme is negligible function of λ (a function $f(\lambda)$ is called negligible if for each $\ell > 0$, there exists λ_0 such that $f(\lambda) < \frac{1}{\lambda^\ell}$ for all $\lambda > \lambda_0$).

In this paper a message (or data or document) will always be treated as a unordered set of blocks. Assume that a message $\mathbf{M}$ can be split into $n \in \mathbb{N}$ different blocks, each block $m_i \in \{0,1\}^*$ is the smallest modifiable unit. Notation $|\mathbf{M}|$ denotes the number of blocks, i.e., $|\mathbf{M}| = n$.

2.2 Standard Cryptographic Primitives

The definitions of standard cryptographic primitives which are used as building blocks to construct our scheme in Sect. 4 as following.

Short Signatures based on bilinear maps: Our scheme is based on the short signature, as developed by Boneh, Lynn, and Shacham in [21]. We use the following notation in this paper.

- G_1, G_2, and G_T are three multiplicative cyclic groups of prime order p.
- g_1 and g_2 are respectively generator of G_1 and G_2.
- ψ is an isomorphism from G_2 to G_1 with $\psi(g_2) = g_1$.
- e is a computable bilinear map $e: G_1 \times G_2 \rightarrow G_T$, which satisfies properties: (i) Bilinear: for all $u \in G_1$, $v \in G_2$ and $a, b \in \mathbb{Z}$, $e(u^a, v^b) = e(u,v)^{ab}$; (ii) Non-degenerate: $e(g_1, g_2) \neq 1$.

A short signature scheme employs a (t, ϵ)-Gap co-Diffie-Hellman group pair (G_1, G_2), where $|G_1| = |G_2| = p$. The signature σ in this scheme is an element of G_1. In this scheme, a full-domain hash function $H : \{0,1\}^* \rightarrow G_1$ is also employed, which is viewed as a random oracle [22], that can be instantiated by a cryptographic hash function such as SHA-1 [23] in practical use, or much more stronger like SHA-224, 256, 384 and 512 [24]. A *short signature scheme* consists of three algorithms: (KeyGen, Signing, Verification), as follows:

1. The key generation algorithm KeyGen picks randomly $x \xleftarrow{R} \mathbf{Z}_p$ and computes $v \leftarrow g_2^x \in G_2$. The signer's private key is x and public key is v.
2. The signing algorithm Signing takes as input the signer's private key x and a message $M \in \{0,1\}^*$, computes $h \leftarrow H(M) \in G_1$, and outputs the signature $\sigma \leftarrow h^x \in G_1$.
3. The verification algorithm Verification takes as input a public key $v \in G_2$, a message $M \in \{0,1\}^*$, a signature $\sigma \in G_1$, and computes $h \leftarrow H(M) \in G_1$. If (g_2, v, h, σ) is a valid co-Diffie-Hellman tuple, i.e., $e(\sigma, g_2) = e(h, v)$, algorithm Verification outputs True; if not, outputs $\perp$.

The short signature scheme on (G_1, G_2) described above is secure against existential forgery under adaptive chosen-message attacks in the random oracle model [21].

Message Commitment Schemes: A *message commitment scheme* allows one party to "commit" to a message m by sending a commitment value com, and allows another party to verify whether the given commitment value com for the message m is valid. A *message commitment scheme* consists of two algorithms (Gen, Com) such that:

1. The generation algorithm Gen takes as input the security parameter λ and outputs the commitment parameter string sp, i.e., sp $\leftarrow$ Gen(λ). For convenience, we assume that sp has length at least λ, and that λ can be determined from sp.
2. The commitment algorithm Com takes as input the commitment parameter string sp, a message string m, and a random string r which can not be too short. It outputs a commitment string com for the message m, and we write this as com $\leftarrow$ Com(sp, m; r). In the following, we will write Com(m; r) as the abbreviated formula of Com(sp, m; r).

The commitment algorithm Com is also used to *verify* whether the given commitment value com is a valid commitment of the message m under random string r. In detail, the committer de-commit com and reveal the message m by sending m, r to the receiver; the receiver recomputes com$' = $ Com(m; r), and verifies this by checking that com$' \overset{?}{=}$ com. A *message commitment scheme* has two main properties: (1) *Hiding*: The commitment com reveals nothing about the message m under random string r, if r is not given. (2) *Binding*: It is infeasible for the committer to find a matching random string r' for a new message $m' \neq m$, who satisfies Com(m'; r') = Com(m; r). A more detailed introduction to the security properties of a message commitment scheme, hiding and binding, please refer to [9].

Quasi-Commutative Hash Functions: Benaloh and Mare introduced a cryptographic hash-function which satisfies a special quasi-commutative property in paper [25].

Let $\mathcal{QCHF}_K : \mathcal{X}_K \times \mathcal{Y}_K \rightarrow \mathcal{X}_K$ denotes a keyed one-way quasi-commutative hash-function family, it satisfies the following properties:

- *Quasi-Commutativity*: For any $k \in K$, and for $\forall x \in \mathcal{X}_k$, $\forall y_1, y_2 \in \mathcal{Y}_k$, there exists $\mathcal{QCHF}_k(\mathcal{QCHF}_k(x, y_1), y_2) = \mathcal{QCHF}_k(\mathcal{QCHF}_k(x, y_2), y_1)$. It is computationally infeasible for a PPT adversary to distinguish the distributions of arbitrary $x \in \mathcal{X}_k$ and $\mathcal{QCHF}_k(x, y) : \forall x \in \mathcal{X}_k, \forall y \in \mathcal{Y}_k$.
- *Second-preimage resistance*: If given $k \xleftarrow{R} K$ and $x \xleftarrow{R} \mathcal{X}_k$, $y \xleftarrow{R} \mathcal{Y}_k$, it is computationally infeasible for a PPT adversary to find a pair of $x' \in \mathcal{X}_k$, $y' \in \mathcal{Y}_k$ ($x' \neq x$ or $y' \neq y$) such that $\mathcal{QCHF}_k(x', y') = \mathcal{QCHF}_k(x, y)$.
- *Preimage resistance*: If given $k \xleftarrow{R} K$ and a uniform hash value $h \in \mathcal{X}_k$, it is computationally infeasible for a PPT adversary to find a pair of string $x' \in \mathcal{X}_k$, $y' \in \mathcal{Y}_k$, such that $\mathcal{QCHF}_k(x', y') = h$.

An example of a one-way $\mathcal{QCHF}_k$ can be constructed by using modular exponentiation [25]. In details, let $N = pq$, where $p = 2p' + 1$, $q = 2q' + 1$, q, p, q', p' are all primes. On input of $r \xleftarrow{R} (\mathbb{Z}/n\mathbb{Z})^\times$ and the set of $\{m_1, m_2, \cdots, m_n\}$, we compute $d \leftarrow r^{\prod_{i=1}^{i=n} \mathcal{H}_p(m_i)} \pmod{N}$, where $\mathcal{H}_p : \{0,1\}^* \rightarrow \mathbb{P} \bigcap \mathbb{Z}_{N/4}$ is a cryptographic hash-function, modeled as a random oracle. More details about how to construct such a function can be found in paper [26].

The quasi-commutative property of $\mathcal{QCHF}_K$ allows it to be used as an accumulator. In this paper, we will denote $\mathcal{QCHF}_K(r, m_1; m_2; \cdots ; m_n)$ as the accumulation of message set $\{m_1, m_2, \cdots, m_n\} \in \mathcal{Y}_k$, where the initial value $r \in \mathcal{X}_k$. Any PPT adversary can not decide how many members m_i have been digested.

3 Definition of Redactable Signature Schemes

This section presents a general definition of a RSS, and then informally explains the requirements of a RSS scheme. The definitions of security notions for a RSS are also given thereinafter.

3.1 Definition of a RSS

Using the above terminology in Sect. 2, a Redactable Signature Scheme (RSS) is defined as follows.

Definition 1 (RSS). *A Redactable Signature Scheme RSS consists of four algorithms (Gen, Sig, Redct, Ver):*

1. *The key generation algorithm* Gen *takes a security parameter λ as input and generates a secret/public key pair $(sk; pk)$.*
2. *The signing generation algorithm* Sig *takes as input the signer's private key sk, a message $\boldsymbol{M} \in \{0,1\}^*$, a submessage redaction control structure $SRCS$, and outputs a redactable signature σ.*
3. *The signature redaction algorithm* Redact *takes a public key pk, a message $\mathbf{M}$, a redact submessage $\mathbf{M}'$ of message $\mathbf{M}$, a redactable signature σ, and outputs a redacted signature σ'.*

4. The signature verification algorithm Ver *takes a public key pk, a redacted submessage* $\mathbf{M}'$*, and a redacted signature* σ'*, and outputs a verification decision* $d \in \{Acc; Rej\}$.

The "Submessage Redaction Control Structure" (SRCS for short) is a dynamically updated coarse-grained access control structure, it controls which submessage blocks of the signed original message can be redacted for valid signatures. The SRCS contains three control statuses, they are respectively "Removed" (REM for short), "Redactable" (RED for short) and "Prohibited to be removed" (PRE for short). In detail, those submessages with REM status means that they have been removed from original message, those submessages with PRE status means that they must be left anytime, and those submessages with RED status means that they can be removed or prohibited to be removed afterwards. The SRCS is under the common control of the signer and redactors. Specifically, the original signer and the first $N - 1$ redactors together assign which submessage blocks can be modified by the subsequent N-th redactor.

3.2 Security Definitions of a RSS

This subsection discusses the security definitions of a RSS, i.e. those which prevent undesirable dishonest operations.

Redactable signature is existential forgery under the standard notion of EUF-CMA. Because redactor can generate a valid signature for any authorized submessage of the signed message. The definition of unforgeability for the RSS we proposed in Sect. 4 can be informally stated as follows.

Definition 2 (Unforgeability). *It is infeasible for an attacker to produce a message/signature pair* $(\mathbf{M}^*, \sigma^*)$*, such that: (i)* σ^* *passes the verification test for* $\mathbf{M}^*$*, and (ii)* $\mathbf{M}^*$ *is either (A) Not a submessage of any message queried to the signing oracle, or (B) Is a submessage of any message queried to the signing oracle, but contains no the submessage whose redactable control condition is "PRE" in original message queried to the signing oracle. We say that a redactable signature scheme for sets is unforgeable, if for any efficient (PPT) adversary* $\mathcal{A}$*, the probability that the game depicted in* **Experiment 1** *returns 1 is negligible (as a function of* λ*).*

> **Experiment 1: Unforgeability**$_{\mathcal{A}}^{RSS}(\lambda)$
> $(pk, sk) \leftarrow$ **KeyGen**(1^λ)
> $(\mathbf{M}^*, \sigma^*) \leftarrow \mathcal{A}(1^\lambda, pk, \mathbf{Sign}(sk, \cdot))$
> $d \leftarrow$ **Verify**$(pk, \mathbf{M}^*, \sigma^*)$
> if $d = Acc$ and for all j,
> either $\mathbf{M}^* \not\subset \mathbf{M}_j$ or $PRE \in \mathbf{C}(\mathbf{M}_j \setminus \mathbf{M}^*)$ return 1
> else   return 0

A secure redactable signature scheme should not leak any information about the content of the removed submessages. We note that a similar requirement has been defined in the context of CES [9]. The definition of privacy can be informally stated as follows.

Definition 3 (Privacy). *An adversary should not be able to derive any additional information besides what can be derived from the received message/signature pair. We say that a redactable signature scheme for sets with submessage redaction control structure is private, iff for any efficient PPT adversary $\mathcal{A}$, the probability that the game depicted in* **Experiment 2** *returns 1 is negligible close to $\frac{1}{2}$ (as a function of λ).*

> **Experiment 2: Privacy$_{\mathcal{A}}^{RSS}(\lambda)$**
> $(pk, sk) \leftarrow \mathbf{KeyGen}(1^\lambda)$
> $(\mathbf{M_0}, \mathbf{M_1}, m_0, m_1) \leftarrow \mathcal{A}(1^\lambda, pk)$
> if $\mathbf{M_0} \setminus \{m_0\} \neq \mathbf{M_1} \setminus \{m_1\}$, return $\perp$
> $b \xleftarrow{R} \{0, 1\}$
> $\sigma_S \leftarrow \mathbf{Sign}(sk, \mathbf{M_b}); \sigma_R \leftarrow \mathbf{Redact}(pk, \mathbf{M_b}, m_b)$
> $b' \leftarrow \mathcal{A}(1^\lambda, pk, \sigma_R)$
> if $b = b'$ then   return 1
> else   return 0

Except for unforgeability and privacy, a secure RSS should also have transparency, i.e. a verifier can not judge whether a signature is created by the original signer or by the subsequent redactors. The definition of transparency can be informally stated as follows.

Definition 4 (Transparency). *An attacker should not be able to decide whether a signature has been created by the signer, or through the redaction algorithm* **Redaction***. It is also difficult for verifier to know how many submessage blocks of the original signed message are redacted. We say that a scheme RSS for sets is transparent, iff for any efficient (PPT) adversary $\mathcal{A}$, the probability that the game depicted in* **Experiment 3** *returns 1 is negligible (as a function of λ).*

> **Experiment 3: Transparency$_{\mathcal{A}}^{RSS}(\lambda)$**
> $(pk, sk) \leftarrow \mathbf{KeyGen}(1^\lambda)$
> $(\mathbf{M^*}, \mathbf{M'}) \leftarrow \mathcal{A}(1^\lambda, pk, \mathbf{Sign}(sk, \cdot), \mathbf{Redact}(pk, \cdot, \cdot, \cdot))$
> $b \xleftarrow{R} \{0, 1\}$
> if $b = 0$
> $\sigma_S \leftarrow \mathbf{Sign}(sk, \mathbf{M^*}); \sigma' \leftarrow \mathbf{Redact}(pk, \sigma_S, \mathbf{M^*}, \mathbf{M'})$
> if $b = 1$
> $\sigma' \leftarrow \mathbf{Sign}(sk, \mathbf{M^*} \setminus \mathbf{M'})$
> $d \leftarrow \mathcal{A}(1^\lambda, pk, \sigma', \mathbf{M^*}, \mathbf{M'})$
> if $d = b$ return 1
> else   return 0

4   Our Construction

In this section, we present an efficient and secure redactable signature scheme with submessage blocks redaction control structure (SRCS). In this scheme, the signature runs the key generation algorithm and gets the private key and public key pair. Assume there exists a message $\mathbf{M}'$ which need the signer to sign, the signer computes some additional information for each submessage and then signs the hash of the concatenate information. Apart from that, the signer also allocates a redaction condition for each submessage. The redactor can execute the redaction operation only if it satisfies the redaction condition set by the signer. Our proposed scheme consists four algorithms: Key Generation, Signing, Redaction and Verification.

Key Generation. The signer picks random $x \xleftarrow{R} \mathbf{Z}_p$ and computes $v \leftarrow g_2{}^x$. The signer's private key is x and public key is v. Additionally, the signer also chooses a cryptographic and quasi-commutative hash-function $\mathcal{QCHF}_k \leftarrow \mathcal{QCHF}_{\mathcal{K}}$.

Signing. To sign an unordered message set $\mathbf{M}'$, the signer performs the following steps:

1. Divide original message set into n' submessages set $\mathbf{M}' = \{m_1, \cdots, m_{n'}\}$. Choose $n - n'$ random submessage $m_j \in \{0,1\}^*$, where $n' \leq n$. Then the signer insert them into $\mathbf{M}'$, and get message set $\mathbf{M} = \{m_1, \cdots, m_n\}$.
2. Choose a random nonce $id \leftarrow \{0,1\}^\lambda$ as the ID of the message set $\mathbf{M}$. Set $\tilde{m}_0 := id$ and $\tilde{m}_i := id \parallel m_i$ $(1 \leq i \leq n)$, where $\parallel$ denotes a concatenation, which is uniquely reversible.
3. Choose $r \xleftarrow{R} \mathcal{X}_k$, i.e., $r \xleftarrow{R} (\mathbb{Z}/n\mathbb{Z})^\times$ for the hash-function by Benaloh et al.
4. Generate two λ-bit length random numbers r_i for each submessage $\tilde{m}_i$ and S_i $(0 \leq i \leq n)$, where λ is the security parameter.
5. Assign redaction control condition c_i for each submessage $\tilde{m}_i$, i.e., $c_j = PRE$ is assigned to $\tilde{m}_0$ and those submessages m_j of original message must be left anytime considered by the signer. $c_j = REM$ is assigned to two types of submessages: (i) Those $n - n'$ submessages m_j chosen by the signer randomly; (ii) Those sensitive submessages considered by signer should be removed. Besides, other submessages are assigned by RED. Thus, $c_i \in \{REM, RED, PRE\}$ $(1 \leq i \leq n)$. We set the submessage redaction control structure $SRCS = \{c_0, c_1, \cdots, c_n\}$, which is dynamically updated.
6. Calculate two points $A_i = (0, \mathsf{Com}(\tilde{m}_i, r_i))$ and $B_i = (2, H(S_i))$ $(0 \leq i \leq n)$. Then the signer calculates the circle O_i whose diameter is $A_i B_i$. The center and radius of the circle O_i respectively are $(1, Q_i)$ and R_i.
7. Accumulate each element $Q_i \parallel R_i$ and r using $\mathcal{QCHF}_k$, the accumulate value $d \leftarrow \mathcal{QCHF}_k(r, Q_0 \parallel R_0, Q_1 \parallel R_1, \cdots, Q_n \parallel R_n)$.
8. Computer $h \leftarrow H(d \parallel id \parallel r)$, where the full-domain hash function $H : \{0,1\}^* \rightarrow G_1$, viewed as a random oracle. Thus, $h \in G_1$. Then, sign the hash value $\sigma_S \leftarrow h^x$, where $\sigma_S \in G_1$.
9. If $c_i = PRE$, the signer removes S_i. If $c_i = RED$, the redactor removes m_i and r_i.
10. Output σ_S, id, r, Q_i $(0 \leq i \leq n)$, $m_i \| r_i$ $(c_i = PRE$ or RED, $1 \leq i \leq n)$, S_i $(c_i = RED$ or REM, $1 \leq i \leq n)$, and the dynamically updated submessage redaction control structure $SRCS$.

Redaction. To redact a subset $\mathbf{M}^*$ of message set $\mathbf{M}$, the redactor performs:

1. Check the validity of σ_S using Verification algorithm. If the signature is not valid, return $\bot$.
2. If $\mathbf{M}^* \not\subseteq \mathbf{M}$, return $\bot$.
3. If $\mathbf{M}^* \subseteq \mathbf{M}$, and the redaction control condition c_j according to each submessage $m_j \in \mathbf{M}^*$ is not "RED", return $\bot$. It means that the redactor only can redact those submessages whose redactable control condition is "RED".
4. Assign one of the three redaction control conditions (REM, RED, PRE) to each submessage $m_j \in \mathbf{M}^*$.
5. If $c_j = REM$, the redactor removes $m_j \parallel r_j$. If $c_j = PRE$, the redactor removes S_j. If $c_j = RED$, the redactor does nothing.
6. Output σ_S, id, r, Q_t $(0 \le t \le n)$, $m_t \parallel r_t$ $(c_t = PRE$ or RED, $1 \le t \le n)$, S_t $(c_t = RED$ or REM, $1 \le t \le n)$, and the updated submessage redaction control structure $SRCS$.

Verification. The verifier receives the original signed message (or one redacted by any other redactors), which consists of $\sigma_S{}'$, id', r', $Q_i{}'$ $(0 \le i \le n)$, $m_i{}' \parallel r_i{}'$ $(c_i{}' = PRE$ or RED, $1 \le i \le n)$, $S_i{}'$ $(c_i{}' = RED$ or REM, $1 \le i \le n)$, and $SRCS'$. To verify the validity of the signature, the verifier performs:

1. If $c_i{}' = RED$, the verifier firstly computes two points $A_i{}' = (0, \mathsf{Com}(\tilde{m}_i{}', r_i{}'))$ and $B_i{}' = (2, H(S_i{}'))$. Then he/she calculates the circle $O_i{}'$ whose diameter is $A_i{}' B_i{}'$. $(1, Q_i{}'')$ and $R_i{}'$ are respectively the center and radius of the circle $O_i{}'$. If $Q_i{}'' \ne Q_i{}'$, return $\bot$.
2. If $c_i{}' = PRE$, the verifier computes one point $A_i{}' = (0, \mathsf{Com}(\tilde{m}_i{}', r_i{}'))$, then calculates the distance $R_i{}'$ between points $A_i{}'$ and $(1, Q_i{}')$.
3. If $c_i{}' = REM$, the verifier computes one point $B_i{}' = (2, H(S_i{}'))$, then calculates the distance $R_i{}'$ between points $B_i{}'$ and $(1, Q_i{}')$.
4. Accumulate each element $Q_i{}' \parallel R_i{}'$ and r' using $\mathcal{QCHF}_k$, the accumulate value $d' \leftarrow \mathcal{QCHF}_k(r, Q_0{}' \parallel R_1{}', Q_1{}' \parallel R_1{}', \cdots, Q_n{}' \parallel R_n{}')$.
5. Compute $h' \leftarrow H(d' \parallel id' \parallel r')$, and verify whether $e(\sigma_S{}', g_2) = e(h', v)$ or not. Return 1, iff the equality holds, otherwise, return $\bot$.

5 Security and Performance Analysis of the Proposed Scheme

The correctness of our proposed scheme in Sect. 4 is obvious. In addition, the operations of signer/redactors assigning one of the three redactable control conditions to each submessage m_i are the same. Therefore, an attacker can not be able to decide whether a signature has been created by the signer, or redacted by a redactor. In addition, the signer insets some random submessages into the original message, so any redactors can not derive there are how many submessages in original message. Specifically, the proposed scheme does not reveal the number of original submessage blocks. Thus the transparency of our proposed scheme is also obvious.

5.1   Unforgeability of Our Proposed Scheme

In this subsection, a related theorem will be given and proven to show the unforgeability of our proposed scheme.

Theorem 1. *If the hash function* H *and* $QCHF_k$ *are second-pre-image resistant and pre-image resistant, the commitment scheme* Com *has the relaxed-binding property (the commitment random number* r *is randomly chosen, and not under the control of the attacker), and the signature scheme based on Gap Diffie-Hellman groups is existentially unforgeable under adaptive chosen message attacks in the random oracle model, then our proposed scheme is unforgeable, as defined in Definition 2.*

Proof. The proposed scheme uses a cryptographic hash function H such as SHA1, thus the proof of security of cryptographic hash function is omitted. A message commitment scheme can be constructed with a cryptographic hash function. The proof of the relaxed-binding of message commitment scheme, a similar proof can be found in paper [9]. In addition, the detail proof process about second-pre-image resistent and pre-image resistent of $QCHF_K$, is similar to the proof of [13]. Due to space limitations, this article also omits it here.

If there is an attacker $\mathcal{A}$ for proposed scheme succeeds to forge a signed message with non-negligible probability, then an attacker $\mathcal{A}_{co-CDH}$ to break the signature scheme based on Gap Diffie-Hellman groups with non-negligible probability. We construct an attacker $\mathcal{A}_{co-CDH}$ for signature scheme based on Gap Diffie-Hellman groups by using an attacker $\mathcal{A}$ for proposed scheme, i.e., attacker $\mathcal{A}_{co-CDH}$ simulates the challenger and interacts with forger $\mathcal{A}$ as follows:

Setup. g_2 is a generator of G_2. Attacker $\mathcal{A}_{co-CDH}$ is given g_2, $u \in G_2$ and $h \in G_1$, where $u = g_2{}^a$. Its goal is to output $h^a \in G_1$. In order to achieve this, attacker $\mathcal{A}_{co-CDH}$ chooses a hash-function $QCHF_k \in QCHF_K$, and passes k to forger $\mathcal{A}$ to use the same hash-function. Besides $\mathcal{A}_{co-CDH}$ gives forger $\mathcal{A}$ the generator g_2 and the public key $u \cdot g_2{}^\alpha \in G_2$, where $\alpha \xleftarrow{R} \mathbb{Z}_p$.

H-queries. Firstly, forger $\mathcal{A}$ gets $F = d\|id\|r$ about message $\mathbf{M} = \{m_1, \cdots, m_n\}$ from Signature queries stage. At any time forger $\mathcal{A}$ can query F to the random oracle H. To respond to these queries, attacker $\mathcal{A}_{co-CDH}$ maintains a list of tuples $< F_j, \omega_j, \beta_j, \gamma_j >$ as explained below. We refer to this list as the H-list, which is initially empty. When forger $\mathcal{A}$ queries the oracle H by using F_i, attacker $\mathcal{A}_{co-CDH}$ responds as follows:

1. If the query F_i already appears on the H-list in a tuple $< F_i, \omega_i, \beta_i, \gamma_i >$, then $\mathcal{A}_{co-CDH}$ responds with $H(F_i) = \omega_i \in G_1$. Otherwise, $\mathcal{A}_{co-CDH}$ generates a random coin $\gamma_i \in \{0, 1\}$ such that $Pr[\gamma_i = 0] = \frac{1}{q_s+1}$. $\mathcal{A}_{co-CDH}$ picks a random $\beta_i \xleftarrow{R} \mathbb{Z}_p$.
2. If $\gamma_i = 0$, $\mathcal{A}_{co-CDH}$ computes $\omega_i \leftarrow h \cdot \psi(g_2)^{\beta_i} \in G_1$. If $\gamma_i = 1$, $\mathcal{A}_{co-CDH}$ computes $\omega_i \leftarrow \psi(g_2)^{\beta_i} \in G_1$.
3. $\mathcal{A}_{co-CDH}$ adds the tuple $< F_i, \omega_i, \beta_i, \gamma_i >$ to the H-list and responds to forger $\mathcal{A}$ by setting $H(F_i) = \omega_i \in G_1$.

Note that either way ω_i is uniform in G_1 and is independent of forger $\mathcal{A}$'s current view as required.

Signature queries. Let $\mathbf{M} = \{m_1, \cdots, m_n\}$ be a signature query issued by $\mathcal{A}$. $\mathcal{A}_{co-CDH}$ responds to this query as follows:

1. $\mathcal{A}_{co-CDH}$ runs the same as the Signing algorithm of our proposed scheme from step 1 to step 7, and gets $F = d\|id\|r$.
2. $\mathcal{A}_{co-CDH}$ runs the same as the above H-queries algorithm from step 1 to step 5 for responding to H-queries to obtain a $\omega_i \in G_1$ such that $H(F_i) = \omega_i$. Let $< F_i, \omega_i, \beta_i, \gamma_i >$ be the corresponding tuple on the H-list. If $\gamma_i = 0$, then $\mathcal{A}_{co-CDH}$ reports failure and terminates.
3. Otherwise, we know $\gamma_i = 1$ and hence $\omega_i = \psi(g_2)^{\beta_i} \in G_1$. Define $\sigma_i = \psi(u)^{\omega_i} \cdot \psi(g_2)^{\alpha \cdot \beta_i}$. Observe that $\sigma_i = \omega_i^{a+\alpha}$ and therefore σ_i is a valid signature on F_i under the public key $u \cdot g_2^{\alpha} = g_2^{a+\alpha}$. $\mathcal{A}_{co-CDH}$ gives σ_i to forger $\mathcal{A}$.

Output. Forger $\mathcal{A}$ eventually produces a forged signed message document, which consists of $\sigma_S{}^*$, id^*, r^*, Q_i^* $(0 \le i \le n)$, $m_i^*\|r_i^*$ $(c_i^* = PRE$ or RED, $1 \le i \le n)$, S_i^* $(c_i^* = RED$ or REM, $1 \le i \le n)$, and the redaction control structure $SRCS$. The message set $\mathbf{M}^* = \{m_1^*, \cdots, m_n^*\}$ is not a subset of any message set queries to signing oracle.

$\mathcal{A}_{co-CDH}$ runs its hash algorithm at each $\tilde{m}_i^*$ and obtains its corresponding tuples $< F_i{}^*, \omega_i{}^*, \beta_i{}^*, \gamma_i{}^* >$. If there is no tuple on the H-list containing $F_i{}^*$ then $\mathcal{A}_{co-CDH}$ issues a query itself for $H(F_i{}^*)$ to ensure that such a tuple exists. We assume $\sigma_S{}^*$ is a valid signature on $F_i{}^*$ under the given public key; if it is not, $\mathcal{A}_{co-CDH}$ reports failure and terminates. Now $\mathcal{A}_{co-CDH}$ proceeds only if $\gamma_i{}^* = 0$, otherwise $\mathcal{A}_{co-CDH}$ declares failure and halts. Since $\gamma_i{}^* = 0$, it follows that $H(F_i{}^*) = \omega_i{}^* = h \cdot \psi(g_2)^{\beta_i{}^*}$. Hence, $\sigma_S{}^* = h^{a+\alpha} \cdot \psi(g_2)^{\beta_i{}^*(a+\alpha)}$. Then, $\mathcal{A}_{co-CDH}$ outputs the required h^a as $h^a \leftarrow \sigma_S{}^*/(h^{\alpha} \cdot \psi(u)^{\beta_i{}^*} \cdot \psi(g_2)^{\alpha \cdot \beta_i{}^*})$.

This completes the description of the attacker $\mathcal{A}_{co-CDH}$ using the forger $\mathcal{A}$. It remains to be shown that attacker $\mathcal{A}_{co-CDH}$ solves the given instance of the co-CDH problem in (G_1, G_2) with probability at least ϵ'. To do so, we analyze the three events needed for $\mathcal{A}_{co-CDH}$ to succeed:

- ε_1: $\mathcal{A}_{co-CDH}$ does not abort as a result of any of $\mathcal{A}$'s signature queries.
- ε_2: $\mathcal{A}$ generates a valid but forged signature.
- ε_3: Event ε_2 occurs and $\gamma_i{}^* = 0$ for the tuple containing $F_i{}^*$ on the H-list.

$\mathcal{A}_{co-CDH}$ succeeds if all of these events happen. The probability $Pr[\varepsilon_1 \wedge \varepsilon_3]$ is:

$$Pr[\varepsilon_1 \wedge \varepsilon_3] = Pr[\varepsilon_1] \cdot Pr[\varepsilon_2 \mid \varepsilon_1] \cdot Pr[\varepsilon_3 \mid \varepsilon_1 \wedge \varepsilon_2] \ge (1 - \tfrac{1}{q_s+1})^{q_s} \cdot \epsilon \cdot \tfrac{1}{q_s+1}.$$

This inequality shows that if the attacker $\mathcal{A}$ succeeds in forging a signed message with non-negligible probability ϵ, then the attacker $\mathcal{A}_{co-CDH}$ for computational co-Diffie-Hellman problem in G_1, G_2 succeeds with non-negligible probability at least $(1 - \tfrac{1}{q_s+1})^{q_s} \cdot \epsilon \cdot \tfrac{1}{q_s+1}$. Its running time t' is at most $t + c_{G_1}(q_H + 2q_s)$, where c_{G_1} is the running time required for an exponentiation in G_1, t is $\mathcal{A}$'s running time. This completes the proof. $\qquad\square$

5.2   Privacy of Our Proposed Scheme

In this subsection, in order to show the privacy of our proposed scheme, a related theorem will be given first and the proof follows.

Theorem 2. *If the message commitment scheme* Com *has the hiding property, then our proposed scheme has the privacy property, as defined in Definition 3.*

Proof. The detail proof process about the hiding property of message commitment scheme Com can be found in paper [9]. Due to space limitations, we omit it here. □

5.3   Performance Analysis

In this subsection, we compare the performance of our proposed scheme with schemes [11,12]. Without loss of generality, we assume that the length of all auxiliary points are equal, i.e., $P_i \in \{0,1\}^\lambda$ [11] and $Q_i \in \{0,1\}^\lambda$ [12] for some fixed $\lambda \in \mathbb{N}$. λ is security parameter of the system. We also assume that 320 bits DSA signature is used in scheme [11]. Schemes [12] and ours adopt 170 bits short signature [21]. This does not impose any restriction, but makes the performance analysis clearer.

Table 1. Comparison of efficiency and functionality

Schemes	Original signature size	Signature computation cost		
		Original	Redact	Verify
[11]	$4n\lambda + l[\mathbf{M}] + l[DS] + l[SRCS]$	$2nt[H] + t[DS] + nt[Lin]$	1	$2nt[H] + t[Ver]$
[12]	$l[\mathbf{M}] + l[ID] + (1+n)l[SS] + l[SRCS]$	$(n+1)(t[H] + t[SS]) + nt[Mul]$	$\varsigma t[Div]$	$nt[H] + (n+1)t[Pair]$
Ours	$(n+1)\lambda + l[\mathbf{M}] + l[ID] + l[SS] + l[SRCS]$	$(2+2n)t[H] + t[SS] + nt[Lin]$	1	$(2+2n)t[H] + t[Pair]$

($l[*]$ is the length of $*$; Lin represents linear operation; Mul represents multiply operation; Div represents division operation; $t[*]$ is the running time of the algorithm $*$; ς denotes the number of removed submessages; Ver is the verification algorithm of a standard digital signature scheme DS;
n is the number of submessages in the original message; $Pair$ represents bilinear pairing verification algorithm of short signature SS.)

The comparison result of schemes [11,12] and ours in terms of signature size, signature computation costs is listed in Table 1. The results show that the signature length of our proposed scheme is shorter than that of schemes [11,12]. Furthermore, with the same properties, the signature computation cost of our proposed scheme is smaller than that of scheme [12]. The results of comparison show that our scheme is much more efficient and practical, with a higher performance.

6 Conclusion

In this paper, we present an efficient and secure redactable signature scheme with submessage blocks redaction control structure (SRCS). This scheme has the security properties of unforgeability, privacy, and transparency, which are formally defined and proved. Compared with state-of-the-art redactable signature schemes, the proposed scheme has a low communication overhead and computational cost. Therefore, this scheme can be successfully guarantee the privacy and unforgeability of signed messages and the transparency of redactable signature in a more efficient and flexible way.

Acknowledgment. This work is supported by National Natural Science Foundation of China (61472083, 61402110), Program for New Century Excellent Talents in Fujian University (JA14067), Distinguished Young Scholars Fund of Fujian (2016J06013), and Fujian Normal University Innovative Research Team (No. IRTL1207).

References

1. Diffie, W., Hellman, M.: New directions in cryptography. IEEE Trans. Inf. Theory **22**(6), 644–654 (1976)
2. Goldwasser, S., Micali, S., Rivest, R.L.: A digital signature scheme secure against adaptive chosen-message attacks. SIAM J. Comput. **17**(2), 281–308 (1988)
3. Miyazaki, K., Susaki, S., Iwamura, M., Matsumoto, T., Sasaki, R., Yoshiura, H.: Digital documents sanitizing problem. Inst. Electron. Inf. Commun. Eng. Tech. Rep. **103**(195), 61–67 (2003)
4. Rivest, R.L.: Two signature schemes. Talk given at Cambridge University, 17 October 2000. http://people.csail.mit.edu/rivest/pubs.html
5. Johnson, R., Molnar, D., Song, D., Wagner, D.: Homomorphic signature schemes. In: Preneel, B. (ed.) CT-RSA 2002. LNCS, vol. 2271, pp. 244–262. Springer, Heidelberg (2002). doi:10.1007/3-540-45760-7_17
6. Becker, G.: Merkle signature schemes, merkle trees and their cryptanalysis. Ruhr-University Bochum, Technical report (2008)
7. Goldreich, O., Goldwasser, S., Micali, S.: How to construct random functions. J. ACM (JACM) **33**(4), 792–807 (1986)
8. Derler, D., Hanser, C., Slamanig, D.: Revisiting cryptographic accumulators, additional properties and relations to other primitives. In: Nyberg, K. (ed.) CT-RSA 2015. LNCS, vol. 9048, pp. 127–144. Springer, Cham (2015). doi:10.1007/978-3-319-16715-2_7
9. Steinfeld, R., Bull, L., Zheng, Y.: Content extraction signatures. In: Kim, K. (ed.) ICISC 2001. LNCS, vol. 2288, pp. 285–304. Springer, Heidelberg (2002). doi:10.1007/3-540-45861-1_22
10. Ateniese, G., Chou, D.H., Medeiros, B., Tsudik, G.: Sanitizable signatures. In: Vimercati, S.C., Syverson, P., Gollmann, D. (eds.) ESORICS 2005. LNCS, vol. 3679, pp. 159–177. Springer, Heidelberg (2005). doi:10.1007/11555827_10
11. Miyazaki, K., Iwamura, M., Matsumoto, T., et al.: Digitally signed document sanitizing scheme with disclosure condition control. IEICE Trans. Fundam. Electron. Commun. Comput. Sci. **88**(1), 239–246 (2005)

12. Miyazaki, K., Hanaoka, G., Imai, H.: Digitally signed document sanitizing scheme based on bilinear maps. In: Proceedings of the 2006 ACM Symposium on Information, Computer and Communications Security, pp. 343–354. ACM (2006)
13. Pohls, H.C., Samelin, K., Posegga, J., et al.: Length-hiding redactable signatures from one-way accumulators in O(n). Technical report MIP-1201, Faculty of Computer Science and Mathematics (FIM), University of Passau (2012)
14. Derler, D., Pöhls, H.C., Samelin, K., Slamanig, D.: A general framework for redactable signatures and new constructions. In: Kwon, S., Yun, A. (eds.) ICISC 2015. LNCS, vol. 9558, pp. 3–19. Springer, Cham (2016). doi:10.1007/978-3-319-30840-1_1
15. Chang, E.-C., Lim, C.L., Xu, J.: Short redactable signatures using random trees. In: Fischlin, M. (ed.) CT-RSA 2009. LNCS, vol. 5473, pp. 133–147. Springer, Heidelberg (2009). doi:10.1007/978-3-642-00862-7_9
16. Brzuska, C., et al.: Redactable signatures for tree-structured data: definitions and constructions. In: Zhou, J., Yung, M. (eds.) ACNS 2010. LNCS, vol. 6123, pp. 87–104. Springer, Heidelberg (2010). doi:10.1007/978-3-642-13708-2_6
17. Kundu, A., Bertino, E.: How to authenticate graphs without leaking. In: Proceedings of the 13th International Conference on Extending Database Technology, pp. 609–620. ACM (2010)
18. Kundu, A., Bertino, E.: Privacy-preserving authentication of trees and graphs. Int. J. Inf. Secur. 12(6), 467–494 (2013)
19. Meer, H., Pöhls, H.C., Posegga, J., Samelin, K.: On the relation between redactable and sanitizable signature schemes. In: Jürjens, J., Piessens, F., Bielova, N. (eds.) ESSoS 2014. LNCS, vol. 8364, pp. 113–130. Springer, Cham (2014). doi:10.1007/978-3-319-04897-0_8
20. Slamanig, D., Derler, D., Hanser, C., et al. (TUG): Overview of Functional and Malleable Signature Schemes (2015)
21. Boneh, D., Lynn, B., Shacham, H.: Short signatures from the Weil pairing. In: Boyd, C. (ed.) ASIACRYPT 2001. LNCS, vol. 2248, pp. 514–532. Springer, Heidelberg (2001). doi:10.1007/3-540-45682-1_30
22. Eastlake 3rd, D., Jones, P.: US secure hash algorithm 1 (SHA1) (2001)
23. Dang, Q.H.: Secure hash standard. National Institute of Standards and Technology, Gaithersburg, MD, Technical report, August 2015
24. Bellare, M., Rogaway, P.: Random oracles are practical: a paradigm for designing efficient protocols. In: Proceedings of the 1st ACM Conference on Computer and Communications Security, pp. 62–73. ACM (1993)
25. Benaloh, J., Mare, M.: One-way accumulators: a decentralized alternative to digital signatures. In: Helleseth, T. (ed.) EUROCRYPT 1993. LNCS, vol. 765, pp. 274–285. Springer, Heidelberg (1994). doi:10.1007/3-540-48285-7_24
26. Barić, N., Pfitzmann, B.: Collision-free accumulators and fail-stop signature schemes without trees. In: Fumy, W. (ed.) EUROCRYPT 1997. LNCS, vol. 1233, pp. 480–494. Springer, Heidelberg (1997). doi:10.1007/3-540-69053-0_33

New Publicly Verifiable Computation for Batch Matrix Multiplication

Xiaoyu Zhang[1]($\boxtimes$), Tao Jiang[1], Kuan-Ching Li[2], and Xiaofeng Chen[1]

[1] State Key Laboratory of Integrated Service Networks (ISN),
Xidian University, Xi'an, People's Republic of China
moliyanyan@163.com, jiangt2009@gmail.com, xfchen@xidian.edu.cn
[2] School of Computer Science and Information Engineering,
Providence University, Taichung, Taiwan
kuancli@gm.pu.edu.tw

Abstract. With the prevalence of cloud computing, the resource constrained clients are trended to outsource their computation-intensive tasks to the cloud server. Although outsourcing computation paradigm brings many benefits for both clients and cloud server, it causes some security challenges. In this paper, we focus on the outsourcing computation of matrix multiplication, and propose a new publicly verifiable computation scheme for batch matrix multiplication. Different from traditional matrix computation outsourcing model, the outsourcing task of our scheme is to compute MX_i for group of clients, where X_i is a private matrix chosen by different clients and M is a public matrix given by a data center beforehand. Based on the two techniques of privacy-preserving matrix transformation and matrix digest, our scheme can protect the secrecy of the client's private matrix X_i and dramatically reduce the computation cost in both the key generation and the compute phases. The security analysis shows that the proposed scheme can also achieve the desired security properties under the co-CDH assumption.

Keywords: Publicly verifiable computation · Public delegation · Batch matrix multiplication · Privacy protection

1 Introduction

In recent years, cloud computing has been widely applied to various information systems [1–6], where clients can outsource heavy computing tasks to the cloud, and realizes the dream of computing as a service. However, the computing tasks in cloud computing usually contain some sensitive information, which inevitably suffer from security challenge. More seriously, in cloud computing, clients will lose local control of their personal data, which makes the protection of private information and the verification of computing results more difficult. Therefore, the security and privacy preservation become more and more important and new solutions are needed in this area.

© Springer International Publishing AG 2017
M.H.A. Au et al. (Eds.): GPC 2017, LNCS 10232, pp. 53–65, 2017.
DOI: 10.1007/978-3-319-57186-7_5

Matrix computation is a basic computational problem in scientific and engineering fields, which has large quantities of applications [7–10]. Specially, the security and privacy of outsourcing matrix computation, including correctness, confidentiality and verifiability of cloud computing results, become two of the most important challenges. The research on secure and privacy-preserving outsourcing matrix computation and designing efficient and verifiable schemes to thwart the challenge is of both theoretical and practical significance in cloud computing. Recently, Fiore et al. [11] and Zhang et al. [12] exploit algebraic PRFs for publicly verifiable matrix computing. However, the two solutions above only allow the client who outsourced the computing task to submit the matrices as inputs for outsourcing matrix multiplication. Therefore, their schemes support private matrix multiplication while not the public delegation requirement. Zhang et al. [13] propose a scheme to provide public delegation and public verification for outsourcing of matrix multiplication. Instead of using algebraic PRFs, the scheme in [13] uses mathematical properties of matrices. The scheme in [13] is secure under the multiple decisional Diffie-Hellman and eXternal Diffie-Hellman assumptions. Very recently, different from traditional outsourcing matrix multiplication computation, where clients need to provide two private matrices to the cloud server [8], Elkhiyaoui et al. [14] firstly focus on the scenario where clients share a public matrix M and each of them only outsources one private matrix X_i for matrix multiplication. Moreover, Elkhiyaoui et al. [14] design an efficient scheme to provide publicly verifiable matrix multiplication, which they call verifiable delegation of computation. However, they do not consider the secrecy of client's matrix, where the client send the plaintext matrix to the server without any blinding treatment. In some situation, such as in the fields of genetic research and educational administration system, the confidential protection of clients' private data and providing verifiable computation result are necessary.

Thus, in this paper, we investigate the outsourcing matrix multiplication among multiple clients in cloud computing environment. We consider both the security and delegation of matrix computation of outsourcing computing in cloud computing and design a secure and verifiable matrix multiplication scheme to protect the confidentiality of client's private matrix and guarantee the correctness of the computing results. However, we find that an auxiliary matrix has to be computed for the cloud to compute the proof, which is inefficient in computation at public matrix provider. To further reduce the computing overhead, we introduce matrix digest technique [15] into our scheme. It can convert the two-dimensional matrix into a one-dimensional vector and the process is irreversible, which can provide security guarantee while significantly reduce the computation overhead of our scheme.

Our Contributions. The contributions of this paper are two folds:

- We design a delegable outsourcing matrix multiplication scheme supporting public verification and public delegation. Moreover, the privacy-preserving matrix transformation technique is firstly leveraged to blind the clients' private matrices in this scenario, which can protect the secrecy of clients' sensitive content in the matrices. Besides, we provide the security analysis of our

scheme, which reveal that our scheme is provable secure under the co-CDH assumption.
- We exploit the matrix digest technique to transform two-dimensional matrices into one-dimensional vectors, which can dramatically reduce the computation overhead both in the key generation phase of the data center and matrices multiplication phase of the cloud server.

Organization. The rest of our paper is organized as follows: in Sect. 2, we provide some necessary definitions and preliminaries. The system model and the detailed construction of our scheme are given in Sect. 3. Following, we conduct the security and efficiency analysis of our scheme in Sect. 4. Finally, we give our conclusion in Sect. 5.

2 Preliminaries

In this section, we describe the general definition of verifiable computation scheme, and some cryptographic tools and techniques used in our scheme.

2.1 Publicly Verifiable Computation

A verifiable computation scheme empowers a client to outsource his evaluation function F to a server, and can verify the correctness of the results returned by the server. Gennaro et al. [16] present a formal definition for securely outsourcing computation.

Definition 1. *A verifiable computation scheme* $\mathcal{VC} = (\textbf{KeyGen}, \textbf{ProbGen},$ *$\textbf{Compute}, \textbf{Verify}, \textbf{Solve})$ contains five algorithms defined as follows.*

- $\textbf{KeyGen}\ (F, \lambda) \rightarrow (PK, SK)$: *Given the security parameter λ, the key generation algorithm randomly generates a public key used to encode the target function F while computing a matching secret key, which is kept private by the client.*
- $\textbf{ProbGen}_{SK}(x) \rightarrow (\sigma_x, \tau_x)$: *The problem generation algorithm uses the secret key SK to encode the function input x and output σ_x which is given to the server to compute with, and a secret value τ_x which is kept private by the client.*
- $\textbf{Compute}_{PK}(\sigma_x) \rightarrow \sigma_y$: *By using the client's public key PK and the encoded input σ_x, the server computes with and outputs the encoded result of function F.*
- $\textbf{Verify}_{SK}(\tau_x, \sigma_y) \rightarrow y \cup \bot$: *Using the secret key SK and the secret decoding τ_x, the verification algorithm transforms the server's encoded output into the output of the function, e.g., $y = F(x)$ or outputs $\bot$, which indicates that σ_y does not represent the valid output of F.*
- $\textbf{Solve}(\tau_x, \sigma_y) \rightarrow y$: *Given the secret key SK, the encoded value σ_y and the secret decoding τ_x, the solving algorithm computes and outputs the result $y = F(x)$.*

Definition 2 *(Correctness). A verifiable computation scheme $\mathcal{VC}$ is correct if for any function F, the key generation algorithm produces keys $(PK, SK) \leftarrow$ **KeyGen**(F, λ) such that, $\forall x \in Domain(F)$, if $(\sigma_x, \tau_x) \leftarrow$ **ProbGen**$_{SK}(x)$ and $\sigma_y \leftarrow$ **Compute**$_{PK}(\sigma_x)$ then $y = F(x) \leftarrow$ **Verify**$_{SK}(\tau_x, \sigma_y)$.*

Definition 3 *(Security). Intuitively, a verifiable computation scheme is a malicious adversary cannot convince the verification algorithm to pass an incorrect output. In the following, we will formalize this intuition with an experiment, where $poly(\cdot)$ is a polynomial.*

$$\text{Experiment } \boldsymbol{Exp}_A^{Verify}[\mathcal{VC}, F, \lambda];$$

$$(PK, SK) \xleftarrow{R} \boldsymbol{KeyGen}(F, \lambda);$$

$$\text{For } i = 1, ..., \mathbb{L} = poly(\lambda);$$

$$x_i \leftarrow A(PK, x_1, \sigma_1, ...x_{i-1}, \sigma_{i-1});$$

$$(\sigma_i, \tau_i) \leftarrow \boldsymbol{ProbGen}_{SK}(x_i);$$

$$(i, \hat{\sigma}_y) \leftarrow A(PK, x_1, \sigma_1, ..., x_{\mathbb{L}}, \tau_{\mathbb{L}});$$

$$\hat{y} \leftarrow \boldsymbol{Verify}_{SK}(\tau_i, \hat{\sigma}_y);$$

$$\text{If } \hat{y} \neq \perp \text{ and } \hat{y} \neq F(x_i), \text{output } 1, \text{else } 0;$$

In fact, the adversary is given oracle access to generate the encoding of multiple problem instances. If the adversary produces a wrong output and persuades the verifier to pass the examination, we say that the adversary succeed. Now, we define the security of the system based on the adversary's success in the experiment above as below.

For a verifiable computation scheme $\mathcal{VC}$, we define the advantage of an adversary A in the experiment above as:

$$Adv_A^{Verif}(\mathcal{VC}, F, \lambda) = Prob[\boldsymbol{Exp}_A^{Verif}[\mathcal{VC}, F, \lambda] = 1]$$

For a function F, we say that a verifiable computation scheme $\mathcal{VC}$ is secure if for any adversary A running in probabilistic polynomial time the following formula holds.

$$Adv_A^{Verif}(\mathcal{VC}, F, \lambda) \leq negli(\lambda)$$

Definition 4 *(Efficiency). The final requirement of a verifiable computation scheme is efficiency. In other words, the time for encoding the input and verifying the output must be shorter than the time for accomplishing the local computation by itself.*

Following, we also need to introduce some necessary definitions used in our scheme. As discussed in [17], two new properties of verifiable computation scheme were firstly proposed, namely public delegation and public verifiability.

Definition 5 *(Public Delegation). The scheme allows not only the entity who conducts the original system setting up but also other clients are able to submit their inputs to accomplish the evaluation of the function.*

Definition 6 *(Public Verifiability). Without loss of generality, any verifier independent of clients can check whether the result returned by the server is correct or not.*

2.2 Bilinear Pairings

Let $\mathbb{G}_1$, $\mathbb{G}_2$ and $\mathbb{G}_T$ be three multiplicative cyclic groups of the same order p, here p is a large prime. And g_1, g_2 are generators of $\mathbb{G}_1$ and $\mathbb{G}_2$, respectively. A bilinear pairing is a map $e\colon \mathbb{G}_1 \times \mathbb{G}_2 \to \mathbb{G}_T$, which has the following properties:

- **Computability:** There is an efficient computable algorithm for computing $e(g, h)$ for any $(g, h) \in \mathbb{G}_1 \times \mathbb{G}_2$.
- **Bilinearity:** For any $\alpha, \beta \in \mathbb{Z}_p$, and $g \in \mathbb{G}_1, h \in \mathbb{G}_2, e(g^\alpha, h^\beta) = e(g, h)^{\alpha\beta}$.
- **Non-degeneracy:** For any $g \in \mathbb{G}_1$, if for all $h \in \mathbb{G}_2$ equation $e(g, h) = 1$ is true, $g = 1$ (where it is also true for the case of exchanging their position).

Definition 7. *Let $\mathbb{G}_1$, $\mathbb{G}_2$ and $\mathbb{G}_T$ be three multiplicative cyclic groups of the same order p, here p is a large prime. And there exists a bilinear pairing map $e\colon \mathbb{G}_1 \times \mathbb{G}_2 \to \mathbb{G}_T$.*

(co-CDH Problem) Given $g, g^\alpha \in \mathbb{G}_1$, $h, h^\beta \in \mathbb{G}_2$, $\alpha, \beta \in_R \mathbb{F}_p{}^*$, compute $g^{\alpha\beta}$.

(co-CDH Assumption) Given $g, g^\alpha \in \mathbb{G}_1, h, h^\beta \in \mathbb{G}_2$, for any random $\alpha, \beta \in \mathbb{F}_p{}^*$, if the probability to compute $g^{\alpha\beta}$ is negligible, we say that the co-computational Diffie-Hellman assumption holds in $\mathbb{G}_1$.

2.3 Privacy-Preserving Matrix Transformation

Privacy-preserving matrix transformation scheme has been researched for many years. It was firstly proposed by Salinas et al. [18], which allows client to disguise his private matrix by adding a matrix in the sense of computational indistinguishability in order to prevent information leakage.

In particular, we assume that client holds his private information in the matrix $\mathbf{X}$, where the values of matrix $\mathbf{X}$ are within the range $[-K, K]$, and $K = 2^l (l > 0)$ is a positive constant. Before delegating the computing task to the server, it is of vital importance to hide private matrix by applying a matrix addition as follow:

$$\hat{\mathbf{X}} = \mathbf{X} + \mathbf{Z}$$

Here, it must be remarked that matrix $\mathbf{Z}$ is formed by a vector outer-produce, i.e.

$$\mathbf{Z} = \mathbf{u}\mathbf{v}^T$$

where $\mathbf{u} \in \mathbb{R}^{m \times 1}$ is a vector of uniformly distributed random variables ranged $[-2^p, 2^p](p > 0)$. And $\mathbf{v} \in \mathbb{R}^{n \times 1}$ is another vector of arbitrary positive constants ranging from 2^l to $2^{l+q}(q > 0)$.

Salinas et al. [18] have proved that matrices $\mathbf{R}$ and $\hat{\mathbf{X}}$ are computationally indistinguishable. Here, let $\mathbf{R}$ be a random matrix whose elements in its jth column are sampled from a uniform distribution with interval $[-2^p v_j, 2^p v_j]$ ($\forall j \in [1, n]$).

2.4   Matrix Digest Technique

Matrix digest [15] is a novel technique which in fact is one vector generated by a matrix together with some chosen parameters. A matrix can be viewed as a set of column vectors. Then, for a matrix $\mathbf{M} \in \mathbb{Z}^{n \times d}$, we have $\mathbf{M} = (\mathbf{m}_1, ..., \mathbf{m}_d)$, where for $i = 1$ to d, $\mathbf{m}_i \in \mathbb{Z}^n$ is a column vector.

Then, for a matrix $\mathbf{M} \in \mathbb{Z}^{n \times d}$ and a vector $\mathbf{s} = (s_1, ..., s_n) \in \mathbb{Z}^n$, the matrix digest $\mathbf{m}$ of $\mathbf{M}$ can be obtained by

$$\mathbf{m} = \mathbf{s} \cdot \mathbf{M}$$

The properties of matrix digest technique include three folds:

- **Deterministic:** On the input of a matrix, the matrix digest is determined only by the parameters, i.e. the vector $\mathbf{s}$ is determined.
- **Computable:** The obtained matrix digest is essentially a vector, which owns all the properties of vector.
- **Irreversible:** The computation of matrix digest is a one-way mapping. Given a matrix digest and the parameters simultaneously, the matrix cannot be detected.

3   The Proposed Scheme

3.1   System Model

Since we consider the public delegation and the public verification properties in the outsourcing computing model, the system model of our scheme contains four entities: *data center, client, server* and *verifier*.

- *data center:* The *data center* provides the *client* with a public matrix which is needed in multiplication operation. The *data center* initializes parameters and produces a key pair. At the same time, it also produces an evaluation key in order to assist the *server* in computing the proof.
- *client:* The *client* wants to outsource large-scale matrix multiplication operation to the *server*. In order to blind the input private matrix, the *client* encodes the private matrix $\mathbf{X}$ into $\hat{\mathbf{X}}$. Besides, the *client* produces a public verification key VK. After receiving the result returned by the *server*, the *client* decrypts the result $\hat{\mathbf{Y}}$.

- *server:* The *server* is a honest but curious cloud service provider deployed with abundant computing resources. When the *server* receives the request from the *client*, it will produce the blinding result $\widehat{\mathbf{Y}}$. Meanwhile, it computes the corresponding proof in order to prove its work.
- *verifier:* The main task of the *verifier* is to check whether the returned blinding result $\widehat{\mathbf{Y}}$ is correct or not. It should be remarked that the *verifier* could be arbitrary entity.

3.2   New Publicly Verifiable Computation Scheme

In this section, we present a new publicly verifiable computation scheme for batch matrix multiplication in the same group. The new publicly verifiable computation scheme $\mathbf{NPVC} = (\mathbf{KeyGen}, \mathbf{ProbGen}, \mathbf{Compute}, \mathbf{Verify}, \mathbf{Solve})$ consists of five algorithms defined as follows:

- $\mathbf{KeyGen}(1^k, F)$: This algorithm is conducted by the *data center*. Considering a *client* who wants to outsource two large-scale matrices multiplication operations to a *server*, where involving one public matrix $\mathbf{M}$. $\mathbf{M}_{i,k} \in \mathbb{F}_p$ ($1 \leq i \leq m$ and $1 \leq k \leq n$) is the element of $\mathbf{M}$, where p is a large prime. It generates two cyclic groups $\mathbb{G}_1$, $\mathbb{G}_2$ of the same prime order p, which admits a bilinear pairing $e: \mathbb{G}_1 \times \mathbb{G}_2 \rightarrow \mathbb{G}_T$. Then, it randomly chooses two generators $g \in \mathbb{G}_1$, $h \in \mathbb{G}_2$, respectively and $\delta \in \mathbb{F}_p^*$, and then computes $\tilde{h} = h^\delta$. The *data center* publishes the public parameter: param=$(p, \mathbb{G}_1, \mathbb{G}_2, \mathbb{G}_T, g, h, \tilde{h})$.
  Next, it produces the evaluation key EK as follows:
  - Firstly, it randomly picks up one vector $\mathbf{s}$, here $s_i \in \mathbb{F}_p^*$ ($1 \leq i \leq m$) and another one vector $\mathbf{r}$. We take $r_k \in \mathbb{F}_p^*$, ($1 \leq k \leq n$) as the secret key pair.
  - Secondly, it computes

    $$\mathbf{m} = \mathbf{s} \cdot \mathbf{M}$$

    where $\mathbf{m} = (m_1, ... m_n), (1 \leq k \leq n)$.
  - Thirdly, it calculates an assistant vector $\mathbf{n}$, where $n_k = g^{\delta m_k + r_k}$ ($1 \leq k \leq n$).
  - Finally, it sets the evaluation key as $EK = (\mathbf{M}, \mathbf{n})$.
  Meanwhile, it determines the public key $PK = (PK_1, PK_2)$ where
  $PK_1 = (g^{s_1}, g^{s_2}, ... g^{s_m})$ $PK_2 = (PK_{21}, PK_{22}, ..., PK_{2n})$, here, we define
  $PK_{2k} = e(g^{r_k}, h)$ ($1 \leq k \leq n$). Afterwards, both the public key PK and the evaluation key EK are delivered to the *server*.
- $\mathbf{ProbGen}(\mathbf{X}, \mathbf{Z}, PK_2)$: This algorithm is conducted by the *client*. On input the private matrix $\mathbf{X} \in \mathbb{F}_p^{n \times m}$ and the additional matrix $\mathbf{Z}$ which is described in [18], the *client* conducts the following operations:
  - In order to hide its private matrix, the *client* conducts the following operation:

    $$\widehat{\mathbf{X}} = \mathbf{X} + \mathbf{Z}$$

    where $\mathbf{Z}$ and $\mathbf{X}$ are of the same size. And $\hat{x}_{i,j} = x_{i,j} + z_{i,j}$, where $\hat{x}_{i,j}$ is the element in the ith row and jth column of matrix $\widehat{\mathbf{X}}$.

- Subsequently, it derives the public verification key
$VK = (VK_1, VK_2, ..., VK_m)$, where $VK_j = \prod_{k=1}^{n} PK_{2k}{}^{\hat{x}_{k,j}}$.
- **Compute**$(\hat{\mathbf{X}}, EK)$: This algorithm is conducted by the *server*. It takes the blinding matrix $\hat{\mathbf{X}}$ and the evaluation key EK as inputs. And then it multiplies matrix $\mathbf{M}$ with matrix $\hat{\mathbf{X}}$ which yields a result matrix $\hat{\mathbf{Y}}$ and a proof $\pi = (\pi_1, \pi_2, ..., \pi_m)$, where

$$\pi_j = \prod_{k=1}^{n} n_k^{\hat{x}_{k,j}}, \ 1 \le j \le m.$$

- **Verify**$(\hat{\mathbf{Y}}, \pi, PK_1)$: On input the result matrix $\hat{\mathbf{Y}}$ associated with π, the public key PK_1 and the verification key VK, the *verifier* checks whether the following m $(1 \le j \le m)$ equations hold:

$$e(\pi_j, h) \overset{?}{=} e(\prod_{i=1}^{m} (PK_{1i})^{\hat{y}_{i,j}}, h^\delta) \cdot VK_j$$

If these n equations hold then it outputs $\hat{\mathbf{Y}}$ meaning that $\mathbf{M}\hat{\mathbf{X}} = \hat{\mathbf{Y}}$, otherwise it outputs $\perp$.
- **Solve**$(\hat{\mathbf{Y}}, \mathbf{Z})$: On input the result $\hat{\mathbf{Y}}$, the *client* runs this algorithm and derives the result of $\mathbf{MX}$.

$$\mathbf{MX} = \hat{\mathbf{Y}} - \mathbf{MZ} = \hat{\mathbf{Y}} - (\mathbf{Mu})\mathbf{v}^T$$

4 Security Analysis

4.1 Correctness

Obviously, our NPVC scheme described above is correct.

$$\pi_j = \prod_{k=1}^{n} n_k^{x\hat{k},j} = \prod_{k=1}^{n} g^{(\delta m_k + r_k)\hat{x}_{k,j}} = g^{\sum_{k=1}^{n} \delta m_k \hat{x}_{k,j} + \sum_{k=1}^{n} r_k \hat{x}_{k,j}}$$

Here, we remark that the main trick is that the following equation holds (for $1 \le j \le m$):

$$\sum_{k=1}^{n} m_k \hat{x}_{k,j} = \sum_{i=1}^{m} s_i \hat{y}_{i,j}$$

Therefore, we have

$$e(\pi_j, h) = e(g, h)^{\sum_{k=1}^{n} \delta m_k \hat{x}_{k,j} + \sum_{k=1}^{n} r_k \hat{x}_{k,j}}$$

$$= e(g, h)^{\sum_{k=1}^{n} \delta m_k \hat{x}_{k,j}} \cdot e(g, h)^{\sum_{k=1}^{n} r_k \hat{x}_{k,j}}$$

$$= e(g, h^\delta)^{\sum_{i=1}^{m} s_i \hat{y}_{i,j}} \cdot \prod_{k=1}^{n} PK_{2k}{}^{\hat{x}_{k,j}}$$

$$= e(\prod_{i=1}^{m} PK_{1i}{}^{\hat{y}_{i,j}}, h^\delta) \cdot VK_j$$

4.2 Security Analysis

Theorem 1. *The proposed scheme for batch matrix multiplication is proved to be secure under the co-CDH assumption holds.*

Proof. We will analysis the security of our scheme. We assume that there exists an adversary A who can break the proposed scheme with a non-negligible advantage ε. In the following, we will prove that the co-CDH assumption can be broken by an adversary B who uses adversary A with a non-negligible probability ε', where we denote that $\varepsilon' \approx \varepsilon$.

First of all, in order to break the co-CDH assumption, adversary B calls the oracle O_{co-CDH} to generate $g, g^{\alpha} \in \mathbb{G}_1$ and $h, h^{\beta} \in \mathbb{G}_2$. Next, the adversary B imitates adversary A to complete the soundness experiment:

- Adversary B selects $\alpha, \beta \in \mathbb{F}_p^*$, later it lets $g' = g^{\alpha}$, $h' = (h^{\beta})^{\delta}$, and sets up $param' = (p, \mathbb{G}_1, \mathbb{G}_2, \mathbb{G}_T, e, g', h, h')$.
- It randomly produces one vector $\mathbf{n}' \in \mathbb{G}_1^{n \times 1}$.
- For all $1 \leq k \leq n$ it computes

$$PK'_{2k} = \frac{e(n_k', h)}{e(\prod_{i=1}^{m} PK'_{1i}{}^{M_{i,k}}, h')}$$

  we denote that $PK'_{1i} = g'^{s_i}$ ($1 \leq i \leq m$).
- It defines:
$PK'_2 = (PK_{21}', ..., PK_{2n}')$
$PK'_1 = (PK_{11}', ..., PK_{1m}')$
Additionally, it sets the evaluation key EK' to $(\mathbf{M}, \mathbf{n}')$.

Therefore, adversary B achieves the public key PK'_2, the public parameters $param'$ and the corresponding evaluation key EK'.

We remark that the output of oracle O_{KeyGen} is statistically indistinguishable from the distribution of the output of algorithm **KeyGen** in the experiment. In other words, the two following are true:

- For each column of the input private matrix $\hat{\mathbf{X}}$ and the blinding result matrix $\hat{\mathbf{Y}} = \mathbf{M}\hat{\mathbf{X}}$, the public key PK'_2 makes the following m equations hold:

$$e(\prod_{k=1}^{n} n_k'^{\hat{x}_{k,j}}, h) = e(\prod_{i=1}^{m} (PK'_{1i})^{\hat{y}_{i,j}}, h') \cdot VK'_j$$

Here,

$$VK'_j = \prod_{k=1}^{n} PK'_{2k}{}^{\hat{x}_{k,j}}$$

- The statistical distribution of auxiliary vector $\mathbf{n}'$ and public key $PK' = (PK'_1, PK'_2)$ are the same as the distribution of $\mathbf{n}$ and public key $PK = (PK_1, PK_2)$ respectively.

Next, adversary A queries the oracle $O_{ProbGen}$ with the input $(\hat{\mathbf{X}}, PK_2')$, adversary B imitates the oracle $O_{ProbGen}$ and takes $(\hat{\mathbf{X}}, VK')$ as output with $VK' = (VK_1', VK_2', ..., VK_m')$.

Finally, adversary A returns fake results $(\hat{\mathbf{Y}}^*, \pi)$ with $\hat{\mathbf{Y}}^* \neq \mathbf{M}\hat{\mathbf{X}}$. Following adversary B verifies whether $\hat{\mathbf{Y}}^* = \hat{\mathbf{Y}}$ (we denote that $\hat{\mathbf{Y}} = \mathbf{M}\hat{\mathbf{X}}$). If the result passes the verification, it means that adversary B fails, otherwise it returns the following result and breaks the co-CDH assumption. We define the jth column of matrix $\hat{\mathbf{Y}}$ and matrix $\hat{\mathbf{Y}}^*$ as $\hat{\mathbf{y}}_j$ and $\hat{\mathbf{y}}_j^*$ respectively.

$$g^{\alpha\beta} = (\frac{\pi_j}{\prod_{k=1}^{n} n_k'^{\hat{x}_{k,j}}})^{(\delta \mathbf{s}(\hat{\mathbf{y}}_j - \hat{\mathbf{y}}_j^*))^{-1}}$$

Afterwards, we will give the details of the result. If the fake results $(\hat{\mathbf{Y}}^*, \pi)$ pass the verification, it means that the following m equations hold:

$$e(\pi_j, h) = e(\prod_{i=1}^{m} PK_{1i}'^{\hat{y}_{i,j}^*}, h') \cdot VK_j', (1 \leq j \leq m)$$

And according to the expression of PK_{2k}', we also have the jth equation holds:

$$e(\prod_{k=1}^{n} n_k'^{\hat{x}_{k,j}}, h) = e(\prod_{i=1}^{m} (PK_{1i}')^{\hat{y}_{i,j}}, h') \cdot VK_j'$$

According to the two equations above, we achieve:

$$e(\frac{\pi_j}{\prod_{k=1}^{n} n_k'^{\hat{x}_{k,j}}}, h) = e(\prod_{i=1}^{m} PK_{1i}'^{(\hat{y}_{i,j}^* - \hat{y}_{i,j})}, h')$$

$$= e(\prod_{i=1}^{m} g'^{s_i(\hat{y}_{i,j}^* - \hat{y}_{i,j})}, h')$$

$$= e(g'^{\sum_{i=1}^{m} s_i(\hat{y}_{i,j}^* - \hat{y}_{i,j})}, h')$$

$$= e(g'^{\mathbf{s}(\hat{\mathbf{y}}_j - \hat{\mathbf{y}}_j^*)}, h')$$

Since $g' = g^\alpha$ and $h' = h^{\beta\delta}$, we conclude that:

$$e(\frac{\pi_j}{\prod_{k=1}^{n} n_k'^{\hat{x}_{k,j}}}, h) = e(g^{\alpha \mathbf{s}(\hat{\mathbf{y}}_j - \hat{\mathbf{y}}_j^*)}, h^{\beta\delta})$$

$$= e(g^{\alpha\beta}, h)^{\delta \mathbf{s}(\hat{\mathbf{y}}_j - \hat{\mathbf{y}}_j^*)}$$

If $\mathbf{s}(\hat{\mathbf{y}}_j - \hat{\mathbf{y}}_j^*) \neq 0$, since $\delta \neq 0$ ($\delta \in \mathbb{F}_p^*$), therefore $\delta \mathbf{s}(\hat{\mathbf{y}}_j - \hat{\mathbf{y}}_j^*) \neq 0$, we obtain:

$$g^{\alpha\beta} = (\frac{\pi_j}{\prod_{k=1}^{n} n_k'^{\hat{x}_{k,j}}})^{(\delta \mathbf{s}(\hat{\mathbf{y}}_j - \hat{\mathbf{y}}_j^*))^{-1}}$$

4.3 Efficiency Analysis

In order to simplify expression, we analysis the performance of multiplying matrix $\mathbf{M}$ with one column of blinding matrix $\hat{\mathbf{X}}$. We will give the elaborate comparison between article [14] and our scheme in following table.

The algorithm **KeyGen** randomly generates two vectors $\mathbf{s}$ and $\mathbf{r}$ that requires the generation of $(n+m)$ random numbers in group operation. Next, it applies matrix digest technique to produce a blinding vector $\mathbf{m}$ which costs mn multiplication operations in $\mathbb{F}_p^*$. In order to generate an auxiliary vector $\mathbf{n}$, algorithm **KeyGen** performs m multiplication and m exponentiation operations in $\mathbb{F}_p$. Furthermore, the generation of public key PK costs $(m+n)$ exponentiations and m pairings. We adopt the matrix digest technique to our scheme which dramatically reduce the computation cost from mn exponentiations in [14] to $(m+n)$ exponentiations.

The algorithm **ProbGen** consists of two operations: firstly, it performs matrix transformation in order to provide privacy with *clients* which costs the generation of $(m+n)$ random numbers, mn multiplication and mn addition operations. Secondly, it computes the evaluation key VK which involves m exponentiations and $(m-1)$ multiplications. Since we consider the secrecy of the private matrix $\mathbf{X}$, in this phase, the computation overhead of our scheme is more than the scheme in article [14].

Following, the algorithm **Compute** to generate the result as well as the proof π which involves m exponentiations and $(m-1)$ multiplications. In this phase, the computation overhead of our scheme is less than the scheme in article [14] which needs mn multiplications and $((m-1)(n-1)+mn)$ exponentiations.

The algorithm **Verify** evaluates whether the equation holds or not, which needs m exponentiations, m multiplications and two pairings. And in this phase, the computation overhead of our scheme is the same as in [14].

Finally, the *client* runs algorithm **Solve** to decode the blinding result $\hat{\mathbf{Y}}$ which needs to perform mn additions and therefore achieves the final result.

Table: Efficiency Comparison

Scheme	Scheme[14]	Our Scheme
Computational Model	Amortized Model	Amortized Model
Privacy protection	No	Yes
Computation (**KeyGen**)	$(2mn-m)M + 2mnE + mP$	$(mn+m)M + (2m+n)E + mP$
Computation (**ProbGen**)	$(m-1)M + mE$	$((m-1)+mn)M + mE + (m+n)G + mnA$
Computation (**Compute**)	$mnM + ((m-1)(n-1)+mn)E$	$(m-1)M + mE$
Computation (**Verify**)	$nE + nM + 2P$	$nE + nM + 2P$
Computation (**Solve**)	–	mnA

5 Conclusion

In this paper, we present a new publicly verifiable computation scheme for batch matrix multiplication which considers the privacy protection of clients. In our scheme, any client belonging to the same group can submit the private matrix to the cloud server and the latter can help to compute the matrix multiplication operation with the private matrix and a public matrix from the data center. To further reduce the computation cost, we introduce matrix digest technique which can convert the two-dimensional matrix into the one-dimensional vector. Finally, we prove that our scheme is secure under the co-CDH assumption and provide the theoretical computation analysis and the comparison with the state-of-the-art work. The comparison results indicate that our scheme can greatly reduce computation overhead in both the key generation and the compute phases.

References

1. Chen, X.: Introduction to secure outsourcing computation. Synth. Lect. Inf. Secur. Priv. Trust **8**, 1–93 (2016)
2. Joshi, K.P., Yesha, Y., Finin, T.: Automating cloud services life cycle through semantic technologies. IEEE Trans. Serv. Comput. **7**, 109–122 (2012)
3. Paik, I., Chen, W., Huhns, M.N.: A scalable architecture for automatic service composition. IEEE Trans. Serv. Comput. **7**, 82–95 (2014)
4. Park, K.W., Han, J., Chung, J.W., Park, K.H.: Themis: a mutually verifiable billing system for the cloud computing environment. IEEE Trans. Serv. Comput. **6**, 300–313 (2013)
5. Wang, C., Wang, Q., Ren, K., Cao, N., Lou, W.: Toward secure and dependable storage services in cloud computing. IEEE Trans. Serv. Comput. **5**, 220–232 (2012)
6. Wang, C., Zhang, B., Ren, K., Roveda, J.M.: Privacy-assured outsourcing of image reconstruction service in cloud. IEEE Trans. Emerg. Top. Comput. **1**, 166–177 (2013)
7. Chen, X., Huang, X., Li, J., Ma, J.: New algorithms for secure outsourcing of large-scale systems of linear equations. IEEE Trans. Inf. Forensics Secur. **10**, 69–78 (2015)
8. Lei, X., Liao, X., Huang, T., Heriniaina, F.: Achieving security, robust cheating resistance, and high-efficiency for outsourcing large matrix multiplication computation to a malicious cloud. Inf. Sci. **280**, 205–217 (2014)
9. Lei, X., Liao, X., Huang, T., Li, H.: Outsourcing large matrix inversion computation to a public cloud. IEEE Trans. Cloud Comput. **1**, 1 (2013)
10. Lei, X., Liao, X., Huang, T., Li, H.: Cloud computing service: the case of large matrix determinant computation. IEEE Trans. Serv. Comput. **8**, 688–700 (2015)
11. Fiore, D., Gennaro, R.: Publicly verifiable delegation of large polynomials and matrix computations, with applications. In: ACM Conference on Computer and Communications Security, pp. 501–512(2012)
12. Zhang, L.F., Safavi-Naini, R.: Verifiable delegation of computations with storage-verification trade-off. In: Kutyłowski, M., Vaidya, J. (eds.) ESORICS 2014. LNCS, vol. 8712, pp. 112–129. Springer, Cham (2014). doi:10.1007/978-3-319-11203-9_7

13. Zhang, Y., Blanton, M.: Efficient secure and verifiable outsourcing of matrix multiplications. In: Chow, S.S.M., Camenisch, J., Hui, L.C.K., Yiu, S.M. (eds.) ISC 2014. LNCS, vol. 8783, pp. 158–178. Springer, Cham (2014). doi:10.1007/978-3-319-13257-0_10
14. Elkhiyaoui, K., Önen, M., Azraoui, M., Molva, R.: Efficient techniques for publicly verifiable delegation of computation. In: Proceedings of the 11th ACM on Asia Conference on Computer and Communications Security, AsiaCCS 2016, Xi'an, China, 30 May–3 June 2016, pp. 119–128 (2016)
15. Sheng, G., Tang, C., Gao, W., Yin, Y.: MD-$\mathcal{VC}_{Matrix}$: an efficient scheme for publicly verifiable computation of outsourced matrix multiplication. In: Chen, J., Piuri, V., Su, C., Yung, M. (eds.) NSS 2016. LNCS, vol. 9955, pp. 349–362. Springer, Cham (2016). doi:10.1007/978-3-319-46298-1_23
16. Gennaro, R., Gentry, C., Parno, B.: Non-interactive verifiable computing: outsourcing computation to untrusted workers. In: Rabin, T. (ed.) CRYPTO 2010. LNCS, vol. 6223, pp. 465–482. Springer, Heidelberg (2010). doi:10.1007/978-3-642-14623-7_25
17. Parno, B., Raykova, M., Vaikuntanathan, V.: How to delegate and verify in public: verifiable computation from attribute-based encryption. In: Cramer, R. (ed.) TCC 2012. LNCS, vol. 7194, pp. 422–439. Springer, Heidelberg (2012). doi:10.1007/978-3-642-28914-9_24
18. Salinas, S.: Efficient secure outsourcing of large-scale linear systems of equations, pp. 1035–1043 (2015)

A Multi-source Homomorphic Network Coding Signature in the Standard Model

Wenbin Chen[1,2(✉)], Hao Lei[3], Jin Li[1,2], Chongzhi Gao[1,2], Fufang Li[1], and Ke Qi[1]

[1] Department of Computer Science, Guangzhou University, Guangzhou, People's Republic of China
`cwb2011@gzhu.edu.cn`
[2] State Key Laboratory of Cryptology, P.O. Box 5159, Beijing, China
[3] Huawei Technologies Co., Ltd., Beijing institute, Beijing, China

Abstract. We study the problem of designing secure network coding signatures in the network with multiple sources. At present, there exists some multi-source homomorphic network coding signatures in the random oracle model. But there are still no multi-source homomorphic network coding signatures in the standard model. How to construct it remains an open problem. In this paper, we propose the first multi-source homomorphic network coding signature in the standard model.

1 Introduction

In the traditional network routing, every node simply stores the received packets and forwards them to other nodes. A new routing method called network coding appears [2,22] and develops in the past fifteen years, in which intermediate nodes can modify received data packets and transit them. But it is still needed to make sure that the final recipients to get the original information. It has wide application [13–15,18,24–27,31,32].

We consider the case of networks with multi-source. The adversary might put into some polluted packets which are not a valid linear combination of original packets. The multi-source networking coding signature is used to prevent pollution attack from some adversarial nodes.

M. Krohn et al. introduced the homomorphic hash function [11] and C. Gkantsidis et al. extent it to network coding [17]. But it is generally not practical to use the homomorphic hash function for integrity protection in the multi-source case.

For the single source case, some linearly homomorphic signature scheme were proposed in some papers. Johnson et al. proposed the first linearly homomorphic signature scheme in [19]. Combining the RSA-based signature with the homomorphic hash function, Yu et al. gave a homomorphic signature scheme [29] for which some security flaw and errors were found in [28,30]. For a P2P system, Kang et al. designed a secure network coding signature [20]. Zhao et al. proposed a homomorphic network coding signature scheme for content distribution in [33]. Lauter et al. gave a homomorphic network coding signature scheme

© Springer International Publishing AG 2017
M.H.A. Au et al. (Eds.): GPC 2017, LNCS 10232, pp. 66–74, 2017.
DOI: 10.1007/978-3-319-57186-7_6

based on bilinear mapping [21]. In [6], Boneh et al. also designed a homomorphic network coding signature scheme with the property of signing unlimited number of messages. In [16], Gennaro et al. propose a linearly homomorphic signature whose security is based on RSA assumption. Based on the complexity of lattice problems, Boneh et al. introduced the k-SIS problem and used it to construct a linear homomorphic signature scheme over binary fields [5]. Previous homomorphic signatures schemes are proven secure in the random oracle model.

There are some linearly homomorphic signatures schemes which are proven secure in the standard model, such as the scheme of Attrapadung et al. [1], the scheme of Catalano et al. [8] and the scheme of Chen et al. [9]. Based on the idea of the identity-based encryption scheme of Lewko et al. [23] and bilinear groups, Attrapadung et al. [1] proposed a linearly homomorphic signature scheme. Based on the adaptive pseudo-free groups [7], Catalano et al. design their linearly homomorphic signature scheme. These two signature schemes are linearly homomorphic over the integers or over $\mathbb{F}_p$ for some large p and their security is based on that the factoring problem or the discrete logarithm problem is hard. Independent of Catalano et al.'s work, Freeman proposed a method that transforms standard signature schemes to linearly-homomorphic signatures in the standard model [10]. Chen et al. proposed the first lattice-based homomorphic signature in the standard model which is linearly homomorphic over a small field such as $\mathbb{F}_2$ [9].

For the multi-source case, Boneh et al. proposed a network coding signature which combines homomorphic hashing function with a signature scheme and whose security is based on the oracle model [3]. But there are still no linearly homomorphic network coding signature schemes in the standard model.

In this paper, we answer the above open problems. Based on the scheme of Catalano et al. [8], we propose the first the multi-source linearly homomorphic network coding signature scheme in the standard model.

The rest of this paper is organized as follows. Section 2 overviews some definitions. Section 3 describes our multi-source linearly homomorphic network coding signature scheme. In Sect. 4 we summarize the paper.

2   Preliminaries

The formal definition of homomorphic linearly homomorphic network coding signature is given as follows.

Definition 1 (*Linearly Homomorphic Network Coding Signatures adapted from [8]*). *A linearly homomorphic network coding signature scheme $\mathcal{LS}$ consists of a tuple of probabilistic, polynomial-time algorithms (NetKG, NetSign, NetVer, NetEval) with the following functionality:*

NetKG$(1^k, m, n)$. *Given the security parameter k and two integers $m, n \geq 1$, this algorithm outputs (sk, pk) where sk is the secret key and pk is the public verification key. Here, m is the dimension of the vector spaces and $n+m$ is an upper* *bound to the size of the signed vectors. We assume that the public key implicitly defines the field $\mathbb{F}_p$ over which vectors and linear combinations are defined, and that it contains the description of an efficiently samplable distribution for $Id \in \mathbb{F}_p$.*

NetSign(*sk, Id, w*)*. The signing algorithm takes as input the secret key sk, a file identifier $Id \in \mathbb{F}_p$ and a vector $w \in \mathbb{F}_p^{n+m}$ and outputs a signature σ.*

NetVer(*pk, Id, w, σ*)*. Given the public key pk, a file identifier Id, a vector $w \in \mathbb{F}_p^{n+m}$ and a signature σ, the algorithm outputs 1 (accept) or 0 (reject).*

NetEval(*pk, Id, $\{(w_i, \alpha_i, \sigma_i)\}_{i=1}^t$*)*. Given a public key pk, a file identifier Id, and a set of tuples $(w_i, \alpha_i, \sigma_i)$ where σ_i is a signature, $w_i \in \mathbb{F}_p^{n+m}$ is a vector and $\alpha_i \in \mathbb{F}_p$ is a scalar. This algorithm outputs a new signature σ such that: if each σ_i is a valid signature on vector w_i, then σ is a valid signature for w obtained from the linear combination $\sum_{i=1}^t \alpha_i w_i$.*

*For correctness, we require that for each (sk, pk) output by **NetKG**$(1^k, m, n)$, the following hold:*

1. *Let $Id \in \mathbb{F}_p$, $w \in \mathbb{F}_p^{n+m}$, if $\sigma \leftarrow$ **NetSign**(sk, Id, w), then* **NetVer**$(pk, Id, w, \sigma) = 1$.
2. *For all Id, any $t > 0$, and all sets of triples $\{(w_i, \alpha_i, \sigma_i)\}_{i=1}^t$, if **NetVer**$(pk, Id, w_i, \sigma_i) = 1$ for all i, then*

$$\textbf{NetVer}(pk, Id, \sum_{i=1}^t \alpha_i w_i, \textbf{NetEval}(pk, Id, \{(w_i, \alpha_i, \sigma_i)\}_{i=1}^t)) = 1.$$

For the unforgeability of linearly homomorphic signature, its definition is given as follows.

Definition 2 *(Unforgeability adapted from [5]). For a linearly homomorphic network coding signature scheme*
$\mathcal{LS} = ((NetKG, NetSign, NetVer, NetEval))$*, we consider the following game:*

Setup: *The challenger runs $NetKG(1^k, m, n)$ to obtain (sk, pk) and gives pk to $\mathcal{A}$.*

Queries: *Proceeding adaptively, $\mathcal{A}$ specifies a sequence of data sets $\overrightarrow{w}_i$. For each i, the challenger chooses Id_i uniformly from $\mathbb{F}_p$ and gives to $\mathcal{A}$ the tag Id_i and the signatures $\sigma_{ij} \leftarrow NetSign(sk, Id_i, w_{ij})$ for $j = 1, \ldots, k$.*

Output: *$\mathcal{A}$ outputs a file identifier Id^*, a message m^*, and a signature σ^*. The adversary wins if $NetVer(pk, Id^*, w^*, \sigma^*) = 1$, and either*

(1) $Id^* \neq Id_i$ for all i (a type 1 forgery), or
(2) $Id^* = Id_i$ for some i but $w^* \notin span(\overrightarrow{w}_i)$ (a type 2 forgery), where $span(\overrightarrow{w}_i)$ is the subspace generated by all $\overrightarrow{w}_i$.

The advantage of $\mathcal{A}$ is defined to be the probability that $\mathcal{A}$ wins the security game.

$\mathcal{LS}$ is called $(t(n), \epsilon(n))$-unforgeable if there is no $t(n)$-time adversary $\mathcal{A}$ with advantage at least $\epsilon(n)$ in the game.

Let $e : \mathbb{G} \times \mathbb{G}' \to \mathbb{G}_T$ be a bilinear map, where $\mathbb{G}, \mathbb{G}'$ and $\mathbb{G}_T$ are bilinear groups of prime order p. In [4], Boneh and Boyen introduced the definition of the q-Strong Diffie-Hellman Assumption (q-SDH for short). We give it as follows.

Definition 3 *(q-SDH Assumption [4]). Let $k \in \mathbb{N}$ be the security parameter, $p > 2^k$ be a prime, and $\mathbb{G}, \mathbb{G}', \mathbb{G}_T$ are bilinear groups of prime order p. Let g be a generator of $\mathbb{G}$ and g' be a generator of $\mathbb{G}'$ respectively. Then we say that the q-SDH Assumption holds in $\mathbb{G}, \mathbb{G}', \mathbb{G}_T$ if for any PPT algorithm $\mathcal{A}$ and any $q = poly(k)$, the following probability (taken over the random choice of x and the random coins of $\mathcal{A}$) is negligible in k:*

$$Pr[\mathcal{A}(g, g^x, g^{x^2}, \ldots, g^{x^q}, g', (g')^x)] = (c, g^{\frac{1}{x+c}})]$$

3 A Multi-source Homomorphic Network Coding Signature Scheme in the Standard Model

In this section, we design a multi-source homomorphic network coding signature scheme in the standard model. We assume that there are t unit-capacity source nodes and any number of receivers. Furthermore, for simplicity, we suppose that source nodes break their data into equal size packets which is a vector $\vec{v}$. Each packet is assigned with an Id such that packets that need be encoded together are assigned with the same Id.

Furthermore, it is assumed in the system that every source node has its own public-private key pair. For source i, it use its private key to sign its data packet. When intermediate nodes receive the signed data packets, they first verify the signatures of the signed data packets. Then, intermediate nodes make linear combinations of the verified data packets and produce a signature for the encoded packet based on the received signatures without accessing the private keys. A tuple (Id, β, Y, σ) denote a signed data packet, where σ is the signature of encoded data packet $Y = \sum_{i=1}^{t} \beta_i D_i$. With the signature σ, a signed data packet can be verified even though it is linear combinations of vectors that are originated from different sources. An adversary's attack is successful if it can produce a forged data packet $(Id^*, \beta^*, Y^* = \sum \beta_i^* D_i^*, \sigma^*)$, where $Y^* \neq 0$ and the verification algorithm output 1, i.e. either $Id^* \neq Id$ or $Id^* = Id$ and $Y^* \neq \sum \beta_i^* D_i$.

In the following, we give a multi-source homomorphic network coding signature scheme in the standard model based on the signature scheme CFW in [8].

Public system parameters. Let e be a bilinear map: $\mathbb{G} \times \mathbb{G}' \to \mathbb{G}_T$, where $\mathbb{G}, \mathbb{G}', \mathbb{G}_T$ are bilinear groups of prime order p. Let g be a generator of $\mathbb{G}$ and g' be a generator of $\mathbb{G}'$. Randomly choose elements $h, h_1, \ldots, h_n, g_1, \ldots, g_m$

from $\mathbb{G}$. Output these public system parameters which all source nodes share: $(p, g, g', h, h_1, \ldots, h_n, g_1, \ldots, g_m)$.

NetKG$(1^k, m, n)$. For every source i, it sets up its own key pair. Source i randomly selects a number a_i from $\mathbb{F}_p$ and sets its private key $sk_i = a_i$. Let $P_i = (g')^{a_i}$ be its public key pk_i.

NetSign(sk, Id, w). Each source node can generate its signature as if the single source signature scheme CFW in [8] was used, but their Id is the same. For the message vector $D_i = (u_1, \ldots, u_n, v_1, \ldots, v_m) \in \mathbb{F}_p^{n+m}$, source i compute its signature: let Id be a number of $\mathbb{F}_p^*$; Randomly select a number $s_i \in \mathbb{F}_p$, compute

$$X_i = (h^{s_i} \prod_{i=1}^{n} h_i^{u_i} \prod_{i=1}^{m} g_i^{v_i})^{\frac{1}{a_i+Id}} \text{ and output its signature } \sigma_i = (X_i, s_i).$$

NetEval(pk, Id, $\{(w_i, \alpha_i, \sigma_i)\}_{i=1}^t$). The signature of an intermediate node is as follows. If an intermediate node receive t data D_i from the same Id, where D_i's signature is $\sigma_i = (X_i, s_i)$. Let the intermediate node's data form be (Id, β, Y), where $Y = \sum_{i=1}^{t} \beta_i D_i$, $\beta = (\beta_1, \ldots, \beta_t)$. Then the signature of the intermediate node is a $t + 1$-dimension vector $\sigma = (X_1, \ldots, X_t, s^{**})$, where $s^{**} = \sum_{i=1}^{t} \beta_i s_i$ mod p.

Public (Id, β, Y, σ) and transfer it to other nodes.

NetVer(pk, Id, w, σ). The verification algorithm is given as follows.

Let $Y = (y_1, \ldots, y_n, w_1, \ldots, w_m)$, $\beta = (\beta_1, \ldots, \beta_t)$, $\sigma = (X_1, \ldots, X_t, s^{**})$. Verification process is as follows:

If $\prod_{j=1}^{t} e(X_j^{\beta_j}, P_j(g')^{Id}) = \prod_{j=1}^{t} e(h^{s^{**}} \prod_{i=1}^{n} h_i^{y_i} \prod_{i=1}^{m} g_i^{w_i}, g')$, output 1. Otherwise, output 0.

Theorem 1. *The above multi-source homomorphic network coding signature scheme is correct.*

Proof. For any $1 \le i \le n$ and $1 \le j \le t$, let u_i^j and v_i^j denote the i-th vector of D_j. Since $X_j = (h^s \prod_{i=1}^{n} h_i^{u_i^j} \prod_{i=1}^{m} g_i^{v_i^j})^{\frac{1}{a_j+Id}}$, $X_j^{\beta_j} = (h^s \prod_{i=1}^{n} h_i^{u_i^j} \prod_{i=1}^{m} g_i^{v_i^j})^{\frac{\beta_j}{a_j+Id}}$, $P_j(g')^{Id} = (g')^{a_j+Id}$. Thus, $\prod_{j=1}^{t} e(X_j^{\beta_j}, P_j(g')^{Id}) = \prod_{j=1}^{t} e(h^s \prod_{i=1}^{n} h_i^{u_i^j} \prod_{i=1}^{m} g_i^{v_i^j}, g')^{\beta_j}$.

On the other hand, since $s^{**} = \sum_{j=1}^{t} \beta_j s_j$ mod p, $y_i = \sum_{j=1}^{t} \beta_j u_i^j$ and $w_i = \sum_{j=1}^{t} \beta_j v_i^j$ for any $1 \le i \le n$ and $1 \le j \le t$. So, $h^{s^{**}} \prod_{i=1}^{n} h_i^{y_i} \prod_{i=1}^{m} g_i^{w_i} = \prod_{j=1}^{t} (h^{s_j} \prod_{i=1}^{n} h_i^{u_i^j} \prod_{i=1}^{m} g_i^{v_i^j})^{\beta_j}$. Thus, $\prod_{j=1}^{t} e(h^{s^{**}} \prod_{i=1}^{n} h_i^{y_i} \prod_{i=1}^{m} g_i^{w_i}, g') = \prod_{j=1}^{t} e(h^{s_j} \prod_{i=1}^{n} h_i^{u_i^j} \prod_{i=1}^{m} g_i^{v_i^j}, g')^{\beta_j}$.

Hence, $\prod_{j=1}^{t} e(X_j^{\beta_j}, P_j(g')^{Id}) = \prod_{j=1}^{t} e(h^{s^{**}} \prod_{i=1}^{n} h_i^{y_i} \prod_{i=1}^{m} g_i^{w_i}, g')$.

Theorem 2. *The above multi-source homomorphic network coding signature scheme is secure under the q-SDH assumption.*

Proof. In the following, we prove that if an adversary has an efficient attacking algorithm $\mathcal{B}^*$ which can produce a forged signed packet for above multi-source signature scheme, we can use $\mathcal{B}^*$ to construct an efficient attacking algorithm $\mathcal{B}$ which produces a forged signed packet for CFW signature scheme in [8].

For algorithm $\mathcal{B}^*$, its input is the following parameters: the public system parameters, the public keys of all the t sources with a valid identifier Id, and the set of corresponding signed packets from these sources. The signed packet from the i-th source is: (Id, E_i, V_i, σ_i), where E_i is the i-th unit vector.

According to the received data signed packets $(Id, E_i, V_i, \sigma_i)(1 \leq i \leq t)$ from the t sources, algorithm $\mathcal{B}^*$ outputs a forged signed packet $(Id^*, \beta^*, Y^* = \sum \beta_i^* V_i^*, \sigma^*)$, where $Y^* \neq 0$ and the verification algorithm output 1, i.e. either $Id^* \neq Id$ or $Id^* = Id$ and $Y^* \neq \sum \beta_i^* V_i$.

We assume that the CFW signature algorithm of one source node uses the following public system parameter: Let $\mathbb{G}, \mathbb{G}', \mathbb{G}_{\mathbb{T}}$ be bilinear groups of prime order p such that e is a bilinear map: $\mathbb{G} \times \mathbb{G}' \to \mathbb{G}_{\mathbb{T}}$. g is a generator of $\mathbb{G}$ and g' is a generator of $\mathbb{G}'$. Choose random elements $h, h_1, \ldots, h_n, g_1, \ldots, g_m$. Suppose a is the private key and $P = (g')^a$ is the public key.

Based on $\mathcal{B}^*$ algorithm, we construct a polynomial time algorithm $\mathcal{B}$ which produces a forged signature packet for the CFW signature scheme.

First, we construct t source nodes. The first source node uses (a, P) as its private and public keys, i.e. $sk_1 = a$ and $pk_1 = P$. We will add $t - 1$ source nodes whose private and public keys are generated as follows. Randomly select $t - 1$ numbers from $\mathbb{F}_p$: $x_1, \ldots, x_{t-1}$. Set the private key of the i-th source $a_i = x_{i-1}(a + Id) - Id$ and its public key $P_i = (g')^{a_i}$. Thus, each source node outputs its signature $\sigma_i = (X_i, s_i)$.

For this t source nodes, we call $\mathcal{B}^*$ algorithm, which outputs a forged signature packet as follows. $(Id^*, \beta^*, Y^* = \sum \beta_i^* V_i^*, \sigma^* = (\sigma_1^*, \ldots, \sigma_t^*))$.

Thus, we output a forged signature packet for CFW as follows: $(Id^*, \beta^*, Y^*, \sigma^{**})$, where $\sigma^{**} = (X^{**}, s^{**})$, $X^{**} = (X_1^*)^{\beta_1^*} \prod_{i=2}^{t} (X_i^*)^{\beta_i^* x_{i-1}}$, $s^{**} = \prod_{i=1}^{t} \beta_i^* s_i^* \mod p$.

It is easy to get:

$$e(X^{**}, P \cdot (g')^{Id}) = e((X_1^*)^{\beta_1^*} \prod_{i=2}^{t} (X_i^*)^{\beta_i^* x_{i-1}}, P \cdot (g')^{Id})$$

$$= e((X_1^*)^{\beta_1^*}, P \cdot (g')^{Id}) \cdot e(\prod_{i=2}^{t} (X_i^*)^{\beta_i^* x_{i-1}}, P \cdot (g')^{Id})$$

$$= e((X_1^*)^{\beta_1^*}, P \cdot (g')^{Id}) \cdot e(\prod_{i=2}^{t} (X_i^*)^{\beta_i^*}, P \cdot (g')^{Id})^{x_{i-1}}$$

$$= e((X_1^*)^{\beta_1^*}, P \cdot (g')^{Id}) \cdot e(\prod_{i=2}^{t} (X_i^*)^{\beta_i^*}, (P \cdot (g')^{Id})^{x_{i-1}})$$

$$= e((X_1^*)^{\beta_1^*}, P \cdot (g')^{Id}) \cdot e(\prod_{i=2}^{t} (X_i^*)^{\beta_i^*}, (g')^{a_i+Id})$$

$$= e((X_1^*)^{\beta_1^*}, P \cdot (g')^{Id}) \cdot e(\prod_{i=2}^{t} (X_i^*)^{\beta_i^*}, (P_i \cdot (g')^{Id})$$

$$= e(\prod_{i=1}^{t} (X_i^*)^{\beta_i^*}, P_i \cdot (g')^{Id}) = e(h^{s^{**}} \prod_{i=1}^{n} h_i^{u_i} \prod_{i=1}^{m} g_i^{v_i}, g')$$

Since either $Id^* \neq Id$, or $Y^* \neq \sum \beta_i^* V_i$, it is a forged signature for CFW signature scheme.

But CFW signature scheme is security under q-SDH assumption. Hence, our multi-source homomorphic network coding signature scheme is secure under the q-SDH assumption.

4 Conclusion

In this paper, we propose the first multi-source homomorphic network coding signature in the standard model and show that our signature scheme is security under q-SDH assumption holds.

There are some problems that are required to studied, such as how to design a multi-source homomorphic network coding signature over lattice whose security is based on the hard lattice problems.

Acknowledgments. We would like to thank the anonymous referees for their careful readings of the manuscripts and many useful suggestions.

Wenbin Chen's research has been partly supported by the science research funding of Huawei Technologies Co., Ltd. under Grant No. YBCB2012055, by the National Natural Science Foundation of China (NSFC) under Grant No. 11271097, and by the Program for Innovative Research Team in Education Department of Guangdong Province Under No. 2015KCXTD014. Jin Li's research has been supported by National Natural Science Foundation of China (No. 61472091), by Natural Science Foundation of Guangdong Province for Distinguished Young Scholars (2014A030306020), by Guangzhou scholars project (No. 1201561613), by Science and Technology Planning Project of Guangdong Province, China (2015B010129015) and by the program of the State Key Laboratory for Cryptology. FuFang Li's work had been co-financed by: National Natural Science Foundation of China under Grant No. 61472092; Guangdong Provincial Science and Technology Plan Project under Grant No. 2013B010401037; and GuangZhou Municipal High School Science Research Fund under grant No. 1201421317. Ke Qi's research has been supported by the Guangzhou Science and Technology Plan Project under Grant No. 201605061403261 and 2014 State Scholarship Fund (201408440338).

References

1. Attrapadung, N., Libert, B.: Homomorphic network coding signatures in the standard model. In: Catalano, D., Fazio, N., Gennaro, R., Nicolosi, A. (eds.) PKC 2011. LNCS, vol. 6571, pp. 17–34. Springer, Heidelberg (2011). doi:10.1007/978-3-642-19379-8_2
2. Ahlswede, R., Cai, N., Li, S.-Y.R., Yeung, R.W.: Network information flow. IEEE Trans. Inf. Theor. 46(4), 1204–1216 (2000)
3. Agrawal, S., Boneh, D., Boyen, X., Freeman, D.M.: Preventing pollution attacks in multi-source network coding. In: Nguyen, P.Q., Pointcheval, D. (eds.) PKC 2010. LNCS, vol. 6056, pp. 161–176. Springer, Heidelberg (2010). doi:10.1007/978-3-642-13013-7_10
4. Boneh, D., Boyen, X.: Short signatures without random oracles. In: Cachin, C., Camenisch, J.L. (eds.) EUROCRYPT 2004. LNCS, vol. 3027, pp. 56–73. Springer, Heidelberg (2004). doi:10.1007/978-3-540-24676-3_4
5. Boneh, D., Freeman, D.M.: Linearly homomorphic signatures over binary fields and new tools for lattice-based signatures. In: Catalano, D., Fazio, N., Gennaro, R., Nicolosi, A. (eds.) PKC 2011. LNCS, vol. 6571, pp. 1–16. Springer, Heidelberg (2011). doi:10.1007/978-3-642-19379-8_1
6. Boneh, D., Freeman, D., Katz, J., Waters, B.: Signing a linear subspace: signature schemes for network coding. In: Jarecki, S., Tsudik, G. (eds.) PKC 2009. LNCS, vol. 5443, pp. 68–87. Springer, Heidelberg (2009). doi:10.1007/978-3-642-00468-1_5
7. Catalano, D., Fiore, D., Warinschi, B.: Adaptive pseudo-free groups and applications. In: Paterson, K.G. (ed.) EUROCRYPT 2011. LNCS, vol. 6632, pp. 207–223. Springer, Heidelberg (2011). doi:10.1007/978-3-642-20465-4_13
8. Catalano, D., Fiore, D., Warinschi, B.: Efficient network coding signatures in the standard model. In: Fischlin et al. [12], pp. 680–696
9. Chen, W., Lei, H., Qi, K.: Lattice-based linearly homomorphic signatures in the standard model. Theor. Comput. Sci. 634, 47–54 (2016)
10. Freeman, D.M.: Improved security for linearly homomorphic signatures: a generic framework. In: Fischlin, M., Buchmann, J., Manulis, M. (eds.) PKC 2012. LNCS, vol. 7293, pp. 697–714. Springer, Heidelberg (2012). doi:10.1007/978-3-642-30057-8_41
11. Krohn, M.N., Freedman, M.J., Mazieres, D.: On-the-fly verification of rateless erasure codes for efficient content distribution. In: Proceedings of 2004 IEEE Symposium on Security and Privacy, Berkeley, California, USA, pp. 226–240, 9–12 May 2004
12. Fischlin, M., Buchmann, J., Manulis, M. (eds.): PKC 2012. LNCS, vol. 7293. Springer, Heidelberg (2012)
13. Fu, Z., Ren, K., Shu, J., Sun, X., Huang, F.: Enabling personalized search over encrypted outsourced data with efficiency improvement. IEEE Trans. Parallel Distrib. Syst. 27, 2546–2559 (2015). doi:10.1109/TPDS.2015.2506573
14. Fu, Z., Sun, X., Liu, Q., Zhou, L., Shu, J.: Achieving efficient cloud search services: multi-keyword ranked search over encrypted cloud data supporting parallel computing. IEICE Trans. Commun. E98-B(1), 190–200 (2015)
15. Fu, Z., Wu, X., Guan, C., Sun, X., Ren, K.: Towards efficient multi-keyword fuzzy search over encrypted outsourced data with accuracy improvement. IEEE Trans. Inf. Forensics Secur. 11(12), 2706–2716 (2016)
16. Gennaro, R., Katz, J., Krawczyk, H., Rabin, T.: Secure network coding over the integers. In: Nguyen, P.Q., Pointcheval, D. (eds.) PKC 2010. LNCS, vol. 6056, pp. 142–160. Springer, Heidelberg (2010). doi:10.1007/978-3-642-13013-7_9

17. Gkantsidis, C., Rodriguez, P.: Cooperative security for network coding file distribution. In: Proceedings of the 24th Annual Joint Conference of the IEEE Computer and Communications Societies (INFOCOM) (2006)
18. Guo, P., Wang, J., Li, B., Lee, S.: A variable threshold-value authentication architecture for wireless mesh networks. J. Internet Technol. **15**(6), 929–936 (2014)
19. Johnson, R., Molnar, D., Song, D., Wagner, D.: Homomorphic signature schemes. In: Preneel, B. (ed.) CT-RSA 2002. LNCS, vol. 2271, pp. 244–262. Springer, Heidelberg (2002). doi:10.1007/3-540-45760-7_17
20. Kang, H.J., Vasserman, E.Y., Lee, H.T., Cheon, J.H., Kim, Y.: Secure network coding for a P2P system. In: ACM Conference on Computer and Communications Security, Poster (2009)
21. Lauter, K.E., Charles, X.D., Jain, K.: Signatures for network coding. In: Proceedings of the 40th Annual Conference on Information Sciences and Systems (CISS 2006), pp. 857–863 (2006)
22. Robert-Li, S.-Y., Yeung, R.Y., Cai, N.: Linear network coding. IEEE Trans. Inf. Theor. **49**(2), 371–381 (2003)
23. Lewko, A., Waters, B.: New techniques for dual system encryption and fully secure HIBE with short ciphertexts. In: Micciancio, D. (ed.) TCC 2010. LNCS, vol. 5978, pp. 455–479. Springer, Heidelberg (2010). doi:10.1007/978-3-642-11799-2_27
24. Ma, T., Zhou, J., Tang, M., Tian, Y., Al-Dhelaan, A., Al-Rodhaan, M., Lee, S.: Social network and tag sources based augmenting collaborative recommender system. IEICE Trans. Inf. Syst. **E98–D**(4), 902–910 (2015)
25. Shen, J., Tan, H., Wang, J., Wang, J., Lee, S.: A novel routing protocol providing good transmission reliability in underwater sensor networks. J. Internet Technol. **16**(1), 171–178 (2015)
26. Xia, Z., Wang, X., Sun, X., Wang, Q.: A secure and dynamic multi-keyword ranked search scheme over encrypted cloud data. IEEE Trans. Parallel Distrib. Syst. **27**(2), 340–352 (2015)
27. Xie, S., Wang, Y.: Construction of tree network with limited delivery latency in homogeneous wireless sensor networks. Wirel. Pers. Commun. **78**(1), 231–246 (2014)
28. Yun, A., Cheon, J., Kim, Y.: On homomorphic signatures for network coding. IEEE Trans. Comput. **59**(9), 1295–1296 (2010)
29. Yu, Z., Wei, Y., Ramkumar, B., Guan, Y.: An efficient signature-based scheme for securing network coding against pollution attacks. In: Proceedings of the Conference of the IEEE Computer and Communications Societies (INFOCOM) (2008)
30. Wang, Y.: Insecure provable secure network coding. http://eprint.iacr.org/2009/504
31. Xia, Z., Wang, X., Zhang, L., Qin, Z., Sun, X., Ren, K.: A privacy-preserving and copy-deterrence content-based image retrieval scheme in cloud computing. IEEE Trans. Inf. Forensics Secur. **11**, 2594–2608 (2016). doi:10.1109/TIFS.2016.2590944
32. Zhou, Z., Wang, Y., Wu, Q.M.J., Yang, C.-N., Sun, X.: Effective and efficient global context verification for image copy detection. IEEE Trans. Inf. Forensics Secur. **12**, 48–63 (2016). doi:10.1109/TIFS.2016.2601065
33. Zhao, F., Kalker, T., Médard, M., Han, K.J.: Signatures for content distribution with network coding. In: Proceedings of 2007 IEEE International Symposium on Information Theory (ISIT 2007), pp. 556–560 (2007)

Trust-ABAC Towards an Access Control System for the Internet of Things

Hamdi Ouechtati(✉) and Nadia Ben Azzouna

ISG, LR11ES03 SMART Lab, Universite de Tunis,
41, Rue de la Liberté, Cité Bouchoucha, 2000 Le Bardo, Tunis, Tunisia
Hamdiouechtati@gmail.com, nadia.benazzouna@ensi.rnu.tn

Abstract. In order to cope with certain challenges posed by device capacity and the nature of IoT networks, a lightweight access control model is needed to resolve security and privacy issues. The use of complex encryption algorithms is infeasible due to the volatile nature of IoT environment and pervasive devices with limited resources. In this paper, we present the Trust-ABAC, an access control model for the Internet of Things, in which a coupling between the access control based on attributes and the trust concept is done. We evaluated the performance of Trust-ABAC through an experiment based on a simulation. We used the OMNeT++ simulator to show the efficiency of our model in terms of power consumption, response time and the average number of messages generated by an access request. The obtained results of simulation prove the good scalability of our Trust-ABAC model.

Keywords: Internet of Things · Access control · Attribute-Based Access Control · Trust

1 Introduction

The concept of the Internet of Things (IoT) has evolved over the last few years following the integration of smart objects in the current Internet infrastructure [1]. It is based on the idea that all objects can be connected to the Internet and are able to transmit information and possibly receive commands. The IoT proposes to create a continuity between the real world and the digital world: it gives existence to physical objects in the digital world [1]. In the IoT, there is no single strategy for realizing the vision of the IoT because it is a complicated challenge, since it must meet many requirements such as scalability, reliability, security, etc. [2]. Thus, in the literature, we can find different visions of the future architecture for the IoT [3].

Centralized IoT: It is characterized by having a single central entity which stores updated information from the network of things in order to provide it to the user. For example, the central entity can be instantiated using a simple server or a cluster of devices forming a cloud.

© Springer International Publishing AG 2017
M.H.A. Au et al. (Eds.): GPC 2017, LNCS 10232, pp. 75–89, 2017.
DOI: 10.1007/978-3-319-57186-7_7

Collaborative IoT: It is similar to the centralized IoT but having several central entities which collaborate with each other by exchanging information in order to create new services. For example, the Collaborative IoT can be used by IoT service providers that analyze the weather condition of different cities that collaborate in order to provide a snapshot of the weather in the whole country.

Connected Intranets of Things: In this case, the intranet provide information and data to the central entity as well as to the user. For example, the connected intranets of Things can be used in hospitals (intranets) which sometimes need to access the services of a central IoT entity to obtain global information (e.g. overall bed occupancy).

Distributed IoT: This scenario describes fully interconnected systems where all entities can provide information/data and services to the other entities. Distributed IoT can be applied in smart city infrastructures (e.g. Vehicular Ad-hoc Networks (VANETs)).

The increasing number of existing heterogeneous objects and the complexity related to managing the wealth of information provided by these objects, represent one of the crucial challenges. Therefore, the number of threats and their sources increases proportionally. Accordingly, in this paper, we put more focus on solving the access control problem in the IoT. Our Trust-ABAC model for the IoT is a combination between the Attribute Based Access Control (ABAC) model [4] and the trust mechanism. ABAC is presented as a contextual access control model which defines the access permissions based on the characteristics of each entity, called attributes. Furthermore, in an open environment such as the IoT, objects are sometimes unknown. To this end, the concept of trust and ABAC model should be combined in order to provide access control in such an open environment.

The remainder of this paper is organized as follows. The second section briefly discusses the main existing access control models. The third section presents the description of our model of access control Trust-ABAC. In this section we will take a closer look on the architecture and the interactions between the various components of our Trust-ABAC model. The Sect. 4 focuses on the description of the experimental study and the results are used to evaluate our model. In the Sect. 5 the conclusion is given and the future work is pointed out.

2   Related Works

In the literature, there exist a large number of access control models which have been proposed to ensure the protection and the confidentiality of data. There are three major categories of access control models namely, Discretionary Access Control models (DAC) [5], Mandatory Access Control model (MAC) [6] and Role Based Access Control model (RBAC) [7]. Other access control models such as TCAC [8] and Or-BAC [9] have been defined to be better adapted to specific organizations. Subsequently, we present the main access control models to determine the most relevant ones for the IoT.

Different models have been proposed to enforce an efficient access control. These models include DAC which is a model based on the identity notion. This latter is called discretionary because the object owner can grant rights to other subjects [5]. This basic principle make the access control vulnerable to malicious programs that can lead to an information leak to unauthorized users. Moreover, in an open environment such as IoT, objects are sometimes unknown, so we can not apply the DAC models for an access control in the IoT. MAC is a model which regulates access based on the classification of subjects and objects in the system. Although MAC solves the problem of information leakage of DAC models, it is very rigid, suitable for organizations where the need for security is very strict and will-suited to distributed systems and then to the IoT. RBAC is another different control model which is not based directly on users, but on the roles assigned to them, so we move from a large number of users to just a few well-defined roles. However, RBAC model is not suitable for highly opened dynamic environments as the Internet of Things because there is a very large number of objects, so that RBAC can loose its ease of administration. It is worth noting that DAC, MAC and RBAC models only allow to model security policies with static permissions.

The access control based on the organization, Or-BAC, (Organization Based Access Control) aims to establish a more abstract access control policy which deals with permissions, prohibitions, requirements and recommendations. In Or-BAC model, it is possible to use the notion of inheritance of roles when there is an organization with sub organizations. However, the Or-BAC model does not meet the collaboration needs, distribution and interoperability between different organizations. So, we can not apply the Or-BAC model for an access control in the IoT. The access control model based on trust and context TCAC (Trust and Context based Access Control) is an RBAC using the concepts of trust and context to give access to system resources [8]. TCAC model is based on roles but it is more flexible than RBAC because it is better adapted to dynamic environments. In [10], Thomas and Sekaran propose an agent based approach for distributed access control in cloud computing environments. The proposed solution is an effective and safe approach that combines two paradigms (cloud computing and agent based systems). However, this centralized solution is difficult to apply in an IoT environment. ABAC has been proposed to address the web services security needs. In the ABAC model, the access to resources can be done based on several attributes characterizing a subject and on policy rules specifying the conditions under which access is granted or refused. The major difference between the ABAC model and the other conventional models is the inclusion of the system execution context through the definition of environmental attributes. Moreover, in the ABAC model, the access control process is based on the attributes of the subjects and not their identifiers, which allows to use this model in open environments such as IoT. Many research in the area of computer security have been drawn to ABAC model. In [11], Waleed W. Smari et al. incorporate trust and privacy in the ABAC model for collaboration environments. The proposed solution provides good scalability and flexibility, but it only focuses on the preliminary model and there is no implementation architecture.

In the literature, there are several access control solutions that allow dynamic access management which have been proposed for different application scenarios of the IoT. The work presented in [12] proposes a decentralized approach for security and privacy challenges in the Internet of Things founded on the delegates capabilities and based on the User Datagram Protocol (UDP) and the Constrained Application Protocol (CoAP). In the CapBAC Approach, the access tokens are provided by the issuer to a customer with an ECC digital signing (Elliptic Curve Cryptography) JSON format (JavaScript Object Notation). A token contains information about access to the resource, actions that can be executed, and additional conditions which are assumed to be verified by the device. When the device receives an access request, the authorization process is established through the validation of the token as well as the rights and conditions. The authors also evaluated their approach and found that each operation requires 480.96 ms in total, of which 89.1 % is dedicated to cryptographic calculations. Taking into account that access control verification is necessary for each request, this overload is quite large in terms of energy efficiency and calculation time. In [13], the authors propose a new regime for authentication and access control IACAC (Identity Authentication and Capability based Access Control). It is compatible with access technologies like Bluetooth, 4G, and Wi-Fi. The IACAC algorithm deals with both authentication and access control that are divided into three parts: (1) The generation of a secret key based on Elliptical Curve Cryptography-Diffie Hellman, (2) The identification process between two devices, (3) The creation of access control capability. The protocol is also analyzed from the point of view of performance and security for various possible attacks within the framework of IoT. The evaluation of the protocol shows that it can defy effectively the DoS attacks, the man in the middle attack and the replay attack.

Concerning the access control models for dynamic environments, Arcangelo et al. in their paper [14] provided new results on the AklTaylor [15] scheme, by carefully analyzing the problem of supporting dynamic updates, as well as key replacement operations. They also perform a rigorous analysis of the AklTaylor scheme in the dynamic setting characterizing cloud storage, by considering different key assignment strategies and proving that the corresponding schemes are secure with respect to the notion of key recovery. In [16], the authors define the concept of hierarchical key assignment schemes supporting dynamic updates, formalizing the relative security model. In particular, they provide the notion of security with respect to key indistinguishability, by taking into account the dynamic changes in the hierarchy. Moreover, they show how to construct a hierarchical key assignment scheme supporting dynamic updates, by using as a building block a symmetric encryption scheme. In [17], Hitesh and al has introduced a security framework called AEGIS to prevent controller APIs from being misused by malicious network applications. Through the run-time verification of API calls, AEGIS performs a finegrained access control for important controller APIs that can be misused by malicious applications. AEGIS provides three core functions including data generation, security rule generation, and decision making to protect controller APIs. At runtime, AEGIS automatically checks applications behaviors when they call APIs and prevents APIs on the controller from being misused.

With the emergence of web 2.0 and semantic web, new content management systems have emerged that rely on these new approaches to manage access to content. In particular, Alam et al. demonstrate the limitations of access rights management solutions using non-semantic description languages. They propose an OWL ontology [18] to describe access to web services, inspired by the XACML model. In [19], the authors propose an ontological approach to let different access control models coexist into large-scale integrated infrastructures for the health-care domain. This solution is generic enough to be adopted in other similar domains where sensitive information has to be properly exchanged among a large number of interested destinations.

3   The TRUST-ABAC model

Our Trust-ABAC model for the IoT is a combination between the access control model based on attributes (ABAC) and the trust mechanism. This section defines all the specifications necessary to configure our Trust-ABAC model. In our model, the authorization decision is based on the attributes of the various entities involved in making access control decisions. When an object sends a request for access, the system evaluates this request based on the corresponding access control policy and the confidence value of the object in question. If the conditions on the attributes and on the trust value are met, the access request is accepted, otherwise it is rejected. In order to specify our Trust-ABAC model, we define some related notions in the following:

Definition 1 (IoT Service): An IoT service is an abstraction of transactions contemplated by the IoT system on its objects. We use srv to represent an IoT Service and $SRVS$ to represent a set of IoT services: SRVS = $\{srv_1, srv_2, ..., srv_n\}$ where srv_i $(1 \leq i \leq n)$ is an IoT service.

Definition 2 (Object): An object is an instance of a protected resource. We use o to represent an object and O to represent a set of objects: O = $\{o_1, o_2, ..., o_n\}$, where o_i $(1 \leq i \leq n)$ is an IoT object.

Definition 3 (Attributes): A set of variables which include the characteristics of an object. We use $attr$ to represent an attribute and $ATTR$ to represent the set of attributes: ATTR = $\{attr_1, attr_2, ..., attr_n\}$, where $attr_i$ $(1 \leq i \leq n)$ is an attribute.

An attribute is defined as a property related to each object in an IoT environment when it is running. An attribute can be a concrete property, like object-ID or a service parameter (the input parameters when calling an IoT service such as time, location, age, etc.). Based on system security requirements, system administrators can determine which attributes will be used to specify access and can dynamically add new attributes if needed. For example, $ATTR$ = $\{identity, time, location\}$.

Definition 4 (Attribute Condition): An attribute condition AC is an expression of the form: $AC = < type >< attr >< LOp >< Val >$; where $type \in$ (int, string, bool, etc.) is the type of $attr$, $attr \in ATTR$, for example (service, time, place, age); LOp is a logical operator in the set $\{\leq, \geq, <, >, =, \neq, \forall, \in, \vee, \wedge\}$; Val is a specific value of $attr$, for example srv = temperature, Age = 40, times $\in$ [9 AM, 17 PM], place = Office.

Definition 5 (Attribute Constraint): An attribute constraint C is a regular expression that refers to a logical combination of AC on a set of attributes.

Attribute constraint: $C = Clause_1 \cup Clause_2 \cup ... \cup Clause_n$;
Regular expression: Clause $= AC_1 \cap AC_2 \cap ... \cap AC_n$;
Based on this format, our access control schema is capable of specifying complex attributes related to the majority of security requirements. For example, the security policy "the temperature service can be accessed by family members outside the home from 9:00 to 7:00 p.m." may be expressed as: $C = $ Times $\geq$ 09:00 $\cap$ Times $\leq$ 19:00 $\cap$ Place = "Outside" $\cap$ Identity = "family members" $\cap$ Trust value $\geq 0,5$.

Definition 6 (Access policy): An access policy AP is defined as a combination of three elements: AP = <srv, C, Trust>, where $Trust$ is the confidence value required to access the IoT service srv in this policy.

Definition 7 (Access Request): An access request to the IoT service is defined as a triple $AR = < ID, srv, AV >$; where ID is the identifier of th object which transmits the access request to the IoT service whose identifier is srv and AV is the attribute value which represents the set of the needed attributes to access the requested service, $AV = \{v_1$ of $attr_1, v_2$ of $attr_2, ..., v_n$ of $attr_n\}$. Based on the access request AR and on the access policy associated to the requested service, Trust-ABAC model either grants or refuses the access.

4   Trust-ABAC Architecture

The architecture of our Trust-ABAC system for the IoT is composed of a set of features and functional components that enforce authorization decisions based on attributes and policies. Our architecture is adapted to the Intranets of Things architecture, which is very widespread in the smart cities (e.g. smart homes, smart hospitals, Smart factories, etc.). In this approach, the data acquisition networks (Intranets of Things) can effectively treat local information, and also provide it not only to central entities but also to local and distant users. Accordingly, the access control process is performed at the point of access to the Intranet which reduces the computational load at the requested object and make our model more flexible and scalable.

4.1   Architecture Components

An overview of the main components of the architecture of our access control system is shown in Fig. 1. The set of components is inspired by a generic computer markup meta-language XACML (eXtensible Access Control Markup Language) [20], an open standard of ABAC proposed by OASIS and widely used in research. In our architecture, there are nine main components described below:

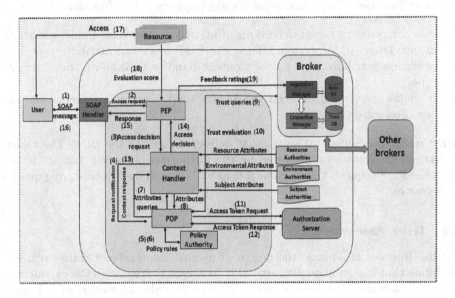

Fig. 1. TRUST-ABAC implementation architecture for the Internet of Things.

SOAP Handler: This module is in charge of accepting SOAP messages and verifies the digital signature of the message presented in the request. If this control is successfully completed, the message is sent to the PEP.

PEP (Policy Enforcement Point): The PEP receives the access requests, sends an authorization request to the PDP and applies the decisions of the PDP (allows or refuses the access to resources). Furthermore, the PEP sends the resources evaluation feedback to the reputation manager to update his reputation database.

PDP (Policy Decision Point): This module is in charge of taking the access decision based on (i) the attributes obtained from the request for authorization, (ii) the policies and the rule sets obtained from the policy authority, and (iii) the requester trust value obtained from the reputation manager.

Subject Authorities: This component defines and provides subject attributes necessary for the authorization decision.

Resource Authorities: This component defines and provides resources attributes necessary for the authorization decision.

Environment Authorities: This component defines and provides environment attributes necessary for the authorization decision.

Policy Authority: This component allows defining access policies, and feeds the access control rules in the PDP.

Context handler: This component should implement two functions:

(1) It is a repository for all definitions of attributes and their implementations in our Trust-ABAC system. When the PDP meets an attribute type in a condition attribute, it calls the Context handler to validate this attribute type.
(2) It makes conversion between the format used outside the system and the one used inside it.

Authorization Server: A server that delivers tokens to the PDP. The tokens are strings of characters generated by the authorization server and are issued when the PDP requests them. These tokens will be used by objects during queries to resources.

4.2 Trust Assessment

For the Internet of Things, the design of a trust management framework is a discipline that has gained much attention in recent years due to the exponential growth of services that heterogeneous devices provide. Moreover, in IoT environments, it is impossible to know in advance all objects hence the usefulness of using the trust to establish the trust relationship progressively with arrivals of objects. In [21], Kwei-Jay Lin et al. propose a reputation and trust management Broker framework for web applications. We will rely on some principles of this architecture to achieve the trust part of our model of access control, Trust-ABAC. Our access control system is based on a distributed trust management system. A broker contains two components, namely the reputation manager and the connection manager:

(1) **Reputation Manager:** The reputation Manager has three features. First, it manages the requests for trust values of the PDP and the other brokers. Second, it sends requests to the connection manager if necessary. Third, it is responsible for backing up feedback information received from objects after each transaction in its reputation database (Repu DB).
(2) **Connection Manager:** In an IoT system, brokers can not rely on its resources to evaluate all objects during the interaction. The connection manager acts as an interface between the broker and the trusting network, and it is responsible for sending requests to the other brokers. Therefore, each broker maintains a list of the other trusting brokers and its trust values in its trust database (trust DB).

The connection manager keeps all the recent recommendations from the broker list in its database. All recommendations received for the same request share the same request ID. The connection manager uses the following method to aggregate the recommendations:

$$R = \sum \frac{X_i * N_i * R_i}{N} * F(\Delta t) \ with \ N = \sum X_i * N_i * F(\Delta t) \qquad (1)$$

Each recommendation R_i is evaluated by the number of transactions N_i used by the broker X_i to calculate the trust value, the time differential factor $F(\Delta t)$, and the trust value of this broker X_i. Each broker uses a differential threshold to decide whether the recommendation should be taken to the full value to ensure the timeliness of the recommendation. If R_i has been reported with a deviation below the time threshold, the value of the time differential factor $F(\Delta t)$ is 1, otherwise it is $e^{-\beta \Delta t}$, with β is a constant set by the administrator.

After each transaction, the reputation manager collects feedback evaluations from PEP. Let N be the number of transactions used to generate the current reputation value R_{old}. After the PEP submission of a feedback rating r concerning the object in question, the reputation manager updates the trust value of the object x stored in its local database of R_{old} to R_{new}. The trust value of an object x is updated using the following formula:

$$R_{new} = e^{-\beta \Delta t} \frac{N}{N+1} R_{old} + (1 - e^{-\beta \Delta t} \frac{N}{N+1}) r \qquad (2)$$

The feedback time difference between r and R_{old} is denoted by Δt, while $e^{-\beta \Delta t}$ represents the reduction factor of R_{old}.

Moreover the connection manager updates the trust value for the brokers that sent the recommendations. The trust value of a broker is not static, it is based on the number of exact recommendations that have been provided. It is updated after each received recommendation by comparing this latter with the result of the real operation. At the beginning, all other brokers receive a neutral trust value X = 0.5. After each transaction, the trust value of a broker is updated as follows:

− If the recommendation correspond to the real experience:

$$X = X + F * (1 - X) \qquad (3)$$

− If the recommendation does not correspond to the real experience:

$$X = X * (1 - F) \qquad (4)$$

In the Eqs. 3 and 4, F is a positive index with a value less than 1. For example, if F is 0.2 and X is 0.6, the new value of X is 0.68 when the recommendation corresponds to the real experience. On the other hand, if the recommendation does not correspond to the real experience X is reduced to a new value of 0.4. The update equations are designed in such a way that X always has a value between 0 and 1. Moreover, it is difficult to gain additional trust, but easy to lose trust when X has a great value.

4.3   Trust-ABAC Architectural Components Interactions

The various steps performed by the components of Trust-ABAC architecture illustrated in Fig. 2, are as follows:

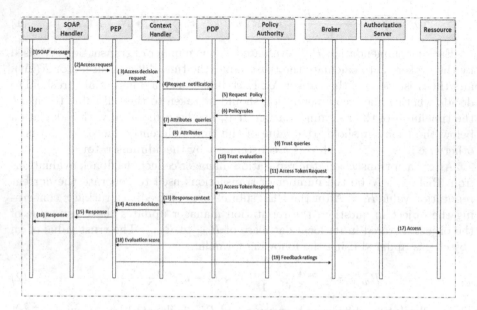

Fig. 2. Workflow of the TRUST-ABAC model.

(1) The subject sends an access request to the SOAP Handler as a SOAP message.
(2) The SOAP Handler accepts the SOAP message and verifies the digital signature contained in the request. If this check is successfully completed the message will be sent to PEP, otherwise, the access request is denied.
(3) The PEP receives the access request and sends the information of the access request to the Context Handler.
(4) The Context Handler builds the context of the access request in a XACML format using the information provided by the PEP and sends it to the PDP.
(5) The PDP receives the context of the access request, and facts a call to the Policy Authority in order to send the necessary access policy evaluation.
(6) The policy Authority, in turn, transmits the necessary access policy evaluation.
(7) The PDP asks the context handler, if necessary, for additional attributes to perform the evaluation.
(8) The context handler, in turn, passes the additional attributes (e.g. environmental attributes, etc.) needed for the evaluation of the PDP access control policy. If attributes do not check with the access policy, the access request is denied.

(9) Otherwise, the PDP uses the trusting broker which sends the confidence value of the requester.

(10) The trusting broker, in turn, transmits the value of trust to the PDP. If the confidence value is below the threshold mentioned in the access policy, the access request is denied.

(11) Otherwise, the PDP uses the authorization server to obtain an access token.

(12) The authorization server, in turn, transmits an access token to the PDP.

(13) The PDP returns its authorization decision to the Context Handler in a XACML message.

(14) The Context Handler transmits the authorization decision and eventually the access token to the PEP. This latter allows or denies access to the resource according to the issued authorization decision.

(15) The PEP sends the authorization decision to the SOAP Handler.

(16) The SOAP Handler, in turn, transmits the authorization decision to the subject requesting access.

(17) The subject uses the token to access the IoT service.

(18) After the interaction with the subject, the resource sends a note of evaluation to the PEP.

(19) Finally, the PEP, in turn, transmits the assessment score to the reputation manager to update its reputation database.

5 Validation

To evaluate our Trust-ABAC access control model for the IoT, we conducted an experiment based on a simulation. Therefore, we used the simulator OMNeT++ [22] and MIXIM framework [23] for wireless networks.

5.1 Performance Metrics

Unlike the current Internet, the IoT environments should be formed by heterogeneous devices with a low processing power and storage capabilities, so our access control system should not be costly in terms of resource consumption. Specifically, to assess our access control system performance, we focus on the average response time, the energy consumption, and the average number of exchanged messages.

Average Response Time. The Response Time (RT) of an access request is defined as the time difference between the transmission time of a request and the arrival time of the access authorization. The Average Response Time (ART) is used to quantify the rapidity of our Trust-ABAC access control system and may be calculated as follows:

$$ART = \frac{\sum_{i=1}^{n} RT_i}{n} \tag{5}$$

where RT_i is the response time of the i-th request and n represents the full number of requests for access.

Energy Consumption. The key criteria for the design of an access control model for IoT is the energy consumption of wireless nodes. We define the metric of energy consumption by the requested object as follows:

$$EC = \frac{\sum_{i=1}^{n} consume_i}{\sum_{i=1}^{n} send_i + recv_i + \tau} \tag{6}$$

where $send_i$ and $recv_i$ denote the energy consumption, when the i-th node respectively sends a message and receives a message. $Consume_i$ is the energy consumed by the i-th node during the access control process. And τ represents the energy used to maintain the normal operation of the node in question.

Average Number of Exchanged Messages. The Average Number of Exchanged Messages (ANEM) is defined as the ratio between the total number of exchanged messages and the number of access requests. The average number of exchanged messages can be calculated as follows:

$$ANEM = \frac{\sum_{i=1}^{n} M_{Generated\,i}}{n} \tag{7}$$

In Eq. (7), $M_{Generated\,i}$ is the total number of exchanged messages due to the i-th access request, and n is the total number of access requests.

5.2   Simulation Parameters

The simulation parameters used in our work are presented in Table 1.

Table 1. Simulation parameters in OMNET++.

Parameters	Values
Number of objects	20
Number of services	20
Number of access requests	50
Simulation time	3000 s
Zone of simulation	1500 m × 1500 m
Channel capacity	54 Mbps
Transmission Range	100 m
Energy consumption for reception	0.395 (W)
Energy consumption for transmission	0.660 (W)
Initial energy level	100 (j)

The requests of access to the IoT services are generated in a random way. The interarrival time between two consecutive access requests is distributed according to an exponential distribution of parameter λ. In the simulation of our access control model Trust-ABAC, where the access requests are random and uniformly distributed between the different objects, tests were conducted with $\lambda = 0,02$.

5.3   Performance Evaluation

In order to evaluate the performance of the implemented Trust-ABAC system, we first evaluate the average response time, secondly the energy consumption and finally the average number of exchanged messages by varying each time the number of consulted brokers. The Fig. 3a presents the average response time of an access request according to the number of consulted brokers. The curve of linear trend of the average response time corresponds to the equation $Y = ax + b$ with, a = 0,0156 and b = 0,2726. Thus, the results of simulation prove the good scalability of our model of access control Trust-ABAC for IoT. The Fig. 3b shows the energy consumption according to the number of consulted brokers. This growth of energy consumption is slow because the curve of linear trend of consumption has an equation of the form $Y = ax + b$, with a = 0,0825 and b = 0,2364. Indeed, the simulation results well justify the advantage of our Trust-ABAC access control system for IoT in terms of consumed energy. The Fig. 3c presents the average number of exchanged messages according to the number of consulted brokers. The curve of linear trend of the average number of exchanged messages corresponds to the equation $Y = ax + b$, with a = 1,3861 et b = 2,8667. Accordingly, this increase in the number of exchanged messages do not threaten the performance of our access control system.

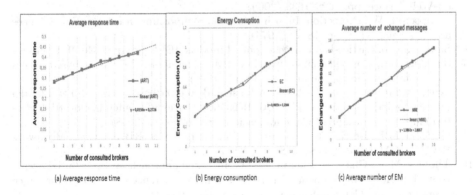

(a) Average response time   (b) Energy consumption   (c) Average number of EM

Fig. 3. Performance evaluation.

6   Conclusion

In this work, our basic contribution is to integrate trust in the ABAC model to enhance the access control level in the IoT environment. We evaluated the performance of our Trust-ABAC model for IoT through an experiment based on a simulation. We used the simulator OMNeT++ to show the effectiveness of our model in terms of energy consumption, response times and the average number of messages generated by an access request. The simulation results show the good scalability of our Trust-ABAC system when the number of brokers increases. The realised model and the obtained results leave the door open to many perspectives for future work. Firstly, we plan to design and implement a mechanism capable to achieve the identification of objects in an IoT system. Secondly, we aim to tackle the problem of the management and the exchange of keys by providing lightweight cryptographic means to protect the exchange of messages between IoT objects. Finally, our Trust-ABAC model will be extended in order to be more adaptive to better meet user's needs by taking into account his context and his behavior.

References

1. Atzori, L., Iera, A., Morabito, G.: The internet of things: a survey. Comput. Netw. **54**, 2787–2805 (2010)
2. Khan, R., Khan, S.U., Zaheer, R., Khan, S.: Future internet: the internet of things architecture, possible applications and key challenges. In: Proceedings of the 10th International Conference on Frontiers of Information Technology, pp. 257–260 (2012)
3. Roman, R., Zhou, J., Lopez, J.: On the features and challenges of security and privacy in distributed internet of things. Comput. Netw. **57**, 2266–2279 (2013)
4. Yuan, E., Tong, J.: Attribute based access control, a new access control approach for service oriented architectures (SOA). In: 2005 IEEE International Conference on Web Service, pp. 1628–1633 (2005)
5. Lampson, B.W.: Protection. In: 5th Princeton Symposium on Information Sciences and Systems, vol. 8, pp. 18–24 (1974)
6. Sandhu, R.S.: Lattice-based access control models. IEEE Comput. **26**, 9–19 (1993)
7. Sandhu, R.S., Coynek, E.J., Feinsteink, H.L., Youmank, C.E.: Role-based access control models. IEEE Comput. **29**, 38–47 (1996)
8. Feng, F., Lin, C., Peng, D., Li, J.: A trust and context based access control model for distributed systems. In: The 10th IEEE International Conference on High Performance Computing and Communications, pp. 629–634 (2008)
9. Damiani, M.L., Bertino, E., Catania, B., Perlasca, P.: Geo-RBAC: a spatially aware RBAC. ACM Trans. Inf. Syst. Secur. **10**, 1–34 (2006)
10. Thomas, M.V., Chandra Sekaran, K.: Agent-based approach for distributed access control in cloud environments. In: International Conference on High Performance Computing and Communications, pp. 1628–1633 (2013)
11. Smari, W.W., Zhu, J., Clemente, P.: Trust and privacy in attribute based access control for collaboration environments. In: International Conference on Information Integration and Web-based Applications and Services, pp. 49–55 (2009)
12. Skarmeta, A.F., Hernandez-Ramos, J.L., Victoria Moreno, M.: A decentralized approach for security and privacy challenges in the internet of things. In: IEEE World Forum on Internet of Things (WF-IoT), pp. 67–72 (2014)
13. Mahalle, P.N., Anggorojati, B., Prasad, N.R., Prasad, R.: Identity authentication and capability based access control (IACAC) for the internet of things. J. Cyber Secur. Mobility **1**, 309–348 (2013)

14. Castiglione, A., De Santis, A., Masucci, B., Palmieri, F., Huang, X., Castiglione, A.: Supporting dynamic updates in storage clouds with the Akl-Taylor scheme. Inf. Sci. **387**, 56–74 (2017)
15. Akl, S.G., Taylor, P.D.: Cryptographic solution to a problem of access control in a hierarchy. ACM Trans. Comput. Syst. **1**(3), 239–248 (1983)
16. Castiglione, A., De Santis, A., Masucci, B., Palmieri, F., Castiglione, A., Huang, X.: Cryptographic hierarchical access control for dynamic structures. IEEE Trans. Inf. Forensics Secur. **11**(10), 2349–2364 (2016)
17. Padekar, H., Park, Y., Hu, H., Chang, S.-Y.: Enabling dynamic access control for controller applications in software-defined networks. In: Proceedings of the 21st ACM on Symposium on Access Control Models and Technologies, SACMAT 2016, Shanghai, China, 5–8 June, 2016, pp. 51–61 (2016)
18. Alam, A., Subbiah, G., Thuraisingam, B., Khan, L.: Reasoning with semantics-aware access control policies for geospatial web services. In: Proceedings of the 3rd ACM Workshop on Secure Web Services, SWS 2006, pp. 69–76. ACM, New York (2006)
19. Esposito, C., Castiglione, A., Palmieri, F.: Interoperable access control by means of a semantic approach. In: 2016 30th International Conference on Advanced Information Networking and Applications Workshops (WAINA), pp. 280–285 (2016)
20. Godik, S., Moses, T.: Extensible access control markup language (xacml) version 1.0. OASIS Standard (2003)
21. Lin, K.-J., Lu, H., Yu, T., Tai, C.: A reputation and trust management broker framework for web applications. In: Proceedings of the 2005 IEEE International Conference on e-Technology, e-Commerce and e-Service, EEE 2005, pp. 262–269 (2005)
22. Varga, A.: Using the OMNet++ discrete event simulation system in education. IEEE Trans. Educ. **42**, 1–11 (1999)
23. Calandriello, G., Papadimitratos, P., Hubaux, J.-P., Lioy, A.: Efficient and robust pseudonymous authentication in VANET. In: Proceedings of the Fourth ACM International Workshop on Vehicular Ad Hoc Networks, pp. 19–28 (2007)

Privacy Preserving Multimodal Biometric Authentication in the Cloud

Neyire Deniz Sarier$^{(\boxtimes)}$

B-IT, cosec, Dahlmannstr. 2, 53113 Bonn, Germany
denizsarier@yahoo.com

Abstract. In this paper, we describe the first privacy preserving multimodal biometric authentication protocol resistant to hill climbing attacks. Due to the encrypted storage and processing in the encrypted domain, the biometric database can be outsourced to the cloud. Our scheme is based on the combination of two different cryptographic primitives operating on encrypted biometric templates generated either from a single trait such as fingerprint or multimodal biometrics. For the former, the scheme employs multiple matchers working on set overlap and euclidean distance resulting in two different matching scores. In both cases, quantized scores are combined privately, to prevent any party accessing the final fused matching score. This way, hill climbing attacks are prevented that are applicable even if the templates are stored as encrypted. Finally, the scheme benefits from the advantages of multimodal biometrics and the efficiency of the underlying primitives with linear computation and communication overhead.

Keywords: Privacy Preserving Biometric Authentication (PPBA) · Cloud security · Set overlap distance · Euclidean distance · Hill climbing attacks · Multi modal biometrics · Fingerprints

1 Introduction

Biometrics have been used for secure identification and authentication for more than two decades since biometric data is non-transferable, unforgettable, and always handy. In this context, multi-modal systems such as fusion of multiple biometrics (i.e. face and fingerprints) or multiple matching of the same biometric trait gained increasing popularity for practical applications, mainly due to the increased recognition performance and enhanced level of security. However, biometrics is sensitive data, thus the privacy of biometric stored on a central database should be guaranteed using cryptographic techniques. This is especially vital if the database that stores the biometric data of each user is outsourced to a cloud to reduce the storage costs. The challenge arises due to several well documented security risks faced by existing cloud service providers such as exposure

---

Dr. N. Deniz Sarier is an external researcher in Bonn-Aachen International Center for Information Technology (B-IT), Computer Security Group (cosec).

© Springer International Publishing AG 2017
M.H.A. Au et al. (Eds.): GPC 2017, LNCS 10232, pp. 90–104, 2017.
DOI: 10.1007/978-3-319-57186-7_8

of user data stored in the clear (i.e. not encrypted) to malicious parties [5]. To avoid this privacy concern, privacy-preserving biometric authentication (PPBA) protocols for unimodal setting are developed [4,5,8,18,20], some of which store biometric data in clear [4,18,20], hence not suitable for cloud storage.

Apart from these risks, biometric authentication systems are vulnerable to various attacks with respect to user and data privacy. Despite the provable security guarantees in semi-honest security level, where the internal attackers such as servers are honest-but-curious following the protocol specifications, much more complex attacks in the malicious adversary model can affect the privacy of data and users [13,17,21]. In particular, hill-climbing attacks can be performed, which can be perpetrated both at the feature extraction module and at the matcher module. When considering the former scenario, hill-climbing attacks generate data resembling the originally acquired biometrics. In alternative, hill-climbing attacks can be also performed by targeting the matcher module, with the aim of generating synthetic templates allowing successful recognition [13]. This attack is performed iteratively, each time updating the data generated at a given step trying to improve the resulting matching output, till a successful recognition is achieved. Here, the malicious (internal) attacker does not need any specific a priori knowledge about the biometrics of the targeted user [13]. In summary, hill climbing can be used to obtain templates with increased scores, however, recovering stored biometric templates has more severe impact than just finding an acceptable biometric template, as the same stored template might be used in multiple biometric authentication systems. Hence, we need to design efficient PPBA systems adaptable to different settings such as multimodal/cloud, at the same time preventing impersonation, malicious attacks and disclosure of biometric data/matching scores to the participating parties.

1.1 Related Work

Traditionally, biometrics is used for identification/authentication purposes, although recently, biometric data have emerged as a tool for fuzzy Identity Based Cryptography or to generate/bind a *key*, where this *key* could be used in encryption. For the latter, there is a number of biometric cryptosystems that aim to guarantee biometric template protection such as fuzzy commitment, fuzzy extractors and fuzzy vault. Juels and Wattenberg [11] introduce the fuzzy commitment scheme, which is suitable for hamming distance and specific for biometrics that can be represented as an ordered set of features, i.e. a feature vector. However, biometrics can be affected from two types of noise, i.e. *white noise* that represents the slight perturbation of each feature and the *replacement noise* caused by the replacement of some features. Thus, Juels and Sudan have developed the *fuzzy vault* [10], which assumes that biometrics consists of an unordered set of features and is designed for the set difference metric. The first attack against biometric encryption was presented in [2], which regenerates the enrolled biometric image from a random template by using a hill climbing attack, which depends on the matching score. An overview of various attacks against fuzzy vault is presented in [14], where implementations for multiple fingers (or even multiple biometric modalities) is suggested as a solution to effectively improve resistance against some of the attacks.

Similar to the above biometric template protection systems, biometric authentication/identification schemes are also vulnerable to various attacks, which are analyzed in [8,17,21]. To prevent these attacks, several privacy preserving biometric authentication/identification (PPBA) schemes are designed based on various architectures (distributed with additional non-colluding parties/client-server) or security models (semi-honest/malicious). An overview of research on PPBA is given in [5,17]. Current research focuses on PPBA schemes that can be outsourcable both in terms of storage and/or computation [5], resisting hill climbing attacks [8] with a distributed architecture as in [4] or providing private matching [18,20] within a simple client/server model. Although [18,20] consider malicious security level in standard model, these schemes store fingerprint data in clear. In [18], the scheme extends the private set intersection cardinality (PSI-CA) protocol of [6], which is based on the private matching scheme of [9] that was in fact the first and currently the most efficient PSI-CA scheme w.r.t. communication (when implemented using elliptic-curve crypto) [15]. As different from the PPBA schemes designed for euclidean or hamming distance, the protocol of [18] works for unordered set of features as in fuzzy vault. Therefore, it is suitable for set overlap distance (and thus any unordered set of biometric features) and for settings with distant parties which have limited connectivity.

Recently, [8] designed a new protocol for fingerprint minutia using the oblivious polynomial evaluation method of [20]. The main difference of [8] is the encrypted storage of biometric data and its architecture involving an additional non-colluding decryptor as in [4]. The authors define security against hill climbing attacks as hiding the matching distance from the decryptor, which stores the secret key of the system and thus, it is the most powerful entity.

1.2 Motivation and Contributions

Early biometric cryptosystems such as fuzzy vault were implemented on fingerprints, where we need query fingers to be pre-aligned so that stored minutiae matching with query minutiae are of sufficient similarity, namely stored minutiae significantly overlap fresh minutiae. Next, prealigned minutia data are quantized and mapped to a fixed finite field before the encoding of the secret *key* [14]. Fingerprint matching can also be performed using a different type of information extracted from fingerprint image, i.e. FingerCode, that uses texture information from a fingerprint scan to form fingerprint representation. Although FingerCodes are not as distinctive as minutiae-based representations, there exists various biometric authentication protocols for FingerCodes due to the efficient implementation within the euclidean distance [18]. Within multimodal setting, minutia and non-minutia based matchers are combined to increase recognition performance as shown in Fig. 2.

However, the similarity measures for many known biometric templates can be quite different from those considered in many theoretical works due to the nature of biometric templates [12]. For instance, a fingerprint template usually consists of a set of minutiae (feature points in 2-D space), and two templates are considered as similar if more than a certain number of minutiae in one template are near distinct minutiae in the other. In this case, the similarity measure has to consider both Euclidean distance and set difference at the same time [12]. For common features, matching could be performed using set overlap metric and for the remaining non-overlapping features, Euclidean distance could be applied on the two biometric templates. Here, one should benefit from the advantages of both distance measures: Set overlap gives exact results on the overlapping features but insufficient for features affected from white noise, whereas euclidean distance gives no clue on the number of overlapping features if performed in the encrypted domain. The reason is that the PPBA protocols for euclidean distance return only the final encrypted distance (or an oblivious evaluation of it resulting in zero/nonzero value), which is then decrypted for the accept/reject decision. However, employment of both distance measures is possible using multiple matchers within multimodal setting. In a recent publication of [19], this property has been realized in a completely different setting, i.e. biometric Identity Based Encryption (IBE), which is restricted for fingerprint biometrics represented using a single unit. Although PPBA and biometric IBE have different goals (authentication vs encryption) with opposing assumptions on the biometric data (secret vs public), they both benefit from the simultaneous use of two distance metrics.

Similarly, to benefit from the advantages of multimodal biometric authentication, two different biometric traits can be combined, which may require again multiple matchers for the different similarity measures of the traits. In particular, multimodal biometric systems are deployed in order to address some of the limitations of unimodal systems such as noisy data, intra-class variations, restricted degrees of freedom, non-universality, spoof attacks, and unacceptable error rates [16]. Hence, we need a fusion of either features, matching scores or decisions based on the fusion mode.

As noted in the Introduction, the vulnerabilities of biometric authentication protocols are analyzed with respect to user and data privacy. The goal of an adversary in such context is not only to bypass the authentication but to learn information either on biometric data or on users that are in the system focusing on internal adversaries to encompass the situation where one or a combination of these entities would be malicious [21]. When going beyond the usual honest-but-curious assumption much more complex attacks can affect the privacy of data and users [21]. Hence, this leakage of information enables a hill-climbing attack against any biometric scheme designed according to semi-honest security model such that, given a sample that matches the template, could lead to the full recovery of the reference biometric template even if it is stored as encrypted.

In this context, multimodal biometrics offers a possible solution, at least by increasing the number of attempts of an attacker for impersonation or hill climbing attacks [13]. These efforts are further affected by the choice of the fusion mode, quantization of the matching scores, rules of decision fusion.

In this paper, we describe the first privacy preserving multimodal biometric authentication (PPMBA) protocol resistant to hill climbing attacks. Due to the encrypted storage of biometric data, the biometric database can be outsourced to the cloud. We present an instantiation of our design on fingerprints with multiple units/matchers, but it can be generalized to have bimodality. We follow a similar strategy presented in [8], where the authors define security against hill climbing attacks as hiding the matching distance from the decryptor, which stores the secret key of the system. Since we design our scheme within the framework of multimodal biometrics and outsourced data storage, our main goal is to achieve security against hill climbing attacks by hiding the final fused matching distance from any party in the system, including the biometric database outsourced to the cloud and the non-colluding decryptor. To the best of our knowledge, our protocol is the first one providing privacy preserving matching of multimodal biometrics with outsourced storage. We describe the security model for PPMBA by defining server and client privacy considering the malicious attack scenarios in score-level fusion. The decryptor can be implemented as a private cloud server as in [5] that does not collude with any party in the system as in [4,5,8]. We instantiate our construction on fingerprints using multiple matchers (for different units) by considering two distance measures at the same time: set difference and euclidean distance. For the latter, we apply a special transformation of the feature vector that will lead to the computation of the euclidean distance obliviously using the Inner Product Encryption (IPE) scheme of [1], which is currently the most practical IPE scheme for computing the inner product of two vectors. Its DDH instantiation gives short ciphertexts and keys using an elliptic curve group [1], on which the matching scheme of the unordered biometrics (i.e. a feature set) also operates. In particular, we employ the scheme of [18], which is based on the currently most efficient private set intersection scheme of [9] w.r.t. communication (when implemented using elliptic-curve crypto) as noted in [15]. To the best of our knowledge, we present the first instantiation of [1] within PPBA setting. After computing the quantized matching scores of the two distance metrics, the final fused score is obtained and compared to the threshold by employing a secure two-party computation protocol that outputs either 1 or 0 denoting accept/reject of the user. This way, neither party in the system can access the final fused score, which is the main goal of the new system. Finally, we compare PPMBA to other biometric authentication schemes designed for fingerprint minutia and show that PPMBA outperforms them due to its linear computation/communication overhead.

2   Background on Biometrics and Crypto

2.1   Minutia-Based Fingerprint Representation

Although our system can operate on two different biometric traits, we instantiate the new system for fingerprints since it can be represented both as a set of minutia locations and/or as a feature vector, i.e. the fingercode. Due to page limitations, the details of the feature set/vector extraction can be found in [19].

After generating the feature sets, matching could be performed as in [14], which reveals set correspondences generated from absolutely pre-aligned minu- tiae templates. As shown in Fig. 1, they share at least $k = 7$ common elements

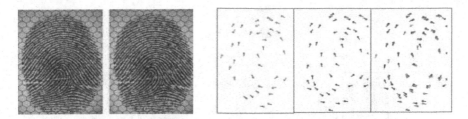

Fig. 1. (a) The minutiae (blue) are rounded to hexagonal grid points (red) extracted from the same fingerprint [14]. (b) Two images with extracted minutia data encoding fingerprint minutia Third image is their overlapping (Color figure online)

overlapping although there are features which are near to each other. In this case, the similarity measure has to consider both Euclidean distance and set difference at the same time. Similar to fingercode representation, other biometrics modalities such as face, online handwritten signatures, iris, voice, etc. can be represented as an ordered set of features (i.e. a sequence of n points) [12,17].

2.2 Multimodal Biometrics

In order to address some of the limitations of unimodal systems such as noisy data, intra-class variations, restricted degrees of freedom, non-universality, spoof attacks, and unacceptable error rates, multimodal biometric systems are deployed [16]. Multiple traits ensure sufficient population coverage and deter spoofing since it would be difficult for an impostor to spoof multiple biometric traits of a genuine user simultaneously. Besides, they ensure that liveliness assumption holds by facilitating a challenge-response type of mechanism that requires the user to present a random subset of biometric traits during each authentication.

Multi-modal biometric systems can be classified in three levels [16]. (a) Fusion at the data or feature level: Either the data itself or the feature sets originating from multiple sensors/sources are fused. (b) Fusion at the match score level: The scores generated by multiple classifiers pertaining to different modalities are combined. (c) Fusion at the decision level: The final output of multiple classifiers are consolidated via techniques such as majority voting, AND rule or OR rule.

Score Fusion [13]: In fact, score-level fusion is a relatively easy operation, not requiring any specific knowledge about the underlying feature extraction and matching algorithms. Score fusion typically requires a two-phase processing:

(1) A normalization step managing potentially not homogeneous matching scores. Several approaches can be evaluated for carrying out this task, such as min-max, z-score, median, double sigmoid or tanh-estimator normalization techniques.
(2) A fusion rule combining the available normalized scores. The use of the sum or the product between the available measures, or the selection of their minimum or maximum, are possible strategies. A weighted sum of the available scores, where each modality contributes proportionally on its accuracy, can be also performed to this aim [13].

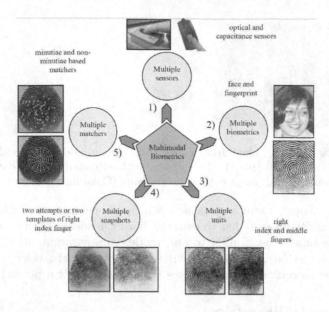

Fig. 2. Scenarios in a multimodal biometric system [16]

In [13], two distinct scenarios are considered for hill-climbing attacks against systems based on score-level fusion. Either both of the scores are available, where we have to assume that an attacker is able to access the scores before their fusion is performed. Or the attacker can only access the fused score and tries to exploit this limited information for impersonation.

Quantization: As for the hill-climbing attacks, uniform or non-uniform score quantization has been proposed as a possible countermeasure [13] since the effectiveness of hill-climbing attacks is negatively affected by the loss of some information about the outcome of the matching process, as it happens when the produced scores are quantized to a limited set of admissible values without significantly affecting the achievable recognition rates. When considering a score-level fusion scheme, we can quantize the produced scores either before or after their fusion. The latter strategy results in a reduced number of admissible operating points with respect to the use of quantization before fusion. In [13], three different scenarios are taken into account when analyzing score-level fusion schemes: (1) the scores are nonuniformly quantized prior to the fusion and the attacker can access the quantized scores to drive his hill-climbing strategy; (2) the scores are fused and then the final output is non-uniformly quantized according to its estimated distribution, being also accessible to the attacker; (3) non-uniform quantization is applied to the original scores, while the attacker is able to capture only the fused score. As for the implemented score-level fusion strategies, the authors suggest the case in which the fused score is quantized and made available to the attacker is the most resilient against hill-climbing attacks.

2.3   Cryptographic Tools

For biometrics whose similarity is measured within the set difference metric, we compare/match aligned query template to the registered template in a private manner using the protocol of [18], which executes in the group $\mathbb{G}$ implemented on a group of points on a certain elliptic curve with generator g of prime order q, a hash function H: $\{0.1\}^* \to \mathbb{G}$ and two random permutations $\mathbf{P}$ and $\mathbf{P'}$.

The client C registers his biometric features b_i for $i \in [1, n]$ at the server S. For verification, the client presents his fresh biometrics $\{b'_i\}$ for $i \in [1, m]$. The client makes an authentication request and the server replies by masking the hashed biometric feature set items corresponding to the client C with a random exponent $k \in \mathbb{Z}_q$ and sends resulting H$(b_i)^k$s to C, which blindly exponentiates them with its own random value $\alpha \in \mathbb{Z}_q$. Next, C shuffles these H$(b_i)^{k\alpha}$s and sends them to S together with the exponentiations of H$(\underline{b}'_j)$s to randomness $\alpha \in \mathbb{Z}_q$. Finally, the server tries to match these H$(\underline{b}'_j)^\alpha$ values received from C with the shuffled H$(b_i)^{k\alpha}$s, stripped of the initial randomness $k \in \mathbb{Z}_q$. Server learns the set intersection cardinality (and nothing else) by counting the number of such matches and notifies the client based on the system threshold t with an accept/reject decision. This PSI-CA scheme is analyzed both in random oracle and standard model, but for simplicity, we employ the former version.

Lemma 1 [18]. *The scheme achieves client privacy (server privacy) against a semi-honest server (client).*

Recently, [1] design a non-pairing-based scheme for the computation of the inner product $\langle \mathbf{w}, \mathbf{w'} \rangle$. Specifically, [1] describes a functional encryption scheme where input messages are represented as a vector $\mathbf{w} = (w_1, ..., w_n) \in \mathbb{Z}_q^n$ that are encrypted in a ciphertext and receiver has a secret key for another vector $\mathbf{w'} = (w'_1, ..., w'_n)$. A ciphertext for a vector $\mathbf{w}$ consists of ElGamal ciphertexts $g^{rx_i} \cdot g^{w_i}$ under public keys g^{x_i}, sharing the same randomness r. The scheme can easily be adapted to PPBA setting using the below transformation as follows. We note that this scheme must be designed for $n + 2$ length vectors, but for simplicity we describe it for n length vectors which can be directly extended to $n + 2$ length vectors. The IPE scheme of [1] adapted to PPBA is as follows:

$$\mathbf{w} = (u_1, u_2, ..., u_n, \sum_{i=1}^{n} f_i u_i^2, 1) \quad \mathbf{w'} = (-2f_1 v_1, -2f_2 v_2, ..., -2f_n v_n, 1, \sum_{i=1}^{n} f_i v_i^2)$$

The transformation satisfies the relationship between inner product and euclidean distance $\langle \mathbf{w}, \mathbf{w'} \rangle = dis_E(\mathbf{u}, \mathbf{v})$, where $\mathbf{u}$ and $\mathbf{v}$ denote biometric feature vectors and dis_E denotes (weighted squared) Euclidean distance $dis_E(\mathbf{w}, \mathbf{w'}) = \sum_{i=1}^{n} f_i (w_i - w'_i)^2$. In [1], each feature vector element is assumed as $w_i \in \mathbb{Z}_q^*$. The modified scheme is as follows:

IPE.User_Setup: For each user, the trusted authority (i.e. the private key generator (PKG)) picks random $(x_1, ..., x_n) \in \mathbb{Z}_q^*$ and sets IPE.User_mpk=$\{g^{x_1}, ..., g^{x_n}\}$ to be stored in the cloud and IPE.User_msk=$(x_1, ..., x_n)$. As different from [1], IPE.User_mpk is user-specific and is not publicly stored.

IPE.User_Extract: Given a user's biometrics $\mathbf{w}$, IPE.User_sk$_\mathbf{w} = \sum_{i=1}^{n} x_i w_i$ is returned by the PKG to the decryptor.

IPE.Encrypt: Pick $r \xleftarrow{\text{R}} \mathbb{Z}_q$. Compute $g^r, U_i = g^{r x_i} \cdot g^{w_i'}$ for $w_i' \in \mathbf{w}'$. The ciphertext IPE.CT$= (g^r, \{U_i : w_i' \in \mathbf{w}'\})$ is generated and stored in the cloud.

IPE.Decrypt: Suppose that IPE.CT$=(C_0, C_1, ..., C_n)$ is a ciphertext encrypted with $\mathbf{w}'$. Decryption works by the ElGamal scheme's homomorphic properties

$$(\prod_{i=1}^{n} C_i^{w_i})/C_0^{\text{IPE.User\_sk}_\mathbf{w}} = (\prod_{i=1}^{n}(g^{r x_i w_i} \cdot g^{w_i' w_i}))/g^{r \sum_{i=1}^{n} x_i w_i}$$

$$= \prod_{i=1}^{n} g^{w_i' w_i} = g^{\sum_{i=1}^{n} w_i' w_i} = g^{\langle \mathbf{w}, \mathbf{w}' \rangle} = g^{dis_E(\mathbf{u}, \mathbf{v})}$$

where $d' = dis_E(\mathbf{u}, \mathbf{v})$ should be less than the threshold t' of Euclidean distance. Here, one requires the computation of a discrete logarithm in the decryption, which makes it usable for small message space only [1]. However, this is exactly the case for an legitimate user, who will have a small distance when his fresh biometrics is compared to the stored one.

Lemma 2. *The IPE scheme of [1] achieves indistinguishability-based security.*

The reader is referred to [1,18] for the proofs of Lemmas 1 and 2, where the protocol of [1] is further improved to have simulation-based security in a recent work of the authors. For simplicity, we employ the version in [1].

3   The New PPMBA Protocol

The new protocol is designed against semi-honest adversaries within the score-level fusion framework. PPMBA executes in the group $\mathbb{G}$ described in Sect. 2.3, which is common both for IPE and PSI-CA scheme. Additionally, a cryptographic hash function H and two random permutations $(\mathbf{P}, \mathbf{P}')$ to mask any ordering of the features are required. Public parameters of PPMBA are $(q, g, \mathbb{G}, \text{H}, t, t')$. Since our protocol can be instantiated on fingerprints, we combine the matching scores associated to two different representations of it, set difference score d and euclidean distance score d' with the thresholds t and t', respectively. E$(\cdot)$ denotes encoding of stored biometrics either by hashing and exponentiating (i.e. E(B)) or encryption using the IPE scheme of Sect. 2.3 (i.e. E(w)).

The client C registers his biometric set $B = \{b_i\}_{1 \leq i \leq n}$ together with another unit of the same modality (or of a different trait) in form of a feature vector w both as encrypted at the server S and stores the helper data aux publicly if alignment-free features are not employed. For verification, the client presents his fresh biometrics, aligns it with the help of aux, and obtains $B' = \{b_i'\}_{1 \leq i \leq m}$ and his feature vector w' associated either to a different unit of the same modality or a different trait, where we assume B and w have the same length n for

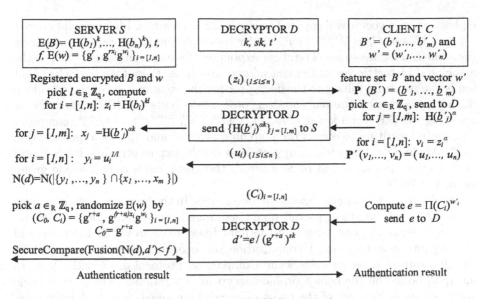

Fig. 3. Our new PPMBA protocol

simplicity. The client makes an authentication request and the protocol operates on the following sub-components with the non-colluding cloud servers S and D, S storing encrypted biometrics and the decryptor D the secret keys/parameters. An overview is presented in Fig. 3 with a single client registered as a user.

3.1 Sub-components of PPMBA

1. *Set Difference distance computation:* After the authentication request of the client C, the server S replies by masking the encrypted biometric feature set $E(B) = \mathrm{H}(b_i)^k$ corresponding to C with a random exponent $l \in \mathbb{Z}_q$ and sends resulting z_is to C, which blindly exponentiates them with its own random value $\alpha \in \mathbb{Z}_q$. Next, C shuffles these v_is and sends to S the resulting u_is and to D the exponentiations of client's items $(\mathrm{H}(\underline{b}'_j)s)$ to randomness $\alpha \in \mathbb{Z}_q$. Next, the decryptor D applies to each $\mathrm{H}(\underline{b}'_j)^\alpha$ the secret value k and sends them to S as x_js. Finally, S tries to match these x_j values with the shuffled u_i values, stripped of the randomness $l \in \mathbb{Z}_q$. Server learns the set intersection cardinality d by counting the number of such matches and applies a normalization step N on d and a quantization as described in Sect. 2.2 to make the set difference score d homogeneous with the euclidean distance score d' that will be computed in the next stage. Here, $\mathrm{O}(m)$ denotes an upperbound on the exponentiations and the communication cost for each party.

2. *Euclidean Distance computation:* After the set difference matching score computation, the server S rerandomizes the encrypted feature vector $E(w)$ with a random exponent $a \in \mathbb{Z}_q$ (i.e. by multiplying $E(w)$ with g^a) and sends resulting $\{C_i\}_{1 \leq i \leq n}$ to the client C and C_0 to the decryptor. Here, a rerandomized IPE ciphertext for a vector $\mathbf{w}$ computed as in Sect. 2.3 consists of ElGamal ciphertexts $C_0 = g^{r+a}$ and $C_i = g^{(r+a)x_i} \cdot g^{w_i}$ under user-specific parameters g^{x_i}s, sharing the same randomness $r+a$. The client exponentiates each component of C_i to the associated biometric vector element w'_i and multiplies them together. The client sends the resulting value e to the decryptor for the computation of the euclidean distance matching score d'. The decryptor D decrypts the IPE ciphertext by applying the IPE secret key of C as $(\prod_{i=1}^{n} C_i^{w_i})/C_0^{\text{IPE.User\_sk}_{\mathbf{w}}} = e/C_0^{sk}$, computes a discrete logarithm to obtain the matching score d' and applies a quantization to d'. Again, $O(m)$ denotes an upperbound on the exponentiations for S,C and on the communication cost of S, whereas the client sends only a single group element e to D.

3. *Secure Fusion of quantized matching scores:* In the final stage, cloud servers S and D, each having a partial quantized matching score, perform a secure computation of the comparison of the final fused score to the fusion threshold f using an efficient two-party computation protocol such as an efficient garbled circuit protocol similar to the SecureComparison protocol of [5] with $O(m)$ as an upperbound on the homomorphic encryption operations. Here, a fusion rule such as sum or product of the two scores can be applied. For the former case, let $N(d) + d'$ be the fused score, where $N(d)$ denotes the normalized distance d. The output of this component is either 1 if $N(d) + d' < f$ or 0, otherwise. The server notifies the client with an accept/reject decision based on this output. The total computation complexity of PPMBA is bound by $O(m)$ encryption operations. Matching and quantization can be performed by a separate non-colluding matcher M implemented as a hardware security module in order to remove this final stage as described in Sect. 4.2. The tradeoff is a more complex architecture and increased success rate for hill climbing attacks performed by a malicious M that is able to access both of the scores before their fusion.

4   Security Analysis

Our protocol is presented in the semi-honest model, i.e. adversaries that are honest-but-curious, who follow the protocols and try to gain more information than they should on the other parties' inputs. Here, the term adversary refers to insiders, i.e., protocol participants. Outside adversaries are not considered, since their actions can be mitigated via standard network security techniques.

4.1   Security Against Honest-but-curious Adversaries

In this case, the traditional real-versus-ideal definition is applied in the security proof. Basically, the protocol privately computes a function for an honest-but-curious Client (resp. Server) if there exists a PPT algorithm SIM that is able to simulate the view of Client (resp. Server), given only Client's (resp. Server's) (private and public) input and output. We have the following goals for PPMBA:

Client Privacy: No information is leaked about client biometrics, except an upper bound on its size m and the matching score of either the set difference metric obtained by the cloud server S, or the euclidean distance score obtained by the decryptor D. Due to the non-colluding S and D, the final fused score is hidden from any party in the protocol.

This goal directly corresponds to the notion of *security against hill climbing attacks* introduced in [8], which is defined via a game between the decryptor and a challenger in the semi-honest model. This notion can only be achieved by hiding the final fusion distance from the decryptor similar to [8], which works for a single fingerprint template that is represented in form of polynomials evaluated in encrypted domain (i.e. obliviously) without leaking distance and minutia data.

Besides, the notions of *template protection against the server and decryptor* as introduced in [8] against semi-honest adversaries, namely hiding biometric features from the server and decryptor, can be achieved through the use of secure encryption schemes (i.e. PSI-CA [18] and IPE [1]) similar to the PPBA protocol of [8], whose security is reduced to the modified Elgamal encryption scheme.

Server Privacy: Client learns no information beyond an upper bound on the size of his registered feature set n at the cloud server and the accept/reject notification. This goal directly corresponds to the notion of *security for authentication* as introduced in [8] in the semi-honest model.

Theorem 1. *PPMBA achieves client privacy (server privacy) against a semi-honest server (client) based on the security of the PSI-CA, IPE and secure two-party comparison sub-protocols.*

Since the sub-protocols produce random values as intermediate results, according to the Sequential Composition Theorem [7], the PPMBA is also secure under semi honest model. The proof will be presented in the full version of the paper.

4.2   Security Against Malicious Attacks

To provide client and server privacy against malicious attacks, one employs standard techniques of cryptography such as zero knowledge proof of knowledge (PoK) as in [18]. We consider one type of malicious attack (i.e. hill-climbing attack) against PPMBA designed in semi-honest model. This attack is based on the assumption that the scores produced by the matcher can be accessed by an attacker and exploited with the aim of generating either synthetic biometric samples used as inputs of the feature extractor module or synthetic biometric templates used as inputs to the matcher allowing successful recognition. At each step the employed data are modified according to the results of previous attempts, expressed in terms of matching scores, assumed to be known to the attacker, with the aim of improving the resulting matching output.

Considering the security model for hill-climbing attacks, which are in fact malicious attacks against schemes designed in semi-honest security model, we combine the means of the adversary A running against our scheme with the goals, namely hill climbing attacks. For the means of the attacker A, we allow the (internal) attacker to compromise either the server S or the decryptor D since they are non-colluding cloud servers. Hence, A can perform either Attack 1 or Attack 2 against our PPMBA in the sense of hill-climbing attacks for multimodal biometrics with score-level fusion as shown in Fig. 4. Here, we do not need the client as a party in the attack game, since the internal attacker A (which is either the server or the decryptor) can generate synthetic biometric samples $\mathbf{b}^{(1)}, \mathbf{b}^{(2)}$ in place of the client. The associated transformed templates $\mathbf{x}^{(1)}, \mathbf{x}^{(2)}$ that enter the template matching procedures performed either by the server or the decryptor are partially computed by the client, hence the attacker A does not have full control on either $\mathbf{x}^{(1)}$ or $\mathbf{x}^{(2)}$. To improve the efficiency by removing the secure fusion protocol, matching and quantization can be performed by a separate non-colluding Matcher M implemented as a hardware security module. For this, S and D forward the data received from C to the matcher, which computes the quantized matching score $\mathbf{s}^{(1)}$ after normalization. Similarly, D and C forward the data to the matcher that computes the quantized matching score $\mathbf{s}^{(2)}$ after a division operation. This way, S and D has access to a single quantized partial score and the authentication result, which is either 1 or 0. The inclusion of the matcher also allows for the removal of the Score Fusion module if the quantized matching scores $\mathbf{s}^{(1)}$, $\mathbf{s}^{(2)}$ are kept private by the matcher and the comparison of the fused score to the threshold f is performed by M instead of S and D. However, this leads to a decrease in the security as verified in [13] since a malicious matcher will have access to both matching scores before fusion.

Theorem 2. *PPMBA achieves security against hill-climbing attacks based on the non-collusion of S and D and the security of the comparison protocol.*

In our scheme, the attacker has access only one of the scores $s^{(1)}$, $s^{(2)}$, due to the non-collusion assumption. However, neither party has access to the fused score as a result of the secure two-party computation for testing $s^{(1)} + s^{(2)} < f$. In case of a single trait, we assume that the two templates differ from each other (i.e. multiple units) so that an internal attacker (S or D) cannot have extra advantage even if he obtains either $s^{(1)}$ or $s^{(2)}$ before quantization. The proof will be presented in the full version of this paper.

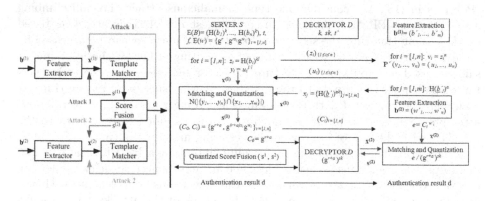

Fig. 4. (a) Hill-climbing attack (b) Modules of PPMBA adapted to the attack scenario

5   Conclusion

In this paper, we describe the first PPMBA protocol resistant to hill climbing attacks. In fact, the effectiveness of hill-climbing attacks is negatively affected by limiting the number of requests and by the loss of some information about the outcome of the matching process, as it happens when the produced scores are quantized to a limited set of admissible values [13]. In our case, the final matching score is hidden as in [8,20] in addition to the increased recognition performance due to the multimodal biometrics. Also, ensuring the aliveness of the biometric inputs provided by the user and increasing the entropy of the input data via feature-level fusion -all of which can be achieved through the use of multimodal biometrics- are other defense mechanisms against these attacks.

Table 1. Properties of various schemes designed for fingerprint minutia

	Computational cost	Outsourcing	Multimodality
Blanton et al. [3] $(m \approx n)$	$O(m^2)$	No	No
Shahandashti et al. [20]	$O(mn)$	No	No
Higo et al. [8]	$O(mn)$	Yes	No
Our Construction $(m \approx n)$	$O(m)$	Yes	Yes

In Table 1, we compare provably secure private minutia-based fingerprint matching protocols. The total computation/communication costs of PPMBA are both bound of $O(m)$ and due to the encrypted storage of biometric data, the biometric database can be outsourced to the cloud. Except for PPMBA, the remaining protocols work only for euclidean distance and cannot be adapted to different settings. We assume $m \approx n$ for the authentication mode since the total number of minutia m registered in S and captured at the client side n will be close to each other as opposed to the identification mode in [3]. Future work could be describing efficient PPMBA schemes in decision-level fusion mode.

Acknowledgement. The author is grateful to Prof. Dr. Joachim von zur Gathen for his valuable support, encouragement and guidance.

References

1. Abdalla, M., Bourse, F., Caro, A., Pointcheval, D.: Simple functional encryption schemes for inner products. In: Katz, J. (ed.) PKC 2015. LNCS, vol. 9020, pp. 733–751. Springer, Heidelberg (2015). doi:10.1007/978-3-662-46447-2_33
2. Adler, A.: Vulnerabilities in biometric encryption systems. In: Kanade, T., Jain, A., Ratha, N.K. (eds.) AVBPA 2005. LNCS, vol. 3546, pp. 1100–1109. Springer, Heidelberg (2005). doi:10.1007/11527923_114
3. Blanton, M., Gasti, P.: Secure and efficient protocols for iris and fingerprint identification. In: Atluri, V., Diaz, C. (eds.) ESORICS 2011. LNCS, vol. 6879, pp. 190–209. Springer, Heidelberg (2011). doi:10.1007/978-3-642-23822-2_11

4. Bringer, J., Chabanne, H., Izabachène, M., Pointcheval, D., Tang, Q., Zimmer, S.: An application of the Goldwasser-Micali cryptosystem to biometric authentication. In: Pieprzyk, J., Ghodosi, H., Dawson, E. (eds.) ACISP 2007. LNCS, vol. 4586, pp. 96–106. Springer, Heidelberg (2007). doi:10.1007/978-3-540-73458-1_8
5. Chun, H., Elmehdwi, Y., Li, F., Bhattacharya, P., Jiang, W.: Outsourcable two-party privacy preserving biometric authentication. In: ACM ASIACCS 2014, pp. 401–412 (2014)
6. Cristofaro, E., Gasti, P., Tsudik, G.: Fast and private computation of cardinality of set intersection and union. In: Pieprzyk, J., Sadeghi, A.-R., Manulis, M. (eds.) CANS 2012. LNCS, vol. 7712, pp. 218–231. Springer, Heidelberg (2012). doi:10.1007/978-3-642-35404-5_17
7. Goldreich, O.: Foundations of Cryptography. Basic Applications, vol. 2. Cambridge University Press, Cambridge (2004)
8. Higo, H., Isshiki, T., Mori, K., Obana, S.: Privacy-preserving fingerprint authentication resistant to hill-climbing attacks. In: Dunkelman, O., Keliher, L. (eds.) SAC 2015. LNCS, vol. 9566, pp. 44–64. Springer, Cham (2016). doi:10.1007/978-3-319-31301-6_3
9. Huberman, B.A., Franklin, M., Hogg, T.: Enhancing privacy and trust in electronic communities. In: ACM EC 1999, pp. 78–86. ACM (1999)
10. Juels, A., Sudan, M.: A fuzzy vault scheme. Des. Codes Crypt. **38**(2), 237–257 (2006)
11. Juels, A., Wattenberg, M.: A fuzzy commitment scheme. In: ACM CCS, pp. 28–36 (1999)
12. Li, Q., Sutcu, Y., Memon, N.: Secure sketch for biometric templates. In: Lai, X., Chen, K. (eds.) ASIACRYPT 2006. LNCS, vol. 4284, pp. 99–113. Springer, Heidelberg (2006). doi:10.1007/11935230_7
13. Maiorana, E., Hine, G.E., Campisi, P.: Hill-climbing attacks on multi-biometrics recognition systems. IEEE TIFS **10**(5), 900–915 (2015)
14. Mihăilescu, P., Munk, A., Tams, B.: Security considerations in minutiae-based fuzzy vaults. IEEE TIFS **10**(5), 985–998 (2015)
15. Pinkas, B., Schneider, T., Zohner, M.: Faster private set intersection based on ot extension. In: USENIX 2014, pp. 797–812. USENIX Association (2014)
16. Ross, A., Jain, A.K.: Multimodal biometrics: an overview. In: EUSIPCO 2004, pp. 1221–1224. IEEE (2004)
17. Sarier, N.D., Cryptosystems, B.: Authentication, encryption and signature for biometric identities. Ph.D. thesis, Bonn University, Germany (2013)
18. Sarier, N.D.: Private minutia-based fingerprint matching. In: Akram, R.N., Jajodia, S. (eds.) WISTP 2015. LNCS, vol. 9311, pp. 52–67. Springer, Cham (2015). doi:10.1007/978-3-319-24018-3_4
19. Sarier, N.D.: Efficient biometric-based encryption for fingerprints. In: ICITST 2016, pp. 127–132. IEEE (2016)
20. Shahandashti, S.F., Safavi-Naini, R., Ogunbona, P.: Private fingerprint matching. In: Susilo, W., Mu, Y., Seberry, J. (eds.) ACISP 2012. LNCS, vol. 7372, pp. 426–433. Springer, Heidelberg (2012). doi:10.1007/978-3-642-31448-3_32
21. Simoens, K., Bringer, J., Chabanne, H., Seys, S.: A framework for analyzing template security and privacy in biometric authentication systems. IEEE TIFS **7**(2), 833–841 (2012)

MOHAB: Mobile Hand-Based Biometric Recognition

Silvio Barra[1], Maria De Marsico[2], Michele Nappi[1], Fabio Narducci[1(✉)], and Daniel Riccio[3]

[1] BipLab, University of Salerno, Salerno, Italy
barra.silvio@gmail.com, {mnappi,fnarducci}@unisa.it
[2] Sapienza University of Rome, Rome, Italy
demarsico@di.uniroma1.it
[3] University "Federico II" of Naples, Naples, Italy
daniel.riccio@unina.it

Abstract. This paper presents a novel approach to hand-based biometrics that uses mobile devices. Hand-based recognition has been explored via different research lines and taking into consideration different traits. On the other hand, few studies tackle its feasibility on mobile devices. Given their diffusion and availability, their use in this context appears particularly attractive. The work presented in this study aims at investigating at an high level the limitations of using hand geometry to enable biometric recognition on mobile. The first results obtained were encouraging let supposing potential margins of improvement of the proposed method.

Keywords: Hand geometry · Hand recognition · Mobile devices

1 Introduction

Hand-based recognition has been explored via different research lines and taking into consideration different hand-related traits. Fingerprints represent the most popular and investigated of these traits, but other possibilities have been also explored. In most cases, they concern static features, as hand geometry, palmprints and palm vein patterns. More recent proposals rather rely on dynamics, namely hand gestures. Apart from the specific biometric trait taken into account, the most recent research lines deal with the way to capture (and possibly process) them. In particular, some few recent works investigate the possibility to exploit mobile devices for hand-based recognition. Smartphones and tablets are nowadays practically ubiquitous, and represent a viable alternative to special-purpose capture devices. However, this raises a number of issues. These are related to both the limitations caused by the still limited computational resources of such devices, and to the uncontrolled and/or adverse conditions usually characterizing image capture through them.

ⓒ Springer International Publishing AG 2017
M.H.A. Au et al. (Eds.): GPC 2017, LNCS 10232, pp. 105–115, 2017.
DOI: 10.1007/978-3-319-57186-7_9

2   Related Work

Biometric hand recognition systems can use a broad set of parameters computed by processing an acquired hand image. These systems generally either measure and analyze the overall structure, shape and proportions of the hand (e.g., length, width and thickness of hand, fingers and joints), or extract characteristics of the skin surface such as creases and ridges (i.e., the palmprint), or rely on the vein pattern. Earlier methods proposed in literature require the user to keep the hand in a predefined position [12,16]. In [14] an ordinary CCD color camera is placed over a plate that is equipped with some driving pegs to guide the user to put the hand in a specific position. Pins are activated by the pressure of the user hand. Once all of them are activated, the system acquires the biometric trait for processing. These systems benefit from the strictly controlled acquisition. Consequently, measures and characteristics stay quite robust across users. The reverse of the medal is that these systems require controlled settings, full collaboration by the users, and special equipment. Moreover, the implementations that have been used for years required the physical contact with the acquisition device (contact-based solution). This further poses several other problems related to the personal hygiene and health of the user. Palmprint is the typical well-known biometric trait used for full hand recognition [8]. Present palmprint scanners simplify the development of the recognition algorithms, with respect to traditional peg-equipped plates, but also require a suitable selection of lens, camera, and light sources [18], and, most of all, still work by direct contact. Apart from health issues, the physical contact may lead to distortions of the characteristics of the hand (e.g., due to the pressure exerted by the user on the glass of the scanner). Moreover, the palmprint scanners cannot be easily moved from one position to another. Last but not least, they can be hardly used in real-time operations due to the scanning time. Therefore, in many environments they result in completely inappropriate solutions. Digital and video cameras have been demonstrated effective to be used to collect palmprint images without contact [2,6]. The system described in [4] uses two commercial cameras (i.e., a RGB camera and an IR camera) placed beside to each other. The illumination is controlled by an external light source (composed of white and infrared leds), which ensures a global illumination of the hand. This must be placed in front of the cameras. The proposed system exploits a score fusion over results from matching hand geometric features and palmprint features, in order to achieve a high recognition accuracy. In [1] has been proposed a method to hand segmentation from complex background by a stereo acquisition system which involves two RGB cameras. On the contrary, the work by Sanches et al. [13] proposes a single RGB camera approach to hand segmentation and recognition. Hand geometry, palmprint and finger surface biometric features are fused at decision level, to come to a recognition rate that is above 98%. The possibility of using ordinary RGB cameras for palmprint recognition suggests that these solutions might be feasible for mobile devices too. However, the mobile cameras can cause recognition problems. Their resolution is generally low, and their preferred use would be to acquire images in an uncontrolled environment, with illumination variations and distortions due to the hand movements. The latter represent with no doubt the most challenging aspects of contact-less hand recognition, due to the lack of constraints for the user on how and where to place the hand in front of the camera. In fact, also the distance between the camera and the hand may vary significantly among successive acquisitions by the same subject. In a similar way, if the hand surface is not perfectly planar (e.g., perpendicular to the camera view axis), inclination may lead to bad measures of geometry. The proposed system is inspired by the work by De Santos-Sierra et al. [15], who designed a human identification system in contact-less scenarios. It is based exclusively on the use of hand shape and geometry, providing a feasible solution for devices with limited hardware resources. In fact, contact-less palmprint recognition can be considered hard to carry out with limited camera resolution. This work therefore aims at investigating if silhouette of hands can inspire a reasonable approach to mobile recognition.

3   Proposed System

The proposed system is built for Android mobile devices and uses the rear camera to acquire the user hand. The application is written in Java through the native Android Software Development Kit (SDK) and OpenCV for mobile, which allowed to achieve a clean, light and versatile programming.

Figure 1 depicts the few steps making up the user enrollment. The first one is the acquisition of the hand image. The user is asked to put the hand in front of the camera, and to ensure that five reference areas displayed on the screen are filled with the color of the skin. The aim of these reference areas is twofold. They help the user to understand how to properly place the hand in front of the camera, and are also used to generate five different segmentation of the hand. The acquired RGB frame is first converted into the HSV color space. The Hue channel is used to filter the image and to produce a distinct segmentation for each of the five areas mentioned above. These segmentation are computed according to a corresponding set of thresholds, which are determined as follows. For each area, the arithmetic mean m_i (for $i = 1, ..., 5$), of the hue values of its pixels is computed. Given the obtained mean mi, a segmentation mask S_i is generated according to the following rule:

$$S_i(p_j) = \begin{cases} 1 \text{ if } m_i - k_i \leq H(p_j) \leq m_i + k_i \\ 0 \text{ otherwise} \end{cases} \tag{1}$$

where $H(p_j)$ is the hue value of the pixel in the original image and k is a constant that defines the amplitude of the hue range for the skin, According to the results of an empirical study, we set this value to k = 4. However, it can be customized by the users to improve the quality of the segmentation. The five obtained segmentation masks are then post-processed by morphological operators to further improve their accuracy, by removing noise and blobs. Finally, they are combined by a union operation (a bitwise OR), to generate a single final one. During the experimentation, several measures have been extracted from the shape of the hand. Before using the final segmentation mask to get these measures related to the hand geometry, the system first checks if the obtained segmentation can represent a hand. It simply determines the concavities ($P1, ..., P5$ in Fig. 2) and convexities ($V1..., V4$ in Fig. 2) from the mask to count the possible fingers, that should be a complete set of 5. If the control succeeds, the application uses the points identified in the previous step to compute the measures needed for the following matching experiments.

Measures can be divided into four classes: (1) lengths; (2) ratios; (3) areas; and (4) angles. Figure 2 shows all the measures that have been computed from the shape of the segmented hand, while Table 1 provide details on these measures, which have been labeled with a code to improve the readability of the results (e.g. f1, f2, f3).

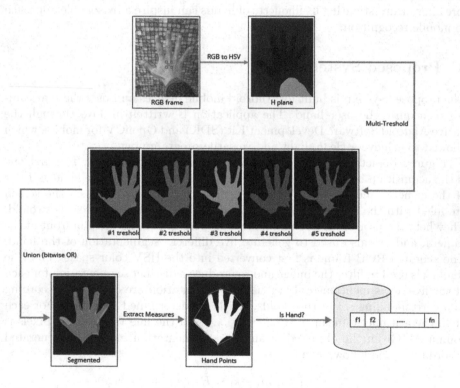

Fig. 1. The overall view of the process of segmentation and features extraction.

4 Experimental Results

The experimentation has been carried out using a Samsung Galaxy Note 4 (N910F) equipped with a Sony IMX240 camera. The system uses a resolution of 800 x 600 for the acquired frame. With this setting, the proposed method segments each frame and extracts features in about 250 ms. In the same conditions, the verification time (1:1 matching) is lower than 1 ms (precisely about 0.33 ms).

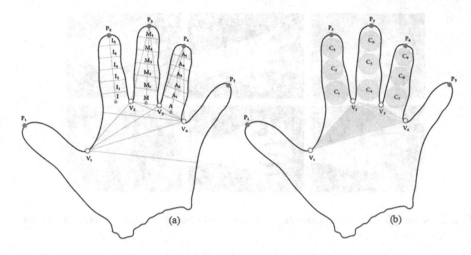

(a)   (b)

Fig. 2. The measures over the hand shape. (a) The reference points P_i and V_i from which lengths are computed, and further segments determined over the fingers and the palm. (b) Triangular and circular areas extracted from the reference points in (a)

Table 1. List of the measurements computed over the segmented hand.

Lengths	f1: $\overline{V_1V_2}$	f7: $\overline{P_2I}$	f13: $\overline{P_3M}$	f19: $\overline{P_4A}$	f25: $\overline{V_2P_3} + \overline{P_3V_3}$
	f2: $\overline{V_1V_3}$	f8: $width(I_1)$	f14: $width(M_1)$	f20: $width(A_1)$	f26: $\overline{V_3P_4} + \overline{P_4V_4}$
	f3: $\overline{V_1V_4}$	f9: $width(I_2)$	f15: $width(M_2)$	f21: $width(A_2)$	f27: $f_8 + \cdots + f_{12}$
	f4: $\overline{V_2V_3}$	f10: $width(I_3)$	f16: $width(M_3)$	f22: $width(A_3)$	f28: $f_{14} + \cdots + f_{18}$
	f5: $\overline{V_3V_4}$	f11: $width(I_4)$	f17: $width(M_4)$	f23: $width(A_4)$	f29: $f_{20} + \cdots + f_{24}$
	f6: $\overline{V_2V_4}$	f12: $width(I_5)$	f18: $width(M_5)$	f24: $width(A_5)$	f30: $width(V_1)$
Ratios	f31: f_1/f_6	f33: f_3/f_6	f35: f_7/f_6	f37: f_{19}/f_6	f39: f_{30}/f_{13}
	f32: f_2/f_6	f34: f_6/f_4	f36: f_{13}/f_6	f38: $(f_7 + f_{13} + f_{19})/f_6$	f40: f_{50}/f_{51}
Areas	f41: A_{C_1}	f43: A_{C_3}	f45: A_{C_5}	f47: A_{C_7}	f49: A_{C_9}
	f42: A_{C_2}	f44: A_{C_4}	f46: A_{C_6}	f48: A_{C_8}	f50: $A_{V_1V_2V_4}$
	f51: $A_{V_2V_3V_4}$				
Angles	f52: $\widehat{V_2V_3V_4}$	f53: $\widehat{V_3V_4V_2}$	f54: $\widehat{V_4V_2V_3}$	f55: $\widehat{V_1V_2V_4}$	f56: $\widehat{V_2V_4V_1}$
	f57: $\widehat{V_4V_1V_2}$				

The user has to hold the mobile device by one hand, and to place the other hand in front of the camera. It was possible to design the system so to ask the user to exhibit either the palm or the back of the hand. We chose the second option because of a more natural user feeling. A minimal and simple Graphical User Interface (GUI) guides the user during image acquisition. In order to allow comparison with other proposals in literature, we searched for a public dataset including images with characteristics similar to those handled by our system. Therefore, the experimental results have been obtained using Technocampus Hand Image Database [3,5] (Fig. 3). We chose this dataset because it is one of the few examples of publicly available ones that include images of the back of the hand.

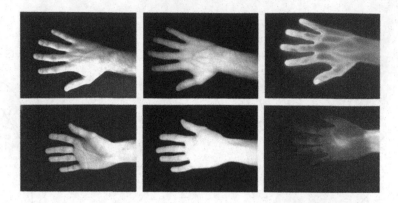

Fig. 3. A sample of the acquisitions from the Technocampus Hand Image Database.

In fact, most hand datasets used for biometric recognition in literature are rather collected using scanners, or cameras mounted on a support, suitable for the acquisition of images of the palm. Moreover, the acquisition conditions in the chosen dataset match those we considered for our system, since no pegs or special tips have been used, the areas used for segmentation are correctly filled in all images, and the resolution is compatible with the one we chose. The Technocampus Hand Image Database contains pictures of the back and of the palm of the right hand of 100 users acquired with a resolution of 640 x 480 pixels. This resolution is the same achievable by a broad range of cheap mobile devices with limited processing power and low resolution cameras. Each subject has been acquired in five different successive sessions with two acquisitions per session. A session contains images in the visible spectrum, a thermal image and an infrared image, of both back and palm (a sample is shown in Fig. 3). The acquisition device is a thermal commercial camera (Testo 882-3). Another similar dataset is the UST hand dataset [9], which contains hands of 287 people acquired in a contactless scenario with an Olympus C-3020 digital camera. No special illumination or pegs have been exploited, but the resolution is 1,280 x 960 pixels, therefore too high to test the performance achievable on most present mobile devices. To the best of our knowledge, it is not possible to find further datasets with similar features to allowing a fair comparison with other state-of-the-art methods. Quite often, researchers rather use private (and small) dataset like in [7,10,17]. This increases the difficulties of a fair comparison with other methods, and this causes in turn the lack of a broad investigation on hand recognition on mobiles. For these reasons, we compared our proposal with works that used the following criteria at least: (1) the acquisition does not involve pegs or constraints; (2) users place naturally their hands in front of the camera; (3) users are asked to open their hand so that fingers are clearly separable (this generally substitutes the condition to fill the highlighted areas). Reasonably, not all of the 57 features that we collected from the hand shape have the same robustness and discriminative power. We firstly computed the robustness per class of features

Table 2. The EER per class of features extracted from hand shapes in the chosen dataset.

Measure	Features set	EER (%)
Length	$f_1, ..., f_{30}$	7%
Ratio	$f_{31}, ..., f_{40}$	18%
Area	$f_{41}, ..., f_{51}$	10%
Angle	$f_{52}, ..., f_{57}$	13%

in order to have a rough estimation of the most reliable ones. Table 2 summarizes the recognition results obtained by the four classes separately. Matching is carried out using the standardized Euclidean distance after a-priori 1-norm normalization of the measures. Performances are reported in terms of Equal Error Rate (EER). The table shows that the class of normalized lengths represents the set of features that better identifies the user. The above results refer to homogeneous sets of features. Our aim was to rather identify the best (reduced) group of possibly heterogeneous measures, able to support recognition. For this reason, we carried out a more detailed experimentation to obtain a finer assessment of the robustness of the single measures. We compared intra/inter-subject variability characterizing single features. In fact, it is preferable to adopt features according to their stability within the same subject as compared with their variability across different subjects. We compared intra/inter-subject variability characterizing single features. In fact, it is preferable to adopt features according to their stability within the same subject as compared with their variability across different subjects. Given a set of hand images $I = I_1, ..., I_n$, which belong to a set of gallery subjects $G = G_1, ..., G_g$, we compute an all-against-all distance matrix M_i for each feature f_i, where each element $M_i(l, j)$ is the absolute difference of the measure of f_i computed for I_l and I_j: $M_i(l, j) = |f_i(I_l) - f_i(I_j)|$. Let us assume to have a total of k comparisons involving samples belonging to the same subject, and a total of m comparisons involving samples belonging to different subjects. This allows us to avoid any assumption on the number of samples per subject, either equal or not. We then define:

$$\Delta_{INTRA_i} = \frac{1}{k} \sum_{I_l, I_j \text{same subjects}} M_i(l, j) \tag{2}$$

and

$$\Delta_{INTER_i} = \frac{1}{m} \sum_{I_l, I_j \text{different subjects}} M_i(l, j) \tag{3}$$

and finally:

$$rank_i = \frac{\Delta_{INTRA_i}}{\Delta_{INTER_i}} \tag{4}$$

Lower values of the rank identify features for which the differences among acquisitions of the same individual have an overall value much lower than those of different individuals. This is a desirable characteristic of a biometric trait which allowed to select the best features to consider for the matching. We grouped features in subsets of decreasing size according to the condition:

$$F_j = \{f_i : rank_i < \tau_j\} \quad with \quad 0 \leq \tau_j \leq 1 \tag{5}$$

Table 3. The EER of the eight subsets of features identified by *rank*. For each subset, the table columns report the threshold used to identify its components, the features included the size of the subset, and the EER achieved. The F4 subset, which minimizes the EER, is mainly built around the computed segments of the hand, but contains some ratios and an angle too.

FV	τ	Features	N.	EER (%)
F0	0.05	$f_8, f_{13}, f_{19}, f_{25-27}, f_{30}, f_{55}$	7	7.6
F1	0.09	$f_8, f_{13}, f_{18-19}, f_{25-28}, f_{30}, f_{55}$	9	6.5
F2	0.11	$f_{7-8}, f_{11}, f_{13}, f_{17-19}, f_{22}, f_{25-28}, f_{30}, f_{55}$	13	5.6
F3	0.128	$f_{7-8}, f_{11-13}, f_{16-19}, f_{22-23}, f_{25-28}, f_{30}, f_{38}, f_{55}$	16	5.2
F4	0.15	$f_{7-8}, f_{11-13}, f_{15-19}, f_{22-30}, f_{37-38}, f_{40}, f_{55}$	22	4.9
F5	0.2	$f_{7-13}, f_{15-19}, f_{22-30}, f_{36-38}, f_{40}, f_{50}, f_{55-56}$	28	5.4
F6	0.4	$f_{6-13}, f_{15-19}, f_{21-38}, f_{40}, f_{46}, f_{49-51}, f_{55-57}$	39	7.7
F7	1	f_{1-57} (all features)	57	7.8

It is easy to deduce that F_i is contained in F_{i+1}, $i = 0, ..., 7$. In practice, each set of features is contained in the following one, strictly or not depending on the choice of the thresholds. In particular, in our case, F_i is strictly contained in F_{i+1}. Our aim was to identify sets of features (the lower their number, the better) able to effectively support an accurate identity verification. We studied the effect of τ on the achieved Equal Error Rate (EER) obtained with sets of features according to the rule 5. The 8 sets of features are summarized in Table 3. The subset achieving the best result is F_4 (EER = 4.9%), that mainly contains lengths of hand segments. This confirms their important role in recognition. In fact, this result confirms the rough comparison between the EERs (reported in Table 2) of the features divided per class, where the subset of lengths was the best one. Moreover, both sets with "too many" features and sets with "too few" of them achieve sub-optimal results.

The best preliminary results obtained so far are comparable to similar approaches in literature. As we said, the lack of datasets of the back of the hand makes a fair comparison particularly difficult to carry out. Table 4 summarizes some of the recent works in literature that deal with the contact-less biometric recognition of hand based on hand geometry in the visible light. As we can notice, most of the method uses proprietary datasets of different size that makes even harder the comparison among them. In any case, the result achieved at the preliminary stage of this work seems encouraging and useful to drive

Table 4. Literature review on recent works that deal with contact-less biometrics based on hand geometry. (*) When the compared approaches use and combine further features besides those extracted by the hand geometry, the EER reported refers to hand geometry only (when available).

Proposal	Method	Dataset	Population	EER (%)
Sanches et al. [13]	Fusion of features from hand geometry (25 features), palmprint and finger surface	UST Database	287	3 *
de Santos-Sierra et al. [15]	Recognition based on hand contour	Proprietary	45	3.7
Kanhangad et al. [7]	Acquisition and combination of 3-D and 2-D features from the hand	Proprietary	177	6.3 *
Goh Kah Ong et al. [10]	Multi-modal biometric approach which includes hand geometry, palm print, palmar knuckle print, palm vein, and finger vein	Proprietary	100	3.61
Morales et al. [11]	SVM on features from hand geometry in the visible spectrum	Proprietary	20	6.3
Ours	Recognition based on 17 measures from hand geometry.	Technocampus Hand Dataset	100	4.9

a further investigation of the proposed approach. In fact, as a future improvement of the proposed results we will explore in more detail the selection of features in order to assess if exists a collection of features that optimizes the performance achievable.

5   Conclusions

In this paper, we have presented a biometric system based on hand geometry, which is suitable to be used on mobile devices. The strength of the proposed approach is that it is oriented to contact-less scenarios, and this is a key aspect for mobile devices. Consequently, it does not use any support or driving pegs to help the user to place his/her hand in the desired position during the acquisition.

The results obtained on a public dataset show that the feature extraction and selection method is able to achieve a level of performance comparable with the state-of-the-art. Together with the low computational demand for human identification, the proposed method represents a viable solution for devices with low hardware profile and is thus applicable to a wider number of different scenarios, not necessarily limited by the constraints of mobile settings.

As a further improvement of the proposed study, we plan to analyze in more detail possible alternative combinations of features, or to compute new features as well, in order to try to increase the achieved recognition performance. To this regards, we are in the process of more formally evaluating the contribution of each feature over the level of performance obtained. We expect that, by involving new metrics and formal quality measurements of the features, we will be able to discover alternative sets (the smallest, if possible) of features that maximise the performances. In addition we plan to carry out a comprehensive formal experimentation in order to extensively assess the weaknesses and strengths of the method proposed in this study.

References

1. Abate, A.F., Narducci, F., Ricciardi, S.: An image based approach to hand occlusions in mixed reality environments. In: Shumaker, R., Lackey, S. (eds.) VAMR 2014. LNCS, vol. 8525, pp. 319–328. Springer, Cham (2014). doi:10.1007/978-3-319-07458-0_30
2. Doublet, J., Revenu, M., Lepetit, O.: Robust grayscale distribution estimation for contactless palmprint recognition. In: Proceedings of 2007 First IEEE International Conference on Biometrics: Theory, Applications, and Systems, BTAS 2007, pp. 1–6. IEEE (2007)
3. Faundez-Zanuy, M., Mekyska, J., Font-Aragonès, X.: A new hand image database simultaneously acquired in visible, near-infrared and thermal spectrums. Cogn. Comput. **6**(2), 230–240 (2014)
4. Ferrer, M.A., Vargas, F., Morales, A.: Bispectral contactless hand based biometric system. In: 2011 2nd National Conference on Telecommunications (CONATEL), pp. 1–6. IEEE (2011)
5. Font Aragonés, X., Faúndez Zanuy, M., Mekyska, J.: Thermal hand image segmentation for biometric recognition. IEEE Aerosp. Electron. Syst. Mag. **28**(6), 4–14 (2013)
6. Han, Y., Tan, T., Sun, Z., Hao, Y.: Embedded palmprint recognition system on mobile devices. In: Lee, S.-W., Li, S.Z. (eds.) ICB 2007. LNCS, vol. 4642, pp. 1184–1193. Springer, Heidelberg (2007). doi:10.1007/978-3-540-74549-5_123
7. Kanhangad, V., Kumar, A., Zhang, D.: A unified framework for contactless hand verification. IEEE Trans. Inf. Forensics Secur. **6**(3), 1014–1027 (2011)
8. Kong, A., Zhang, D., Kamel, M.: A survey of palmprint recognition. Pattern Recogn. **42**(7), 1408–1418 (2009)
9. Kumar, A., Wong, D.C.M., Shen, H.C., Jain, A.K.: Personal verification using palmprint and hand geometry biometric. In: Kittler, J., Nixon, M.S. (eds.) AVBPA 2003. LNCS, vol. 2688, pp. 668–678. Springer, Heidelberg (2003). doi:10.1007/3-540-44887-X_78
10. Michael, G.K.O., Connie, T., Teoh, A.B.J.: A contactless biometric system using multiple hand features. J. Vis. Commun. Image Represent. **23**(7), 1068–1084 (2012)

11. Morales, A., Ferrer, M.A., Alonso, J.B., Travieso, C.M.: Comparing infrared and visible illumination for contactless hand based biometric scheme. In: 2008 42nd Annual IEEE International Carnahan Conference on Security Technology, pp. 191–197. IEEE (2008)
12. Ross, A., Jain, A.: A prototype hand geometry based verification system. In: Proceedings of 2nd Conference on Audio and Video Based Biometric Person Authentication, pp. 166–171 (1999)
13. Sanches, T., Antunes, J., Correia, P.L.: A single sensor hand biometric multimodal system. In: 2007 15th European Signal Processing Conference, pp. 30–34. IEEE (2007)
14. Sanchez-Reillo, R., Sanchez-Avila, C., Gonzalez-Marcos, A.: Biometric identification through hand geometry measurements. IEEE Trans. Pattern Anal. Mach. Intell. **22**(10), 1168–1171 (2000)
15. de Santos-Sierra, A., Sánchez-Avila, C., del Pozo, G.B., Guerra-Casanova, J.: Unconstrained and contactless hand geometry biometrics. Sensors **11**(11), 10143–10164 (2011)
16. Varchol, P., Levicky, D.: Using of hand geometry in biometric security systems. RADIOENGINEERING-PRAGUE- **16**(4), 82 (2007)
17. Wong, A.L., Shi, P.: Peg-free hand geometry recognition using hierarchical geometry and shape matching. In: MVA, pp. 281–284. Citeseer (2002)
18. Wong, M., Zhang, D., Kong, W.K., Lu, G.: Real-time palmprint acquisition system design. IEE Proc. Vis. Image Sig. Process. **152**(5), 527–534 (2005)

Further Improvement on An Efficient and Secure Three-factor Based Authenticated Key Exchange Scheme Using Elliptic Curve Cryptosystems

Chun-Ta Li[1], Chin-Ling Chen[2]($\boxtimes$), Cheng-Chi Lee[3,4]($\boxtimes$),
and Chien-Ming Chen[5]

[1] Department of Information Management, Tainan University of Technology,
No. 529, Zhongzheng Road, Tainan City 71002, Taiwan, R.O.C.
th0040@mail.tut.edu.tw
[2] Department of Computer Science and Information Engineering, Chaoyang
University of Technology, 168 Jifeng East Road, Taichung City 41349, Taiwan, R.O.C.
clc@mail.cyut.edu.tw
[3] Department of Library and Information Science, Fu Jen Catholic University,
No. 510, Jhongjheng Road, New Taipei City 24205, Taiwan, R.O.C.
cclee@mail.fju.edu.tw
[4] Department of Photonics and Communication Engineering, Asia University,
500 Lioufeng Road, Taichung City 41354, Taiwan, R.O.C.
[5] School of Computer Science and Technology, Harbin Institute of Technology
Shenzhen Graduate School, Shenzhen University Town, Nanshan District,
Shenzhen 518055, People's Republic of China
chienming.taiwan@gmail.com

Abstract. Nowadays users can access various online services and resources from distributed information systems remotely via Internet or other public networks. However, remote online systems are vulnerable to many security attacks due to they are built on public networks. Therefore it is necessary to design an authentication scheme for securing network communications between a login user and a remote server. In 2016, Han et al. proposed a secure three-factor authentication scheme based on elliptic curve cryptography (ECC) to achieve this goal. Unfortunately, we analyzed Han et al.'s scheme and demonstrated that their authentication scheme cannot satisfactory to be implemented in practice because it fails to ensure the property of unlinkability between the login user and the remote server and is unable to withstand account duplication attack. In this paper, we suggest an enhanced anonymous authentication scheme to repair the security flaws in Han et al.'s scheme. We give the security analysis and performance evaluation to demonstrate that the proposed scheme not only resists the aforementioned security weaknesses on Han et al.'s scheme but also inherits the functionality merits and performance efficiencies of their authentication scheme.

Keywords: Authentication · Biometric · Cryptanalysis · Elliptic curve cryptography · Password · Smart card

© Springer International Publishing AG 2017
M.H.A. Au et al. (Eds.): GPC 2017, LNCS 10232, pp. 116–126, 2017.
DOI: 10.1007/978-3-319-57186-7_10

1   Introduction

Along with the explosive advance of Internet and network communication technologies, it enables the network users to gain various online services at anywhere and access remote resources and servers at anytime. Considering the security issues (e.g., user authentication, communication privacy, data confidentiality, system availability etc.) for public networks, it is critical to ensure a secure communication over any insecure channel and many three-factor (including: password, smart card and biometrics) based authentication mechanisms have been proposed in the literatures [1,4–8,10–15]. In 2010, Li and Hwang [10] proposed the first biometrics-based remote user authentication scheme using smart cards. As compared to traditional easy-to-remember passwords, the major advantages of using biometric keys (such as palmprints, fingerprints, irises, faces, hand geometry and so on) are listed in the following:

– Biometric keys cannot be lost or forgotten.
– Biometric keys are very difficult to copy or share.
– Biometric keys are extremely hard to forge or distribute.
– Biometric keys cannot be guessed easily.
– Someone's biometrics is not easy to break than others.

In 2011, Das [4] pointed out that Li and Hwang's authentication has some security problems and proposed an improved solution. However, in 2012, An [1] pointed out that Das's solution is vulnerable to user impersonation, server masquerading, password guessing and insider attacks when the secret parameters stored in the smart card are revealed to a malicious attack. To resist those security weaknesses, An further introduced the enhanced scheme to withstand these security attacks. In 2015, Das and Goswami [5] showed that An's scheme has some serious design flaws and proposed a new biometric-based authentication scheme with user anonymity. In the same year, Lu et al. [11] proposed a biometric-based authentication scheme for telecare medicine information systems using elliptic curve cryptosystem [3]. Unfortunately, in 2016, Han et al. [8] observed that Lu et al.'s authentication scheme can't protect user anonymity and failed to resist user impersonation and server masquerading attacks. In order to overcome these drawbacks, Han et al. introduced their modified scheme based on Lu et al.'s scheme and the security of their scheme is proven by BAN logic tool [2] and robustly secure under a random oracle model. In this paper, we analyze the security of Han et al.'s ECC and three-factor based authentication scheme and demonstrate that their scheme fails to protect the property of unlinkability between the login user and the remote server. Additionally, we show that a legitimate user may quietly duplicate his/her login parameters and intentionally expose them to other non-registered users. This design flaw may lead multiple adversaries to login the remote server and the remote server is not aware of having caused problems. So as to overcome the aforementioned flaws of the scheme in [8], we put forward an improved version of Han et al.'s authentication scheme while preserving the merits and maintaining the efficiency of their scheme.

The remainder of the paper is organized as follows. In Sect. 2, we briefly review Han et al.'s ECC and three-factor based authenticated key exchange scheme. We further demonstrate two weaknesses of Han et al.'s scheme in Sect. 3. In Sect. 4, we suggest a security enhanced scheme. The security analysis and the performance evaluation are presented in Sects. 5 and 6, respectively. Section 7 concludes this paper.

2 Han et al.'s Three-Factor Based Authenticated Key Exchange Scheme

In this section, we review Han et al.'s three-factor based authenticated key exchange scheme [8]. Two roles participate in this scheme: the login user (U) and the remote server (S). In addition, three phases involve in their scheme: registration phase, login and authentication phase, and password change phase. The notations used throughout this paper are summarized as follows:

- U_i: The login user.
- S: The remote server.
- (ID_i, PW_i, B_i, SC_i): The identity, password, biometric and smart card of U_i.
- $H(\cdot)$: The biometric hash function [9].
- $h(\cdot)$: The cryptographic one-way hash function and it can be represented as $h : \{0,1\}^* \rightarrow \{0,1\}^n$.
- x: The private key maintained by S.
- SK: The common session key shared between U_i and S.
- $\oplus$: The bitwise exclusive OR operation.
- $||$: The string concatenation operation.
- $E_k(\cdot)/D_k(\cdot)$: The symmetric encryption/decryption with key k.
- P: The elliptic curve point $P = (x, y)$ as a value $x||y$.

2.1 Registration Phase

In this phase, the user U_i needs to perform the user registration procedure with the remote server S via a secure channel. The detailed steps are described as follows.

Step 1. U_i chooses a random number r, his identity ID_i, password PW_i and his biometric B_i and computes $MP_i = PW_i \oplus H(B_i) \oplus r$. Then U_i sends $\{ID_i, MP_i\}$ to S via a secure channel.

Step 2. After receiving the registration request from U_i, S generates a random number a and computes $AID_i = h(ID_i||x)$, $K_i = h(AID_i)$, $V_i = AID_i \oplus MP_i$ and $CID_i = E_x(ID_i||a)$. Then S stores $\{K_i, V_i, CID_i, h(\cdot), H(\cdot)\}$ into U_i's smart card SC_i and issues it to U_i via a secure channel.

Step 3. After receiving SC_i from S, U_i computes $R_i = r \oplus h(ID_i||PW_i||H(B_i))$ and stores R_i into SC_i.

2.2 Login and Authentication Phase

The login and authentication phase of Han et al.'s scheme is described as follows.

Step 1. U_i inserts SC_i into a card reader and inputs his identity ID_i, password PW_i and biometric B_i. Next, SC_i computes $r = R_i \oplus h(ID_i||PW_i||H(B_i))$, $MP_i = PW_i \oplus H(B_i) \oplus r$ and $AID_i = V_i \oplus MP_i$ and checks whether $h(AID_i) \overset{?}{=} K_i$. If it is valid, SC_i goes to Step 2.

Step 2. SC_i generates a random nonce $d_u \in Z_p$ and computes $D = d_u P$, $M_1 = AID_i \oplus D$ and $M_2 = h(AID_i||D||T_1)$, where T_1 is the current timestamp of SC_i. Then SC_i submits the login request $\{M_1, M_2, CID_i, T_1\}$ to S via a public channel.

Step 3. After receiving the login request from U_i, S checks the validity of T_1. If it holds, S retrieves ID_i by computing $D_x(CID_i)$ and further computes $AID_i = h(ID_i||x)$ and $D = AID_i \oplus M_1$. Then S checks whether $M_2 \overset{?}{=} h(AID_i||D||T_1)$. If it holds, S generates a' and $d_s \in Z_p$ and computes $E = d_s P$, $CID_i' = E_x(ID_i, a')$, $M_3 = AID_i \oplus E$, $SK = h(AID_i||d_s D||CID_i)$ and $M_4 = h(CID_i'||SK||E||T_2)$, where T_2 is the current time of S. Then S responses $\{M_3, M_4, CID_i', T_2\}$ to SC_i via a public channel.

Step 4. After receiving the response from S, SC_i checks the validity of T_2. If it holds, SC_i extracts E by computing $M_3 \oplus AID_i$ and computes $SK = h(AID_i||d_u E||CID_i)$, $M_4' = h(CID_i'||SK||E||T_2)$. Then SC_i checks whether $M_4' \overset{?}{=} M_4$. If it holds, SC_i replaces CID_i with CID_i' and responses $\{M_5, T_3\}$ to S via a public channel, where $M_5 = h(E||SK||T_3)$ and T_3 is the current time of SC_i.

Step 5. S checks the validity of T_3 and verifies whether $h(E||SK||T_3) \overset{?}{=} M_5$. If they are both correct, S authenticates U_i and convinces SK as the session key shared between U_i and S.

2.3 Password Change Phase

In this phase, U_i can freely change the original password PW_i to a new password PW_i^{new}. The password change phase of Han et al.'s scheme is described as follows.

Step 1. U_i inserts his SC_i into a card reader and inputs ID_i, PW_i and B_i.

Step 2. SC_i computes $r = R_i \oplus h(ID_i||PW_i||H(B_i))$, $MP_i = PW_i \oplus H(B_i) \oplus r$ and $AID_i = V_i \oplus MP_i$ and checks whether $h(AID_i) \overset{?}{=} K_i$. If it holds, U_i inputs the new password PW_i^{new}, the new biometric B_i^{new} and a new random number r^{new}.

Step 3. SC_i computes $MP_i^{new} = PW_i^{new} \oplus H(B_i^{new}) \oplus r^{new}$, $V_i^{new} = AID_i \oplus MP_i^{new}$ and $R_i^{new} = r^{new} \oplus h(ID_i||PW_i^{new}||H(B_i^{new}))$. Finally, SC_i replaces R_i and V_i with R_i^{new} and V_i^{new}, respectively.

3 Weaknesses of Han et al.'s Scheme

To analyze the security of Han et al.'s three-factor based authentication scheme, we assume that an adversary U_A has the ability of controlling over the communication channel and he may eavesdrop, intercept, insert, delete or modify the transmitted messages between U_i and S. Although Han et al.'s scheme is claimed to be secure against various attacks, we observe that their scheme fails to ensure unlinkability. Moreover, a legitimate user may intentionally duplicate his/her account to multiple non-registered users by using the same identity with different encrypted value CID_i and the remote server S is not aware of having caused problem. In the following, we will demonstrate the security flaws of Han et al.'s scheme in detail.

3.1 Fails to Ensure Unlinkability

In Han et al.'s scheme, U_i's identity ID_i is obscured by computing $M_1 = h(ID_i||x) \oplus D$, which is transmitted via a public channel in step 2 of login and authentication phase. Therefore, it is impossible to recover U_i's identity without knowing the knowledge of the secret values x and d_u. However, in step 3 of login and authentication phase, the masked value CID_i' transmitted from S to U_i will be used in next login session. Thus, the unlinkability will not be ensured even U_i's real identity ID_i is encrypted by an alias $CID_i' = E_x(ID_i, a')$. For example, if there is a login parameter transmitted between U_i and S containing CID_i'. It means that U_i is involved in some login session. Finally, Han et al.'s scheme is failed to ensure unlinkability and the adversary U_A can discover the relation of a connection between U_i and S as long as the login requests transmitted over the public channels contains CID_i'. For clarity, the details of this weakness are given in Fig. 1.

3.2 Account Duplication Attacks

In Han et al.'s scheme, we found that a legitimate user may intentionally duplicate his login account to multiple non-registered users by using the same identity $AID_i = h(ID_i||x)$ with different encrypted values (e.g. $CID_i, CID_i', CID_i'', \ldots$). The detailed steps of this attack are described as follows.

1. In i-th login session of Han et al.'s scheme, a login user U_i submits the i-th login request $\{M_1, M_2, CID_i, T_1\}$ to S, where $CID_i = E_x(ID_i||a)$. Then S responses $\{M_3, M_4, CID_i', T_2\}$ to U_i, where $CID_i' = E_x(ID_i||a')$ will be used in $i+1$-th login session.
2. In $i+1$-th login session of Han et al.'s scheme, a login user U_i submits the $i+1$-th login request $\{M_1', M_2', CID_i', T_1'\}$ to S. Then S responses $\{M_3', M_4', CID_i'', T_2'\}$ to U_i, where $CID_i'' = E_x(ID_i||a'')$ will be used in $i+2$-th login session.

Afterwards, U_i can duplicate three accounts $\{AID_i, CID_i, h(\cdot), H(\cdot)\}$, $\{AID_i, CID_i', h(\cdot), H(\cdot)\}$ and $\{AID_i, CID_i'', h(\cdot), H(\cdot)\}$ for other three non-registered users. Therefore, Han et al.'s scheme cannot resist account duplication attacks.

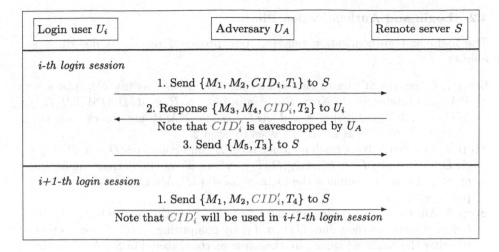

Fig. 1. Han et al.'s scheme failed to ensure unlinkability

4   The Proposed Scheme

In order to repair the identified security flaws of Han et al.'s three-factor based authentication scheme with privacy preserving, in this section, we suggest an improved scheme for preventing linkability problems and user duplication attacks. The improved scheme can be described in the following phases.

4.1   Registration Phase

In this phase, the executed steps are almost the same as in Han et al.'s scheme. The only difference is that S maintains the access control table (ACT) for a registration service and the format of ACT is shown in Table 1. Note that the first field records U_i's real identity, the second field records the pseudo number for U_i's initial registration, and the third field records U_i's latest login time and it records T_0 if it is U_i's initial registration.

Table 1. ACT of S after finishing the registration phase

User identity	Latest pseudo number	Latest login time
$\vdots$	$\vdots$	$\vdots$
ID_i	a	T_0
$\vdots$	$\vdots$	$\vdots$

4.2 Login and Authentication Phase

The login and authentication phase of our proposed scheme is described as follows.

Step 1. U_i inserts SC_i into a card reader and inputs his identity ID_i, password PW_i and biometric B_i. Next, SC_i computes $r = R_i \oplus h(ID_i||PW_i||H(B_i))$, $MP_i = PW_i \oplus H(B_i) \oplus r$ and $AID_i = V_i \oplus MP_i$ and checks whether $h(AID_i) \stackrel{?}{=} K_i$. If it is valid, SC_i goes to Step 2.

Step 2. SC_i generates a random nonce $d_u \in Z_p$ and computes $D = d_u P$, $M_1 = AID_i \oplus D$ and $M_2 = h(AID_i||D||T_1)$, where T_1 is the current timestamp of SC_i. Then SC_i submits the login request $\{M_1, M_2, CID_i, T_1\}$ to S via a public channel.

Step 3. After receiving the login request from U_i, S checks the validity of T_1. If it holds, S retrieves the values (ID_i, a, T_0) by computing $D_x(CID_i)$ and checks whether the retrieved values are the same as them stored in S's ACT. If they are match, S further computes $AID_i = h(ID_i||x)$ and $D = AID_i \oplus M_1$ and checks whether $M_2 \stackrel{?}{=} h(AID_i||D||T_1)$. If it holds, S generates a' and $d_s \in Z_p$ and computes $E = d_s P$, $CID_i' = E_x(ID_i, a', T_2)$, $M_3 = AID_i \oplus E$, $SK = h(AID_i||d_s D||CID_i)$, $M_4 = h(CID_i'||SK||E||T_2)$ and $M_5 = h(SK) \oplus CID_i'$, where T_2 is the current time of S. Then S responses $\{M_3, M_4, M_5, T_2\}$ to SC_i via a public channel.

Step 4. After receiving the response from S, SC_i checks the validity of T_2. If it holds, SC_i extracts E by computing $M_3 \oplus AID_i$ and computes $SK = h(AID_i||d_u E||CID_i)$, $CID_i' = M_5 \oplus h(SK)$ and $M_4' = h(CID_i'||SK||E||T_2)$. Then SC_i checks whether $M_4' \stackrel{?}{=} M_4$. If it holds, SC_i replaces CID_i with CID_i' and responses $\{M_6, T_3\}$ to S via a public channel, where $M_6 = h(E||SK||T_3)$ and T_3 is the current time of SC_i.

Step 5. S checks the validity of T_3 and verifies whether $h(E||SK||T_3) \stackrel{?}{=} M_6$. If they are both correct, S authenticates U_i and replaces a and T_0 with a' and T_2 in its ACT. After finishing this step, S convinces SK as the session key shared between U_i and S and the current format of S's ACT is shown in Table 2.

Table 2. ACT of S after finishing the login and authentication phase

User identity	Latest pseudo number	Latest login time
⋮	⋮	⋮
ID_i	a'	T_2
⋮	⋮	⋮

The details of login and authentication phase of the proposed scheme are shown in Fig. 2.

Login user U_i	Remote server S

Input ID_i, PW_i, B_i

$r = R_i \oplus h(ID_i||PW_i||H(B_i))$

$MP_i = PW_i \oplus H(B_i) \oplus r$

$AID_i = V_i \oplus MP_i$

$h(AID_i) \overset{?}{=} K_i$

$D = d_u P$

$M_1 = AID_i \oplus D$

$M_2 = h(AID_i||D||T_1)$

$$\xrightarrow{\text{Send } \{M_1, M_2, CID_i, T_1\} \text{ to } S}$$

Check the validity of T_1

$D_x(CID_i) = (ID_i, a, T_0)$

Compare (ID_i, a, T_0) with ACT

$AID_i = h(ID_i||x)$

$D = AID_i \oplus M_1$

$M_2 \overset{?}{=} h(AID_i||D||T_1)$

$E = d_s P$

$CID_i' = E_x(ID_i, a', T_2)$

$M_3 = AID_i \oplus E$

$SK = h(AID_i||d_s D||CID_i)$

$M_4 = h(CID_i'||SK||E||T_2)$

$M_5 = h(SK) \oplus CID_i'$

$$\xleftarrow{\text{Send } \{M_3, M_4, M_5, T_2\} \text{ to } U_i}$$

Check the validity of T_2

$E = M_3 \oplus AID_i$

$SK = h(AID_i||d_u E||CID_i)$

$CID_i' = M_5 \oplus h(SK)$

$M_4' = h(CID_i'||SK||E||T_2)$

$M_4' \overset{?}{=} M_4$

Replace CID_i with CID_i'

$M_6 = h(E||SK||T_3)$

$$\xrightarrow{\text{Send } \{M_6, T_3\} \text{ to } S}$$

Check the validity of T_3

$h(E||SK||T_3) \overset{?}{=} M_6$

Replace (a, T_0) with (a', T_2) in ACT

Fig. 2. The details of login and authentication phase of the proposed scheme

4.3   Password Change Phase

In this phase, the executed steps are the same as in Han et al.'s scheme.

5   Security Analysis of the Proposed Scheme

As shown in previous subsections, we can see that our proposed scheme is similar to the original Han et al.'s scheme. The two differences are the step 3 and step 4 of login and authentication phase. Therefore, our suggested scheme inherits the auxiliary functions of Han et al.'s scheme. In the following, we analyze why the proposed scheme can resist our proposed attacks in Sect. 3.

Remark 1. *In order to put emphasis on describing the security of our proposed scheme, we assume that the common session key SK shared between U_i and S has been well-protected by themselves.*

During the login and authentication phase of the proposed scheme, as pointed out by our attacks in Sect. 3.1, an adversary U_A may trace CID_i' with all of the eavesdropped messages transmitted between U_i and S and thus the unlinkability property of their scheme may be compromised. However, as suggested by our improvement in step 3 of login and authentication phase, U_A can't trace the specific session from S to U_i by comparing CID_i' in our improved scheme. Due to the use of hashed key $h(SK)$ and $h(SK)$ is computed freshly in each session, U_A can't derive CID_i' by computing $M_5 \oplus h(SK)$ and compare it with the eavesdropped messages unless U_A knows $h(SK) = h(h(AID_i||d_sD||CID_i))$. Therefore, it can be rightly said that the proposed scheme achieves the properties of user anonymity and unlinkability.

On the other hand, we further analyze why the proposed scheme can resist our proposed attack in Sect. 3.2. We assume that a registered user's duplicate accounts $\{AID_i, CID_i, h(\cdot), H(\cdot)\}$, $\{AID_i, CID_i', h(\cdot), H(\cdot)\}$ and $\{AID_i, CID_i'', h(\cdot), H(\cdot)\}$ are intentionally exposed to three non-registered users. Thus each one who knows U_i's AID_i and its corresponding encrypted value can login to S at the same time. However, as suggested by our improvement in login and authentication phase, the remote server S maintains an access control table and only one who knows the latest pseudo number and the latest login time can successfully login to S. As a result, the proposed scheme can prevent account duplication attack.

6   Performance Evaluation of the Proposed Scheme

In this section, we evaluate the performance of our proposed scheme with other related three-factor authentication schemes [8,14]. Table 3 shows the computation overhead of ours, Wu et al.'s and Han et al.'s schemes in login and authentication phase. It is noted that, the computation complexity associated with T_h, T_{sym} and T_{ecc} can be more or less expressed as $T_{ecc} \gg T_{sym} \gg T_h$. Also, due to

Table 3. Performance comparisons

	User side	Server side
Wu et al.'s scheme [14]	$6T_h+2T_{sym}+2T_{ecc}$	$6T_h+2T_{sym}+2T_{ecc}$
Han et al.'s scheme [8]	$6T_h+2T_{ecc}$	$5T_h+2T_{sym}+2T_{ecc}$
The proposed scheme	$7T_h+2T_{ecc}$	$6T_h+2T_{sym}+2T_{ecc}$

T_h: The time for executing a one-way hash function.
T_{sym}: The time for executing a symmetric en/decryption computation.
T_{ecc}: The time for executing an elliptic curve point multiplication.

the computational overhead of the exclusive OR operation is negligible as compared with above-mentioned cryptographic notations, we did not take exclusive OR operation into account. The computation overhead of server side of our proposed scheme is almost the same as Han et al.'s scheme because we only add one T_h in M_5 and replace Han et al.'s CID_i' with our $M_5 = h(SK) \oplus CID_i'$. Similarly, the computation overhead of user side of our proposed scheme is almost the same as in Han et al.'s scheme because we only add one T_h to reveal CID_i' by computing $M_5 \oplus h(SK)$. Therefore, the efficiency of the proposed scheme is similar to Han et al.'s scheme.

7 Conclusions

In this paper, we have first reviewed Han et al.'s three-factor based authenticated key exchange and user anonymity scheme and shown that the process of login and authentication phase is insecure, that is, an adversary can maliciously eavesdrop the transmitted message, discover the relation of a connection between U_i and S and damage the property of unlinkability. Moreover, we found that Han et al.'s scheme is vulnerable to account duplication attack. To avoid the security flaws on Han et al.'s scheme, we have proposed security improvements to prevent the aforementioned security weaknesses on Han et al.'s scheme, while inheriting all their merits and efficiencies of their scheme.

Acknowledgements. The authors would like to thank the anonymous reviewers for their valuable comments and suggestions. This research was supported in part by the Ministry of Science and Technology, Taiwan, R.O.C., under Grand number MOST 105-2221-E-165-005 and MOST 105-3314-C-165-001-ES.

References

1. An, Y.: Security analysis and enhancements of an effective biometric-based remote user authentication scheme using smart cards. J. Biomed. Biotechnol. **2012**, 1–6 (2012). Article no. 519723
2. Burrows, M., Abadi, M., Needham, R.: A logic of authentication. ACM Trans. Comput. Syst. **8**(1), 18–36 (1990)
3. Koblitz, N.: Elliptic curve cryptosystems. Math. Comput. **48**, 203–209 (1987)

4. Das, A.K.: Analysis and improvement on an efficient biometricbased remote user authentication. IET Inf. Secur. **5**(3), 145–151 (2011)
5. Das, A.K., Goswami, A.: A robust anonymous biometric-based remote user authentication scheme using smart cards. J. King Saud Univ. Comput. Inf. Sci. **27**(2), 193–210 (2015)
6. Das, A.K.: A secure user anonymity-preserving three-factor remote user authentication scheme for the telecare medicine information systems. J. Med. Syst. **39**(3), 1–20 (2015). Article no. 30
7. Guo, D., Wen, Q., Li, W., Zhang, H., Jin, Z.: An improved biometrics-based authentication scheme for telecare medical information systems. J. Med. Syst. **39**(3), 1–10 (2015). Article no. 20
8. Han, L., Tan, X., Wang, S., Liang, X.: An efficient and secure three-factor based authenticated key exchange scheme using elliptic curve cryptosystems. Peer-to-Peer Netw. Appl. (2016). doi:10.1007/s12083-016-0499-3
9. Jin, A.T.B., Ling, D.N.C., Goh, A.: Biohashing: two factor authentication featuring fingerprint data and tokenised random number. Pattern Recogn. **37**(11), 2245–2255 (2004)
10. Li, C.T., Hwang, M.S.: An efficient biometrics-based remote user authentication scheme using smart cards. J. Netw. Comput. Appl. **33**(1), 1–5 (2010)
11. Lu, Y., Li, L., Peng, H., Yang, Y.: An enhanced biometric-based authentication scheme for telecare medicine information systems using elliptic curve cryptosystem. J. Med. Syst. **39**(3), 1–9 (2015). Article no. 32
12. Mishra, D., Das, A.K., Mukhopadhyay, S.: A secure user anonymity-preserving biometric-based multi-server authenticated key agreement scheme using smart cards. Expert Syst. Appl. **41**(8), 8129–8143 (2014)
13. Moon, J., Choi, Y., Kim, J., Won, D.: An improvement of robust and efficient biometrics based password authentication scheme for telecare medicine information systems using extended chaotic maps. J. Med. Syst. **40**(3), 1–11 (2016). Article no. 70
14. Wu, F., Xu, L., Kumari, S., Li, X.: A novel and provably secure biometrics-based three-factor remote authentication scheme for mobile client-server networks. Comput. Electr. Eng. **45**, 274–285 (2015)
15. Yeh, H.L., Chen, T.H., Hu, K.J., Shih, W.K.: Robust elliptic curve cryptography-based three factor user authentication providing privacy of biometric data. IET Inf. Secur. **7**(3), 247–252 (2013)

Advanced Network Services, Algorithms and Optimization

A Study of Interference Cancellation for NOMA Downlink Near-Far Effect to Support Big Data

Shaoyu Dou[1], Xin Su[1(✉)], Dongmin Choi[2], Pankoo Kim[3], and Chang Choi[3]

[1] College of IOT Engineering, Changzhou Key Laboratory of Robotics and Intelligent Technology, Hohai University, Changzhou, China
shaoyudou1122@gmail.com, leosu8622@163.com
[2] Division of Undeclared Majors, Chosun University, Gwangju, Korea
jdmcc@chosun.ac.kr
[3] Department of Computer Engineering, Chosun University, Gwangju, Korea
pkkim@chosun.ac.kr, enduranceaura@gmail.com

Abstract. Non-orthogonal Multiple Access (NOMA) is proposed as a new multiple access for 5G communication. However, one of the crucial constraints is near-far effect that occurs to the NOMA downlink and serial interference cancellation (SIC). To avoid near-far effect, we propose 3D beam forming application based on antenna polarization in M-MIMO systems to re-group users. The proposed scheme effectively reduces the number of users within the beam coverage. On the other hand, we propose a method that adaptively selects channel estimation method according to the power of the user in SIC process to eliminate the effect.

Keywords: Non-orthogonal multiple access · Serial interference cancellation · 3D beam-forming · Near-far effect

1 Introduction

Higher downlink data rate (more than 10G bit/s) provided by the next generation of cellular network (i.e., 5G) will bring considerable benefits to all walks of life. However, how to deal with such a large communications volume on network has become a key issue to be solved in the 5G systems. Generally, Higher transmission rate (> 10G bit/s), Lower network latency and less user cost are required to enhance the performance of wireless transmission [1–6].

In current research, several novel technologies are proposed by the Mobile and wireless communications Enablers for Twenty-twenty Information Society (METIS) and 5GNOW, for instance, Massive-MIMO (multiple-input and multiple-output), mmWAVE, Device-to-Device (D2D), Filter-band Multicarrier (FBMC), Non-orthogonal Multiple Access (NOMA). The NOMA proposed by DoCoMo and Tokyo University has been regarded as a new method to improve the performance of multiple access in the future. Different from Orthogonal Multiple Access (OMA) adopted in the 4th generation mobile communication systems, NOMA utilizes the power domain to increase overall system throughput, even if the signal modulation is still bases on

© Springer International Publishing AG 2017
M.H.A. Au et al. (Eds.): GPC 2017, LNCS 10232, pp. 129–137, 2017.
DOI: 10.1007/978-3-319-57186-7_11

orthogonal frequency division multiple access (OFDMA) in uplink and Orthogonal Frequency Division Multiplexing (OFDM) in downlink. For the base station, non-orthogonality is achieved by introducing power domain and bring interference to the signal, for user equipment (UE), user de-multiplexing is obtained by the application of Successive Interference Cancelation (SIC). Although the application of SIC increase the complexity of cellular, higher spectrum efficiency could be achieved by using this method. According to [7], NOMA compared with OMA, can effectively improve nearly 30% of the system spectral efficiency.

Considering the situation of basic NOMA with SIC for two users (Fig. 1), the base station (BS) transmit x_1 to nearly UE (UE_1) with lower power, and utilizes higher power to transmit x_2 for UE_2. In the NOMA downlink, the order of decoding is depend on the inter-cell interference power and the increasing channel gain normalized by the noise. As for UE_1, it decode x_2 firstly and eliminate x_2 from received signal, for UE_2, it can decode x_2 directly without interference cancellation because x_2 has the first decode order.

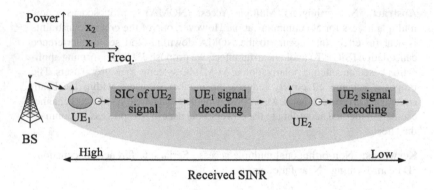

Fig. 1. Basic NOMA scheme applying SIC in downlink.

As a newly-developing concept, the performance of NOMA so far is discussed and evaluated in the context of assuming perfect SIC and with small number of users. Actually, UEs can't be clarified precisely via NOMA because the transmission power differences among crowded users are tiny. That will result in chaotic decoding order, so that the received signal probably cannot be decoded correctly. To solve the aforementioned problem (near-far effect in NOMA), we propose the solution from two aspects in this paper. For base station, we introduce 3D beamforming technology to reduce near-far effect; at user side, we optimize the signal detection scheme in order to overcome the near-far effect as well.

The remaining parts of this paper are organized as follows: Sect. 2 describes the near-far effect in NOMA and another factors hindering the practical application of NOMA. In Sect. 2.1, user regrouping achieved by 3D Beam Forming are introduced and we discuss the optimized SIC Scheme. Finally, our conclusions are drawn in Sect. 3.

2 NOMA Application Constrains

For conventional multiple access schemes, the power domain multiplexing technology is not used to fully exploit the spectrum efficiency. Outperforming the orthogonal multiple access, the non-orthogonal system are expected to get a great performance gain by introducing power domain multiplexing, e.g., in use of 5G Enhance Mobile Broadband (eMBB) scenario. However, the NOMA 'near-far effect' has become a crucial constraint to realize NOMA in practice.

As we know, the CDMA systems use orthogonal transmission and all users share same channel, pseudorandom spreading code is adopted to distinguish different users. Users near the base station affect cell-edge user's performance because of excessive transmission power produced in case without an efficient power allocation scheme. In this situation, the so-called 'near-far effect' occurred in uplink limits the CDMA system performance. Different from the CDMA system, as depicted in Fig. 2, the NOMA system detects users by transmission power. When $Beam_A$ is steered to cover UE_1, UE_2 and UE_3, UE_1 is unable to differentiate the data for UE_2 and UE_3 accurately. This is because the base transmission power difference between UE_2 and UE_3 is small, that yields the near-far effect in downlink of NOMA system.

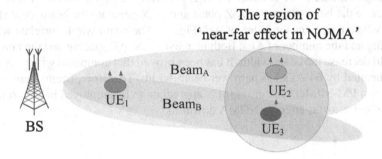

Fig. 2. The near-far effect occurs on NOMA downlink.

In summary, the near-far effect in CDMA systems occurs on the uplink, users close to the base station affect the users away from it. Power control should be applied at mobile terminals in order to overcome the near-far effect. The near-far effect in NOMA systems occurs on the downlink, distant users could interfere cell-center users. The Power control and user grouping scheme should be designed to avoid NOMA near-far effect. In this paper, we suggest a user grouping scheme base on the 3D Beamforming (3D-BF). The proposed scheme uses a polarized massive MIMO (PM-MIMO) system associated with 3D-BF to generate steerable narrow beam, e.g., $Beam_B$ in Fig. 2, which can be steered and varied separately on the X-Y, X-Z, and Y-Z planes to cover UE1 and UE3 only. Interference from UE2 then can be removed by this way.

Besides that, NOMA system has to face other challenges, such as the multi-user detection achieved via the SIC process. On one hand, a complicated SIC scheme is required to distinguish users in high-density transmission scenario. On the other hand, the receiver's SIC process need to report base station to rearrange the users' power continually that accommodates the mobility of users. This inevitably leads to a high power consumption for smart devices. The SIC generates latency during the interference cancellation process; an appropriate NOMA-SIC algorithm thus is required to reach a desired performance. In this paper, we also discuss the SIC complexity for different channel estimation (CE) schemes, and the NOMA-SIC process should consider the tradeoff between the receive power and estimation approach complexity.

2.1 NOMA with 3D Beamforming

We assume a beam is steered to K users, in the worst situation, a UE has to perform K-1 times SIC process to ensure the correct demodulation. Therefore, keeping a rational number of users covered by a same beam can reduce the near-far effect in NOMA downlink.

As discussed in Su and Chang [8], a PM-MIMO array system, where three orthogonally collocated antenna branches are applied to each array element (AE) (Fig. 3), can generate a 3D beam, which can be steered and varied at X-Y, X-Z and Y-Z planes respectively. Corresponding cross array branches should be used to generate beam instead of an AE, because the AE generate beam with a beam-width of 360°. Therefore three orthogonal beams are obtained as: A_pZ generate the beam steered in X-Y plane, A_pY generate the beam steered in X-Z plane and A_pX generate the beam steered in Y-Z plane, where p denotes the index of AE (Fig. 3). The beam-width correlate with the AE spacing and the number of AEs. Both increasing the AE spacing and the number of AEs could decrease the beam-width. It has been proved that compared with 8 AEs case, beam generated by 64 AEs has narrower beam-width. Therefore, beams generated by the proposed PM-MIMO systems in [8] is appreciate to be employed in base station in order to avoid near-far effect in NOMA downlink.

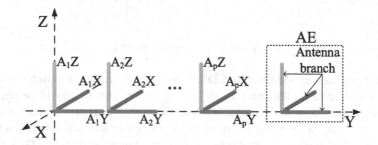

Fig. 3. PM-MIMO array system.

To realize PM-MIMO scenario in practice, we introduce factors D, d, ρ which denote the distance between UE and the BS, distance between UEs and the intensity of the spatial Poisson process followed by UEs respectively to describe a situation of two beams toward two adjacent pieces of UEs, as depicted as Fig. 4. We assume that there a number of UEs in a cell which have high density,

$$d_i \approx v_i. \tag{1}$$

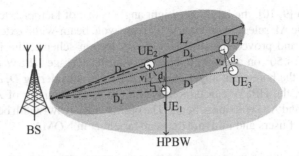

Fig. 4. Two beams steer toward two adjacent pieces of UE.

We use the model depicted in [8] to calculate D and d. The sum of UEs in a cell is

$$K = \rho L^2. \tag{2}$$

L is defined as beam coverage,

$$
\begin{aligned}
D &= \iint_{L^2} \frac{1}{L^2} r dr d\theta = \frac{2}{L^2} \left(\int_0^\omega \int_0^{a/\cos\theta} r^2 dr d\theta + \int_\omega^{\pi/2} \int_0^{2a/\sin\theta} r^2 dr d\theta \right) \\
&= \frac{\xi L}{2},
\end{aligned}
\tag{3}
$$

Where $\xi \approx 1.187$. d is calculated by

$$d = \iint_A \frac{1}{A} r dr d\theta = \int_0^{2\pi} \int_0^{r_{UE}} \frac{r^2}{\pi r_{UE}^2} dr d\theta = \frac{2}{3} r_{UE}, \tag{4}$$

where A declares the local coverage area depending on ρ.

To avoid BF interference, in the case of UEs in a half power beam-width (HPSW) area, like UE_2 and UE_1 in Fig. 4, HPSW should be limited less than $2d_1$. For UEs at beam peak area (UE_3 and UE_4), HPSW could scale up to $2d_2$. Therefore, the HPSW can be calculated as

$$HPSW \approx 2 \left| \sin^{-1} \left(1.391 \frac{\varepsilon}{\pi P} + \sin\theta_0 \right) \right| < 2d = \frac{4}{3} r_{UE}, \tag{5}$$

where θ_0 is the signal incidence angle shifted from the bore-sight direction, ε is the array spacing factor and is calculated by

$$\varepsilon = \lambda / s, \tag{6}$$

Where λ is signal wave length and s is array spacing. Usually, d and r_{UE} could be calculated after cellular communication model is fixed, the requested antenna array configuration could be derived by HPSW and ε.

As studies in [9, 10], the large bore-sight angle is one of factors extends the beam-width. A dynamic AE selection scheme which can avoid beam-width extension has been provided in [9] and proved that by using this selection scheme, the HPBW can be effectively kept as 50° on average. In contrast that the average HPSW extends to 65° when we ignore the bore-sight angel effect (Fig. 5). By considering D, d, K, ρ and the bore-sight angle, the HPSW can be jointly limited by the number of AEs, the array spacing factor ε and AE selection scheme. The optimized narrow-width beams can cover a small number of users and mitigate the near-far effect in NOMA.

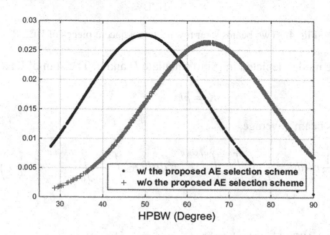

Fig. 5. Performance of AE selection scheme.

2.2 NOMA-SIC Optimization

The channel estimation approach employed in multi-carrier communication system should consist of channel estimation filtering, such as 1-D Least Square Interpolation, Maximum Likelihood Estimation, Wiener Filter (including 2-D Wiener filter, 2×1D Wiener filter and Time Wiener filter), etc. [11, 12]. The computation complexity of channel estimation is proportional to its performance. However, high-complexity esti-mate method can lead to a high power consumption for device if it is used indiscrimin-ately in various case; that is, the NOMA-SIC process should consider the tradeoff between the receive power and estimation approach complexity.

The computational complexity for various channel estimation methods are listed as Table 1. Three variables are adopted in analysis: L is channel length, N_p is the number of pilots and N_s is the number of subcarrier. We propose that difference channel esti-mation approaches can be chosen adaptively according to receive power.

Refer to [13], signal modulation bases on OFDM although UEs access network via NOMA. Figure 6 illustrates the downlink NOMA scheme of 2-UE case. For UE_1, the received signal y_1 is

$$y_1 = H_{11}\sqrt{p_1}s_1 + H_{21}\sqrt{p_2}s_2 + n_1,\tag{7}$$

Table 1. Computational complexity for various channel estimation methods.

Channel Estimation	Computational Complexity
LS Interpolation	$9N_s$
MLE	$4L\left(\dfrac{N_p}{2}(L+1)+N_s+\dfrac{L^2}{2}\right)+7N_s$
MLE + Time Wiener Filter	$4L\left(\dfrac{N_p}{2}(L+1)+N_s+\dfrac{L^2}{2}\right)+68N_s$
Time Wiener Filter + MLE	$7L\left[L^2+2LN_p+(2N_p+N_s)\right]+23N_p$
2×1D Wiener Filter	$N_p\left[\left(\dfrac{N_p}{2}\right)^2+(N_s+1)\dfrac{N_p}{2}+2N_s\right]+68N_s$
2D Wiener Filter	$N_p\left[N_p^2+3N_p+(28+N_p)N_s\right]$

where S_i is the data for UE_i and p_i is the allocated power. UE_1 should estimate H_{21} using low-complexity estimation method before demodulate s_2. Since the signal power for UE_2 is large, H_{21} can be correctly estimated even if a low performance algorithm is employed. On the contrary, UE_2 should use a great performance estimation method to estimate H_{22} in spite of high power is distributed to the signal for UE_2.

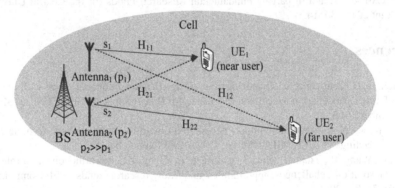

Fig. 6. NOMA-MIMO system for 2-UE case.

Besides above several methods, an efficient channel estimation method in NOMA should also focus on reducing the complexity of channel detector to ease the energy burden for UEs. For instance, the complexity of Wiener filter, mainly deriving from inversing operation of matrix when calculate minimum mean square error, is $O\left(N_{BS}N_{UE}^3\right)$. We can simplify the matrix inversion process to reduce its complexity to $O\left(N_{BS}N_{UE}^2\right)$ [14] by effectively select the weighting coefficient; threshold and other parameters based on the transmit power of the mobile terminal, where N_{BS} and N_{UE} denote the number of antenna equipped on BS and the number of mobile terminals respectively.

3   Conclusion

In this paper, to overcome the near-far effect occurs in NOMA downlink, we proposed employing 3D Beamforming at the base station. Unlike current studies in which beamforming and NOMA are combined to group users, the proposed scheme can steer and vary beams at X-Y, Y-Z and X-Z planes to avoid near-far effect in NOMA. In addition, we propose an idea that optimize channel estimation method selection in SIC process to overcomes the near-far effect, while also reducing the user's energy cost. We optimistically believe that, the system capacity will be greatly improved in the future when M-MIMO technology is widely utilized in practical communication. That will also provide a solid basis for 3D-BF. Moreover, NOMA with 3D-BF and other advanced technologies will overcome existing constraints in future 5G communications, providing us with high-speed, low-latency and low-cost communications and will become a new technology which are prioritized for development.

Acknowledgements. This work was supported in part by the Basic Science Research Program through National Research Foundation of Korea funded by the Ministry of Science, ICT & Future Planning under Grant 2015R1C1A1A02037515, and by the National Research Foundation of Korea (NRF) grant funded by the Korea government (MSIP) (No. NRF-2016R1A2B4012638). Also, This work is also supported by the Natural Science Foundation of Jiangsu Province under Grant BK20160287, and in part by Fundamental Research Funds for the Central Universities under Grant 2015B30614.

References

1. Umehara, J., Kishiyama, Y.: Enhancing user fairness in non-orthogonal access with successive interference cancellation for cellular downlink. In: Proceedings of IEEE CCS, pp. 324–328, November 2012
2. Beomju, K.: Non-orthogonal multiple access in a downlink multiuser beamforming system. In: Proceedings of IEEE MILCOM, pp. 1278–1283, November 2013
3. Dai, L., Wang, B., Yuan, Y., Han, S., Chih-Lin, I., Wang, Z.: Non-orthogonal multiple access for 5G: solutions, challenges, opportunities, and future research trends. IEEE Commun. Mag. **53**(9), 74–81 (2015)
4. Wang, Y.P., Su, X., Choi, D.M., Choi, C.: Coordinated scheduling algorithm for system utility maximization with heterogeneous QoS requirements in wireless relay networks. IEEE Access **4**, 8351–8361 (2016). (WOS: 000391487700017)
5. Su, X., Liang, C.C., Choi, D.M., Choi, C.: Power allocation schemes for femto-to-macro downlink interference reduction for smart devices in ambient intelligence. Mobile Inf. Syst. **2016**, 10 (2016). (WOS: 00039161870000)
6. Su, X., Wang, Y., Choi, D.M., Kim, P.K., Choi, C.: Channel allocation and power control schemes for cross-tier 3GPP LTE networks to support multimedia applications. Multimedia Tools Appl. (2017). doi:10.1007/s11042-016-4320-3
7. Li, Q., Niu, H.N., Papathanassiou, A., Wu, G.: 5G network capacity: key elements and technologies. IEEE Veh. Technol. Mag. **9**(1), 71–78 (2014)
8. Su, X., Chang, K.H.: Diversity and multiplexing technologies by 3D beams in polarized massive MIMO systems. Mobile Inf. Syst. **2016**, 15 (2016). Article ID 2318287

9. Su, X., Chang, K.H.: Polarized uniform linear array system: beam radiation pattern, beamforming diversity order, and channel capacity. Int. J. Antenna Propag. **2015**, 9 (2015). Article ID 371236
10. Liu, W.: Adaptive wideband beamforming with sensor delay lines. Sign. Proces. **89**(5), 876–882 (2009)
11. Liu, X., Miao, H., Huang, X.D.: A novel approach for blind estimation of a MIMO channel including phase unwrapping ambiguity elimination. IT Convergence Practice (INPRA) **1**(2), 20–33 (2013)
12. Su, X., Yu, H.F., Chang, K.H., Kim, S.G., Lim, Y.K.: Case study for ship ad-hoc networks under a maritime channel model in coastline areas. KSII Trans. Internet Inf. Syst. **9**(10), 4002–4014 (2015)
13. Su, X., Yu, H.F.: Non-orthogonal multiple access with practical interference cancellation for MIMO systems. IT Convergence Pract. (INPRA) **3**(4), 34–40 (2015)
14. Omori, H., Asai, T., Matsumoto, T.: A matched filter approximation for SC/MMSE iterative equalizers. IEEE Commun. Lett. **5**(7), 310–312 (2001)

Dynamic Latency Sensitivity Recognition: An Application to Energy Saving

S. Al Haj Baddar[1], A. Merlo[2], M. Migliardi[3,4(✉)], and F. Palmieri[5]

[1] The University of Jordan, Amman, Jordan
s.baddar@ju.edu.jo
[2] DIBRIS, University of Genoa, Genoa, Italy
a.merlo@dibris.unige.it
[3] DEI, University of Padua, Padua, Italy
mauro.migliardi@unipd.it
[4] CIPI, University of Genoa, Genoa, Italy
mauro.migliardi@cipi.unige.it
[5] DI, University of Salerno, Fisciano, Italy
francesco.palmieri@unisa.it

Abstract. In the world of connected everything, network attacks and cyber-security breaches may cause huge monetary damages and even endanger lives; hence, full sanitization of the Internet traffic is a real necessity. In this paper we will apply a dynamic statistical analysis to separate latency sensitive traffic from the latency insensitive one at the source. Then, we will calculate the energy savings that can be achieved by identifying and dropping all the unwanted portion of the latency insensitive traffic directly at the source. This value represents an upper-bound to the actual amount of energy that can be saved by applying our adaptive aggressive intrusion detection technique to latency insensitive traffic, in fact the actual value depends on the actual load of the network and its capability to spread the hunt for malicious packet among all the network nodes. The main contribution of this paper is to show that energy savings through aggressive intrusion detection may be achieved without burdening latency sensitive traffic with delays that may render it unusable, nonetheless, as a side effect of early removal of unwanted traffic from the network flows is to reduce the network load, the traffic reduction so obtained allows sanitizing even the latency sensitive traffic with a reduced risk of excessive delays due to resources allocation and traffic forecasting errors.

Keywords: Dynamic traffic classification · Network greenification · Aggressive intrusion detection · Distributed intrusion detection

1 Introduction

The prospective of *everything connected* makes the thorough sanitization of Internet traffic a real necessity. As a matter of fact, network attacks and cyber-security breaches have turned from a major nuisance in the past, to a source

© Springer International Publishing AG 2017
M.H.A. Au et al. (Eds.): GPC 2017, LNCS 10232, pp. 138–151, 2017.
DOI: 10.1007/978-3-319-57186-7_12

of monetary damage in the present and will become capable of endangering lives as soon remote control of physical devices will become widespread. At the same time, the fact that malicious traffic has a significant effect on networks' behavior has been demonstrated in several studies [5,12]. Finally, many recent studies dedicated to network threats ([9] [1, 2]) suggest that an increasing number of zombie nodes produce increasing amounts of malicious traffic. We claim that the combination of the need for thorough sanitization of the Internet traffic together with the fact that the amount of unwanted, purely malicious traffic roaming the network is significant, calls for the opportunity to merge the need for security with an energy saving activity. Past work [13,14] shows that early removal of unwanted traffic may produce significant energy savings, however it also showed that the risk of burdening some flows with undesired delays due to mis-prediction of the incoming traffic is non-negligible. In this paper we propose to tackle this problem introducing a mechanism to dynamically identify *Latency Sensitive Traffic* (LST) as opposed to *Latency Insensitive Traffic* (LIT). This allows focusing on LIT first guaranteeing undelayed delivery of LST, while the removal of unwanted LIT frees more resources that may be used later along the LST traffic flow to complete the sanitization without compromising the timing characteristics of LST. We first calculate the size of the energy saving deriving from immediate sanitization of LIT alone. This represent an upper bound of the amount of energy that can be saved by early dropping of unwanted LIT, in fact, even if LIT can be freely delayed to complete the Intrusion Detection phase as soon as possible, the amount of buffer space required to do so would be unbounded. Hence, a realistic approach requires to distribute the Intrusion Detection phase over the nodes along the traffic path. The calculation of this upper bound takes into account the energy cost of the classification of the Internet traffic into LIT and LST as it is instrumental only to our approach and thus has to be subtracted from the amount of energy that can be saved. The paper is structured as follows: in Sect. 2 we describe past relevant studies in the field, while in Sect. 3 we describe our mechanism dedicated to the dynamic identification of *Latency Sensitive Traffic* and *Latency Insensitive Traffic*. In Sect. 4 we describe the application of our scheme to a sample of a real world dataset, namely the traffic generated in a month at the department of Ingegneria dell'Informazione of the Universita' degli Studi di Padova, and we discuss our results; finally, in Sect. 5 we draw some conclusion and describe our future work in this field.

2 Related Work

Several Recent studies approached the problem of developing effective Network Intrusion Detection Systems (NIDS) from different perspectives. For example, some well-known NIDSs choose to consider a given behavior an intrusion if it

---

[1] http://securityaffairs.co/wordpress/8130/cyber-crime/
    botnet-around-us-are-we-nodes-of-the-matrix.html.
[2] http://www.mcafee.com/us/resources/reports/rp-quarterly-threats-dec-2016.pdf.

happens to fit in either one of its pre-defined intrusion molds. Such systems are commonly referred to as signature-based NIDSs, and include some of the most well-known NIDSs like Snort[3], Bro[4], and Suricata[5]. While Snort is popular, it is single-threaded and typically incapable of distinguishing application-level protocols. Bro, on the other hand, has a more elaborate system to define signatures, yet, is limited to Unix-based platforms. Unlike either one of these two NIDSs, Suricata is multi-threaded, and platform independent [13]. While signature-based NIDSs are potentially fast, they fall short of identifying any intrusion outside the scope of their signatures; which renders them incapable of addressing new intrusions. Another approach to detecting intrusions is behavioral, in the sense that normal network operations get modeled such that intrusions will be singled out immediately. Recent examples include [1,8,11]. As behavioral NIDSs are essentially capable of identifying unseen behaviors, they are hard to develop as it can be challenging to define what normal network behavior means. Consequently, they are prone to false alarms, as behaviors deviating from the modeled normal behavior may not necessarily be intrusions. As a result, we can hardly find effective behavioral NIDSs in the market.

Network intrusion detection systems can come in multiple flavors; some are statistical while others are based on one or more machine learning techniques, including clustering, classification, nearest neighbor algorithms, and even an ensemble of such algorithms. Several examples are surveyed in [4,10,16]. Furthermore, some NIDSs adopt an information theoretic approach to the problem like the examples surveyed in [24], and others utilize the streaming approach [6,18,23].

One emerging problem in this area is identifying intrusions in massively large datasets; this prompted the development of distributed intrusion detection systems. Several examples exist in literature including the studies in [14,15,17,19].

Another emerging problem in designing NIDSs is energy-effectiveness; it has become vital for various kinds of computational operations to become energy-saving. Thus, several recently developed NIDSs device energy-aware mechanisms to detect intrusions timely, albeit the large amounts of data that need to be processed along the way [7,20,21]. One example is illustrated in [14], where a distributed intrusion detection technique was introduced. The authors contrasted energy-savings obtained from early and later discovery of intrusion and used simulation to show that their approach is beneficial in terms of network energy savings. Another example is depicted in [22] where authors argued that implementing security algorithms in hardware saves considerable amounts of energy compared to implementing the same algorithm in software. In their work, the authors introduced energy-efficient feature selection and extraction algorithms. They also compared the energy profiles of hardware and software implementations of their approach compared to three machine learning classifiers Decision Tree, NaiveBayes, and k-Nearest Neighbors (kNN). Their experiments showed

---

[3] http://snort.org.
[4] http://bro.org.
[5] http://suricata-ids.org.

that their approach saved energy compared to the other approaches they studies; in particular, the energy consumption of the hardware implementation of their approach is only 12% of the hardware implementations of the 3 machine learning classifiers. Their results also showed that their approach's software implementation consumed only 22% of the energy consumed by its machine learning counterparts. Some solutions addresses intrusion detection in delay/disruption tolerant networks (DTNs). For example, the work depicted in [25] discusses a probabilistic misbehavior detection scheme, for secure routing in DTNs. The technique they introduced, referred to as iTrust, uses a Trusted Authority (TA) to evaluate the node's behavior based on the collected routing evidences and probabilistic checking, on a regular basis. The authors illustrated that by choosing the appropriate investigation probability, their technique ensures the security of DTN routing at a reduced cost.

3 Adaptive Intrusion Detection: Traffic Prioritization and Energy Saving

The main idea behind our approach to aggressive intrusion detection is to capitalize on the fact that while LST cannot afford to be delayed, LIT can. Thus, our approach prioritizes routing LST over its security analysis, whereas for LIT, it chooses to prioritize its security analysis over routing. In this sense, our approach to intrusion detection is adaptive. As we distribute the task of identifying malicious packets over multiple routers and have them drop such packets as soon as possible, we achieve energy savings. In this section we illustrate how adaptive intrusion detection is implemented using F-Sketure, a per-flow version of Sketure; the sketch-based packet analysis tool described in [2,3]. We demonstrate how F-Sketure classifies traffic into LST and LIT classes, and show how this approach helps save energy.

3.1 LST vs. LIT Traffic: Classifying Traffic Using F-Sketure

In order to be able to implement our adaptive approach to intrusion detection, we first need to be able to identify LST vs. LIT classes, and process each accordingly. To do so, we developed a per-flow version of Sketure, F-Sketure that is capable of splitting incoming traffic to LST and LIT classes and tag each packet accordingly. Each incoming packet's header, pheader is assumed to have the following format: $p_{header} = (source, destination, t_i, v^0(t_i), v^1(t_i), \ldots, v^{|\mathcal{F}|-1}(t_i), T, Checked)$ where source, and destination designate the packet's sender and receiver respectively, $v^j(t_i)$ denotes the value of the jth feature at time t_i, with $i \in 0, 1, 2, \ldots$), and T denotes the packet's tag. The packet' tag denotes the class of traffic to which the packet belongs, i.e. either LST or LIT. Initially, T is set to undefined. Finally, the checked field is a binary status field that designates whether or not the packet undergone security check. Intuitively, a packet needs only to be checked exactly once during its life span. To achieve its goal, Sketure first identifies traffic flows, and for each such flow it summarizes some features of the flows' packet headers in order to be able to distinguish LST from LIT. Let us assume that time is split into equal units, each of which is denoted by g. Then, a typical flow, f, in F-Sketure, comprises a set of aggregates, denoted by γ_g^f, where each such aggregate summarizes f's packets during g. In particular, each aggregate summarizes flow f's behavior in terms of three features; packet size, denoted by s, and packet count denoted by c. The aggregate also comprises a tag field denoted by T, which designates the traffic class to which the packets comprising the aggregate belong to. Similarly, each flow comprises a tag field, denoted by T, which designates the class to which the flow currently belongs. All such tag fields are initially undefined. Thus,

$$\gamma_g^f = < g, s, c, T > \tag{1}$$

and

$$f = (source, destination, T, \{\gamma_g^f, g \in \{0, 1, 2, \dots\}\}) \tag{2}$$

While flow f designates the communication from node source to nodes destination, we define f', the inverse of flow f to be on the form

$$f' = (destination, source, T, \{\gamma_g^{f'}, g \in \{0, 1, 2, \dots\}\}) \tag{3}$$

We also denote a given aggregate in f' by $\gamma_g^{f'}$ where

$$\gamma_g^{f'} = < g, s', c', T > \tag{4}$$

Upon recognizing a new flow, F-Sketure summarizes its behavior for $|g|$ time units, and generates the corresponding aggregate γ_g^f comprising the corresponding s, and c values. Then, it performs two tests on these values in flow f, and in ts inverse f', as LST flows are typically two-way, compared to, for example, streaming flows, which are not LST according to our definition. To decide whether aggregate γ_g^f is LST or LIT. Namely, F-Sketure considers an aggregate to be LST if it meets either one of the two following conditions:

1. If s and $s' \in [\delta_1 \bar{S}_{voip}, \delta_2 \bar{S}_{voip}]$ and c and $c' \in [\delta_1 \bar{C}_{voip}, \delta_2 \bar{C}_{voip}]$, where $\bar{S}_{voip}$ and $\bar{C}_{voip}$ are the average packet size and average packet count of the VOIP classes depicted in[6] respectively, while δ_1 and δ_2 denote the error margins.
2. If s and $s' \in [\delta_1 \bar{S}_{data}, \delta_2 \bar{S}_{data}]$ and c and $c' \in [\delta_1 \bar{C}_{data}, \delta_2 \bar{C}_{data}]$, where $\bar{S}_{data}$ and $\bar{C}_{data}$ are the average packet size and average packet count from the previous three aggregates respectively, while δ_1 and δ_2 denote the error margins.

As illustrated from the two conditions specified above, an aggregate is considered latency sensitive if both itself and its corresponding instance in the inverse flow exhibits a VOIP typical behavior, and/or if they exhibit a temporal regularity pattern. Otherwise, the aggregate is considered latency insensitive. The aggregates tag field T, is set to LST if either one of the aforementioned conditions is met, and set to LIT otherwise. When a given aggregate is tagged as

---

[6] http://www.cisco.com/c/en/us/support/docs/voice/voice-quality/7934-bwidth-consume.html.

either LST or LIT, its corresponding flow alongside all the packets that comprise the aggregate are tagged accordingly. After tagging the very first aggregate, all subsequent aggregates together with their comprising packets retain the same tag, until the next classification window arrives after t time units, where the two LST conditions are checked using the current aggregate, and the aggregate's tag, together with the flow and its current and upcoming packets either retain the previous value or obtain a new one.

3.2 Adaptive Intrusion Detection Architecture

Our intrusion detection architecture comprises a head router node that operates the F-Sketure tool followed by a set of Intrusion Prevention routers (IP). To clarify the operations of our approach, we assume time is split into slices, denoted by t.

The role of the head node is to tag each incoming packet as either LST or LIT, and then forward it to the next IP node. On the other hand, a typical IP node routes, and possibly, analyzes incoming. As proposed in [13], an IP router not only routes packets, but is also capable of identifying malicious incoming packets. A pre-processing unit, is dedicated to the estimation of the maximum number of packets that can be analyzed by router i at a given time slice t, whereas the Intrusion Prevention System (IPS) unit is responsible for identifying malicious incoming packets. LIT traffic has a higher priority at being analyzed. Therefore, LST traffic gets analyzed before routed, only after all LIT traffic within the same slice has been analyzed.

Each router, i, has an amount of energy that is equally split among time slices t. Thus, the amount of energy a router can consume at t, is denoted by $E_i(t)$. As each packet gets routed and/or analyzed $E_i(t)$ decreases accordingly. The main priority of a given IP router is to route rather than analyze packets. Thus, it is not typically possible to analyze all incoming packets within a slice at router i, Therefore, different packets get analyzed at different routers which renders our adaptive intrusion detection process distributed.

3.3 Modeling IP-Routers

Let us denote the maximum number of packets that can be analyzed by router i at a given time slice t by $M_i(t)$. Let us also denote router's i capacity at slice t by $C_i(t)$, and denote the expected number of incoming packets at slice t by $X_i(t)$. Furthermore, let us assume that routing one packet consumes R energy units. According to the work in [oxford paper], we know that the energy cost of performing security checks on a packet is more than the energy cost of routing the same packet, Thus, let the energy cost of analyzing a packet to be α times the energy cost of routing the packet, such that $\alpha > 1$. If we also denote the amount of packets in router's i buffer at the beginning of time slice t by $B_i(t)$, then can calculate $M_i(t)$ as follows

$$M_i(t) = \frac{C_i(t) - (X_i(t) + B_i(t))}{\alpha} \tag{5}$$

Upon calculating $M_i(t)$, at the beginning of time slice t, router i will undergo either one of the following energy consumption possibilities, provided that $A_i(t)$ denotes the number of analyzed packets during t so far, $K_i(t)$ denotes the number of checked packets observed during t, $N_i(t)$ denotes the number of incoming packets observed during t so far, and r_{LIT} is the ratio of LIT packets. Upon receiving new packet p with header of the form

$$(source, destination, i, v^0(t_i), v^1(t_i), \ldots, v^{|\mathcal{F}|-1}(t_i), T, Checked),$$

then either one of the following scenarios will happen:

1. If $Checked = 0$ or 1, $T = $ LST or LIT, and $E_i(t) < R$, then packet p is buffered until the next time slice, and $N_i(t)$ is incremented by 1.
2. If $Checked = 1$, $T = $ LST or LIT, and $E_i(t) \geq R$, then packet p is routed. Remaining energy $E_i(t) = E_i(t) - R$, while $N_i(t)$ and $K_i(t)$ are each incremented by 1.
3. If $Checked = 0$, $T = $ LST or LIT, $A_i(t) = M_i(t)$, and $E_i(t) \geq R$, then packet p is routed without being analyzed, $E_i(t) = E_i(t) - R$, while $N_i(t)$ is incremented by 1.
4. If $Checked = 0$, $T = $ LIT, $A_i(t) < M_i(t)$, and $E_i(t) \geq (1 + \alpha)R$, then packet p is analyzed, if it is malicious router i drops it, otherwise, its $Checked$ flag is set to 1, and the packet is routed. Remaining energy $E_i(t) = E_i(t) - (1 + \alpha)R$, while $A_i(t)$, $N_i(t)$, and $K_i(t)$ are each incremented by 1.
5. If $Checked = 0$, $T = $ LST, $A_i(t) < M_i(t)$, and $E_i(t) \geq (1 + \alpha) * R$, and $K_i(t) < r_{LIT}N_i(t)$, then packet p is routed without analysis, as $K_i(t) < r_{LIT} * N_i(t)$ implies that not all LIT traffic has been already analyzed. Remaining energy $E_i(t) = E_i(t) - R$, while $N_i(t)$ is incremented by 1.
6. If $Checked = 0$, $T = $ LST, $A_i(t) < M_i(t)$, and $E_i(t) \geq (1 + \alpha)R$, and $K_i(t) \geq r_{LIT}N_i(t)$ then packet p is analyzed, as $K_i(t) \geq r_{LIT}N_i(t)$ implies that all LIT traffic has been already analyzed. If packet p is found to be malicious, router i drops it, otherwise, its $Checked$ flag is set to 1, and the packet is routed. Remaining energy $E_i(t) = E_i(t) - (1 + \alpha)R$, while $A_i(t)$, $N_i(t)$, and $K_i(t)$ are each incremented by 1.

In summary, the behavior of a given IP router depends on the incoming traffic compared to the router's own capacity. If incoming packets are less than the router's maximum routing capacity, then it immediately routes incoming LST packets, and then applies an intrusion detection technique to as much as it can handle from remaining LIT packets. However, when the router falls short of energy, it limits its actions to only routing incoming packets without analysis. This implies that malicious packets get dropped as soon as they are discovered which is expected to reduce the overall energy expenditure. As for calculating the expected amount of traffic at a given time slice, denoted by $x_i(t)$, it is calculated using the average of the actual incoming packets from the two most recent $N_i(t)$ values. That is $X_i(t) = \frac{N_i(t-1) + N_i(t-2)}{2}$. During the two first slices, $X_i(t)$ is set to $\frac{C_i(t)}{2}$.

3.4   Modeling the Head Router

It is worth noting that the head router uses a similar model; it caps the number of packets it can tag at the beginning of each time slice, and behaves accordingly. More precisely, the head node calculates the maximum number of packets it can tag at a given time slice, denoted by $M_h(t)$ as follows

$$M_h(t) = \frac{C_h(t) - (X_h(t) + B_h(t))}{\beta}$$

where $C_h(t)$ denotes the head node's capacity, $X_h(t)$ denotes the expected number of packets at time slice t, and $B_h(t)$ denotes the number of packets buffered at the head router at the beginning of t. Moreover, beta designates the ratio of the energy cost of tagging one packets to the energy cost of routing such a packet. Yet, the behavior of the head router is a bit different, since it needs to tag all incoming packets before they get routed. The head router is presumably the first node to observe packets, thus, all its incoming packets arrive initially untagged. As we need all packets to be tagged and use IP routers with capacity $C_i(t)$, we need to use a more capable header node in order to be able to deliver tagged packets at the IP routers maximum capacity. To achieve this goal, the following inequality must be satisfied

$$C_h(t) > (1 + \beta)C_i(t)$$

As energy preserving is pursued, it is recommended to choose a head router with capacity $C_h(t)$ equal to $(1 + \beta)C_i(t)$. It is also noted that the smaller the value of β is, the more energy will be saved.

4   Experimentation and Performance Evaluation

In this section we illustrate the experiments conducted to evaluate the performance of our adaptive intrusion detection strategy. In order to measure the performance of F-Sketure on a real dataset and also identify the LST within that set, we used 10 h worthy of packet traces from Friday April 10th 2015 taken from the Padua dataset [2]. For each observed packet the following header information was provided:

- Packet timestamp in the form hh:mm:ss.
- Obfuscated source and destination addresses
- Packet size

This sample dataset comprised 1.48 GB packet header information spanning the interval from 1:00 am until 10:00 am.

We implemented the F-Sketure behavior as illustrated in Subsect. 3.1 using Java and fed it with the Padua dataset sample describe in Sect. 4. We choose the error margins δ_1 and δ_2 to be 0.95 and 1.05, respectively. Our implementation of F-Sketure produced aggregates once every second, and re-evaluated their tags once every 3 s.

The results of our implementation revealed that almost 3% of the traffic was classified as LST. The results also revealed that tagging a packet without re-evaluation consumed 0.5 nsec on average, while tagging a packet after re-evaluating its aggregate's class consumed 0.273 μs.

The time it took F-Sketure to read packet headers, identify flows, generate aggregates, and tag packets ranged from 8 s to handle 4M packets up to 94 s to handle 32M packets. As for F-Sketure's memory consumption, the amount of memory consumed to process packets ranged from 2.5 GB to 4.5 GB.

To simulate the operations of our adaptive intrusion detection system, we considered a path that comprises one head router and 10 IP routers. While F-Sketure operates in the head router to feed the next routers with tagged packets, the remaining IP routers route packets, and if possible, analyze them according to the process depicted in Subsect. 3.3. We implemented our simulation tool in Java, and assumed the capacity of IP routers to be 20 Gbps each. We also assumed the header router to be a more capable router with 30 Gbps capacity. At the maximum capacity of IP routers, the header router would be still able to tag and route all incoming packets. We split simulation time into 1 ms slices. In order to simulate incoming traffic we modulated a set of incoming packets from the total traffic at MIX premises as illustrated in[7]. As for the intrusion detection technique deployed in simulated IP routers, we use Suricata's signature-based intrusion detection system, and according to [13], α is set to 4.5. As for β, according to the experiments executed using F-Sketure, it was set to 0.35.

We ran our simulation for 18 min with a malicious packet ratio of 6%. In the real dataset, LST is just 3% of the whole traffic; such a low percentage of LST suits perfectly our scheme, in fact it is very easy to guarantee the forwarding of 3% of the traffic while performing aggressive security analysis of the remaining 97%. In order to stress our scheme, we varied LST ratio from 5% to 20%. In each experiment, we calculated average number of routed packets, average number of analyzed packets, average number of malicious packets dropped, and average amount of energy consumed per router. We also calculated the number of malicious packets identified and the total amount of energy consumed. We also compared the amount of energy consumed by our approach to the amount of energy consumed in a typical routing scenario where malicious packets are discovered and dropped only at the destination node.

Figure 1 through 4 depict the results we obtained, and we discuss them in this section.

Figure 1 shows that while a router receives and routes 1.5M packets, it is capable of analyzing around 1M packets on average. This implies that 66% of the traffic is potentially analyzed in the first router. From this follows that, on the average, 66% of the malicious traffic can be dropped immediately, i.e., 4% of the whole traffic when 6% of packets were malicious.

The simulation ran for periods ranging from 1.5 min to 18 min. Figure 2 illustrates the average number of malicious packets identified during each period with

---

[7] http://www.mix-it.net/statistics/cgi-bin/14all-Totale_globale.cgi?
log=totaltraffic_global.

LST percentages ranging from 5% to 20%. With the statistical variability, there is obviously no relation between the percentage of LST traffic and the number of bad packets in the traffic flow. Furthermore, as the percentage of LST is lower than the routing capability of the router, there is no reduction in the amount of traffic analyzed.

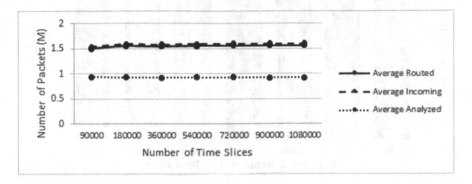

Fig. 1. Average number of incoming, routed, analyzed packets using $\lambda= 6\%$

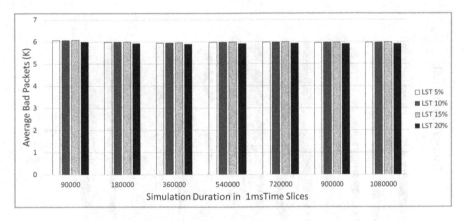

Fig. 2. Number of malicious packets using $\lambda= 6\%$

As for the amount of energy consumed for routing and analyzing packets, Fig. 3 illustrates the total amount of energy consumed for each simulation duration, averaged over the simulation duration and with varying LST ratios. While the shortest simulation used a slightly lower amount of energy as the initial phase, all the others show that, at the steady state where the nodes are always working in full, the amount of energy consumed is stable. Furthermore, the results show no dependency from the percentage of LST in the packet flow. This latter results depends from the fact that in our simulation the analysis and routing capability of the nodes always guaranteed the forwarding of LST.

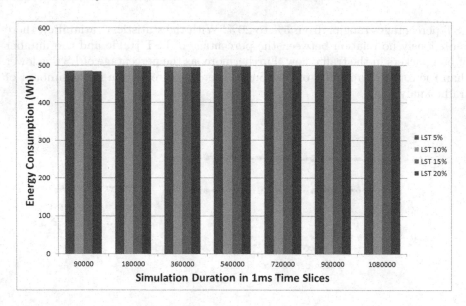

Fig. 3. Energy consumed using $\lambda = 6\%$

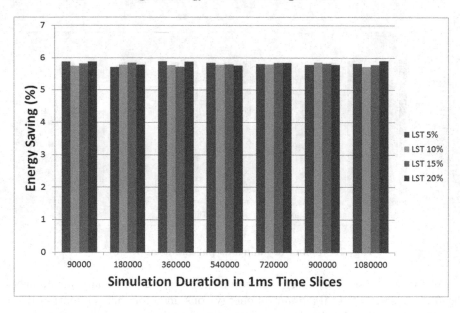

Fig. 4. Energy saved using $\lambda = 6\%$

We also compared between our approach and the classical approach where no traffic filtering is used and where bad packets were identified and dropped only at the destination nodes. Figure 4 depicts energy savings. The simulation shows that our scheme guarantees a level of energy saving very close to the optimal level, i.e., the amount that could be obtained by dropping all the malicious traffic at the network access node. While our simulation shows no dependency from the amount of LST present in the whole packet flow, we argue that a situation where the nodes are closer to their full load could require a more conservative approach in dealing with LST and thus could expose a different behavior. In future work we will analyze with situation in much deeper detail.

5   Conclusions and Future Work

In this work we introduce and evaluate an adaptive aggressive intrusion detection technique, that saves energy not only by distributing the task of malicious packet identification among router nodes, but also by prioritizing the type of traffic that gets examined first. More precisely, our approach classifies traffic into latency sensitive traffic (LST) and latency insensitive traffic (LIT) classes at the source node, then identifies and drops malicious packets from LIT traffic while LST gets routed. After all LIT traffic is examined, LST traffic is examined in order to locate and drop its share of malicious packets while avoiding burdening it with excessive delays. We applied our approach to a real dataset comprising 12 h of traffic recorded within a university campus, and developed a flow-based version of the packet analysis tool Sketure to classify the traffic into LST and LIT classes. Then, we developed a simulation environment and calculated traffic and energy consumption while varying the ratios of malicious and LST packets. Our simulation showed that our approach saved up to 30% of the energy compared to non-distributed intrusion detection that takes place at the destination node. In future work we will provide a detailed analysis of the capability of our scheme to prevent delays to LST. As in this work we focused on a subset of commonly-used symmetric VOIP traffic classes, we plan on including additional categories of real-time LST traffic classes. Moreover, we plan to enhance our approach by reducing the amount of computations needed to identify malicious packets so that more energy can be saved. We will also improve our approach to off-load the process of tagging packets to a co-processor unit so that packet tagging and analysis can happen simultaneously.

References

1. Ashfaq, R.A.R., Wang, X.-Z., Huang, J.Z., Abbas, H., He, Y.-L.: Fuzziness based semi-supervised learning approach for intrusion detection system. Inf. Sci. **378**, 484–497 (2017)
2. Al-Haj Baddar, S.W., Mauro, A., Migliardi, M.: SKETURE: a sketch-based packet analysis tool. In: Proceedings of the 7th ACM CCS International Workshop on Managing Insider Security Threats, MIST 2015, Denver, Colorado, USA, October 16, pp. 67–70 (2015)
3. Al-Haj Baddar, S.W., Merlo, A., Migliardi, M.: Generating statistical insights into network behavior using SKETURE. J. High Speed Netw. **22**(1), 65–76 (2016)
4. Bhuyan, M.H., Bhattacharyya, D.K., Kalita, J.K.: Network anomaly detection: methods, systems and tools. IEEE Commun. Surv. Tutorials **16**(1), 303–336 (2014)

5. Lan, K.C., Hussain, A., Dutta, D.: Effect of malicious traffic on the network (2003)
6. Desale, K.S., Kumathekar, C.N., Chavan, A.P.: Efficient intrusion detection system using stream data mining classification technique. In: 2015 International Conference on Computing Communication Control and Automation, pp. 469–473, February 2015
7. Hassanzadeh, A., Altaweel, A., Stoleru, R.: Traffic-and-resource-aware intrusion detection in wireless mesh networks. Ad Hoc Netw. **21**, 18–41 (2014)
8. Ji, S.-Y., Jeong, B.-K., Choi, S., Jeong, D.H.: A multi-level intrusion detection method for abnormal network behaviors. J. Netw. Comput. Appl. **62**, 9–17 (2016)
9. Leder, F., Werner, T., Martini, P.: Proactive botnet countermeasures - an offensive approach. In: Cooperative Cyber Defence Centre of Excellence (2009)
10. Liao, H.-J., Lin, C.-H.R., Lin, Y.-C., Tung, K.-Y.: Intrusion detection system: a comprehensive review. J. Netw. Comput. Appl. **36**(1), 16–24 (2013)
11. Lin, W.-C., Ke, S.-W., Tsai, C.-F.: CANN: an intrusion detection system based on combining cluster centers and nearest neighbors. Knowl.-Based Syst. **78**, 13–21 (2015)
12. Mallikarjunan, K.N., Muthupriya, K., Shalinie, S.M.: A survey of distributed denial of service attack. In: 2016 10th International Conference on Intelligent Systems and Control (ISCO), pp. 1–6, January 2016
13. Merlo, A., Spadacini, E., Migliardi, M.: IPS-based reduction of network energy consumption. Logic J. IGPL **24**(6), 982 (2016)
14. Migliardi, M., Merlo, A.: Improving energy efficiency in distributed intrusion detection systems. J. High Speed Netw. **19**(3), 251–264 (2013)
15. Mitchell, R., Chen, I.-R.: A survey of intrusion detection in wireless network applications. Comput. Commun. **42**, 1–23 (2014)
16. Modi, C., Patel, D., Borisaniya, B., Patel, H., Patel, A., Rajarajan, M.: Review: a survey of intrusion detection techniques in cloud. J. Netw. Comput. Appl. **36**(1), 42–57 (2013)
17. Modi, C., Patel, D., Borisaniya, B., Patel, H., Patel, A., Rajarajan, M.: A survey of intrusion detection techniques in cloud. J. Netw. Comput. Appl. **36**(1), 42–57 (2013)
18. Noorbehbahani, F., Fanian, A., Mousavi, R., Hasannejad, H.: An incremental intrusion detection system using a new semi-supervised stream classification method. Int. J. Commun. Syst. **30**(4) (2017). e3002-n/a, e3002 IJCS-15-0106.R1
19. Patel, A., Taghavi, M., Bakhtiyari, K., Júnior, J.C.: An intrusion detection and prevention system in cloud computing: a systematic review. J. Netw. Comput. Appl. **36**(1), 25–41 (2013)
20. Şen, S., Clark, J.A., Tapiador, J.E.: Power-aware intrusion detection in mobile ad hoc networks. In: Zheng, J., Mao, S., Midkiff, S.F., Zhu, H. (eds.) ADHOCNETS 2009. LNICSSITE, vol. 28, pp. 224–239. Springer, Heidelberg (2010). doi:10.1007/978-3-642-11723-7_15
21. Tsikoudis, N., Papadogiannakis, A., Markatos, E.P.: LEoNIDS: a low-latency and energy-efficient network-level intrusion detection system. IEEE Trans. Emerg. Top. Comput. **4**(1), 142–155 (2016)
22. Viegas, E., Santin, A.O., França, A., Jasinski, R., Pedroni, V.A., Oliveira, L.S.: Towards an energy-efficient anomaly-based intrusion detection engine for embedded systems. IEEE Trans. Comput. **66**(1), 163–177 (2017)
23. Wang, W., Guyet, T., Quiniou, R., Cordier, M.-O., Masseglia, F., Zhang, X.: Autonomic intrusion detection: adaptively detecting anomalies over unlabeled audit data streams in computer networks. Knowl.-Based Syst. **70**, 103–117 (2014)

24. Weller-Fahy, D.J., Borghetti, B.J., Sodemann, A.A.: A survey of distance and similarity measures used within network intrusion anomaly detection. IEEE Commun. Surv. Tutorials **17**(1), 70–91 (2015)
25. Zhu, H., Du, S., Gao, Z., Dong, M., Cao, Z.: A probabilistic misbehavior detection scheme toward efficient trust establishment in delay-tolerant networks. IEEE Trans. Parallel Distrib. Syst. **25**(1), 22–32 (2014)

TPS: An Efficient VM Scheduling Algorithm for HPC Applications in Cloud

Duoqiang Wang$^{(\boxtimes)}$, Wei Dai, Chi Zhang, Xuanhua Shi, and Hai Jin

Services Computing Technology and System Lab,
Cluster and Grid Computing Lab, School of Computer Science and Technology,
Huazhong University of Science and Technology, Wuhan 430074, China
{dqwang,weidai,ciba,xhshi,hjin}@hust.edu.cn

Abstract. Cloud computing platforms are becoming viable alternative for running high performance parallel applications. However, when running these applications in cloud platforms, VMs (*virtual machines*) are easily affected by the synchronization latency problem which leads to serious performance degradation. There are two main reasons. The first is that a host is unaware of the synchronization requirements of the guest OS. The second is that the synchronization requests of VMs on a physical host are unknown to VMs on the other physical host. It is a great challenge to mitigate the negative influence of virtualization on synchronization and accelerate the synchronization response of HPC applications. In this paper, we propose a *two − phase synchronization-aware* (TPS) scheduling algorithm to solve the problem above. The TPS algorithm takes both intra-VMs' and inter-VMs' synchronization demands into consideration. Spin-locks and network packets are used as the metrics to detect the synchronization demands of VMs and VMs are scheduled based on spinlock-aware and communication-aware strategies. The algorithm is implemented on the base of KVM and experiments are conducted in a cluster environment. The experimental results show that our TPS algorithm obtains a better performance for HPC applications and reduces negative impacts on non-HPC applications simultaneously. Therefore, our approach is an effective solution to the HPC synchronization issues in cloud platforms.

Keywords: High performance computing · Synchronization · Scheduling · Virtualization · Cloud computing

1 Introduction

Cloud computing provides a new usage pattern for symmetric multi-processor power. Resource utilization and hardware flexibility are greatly improved by cloud computing based on virtualization technology. Cloud platforms have become a suitable choice for HPC (*high performance computing*) applications. Parallel HPC applications such as biological macromolecules and hydromechanics usually require lots of computing resources and high degree parallelism.

© Springer International Publishing AG 2017
M.H.A. Au et al. (Eds.): GPC 2017, LNCS 10232, pp. 152–164, 2017.
DOI: 10.1007/978-3-319-57186-7_13

However, running HPC applications in cloud environment may lead to significant performance degradation because of the characteristics of virtualization technology and HPC applications' synchronization demands. First, all vCPUs in the overcommitted cloud environment are not always online and the sibling vCPUs in a VM are not always online simultaneously. Therefore, if an online vCPU wants to get the spinlock held by an offline vCPU, it will lead to a nontrivial CPU busy-wait problem which could be solved by synchronization operations. Second, large-scale HPC applications require lots of *virtual machines* (VMs) when running in cloud. A cluster which consists of VMs distributed on different physical hosts is called virtual cluster [4]. Applications running in a virtual cluster also need synchronization operations.

Previous works such as co-scheduling [15,17], dynamic adaptive scheduling [16], and balance scheduling [13] have made many improvements on mitigating synchronization latency problems. However, most of them concentrated on solving the synchronization problems in a single SMP VM, while solving synchronization latency problems between VMs located on different hosts was neglected. In this paper, we propose a scheduling strategy called two-phase synchronization-aware scheduling algorithm (TPS for short), to efficiently reduce synchronization latency of both intra-VMs and inter-VMs. This scheduling strategy also has performance improvement on non-HPC applications. We implement TPS by extending KVM's default scheduler and *completely fair scheduling* (CFS). The main contributions of this paper are as follows.

1. We make a detailed analysis about the impact of virtualization on synchronization in HPC applications. We find out that HPC applications running in cloud can lead to two kinds of synchronization latency problems. The first is lock-holder preemption [2,14], and the second is data synchronization among sibling tasks such as MPI_Barrier().
2. We present our TPS strategy based on the analysis above. The strategy has two key aspects. First, a communication-aware approach is used to mitigate the synchronization latency between VMs [18]. Second, the waiting time of spinlocks is utilized as the metric to detect lock-holder preemption in a single VM.
3. A comprehensive comparison is performed between TPS and CFS, balance scheduling and co-scheduling. The experimental results illustrate that TPS is more efficient in solving the synchronization problem and improving the performance of HPC applications in virtual clusters.

The rest of this paper is organized as follows. Section 2 describes the background and motivation. Section 3 presents our TPS scheduling algorithm. Section 4 describes the detail implementation of TPS. In Sect. 5 we discuss the evaluation results. Section 6 introduces related work. We conclude our work in Sect. 7.

2   Background and Motivation

It is well-known that virtualization platforms, such as KVM and Xen, add an extra layer between hardware layer and guest operation system, named hypervisor or VMM (*Virtual Machine Monitor*), which mainly schedules hosts' resources and maps them to VMs. The complexity of virtualization architecture forces the hypervisor's CPU scheduler to consider two issues when running HPC applications on virtual cluster: first, how to schedule the vCPUs of a VM to solve the lock-holder preemption problem, and second, how to mitigate the synchronization overheads of inter-VMs caused by mutex locks. Mutex locks are usually used to access critical sections and ensure data consistency. Compared to spinlocks, mutex locks do not lead to CPU busy-wait, but it can add extra execution time of the program. Hence, we need to find an approach to detect the synchronization demands between different VMs and reduce the skew among sibling tasks so that the lock can be released faster. However, most researches [16–18] only take one aspect into consideration and cannot satisfy all the requirements of parallel HPC applications.

2.1   Synchronization Overheads of Intra-VMs

Previous researches have demonstrated that the synchronization overheads in SMP VM are mainly caused by lock-holder preemption. We use Fig. 1 to illustrate this situation. Assume that there is a VM running a HPC application in a dual-core physical machine, and the VM has two vCPUs (virtual CPUs) named vCPU0 and vCPU1. These two vCPUs are mapped to different pCPUs (physical CPUs) . The host will run other vCPUs when vCPU0 and vCPU1 are de-scheduled. From time $t0$ to $t3$, vCPU0 is the lock holder. As a lock waiter, vCPU1 has to spin to wait for the lock to be released. At time $t1$, vCPU0 is preempted by other VMs, if vCPU1 restarts at time $t2$. Then vCPU1 will waste an extra time slice to get the lock, which is the main reason of the SMP VM synchronization latency problem. If there are N vCPUs in the run-queue before vCPU0, then the latency time will be as long as $N \times T_{slice\_i}$.

In order to verify this conclusion, a simple experiment is performed on a physical machine which boasts 16 cores and 64 GB memory. We start 4 VMs with the same configuration on the physical machine, each VM consists of 8 cores. In each VM, we run a $lu.C.8$ (lu is a benchmark from NAS Parallel Benchmark,

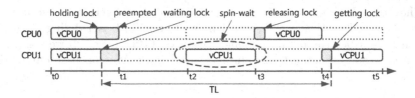

Fig. 1. Synchronization latency when running parallel HPC applications

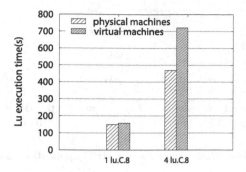

Fig. 2. The execution time of $lu.C.8$ on physical machines and virtual machines

class C, with 8 processes). The ratio of vCPU-to-pCPU is 2:1. As a comparison, we also run 4 $lu.C.8$ programs on another same physical machine. From Fig. 2 we find that the execution time of running four same benchmarks is 3.1 times longer than that of running one benchmark on the physical machine, while the time of running $lu.C.8$ programs on 4 VMs simultaneously is 4.6 times longer than that of running only one $lu.C.8$ on one VM. From the conclusion of Friebel et al. [2], the phenomenon is mainly resulted by spinlock latency of intra-VMs.

2.2 Synchronization Demands in Virtual Cluster

Consider the scenario that a virtual cluster with 3 VMs (each has 2 vCPUs) is deployed on 3 physical machines. Each physical machine has two processors, named CPU0 and CPU1, each of which has 8 cores. So there are 16 cores in total. Lots of VMs are running on a physical machine and VMs of the virtual cluster are some of them. A HPC application with six threads is running in this virtual cluster. The ordering of sibling vCPUs are from 1 to 6. At the end of each time slice, the HPC application needs a synchronization operation. Figure 3(a) presents a possible scenario when running such a HPC application under CFS. It is the extreme situation that all the vCPUs are running serially. In Fig. 3(a), an iteration cycle from time $t0$ to $t6$ costs six time slices. The next iteration has to start after time $t6$. In the ideal situation, there is a global scheduler to force all the vCPUs to co-start and co-stop, and the cost of an iteration can be optimized to a single time slice. However it is unrealistic because the network communication is measured with the basic unit of us level, while the basic time unit of cpu scheduler is at the level of ns.

The second scheduling strategy, co-scheduling, is shown in Fig. 3(b). An iteration cycle is reduced to 5 time slices because co-scheduling is unable to run all vCPUs simultaneously. The next iteration cycle starts at time $t5$. If vCPU5 and vCPU6 could be run earlier, lots of time would have been saved. If we only consider the characteristics of HPC applications, VM3 is the crucial factor for minimizing the execution time, while VM1 and VM2 are secondary factors. This phenomenon is usually called "Cask Effect". Therefore its additional

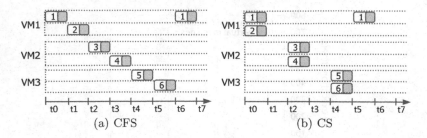

Fig. 3. Possible scheduling sequences of a HPC application under CFS and CS

effects during the execution of the program should not be neglected. Though co-scheduling does not play a major role in this phenomenon, it leads to priority inversion and CPU fragmentation [13]. Frequent context-switch is also inevitable when using *inter − processor interrupt* (IPI), which will cost extra CPU time and reduce the cache hit ratio of CPU. As the scale grows, the performance of co-scheduling will be worse.

Though there are some approaches considering the synchronization of inter-VMs, they do not handle the lock-holder preemption problem precisely. For example, SVS [18] scheduling uses network packets as a signal to detect synchronization requests of inter-VMs. However, when the application in VM uses a MPI+pthread framework, the performance of SVS will be poor for the reason that multiple threads in pthread almost share the same process resources and do not need to communicate through TCP/IP. Hence, the SVS algorithm is unable to solve the synchronization problem of intra-VMs accurately.

In summary, reducing synchronization overheads of inter-VMs and intra-VMs requires the scheduler to be more efficient. On the basis of above analysis, we propose our solution: a *Two-Phase Synchronization-aware Scheduling* (TPS).

3   Two-Phase Synchronization-Aware Scheduling

TPS algorithm consists of two phases, coarse-grained communication-aware synchronization and fine-grained spinlock-aware synchronization. The key point of communication-aware is how to choose a suitable signal to indicate the synchronization requests between VMs on different nodes. It is well known that HPC applications in distributed system mainly employ MPI as the tool of parallelization. Data transmissions are required before synchronization during each iteration cycle. Therefore, we can utilize the speed of receiving packets as the metric of synchronization demands between VMs [18]. In the second phase, we utilize relaxed co-scheduling rather than strict co-scheduling to solve the lock-holder preemption problem. If the last spinlock time is longer than normal time, we think that a synchronization operation should be performed among the sibling vCPUs of the VM. This approach makes the synchronization overheads decreased dramatically by slowing down the frequency of unnecessary synchronization of intra-VMs.

Moreover, inspired by affinity-based scheduling that handling vCPU stacking problem [13], we map vCPUs to different pCPUs if the VM is going to run a HPC application, and load balance will be performed if the VM is going to run non-HPC applications.

We use Formula 1 to express the time saved by TPS compared with CFS when running HPC applications.

$$\Delta T = \sum T_{packet} + \sum T_{spinlock} - \sum T_{repeat} \qquad (1)$$

For the convenience of our analysis, some variables are defined as follows.

(a) T_{packet} is the time saved by a synchronization operation of inter-VMs.
(b) $T_{spinlock}$ is the time saved by a synchronization operation of intra-VMs.
(c) T_{repeat} is the time saved when there is a phenomenon of (a) and (b) occurring simultaneously.

Algorithm 1 simply describes the main idea of TPS using pseudo-code. In the algorithm, N is the number of vCPUs, S is the set of sibling vCPUs in a single VM, v_i is the ith scheduled vCPU of a VM, $tgid$ is the parent pid of a vCPU, syn_vm is the VM which needs to be synchronized, max_P and max_S are the thresholds of the received packets and spinlocks repectively. When the rate of receiving packets in a HPC-VM exceeds the thresholds, the first scheduled vCPU will send IPI to inform all the sibling vCPUs. Then each vCPU will preempt the pCPU and run the HPC application simultaneously. Otherwise it just sends IPI information according to the time of spinlocks. For non-HPC

Algorithm 1. The TPS VM scheduling algorithm

```
 1: if v_i ∈ HPC then
 2:      if v_i is the first vCPU of a VM then
 3:          if !syn_vm and v_i.packets ≥ max_P then
 4:              syn_vm ← v_i.tgid
 5:              for j ← 1 to N do
 6:                  if j ≠ i and v_j ∈ S then
 7:                      schedule v_j
 8:                  end if
 9:              end for
10:              syn_vm ← NULL
11:          else if !syn_vm and v_i.spinlocks ≥ max_S then
12:              syn_vm ← v_i.tgid
13:              for j ← 1 to N do
14:                  if j ≠ i and v_j ∈ S then
15:                      schedule v_j
16:                  end if
17:              end for
18:              syn_vm ← NULL
19:          else if syn_vm ≠ NULL then
20:              schedule v_i as CFS
21:          end if
22:      else if v_i ≠ v_1 and syn_vm ≠ NULL then
23:          schedule v_i as CFS
24:      end if
25: else if v_i ∉ HPC then
26:      schedule v_i as CFS
27: end if
```

applications, they will be scheduled by default asynchronous algorithm, CFS. The time complexity of our algorithm is $O(N)$.

4   Implementation

We implement TPS scheduler based on the CFS scheduler of KVM. The linux kernel version is 3.17.4. We slightly modify the kernel of both guest OS and host OS by extending the CFS scheduler with a new scheduler called TPSched.

4.1   Modification to the Kernel

In our system, VMs are divided into two kinds, those running HPC applications and those running non-HPC applications. We add a variable *type* into *task_struct* to distinguish the type of VMs. *task_struct* is the VM description of KVM scheduler. If the value of *type* is one, the VM is HPC VM, and zero indicates a non-HPC VM. The default value of *type* is zero.

As shown in Fig. 4, we modify the guest OS to collect the information of spinlocks and packets in the VMs. Spinlocks are counted in the guest's kernel function named *_raw_spin_lock*, and packets are also counted using the struct *net_device_stats*. Then information is sent to hosts by KVM hyper call named *kvm_hypercall*. All the functions implemented in guest OS are called Sensors. In the host OS, we use a Collector to receive the information coming from VMs. The main codes are implemented in the kernel function *kvm_emulate_hypercall*. We handle the guest information in Collector instead of Sensor to decouple this function from the dependencies on the guest OS and host OS. In our system, the threshold of packets received is set as 10K/s and the threshold of spinlocks is set as 2^{15} cycles due to the characteristics of HPC applications.

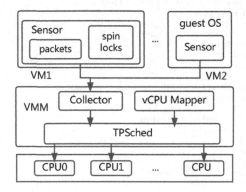

Fig. 4. Overall architecture of the system

4.2   Modification to CFS

TPS requires some modifications to CFS in KVM hypervisor. First, we employ two constants named max_P and max_S as the flags of selecting different scheduling strategies. In $task\_struct$, we use $spinlock\_count$ and $packet\_count$ to indicate the number of spinlocks and packets. Second, a vCPU Mapper is used to distribute vCPUs to different pCPUs. It mainly amends the vCPUs' $cpus\_allowed$, a bit mask to identify which pCPU a vCPU can be mapped to. Last and most, we add our core algorithm in the function $pick\_next\_task\_fair$. When the system needs synchronization operations, the sponsor vCPU will use IPI to make all sibling vCPUs invoke $resched\_cpu$. The detailed code inevitably uses bit operations and locks to access critical sections among all vCPUs.

5   Evaluation

5.1   Experimental Setup

We run all the experiments on 8 nodes (physical machines). Each node boasts 16 cores clocked at 2.6 GHz and 64 GB memory. The host OS is Redhat Enterprise Linux 6.2 with kernel 3.17.4. The guest OS is CentOS 7 with the same kernel. We use vncviewer to display the user interface of all VMs.

We have run HPC applications like NPB ($NAS\ Parallel\ Benchmark$) [9] and non-HPC applications, such as httperf [5], bonnie++ [1], SPEC CPU 2006 [11], stream [12], to evaluate the actual performance of our TPS scheduler. For comparisons, we also run these applications using some other well-known scheduling approaches: $complete\ fair\ scheduling$ (CFS), $balancescheduling$ (BS), and $relaxed\ co\text{-}scheduling$ (CS).

There are four non-ignorable issues that should be considered when we design the VM scheduler: fairness, adaptiveness, scalability, and performance. These four factors will be covered in our experiments.

5.2   Experiment for Performance

The main target of our design is to improve the performance of HPC applications. Therefore our first experiment is to evaluate whether our algorithm is efficient. We use cg, is, ep from NPB suite as the benchmark. The experiment platform is set up with 8 physical machines mentioned above, each physical machine hosts 4 VMs and each VM consists of 8 vCPUs. The fixed vCPU-to-pCPU ratio is 2:1. The virtual clusters are deployed as follows.

Eight 8-vCPU independent VMs (called **VM1**).

Four 16-vCPU virtual clusters (called **VC1**).

Two 32-vCPU virtual clusters (called **VC2**).

One 64-vCPU virtual cluster (called **VC3**).

The architecture of VC1 is shown in Fig. 5(d), it has 8 vCPUs on both node1 and node2. VC1 consists of two VM1s, VC2 consists of two VC1s and VC3

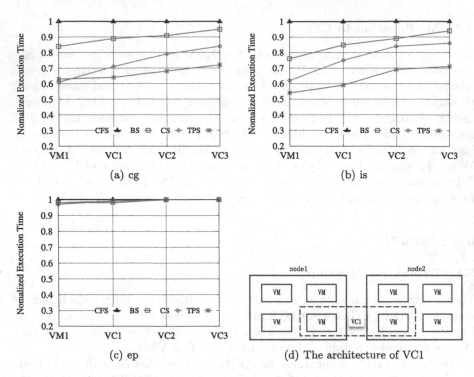

Fig. 5. The normalized execution time of cg, is, ep under different scheduling strategies

consists of two VC2s. Each node hosts one VM1, one VM of VC1, one VM of VC2, and one VM of VC3.

On these four kinds of virtual clusters, we run benchmark cg simultaneously for five times and record the average execution time on each virtual cluster. We perform the same operation with is, and ep, respectively. The experimental results are shown in Fig. 5. The average execution times of cg, is, and ep are normalized based on CFS. Figure 5(a) illustrates that, compared with CFS, TPS algorithm has a performance improvement from 28% to 37% for the benchmark $cg.C$. As the application's scale grows, the performance hardly improves because the synchronization overheads between VMs are increased. Compared with CFS, the normalized execution times of BS, CS, and TPS are 0.95, 0.84, and 0.72, respectively, when running $cg.C.64$ in VC3. It means that TPS has 23% and 12% performance improvements over BS, and CS. These results imply that our coarse-grained communication-aware strategy is effective. Compared with CFS, BS, and CS, TPS scheduler is a better approach to reduce the synchronization overheads between VMs.

When we run $cg.C.8$ in VM1, the execution times of CFS, BS, CS, TPS are 179 s, 152 s, 109 s, 112 s. The performance of TPS is better than CFS and BS, which illustrates that our fine-grained spinlock-aware strategy is also effective. However, CS is 3 s faster than TPS. According to the strategy of TPS, VM1 may

Table 1. The average speed of receiving packets of different benchmarks

Benchmarks	cg	is	ep
Packets/s	15408	23055	4725

be preempted by other virtual clusters if there are some intensive TCP/IP communications in VC1, VC2, or VC3. It means TPS provides virtual clusters a higher priority than independent VMs while CS provides all the VMs the same priority. That's why CS is better than TPS in independent VMs.

From Fig. 5, we can observe that all schedulers hardly improve the performance of benchmark *ep*. NAS describes the *ep* benchmark as embarrassing parallel. According to the introduction from NAS and the results of Table 1, we know that *ep* is a loosely coupled application and requires a little data transmission, and hence the packets received and the spinlocks of *ep* will not reach the threshold to trigger the TPS scheduling. In other words, the *ep* benchmark likes a non-HPC application, which leads to no performance improvements as BS and CS.

According to the experiment results, the TPS scheduler is more efficient reducing synchronization overheads and improves the performance of HPC applications in cloud environment.

5.3 Experiment for Adaptiveness

In order to confirm that our TPS scheduler does not have much negative impacts on non-HPC applications. We use 4 nodes, each of which has an independent VM running non-HPC applications selected from bonnie++, stream, httperf, and SPEC CPU 2006. These four applications represent I/O-bound application, memory-bound application, latency-sensitive application, and CPU-bound application, respectively. We also create several virtual clusters on 8 nodes (similar as in Sect. 5.2) and the HPC parallel applications selected from NPB suite are running on these virtual clusters.

As depicted in Fig. 6, we normalize the average performance of Bonnie++, stream, httperf, and SPEC CPU 2006 based on CFS. The average throughput of BSO, BSI, stream copy, stream add, gcc, and bzip2 are almost identical. This indicates that modifications for HPC applications have little impact on this type of applications.

However, the response time of httperf under TPS is 21% longer than CFS. This phenomenon can be explained by our scheduling strategy. Using IPI to enforce the sibling VMs to run synchronously will break the priority of runqueues and lead to some VMs' priority declining. It has negative impacts on the latency-sensitive applications such as ping and web server, while has little influence on non-HPC applications such as stream and bonnie++. Because our TPS scheduler needs more synchronization operations among different nodes, the response time of httperf under TPS is longer than CS. In terms of the experimental results, our strategy is suitable for a variety kinds of applications even though it has a little performance degradation for latency-sensitive applications.

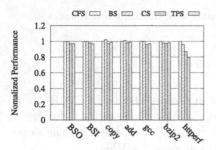

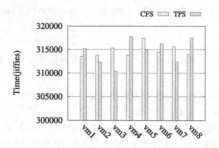

Fig. 6. The performance of different benchmarks under different strategies

Fig. 7. The average time of all the VMs in a fixed time interval

5.4 Experiment for Fairness

In this testing scenario, a variety of benchmarks are running on 16 VMs. These 16 VMs are located in two physical machines and each VM consists of 4 vCPUs, 4 GB memory and 10 GB disk.

We randomly select a physical machine as the test machine. During a fixed time interval, 1500s, the execution time of 8 VMs is shown in Fig. 7. The VMs' running time is measured through reading the file */proc/pid/stat*. We repeatedly run the application for 10 times and choose the one whose standard deviation is the largest. Taking CFS as reference, Table 2 records the Jain's fairness index [6]. The results illustrate that our TPS scheduling almost has the same fairness as CFS.

Table 2. Jain's fairness index of CFS and TPS

Metric	CFS	TPS
Jain's fairness index	0.99998	0.99971

6 Related Work

In symmetric multi-processor systems, we use spinlocks to access critical sections in sequence. There is a lock-holder preemption phenomenon in cloud environment, which leads to the CPU busy-wait problem [2]. This phenomenon will be worse when running high performance parallel applications. There are many works [7,8,19] related to virtual machine scheduling. Some of them focus on the synchronization problem. Uhlig et al. [2] presented some approaches to solve the problem, such as lock-aware and time ballooning. Co-scheduling is also effective in avoiding lock-holder preemption, which forces all sibling vCPUs co-start and co-stop simultaneously. Weng et al. [16] improved the co-scheduling by triggering the co-start once the waiting time of spinlocks exceeds a threshold. Sukwong et al. [13] proposed that co-scheduling was too expensive for SMP VMs and designed balance scheduling to compensate the co-scheduling's drawbacks. Combined with applications' own characteristics, Weng et al. [17] designed a hybrid scheduling framework to choose different strategies based on the applications' types. Francesco Palmieri [10] proposed a network-aware scheduling for real-time execution in data-intensive optical grids.

However, researches mentioned above are only applicable for SMP VMs, and they did not take the global information of virtual cluster into account. Govindan et al. [3] studied the I/O virtualization overheads of Xen and analyzed the communication procedure between VMs, and then proposed an approach named communication-aware scheduling. Wu et al. [18] designed a *synchronization-aware scheduling* (SVS) for virtual clusters based on the correlation of network packets and synchronizations on cloud. However, network packets cannot reflect the synchronization requests between threads in same process.

7 Conclusion

In this paper, we comprehensively analyzed the virtual machine synchronization problem and found that the existing VM schedulers are not suitable for HPC applications. Running high performance parallel applications in VMs raises two kinds of synchronization problems as mentioned before. It is not sufficient for us to just consider one aspect. Therefore, we propose a two-phases synchronization-aware scheduling strategy.

The TPS scheduler can adapt several kinds of applications dynamically by different scheduling strategies. It is able to carry out synchronization operations with various granularities according to different metrics. When there are frequent information transmissions between VMs, the TPS algorithm will take synchronization operations depending on the packets received. It will perform synchronization in a single VM when the number of spinlocks exceeds the threshold. Otherwise, the default scheduler, CFS will be used. At last, we evaluate the performance of the TPS algorithm based on our cluster platform. The experimental results show that TPS outperforms the traditional schedulers and is feasible to improve the performance of HPC applications running in cloud.

Acknowledgements. This research was supported by National Key Research and Development Program under grant 2016YFB1000501, 863 Hi-Tech Research and Development Program under grant No. 2015AA01A203, National Science Foundation of China under grant No. 61232008, and Fundamental Research Funds for the Central Universities under grant HUST: 2016YXZD016.

References

1. Bonnie++: http://www.coker.com.au/bonnie++/
2. Friebel, T., Biemueller, S.: How to deal with lock holder preemption. Xen Summit North America (2008)

3. Govindan, S., Choi, J., Nath, A.R., Das, A., Urgaonkar, B., Sivasubramaniam, A.: Xen and Co.: Communication-aware CPU management in consolidated Xen-based hosting platforms. IEEE Trans. Comput. **58**(8), 1111–1125 (2009)
4. Hacker, T.J., Mahadik, K.: Flexible resource allocation for reliable virtual cluster computing systems. In: Proceedings of 2011 International Conference for High Performance Computing, Networking, Storage and Analysis, SC 2011, NY, USA, New York, pp. 48:1–48:12. ACM (2011)
5. Httperf: https://github.com/httperf/httperf
6. Jain, R., Durresi, A., Babic, G.: Throughput fairness index: an explanation. ATM Forum/99-0045 (1999)
7. Jang, J.W., Jeon, M., Kim, H.S., Jo, H., Kim, J.S., Maeng, S.: Energy reduction in consolidated servers through memory-aware virtual machine scheduling. IEEE Trans. Comput. **60**(4), 552–564 (2011)
8. Kim, H., Lim, H., Jeong, J., Jo, H., Lee, J.: Task-aware virtual machine scheduling for I/O performance. In: Procedings of International Conference on Virtual Execution Environments, VEE 2009, Washington, DC, USA, pp. 101–110. ACM Press (2009)
9. NPB2.4: http://www.nas.nasa.gov/publications/npb.html/
10. Palmieri, F.: Network-aware scheduling for real-time execution support in data-intensive optical grids. Future Gener. Comput. Syst. **25**(7), 794–803 (2009)
11. SPEC: http://www.spec.org/cpu2006/
12. Stream: https://www.cs.virginia.edu/stream/
13. Sukwong, O., Kim, H.S.: Is co-scheduling too expensive for SMP VMs? In: Proceedings of the Sixth European Conference on Computer Systems, EuroSys 2011, Alzburg, Austria, pp. 257–272. ACM Press (2011)
14. Uhlig, V., Levasseur, J., Skoglund, E., Dannowski, U.: Towards scalable multiprocessor virtual machines. Proc. Virtual Mach. Res. Technol. Sympo. **3**, 43–56 (2004)
15. VMware: Vmware vsphere: The CPU scheduler in VMware ESX 4.1. https://www.vmware.com/files/pdf/techpaper/VMW_vSphere41_cpu_schedule_ESX.pdf
16. Weng, C., Liu, Q., Yu, L., Li, M.: Dynamic adaptive scheduling for virtual machines. In: Procedings of ACM International Symposium on High Performance Distributed Computing, HPDC 2011, San Jose, CA, USA, pp. 239–250. IEEE Press (2011)
17. Weng, C., Wang, Z., Li, M., Lu, X.: The hybrid scheduling framework for virtual machine systems. In: Procedings of International Conference on Virtual Execution Environments, VEE 2009, Washington, DC, USA, pp. 111–120. ACM Press (2009)
18. Wu, S., Chen, H., Di, S., Zhou, B., Xie, Z., Jin, H., Shi, X.: Synchronization-aware scheduling for virtual clusters in cloud. IEEE Trans. Parallel Distrib. Syst. **26**(10), 2890–2902 (2015)
19. Zhou, L., Wu, S., Sun, H., Jin, H., Shi, X.: Virtual machine scheduling for parallel soft real-time applications. In: Proceedings of 21st International Symposium on Modelling, Analysis and Simulation of Computer and Telecommunication Systems, MASCOTS 2013, pp. 525–534. IEEE Press (2013)

Improved Upper and Lower Bounds for the Close Enough Traveling Salesman Problem

Francesco Carrabs[1], Carmine Cerrone[2(✉)], Raffaele Cerulli[1],
and Ciriaco D'Ambrosio[1]

[1] Department of Mathematics, University of Salerno, Fisciano, Italy
{fcarrabs,raffaele,cdambrosio}@unisa.it
[2] Department of Biosciences and Territory, University of Molise, Campobasso, Italy
carmine.cerrone@unimol.it

Abstract. This paper studies the close-enough traveling salesman problem, a variant of the Euclidean traveling salesman problem in which the traveler visits a node if it passes through the neighborhood of that node. We introduce an improved version of the adaptive internal discretization scheme, recently proposed in the literature, and a heuristic that combines this scheme with to a second-order cone programming algorithm. Our heuristic is able to compute tight bounds for the problem. The computational results, carried out on benchmark instances, confirm the improvements of the bounds computed with respect to the other algorithms proposed in the literature.

Keywords: Close-enough · Traveling salesman problem · Discretization scheme · Second-order cone programming

1 Introduction

This paper concerns a variant of the traveling salesman problem (TSP) called close-enough traveling salesman problem (CETSP). The TSP is one of the most studied optimization problems. Given a set of target points, in an Euclidean space, the TSP consists of finding a minimum length tour that starts and ends at a depot while visiting each target point exactly once. In CETSP to each target point v is associated a neighborhood, that is a compact region of the space containing v. The CETSP consists of finding the shortest tour that starts and ends at the depot and intersects each neighborhood once. In this work we assume that the neighborhoods shape is a disc.

The CETSP has several practical applications in the context of Unmanned Aerial Vehicles that are vehicles without crew used for military and civil missions like aerial forest fire detection, supply delivering (food, munition, etc.) to targets, geographic region monitoring and military surveillance. Moreover, even the robot monitoring wireless sensor networks can be modeled as a CETSP [17]. Furthermore some classical wireless sensor networks problems such as those presented in [6,7] can be obtain useful hint by considering the Convex Hull construction proposed in this paper. Finally, the CETSP arises in the context of the

© Springer International Publishing AG 2017
M.H.A. Au et al. (Eds.): GPC 2017, LNCS 10232, pp. 165–177, 2017.
DOI: 10.1007/978-3-319-57186-7_14

reading process of water (electricity or gas) consumption. Indeed, by using radio frequency identification readers, it is possible to catch the information about the consumption by using a drone flying within the range of each reader. This methodology is much faster than the classical door-by-door reading process and requires the resolution of CETSP.

The CETSP was introduced by Gulczynski et al. [14] that proposed several heuristics to face the problem. Afterwards, other heuristics were introduced in [12,15,16] while an effective evolutionary approach was implemented in [17].

Very recently, a branch-and-bound algorithm was proposed in [11] in which the subproblem, solved in each node of the search tree, consists of a Second Order Cone Programming. The authors carried out computational tests on several instances proving that their branch and bound often finds the optimal solution. To the best of our knowledge, the idea to use the second order cone programming for the CETSP was introduced the first time in [16].

In this paper we propose a more effective version of the internal discretization scheme introduced in [5]. Moreover, we propose a new heutistic obtained by combining this new scheme with the second-order cone programming algorithm [16] to obtain a heuristic able to compute tight bounds for the CETSP problem. The computational results reveal that our approach produces better bounds with respect to the ones proposed in [2,5].

The remainder of the paper is organized as follows. Section 2 introduces the definitions and the notations that are throughout the paper. Section 3 contains a brief overview of the algorithm based on the internal discretization scheme [5] while Sect. 4 reports a mixed-integer programming model for CETSP. The second-order cone programming algorithm [16] is described in Sect. 5. Finally, computational results are presented in Sect. 6 followed by conclusions in Sect. 7.

2   Definitions and Notation

Given a two-dimensional plane, let N be a set of *target points* placed in the plane, with $|N| = n$, and let $v_0 \notin N$ be the depot point. A circumference C_v, with center v and radius r_v, is associated to each target point $v \in N$ (Fig. 1(a)). The set of points within and on C_v compose the *neighborhood* $N(v)$ of v. W.l.o.g., we suppose that $v_0 \notin N(v), \forall v \in N$. Given the neighborhood $N(v)$ depicted in Fig. 1(a), let d_i and d_j be two points on C_v. We denote by $\overline{d_i, d_j}$ the *chord* between these two points and by $\overparen{d_i, d_j}$ the *circular arc* from d_i to d_j in the clockwise direction.

The CETSP consists in finding a shortest tour T^* that starts and ends into the depot v_0 and intersects the neighborhoods of all target points. Given a tour T, its *turn points* are the points where a direction change occurs. For instance, in Fig. 1(b) it is shown a feasible tour for the CETSP with the turn points v_0, p_1, p_2 and p_3. Note that any tour can be uniquely identified through the sequence of its turn points. Given a couple of turn points p_i and p_j, the length of the edge (p_i, p_j) is given by the euclidean distance between p_i and p_j and it is denoted by $w(\overline{p_i, p_j})$. The total cost of a tour T is denoted by $w(T)$ and it is equal to the sum of the edge lengths in T.

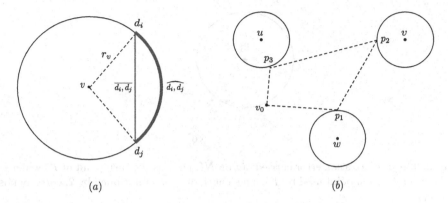

Fig. 1. (a) Circumference C_v of the target point v. The points in and on C_v compose the neighborhood $N(v)$. (b) A feasible tour, for the CETSP, composed by turn points v_0, p_1, p_2 and p_3.

3 The Adaptive Internal Discretization Algorithm

In this section we briefly describe the *internal point discretization* scheme (IP) and the steps of the *internal discretization algorithm*, based on IP, that finds upper bounds for CETSP. See [5] for a detailed explanation of both the discretization scheme and the algorithm.

It is easy to see that the number of feasible tours for CETSP is infinite because each neighborhood $N(v)$, with $v \in N$, contains an infinite number of turn points usable to create the tours. However, any single tour can be identified by using a finite set of turn points. For this reason, we discretize the neighborhoods by using a finite number of discretization points and we use only these points to build the tours. Obviously, this choice implies that our algorithm will consider only a subset of infinite feasible tours of the problem. In more details, each neighborhood $N(v)$ is discretized by using a fixed number k of discretization points denoted by $\hat{N}(v)$. After the discretization, we build the *discretized graph* $G = (V, E)$, where $V = \bigcup_{v \in N} \hat{N}(v)$ and $E = \{(x, y) : x \in N(u), y \in N(v), u \neq v\}$.

From now on, we will denote by T and $\hat{T}$ the feasible tours of the CETSP computed by using the points of $N(v)$ and of $\hat{N}(v)$, $v \in N$, respectively. It is easy to see that the weight of any tour $\hat{T}$ of G, that starts and ends at the depot and that visits exactly one discretization point in each neighborhood, is an upper bound to $w(T^*)$. However, in order to find tighter upper bound of $w(T^*)$ we solve the Generalized Traveling Salesman Problem (GTSP) [13] on G obtaining the shortest tour $\hat{T}^*$. The tightness of $w(\hat{T}^*)$ with respect to $w(T^*)$ heavily depends (i) on the number of points k used to carry out the discretization and (ii) on their placement in each neighborhood. Obviously, as the number of discretization points increases as the quality of the upper bound improves. However, by increasing the discretization points used we increase the size of the graph G too and then the computational time required to solve the GTSP on G. For this

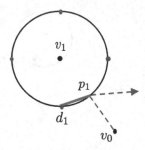

Fig. 2. The discretization error carried out on $\hat{N}(v_1)$. p_1 is the turn point of T^* while d_1 is the discretization point used by $\hat{T}^*$. The length of $\overline{p_1, d_1}$, multiplied by 2, corresponds to $\xi(v_1)$.

reason, the number of discretization points, to use for each neighborhood, has to be wisely defined in order to obtain an appropriate trade-off between the quality of the upper bound and the time spent to compute it.

Fixed the number k of discretization point to use for each neighborhood the next question is: where are the best positions where to place these discretization points in order to obtain an upper bound as tight as possible? There are various *discretization scheme*, proposed in literature, that state the positions of the discretization points in each neighborhood. In this work we use IP scheme introduced in [5]. However, before describing this scheme, let us see why the positions of discretization points can significantly change the quality of the upper bound computed.

Since the construction of $\hat{T}^*$ is carried out by using only the discretization points then a *discretization error* $\xi(v_i)$ occurs, on each neighborhood $\hat{N}(v_i)$, with respect to the turn point p_i of T^* in $N(v_i)$. If d_i is the discretization point of $\hat{N}(v_i)$ closest to the turn point p_i, then $\xi(v_i)$ is equal to two times the length of $\overline{p_i, d_i}$. For instance, in Fig. 2 the neighborhood $N(v_1)$ is discretized by using four points that are placed on C_{v_1}. Since the tour T^* intersects $N(v_1)$ in the turn point p_1 then $\xi(v_i)$ is equal to two times the length of $\overline{p_1, d_1}$, one time to come from p_1 to d_1 and another one to come back. Let Q be a walk composed by edges of T^* and by discretization errors of all the neighborhoods. This means that $w(Q) = w(T^*) + \sum_{v \in N} \xi(v)$. Moreover, since Q starts and ends at the depot v_0 and visits one discretization point for each neighborhood, then $w(\hat{T}^*) \leq w(Q)$. This means that the lower is the discretization error carried out in each neighborhood, the tighter will be $w(\hat{T}^*)$. For this reason, it is very important to apply a discretization scheme that minimizes $\sum_{v \in N} \xi(v)$. Of course, the best situation occurs when $\xi(v_i) = 0$ that is when p_1 coincides with d_1 in Fig. 2 but, in general, $\xi(v_i) > 0$ and it will affect the quality of the upper bounds found.

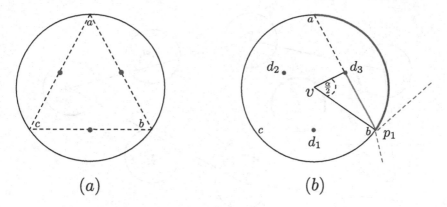

$$(a) \qquad\qquad\qquad (b)$$

Fig. 3. (a) The internal discretization scheme for $k = 3$. (b) Computation of the maximum error $\xi(v)$ for IP scheme.

3.1   Internal Point Discretization Scheme

The internal point discretization (IP) scheme was introduced in [5] with the aim to minimize the discretization error carried out during the construction of $\hat{T}^*$ whatever are the turn points of T^*. Given k discretization points, the IP scheme divides C_v in k equal circular arcs and, for each arc $\widehat{a,b}$, places a discretization point in the middle of the chord $\overline{a,b}$. In Fig. 3(a) the IP scheme is shown for $k = 3$.

In order to compute the discretization error $\xi(v)$, produced by IP scheme, let us consider the example in Fig. 3(b). If the turn point p_1 of T^* intersects $N(v)$ on the circular arc $\widehat{a,b}$ then the maximum distance between p_1 and the discretization point d_3 occurs when p_1 coincides with the point a or b. Therefore, the discretization error $\xi(v)$ is equal to $2(\frac{1}{2}w(\widehat{a,b})) = w(\widehat{a,b})$. The same reasoning holds for the circular arc $\widehat{b,c}$ with the discretization point d_1 and for the circular arc $\widehat{c,a}$ with the discretization point d_2.

Now, from trigonometry, we know that $w(\widehat{a,b}) = 2r_v \sin(\frac{\alpha}{2})$, where α is the central angle associated to the circular arc $\widehat{a,b}$. Note that, by definition, $\alpha = \frac{2\pi}{k}$. As consequence, fixed the number k of discretization points, the maximum error associated to the IP scheme in $\hat{N}(v)$ is $\xi(v) = 2r_v \sin(\frac{\pi}{k})$.

3.2   Convex Hull Strategy

In [2] the authors proved that the turn points of T^* are always on the circular arcs belonging to the convex hull generated by target points. This means that all the points of the circular arcs outside $conv(N \cup \{v_0\})$ can be discarded because they cannot belong to the optimal solution. In Fig. 4 the convex hull, generated by depot and target points $p_1, \ldots, p_8$ is depicted. The circular arcs within the convex hull are highlighted in blue and, from now on, are referred to as *feasible circular arcs* (fca). Given a target point v_i, we denote by $\widehat{v_i', v_i''}$ the fca of C_{v_i} and by α_i the central angle associated to $\widehat{v_i', v_i''}$.

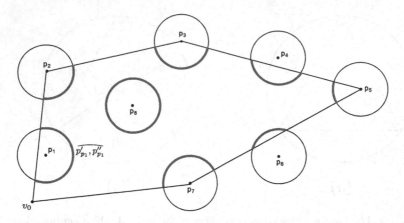

Fig. 4. In blue the circular arcs discretized after the construction of the convex hull. (Color figure online)

Since the turn points of T^* can be only on the *fca*, rather than wasting discretization points on whole circumference C_v, in [5] the author discretized only the *fca*. Moreover, rather than using the same number k of points for each *fca*, they assigned the number of discretization points to be used for each *fca* according to its length. For instance, the length of $\widehat{p'_{p_1}, p''_{p_1}}$, in Fig. 4, is much longer than the length of $\widehat{p'_{p_5}, p''_{p_5}}$ and then the number of discretization points assigned to the former *fca* should be greater than the number of discretization points assigned to the latter *fca* in order to minimize the discretization errors.

The number of discretization points, assigned to each neighborhood, is defined as follows. Given a neighborhood $N(v_i)$, let $\hat{\alpha}$ be the *degree step* given by the ratio between the sum of all central angles α_i and the total number of discretization points $k|N|$. Formally, $\hat{\alpha} = \dfrac{\sum_{v_i \in N} \alpha_i}{k|N|}$. Then, the *fca* $\widehat{v'_i, v''_i}$ is discretized by using $\lfloor \frac{\alpha_i}{\hat{\alpha}} \rfloor$ points. According to this idea, the discretization error $\xi(v_i)$, carried out on $\hat{N}(v_i)$, is expressed as: $\xi(v_i) = 2r_{v_i} \sin(\frac{\alpha_i}{2k_i}) = 2r_{v_i} \sin(\frac{\hat{\alpha}}{2})$ where $k_i = \frac{\alpha_i}{\hat{\alpha}}$.

Here we introduce a new modification to the previous scheme that can significantly improve the lower bounds computed. The idea behind this modification is the following. Since k_i is an integer value and $k_i = \frac{\alpha_i}{\hat{\alpha}}$ then a truncation operations is often carried out when we compute k_i. Due to this truncation, the total number of discretization points used could be lower than $k|N|$. When this event occurs, we have discretization points that can be used to further reduce the discretization errors. Let ℓ be the number of remaining discretization points available. Then we apply a greedy algorithm, named *residual points assignment* (RPA) to assign even these points. The pseudocode of RPA is reported in Algorithm 1.

Algorithm 1. Residual Points Assignment
1: Input: The value ℓ.
2: **while** $\ell > 0$ **do**
3:    Select vertex v_i such that $\xi(v_i) \geq \xi(v_j)$ $\forall j \in N$
4:    $k_i \leftarrow k_i + 1$
5:    $\ell \leftarrow \ell - 1$
6: **end while**

For each residual point available, the algorithm finds the vertex v_i with maximum discretization error (line 3) and try to reduce this last error by increasing by one the number of discretization point used for $\widehat{p'_{v_i}, p''_{v_i}}$ (line 4). The process is repeated until all the residual points are assigned.

4 Mathematical Formulation

In this section we report the mathematical formulation of the GTSP problem that is used to compute $\hat{T}^*$. Since the resolution of GTSP is expensive, we reduce the complexity of the problem by reducing the size of the graph $G(V, E)$. To this end, we apply on G the graph reduction algorithm described in [5]. This algorithm looks for useless edges in G, that is edges that cannot belong to $\hat{T}^*$, and it removes them. Often the number of edges in G is reduced by 50%, thanks to this algorithm, making the individuation of $\hat{T}^*$ less expensive.

To formulate the GTSP problem, we associate to each edge $(i, j) \in E'$ a binary variable x_{ij} taking value 1 if and only if (i, j) belongs to the solution. Moreover, we associate to each discretization node i the binary variable y_i taking value 1 if and only if i belongs to the solution. Finally, we let c_{ij} be the euclidean distance between the discretization points i and j and define the set $E(S)$ as follows:

$$E(S) = \{(i, j) \in E' : i, j \in \bigcup_{v \in S} \hat{N}(v)\}$$

for $S \subseteq N$. Our integer linear programming model for the GTSP is the following:

$$(\textbf{MIP}) \quad \min \sum_{(i,j) \in E'} c_{ij} x_{ij} \tag{1}$$

$$\sum_{i \in \hat{N}(v)} y_i = 1 \qquad \forall v \in N \tag{2}$$

$$\sum_{i \in \hat{N}(u), j \in \hat{N}(v)} x_{ij} \leq 1 \qquad u, v \in N, u \neq v \tag{3}$$

$$\sum_{(i,j) \in E'} x_{ij} = 2y_i \qquad \forall i \in V \tag{4}$$

$$\sum_{(i,j) \in E(S)} x_{ij} \leq |S| - 1 \qquad \forall S \subseteq N, |S| \geq 2 \tag{5}$$

The objective function (1) minimizes the cost of the tour. Constraints (2) guarantee that a discretization point of each neighborhood is visited while Constraints (3) ensure that at most one edge connecting two neighborhoods is selected. Constraints (4) bind the two sets of variables by letting y_i equal to 1 if and only if v_i belongs to the solution. Finally, constraints (5) are the subtour elimination constraints adapted to the Generalized TSP [13].

The MIP model returns the optimal tour $\hat{T}^*$ with $w(\hat{T}^*)$ being our upper bound to the optimal solution T^* of CETSP. A lower bound for T^* can be found too by removing from $w(\hat{T}^*)$ the maximum discretization error value $\xi(v)$ for each target point v. Formally, $LB = w(\hat{T}^*) - \sum_{v \in V} \xi(v)$.

Finally, once the solution $\hat{T}^*$ has been found, we carry out an additional step to improve the upper bound, this additional step is introduced in the next section.

5   Second-Order Cone Programming Algorithm

The solution $\hat{T}^*$ computed by MIP model in the previous section, can be further improved by modifying the position of the discretization points used. More in details, when the visiting sequence of target points is fixed a priori, the CETSP corresponds to the Touring Steiner Zones Problem (TSZP). This problem can be formulated as a second-order cone programming (SOCP) [15] and solved in polynomial time [1]. In the following we briefly describe the formulation proposed in [15] and that is implemented in our algorithm to further improve the upper bounds computed.

$$(\textbf{SOCP}) \quad \min \sum_{i=0}^{|N|} z_i \tag{6}$$

$$w_i = x_i - x_{i+1} \qquad \forall\, i \in \{0, \dots, |N|\} \tag{7}$$

$$u_i = y_i - y_{i+1} \qquad \forall\, i \in \{0, \dots, |N|\} \tag{8}$$

$$s_i = \bar{x}_i - x_i \qquad \forall\, i \in \{0, \dots, |N|\} \tag{9}$$

$$t_i = \bar{y}_i - y_i \qquad \forall\, i \in \{0, \dots, |N|\} \tag{10}$$

$$z_i^2 \geq w_i^2 + u_i^2 \qquad \forall\, i \in \{0, \dots, |N|\} \tag{11}$$

$$s_i^2 + t_i^2 \leq r_i^2 \qquad \forall\, i \in \{0, \dots, |N|\} \tag{12}$$

$$z_i \geq 0 \qquad \forall\, i \in \{0, \dots, |N|\} \tag{13}$$

$$w_i,\, u_i,\, s_i,\, t_i,\, x_i,\, y_i, free \qquad \forall\, i \in \{0, \dots, |N|\} \tag{14}$$

The tour $\hat{T}^*$, computed by MIP, defines a visiting sequence of the target points. W.l.o.g. let us suppose that such a sequence is $(v_1, v_2, \dots, v_{|N|})$. We replicate the first target point v_1 in the last position of the sequence obtaining the new sequence $(v_1, v_2, \dots, v_{|N|}, v_1)$. To each target point v_i in the sequence are associated the variables x_i and y_i representing the coordinates of the discretization point that covers v_i in the tour. For each target point v_i, we want to find the best position where to place the discretization point in order to mini-mize the tour length. The z_i variables represents the Euclidean distance between the discretization points associated to v_i and v_{i+1}. The objective function (6) minimizes the sum of Euclidean distances among the discretization points of the tour. Finally, the variables w_i and u_i are used in constraints (11), to compute the Euclidean distance between the vertex v_i and v_{i+1} while the variables s_i and t_i are used in constraints (12), to ensure that the position of discretization point (x_i, y_i) is inside the circumference C_{v_i}.

6 Computational Results

This section presents the computational results of our algorithm, named IULB on the largest benchmark instances proposed in [2,5]. IULB was coded in Java on a OSX platform running on an Intel Core i5 2.9 GHz processor with 16GB RAM, equipped with the IBM ILOG CPLEX 12.5.1 solver and the Concert Technology Library for the mathematical formulations. In order to verify both the effectiveness and the performance of IULB we will compare it with the Bender Decomposition (BD) proposed in [2] and the ULB algorithm proposed in [5].

In Table 1 the results of BD, ULB and IULB algorithms, on the instances from 14 to 20 target points and with a radius equal to 0.25 and 0.5, are reported. To each algorithm are associated two columns: Gap and Time. The Gap value represents the gap in percentage between the upper (UB) and lower (LB) bound values and it is computed with the formula: $100 \times \frac{(UB-LB)}{UB}$. The Time value is the CPU Time, in seconds, spent by algorithms to compute the bounds. Finally, the average Gap and Time values are reported in the last line of the table.

On the scenarios with $r = 0.25$, IULB is much more effective and faster than BD. Indeed, the Gap values of IULB are always better than the ones of BD and the improvements ranges from 49.4 % (CETSP-16-06) to 57.48% (CETSP-18-04). With so high improvements, it is easy to state that, at least on these instances, IULB is much more effective than BD. Regarding the performance, IULB is always faster than BD and it results at least 50% faster than BD in 29 out of 40 instances.

More interesting is the comparison between IULB and ULB because allow us to evaluate the impact of ideas proposed in this paper on the effectiveness and the performance of original algorithm ULB. Obviously, due to the kind of ideas used in IULB, its Gap values should be always better than or equal to the Gap values of ULB. For this reason, thanks to the computational tests, we are interested to quantify the quality improvement of the solution found by IULB with respect to ULB and to evaluate the performance of new algorithm. The results show that the Gap values of IULB are always better than the Gap values of ULB. These improvements range from 1.15% (CETSP-14-09) to 9.36% (CETSP-14-06). It is interesting to observe that, despite the use of a greedy algorithm to introduce more discretization points and the application of an exact approach instead of the elastic force heuristic, IULB results slower than ULB only in 4 out of 40

Table 1. Test results of the Bender Decomposition, ULB and IULB algorithms on the instances up to 20 target points.

Instance	r = 0.25						r = 0.5					
	BD		ULB		IULB		BD		ULB		IULB	
	Gap	Time	Gap	Time	Gap	Time	Gap	Time	Gap	Time	Gap	Time
CETSP-14-01	9.3	2.5	4.4	2.6	4.3	2.1	21.3	5.3	9.3	3.8	9.0	3.8
CETSP-14-02	9.5	1.5	4.5	1.3	4.4	1.2	19.8	2.2	10.1	3.2	9.7	2.4
CETSP-14-03	9.2	6.4	4.3	1.6	4.2	1.2	18.9	11.7	8.6	4.2	8.2	4.2
CETSP-14-04	8.5	2.6	4.5	1.3	4.3	1.0	18.6	4.5	8.9	3.4	8.7	2.5
CETSP-14-05	9.3	2.1	4.2	1.1	4.0	0.7	16.3	3.3	8.6	1.5	8.4	1.7
CETSP-14-06	9.6	3.7	4.9	2.0	4.4	1.5	21.9	2.5	10.0	3.3	9.1	2.6
CETSP-14-07	7.8	2.4	4.0	1.0	3.9	0.8	18.9	2.8	8.7	2.2	8.5	1.8
CETSP-14-08	9.8	6.3	4.7	1.3	4.5	1.1	20.2	7.4	9.9	2.9	9.6	3.0
CETSP-14-09	11.5	2.9	5.0	1.4	4.9	1.2	22.3	1.9	10.0	3.5	9.7	2.8
CETSP-14-10	10.2	3.4	4.9	2.0	4.8	1.1	20.5	6.0	10.3	4.5	10.0	3.3
CETSP-16-01	9.4	5.0	4.7	2.4	4.5	2.1	21.9	8.3	9.5	7.1	9.2	6.2
CETSP-16-02	11.5	1.8	5.6	1.1	5.5	0.9	22.8	8.7	11.8	3.5	11.4	2.5
CETSP-16-03	10.9	6.7	5.2	1.5	5.1	1.3	22.1	9.7	10.6	5.3	10.3	3.9
CETSP-16-04	9.7	3.0	5.0	1.3	4.9	1.1	20.0	13.8	10.9	4.8	10.7	5.2
CETSP-16-05	11.1	3.2	5.7	2.3	5.3	1.9	25.0	8.4	12.0	5.9	11.3	4.9
CETSP-16-06	8.3	4.0	4.3	3.2	4.2	1.9	19.9	14.2	9.3	3.6	8.9	3.4
CETSP-16-07	9.9	7.5	4.7	3.1	4.6	6.1	21.6	15.6	10.3	14.5	10.1	3.8
CETSP-16-08	9.9	2.0	5.2	1.1	4.9	1.0	19.9	7.2	10.7	2.5	10.3	1.3
CETSP-16-09	12.0	11.6	5.8	3.0	5.6	2.3	25.9	520.1	12.0	10.6	11.7	6.6
CETSP-16-10	11.7	5.2	5.6	2.2	5.4	3.5	24.8	15.8	11.5	6.8	11.3	6.9
CETSP-18-01	10.3	8.1	5.1	4.0	4.9	2.8	24.0	35.6	10.7	8.4	10.4	7.6
CETSP-18-02	12.8	12.8	5.7	4.6	5.5	2.3	24.3	202.0	12.0	8.9	11.6	7.8
CETSP-18-03	10.7	9.1	5.6	4.7	5.4	4.3	24.5	102.9	12.2	13.9	11.8	6.6
CETSP-18-04	11.8	2.7	5.2	2.4	5.0	2.0	22.7	11.0	11.0	4.7	10.7	5.1
CETSP-18-05	11.7	4.7	5.8	3.9	5.6	2.2	22.5	28.0	11.7	5.7	11.5	4.2
CETSP-18-06	12.5	13.4	5.8	5.4	5.6	4.4	28.0	173.9	12.6	11.9	12.0	15.2
CETSP-18-07	13.5	4.2	6.1	3.3	5.9	2.7	27.7	11.4	12.2	7.3	11.9	3.5
CETSP-18-08	12.9	22.0	6.3	4.5	6.1	4.1	33.4	1501.0	13.2	12.5	12.8	7.8
CETSP-18-09	13.0	5.7	6.3	2.2	6.1	1.7	27.3	38.4	13.3	9.0	12.9	6.8
CETSP-18-10	10.4	4.7	5.2	3.9	5.1	2.3	22.8	36.2	11.4	9.8	11.1	6.1
CETSP-20-01	11.9	11.7	5.6	4.0	5.4	3.9	23.8	556.4	12.1	12.5	11.7	12.5
CETSP-20-02	13.2	11.8	6.1	5.1	5.9	6.4	28.7	135.4	13.2	10.0	12.7	9.7
CETSP-20-03	10.2	8.3	5.3	1.9	5.1	4.3	24.6	41.5	11.7	13.6	11.3	7.8
CETSP-20-04	12.6	9.2	6.5	5.2	6.1	4.2	28.1	84.6	14.1	11.0	13.6	7.2
CETSP-20-05	12.3	8.2	6.2	4.4	5.9	2.4	25.7	716.9	13.3	8.4	12.7	8.1
CETSP-20-06	11.7	15.0	5.7	4.0	5.5	13.2	24.4	177.3	12.2	11.1	12.0	15.8
CETSP-20-07	13.7	15.8	7.0	6.8	6.8	3.7	31.9	1501.3	14.9	23.5	14.4	15.2
CETSP-20-08	13.4	39.4	6.6	7.5	6.4	8.0	30.8	1501.0	14.0	78.5	13.6	48.8
CETSP-20-09	11.5	17.4	5.8	3.1	5.7	5.0	27.3	57.0	12.7	8.3	12.4	9.5
CETSP-20-10	11.3	10.1	5.8	5.7	5.6	1.9	26.6	21.4	12.8	10.6	12.4	10.7
AVG	**11.0**	**8.0**	**5.4**	**3.1**	**5.2**	**2.9**	**23.8**	**190.1**	**11.4**	**9.4**	**11.0**	**7.2**

Table 2. Computational results of ULB and IULB algorithms on the the larger instances with $r = 0.5$.

Instance	ULB		IULB	
	GAP	Time	Gap	Time
CETSP-25-01	16.17%	95.63	15.59%	95.24
CETSP-25-02	14.02%	16.64	13.69%	17.58
CETSP-25-03	14.34%	102.01	13.98%	92.04
CETSP-25-04	15.08%	21.19	14.64%	21.96
CETSP-25-05	14.91%	55.11	14.54%	46.81
CETSP-25-06	15.39%	93.91	14.89%	33.45
CETSP-25-07	14.06%	28.70	13.54%	61.53
CETSP-25-08	13.79%	57.22	13.13%	22.08
CETSP-25-09	15.41%	132.46	14.07%	61.20
CETSP-25-10	16.15%	49.67	16.04%	22.93
CETSP-30-01	17.89%	82.28	17.00%	98.13
CETSP-30-02	18.80%	78.37	17.56%	39.26
CETSP-30-03	15.86%	334.09	14.93%	240.33
CETSP-30-04	19.31%	866.01	18.19%	1005.15
CETSP-30-05	18.15%	129.34	17.59%	59.04
CETSP-30-06	16.78%	56.07	16.23%	79.40
CETSP-30-07	16.58%	537.38	16.28%	94.79
CETSP-30-08	16.23%	76.08	15.80%	93.93
CETSP-30-09	18.04%	331.81	17.47%	307.89
CETSP-30-10	17.69%	232.45	16.80%	95.57

instances (CETSP-16-07, CETSP-20-02, CETSP-20-06, CETSP-20-08) while it is from 14% to 84% faster than ULB in the remaining 36 instances.

By increasing the radius to 0.5 the instances become harder to solve as proven by the increment of both the Gap values and Time of all the algorithms. Again, the Gap values of IULB are always better than the Gap values of BD with an improvement that reaches 61.82% (CETSP-18-08). Hence, the increment of radius amplifies the gap effectiveness between these two algorithms. Regarding the performance, only in three cases BD results faster than IULB but the gap time in these cases is lower than a second and then negligible. On the contrary, on the remaining 37 instances there are cases where IULB is orders of magnitude faster than BD, in particular on the instances with 20 target points. Moreover, there are three scenarios (18-08, 20-07 and 20-08) where BD reaches the time limit of 1500 s while IULB solves these scenarios in less than 50 s.

Even on the instances with $r = 0.5$ the Gap values of IULB are always better than the Gap values of ULB with the improvements that range from 1.45% to 9.05%. These results are very similar to the ones observed for the case with

$r = 0.25$ and then increasing the radius value does not change the effectiveness gap between IULB and ULB. More interesting is to analyze the computational time of IULB on these instances because it appears more expensive. Indeed, as the radius increases as the Time value of IULB increases and there are more instances in which IULB is slower than ULB. However, this gap time never exceeds 5 s then it is not so relevant.

Finally, from the average values reported in the last line of the table, it is evident that IULB is the more effective and efficient algorithm. Moreover, these values further certify that the greater is the radius r the higher is the complexity of the instances.

In Table 2 the results of ULB and IULB on the largest instances with 25 and 30 target points and radius $r = 0.5$ are reported. As expected, the Gap values show that as the size of the instances increases as the quality of the bounds found by two algorithms decreases. However, once again IULB results more effective than ULB in all the instances with an improvement that ranges from 0.66% (CETSP-25-10) to 8.71% (CETSP-25-09). These further results definitively state that, whatever are the size of the instances and the radius considered, the new ideas implemented in IULB make this new algorithm always more effective than ULB. Surprisingly, the improvements concern even the performance. Indeed, IULB is faster than ULB in 13 out of 20 instances and in 8 cases its computational time is the half of the computational time of ULB. Finally, IULB solves 17 instances in less than 100 s while ULB, in the same time, solves only 12 instances.

7   Conclusions

In this article, we have presented an improved version of the adaptive internal discretization scheme and a heuristic that combines this scheme with a second-order cone programming algorithm. The computational results carried out on benchmark instances revealed that the new algorithm outperforms previous approaches to CETSP, in terms of quality of the bounds and, often, of the computational time. A possible direction for future work is to improve Algorithm 1 with the Carousel Greedy [10] or to develop new effective meta-heuristics like Tabu Search [4,9] and Genetic Algorithm [3,8] without applying discretization schemes.

References

1. Andersen, E.D., Roos, C., Terlaky, T.: On implementing a primal-dual interior-point method for conic quadratic optimization. Math. Program. **95**(2), 249–277 (2003)
2. Behdani, B., Smith, J.C.: An integer-programming-based approach to the close-enough traveling salesman problem. INFORMS J. Comput. **26**(3), 415–432 (2014)
3. Carrabs, F., Cerrone, C., Cerulli, R.: A memetic algorithm for the weighted feedback vertex set problem. Networks **64**(4), 339–356 (2014)

4. Carrabs, F., Cerrone, C., Cerulli, R.: A tabu search approach for the circle packing problem. In: 2014 17th International Conference on Network-Based Information Systems, pp. 165–171. IEEE (2014)
5. Carrabs, F., Cerrone, C., Cerulli, R., Gaudioso, M.: A novel discretization scheme for the close enough traveling salesman problem. Comput. Oper. Res. **78**, 163–171 (2017)
6. Carrabs, F., Cerulli, R., D'Ambrosio, C., Raiconi, A.: Extending lifetime through partial coverage and roles allocation in connectivity-constrained sensor networks. IFAC-PapersOnLine **49**(12), 973–978 (2016)
7. Carrabs, F., Cerulli, R., D'Ambrosio, C., Raiconi, A.: An exact algorithm to extend lifetime through roles allocation in sensor networks with connectivity constraints. Optimi. Lett., 1–16 (2016)
8. Cerrone, C., Cerulli, R., Gaudioso, M.: Omega one multi ethnic genetic approach. Optim. Lett. **10**(2), 309–324 (2016)
9. Cerrone, C., Cerulli, R., Gentili, M.: Vehicle-id sensor location for route flow recognition: models and algorithms. Eur. J. Oper. Res. **247**(2), 618–629 (2015)
10. Cerrone, C., Cerulli, R., Golden, B.: Carousel greedy: a generalized greedy algorithm with applications in optimization. University of Maryland (submitted for publication)
11. Coutinho, W.P., Do Nascimento, R.Q., Pessoa, A.A., Subramanian, A.: A branch-and-bound algorithm for the close-enough traveling salesman problem. INFORMS J. Comput. **28**(4), 752–765 (2016)
12. Dong, J., Yang, N., Chen, M.: Heuristic approaches for a TSP variant: the automatic meter reading shortest tour problem. Oper. Res./Comput. Sci. Interf. Ser. **37**, 145–163 (2007)
13. Fischetti, M., Salazar-Gonzalez, J., Toth, P.: The generalized traveling salesman and orienteering problems. In: Gutin, G., Punnen, A.P. (eds.) The Traveling Salesman Problem and Its Variations. Combinatorial Optimization, vol. 12, pp. 609–662. Springer, New York (2007)
14. Gulczynski, D., Heath, J., Price, C.: Close enough traveling salesman problem: a discussion of several heuristics. In: Alt, F.B., Fu, M.C., Golden, B.L. (eds.) Perspectives in Operations Research. Operations Research/Computer Science Interfaces Series, vol. 36, pp. 271–283. Springer, New York (2006)
15. Mennell, W.K.: Heuristics for solving three routing problems: close-enough traveling salesman problem, close-enough vehicle routing problem, sequence-dependent team orienteering problem. PhD thesis, The Robert H. Smith School of Business, University of Maryland, College Park (2009)
16. Mennell, W.K., Golden, B., Wasil, E.: A steiner-zone heuristic for solving the close-enough traveling salesman problem. In: 2nd INFORMS Computing Society Conference: Operations Research, Computing, and Homeland Defense (2011)
17. Yuan, B., Orlowska, M., Sadiq, S.: On the optimal robot routing problem in wireless sensor networks. IEEE Trans. Knowl. Data Eng. **19**(9), 1252–1261 (2007)

Object Storage in Cloud Computing Environments: An Availability Analysis

Giuliana Carullo[2], Mario Di Mauro[1(✉)], Michele Galderisi[1], Maurizio Longo[1], Fabio Postiglione[1], and Marco Tambasco[2]

[1] Department of Information and Electrical Engineering and Applied Mathematics (DIEM), University of Salerno, Fisciano, SA, Italy
{mdimauro,longo,fpostiglione}@unisa.it, m.galderisi@studenti.unisa.it
[2] Research Consortium on Telecommunication (CoRiTeL), Fisciano, SA, Italy
{giuliana.carullo,marco.tambasco}@coritel.it

Abstract. Object Storage Systems (OSSs) have been conceived to manage a bulk of highly unstructured data (videos, images, social resources etc.) by storing them in the form of objects accessible via REST APIs. An interesting implementation of OSS is based on Swift, a component of OpenStack, the most important platform exploited to deploy the Infrastructure as a Service (IaaS) paradigm. The present work is aimed at characterizing a Swift-based OSS from the availability point of view, namely at finding out the best configuration able to guarantee the so-called "five nines" availability requirement allowing a maximum system downtime of a little more than five minutes per year. The availability analysis is faced by exploiting the Stochastic Reward Nets (SRNs) formalism, accounting for the probabilistic behavior of the underlying structure of the Object Storage System. More specifically, the OSS availability has been assessed by performing a steady-state analysis whereas a sensitivity analysis has been carried out to evaluate the robustness of the overall system with respect to variations of some key parameters.

Keywords: Object Storage Systems · OpenStack · Swift · Availability analysis · Sensitivity analysis · Stochastic Reward Nets

1 Introduction

In the era of massive communications, network and content providers have to deal with a huge amount of data coming from a variety of resources: high-quality video, social media, gaming, user-uploaded content and so forth. Such data have the common characteristic of being highly unstructured, namely, do not rely on a specific data model resulting in a complete rethinking of the classical database structures. At this aim, an emerging paradigm speaking the web language is raising: the object storage. Typically, Object Storage Systems do not provide access to raw blocks of data nor files, whilst they offer some specific APIs allowing a direct access to the objects via URLs on behalf of the HTTP protocol [1]. Furthermore, the OSSs can greatly benefit from the new paradigms emerging in fifth

© Springer International Publishing AG 2017
M.H.A. Au et al. (Eds.): GPC 2017, LNCS 10232, pp. 178–190, 2017.
DOI: 10.1007/978-3-319-57186-7_15

generation (5G) telecommunication environments, such as Software Defined Networking (SDN) and Network Function Virtualization (NFV), by inheriting some interesting features: SDN inspired the software-defined storage systems that are based on the separation of the logical intelligence from the underlying physical hardware, whereas, virtualization concepts offered by NFV make such systems easily suitable for telecommunication scenarios [2]. One of the most promising frameworks in the world of Object Storage Systems is Swift, born as a module of OpenStack, a valuable project aimed at designing IaaS architectures. Due to the specific role, Object Storage Systems need to meet some requirements: (*i*) *durability*, namely, the ability to guarantee that the data will never permanently corrupted or lost; (*ii*) *manageability*, namely, the effort required to have a system properly functioning in the long run; (*iii*) *availability*, namely, the capability of the system being available when called upon for use. In this work, we specifically focus on the last requirement by performing an availability evaluation of a Swift-based OSS aimed at finding the best configuration guaranteeing the so-called "five nines" requirement more and more demanded by content and network providers, and allowing a maximum downtime of 5 min and 2 s per year for the overall system. Such an analysis has been carried out by exploiting the Stochastic Reward Net (SRN) formalism, a state-space model accounting for the probabilistic behavior of the underlying structure of each single component.

The remaining part of this paper is organized as follows. In Sect. 2 some related works are presented and in Sect. 3 more details about Swift features are provided. Section 4 is the core of this paper and describes the proposed availability model, while Sect. 5 discusses the outcoming experimental results. Section 6 ends this paper by providing conclusions and some future work directions.

2 Related Work

Nowadays, Object Storage Systems are attracting many specialized operators but also industrial and academical researchers due to the increasing opportunities in developing novel strategies, procedures and algorithms able to deal with a huge amount of non structured data. In [3], the authors propose *IOFlow*, an infrastructure relying on a centralized control plane aimed at enabling specific flow policies and adding a queueing abstraction at data plane. Inspired by this work, the authors in [4] introduce *IOStack*, a software-defined storage framework based on OpenStack Swift, aimed at enabling policy-based provisioning. Such a solution envisages both a control and a data plane. The former is exploited by administrators to offer specific services to tenants in accordance with defined policies; the latter is used to build filters performing data transformations on object requests. In [5] a detailed analysis of a cloud storage system based on Swift, with a focus on object synchronization protocol has been carried out. In particular, the authors consider data-intensive scenarios, characterized by a number of replicas for each object greater than 3 and a number of objects hosted by each storage element much greater than 1000. In such scenarios, a significant delay during the operations is related to the synchronization protocol; in order to overcome this issue, a lightweight protocol is proposed for object synchronization. The work in [6] reports an analysis of an object storage system exploiting a Swift implementation, by analyzing different configurations aimed at understanding on one hand, how the various Swift components influence the performance of the whole system, and on the other hand, how to improve the files size processing by leveraging optimization methods. In [7], the authors focus on the placement and replication of multimedia objects in order to guarantee reliability and load balancing requirements. At this aim, a load balancing strategy based on the cooperation of multiple object storage servers modeled as $M/G/m$ systems has been designed. An interesting perspective concerning the availability issues of cloud infrastructures (hence including OSSs) is emerging in some recent works. A Markov chain approach is adopted in [8] to compute the availability of a large-scale IaaS cloud system characterized by failure events mitigated by the migration of physical machines. In particular, three pools of machines involved in the migration process, namely, hot (running), warm (not ready but turned on) and cold (turned off) have been considered as interacting sub-models with dependencies resolved with fixed-point iteration. In [9], the authors analyze the reliability of geo-replicated cloud storage systems based on the OpenStack Swift characterized by different bandwidth resources. Such a reliability analysis has been carried out by considering a recovery scheme designed from scratch. Authors in [10] present a strategy relying on a hierarchical and heterogeneous approach aimed at designing a cloud infrastructure that meet both reliability and cost requirements. In particular, a two-level methodology has been applied: the first level exploits the Reliability Block Diagram method to highlight the dependencies among the functional blocks composing the system; the second level relies on Stochastic Petri Nets formalism in order to express each block as an interconnection of failure-prone sub-blocks. In [11], a novel restoration method of virtual resources running on OpenStack platform when physical machines fail has been proposed by acting on Pacemaker service. Authors in [12] perform an availability analysis of a Virtualized Infrastructure Manager (VIM) based on the OpenStack implementation, aimed at obtaining the best system configuration respecting the "five nines" availability requirement. Although the availability evaluation of some cloud infrastructures is already available (see [8], [10]), to the best knowledge of the authors the availability of an object storage system has not been assessed yet. The main contribution of the present paper is the definition and the evaluation of a stochastic availability model of an object storage system based on a Swift implementation, useful to find out its optimal configuration able to guarantee high availability requirements in long runs.

3   Overview of OpenStack Swift Object Storage

Object storage in OpenStack is provided by the Swift framework, a highly distributed, eventually consistent system meant to guarantee high availability and scalability requirements and it is designed for managing a huge amount of data. It is worth recalling that Swift has not been conceived as a traditional file system or a raw block device, but rather, as a highly scalable system able to store,

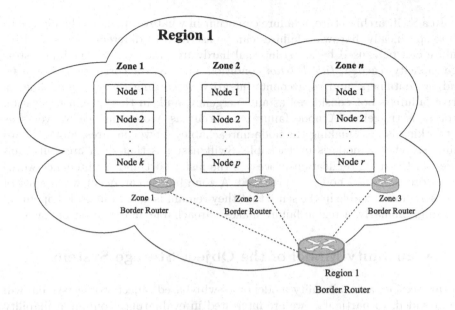

Fig. 1. Swift high-level architecture

recover and delete objects along with their associated metadata by using REST-ful HTTP API. Such a system can distribute the bulk of data across different data centers in order to guarantee on one hand high availability of data accessible from multiple sites (with different latencies) and, on the other hand, to implement robust backup policies in order to fulfill disaster recovery procedures. The Swift data model relies on a hierarchical structure including the *account*, the root data storage location, the *container*, a user-defined area providing storage locations similarly to folders or directories, the *object*, the stored (unstructured) data including the data itself and the respective metadata. For the purposes of the present work, we simply refer to the objects without considering the underlying structure. From an architectural perspective, Swift is organized as shown in Fig. 1 and it is made up of:

- Nodes: are physical servers that host the full set of Swift processes (e.g., proxy, containers, accounts and so on) in order to implement the distributed storage system. A collection of nodes running such processes is often called cluster. Typically, a node contains one or more hardware drives.
- Regions: are parts of the cluster. They are physically separated and often, delimited by geographical boundaries. A cluster should have a minimum of one region.
- Zones: are parts of regions. A zone is intended to offer a failure isolation service, by including a set of physical nodes separated from nodes within other zones. In the most common deployments, each zone has its own rack, power supply and zone border router.

In a Swift architecture, a failure can occur in whatever point of the hierarchy. More specifically, hardware failures can be ascribed to different events. A drive failure can be caused by a: *(i)* internal hardware damage, *(ii)* maximum storage capacity reached, *(iii) Bit-Rot* condition, namely, the corruption of objects, and/or containers, and/or accounts integrity. According to Swift guidelines, a drive failure is not considered as an emergency, and, in this case, a replication process is triggered. A node failure can occur as a consequence of events as networking issues (making the node unreachable), power failures, motherboard failures. When a node is unreachable, Swift assumes that data are still available, so, the node replication process is the last resort and maintenance works to restore the failed node are preferred. A zone failure can occur when a set of nodes are unreachable in the sense that they remain isolated but still (hopefully) working. Similarly, a region failure makes unreachable an entire set of zones.

4   Availability Model of the Object Storage System

In this section, an availability model of a Swift-based object storage system will be provided. In particular, we are interested in evaluating, from an availability point of view, the distribution of object replicas in respect of the high-level Swift architecture composed by drives, nodes, zones and regions. More specifically, in line with the most common settings, we consider two deployment scenarios, often referred to as *storage policies*: (*i*) *Off-Site Disaster Recovery* (OSDR) consisting in storing $N - 1$ object replicas in the primary region and 1 object replica in the secondary (off-site) region; (*ii*) *Multi-Region Sharing* (MRS) consisting in having R regions each one storing 1 object replica. Before examining in depth the model structure, we consider worthwhile to provide some details about the adopted approach, namely, the Stochastic Reward Network (SRN) formalism.

4.1   The Stochastic Reward Nets Formalism

The SRN formalism [13] can be considered as a state-space model that takes into account the probabilistic behavior of single blocks in an architectural model. Recently, SRN has emerged as a robust modeling paradigm for reliability, performance and availability analysis of last generation systems (SDN, NFV, Cloud-based architectures etc.) as it enables the automated generation and solution of large Markov reward models [14]. In other words, SRN has the main benefit of providing a more compact representation of the underlying Markov reward model (an extension of the classical Markov model where a reward rate is attached to each state of the Markov chain) whose major drawback is the largeness of its state space. Besides, such a representation allows to interpret in a more intuitive way the results in terms of entities that model the system.

SRN can be considered an extension of the Stochastic Petri Nets (SPNs), a formalism able to capture the structure of a complex system in the form of a bipartite directed graph where the *places* identify a particular condition of the system (e.g. a node *up* or *down*), the *transitions* identify an action (e.g. a node that crashes) and the *arcs* are directed edges that connect places and transitions. In the SPNs we consider the transition times modeled as exponentially distributed random variables. SRNs introduce the concept of *reward*, a numerical value associated with specific conditions of the underlying Petri Net that allows to evaluate the system availability by exploiting simple boolean expressions. The SRN model associated to the high-level architecture of an object storage system implemented according Swift specifications is shown in Fig. 2, where four failure domains emerge: *drive domain, node domain, zone domain* and *region domain*. We want to highlight that such domains are separated in the sense that a zone failure, for example, does not compromise the regular working of pertaining nodes but simply make them unreachable. A description of the elements composing the model and their respective roles follows:

– *Places* (circles): the place P_{up} takes into account a fully working system condition and the parameter N inside it identifies the number of *tokens*, namely, the number of initial working object replicas; the place P_d models the drive failure condition while P_{repd} models the drive replication condition, namely, the necessity of setting another working drive replica to replace the failed one. Place P_n takes into account a node failure condition whereas the places P_{sn} and P_{hn} model a *soft failure condition* (e.g., a disconnected network cable, a temporary reboot of the system etc.) and a *hard failure condition* (e.g., a damaged power supply, a failed motherboard etc.) respectively. The place P_{repn1} represents a condition indicating that an object replication process is waiting for being activated; P_{repn2} takes into account the most critical condition of a node completely unrecoverable (e.g. whole internal hardware failure caused by a short circuit) that forces Swift to initiate a replication of the damaged node; such a condition is invasive as well, because of the load managed by the out-of-work node has now to be distributed among remaining working nodes. Places P_z and P_r model a zone and a region failure respectively, intended as conditions preventing the internal nodes reachability (e.g., a zone/region router failure) although such nodes should remain fully working.
– *Timed Transitions* (unfilled rectangles): are characterized by an exponentially distributed time with a specific rate parameter (λ, δ or μ in our model), also known as *firing rate*. If the firing rate depends on the number of tokens in the starting place, the symbol $\#$ appears close to the transition and we refer to it as a *Place Dependent Transition* (PDT). The timed transitions in our model are: T_{fd} (drive failure), T_{repd} (drive replication), T_{fn} (node failure), T_{repn} (node replication), T_{hrn} (node hard repair), T_{srn} (node soft repair), T_{fz} (zone failure), T_{rz} (zone repair), T_{fr} (region failure), T_{rr} (region repair).
– *Immediate Transitions* (thin and filled rectangles): are characterized by a zero transition time, and take into account instantaneous actions. Such transitions are: $t_{rd}, t_{rn1}, t_{rn2}, t_h$ and t_s.

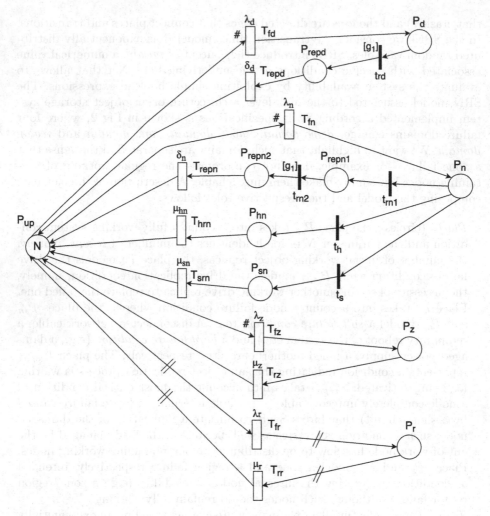

Fig. 2. SRN model of the high-level architecture of an object storage system based on a Swift implementation

4.2   SRN Model Evolution of the OSS

Let us now describe the dynamics of the SRN model by reasonably assuming that the probability of failure during repair and/or replication operations is negligible. By starting from an initial fully working system with N tokens (object replicas) in P_{up} place, in case of a failure of a drive hosting the object, the T_{fd} transition with failure rate λ_d is fired and a token is moved from P_{up} to P_d. According to Swift implementation, a drive failure immediately triggers a replication so t_{rd} is fired and the token is deposited in P_{repd}. The transition T_{repd} with rate δ_d governs the replication process and hence the return in P_{up}. In case of node failure, T_{fn} is fired with failure rate λ_n and a token is deposited in P_n. At this time three cases can arise: (i) in case soft failure t_s is fired, P_{sn} is reached with probability p_{sf} and the soft repair is ruled by T_{srn} with a repair rate μ_{sn} to come back in P_{up}; (ii) in case of hard failure t_h is fired, P_{hn} is entered with probability p_{hf} and the hard repair is governed by T_{hrn} with a repair rate μ_{hn}; (iii) in case of critical failure t_{rn1} is fired and P_{repn1} is reached with probability p_{rep}; at this time t_{rn2} is fired and place P_{repn2} is reached indicating that a node is performing a replication process. At last, the transition T_{repn} with rate δ_n is fired when the replication process occurs and, when terminated, the token can come back in P_{up}. In case of a zone failure (e.g. the border router of the zone crashes and the working nodes become unreachable), the transition T_{fz} is fired with rate λ_z to reach the failure condition P_z; the repair process is ruled by T_{rz} with a repair rate μ_z that allows to come back in the working condition P_{up}. Similarly, when a region fails (e.g. the region router crashes and zones remain isolated), the transition T_{fr} is fired with rate λ_r to reach the failure condition P_r and the initial condition is reached on behalf of T_{rr} transition characterized by a repair rate μ_r. In the SRN model has also been added a *guard function* g_1 associated to t_{rd} and to t_{rn2} aimed at preventing that replication processes could be activated simultaneously when $(\#P_{repn2} + \#P_{repd}) > 0$. Such a condition in fact, imposes a block when there is at least one token in P_{repn2} or in P_{repnd}.

We recall that the main purpose of the present work remains in performing an availability analysis of the system in two configurations: MRS and OSDR. More specifically, in the MRS configuration, we are interested in evaluating the availability in the case that each object replica would be contained in a "backup" region R (in such a case $N = R$) resulting in finding out the minimum number of object replicas (and then of regions) that guarantees the "five nines" requirement. It corresponds in evaluating N SRN models reported in Fig. 2.

In the OSDR case instead, we are interested in finding the minimum number of object replicas $N - 1$ contained in the primary region (and in different zones) by leaving only a backup replica in the secondary region (in such a case we have $R = 2$). It corresponds in evaluating 2 SRN models (one for the primary region and one for the secondary region) where the model representative of primary region contemplates the arcs of T_{fr} and T_{rr} transitions having multiplicity ≥ 1 and marked with a double stick symbol; this is useful accounting the condition that if the primary region fails, all the replicas fail.

In order to cope with multiple SRN models, we generalize the model shown in Fig. 2 by considering N_h tokens in $P_{up}^{(h)}$, $h = 1, ...R$, where h indicates the region, and by introducing the generalized guard function that enables the associated transitions only when it returns one:

$$g_1 = \begin{cases} 0 & \text{if } \left(\sum_{h=1}^{R} (\#P_{repn2}^{(h)} + \#P_{repd}^{(h)}) > 0 \right) \\ 1 & \text{otherwise} \end{cases} \tag{1}$$

Let us define the *marking* of the SRN as the distribution of tokens in the various places of SRN. Said r_i the reward rate assigned to marking i and $p_i(t)$ the probability of SRN to be in the marking i at time t, the instantaneous availability $A(t)$ can be expressed as

$$A(t) = \sum_{i \in I} r_i p_i(t) \tag{2}$$

where I identifies the set of *tangible markings* (markings where only timed transitions are enabled).

The reward rate r_i associated to the tangible marking i is given by

$$r_i = \begin{cases} 1 & \text{if } \left(\sum_{h=1}^{R} \#P_{up}^{(h)} \geq 1 \right) \\ 0 & \text{otherwise} \end{cases} \tag{3}$$

It is worth noting that the tangible markings of the SRN and the transition rates among them can be considered equivalent to states and transitions of the underlying continuous-time Markov chain, respectively. Besides, the reward rate can be thought as conceived to quantify the "value" of the system in a specific state. Therefore, steady-state availability of the Object Storage System can be expressed as:

$$A_{OSS} = \lim_{t \to +\infty} A(t) = \sum_{i \in I} r_i p_i \tag{4}$$

where p_i is the steady-state probability given by $p_i = \lim_{t \to +\infty} p_i(t)$. The availability of the OSS system is evaluated for both OSDR and MRS strategies.

5   Numerical Analysis

The modeling and the assessment of the proposed OSS have been faced by exploiting the language model offered by SHARPE [15] (Symbolic Hierarchical Automated Reliability and Performance Evaluator), a powerful tool providing a series of formalisms to perform reliability analyses of complex systems. The availability analysis of the aforementioned strategies is carried out by considering numerical values of the model parameters drawn from technical literature as well from in-field experience. Those values are reported in Table 1.

Two remarks are necessary: *(i)* the value of mean time for hard node repair takes into account various contributions (e.g. components order, specialized manpower etc.); *(ii)* being the replication of nodes and drives similar processes, we assume the same values of δ parameters but we differentiate the *intra-region* replication (object replicas located in the same region) from *inter-region* replication (object replicas located in the different regions). In the former case we use the δ symbol, while in the latter case the δ^* symbol. The final goal of the availability analysis is to characterize the OSS in terms of the minimal number of object replicas (optimal configuration) guaranteeing the "five nines" availability requirement for both OSDR and MRS strategies. Table 2 summarizes the obtained results.

In the OSDR strategy with 1 object replica in the primary region and 1 object replica in secondary region expressed as $(1,1)$, the system exhibits a not acceptable "four nines" availability condition. With a total of 3 replicas distributed

Table 1. Input parameters for the OSS model

Parameter	Description	Value
$1/\lambda_d$	Mean time for drive failure	28000 h
$1/\lambda_n$	Mean time for node failure	10000 h
$1/\delta_d = 1/\delta_n$	Mean time for replication intra-region	3 h
$1/\delta_d^* = 1/\delta_n^*$	Mean time for replication inter-region	12 h
$1/\mu_{hn}$	Mean time for hard node repair	240 h
$1/\mu_{sn}$	Mean time for soft node repair	3 h
$1/\lambda_z$	Mean time for zone failure	10000 h
$1/\mu_z$	Mean time for zone repair	6 h
$1/\lambda_r$	Mean time for region failure	18000 h
$1/\mu_r$	Mean time for region repair	10 h
p_{rep}	Probability that node needs a replication	0.1
p_{hf}	Probability that node needs a hard repair	0.3
p_{sf}	Probability that node needs a soft repair	0.6

Table 2. Availability results of the overall OSS model

OSDR configuration	A_{OSDR}	MRS configuration	A_{MRS}
N = 2 (1,1)	0.9999186	N = R = 2	0.9999186
N = 3 (2,1)	0.9999940	N = R = 3	0.9999992
N = 4 (3,1)	0.9999951	N = R = 4	0.9999999

as 2 replicas in primary region and 1 replica in secondary region (configuration $(2, 1)$), the system satisfies the desirable condition. The same condition is also satisfied in the OSDR configuration $(3, 1)$ but it is paid in the coin of higher cost.

In the case of MRS strategy instead, the configuration with 2 replicas distributed over 2 regions corresponds (for hypothesis) to the $(1, 1)$ configuration of the OSDR scenario and results again in an unacceptable "four nines" condition. In the case of 3 replicas distributed over 3 regions instead, the system availability rises up to a "six nines" condition that in some cases is required for strict robustness demands. The last configuration with 4 replicas in 4 regions is obviously excessive, leading to a steady-state availability $A_{MRS} \geq 1 - 10^{-7}$.

Furthermore, we evaluated the robustness of the system by changing the values of some critical parameters in order to pinpoint a feasible range of values in which the "five nines" condition continues to hold at least for OSDR strategy (whereas is typically exceeded in the MRS case). This sensitivity analysis considers the critical parameters λ_r and μ_r (expressed in terms of mean time to failure of the region $1/\lambda_r$ and mean time to repair of the region $1/\mu_r$ respectively) in the two relevant cases: OSDR strategy in configuration $2, 1$ and MRS strategy

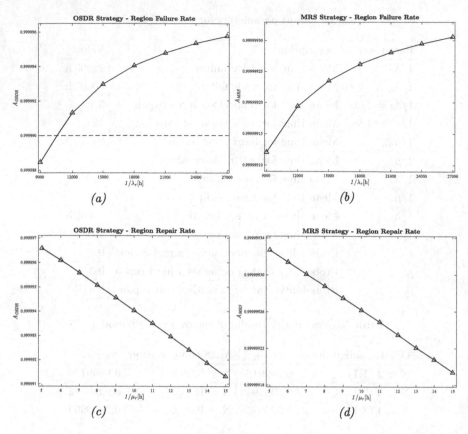

Fig. 3. Sensitivity analysis. *(a)* Influence of the region failure rate (expressed in terms of $1/\lambda_r$) on the object storage system in OSDR configuration; *(b)* influence of the region failure rate on the object storage system in MRS configuration; *(c)* influence of the region repair rate (expressed in terms of $1/\mu_r$) on the object storage system in OSDR configuration; *(d)* influence of the region repair rate on the object storage system in MRS configuration.

in the configuration envisaging $N = 3$ object replicas (that corresponds to have $R = 3$ regions as well). Figure 3*(a)* reveals that the mean time to failure of the region domain in the OSDR strategy can be relaxed from 18000 h (working hypothesis) to almost 10000 h by still guaranteeing $A_{OSDR} \geq 0.99999$ indicated by the horizontal dashed line. Thus, the system is able to tolerate more failures (by choosing greater values of λ_r) with no side-effects. Similar considerations hold in case of MRS strategy. In this case, Fig. 3*(b)* shows that the working condition can be relaxed more considerably by lowering the mean time of failure value considerably under 10000 h. Such expected behavior is in line with results of the steady-state availability analysis that highlights how being equal the number of replicas (3) for OSDR and MRS strategies, the latter is definitely more robust. As regards of repair parameters, Fig. 3*(c)* reveals that it is possible to relax the mean time to repair of the region for OSDR strategy up to 15 h whereas in Fig. 3 *(d)* it is possible to notice that the same parameter considered for MRS strategy can be relaxed up to (not displayed in the plot) 240 h (10 days) confirming once more the expected robustness of MRS schema.

6 Conclusions

Nowadays, the Object Storage Systems (OSSs) are becoming crucial platforms for network and content providers in order to deal with a massive bulk of unstructured data (e.g. multimedia content) difficult to manage with traditional database systems. The Swift project, a part of the IaaS-based platform OpenStack, definitely constitutes one of the most interesting object storage systems. Being the OSSs availability a key issue in design and management of such systems, in this work we perform an availability analysis aimed at pointing the optimal configuration in terms of minimal object replicas being present in the system in order to guarantee the so-called "five nines" availability requirement. Such an analysis takes into account two redundancy strategies called Off-Site Disaster Recovery and Multi-Region Sharing. By the Stochastic Reward Nets (SRNs) methodology we model the high-level architecture of an object storage system based on Swift guidelines. A steady-state analysis and a sensitivity analysis have been carried out. Future works will be devoted at specializing the behavior of the system sub-components by using continuous time Markov chains.

References

1. Arnold, J.: OpenStack Swift: Using, Administering, and Developing for Swift Object Storage, 1st edn. O'Reilly Media Inc., Sebastopol (2014)
2. Kavanagh, A.: OpenStack as the API framework for NFV: the benefits, and the extensions needed. Ericsson Rev. (Engl. Ed.) **92**(1), 44–51 (2015)
3. Thereska, E., Ballani, H., O'Shea, G., Karagiannis, T., Rowstron, A., Talpey, T., Black, R., Zhu, T.: IOFlow: a software-defined storage architecture. In: Kaminsky, M., Dahlin, M. (eds.) The 24th ACM Symposium on Operating Systems Principles, pp. 182–196. ACM (2013)
4. Gracia-Tinedo, R., Garcia-Lopez, P., Sanchez-Artigas, M., Sampe, J., Moatti, Y., Rom, E., Naor, D., Nou, R., Cortes, T., Oppermann, W., Michiardi, P.: IOStack: software-defined object storage. IEEE Internet Comput. **20**(3), 10–18 (2016)
5. Chekam, T.T., Zhai, E., Li, Z., Cui, Y., Ren, K.: On the synchronization bottleneck of OpenStack Swift-like cloud storage systems. In: IEEE INFOCOM 2016 - The 35th Annual IEEE International Conference on Computer Communications, pp. 1–9 (2016)
6. Li, L., Li, D., Su, Z., Jin, L., Huang, G.: Performance analysis and framework optimization of open source cloud storage system. China Commun. **13**(6), 110–122 (2016)
7. Zeng, Z., Veeravalli, B.: On the design of distributed object placement and load balancing strategies in large-scale networked multimedia storage systems. IEEE Trans. Knowl. Data Eng. **20**(3), 369–382 (2008)

8. Ghosh, R., Longo, F., Frattini, F., Russo, S., Trivedi, K.S.: Scalable analytics for IaaS cloud availability. IEEE Trans. Cloud Comput. **2**(1), 57–70 (2014)
9. Iliadis, I., Sotnikov, D., Ta-Shma, P., Venkatesan, V.: Reliability of geo-replicated Cloud storage systems. In: 2014 IEEE 20th Pacific Rim International Symposium on Dependable Computing, pp. 169–179 (2014)
10. Sousa, E., Lins, F., Tavares, E., Cunha, P., Maciel, P.: A modeling approach for cloud infrastructure planning considering dependability and cost requirements. IEEE Trans. Syst. Man Cybern. **45**(4), 549–558 (2015)
11. Yamato, Y., Nishizawa, Y., Nagao, S., Sato, K.: Fast and reliable restoration method of virtual resources on OpenStack. IEEE Trans. Cloud Comput. **PP**(99), 1 (2015)
12. Di Mauro, M., Postiglione, F., Longo, M., Restaino, R., Tambasco, M.: Availability evaluation of the virtualized infrastructure manager in network function virtualization environments. In: Walls, L., Revie, M., Bedford, T. (eds.) Safety and Reliability of Complex Engineered Systems: ESREL2016, pp. 2591–2596. Taylor & Francis Group (2016)
13. Muppala, J.K., Ciardo, G., Trivedi, K.S.: Stochastic reward nets for reliability prediction. Commun. Reliab. Maint. Serv. **1**, 9–20 (1994)
14. Entezari-Maleki, R., Trivedi, K.S., Movaghar, A.: Performability evaluation of grid environments using stochastic reward nets. IEEE Trans. Dependable Sec. Comput. **12**(2), 204–216 (2015)
15. Sahner, R.A., Trivedi, K.S.: Reliability modeling using SHARPE. IEEE Trans. Reliab. **36**(2), 186–193 (1987)

Energy-Efficient Dynamic Consolidation of Virtual Machines in Big Data Centers

Shuting Xu[1], Chase Q. Wu[1,2]($\boxtimes$), Aiqin Hou[1], Yongqiang Wang[1], and Meng Wang[1]

[1] School of Information Science and Technology,
Northwest University, Xi'an 710127, Shaanxi, China
{xushuting,xidawm}@stumail.nwu.edu.cn, {houaiqin,yqwang}@nwu.edu.cn
[2] Department of Computer Science, New Jersey Institute of Technology,
Newark, NJ 07102, USA
chase.wu@njit.edu

Abstract. There is a rapidly growing demand for computing power driven by big data applications, which is typically met by constructing large-scale data centers provisioning virtualized resources. Such data centers consume an enormous amount of energy, resulting in high operational cost and carbon dioxide emission. Meanwhile, cloud providers need to ensure Quality of Service (QoS) in the computing solution delivered to their customers, and hence must consider the power-performance trade-off. We propose a virtual machine (VM) consolidation optimization framework, consisting of three optimization processes in big data centers: (i) VM allocation, (ii) overloaded physical machine (PM) detection and consolidation, and (iii) underloaded PM detection and consolidation. We show that the optimization problem is NP-complete, and design a resource management scheme that integrates three algorithms, one for each optimization process. We implement and evaluate the proposed resource management scheme in CloudSim and conduct simulations on a real workload trace of PlanetLab. Extensive simulation results show that the proposed solution yields up to 21.5% reduction in energy consumption, 34.2% reduction in performance degradation due to migration, 70.2% reduction in SLA violation time per active host, and 68% reduction in Energy and SLA Violations (ESV), respectively, in comparison with state-of-the-art solutions.

Keywords: Big data centers · VM consolidation · Energy consumption

1 Introduction

Big data applications in various domains are the main drive for a rapidly growing demand for computing power, which is currently met by constructing large-scale data centers provisioning virtualized resources. Such data centers consume an enormous amount of energy, resulting in high operational cost and carbon dioxide emission [1,2], which have become a major economical factor and also led

© Springer International Publishing AG 2017
M.H.A. Au et al. (Eds.): GPC 2017, LNCS 10232, pp. 191–206, 2017.
DOI: 10.1007/978-3-319-57186-7_16

to performance degradation. Over the past few years, dynamic virtual machine (VM) provisioning and physical machine (VM) consolidation have emerged as a promising solution and their significance has been well recognized in both academic and industrial communities [3,4].

The sharing of PM resources among multiple VMs is a major feature of virtualization [5]. Generally, a Virtual Machine Monitor keeps track of workload variation on VMs in real time and detects overloaded and underloaded PMs. The general optimization goal is to minimize the number of PMs and meanwhile ensure the Quality of Service (QoS) promised to customers. According to the virtualization process, it is natural to divide the VM dynamic consolidation problem into a number of sequential steps and design an energy-efficient approach for each [6]. However, the energy consumption management of VMs may also lead to certain performance degradation in big data centers. In general, the QoS requirements are formalized via Service Level Agreements (SLAs) that describe the required characteristics, such as performance degradation due to migration and the time period, during which the PMs achieve 100% resource utilization.

In this paper, we consider the VM consolidation problem with a goal to reduce the energy consumption of a data center while satisfying QoS requirements. We formulate an optimization framework consisting of three optimization processes: (i) VM allocation, (ii) overloaded PM detection and consolidation, and (iii) underloaded PM detection and consolidation. We show that this optimization problem is NP-complete, and design a resource management scheme that integrates three algorithms, one for each process. We implement and evaluate the proposed resource management scheme in CloudSim and conduct simulations of a real workload trace of PlanetLab. Extensive results show that the proposed solution outperforms existing ones in terms of reducing energy consumption, performance degradation due to migration, SLA violation time per active host, and Energy and SLA Violations.

The rest of the paper is organized as follows. Section 2 conducts a survey of related work. Section 3 constructs cost models and proposes the optimization framework. Section 4 designs heuristic algorithms and Sect. 5 evaluates their performances. Section 6 concludes our work.

2   Related Work

Several studies investigated the VM consolidation problem and considered the energy efficiency in data centers. Arianyan et al. divided the basic online consolidation problem in cloud data centers into four parts: (i) determining overloaded hosts; (ii) determining underloaded hosts; (iii) selecting VMs for migration from an overloaded host; and (iv) deciding a new placement for a VM migrated from an overloaded or underloaded host. They focused on the second and the fourth phases and proposed a heuristic, TPSA, based on a multi-criteria decision making method [7]. Farahnakian et al. employed a distributed controller to decompose the VM consolidation problem into two sub-problems: PM status detection and VM placement optimization. Since the VM placement optimization problem is NP-complete, they used the ant colony system to find a near optimal solution to improve resource utilization of PMs and reduce energy consumption [8]. Afterwards, they presented a distributed system architecture and used an on-line Ant Colony System (ACS) algorithm to reduce energy consumption of cloud data centers while maintaining the desired QoS [9]. Xiao *et al.* proposed an optimization algorithm of VPPEO based on the evolutionary game theory, which takes the initial solution into account and guarantees an executable list of VM migrations from the initial solution to the target solution [10]. Beloglazov *et al.* proposed a local regression based algorithm combined with the MMT VM selection policy for dynamic consolidation of VMs based on the analysis of historical data from the resource usage by VMs [11]. In [12], Marotta *et al.* built a consolidation problem model, which was solved through a simulated annealing (SA)-based algorithm, which takes into account a value of attractiveness of a VM migration, which is computed through the resource utilization and the energy efficiency of physical servers.

There also exist several research efforts on the design of scheduling algorithms on Big Data platforms. Sfrent *et al.* designed a hybrid algorithm to address the problem of scheduling a set of jobs across a set of machines and analyzed the system behaviors at very high loads for Big Data processing [13]. In [14], Vasile *et al.* proposed a resource-aware hybrid approach for task scheduling in HDC considering both tasks and resources. To predict provisioning and booting time in an MaaS system, Sirbu *et al.* proposed a solution based on platform monitoring and a multi-variate regression algorithm [15].

Different from most of the aforementioned work that considers a static threshold in PM utilization, we propose a dynamic method to determine when a host is considered overloaded on the fly. This dynamic threshold policy would also lead to more efficient VM reallocation in a big data computing environment. Also, we design a heuristic algorithm to solve each optimization problem in the VM consolidation framework to ensure that service requests be satisfied at a high level of energy efficiency.

3 Problem Formulation

In this section, we formulate dynamic VM consolidation optimization problems. We first construct the data center and energy cost models, and then define performance metrics in terms of energy consumption and SLA violation. Based on these models and metrics, we propose a dynamic VM consolidation optimization framework that integrates three optimization processes.

3.1 Data Center Model

System Model: We consider an IaaS cloud computing model, as commonly adopted by big data centers, consisting of a set of heterogeneous physical machines (PM) connected via high-speed switches with an initial power consumption. Each physical machine pm_i is equipped with a set CR_i of homogeneous CPU cores $\{cr_{i,n} \mid 1 \leq n \leq H_i, n \in \mathbb{N}\}$ characterized by the CPU processing performance p_i defined in Millions Instructions Per Second (MIPS).

VM Model: The energy consumption of a PM is mainly caused by the workloads of various applications running on it. We consider an application request in the form of a VM execution request $VM_i(c_i, t_i)$, which specifies the maximum CPU resource request and its running time. In general, each vm carries a time-varying workload from a real application.

3.2   Energy Cost Model

Power Model: Recent studies [16, 17] show that the power consumption by physical machines can be approximated by a linear relationship with CPU utilization. Also, the results of the SPEC power benchmark [18] indicate that the power consumption of servers can be described using a power model, defined as

$$P(u) = k \cdot P_{max} + (1 - k) \cdot P_{max} \cdot u, \tag{1}$$

where P_{max} is the maximum consumed power when the server is fully utilized, k is the fraction of power consumed by the idle server, and u is the CPU utilization. Obviously, the CPU utilization is time varying and is oftentimes denoted by a function $u(t)$ of time. Hence, the total energy consumption of a PM can be calculated as follows, as widely adopted in the literature such as [16]:

$$E(t) = \int_{t_0}^{t_1} p(u(t)) dt. \tag{2}$$

Service Level Agreement Violation Metrics: Service Level Agreement Violation (SLAV) is the common form of Quality of Service (QoS), which can be defined as a workload independent metric [11]. SLAs are delivered if the performance of the application is bounded by the capacity of the PM and the corresponding VM is not being provided with the required performance level. We consider the SLAV metric in [11]:

$$SLAV = SLATAH \cdot PDM, \tag{3}$$

which contains two metrics: i) SLA violation time per active host (SLATAH), which describes the average percentage of time when active hosts achieve 100% CPU utilization:

$$SLATAH = \frac{1}{M} \sum_{i=1}^{M} \frac{T_{s_i}}{T_{a_i}}, \tag{4}$$

where M denotes the number of PMs, T_{s_i} is the total time, during which pm_i achieves 100% utilization, and T_{a_i} is the total time of pm_i being in the active mode; and ii) performance degradation due to migration (PDM):

$$PDM = \frac{1}{N} \sum_{j=1}^{N} \frac{C_{d_j}}{C_{r_j}}, \tag{5}$$

where N is the number of VMs, C_{d_j} is the estimated performance degradation of vm_j caused by migration, which is generally estimated as 10% of the average CPU utilization in MIPS during all migrations of vm_j, and C_{r_j} is the total CPU capacity requested by vm_j during its lifetime.

Performance Metrics: We consider PM energy consumption and SLAV as performance metrics, which, however, are typically negatively correlated as energy could be reduced at the cost of increasing the level of SLA violations. The main objective of resource management in cloud-based data centers is to minimize both energy cost and SLA violation. Therefore, we consider a combined metric in [11] to take into account both energy cost and the level of SLA violations, which are commonly denoted as Energy and SLA Violations (ESV):

$$ESV = Energy \cdot SLAV. \tag{6}$$

3.3 Problem Definition

For a data center built on a cluster of $PM(cr_{i,n}, p_i)$ and a set of VM requests (c_j, t_j), we propose a dynamic VM consolidation optimization framework. Within this framework, the system starts from allocating VM requests to PMs as they arrive. The workloads of PMs vary over time due to the dynamics of the VMs residing on them. To meet the requirements of QoS and energy efficiency, this framework detects the workload condition of live PMs in the data center and consolidates the VMs during their lifetime. On overloaded PMs, we want to select VMs that can be migrated and reallocated to mitigate the overloading risk of each PM. On underloaded PMs, we want to reallocate VMs to shut down unnecessary PMs for energy saving. In general, this optimization framework consists of three optimization processes as described below.

- **VMOAEE** (VM Optimal Allocation for Energy Efficiency): Given a data center and a set of VM requests, the objective is to allocate each VM on the most suitable PM such that the number of PMs is minimized. The VM allocation strategy has a holistic view with the goal to make a positive contribution to the overall performance evaluation metric ESV.
- **MVMDOPM** (Migrated VM Determination on Overloaded PMs): In data centers, there exist many time-varying factors that prevent a static VM placement method from achieving satisfactory performance. Since the mapping between VMs and PMs should be dynamically adjusted, we propose a dynamic scheme for VM placement, which adaptively adjusts the mapping at a certain time interval in accordance with all variations to guarantee SLA (Service Level Agreement) and optimize system performance. Accordingly, we use a dynamic threshold to determine overloaded PMs, and the goal is to determine which set of VMs should be migrated from each overloaded PM to avoid a performance degradation due to overloading.

– **UPMC** (Underloaded PM Consolidation): Given a set of active PMs in the system, the goal is to consolidate the underloaded PMs, i.e. migrate all of the VMs on one underloaded PM to other existing PMs without affecting the performance of the destination PMs, and then shut down the idle PM without any VMs to save energy.

It is straightforward to show that VMOAEE is an NP-complete problem as it is a generalized version of the NP-complete bin-packing problem. We can restrict VMOAEE to the bin packing problem by only considering those instances in which, the physical machines (PMs) are homogeneous with the same capacity C and the VM requests are constant over time, and only considering a performance goal to pack a minimum number of PMs. Under this circumstance, the bin packing problem is a special case of VMOAEE. Since the bin packing problem is NP-complete [19], so is VMOAEE. Therefore, there does not exist any polynomial-time solution to the optimization problem unless $P = NP$, and we design a heuristic approach for each of the three optimization processes.

4   Algorithm Design

In this section, we design three heuristic algorithms. The first heuristic is to solve VMOAEE. Due to the time-varying nature of workloads, a PM could be either overloaded or underloaded. We design an algorithm to determine the candidate VMs for migration from overloaded PMs and another algorithm to determine the set of PMs that should be shut down. Finally, we propose a resource management scheme that integrates these three algorithms within a unified optimization framework for dynamic VM consolidation. For the convenience of reference, we provide all notations used in algorithm design in Table 1.

4.1   OVMA Algorithm for VMOAEE

For the problem of VMOAEE, we design a heuristic algorithm for optimal VM allocation, referred to as OVMA. The pseudocode of this algorithm is provided in Algorithm 1.

In Lines 1–8, it computes evaluated scores for all living PMs using a three-parameter method in [7] to quantify the advantages of a pm hosting a vm. The three parameters, denoted by ac, ei, and nv, are transformed into different numbers between 0 and 1: ac is a type of benefit, which increases the probability of candidate pm_i to be selected, while ei and nv are a type of cost, which reduces the probability of candidate pm_i to be selected. Hence, the numerator of the formula for ac_i calculates the distance from ac_i to ac_{min}, while the numerators of the formulas for ei_i and nv_i calculate the distances from ei_i and nv_i to ei_{max} and nv_{max}, respectively. It sorts the list of living PMs in a descending order according to the scores in Line 9. In Lines 10–17, it takes pm from the list in the descending order to determine the most appropriate destination pm. In Lines 10–12, it computes the average variation of the requested resources of VMs

Table 1. Notations used in the algorithm design.

Parameters	Definitions
M	The number of living PMs in the data center
N_i	The number of VMs in the i-th PM
G	The number of VM requests
pml	The living PM list in the datacenter
vml_i	The vm request list on the i-th PM
vm_i	The i-th vm request
r_{vm}	The requested resource of vm
r_k	The requested resource of vm_i on the k-th time slot
ac_i	The available capacity of the i-th living PM
ei_i	The energy increase caused by the allocation of vm on the i-th living PM
nv_i	The number of VMs in the i-th living PM
acn_i	The available capacity of the i-th type of PM
ein_i	The energy increase caused by the allocation of vm to the i-th type of PM
nvn_i	The number of VMs in the i-th type of PM
$score_i$	The evaluated score of the i-th PM
ai_{ij}	The average increase of the requested resource of vm_j in the i-th PM
t_{ij}	The running time of vm_j in the i-th PM
av_i	The average variation of the requested resources of the i-th PM
ut_i	The upper utilization ratio threshold of the i-th PM
nu_i	The new utilization ratio of the i-th PM
u_i	The current utilization ratio of the i-th PM
du_i	The difference between the current utilization ratio and the upper utilization ratio threshold
c_i	The capacity of the i-th PM
ar_{ij}	The average requested resource of vm_j in the i-th PM
vml_i	the VM list in the i-th PM
$qes(pm, vm)$	The Quadratic Exponential Smoothing forecast function
ml	The migrated VM list
wml	The whole migrated VM list
$updateUT$	The function updating the upper utilization ratio threshold of all living PMs
lt_{vm_i}	The lifetime of the i-th vm

Algorithm 1. OVMA

Input: the vm for allocation and pml

Output: the destination pm for vm allocation

1: $M = sizeof(pml)$;

2: $N_i = sizeof(pml_i)$;

3: **for** $(i = 0; i < M; i + +)$ **do**

4:    **if** $ac_i > r_{vm}$ **then**

5:        $ac_i = \dfrac{\sqrt{ac_i - ac_{min}}^2}{\sqrt{(ac_i - ac_{min})^2} + \sqrt{(ac_i - ac_{max})^2}}$;

6:        $ei_i = \dfrac{\sqrt{ei_i - ei_{max}}^2}{\sqrt{(ei_i - ei_{max})^2} + \sqrt{(ei_i - ei_{min})^2}}$;

7:        $nv_i = \dfrac{\sqrt{nv_i - nv_{max}}^2}{\sqrt{(nv_i - nv_{max})^2} + \sqrt{(nv_i - nv_{min})^2}}$;

8:        $score_i = ac_i + ei_i + nv_i$;

9: $DecreasingSort(pml, s)$;

10: **for** $(i = 0; i < M; i + +)$ **do**

11:    **for** $(j = 0; j < N_i; j + +)$ **do**

12:        $ai_{ij} = |\sum\limits_{k=0}^{t_{ij}-2} r_k / (t_{ij} - 1) - r_{t_{ij}-1}|$;

13:    $av_i = \sum\limits_{h=0}^{N_i-1} ai_h / N_i$;

14:    $ut_i = 100\% - av_i \cdot \dfrac{(N_i+1)}{2} / c_i$;

15:    $nu_i = u_i + r_{vm} / c_i$;

16:    **if** $nu_i < ut_i$ **then**

17:        **return** pm_i;

18: **if** vm can not be allocated on living pms **then**

19:    **for** $(i = 0; i < sizeof(newType); i + +)$ **do**

20:        **if** $acn_i > r_{vm}$ **then**

21:            $acn_i = \dfrac{\sqrt{acn_i - acn_{min}}^2}{\sqrt{(acn_i - acn_{min})^2} + \sqrt{(acn_i - acn_{max})^2}}$;

22:            $ein_i = \dfrac{\sqrt{ein_i - ei_{max}}^2}{\sqrt{(ein_i - ei_{max})^2} + \sqrt{(ein_i - ein_{min})^2}}$;

23:            $nvn_i = \dfrac{\sqrt{nvn_i - nv_{max}}^2}{\sqrt{(nvn_i - nv_{max})^2} + \sqrt{(nvn_i - nvn_{min})^2}}$;

24:            $score_i = acn_i + ein_i + nvn_i$

25:    $DecreasingSort(pml, score)$;

26:    **return** pm_0;

based on the absolute difference between the average requested resource from 0 time-slot to $t - 1$ time-slot and the requested resource of the last time-slot. It then calculates the average variation of the VMs' requested resource on pm_i in Line 13. It sets ut_i for every living pm and calculates the new utilization ratio of pm if it hosts the vm. In Lines 16–17, if nu_i is less than ut_i, then this pm_i would be the destination pm; otherwise, if this vm can not be allocated on living pms, it scores all the new pm's using the above method and select the pm with the highest score.

4.2 OPMCEE Algorithm for MVMDOPM

We design an algorithm to solve the overloaded PM consolidation problem for energy efficiency, referred to as OPMCEE. The pseudocode is provided in Algorithm 2. It computes the average requested resource of vms' on pm_i in Lines 1–3. Then, it sorts the vm list in a descending order according to the average requested resource. In Lines 5–8, it processes the vm's one at a time. It first applies the second exponential smoothing method to predict the new utilization ratio of pm_i without vm_j. If the new utilization is lower than the upper utilization ratio threshold of pm_i, it adds vm_j on the migrated list ml and returns ml, which should be migrated from the overloaded pm_i to avoid the risk of overloading. However, if removing every single vm can not resolve the overloading problem, it removes the first vm, then repeats the above process to determine which vm should be migrated until the predicted outcome of the quadratic exponential smoothing function qes is lower than the upper utilization ratio threshold of pm_i.

The process of dynamic quadratic exponential smoothing prediction for the utilization of pm is as follows. Suppose that $D = (d_1, ... d_n)$, $n \in \mathbb{N}$, denotes a time series of utilization ratios of pm. The single exponential smoothing method calculates the single exponential smoothing value of the n-th time slot's utilization ratio of pm as:

$$S_n^{(1)} = \alpha d_n + (1 - \alpha) S_{n-1}^{(1)}, \tag{7}$$

where d_n is the actual value of the n-th time slot's utilization ratio of pm, S_{n-1} is the single exponential smoothing value of the $(n-1)$-th time slot's utilization ratio of pm, and α is a smoothing parameter, which affects the error range. Eq. (7) can be rearranged as:

$$S_n^{(1)} = \sum_{i=1}^{n} \alpha(1-\alpha)^{n-i} d_i + (1-\alpha)^n S_0, \tag{8}$$

where S_0 is the initial smoothing value, which is the arithmetic mean value of D. The second exponential smoothing value is calculated as

$$S_n^{(2)} = \alpha S_n^{(1)} + (1 - \alpha) S_{n-1}^{(2)}, \tag{9}$$

where $S_n^{(1)}$ is the single exponential smoothing value of the $(n-1)$-th time slot's utilization ratio of pm, and $S_{n-1}^{(2)}$ is the second exponential smoothing value of the $(n-1)$-th time slot's utilization rate of pm. Then, the predicted value of the $(n+1)$-th time slot's utilization rate of pm is calculated as

$$\widetilde{d_{n+1}} = (2S_n^{(1)} - S_n^{(2)}) + \frac{\alpha}{1-\alpha}(S_n^{(1)} - S_n^{(2)}). \tag{10}$$

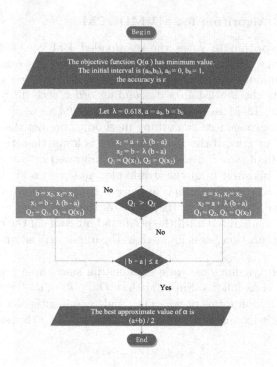

Fig. 1. The flowchart for dynamically determining α using the golden section method.

To improve the prediction accuracy, it dynamically determines the optimal value of α before prediction. The value of α is estimated by minimizing the mean square error (MSE) between the actual and estimated values of the utilization ratio in D. The objective function is defined as:

$$Q(\alpha) = MSE = \frac{\sum_{i=1}^{n}(d_n - \widetilde{d_n})^2}{n}, \tag{11}$$

where d_n is the actual value of the n-th time slot's utilization ratio of pm, and $\widetilde{d_n}$ is the corresponding predicted value. The flowchart for determining α using $minQ(\alpha)$ based on the golden section method in [20] is shown in Fig. 1.

4.3   UPMCEE Algorithm for UPMC

We design an algorithm for the underloaded PM consolidation problem for energy efficiency, referred to as UPMCEE. The pseudocode is provided in Algorithm 3. For each pm in the data center, it firstly calculates the difference value between the upper utilization ratio threshold and the current resource utilization of pm_i and sort the results in a descending order in Lines 1–5. In Lines 6–15, it calls OVMA method to determine whether all the vms on pm_i can be reallocated to

---

Algorithm 2. OPMCEE

Input: overloaded pm_i
Output: the vm list ml for migration
1: $N_i = sizeof(pm_i)$;
2: **for** $(j = 0; j < N_i; j++)$ **do**
3:    $ar_{ij} = \sum_{k=0}^{t_{ij}-1} r_k/(t_{ij})$;
4: $DescendingSort(vml_i, ar)$;
5: **for** $(j = 0; j < N_i; j++)$ **do**
6:    **if** $qes(pm_i, vm_j) < ut_i$ **then**
7:       $ml.add(vm_j)$;
8:       **return** ml;
9:    **if** $(j == N_i)$ **then**
10:       $ml.add(vm_0)$;
11:       $--N_i$;
12:       $j = 0$;

Algorithm 3. UPMCEE

Input: pml
Output: pm in which all vm's need to be migrated
1: $M = sizeof(pml)$;
2: $N_i = sizeof(pml_i)$;
3: **for** $(i = 0; i < M; i++)$ **do**
4:    $du_i = ut_i - u_i$;
5: $DescendingSort(pml, du)$;
6: **for** $(i = 0; i < M; i++)$ **do**
7:    **for** $(j = 0; j < N_i; j++)$ **do**
8:       **if** $(OVMA(vm_{ij}) \in pml$ && $OVMA(vm_{ij})! = pm_i)$ **then**
9:          continue;
10:      **else**
11:         break;
12:    **if** $(j == N_i)$ **then**
13:       **return** pm_i;
14: **if** $(i == M)$ **then**
15:    **return** $null$;

---

another living pm without provisioning a new pm. If the answer is yes, it returns pm_i; otherwise, if none of the pms meets the condition, it returns null, which means that no pm should be shut down.

4.4 OptEE Algorithm for the Entire Optimization Framework

For the entire optimization framework, we propose a resource management scheme, referred to as OptEE, which integrates the above three component algorithms. The pseudocode of OptEE is provided in Algorithm 4. In Lines 1–4, for each VM request, it employs the $OVMA$ algorithm to allocate it to an appropriate PM. If there is still any running VM, it detects the conditions of living PMs.

Algorithm 4. OptEE

Input: vml
 1: $G = sizeof(vml)$;
 2: $M = sizeof(pml)$;
 3: **for** $(i = 0; i < G; i++)$ **do**
 4:    $OVMA(vm_i)$;
 5: **while** $(!G)$ **do**
 6:    $updateUT(pml)$;
 7:    **for** $(i = 0; i < M; i++)$ **do**
 8:      **if** $(ut_i < u_i)$ **then**
 9:        $wml.add(OPMCEE(pm_i))$;
10:    **for** $(j = 0; j < sizeof(wml); j++)$ **do**
11:      $OVMA(vm_j)$;
12:    **if** $(sizeof(wml) == 0)$ **then**
13:      $UPMCEE(pml)$;
14:    **for** $(i = 0; i < G; i++)$ **do**
15:      $--lt_{vm_i}$;
16:      **if** $(lt_{vm_i} == 0)$ **then**
17:        $--G$;
18:    $wml.clear()$;

In every time-step, it updates the upper utilization ratio threshold of PMs according to the historical data. If a PM is considered as overloaded, it employs the OPM-CEE algorithm to acquire the targeted migration list and adds the list to the wml in Lines 7–9. Then, it employs OVMA to reallocate all the VMs in the wml in Lines 10–11. If there is no overloaded PM for processing, it invokes UPMCEE to detect underloaded PMs and tackle the underloading problem in Lines 12–13. The lifetime of every VM request decreases in every time-step. The total number of VM requests decreases when the lifetime of a VM ends.

5   Performance Evaluation

We evaluate the performance of the proposed optimization framework in the CloudSim toolkit [21], which is a commonly used simulation framework in cloud computing environments.

5.1   Simulation Setup

For performance evaluation, we consider two types of physical nodes and five types of VMs in the simulator. The physical nodes include HP ProLiant ML110 G4 servers and HP ProLiant ML110 G5 servers, whose configurations are shown in Table 3, and whose power consumption is shown in Table 2. The five types of VMs are shown in Table 4. VMs utilize less resources according to the workload, hence creating opportunities for dynamic consolidation. To conduct our experiments in a more practical setting, we use the workload traces from a real system,

Table 2. Power consumption of considered servers for different loads (kw) [7].

Server	Idle	10%	20%	30%	40%	50%	60%	70%	80%	90%	100%
HP ProLiant G4	86	89.4	92.6	96	99.5	102	106	108	112	114	117
HP ProLiant G5	93.7	97	101	105	110	116	121	125	129	133	135

Table 3. Configuration of servers [7].

Server	CPU model	Cores	Frequency (MHz)	RAM (GB)
HP ProLiant G4	Intel Xeon 3040	2	1860	4
HP ProLiant G5	Intel Xeon 3075	2	2660	4

Table 4. VM types (five Amazon EC2 VM types) [23].

VM type	CPU (MIPS)	RAM (GB)
High-memory extra large	3000	6
High-CPU medium instance	2500	0.85
Extra-large instance	2000	3.75
Small instance	1000	1.7
Micro instance	500	0.613

which are provided as part of the CoMon project, a monitoring infrastructure for PlanetLab [22]. The characteristics of the VM types we consider correspond to Amazon EC2 instance types with only one exception that every VM has a single core, which is to match the fact that the workload data used for the simulations came from single-core VMs. For each *vm* request, we specify the running time and VM type in a random manner, and assign a workload trace from the CoMon project to it also randomly.

5.2 Performance Comparison of the Algorithms

We compare the proposed VM consolidation solution with the state-of-the-art method through simulations. The VM consolidation framework in a data center typically consists of three key processes: (i) allocating VMs; (ii) determining migrated VMs from an overloaded PM; and (iii) detecting and consolidating an underloaded PM. Our proposed resource management scheme OptEE integrates three algorithms, i.e. OVMA, OPMECC and UPMCEE, one for each process. We compare the performance of OptEE with that of the ConEE policy, including First Fit, LR, SM and RC algorithms proposed in [11].

We conduct ten different scales of experiments from 10 VM requests to 100 VM requests. We generate VM requests with 30 execution time units. The energy consumption measurements of the OptEE policy and the ConEE policy in different VM request scales are plotted in Fig. 2. The performance degradation

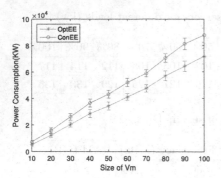

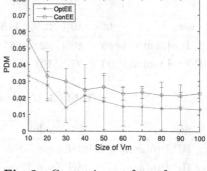

Fig. 2. Comparison of energy consumption between the OptEE policy and the ConEE policy in different virtual machine request scales.

Fig. 3. Comparison of performance degradation due to migration between the OptEE policy and the ConEE policy in different virtual machine request scales.

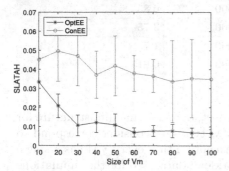

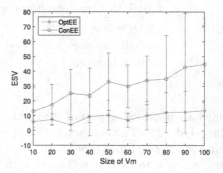

Fig. 4. Comparison of SLA violation time per active host between the OptEE policy and the ConEE policy in different virtual machine request scales.

Fig. 5. Comparison of ESV between the OptEE policy and the ConEE policy in different virtual machine request scales.

measurements due to migration achieved by the OptEE policy and the ConEE policy in different VM request scales are plotted in Fig. 3. The performance measurements of SLA violation time per active host achieved by the OptEE policy and the ConEE policy in different VM request scales are plotted in Fig. 4. The ESV performance measurements achieved by the OptEE policy and the ConEE policy in different VM request scales are plotted in Fig. 5. These results show that the the proposed OptEE policy consistently achieve a better performance than the ConEE policy.

6   Conclusion

We formulated a dynamic virtual machine consolidation optimization framework and showed that the VM allocation problem is NP-complete. We designed a resource management scheme, OptEE, which integrates three algorithms to address each of the three optimization problems in the consolidation process. The performance superiority of the proposed framework was verified by extensive simulations in a large-scale experimental setup using real-life workload traces from more than one thousand PlanetLab VMs. The proposed scheme demonstrated a superior performance in terms of ESV due to a substantially reduced level of SLA violations and energy consumption. It is of our future interest to implement these algorithms as an extension of the VM manager within the OpenStack Cloud platform to evaluate the proposed VM consolidation strategy in real cloud environments.

Acknowledgment. This research is sponsored by U.S. National Science Foundation under Grant No. CNS-1560698 with New Jersey Institute of Technology and National Nature Science Foundation of China under Grant No. 61472320 with Northwest University, P.R. China.

References

1. Luo, J.P., Li, X., Chen, M.R.: Hybrid shuffled frog leaping algorithm for energy-efficient dynamic consolidation of virtual machines in cloud data centers. Expert Syst. Appl. **41**(13), 5804–5816 (2014)
2. Beloglazov, A., Buyya, R., Lee, Y.C., Zomaya, A.: A taxonomy and survey of energy-efficient data centers and cloud computing systems. Adv. Comput. **82**, 47–111 (2010)
3. Esfandiarpoor, S., Pahlavan, A., Goudarzi, M.: Structure-aware online virtual machine consolidation for datacenter energy improvement in cloud computing. Comput. Electr. Eng. **42**, 74–89 (2014)
4. Ashraf, A.: Cost-efficient virtual machine management: provisioning, admission control, and consolidation. Turku Centre for Computer Science (2014)
5. Horri, A., Mozafari, M.S., Dastghaibyfard, G.: Novel resource allocation algorithms to performance and energy efficiency in cloud computing. J. Supercomput. **69**(3), 1445–1461 (2014)
6. Beloglazov, A., Buyya, R.: Managing overloaded hosts for dynamic consolidation of virtual machines in cloud data centers under quality of service constraints. IEEE Trans. Parallel Distrib. Syst. **24**(7), 1366–1379 (2013)
7. Arianyan, E., Taheri, H., Sharifian, S.: Novel energy and sla efficient resource management heuristics for consolidation of virtual machines in cloud data centers. Comput. Electr. Eng. **47**, 222–240 (2015)
8. Farahnakian, F., Ashraf, A., Liljeberg, P., Pahikkala, T., Plosila, J., Porres, I., Tenhunen, H.: Energy-aware dynamic VM consolidation in cloud data centers using ant colony system. In: IEEE International Conference on Cloud Computing, pp. 104–111 (2014)
9. Farahnakian, F., Ashraf, A., Pahikkala, T., Liljeberg, P., Plosila, J., Porres, I., Tenhunen, H.: Using ant colony system to consolidate VMs for green cloud computing. IEEE Trans. Serv. Comput. **8**(2), 187–198 (2015)

10. Xiao, Z., Jiang, J., Zhu, Y., Ming, Z., Zhong, S., Cai, S.: A solution of dynamic VMs placement problem for energy consumption optimization based on evolutionary game theory. J. Syst. Softw. **101**, 260–272 (2015). http://www.sciencedirect.com/science/article/pii/S016412121400288X
11. Beloglazov, A., Buyya, R.: Optimal online deterministic algorithms and adaptive heuristics for energy and performance efficient dynamic consolidation of virtual machines in cloud data centers. Concurrency Comput. Pract. Experience **24**(13), 1397–1420 (2012)
12. Marotta, A., Avallone, S.: A simulated annealing based approach for power efficient virtual machines consolidation. In: IEEE International Conference on Cloud Computing, pp. 445–452 (2015)
13. Sfrent, A., Pop, F.: Asymptotic scheduling for many task computing in big data platforms. Inf. Sci. **319**, 71–91 (2015)
14. Vasile, M.A., Pop, F., Tutueanu, R.I., Cristea, V., Kolodziej, J.: Resource-aware hybrid scheduling algorithm in heterogeneous distributed computing. Future Gener. Comput. Syst. **51**(C), 61–71 (2015)
15. Sirbu, A., Pop, C., Serbanescu, C., Pop, F.: Predicting provisioning and booting times in a metal-as-a-service system. Future Gener. Comput. Syst. (2016)
16. Beloglazov, A., Abawajy, J., Buyya, R.: Energy-aware resource allocation heuristics for efficient management of data centers for cloud computing. Future Gener. Comput. Syst. **28**(5), 755–768 (2012)
17. Kusic, D., Kephart, J.O., Hanson, J.E., Kandasamy, N., Jiang, G.: Power and performance management of virtualized computing environments via lookahead control. Cluster Comput. **12**(1), 1–15 (2009)
18. Spec power benchmarks, standard performance evaluation corporation. http://www.spec.org/benchmarks.html
19. Korte, B., Vygen, J.: Combinatorial Optimization: Theory and Algorithms. Springer, Heidelberg (2000)
20. Golden-section search. https://en.wikipedia.org/wiki/Golden-section_search
21. Calheiros, R.N., Ranjan, R., Beloglazov, A., Rose, C.A.F.D., Buyya, R.: CloudSim: a toolkit for modeling and simulation of cloud computing environments and evaluation of resource provisioning algorithms. Softw. Pract. Experience **41**(1), 23–50 (2011)
22. CoMon: a mostly-scalable monitoringsystem for PlanetLab. ACM SIGOPS Operating Syst. Rev.
23. Amazon elastic computing cloud (EC2). http://aws.amazon.com/ec2/instance-types

Influence Maximization in Social Media Networks Using Hypergraphs

Flora Amato[1,2], Vincenzo Moscato[1,2], Antonio Picariello[1,2],
and Giancarlo Sperlí[1(✉)]

[1] DIETI - Department of Electrical Engineering and Information Technology,
University of Naples "Federico II", Naples, Italy
{flora.amato,vmoscato,picus,giancarlo.sperli}@unina.it
[2] CINI ITEM Lab, Naples, Italy

Abstract. In this paper, inspired by hypergraph-based approaches, we
propose a novel data model for social media networks: it allows to represent in a simple way all the different kinds of relationships that are
typical of these environments (among multimedia contents, among users
and multimedia content and among users themselves) and to enable several kinds of analytics and applications. From the other hand, we have
tested several influence maximization algorithms leveraging the introduced network structure in order to show the advantages to consider
also "user-to-multimedia" relationships (in addition to the "user-to-user"
ones) in the influence analysis problem. Preliminary experiments using
data of several social media networks shows how our approach obtains
very promising results.

1 Introduction

Nowadays, multimedia data allow fast and effective communication and sharing
of information about peoples' lives, their behaviors, works, interests, but they
are also the digital testimony of facts, objects, and locations.

In such a context, *Social Media Networks* actually represent a natural environment where users can create and share multimedia content such as text,
image, video, audio, and so on. Just as an example, each minute thousands of
tweets are sent on Twitter, several hundreds of hours of videos are uploaded to
YouTube, and a huge quantity of photos are shared on Instagram or uploaded
to Flickr.

Indeed, using multimedia content each user interacts with the others generating "social links" that well characterize the behaviors of users in the network.
In particular, the links in a social media network could represent anything from
intimate friendships to common interests for a given multimedia object (e.g.,
tweet, post, video, photo, etc.): they determine the "flow" of information and
hence indicate a user's *influence* on the others, a concept that is crucial in soci-
ology and viral marketing.

As well known, studying influence patterns can help us better understand
why certain trends or innovations are adopted faster than others and how we

© Springer International Publishing AG 2017
M.H.A. Au et al. (Eds.): GPC 2017, LNCS 10232, pp. 207–221, 2017.
DOI: 10.1007/978-3-319-57186-7_17

could help advertisers and marketers design more effective campaigns. Traditional communication theory states that a minority of users, called *influentials*, excel in persuading others; a more modern view, in contrast, de-emphasizes the role of influential and posits that the key factors determining influence are: the interpersonal relationship among ordinary users and the readiness of a society to adopt an innovation [1]. Moving from theory into practice, in social networks influence of a user is usually correlated to her/his *popularity* that is usually measured considering "user-to-user" relationships [2]: as an example in Twitter the most diffused measures of influence are indegree, retweets, and mentions [3].

In turn, if we consider a social media network in our opinion also multimedia data can play a "key-role" in the influence analysis task: representing and understanding all the possible "user-to-multimedia" interaction mechanisms can be useful to better predict user behavior and estimated the related influence in the network [4,5]. In this case, additional research questions have to be addressed in according to the *Social Network Analysis* (SNA) perspective:

- It possible to exploit multimedia features and the notion of similarity among multimedia contents to discover more useful social links?
- Can all the different types of user annotations (e.g. tag, comment, review, etc.) [6] and interactions with multimedia objects provide a further support for an advanced network analysis?
- Is it possible to integrate and efficiently manage in a unique network [7] the information coming from heterogeneous social media networks (for example, a Instagram user has usually an account also on Flickr)?
- How can we deal with a very large volume of data?
- In this context, how is possible to model all the various relationships among users and multimedia objects? Are the "graph-based" strategies still the most suitable solutions?

To capture the described issues, we adopt the term *Multimedia Social Networks* (MSNs) to indicate: *"integrated social media networks that combine the information on users, belonging to one or more social communities, together with all the multimedia contents that can be generated and used within the related environments"*.

In this paper, inspired by hypergraph based approaches, we propose a novel data model for Multimedia Social Networks and test several influence maximization algorithms leveraging the introduced network structure. More in details, our model provides a solution for representing MSNs sufficiently general with respect to: (i) a particular social information network, (ii) the different kinds of entities, (iii) the different types of relationships, (iv) the different applications. Exploiting hypergraphs, the model allows us to represent in a simple way all the different kinds of relationships that are typical of a MSN (among multimedia contents, among users and multimedia content and among users themselves) and to enable several kinds of analytics and applications by means of the introduction of some user and multimedia (*global* and *topic sensitive*) "ranking" functions [8].

We also use a strategy for hypergraph building from data coming from different social media networks (e.g. Facebook, Twitter, Flickr, Instagram, Last.fm, Youtube). Eventually, we report some experiments using a dataset of Flickr, showing how our model can support the most diffused algorithms for determining user influence and how this problem can take some advantages considering also "user-to-multimedia" interactions.

The paper is organized as the following. Section 2 reports a brief state of the art of the most different models and influence analysis approaches for social media networks. Sections 3 and 4 describe the proposed model for MSN and the strategy for computing user influence, respectively. Section 5 provides some implementation details and the preliminary experimental results. Finally, Sect. 6 discusses conclusions and the future work.

2 Related Work

2.1 Models for Social Media Networks

In the last decade, the huge amount of heterogeneous data that could be extracted from social media networks (such as Youtube, Flickr and so on) led to a continued growth of interest in the modeling of such networks taking in account jointly social and multimedia features.

The first approaches for modeling these networks represent the underlying network [9] as a graph which vertices correspond to users and the relationships among them have different meaning on the base of specific applications of interest: influence analysis, lurker identification, expert finding and so on.

Successively, other approaches have been introduced for including multimedia content into social media network models: they are usually classified in four groups.

The first group models a social media network as a *graph* composed by heterogeneous vertices such as users, tags and multimedia objects. Jin et al. [10] develop an algorithm to take in account jointly link-based and content-based similarities by considering network structure [11,12], mutually reinforcing link similarity and feature weight learning.

A *bi-partite graph* is exploited by the second category to model the relationship established among user and contents and to support several applications: computing influence diffusion in social networks [13], consensus maximization problem [14] and so on.

The third category is based on the adoption of a *three-partite graph* for different applications: clustering [15] and personalized recommendation [16].

Eventually, the last group leverage *hypergraph* theory to represent the heterogeneous and complex relationships [17] that could be established in social media networks [18,19]. A music recommendation approach based on hypergraph, exploiting both social and acoustic based information, is proposed by Bu et al. [20]. In [21], the authors develop an approach based on tensor decomposition for guaranteed learning of communities in 3-uniform hypergraph.

2.2 Strategies for Influence Analysis

Deciding whether to adopt an innovation (such as a political idea or product), individuals are frequently influenced, explicitly or implicitly, by their social contacts.

Indeed, the way in which new practices spread through a population depends mainly on the fact that people influence each others behavior. It is essential for companies to target "opinion leaders", as influencing them will lead to a large cascade of further recommendations [22]. This is the goal of each viral marketing and social advertisement campaigns, and corresponds in solving the *influence maximization problem*.

Richardson and Domingos [23] are the first to deal with a problem of influence maximization related to viral marketing applications. In particular, they examine a particular market as a social network composed by different interconnecting entities and model it as a *Markov Random Field* (MRF) in order to identify a subset of users to convince to adopt a new technology for maximizing the adoption of the technology itself. The choosing of the most influence nodes is an optimization problem that has been proven by Kempe et al. [24] to be NP-Hard. For this reason, the authors provides a greedy strategy exploiting a sub-modular influence function that allows to obtain a solution that is no worse than $(1 - 1/e)$ w.r.t. optimal solution.

Different models have been then proposed in the literature to deal with influence analysis problems: *Threshold* model [25], in which a node is activated only if the sum of influence provided by its neighbor is greater than specific node threshold, *Indipendent Cascade* model [26], in which a node has only one chance to activate its neighbor.

Other approaches have been developed to analyze the influence spread related to specific topics. A first attempt to analyze the strength of social influence based on different topics is proposed by Tang et al. [2]. They propose an approach, called *Topical Affinity Propagation*, taking in input the network structure and distribution topic for each node that models the topic-level social influence. In order to derive the indirect influence between nodes, Liu et al. [27], also, propose a topic-level influence propagation approach based on direct influence learned by a generative graphical model, exploiting jointly heterogeneous link information and textual information.

Summarizing, in the influence maximization problem, it is mandatory to accomplish two tasks:

- a detailed modeling of the influence diffusion process in the network;
- efficient identification of the target nodes given a diffusion model.

In [28], the state of the art with the related comparison of the most diffused algorithms for an influence maximization problem is reported.

3   Modeling Social Media Networks via Hypergraph

3.1   Basic Concepts

In our vision, a MSN is basically composed by three different entities:

- **Users** - the set of persons and organizations constituting the particular social community. Several information concerning their profile, interests, preferences, etc. can be opportunely exploited by our model.
- **Multimedia Objects** - the set of multimedia resources (i.e. texts, images, video, audio, etc.) that can be shared within a MSN community. High level (*metadata*) and low level information (*features*) can be properly and jointly used in our model.
- **Annotation Assests** - the most significant terms or named entities - whose definition can be retrieved from dictionaries, ontologies and so on - of a given domain, namely *topics*, exploited by users to annotate multimedia data and derived from the analysis of textual information such as keywords, labels, tags, comments etc.

Several types of relationships can be established among the described entities: for example, a user can annotate an image with a particular tag, two friends can comment the same post, a user can tag another user in a photo, a user can share some videos within a group and so on.

Due to the variety and complexity of these relationships, we decided to leverage the *hypergraph* formalism to model a MSN [8,29].

In particular, our model relies on several concepts, *Multimedia Social Network* (seen as particular a weighted *hypergraph*) (see Fig. 1) and *social paths* (i.e. *hyperpaths*), which basic definitions are provided in the following.

Definition 31 (MSN). *A Multimedia Social Network MSN is a triple $(V; H_e = \{e_i : i \in I\}; \omega)$, V being a finite set of vertices, H_e a set of hyperedges with a finite set of indexes I and $\omega : H_e \rightarrow [0,1]$ a weight function. The set of vertices is defined as $V = U \cup M \cup A$, U being the set of MSN users, M the set of multimedia objects and A the set of annotation assets. Each hyperedge $e_i \in H_e$ is in turn defined by a ordered pair $e_i = (e_i^+ = (V_{e_i}^+, i); e_i^- = (i, V_{e_i}^-))$. The element e_i^+ is called the tail of the hyperarc e_i whereas e_i^- is its head, $V_{e_i}^+ \subseteq V$ being the set of vertices of e_i^+, $V_{e_i}^- \subseteq V$ the set of vertices of e_i^- and $V_{e_i} = V_{e_i}^+ \cup V_{e_i}^-$ the subset of vertices constituting the whole hyperedge.*

Actually, vertices and hyperedges are *abstract data types* with a set of properties (attributes and methods) that permit to support several applications. As an example, each hyperdge is characterized by tthe following attributes: id, name, timestamp, source (social network) and type. In turn, the weight function can be used to define the confidence or uncertainty of a given relationship in terms of probability, fuzzy membership, etc.

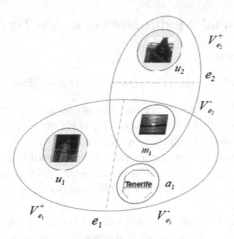

Fig. 1. An hypergraph example.

Definition 32 (Social path). *A social path between vertices v_{s_1} and v_{s_k} of a MSN is a sequence of distinct vertices and hyperedges $v_{s_1}, e_{s_1}, v_{s_2}, ..., e_{s_{k-1}}, v_{s_k}$ such that $\{v_{s_i}, v_{s_{i+1}}\} \subseteq V_{e_{s_i}}$ for $1 \le i \le k - 1$. The length of the hyperpath is $\alpha \cdot \sum_{i=1}^{k-1} \cdot \frac{1}{\omega(e_{s_i})}$, α being a normalizing factor. We say that a social path contains a vertex v_h if $\exists e_{s_i} : v_h \in V_{e_{s_i}}$.*

Social paths between two nodes leverage the different kinds of relationships (see Sect. 3.2): a given path can "directly" connect two users because they are "friends" or members of the same group, or "indirectly", as they have shared the same picture or commented the same video.

3.2 Relationships

Analyzing the different types of relationships that can be established in the main social media networks, we have identified three categories:

- **User to User** relationships, describing user actions towards other users;
- **Similarity** relationships, describing a relatedness between two multimedia objects, users or annotation assets;
- **User to Multimedia** relationships, describing user actions on multimedia objects, eventually involving some annotation assets or other users.

Definition 33 (User to user relationship). *Let $\widehat{U} \subseteq U$ a subset of users in a MSN, we define* user to user relationship *each hyperedge e_i with the following properties:*

1. $V_{e_i}^+ = u_k$ such that $u_k \in \widehat{U}$,
2. $V_{e_i}^- \subseteq \widehat{U} - u_k$.

Examples of "user to user" relationships are properly represented by *friendship*, *following* or *membership* in On-line Social Networks. To better explain this type of relationships, we provide in Fig. 2 an example of *friendship* relationship. For this kind of relationships, we set $\omega(e_i)$ to a value in $[0,1]$ that is function of the specific relationship (e.g. a friendship has a more high value than a membership).

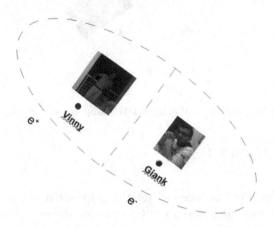

Fig. 2. Friendship relationship between two users.

Definition 34 (Similarity relationship). *Let* $v_k, v_j \in V$ *(k ≠ j) two vertices of the same type of a MSN, we define* similarity relationship *each hyperedge* e_i *with* $V_{e_i}^+ = v_k$ *and* $V_{e_i}^- = v_j$. *The weight function for this relationship returns similarity value between the two vertices.*

Similarity relationships are defined on the top of a *similarity function* that associates to a couple of vertices of the same type a value in $[0,1]$. It is possible to compute a similarity value:

- between two users by considering different types of features (interests, profile information, preferences, etc.);
- between two multimedia objects using the well-known (high and low level) features and metrics proposed in the literature;
- between two annotation assets exploiting the related topics and the well-known metrics on vocabularies or ontologies.

In our model, a similarity hyperedge is effectively generated if $\omega(e_i) \geq \theta$, θ being a given threshold. To better explain this type of relationships, we provide in Fig. 3 an example of *multimedia similarity* relationship.

Definition 35 (User to Multimedia relationship). *Let* $\widehat{U} \subseteq U$ *a set of users in a MSN and* $\widehat{M} \subseteq M$ *a set of multimedia objects, we define* user to multimedia relationship *each hyperedge* e_i *with the following properties:*

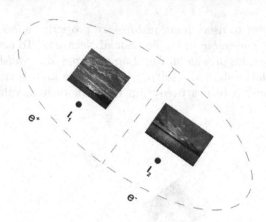

Fig. 3. Multimedia similarity relationship among two images.

1. $V_{e_i}^+ = u_k$ such that $u_k \in \widehat{U}$,
2. $V_{e_i}^- \subseteq \widehat{M} \cup A$.

Examples of "user to multimedia" relationships are represented, as an example, by *publishing, reaction, annotation* (in this case the set $V_{e_i}^-$ also contains one or more annotation assets) or *user tagging* (involving also one ore more users) activities.

To better explain this type of relationships, we provide in Fig. 4 an example of *multimedia tagging* relationship. For this kind of relationships, we set $\omega(e_i)$ to a value in [0,1] that is function of the specific relationship (e.g. a publishing has a more high value than a comment or reaction).

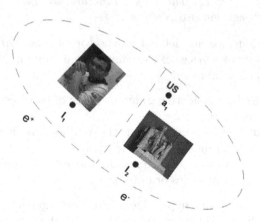

Fig. 4. Multimedia tagging of an image.

Figure 5 shows as the different relationships can be easily represented in our model using hypergraphs.

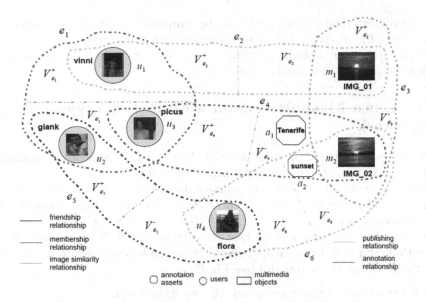

Fig. 5. An example of MSN constituted by six hyperedges.

3.3 Hypergraph Building

The proposed hypergraph building process is in part inspired by the methodology proposed in [30]. It consists of three different stages:

- hypergraph structure construction,
- topic distribution,
- similarity learning.

First, extracted data related to relationships between multimedia contents, users and multimedia content and users themselves are initially used to construct the hypergraph structure in terms of nodes and hyperedges. For the annotation relationships, textual annotations are then analyzed by the LDA approach - proposed in [31] - to learn the most important topics and to infer relations between topics and annotation assets. From the other hand, similarity values between users, multimedia objects and topics are eventually determined using proper strategies [32,33].

3.4 Ranking Functions

Ranking functions can be profitably used to "rank" users and multimedia objects in a MSN in an absolute way or with respect to a given topic of interest. In our model the *rank* of a given node can be measured by the number of user nodes that are "reachable" within a certain number of steps using social paths (see [8] for more details).

By similarity relationships paths can be "implicitly" instantiated: two users (that are not friend, do not belong to any group and do not share any multimedia object) have annotated two images that are very similar, or they have commented two posts which concern similar topics.

4 Influence Maximization on a Multimedia Social Network

We implemented some of the most diffused algorithms for influence analysis and maximization on the top of our hypergraph-based model.

Generally, hypergraphs are very complex data structures to manage, and for computational reasons, several approaches have been introduced to deal with their intrinsic complexity [34], especially for large graphs. In this work, we have chosen to adopt the methodology that transforms the MSN hypergraph into a *bi-partite* graph [35]. In particular, each hyperedge is mapped into a subgraph with the following characteristics (see Fig. 6):

- each hypergraph vertex corresponds to a subgraph vertex;
- the hyperedge generates a new vertex: each vertex in $V_{e_i}^+$ and $V_{e_i}^-$ is separately connected to the new vertex by a directed edge;
- the hyperdge weight is uniformly distributed over each path connecting the vertex in $V_{e_i}^+$ to the vertices in $V_{e_i}^-$.

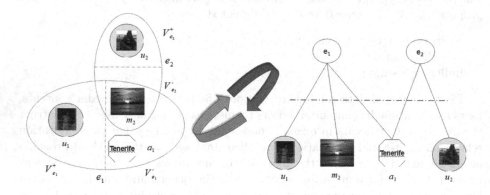

Fig. 6. Mapping on bi-partite graph

In particular, we exploited the following algorithms to determine the most influentials nodes of a MSN:

- TIM+ [36]: a two-phase influence maximization algorithm based on a *sketch* method. In the first phase the θ parameter is derived using a lower bound respect to the maximum expected spread; in the second phase the computed θ value is exploited to derive a k-size set of nodes that covers a large number of Reverse Random (RR) sets.

- IMM [37]: an algorithm leveraging the two-phases approach of TIM that exploits a set of estimation probabilistic techniques [38] to compute a lower bound of the maximum expected influence of any size-k set of nodes that is asymptotically tight.

5 Preliminary Experiments

We used as dataset for our experiments the *Yahoo Flickr Creative Commons 100 Million Data* (YFCC100M)[1] multimedia collection, provided by Yahoo in 2014.

In particular, we considered images about animal, landscape and nature domains and leveraged the Flickr API[2] to gather users' social information and actions (tags, comments, favorites). Successively, we generated the related Multimedia Social Network using the proposed hypergraph building strategy. In particular, we computed the similarity relationships between two tags and two images using respectively the Wu&Palmer distance on *WordNet* [39] vocabulary and the *Image Path* distance [40].

Table 1 provides the characterization of our dataset.

Table 1. Dataset characterization

Dataset	Vertices			Hyperedges
	Users	Topics	Images	
YFCC100M	1K	30	1.3K	4K

Our experiment protocol has two different goals: evaluating efficiency and effectiveness of the described influence maximization algorithms over the considered MSN.

From one hand, we measured the execution times of the two influence maximization algorithms varying the related seed set k and the desired accuracy ϵ. From the other one, we analyzed how materialized tag and multimedia objects in the network can affect influence spread by comparing results of the TIM+ and IMM algorithms with respect to a given ground-truth.

In particular, the influentials composing the ground-truth have been computed using a strategy that takes into how many popular photos have been published by each user. We note that the *popularity* of an image is obtained as a combination of the related numbers of favorite, comments and visualizations.

5.1 Implementation Details

This experiments were performed using a machine with Intel Core i7-67000HQ 2.59 GHz CPU and 8 GB memory with a 64-bit Ubuntu 14.04 operating system. All the algorithms have been implemented in Apache Spark using Scala 2.11.

---

[1] https://webscope.sandbox.yahoo.com.
[2] https://www.flickr.com/services/api.

5.2 Experimental Results

Here, we show the results of our experimental evaluation.

Figure 7a reports the running time comparison between the TIM+ and IMM algorithms varying the cardinality k of seed set from 1 to 50 and considering $\epsilon = 0.2$. It's possible to note that *IMM* outperforms TIM+ algorithm due to the exploited optimization techniques. Moreover, in the Fig. 7b it's possible to note that *IMM* algorithm outperforms TIM+ algorithm also varying the ϵ parameter.

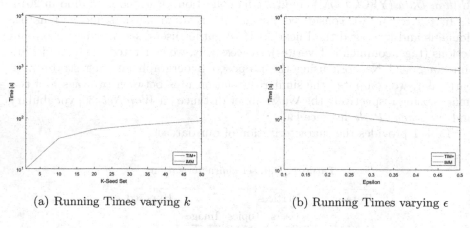

(a) Running Times varying k (b) Running Times varying ϵ

Fig. 7. Efficiency of the TIM+ and IMM algorithms on the considered MSN

Concerning the effectiveness, we compared the results of the TIM+ and IMM algorithms with respect to the generated ground-truth using a recall based measure:

$$R = \frac{|\hat{U} \cap \tilde{U}|}{|\hat{U}|}$$

where $\hat{U}$ corresponds to the set of influentials in the ground-truth and $\tilde{U}$ is the set of influentials computed by a specific influence maximizations algorithm.

Table 2 shows the obtained results of recall using as influence analysis algorithm TIM+ and IMM considering the whole MSN and an its part MSN* (generated considering only hyperedges connecting users or by means user to user relationships or by comment and favorite relationships).

Table 2. Recall evaluation

	TIM (MSN) +	IMM (MSN)	TIM (MSN*) +	IMM (MSN*)
Recall	78%	81%	59%	63%

6 Conclusions and Future Work

In this paper we described a data model for Multimedia Social Networks, combining information on users together with the multimedia content. Preliminary experiments have shown how some influence maximization algorithms can take advantages from the adoption the introduced hypergraph data structure. Future work will be devoted to extend the proposed experimentation considering other influence analysis algorithms and big data coming form heterogeneous networks.

References

1. Watts, D.J., Dodds, P.S.: Influentials, networks, and public opinion formation. J. Consum. Res. **34**(4), 441–458 (2007)
2. Tang, J., Sun, J., Wang, C., Yang, Z.: Social influence analysis in large-scale networks. In: Proceedings of the 15th ACM SIGKDD International Conference on Knowledge Discovery and Data Mining, pp. 807–816. ACM (2009)
3. Cha, M., Haddadi, H., Benevenuto, F., Gummadi, P.K.: Measuring user influence in twitter: The million follower fallacy. In: ICWSM, vol. 10, issue (10–17), p. 30 (2010)
4. Di Lorenzo, G., Moscato, F., Mazzocca, N., Vittorini, V.: Automatic analysis of control flow in web services composition processes. In: 2007 15th EUROMICRO International Conference on Parallel, Distributed and Network-Based Processing, PDP 2007, pp. 299–306. IEEE (2007)
5. Di Lorenzo, G., Mazzocca, N., Moscato, F., Vittorini, V.: Towards semantics driven generation of executable web services compositions. JSW **2**(5), 1–15 (2007)
6. Amato, F., Mazzeo, A., Penta, A., Picariello, A.: Using NLP and ontologies for notary document management systems. In: 2008 19th International Workshop on Database and Expert Systems Application, DEXA 2008, pp. 67–71. IEEE (2008)
7. Amato, F., Mazzeo, A., Moscato, V., Picariello, A.: A framework for semantic interoperability over the cloud. In: 2013 27th International Conference on Advanced Information Networking and Applications Workshops (WAINA), pp. 1259–1264. IEEE (2013)
8. Sperlì, G., Amato, F., Moscato, V., Picariello, A.: Multimedia social network modeling using hypergraphs. Int. J. Multimedia Data Eng. Manage. (IJMDEM) **7**(3), 53–77 (2016)
9. Palmieri, F.: Network-aware scheduling for real-time execution support in data-intensive optical grids. Future Gener. Comput. Syst. **25**(7), 794–803 (2009)
10. Jin, X., Luo, J., Yu, J., Wang, G., Joshi, D., Han, J.: Reinforced similarity integration in image-rich information networks. IEEE Trans. Knowl. Data Eng. **25**(2), 448–460 (2013)
11. Palmieri, F.: Bayesian resource discovery in infrastructure-less networks. Inf. Sci. **376**, 95–109 (2017)
12. Palmieri, F.: Scalable service discovery in ubiquitous and pervasive computing architectures: A percolation-driven approach. Future Gener. Comput. Syst. **29**(3), 693–703 (2013)
13. Zhu, Z., Su, J., Kong, L.: Measuring influence in online social network based on the user-content bipartite graph. Comput. Hum. Behav. **52**, 184–189 (2015)

14. Gao, J., et al.: A graph-based consensus maximization approach for combining multiple supervised and unsupervised models. IEEE Trans. Knowl. Data Eng. **25**(1), 15–28 (2013)

15. Qi, G.-J., Aggarwal, C.C., Huang, T.S.: On clustering heterogeneous social media objects with outlier links. In: Proceedings of the Fifth ACM International Conference on Web Search and Data Mining, pp. pp. 553–562. ACM (2012)

16. Chen, B., Wang, J., Huang, Q., Mei, T.: Personalized video recommendation through tripartite graph propagation. In: Proceedings of the 20th ACM International Conference on Multimedia, pp. pp. 1133–1136. ACM (2012)

17. Carullo, G., Castiglione, A., De Santis, A., Palmieri, F.: A triadic closure and homophily-based recommendation system for online social networks. World Wide Web **18**(6), 1579–1601 (2015)

18. Castiglione, A., Cattaneo, G., De Santis, A.: A forensic analysis of images on online social networks. In: 2011 Third International Conference on Intelligent Networking and Collaborative Systems, pp. 679–684, November 2011

19. Castiglione, A., D'Alessio, B., De Santis, A.: Steganography and secure communication on online social networks and online photo sharing. In: 2011 International Conference on Broadband and Wireless Computing, Communication and Applications, pp. 363–368, October 2011

20. Bu, J., Tan, S., Chen, C., Wang, C., Wu, H., Zhang, L., He, X.: Music recommendation by unified hypergraph: Combining social media information and music content. In: Proceedings of the International Conference on Multimedia, pp. 391–400. ACM (2010)

21. Anandkumar, A., Sedghi, H.: Learning mixed membership community models in social tagging networks through tensor methods (2015). arXiv preprint arXiv:1503.04567

22. Colace, F., De Santo, M., Greco, L., Moscato, V., Picariello, A.: A collaborative user-centered framework for recommending items in online social networks. Comput. Hum. Behav. **51**, 694–704 (2015)

23. Domingos, P., Richardson, M.: Mining the network value of customers. In: Proceedings of the Seventh ACM SIGKDD International Conference on Knowledge Discovery and Data Mining, pp. 57–66. ACM (2001)

24. Kempe, D., Kleinberg, J., Tardos, É.: Maximizing the spread of influence through a social network. In: Proceedings of the Ninth ACM SIGKDD International Conference on Knowledge Discovery and Data Mining, pp. 137–146. ACM (2003)

25. Granovetter, M.: Threshold models of collective behavior. Am. J. Sociol. **83**(6), 420–1443 (1978)

26. Goldenberg, J., Libai, B., Muller, E.: Talk of the network: A complex systems look at the underlying process of word-of-mouth. Mark. Lett. **12**(3), 211–223 (2001)

27. Liu, L., Tang, J., Han, J., Jiang, M., Yang, S.: Mining topic-level influence in heterogeneous networks. In: Proceedings of the 19th ACM International Conference on Information and Knowledge Management, pp. 199–208. ACM (2010)

28. Kempe, D., Kleinberg, J.M., Tardos, É.: Maximizing the spread of influence through a social network. Theory Comput. **11**(4), 105–147 (2015)

29. Amato, F., Moscato, V., Picariello, A., Sperlí, G.: Multimedia social network modeling: A proposal. In: 2016 IEEE Tenth International Conference on Semantic Computing (ICSC), pp. 448–453. IEEE (2016)

30. Fang, Q., Sang, J., Xu, C., Rui, Y.: Topic-sensitive influencer mining in interest-based social media networks via hypergraph learning. IEEE Trans. Multimedia **16**(3), 796–812 (2014)

31. Colace, F., De Santo, M., Greco, L., Amato, F., Moscato, V., Picariello, A.: Terminological ontology learning and population using latent dirichlet allocation. J. Vis. Lang. Comput. **25**(6), 818–826 (2014)
32. Amato, F., Barbareschi, M., Casola, V., Mazzeo, A.: An FPGA-based smart classifier for decision support systems. In: Zavoral, F., Jung, J.J., Badica, C. (eds.) Intelligent Distributed Computing VII. Studies in Computational Intelligence, vol. 511, pp. 289–299. Springer, Heidelberg (2014)
33. Colace, F., De Santo, M., Greco, L.: A probabilistic approach to tweets' sentiment classification. In: 2013 Humaine Association Conference on Affective Computing and Intelligent Interaction (ACII), pp. 37–42. IEEE (2013)
34. Heintz, B., Chandra, A.: Beyond graphs: Toward scalable hypergraph analysis systems. ACM SIGMETRICS Perform. Eval. Rev. **41**(4), 94–97 (2014)
35. Zhou, D., Huang, J., Schölkopf, B.: Learning with hypergraphs: Clustering, classification, and embedding. In: NIPS, vol. 19, pp. 1633–1640 (2006)
36. Tang, Y., et al.: Influence maximization: Near-optimal time complexity meets practical efficiency. In: SIGMOD 2014 Proceedings of 2014 ACM International Conference on Management of Data, pp. 75–86. ACM, New York (2014)
37. Tang, Y., Shi, Y., Xiao, X.: Influence maximization in near-linear time: A martingale approach. In: Proceedings of the 2015 ACM SIGMOD International Conference on Management of Data, SIGMOD 2015, pp. 1539–1554. ACM, New York (2015)
38. Williams, D.: Probability with Martingales. Cambridge University Press, Cambridge (1991)
39. Miller, G.A.: Wordnet: A lexical database for english. Commun. ACM **38**(11), 39–41 (1995)
40. Boccignone, G., Chianese, A., Moscato, V., Picariello, A.: Context-sensitive queries for image retrieval in digital libraries. J. Intell. Inf. Syst. **31**(1), 53–84 (2008)

A Modified Segmentation Approach for Overlapping Elliptical Objects with Various Sizes

Guanghui Zhao[1], Xingyan Zi[1], Kaitai Liang[2], Panyi Yun[1],
and Junwei Zhou[1(✉)]

[1] Computer Science and Technology, Wuhan University of Technology,
Wuhan, People's Republic of China
junweizhou@msn.com
[2] School of Computing, Mathematics and Digital Technology,
Manchester Metropolitan University, Manchester, UK

Abstract. Segmentation of elliptical objects has many real-world applications including morphology analysis on biological cell, material particles and other objects which need quantitative analysis according to size and shape. However, overlapping and varying in size may make the objects segmentation extremely challenging. In this paper, a modified segmentation approach for overlapping objects with different sizes is proposed. Specifically, we extract all the concave points for each connected region from the object's silhouette. We next fit all of the circles by two adjacent concave points and an arbitrary point which is on the edge right between the two concave points. A radius set is extracted from all the circles, and a segments set is determined by the edge fragments between all the two adjacent concave points. Based on the radius set and the segments set, we can determine if there is a large gap in the radius set and the length of segments corresponding to the radius. The edge segments and radius set are divided into two subsets, while the appropriate radius range and threshold are selected respectively from the two subsets to execute the Bounded Erosion-Fast Radial Symmetry transform to get the seed point for each object. Our experiments are taken under synthetic and real datasets, in which the overlapping objects in these datasets are with different size. The experimental outcomes show that the proposed approach outperforms other existing schemes.

Keywords: Segmentation · Bounded erosion-fast radial symmetry transform · Overlapping elliptical objects · Convex objects

1 Introduction

Elliptical object segmentation has many real-world applications including morphology analysis on biological cell, material particles and other objects which need quantitative analysis according to size and shape [1–3]. In material analysis, the functional behavior of particles is tightly linked to the surface morphology

© Springer International Publishing AG 2017
M.H.A. Au et al. (Eds.): GPC 2017, LNCS 10232, pp. 222–236, 2017.
DOI: 10.1007/978-3-319-57186-7_18

of the particles. Accurate particles segmentation and estimating silhouette are significant for characterizing the particle's behaviors [4–6]. The current state-of-art approach for segmentation is divided into watershed transform, graph-cut, active contours and other sophisticated morphological segmentation, such as a modified Ultimate Erosion for Convex Sets (UECS) [3] and Bounded Erosion-Fast Radial Symmetry (BE-FRS) [7].

The watershed transformation is a very useful segmentation for digital image. However, when the pixels with similar gray value, this method is over-segmented. In order to tackle the problem of over-segmentation, many improvements have been proposed in the literature, such as predicting the end boundary of the segmentation by using Radial Bases Function [8], combining color deconvolution with gradient vector flow [9] and initiating with H-minima [10]. Graph-cut is a commonly used approach that can also be applied for segmenting overlapping objects [11]. It takes two phases. In the first one, a set of initial region pixels and background are specified by interactive graph-cut model. Later, the final segmentation is executed based on Bayes theorem, which combines the prior information with data. Active contour can be used to segment overlapping objects within a changed framework. An adaptive contour model [12] has been proposed to segment nucleus. Its basic idea is to make contour adaptive deformation to obtain the minimized given region energy function. To segment cells, the local competitive active contour model is used to get contours of each cell [13].

For morphological segmentation methods, UECS [3] with an earlier stopping criterion has been used to get marker for each object. It can be used to split all shapes of particles as well as processing information automatically. But if the degree of overlapping is high, the segment result may suffer from under-segmentation. The BE-FRS [7] is recently proposed to segment overlapping objects with elliptical shape. The first step of this method is to mark each object using the seed points extracted by FRS, where the FRS is every edge pixel in the image giving a vote for the plausible radial symmetry at some specific distance from that point. This step relies on two parameters R and T, $R = [R_{min}, R_{max}]$ which represents the range of the vote of each point, while T indicates the threshold for the distance between two adjacent seed points. The seed points are used to segment the edges of the image and determine which seed points each fragment of the edge belongs to. Finally, ellipse fitting is applied to each segmented edge. It has been well-known that BE-FRS has a high accuracy in overlapping particles segmentation. However, this method is only applicable to the case where the particles are with similar size and the radius of particles is already known. If the overlapping particles varies in size, the method will fail to segment overlapping particles. As shown in Fig. 1, (a) is overlapping particles with different sizes, (b) and (c) are segmentation results using BE-FRS with appropriate parameters R and T. From (b), it can be seen that if a small radius range and threshold are preset, the biggest object is over-segmented to three small objects. Take another example in (c), if a larger radius range and threshold are preset, the small overlapping objects cannot be segmented.

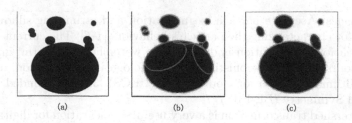

(a)   (b)   (c)

Fig. 1. Performed by BE-FRS: (a) Original image; (b) Result of the parameters $R = [5 : 6]$ and $T = 16$; (c) Result of the parameters $R = [20 : 30]$ and $T = 20$.

In this paper, to support segmenting overlapping objects with various sizes, we locally perform BE-FRS on overlapping objects with similar size. Figure 2 illustrates the framework of the proposed method, which has four sequential steps: concave point extraction, circle fitting, edge segmentation and BE-FRS. The input image is firstly converted to binary image, which can distinguish the foreground from the background and normalize the pixel value for the BE-FRS. The binarization of the image is obtained by background suppression based on the Otsu's method. Then connected regions are extracted from the binary image cyclically, thus all the concave points on the outer edge can be obtained. If there is no concave points, meaning that the connect region is a individual object with non-overlapping, and the object is fitted by applying the numerically stable direct ellipse fitting. If there exists one concave point, there are overlapping objects. Since the objects we deal with are convex, we can separate the edge points into two sets according to the concave point, and apply the direct ellipse fitting separately. If two or more concave points are extracted, we select two adjacent concave points and a point on the contour between them, and fit a circle based on these three points and calculate the radius. After all adjacent concave points are proceeded, a set of radii α and a set of contour fragments β can be obtained. We set the thresholds r_{t1} for radius and c_t for length of contour to determine if there are objects with large differences in size in this connected region, and we also set a threshold r_{t2} for segmenting the contours. If there are objects with large differences in size, we segment the contour of overlapping objects into two parts, the BE-FRS is employed to each part to mark each individual object. Otherwise, we execute BE-FRS on the whole contour with parameters R and T from radius set α. In this way, when there is a large difference in the size of the objects in a connected region, we divide the connected region into two parts to execute BE-FRS locally, and finally achieve the purpose of segmenting the objects.

This paper organized as follows: Related Work is reviewed in Sec. 2. Section 3 introduces the modified scheme in details. The method is applied to synthetic and real datasets compared with other methods in Sec. 4. And the conclusions are drawn in Sec. 5.

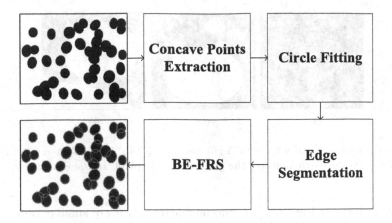

Fig. 2. The framework of the proposed method

2   Related Work

The BE-FRS [7] uses three sequential steps: seed point extraction, contour evidence extraction and contour estimation to segment overlapping objects. It applies a hybrid model consisting of morphological erosion and the FRS in a silhouette image to obtain the seed points of each object, while each seed point is used to mark an individual object. In particular, it makes each edge point vote in the gradient direction according to the current distance $d \in R$. The center of gravity of each vote region is taken as its seed point, which is used to mark each object in the image. The main idea of the contour evidence extraction is determining edge pixel belongs to which seed point. To separate overlapping objects, contour estimation is performed using numerically stable direct ellipse fitting based on the edge segments obtained from the contour evidence.

As shown in Fig. 1, when overlapping objects have various sizes, BE-FRS suffers from over-segmentation if small radius and threshold are selected. On the contrary, it suffers from under-segmentation while large radius and threshold are set. Since each edge point in FRS transform gives a vote at some specific distance, if there are small overlapping objects in the image, we may reset the parameters R and T according to the radius of the smallest object. When we set $R = [5 : 6]$, the vote result is shown in Fig. 3(a). According to the BE-FRS, we can extract the center of gravity of each vote region which is taken as the seed point. As shown in Fig. 3(a), we can find that there are 16 connected regions, so that we can get 16 seed points. Since the parameter T is used to merge over-detective seed points, we only need extract 11 seed points, and three of them are false results as shown in Fig. 3(b). The next step is to segment the edge according to the seed points. Since the result of seed points is not precise, it may cause the flaw in following steps as shown in Fig. 1(b). The reason of the false output is that the filtering does not remove the useless results. Since the pixels in the overlap area will be in a ladder-like arrangement, and the direction of the

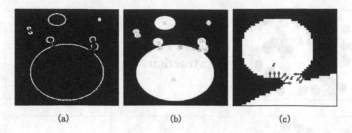

      (a)   (b)   (c)

Fig. 3. The result of FRS with $R = [5:6]$ and $T = 16$: (a) The result of vote; (b) the result of seed point extraction; (c) the gradient of the pixels in the enlarged view.

gradient as shown in Fig. 3(c), it means no matter how big or small parameters we choose, there always exists false connected regions. In the BE-FRS, the method of eliminating the false connected regions is filtering, and it uses the Gaussian convolution which is defined according to the current $d \in R$. The false results mean that the convolution cannot filter the false connected regions, however if we set Gaussian kernel regardless the d, it might affects the true vote result. From the result in Fig. 3(b), we need a bigger R to filter the false result. But if we set a bigger parameters R and T to get the correct result in the big object, however we cannot segment the small overlapping objects correctly as shown in Fig. 1(c). Therefore, no matter how we select the parameters, we still cannot separate the overlapping objects correctly.

A method named Concave-point Extraction and Contour Segmentation (CECS) [2], which uses concave point to segment the overlapping elliptical bubble, has been proposed recently. The process of recognizing overlapping elliptical bubbles can be divided into three steps: image pre-processing, contour segmentation and segment grouping. Firstly, it converts the image into the binary image, and next extracts the contour and smooths the contour. Secondly, it detects the dominant points on the smoothed contour by polygonal approximation method, and segments the contour through the concave points in the dominant point sequence. Finally, it groups the candidate segments according to average distance deviation criterion and two constraint conditions. The constraint conditions are grouping the nearest segment in one direction and grouping the segments whose total angle is no smaller than 90°. The process of segment grouping can determine which segments belong to a same object. This method has been improved in [14] and been applied in the overlapping nano-particles segmentation. The improved method modifies the stage of contour segmentation by adopting modified Curvature Scale Space (CSS) method to detect the corner points on the edge, and selects the concave points from the corner points to segment the contour.

3   Our Proposed Method

To segment overlapping objects with various sizes, a modified scheme is proposed in this paper. In this modified version, concave points are used to determine the radii of overlapping objects in the sense that the objects with similar size can be processed locally with BE-FRS. Our method can be divided into four steps: concave point extraction, circle fitting, edge segmentation and BE-FRS.

3.1   Concave Point Extraction

After obtaining the binary image of input image, each independent connected region and the image edge can be obtained by using canny edge detector, all the concave points on the edge can be extracted. In some case, since the overlapping region may cause background to be presented inside the connected region, and it can create holes in the binary image. The edges of such voids will have an effect on the concave point extraction as well as the circle fitting result. These inner edges need to be eliminated. The original image and the binary image without hole are shown in Fig. 4(a) and Fig. 4(b) respectively. However, the FRS marks each object by making each edge point vote in the gradient direction, which means the inner edges are essential in FRS. The binary image with hole as shown in Fig. 4(c).

We use the modified CSS method based on curvature analysis [15] to detect all the corner points of this connected region. The corner points are defined as the maximum curvature points on the edge. The original CSS only uses one scale to detect the corner points, and make use of a global threshold to filter the detected points, which results in wrong corners. The modified CSS retains all true corners at a relatively low scale, and the curvature of corner candidates are compared with an adaptive local threshold to remove the rounded corners. Among the candidates for the corners, although some points are numerically

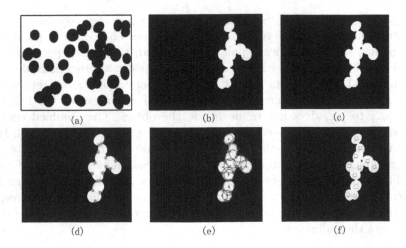

Fig. 4. The output of our scheme's four steps: (a) The original image; (b) the binary image of a connected region with no hole; (c) the binary image of a connected region with hole; (d) the result of concave point extraction; (e) the result of circle fitting; (f) the result of seed point extraction.

detected as local maximum, the difference between adjacent points in the region of support (ROS) is usually very small, such as rounded corners. In this case, the rounded corners can be removed by using the adaptive local curvature threshold. In principle, the adaptive local threshold for a candidate is determined according to its neighborhood region's curvature. The candidate corner whose absolute curvature is under its local threshold is eliminated. The adaptive local threshold in Eq. (1).

$$T(p) = C * \bar{k} = 1.5 * \frac{1}{R_1 + R_2 + 1} \sum_{i=p-R_2}^{p+R_1} k(i) \tag{1}$$

where the value $\bar{k}$ represents the curvature of a neighborhood region, p is the position of corner candidate in the curve, R_1 and R_2 are the sizes of the ROS, and C is a coefficient. In this case, the ROS is defined as from one of the neighboring local curvature minimal to the next, where the curvature is strictly decreasing from the candidate point to both ends. If the adaptive local threshold is used, a proper ROS also is needed to calculate the curvature. To a corner candidate, the ROS is determined by its two adjacent corner candidates, and the corner checking is given by $\angle C_i$, where $\angle C_i$ is given by

$$\angle C_i = |tan^{-1}(\Delta y_1 / \Delta x_1) - tan^{-1}(\Delta y_2 / \Delta x_2)|$$

$$\Delta x_1 = \frac{1}{R_1} \sum_{i=p+1}^{p+R_1} x(i) - x(p); \Delta y_1 = \frac{1}{R_1} \sum_{i=p+1}^{p+R_1} y(i) - y(p)$$

$$\Delta x_2 = \frac{1}{R_2} \sum_{i=p-R_2}^{p-1} x(i) - x(p); \Delta y_2 = \frac{1}{R_2} \sum_{i=p-R_2}^{p-1} y(i) - y(p) \tag{2}$$

if $162° \leq \angle C_i \leq 198°$, the C_i is a false corner, else C_i is a true corner.

Because the result of the corner detector includes both concave points and convex points, and only concave points are needed, the convex points can be removed by subsequent processing. We use p_i to represent a corner point detected by the modified CSS, and its two lth adjacent contour points are represented by p_{i-l} and p_{i+l}. The corner point p_i is qualified as concave if the line connecting p_{i-l} to p_{i+l} does not reside inside the object. The obtained concave points are used to split the contour into contour segments as in Fig. 4(d). If there is no concave point in the edge, it means that this connected region is a non-overlapping individual object, so that we can use numerically stable direct ellipse fitting directly. If there is one concave point, we segment the edge into two parts according to the concave point, and use the edge fitting ellipse respectively. But if there are two or more concave points on the edge, we use the circle fitting to get the radius set.

3.2   Circle Fitting

In this stage, the radius set is produced by the circle fitting to roughly determine the parameters including R and T. Based on a fact that three points (being not on the same line) can determine a circle, two adjacent concave points (x_1, y_1), (x_2, y_2) and a point (x_3, y_3) on the contour between these two concave points are used to fit a circle. The center of the circle (x_0, y_0) is determined by Eq. (3).

$$x_0 = -\frac{de - bf}{bc - ad}; y_0 = -\frac{af - ce}{bc - ad}$$

$$a = x_1 - x_2; b = y_1 - y_2$$

$$c = x_3 - x_2; d = y_3 - y_2 \tag{3}$$

$$e = \frac{(x_1^2 - x_2^2) - (y_2^2 - y_1^2)}{2}; f = \frac{(x_3^2 - x_2^2) - (y_2^2 - y_3^2)}{2}$$

The radius can be calculated through the Euclidean distance between (x_0, y_0) and (x_1, y_1).

After fitting all the circles, a radius set $\alpha = \{r_1, r_2, ..., r_n\}$ can be obtained. We can also get a set of contour that holds segments between two concave points, $\beta = \{c_1, c_2, ..., c_n\}$, which $c_i = \{p_1, p_2, ..., p_m\}$, $p_j \in c_i$ represents a point on the contour c_i. The result of circle fitting is shown in Figs. 4(e) and 5(a).

3.3   Edge Segmentation

In the BE-FRS, we cannot find proper R and T to segment overlapping objects if objects vary in size. Here, we set threshold r_{t1} to determine if a connected region incurs the same phenomenon. Since some concave points may be missing, we need another threshold c_t to increase robustness. We find the minimum radius $r_{min} \in \alpha$ and the corresponding segment $c_{r_{min}} \in \beta$. If there is a radius $r_i \in \alpha$ and its corresponding segment $c_i \in \beta$ that hold in Eq. (4).

$$\frac{r_i}{r_{min}} > r_{t1}; \frac{length(c_i)}{length(c_{r_{min}})} > c_t \tag{4}$$

We consider that there are overlapping objects with large size gaps in the image. Another threshold r_{t2} is set to segment α into two subsets α_b and α_m according to if the radius $r_i \in \alpha$ is greater than r_{t2}. And the set of β is also divided into β_b and β_m corresponding to α_b and α_m. The result of contour segmentation is shown in Fig. 5(b) and (c), and the parameters R and T are selected from α_b and α_m, respectively, and execute BE-FRS on the segment set of β_b and β_m. Figure 5(d) indicates the result of seed point on the small segment set β_m, and Fig. 5(e) shows the segment result on the big segment set β_b. The segment result is shown in Fig. 5(f). If all the radius $r_i \in \alpha$ and the corresponding segment c_i don't satisfy the Eq. (4), which means the overlapping objects are similar in size. The parameters R and T are determined according to the minimum radius in the set of α automatically for BE-FRS. The result of seed point extraction for the connected region is shown in Fig. 4(f).

3.4   BE-FRS

The BE-FRS consists of three stages: seed point extraction, contour evidence extraction and contour estimation. For the seed point extraction, the main idea

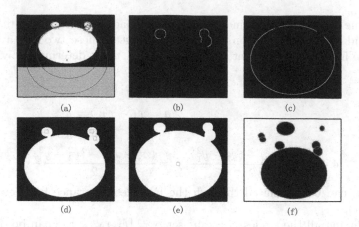

Fig. 5. The process of edge segmentation and BE-FRS: (a) The result of circle fitting; (b) the subset of contour for small objects; (c) the subset of contour for big objects; (d) BE-FRS on small objects; (e) BE-FRS on big objects; (f) the result of segmentation.

is that every edge point of the image space gives a vote for the plausible radial symmetry at some specific distance from that point. Given the distance value $d \in R$, for every piexl (x, y) of the gradient image g, FRS determines the positively-affected p_{+g} and negatively-affected p_{-g} pixels, and sequentially constructs the orientation projection image O_d and the magnitude projection image M_d as follows:

$$p_{+g}(x, y) = (x, y) + round(\frac{g(x, y)}{||g(x, y)||} * d)$$

$$p_{-g}(x, y) = (x, y) - round(\frac{g(x, y)}{||g(x, y)||} * d) \tag{5}$$

$$O_d(p_{+g}(x, y)) = O_d(p_{+g}(x, y)) + 1$$

$$O_d(p_{-g}(x, y)) = O_d(p_{-g}(x, y)) - 1 \tag{6}$$

$$M_d(p_{+g}(x, y)) = M_d(p_{+g}(x, y)) + ||g(x, y)||$$

$$M_d(p_{-g}(x, y)) = M_d(p_{-g}(x, y)) - ||g(x, y)|| \tag{7}$$

Upon constructing the orientation and magnitude images, the radial symmetry contribution S_d for the radius $d \in R$ is calculated by the convolution of F_d with a 2D Gaussian A_d:

$$S_d = F_d * A_d \tag{8}$$

where F_d is formulated as

$$F_d(x, y) = \frac{M_d(x, y)}{k_m} (\frac{|O_d(x, y)|}{k_m})^\alpha \tag{9}$$

α and k_m are the radial strictness and the scaling factor that normalizes M_d and O_d across different radii respectively. The full FRS transform S by which the interest symmetric regions are defined is given by the average of the symmetry contributions over all the radii $d \in R$ considered:

$$S = \frac{1}{|N|} \sum_{d \in R} S_d \qquad (10)$$

The contour evidence is constructed by an edge-to-seed point association method [3]. Specifically, the contour evidence consists of the Euclidean distance between the seed points and edge points, combined with the cosine distance between the gradient and seed-to-edge vectors. After the process of seed point extraction, a set of seed points $S = \{s_1, s_2, ..., s_n\}$ can be obtained. For each edge pixel point e_k in $E = \{e_1, e_2, ..., e_m\}$, if all the pixel points on the line connecting the edge point to the seed point $l(e_k, s_j)$ reside in the image foreground, the Euclidean distance $dist(e_k, s_j)$ and divergence functions $div(e_k, s_j)$ can be calculated. The relevance metric $rel(e_k, s_j)$ is defined as

$$rel(e_k, s_j) = \frac{1 - \lambda}{1 + dist(e_k, s_j)} + \lambda \frac{div(e_k, s_j)}{2} \qquad (11)$$

If the edge point e_k belongs to the seed point s_j, the value of $dist(e_k, s_j)$ is small while the one of $div(e_k, s_j)$ is large. After all the edge points are processed and location of seed point is found, contour estimation is performed to separate overlapping objects by using numerically stable direct ellipse fitting on the contour evidence.

4   Result Analysis

The experiments are implemented in two synthetically generated datasets and two real datasets. The performance of our method is compared with three existing methods including BE-FRS [7], UECS [3] and CECS [2].

Here, we use True Positive Rate (TPR) and Positive Predictive Value (PPV) to measure the performance, where TPR and PPV are defined by following equations:

$$TPR = \frac{TP}{TP + FN}; PPV = \frac{TP}{TP + FP} \qquad (12)$$

True Positive (TP) denotes the number of correctly detected segmented objects, and False Positive (FP) represents the number of incorrectly detected segmentation result, and False Negative (FN) is the number of missed objects.

We use Jaccard Similarity coefficient (JSC) [16] to decide if the segmentation result is correct. Given a binary map of the segmented object M_s and the ground true particle M_g, JSC can be calculated by

$$JSC = \frac{M_s \cap M_g}{M_s \cup M_g} \qquad (13)$$

We use the average JSC (AJSC) in the datasets to measure the segmentation performance.

As shown in Fig. 4(a), the synthetic dataset I is collected from [7], which consists of images with overlapping ellipse-shape objects that are uniformly randomly scaled, rotated, and translated. The dataset are with 150 sample images which can be divided into three classes based on overlapping degree. The maximum overlapping rates of three classes are 40%, 50% and 60%, respectively. Each class contains 50 images with 40 objects and the size of image is 300×400 pixels. The performance of segmentation is shown in Table 1.

The dataset II is synthetic, which has 40 sample images with overlapping ellipse-shape objects varying in size. The size of each image is 466×443 pixels. The segment performance on the dataset II is shown in Table 2, and the examples of typical segmentation results are presented in Fig. 6.

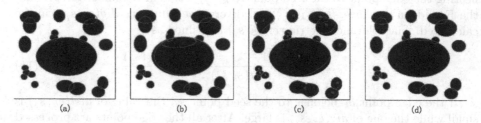

| (a) | (b) | (c) | (d) |

Fig. 6. Examples of segmentation result on the synthetic dataset II: (a) Proposed method; (b) BE-FRS; (c) UECS; (d) CECS.

From Table 1, we can find that our method enjoys the best segmentation performance in the first two subsets. This is because the proposed method selects a more accurate local parameters to execute the BE-FRS for extracting seed points. But for the subset whose overlapping rate is 60%, the performance of the BE-FRS is better than ours. The reason behind that is that the higher overlapping rate is, more true concave points are missing, indicating more mistakes in the result of radius set and segments set will be appeared. Note the parameters of the BE-FRS are selected manually, it will be more robust for segmentation.

Our method outperforms others in each metric of Table 2. We note that the performance of the CECS with an higher accuracy than the BE-FRS, which contradicts to the result shown in Table 1. This is because the overlapping objects in the first synthetic dataset are similar in size, the BE-FRS has a higher accuracy to segment the overlapping objects. However, the CECS suffers from undersegmentation due to the missing concave points. In the synthetic dataset II, since the overlapping objects varies in size, it is difficult for the BE-FRS to segment correctly. But for the CECS, although missing concave points, its result is still better than that of the BE-FRS.

The real dataset I consists of 3 nano-particles images captured by transmission electron microscopy. One of them is golden nano-particles [17] with size is 3340×3000 pixels, and 63 particles are marked manually by an expert. Other images are nickel nano-particles [18] with 1052×1052, and around 85 particles are marked manually in each image. The performance of segmentation is shown

Table 1. Comparison of the performance of the proposed method with existing schemes on the synthetic dataset I

Methods	Overlapping rate (%)	TPR (%)	PPV (%)	AJSC (%)
Ours		94.5	97	91.9
BE-FRS	40%	93	95	89
UECS		68	80	60
CECS		89	91	83
Ours		90.4	94.3	85.6
BE-FRS	50%	88	92	83
UECS		61	76	53
CECS		82	87	73
Ours		83.5	90.8	76.3
BE-FRS	60%	87	91	80
UECS		53	71	44
CECS		75	83	65

Table 2. Comparison of the performance of the proposed method with existing schemes on the synthetic dataset II

Methods	Total number	TPR (%)	PPV (%)	AJSC (%)	Accuracy (%)
Ours		90.7	92.3	84.3	96.2
BE-FRS	687	80.7	82	68.6	79.2
UECS		58.6	70.7	47.1	41.5
CECS		81.3	80.6	68.1	82.4

in Table 3, and the examples of typical segmentation results are presented in Fig. 7.

From the Table 3 we can notice that the result of the proposed method is better than other three methods in total true detection. An example of segmentation on the first real dataset is presented in Fig. 7, and we can find that BE-FRS suffers from over-segmentation, and it also misses some small nano-particles. We can see that UECS suffers from under-segmentation as shown in Fig. 7(c), and some fitting results are false. Since the false result of concave points extraction, the result of CECS as shown in Fig. 7(d).

Table 4 presents the results for the second real dataset (nano-particles dataset) from [3] updated with the proposed method. The dataset includes 9 micrograph images of nano-particles divided into two classes, medium and high degree of overlap. The other method as BE-FRS, UECS, watershed segmentation with h-dome transform (WHD) [19], marker-controlled watershed with h-maxima transform (WHM) [20], normalized-cut (N-Cut) [21], multiphase active contour (MPAC) [22], sliding band filter (SBF) [23], morphological multi scale method (MSD) [24], and iterative voting method (IVM) [25]. The performance

Table 3. Comparison of the performance of the proposed method with existing schemes on the nano-particles dataset I

Samples	Ground truth	Ours	BE-FRS	UECS	CECS
Sample1	63	54	40	47	49
Sample2	84	64	60	57	58
Sample3	90	65	67	58	68
Total	237	183	167	162	175

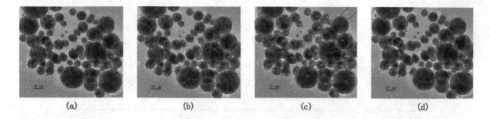

(a)   (b)   (c)   (d)

Fig. 7. The segment result on real dataset I: (a) Our proposed method; (b) BE-FRS; (c) UECS; (d) CECS.

Table 4. Comparison of the performance of the proposed method with existing schemes on the nano-particles dataset II

Sample	Degree of overlap	Total # of particles	Ours method	BE-FRS	UECS	N-Cut	MPAC	SBF	IVM	MSD	WHM	WHD
Sample1	Medium	28	28	28	26	6	2	28	25	20	20	20
Sample2	Medium	52	50	46	48	29	22	43	45	48	45	39
Sample3	Medium	459	419	425	437	298	147	262	227	429	424	421
Sample4	Medium	19	18	18	17	10	8	6	16	16	15	6
Sample5	Medium	108	104	104	103	56	44	99	85	92	82	70
Sample6	Medium	29	29	25	25	12	13	19	21	23	18	14
Sample7	High	63	56	52	54	31	12	42	42	40	38	61
Sample8	High	44	35	37	34	23	11	28	27	28	28	28
Sample9	High	45	30	33	33	20	6	25	24	22	19	20
AVG [%]			90	88	87	48	29	68	71	75	70	60

is quantified by the total number of correctly identified objects. From the result we can learn that the proposed method achieves the highest segmentation rate in six images, second-highest rate in two images, and the average rate of correct detecting is 90%.

5   Conclusion

This paper introduced a modified method to select local radius R and threshold T for Bounded Erosion-Fast Radial Symmetry (BE-FRS) transform automatically.

The main idea of our method is to automatically select local parameters for overlapping objects of similar size and perform BE-FRS. The method includes four stages, namely concave point extraction, circle fitting, edge segmentation and BE-FRS. If there are overlapping objects with large range of size, we segment the edge and radius set obtained from circle fitting to execute FRS respectively. Otherwise, we use FRS on all of the edge points. The experimental results showed that our method outperformed the original BE-FRS and other methods in the test bed. It would be interesting to employ our method to deal with more complex convex objects.

Acknowledgement. The work described in this paper was supported in part by the National Natural Science Foundation of China [grant number 61601337], by the Fundamental Research Funds for the Central Universities (Grant No. WUT: 2017IVB025) and by Key Project of Nature Science Foundation of Hubei Province [grant number ZRZ2015000393].

References

1. Kothari, S., Chaudry, Q., Wang, M.D.: Automated cell counting and cluster segmentation using concavity detection and ellipse fitting techniques. In: 2009 IEEE International Symposium on Biomedical Imaging: From Nano to Macro, pp. 795–798 (2009)
2. Zhang, W.-H., Jiang, X., Liu, Y.-M.: A method for recognizing overlapping elliptical bubbles in bubble image. Pattern Recogn. Lett. **33**(12), 1543–1548 (2012)
3. Park, C., Huang, J.Z., Ji, J.X., Ding, Y.: Segmentation, inference and classification of partially overlapping nanoparticles. IEEE Trans. Pattern Anal. Mach. Intell. **35**(3), 669–681 (2013)
4. Nehl, C.L., Liao, H., Hafner, J.H.: Optical properties of star-shaped gold nanoparticles. Nano Lett. **6**(4), 683–688 (2006)
5. Wang, Z.L., Petroski, J.M., Green, T.C., El-Sayed, M.A.: Shape transformation and surface melting of cubic and tetrahedral platinum nanocrystals. J. Phys. Chem. B **102**(32), 6145–6151 (1998)
6. Pan, Y., Neuss, S., Leifert, A., Fischler, M., Wen, F., Simon, U., Schmid, G., Brandau, W., Jahnen-Dechent, W.: Size-dependent cytotoxicity of gold nanoparticles. Small **3**(11), 1941–1949 (2007)
7. Zafari, S., Eerola, T., Sampo, J., Kälviäinen, H., Haario, H.: Segmentation of overlapping elliptical objects in silhouette images. IEEE Trans. Image Process. **24**(12), 5942–5952 (2015)
8. Husain, R.A., Zayed, A.S., Ahmed, W.M., Elhaji, H.S.: Image segmentation with improved watershed algorithm using radial bases function neural networks. In: 2015 16th International Conference on Sciences and Techniques of Automatic Control and Computer Engineering, pp. 121–126 (2015)
9. Wdowiak, M., Slodkowska, J., Markiewicz, T.: Cell segmentation in desmoglein-3 stained specimen microscopic images using GVF and watershed algorithm. In: 2016 17th International Conference Computational Problems of Electrical Engineering, pp. 1–3 (2016)
10. Shen, P., Qin, W., Yang, J., Hu, W., Chen, S., Li, L., Wen, T., Gu, J.: Segmenting multiple overlapping nuclei in histopathology images based on an improved watershed. In: 2015 IET International Conference on Biomedical Image and Signal Processing, pp. 1–4 (2015)

11. Browet, A., De Vleeschouwer, C., Jacques, L., Mathiah, N., Saykali, B., Migeotte, I.: Cell segmentation with random ferns and graph-cuts. In: 2016 IEEE International Conference on Image Processing, pp. 4145–4149 (2016)
12. Zhang, L., Kong, H., Chin, C.T., Liu, S., Wang, T., Chen, S.: Automated segmentation of abnormal cervical cells using global and local graph cuts. In: 2014 IEEE 11th International Symposium on Biomedical Imaging (ISBI), pp. 485–488 (2014)
13. Wu, P., Yi, J., Zhao, G., Huang, Z., Qiu, B., Gao, D.: Active contour-based cell segmentation during freezing and its application in cryopreservation. IEEE Trans. Biomed. Eng. **62**(1), 284–295 (2015)
14. Zafari, S., Eerola, T., Sampo, J., Kälviäinen, H., Haario, H.: Segmentation of partially overlapping nanoparticles using concave points. In: Bebis, G., Boyle, R., Parvin, B., Koracin, D., Pavlidis, I., Feris, R., McGraw, T., Elendt, M., Kopper, R., Ragan, E., Ye, Z., Weber, G. (eds.) ISVC 2015. LNCS, vol. 9474, pp. 187–197. Springer, Cham (2015). doi:10.1007/978-3-319-27857-5_17
15. He, X.C., Yung, N.H.C.: Curvature scale space corner detector with adaptive threshold and dynamic region of support. In: Proceedings of the 17th International Conference on Pattern Recognition, vol. 2, pp. 791–794 (2004)
16. Loy, G., Zelinsky, A.: Fast radial symmetry for detecting points of interest. IEEE Trans. Pattern Anal. Mach. Intell. **25**(8), 959–973 (2003)
17. Andreev, S.: Russia - the leader of the scientific revolution. why whisper? https://regnum.ru/news/innovatio/2165960.html/
18. NANO-LAB. Nickel nanoparticles. http://www.nano-lab.com/nanoparticles.html/
19. Malpica, N., de Solorzano, C.O., Vaquero, J.J.: Applying watershed algorithms to the segmentation of clustered nuclei. Cytometry **28**(4), 289–297 (1997)
20. Bengtsson, E., Wahlby, C., Lindblad, J.: Robust cell image segmentation methods. Pattern Recogn. Image Anal. **14**(2), 157–167 (2004)
21. Shi, J., Malik, J.: Normalized cuts and image segmentation. IEEE Trans. Pattern Anal. Mach. Intell. **22**(8), 888–905 (2000)
22. Vese, L., Chan, T.: A multiphase level set framework for image segmentation using the mumford and shah model. Int. J. Comput. Vis. **50**(3), 271–293 (2002)
23. Pereira, C.S., Fernandes, H., Mendonça, A.M., Campilho, A.: Detection of lung nodule candidates in chest radiographs. In: Martí, J., Benedí, J.M., Mendonça, A.M., Serrat, J. (eds.) IbPRIA 2007. LNCS, vol. 4478, pp. 170–177. Springer, Heidelberg (2007). doi:10.1007/978-3-540-72849-8_22
24. Schmitt, O., Hasse, M.: Morphological multiscale decomposition of connected regions with emphasis on cell clusters. Comput. Vis. Image Underst. **113**(2), 188–201 (2009)
25. Parvin, B., Yang, Q., Han, J., Chang, H., Rydberg, B., Barcellos-Hoff, M.H.: Iterative voting for inference of structural saliency and characterization of subcellular events. IEEE Trans. Image Process. **16**(3), 615–623 (2007)

Privacy and Temporal Aware Allocation of Data in Decentralized Online Social Networks

Andrea De Salve[1,2]([envelope]), Barbara Guidi[2], Paolo Mori[1], Laura Ricci[2], and Vincenzo Ambriola[2]

[1] Istituto di Informatica e Telematica, Consiglio Nazionale delle Ricerche, Via G. Moruzzi, 1, Pisa, Italy
{andrea.desalve,paolo.mori}@iit.cnr.it
[2] Department of Computer Science, University of Pisa, Largo Bruno Pontecorvo, Pisa, Italy
{desalve,guidi,ricci,ambriola}@di.unipi.it

Abstract. Distributed Online Social Networks (DOSNs) have recently been proposed to grant users more control over the data they share with the other users. Indeed, in contrast to centralized Online Social Networks (such as Facebook), DOSNs are not based on centralized storage services, because the contents shared by the users are stored on the devices of the users themselves. One of the main challenges in a DOSN comes from guaranteeing availability of the users' contents when the data owner disconnects from the network. In this paper, we focus our attention on data availability by proposing a distributed allocation strategy which takes into account both the privacy policies defined on the contents and the availability patterns (online/offline) of the users in order to allocate their contents on trusted nodes. A linear predictor is used to model and to predict the availability status of the users in a future time interval, on the basis of their past temporal behaviour. We conduct a set of experiments on a set of traces taken from Facebook. The results prove the effectiveness of our approach by showing high availability of users' profiles.

Keywords: Decentralized Online Social Networks · Data availability · Data privacy · Availability prediction

1 Introduction

Online Social Networks (OSNs) [13] have become crucial for communication and contents sharing between users of the Internet. According to different statistics[1] the use of OSN platforms has spread at an impressive rate across the world and users generate a high-volume of valuable information. As a result, the presence of a such large amount of personal information about users has created new business models.

---

[1] International Telecommunication Union (ITU) - Measuring the Information Society Report 2016 http://www.itu.int/en/ITU-D/Statistics/Documents/publications/misr2016/MISR2016-w4.pdf.

© Springer International Publishing AG 2017
M.H.A. Au et al. (Eds.): GPC 2017, LNCS 10232, pp. 237–251, 2017.
DOI: 10.1007/978-3-319-57186-7_19

Nowadays, popular OSNs are mainly based on centralized architectures and information shared by the users on the platform may be exploited for targeting advertisements or for other purposes. Such centralized architectures of current OSNs have raised several problems related to both privacy risks and performance issues [14, 19, 27].

Distributed Online Social Networks (DOSNs) [8] have been proposed as an alternative to the centralized solutions to allow a major control of the users over their own contents. A DOSN is made up of a (dynamic) set of peers, such as a network of trusted servers, a P2P system or an opportunistic network, which collaborate with each other in order to provide the social services. Even though DOSNs solve the problem of control over user contents, the decentralization of the OSN introduces new security issues related to the availability of user contents and privacy of those contents with respect the other users of the DOSNs. In fact, DOSNs allow their users to create different types of contents (such as posts, images, comments, likes, etc.) and to organize them under relevant categories in their profiles. In order to support fine-grained access control, current DOSNs enable users to regulate the access to the contents shared in their profile by using privacy policies. Such policies are statements that specify the users authorized to access the contents in terms of a set of features, modeled by the attributes (such friendship, friendship type, etc.).

An important challenge of DOSNs is to guarantee the availability of such contents even when the user who published them is offline. Replication is the most widely used technique to ensure data availability and it consists of storing multiple copies of the same content on several devices available in the system. In DOSNs, the classical replication approach consists in selecting random peers, where the contents should be stored, from the users' devices available in the network. Other replication approaches set specific performance objectives for the selection of replica peers (such as online-online correlation between time spent online by users [22] and the average time spent online by users [6, 12]). However, confidentiality of contents must be protected in order to avoid disclosure of information to unauthorized users that store the contents. Indeed, it is possible that the device selected as a replica peer for a content belongs to a user who is not authorized to access it. As a result, the solution typically adopted by existing DOSNs [1, 5, 7] consists in encrypting the contents before being stored on user devices, in such a way that only the users who have the access right can access them. Although this kind of design ensures high data availability, it suffers from performance issues due to the overhead introduced by the encryption mechanisms [3, 9].

In this paper, we propose a strategy for a privacy aware allocation of the contents to the peers of the DOSN which improves the results presented in [12]. Our solution ensures high availability of contents by exploiting the availability patterns of the users to define the content allocation. In particular, the allocation strategy we propose enhances the availability of contents by replicating them on the peers which belong to the users authorized to access them. In addition, the strategy also evaluates the availability patterns of the related users in order to choose the devices where contents can be stored. For this purpose, we use a linear predictor which predicts the availability status of the users (i.e., online or offline) in a future time interval on the basis of their past behavior. Summarizing, the proposed allocation strategy can effectively improve the content availability because each content is replicated on the peers of users who are both *(i)* authorized to access it, and *(ii)* most likely to be online for a period of time in the future. We conducted a number of simulations based on the real behavior of users extracted from a Facebook dataset, and we demonstrated that our allocation strategy ensures a higher level of content availability compared to the classical approaches proposed by current DOSNs.

This paper is organized as follows. Section 2 reviews related work about privacy protection and data availability in DOSNs. Section 3 presents preliminary concepts on modeling OSNs contents. Section 4 discusses the general architecture of our system, while Sect. 5 introduces the new strategy we propose for replica management. Section 6 reports the experimental results. Finally, conclusions and future work are presented in Sect. 7.

2   Related Work

In this section, we provide an overview of current DOSN's approaches used to enforce privacy control over users' data. Current DOSNs use simple privacy policies by coupling distributed approaches with encryption techniques, mostly the Public Key Infrastructure (PKI) and the Attribute Based Encryption (ABE).

The first proposed DOSN is Diaspora[2], where users are able to act as local servers in order to keep complete control over their data. In Safebook [7] users can specify, for each friend, a trust level used to select closely related contacts that will store user's data. A similar approach is proposed also by My3 [22], where users are able to choose a set of trusted friends where the contents can be stored. Authors of [2] propose to store data on the set of trusted friends, chosen by using the Dunbar's approach. PeerSoN [5] exploits local users devices to store their data securely. Users data are encrypted with the public keys of the users who have access to it. LotusNet [1] exploits a combination of both symmetric and asymmetric encryption. In SuperNova [26] users' data may be stored on untrusted peers or on users' friends peers. The data stored on untrusted peers (or on friend peers) are encrypted by using a threshold-based secret sharing approach. LifeSocial.KOM [18] uses a DHT to store and replicate users' data and each content is protected with an individual symmetric key. Then, this symmetric key is encrypted individually with the public key of the users able to access the data and attached to the users content. In Cachet [24] users' data are securely stored and replicated on the peers of a DHT by using a cryptography hybrid structure which leverages ABE and symmetric key. Only users that meet the policy can decrypt the private key used to encrypt the content. In SOUP [21] users can store private data on other participants without the usage of a DHT by creating mirror replicas and every replica must be encrypted. Authors

---

[2] http://joindiaspora.com.

of [25] build a replication strategy by considering the underlying social graph and they evaluate two types of availability: pure and friend availability. Other possible selection strategies and a comparison between them have been proposed in [6,22].

3   Modeling Social Profiles

In our system, the social profile P_u of a user u is modeled by a tree whose nodes correspond to the contents belonging to P_u. The structure of the information contained in the user's profile (images, albums, posts, comments, likes, blogs, pages, etc.) is well suited to be represented by using a hierarchical data structure, such as a tree. A detailed explanation of the hierarchical profile structure we defined is reported in [11]. The root of the tree is considered as the entry point for all the contents related to a profile owner. Each node of the profile tree embeds information about the identifiers of the children and parent nodes and it is paired with the privacy preferences chosen by the owner. Note that, since we have a one to one mapping between the nodes of the tree P_u and the user's contents, we use interchangeably the terms node or content to refer them. Furthermore, we suppose that an unique identifier is assigned to each node of the user's content tree.

To achieve fine-grained access control, users can specify the authorization on the contents of their profile by defining privacy policies. The privacy policies defined by a user for his contents are collected in the *privacy policy repository* of the user.

We exploit the authorization framework proposed in [11] to support users in the management of their privacy preferences. The framework allows its users to define flexible privacy policies to regulate the accesses to the content they have shared by means of a proper Privacy Policy Language.

4   System Architecture

This section summarizes the general architecture of our system, which has been proposed in [12]. We assume a one-to-one mapping between users and their peers and we use interchangeably the terms peer or user to refer them.

The system we propose is based on a multi-layered architecture, exploiting both a DHT and direct communications between the peers. The profile of a user is replicated on a set of peer, as described in the following.

Each user u is bound to its user descriptor D_u which contains information about the IP address of the corresponding peer, the online/offline status of the peer, the identifier of the root of its profile tree and the current replicas available for all contents of the profile. Since the descriptor D_u must be available to all the peers which are going to access the profile of u when it is offline, it is stored on a DHT and may be retrieved by exploiting the identifier of the u. The DHT provides a secure storage layer and look-up service which is used to store information required to identify users and their devices (such as the current IP

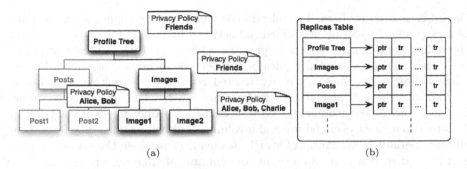

(a)   (b)

Fig. 1. Figure 1(a) shows the general profile tree data structure which contains posts and images of the user U. The root of the profile tree and the *Images* node are intended to be shared with the entire circle of U's friends. Finally, the privacy policies specified by U for the contents *Image1* and *Image2* allow access to the set of users {*Alice, Bob*} and {*Alice, Bob, Charlie*}, respectively. The Fig. 1(b) shows the replicas table for the profile tree of U where names of the nodes are used as content ids. A primary trusted replica (ptr) and a set of further trusted replicas (tr) are defined for each node.

address of the user) and to find the replicas where contents are stored. Users and contents are identified by using the DHT identifier space. Note that the DHT is exploited not only to keep track of the content replicas, but it is also indispensable for peer bootstrapping, addressing and for supporting the search of new friends.

The association between the contents of a profile tree P_u and the trusted replica peers that store such contents are maintained in the *replicas table* R_u (see Fig. 1(b)) which is located in the user's descriptor D_u of the profile owner.

In order to ensure higher data availability, each content of a profile tree is replicated on k peers, where k is an input parameter of the system. The replicas table R_u provides information about the current trusted replicas available for the profile P_u and it contains, for each content c of P_u, the trusted replica list $R_u(c) = \{ptr, tr_1 \ldots, tr_{k-1}\}$, where ptr is the primary trusted replica, while $\{tr_1 \ldots, tr_{k-1}\}$ are the other replicas of the content. Let us denote by $tr(c)$ and $ptr(c)$ respectively, the set of trusted replicas and the primary trusted replica for the content c. For maintaining replication transparency, the trusted replica lists are managed according to a *passive replication model* [15] where every user communicates only with ptr, the *primary trusted replica*. When the profile owner is online, it becomes primary trusted replica of his contents. Primary trusted replicas are responsible for the availability of the contents, for enforcing privacy policies every time a user tries to access a content, and for the selection of the new trusted replicas. Specifically, when a user v requests access to the content c of P_u, the replica storing c evaluates the privacy policies of u (linked to the profile P_u) in order to decide whether to permit or deny the access to c

Only the primary replica can elect new replicas for the content and it can add them at the end of the trusted replica list. If the primary replica crashes abruptly or voluntary leaves the DOSN, the availability of their contents is guaranteed by the other trusted replicas. The selection of a new trusted replica for a content c of user profile P_u can be performed: *(i)* actively by the content owner u during the online periods since it acts as primary replicas for their contents or *(ii)* by the current primary trusted replica of c, when the owner is not online. Indeed, when a user u becomes a primary trusted replica for a content c, it has to periodically check if new trusted replicas are needed and, in this case, it has to find another peer who is allowed to access c according to u's privacy policy. Robustness against peers failure and involuntary disconnections may be ensured through periodical exchanges of heartbeat messages between the primary replica and trusted replica peer. As a result, the amount of time data is kept available depends on both the effectiveness and complexity of the strategy with which the trusted replicas are chosen.

5   Replica Selection: Our Proposal

This paper proposes an enhancement of the framework we proposed in [11] by exploiting a new replica selection strategy which, besides preserving the privacy preferences defined by the users, also guarantees a high level of data availability. In particular, the data allocation strategy exploits both online pattern of users and privacy policies defined by the users on their contents in order to decide on which user's device a content should be replicated. As proposed in our previous work [12], the privacy policy specified for the content c is used by the primary trusted replica to retrieve the set of users authorized to access the content c. The privacy policy is evaluated by using the authorization component of the privacy-preserving framework and by simulating an access to the content in order to define set of possible *trusted peers* to host replicas for a content c, i.e., the peers who are allowed to read the content of the profile according to the privacy policy defined by u.

The criteria considered for the selection of a trusted peer from the set of possible candidate heavily affects the availability of data. Indeed, a first proposal was to select at random the peers on which the data are placed from the set of possible candidate trusted replicas [23]. However, replicating data on different random users' devices is not enough to ensure high data availability because peers participating in the network are heterogeneous in terms of demands and online behavior. To take into account the dynamic behavior of the users of the DOSNs, simple temporal information related to users can be considered by the replication strategies (such as average session length or online-offline correlation [17,20]). In contrast, the periodic behavior of users in DOSNs has not been exploited yet in replica selection strategies. However, the availability patterns of the users of the DOSNs are crucial to better design the data replication strategies of the DOSN infrastructure. For example, as shown in [4,16], users of the OSNs seem to connect to the service with a periodic trends. This suggest the existence of a periodic pattern where each user is connected at similar times each day. We believe that such availability patterns of users can be exploited to achieve accurate predictions about availability of users contents.

For this purpose, we used a linear predictor to predict the availability status of the user (online or not) during a certain future time interval, on the basis of his past behavior. A linear predictor is defined as a linear combination $f(x^t)$ constructed from a set of k terms $x^{t_1}, \cdots, x^{t_k}$ by multiplying each term x^{t_i} with the corresponding weight β_i:

$$f(x^t) = \frac{\beta_1 x^{t_1} + \beta_2 x^{t_2} + \cdots + \beta_k x^{t_k}}{\sum_{j=1}^{k} \beta_j} \qquad (1)$$

In particular, weights β_i for $i = 1 \cdots k$ are named *coefficients* and they are used to specify the weights reflecting the importance of each element. For the purposes of data availability, linear predictors are used to calculate the probability that a candidate trusted peer u is online/offline in a given future period t by taking into account the past availability status of the same user u in k different time instants. The coefficient vector can be used in the fitting process to indicate how much each day contributes to the prediction of the availability status. To be able to compare probability measures, we performed a normalization by dividing it for the sum of the weights β, obtaining a normalized value between 0 and 1. Given the vector of probabilities resulting from the application of Eq. 1 on each candidate trusted replica, the framework selects the user who has the highest probability of being online.

We describe the algorithm utilized by the primary trusted replica o to select a new trusted replica peer p for a content c created by the user u, in more details. The peer p must be currently online and be allowed to access c according to the privacy policy defined on c. Furthermore, we consider the probability that p remains online for some time. Initially, we assume that o is authorized to access the content c (optionally, we can consider $o = u$). As specified in Algorithm 1, user o retrieves the user descriptor D_u in order to get the replica table R_u and to have information about the replicas available for the content c (line [2–4]). Then, user o executes an election procedure which selects a new trusted replica for c. User u get the set of online users F having a friendship relation with u (the owner of the content) and then uses the authorization module of the privacy preserving framework to evaluate whether the user $f \in F$ is authorized to read the content c of u (line 5–8).

The privacy policy of c is evaluated on each user f in the set of neighbors by simulating an access request on a user's content c and it may only return permit or deny (line 9). The linear predictor is evaluated only on the users who have obtained a permit authorization decision (line 10) and in such a case, availability status of f (online/offline) during the last k time instants is exploited for prediction. The selection procedure chooses as trusted replica peer, the user f who has the maximum probability to be online, based on the result of the linear predictor. To make availability predictions for t time steps into the future, we iteratively evaluate the linear combination using the k most recent availability samples of each user.

Algorithm 1. User o executes the selection of a replica for the content c of user u.

```
1: procedure SELECT
2:     Du=getUserDescriptor(u);
3:     Ru=getReplicaTable(Du);
4:     tr=getTrustedReplicas(c);
5:     auth =getAuthorization(Dn);                    ▷ init authorization component
6:     F =getOnlinePeer(Dn);
7:     candidates = ∅,maxVal = 0;
8:     for f ∈ F do
9:         result = auth.evaluateAccess(c,READ, f);
10:         if result = PERMIT then
11:             val = predict(f, xᵗ) = (β₁xᵗ¹ + β₂xᵗ² + ··· + βₖxᵗᵏ)/∑ᵏⱼ₌₁ βⱼ
12:             if maxVal > val then
13:                 candidate = f;
14:             end if
15:         end if
16:     end for
17:     tr(c) = tr(c) · candidate;                          ▷ trusted replica selection
18: end procedure
```

6   Evaluation

In order to validate our approach in a real scenario, we have implemented a Facebook application, called *SocialCircles!*[3], which exploits the former Facebook API (supported till 1st May 2015) to retrieve different information from the registered users.

6.1   The Dataset

We used a dataset containing the same information described in [10] but collected during a larger period of 32 days. In detail, we sampled all the registered users and their friends every 5 min, for 32 days (from 9 March to 10 April 2015). Using this methodology we were able to access the temporal status of about 204 registered users and of their friends (for a total of 44.200 users). A discrete time model is used to represent the availability status (i.e. online/offline) of the users during the simulation. In particular, each day of the monitored period consists of a finite number of time slots (i.e., 288 time slots each of 5 min), for a total number of about 9200 time slots in the whole monitored period.

In order to apply all our privacy policies, we used a subset of 62 registered users and of their friends (for a total of 23.428 users). In Fig. 2 we show temporal information of such users by plotting at each time slot the number of online/offline registered users (first plot), the average number of online friends (the second plot), and the total number of online/offline users (the third plot).

---

[3] https://www.facebook.com/SocialCircles-244719909045196/.

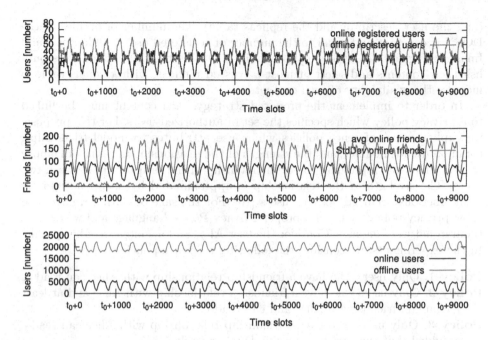

Fig. 2. Number of online/offline registered users, friends of the registered users, and total number of user over the time.

As shown by the first plot, the number of registered users connected at the same time to the OSN ranges between 5 and 40 and it clearly exhibits a periodic pattern which depends on the time of the day. As we expected, users are more connected to Facebook during the daylight hours, while at most 10 registered users are simultaneously connected during the nighttime hours. The second plot of Fig. 2 shows that registered users have an average number of online friends ranging between 20 and 100. In addition, the values of the Standard Deviation (StdDev) indicated a large variation and heterogeneity of our analyzed sample. As showed by the third plot, the overall number of users connected to the OSN ranges between 600 and 5000.

6.2 Experimental Methodology

In order to evaluate the proposed approach we used the PeerSim Simulator[4], a P2P simulator written in Java. We developed a set of simulations, based on the dataset previously described, that implement the proposed replication strategy. The duration of the simulation is equal to the length of the monitored period (i.e., 9200 time slots) and the availability status of a peer corresponds to the availability status of a user. A simple DHT-like implementations is used to bootstrap peers and to track where the contents of a user's profile are stored

---

[4] http://peersim.sourceforge.net/.

(i.e., the user descriptor and the replicas table). The number of profiles in the DOSN is constant and equal to the number of registered users, while Posts and Images are generated with equal probability. During the simulation, users publish their contents and select at most k trusted replicas, with k equals to 4, to increase the availability of each content.

In order to implement the proposed strategy, each content must be linked to a privacy policy which specifies the set of authorized users. For this purpose, we exploit some reference policies which use attributes to model friendships, common friends number, and the strength of the relationship in terms of Dunbar circles, which is a representation of the intensity of the relationship between two users. The strength of the relationship is approximated by using the number of interactions occurred between users [10]. For the sake of clarity, we avoid to show privacy policy by using a proper Privacy Policy Language and we express them in natural language. Consider the user Alice and a content c of her profile. In the experiments, we consider the following reference policies:

Policy 1. Only users who have a friendship relationship with Alice can read c.
Policy 2. Only users who have a friendship relationship with Alice and at least f common friends with Alice and can read c.
Policy 3. Only users who have a friendship relationship with Alice can read c provided that they are in a specific Dunbar circle C.

6.3 Experimental Results

From time t_0 to time $t_0 + 3500$ the simulation is initiated and each user registered to our Facebook application creates an empty profile which can be used to publish the shared contents. The future online presence of a user u at a certain time unit t is computed by using a linear predictor, which exploits the availability patterns of user u during the previous 12 days to predict the availability status of u in a future time intervals. For this reason, the first 12 days of the monitoring periods (from time slot t_0 to $t_0 + 3500$) are considered as training set. We introduce also a coefficient vector that specifies the importance of each of the previous 12 days. In our simulation, each past day $j = 1 \ldots 12$ has the same importance in predicting the user's availability and each weight β_j of the coefficient vector is equal to 1.

At time $t_0 + 3500$ the set-up phase is finished and users start to publish either Posts or Images with a probability of 0.5. Figure 3(a) shows the total number of Profile objects created during the simulation as well as the total number of Posts and Images published. The number of profiles in the DOSN is constant and equal to the number of registered users (i.e., 62), which amount to 189 data objects. The total number of Posts and Images published on these profiles does not exceed 3.145 contents (1.581 Posts and 1.564 Images, respectively) and each registered user publishes an average number of 25 Posts and 25 Images on its profile. When the user creates a content, it assigns to the generated content a privacy policy randomly chosen among those previously defined. In Policy 2, the number of common friends (f) is equal to 1. Figure 3(b) shows that the

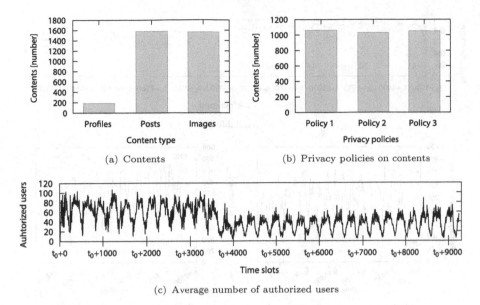

(a) Contents

(b) Privacy policies on contents

(c) Average number of authorized users

Fig. 3. Statistics on the contents created by users during the simulations.

three policies are uniformly distributed among the contents. Figure 3(c) shows the average number of users that can access a content. Initially (from time t_0 until $t_0 + 3500$), each user's profile is empty and it can be accessed by all the user's friends. Thereafter (i.e., from time $t_0 + 3500$), new contents are created and only a subset of the users' friends are enabled to access them, according to the selected privacy policies.

With the previous set up, we investigated the availability resulting from our approach with respect to other peer selection strategies. In particular, during the simulation, users select at most $k = 4$ trusted replicas to increase the availability of each content c. Each trusted peer hosting a replica for c is chosen by using the following strategies:

RND: Randomly selects a trusted replica from the set of user's peers authorized to access c.

SL: Selects as trusted replica a user's peer that is authorized to access c and that has the highest average session length.

LP: Selects as trusted replica the user's peer authorized to access c and that has the highest probability of remaining online (see Algorithm 1).

We measured the number of trusted replicas and the availability of contents at each time slot and for each of the proposed strategies. Figure 4(a) shows the percentage of contents available on the DOSN for each time slot of the simulation period. The LP selection strategy outperform over the SL and RND strategies by reaching the availability of the most part of the contents (about 95%) during the daylight hours. Clearly, the availability of the contents depends on the number

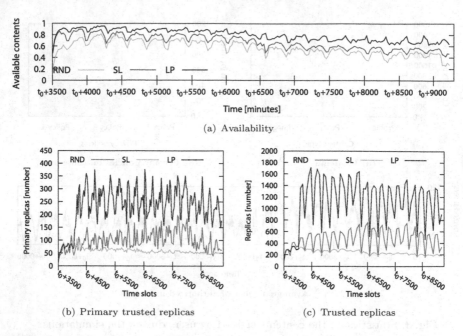

(a) Availability

(b) Primary trusted replicas

(c) Trusted replicas

Fig. 4. Statistics on the availability of the contents created by users during the simulations.

of users connected at the time of the day and it decreases of about 10% during the nighttime hours. The availability of the contents provided by the SL strategy is lower than LP: at most 80% of the contents were kept available. In particular, the plot indicates clearly that during the night periods the LP strategy has a gain of about 30% with respect the SL strategy. Indeed, the LP strategy exploits availability patterns of users to predict the users' peers that will be online (with high probability) during the nighttime hours. In contrast, the SL strategy chooses the user's peer with the highest average session length, regardless of the time of the day in which the user spends this time.

Since the simulation selects at most 4 trusted replicas for each content, the total number of trusted replicas available in the DOSN is bounded by $4 \cdot \#Contents$, where $\#Contents$ represents the total number of contents created by users (i.e. 3334 contents). Figure 4(b) and (c) show, respectively, the number of primary trusted replicas and trusted replicas. The LP strategy employs at most 400 primary trusted replicas for providing the users' contents, while trusted replicas created as support for availability of such contents ranges between 600 and 1600. Instead, the total number of primary trusted replicas and trusted replicas of the RND strategy is quite low (about 100 primary trusted replicas and less than 600 trusted replicas) as the most part of the contents are not provided. The SL strategy uses the fewest number of primary trusted replicas and trusted replicas because it always selects as replicas the users' peers with the highest average session length. We investigated the average session length of the trusted

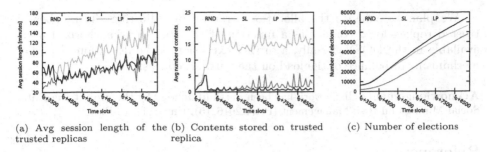

(a) Avg session length of the trusted replicas (b) Contents stored on trusted replica (c) Number of elections

Fig. 5. Statistics on the number of the messages and the storage load taken by the trusted replicas.

replicas selected by each allocation strategy. As expected, the Fig. 5(a) clearly indicates that trusted replicas selected by the SL strategy have the highest average session length while trusted replicas selected by the RND and LP strategy have very similar average session length. This facts indicate that LP strategy provides higher availability of contents with respect to SL and RND, despite the average session length of the trusted replicas is lower. We investigated the load of replicas by measuring the average number of contents stored on each trusted replicas. The results given by Fig. 5(b) indicate that the SL allocation strategy has the highest average load (about 20 contents stored on each trusted replica) because the contents are mainly stored on the same trusted replicas, i.e. those with the highest average session length. Indeed, the LP and RND strategies balance the load uniformly between the different trusted replicas.

Finally, we assessed the number of trusted replica elections. Figure 5(c) shows the sum of the number of the trusted replicas selected by each strategy during the simulation. The LP and the SL allocation strategy take about the same number of trusted replica selection while the RND strategy perform less elections of trusted replica peers.

7   Conclusion and Future Works

In this paper we have presented the design and evaluation of allocation strategies for data in DOSNs using the privacy policies defined on content and the availability patterns of users. In particular, the proposed replication strategy selects the peers that will store a replica of the content c of a user u among the set of users authorized to access c and it uses linear predictor, which exploits past availability status (online/offline) of these peers to predict their online status in a future time. We evaluated the proposed strategy by using a real Facebook dataset and by comparing it with the other allocation strategies used by the current DOSNs. The results indicate that the proposed allocation strategy increases data availability of contents of about 30% with respect to ours competitors. In addition, the proposed allocation strategy gives back to users more control over their contents since they are stored and maintained according to the users' privacy preferences.

We plan to enhance the allocation strategy by adjusting the number of trusted replica for a content as a function of the number of authorized users available in the DOSN. Finally, a further extension is the definition of proper mechanisms to balance of the load on the trusted replicas.

Acknowledgements. This work has been partially funded by the project Big Data, Social Mining and Risk Management (PRA_2016_15), University of Pisa.

References

1. Aiello, L.M., Ruffo, G.: Lotusnet: tunable privacy for distributed online social network services. Comput. Commun. **35**(1), 75–88 (2012)
2. Barbara, G., Tobias, A., Andrea, D.S., Kalman, G., Laura, R.: DiDuSoNet: A P2P architecture for distributed dunbar-based social networks. Peer-to-Peer Netw. Appl. **9**(6), 1177–1194 (2016)
3. Bodriagov, O., Buchegger, S.: Encryption for peer-to-peer social networks. In: Altshuler, Y., Elovici, Y., Cremers, A.B., Aharony, N., Pentland, A. (eds.) Security and Privacy in Social Networks, pp. 47–65. Springer, New York (2013)
4. Boutet, A., Kermarrec, A.M., Le Merrer, E., Van Kempen, A.: On the impact of users availability in osns. In: Proceedings of the Fifth Workshop on Social Network Systems, pp. 4:1–4:6. ACM (2012)
5. Buchegger, S., Schiöberg, D., Vu, L.H., Datta, A.: PeerSoN: P2P social networking: Early experiences and insights. In: Proceedings of the Second ACM EuroSys Workshop on Social Network Systems, SNS 2009, pp. 46–52 (2009)
6. Conti, M., De Salve, A., Guidi, B., Pitto, F., Ricci, L.: Trusted dynamic storage for dunbar-based P2P online social networks. In: Meersman, R., Panetto, H., Dillon, T., Missikoff, M., Liu, L., Pastor, O., Cuzzocrea, A., Sellis, T. (eds.) OTM 2014. LNCS, vol. 8841, pp. 400–417. Springer, Heidelberg (2014). doi:10.1007/978-3-662-45563-0_23
7. Cutillo, L.A., Molva, R., Strufe, T.: Safebook: a privacy preserving online social network leveraging on real-life trust. IEEE Commun. Mag. **47**(12), 94–101 (2009)
8. Datta, A., Buchegger, S., Vu, L.H., Strufe, T., Rzadca, K.: Decentralized online social networks. In: Furht, B. (ed.) Handbook of Social Network Technologies and Applications, pp. 349–378. Springer, Heidelberg (2010)
9. De Salve, A., Di Pietro, R., Mori, P., Ricci, L.: Logical key hierarchy for groups management in distributed online social network. In: IEEE Symposium on Computers and Communication, ISCC 2016, Messina, Italy, 27–30 June 2016, pp. 710–717 (2016)
10. De Salve, A., Dondio, M., Guidi, B., Ricci, L.: The impact of user's availability on on-line ego networks: a Facebook analysis. Comput. Commun. **73**, 211–218 (2016)
11. De Salve, A., Mori, P., Ricci, L.: A privacy-aware framework for decentralized online social networks. In: Chen, Q., Hameurlain, A., Toumani, F., Wagner, R., Decker, H. (eds.) DEXA 2015. LNCS, vol. 9262, pp. 479–490. Springer, Cham (2015). doi:10.1007/978-3-319-22852-5_39
12. De Salve, A., Mori, P., Ricci, L., Al-Aaridhi, R., Graffi, K.: Privacy-preserving data allocation in decentralized online social networks. In: Jelasity, M., Kalyvianaki, E. (eds.) DAIS 2016. LNCS, vol. 9687, pp. 47–60. Springer, Cham (2016). doi:10.1007/978-3-319-39577-7_4

13. Ellison, N.B., et al.: Social network sites: definition, history, and scholarship. J. Comput. Mediat. Commun. **13**(1), 210–230 (2007)
14. Gao, H., Hu, J., Huang, T., Wang, J., Chen, Y.: Security issues in online social networks. IEEE Internet Comput. **15**(4), 56–63 (2011)
15. Ghosh, S.: Distributed Systems: An Algorithmic Approach. CRC Press, Boca Raton (2014)
16. Golder, S.A., Wilkinson, D.M., Huberman, B.A.: Rhythms of social interaction: messaging within a massive online network. In: Steinfield, C., Pentland, B.T., Ackerman, M., Contractor, N. (eds.) Communities and Technologies 2007, pp. 41–66. Springer, Heidelberg (2007)
17. Gracia-Tinedo, R., Artigas, M.S., Lopez, P.G.: Analysis of data availability in f2f storage systems: when correlations matter. In: 2012 IEEE 12th International Conference on Peer-to-Peer Computing (P2P), pp. 225–236. IEEE (2012)
18. Graffi, K., Gross, C., Stingl, D., Hartung, D., Kovacevic, A., Steinmetz, R.: LifeSocial.KOM: a secure and P2P-based solution for online social networks. In: Consumer Communications and Networking Conference (CCNC), pp. 554–558. IEEE (2011)
19. Gross, R., Acquisti, A.: Information revelation and privacy in online social networks. In: Proceedings of the 2005 ACM Workshop on Privacy in the Electronic Society, pp. 71–80. ACM (2005)
20. Kermarrec, A.M., Le Merrer, E., Straub, G., Van Kempen, A.: Availability-based methods for distributed storage systems. In: 2012 IEEE 31st Symposium on Reliable Distributed Systems (SRDS), pp. 151–160. IEEE (2012)
21. Koll, D., Li, J., Fu, X.: Soup: an online social network by the people, for the people. In: Proceedings of the 15th International Middleware Conference, Middleware 2014, pp. 193–204 (2014)
22. Narendula, R., Papaioannou, T.G., Aberer, K.: A decentralized online social network with efficient user-driven replication. In: 2012 International Conference on Privacy, Security, Risk and Trust (PASSAT) and 2012 International Confernece on Social Computing (SocialCom), pp. 166–175. IEEE (2012)
23. Narendula, R., Papaioannou, T.G., Aberer, K.: Towards the realization of decentralized online social networks: an empirical study. In: 2012 32nd International Conference on Distributed Computing Systems Workshops, pp. 155–162. IEEE (2012)
24. Nilizadeh, S., Jahid, S., Mittal, P., Borisov, N., Kapadia, A.: Cachet: a decentralized architecture for privacy preserving social networking with caching, pp. 337–348 (2012)
25. Schiöberg, D., Schneider, F., Trédan, G., Uhlig, S., Feldmann, A.: Revisiting content availability in distributed online social networks. CoRR abs/1210.1394 (2012)
26. Sharma, R., Datta, A.: Supernova: super-peers based architecture for decentralized online social networks. In: 2012 Fourth International Conference on Communication Systems and Networks (COMSNETS 2012), pp. 1–10 (2012)
27. Zhang, C., Sun, J., Zhu, X., Fang, Y.: Privacy and security for online social networks: challenges and opportunities. IEEE Netw. **24**(4), 13–18 (2010)

A Unifying Orchestration Operating Platform for 5G

Antonio Manzalini[1], Marco Di Girolamo[2], Giuseppe Celozzi[3], Fulvio Bruno[3],
Giuliana Carullo[4(✉)], Marco Tambasco[4], Gino Carrozzo[5], Fulvio Risso[6],
and Gabriele Castellano[6]

[1] Telecom Italia Mobile, Milan, Italy
[2] HPE, Rome, Italy
[3] Ericsson, Rome, Italy
[4] CoRiTeL, Rome, Italy
giuliana.carullo@coritel.it
[5] Nextworks, Pisa, Italy
[6] Politecnico di Torino, Turin, Italy

Abstract. 5G will revolutionize the way ICT and Telecommunications infrastructures work. Indeed, businesses can greatly benefit from innovation introduced by 5G and exploit the new deep integration between ICT and networking capabilities to generate new value-added services. Although a plethora of solutions for virtual resources and infrastructures management and orchestration already exists (e.g., OpenDaylight, ONOS, OpenStack, Apache Mesos, Open Source MANO, Docker Swarm, LXD/LXC, etc.), they are still not properly integrated to match the 5G requirements. In this paper, we present the 5G Operating Platform (5G-OP) which has been conceived to fill in this gap and integrate management, control and orchestration of computing, storage and networking resources down to the end-user devices and terminals (e.g., smart phone, machines, robots, drones, autonomous vehicles, etc.). The 5G-OP is an overarching framework capable to provide agnostic interfaces and a universal set of abstractions in order to implement seamless 5G infrastructure control and orchestration. The functional structure of the 5G-OP, including the horizontal and vertical interworking of functions in it, has been designed to allow Network Operators and Service Providers to exploit diverse roles and business strategies. Moreover, the functional decoupling of the 5G-OP from the underneath management, control and orchestration solutions allows pursuing faster innovation cycles, being ready for the emergence of new service models.

Keywords: 5G · SDN · NFV · Cloud · Management · Control · Orchestration · API

1 Introduction

In the era of massive explosion of pervasive powerful devices and the high diffusion of fixed and mobile ultra-broadband, both ICT and Telecommunications

© Springer International Publishing AG 2017
M.H.A. Au et al. (Eds.): GPC 2017, LNCS 10232, pp. 252–266, 2017.
DOI: 10.1007/978-3-319-57186-7_20

infrastructures are evolving towards 5G. A systemic trend, usually termed as network Softwarization, is in place, where ICT and Telecommunication infrastructures are radically leveraging on software decoupling and virtualization technologies. In this context, Cloud, Edge and Fog Computing [1], Network Function Virtualization (NFV) [2] and Software Defined Networking (SDN) [3] are the most important enabling technology frameworks, which can be seen as different dimensions of an overall effort to implement the 5G paradigm. Indeed, the design of 5G infrastructure is looking much beyond a simple evolution of current 4G/LTE mobile networks. 5G will not only provide higher radio bit rates or reduced end-to-end latency: it will be based on a true fixed-mobile convergence and a deeper integration of IT and networking capabilities. Eventually, the overall 5G infrastructure will be simplified, for example, by reducing the number of layers and overcoming the need for silos; 5G functionalities will be virtualized and dynamically allocated onto horizontal network-service platforms, pervasively deployed, including the access segments (e.g., SoftRAN, CloudRAN [4]). This will improve the levels of pervasivity, dynamicity, programmability and robustness of 5G infrastructures, whilst increasing the degrees of complexity, volatility and unpredictability. Indeed, human-made operations will not be able to face the emerging control and management challenges, especially in highly dynamic environments, highlighting - as a consequence - the urgent need to redesign the processes for infrastructure control, management and orchestration, namely by introducing higher levels of automation. The provisioning of 5G end-to-end services, allocated and executed in network slices, will require orchestration capabilities, a universal set of abstractions and standard Open APIs. By filling this gap, it will be possible to achieve network services separation as well as proper isolation required to ensure both service quality and security. Multiple levels of orchestration are needed for service and resource (network and computing) provisioning, to ensure that the network slices deliver services at the required quality levels and with optimal resource utilization. Furthermore, a policy-based control can be used to validate the performance of network slices, and more widely to enact service monitoring. The first concrete exploitations of 5G Software Networks implementing the functionalities introduced above are expected to be rolled-out by 2020.

Within this research framework, the authors of this paper have elaborated a reference functional architecture for a unifying Operating Platform for 5G (5G-OP), which integrates management, control and orchestration of computing, storage and networking resources down to the end-user devices and terminals (e.g., smart phone, machines, robots, drones, autonomous vehicles, etc.). Despite numerous research and development efforts in the area of SDN and NFV have been going on for many years, with a number of products now in the market and a significant steering role of large-scale open source development communities (e.g. those behind the developments of OpenDaylight [5], ONOS [6], OpenStack [7,8], Apache Mesos [9], OpenSource MANO [10], Docker Swarm, LXD/LXC, etc.), no consolidated control and orchestration solutions exist. For instance, SDN controllers lack common application interfaces (northbound Interfaces), NFV orchestrators rely on different infrastructure models, etc. The heterogeneity of the implemented solutions is heading for complex and costly situations, with high fragmentation, which in turn creates uncertainty and the risk of delaying 5G innovations.

5G-OP originates from the observation of the state of the art, to address this issue, by providing a platform that can easily taken up by Telcos and service providers to implement in an end-to-end way the various 5G scenarios for their vertical customers. The main innovation of the 5G-OP lies in its overarching characteristics. 5G-OP does not intend to develop one more control-orchestration platform to replace the ones in current state of the art (OpenDaylight, ONOS, CORD [11], M-CORD [12], OpenStack, etc.). Contrarily, 5G-OP sits on top of them, exposing orchestrated services across multiple different network and non-network domains through unified interfaces, providing a set of abstractions and adaptation functions. The agnostic and overarching characteristics of the 5G-OP allows true decoupling from the underneath control-orchestration platforms, which thus becomes pluggable into the 5G-OP. Therefore, 5G-OP does not add another layer of complexity; contrarily, it is radically simplifying the integration of current and future platforms in the 5G-OP in a way to provide end-to-end services spanning across heterogeneous technological infrastructures (e.g., cloud, network, fog, terminals), and that can evolve over time.

The outline of the paper is the following. Section 2 presents the master design guidelines of the 5G-OP, while Sect. 3 reports some of the possible application scenarios in which the 5G-OP can definitely impact and create value. A brief description of a preliminary prototype is presented in Sect. 4, while Sect. 5 provides some results from the experimental validation we performed. Finally, Sect. 6 reports our closing remarks and sketches some future evolutions of the 5G-OP.

2   The 5G Operating Platform

The 5G-OP is an overarching architecture, with agnostic interfaces and a rich set of abstractions, offering seamless integration of current and future infrastructure management, control and orchestration solutions (e.g., ONOS, OpenDaylight, OpenStack and even Robot Operating System [13], etc.). In 5G-OP, each service orchestrator exposes its resources and services via a Northbound API (NBI) to a consumer and a Southbound API (SBI) to use resources and services from underlying serving orchestrators. In order to keep the overall control architecture manageable across multiple distributed and chained instances, it is fundamental to design Northbound APIs that can abstract the various primitive functions of each Orchestrator instance, and that can allow the formulation of the typical actions on resources and services like composition, chaining and so on, in the form of "intents". Interfaces are defined towards the Infrastructure controllers (Southbound APIs) and intent-based APIs are defined towards the Application/tenant (Northbound API). NBI API is meant to make this available to the verticals and Over-The-Top (OTT), that will use them to implement their applications.

The technical approach we propose aims at enabling a flexible coupling with the underlying infrastructure control and orchestration platforms. In particular, we focus on the aspects that are involved when an application wants to make use of 5G-OP and leverage the best of the underlying infrastructure, which translates in the possibility to exploit the peculiar characteristics available in each domain. This implies that an overarching orchestrator based on the *minimum common denominator* is not appropriate, as it hides possible unique features available in some portions of the infrastructure. Instead, the 5G-OP must export the above capabilities to the upper layers in order to allow potential usage of them.

Open APIs are a key aspect of this approach that guarantees an easy integration of infrastructure platforms, thus allowing the boost and quick exploitation of open innovations creation of vertical application services on 5G. In other words, the core of the 5G-OP consists in an overarching orchestration framework operating over different 5G infrastructures including core/edge/access networks, cloud, and end-user devices and terminals, while leveraging unified service and infrastructure abstractions to support end-to-end orchestration across different technology domains as well as generalized orchestration of infrastructure and application services.

2.1   Unified Service Model and 5G Abstractions

5G-OP seamlessly supports new capabilities (e.g., a new type of network infrastructure) and services (e.g., application-specific orchestrators, or a module that can handle a new type of IoT sensor). 5G-OP offers allows new capabilities and adds support for new technological domains and various administrative domains (i.e., with technology agnostic and business federation mechanisms) by a plug-and-play approach. This way, new services and applications can easily access and use such new features.

2.2   A Generalized Orchestration Space

With the concept of the "shared orchestration space" (shown in Fig. 1), the 5G-OP brings together two problems that are usually considered separately: infrastructure-level and application-layer orchestration. A generalized orchestration workflow/process should be devised that involves the composition of both application and infrastructural resources, capabilities and services while adapting the composite services to the different and/or ever-changing contextual information [14].

5G-OP aims to achieve a model-driven provisioning of services through the different levels of orchestration. Thus one of its key features is the availability of a common data model based on graphs correlating and merging together services, resources and capabilities to represent relationships and workflows, as shown in the example in Fig. 2. The relations between orchestration modules can be defined as a set of transformations and be formally verified. In order to improve performance and scalability of services, the transition across multiple layers can be optimized through an equivalent and formally verified graph-based model,

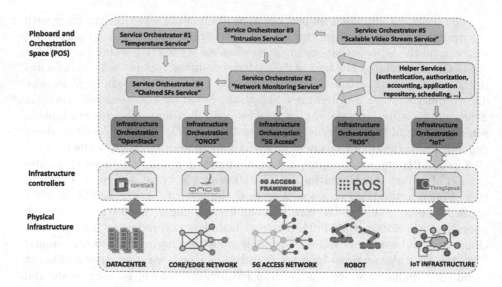

Fig. 1. 5G-OP architecture.

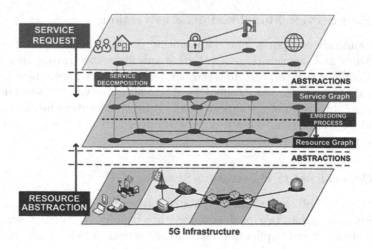

Fig. 2. Service and resource graphs.

enabling the definition of an allowed set of transformations. The API exposed by this consistent approach between design and runtime phases will enable 5G-OP to reduce capacity churn, eliminating isolated under/unused capacity and delivering the best user experience.

2.3   Architectural Principles

5G-OP allows a generalized, flexible and de-structured orchestration workflow in which orchestrators can decompose a service request into more elementary ones. The generalized orchestration is assured by proper abstractions and interfaces offered by orchestrators while interacting each other to address service requests in a structured service producer-consumer relationship. In 5G-OP, each service orchestrator exposes a Provider API for the northbound interface and a Consumer API for the southbound interface. Composition is achieved by attaching a Provider to a Consumer, thus providing the additional advantage of allowing horizontal composition, not requiring strict vertical hierarchies. At the Provider API, different logical views of the underlying resource and service capabilities (for network and non-network components) are provided to the service consumers, thus realizing the slicing concept.

The 5G-OP Provider API supports the concept of intents to ease the way a service consumer can request a service from the underlying layer, ignoring technological details on how the actual resources are configured and how the service is provisioned. At the Consumer API, abstraction is mainly aimed at wrapping details of different devices and resources in the underlying layer, controlled as objects with generalized capabilities across various technology domains.

2.4   5G-OP and New Benchmarking Principles

Benchmarking is important both in selecting and purchasing components and solutions but even more for planning, deployment and in-operation optimization where knowledge about performance benchmarks is non-negligible. We have to go beyond designing traffic traces for benchmarking of one virtualized node or network function (e.g., as suggested in [15]) and consider the definition of complex usage scenarios encompassing a mix of services across multiple carrier-grade data centers instances and controllers. Ultimate goal is benchmarking and comparing deployment options for different sets of network applications and their combined usage patterns, as well as taking into account different scaling scenarios. As a result, it will be possible to obtain performance knowledge which is comparable across - and from - different sources and cases to better appraise the resource footprint and performance achievements, and to detect the most efficient algorithms for mapping services to resources. Advances in benchmarking definitions, methods and supporting tools, and the corresponding standardization (see for instance [16]) will be greatly beneficial to the 5G-OP vision. Furthermore, the 5G-OP architectural principles are also important for enabling such advanced benchmarking scenarios.

2.5   5G-OP Security Perspective

While 5G-OP provides significant advantages in terms of flexibility, automation and efficiency of network controls, possible security threats need to be successfully addressed and mitigated by enforcing protection measures. In particular, since services, SDN controllers and data are hosted in the cloud, the infrastructure itself can offer a potential target to attacks. For example, an SDN controller in the cloud may not only be compromised via security breaches in the virtualization layer, but also via Application Programming Interfaces (APIs) exposed to overarching applications. As a result, APIs are a topic of great interest - in general - in the information security community: they are still affected by security issues, often caused by poorly written code that can quickly become dangerous, especially when it involves Open APIs. Insecure Open APIs come with major risks for both applications and underlying data. 5G-OP will consider this issues and will thus apply, when possible, best practices to deliver secure APIs.

More in general, 5G-OP will exploit both scalable allocation of resources and the programmability provided by SDN to enable the deployment of security solutions in a flexible and efficient manner.

3   5G Application Scenarios

In this Section we propose some key application scenarios in which 5G-OP would greatly impact control and orchestration.

3.1   5G Enabling Cloud Robotics and Industry 4.0

The development of increasingly complex cognitive capabilities spanning across the 5G infrastructure up to the terminals (e.g., robots, drones or autonomous machines), will offer benefits in terms of automated operational processes and optimized costs, as well as enabling the development of new service scenarios. This will pose challenging requirements for ensuring ultra-low latencies in "closing" the "interaction loop" made of sensors, processing-storage-networking nodes, systems and actuators. 5G for Cloud robotics offers several examples of use cases for Industry 4.0 and Precision Agriculture. Moreover, it is likely that remotely controlled and operated robots will enable remote surgery and will open up a new world of domestic applications. The benefits of a 5G-OP overarching orchestration framework in this context are quite important, since 5G-OP allows to control the end-to-end service provisioning and lifecycle across the various network and non-network domains while matching the challenging KPIs on latency, bandwidth, mobility and fast adapting service chain.

3.2   Media Content Everywhere and Home Services

Delivery of content is subject to a massive growth, due to a variety of devices and the demand for increased video quality in terms of resolution and frame rate. To this end, cloud offers the possibility to increase the amount of contents to be stored, but Live and On-demand content services need to be delivered as if they were stored locally and that is where a Content Delivery Network (CDN) is needed. Traditional CDN cache nodes offered as dedicated physical appliances or software with standard but dedicated hardware, come with disadvantages like the capacity of the devices that needs to be designed for peak hours on weekends, while on weekdays and business hours, they are almost unused. Furthermore, they do not scale well to deal with unforeseen capacity needs (e.g., live events). Integrating nodes of Content Delivery Networks via NFV orchestration into operator networks can be the most effective and cost-efficient way to answer the challenges imposed by Video Traffic Delivery scenario. Content streams will steam out of compute/storage nodes nearer to the end customer, saving upper network links and equipment and delivering, at the same time, higher bandwidth and quality.

Moreover, the availability of high bandwidth access and NFV technology can facilitate the virtualization of the home environment, built on top of simple, low cost and low maintenance devices at the customer premises. NFV technologies are ideal to support this shift of computational workload from formerly dispersed functions with minimal cost introduced on a grow-as-you-need basis. Even more important, 5G-OP could seamlessly integrate the home environment, with the foreseen IoT-oriented services, into the whole world of services delivered by the Telco provider. This can enable the seamless deployment of virtual appliances and services (e.g., analytics) on a virtual platform that can take care of decomposing the requested service (and the associated data) and relocating its components on the best location based on service and user constraints.

3.3 Remote Control of Critical Operations

The possible scenarios of remote operations in industry are numerous, and each scenario brings its unique set of challenges. Power plants, mines, construction sites, and oil platforms can be target environments for remote control, which will reduce personnel exposure to an abundance of risks associated including, for example, the presence of heavy machinery and chemicals. Remote operation solutions allow people to operate machinery from a control centre at another site. Anyway, the distance between these sites puts challenges in terms of both delay and connection reliability that can be solved with proper orchestrated solutions.

In order to be as productive as on-site manual operators, it is needed to reproduce the sense of a surrounding environment, including all the real-time feedback that we can obtain when the operator is physically located in the (dangerous) environment.

The requirements set by some use cases, which are of interest of both society and industries, cannot easily be met by existing communication technologies. Instead, remote operation solutions with 5G connectivity must be used, which can offer a number of benefits as it can provide connectivity to mobile machinery and devices. Furthermore, orchestration of 5G slices can deliver high reliability, and the required level of security.

4 5G-OP Prototype

A preliminary version of our 5G-OP has been implemented in the FROGv4 opensource prototype [17]. It includes six modules: a main orchestrator (called *telco orchestrator*), three *domain orchestrators* each one supporting a different technological infrastructure, and two *helper services*. Our prototype addresses the requirement from Telco operators to split their network infrastructure across different domains, either because of technical diversities (i.e., a data center requires a different controller compared to a transport SDN network) or scalability reasons. Thus, we designed the Telco orchestrator as the entry point for any service request targeting the infrastructure. Upon an incoming service request from the northbound interface, the Telco orchestrator is in charge to determine how the service is mapped on the available domains based on the capabilities exposed by each domain controller. If needed, the service request will be broken down into smaller requests targeting individual domains (e.g., a set of VMs to be allocated in the data center, a set of "virtual wires" established in a SDN domain), which are then sent to the selected domain controllers. In addition, the Telco orchestrator will create the proper logical connections (e.g., by setting up point-to-point VLANs, IPsec/GRE tunnels, etc.) that allow the portion of the service instantiated in a first domain to deliver the traffic to the following network functions, installed in a different domain. The Telco orchestrator interacts with three domain orchestrators. These orchestrators provide the interface between the Pinboard and Orchestration Space (POS) and technology-specific individual domain controllers, which will be presented with more details in the next sections. Finally, we designed two helper services: one that is dedicated to authentication and security purposes, the other that provides storage for all the above modules.

These six modules constitute the first implementation of a 5G-OP. Each module exposes a northbound interface that includes both a REST API for direct service invocation and an access to a message bus, where publish/subscribe primitives are used. The message bus is implemented with DoubleDecker [18], a ZeroMQ based distributed message solution, that provides a hierarchical brokering system. It allows different modules to be notified when a given event happens (*subscribe* primitive) and enables a module to send a given information to an unknown set of consumers (*publish* primitive). This feature, coupled with the YANG-derived [19] common data module across all the services, creates a common ground between modules that allows to produce and consume data, and to interact each other in a seamless way.

Each domain orchestrator has been implemented as a software module that receives service requests through its northbound interface, and that interacts (e.g., to deploy NFs, create network paths, retrieve information on available services and network topology) with the technology-specific controller (e.g., OpenStack or ONOS) of the underlying domain through the controller-specific APIs. Thus, the prototype can leverage existing vanilla infrastructure controllers, which can be integrated in our orchestration framework by simply writing the proper domain orchestrator on top of them. In the following we describe the three domain orchestrators we developed: the SDN domain orchestrator, the Openstack domain orchestrator and the Universal Node domain orchestrator.

4.1 SDN Domain Orchestrator

The *SDN domain orchestrator* sits on top of the ONOS (Falcon release) controller and aims at supporting SDN domains. This orchestrator queries the ONOS controller to retrieve the underlying network topology (consisting of OpenFlow switches) and to detect all the available software bundles. The former is exported as unique "big switch" through the orchestrator northbound interface, while the latter are advertised as potential services that can be turned on upon request. Currently, the list of available actions is limited to the possibility to (*i*) control software switches (e.g., creating logical switching instances, adding/removing ports), (*ii*) handle network paths (e.g., creating, redirecting, and tearing down a path between two ports of the "big switch"), and (*iii*) start one of the advertised service[1]. Network paths are implemented by installing OpenFlow rules in any hardware/software switch; however, this is considered an internal detail and hence it is not exported to the POS, which can control the infrastructure with more abstract primitives such as end-to-end (logical) paths.

When the SDN orchestrator receives a service request from its northbound interface, it calls the proper set of ONOS functions in order to set up the required paths and, if needed, starts the requested application (i.e., software bundle). Moreover, the SDN domain orchestrator receives also the precise ingress/egress traffic characterization of the endpoints that are part of the service graph, which are used, between all, to recognize where the traffic comes from (and the possible encapsulation, e.g., in a specific VLAN ID) and handle it accordingly. In this respect, the SDN orchestrator has to inject the proper flow-rules in the underlying OpenFlow domain border switches, which are used to properly tag/untag packets entering in (and exiting from) the domain as indicated by the endpoints.

Finally, since ONOS does not support the parallel execution of multiple instances of the same bundle, applications must also manage multi-tenancy by themselves in order to support service chains deployed at the same time and requiring the same bundle.

4.2 OpenStack Domain Orchestrator

This domain orchestrator is responsible for the deployment of service requests in OpenStack-based data centers, solving the necessity to handle services that spans across multiple domain. In particular, it enables a complete control on the traffic that enters in (or exits from) the considered domain. As an example, a service chain split across two domains may require the setup of a GRE tunnel between two boundary interfaces of the involved domains. This behavior is not supported by the vanilla OpenStack software, which does not allow a fine control of the network traffic coming from the external world. The Openstack domain orchestrator solves this issue, as shown in Fig. 3. Upon receiving a service request, the OpenStack domain orchestrator sends part of the service

---

[1] In SDN networks, the creation of a chain of applications is not trivial; hence, the current prototype supports only service requests that include at most *one* application in this domain; the support for more complex services is left to our future work.

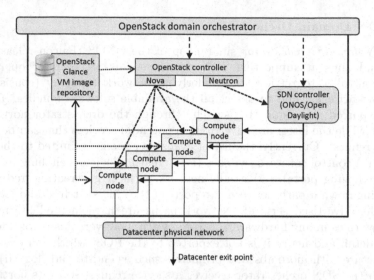

Fig. 3. Logical structure of the OpenStack domain.

to the OpenStack controller that takes care of starting the NFs and creating connections among them. It also interacts directly with the SDN controller to set up the inter-domain traffic steering (e.g., create a GRE tunnel linked to the external domain). Finally, the OpenStack domain orchestrator creates the list of available services based on the content of the OpenStack image repository, which allows the Telco orchestrator to recognize whether the considered domain supports a given application.

4.3 Universal Node Domain Orchestrator

The Universal Node (UN) [20] orchestrator can be considered as a "data center in a box", and it handles the orchestration of compute and network resources within a single physical node, such as a standalone server or a resource-constrained Customer Premises Equipment. The UN supports multiple types of NFs that can be mixed together when creating a service chain, such as VMs, Docker, DPDK processes, and Native Network Functions (NNF) [21]. Particularly, NNFs exploit the presence of native software modules (e.g., `iptables`) and (often) hardware accelerator (e.g., crypto hardware, integrated L2 switch) that are often available in Linux-based embedded devices. Since, in our model, NFs are exported as *capabilities* to the overarching orchestrator, no matter how the actual implementation is (e.g., VM/Docker/NNF), NNF provides a way to implement NFs with reduced overhead compared to VMs and containers, while still being transparent to the service requester. Thus, a service request can be served by instantiating at least a portion of it at the very edge of the network, on the user residential gateway, while other NFs (e.g., the ones that require more resources) can be allocated in data centers, hence enabling the users to experience a better service given its proximity to the requested NFs.

5   Validation

The prototype of our 5G-OP has been validated on the experimental JOL-NET [22] facility. JOLNET is an Italian geographical testbed consisting of a set of nodes that represent the access side (e.g., residential gateways) and a set of OpenStack domains, connected through a pure OpenFlow network; the Internet can be emulated by installing "public" services on one of the JOLNET POPs, as shown in Fig. 4.

The service chain deployed in the testbed is shown in Fig. 4(a). It operates between the user U at the edge of the network and the server S on the Internet and includes two NFs, a firewall and a NAT that can have different implementations in each domain. Indeed, the firewall is a NNF exploiting a simple `iptables` executed on the UN, while the NAT can be either an ONOS bundle running in SDN domain or a KVM-based VM in the data center. The specific domain where to start each NF is up to the Telco orchestrator, whose current logic aims at allocating NFs as close as possible to the traffic source (user U), subject to the availability of that NF in the given domain, according to the information exported by each domain controller and shown with (1) in Fig. 4.

In the first validation scenario, shown in Fig. 4(a), the firewall is deployed in the UN because this domain represents the entry point of the user's traffic and the domain orchestrator exports this capability. Instead, the NAT is deployed in the data center in Venice, as this is the only domain advertising such a capability; the SDN network is used only to create the logical connection (through the proper VLAN ID) between the two portions of the service. In the second validation scenario, shown in Fig. 4(b), the NAT capability is exported also by SDN domain orchestrator, hence the Telco orchestrator selects this domain for the execution of this NF, thus reducing the distance between chained NFs and freeing up all the consumed resources in the OpenStack domain.

In both cases, we measured the end-to-end latency (using the `ping` command) and the throughput (generating TCP traffic through `iperf`) between the user U and the server S.

As shown in Table 1, performance results improve when the NAT is executed in the SDN domain (case (b)), with respect to the case in which such a NF is deployed in the data center (case (a)). It happens because (i) the traffic does not need to be forwarded to the distant data center before being actually delivered to S, and (ii) the NAT is actually implemented as a set of Openflow rules installed by the ONOS NAT bundle in the hardware switches (only the first packet of a flow is processed in the software bundle, while the following packets are directly processed in hardware by the switches). Notably, the result achieved in case (b) are very close to the case in which no network function is present (*baseline*). In all cases, the throughput is limited by the speed of the geographical connections (100 Mbps).

An early version of the prototype has been showcased at the ITU IMT2020 Workshop and Demo Day [23].

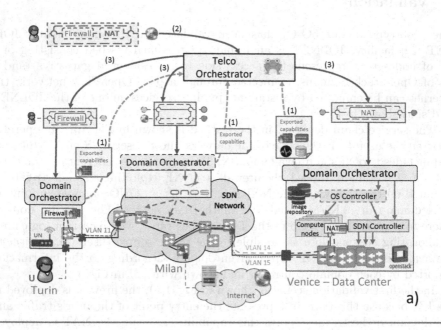

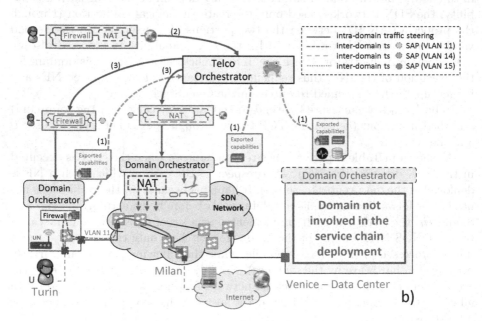

Fig. 4. Validation scenario: (a) service chain split across three domains; (b) service chain deployed in two domains.

Table 1. Comparing the throughput when different domains are involved in the service deployment.

Test case	TCP throughput	End-to-end latency
Baseline: direct connection to Internet, no NFs	88.59 Mbit/s	10.96 ms
Case (a): NFs spanning across three domains	67.04 Mbit/s	27.10 ms
Case (b): NFs spanning across two domains	81.34 Mbit/s	14.99 ms

6 Conclusions

This paper presents the reference functional architecture of a unifying Operating Platform for 5G (5G-OP) integrating management, control and orchestration of computing, storage and networking resources down to the end-user devices and terminals (e.g., smart phone, machines, robots, drones, autonomous vehicles, etc.). 5G-OP represents an attempt to overcome the fragmentation in Standardization Bodies and large-scale open source development communities, where it is still difficult to find consolidated control and orchestration solutions that can be easily taken up by Telco operators and service providers. The agnostic and overarching characteristics of the 5G-OP will allow decoupling from the underneath control-orchestration platforms, which thus become pluggable in the proposed platform.

Future work on 5G-OP is planned to evolve the FROGv4 open-source prototype and add more 5G-OP functions across more technological network and non-network domains. The enhanced prototype will be validated against some of the most challenging 5G use cases briefly introduced in this paper, thus providing a solid reference framework for Telcos to efficiently operate the 5G networks.

References

1. Manzalini, A., Minerva, R., Callegati, F., Cerroni, W., Campi, A.: Clouds of virtual machines in edge networks. IEEE Commun. Mag. **51**(7), 63–70 (2013)
2. Mijumbi, R., Serrat, J., Gorricho, J.-L., Bouten, N., De Turck, F., Boutaba, R.: Network function virtualization: State-of-the-art and research challenges. IEEE Commun. Surv. Tutorials **18**(1), 236–262 (2016)
3. Kreutz, D., et al.: Software-defined networking: A comprehensive survey. Proc. IEEE **103**(1), 14–76 (2015)
4. Checko, A., Christiansen, H.L., Yan, Y., Scolari, L., Kardaras, G., Berger, M.S., Dittmann, L.: Cloud RAN for mobile networks - A technology overview. IEEE Commun. Surv. Tutorials **17**(1), 405–426 (2015)
5. The OpenDayLight open source project. http://www.opendaylight.org/
6. Berde, P., et al.: ONOS: towards an open, distributed SDN OS. In: Proceedings of the Third Workshop on Hot Topics in Software Defined Networking, pp. 1–6 (2014)

7. The OpenStack project. http://www.openstack.org/
8. Di Mauro, M., Postiglione, F., Longo, M., Restaino, R., Tambasco, M.: Availability evaluation of the virtualized infrastructure manager in network function virtualization environments. In: Walls, L., Revie, M., Bedford, T. (eds.) Risk, Reliability, Safety: Innovating Theory and Practice, pp. 2591–2596 (2016)
9. Kakadia, D.: Apache Mesos Essentials. Packt Publishing, Birmingham (2015)
10. The OpenSouce MANO project. https://osm.etsi.org/
11. Peterson, L., et al.: Central office re-architected as a data center. IEEE Commun. Mag. **54**(10), 96–101 (2016)
12. Yoon, M., Tofigh, T., Parulkar, G.: Rethinking the Mobile Edge Network with CORD (Mobile-CORD). IEEE SDN Newsletter, March 2016
13. The Robot Operating System (ROS). http://wiki.ros.org/ROS/Introduction
14. Paganelli, F., Ulema, M., Martini, B.: Context-aware service composition and delivery in NGSONs over SDN. IEEE Commun. Mag. **52**(8), 97–105 (2014)
15. Csikor, L., Szalay, M., Sonkoly, B., Toka, L.: NFPA: Network function performance analyzer. In: IEEE Conference on Network Function Virtualization and Software Defined Network (NFV-SDN), pp. 15–17 (2015)
16. IETF Benchmarking Methodology WG. https://tools.ietf.org/wg/bmwg/
17. The FROG open source project. https://github.com/netgroup-polito/frog4
18. The DoubleDecker project. http://acreo.github.io/DoubleDecker/
19. Bjorklund, M.: The YANG 1.1 Data Modeling Language. RFC 7950, August 2016
20. Cerrato, I., Palesandro, A., Risso, F., Suñé, M., Vercellone, V., Woesner, H.: Toward dynamic virtualized network services in telecom operator networks. Comput. Netw. **92**, 380–395 (2015)
21. Bonafiglia, R., Miano, S., Nuccio, S., Risso, F., Sapio, A.: Enabling NFV services on resource-constrained CPEs. In: 5th IEEE International Conference on Cloud Networking (Cloudnet), pp. 83–88. IEEE (2016)
22. JOLNET: A geographical SDN network testbed. https://www.softfire.eu/jolnet/. Accessed 06 Feb 2017
23. Manzalini, A., Castellano, G., Risso, F.: 5G operating platform: Infrastructure-agnostic orchestration. In: IMT2020 Workshop and Demo Day: Technology Enablers for 5G. ITU, December 2016. Youtube video recording available https://www.youtube.com/watch?v=N6SBo2f6Lyc

Identification of Energy Hotspots:
A Case Study of the Very Fast Decision Tree

Eva Garcia-Martin[✉], Niklas Lavesson, and Håkan Grahn

Blekinge Institute of Technology, Karlskrona, Sweden
eva.garcia.martin@bth.se

Abstract. Large-scale data centers account for a significant share of the energy consumption in many countries. Machine learning technology requires intensive workloads and thus drives requirements for lots of power and cooling capacity in data centers. It is time to explore green machine learning. The aim of this paper is to profile a machine learning algorithm with respect to its energy consumption and to determine the causes behind this consumption. The first scalable machine learning algorithm able to handle large volumes of streaming data is the Very Fast Decision Tree (VFDT), which outputs competitive results in comparison to algorithms that analyze data from static datasets. Our objectives are to: (i) establish a methodology that profiles the energy consumption of decision trees at the function level, (ii) apply this methodology in an experiment to obtain the energy consumption of the VFDT, (iii) conduct a fine-grained analysis of the functions that consume most of the energy, providing an understanding of that consumption, (iv) analyze how different parameter settings can significantly reduce the energy consumption. The results show that by addressing the most energy intensive part of the VFDT, the energy consumption can be reduced up to a 74.3%.

Keywords: Machine learning · Big data · Very Fast Decision Tree · Green machine learning · Data mining · Data stream mining

1 Introduction

Current advancements in hardware together with the availability of large volumes of data, have inspired the field of machine learning into developing state-of-the-art algorithms that can process these volumes of data in real-time. For that reason, many machine learning algorithms are being implemented in big data platforms and in the cloud [22]. Examples of such applications are Apache Mahout and Apache SAMOA [4], frameworks for distributed and scalable machine learning algorithms.

There are several desired properties for an algorithm to handle large volumes of data: processing streams of data, adaptation to the stream speed, and deployment in the cloud. The Very Fast Decision Tree (VFDT) algorithm [6] is the first machine learning algorithm that is able to handle potentially infinite streams of

© Springer International Publishing AG 2017
M.H.A. Au et al. (Eds.): GPC 2017, LNCS 10232, pp. 267–281, 2017.
DOI: 10.1007/978-3-319-57186-7_21

data, while obtaining competitive predictive performance results in comparison to algorithms that analyze static datasets. Since these algorithms often run in the cloud, an energy efficient approach to the algorithm design could significantly affect the overall energy consumption of the cluster of servers.

The VFDT and other streaming algorithms are only evaluated in terms of scalability and predictive performance. The aim of this paper is to profile the Very Fast Decision Tree algorithm with respect to its energy consumption and to determine the causes behind this consumption. Our objectives are to: (i) establish a methodology that profiles the energy consumption of decision trees at the function level, (ii) apply this methodology in an experiment with four large datasets (10M examples) to obtain the energy consumption of the VFDT, (iii) conduct a fine-grained analysis of the functions that consume most of the energy, providing an understanding of that consumption, (iv) analyze how different parameter settings can significantly reduce the energy consumption. We have identified the part of the algorithm that consumes the most amount of energy, i.e. the energy hotspot. The results suggest that the energy can be reduced up to a 74.3% by addressing the energy hotspot and by parameter tuning the algorithm.

The paper is organized as follows. In Sect. 2 we give a background explanation of decision trees and the VFDT, continuing with a review of related work. In Sect. 3 we explain the proposed method to profile energy consumption and how to apply it to the VFDT. Sections 4 and 5 present the experiment and the results and analysis of the experiment. Finally, we present the conclusions and pointers to future work in Sect. 6.

2   Background

2.1   Decision Trees and Very Fast Decision Tree (VFDT)

In a classification problem, we have a set of examples in the form (x, y). x represents the features or attributes, and y represents the label to be predicted. The goal is to find the function, or model, that predicts y given x $(y = f(x))$ [6]. Decision trees are a common type of algorithms used in machine learning that represent f in the form of a tree. A node in the tree represents a test on an attribute, and the branches of such node, known as literals, represent the attribute values. The leaves represent the labels y. When the model is built, in order to predict the label of a new example x_i, the example passes through the nodes based on the different attribute values, until it reaches a leaf. That leaf will be the label y. In order to build the model, the algorithm uses a divide-and-conquer approach. The dataset is passed to the first node, and based on that data chunk, the attribute with the highest information gain is chosen as the root node. The dataset is then **split** based on that attribute choice, and each chunk of data is passed to the corresponding child. The process is repeated recursively on each node, until the information is **homogeneous** enough, then the leaf is **labeled** with the appropriate class.

Very Fast Decision Tree (VFDT) [6] is a decision tree algorithm that builds a tree incrementally. The data is analyzed sequentially and only once. The algorithm analyzes the first n instances of the data stream, and chooses the best attribute as the root node. This node is updated with the literals, each being a leaf. The following examples will be passed to the next leaves and follow the same procedure of replacing leaves by decision nodes. On each iteration, the statistics on each leaf are updated with the new example values. This is done by first sorting an example to a leaf l, based on the attribute values of that example and on the parent nodes, and then updating the times each attribute value is observed in l. After a minimum number of examples n are seen in l, the algorithm calculates the two attributes with the highest information gain (G). Let $\Delta G = G(X_a) - G(X_b)$ be the difference between the information gain of both attributes. If $\Delta G > \epsilon$ the leaf is substituted by an internal node with the attribute with highest G. ϵ represents the Hoeffding Bound [10], shown in Eq. 1. This bound states that the chosen attribute at a specific node after seeing n number of examples, will be the same attribute as if the algorithm had seen infinite number of examples, with probability $1 - \delta$.

$$\epsilon = \sqrt{\frac{R^2 \ln(1/\delta)}{2n}} \tag{1}$$

2.2 Related Work

This section focuses on two areas. The first area regarding energy efficiency in computing and the second relating machine learning, big data and energy efficiency.

Many energy-aware hardware solutions have been implemented. For instance, the Dynamic Voltage Frequency Scaling (DVFS) power saving technique is used in many contemporary processors. Several energy-saving approaches present energy efficient solutions for computation [21]. Regarding green computing at the software level, several publications [8,11,19] address the importance of developing energy-aware solutions, applications and algorithms. One of the key points is that still there is a very abstract-level research that aims at making energy efficient computations. Companies such as Google, Microsoft, and Intel, are committed to build software, hardware and data centers that are sustainable, energy efficient and environmentally friendly[1]. The Spirals[2] research group builds energy efficient software, showing different factors that affect energy consumption at the processor level [20].

Moving on to machine learning, there have been different approaches and studies to evaluate machine learning algorithms on large scale datasets. We have identified three studies that we consider to be the most relevant in terms of large scale experiments that follow a fine-grained analysis. The first comparison between different algorithms on large scale datasets was conducted in terms of predictive performance [13] in 1995. This study empirically compares 17 machine learning algorithms across 12 datasets using time and accuracy. More than a decade later, a study was conducted that empirically compared ten supervised

---

[1] http://www.theverge.com/2016/7/21/12246258/google-deepmind-ai-data-center-cooling.

[2] https://team.inria.fr/spirals/.

learning algorithms across 11 different datasets [3] by using eight accuracy-based performance measures. While these studies analyzed the total or average algorithm performance, another study was presented that evaluated algorithms in terms of time, by using a more detailed approach [1]. More specifically, the authors empirically compare eight machine learning algorithms for time series prediction and with respect to accuracy and the computation time for every function per time series. In the past years there has been an increase in designing machine learning algorithms in distributed systems that are able to analyze big data streams [4,18]. The Vertical Hoeffding Tree (VHT) [15] algorithm has been recently implemented to extend the VFDT. It is the first distributed streaming algorithm for learning decision trees. There is also a different perspective on how to use machine learning to make cloud computing environments more energy efficient [5].

There is a current increase of interest on energy efficiency algorithm design starting from the deep learning community, where they try to reduce the overall consumption of a neural networks by pruning several nodes in the different layers while minimizing the error [23]. In the field of data stream mining, although several algorithms have been published that can handle large amounts of data, such as the VFDT [6] and its extensions, we have yet to find an empirical evaluation of these algorithms with respect to energy consumption at the same detailed level. We believe that reducing the energy consumption of these kind of algorithms will have a significant impact in the overall consumption of data centers. In a previous work [16], we evaluated the impact on energy consumption of tuning the parameters of the VFDT. This work was extended [17] to choose more relevant parameters that could impact energy consumption based on a theoretical analysis of such parameters. For this paper, we focus on investigating the causes behind the energy consumption, by doing a fine-grained analysis of the energy consumption at the function level of the same algorithm.

3 Energy Profiling of Decision Trees

In order to analyze the energy consumption of the VFDT, we present a methodology to profile the energy consumption of decision tree learners at the function level. This approach allows us to: identify the energy hotspot of the algorithm, by discovering which functions are consuming most of the energy; and compare the energy consumption of different algorithms of the same class. The goal is to break down a specific algorithm into its specific functions, to then map them to the generic functions of the same algorithm class. We apply this to the VFDT in the following subsections. The method is divided in the following four steps:

1. Identification of the generic functions of a decision tree.
2. Identification of the specific functions of the algorithm to be profiled.
3. Mapping the specific functions of step 2 to generic functions of step 1.
4. Energy consumption measurement of the specific functions, to then aggregate those values into the generic functions.

3.1 Generic Decision Tree Breakdown

This is the first step in the proposed methodology where we identify the generic functions of a decision tree obtained from analyzing the *GrowTree* algorithm presented by Peter Flach [7]. Flach has identified four key functions: *homogeneous()*, *label()*, *bestSplit()* and *split()*. The *homogeneous()* function returns true if all the instances of the tree can be labeled with a single class. The *label()* function returns the label for the leaf node. There are different techniques to predict the value of the leaf node, e.g. using the majority class observed. The *bestSplit()* function returns the best attribute to split on. This can be achieved in different ways, such as using the *information gain* function. The *split()* function covers all the functions that are responsible for making the split of an internal node into different children.

3.2 Specific Function Breakdown

In the second step of the methodology we identify the specific functions of the VFDT. Specifically, we study the VFDT implementation from MOA (Massive Online Analysis) [2] version 2014.11. We have identified the structure of functions presented in Fig. 1.

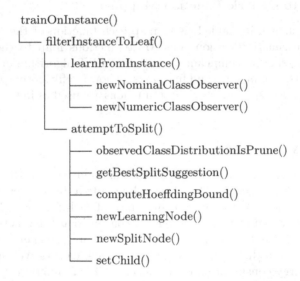

Fig. 1. Functions structure of the VFDT implementation.

The training phase starts by calling the function `trainOnInstance()`, which reads each instance sequentially, and updates the tree by updating the statistics at the leaf after reading the instance. To do so, it calls `filterInstanceToLeaf()`, which sorts the instance to the leaf by following the tests at the nodes. Then, the function `learnFromInstance()` updates the statistics and labels the leaf based on the option set by the user (majority class, Naive Bayes or a hybrid between both). Depending on the type of attribute (numerical or nominal) `newNominalClassObserver()` or `newNumericClassObserver()` will be used to keep track of the attribute values at that leaf. `attemptToSplit()` will then decide between substituting the leaf with an internal node or keeping the leaf with the previously predicted class.

Inside `attemptToSplit()`, they first calculate if all instances observed so far belong to the same class with `observedClassDistributionIsPrune()`. If they do not belong to the same class, the Hoeffding Bound [10] is computed, by calling `computeHoeffdingBound()`. The two best attributes are obtained by calling the function `getBestSplitSuggestion()`. The difference between those attributes is compared with the Hoeffding Bound previously calculated. Thus, if such difference is higher than the Hoeffding Bound, there will be a split on the tree by replacing the leaf with a new internal node with the best attribute. This internal node is created by calling `newSplitNode()` and updated with the literals by creating new leaves calling `newLearningNode()` and `setChild()`. There are some functions specific to the MOA implementation that were not measured since we consider them a baseline: `estimateModelByteSizes()`, `calculateByteSizes()`, `findLearningNodes()`, `enforceTrackerLimit()`.

3.3 Specific to Generic Function Mapping

The third step, shown in Table 1, is to map each function of the VFDT to the functions of the generic decision tree. Most functions map to the *split()* and *label()* functions, since a significant part of the VFDT algorithm and implementation addresses different ways and functions on how to efficiently split the nodes. Both the *homogeneous()* and *bestSplit()* functions are used as in the generic decision tree.

3.4 Energy Measurement

To estimate the energy consumption at the function level of the VFDT algorithm, we use the tool Jalen [20]. This tool accepts a Java or jar file as input, and outputs the energy consumption (in joules) of each function. Jalen outputs enough granularity to understand the energy consumed at the function level. The main limitation of the tool is the inability to estimate the energy consumption of programs that run during a short period of time, e.g. 5 s. We aggregate and combine the energy consumption of the specific VFDT functions to understand where the energy is being consumed in the generic decision tree functions.

4   Experimental Design

This experiment has been designed with two objectives:

- To understand which functions of the VFDT (mapped to generic decision tree functions) consume more energy than others.

Table 1. Mapping of functions between the generic decision tree and the VFDT algorithm. First column = implementation functions (Sect. 3.2). Second column = functions of the VFDT original algorithm [6]. Third column = generic functions of the decision tree (Sect. 3.1).

VFDT implementation	VFDT algorithm	Decision tree
filterInstanceToLeaf()	*Sort (x,y) into a leaf l ...*	*label()*
learnFromInstance()	*Label l and update statistics*	*label()*
newNominalClassObserver()	*Update statistics*	*label()*
newNumericClassOsserver()	*Update statistics*	*label()*
observedClassDistributionIsPrune()	*If the examples seen so far ...*	*homogeneous()*
getBestSplitSuggestions()	*Comp. $\overline{G}_l(X_i)$. Let X_b be the attribute...*	*bestSplit()*
computeHoeffdingBound()	*Compute ϵ using Eq. 1*	*split()*
newSplitNode()	*Replace l by an internal node*	*split()*
newLearningNode()	*Add a new leaf l_m ...*	*split()*
setChild()	*Add a new leaf l_m ...*	*split()*

- To understand the links between parameter configurations and the energy consumption, distributed across the generic functions. For instance, there could be some cases in which modifying the *tie threshold* parameter will affect the energy consumption of one specific function, and this function is the one that consumes more energy on average.

This knowledge makes it possible to make informed choices regarding parameter tuning to reduce energy consumption while retaining the same level of predictive accuracy.

4.1 Experimental Setup

The experiment is conducted as follows: The VFDT algorithm has been tuned with a total of 14 parameters setups (labeled A-N) and tested in four different datasets. Each configuration is an execution of the VFDT algorithm with such a parameter configuration. All 14 configurations have been tested on all four datasets. Therefore, there have been a total of $14 \times 4 = 56$ executions. Each execution has been repeated 5 times and averaged. The datasets and parameter tuning are further explained in Sects. 4.2 and 4.3.

We evaluate the predictive performance and energy consumption of the VFDT under the different parameter setups and datasets. The training and testing of the algorithm are carried out in MOA (Massive Online Analysis) [2], and the energy is measured with Jalen (explained in Sect. 3.4). The experiment is run on a Linux machine with an i7@2.70 GHz and 8 GB of RAM.

4.2 Datasets

Our experiment features four different datasets, summarized in Table 2. The datasets have been synthetically generated from MOA. The Random Tree generator creates a tree, following the explanation from the VFDT original authors [6]. We consider this dataset as the default behavior of the algorithm. The Hyperplane generator uses a function to generate data that follows a plane in several dimensions [12]. This dataset is often used to test algorithms that can handle concept drift, making it a more challenging synthetic dataset in comparison to the first one. The LED generator predicts the digit displayed on a LED display. Each attribute has a 10% chance of being inverted, and there a total of 7 segments in the display. Finally, the Waveform generator creates three different types of waves as a combination of two or three base waves. The goal is that the algorithm should be able to differentiate between these three types of waves [2].

Table 2. Dataset summary.

Dataset	Name	Type	Instances	Attributes	Numeric	Nominal
1	Random tree	Synthetic	10,000,000	10	5	5
2	Hyperplane	Synthetic	10,000,000	10	10	-
3	LED	Synthetic	10,000,000	24	-	24
4	Waveform	Synthetic	10,000,000	21	21	-

4.3 Parameter Tuning

The parameters that have been varied are shown in Table 3. The $nmin$ parameter represents the number of instances that the algorithm observes before calculating which attribute has the highest information gain. Theoretically, increasing this value will speed up the computations and lower the accuracy [6]. The τ parameter represents the tie threshold. Whenever the difference between the two best attributes is calculated, if this difference is smaller than τ, then there will be a split on the best attribute since the attributes are equally good. The absence of this parameter slows down the computation and decreases accuracy in theory [6]. The δ parameter represents one minus the confidence to make a split. In theory, the higher the confidence the higher the accuracy. The $Memory$ parameter represents the maximum memory the tree can consume. When the memory limit is reached, the algorithm will deactivate less promising leaves. The last parameter is the leaf prediction parameter. This parameter was introduced in the VFDTc, an extension of the VFDT [9] that is able to handle numeric attributes and that features a Naive Bayes classifier to label the leaves. We test between majority class, Naive Bayes, or a hybrid between both (Naive Bayes Adaptive [14]). The hybrid calculates both the majority class and the Naive Bayes prediction, and chooses the one that outputs higher predictive performance. The goal is to discover if the extra computation done by calculating both Naive Bayes and the majority class in comparison to calculating only one of them, trades-off with a significant increase in accuracy.

Table 3. Parameter configuration index. Different configurations of the VFDT. The parameters that are changed are represented in bold.

IDX	$nmin$	τ	δ	Memory	Leaf prediction
A	200	0.05	10^{-7}	30 MB	NBA
B	**700**	0.05	10^{-7}	30 MB	NBA
C	**1,200**	0.05	10^{-7}	30 MB	NBA
D	**1,700**	0.05	10^{-7}	30 MB	NBA
E	200	**0.01**	10^{-7}	30 MB	NBA
F	200	**0.09**	10^{-7}	30 MB	NBA
G	200	**0.13**	10^{-7}	30 MB	NBA
H	200	0.05	$\mathbf{10^{-1}}$	30 MB	NBA
I	200	0.05	$\mathbf{10^{-4}}$	30 MB	NBA
J	200	0.05	$\mathbf{10^{-10}}$	30 MB	NBA
K	200	0.05	10^{-7}	**100 KB**	NBA
L	200	0.05	10^{-7}	**2 GB**	NBA
M	200	0.05	10^{-7}	30 MB	**NB**
N	200	0.05	10^{-7}	30 MB	**MC**

NB = Naive Bayes. NBA = NB Adaptive. MC = Majority Class.

5   Results and Analysis

The results of the experiment are shown in Tables 4 and 5. These values are presented per parameter setup and in average. The values with higher accuracy and lower energy consumption are shown in bold. Setup K is not considered as the one with the lowest energy since its accuracy is significantly lower than the rest. Table 6 summarizes Tables 4 and 5 by averaging all setups. Each setup and dataset consume different amounts of energy. By comparing the parameters with the highest energy consumption and the lowest, we can have an energy saving of 52.18%, 47.76%, 74.22%, 76.24%, respectively per dataset.

Figure 4 shows the trade-off between accuracy and energy. The correlation between these two variables is of -0.79, which suggests that the higher the accuracy the lower the energy consumption, calculated from Table 6. The reason for this correlation is that datasets such as the LED dataset are complicated to analyze, thus consuming a lot of energy and obtaining low accuracy results. The opposite occurs in the Random Tree, that is easy to analyze, thus consuming less energy to do so, outputting higher accuracy results.

5.1   Energy Hotspot

The aim of this paper is to profile the energy consumption of the VFDT by showing which part of the algorithm is consuming most of the energy. Figure 3 shows the functions that consume the most amount of energy in the algorithm.

Table 4. Results for dataset 1 (random tree) and dataset 2 (hyperplane). In both datasets the energy is consumed in labeling (E1). The setup with lowest energy consumption and high accuracy is N: labeling with majority class. The random tree dataset outputs high accuracy in almost all setups.

I	Random tree dataset						Hyperplane dataset					
	ACC	#Leaves	E1	E2	E3	ET	ACC	#Leaves	E1	E2	E3	ET
A	99.82	11,443	96.11	0.01	1.70	97.83	91.40	22,429	230.58	1.10	18.67	250.36
B	99.78	8,061	98.48	0.02	0.36	98.85	91.38	21,331	235.61	0.86	5.46	241.93
C	99.73	6,746	101.09	0.02	0.21	101.33	91.47	20,433	238.90	0.80	3.24	242.94
D	99.69	5,832	97.83	0.01	0.19	98.03	91.73	19,366	256.26	0.65	2.59	259.51
E	99.50	7,518	99.83	0.02	3.57	103.42	91.82	1,854	231.76	0.00	35.03	266.79
F	99.87	13,372	86.41	0.01	0.81	87.24	89.33	44,817	199.80	9.01	8.99	217.81
G	99.88	15,734	80.54	0.14	0.62	81.30	88.90	60,398	197.61	19.61	6.39	223.62
H	**99.90**	16,920	76.12	0.01	0.62	76.75	88.93	60,911	195.29	19.59	6.06	220.96
I	99.87	12,928	88.04	0.03	1.02	89.09	90.18	31,316	202.99	3.08	12.45	218.52
J	99.78	10,368	102.70	0.02	1.44	104.15	92.04	18,723	258.59	0.02	22.79	281.42
K	94.94	806	10.89	0.00	0.00	10.89	83.06	524	15.14	0.00	0.00	15.14
L	99.82	11,444	100.99	0.01	1.21	102.20	**92.29**	33,549	420.43	0.05	35.38	455.87
M	99.67	11,443	49.49	0.01	1.22	50.72	87.41	22,442	128.49	1.06	17.47	**147.04**
N	99.83	11,443	48.52	0.02	1.27	**49.81**	91.41	22,442	132.57	1.06	16.74	150.39
AVG	99.43	10,289	81.22	0.02	1.02	82.26	90.10	27,181	210.29	4.06	13.66	228.02

E1(J) = Energy in *label()*, E2(J) = Energy in *split()*, E3(J) = Energy in *bestSplit()*, E4(J) = Energy in *homogeneous()*, ET(J) = E1 + E2 + E3 + E4. E4 $\simeq$ 0 across all setups, thus it's omission.

Table 5. Results for dataset 3 (LED) and dataset 4 (waveform). In the LED dataset, accuracy is constant and the energy consumption very high, most of it consumed in labeling when there are less splits on the nodes. In the Waveform dataset energy is consumed between labeling (E1) and calculating the best split (E3).

I	LED dataset						Waveform dataset					
	ACC	#Leaves	E1	E2	E3	ET	ACC	#Leaves	E1	E2	E3	ET
A	74.02	2,789	835.91	0.01	35.38	871.31	84.98	11,852	30.98	0.02	41.13	72.14
B	74.02	2,788	836.07	0.01	10.09	846.17	85.04	11,262	29.35	0.00	12.09	41.44
C	74.01	2,772	832.26	0.01	6.20	838.47	85.06	10,794	29.38	0.00	6.85	36.23
D	74.02	2,780	833.92	0.01	4.37	838.31	85.04	10,377	27.70	0.01	5.02	**32.73**
E	**74.03**	176	490.50	0.00	45.32	535.81	85.42	868	6.77	0.01	90.33	97.11
F	74.00	7,437	549.87	0.01	19.71	569.59	84.45	24,557	58.23	0.00	21.57	79.81
G	74.02	13,337	388.73	0.01	12.00	400.75	84.25	36,935	81.10	0.00	13.36	94.46
H	74.00	13,498	384.36	0.02	11.58	395.97	84.24	37,839	79.86	0.00	13.20	93.05
I	74.00	4,466	720.77	0.01	27.44	748.23	84.74	17,027	43.52	0.01	31.08	74.62
J	74.02	2,331	831.28	0.00	37.33	868.60	85.24	9,035	25.08	0.01	52.41	77.50
K	74.02	285	17.73	0.00	0.06	17.79	81.12	438	0.39	0.00	0.08	0.48
L	74.02	2,789	860.54	0.01	36.19	896.75	**85.59**	19,029	58.56	0.04	79.16	137.75
M	74.01	2,789	186.68	0.00	37.97	**224.65**	83.58	11,866	28.83	0.01	39.04	67.89
N	74.01	2,789	204.14	0.00	37.40	241.54	84.95	11,866	30.10	0.23	38.88	69.21
AVG	74.01	4,359	569.48	0.01	22.93	592.42	84.55	15,267	37.85	0.02	31.73	69.60

E1(J) = Energy in *label()*, E2(J) = Energy in *split()*, E3(J) = Energy in *bestSplit()*, E4(J) = Energy in *homogeneous()*, ET(J) = E1 + E2 + E3 + E4. E4 $\simeq$ 0 across all setups, thus it's omission.

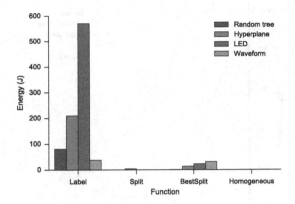

Fig. 2. Energy consumption, of the generic functions of a decision tree mapped from the VFDT algorithm, per dataset.

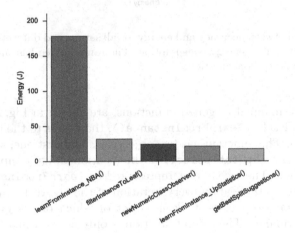

Fig. 3. Five functions with highest energy consumption.

Table 6. Averaged accuracy, leaves and energy results, from executing the VFDT algorithm in the four datasets shown in Table 2. Averaged from Tables 4 and 5.

Dataset	ACC(%)	#Leaves	E1(J)	E2(J)	E3(J)	E4(J)	ET(J)
Random tree	99.43	10, 289	81.22	0.02	1.02	0.00	82.26
Hyperplane	90.10	27, 181	210.29	4.06	13.66	0.01	228.02
LED	74.01	4, 359	569.48	0.01	22.93	0.00	592.42
Waveform	84.55	15, 267	37.85	0.02	31.73	0.00	69.60

E1 = Energy in *label()*, E2 = Energy in *split()*, E3 = Energy in *bestSplit()*, E4 = Energy in *homogeneous()*, ET = E1 + E2 + E3 + E4.

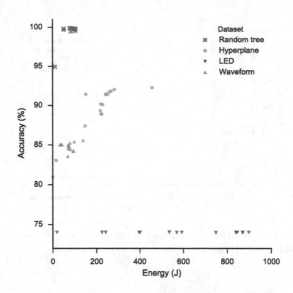

Fig. 4. Trade-off between accuracy and energy for all setups and datasets. Each dataset has a different pattern of energy consumption. The random tree has the highest accuracy and lowest energy consumption.

These functions, mapped to generic functions, are shown in Fig. 2. The energy hotspot of the VFDT is `learnFromInstance()`, that maps to the labeling phase of the algorithm. This function has two objectives. The first one, represented by `learnFromInstance_UpStatistics()` in the mentioned figure, updates the statistics of every leaf. The second one, represented by `learnFromInstance_NBA()`, predicts the class at the leaf on every iteration of the algorithm applying Naive Bayes and the majority class, to keep count of which one is giving a better predictive performance. The second function is only active when the parameter NBA (Naive Bayes Adaptive) is set (by default in the implementation). Based on the results, it is more energy efficient to split on a node rather than to delay the splitting, because updating the statistics at a leaf and applying Naive Bayes is more expensive on leaves that have already seen many examples. This phenomena can be observed in datasets 1, 2 and 3.

Dataset 4 has a different behavior than datasets 1–3 because it contains only numeric attributes whose values are not close to each other. The energy consumed in the labeling phase of this dataset is mainly done by the function `newNumericClassObserver()`, because updating the statistics of such attributes is quite expensive. However, this function consumes less energy when there are less splits on the leaves, as opposed to the behavior of `learnFromInstance()`. That is why in dataset 4, more splits lead to a higher energy consumption.

In summary, updating the statistics and setting the leaf prediction to Naive Bayes Adaptive are the energy hotspots of the algorithm. They are very expensive operations, and their energy consumption is higher when the splits on the leaves are delayed. There is a trade-off regarding the numeric estimator, since it consumes less energy whenever the splits are delayed. So, if the data has numeric attributes that are complicated to keep track of, it might be better to have smaller trees, since this can reduce the energy of the numeric estimator, and this function might be consuming more energy than the others in `learnFromInstance()`.

5.2 Parameter Analysis

We focus the parameter analysis on such parameters that can reduce the energy consumption of the labeling phase, and in particular of `learnFromInstance()`, since that is the energy hotspot. The longer it takes to make a decision to split on a leaf (by substituting it with a node), the higher the energy consumption. τ and δ are two parameters that have a great impact on how the tree expands. $1 - \delta$ represents the confidence on making the correct split. The higher the δ, the lower the confidence, leading to more splits and a reduction in energy. τ represents how separate the attributes can be in order to split. The higher the τ, the easier it is to make a split, thus lowering the energy consumption. For this reason, $\tau = 0.13$ and $\delta = 10^{-1}$ lead to very similar energy patterns. This occurs in datasets 1–3, for the reasons explained in the previous subsection.

In relation to *leaf prediction*, the default setup for this parameter (*Naive Bayes Adaptive*) is, on average, a worse choice than the other possible setups: *Naive Bayes* or *majority class*. For all datasets, the choice of one of these two setups showed a reduction in energy, hardly affecting accuracy. NBA computes the leaf prediction by applying Naive Bayes and majority class on every iteration of the algorithm for each instance, thus being very computationally and energy inefficient. On the other hand, *Naive Bayes* and *Majority class* predict the leaf value on the testing phase, reducing the energy consumption significantly. Moving on to *memory consumption*, we observe that reducing the amount of memory allocated for the tree drastically decreases energy consumption, but it also significantly reduces accuracy. We propose for future work to tune different values of memory consumption to see if there are important savings without having to reduce the accuracy of the model. Finally, when increasing the *nmin* parameter the accuracy and energy consumption are not significantly affected.

5.3 Suggestions to Improve Energy Efficiency

Based on this analysis, we can extract some suggestions to significantly reduce the energy consumption of the VFDT.

- Avoiding using the parameter Naive Bayes Adaptive since it marginally increases accuracy and it consumes a lot of energy. The reason is that Naive Bayes and majority class are computed every time an instance is processed.
- Splitting the leaf into a node is more energy efficient than delaying the split, since updating the statistics at the leaves that have already observed many instances is very expensive.

- Increasing the δ and τ has positive effects on energy consumption, creating more splits and avoiding delaying the splits.
- If the data is numerical and complicated to keep track of, delaying the splits can be more energy efficient.

6   Conclusions and Future Work

The aim of this paper is to profile the energy consumption of the Very Fast Decision Tree algorithm. To achieve that, we have presented the following: (i) a methodology that profiles the energy consumption of decision trees at the function level, (ii) an experiment that uses this methodology to discover the most energy consuming functions of the VFDT, (iii) a thorough analysis to understand the reasons behind the functions energy consumption, and (iv) which parameter settings decrease the energy consumption of such functions.

The analysis of the results show that the functions responsible for the labeling of the decision tree are the main energy hotspots. Specifically, updating the statistics in the leaves and predicting the class at the leaf with parameter NBA are the main reasons for the amount of energy consumed in the algorithm. The energy consumption in labeling is significantly reduced if there are more splits on the leaves, rather than delaying the splitting to gain a higher confidence. Additionally, the results show that the energy can be reduced up to a 74.3% by tuning the parameters of the VFDT.

The planned future work is to make an energy efficient extension of the VFDT with the knowledge extracted from this study. We will also investigate in more depth different parameter combinations to see if energy can be reduced further. We also plan to compare the predictive performance and the energy consumption of other tree learners with the VFDT.

Acknowledgments. This work is part of the research project "Scalable resource-efficient systems for big data analytics" funded by the Knowledge Foundation (grant: 20140032) in Sweden.

References

1. Ahmed, N.K., Atiya, A.F., Gayar, N.E., El-Shishiny, H.: An empirical comparison of machine learning models for time series forecasting. Econometric Rev. **29**(5–6), 594–621 (2010)
2. Bifet, A., Holmes, G., Kirkby, R., Pfahringer, B.: MOA: Massive Online Analysis. J. Mach. Learn. Res. **11**, 1601–1604 (2010)
3. Caruana, R., Niculescu-Mizil, A.: An empirical comparison of supervised learning algorithms. In: Proceedings of the 23rd International Conference on Machine Learning, pp. 161–168. ACM (2006)
4. De Francisci Morales, G.: SAMOA: a platform for mining big data streams. In: Proceedings of the 22nd International Conference on World Wide Web, pp. 777–778. ACM (2013)

5. Demirci, M.: A survey of machine learning applications for energy-efficient resource management in cloud computing environments. In: IEEE 14th International Conference on Machine Learning and Applications (ICMLA), pp. 1185–1190 (2015)
6. Domingos, P., Hulten, G.: Mining high-speed data streams. In: Proceedings of the 6th ACM SIGKDD International Conference on Knowledge Discovery and Data Mining, pp. 71–80 (2000)
7. Flach, P.: Machine Learning: The Art and Science of Algorithms that Make Sense of Data. Cambridge University Press, New York (2012)
8. Freire, A., Macdonald, C., Tonellotto, N., Ounis, I., Cacheda, F.: A self-adapting latency/power tradeoff model for replicated search engines. In: 7th ACM International Conference on Web Search and Data Mining, pp. 13–22 (2014)
9. Gama, J., Rocha, R., Medas, P.: Accurate decision trees for mining high-speed data streams. In: Proceedings of the Ninth ACM SIGKDD International Conference on Knowledge Discovery and Data Mining, pp. 523–528. ACM (2003)
10. Hoeffding, W.: Probability inequalities for sums of bounded random variables. J. Am. Stat. Assoc. **58**(301), 13–30 (1963)
11. Hooper, A.: Green computing. Commun. ACM **51**(10), 11–13 (2008)
12. Hulten, G., Spencer, L., Domingos, P.: Mining time-changing data streams. In: Proceedings of the Seventh ACM SIGKDD International Conference on Knowledge Discovery and Data Mining, pp. 97–106 (2001)
13. King, R.D., Feng, C., Sutherland, A.: Statlog: comparison of classification algorithms on large real-world problems. Appl. Artif. Intell. Int. J. **9**(3), 289–333 (1995)
14. Kirkby, R.B.: Improving hoeffding trees. Ph.D. thesis, The University of Waikato (2007)
15. Kourtellis, N., Morales, G.D.F., Bifet, A., Murdopo, A.: VHT: Vertical Hoeffding Tree. arXiv preprint arXiv:1607.08325 (2016)
16. Martín, E.G., Lavesson, N., Grahn, H.: Energy efficiency in data stream mining. In: Proceedings of the 2015 IEEE/ACM International Conference on Advances in Social Networks Analysis and Mining 2015, pp. 1125–1132. ACM (2015)
17. Garcia-Martín, E., Lavesson, N., Grahn, H.: Energy efficiency analysis of the very fast decision tree algorithm. In: Missaoui, R., Abdessalem, T., Latapy, M. (eds.) Trends in Social Network Analysis - Information Propagation, User Behavior Modelling, Forecasting, and Vulnerability Assessment(2017, to appear)
18. Murdopo, A.: Distributed decision tree learning for mining big data streams (2013)
19. Murugesan, S.: Harnessing green IT: principles and practices. IT Prof. **10**(1), 24–33 (2008)
20. Noureddine, A., Rouvoy, R., Seinturier, L.: Monitoring energy hotspots in software. Autom. Softw. Eng. **22**(3), 291–332 (2015)
21. Reams, C.: Modelling energy efficiency for computation. Ph.D. thesis, University of Cambridge (2012)
22. Wu, X., Zhu, X., Wu, G.Q., Ding, W.: Data mining with big data. IEEE Trans. Knowl. Data Eng. **26**(1), 97–107 (2014)
23. Yang, T.J., Chen, Y.H., Sze, V.: Designing energy-efficient convolutional neural networks using energy-aware pruning. arXiv preprint arXiv:1611.05128 (2016)

Mobile and Pervasive Computing

Prolonging Lifetime in Wireless Sensor Networks with Interference Constraints

Francesco Carrabs, Raffaele Cerulli, Ciriaco D'Ambrosio$^{(\boxtimes)}$, and Andrea Raiconi

Department of Mathematics, University of Salerno,
Via Giovanni Paolo II 132, 84084 Fisciano, SA, Italy
{fcarrabs,raffaele,cdambrosio,araiconi}@unisa.it

Abstract. In this work, we consider a scenario in which we have to monitor some locations of interest in a geographical area by means of a wireless sensor network. Our aim is to keep the network operational for as long as possible, while preventing certain sensors from being active simultaneously, since they would interfere with one another causing data loss, need for retransmissions and overall affecting the throughput and efficiency of the network. We propose an exact approach based on column generation, as well as a heuristic algorithm to solve its separation problem. Computational tests prove our approach to be effective, and that the introduction of our heuristic in the Column Generation framework allows significant gains in terms of required computational effort.

Keywords: Wireless sensor network · Column generation · Maximum lifetime · Interference constraints · Greedy algorithm

1 Introduction

Wireless Sensor Networks (WSNs) represent nowadays an ubiquitous technology. The rapid advancements in the technologies involved in the production of cost-effective embedded hardware greatly contributed to this trend, enabling the development of new related concepts such as the Internet of Things [1] and flying drones [9], and also raising concerns about the security of wireless communications ([15–17]). Among their many applications, monitoring and surveillance are very relevant in several contexts, with applications varying from natural disasters forecasting to personal safety and city management ([5,18,20]). One may consider, for instance, monitoring of environmental parameters such as temperature, sound, soil movements or pollution levels, or surveillance and motion detection in urban, military or domestic environments.

One of the main drawbacks is represented by the batteries installed in the individual sensor devices, which due to cost and size reasons have often a limited capacity. Hence, finding means to efficiently coordinate their activity to prolong the amount of time over which the network can remain operational is a crucial issue. To this end, many scientific efforts have been focused on proposing solutions for the *Maximum Network Lifetime Problem* (MLP) and variants. The aim

© Springer International Publishing AG 2017
M.H.A. Au et al. (Eds.): GPC 2017, LNCS 10232, pp. 285–297, 2017.
DOI: 10.1007/978-3-319-57186-7_22

of the problem is to individuate multiple and possibly overlapping sensor subsets (*covers*) that can individually provide coverage for all the considered points of interest (*targets*), as well as an appropriate amount of activation time for each of them. Since each cover is able to provide the necessary coverage, all sensors that do not belong to it can be kept in a battery-preserving idle state while it is active. If a sensor belongs to more than one cover, the sum of their chosen activation times should not exceed the battery lifetime of the sensor. Under these assumptions, a continuous monitoring of the region of interest can be performed by activating covers one by one, and the overall network lifetime is given by the sum of the individual activation times. MLP was proven to be NP-Complete in [7], in which the authors also show that considering overlapping covers can greatly improve the optimal solution with respect to disjoint ones.

The main issue to be faced to solve a Maximum Network Lifetime problem is given by the number covers, which can be exponential with respect to the size of the considered instance (theoretically, any subset of the set of sensors may be a cover). The Column Generation (CG) technique has proved to be an effective tool to tackle this issue. This technique decomposes the problem in two components, a so-called *master problem* that only considers a subset of covers and assigns appropriate lifetime durations to each of them, and a *separation problem* whose aim is to produce new promising covers to be used by the master problem. A CG approach for the classical version of the problem was proposed by [21]. Since the separation problem is a hard problem itself, the author also proposed a heuristic algorithm to face it.

As mentioned, several variants of the problem have been proposed as well, to adapt it to different application contexts. For instance, there are works that consider cases in which not all targets must be continuously covered, but rather a given percentage of them ([12,23,30]), sensors that can adjust their radii to find optimal trade-offs between coverage and energy consumption ([8,19,22,28]), heterogeneous networks with multiple sensor types ([3,10]), and works considering connectivity issues in order to transmit the collected information to a central processing unit ([2,6,11,13,14,24,27,31]).

Another relevant issue in the WSNs literature is related to interferences among the sensors of the network. The sudden increase in the number of connected devices has raised concern on this topic, due for instance to the coexistence of different wireless technologies operating in the same frequency band [4]. Even within sensors of the same type, concurrent transmission of sensors that are close enough to interfere may limit the network throughput and cause additional energy expense due to collisions, which cause data loss and hence require retransmissions [26]. Some works attempt to produce a connected topology that minimizes the interferences ([25,26,29]).

In this work we address the problem of maximizing the network lifetime on a wireless sensor network with interference constraints. In this variant of the problem, we are given a collection of pairs of *conflicting* sensors. Two sensors are said to be conflicting if each of them should be in idle mode while the other is in sensing mode, since they would generate interference if used together. It follows that by allowing covers to contain at most a sensor for each conflicting pair, we are able to find the maximum network lifetime that can be obtained without interferences.

To solve the problem, we propose a Column Generation exact approach. An appropriately designed heuristic algorithm to speed up the separation problem resolution is also proposed.

It should be noted that our definition of conflicting sensors is perfectly fit to model the case in which sensors interfere with each other because they are too close; in this case, there will be a conflicting pair for each couple of sensors that are contained in each other's sensing or transmission range (in the following, this conflict-defining range will be called *conflict range*). This will also be our assumption in the computational tests carried out for this work. However, it is also general enough to be adaptable to other interference definitions, or any other cases in which specific sensor subsets should not be used together.

The rest of the work is organized as follows. In Sect. 2 we formally define the problem. Section 3 describes in detail the proposed algorithm. Section 4 summarizes the results of our computational tests. Finally, Sect. 5 contains some final remarks.

2 Problem Definition

Let $W = \{S, T, \tau, \delta, \gamma\}$ be a wireless sensor network, where:

- $S = \{s_1, \ldots s_n\}$ is the set of sensors (let $|S| = n$);
- $T = \{t_1, \ldots t_m\}$ is the set of targets (let $|T| = m$);
- $\tau : S \to \mathbb{R}^+$ is a function assigning to each sensor the maximum amount of time for which it can be kept in active (sensing) mode before exhausting its battery. In the following, we will use the notation τ_i to refer to $\tau(s_i)$;
- $\delta : S \times T \to \{0, 1\}$ is a function such that $\delta(s_i, t_j)$ is equal to 1 if sensor t_j is located within the sensing range of sensor s_i and can therefore be monitored by it (in which case we say that s_i *covers* t_j), and 0 otherwise. In the following, we will use the notation δ_{ij} to refer to $\delta(s_i, t_j)$;
- $\gamma : S \times S \to \{0, 1\}$ is a function such that $\gamma(s_i, s_j)$ is equal to 1 if sensors s_i and s_j are in conflict, and therefore at most one of them can be active in any given time instant, and 0 otherwise. In the following, we will use the notation γ_{ij} to refer to $\gamma(s_i, s_j)$. By definition, $\gamma_{ij} = \gamma_{ji} \; \forall (s_i, s_j) \in S \times S$.

A cover $C \subseteq S$ is a subset of sensors satisfying the following two properties:

1. $\sum_{s_i \in C} \delta_{ij} \geq 1 \; \forall t_j \in T$. That is, each target of the network can be monitored by at least a sensor belonging to the cover;
2. $\gamma_{ij} = 0 \; \forall (s_i, s_j) \in C \times C$. That is, the cover contains at most one sensor for each conflicting pair.

It follows that, by activating all sensors in C while keeping those in $S \setminus C$ in idle mode, the whole set of targets can be monitored without generating interference.

The Maximum Lifetime problem with Interferences Constraints (MLIC) requires to find a collection of pairs $(C_1, w_1), \ldots, (C_z, w_z)$, where each C_k is a cover and the related $w_k \geq 0$ is a value representing the *activation time* assigned to it, such that:

1. $\sum_{C_k : s_i \in C_k} w_k \leq \tau_i \ \forall s_i \in S$. That is, each sensor is not scheduled to be active for an amount of time that exceeds its battery capacity;
2. $\sum_{k=1}^{z} w_k$ (that is, the overall network lifetime) is maximized.

Assuming to be able to identify and enumerate all covers $C_1, \ldots, C_\ell$, the problem is described by the following linear programming mathematical model:

$$[\mathbf{P}] \max \sum_{k=1}^{\ell} w_k \tag{1}$$

$$\sum_{C_k : s_i \in C_k} w_k \leq \tau_i \qquad\qquad \forall s_i \in S \tag{2}$$

$$w_k \geq 0 \qquad\qquad \forall k = 1, \ldots, \ell \tag{3}$$

The model contains one constraint (row) for each sensor of the network, and one variable (column) for each cover; each variable w_k has coefficient 1 in the ith constraint if $s_i \in C_k$, and is not in the constraint otherwise.

It is easy to see that the objective function (1) and constraints (2) correspond to the lifetime maximization and to the enforcement of battery capacity constraints, respectively.

However, as mentioned in Sect. 1, the number of covers (and hence, the number of variables) is potentially exponential, therefore using an optimization software such as IBM ILOG CPLEX to find the optimal solution of this model is not generally possible in practice. For this reason, we developed the Column Generation approach presented in next section.

3 Column Generation Approach

Our CG approach starts by finding an optimal solution for a variant of the [$\mathbf{P}$] formulation that only considers a subset of all covers, called the master problem or [$\mathbf{MP}$] from now on. Ideally, in order to understand if this solution is optimal for the original problem as well, one should compute all reduced costs for the variables that were not taken into account by [$\mathbf{MP}$].

In order to avoid to explicitly consider all these variables, we instead define and solve another problem (called separation problem) whose aim is to build the column (representing, in our case, a cover) of the variable with minimum reduced cost. If this reduced cost is negative, the related variable is then introduced into [$\mathbf{MP}$], since it may improve the current solution (we define such a variable and the related cover to be *attractive*), and [$\mathbf{MP}$] is solved again. This procedure is iterated until the optimal solution for the separation problem corresponds to

---

Algorithm 1. GreedySP

Input: Wireless network, dual prices vector π;
Output: Attractive cover C or failure;

1 $C \leftarrow \emptyset$;
2 $S_c \leftarrow S$;
3 $T_u \leftarrow T$;
4 $\underline{\omega}_c \leftarrow updateWeights(S_c)$;
5 **while** $|T_u| > 0$ **do**
6   **if** $S_c == \emptyset$ **then**
7   ⌊ **return** failure;
8      $s \leftarrow ChooseBest(S_c, \underline{\omega}_c)$;
9      $C \leftarrow C \cup \{s\}$;
10     $T_u \leftarrow RemoveCovered(s)$;
11     $S_c \leftarrow RemoveConflicts(s)$;
12     $S_c \leftarrow RemoveUseless(T_u)$;
13   ⌊ $\underline{\omega}_c \leftarrow updateWeights(S_c)$;
14 **if** $Attractive(C)$ **then**
15   ⌊ **return** C;
16 **else**
17   ⌊ **return** failure;

---

a cover with a nonnegative reduced cost. Indeed, in this case, the last optimal solution found for [**MP**] is also optimal for the original problem [**P**].

Let π_i, $\forall s_i \in S$, be the dual prices of the sensors associated to the optimal solution of an instance of [**MP**]. The separation problem requires to find the cover C_k that minimizes the quantity $\sum_{s_i \in C_k} \pi_i - c_k = \sum_{s_i \in C_k} \pi_i - 1$, since the coefficient c_k of each variable w_k in the objective function (1) of [**P**] is 1. Being a set cover problem, the separation problem is NP-Hard. Moreover, it can be noted that any attractive cover (not necessarily the optimal one) can improve the current solution. For these reasons, we propose a greedy heuristic (called GreedySP) to solve this problem, which is described in Sect. 3.1.

However, whenever GreedySP fails (meaning that it either does not find a cover, or does not find an attractive one) there is no guarantee that the optimality condition has been reached. Therefore, we also propose an integer programming formulation called [**SP**] to solve the separation problem to optimality. In more detail, after solving [**MP**], in each CG iteration the procedure first solves the separation problem heuristically using our greedy algorithm. If it succeeds in finding an attractive cover, the cover is added to the set considered by [**MP**], and the current CG iteration ends. Otherwise, [**SP**] is used to solve the separation problem to optimality. The [**SP**] model is presented in Sect. 3.2.

As will be shown in Sect. 4, our algorithm is an effective method to solve the MLIC problem. On the one hand, it allows to solve the problem optimally; on the other hand, the introduction of GreedySP allows to significantly reduce the required computational effort.

3.1 Heuristic for the Separation Problem

The pseudocode for GreedySP is reported in Algorithm 1. The algorithm takes as input the wireless sensor network and the dual prices vector π. In the first step, the algorithm initializes the sets C, S_c, T_u and the vector $\underline{\omega_c}$. The C set represents the cover that GreedySP is attempting to build, and therefore it is initialized with the empty set. The S_c set contains the candidate sensors, that is, sensors that do not belong to C but are not in conflict with any element of C, and is initialized with the S set. The T_u set contains the uncovered targets, meaning that they are not within the sensing range of any sensor in C; therefore, when C is empty, T_u is equal to T. The $updateWeights$ function attributes a weight to each element of S_c. The weights are computed as follows:

$$\omega_c(s_i) = \frac{\pi_i}{\sum_{t_j \in T_u} \delta_{ij}} \qquad \forall s_i \in S_c \tag{4}$$

The weighting function balances the dual price of each candidate sensor and the number of uncovered targets that are covered by it. Since we are interested in minimizing the sum of the dual prices belonging to the cover, and selecting sensors that cover many targets may lead to needing less of them in C, it follows that the smaller is $\omega_c(s_i)$, the better is the sensor evaluation. Note that the weight is undefined if s_i does not cover any target in T_u; we assume this to never be the case in the initialization phase, since it would mean that the sensor is useless (no target in T is within its sensing range) and therefore it should be removed in preprocessing.

The while loop adds new sensors to C one by one, and iterates until there are no uncovered targets, meaning that C is indeed a cover. Inside the loop, we first check whether S_c is empty, in which case C cannot be completed and the algorithm ends, reporting a failure. If S_c is not empty, the $ChooseBest$ function selects its minimum-weight element s and removes it from S_c. The new sensor is added to C, and all targets that are covered by it are removed by T_u. The $RemoveConflicts$ and $RemoveUseless$ functions update S_c by removing all sensors that cannot be chosen in future iterations since they are either in conflict with the new sensor, or do not cover uncovered targets any more. Finally, since the T_u set was updated, the $\underline{\omega_c}$ weights are recomputed for the remaining elements of S_c.

At the end of the while loop, as mentioned, the set C constitutes a cover. However, in order to understand if it is an attractive one, we check whether $\sum_{s_i \in C} \pi_i < 1$. If C is attractive, it is retuned by GreedySP and the current CG iteration ends, otherwise the heuristic reports a failure.

3.2 Integer Programming Formulation for the Separation Problem

The following formulation describes the separation problem:

$$[\mathbf{SP}] \min \sum_{s_i \in S} \pi_i y_i \tag{5}$$

$$\sum_{s_i \in S: \delta_{ij}=1} y_i \geq 1 \qquad\qquad \forall t_j \in T \tag{6}$$

$$y_i + y_j \leq 1 \qquad \forall (s_i, s_j) \in S \times S : \gamma_{ij} = 1, i < j \tag{7}$$

$$y_i \in \{0,1\} \qquad\qquad \forall s_i \in S \tag{8}$$

For each sensor $s_i \in S$, the binary variable y_i will be equal to 1 if the sensor is chosen to be part of the cover, 0 otherwise. The objective function (5) minimizes the sum of the dual prices of the chosen sensors. Constraints (6) impose for each target t_j the selection of at least a sensor among those that can cover it, while constraints (7) make sure that at most a sensor is selected for each conflicting pair.

As mentioned, [**SP**] is used within the CG framework to solve the subproblem to optimality whenever GreedySP fails. If the objective function value is greater than or equal to 1, the optimality condition has been reached and CG ends, otherwise the cover found by the model is attractive and CG must be iterated again.

3.3 Initializing the CG Method

We need a procedure to build the set of covers considered by [**MP**] in the first iteration of the CG method. In our algorithm, we initialize this set with a single cover, produced by a variant of GreedySP. Since in this case we do not have dual prices associated to the sensors, the weights in this variant are computed as follows:

$$\omega_c(s_i) = \frac{\sum_{s_k \in S} \gamma_{ki}}{\sum_{t_j \in T_u} \delta_{ij}} \qquad \forall s_i \in S_c \tag{9}$$

That is, in this case the weighting function balances the number of conflicts of the sensor in the network and the number of uncovered targets that are covered by it. Note that, since we do not have dual prices, the concept of attractive cover is not defined for this initialization step, therefore if GreedySP produces a cover, it is always returned and used to initialize [**MP**]. If GreedySP fails to build a cover, we use the [**SP**] formulation with random dual price values to initialize [**MP**].

4 Computational Results

In this section, in order to evaluate the effectiveness of our CG approach that uses GreedySP (called CG+GSP from now on), we compare it with a version that always solves the separation problem exactly by means of the [**SP**] formulation. In the following, we will refer to this second version with the name SimpleCG.

Our algorithms were coded in C++, and the tests were executed on a Linux platform with an Intel Xeon E5-2650 CPU running at 2.30 GHz and 128 GB of RAM. The mathematical formulations embedded in the CG framework were solved using the Concert library of IBM ILOG CPLEX 12.6.1. All tests were run in single thread mode, and we fixed a time limit equal to 1 hour for each test. When a certified optimal solution is not found within this amount of time, the best solution found is returned and used for our comparisons. In these cases, a "*" symbol is added near the related values in Tables 1 and 2.

We considered two different groups of instances. The first group was proposed in [14] for a different variant of the maximum lifetime problem. In this work, the authors proposed instances with a number of sensors varying in the set $\{100, 200, 300, 400, 500\}$, and 15 or 30 targets. However, here we only considered instances with a number of sensors greater than or equal to 300, as the smaller ones resulted to be too easily solvable for the MLIC problem. All sensors have the same battery duration, normalized to 1 time unit. Sensors and targets are disposed in a square area with size 500×500. The sensing range (RS) is equal to either 100 or 125, meaning that any sensor with an euclidean distance within this value from a given sensor is considered to be covered by it. Additionally, for these instances we consider a conflict range (RC) equal to either 125 or 175, meaning that two sensors that are within this distance from each other form a conflicting pair. There are 4 different instances for each combination of parameters, leading to 96 instances.

In order to test our approach on more challenging instances, we propose a second group, generated similarly to the ones in [14]. The new set of instances have a number of sensors equal to either 750, 1000, or 1250, while all other parameters are the same as the previous group. Hence, the second group is composed of 96 instances as well.

The results of the comparison on the first group are reported in Table 1. The table contains 12 rows divided in two groups of six rows each, associated to the sensing ranges $RS = 100$ and $RS = 125$, respectively. The first two columns show the number of sensors ($|S|$) and targets ($|T|$) in the scenarios. The next 10 columns are divided in two groups associated to the conflict ranges $RC = 125$ and $RC = 175$, respectively. Under these columns, we report in each entry an average value related to a scenario composed of four instances with the same characteristics. In more detail, we report for each algorithm the lifetime (LF) rounded to the second decimal digit, the computational time ($Time$) in seconds and the percentage gap between these computational times (Gap), evaluated as $\frac{Time(SimpleCG) - Time(CG+GSP)}{Time(SimpleCG)}$. When the time gap between the two algorithms is lower then 5 s, we do not report its percentage value, since we consider it negligible.

On the scenarios with $RS = 100$ and $RC = 125$, CG+GSP is always faster than SimpleCG with a gap value that ranges from about 43% to 92%. However, both algorithms are very effective on these scenarios, since they are solved to

Table 1. Comparison between CG+GSP and SimpleCG on the smaller instances.

	$|S|$	$|T|$	RC=125					RC=175				
			CG+GSP		SimpleCG		Gap	CG+GSP		SimpleCG		Gap
			LF	Time	LF	Time		LF	Time	LF	Time	
RS = 100	300	15	16.25	0.98	16.25	4.05		13.75	4.57	13.75	6.56	
	300	30	13.25	1.38	13.25	4.58		9.16	9.35	9.16	9.93	
	400	15	20.75	0.73	20.75	9.44	92.27%	18.25	12.11	18.25	19.58	38.15%
	400	30	19.00	5.41	19.00	13.35	59.48%	14.25	34.84	14.25	36.19	
	500	15	28.75	4.72	28.75	26.54	82.22%	25.50	42.36	25.50	55.12	23.15%
	500	30	26.00	20.49	26.00	35.92	42.96%	19.00	118.05	19.00	122.02	
RS = 125	300	15	23.25	0.19	23.25	5.36	96.46%	23.25	3.89	23.25	11.40	65.88%
	300	30	18.25	0.36	18.25	5.39	93.32%	18.25	7.17	18.25	10.80	
	400	15	32.50	0.24	32.50	14.97	98.40%	32.50	5.59	32.50	36.80	84.81%
	400	30	27.25	0.31	27.25	16.77	98.15%	26.75	30.48	26.75	40.76	25.22%
	500	15	41.25	0.55	41.25	38.28	98.56%	41.25	35.52	41.25	90.10	60.58%
	500	30	38.00	3.63	38.00	40.78	91.10%	38.00	85.67	38.00	107.35	20.20%

optimality in less than a minute. By increasing the conflict range RC to 175, it can be observed that computational times increase for both algorithms. Indeed, while all scenarios are still optimally solved by them, the requested computational time grows up to about two minutes. On these instances, CG+GSP is again always faster than SimpleCG; however, percentage gaps are smaller, and we report them in just 2 out of 6 cases, in which this value ranges from 23% to 38%. This is due to GreedySP becoming less effective, due to the additional conflicts on these instances.

By considering the instances with sensing range $RS = 125$, the computational times increase for SimpleCG and decrease for CG+GSP. Indeed, on the scenarios with $RS = 125$ and $RC = 125$, the gap values are always higher than 90%, proving that GreedySP is highly effective in finding attractive covers in these denser instances. By increasing the conflict range to 175, we observe a reduction of the gap values with respect to the scenarios with $RC = 125$. However, they remain generally significant, up to 84.81%, and the difference between the computational times of the two algorithms is under 5 s only in 1 case out of 6.

These results suggest that the main factor affecting the complexity of the problem is the size of the conflict range (and hence the number of conflicts), and that CG+GSP appears to relevantly outperform SimpleCG. However, this dataset resulted to be too simple to draw definitive conclusions, since all scenarios were solved within 123 s. For these reasons, we generated the second group of instances with up to 1250 sensors.

The results on these new instances are reported in Table 2. As expected, the computational times are higher than the ones required to solve previous instances, and there are scenarios that are not solved within the time limit. In more detail, on the scenarios with $RS = 100$ and $RC = 125$, CG+GSP requires

Table 2. Comparison between CG+GSP and SimpleCG on the larger instances

	$|S|$	$|T|$	RC=125					RC=175				
			CG+GSP		SimpleCG		Gap	CG+GSP		SimpleCG		Gap
			LF	Time	LF	Time		LF	Time	LF	Time	
RS = 100	750	15	70.25	37.46	70.25	429.89	91.29%	68.50	671.88	68.50	977.29	31.25%
	750	30	43.50	59.64	43.50	208.32	71.37%	43.00	719.42	43.00	729.30	1.35%
	1000	15	60.25	2.53	60.25	814.45	99.69%	60.25	962.01	60.25	1773.15	45.75%
	1000	30	52.50	26.90	52.50	668.10	95.97%	49.00	1704.59	49.00	1757.12	2.99%
	1250	15	89.75	15.95	89.75	1935.21	99.18%	85.91*	2274.69	79.84*	3400.97	33.12%
	1250	30	57.00	342.85	57.00	1307.43	73.78%	52.75	2365.43	52.75	2500.29	5.39%
RS = 125	750	15	72.25	1.51	72.25	279.57	99.46%	72.25	117.82	72.25	701.84	83.21%
	750	30	56.50	2.53	56.50	257.09	99.02%	55.50	419.09	55.50	660.50	36.55%
	1000	15	96.75	3.85	96.75	940.66	99.59%	96.75	796.88	96.75	2338.06	65.92%
	1000	30	79.25	4.21	79.25	733.95	99.43%	79.00	1360.21	79.00	1958.42	30.55%
	1250	15	127.75	8.88	127.75	2393.13	99.63%	127.75	843.91	95.45*	3523.17	76.05%
	1250	30	68.25	4.99	68.25	1378.17	99.64%	68.25	2035.12	68.25	2569.43	20.79%

up to 342 s to solve the problem, while SimpleCG requires 1307 s in the worst case. Percentage gaps range from 71% to over 99%. By increasing the conflict range to 175, similarly to the results of Table 1, the gap values decrease and range from 1.35% to 45.75%. In the scenario with 1250 sensors and 15 targets, both algorithms fail to find all optimal solutions within the time limit. In more detail, this happens for a single instance of the scenario for CG+GSP and for 3 out of 4 instances for SimpleCG. As a consequence, the average solution found by CG+GSP (85.91) is significantly better than the one of SimpleCG (79.84).

On the scenarios with $RS = 125$ and $RC = 125$ the percentage gaps are always higher than 99%. Indeed, CG+GSP is able to solve these scenarios within 10 s, while SimpleCG requires from 257 to 2393 s. Overall, for both the groups of instances, the combination of parameters $RS = 125, RC = 125$ appears to be the one where CG+GSP has the largest advantage over SimpleCG, since the smaller conflict ranges and higher sensing ranges allow GreedySP to find more attractive covers. On the scenarios with $RS = 125$ and $RC = 175$, percentage gaps range from 20.79% and 83.21%. Again SimpleCG fails to optimally solve 3 instances in the scenario with 1250 sensors and 15 targets, while CG+GSP solves to optimality all of them. The average solution returned by SimpleCG for this scenario is equal to 95.45, while the optimal value provided by CG+GSP is significantly better, being equal to 127.75.

Overall, the results reported in Table 2 show that CG+GSP is often one order of magnitude faster than SimpleCG, with percentage time gaps higher than 65% for 15 out of 24 scenarios. Moreover, CG+GSP is more effective, with a single failure out of 96 instances, as opposed to the 6 failures of SimpleCG. Finally, in the single scenario in which both algorithms failed, CG+GSP returned a significantly better solution.

Figures 1 and 2 give a graphical representation of the computational time required by the two algorithms. Again, it can be noticed that the continuous line (representing CG+GSP) is always below the dotted line (SimpleCG), and that the gaps are particularly significant in the scenarios with RC = 125.

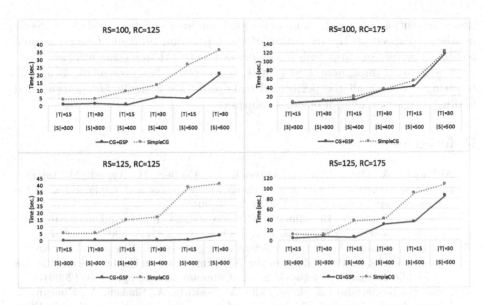

Fig. 1. Computational time for CG+GSP and SimpleCG, on instances with $|S| \leq 500$

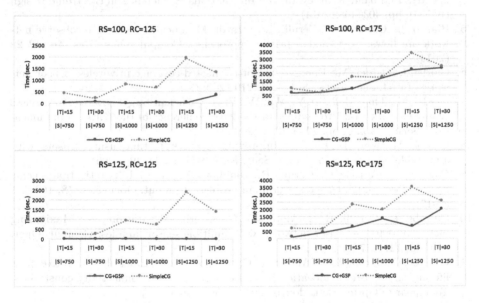

Fig. 2. Computational time for CG+GSP and SimpleCG, on instances with $|S| \geq 750$

5   Conclusions

In this work we addressed a novel variant of the maximum lifetime problem, that takes into account the interference issue. We proposed a column generation-based exact resolution approach, and developed an appropriately designed greedy heuristic to speed up the resolution of the separation problem. Computational results show that our approach is significantly better than a straightforward column generation implementation that does not take advantage of the heuristic, resulting faster on all the performed tests, often by a significant margin, and finding a larger number of optimal solutions.

References

1. Al-Fuqaha, A., Guizani, M., Mohammadi, M., Aledhari, M., Ayyash, M.: Internet of things: a survey on enabling technologies, protocols and applications. IEEE Commun. Surv. Tutorials **17**(4), 2347–2376 (2015)
2. Alfieri, A., Bianco, A., Brandimarte, P., Chiasserini, C.F.: Maximizing system lifetime in wireless sensor networks. Eur. J. Oper. Res. **181**(1), 390–402 (2007)
3. Awada, W., Cardei, M.: Energy-efficient data gathering in heterogeneous wireless sensor networks. In: Proceedings of the IEEE International Conference on Wireless and Mobile Computing, Networking and Communications, pp. 53–60 (2006)
4. Azmi, N., Kamarudin, L., Mahmuddin, M., Zakaria, A., Shakaff, A., Khatun, S., Kamarudin, K., Morshed, M.: Interference issues and mitigation method in WSN 2.4 GHZ ISM band: a survey. In: 2nd International Conference on Electronic Design (ICED), pp. 403–408 (2014)
5. Bianco, L., Cerrone, C., Cerulli, R., Gentili, M.: Locating sensors to observe network arc flows: exact and heuristic approaches. Comput. Oper. Res. **46**, 12–22 (2014)
6. Cardei, I., Cardei, M.: Energy-efficient connected-coverage in wireless sensor networks. Int. J. Sens. Netw. **3**(3), 201–210 (2008)
7. Cardei, M., Thai, M.T., Li, Y., Wu, W.: Energy-efficient target coverage in wireless sensor networks. In: Proceedings of the 24th conference of the IEEE Communications Society, vol. 3, pp. 1976–1984 (2005)
8. Cardei, M., Wu, J., Lu, M.: Improving network lifetime using sensors with adjustable sensing ranges. Int. J. Sens. Netw. **1**(1–2), 41–49 (2006)
9. Carrabs, F., Cerrone, C., Cerulli, R., Gaudioso, M.: A novel discretization scheme for the close enough traveling salesman problem. Comput. Oper. Res. **78**, 163–171 (2017)
10. Carrabs, F., Cerulli, R., D'Ambrosio, C., Gentili, M., Raiconi, A.: Maximizing lifetime in wireless sensor networks with multiple sensor families. Comput. Oper. Res. **60**, 121–137 (2015)
11. Carrabs, F., Cerulli, R., D'Ambrosio, C., Raiconi, A.: An exact algorithm to extend lifetime through roles allocation in sensor networks with connectivity constraints. To appear in Optim. Lett. doi:10.1007/s11590-016-1072-y
12. Carrabs, F., Cerulli, R., D'Ambrosio, C., Raiconi, A.: A hybrid exact approach for maximizing lifetime in sensor networks with complete and partial coverage constraints. J. Netw. Comput. Appl. **58**, 12–22 (2015)
13. Carrabs, F., Cerulli, R., D'Ambrosio, C., Raiconi, A.: Extending lifetime through partial coverage and roles allocation in connectivity-constrained sensor networks. IFAC-PapersOnline **49**(12), 973–978 (2016)
14. Castaño, F., Rossi, A., Sevaux, M., Velasco, N.: A column generation approach to extend lifetime in wireless sensor networks with coverage and connectivity constraints. Comput. Oper. Res. **52**(B), 220–230 (2014)

15. Castiglione, A., D'Arco, P., De Santis, A., Russo, R.: Secure group communication schemes for dynamic heterogeneous distributed computing. To appear in Future Gener. Comput. Syst. http://dx.doi.org/10.1016/j.future.2015.11.026
16. Castiglione, A., Palmieri, F., Fiore, U., Castiglione, A., De Santis, A.: Modeling energy-efficient secure communications in multi-mode wireless mobile devices. J. Comput. Syst. Sci. **81**(8), 1464–1478 (2015)
17. Castiglione, A., De Santis, A., Castiglione, A., Palmieri, F., Fiore, U.: An energy-aware framework for reliable and secure end-to-end ubiquitous data communications. In: 5th International Conference on Intelligent Networking and Collaborative Systems (INCoS), pp. 157–165 (2013)
18. Cerrone, C., Cerulli, R., Gentili, M.: Vehicle-id sensor location for route flow recognition: models and algorithms. Eur. J. Oper. Res. **247**(2), 618–629 (2015)
19. Cerulli, R., Gentili, M., Raiconi, A.: Maximizing lifetime and handling reliability in wireless sensor networks. Networks **64**(4), 321–338 (2014)
20. Chen, D., Liu, Z., Wang, L., Dou, M., Chen, J., Li, H.: Natural disaster monitoring with wireless sensor networks: a case study of data-intensive applications upon low-cost scalable systems. Mob. Netw. Appl. **18**(5), 651–663 (2013)
21. Deschinkel, K.: A column generation based heuristic for maximum lifetime coverage in wireless sensor networks. In: 5th International Conference on Sensor Technologies and Applications, SENSORCOMM 2011, vol. 4, pp. 209–214 (2011)
22. Dhawan, A., Vu, C.T., Zelikovsky, A., Li, Y., Prasad, S.K.: Maximum lifetime of sensor networks with adjustable sensing range. In: Proceedings of the Seventh ACIS International Conference on Software Engineering, Artificial Intelligence, Networking, and Parallel/Distributed Computing, pp. 285–289 (2006)
23. Gentili, M., Raiconi, A.: $\alpha-$coverage to extend network lifetime on wireless sensor networks. Optim. Lett. **7**(1), 157–172 (2013)
24. Gu, Y., Ji, Y., Zhao, B.: Maximize lifetime of heterogeneous wireless sensor networks with joint coverage and connectivity requirement. In: 8th International Conference on Embedded Computing, EmbeddedCom 2009, pp. 226–231 (2009)
25. Moraes, R.E.N., Ribeiro, C.C., Ribeiro, G.M.: Exact formulations for the minimum interference problem in k-connected ad hoc wireless networks. Int. Trans. Oper. Res. **23**(6), 1113–1139 (2016)
26. Moscibroda, T., Wattenhofer, R.: Minimizing interference in ad hoc and sensor networks. In: 2nd ACM SIGACT/SIGMOBILE International Workshop on Foundations of Mobile Computing (DIALM-POMC), pp. 24–33 (2005)
27. Raiconi, A., Gentili, M.: Exact and metaheuristic approaches to extend lifetime and maintain connectivity in wireless sensors networks. In: Pahl, J., Reiners, T., Voss, S. (eds.) Network Optimization. LNCS, vol. 6701, pp. 607–619. Springer, Berlin/Heidelberg (2011)
28. Rossi, A., Singh, A., Sevaux, M.: An exact approach for maximizing the lifetime of sensor networks with adjustable sensing ranges. Comput. Oper. Res. **39**(12), 3166–3176 (2012)
29. Tan, H., Lou, T., Wang, Y., Hua, Q.-S., Lau, F.C.M.: Exact algorithms to minimize interference in wireless sensor networks. Theoret. Comput. Sci. **412**(50), 6913–6925 (2011)
30. Wang, C., Thai, M.T., Li, Y., Wang, F., Wu, W.: Minimum coverage breach and maximum network lifetime in wireless sensor networks. In: Proceedings of the IEEE Global Telecommunications Conference, pp. 1118–1123 (2007)
31. Zhao, Q., Gurusamy, M.: Lifetime maximization for connected target coverage in wireless sensor networks. IEEE/ACM Trans. Netw. **16**(6), 1378–1391 (2008)

An Orchestrated Security Platform
for Internet of Robots

Mehrnoosh Monshizadeh[1,2(✉)], Vikramajeet Khatri[1] ⓘ,
Raimo Kantola[2], and Zheng Yan[2,3]

[1] Nokia Bell Labs, Espoo, Finland
{mehrnoosh.monshizadeh,
vikramajeet.khatri}@nokia-bell-labs.com
[2] Department of Comnet, Aalto University, Espoo, Finland
{mehrnoosh.monshizadeh,raimo.kantola,
zheng.yan}@aalto.fi
[3] The State Key Lab of ISN, Xidian University, Xi'an, China
zyan@xidian.edu.cn

Abstract. Although the research on Internet of Things (IoT) is emerging and getting popular, there are few mobile operators that offer connectivity services for IoT devices such as robots in their networks. One of the reasons is security. Mobile operators who offer connectivity to IoT devices could benefit from an orchestrated security platform by applying data mining and classification based on the data collected to offer more reactive security notifications to owners of robots. For this purpose, we propose a distributed security platform for Mobile Cloud Robot (MCR) to detect and prevent an attack on the mobile network and robots based on the collected information from robots. The proposed platform includes robots, Local Robot Controller (LRC), Mobile Cloud, an IoT anomaly detection module and IoT orchestrator. This platform applies an orchestrated data analysis not only to achieve an accurate anomaly detection for robot security but also improves different aspects such as energy saving, processing time, fault detection etc.

Keywords: Security · Cloud computing · Mobile Virtual Network Operator · Software Defined Networking · Internet of Things · Mobile Cloud Robot · Robot · Drone

1 Introduction

The existing technologies of cloud computing, Internet of Things (IoT), and wireless controlled robots combine to produce a new variant called Cloud Robotics. Cloud robotics uses the big data techniques and computing power of the cloud along with the connectivity provided by Long Term Evolution (LTE) and other wireless technologies to control the actions of wireless robots. We shall refer to this technology as Mobile

The original version of this chapter was revised: For the second author's name, Vikramajeet Khatri, an ORCID was added. The erratum to this chapter can be found at https://doi.org/10.1007/978-3-319-57186-7_59

© Springer International Publishing AG 2017
M.H.A. Au et al. (Eds.): GPC 2017, LNCS 10232, pp. 298–312, 2017.
DOI: 10.1007/978-3-319-57186-7_23

Cloud Robot (MCR) where the robot-cloud connectivity is provided by mobile networks. This technology has the mutual attention of telecommunication vendors as well as different industries including manufacturing, medicine and agriculture.

Because of the operational characteristics of resource sharing and a centralized controller, MCR can act as a potential cost saver. On the other hand, with big data techniques such as data mining and knowledge reuse, efficiency and security could be improved. Using all this computing power has risks and it is critically important to secure the communications path and efficiently use the wireless bandwidth. Big data and the use of data intelligence can be applied to MCR to provide both services and security support to an MCR network. Examples such as fault detection, service issue resolution, network segmentation and security are common. For this purpose, we propose a distributed security platform including robots, Local Robot Controller (LRC), Mobile Cloud, IoT anomaly detection module and IoT Orchestrator. Here, we aim to reach high efficiency from different perspectives to perform data analysis that shall identify improvements for an MCR environment, e.g., processing time, data accuracy, energy saving for different applications such as robot programming, monitoring, security and fault management.

The rest of the paper is organized as follows. Section 2 briefly reviews related work. Section 3 discusses the MCR and its security challenges. Section 4 discusses our distributed security architecture for MCRs that detects anomalies and distribute preventive actions to mitigate identified threats. Further in Sect. 5 we discuss about the data classification and connectivity scenarios for our security platform. Finally, conclusion is presented in the last section.

2 Related Work

Ian et al. [1] have proposed an automated drone security system for surveillance purposes, where on board sensors and an imaging device is used for capturing surveillance data. Drones execute flight operation, store surveillance data and connect to a server for location update and transmission of encrypted surveillance data. In this study, Global Positioning System (GPS) is used for positioning. A user device is connected to server to receive and display surveillance data. The flight operation of drone is controlled by server or a user device. It also covers drone docks that are used for launching, landing and charging drones, as drones are battery powered. Their proposed architecture does not address authentication hijacking scenarios for drones and the server. A malicious drone may get authenticated to server; or server may get hacked. In this case an attacker gains access to data and misguides the drones for surveillance.

Daniel [2] proposed a system for a drone docking station to deliver goods. A drone resides at a docking station and goods from a storage facility are attached to the drone for delivery. The communication between the drone docking station and the drone is via GPS, Wi-Fi, Bluetooth and satellites. The drone can be traced via GPS; however, its flight path cannot be controlled. When the drone reaches the docking station, it may inform the next delivery to the storage facility via Wi-Fi or Bluetooth. Then the storage facility exchanges information about next delivery i.e., what and where to deliver. However, the proposed system is only about flight location update and not applicable to control the drone on the fly.

Shriram et al. [3] have discussed drone delivery assurance, where a drone delivers a package of goods to a destination. Here, assurance refers to delivering to a correct destination after verifying the recipient and its location while taking pictures as evidence. When a drone arrives near the delivery location, a notification is sent to the receiver. The receiver then sends the goods purchase code to the drone using Wi-Fi or Bluetooth. Drone receives the purchase code, authenticates it and after successful authentication, lands and delivers the goods. In case of failed authentication on the purchase code, the drone will not land. Global Navigation Satellite System (GNSS) is used for positioning purposes. In addition, cellular communication is used for establishing connection with other devices. The proposed architecture lacks a security mechanism to verify or authorize the drone; a malicious drone may arrive and take the goods using a fake purchase code to authenticate.

Anthony et al. [4] proposed a system and a method for managing communications in robot competitions. The communication takes place over a wireless network between a network arena controller and a robot controller. The network arena controller provides security keys and firewall policies to robot controllers; and robot controllers execute those firewall policies to secure communications between the brand/operator stations and robots. The network arena controller may also monitor and log communication traffic to verify connectivity and monitor battery level, signal strength and robot status. The brand/operator stations may include any software, hardware, and/or firmware, which are configured to monitor and control robots associated to it. These stations give commands to robots to perform an action. The proposed system prevents one or more intentional or unintentional security risks such as Denial of Service (DoS) attack and spoofing attack via bandwidth monitoring. Upon detection of intentional flooding, the system either imposes bandwidth limitation for the robot or totally blocks the robot using firewall.

The mentioned studies are mostly focused on robot applications such as automated drone security system for surveillance, drone delivery assurance, drone communication management with security keys and firewall policies. Yet there hasn't been specific research that concentrates on MCR security for Mobile Virtual Network Operators (MVNOs); none of the current studies in relevant area has utilized data mining techniques for security threat analysis. This paper applies data mining mechanisms in an orchestrated security platform to detect intrusion in robots belong to MVNOs. The proposed platform could detect and prevent different types of attacks on both robot and LRC that are explained in Sect. 4.

3   Literature Overview and Research Motivation

Diverse industries have been using sensors and robots for years; but their control systems often remain deliberately isolated to avoid any attacks.

Performing data mining on data collected from sensors and robots in the industrial environment helps to detect the anomalies before they occur. The collected data should be made available across each site to perform data mining and classification. Therefore, we introduce a mobile network cloud platform that collects data from IoT robots, performs data mining and data analysis to find out malicious robots and isolate them.

In order to perform efficient intrusion detection, we introduce a platform comprising of two main parts: LRC and IoT service provider that is a MVNO in this paper. Once the attack is detected in a MVNO, an IoT orchestrator is used to distribute the malicious pattern and information on malicious robot to other MVNOs, so they can also retaliate to the malicious intent without re-analyzing the same kind of robots. This capability enhances the scalability of the proposed platform and makes it an efficient distributed security framework. Therefore, our proposed platform is also a distributed mitigation strategy for malicious robots to prevent its malicious intent to all nearby MVNOs. LRC would directly interact with all connected robots for various functions such as local privacy, security and monitoring, local hardware control, local software manager and local application etc.; while in our proposed architecture LRC concentrates only on local security and monitoring.

Apart from robots that are working in an industrial environment, the flying robots so called drones are increasingly used in a service industry e.g., postal delivery, vaccine delivery, remote surveillance and inspection of terrain for radio network planning, etc. The regulatory authorities have been allocating bands for their operation but who controls where the drones can fly, what they can do and what forbids them are yet challenges to be addressed. In addition, if a drone breaks down while performing assigned task such as delivering vaccines; the control platform for drones should guide another drone to replace it and recover the failed drone so it is not stolen to be used later to gain unauthorized access to the platform of drone. One can attack, gain unauthorized access, and divert the mobile robot to an improper location or steal the data collected. Therefore, security for such an environment (MCR) is very important. However, the overall scope of the proposed architecture is on security related functions which covers three main security requirements: authentication, authorization, accounting (AAA), integrity and availability of data. To fulfil these security requirements, the data should be collected and sent from LRC to a service provider for further analysis.

4   A Distributed Security Platform

Various communication systems may benefit from increased security. For example, communication systems that include machine type communications may benefit from improved security and fault detection. This paper proposes a platform for enhancing robots and MVNO security where robots refer to both fixed robots and drones. The platform includes detecting an attack based on the robot information and determining a preventive action. Furthermore, the architecture includes sending an indication of an attack to LRCs or MVNOs via an IoT orchestrator. An MVNO receives data at an IoT anomaly detection module from a LRC. The data includes robot information from a plurality of machine type communication devices.

4.1   Robot Data Classification

Collected data from robots could be on different protocols such as hypertext transfer protocol (HTTP) and user datagram protocol (UDP). The chosen protocol is robot vendor specific and based on the robot application. Particularly our model could be tuned based on robot vendor proprietary protocols when their protocol specifications are known. But in general, and for all protocols, data is categorized in two groups: control plane data and user plane data.

Control plane data includes signaling data such as non-access stratum (NAS), authentication-security, bearer request, paging, location area update, etc. User plane data covers telemetry and command-control data. Telemetry data is related to application of the robot and geographical location. For example, images, video, measurements (temperature, speed, etc.) and HTTP traffic. Command-control data is related to control of the robot such as status check, software update and task management. All user plane data should be normalized before being processed for anomaly detection.

MVNOs can deny access to their networks for vendors that do not open their data specifications to the operator and export only normalized data using commonly agreed data model, thus hiding vendor proprietary protocol design from other operators and vendors. However, legislation mandates that vendor protocols are open as perquisite for approval for license to enter markets. Another way for tuning our model to process different types of robots' data is reverse engineering the vendor protocols, in case the specifications are not communicated.

4.2   Robot Attack Classification

The victim is either a mobile network or a robot. In case a robot attacks another robot, as it is shown in Figs. 1 and 2, the attack can be done either through the LRC, where a malicious robot and a target victim robot belong to a same brand or they belong to different brands and the attack is issued through MVNOs.

Fig. 1. Attack scenario for robots belong to a same brand

Fig. 2. Attack scenario for robots belong to different brands

Examples of attacks include corrupting and tampering other robots' data and mission, stealing other robots' data and overloading other robots with consecutive requests. The attacks on mobile network include any kinds of malicious behaviors that cause unavailability or degradation of network services or stealing network information. A concrete example is the DoS attack on mobility management entity

(MME) through burst of signaling message (paging, status transition, etc.), configuration corruption and stealing home subscriber server (HSS) information.

In Table 1 different types of attacks that may target robot and LRC are classified based on the three main security requirements [5, 6].

Table 1. Threats classification

AAA	Availability	Integrity
Unauthorized access and privileged access	Data loss and resources unavailability	Data corruption, tampering and leakage
• Probing	• Unexpected system	• Botnet
• Remote access	failure	• Malware
• Man-in-the middle	• DoS	• Application corruption
• IP Spoofing	• Image loss	• Ransomware
• Spyware	• Configuration loss	
• Service injection	• Misconfiguration	

Some of the threats listed in Table 1 are described here.

- Probing: It is an attempt to monitor a robot and steal information such as open ports and IP addresses of robots connected to network.
- Remote access: This threat tries to access the robot without having a permission. The access is made possible by exploiting a vulnerability.
- Man-in-the middle attack: This attack occurs when an attacker gains access to the communication channel established between robot and LRC or between two robots. The attacker can perform unauthorized activities such as intercepting robot data or modifying communications to change the robot mission.
- IP Spoofing: In this attack, an attacker creates IP packets with a false source IP address to hide the identity of itself to be introduced itself as another robot and steal the data.
- Spyware: Spyware is all kinds of software that monitors and steal robot's information.
- Service injection attack: The attacker targets a robot service and injects malicious code to corrupt the service.
- Botnet: A 'botnet' is a group of connected vulnerable robots in a network, which are remotely controlled by a master computer (hacker). Like robots they automatically perform some functions that are predefined by the botmaster and forward the information like viruses to target LRCs or robots, which could cause denial of service.
- Malware: Malware refers to all kinds of software codes like viruses, worms, Trojans. These attacks are programmed to perform malicious operations on a robot.
- Ransomware: Ransomware is any kind of software that locks a robot and demands some form of payment to make the robot unlocked.

- Denial of Service (DoS): An attacker occupies the network resources by flooding network with consecutive requests and cause denial of services to robots.
- Unavailability of robot or LRC: Based on unexpected failure or any attack, robot's and LRC's firmware or configuration could be lost or corrupted and makes the robot unavailable.

4.3   Robot Security Platform

As it is shown in Fig. 3, the proposed Internet of robot security platform has two sections: robot section and mobile network section.

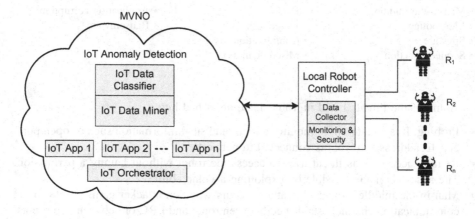

Fig. 3. Internet of robot security platform

The robot section includes robots and local robot controller (LRC). LRC is a central node for all robots and responsible for connectivity between robots and mobile network. The first level of data monitoring and security analysis is done in LRC and before data is forwarded to mobile network. The IoT service provider can be either a mobile network operator or a mobile virtual network operator (MVNO). The MVNO carries out advanced analysis of collected data from various LRCs through data mining mechanisms in IoT anomaly detection module. The analyzed data would be used for intrusion detection in same or different MVNO. While a robot has been identified as malicious in a MVNO, a notification will be sent to all MVNOs by an IoT orchestrator to block the malicious robot and prevent the re-analysis of malicious robot in future communication; since the malicious robot may try to attack the cloud platform using other MVNOs. Therefore, our distributed security platform reduces the computation processing for a malicious robot that has been already identified as malicious in other MVNO. The detailed design is introduced as below.

Robot Section

- A robot with connectivity to a mobile network through a LRC.
- LRC will be a central node for all robots and sensors present in an industrial environment. LRC will be responsible for hardware, software, and security policy for all robots and sensors connected to it. Hardware domain includes controlling engine and its power; whereas software domain includes drivers and its applications.
  - Local Security & Monitoring: All hardware and software key performance indicators (KPIs) as well as some other parameters of interest for all robots and sensors connected in an industrial environment will be monitored via a module called Local Security & Monitoring. Local Security & Monitoring module will send the data to a node called Data Collector.
  - Data Collector: It will act as a gateway for the industrial environment, collect the data from the modules connected to it and will continuously communicate with mobile network for data mining and classification.

In our architecture, there is no direct communication between robots. If robots belong to the same brand, LRC will take care of trust management among the robots and if they belong to different brands then mobile network takes care of trust management (by correlating information between two LRCs).

Mobile network section

- IoT anomaly detection module compromises of IoT Data Miner and IoT Data Classifier.
  - IoT Data Miner: The collected data will be heterogeneous in nature i.e.; data will be from different IoT devices and with different profiles. Therefore, the collected data should be properly combined, processed and correlated. The IoT Data Miner performs data mining on the collected data, and labels the collected data in an efficient way so that it can be easily classified by the IoT Data Classifier. The normalization process is done in this module.
  - IoT Data Classifier: Big data algorithms are applied to label the data. Data classification refers to association of collected data to different classes based on the purpose of anomaly detection. The anomaly detection could be either for attack detection or other application such as traffic safety and so on. In principle, it would be possible to use the described data mining mechanisms to detect all types of anomalies and to feed the information for example to Public Warning System [7] to send a warning as cell broadcast to alarm any robots in an affected area about a potential threat. The classes are defined based on different features. The features are either predefined or extracted based on training data or they would be dynamically defined during analysis process.

In the IoT anomaly detection module, different linear and learning algorithms are combined in a wide range to investigate a hybrid model for achieving high detection performance and yet relatively low detection time, and will be deployed to detect intrusion attempts on IoT robots.

- IoT Application: This refers to an application layer and provides interfaces for various IoT domains such as smart parking, smart home automation and security.

- IoT Orchestrator: IoT orchestrator distributes the information about malicious robots to MVNOs using orchestration module. Once the attack is detected the prevention action should be performed. Prevention includes sending information to local robot collector to identify the malicious robot. Local robot collector traces back the malicious robot and blocks it from authenticating to MCR. The above-mentioned mitigation strategy can be safely applied if the malicious robot is authenticated either to the same IoT service provider (MVNO) or other cloud service providers (MVNOs). Therefore, an IoT orchestrator is used to distribute the malicious patterns and information on malicious robots to all cloud service providers (MVNOs) so they can also retaliate to the malicious intent. This enhances the scalability of the proposed platform and makes it a secure distributed platform.

5 Mobile Cloud Robot Security Scenarios

Machine-type communication is increasingly important to both government entities and enterprises where the private LTE networks are used to support the application of drones and robots for military, transportation and energy industry services. Government entities deploy private LTE networks for emergency and strategic situations, where the anomaly in the original function means the difference between life and death such as in military, national security and emergency services. Therefore, a secure communication is major consideration for government also some enterprise entities such as energy, transportation etc. [8, 9].

In this paper, we propose An Orchestrated Security Platform for Internet of Robots that is applicable for entities that use private LTE networks as well as commercial service providers. On the other hand, based on the robot connectivity to network, two scenarios: robot-with-SIM card and robot-without-SIMcard, are considered for the proposed platform.

5.1   Robot with SIMcard

As it is shown in Fig. 4, we consider "n*m" robots which belong to "n" different brands while robots belong to brand 1 and brand 2 are connected to MVNO1 and robots belong to brand n connected to MVNO2. In this scenario, each robot has a SIM card. If robots are belonging to a commercial network (and not a private LTE network), LRC is installed at Base Transceiver Station (BTS) nodes for cost saving.

As it is shown in Fig. 5, when a robot tries to connect to a mobile network, first robot is authenticated internally by LRC and information is analyzed. Based on the policies or rules which are locally defined in the LRC, the traffic would be either dropped or passed to related MVNO. If the traffic is dropped at LRC, a notification message would be sent to parent MVNO. Later parent MVNO will inform other MVNOs about malicious robot through IoT orchestrator. If the traffic is safe and traffic arrives to MVNO1, IoT anomaly detection module in MVNO1 will analyze whether the traffic is safe or not.

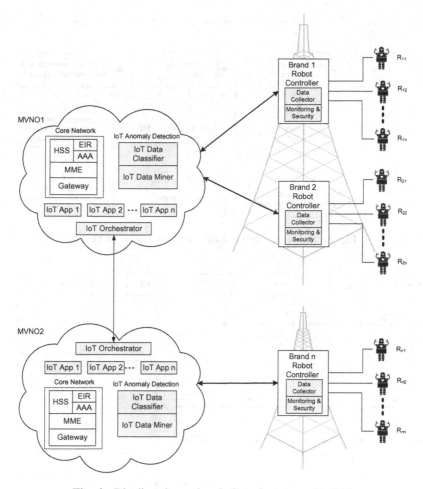

Fig. 4. Distributed security platform for robot with SIM

If the traffic is not safe it would be dropped and a message would be sent to associated LRC and through associated IoT orchestrator to other MVNOs. If the traffic is labeled safe in IoT anomaly detection module, MVNO will forward the robot attach request to MME and HSS/AAA for authentication procedure. After robot is authenticated, the robot user plane (UP) data would be forwarded to mobile network. The same anomaly detection procedure would be applied on UP data. Mentioned procedure is shown in Fig. 6.

5.2   SIMless Robot

In this scenario, robots do not have any SIM cards; they are connected to LRC via Wi-Fi and LRC has a SIM card to connect to mobile networks. LRC acts as a gateway

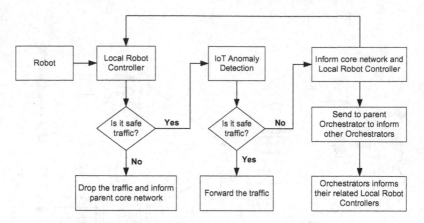

Fig. 5. Robot anomaly detection and mitigation procedure

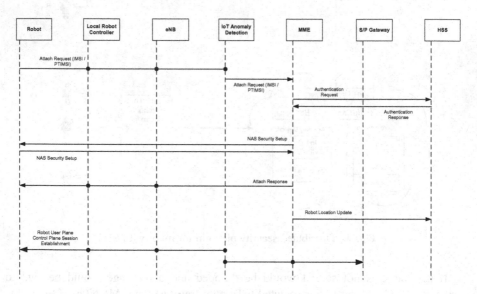

Fig. 6. Robot authentication and session establishment

for all the robots connected to it. The communication via mobile network and anomaly detection procedures are like the above-mentioned scenario.

For a drone communication case, as shown in the Fig. 7, each cell may have multiple LRC that either fixed at a location (Private LTE) or integrated into BTS. LRCs are authenticated with the nearest base station of mobile network operator in that area. The LRC is the primary contact for drones operating in the area. Every drone operating in an area will be first authenticated to the LRC. After authentication with the first LRC, the drone will be assigned with a task. In addition to task assignment, task cancellation, task replacement processes. The LRC periodically collects information from drones

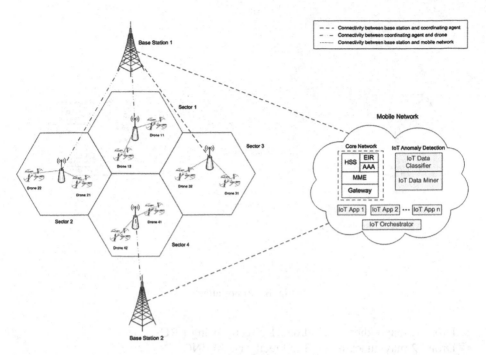

Fig. 7. Distributed security platform for SIMless robots

and sends it to BTS. The received information will be forwarded to IoT anomaly detection module for further analysis. Each LRC has a coverage area and while a drone moves from an area to another, new LRC would be responsible for the connectivity and related procedures.

If IoT anomaly detection module detects a suspicious pattern in data received from any drone, it will inform the associated LRC to initiate a mitigation strategy. The mitigation strategy starts with cancellation of task, and triggering automatic clean-up of malwares or malicious content. If the automatic clean up activity fails, LRC sends message to service center to perform manual clean-up and de-authenticate malicious drones from the network. In case the suspicious drone does not belong to associated MVNO, it will be de-authenticated, blacklisted and a blacklist will be updated to all MVNOs and LRCs in the network. Afterwards that malicious drone will not be authenticated anymore to harm the services or network elements.

5.3   Robot Attack

Figure 8 shows robot attack scenarios, which has been discussed in Sect. 4. Here we only added attack detection considering whole MVNO.

There are 3 drones, drone 2 is an attacker whereas drone 1 and drone 3 are victims. Drone 1 and drone 2 are in one cell and belong to a same LRC but drone 3 belongs to a different sector and with different brand.

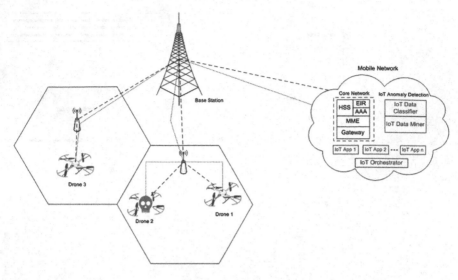

Fig. 8. Robot attack

- Drone 2 may either attack drone 1 directly using LRC
- Drone 2 may attack drone 3 indirectly via MVNO.

5.4   Robot Communication

There are three types of communication between robots:

- Intra MVNO communication: A robot communicates to other robots inside its MVNO
- Inter MVNO communication: A robot communicates to other robots inside other MVNOs.
- Roaming between MVNOs: A robot moves to different MVNOs and tries to communicate to other robots. As it is shown in the Fig. 9, a robot has been earlier at certain location and later has been physically moved to another location. The authentication request will be send to nearby LRC of service provider.

A robot sends a handover request through LRC and source base station for example an eNB, to an IoT anomaly detection module. If received data is safe, IoT anomaly detection module will forward the request to source MME. Then source MME sends the relocation request to a target MME, and source MME receives a relocation response. Source MME returns the handover response to source eNB, which then forward the handover response to robot through LRC. Source eNB sends an eNB status transfer notification to source MME, which indicates to source MME about robot hand over to target eNB. Target MME then informs target eNB of an MME status transfer and a handover confirmation then will be sent to the target eNB via LRC.

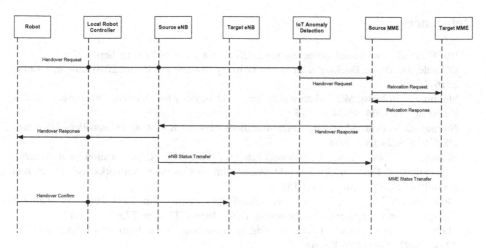

Fig. 9. Robots roaming

6 Conclusion

In this paper, we reviewed mobile cloud robot security challenges and proposed a distributed security platform for mobile cloud robot.

The proposed platform has two sections; robot section and mobile network section. The robot section includes robots and local robot controller (LRC). LRC is a central node for all robots and responsible for connectivity between robots and mobile network. The first level of data monitoring and security analysis is done in LRC and before data is forwarded to mobile network. The IoT service provider can be either a mobile network operator or a mobile virtual network operator (MVNO). The MVNO carries out advanced analysis of collected data from various LRCs through data mining mechanisms in IoT anomaly detection module. The IoT anomaly detection module includes linear and learning algorithms. Linear DM algorithm will extract and provide proper attributes to the next process using a learning algorithm. This mechanism would decrease the load of input data for the learning algorithm that is the most time-consuming part (because of the algorithm complexity). So, the proposed algorithm could label new attacks and detect known ones (e.g., botnet, malware) faster than existing solutions. The analysed data would be used for intrusion detection in same or different MVNO. While a robot has been identified as malicious in a MVNO, a notification will be sent to all MVNOs by an IoT orchestrator to block the malicious robot and prevent the re-analysis of malicious robot in future communication; since the malicious robot may try to attack the cloud platform using other MVNOs. Therefore, our distributed security platform reduces the computation processing for a malicious robot that has been already identified as malicious in other MVNO. An implementation with different attacks for mentioned scenarios is already ongoing by authors to evaluate the performance.

References

1. Ian, C., et al.: Automated Drone Systems. US Patent 2016266579, 15 Sept 2016
2. O'Toole, D.: Drone Docking Station and Delivery System. US Patent 2016159496, 16 June 2016
3. Shiram, G., Roberto, M.J.: Methods, Systems and Devices for Delivery Drone Security. US Patent 2016068264, 10 Mar 2016
4. Norman, D.A., et al.: Managing Communications Between Robots and Controllers. US Patent 2008263628, 24 Dec 2008
5. Monshizadeh, M., Yan, Z., Hippeläinen, L., Khatri.V.: Cloudification and security implications of TaaS. In: 2015 World Symposium on Computer Networks and Information Security (WSCNIS), pp. 1–8 (2015)
6. Monshizadeh, M., Yan, Z.: Security related data mining. In: 2014 IEEE International Conference on Computer and Information Technology (CIT), pp. 775–782 (2014)
7. 3GPP TS 22.268 V13.0.0. Public warning systems. http://www.3gpp.org/ftp/Specs/archive/22_series/22.268/22268-d00.zip
8. Nokia targets industrial IoT with private LTE, RCRWirelessNews. http://www.rcrwireless.com/20160929/internet-of-things/nokia-targets-industrial-iot-with-private-lte-tag4
9. Private 4G/LTE, Duons. http://www.duons.com.au/private-tactical-4g-lte/

A Novel Clustering Solution for Wireless Sensor Networks

Anxi Wang[3], Shuzhen Pan[3], Chen Wang[3], Jian Shen[1,2,3(✉)], and Dengzhi Liu[3]

[1] Jiangsu Engineering Center of Network Monitoring, Nanjing University of Information
Science and Technology, Nanjing, China
s_shenjian@126.com

[2] Jiangsu Collaborative Innovation Center on Atmospheric Environment and Equipment
Technology, Nanjing University of Information Science and Technology, Nanjing, China

[3] School of Computer and Software, Nanjing University of Information
Science and Technology, Nanjing, China
Anxi_wang@126.com

Abstract. Wireless Sensor Network (WSN) deploys a large amount number of
nodes into its monitored range, where watchers can monitor the real-time environment parameter by compressing packets transferred by the cluster head nodes
from local regions. In WSN, the resource of energy is restricted. Energy efficient
clustering solutions are required to keep a long lifetime and enough data packets
by extending the run time of CHs. In this paper, we propose a novel clustering
solution to improve the selection and rotation of CHs. The presented solution
includes two key parts: a new cluster selection based on the distance to the energy-
centroid of the cluster and a new cluster rotation solution based on the residual
energy level of the node in order to evenly distribute the energy load among all
sensors nodes. In particular, the distance between the node and the energy-centroid in EEC when it comes to the rotation of the cluster head node. Our simulation
is based on the platform NS-2. The simulate part presents the performance
comparison among EEC and the conventional protocols such as LEACH and
LEACH-C in terms of energy efficient, the network lifetime and data packets
received by the BS. It is worth noting that EEC outperforms the existing protocols
from our simulation results.

Keywords: Wireless Sensor Network · Energy efficient · Clustering solution ·
Prolong lifetime

1 Introduction

A WSN is a collection of wireless nodes with limited energy capabilities that may be
mobile or stationary and are located randomly on a dynamically changing environment.
The routing strategies selection is an important issue for the efficient delivery of the
packets to their destination [13–25]. Moreover, in such networks, the applied routing
strategy should ensure the minimum of the energy consumption and hence maximization
of the lifetime of the network. The main parts of WSN include sensor node and network
structure. Next, we will introduce the two parts briefly [11, 12].

© Springer International Publishing AG 2017
M.H.A. Au et al. (Eds.): GPC 2017, LNCS 10232, pp. 313–322, 2017.
DOI: 10.1007/978-3-319-57186-7_24

1.1 Network Structure

The nodes in some networks are considered to be deployed uniformly and the distribution probability is equal to each other, or other networks make distinctions between different nodes based on their identity. More specifically, the main attribute of the routing protocols belonging to this category is the way that the nodes are connected and they route the information based on the networks architecture. This addresses two types of node deployments, nodes with the same level of connection and nodes with different hierarchies. Therefore, the schemes on this category can be further classified as follows:

- **Flat Protocols**: All the nodes in the network play the same role. Flat network architecture presents several advantages, including minimal overhead to maintain the infrastructure between communicating nodes.
- **Hierarchical Protocols**: The routing protocols on this scheme impose a structure on the network to achieve energy efficiency, stability, and scalability. In this class of protocols, network nodes are organized in clusters in which a node with higher residual energy, for example, assumes the role of a cluster head. The cluster head is responsible for coordinating activities within the cluster and forwarding information between clusters. Clustering has the potential to reduce energy consumption and extend the lifetime of the network. They have high delivery ratio and scalability and can balance the energy consumption. The nodes around the base station or cluster head will deplete their energy sources faster than the other nodes. Network dysconnectivity is a problem where certain sections of the network can become unreachable. If there is only one node connecting a part of the network to the rest and fails, then this section would cut off from the rest of the network.

1.2 Our Contribution

In this paper, we only take our attention on the selection and rotation of CHs. For the reason that it can provide longer lifetime than the direct communication case. In the Hierarchical Protocols, the core part is to select the suitable CHs and set up a schedule to CH rotate. However, CH node is decided by the base station (BS) which has a steady stream of energy supply, the normal nodes which just report to the local CH instead of reporting to the BS. To achieve the longer lifetime, it is necessary to rotate the CHs, which can load energy consumption evenly to all nodes. Only in this way the nodes can survive a long time. The BS can calculate the position of the energy-centroid. The detail description of energy-centroid calculation is given in the Sect. 3.

The rest of this paper is organized as follows. In Sect. 2, the related work and current research are introduced briefly. In Sect. 3, we introduce the main part of the clustering solution. The simulation is summarized in Sect. 4. Finally, in Sect. 5, we summarize the main conclusions.

2 Related Work

Clustering method in WSNs is very popular to organize and manage the network efficiently since 2000. One major issue is to relieve CH nodes of their high load and energy consumption. LEACH [1] is a typical random clustering protocol in which the CH role is randomly rotated among nodes to achieve the consumption balance. However, LEACH requires all CHs transfer directly to the network's BS, thus it will reduce the survive time because of long distance transmissions. As a result, when the nodes which are have a long distance from the BS their energy consumption is much earlier than others. In order to deal with this issue, EECS [2] allocates fewer number of member nodes in clusters with longer distances to the BS. Nevertheless, it is still based on single-hop transmissions to the BS from the CHs and is not scalable to large-scale networks. To avoid the high cost of long-range transmissions, HEED [3] adopts multi-hop inter-cluster communication and further selects its CHs based on the residual energy level of the nodes. However, in HEED, hot spot matter appears in areas that are near to the BS, as nodes in such areas need to relay incoming traffic from outer parts of the network.

To address the hot-spot issue, UCR [4], EEDUC [5], MRPUC [6] and UCS [7] propose using multi-hop routes to the BS and conclude that the sizes of clusters should be smaller as they approach the sink. The main idea here is to compensate for the high inter-cluster communication load by reducing the cost of intra-cluster communications. With small cluster sizes, the high load of incoming data is claimed to be distributed among more clusters, effectively reducing the load of each CH near the sink. However, this might cause too many clusters to be formed around the sink and a significant number of summary packets to be produced when approaching the sink. The result is a higher traffic load than predicted. Therefore, an analytical study is required to balance the intra-cluster and inter-cluster energy consumption amounts while considering the varying traffic load at different locations of the network.

Although a basic analysis of energy consumption for clustering is conducted in a few existing works, such as [7–9], they have some deficiencies. For example, the analysis of energy consumption in control overhead caused by route discovery and cluster formation is not fully covered. Furthermore, some key parameters are determined via complex experiments [10], which is an impractical technique.

In short, there is a need for a comprehensive analysis of the total energy consumption in multi-hop data delivery in clustered WSNs. Such an analysis should be based on an energy-efficient data routing and clustering protocol that avoids using network-wide broadcasts and reduces control overhead. Furthermore, to establish the load balance in a WSN, this trade-off between the distance to the sink and the cluster sizes should be studied analytically but not experimentally, before setting up the network hierarchy.

3 Clustering Solution

In this section, the details of EEC are going to be discussed. We assume that micro sensor nodes are distributed randomly in the network area [26–37]. Each sensor node has a limited built-in battery, and the battery cannot be replaced after the node has been deployed. Once the deployment of the network is totally completed, the location of the sensor node will not be changed. In addition, the residual energy level is known to the node itself. We also assume each node does know the position of the BS. And its remaining energy can be achieved at any time. The shape of the whole tested area nodes distributed in is a rectangle. We set the lower left corner of the whole region to be the origin point [38–40]. In EEC, CH nodes have direct communication with the BS. We set the number of CH nodes at the percentage of 5% at the beginning of the simulation. According to the time period, the running process of the whole EEC is divided into two stages: Selection phase and Rotation phase.

3.1   Selection Phase

In the field of mathematics, the centroid is the center of mass, which is the imaginary point of mass concentration. Centroid position is important in engineering field, for example, to stabilize the crane, the position of the centroid should satisfy certain conditions. Motion stability of aircraft, ships and vehicles are closely related with the centroid position.

In our study, we use the concept of the cluster energy centroid instead of the traditional concept. The reason of utilization of the cluster energy centroid is analyzed as follows. First and foremost, the quality of sensor nodes in the network is meaningless. Secondly, the center of mass of nodes for the entire cluster is meaningless, for the reason that node location and quality change in the running process of the network. Finally, through the whole network, energy of sensor node is the only factor which changes with time. The energy centroid can intuitively display distribution of residual energy in the network.

Note here that Eqs. (4) and (5) are derived from Eqs. (1), (2) and (3). Equations (8) and (9) are the derivation of Eqs. (6) and (7). In Eqs. (4), (5), μ is the density of the quality in the cluster; S is the measure of cluster area; $d\sigma$ is the differential of quality; d_{Mx} and d_{My} are the static moment to the x-axis and y-axis. In Eqs. (8), (9), E_i rs represents the residual energy level of node i; E_0 is the initial value of energy; X and Y are the X coordinate and the Y coordinate of node i.

If qualities of sensor nodes in the cluster are known and evenly distributed, we can use Eqs. (5), (6) to calculate the position of the centroid. However, compared with node's residual energy, the quality of the node plays less role on the network performance. Hence, with node location information and the energy consumption, we can use the Eqs. (8), (9) to calculate the energy-centroid position.

$$\mu = \frac{S \sum m}{D} \tag{1}$$

$$dM_x = y\mu \, d\sigma \tag{2}$$

$$dM_y = x\mu \, d\sigma \tag{3}$$

$$\bar{X} = \frac{M_y}{M} = \frac{\iint_D x\mu \, d\sigma}{\iint_D \mu \, d\sigma} \tag{4}$$

$$\bar{Y} = \frac{M_x}{M} = \frac{\iint_D y\mu \, d\sigma}{\iint_D \mu \, d\sigma} \tag{5}$$

$$X_{all} = \sum_{i=1}^{N} \frac{E_{i_{rs}}}{E_0} X \tag{6}$$

$$Y_{all} = \sum_{i=1}^{N} \frac{E_{i_{rs}}}{E_0} Y \tag{7}$$

$$\bar{X} = \frac{X_{all}}{N} \tag{8}$$

$$\bar{Y} = \frac{Y_{all}}{N} \tag{9}$$

3.2 Rotation Phase

Then general node is added into the candidate CH sequence. The added nodes must meet the following two conditions.

(1) Its energy is more than average energy level of the clusters.
(2) The distance from the centroid of the network to the node is less than the average distance of the whole cluster nodes to the centroid.

What's more, in the process of CH rotation, the number of CH nodes and dead nodes are taken into consideration. In other words, the amount of cluster decreases with the dead nodes increasing, to keep the value of P unchanged. Note here that P represents the desired percentage, which is defined in previous work. The detail information of P can be seen from [1].

4   Performance Evaluation

The version of NS-2 [41] used in our simulation is NS-2.35. The software platform we run the protocols on is Ubuntu 12.04. The BS is set at (50, 175). The detailed comparisons are shown as follows. We consider a wireless sensor network with N = 100 nodes randomly distributed in a 1000 m × 1000 m field. The energy of each node is set to be 2 J.

4.1   The Number of Nodes Alive

As is shown in Fig. 1, great differences exist between the number of sensor nodes alive of the EEC and typical or improved LEACH protocols. In other word, the number of alive-nodes is the lifetime of the wireless sensor network, which is the most important parameter of routing protocol. First of all, the first node of LEACH-C starts to die at about the 100th round. When it comes to LEACH and EEC, the first nodes start to die at about the 400th round. Second, the nodes of LEACH-C die in a very short time owing to the large amount of communicating control message, while the network using EEC has a very long life time. Almost have more than 60 rounds than LEACH has. Lastly, all nodes of LEACH-C die even earlier than LEACH and EEC.

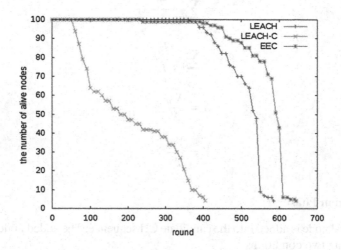

Fig. 1. Number of sensor nodes alive of the three protocols

4.2   The Number of Messages Received by BS

Figure 2 shows that LEACH-C delivers much less messages to BS than any other protocols. The numbers of signals received by BS in the network using EEC are equal to LEACH before the 400th round. But after 400th round EEC's packet delivered is growing slowly. The decrease of information is not influencing the monitor of the whole network.

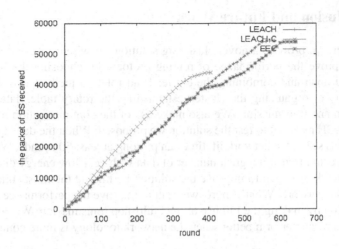

Fig. 2. Number of messages received by BS of the three protocols

4.3 The Energy Dissipation

As shown in Fig. 3, the speed of total energy dissipation of LEACH-C keeps in a very high level. On the other hand, in this aspect, LEACH-C performs not so good compared with LEACH and EEC. In addition, the speed of energy consumption of EEC is slower than that of LEACH after 400th round. That's means in EEC protocol nodes can monitor the network longer than LEACH.

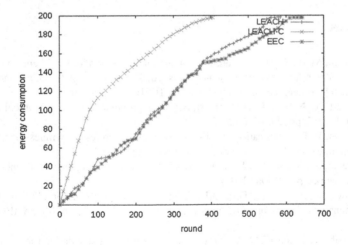

Fig. 3. Total energy dissipation of the three protocols

5 Conclusion and Future Work

In this paper, we propose a novel clustering solution for wireless sensor networks in order to improve the performance of routing protocol by choosing the best suitable cluster head node and combining the cluster head rotation method, which takes the responsibility of organizing the cluster, establishing the rotary table, data collection, compression and transmission. We also make use of the communication model of the typical LEACH protocol to test the solution we proposed. When the density of node in the network is scale, the network lifetime can prolong at least 50 rounds. What's more, the solution could transmit a great number of data with very low energy dissipation. In the further work, we want to improve the solution by finding the most suitable cluster number of the network. What's more, we want to improve the performance of the clustering solution by making the full use of the multi-hop transmission. We hope that our future solution can perform better when the network topology is more complex.

Acknowledgment. This work is supported by the National Science Foundation of China under Grant No. 61300237, No. U1536206, No. U1405254, No. 61232016 and No. 61402234, the National Basic Research Program 973 under Grant No. 2011CB311808, the Natural Science Foundation of Jiangsu province under Grant No. BK2012461, the research fund from Jiangsu Technology & Engineering Center of Meteorological Sensor Network in NUIST under Grant No. KDXG1301, the research fund from Jiangsu Engineering Center of Network Monitoring in NUIST under Grant No. KJR1302, the research fund from Nanjing University of Information Science and Technology under Grant No. S8113003001, the 2013 Nanjing Project of Science and Technology Activities for Returning from Overseas, the 2015 Project of six personnel in Jiangsu Province under Grant No. R2015L06, the CICAEET fund, and the PAPD fund.

References

1. Heinzelman, W.R., Chandrakasan, A., Balakrishnan, H.: Energy efficient communication protocol for wireless micro sensor networks. In: Proceedings of the 33rd Annual Hawaii International Conference on System Sciences. IEEE, p. 10 (2000)
2. Yektaparast, A., Nabavi, F.-H., Sarmast, A.: An improvement on leach protocol (cell-leach). In: ICACT 2012, pp. 992–996 (2012)
3. Heinzelman, W.B.: Application-specific protocol architectures for wireless networks. Ph.D. Dissertation, Massachusetts Institute of Technology (2000)
4. Manjeshwar, A., Agrawal, D.P.: Teen: a routing protocol for enhanced efficiency in wireless sensor networks, p. 30189a (2001)
5. Manjeshwar, A., Agrawal, D.P.: APTEEN: a hybrid protocol for efficient routing and comprehensive information retrieval in wireless sensor networks. In: IPDPS. IEEE, p. 0195b (2002)
6. Wu, Y., Fahmy, S., Shroff, N.B.: Energy efficient sleep/wake scheduling for multi-hop sensor networks: non-convexity and approximation algorithm. In: INFOCOM 2007, pp. 1568–1576 (2007)
7. Sharma, T., Joshi, R., Misra, M.: GBDD: grid based data dissemination in wireless sensor networks. In: Advanced Computing and Communications, ADCOM 2008, pp. 234–240 (2008)

8. Lotf, J.J., Bonab, M.N., Khorsandi, S.: A novel cluster-based routing protocol with extending lifetime for wireless sensor networks. In: WOCN 2008, pp. 1–5 (2008)
9. Cheng, H.-B., Geng, Y., Hu, S.-J.: NHRPA: a novel hierarchical routing protocol algorithm for wireless sensor networks. J. China Univ. Posts Telecommun. **15**(3), 75–81 (2008)
10. Kandris, D., Tsioumas, P., Tzes, A., Nikolakopoulos, G., Vergados, D.D.: Power conservation through energy efficient routing in wireless sensor networks. Sensors **9**(9), 7320–7342 (2009)
11. Lung, C.-H., Zhou, C.: Using hierarchical agglomerative clustering in wireless sensor networks: an energy-efficient and flexible approach. Ad Hoc Netw. **8**(3), 328–344 (2010)
12. Carrabs, F., Cerulli, R., D'Ambrosio, C., Raiconi, A.: Extending lifetime through partial coverage and roles allocation in connectivity-constrained sensor networks. IFAC-PapersOnLine **49**(12), 973–978 (2016)
13. Muruganathan, S.D., Ma, D.C., Bhasin, R.I., Fapojuwo, A.O.: A centralized energy-efficient routing protocol for wireless sensor networks. IEEE Commun. Mag. **43**(3), S8–13 (2005)
14. Ye, F., Zhong, G., Lu, S., Zhang, L.: Gradient broadcast: a robust data delivery protocol for large scale sensor networks. Wireless Netw. **11**(3), 285–298 (2005)
15. Kumar, D., Aseri, T.C., Patel, R.: EEHC: energy efficient heterogeneous clustered scheme for wireless sensor networks. Comput. Commun. **32**(4), 662–667 (2009)
16. Wang, Y., Tsai, C., Mao, H.: HMRP: hierarchy-based multipath routing protocol for wireless sensor networks. J. Sci. Eng. **9**(3), 255 (2006)
17. Nayak, S.P., Rai, S.C., Pradhan, S.K.: MERA: a multi-clustered energy efficient routing algorithm in WSN. In: IEEE ICIT, pp. 37–42 (2015)
18. Zhang, J., Jeong, C.K., Lee, G.Y., Kim, H.J.: Cluster-based multipath routing algorithm for multi-hop wireless network. Future Gener. Commun. Netw. **1**, 67–75 (2007)
19. Chen, M., Leung, V.C., Mao, S., Yuan, Y.: Directional geographical routing for real-time video communications in wireless sensor networks. Comput. Commun. **30**(17), 3368–3383 (2007)
20. Chen, M., Leung, V.C., Mao, S.: Directional controlled fusion in wireless sensor networks. Mobile Netw. Appl. **14**(2), 220–229 (2009)
21. Chao, H.-L., Chang, C.-L.: A fault-tolerant routing protocol in wireless sensor networks. Int. J. Sens. Netw. **3**(1), 66–73 (2008)
22. Luo, H., Ye, F., Cheng, J., Lu, S., Zhang, L.: TTDD: two-tier data dissemination in large-scale wireless sensor networks. Wireless Netw. **11**(1–2), 161–175 (2005)
23. Yuan, Y., He, Z., Chen, M.: Virtual mimo-based cross-layer design for wireless sensor networks. IEEE Trans. Veh. Technol. **55**(3), 856–864 (2006)
24. Al-Karaki, J.N., Ul-Mustafa, R., Kamal, A.E.: Data aggregation in wireless sensor networks-exact and approximate algorithms. In: HPSR 2004, pp. 241–245 (2004)
25. Carrabs, F., Cerulli, R., D'Ambrosio, C., Raiconi, A.: An exact algorithm to extend lifetime through roles allocation in sensor networks with connectivity constraints. Optim. Lett., 1–16 (2016)
26. Liu, A., Zheng, Z., Zhang, C., Chen, Z., Shen, X.: Secure and energy efficient disjoint multipath routing for wsns. IEEE Trans. Veh. Technol. **61**(7), 3255–3265 (2012)
27. Xiong, N., Jia, X., Yang, L.T., Vasilakos, A.V., Li, Y., Pan, Y.: A distributed efficient flow control scheme for multirate multicast networks. IEEE Trans. Parallel Distrib. Syst. **21**(9), 1254–1266 (2010)
28. Lin, X., Lu, R., Shen, X., Nemoto, Y., Kato, N.: SAGE: a strong privacy preserving scheme against global eavesdropping for e-health systems. IEEE J. Sel. Areas Commun. **27**(4), 365–378 (2009)
29. Akyildiz, I.F., Su, W., Sankarasubramaniam, Y., Cayirci, E.: Wireless sensor networks: a survey. Comput. Netw. **38**(4), 393–422 (2002)

30. Liu, A., Ren, J., Li, X., Chen, Z., Shen, X.S.: Design principles and improvement of cost function based energy aware routing algorithms for wireless sensor networks. Comput. Netw. **56**(7), 1951–1967 (2012)
31. Rajput, N., Gandhi, N., Saxena, L.: Wireless sensor networks: apple farming in northern india. In: 2012 Fourth International Conference on Computational Intelligence and Communication Networks (CICN), pp. 218–221. IEEE (2012)
32. Qing, L., Zhu, Q., Wang, M.: Design of a distributed energy-efficient clustering algorithm for heterogeneous wireless sensor networks. Comput. Commun. **29**(12), 2230–2237 (2006)
33. Shen, J., Tan, H., Wang, J., Wang, J., Lee, S.: A novel routing protocol providing good transmission reliability in underwater sensor networks. J. Internet Technol. **16**(1), 171–178 (2015)
34. Xia, Z., Wang, X., Sun, X., Wang, Q.: A secure and dynamic multi-keyword ranked search scheme over encrypted cloud data. IEEE Trans. Parallel Distrib. Syst. **27**(2), 340–352 (2016)
35. Fu, Z., Sun, X., Liu, Q., Zhou, L., Shu, J.: Achieving efficient cloud search services: multi-keyword ranked search over encrypted cloud data supporting parallel computing. IEICE Trans. Commun. **98**(1), 190–200 (2015)
36. Yick, J., Mukherjee, B., Ghosal, D.: Wireless sensor network survey. Comput. Netw. **52**(12), 2292–2330 (2008)
37. Abbasi, A.A., Younis, M.: A survey on clustering algorithms for wireless sensor networks. Comput. Commun. **30**(14), 2826–2841 (2007)
38. Bandyopadhyay, S., Coyle, E.J.: An energy efficient hierarchical clustering algorithm for wireless sensor networks. In: INFOCOM 2003, vol. 3, pp. 1713–1723 (2003)
39. Smaragdakis, G., Matta, I., Bestavros, A., et al.: SEP: a stable election protocol for clustered heterogeneous wireless sensor networks. In: Second International Workshop on Sensor and Actor Network Protocols and Applications (SANPA 2004), vol. 3 (2004)
40. Ye, M., Li, C., Chen, G., Wu, J.: EECS: an energy efficient clustering scheme in wireless sensor networks. In: IPCCC 2005, pp. 535–540 (2005)
41. McCanne, S., Floyd, S., Fall, K., Varadhan, K., et al.: Network simulator ns-2 (1997)

Reliable Data Collection for Wireless Sensor Networks Using Unmanned Aerial Vehicles

Alexandru-Valentin Vlăduță[1], Ion Bica[1], Victor-Valeriu Patriciu[1], and Florin Pop[2,3(✉)]

[1] Military Technical Academy, Bucharest, Romania
{alexandru.vladuta,ibica,vip}@mta.ro
[2] University Politehnica of Bucharest, Bucharest, Romania
florin.pop@cs.pub.ro
[3] National Institute for Research and Development in Informatics, Bucharest, Romania

Abstract. Data gathering is a subject of interest in Wireless Sensor Networks (WSNs). Because these networks use devices with limited resources, to obtain good results, they must be well configured and distributed, while data must be gathered in an efficient manner, without wasting resources. In this paper, the factors used as a trade-off for a reliable transmission are: complexity and latency. In order to obtain reliability, it is mandatory to make more frame exchanges and to employ extra communication between entities, to ensure that data is not corrupted or lost during transmission. The objective of this paper is centered around reliable communication in WSNs and the proposed solution minimizes the risk of losing data when nodes remain without energy. Among energy aspects, a prioritization algorithm that uses the positions of sensors and the trajectory of a collecting unmanned aerial vehicle (UAV) is implemented in this proposition. All these together form a protocol that is intended to be used in critical systems where every bit of information is vital.

Keywords: Wireless Sensor Networks · Data gathering protocols · Cooperative communications · Reliable transmission · NS2 simulations

1 Introduction

Wireless Sensor Networks have been seen as a solution for the mobility factor present in our everyday life. As a result, this technology has evolved greatly in the recent years and is still on a growing path, due to the high demand from vendors. Having such a motivation, different research teams from all over the world have tried over the years to push the limits of these mobile devices to become smaller, more scalable, to increase their power and range of connectivity, to decrease power consumption and to merge them with other technologies to obtain a complex multi-role device.

"*Smart Cities*" is one of the beneficiaries that rely on the development of WSNs. In [1], authors give a wider perspective of the earlier mentioned concept and explain the vision of CISCO on how Internet of Everything (IoE) and Smart Cities go hand in hand.

Authors of [2] underline, among other aspects, the enablers that sustained the development of the Internet-of-Things (IoT). One of these are sensors. Over time, they

© Springer International Publishing AG 2017
M.H.A. Au et al. (Eds.): GPC 2017, LNCS 10232, pp. 323–337, 2017.
DOI: 10.1007/978-3-319-57186-7_25

increased performances while prices decreased significantly. As a result, vendors started to include sensors in their products without increasing costs. With cheap sensors, networks started to increase in size and complexity and how data was collected became a challenge. And for this reason, many research teams developed protocols and solutions to limit collisions and to improve data gathering in dense networks. Other two enablers enumerated in [2] are bandwidth and processing. These two reduced their cost significantly and permitted this area of research to develop greatly. With low costs for bandwidth, networks increased their capacities and complexity. Furthermore, with decreased costs for processing, WSNs obtained not only the capability to collect and forward data, but also to process and filter data to take decisions faster and to remove redundant data. The effect of this action is translated in lower transmission times, energy savings and increased network lifetime [3]. Therefore, devices will not only sense and transmit data, but also process and transform it from raw data into information (as mentioned in [1]). Another factor that contributed to the development of IoT was the concept of big data. It is known that high density WSNs can generate large amounts of data that has to be processed at a certain point. The solution for this challenge relies on the development of big data that comes into aid with its analytics. Finally, the last component that helped IoT reach the actual state is IPv6. It's a known fact that IPv4 was on the point of depletion due to its limited number of addresses (32 bits length, which is translated in only 2^{32} addresses). With the development of mobile devices and the need of more and more devices connected to the Internet, the number of remaining free addresses started to decrease rapidly. In order to counter this limitation, IPv6 was created to aid networks in this situation and offer a solution. The new standard offers a length of 128 bits and a large range of addresses (2^{128}). With this solution, WSNs were able to offer addresses, without restrictions, to all their devices, regardless the size of the network.

The objective of this paper circles around assuring reliability in the communication process, with regards to other two important aspects: energy efficiency and collision avoidance. A trade-off must be made in terms of complexity and latency. No proposed solution offered only advantages, without making compromises on other aspects. In this format, these compromises are in terms of complexity, by adding extra control frames to assure reliability, and in terms of latency, by adding delay in the transmission, when control frames are exchanged before the data transfer.

The remaining of the paper is organized as follows. Related work is presented in Sect. 2, the protocol proposed in [21] is summarized in Sect. 3, the proposition is revealed in Sect. 4, simulation results are detailed in Sect. 5, and, finally, conclusions are drawn in Sect. 6.

2   Related Work

This section presents relevant work of other research teams about data gathering in WSNs. Many solutions have been proposed over the time: some use static or dynamic trees, others use routing data on different paths for distributing energy consumption in an equal manner, others use mobile devices that have the role to gather data from static deployed sensors and many more.

For example, authors of [4] propose in their paper a protocol that uses mobile base stations to gather data from statically deployed sensors. There are two methods to transmit data to a base station: directly, when the distance is short or the trajectory of the moving station is toward the sensor, and indirectly, with the use of other sensors, when the distance is high or the station is increasing its distance from the specific sensor. When nodes send data from one to another, they use a neighbor table that was previously constructed. This is an important point of reference that influenced the development of the proposition mentioned in Sect. 4.

An alternative method to collect data is detailed in [5]. Authors present a protocol that uses an unmanned aerial vehicles (UAV) to collect data from sensors. Sensors are gathered into groups and in each of these a specific device with the highest energy level is selected to be the leader of the group. All surrounding sensors will be kept in sleep mode to conserve their energy level. When the UAV approaches the area of a specific group, it transmits a frame to the leader to inform about its presence. At that moment, the leader will wake up all its neighbors and start the data gathering process. When it finishes, they return to sleep.

A different data gathering method is revealed in [6]. Authors focus on developing a protocol that uses a tree-based structure with the end goal of obtaining a reliable communication with efficiency in terms of energy consumption and duty cycles. The communication is initialized by the parents with the aid of beacon frames. Child nodes respond with a busy tone that enables the contention window and with a request frame that initializes the connection. Afterwards, data is sent and the connection ends.

Another perspective is presented by authors of [7]. Their work centers around hierarchical protocols, like LEACH [8] and PEGASIS [9]. The objective is to obtain a protocol that has an even consumption of energy for all nodes in the network. The offered solution comes in the form of a chain that is constructed with the help of greedy algorithms. The first node in the chain is considered the device that has the highest distance from the base station. The second node will be the device with the closest position and the pattern continues until all nodes in the simulation are included. In each data gathering round, a node that will act as leader is elected. This node aggregates data from the entire chain and forwards it to the sink.

In [10], authors present two protocols that have LEACH at their origin. The two have been developed for critical applications in indoor environments. For this reason, the transmission is considered reliable. The first one is named Randomly clustered Energy Efficient Routing Protocol (R-EERP) and deploys sensors randomly and uniformly on the floors of a building, in a similar manner with the original LEACH protocol. The second one, Sequentially clustered Energy Efficient Routing Protocol (S-EERP) deploys sensors sequentially in every room, on every floor, differently from the first one. With the two thresholds that they both use, R-EERP and S-EERP can schedule when and how to receive data from cluster heads. Additionally, the two protocols can also remove redundant data (gathered from sensors placed at close ranges) by making XOR at cluster heads on raw data. This filter helps the two protocols on lowering traffic in the network and on increasing network lifetime.

Authors of [11] created a protocol that comes as an upgrade to the Bellman-Ford distributed (BFD) asynchronous version [12]. The new protocol received a new name,

Efficient Bellman-Ford (EBF). The key characteristics inherited by the new protocol from its predecessor are: simplicity, low computational demand and tolerance to message/node failures during transmissions. The main difference is that EBF reduces traffic by using a threshold for every request message. If it receives a packet with a higher value, it floods it further in the network, otherwise it ignores the message.

Another approach for data gathering in WSN is presented in [13], where authors underline a protocol that collects data with the aid of an UAV. The name of the proposition is Dual-Stack Single-Radio Communication Architecture (DSSRCA) and, as the name states, the main objective of it is to have two communications types (best effort and reliable) on a single radio antenna. Each type will be used in a specific scenario: when the drone, also known as UAV, needs to communicate with the sink, it will use a reliable connection to transmit all gathered data, while in the case of drone-sensor communication, it will be used a best effort communication. 6LoWPAN [14] is the technology used for the reliable transmission. Another important aspect is the existence of different classes of priorities, which permits different numbers of retransmission. For high priority messages, an unlimited number of retries is set, for normal priority packets, a pre-defined number of retransmissions are permitted, while in the case of low priority frames, no retries are permitted.

In [15], authors propose a protocol that fixes the deficiencies identified at Enhanced-Pegasis [16] (high density networks translate in long chains which lead to increased energy consumption; leaders are elected in a certain order, not by the level of remaining energy, which leads to a decreased network lifetime) and at COSEN [17] (redundant paths are introduced for nodes that are near the base station, making the communication inefficient by wasting time and energy for extra-transmissions between sensors and leaders). The name of the proposition is CHIRON and is a hierarchical chain-based protocol. In the first step, the area is divided into smaller groups to obtain shorter chains, which will reduce traffic and power consumption. Unlike the round-robin method used in [16, 17], in this proposition the leader will be, initially, the first node in the chain and afterwards, the node with the highest level of residual energy. With this method, authors increase the lifetime of the network by evenly distributing the power consumption in the entire network. The data gathering process starts from the other end of a chain and aggregates at the leader. Afterwards, leaders relay between them to transfer data to the base station. As a result, the sensing time and power dissipation are reduced and data delivery is improved, as can be seen from the simulations from [15].

A different approach is revealed in [18]. Authors propose a protocol that uses mobile cluster heads with the role to lower the power consumption and increase the network lifetime. These cluster heads are seen as relays between certain areas and the base station, and have the objective to limit the amount of energy consumed by sensors when transmitting at high distances. The results underlined by authors demonstrate that the proposition increased the network lifetime up to 75%, when compared to similar protocols and decreased the transmission delays down to 40%.

An alternative approach for data gathering is presented in [19, 20]. Both papers focus on using an UAV and a priority based scheme. The key factor used in [19] is that sensors are gathered into groups and each of these obtains a priority from a Prioritized Frame Selection (PFS) scheme which will indicate the order in which groups will communicate with the UAV. Moreover, Time Division Multiple Access (TDMA) is employed in each group for the data gathering process. On the other hand, in [20], authors rely on the use of Carrier Sense Multiple Access with Collision Avoidance (CSMA/CA). The beacon transmitted by the UAV is split into multiple frames with different priorities, based on the distance. For high priority frames are used short contention windows, while for low priority frames, longer contention windows are inserted.

All the previously mentioned papers create a large perspective related to the subject of this paper and increase the level of knowledge. By studying the pros and cons of each given solution, an opinion was shaped on how data should be gathered in a reliable manner, with minimum chance to lose data. It has been underlined and demonstrated that in order to obtain advantages on some aspects, there must be disadvantages on other parts. It is very important to mention from the beginning the objectives and available resources that have to be combined in order to reach the end goal. Without a clear perspective upon all details from the beginning, it will be very difficult to obtain good results. More information related to the proposed solution will be detailed in Sect. 4.

3   Original Data Gathering Protocol

In [21] the original version of our proposed protocol is presented. In this section, the operating mechanism and the limitations identified in the protocol will be shortly described.

The objective is to gather data in a reliable manner, with minimal loss, by offering a fair chance to all sensors to transmit during their communication window with the drone. The key element in the original version is the prioritization mechanism, which uses the location of sensors and of the drone to calculate the priority for each sensing device. A dynamic drone was used to collect data from a number of static sensors due to its independence from ground factors and to its effectiveness in terms of quantity, delay and reliability. A ground unit would have limitations in certain areas, due to terrain factors. Furthermore, the quantity of gathered data is lower when compared to the results obtained by an UAV in the same period. These results are due to the superior speed that comes from the limited number of obstacles that a drone may encounter on its trajectory, to the altitude that offers a wider range of transmission to flying devices and many more factors. For these reasons, many research teams focused in their propositions [5, 13, 19–22] on using drones or other flying devices for data gathering.

The center of the algorithm used in the protocol is, as mentioned earlier, the prioritization mechanism. In dense networks, where multiple sensors compete for transferring data to the flying drone, prioritization must be employed to limit the chance for collisions to appear. This is done with the help of coordinates from which communication windows for sensors are created. Beside the coordinates of static sensors, the trajectory of the drone is also used. The BEAM frame initiates the process that orders the sensors by their position regarding the position of the drone on its trajectory. The earlier mentioned packet contains information about the drone's location when it generated the frame and about the trajectory that it will follow. These coordi-nates are going to be used by all receiving sensors to calculate their priorities. At the expiration of the priority timer, the node sends a PRI frame to establish a reliable connection with the drone, in which it informs about the quantity of packets that it has to transfer. The UAV responds with a BUSY packet that instructs all surrounding sensors to delay their timers because it will start to communicate with the first node, limiting the chance for collision to appear during the transmission. At this point, data and acknowledgement packets are exchanged between the selected sensor and the drone. When the drone receives the amount of packets advised previously with the PRI frame, it broadcasts a CLEAR frame that informs all remaining sensors that they can restart their competition for data transferring. This method limits the amount of time that the drone would waste while waiting to see if it has to receive more data or not, increasing the efficiency of the protocol.

A general limitation specific to WSNs is the energy capacity. Since sensors are placed at various positions and often in isolated places, they are powered with batteries. Therefore, based on how energy is consumed, some sensors may deplete their capacities before the UAV arrives in their vicinity to gather data. In an ideal scenario, all sensors have an equal amount of energy when they are deployed and the consumption is the same in the entire network. But in a real-life scenario, sensors have different levels of energy and based on the amount and type of data that they gather, energy is consumed unevenly among them. Some sensors may start with a lower level of energy and gather more data due to the presence of different events, while others may gather data only at certain regular moments. When the UAV arrives in the coverage area of these sensors, some may already have depleted their batteries or they may have a limited amount, which results in packet loss in certain points of the map, where activities were intensive. In critical application where data is important, this kind of scenario may not be acceptable. This is one limitation of the initial protocol. A solution for this would be to transfer data from a node that detects a low energy level to a neighbor that has sufficient power to transfer its own data and the received packets. One of the mechanisms that can be improved in terms of efficiency is the prioritization. For devices that are in the same region, at close range, prioritization based on coordinates may not be the best option. In some scenarios, there may be two sensors that have been deployed in the same area and gather different types and amounts of data. One would gather very little information, while the other may have three times the number of packets stored. Because of the short distance between the two, the prioritization process will choose the one that has a shorter window to communicate, even though the distance and difference between the two windows would be almost imperceptible. Another criterion should be introduced to handle scenarios where sensors have close positions, to pick the sensor with more data or with lesser energy. If the drone would pick the sensing unit with lower power level it would decrease the chance to lose data due to energy depletion and increase the network lifetime by reducing the energy consumed while waiting its turn to transmit. On the other hand, if the UAV would pick the sensor with more data, it would gather its data firstly and construct a larger perspective about the environment than from the other sensor that has less information. If the drone would not have time to process data from both sensors, it would be preferable to gather from the one that has more data to transmit.

To improve even more the efficiency and results of the proposition, a new protocol has been developed. Some of the drawbacks will remain, since the improved protocol was built on the foundation of the previous version. Next section presents details related to the implementation and operation of the improved protocol.

4 Improved Data Gathering Protocol

This section is centered on presenting an improved version of the data gathering protocol described in [21] that is intended for critical applications, in which every piece of data is important. To obtain a reliable communication between entities, several disadvantages had to be introduced: latency, complexity and delay.

These three are the result of adding extra communication for synchronization, prioritization and acknowledgement of receipt. A reliable communication is mandatory in such a protocol because it guarantees that data has minimum chance to be lost due to collisions, battery exhaustion or unbalanced power consumption. These are the main causes identified in data gathering protocols presented by other research teams over the time. For this reason, the key advantage of this proposition over the version presented in [21] is that it takes into consideration all three aspects mentioned earlier to lower at minimum the chance to lose data due to collisions or battery exhaustion.

The first limitation that was identified in the protocol presented in [21] was related to data loss due to low energy level or battery exhaustion. Sensors may deplete their energy level before receiving a signal from an UAV to start the data transmission. In such a scenario, data would get lost and for critical applications this action is not acceptable. The solution is to transfer data from one sensor to another before the sending device depletes its remaining energy.

The mechanism used in this proposition employs data transfer from one device to another when a minimum level of energy is reached. The receiving device needs to have enough energy to transmit the received packets along with its own data. In order to pick the proper neighbor to forward data, the sending sensor needs a table with relevant information about its surrounding neighbors. Figure 1 illustrates the steps for creating an entry in the neighbors table of a sensor. Tables are periodically updated with information from neighbors to have relevant data regarding the energy level and link quality of a sensor, before the transmission step between two sensing devices starts. The update frequency depends on the environment (for dense and active environments, where data is continuously collected and energy consumption is increased, updates are done frequently, due to the accelerated way events occur, while for static environments where data is sensed at fixed moments of time, updates are done rarely because consumption is lower and changes to the energy levels are insignificant). Furthermore, the update frequency depends on the type of used sensors. For devices with low energy capacity, every transmission and data process is important, therefore updates are done rarely, to not impact the sensing process, while for devices with high energy capacity, updates can be done frequently. It is important to have a balance, to not waste energy on updates and in the same time, to not have outdated values in tables.

A new control frame was introduced with the purpose of updating neighbors' tables with information related to energy level and link quality. The frame is named REQ and is used only in communication between sensors. Transmission is done using TDMA as

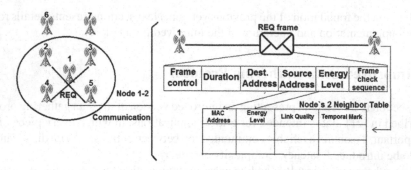

Fig. 1. Steps for processing a REQ frame.

a channel access method and each sensor has its own window to broadcast the REQ packet to all surrounding neighbors. The size of the control frame has a length of only 28 bytes to impact as less as possible the energy consumption. The format of the packet is also illustrated in Fig. 1. Furthermore, in the same figure is detailed the process done by sensor 2 when it receives a REQ frame from sensor 1. The source address from the frame is extracted and checked in the local neighbors table. If it exists, it verifies the temporal mark from the table row to see if it's older and if the check returns positive, it updates the energy level with the one received in the packet. If the address is not present in the table, a new row is created with the values received in the frame. The link quality column contains values that are calculated whenever a REQ packet is received. In (1) can be observed the mathematical equation for the link quality or Signal-to-interference-plus-noise ratio (SINR), where P represents the power of the incoming frame, I the interference power of other signals present in the environment and N the noise, which is a constant value defined at the start of the simulation. Lastly, the temporal mark column contains a value that represents the moment when the REQ frame was received by the processing sensor. This value is required to have only updated values and to prevent obsolete values to remain in the table.

$$SINR = \frac{P}{N + I} \qquad (1)$$

Figure 2 illustrates the activity diagram for the neighbors discovering mechanism. In this step, only REQ frames are used by sensors to update their neighbors' tables. The reason for creating a new discovery mechanism instead of using an existing one is due to the limitations in terms of processing power and energy capacity of the devices. It is more practical to make a custom frame that will contain information regarding the identity and energy level of the transmitter, than using an existing mechanism that will contain other irrelevant information that increases the length of the packet, which translates in an increased energy consumption and latency in the network. For this reason, the mechanism presented in Fig. 2 is used to discover neighbors and update the corresponding table. As mentioned earlier, the discovery mechanism uses TDMA as a channel accessing method, in which each sensor gets a window to send its REQ frame. When the timer expires, a sensor enters its communication window and generates a REQ frame that will be broadcasted to all surrounding sensing devices. A receiving sensor will search its neighbor table to see if the entry corresponding to the source of the frame exists. If it does and the temporal mark is older, then it updates the row in the table. If it does not exist, it creates a new entry.

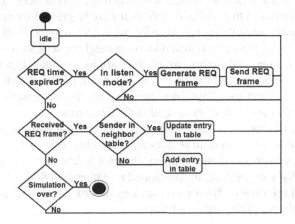

Fig. 2. Activity diagram for neighbor discovery process.

The only cost associated with this method is that it increases the energy consumption by adding an extra control frame between sensors, in order to create and update their neighbors tables. The major advantage that this mechanism offers is that it prevents the loss of data due to low energy and makes the transmission reliable, with redundancy for cases when several nodes deplete their energy.

With all tables updated, the process can move to the next step where all sensors check their own energy level to see if they have enough to send their data. If the level drops below 15% (this value was selected based on a trial and error method in which was verified the percentage for which a sensor can send its data without having the risk to deplete its battery during transfer), the probability to deplete the remaining energy while it transfers to the collecting unit increases. For this reason, it starts sending its data to one of the neighbors that it picks from the table. The criterion of selection includes the neighbor with the highest level of remaining energy. If several nodes meet this criterion, it selects the one with better link quality. The motivation behind this selection criterion is based on the fact that the node with the highest level of energy is most suited because it has to transfer its data and also the information received from the depleted sensor and it needs to have enough energy to complete these tasks. Furthermore, if several sensors have the same level, the one with the highest link quality indicates a node that is better positioned or that it has lesser interference than other nodes in the area, making it more suitable for transfer. We consider transferring data to neighbors only when the energy level drops below 15% in order to limit the number of transmission in the network and to save energy. If one sensor has enough energy to send its own data, it won't overload a neighbor, in terms of energy consumption and delay, to send data on its behalf. Having this mechanism implemented, the risk of losing data due to battery depletion, decreased significantly and therefore, a significant improvement was made to the protocol presented in [21].

A special case had to be taken into account. In the protocol presented in [21], when two sensors are placed at close positions, the prioritization algorithm that uses location coordinates will make a random selection between the two devices, due to a random jitter that was introduced to avoid collisions that may be created by the close position of the two. In the approach that we propose in this work, an extra condition is added. If one of the two sensors have aggregated data from neighbor sensors it will grant higher priority when compared to the other, which has only its own data. If both sensors have aggregated data, the difference is made by the number of nodes for which they forward data. If still both sensors have data from the same number of sensors, the jitter is the factor that prevents the two devices to send in the same time.

In critical applications, it is mandatory to collect firstly from sensors that have data from other neighbors too, then from sensors that send only their own sensed data. There may be situations where the drone's battery depletes before the collection process can finish successfully and therefore, it is indicated to gather data firstly from devices that have aggregated information from more devices, in order to collect as much data as possible within the remaining period of time.

5   Simulation Results

The improved version of data gathering protocol was tested using the Network Simulator (NS) 2, version 2.34, which is detailed in [23]. For simulations was used a two-ray ground reflection model and omnidirectional antennas were equipped on all devices in the virtual environment. Furthermore, more settings are summarized in Table 1.

Table 1. Simulation parameters for NS-2.

Sensors	7–100 nodes	Bandwidth	20 Kbps
SIFS	5 ms	TX Power	0.5 W
DIFS	10 ms	TX Range	250 m
Packet Generation	550 m	Carrier Sense Range	550 m

A first simulation was conducted to demonstrate the efficiency of the improved protocol over the original version in term of success rate, while transferring data packets to the collecting unit. An important factor that has to be mentioned from the beginning is that the energy level of each sensor is not set at 100%. Each device starts with a different level, like in real life situations, where it cannot be set a predefined value to all devices. Some may have different energy capacities, while others may have been deployed with half of their capacities. For this reason, is important to take into consideration the energy level of a device when making a reliable data gathering protocol for critical applications. Figure 3 illustrates a chart that proves the success rate of the proposed protocol. In this comparison are randomly deployed different amounts of sensors, to demonstrate how transfer efficiency is affected by network density.

The deployed sensors was varied from 10 to 25, 50 and until 100 nodes in the same environment.

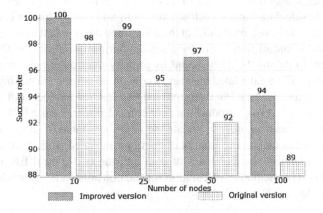

Success rate chart.

At the first test, with only 10 sensors, results had close values, with 100% for the improved protocol and 98% for the original version. The difference is almost imperceptible, but with every network density increase, these values decrease. At 25 nodes the results get to 99% for the improved protocol and 95% for the original version. At this step, the difference is still not critical. Starting with 50 nodes, values drop even more, to the limit of 97% for the proposed protocol and 92% for the original version. The last test was made with 100 sensors and results remained at an acceptable value of 94% success rate for the improved version, while for the original version of the protocol, the rate dropped to 89%. The explanation for these results comes from the fact that one protocol does not consider the energy level of devices, while the other does. If a device depletes its energy, it will communicate with a neighbor that has a higher energy level and therefore, packets are not lost and success rate keeps at high limits. Otherwise, results decrease and packets gets lost. For these reasons, in every scenario, the improved version has better results than the original protocol. Moreover, when the sensor density is increased, the success rate values decreases for both versions. The explanation for these values is that, as the number of sensors increases, the amount of control frames exchanged between sensors and the drone increases as well. This increase is translated in higher energy consumption and in higher chances to deplete sensor battery during transmission. Even with the mechanism that takes into ac-count the energy level of sensors, data can be lost in some scenarios where all neighbors deplete their energy or have low levels that cannot permit them to aggregate data from surrounding nodes. Having all these facts explained, results demonstrate the increased performance of the proposed solution when compared with its predecessor, backing-up the motivation for which the proposed protocol was created.

Energy consumption is another important aspect [24–26]. It was measured for this proposition because devices have limited capacities and the way how energy is consumed is important. Every action needs to be accounted for and the system needs to be optimized as much as possible for the given conditions. Figure 4 depicts an energy consumption comparison that demonstrates the power efficiency of each protocol. In the simulation, each sensor has 512 bytes of data that it has to transfer to the collecting unit. Furthermore, beside data frames, each sensor has to add control frames exchanged with the drone, in order to have a final value of the consumed energy. In the case of the original version, the only control frame sent by a sensor during its lifetime is the PRI frame, through which it informs the drone about its priority over other neighbors. Therefore, for this protocol will be calculated the energy consumed while transmitting a PRI frame and 512 bytes of data frames. For the improved version, the numbers differ a little from the original protocol. It has introduced a new control frame, beside PRI, which is sent periodically by a sensor in order to update the neighbors table of surrounding devices. Therefore, when calculating the amount of energy consumed while transferring data, it takes into consideration the 512 bytes of data and the two control frames exchanged (PRI and REQ). The method of calculation for the consumed energy while transferring packets is detailed in (2).

$$E_{TX} = P_{TX} * t_{TX} \tag{2}$$

where P_{TX} represents the transmission power and is the same for all nodes in the network. The value for P_{TX} is noted in Table 1. The variable t represents the total time required for a node to send all its packets.

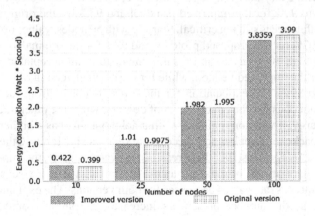

Fig. 4. Energy consumption chart.

It may be obvious that the consumption of the improved version is higher due to the extra frame introduced in the mechanism. When referring to the results depicted in Fig. 4, the first interpretation changes. Simulations were done with different amounts of sensors, like in the previous comparison, in order to show how node density affects the total amount of energy consumed in the network. Four thresholds have been used as amounts of deployed nodes: 10, 25, 50 and 100.

For the simulation where 10 nodes were deployed, the energy consumption for the original version had a smaller value than in the case of the improved version. The difference is of approximately 0.023, not much for a fair comparison between the two.

This difference comes from the extra control frame that was introduced to improve the data gathering mechanism. In the scenario with 25 sensors, the consumption increased because of the number of present nodes in the environment, but the difference between the two protocols decreased to the amount of 0.0125. At this point, still, the original version obtains better results in terms of energy consumption. At the value of 50 nodes, the situation changed significantly. The improved version obtained lower results in term of energy consumption. The difference is almost insignificant, of about 0.01, but it this case, is favorable for the proposed solution. At 100 nodes, the comparison between the two protocols starts to shape up in favor of the improved version, where it obtained better results, with a difference of 0.154. This result proves that the new solution is efficient for high network densities, where the power consumption decreases in comparison with the original protocol. The explanation behind these results is centered on the new mechanism that ensures reliability to communications. In the first two scenarios, where network density was below 50 nodes, the original version had better results because it uses only one control frame, instead of two, for the improved version. When network density increased beyond 50 nodes, the difference between the two changed in favor of the proposed protocol. This change is due to the fact that high density networks generate more traffic, which makes sensors deplete their energy faster. If multiple sensors send their data to a node, which aggregates all received information, then the communication is done between the selected sensor and the collecting unit. This is translated in fewer control frames exchanged between the drone and the sensor, due to the fact that one sensor sends data for multiple devices, which leads to energy savings by eliminating energy consumption for control packets.

With the two charts, one can state that the improved version of the data gathering protocol achieves the proposed goals by making a reliable communication, with fewer risks to lose data due to energy factors. Furthermore, for high density networks, the proposition proves to be energy efficient when compared with the previous version.

6 Conclusions

The goal of the proposed protocol was to improve the original version by adding features that increases the efficiency of the protocol. The new protocol is aimed for critical applications where data is important and therefore, the operating mechanism must be optimized to reduce the risk of losing data. This is achieved by using a prioritization mechanism based on communication windows, where devices that have short communication periods obtain priority over nodes that have longer periods and where the energy level of devices is taken into account. Nodes that deplete their capacities will transfer stored data to neighbors that have enough energy to transmit all data to the collecting unit. Moreover, when nodes are close to each other and a prioritization cannot be established based on their position and communication windows, nodes are ordered by the amount of data received from surrounding neighbors. It is preferable to gather data from several nodes in one step, than to gather from individual nodes. With all these features included, the new proposal reached its goals and improved its data gathering efficiency. Moreover, simulations demonstrated that the transmission efficiency increased for the new protocol by reducing risks for losing data, making it more suitable for critical applications. Not only was the transmission efficiency improved, but also the energy consumption in high density networks. When a high number of nodes is deployed in a certain area, the communication between sensors increases which results in a higher chance for a sensor to deplete its energy. Therefore, when a node transmits data for several sensors, this will reduce the amount of control frames that would have been used for each communication, reducing the overall energy consumption. The results of the simulations demonstrate the features and advantages of the new protocol.

As future work, we intend to study the power constraints and the overhead induced by the proposed protocol and compare the results with those of other similar data gathering protocols.

Acknowledgment. The research presented in this paper is supported by the project: *DataWay - Real-time Data Processing Platform for Smart Cities: Making sense of Big Data* - PN-II-RU-TE-2014-4-2731. We would like to thank the reviewers for their time and expertise, constructive comments and valuable insight.

References

1. Everything for Cities - Connecting People, Process, Data, and Things To Improve the 'Livability' of Cities and Communities. CISCO (2013)
2. Jankowski, S., Covello, J., Bellini, H., Ritchie, J., Costa, D.: The internet of things: Making sense of the next mega-trend. Goldman Sachs (2014)
3. Cerulli, R., Gentili, M., Raiconi, A.: Maximizing lifetime and handling reliability in wireless sensor networks. Netw. Int. J. **64**(4), 321–338 (2014)
4. Bhuyan, B., Sarma, N.: A QoS aware routing protocol in wireless sensor networks with mobile base stations. In: Proceedings of the International Conference on Internet of things and Cloud Computing, Article no 15, March 2016
5. Mianxiong, D., Kaoru, O., Man, L., Zunyi, T., Suguo, D., Haojin, Z.: UAV-assisted data gathering in wireless sensor networks. J. Supercomputing **70**(3), 1142–1155 (2014)
6. Burri, N., von Rickenbach, P., Wattenhofer, R.: Dozer: Ultra-low power data gathering in sensor networks. In: Information Processing in Sensor Networks, pp. 450–459 (2007)
7. Zytoune, O., Aboutajdine, D.: A lifetime extension protocol for data gathering in wireless sensor networks. Int. J. Innov. Appl. Stud. **4**(3), 477–482 (2013)
8. Arumugam, G.S., Ponnuchamy, T.: EE-LEACH: Development of energy-efficient LEACH Protocol for data gathering in WSN. EURASIP J. Wirel. Commun. Networking **76**, 1–9 (2015)
9. Fu, C., Jiang, Z., Wei, W., Wei, A.: An energy balanced algorithm of LEACH protocol in WSN. IJCSI Int. J. Comput. Sci. Issues **10**(1), 354–359 (2013)
10. Nehra, V., Sharma, A.K.: PEGASIS-E: Power efficient gathering in sensor information system extended. Glob. J. Comput. Sci. Technol. Netw. Web Secur. **13**(15), 1–5 (2013). Version 1.0
11. Tumer, A.E., Gunduz, M.: Energy-efficient and fast data gathering protocols for indoor wireless sensor networks. Sens. J. **10**(9), 8054–8069 (2010). Multidisciplinary Digital Publishing Institute (MDPI)
12. Lachowski, R., Pellenz, M.E., Penna, M.C., Jamhour, E., Souza, R.D.: An efficient distributed algorithm for constructing spanning trees in wireless sensor networks. Sens. J. **15**(1), 1518–1536 (2015). Multidisciplinary Digital Publishing Institute (MDPI)
13. Walden, D.: The Bellman-Ford Algorithm and Distributed Bellman-Ford (2008)

14. Sayyed, A., de Araújo, G.M., Bodanese, J.P., Becker, L.B.: Dual-stack single-radio communication architecture for UAV acting as a mobile node to collect data in WSNs. Sens. J. **15**(9), 23376–23401 (2015). Multidisciplinary Digital Publishing Institute (MDPI)
15. Olsson, J.: 6LoWPAN demystified. Texas Instruments, October 2014
16. Kumar, R., Mundra, P.S.: Improved data gathering protocol for WSN. Int. J. Electron. Comput. Sci. Eng. **1**(3), 1208–1213 (2012)
17. Yueyang, L., Hong, J., Guangxin, Y.: An energy-efficient PEGASIS-based enhanced algorithm in WSN. China Communications, Beijing, China, August, pp. 91–97 (2006)
18. Tabassum, N., Mamun, Q., Urano, Y.: COSEN: A chain oriented sensor network for efficient data collection. In: Third International Conference on Information Technology: New Generations (ITNG 2006) (2006)
19. Banerjee, T., Xie, B., Jun, J.H., Agrawal, D.P.: Increasing lifetime of wireless sensor networks using controllable mobile cluster heads. Wirel. Commun. Mobile Comput. **10**(3), 313–336 (2010)
20. Ho, D.T., Shimamoto, S.: Highly reliable communication protocol for WSN-UAV system employing TDMA and PFS scheme. In: GLOBECOM Workshops (GC Wkshps) (2011)
21. Sotheara, S., Aomi, N., Ando, T., Jiang, L., Shiratori, N., Shimamoto, S.: Effective data gathering protocol in WSN-UAV employing priority-based contention window adjustment scheme. In: Proceedings of the Globecom Workshops, pp. 1475–1480, December 2014
22. Vladuta, A.V., Pura, M.L., Bica, I.: MAC protocol for data gathering in wireless sensor networks with the aid of unmanned aerial vehicles. Adv. Electr. Comput. Eng. **16**(2), 51–56 (2016)
23. Carrabs, F., Cerrone, C., Cerulli, R., Gaudioso, M.: A novel discretization scheme for the close enough traveling salesman problem. Comput. Oper. Res. **78**(C), 163–171 (2017)
24. The Network Simulator – ns 2. http://nsnam.sourceforge.net/wiki/index.php/Main_Page
25. Castiglione, A., Palmieri, F., Fiore, U., Castiglione, A., De Santis, A.: Modeling energy-efficient secure communications in multi-mode wireless mobile devices. J. Comput. Syst. Sci. **81**(8), 1464–1478 (2015)
26. Ricciardi, S., Palmieri, F., Fiore, U., Castiglione, A., Santos-Boada, G.: Modeling energy consumption in next-generation wireless access-over-WDM networks with hybrid power sources. Math. Comput. Model. **58**(5–6), 1389–1404 (2013)

Flaw Recovery in Cloud Based Bio-inspired Peer-to-Peer Systems for Smart Cities

Bogdan Mocanu[1(✉)], Florin Pop[1,3], Alexandra Mihaita (Mocanu)[1],
Ciprian Dobre[1,3], Valentin Cristea[1], and Aniello Castiglione[2]

[1] Department of Computer Science,
University Politehnica Bucharest, Bucharest, Romania
{bogdan.mocanu,alexandra.mihaita}@hpc.pub.ro,
{florin.pop,ciprian.dobre,valentin.cristea}@cs.pub.ro
[2] Department of Computer Science, University of Salerno, Fisciano, SA, Italy
castiglione@ieee.org
[3] National Institute for Research and Development in Informatics (ICI),
Bucharest, Romania

Abstract. Internet of Things and Smart Cities concept have become
very well spared in the last years especially with the growth of mobile
data bandwidth from 3G to 4G networks. This evolution have led to
a new type of ubiquitous connectivity through devices in an unconven-
tional manner. The old, client-server approach is not anymore feasible,
therefore the Peer-to-Peer concept must be applied. The most common
approach in this case represents Cloud based Peer-to-Peer services. This
paper presents SPIDER Peer-to-Peer overlay flaws analysis and several
requirements for Peer-to-Peer applications considering those flaws.

Keywords: Peer-to-Peer · Bio-inspired Peer-to-Peer overlays ·
Cyber-physical infrastructures · Flaw management in Peer-to-Peer
systems · Cloud based Peer-to-Peer systems

1 Introduction

Peer-to-Peer systems has become an emerging research topic in the last years.
Many researchers focuses their attention on Cloud systems based on Peer-to-Peer
overlays. This type of system has many applications in various domains like big-
data dissemination, trust management [13], Internet of Things [5], smart cities
[3,11] and cyber physical infrastructures [8].

Flaws management in Peer-to-Peer systems represent a major research topic
due do its impact in the systems availability. Therefore, the most important the
capabilities Peer-to-Peer systems are self-adaption and self-reorganization with
minimal resources keeping the functionality of the system.

The Peer-to-Peer overlay that is taken in consideration for this paper is the
bio-inspired SPIDER Peer-to-Peer overlay, developed in University Politehnica
Bucharest and presented in paper [9]. This overlay is inspired from nature, thus

© Springer International Publishing AG 2017
M.H.A. Au et al. (Eds.): GPC 2017, LNCS 10232, pp. 338–352, 2017.
DOI: 10.1007/978-3-319-57186-7_26

the construction of this overlay is considered to be bio-inspired. The network is constructed similar to spider webs because it has a fixed number of chains and a variable number of rings depending on the size of the system.

The Internet of Things is a new era in the field of computer science research domain. This type of research segment, basically deals with interconnected devices and sensors through a radio network and aggregate the data form those devices in order to provide information that supports the decision making process. One example of the Internet of Things or Internet of Objects is a smart home surveillance system. In this case, based on the information aggregated from different sensors like video cameras, door sensors, window sensors, heat sensors and proximity sensors, the user can be notified in real time in case his house is been robbed and take further legal actions.

In this paper we analyze several flaws in SPIDER Peer-to-Peer overlay and the way that the overlay recovers from those flaws. The rest of the paper is structured in 6 sections. In the second section is presented state of the art review of existing solutions for cyber-physical infrastructures. Section 3 presents the flaws of the SPIDER overlay. Section 4 is about application type for the SPIDER overlay. In this section are presented two type of applications: IoT and live video streaming. The requirements of this type of applications are presented in Sect. 5. Also in this chapter is realized a mapping of application types, flaws and requirements. Finally, in Sect. 6 are drawn the conclusions of this research.

2   Related Work

Smart cities and cyber-physical infrastructures have become very attractive subjects of research in the past years. Trust management in bio-inspired Peer-to-Peer systems has many challenges especially coming from the fact that there is no central authority to trust.

The authors of [12] have presented an emergency situation management system based on a hybrid cloud architecture that manages storage and computing resources for command and control activities. The efficiency of the proposed approach is based on the fact that the system is aggregating information from motion sensors correlated with the signal strength from landmark nodes.

In paper [5], the authors present a model for dynamic fault reduction of devices in an IoT environment. One particular example of this modes takes the advantage of the door sensor and the heat sensor in order to replace the functionality of the video camera.

Paper [14] presents TRANSIT an interesting approach for the transition between different types of mechanisms in live video streaming with respect of performance in an highly dynamic environment from fluctuation point of view. The proposed approach was evaluated through trace-based workloads. The experimental results showed the fact that the proposed solution offers good resilience.

The authors of paper [16] present a very good survey for smart greed communications. In this paper are described several requirements such: QoS expressed in terms of latency, bandwidth, interoperability, scalability, security and standardization.

The authors of paper [1], presents a scheduling algorithm for video broadcasting with maximum stream rate. The hypothesis on their paper is based on the fact that each peer in the system interacts only with a few peers in their neighborhood.

Despite the scientifically contributions of the authors of the papers mentioned above, we have presented and evaluated in terms of performance the auto-recovery mechanisms in case of several flaw scenarios for the SPIDER Peer-to-Peer overlay with direct impact in real Peer-to-Peer systems.

3   Type of Flaws in SPIDER Overlay

This section analyses several types of flaw in the SPIDER Overlay and the impact of the reorganization of the logical structure of the system in order to regain functionality.

For a better understanding of the proposed algorithms for flaw recovery we have decided to use the flowing annotations:

- SPIDER overlay with N nodes organized in nr rings and nc chains : $S[nr, nc]$;
- Number of peers in the SPIDER Overlay : n;
- A node in the SPIDER Overlay named by its coordinates in the overlay (chain and ring) : $*[c, r]$;
- Node N neighbor table : $NTable(N)$;
- Upper neighbor of N : $NTable(N).UP$;
- Lower neighbor of N : $NTable(N).DOWN$;
- Left neighbor of N : $NTable(N).LEFT$;
- Right neighbor of N : $NTable(N).RIGHT$;
- Free position in the SPIDER Overlay : $free$;
- Node in the SPIDER overlay fall : $*[c, r].FALL$;
- Create node with empty neighbor table : $NTable(NewNod[c, r]).EMPTY$;
- Delete node form SPIDER Overlay : $*[c, r].DELETE$;
- Entire chain from SPIDER Overlay fall : $*[*, r].FALL$;
- Entire ring from SPIDER Overlay fall : $*[c, *].FALL$.

3.1   Local Flaws

This types of flaw affect only locally the structure of the overlay. This means, that the changes, the overlay has to make are small and the effects of such flaws are minor. The availability of the overlay in this cases is not affected.

For the analysis of the local flaws we have taken in consideration a SPIDER Peer-to-Peer overlay with N nodes organized in r rings and c chains. In a full SPIDER overlay are $N = nr \times nc$ nodes. The maximum number of nodes on a ring is $NoNodesRing = nc$ and the maximum number of nodes on chain is $NoNodesChain = nr$.

One node randomly fall. Joining and leaving from Peer-to-Peer overlay systems are very common operations. Therefore, leaving from such system is realized without any announcements. One of the reasons why nodes leave the overlay very often might be battery life failure ar loss of radio connectivity.

The algorithm for one node randomly fall is given in Algorithm 1:

Algorithm 1. One node randomly fall

1: Randomly Node $X[c,r].FALL$
2: $NTable(X[c,r+1]).DOWN = free$
3: $NTable(X[c,r-1]).UP = free$
4: $NTable(X[(c-1)\%nc,r]).UP = free$
5: $NTable(X[(c+1)\%nc,r).UP = free$

The impact in this case is very minor because the structure of the SPIDER overlay is not affected. The only changes that must be made are only locally for the neighbors of fallen node. Therefore, there is computed only one operation/node for four nodes in the overlay resulting a total of 4 operations.

In case of one randomly node fall, the overlay does not need to change in order to reestablish its structure. Thus, there is no recovery method needed for this type of flaw.

Two nodes fall from same chain. Another flaw taken in consideration in the SPIDER overlay, might be the falling of two neighbor nodes from the same chain. This type of flaw might happen when the two nodes have a common power supply and it falls. Even though, two nodes fall at the same time, this flaw is still considered to be a local one due to the fact that the structure of the overlay is not affected and the actions that must be done are only local.

The algorithm for two nodes fall from the same chain is Algorithm 2:

Algorithm 2. Two nodes fall from same chain

   $X[c,r].FALL$ and $Y[c,r+1].FALL$
2: $NTable(Y[c,r+2]).DOWN = free$
   $NTable(X[c,r-1]).UP = free$
4: $NTable(X[(c-1)\%nc,r]).RIGHT = free$
   $NTable(Y[(c-1)\%nc,r+1]).RIGHT = free$
6: $NTable(X[(c+1)\%nc,r]).RIGHT = free$
   $NTable(Y[(c+1)\%nc,r+1]).RIGHT = free$

Despite the fact that two nodes from the same chain fall at the same time, this flaw is considered to be a local one. The structure of the overlay is not compromised and the operations that must be realized affect only the neighbor tables neighbor nodes. Therefore, the number of operations in this case increases with 2 from the case of one randomly node failure.

In terms of auto-recovery, the two node fall from the same chain flaw can be reduced in fact to a random node failure, thus the structure of the overlay is not affected and there is no need for the overlay to auto-configure itself.

Two nodes randomly fall. This type of flaw appears when two nodes in the SPIDER overlay fall at the same time from various reasons: power supply failure, physical malfunction etc. In this case, the flaw is considered to be local because it does not affect the structure of the overlay. This issue can be easily divided in 2 random node fall flaw.

When two randomly nodes fall in SPIDER overlay can be used Algorithm 1 for booth nodes resulting an 8 operation process for the overlay.

A particular case of two randomly node failure is two closed nodes from the same ring failure. In this case the flaw is transformed in the same manner mentioned above with the flowing exception. The number of operations realized by the SPIDER overlay nodes is calculated as $noOfOperations = oneRandomNodeFailureOperations * 2 - 2$ because the left and right neighbors have already set their positions to be free.

3.2   Global Flaws

This types of flaws affect the entire overlay structure. This means that the changes that the overlay has to compute are consistent and the effects of such flaw are huge. When this type of flaws appear the overlay availability is affected.

In this section are presented two self-organization algorithms for the SPIDER Peer-to-Peer overlay for critical disaster scenarios:

– Entire Chain lost;
– Entire Ring lost.

Taking in consideration a network formed by N nodes organized in nr rings and nc chains as shown in Fig. 1. Each node is named by its coordinates: chain and ring. The aim of this section is to present how the SPIDER overlay reorganizes it self when the nodes form one chain fall all at the same time or when all the nodes from a ring all fall at the same time. In booth cases the SPIDER Peer-to-Peer network reorganizes itself in order to be totally functional again.

Entire Chain lost Scenario 1. Starting from the scenario overview presented with a n nodes network, the first critical disaster scenario implies the fault of

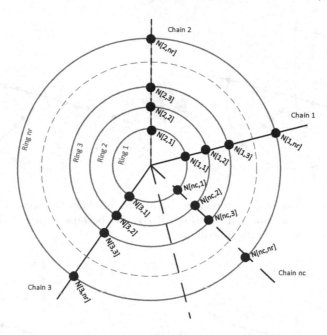

Fig. 1. SPIDER Peer-to-Peer Overlay network organized in nc chains and nr rings.

one chain at the same time. For this scenario it is considered that all nodes $N[2,*]$, from Chain 2 disappears at once along with the chain. Therefore, the overlays have to reconfigure it self from a structure with N nodes and nc chains in one of $N - nr$ nodes and $nc - 1$ chains Fig. 2.

In this scenario the reorganization consists of updating the neighbor table of each node on the chain on the left and on the right the lost chain. Thus, every node on Chain 1 updates its left neighbor to the node on the same Ring and Chain 3, and every node on Chain 3 updates its right neighbor to the node on the same Ring and Chain 1.

The impact in this type of flaw is high because about 66% of the nodes of the overlay are affected and the number of the operations that must be computed for the reconfiguration of the SPIDER overlay is given by $noOfOperations = 2 * noOfRings$.

Entire Chain lost Scenario 2. Starting from the scenario overview presented with a n nodes network, the first critical disaster scenario implies the fault of one chain at the same time. For this scenario it is considered that nodes $N[2,*]$, from Chain 2 disappears at once but the chain remains. Therefore, the overlays have to reconfigure it self from a structure with N nodes and nc chains in one if $N - nr$ nodes and nc chains.

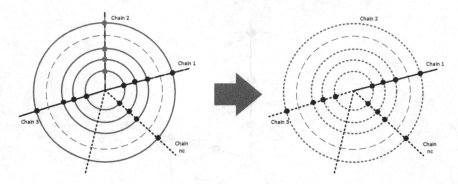

Fig. 2. SPIDER Overlay self-reorganization in case of chain fall scenario 1. The red nodes fall at the same time and the SPIDER Overlay becomes a $nc - 1$ chain overlay with $N - nr$ nodes. (Color figure online)

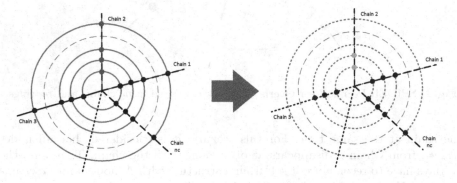

Fig. 3. SPIDER Overlay self-reorganization in case of chain fall scenario 2. The red nodes fall at the same time and the SPIDER Overlay becomes a nc chain overlay with $N - nr$ nodes. The green nodes are the new nodes created from the renaming ones. (Color figure online)

In this scenario the self-adaption technique that the overlay adopts is different from the ones mentioned the previous section. The main difference consists of creating 2 new nodes from the remaining ones on the lost chain as seen in Fig. 3. After the creation of the new nodes the neighbors tables must be updated.

For this scenario we have taken in consideration that the structure of the overlay remains the same in terms of number of chains. Thus, when an flaw where all nodes from a chain fall at the same time the SPIDER overlay is reconstructed by keeping as mush as possible of the initial structure of the overlay. The self-recovery algorithm used in this case is presented in Algorithm 3:

Algorithm 3. Entire chain fall keeping the chain structure of the overlay

$X[*, r].FALL$
$NewNode[c, 1] = X[(c - 1)\%nc, r]$
3: $NTable(NewNode(c, 1)).EMPTY$
$NewNode[c, 2] = X[(c + 1)\%nc, r]$
$NTable(NewNode(c, 1)).EMPTY$
6: $X[(c - 1)\%nc, r].DELETE$
$X[(c + 1)\%nc, r].DELETE$
$NTable(X[(c - 2)\%nc, r - 1]).RIGHT = free$
9: $NTable(X[(c + 2)\%nc, r - 1]).LEFT = free$
$NTable(X[(c - 1)\%nc, r - 1]).UP = free$
$NTable(X[(c + 1)\%nc, r - 1]).UP = free$
12: **for** $i = 1; i < nr - 1; i + +$ **do**
    if $i <= 2$ **then**
        $NTable(X[(c - 1)\%nc, i]).LEFT = X[c, i]$
15:     $NTable(X[(c + 1)\%nc, i]).RIGHT = X[c, i]$
        $NTable(X[c, i]).LEFT = X[(c + 1)\%nc, i]$
        $NTable(X[c, i]).LEFT = X[(c - 1)\%nc, i]$
18:   **else**
        $NTable(X[(c - 1)\%nc, i]).LEFT = free$
        $NTable(X[(c + 1)\%nc, i]).RIGHT = free$
21:   **end if**
    end for
    $NTable(X[c, 1]).UP = X[c, 2]$
24: $NTable(X[c, 2]).UP = free$
$NTable(X[c, 2]).DOWN = X[c, 1]$

The impact in this scenario is the highest. Not only, the number of updates in this scenario is very high but there must be created 2 new nodes on the lost chain. After this construction, a complex neighbor table update schedule must be effectuated. The number of operations in this scenario is given by $noOfOperations = newNodeCreation(1) * 2 + deleteExistingNodes(1) * 2 + 4 + 2 * newNodesUpdates(4) + (nr - 3)nodeUpdateOfTheNeighborChains(2) + 3$.

Entire ring fall. Another frequent flaw in th SPIDER overlay might be the entire ring lost is depicted in Fig. 4. This flaw happen when all the nodes from specific ring fall at the same time. This type of flaw is considered to be a global one because the structure of the overlay is affected and the overlay have to auto-recover in a manner that changes its structure.

For this scenario we are taking in consideration a SPIDER overlay network with N nodes constructed by nc chains and nr rings. If a ring from the overlay fall at the same time the overlay auto-adapts by making the upper and bottom connections of the fallen nodes. Therefore in this case the algorithm that might be uses is presented in Algorithm 4.

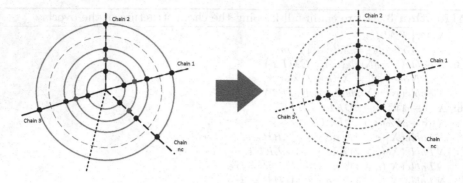

Fig. 4. SPIDER Overlay self-reorganization in case of ring fall. The red nodes fall at the same time and the SPIDER Overlay becomes a nc chain, $nr - 1$ rings overlay with $N - nc$ nodes. (Color figure online)

Algorithm 4. Entire ring fall

   $S[nr, nc]$ with n nodes
   $X[c, *].FALL$
   for $i = 0; i < nc; i + +$ **do**
      $NTable(X[c, r + i + 1]).DOWN = X[c, r - i - 1]$
5:    $NTable(X[c, r - i - 1]).UP = X[c, r + i + 1]$
   end for
   $nr = nr - 1$

This type of flaw is considered a global flow because the overlay has to change its structure. The number of operations needed to be executed in order to auto-recover the SPIDER overlay in this case of flaw is given by $c * 2$, because for each chain there must be realized 2 connections between the upper neighbors to the lower ones and all the way around.

4 Type of Applications of SPIDER Overlay

4.1 Live Video Streaming

A particular type of application that is SPIDER peer-to-peer overlay based is live video streaming for video surveillance of a vegetables Farm. The use case of vegetable farming is coming from ClueFarm project [10], developed in University of Politehnica Bucharest.

The use case taken in consideration is a farm formed by 3 farming zone, and each zone consisting in 3 or 4 green-houses. The overlay in this case consists of 3 chains representing the number of farming zones and 4 rings representing the maxim number of green-houses in each zone.

The flaws that might happen in this particular use case are:

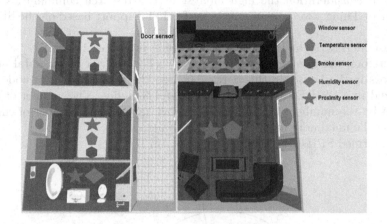

Fig. 5. IoT support use case. Smart-home sensor monitoring. 5 room (1. Kitchen, 2. Living room, 3. Bathroom, 4. First bedroom, 5. Second bedroom).

- One random node fall - in case of a camera malfunction;
- Two random nodes fall - in case weather phenomenon that might affect the green house;
- Two random nodes fall - in case of weather phenomenon that might affect the green houses;
- Entire chain fall - in case farm zones reorganization.

Another use case of live video streaming presented also in paper [8] is river pollution monitoring. This use case is based on [10] developed in University of Politehnica from Bucharest. This use case is based on an logical overlay develop based on the SPIDER overlay. The overlay is formed by 4 chains representing the number of rivers in a specific geographical area, that is monitored and 2 rings representing the number of the observation points placed o that river. Physically the number of observation points vary from the number of tributaries of each river that is monitored.

In this use case the possible flaws that might appear are:

- One random node fall - in case of a observation point failure;
- Two random nodes fall - in case of severe weather phenomenon that might affect the observation points, or blackouts;
- Two random nodes fall - in case of severe weather phenomenon that might affect the observation points or blackouts;
- Entire chain fall - in case of natural hazards like earthquakes or extremely sever weather conditions.

4.2 IoT Support for Smart Houses

Taking in consideration the high interest of the research communities in the Internet of Things, we present a use case for IoT support based on the SPIDER overlay.

The underlay of the IoT support use case is presented in Fig. 5.

Therefore, the number of nodes in the overlay is given by the total number of sensors in the house. In this particular case the total number of nodes is 19 organized in a SPIDER overlay of 5 rings and 5 chains. The number of chains is given by the number of chambers in the overlay and the number of chains is given by the maximum number of sensors in a room.

The formed SPIDER overlay is presented in Fig. 6.

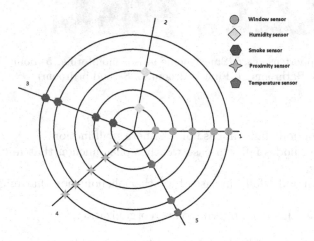

Fig. 6. SPIDER Overlay for the IoT support use case formed by 5 chains and 5 rings. Each ring represents a room and on each chain is only one type of sensor.

Taking in consideration the IoT support use case mentioned above we can present several potential flaws. Therefore, the most common flaw that might happen in a smart home Peer-to-Peer system is the malfunction of one or several sensors. This flaw appears when the sensors have no energy left in their batteries. In this case, the SPIDER Peer-to-Peer overlay flaws, that matches this use case, are the one random node fall or 2 nodes fall. This type of flaws can be frequent and the recovery from this state is realized by replacing the broken sensors with new ones.

Another flaw that might appear in this use case is the entire ring fall. This might happen all the sensors in a room falls at the same time, due to when due to a major problem.

5 Requirements for Peer-to-Peer Applications

The requirements of the live video streaming and IoT Peer-to-Peer applications are presented in Table 1.

Table 1. Peer-to-Peer overlay application requirements

Application type/requirements	Live video streaming	IoT Support
Physical infrastructure	Cable/WiFi	WiFi
Transport protocol	UDP	UDP/TCP
Bandwidth	High	Low
Self-recovery from local flaws	Yes	Yes
Self-recovery from global flaws	Yes	Yes
Throughput	High	High

5.1 Application Type - Flaw Mapping

The mapping of the application types to the flaws self-recovery features of the SPIDER overlay are presented in Table 2.

Table 2. Application type - flaw mapping

Application type	Live video streaming	IoT Support
One random node fault	Yes	Yes
Two nodes fall from the same chain fault	Yes	Yes
Two random nodes fault	Yes	Yes
Two nodes fall from the same ring fault	Yes	Yes
Entire chain fault - scenario 1	Yes	Yes
Entire chain fault - scenario 2	No	No
Entire ring fall	No	Yes

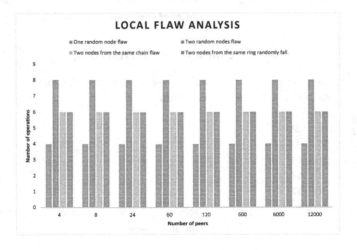

Fig. 7. Number of operations needed for SPIDER self-adaption in case of local flaws.

5.2   Flaw Analysis Experimental Results

The number of operations for each local flaw is presented in Fig. 7.
The number of operations for each global flaw is presented in Fig. 8.

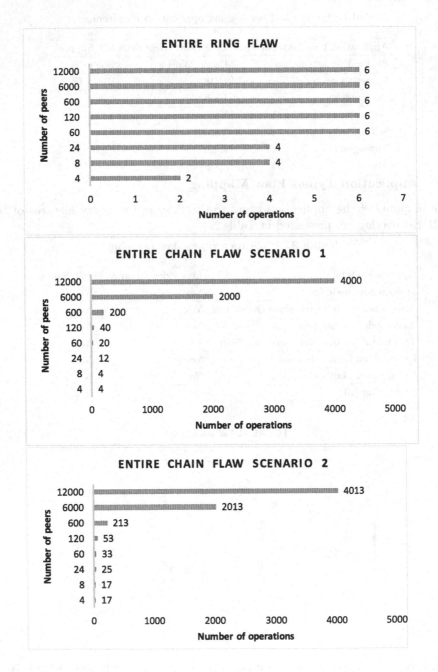

Fig. 8. Number of operations needed for SPIDER self-adaption in case of global flaws.

The most important observation is the fact that SPIDER overlays organized on rings are fault safer than SPIDER overlays organized on chains.

6 Conclusion and Future Work

In this paper we have presented several possible flaws of the SPIDER Peer-to-Peer overlay and the way the system auto-recovers from those state. Also were presented 4 algorithms for fault self-recovery. We have stated the fact that local flaws does not affect the structure of the SPIDER overlay and the only actions that must be executed is the update of the neighbor tables. In case of global flaws the structure of the overlay is affected and it must self-reconstruct. In case of entire chain fall the overlay will be reconstructed with a decremented number of chains by 1. The same behavior is happening when an entire ring falls, but the recovery process is more efficient.

In future research we will focus on researching redundancy and replication techniques for SPIDER overlay in order to achieve availability.

Acknowledgment. The research presented in this paper is supported by projects: *DataWay*: Real-time Data Processing Platform for Smart Cities: Making sense of Big Data - PN-II-RU-TE-2014-4-2731; *MobiWay*: Mobility Beyond Individualism: an Integrated Platform for Intelligent Transportation Systems of Tomorrow - PN-II-PT-PCCA-2013-4-0321; *clueFarm*: Information system based on cloud services accessible through mobile devices, to increase product quality and business development farms - PN-II-PT-PCCA-2013-4-0870. The research presented in this paper is also supported by project Data4Water, H2020-TWINN-2015 ID. 690900.

We would like to thank the reviewers for their time and expertise, constructive comments and valuable insight.

References

1. Alghazawy, B.A., Fujita, S.: A scheme for maximal resource utilization in peer-to-peer live streaming. arXiv preprint arXiv:1510.02138 (2015)
2. Andersen, M.P., Fierro, G., Culler, D.E.: Enabling synergy in iot: platform to service and beyond. In: 2016 IEEE First International Conference on Internet-of-Things Design and Implementation (IoTDI), pp. 1–12. IEEE (2016)
3. Bojan, V.C., Raducu, I.G., Pop, F., Mocanu, M., Cristea, V.: Architecture design of pattern detection system for smart cities datasets. In: 2016 IEEE 12th International Conference on Intelligent Computer Communication and Processing (ICCP), pp. 403–408. IEEE (2016)
4. Brienza, S., Cebeci, S.E., Masoumzadeh, S.S., Hlavacs, H., Özkasap, Ö., Anastasi, G.: A survey on energy efficiency in p2p systems: file distribution, content streaming, and epidemics. ACM Comput. Surv. (CSUR) **48**(3), 36 (2016)
5. Chilipirea, C., Ursache, A., Popa, D.O., Pop, F.: Energy efficiency and robustness for IoT: building a smart home security system. In: 2016 IEEE 12th International Conference on Intelligent Computer Communication and Processing (ICCP), pp. 43–48. IEEE (2016)

6. Coradeschi, S., Cesta, A., Cortellessa, G., Coraci, L., Gonzalez, J., Karlsson, L., Furfari, F., Loutfi, A., Orlandini, A., Palumbo, F., et al.: Giraffplus: combining social interaction and long term monitoring for promoting independent living. In: 2013 6th International Conference on Human System Interactions (HSI), pp. 578–585. IEEE (2013)
7. Magharei, N., Rejaie, R., Rimac, I., Hilt, V., Hofmann, M.: Isp-friendly live p2p streaming. IEEE/ACM Trans. Networking **22**(1), 244–256 (2014)
8. Mocanu, B., Mureean, V., Mocanu, M., Cristea, V.: Cloud live streaming system based on auto-adaptive overlay for cyber physical infrastructure. In: Proceedings of the Third International Workshop on Adaptive Resource Management and Scheduling for Cloud Computing, pp. 52–58. ACM (2016)
9. Mocanu, B., Pop, F., Mocanu, A.M., Dobre, C., Cristea, V.: Spider: a bio-inspired structured peer-to-peer overlay for data dissemination. In: 2015 10th International Conference on P2P, Parallel, Grid, Cloud and Internet Computing (3PGCIC), pp. 291–295. IEEE (2015)
10. Mocanu, M., Cristea, V., Negru, C., Pop, F., Ciobanu, V., Dobre, C.: Cloud-based architecture for farm management. In: 2015 20th International Conference on Control Systems and Computer Science (CSCS), pp. 814–819. IEEE (2015)
11. Morosan, A.-G., Pop, F., Arion, A.-F.: Electric mobility in green and smart cities. In: Xhafa, F., Barolli, L., Amato, F. (eds.) Advances on P2P, Parallel, Grid, Cloud and Internet Computing. LNDECT, vol. 1, pp. 173–184. Springer, Cham (2017). doi:10.1007/978-3-319-49109-7_17
12. Palmieri, F., Ficco, M., Pardi, S., Castiglione, A.: A cloud-based architecture for emergency management and first responders localization in smart city environments. Comput. Electr. Eng. **56**, 810–830 (2016)
13. Pop, F., Dobre, C., Mocanu, B.C., Citoteanu, O.M., Xhafa, F.: Trust models for efficient communication in mobile cloud computing and their applications to e-commerce. Enterp. Inf. Syst. **10**(9), 1–19 (2015)
14. Wichtlhuber, M., Richerzhagen, B., Rückert, J., Hausheer, D.: Transit: supporting transitions in peer-to-peer live video streaming. In: 2014 IFIP Networking Conference, pp. 1–9. IEEE (2014)
15. Xu, K., Wang, X., Wei, W., Song, H., Mao, B.: Toward software defined smart home. IEEE Commun. Mag. **54**(5), 116–122 (2016)
16. Yan, Y., Qian, Y., Sharif, H., Tipper, D.: A survey on smart grid communication infrastructures: motivations, requirements and challenges. IEEE Commun. Surv. Tutorials **15**(1), 5–20 (2013)

DPCAS: Data Prediction with Cubic Adaptive Sampling for Wireless Sensor Networks

Leonardo C. Monteiro, Flavia C. Delicato$^{(\boxtimes)}$, Luci Pirmez,
Paulo F. Pires, and Claudio Miceli

PPGI/DCC-IM - UFRJ, Rio de Janeiro/RJ, Brazil
leonardo.monteiro@ufrj.br, fdelicato@gmail.com,
luci.pirmez@gmail.com, paulo.f.pires@gmail.com,
cmicelifarias@gmail.com

Abstract. The advance of the Wireless Sensor Network (WSN) technology opens many possibilities for several kinds of applications. This kind of network, though, presents as main limitation the lack of a permanent and reliable energy supply. Keep the energy supply of a WSN for long periods may constitute a significant obstacle for its implementation. There are many strategies to prolong the energy supply of a WSN, one of them, knows as Dual Prediction Scheme (DPS) is explored in this article. This work proposes a new DPS technique, called DPCAS (Dual Prediction with Cubic Adaptive Sampling), combining adaptive sampling with prediction models based in exponential time series. Simulations were carry on with the use of this new technique and the results were promising in quality of the generated data and energy save in the sensor nodes.

Keywords: Data prediction · Adaptive sampling · Wireless Sensor Networks

1 Introduction

Recent advances in micro-electromechanical systems and wireless communication technologies have enabled the building of low-cost and small-sized sensors, which are capable of sensing, processing and communicating through wireless links. Wireless Sensor Networks (WSNs), which are composed of tens, hundreds or even thousands of such small devices, are commonly used to monitor a wide range of environmental variables, such as temperature, light intensity, humidity and acceleration [2]. Sensor nodes rely on batteries often non-rechargeable, and the replacement of depleted batteries is not always feasible or desirable. One of the greatest challenges in these networks is to save energy in order to extend their operational lifetime.

Several strategies can be used to save energy in WSNs (see a taxonomy in [5]), some of which can be used simultaneously. In general, the basic strategy for conserving energy in WSNs is: (i) try to keep the sensor nodes in hibernation as long as possible, or at least most of their subsystems; and (ii) try to reduce the data traffic in the network as much as possible, which helps to reduce at least the demand for the communication subsystem, which is generally very energy-intensive [2]. However, any strategy should always be conscientiously employed, keeping in mind the requirements of the applications that make use of the network [3, 4].

© Springer International Publishing AG 2017
M.H.A. Au et al. (Eds.): GPC 2017, LNCS 10232, pp. 353–368, 2017.
DOI: 10.1007/978-3-319-57186-7_27

A strategy that simultaneously increases the hibernation time of the sensors and reduces the data traffic in the network is the so-called "adaptive sampling" [2], that is, to vary the time interval between samplings according to the behavior of the sensed physical variable, in such a way to minimize the number of measurements and data transmissions between the network nodes, trying to keep the sensors as long as possible in a state of low energy consumption. Adaptive sampling methods, however, are usually not adequate to sample physical phenomena that may exhibit significant sudden variations, such as in event detection systems, where, after a period of stability, sudden and expressive variations of a physical variable may indicate the occurrence of an event, such as the detection of an intruder in a protected area in security applications. In general, adaptive sampling methods are more adequate to sample more predictable physical phenomena, with more diluted variations in time, as in the monitoring of environmental variables (temperature, humidity, etc.).

A strategy to minimize this problem is to combine an adaptive sampling method with a data prediction model, which is a model to compute estimates of future sensor readings. This combination is known as DPS (Dual Prediction Scheme) [12]. In this way, queries generated by the application can obtain data continuously from the sink, through the prediction model, without the need to wait for the data transferred irregularly by the sensor nodes. The prediction model, however, needs to be constantly updated with the data coming from the sensors. Overall, a dual prediction strategy can significantly reduce the use of the sensor node subsystems, helping to extend the life of its energy supply. When associated with a time series prediction model, the objective of an adaptive sampling method is to reduce the number of samples per unit of time to the maximum, aiming at reducing the energy consumption of the sensor node to the maximum. Similar behavior is noted in the dynamic tuning of the congestion window of the TCP CUBIC protocol [7, 11], where the size of the congestion window varies in time according to a cubic function. This suits a WSN due to the simplicity of the algorithm, which demands few computations, and low memory consumption.

This paper proposes a new technique of dual prediction for environmental physical variables in WSN. Named DPCAS (Dual Prediction with Cubic Adaptive Sampling), the proposed technique uses a predictive model based on exponential time series and incorporates a greedy method of adaptive sampling based on TCP CUBIC congestion control algorithm [7], the latter being the most innovative aspect of the work.

The rest of this document is organized as follows: Sect. 2 details the proposed dual prediction technique. Section 3 presents the results of simulations to evaluate the proposed technique and to compare it with similar ones. Section 4 presents the main works of the literature related to the study theme. Section 5 concludes the paper and describes future directions.

2   DPCAS: Dual Prediction Technique for WSN

In this section, we present the proposed dual prediction technique, DPCAS. As mentioned, this technique combines a data prediction model based on exponential time series, to be detailed in Sect. 2.1, with an adaptive sampling method based on the

TCP CUBIC congestion control algorithm, detailed in Sect. 2.2. Section 2.3 details how the DPCAS technique should be implemented in a WSN system.

2.1 Data Prediction Model

A prediction model is a model to compute future sensor readings. A One of these models, quite computationally economical (so interesting for WSNs), is called Simple Exponential Smoothing (SES) [7], expressed by the following equation:

$$F_{i+1} = \alpha Y_i + (1 - \alpha)F_i, \ 0 < \alpha < 1 \tag{1}$$

Where Y_i represents the value measured by the sensor at the *i-th* sampling, F_{i+1} is the prediction of the model for the next sampling, F_i the prediction previously performed by the model for the *i-th* sampling and α a smoothing coefficient of the series. Thus, the prediction (F_{i+1}) is simply a weighted sum of the last measurement (Y_i) and the last prediction (F_i).

A SES model, however, is more suitable for predicting stationary variables, that is, with little variation in time around an average value. When the variable presents local trends of growth or decline, a SES model usually does not perform very well, as it may present an excessive lag to respond satisfactorily to the trend changes. Environmental physical variables commonly have local trends, for example, it is reasonable to assume that the temperature of an environment (an office, a forest, etc.) increases during the day and decreases at night. Therefore, a prediction model that is more appropriate to this type of behavior is needed.

Another model of time series prediction, similar to SES, that presents more suitable characteristics for variables that present local trends is called Double Exponential Smoothing (DES), also known as Holt Method [9], expressed by the following equations:

$$L_i = \alpha Y_i + (1 - \alpha)(L_{i-1} + b_{i-1}), \ 0 < \alpha < 1 \tag{2}$$

$$b_i = \gamma(L_i - L_{i-1}) + (1 - \gamma)b_{i-1}, \ 0 < \gamma < 1 \tag{3}$$

$$F_{i+1} = L_i + b_i W, \ W > 0 \tag{4}$$

Where Y_i represents the value measured by the sensor at the *i-th* sampling, W the interval between samplings (sampling interval), F_{i+1} the prediction of the model for the next sampling and α and γ the smoothing coefficients of the exponential series L_i and b_i, which represent, respectively, the level of the prediction and its local trend or slope.

The use of the DES model, however, assumes regular sampling intervals. To fit irregular sampling intervals, characteristic of the adaptive sampling used in the DPCAS technique, an adjustment known as the Wright Extension to Holt Method [17] was adopted in this study, expressed by the following equations:

$$A_i = A_{i-1}/[A_{i-1} + (1 - \alpha)^{W_i - 1}], \ 0 < \alpha < 1 \tag{5}$$

$$G_i = G_{i-1}/[G_{i-1} + (1 - \gamma)^{W_i-1}], \, 0 < \gamma < 1 \tag{6}$$

$$L_i = A_i Y_i + (1 - A_i)(L_{i-1} + W_{i-1} b_{i-1}) \tag{7}$$

$$b_i = G_i(L_i - L_{i-1})/W_{i-1} + (1 - G_i)b_{i-1} \tag{8}$$

$$F_{i+1} = L_i + b_i W_i, \, W_i > 0 \tag{9}$$

Where W_i represents the variable sampling interval computed in the i-th sampling, which will be used as the sensor node's hibernation time until the next sampling. In this study, the calculation of the sample interval W_i should be done through the adaptive sampling method described in Sect. 2.2, based on the TCP CUBIC congestion control algorithm.

Note, however, that in Eq. 8 when $W_{i-1} \to 0$ implies $b_i \to \infty$. This means that for very small values of the sampling interval the slope may fluctuate significantly, which may result in significant distortions in the prediction. In order to avoid this undesirable behavior and to make the prediction model more robust, in this work was adopted the adjustment proposed by Hanzák [8] in the Wright Extension to Holt Method. This adjustment leads to a small modification in Eq. 6, which must be rewritten as follows:

$$H_i = W_{i-2}/W_{i-1} \tag{10}$$

$$G_i = G_{i-1}/[G_{i-1} + H_i(1 - \gamma)^{W_i-1}], \, 0 < \gamma < 1 \tag{11}$$

2.2 Adaptive Sampling Method

An adaptive sampling strategy consists in varying the time interval between samplings in such a way to adapt dynamically to the variability of the sampled physical phenomena. That is, in periods when the physical phenomenon presents little variation the sample interval can be increased, when the physical phenomenon presents greater variation the sampling interval can be reduced. Obviously, this strategy of adapting the sample interval must always be done in such a way to not compromise significantly the accuracy of the sample series.

When associated with a time series prediction model, the objective of an adaptive sampling method is to reduce the number of samples per unit of time to the maximum, aiming at reducing the energy consumption of the sensor node to the maximum, but always trying to maintain the difference (δ) between the sampled values (Y_i) and predicted (F_i) within a tolerance limit acceptable to the application (ε), so as not to compromise the accuracy of the sample series. That is, the application should try to maintain:

$$|Y_i - F_i| = \delta \le \varepsilon \tag{12}$$

A greedy adaptive sampling strategy is always to try to increase the sampling interval at each sampling until the prediction exceeds the tolerance limit of the application, that is, until $\delta > \varepsilon$. When this event occurs, the adaptive sampling method must then reduce the sample interval until the prediction returns to the tolerance limit of the application, that is, until $\delta \leq \varepsilon$. With these increases and decreases, the sample interval then varies in time in a manner similar to that shown in Fig. 1 (similar to a saw tooth). It is interesting to note that this type of adaptive behavior of the sample interval is very similar to the dynamic tuning of the congestion window of the TCP protocol [11].

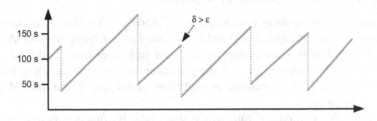

Fig. 1. Variation of the sampling interval in a greedy adaptive sampling

Due to the similarities highlighted above, the purpose of this work is to use the concepts of the TCP congestion control algorithm to adjust the sampling interval of the adaptive sampling. Although there are several congestion control algorithms for TCP (see some in [10]), the proposed adaptive sampling method is based on the TCP CUBIC protocol [7], where the size of the congestion window varies in time according to a cubic function. The reason for this choice is the simplicity of the algorithm, which demands few computations, and low memory consumption. The equations of the adaptive sampling method are as follows:

$$W_i = C(t - K)^3 + W_{max} \tag{13}$$

$$K = (\beta W_{max}/C)^{1/3}, \; 0 < \beta \leq 1 \tag{14}$$

Where W_i represents the sample interval calculated at the i-th sampling, which will be used as the sensor hibernation time until the next sampling, C is a scale factor known as a CUBIC parameter (typically 0.4), t is the elapsed time since the last reduction of the sample interval, W_{max} is the sample interval immediately before the last reduction of the sample interval and β a multiplicative reduction factor (typically 0.2). The factor K, described in Eq. 14, is updated only when an event of reduction of the sample interval occurs.

An event of reduction of the sampling interval occurs whenever the difference (δ) between the sampled value (Y_i) and its respective prediction (F_i) exceeds the tolerance limit of the application (ε), that is, whenever:

$$|Y_i - F_i| = \delta > \varepsilon \tag{15}$$

In addition, the application can also impose a minimum (S_{min}) and maximum (S_{max}) limit for sampling interval variation, that is:

$$S_{min} \leq W_i \leq S_{max} \tag{16}$$

2.3   Proposal: Dual Prediction Algorithm

In this section it is shown how the time series prediction model described in Sect. 2.1 and the adaptive sampling method described in Sect. 2.2 should be combined. The DPCAS technique involves four distinct components distributed in three nodes, as shown in Fig. 2. The components are as follows:

- Sampler – this component runs in the sensor node. Its function is to sampling the physical variable at intervals defined by the adaptive sampling method. At the end of each sampling this component sends to the sink three data: 1. the value of the physical variable sampled (Y_i); 2. the prediction for the next sampling (F_{i+1}), calculated according to the time series prediction model; and 3. the interval until the next sampling (W_i).
- Receiver – this component runs in the sink node. Its function is to continuously receive and store locally the data sent by the sensor nodes, that is, Y_i, F_{i+1} and W_i. At first, there is no need for this component to store all the data series sent by the sensor nodes, only the last values.
- Supplier – this component runs in the sink node. Its function is to supply the application with data of the physical variable. These data should be calculated by interpolating the values of Y_i and F_{i+1} for a given time t.
- Application – user application that consumes the data of the physical variable provided by the sink.

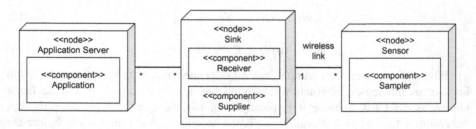

Fig. 2. Nodes and components involved in the use of the DPCAS technique

Figure 3 shows the pseudocode of the Sampler component. The pseudocode follows the format proposed in [13]. Note between lines 48 – 51 of this code that, as an extra measure to further reduce the demand for the communication subsystem, transmissions between the sensor nodes and the sink are only performed when significant variations of the physical variable are detected, that is, only when:

$$|Y_i - Y_{last}| = \theta > \varepsilon \tag{17}$$

Where Y_i corresponds to the current sampled value, Y_{last} to the last value sampled and transmitted to the sink and ε to the tolerance limit of the application.

3   Simulations

In this study were performed simulations with two main objectives: (i) to evaluate the DPCAS technique regarding the quality of the predictions and the energy consumption in the sensor nodes; (ii) comparing the advantages and disadvantages of using the DPCAS technique with the EDSAS and ASTCP techniques, described in Sect. 4. These simulations were performed using routines in C code specifically developed for this study.

3.1   Input Data

As input to all simulations, in this study were used data from real sensor nodes publicly available by the Intel Berkeley Research Lab (IBRL) [14]. These data were collected through 54 Mica2Dot sensor nodes distributed in the IBRL facilities. These observations were performed between February 28 and April 5, 2004 and include temperature, humidity, light, and voltage data, with sampling intervals of approximately 31 s.

In the simulations, only temperature data collected between March 1 and 7, 2004 (one week of data) were considered. Sensor nodes 5, 8 and 15 were not used because they clearly presented problems in the data series.

3.2   Quality Metrics

Four metrics were considered to evaluate the quality of the series generated by the prediction techniques, where lower values indicate better results:

- MAE – Mean Absolute Error: this metric shows how precise was the prediction in absolute values.
- MAPE – Mean Absolute Percentage Error: this metric shows how precise was the prediction in percentage.
- MSE – Mean Square Error: this metric shows how fast the error will increase.
- RMSE – Root Mean Square Error: this metric shows the tendency of the errors.

3.3   Energy Model

The DPCAS technique was also evaluated regarding the sensor nodes energy consumption. For this, the energy consumption of each node was calculated based on a simplified energy model. The formulation of this model was based on the study published in [16].

```
Sensor-Node-Sampler(α, γ, ε, S_min, S_max, C, β)
 1   // Prediction model initialization
 2   Y_1 = Get-Sensor-Value()
 3   Put-Node-To-Sleep(S_min)
 4   Y_2 = Get-Sensor-Value()
 5   Put-Node-To-Sleep(S_min)
 6   A_i = α
 7   G_i = γ
 8   L_i = Y_1
 9   b_i = Y_2 - Y_1
10   F_i = Y_2
11
12   // Adaptive sampling initialization
13   t_CUBIC = 0
14   W_max = S_min/(1 - β)
15   K = (βW_max/C)^(1/3)
16   W_{i-1} = S_min
17   W_i = S_min
18
19   // Sampling loop
20   Y_last = ∞
21   while TRUE
22       Y_i = Get-Sensor-Value()
23       W_{i-2} = W_{i-1}
24       W_{i-1} = W_i
25       δ = |Y_i - F_i|
26       if δ > ε
27           t_CUBIC = 0
28           W_max = W_i
29           K = (βW_max/C)^(1/3)
30       W_i = C(t_CUBIC - K)^3 + W_max
31       if W_i < S_min
32           W_i = S_min
33       else
34           if W_i > S_max
35               W_i = S_max
36           else
37               t_CUBIC = t_CUBIC + 1
38       H_i = W_{i-2}/W_{i-1}
39       A_{i-1} = A_i
40       G_{i-1} = G_i
41       L_{i-1} = L_i
42       b_{i-1} = b_i
43       A_i = A_{i-1}/(A_{i-1} + (1 - α)^{Wi-1})
44       G_i = G_{i-1}/(G_{i-1} + H_i(1 - γ)^{Wi-1})
45       L_i = A_iY_i + (1 - A_i)(L_{i-1} + W_{i-1}b_{i-1})
46       b_i = G_i(L_i - L_{i-1})/W_{i-1} + (1 - G_i)b_{i-1}
47       F_{i+1} = L_i + b_iW_i
48       θ = |Y_i - Y_last|
49       if θ > ε
50           Send-Data-To-Sink(Y_i, F_{i+1}, W_i)
51           Y_last = Y_i
52       Put-Node-To-Sleep(W_i)
```

Fig. 3. Pseudocode of the sampler component

Each sensor node of the energy model is characterized by: (i) Operating system: TinyOS; (ii) Hardware: microcontroller Atmel ATmega 128L 7.3 MHz, 128 KB code memory, 4 KB data memory, 512 KB EEPROM, radio ChipCon CC1000 38.4 Kbps, 3 V battery, sensor board MTS300CA. The current demand of the various hardware components is shown in Table 1.

Table 1. Current demand of the hardware of the energy model

Mode	Current	Mode	Current	Mode	Current
CPU		Radio		Sensor Board	0.7 mA
Active	8.0 mA	Rx	7.0 mA	LEDs	2.2 mA
Idle	3.2 mA	Tx (– 20 dBm)	3.7 mA		
ADC Noise Reduce	1.0 mA	Tx (– 19 dBm)	5.2 mA		
Power-down	103 μA	Tx (– 15 dBm)	5.4 mA		
Power-save	110 μA	Tx (– 8 dBm)	6.5 mA		
Standby	216 μA	Tx (– 5 dBm)	7.1 mA		
Extended Standby	223 μA	Tx (0 dBm)	8.5 mA		
Internal Oscilator	0.93 mA	Tx (+ 4 dBm)	11.6 mA		
EEPROM		Tx (+ 6 dBm)	13.8 mA		
Read	6.2 mA	Tx (+ 8 dBm)	17.4 mA		
Write	18.4 mA	Tx (+ 10 dBm)	21.5 mA		

During a sampling, each sensor node presents five phases of current demand, as shown in Fig. 4. A detail of each phase of the energy model is shown in Table 2. Note in this table that the sensor board is always kept active, permanently draining 0.7 mA of current, during the entire operation of the sensor node.

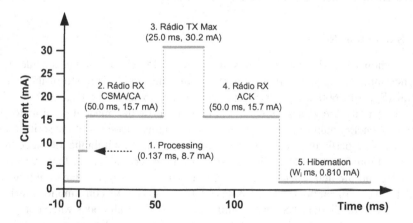

Fig. 4. Current demand in a sample of the energy model

Table 2. Detail of the current demand of the energy model

Phase	Current (mA)				Time (ms)
	CPU	Sensor	Radio	Total	
1. Processing – This phase requires 1000 CPU cycles for reading the sensor data and calculating the prediction.	8.0	0.7	0.0	8.7	0.137
2. Reception CSMA/CA – This phase is required by the link layer CSMA/CA protocol to listen to the communication channel and avoid collisions in the transmission phase.	8.0	0.7	7.0	15.7	50.0
3. Transmission – During this phase the sensor data is transmitted to the sink, assuming maximum radio power.	8.0	0.7	21.5	30.2	25.0
4. Reception ACK – During this phase the sensor node waits for an ACK sent back by the sink.	8.0	0.7	7.0	15.7	50.0
5. Hibernation – After transmitting the data to the sink, the sensor node is put in hibernation (CPU Power-save) until the next sampling, that is, until to elapse the sampling interval W_i calculated in the processing phase.	0.110	0.7	0.0	0.810	W_i

As for energy consumption, the following metrics were calculated:

- ES – Energy consumption in sampling.
- EH – Energy consumption in hibernation.
- ET – Total energy consumption.
- EG – Energy gain with prediction. It represents how much energy was saved with prediction. Higher values indicate better results.

3.4   Simulation Results

Table 3 shows the simulation results using the DPCAS technique considering the tolerance limit of the application (ε) in 0.1°C and the limit of growth of the sampling interval (S_{max}) in 600 s. By varying the coefficients α and γ between 0.0 and 1.0 in decimal intervals, the values shown in Table 3 are those that made it possible to obtain the highest energy gain (EG) for each node. The quality measures of the series presents good results. In particular, note that the MAE has remained within the tolerance limit of the application for all nodes. With respect to energy consumption, there was a clear gain using the prediction technique when compared to using regular sampling of the input database. In particular, it is observed that the energy consumption during the sampling with prediction (ES_p) was significantly lower for all nodes when compared to the technique without prediction (ES_r), up to 10 times smaller, as in the case of the node 7, a very significant reduction.

Table 3. Simulations for all nodes employing DPCAS, ε = 0.1°C and S_{max} = 600 s

Node	Model coefficients		Quality metrics				Energy consumption with prediction (J)			Energy consumption without prediction (J)			EG (%)
	α	β	MAE	MAPE	MSE	RMSE	ES_p	EH_p	ET_p	ES_r	EH_r	ET_r	
1	0.2	0.2	0.06	0.28	0.04	0.21	20.8	1468.4	1489.2	94.5	1465.2	1559.8	4.5
2	0.1	0.1	0.05	0.24	0.03	0.17	12.9	1469.0	1481.9	67.0	1466.6	1533.6	3.4
3	0.2	0.1	0.06	0.26	0.03	0.18	17.8	1468.6	1486.4	93.5	1465.3	1558.8	4.6
4	0.1	0.1	0.05	0.24	0.03	0.17	13.6	1468.9	1482.4	78.1	1466.1	1544.2	4.0
6	0.1	0.1	0.05	0.22	0.01	0.12	11.2	1468.8	1480.0	68.3	1466.3	1534.6	3.6
7	0.1	0.1	0.05	0.25	0.03	0.18	11.5	1469.1	1480.5	116.3	1464.5	1580.8	6.3
9	0.1	0.1	0.05	0.25	0.03	0.18	12.7	1468.9	1481.6	103.8	1464.9	1568.8	5.6
10	0.1	0.1	0.05	0.24	0.02	0.14	12.5	1468.8	1481.3	93.2	1465.3	1558.5	5.0
11	0.1	0.1	0.06	0.29	0.03	0.17	15.7	1468.9	1484.6	92.5	1465.5	1558.0	4.7
12	0.2	0.1	0.06	0.29	0.02	0.14	13.9	1468.4	1482.3	48.0	1467.0	1515.0	2.2
13	0.1	0.2	0.06	0.27	0.01	0.12	17.7	1468.7	1486.4	62.9	1466.7	1529.6	2.8
14	0.1	0.1	0.06	0.29	0.04	0.19	13.7	1468.2	1481.9	57.5	1466.3	1523.8	2.7
16	0.2	0.1	0.07	0.33	0.06	0.24	25.3	1468.4	1493.6	78.4	1466.0	1544.5	3.3
17	0.1	0.2	0.06	0.28	0.03	0.18	14.9	1468.9	1483.8	93.0	1465.5	1558.5	4.8
18	0.1	0.1	0.06	0.25	0.03	0.18	12.1	1469.0	1481.1	109.8	1464.8	1574.6	5.9
19	0.3	0.1	0.07	0.29	0.05	0.23	15.1	1468.7	1483.7	78.8	1465.9	1544.8	3.9
20	0.1	0.1	0.06	0.28	0.05	0.23	16.0	1468.8	1484.8	121.5	1464.2	1585.7	6.4
21	0.2	0.2	0.09	0.35	0.17	0.41	26.9	1468.4	1495.3	119.8	1464.3	1584.1	5.6
22	0.2	0.3	0.09	0.37	0.23	0.48	23.5	1468.5	1491.9	125.1	1464.0	1589.1	6.1
23	0.2	0.6	0.07	0.30	0.09	0.29	19.0	1468.7	1487.7	108.2	1464.8	1573.1	5.4
24	0.2	0.4	0.08	0.33	0.16	0.40	21.4	1468.2	1489.6	94.8	1465.0	1559.8	4.5
25	0.4	0.4	0.08	0.34	0.14	0.37	19.3	1468.7	1487.9	94.8	1465.4	1560.2	4.6
26	0.3	0.1	0.07	0.30	0.06	0.25	22.0	1468.5	1490.5	96.2	1465.3	1561.5	4.5
27	0.2	0.2	0.05	0.23	0.02	0.16	14.5	1468.6	1483.1	49.3	1467.0	1516.4	2.2
28	0.2	0.1	0.07	0.29	0.04	0.19	22.6	1468.6	1491.1	102.1	1465.1	1567.2	4.9
29	0.2	0.2	0.06	0.27	0.05	0.23	15.0	1468.9	1483.9	79.1	1466.1	1545.2	4.0
30	0.1	0.1	0.06	0.27	0.05	0.22	16.8	1468.3	1485.1	53.1	1466.8	1519.8	2.3

(continued)

Table 3. (*continued*)

Node	Model coefficients		Quality metrics				Energy consumption with prediction (J)			Energy consumption without prediction (J)			EG (%)
	α	β	MAE	MAPE	MSE	RMSE	ES_p	EH_p	ET_p	ES_r	EH_r	ET_r	
31	0.1	0.1	0.06	0.28	0.04	0.20	17.6	1468.7	1486.3	111.3	1464.6	1576.0	5.7
32	0.1	0.1	0.07	0.29	0.04	0.21	17.4	1468.8	1486.2	57.1	1467.1	1524.2	2.5
33	0.1	0.1	0.06	0.28	0.02	0.16	21.3	1468.3	1489.6	51.2	1467.0	1518.3	1.9
34	0.4	0.1	0.07	0.31	0.04	0.19	14.7	1468.8	1483.4	69.7	1466.4	1536.1	3.4
35	0.1	0.2	0.07	0.30	0.04	0.20	17.1	1468.8	1485.9	101.3	1465.1	1566.4	5.1
36	0.2	0.2	0.07	0.33	0.05	0.23	21.0	1468.6	1489.6	109.2	1464.7	1573.9	5.4
37	0.2	0.3	0.07	0.29	0.04	0.20	17.7	1468.8	1486.4	101.9	1465.1	1567.0	5.1
38	0.2	0.1	0.07	0.30	0.02	0.13	25.0	1468.5	1493.5	99.4	1465.2	1564.6	4.5
39	0.3	0.1	0.06	0.29	0.04	0.21	14.2	1468.9	1483.1	57.3	1467.0	1524.3	2.7
40	0.2	0.2	0.07	0.30	0.05	0.22	17.0	1468.8	1485.7	88.5	1465.7	1554.2	4.4
41	0.4	0.2	0.08	0.36	0.10	0.32	16.6	1468.7	1485.3	77.3	1466.1	1543.4	3.8
42	0.2	0.1	0.08	0.34	0.11	0.34	17.7	1468.7	1486.5	88.9	1465.6	1554.5	4.4
43	0.1	0.1	0.06	0.28	0.05	0.23	14.6	1468.8	1483.4	79.5	1465.9	1545.4	4.0
44	0.1	0.2	0.07	0.34	0.11	0.33	17.0	1468.7	1485.7	101.4	1465.0	1566.5	5.2
45	0.1	0.1	0.06	0.29	0.06	0.24	14.3	1468.9	1483.2	118.6	1464.4	1582.9	6.3
46	0.2	0.2	0.07	0.33	0.13	0.35	18.5	1468.8	1487.2	115.3	1464.5	1579.9	5.9
47	0.1	0.1	0.07	0.33	0.10	0.31	21.5	1468.5	1490.1	122.4	1464.1	1586.5	6.1
48	0.1	0.2	0.06	0.30	0.07	0.26	12.6	1469.0	1481.5	123.8	1464.1	1588.0	6.7
49	0.1	0.1	0.08	0.37	0.14	0.37	17.2	1468.7	1485.9	82.1	1465.9	1548.0	4.0
50	0.1	0.1	0.07	0.34	0.05	0.22	16.1	1468.8	1484.9	66.4	1466.6	1533.0	3.1
51	0.1	0.1	0.07	0.33	0.11	0.33	16.7	1468.8	1485.5	84.2	1465.8	1550.0	4.2
52	0.1	0.1	0.07	0.31	0.07	0.26	13.5	1468.2	1481.7	68.0	1465.8	1533.8	3.4
53	0.1	0.1	0.07	0.33	0.05	0.22	13.9	1468.9	1482.8	58.1	1467.0	1525.1	2.8
54	0.1	0.1	0.06	0.29	0.04	0.20	11.4	1469.0	1480.5	71.7	1466.4	1538.2	3.8

3.5   Comparison with Other Techniques

In addition to DPCAS technique, in this study were also performed simulations with two other time series prediction techniques, mentioned in Sect. 4, EDSAS [6] and ASTCP [1]. The objective is to evaluate the advantages and disadvantages of these techniques regarding the quality of the predictions and the energy consumption in the sensor nodes.

Figure 5 shows a comparison of these techniques with respect to mean absolute error (MAE). Note that, as mentioned in Sect. 3.4, that the DPCAS technique remained within the application tolerance of 0.1°C for all nodes. The EDSAS technique

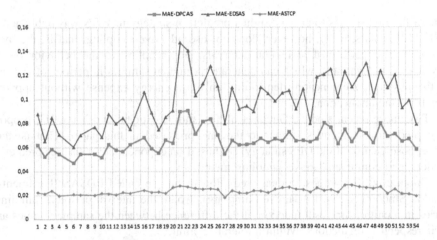

Fig. 5. Mean absolute error (MAE) for each node using DPCAS, EDSAS, and ASTCP, with $\varepsilon = 0.1°C$ and $S_{max} = 600$ s

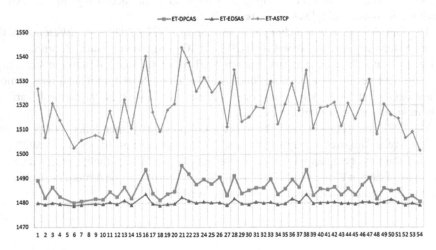

Fig. 6. Total energy consumption (ET_p) in J for each node using DPCAS, EDSAS, and ASTCP, with $\varepsilon = 0.1°C$ and $S_{max} = 600$ s

presented values above this limit for several nodes. The ASTCP technique presented significantly lower values, due to a higher sampling rate.

Figure 6 shows a comparison of total energy consumption (ET_p). It is noted that the DPCAS technique presented intermediate results for all nodes. The EDSAS technique clearly showed lower energy consumption for all nodes. The ASTCP technique presented the highest consumption for all nodes. This happens because these techniques cannot predict data to be used in the sampling as our solution.

4 Related Work

One of the first studies to propose a dual prediction strategy in WSN was published in 2007 [12]. This strategy, however, does not use adaptive sampling, that is, the measurements are performed at regular intervals, not adapting to the behavior of the physical sensed variable, which can generate redundant samples in periods of stability of the physical phenomenon, demanding an extra energy expense without apparent benefit to the application.

Two more recent studies, Gupta et al. [6] and Al-Hoqani and Yang [1], propose dual prediction techniques similar to the one proposed in this paper. That is, they presuppose the use of the DPS strategy, are based on exponential time series predictive models, and combine adaptive sampling methods.

Gupta et al. [6] propose a dual prediction technique called EDSAS (Exponential Double Smoothing-based Adaptive Sampling), where the interval between samplings varies in a unit of time as a function of the difference between the sampled values and their respective predictions, within a tolerance limit.

Based on the study by Gupta et al., Al-Hoqani and Yang [1] propose a similar technique, called ASTCP (Adaptive Sampling TCP), whose adaptive sampling method is based on TCP Reno congestion control algorithm [11], a traditional version of TCP, where the interval between samplings varies in time according to an AIMD (Additive-increase/Multiplicative-decrease) function.

The DPCAS prediction technique is similar to ASTCP, the main difference is the adaptive sampling method, based on TCP CUBIC congestion control algorithm [7], a TCP version widely used in Linux systems [10]. Here, the interval between samplings varies in time according to a cubic function. The DPCAS technique also uses a more robust data prediction model, supporting abrupt variations in the sensed variable without significant distortions in prediction.

The DPCAS technique and the other two previously mentioned (EDSAS and ASTCP) were compared through simulations. The results obtained (shown in Sect. 3.5) were satisfactory, being an intermediate alternative in quality of the generated data and in energy saving in the sensors. Therefore, DPCAS proved to be a more cost-effective solution when negotiating data quality and energy savings.

5 Conclusion

In this paper, we propose a new technique for dual prediction for environmental physical variables in WSN. The proposed solution, called DPCAS, combines a predictive model with exponential time series and a greedy adaptive sampling method, based on the TCP CUBIC congestion control algorithm, the latter being the most innovative aspect of the proposal. As is in general the time prediction algorithms based on time series, the proposed technique is simple to implement, requires little processing and is "Plug & Play", that is, it can be used immediately, not requiring a preliminary training phase to fit a model.

Simulations were performed using this new technique from a database of real sensors, in addition to the use of a simplified energy model. The results obtained were promising, with respect the quality of the generated data and the reduction of the energy consumption in the sensor nodes. When compared to two other similar prediction techniques, EDSAS and ASTCP, were obtained results that present a good balance between the quality of the generated data and the energy consumption in the sensors.

As part of future works, it is still necessary to test the DPCAS technique in practical applications, using real sensor nodes and exploring several types of environmental physical variables. In addition, it is possible to further explore the adaptive sampling method, described in Sect. 2.2, by varying the factors C and β of the TCP CUBIC algorithm, which in this study were set at the typical values, respectively 0.4 and 0.2.

Acknowledgments. This work was partly supported by the Brazilian funding agencies CNPq and FAPERJ. Flavia C. Delicato, Luci Pirmez and Paulo F. Pires as CNPq fellows.

References

1. Al-Hoqani, N., Yang, S.: Adaptive sampling for wireless household water consumption monitoring. Procedia Eng. **119**, 1356–1365 (2015)
2. Anastasi, G., Conti, M., Di Francesco, M., Passarella, A.: Energy conservation in wireless sensor networks: a survey. Ad Hoc Netw. **7**, 537–568 (2009)
3. Carrabs, F., Cerulli, R., D'Ambrosio, C., Raiconi, A.: An exact algorithm to extend lifetime through roles allocation in sensor networks with connectivity constraints. Optim. Lett. (2016)
4. Carrabs, F., Cerulli, R., D'Ambrosio, C., Raiconi, A.: Extending Lifetime Through Partial Coverage And Roles Allocation in Connectivity-Constrained Sensor Networks. IFAC-PapersOnLine **49**, 973–978 (2016)
5. Delicato, F.C., Pires, P.F.: Energy awareness and efficiency in wireless sensor networks: from physical devices to the communication link. In: Energy-Efficient Distributed Computing Systems, pp 673–707 (2012)
6. Gupta, M., Shum, L.V., Bodanese, E., Hailes, S.: Design and evaluation of an adaptive sampling strategy for a wireless air pollution sensor network. In: 2011 IEEE 36th Conference on Local Computer Networks, pp 1003–1010 (2011)

7. Ha, S., Rhee, I.: CUBIC: a new TCP-friendly high-speed TCP variant. ACM SIGOPS Oper. Syst. Rev. - Res. Dev. Linux kernel **42**, 64–74 (2008)
8. Hanzák, T.: Improved Holt method for irregular time series. In: WDS 2008, pp 62–67 (2008)
9. Hyndman, R.J., Athanasopoulos, G.: Forecasting: Principles and Practice (2013)
10. Jamal, H., Sultan, K.: Performance analysis of TCP congestion control algorithms. Int. J. Comput. Commun. **2**, 30–38 (2008)
11. Kurose, J.F., Ross, K.W.: Computer Networking: A Top-Down Approach, 6th edn. (2013)
12. Le Borgne, Y., Santini, S., Bontempi, G.: Adaptive model selection for time series prediction in wireless sensor networks. Sig. Process. **87**, 3010–3020 (2007)
13. Leiserson, C.C.E., Rivest, R.R.L., Stein, C., Cormen, T.H.: Introduction to Algorithms, 3rd edn. MIT Press, Cambridge (2009)
14. Madden, S.: Intel Lab data (2004). http://db.csail.mit.edu/labdata/labdata.html
15. Miret, S.: Storage Wars: Batteries vs Supercapacitors. Berkeley Energy and Resources Collaborative 10 (2013)
16. Shnayder, V., Hempstead, M., Chen, B-R., et al.: Simulating the power consumption of large-scale sensor network applications. In: Proceedings of the 2nd International Conference on Embedded Networked Sensor Systems - SenSys 2004, p. 188 (2004)
17. Wright, D.J.: Forecasting data published at irregular time intervals using an extension of Holts method. Manage. Sci. **32**, 499–510 (1986)

Cybersecurity

Personalized Privacy Preserving Collaborative Filtering

Mengmeng Yang$^{(\boxtimes)}$, Tianqing Zhu, Yang Xiang, and Wanlei Zhou

School of Information Technology, Deakin University, Burwood, Australia
{ymengm,t.zhu,yang.xiang,wanlei.zhou}@deakin.edu.au

Abstract. Recommendation systems are widely applied these years as a result of significant growth in the amount of online information. To provide accurate recommendation, a great deal of personal information are collected, which gives rise to privacy concerns for many individuals. Differential privacy is a well accepted technique for providing a strong privacy guarantee. However, traditional differential privacy can only preserve privacy at a uniform level for all users. When, in reality, different people have different privacy requirements. A uniform privacy standard cannot preserve enough privacy for users with a strong privacy requirement and will likely provide unnecessary protection for users who do not care about the disclosure of their personal information. In this paper, we propose a *personalized privacy preserving collaborative filtering* method that considers an individual's privacy preferences to overcome this problem. A Johnson Lindenstrauss transform is introduced to pre-process the original dataset to improve the quality of the selected neighbours - an important factor for final prediction. Our method was tested on two real-world datasets. Extensive experiments prove that our method maintains more utility while guaranteeing privacy.

Keywords: Personalized privacy preservation · Differential privacy · Johnson-Lindenstrauss transform · Recommendation system

1 Introduction

With the continued expansion of searchable data, recommendation systems arise for the purpose of providing information retrieval services to users' interests using their personal data stored on cloud, which give rise to privacy concerns. The literature shows that continuous observation of recommendations, supplemented by a certain amount of background information, makes it possible for an individual's transaction history to be inferred, especially when using neighbourhood-based methods [1], known as k-nearest neighbor (KNN) attack. Suppose the attacker knows m ratings of the items of an intended victim, the attacker can then compromise the victim's privacy by creating k fake users with the same ratings to replicate their recommendation list.

Differential privacy is a new provable privacy framework developed in recent years. It has become an important standard for evaluating the privacy levels

© Springer International Publishing AG 2017
M.H.A. Au et al. (Eds.): GPC 2017, LNCS 10232, pp. 371–385, 2017.
DOI: 10.1007/978-3-319-57186-7_28

due to its rigorous privacy guarantee. Normally, differential privacy guarantees users' privacy by adding random noise to the results of queries to ensure that the output is insensitive to any individual record in the dataset. Several papers have recently applied differential privacy to solve privacy problems in recommendation systems. Guerraoui et al. [2] provide distance-based differential privacy in a KNN-based CF recommendation system. Shen and Jin [3] provide a novel relaxed admissible mechanism that guarantees differential privacy by injecting relaxed instance-based random noise. In a subsequent work, Shen and Jin [4] also provide a practical privacy framework in an untrusted server setting. User data are perturbed and anonymized before leaving their private devices. All of these methods apply traditional differential privacy to preserve a uniform level of privacy for users.

However, privacy is a personal concept, and users may have different expectations for preserving their personal data. For example, users with particular interests may require a strong privacy guarantee. Therefore, we argue that a uniform level of privacy protection leads to insufficient privacy protection for users who have a strong privacy requirement, while over providing protection to those users who do not. In this paper, we consider personalized privacy in neighborhood-based collaborative filtering.

The main challenge in personalized privacy is engineering the privacy parameters in the method's design to provide different levels of privacy for individual users. To solve this problem, we consider privacy requirements of users who are directly related to the query. Specifically, we make the following contributions:

1. We propose a personalized privacy preservation method based on *Laplace* mechanism for neighborhood-based collaborative filtering. We add personalized *Laplace* noise to the query results according to each user's privacy requirements.
2. We propose a randomized pre-processing method to process a sparse original dataset, which contributes to the improved prediction quality. Given the quality of neighbors selected from sparse datasets is often not very good, our randomized method can help to choose much closer neighbors, which is very important for final prediction.

Extensive testing shows that the proposed privacy method is not only personalized to users' requirements, but also makes better predictions than when using traditional differential privacy.

The rest of this paper is organized as follows: We provide the preliminaries in Sect. 2 and define the personalized privacy in Sect. 3. In Sects. 4 and 5, we introduce the proposed personalized method and analyse the privacy levels and utility provided by our method respectively, followed by a detailed description of the experiments in Sect. 6. At the end of the paper we present our conclusions.

2 Preliminaries

2.1 Notation

We denote the dataset D as an $n \times d$ matrix, where n is the number of users and d is the number of items in the dataset. Let $U = [U_1, U_2, ...U_n]$ be the row vectors of the matrix D, then, $U_i = [r_{u_i1}, r_{u_i2}, ...r_{u_id}]$ is the rating list of user u_i. r_{u_it} is the rating that user u_i gives to item t. The similarity between user u_i and u_j is represented as $s(u_i, u_j)$, while $N_k(u_i)$ is the set of user u_i's k-nearest neighbors. We define two datasets as neighbors if they differ by only one row.

2.2 Collaborative Filtering

Collaborative filtering, a popular method for analysing users' interests, has been widely applied to recommendation systems. The premise of collaborative filtering is that users will obtain good recommendations from people with similar tastes, and therefore these methods make their predictions based on the preferences of the users with the closest common interests. Collaborative filtering systems typically involve two stages: Step 1, select k users with the highest similarity as the closest neighbors and Step 2, predict rating that the predicted user may give to the item. Cosine-based Similarity and Pearson's Correlation Coefficient [5] are used to estimate the similarity between two users in this paper, and the prediction is calculated as follows:

$$r_{u_it} = \frac{\sum_{a \in N_k(b)} s(u_i, u_j) r_{u_jt}}{\sum_{a \in N_k(b)} r_{u_jt}}. \tag{1}$$

2.3 Differential Privacy

The goal of *differential privacy* [6] is to mask the difference in the answer to query f between neighboring datasets. In ϵ-differential privacy, the parameter ϵ is defined as the *privacy budget*, which controls the privacy guarantee level of mechanism $\mathcal{M}$. A smaller ϵ represents a stronger privacy level. The formal definition of differential privacy is presented below:

Definition 1 (ϵ-Differential Privacy). *A randomized algorithm $\mathcal{M}$ gives ϵ-differential privacy for any pair of neighboring datasets D and D^*, and for every set of outcomes Ω, $\mathcal{M}$ satisfies*

$$Pr[\mathcal{M}(D) \in \Omega] \leq \exp(\epsilon) \cdot Pr[\mathcal{M}(D^*) \in \Omega]. \tag{2}$$

Definition 2 (*Laplace* mechanism). *Given a function $f : D \to \mathbb{R}$ over a dataset D, Eq. 2 provides ϵ-differential privacy.*

$$\widehat{f}(D) = f(D) + Laplace(\frac{s}{\epsilon}). \tag{3}$$

Laplace mechanism satisfies differential privacy by adding *Laplace* noise to the true answer.

2.4   Johnson-Lindenstrauss Transform

The Johnson-Lindenstrauss transform is a random projection that transforms the points from a high dimension to lower dimensional space while preserving the Euclidean distance between any pair of points. The Johnson-Lindenstrauss transform results in the powerful Johnson-Lindenstrauss Lemma shown below:

Lemma 1 (Johnson-Lindenstrauss lemma [7]**).** *For any set S of n points in $\mathbb{R}^d$, given $0 \leq \delta \leq 1/2$, $m = \Omega(log(n)/\delta^2)$, there is a matrix $A \in \mathbb{R}^{d \times m}$, and there is a map $f : \mathbb{R}^d \rightarrow \mathbb{R}^m$ for all $u, v \in S$, such that*

$$(1 - \delta)\|u - v\|^2 \leq \|f(u) - f(v)\|^2 \leq (1 + \delta)\|u - v\|^2. \qquad (4)$$

in which $f(u) = uA, f(v) = vA$.

This lemma states that the random matrix A can project the dataset from d dimension to m while maintaining the relative distance. Several constructions for A have been proposed [8,9]. We use Gaussian distribution to generate the random matrix A.

3   Personalized Privacy Definition

In this section, we focus on the problem of preserving privacy in neighborhood-based collaborative filtering. In traditional differential privacy preservation methods, users are given a uniform privacy guarantee. However, in real life, users have different privacy requirements. A uniform privacy guarantee provides over-protection to users who are not concerned about their personal information while providing insufficient protection to users with strong privacy concerns. To solve this problem, we propose a personalized privacy preservation method that considers the differing privacy requirements of all users. Its formal definition is presented as follows:

Definition 3 (Personalized Differential Privacy [10]**).** *A randomized algorithm $\mathcal{M}$ gives Ψ-differential privacy for any pair of neighboring datasets D and D^*, and for every set of outcomes Ω, $\mathcal{M}$ satisfies:*

$$Pr[\mathcal{M}(D) \in \Omega] \leq e^{\varepsilon_\varphi(i)} \cdot Pr[\mathcal{M}(D^*) \in \Omega]. \qquad (5)$$

where $\varepsilon_\varphi(i)$ is the user's privacy requirement.

Definition 4 (Privacy Requirement). *Model the dataset as a set of tuples, where each tuple associated with a user u_i has multiple attributes. There exists a map $\Psi : u_i \rightarrow \varepsilon_\varphi(i)$ from each user to a corresponding self-defined privacy parameter.*

Each user can choose a privacy parameter according to their own privacy requirements. Practically, this may be presented to the user as a choice of labelled buttons, such as 'I don't care about privacy', 'I am a little concerned about

---

Algorithm 1. Personalized Privacy Preserving Collaborative Filtering (PPCF)

Require: Dataset $D \in \mathbb{R}^{n \times d}$, privacy parameter $\varepsilon_\varphi(i)$, number of neighbors k
Ensure: r_i.
1. Pre-process the original dataset;
2. Calculate the similarity between all pairs of users, perturb the similarity by adding $Lap(\frac{IS_{ij}}{\varepsilon_\varphi(i)})$ noise.
3. Select k nearest neighbors based on the perturbed similarity.
4. Predict r_i.

---

privacy', or 'I am very concerned about privacy'. In our work, we define $0.1 \leq \varepsilon_\varphi(i) \leq 1$. If the user doesn't specify a privacy requirement, we would assign a default value of $\varepsilon_\varphi = 1$.

On the assumption that all users in the dataset have the same privacy preference. That is, for all $u_i \in O$, where O is the set of all users in D, $\varepsilon_\varphi(i) = max_i(\varepsilon_\varphi(i))$. In these cases, there would be no objection to providing differential privacy with the same guarantee as traditional methods (i.e., e^ε, where $\varepsilon = max_i(\varepsilon_\varphi(i))$). Consider another situation. Half the users in D do not care about their personal data and are happy for it to be public without reservation. Even though none of the privacy budget has been assigned to these data, their privacy has not been disclosed because the data are not considered private to those users. In this way, we can say that personalized differential privacy not only considers personalized privacy requirements, but also preserves the same level of privacy as traditional methods with much more utility.

4 Personalized Privacy Collaborate Filtering

In this section, we propose a *Personalized Privacy Preserving Collaborative Filtering* algorithm with a pre-processing method that improves the accuracy of prediction. An overview of our method follows.

As rating datasets are very sparse, which can directly affect the neighbor selection, result in inaccurate prediction. we propose a pre-processing method based on the Johnson Lindenstrauss transform to process sparse original datasets. The basic idea is to multiply the dataset with a random matrix that satisfies the Johnson Lindenstrauss lemma. Studies show that a randomization method helps to greatly improve performance.

We implement differential privacy collaborative filtering on a sanitary dataset, then add *Laplace* noise to the similarity to ensure the user's privacy. According to Eq. 2, the amount of *Laplace* noise added is determined by the sensitivity and privacy parameters. We propose a new definition of sensitivity to reduce the amount of noise that is only associated with related users. In addition, the privacy parameter in our method varies from user to user. We assign different values of the privacy parameter to users according to their privacy preferences.

The details of the proposed method are presented in Algorithm 1.

First, we process the original dataset in Step 1, presenting the detail in Sect. 4.1. In Step 2, we calculate the similarity matrix of the users in a sanitized dataset and perturb it using *Laplace* noise. The specific operations are presented in Sect. 4.2. The top-k users with the highest similarity are selected as the active user's neighbor in Step 3. Lastly, we predict the rating that the active user will give to a specific item according to Eq. 1 in Step 4. Steps 3 and 4 are standard collaborative filtering steps that do not require explanation.

4.1 Pre-processing

Ratings datasets are usually of high-dimension and sparse. Therefore, the quality of the neighbors is crucial to neighborhood-based collaborative filtering. As neighbor selection is based on co-rated items, the sparsity of the original dataset means that the selected neighbors are often not the best choices. To solve this problem, we propose a randomized pre-processing method based on the Johnson Lindenstrauss transform that can help to improve prediction. The details are provided in Algorithm 2.

Algorithm 2. Pre-processing

Require: Dataset $D \in \mathbb{R}^{n \times d}$, projected dimension $m \ll d$
Ensure: Matrix X with lower dimension.
    1. Construct a random matrix $A \in \mathbb{R}^{d \times m}$, whose entries are samples from iid Gaussian distribution $N(0, 1/m)$;
    2. Get the low dimension matrix $X = DA$;

In Step 1, we construct a transition matrix A by sampling each entry from a Gaussian distribution $N(0, 1/m)$. Then we calculate the new dataset by multiplying the original dataset with this transition matrix in Step 2. This new dataset is only m dimensions, which reduces the algorithm's complexity significantly. Also, it makes the dataset more compact, which helps to select closer neighbors.

4.2 Perturb the Similarity

To prevent disclosure of the ratings records, we perturb the similarity based on a *Laplace* mechanism. The *Laplace* mechanism preserves differential privacy by adding *Laplace* noise where the naive *Laplace* mechanism cannot provide an accurate prediction. Recall that the noise added by the *Laplace* mechanism follows *Laplace* distribution, $Noise = Laplace(s/\varepsilon)$, which is determined by the sensitivity and privacy parameters.

Sensitivity. Sensitivity answers the question 'How many changes will be made to the result of the query when one record is removed from, or added to, the dataset?'. In addition, it determines how much perturbation should be generated in the mechanism under a certain privacy parameter. Generally, it refers to global sensitivity, which measures the maximum difference between the results of the query from all neighboring datasets. The formal definition is as follows:

Definition 5 (Global sensitivity). *Given a query f to the dataset D, D' is the neighbor dataset of D, the global sensitivity of f is defined as*

$$GS_f = \max_{D,D'} \|f(D) - f(D')\|_1. \tag{6}$$

The sensitivity is independent of the dataset but determined by the query function [11]. However, for some queries, the global sensitivity is too high to provide an accurate answer. Especially for the similarity query. Global sensitivity always considers the worst case, applying the same standard to all other users. In reality, however, the scope of the dataset is so large that the probability of the worst case occurring is very small. In this case, it is almost impossible for two users to even rate the same movie let alone give an identical score. As a result, we consider a much more practical situation in our paper - immediate sensitivity (IS), defined as follows:

Definition 6 (Immediate Sensitivity). *Immediate sensitivity is a dynamic sensitivity, determined by the two users being queried instantly. It is calculated as*

$$IS = f_D(u_i, u_j) - f_{D'}(u_i, u_j). \tag{7}$$

where, $u_j \in D$, and $u_j \notin D'$.

IS is updated with changing queries and reflects real situations, which avoids adding too over-much noise. For example, given a dataset $D = [u_1, u_2, u_3, u_4, u_5]$, when we query the similarity between u_2 and u_3, we would consider how much the result of the query would change if we deleted record u_2 or u_3 from the dataset. We then add *Laplace* noise based on this sensitivity to hide the information that the query might disclosed.

Privacy Parameter. In traditional differential privacy, uniform privacy parameters are provided to all users. For some users who are not concerned about the safety of their personal dataset, uniform parameters provide both too much protection and more noise, which reduces utility to some extent. In the proposed method, we consider individual preferences when adding Laplace noise. We assume that users have chosen their own privacy parameters or selected their privacy level in a user-friendly way, using such options as 'low privacy concern', 'medium privacy concern' and 'high privacy concern'. When we calculate the amount of noise added to the similarity between any two users, we are comparing their privacy concerns. In personalized privacy, the privacy parameter varies according to the user, so choosing the smaller value as the privacy parameter guarantees both users' privacy. More formally,

$$Pp = min_{i,j}\{\varepsilon_\varphi(i), \ \varepsilon_\varphi(j)\}. \tag{8}$$

where, $\varepsilon_\varphi(i), \varepsilon_\varphi(j)$ are the privacy preferences of user u_i and user u_j respectively.

As previously mentioned, three operations in the proposed method contribute to improved performance: randomized pre-processing helps to select high-quality neighbors, while both calibrated sensitivity and personalized privacy parameters reduce added noise. Theoretical analysis and testing have proven the effectiveness of the proposed method.

5   Privacy and Utility Analysis

5.1   Privacy Analysis

We preserve users' rating records by perturbing the similarity between any pair of users. We take the personal privacy requirement into account and add *Laplace* noise using different privacy parameters. Theorem 1 shows that the proposed method satisfies personalized differential privacy.

Theorem 1. *For a given a dataset D, users u_i in D have different privacy preferences, represented as $\varepsilon_\varphi(i)$, the PPCF method can provide personalized differential privacy to users in D.*

Proof. Assume the user's privacy preference is $\varepsilon_\varphi(i)$, the sensitivity is $IS_{i,j}$, $f(D)$ is the query function, and the outcomes are in the set of S. D' is the neighboring dataset. $N(x)$ is the noise added to the similarity, which follows the *Laplace* distribution Laplace(0, b).
   Then,

$$\frac{Pr[f(D) = S]}{Pr[f(D') = S]} = \frac{N(S - f(D))}{N(S - f(D'))} \le exp(\frac{|f(D) - f(D')|}{b}) = exp(IS_{i,j}/b) = e^{\varepsilon_\varphi(i)}.$$

Therefore, the proposed method not only satisfies differential privacy, but also provides corresponding privacy preservation for each user.

5.2   Utility Analysis

In this section, we apply a well known utility definition suggested by Blum et al. [12] to measure the accuracy of prediction, which in turn is based on the quality of the neighbors.

Definition 7 ((α, β)-useful). *A database access mechanism $\mathcal{M}$ is (α, β)-useful with respect to COS query, if for every database D, with probability at least $1 - \beta$, the output of the mechanism $\mathcal{M}$ satisfies:*

$$Pr[max|cos(u', v') - cos(u, v)| \le \alpha] \ge 1 - \beta. \tag{9}$$

Theorem 2. *For COS query on any pair of users, the output error caused by the proposed method (PPCF) is less than α with the probability at least $1-\beta$. The proposed method is satisfied with (α, β)-useful when $\alpha < \dfrac{s(u,v)\sqrt{d}(\ln\frac{2}{\beta} - \frac{1-\delta}{\sqrt{d}})}{2s(u,v)(1-\delta)+\varepsilon_\varphi(i)\sqrt{d}}$.*

Proof. The error caused by the proposed method is the result of the Johnson Lindenstrauss transform and *Laplace* noise. We use E_{JL} and E_{Lap} to represent the error introduced by the Johnson Lindenstrauss transform and *Laplace* noise, respectively. We have

$$Pr(max|cos(u',v') - cos(u,v)| > \alpha) \leq Pr(E_{JL} > \alpha) + Pr(E_{Lap} > \alpha).$$

Referring to the Johnson Lindenstrauss lemma and according to the relationship between l_2 Euclidean distance and cosine similarity, we have

$$cos(u,v) \geq \frac{(\|u\| + \|v\|)(1-\delta) - \|u'-v'\|}{2\|u\|\|v\|(1-\delta)}.$$

Then, we have

$$
\begin{aligned}
E_{JL} &\leq \frac{\|u'\| + \|v'\| - \|u'-v'\|}{2\|u'\|\|v'\|} + \frac{\|u'-v'\| - (\|u\| + \|v\|)(1-\delta)}{2\|u\|\|v\|(1-\delta)} \\
&\leq \frac{\|u'\| + \|v'\| - (\|u\| + \|v\|)(1-\delta)}{2\|u\|\|v\|(1-\delta)} \\
&\leq \frac{\|u'\| + \|v'\|}{2(\|u\| + \|v\|)(1-\delta)} - \frac{1}{2} \leq \frac{(\|u\| + \|v\|)\|X\|}{2(\|u\| + \|v\|)(1-\delta)} - \frac{1}{2} = \frac{\|X\|}{2(1-\delta)} - \frac{1}{2}.
\end{aligned}
$$

Accordingly,

$$Pr(E_{JL} > \alpha) = Pr[\frac{\|X\|}{2(1-\delta)} - \frac{1}{2} > \alpha]$$

$$= Pr[\sqrt{dm}|x| > 2(\alpha + \frac{1}{2})(1-\delta)] = Pr[|x| > \frac{2(\alpha + \frac{1}{2})(1-\delta)}{\sqrt{dm}}].$$

Because variable $x \sim N(0, 1/m)$, according to the property of Gaussian distribution, we have

$$Pr(E_{JL} > \alpha) = 2e^{-\frac{2}{\sqrt{d}}(\alpha + \frac{1}{2})(1-\delta)}.$$

Given the *Noise* $\sim$ *Laplace*$(\frac{s(u,v)}{\varepsilon_\varphi(i)})$, according to the property of *Laplace* distribution, we have

$$Pr(E_{Lap} > \alpha) = e^{-\frac{\varepsilon_\varphi(i)}{s(u,v)}\alpha}.$$

Accordingly,

$$Pr(max|cos(u',v') - cos(u,v)| > \alpha) \leq 2e^{-\frac{2}{\sqrt{d}}(\alpha + \frac{1}{2})(1-\delta)} + e^{-\frac{\varepsilon_\varphi(i)}{s(u,v)}\alpha}. \tag{10}$$

Let Eq. 10 = β, and we have

$$ln2 - \frac{2}{\sqrt{d}}(\alpha + \frac{1}{2})(1 - \delta) - \frac{\varepsilon_\varphi(i)}{s(u,v)}\alpha = ln\beta$$

$$\Rightarrow \alpha = \frac{s(u,v)\sqrt{d}(ln\frac{2}{\beta} - \frac{1-\delta}{\sqrt{d}})}{2s(u,v)(1-\delta) + \varepsilon_\varphi(i)\sqrt{d}}. \tag{11}$$

The result shows that the error is bounded by α, where $\alpha <$ $\frac{s(u,v)\sqrt{d}(ln\frac{2}{\beta} - \frac{1-\delta}{\sqrt{d}})}{2s(u,v)(1-\delta) + \varepsilon_\varphi(i)\sqrt{d}}$. When the privacy parameter $\varepsilon_\varphi(i)$ grows larger and δ becomes smaller, the error introduced by the proposed method becomes much smaller.

6   Experiment and Analysis

In this section, our main goal is to demonstrate that applying a Johnson Lindenstrauss transform and considering personal privacy preferences can both contribute to an accurate prediction.

6.1   Experiment Setting

Datasets. In this experiment, we use Netflix[1] and MovieLens[2] datasets. The Netflix dataset was extracted from the official dataset used in the Netflix Prize competition. Each movie has been rated by at least $20,250$ users, who have each rated at least 20 movies. The MovieLens dataset is a benchmark dataset, used for collaborative filtering research. It has about 1 million ratings of 3900 movies rated by at least 6040 users. We randomly chose one rating by each user as the test dataset and deleted it from the original dataset.

Privacy Configuration. According to Acquisti and Grossklags and Berendt et al. [13,14], users can fall into several groups according to their attitudes regarding privacy. To simulate users' privacy preferences, we divided users randomly into three groups: *low, medium* and *high* privacy concern. The corresponding proportion are p_l, p_m and p_h. The users' preferences are sampled uniformly at the ranges of $[\varepsilon_l, \varepsilon_m]$ and $[\varepsilon_m, \varepsilon_h]$ respectively, where $\varepsilon_L, \varepsilon_M, \varepsilon_H \in [0.1, 1]$. Smaller values represent a stronger privacy requirement. The users in group *low* have a fixed value: $\varepsilon_L = 1$.

Baseline Mechanisms. To prove the effectiveness of our method, we introduce two baseline mechanisms. Both mechanisms satisfy personalized privacy preservation. We use the proposed method without Johnson Lindenstrauss transform

---

[1] http://www.netflixprize.com.
[2] http://www.grouplens.org.

as *Baseline* 1. This baseline was designed to determine whether linear transformation contributes an improvement in utility. *Baseline* 2 is the method that consider the strongest privacy requirement among users, we chose the smallest privacy parameter ε_{min} as the uniform standard to perturb similarity. *Baseline* 2 also satisfies personalized differential privacy but does not take the advantage of it. *Baseline* 2 is designed to confirm the effectiveness of considering personalized privacy preferences.

6.2 Evaluation

We performed a substantial number of experiments to evaluate the performance of our methods. Our objective is to predict the missing test rating by each user using the remaining ratings, by applying $RMSE$ to show the effectiveness of our method. $RMSE$ is defined as follows:

$$RMSE = \sqrt{\frac{\sum_{u_i,t \in T}(r_{u_i t} - r_{\hat{u_i}t})^2}{|T|}}. \tag{12}$$

where $r_{u_i t}$ is the true rating, and $r_{\hat{u_i}t}$ is the predicted rating. T is the test dataset and $|T|$ is its size. A lower $RMSE$ represents a higher accuracy.

Table 1 lists the parameters and default values used in our experiments.

Table 1. Values of various parameters

Parameters	Description	Values
m	New matrix dimension	500
k	Number of neighbours	10
p_l	Proportion of low privacy concern users	0.09
p_m	Proportion of medium privacy concern users	0.37
p_h	Proportion of high privacy concern users	0.54
ε_l	Lower bound of privacy parameter	0.1
ε_m	Median of privacy parameter	0.3
ε_h	Upper bound of privacy parameter	1

Performance Evaluation of the Johnson Lindenstrauss Transform. The performance of the Johnson Lindenstrauss transform was examined by comparing the proposed method with *Baseline* 1. We used default values for all other parameters in this comparison. Put simply, we varied the number of neighbors from 5 to 50 in steps of 5 on both datasets to specify the number of neighbors in the COS and PCC metrics.

Figure 1 shows the results of the comparison. We observe that, no matter which metric was used, increasing the number of neighbors selected improved performance for both mechanisms. This is because the performance of proposed method

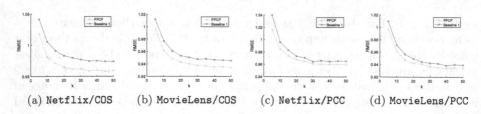

(a) Netflix/COS   (b) MovieLens/COS   (c) Netflix/PCC   (d) MovieLens/PCC

Fig. 1. Performance of Johnson Lindestrauss transform

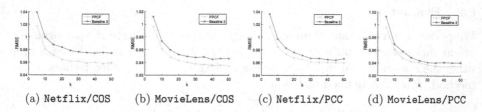

(a) Netflix/COS   (b) MovieLens/COS   (c) Netflix/PCC   (d) MovieLens/PCC

Fig. 2. Performance of personalized privacy setting

is determined mainly by the quality of neighbors. Within a threshold, a higher number of neighbors gives a higher probability that the prediction contains the true close neighbors. In addition, we observe that the performance of proposed method outperforms the baseline without the Johnson Lindenstrauss transform across all k values and in all cases. When $k = 20$, the $RMSE$ was 0.9645 and 0.9430 for the proposed method on the Netflix and MovieLens datasets, respectively, using the COS metric. *Baseline* 1's $RMSE$ was 0.9832 and 0.9531, accordingly. Similar results can be seen on both datasets in terms of the PCC metric. The reason the Johnson Lindenstrauss transform can improve performance is because it tightens the ratings dataset, which increases the accuracy of the selected neighbors. In other words, the Johnson Lindesntrauss transform helps to choose much closer neighbors with more similar tastes.

Performance of Personalized Consideration. To prove the effectiveness of personalized privacy settings, we compared our method with Baseline 2, which assigns all users the same and strongest privacy parameter. While both mechanisms satisfy users' privacy requirements, Baseline 2 does not consider individual privacy preferences, rather it simply provides the strongest privacy guarantee. We use the same settings as outlined in last section.

Figure 3 shows the results of the experiments. We observe, from Fig. 2a, that both methods performed better with an increase in the number of neighbors and that the proposed method always showed better performance than Baseline 2 in terms of $RMSE$, no matter how many neighbors were selected. Similar results can be seen on both datasets in terms of the PCC metric.

The proposed method considers each user's individual privacy preferences. For users who are not sensitive about their personal data, we add less noise to

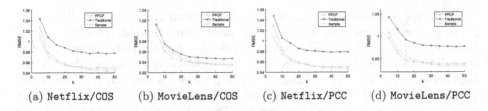

(a) Netflix/COS   (b) MovieLens/COS   (c) Netflix/PCC   (d) MovieLens/PCC

Fig. 3. Compare with other related works

hide their information. Therefore, more real information is preserved and more utility is maintained compared to methods that assign the strongest privacy parameter to all users.

Comparison with Other Related Methods. The performance of the proposed method was also compared to other state-of-the-art methods. Specifically, with both a traditional *Laplace* method, and the *Sample* mechanism introduced by Jorgensen [10]. Jorgensen's method works by sampling records according to a probability calculation of the individual's privacy requirements. We provided them with the same privacy settings and varied the number of neighbors from 5 to 50 in steps of 5 on both datasets.

Figure 3 shows the comparison results. It is observed that both *Sample* mechanism and our method outperform the traditional *Laplace* method significantly in Fig. 3a. And the performance of our method is roughly the same with *Sample* mechanism. Similar results can be seen in other sub-figures as well. Though the performance of our method is without much difference compared to *Sample* mechanism, our method has less computational complexity. For *Sample* mechanism, its computational complexity is $O(n^3 d)$, while our method is $O(\frac{n^2 log(n)}{\delta^2} + \frac{dnlog(n)}{\delta^2})$. Because the Johnson Lindenstrauss transform reduces the data dimension from d to m. However, n times sampling operations need to be done for recommendation purpose.

7 Related Work

The concept of *personalized privacy* was first proposed by Xiao and Tao [15]. They present a generalization framework that take into account personal anonymity requirements, choosing the minimum amount of necessary generalization for each record. Later, Poolsappasit and Ray [16] considered people's different privacy attitudes to location information in various situations. Yuan et al. [17] preserved a labelled social network by generalizing and modifying a graph. Wang [18] achieve personalized privacy preservation using a clustering technique. All of these methods are based on K-anonymity, which has proven to be very weak and open to attack by newly-developed attack models. Differential privacy has since been the much preferred approach for its rigid privacy preservation.

Zach [10] introduced two mechanisms for achieving personalized differential privacy. The first method is a sampling mechanism that samples the records based on a proposed sample probability associated with users' privacy preference. The third mechanism is based on *Exponential* mechanism, which is not applicable to our situation. Mohammad [19] proposed a new concept, called *heterogeneous differential privacy*. First, the data is rescaled by a shrinkage matrix associated with users' privacy preferences. Then the new dataset is queried, and *Laplace* noise is added to the result of the query. However, to satisfy heterogeneous differential privacy, the sensitivity of the query to the rescaled dataset must be equal to, or less than, the product of the privacy preference and the sensitivity of the query to the original dataset. This means that the users' privacy preferences cannot be chosen as they wish, and the method does not strictly provide personalized privacy preservation.

Many work [20–22] focused on privacy perservation recommendation system, while none of them considered the personalized privacy setting.

8   Conclusions

In this paper, we consider users' personal privacy requirements in a recommendation system to provide a personalized privacy preservation method for neighborhood-based collaborative filtering. The method is based on a Laplace mechanism where calibrated noise is added to the query result according to each user's individual privacy requirements. In addition, a Johnson Lindenstrauss transform-based pre-processing method is introduced to improve performance. We show that the proposed method satisfies personalized differential privacy, and maintains more utility, compared to traditional differential privacy methods that provide a uniform level of privacy to all users.

References

1. Calandrino, J.A., Kilzer, A., Narayanan, A., Felten, E.W., Shmatikov, V.: You might also like: privacy risks of collaborative filtering. In: 2011 IEEE Symposium on Security and Privacy, pp. 231–246. IEEE Computer Society, Washington, DC (2011)
2. Guerraoui, R., Kermarrec, A., Patra, R., Taziki, M.: D2P: distance-based differential privacy in recommenders. Proc. VLDB Endowment **8**, 862–873 (2015)
3. Shen, Y., Jin, H.: Privacy-preserving personalized recommendation: an instance-based approach via differential privacy. In: IEEE International Conference on Data Mining, pp. 540–549. IEEE (2014)
4. Shen, Y.L., Jin, H.X.: EpicRec: towards practical differentially private framework for personalized recommendation. In: 2016 ACM SIGSAC Conference on Computer and Communications Security, pp. 180–191. ACM, New York (2016)
5. Adomavicius, G., Tuzhilin, A.: Toward the next generation of recommender systems: a survey of the state-of-the-art and possible extensions. IEEE Trans. Knowl. Data Eng. **17**, 734–749 (2005)

6. Dwork, C.: A firm foundation for private data analysis. Commun. ACM **54**, 86–95 (2011)
7. Johnson, W.B., Lindenstrauss, J.: Extensions of Lipschitz mappings into a Hilbert space. Contemp. Math. **26**, 189–206 (1984)
8. Achlioptas, D.: Database-friendly random projections: Johnson-Lindenstrauss with binary coins. Comput. Syst. Sci. **66**, 671–687 (2003)
9. Indyk, P., Motwani, R.: Approximate nearest neighbors: towards removing the curse of dimensionality. In: 30th Annual ACM Symposium on Theory of Computing, pp. 604–613. ACM, New York (1998)
10. Jorgensen, Z., Yu, T., Cormode, G.: Conservative or liberal? personalized differential privacy. In: 31st International Conference on Data Engineering, pp. 1023–1034. IEEE (2015)
11. Dwork, C.: Differential privacy: a survey of results. In: Agrawal, M., Du, D., Duan, Z., Li, A. (eds.) TAMC 2008. LNCS, vol. 4978, pp. 1–19. Springer, Heidelberg (2008). doi:10.1007/978-3-540-79228-4_1
12. Blum, A., Ligett, K., Roth, A.: A learning theory approach to noninteractive database privacy. J. ACM (JACM) **60**, 12:1–12:25 (2013)
13. Acquisti, A., Grossklags, J.: Privacy and rationality in individual decision making. J. Secur. Priv. **2**, 24–30 (2005)
14. Berendt, B., Günther, O., Spiekermann, S.: Privacy in e-commerce: stated preferences vs. actual behavior. Commun. ACM **48**, 101–106 (2005)
15. Xiao, X.K., Tao, Y.F.: Personalized privacy preservation. In: Proceedings of the 2006 ACM SIGMOD International Conference on Management of Data, pp. 229–240. ACM, New York (2006)
16. Poolsappasit, N., Ray, I.: Towards achieving personalized privacy for location-based services. Transactions on Data Priv. **2**, 77–99 (2009)
17. Yuan, M.X., Chen, L., Yu, P.S.: Personalized privacy protection in social networks. Proc. VLDB Endowment **4**, 141–150 (2010)
18. Wang, P.S.: Personalized anonymity algorithm using clustering techniques. Comput. Inf. Syst. **7**, 924–931 (2011)
19. Laggan, M., Gambs, S., Kermarrec, A.-M.: Heterogeneous differential privacy. arXiv preprint arXiv:1504.06998 (2015)
20. Shripad, K.V., Vaidya, A.S.: Privacy preserving profile matching system for trust-aware personalized user recommendations in social networks. Int. J. Comput. Appl. **122** (2015)
21. Liu, R., Cao, J., Zhang, K., Gao, W., Liang, J., Yang, L.: When privacy meets usability: unobtrusive privacy permission recommendation system for mobile apps based on crowdsourcing. IEEE Trans. Serv. Comput. (2016)
22. Carullo, G., Castiglione, A., De Santis, A., Palmieri, F.: A triadic closure and homophily-based recommendation system for online social networks. World Wide Web **18**, 1579–1601 (2015)

Know Your Enemy: Stealth Configuration-Information Gathering in SDN

Mauro Conti[1], Fabio De Gaspari[2]([✉]), and Luigi V. Mancini[2]

[1] University of Padova, Padua, Italy
conti@math.unipd.it
[2] Sapienza University of Rome, Rome, Italy
{degaspari,mancini}@di.uniroma1.it

Abstract. Software Defined Networking (SDN) is a widely-adopted network architecture that provides high flexibility through the separation of the network logic from the forwarding functions. Researchers thoroughly analyzed SDN vulnerabilities and improved its security. However, we believe important security aspects of SDN are still left uninvestigated.

In this paper, we raise the concern of the possibility for an attacker to obtain detailed knowledge about an SDN network. In particular, we introduce a novel attack, named *Know Your Enemy* (KYE), by means of which an attacker can gather vital information about the configuration of the network. This information ranges from the configuration of security tools, such as attack detection thresholds for network scanning, to general network policies like QoS and network virtualization. Additionally, we show that an attacker can perform a KYE attack in a stealthy fashion, i.e., without the risk of being detected. We underline that the vulnerability exploited by the KYE attack is proper of SDN and is not present in legacy networks.

1 Introduction

Software Defined Networking (SDN) is a network architecture proposed in recent years to address the shortcomings of traditional architectures. SDN posits that the implementation of network functions and the control logic of the network are two separate concepts, and should therefore be separated in different entities. To this end, SDN introduces the concepts of *data plane* and *control plane*: the data plane is comprised of the physical network devices (from here on, called switches) and implements the forwarding functionalities of the network, while the control plane manages the network logic and decision making process. In SDN, the control plane takes the decisions on how traffic flows are managed and pushes these decisions to the data plane, that will in turn enforce them. This separation between logical control and physical implementation of network functions provides a high degree of flexibility, which is one of the main reason for the widespread adoption of SDN even amongst big companies [19].

© Springer International Publishing AG 2017
M.H.A. Au et al. (Eds.): GPC 2017, LNCS 10232, pp. 386–401, 2017.
DOI: 10.1007/978-3-319-57186-7_29

While the programmability of SDN allows for fast prototyping and high adaptability to different scenarios, it also opens new venues for attacks [4,5]. Indeed, while the decision making process is centralized in the control plane, the enforcement of the decision is distributed throughout all switches, which follow the rules pushed by the control plane. We show that, by exploiting this distributed policy-enforcement mechanism, an attacker can gather intelligence about the control logic of the network in a stealthy fashion. In particular, to run the attack we propose in this paper, the adversary needs to have only a *flow table side-channel*, i.e., a way of learning which rules are installed, for a single switch (which we call *entry switch*, see Sect. 2). By analyzing the conditions under which a rule is pushed, and the type of such rule, an attacker can infer sensitive information regarding the configuration of the network. The final result is that through a single switch, the attacker can gather information which, in a classical network, would have required access to numerous distinct devices, such as firewalls, intrusion detection/prevention systems, etc. The information gathered can subsequently be exploited to mount different attacks, tailored to the target network, without being detected.

To summarize, our contribution in this paper is as follows:

- We propose a novel, attack, the *Know Your Enemy* (KYE) attack, that allows stealth intelligence gathering about the configuration of a target SDN network. The information that an adversary can obtain ranges from configuration of security tools, such as attack detection thresholds for network scanning, to general network policies like QoS and network virtualization.
- We prove the feasibility and efficacy of the KYE attack through its implementation and a thorough experimental evaluation on an SDN network based on OpenFlow [1].

2 Assumptions and SDN Issues

Distributing the policy enforcement introduces new problems with regard to information disclosure. Where network functions in legacy networks are relegated to the specific devices implementing them, providing higher control over access to their configuration, in SDN they are distributed throughout the switches. Indeed, network policies and functionalities like intrusion detection/prevention systems (IDS/IPS), network virtualization, or access control, are often enforced by the switches, through the application of the rules installed by the controller [11–13].

As we show in this paper, by having a flow table side-channel on a single switch (called *entry switch*), an attacker can gather a relevant amount of information regarding the configuration of the SDN network the switch belongs to. A flow table side-channel is defined as any mean by which an attacker can learn or infer the rules installed on the *flow table* of a switch by the controller. The KYE attack is independent from how this side-channel is obtained, and the detailed description of how to obtain it is out of the scope of this paper. As an example, the attacker could have compromised a vulnerable switch in the network.

Threat Model. Our threat model assumes that the attacker has a flow table
side-channel for a single switch. His goal is to gather information on the network
without being detected. Therefore, the attacker uses the flow table side-channel
only to read the state of the flow table, without modifying the overall state of
the entry switch in any way. In particular, the only abilities of the attacker are
(*i*) sending packets through the target network and (*ii*) using the side-channel to
learn the rules that are installed on the entry switch. The attacker can be either
internal or external. Furthermore, we assume that the switch only provides the
functionality described in the OpenFlow standard [1]. Therefore, the attacker
does not modify the software nor adds capabilities to the switch in any way.

3 The KYE Attack

The details of the attack vary based on the specific information the attacker
wants to gather (see Sect. 4). However, all instances of the KYE attack share a
common kernel. The KYE attack exploits the on-demand installation of rules
of SDN, allowing an attacker to gather knowledge about which conditions trigger the installation of a given rule, as illustrated in Fig. 1. The KYE attack is
structured in two phases: (*A*) the *probing phase* and (*B*) the *inference phase*.

In the probing phase (*A*), which is repeated numerous times, the attacker
attempts to trigger the installation of rules on the entry switch (steps 1 through
5 in Fig. 1):

- The attacker sends carefully crafted *probing traffic* through the entry switch
  in order to trigger the installation of new rules. The specific characteristics
  of the probing traffic depend on what kind of information the attacker is
  interested in learning (see Sects. 4 and 5).
- Through the flow table side-channel, the attacker obtains the rule (if any)
  installed in response to the probing traffic.

In the inference phase (*B*), the attacker analyzes the correlation between the
probing traffic sent in the probing phase and the corresponding rules installed
(step 6 in Fig. 1). From this analysis, it is possible to infer what network policy is enforced for specific types of network flows (see Sect. 4). Additionally, by
studying the features of the probing traffic, the attacker can potentially infer
the trigger conditions for network policies that require a specific trigger before
being activated (e.g., scanning detection thresholds, see Sect. 5). The attacker
can then exploit this knowledge to perform additional attacks without triggering
detection (see Sect. 5.2).

It is worth noting that introducing probing traffic in the network does not
expose the KYE attack to detection. Indeed, one of the strengths of the KYE
attack is that it is hidden by other attacks: for instance, an attacker performing a
KYE attack to gather information related to DoS countermeasures will generate
DoS traffic through the target network during the probing phase. When the
DoS traffic is detected, the network will categorise it as a DoS attack, and the
KYE attack will remain undetected. Effectively, the probing traffic hides the

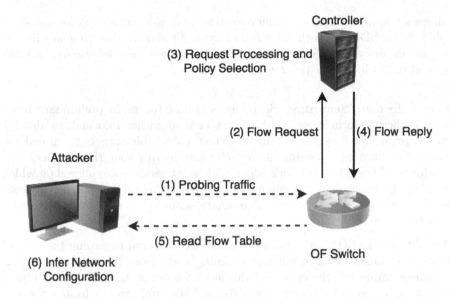

Fig. 1. Overview of a general KYE attack.

real attack to the network, making it extremely hard to detect the KYE attack reliably. Moreover, the attacker can employ IP spoofing or other techniques, such as proxies, during the probing phase, so that it is not possible to link him to the probing traffic.

4   KYE Instances

As we discussed before, the KYE attack is a general attack strategy, and the details of the attack vary based on the specific information the attacker wants to gather. In this section, we discuss different instances of the KYE attack, with respect to what type of information the attacker wants to obtain. Additionally, we provide a non-exhaustive list of concrete examples of KYE attack, showing how an attacker can exploit the flow table side-channel to infer different configuration features of the network. Due to space constraints, we limit our discussion to KYE attacks aimed at disclosing security-related configuration information in Sect. 4.1. However, the KYE attack can be easily used to disclose almost any type of network-configuration information, like for example flow table saturation prevention techniques, network virtualization functions or control plane scalability measures.

4.1   Gathering Network Security Configuration Information

When planning an attack, knowing what detection and defense mechanisms are used by the target network is obviously invaluable to an attacker. In this section we discuss how an attacker can infer detection mechanisms and defense measures in place in an SDN network for different types of attack. Due to space limitations, in our analysis we focus on some popular SDN-based defense mechanisms proposed in the literature [14,25].

Worm Infection/Scanning. Scanning is one of the main preliminary intelligence gathering techniques, used by attackers to gather information about a given target network and by worms to detect vulnerable targets to spread the infection to. Through scanning, an attacker can learn about the number, type and address of hosts in a network, along with what services are offered on which port. This information is a prerequisite for mounting more complex attacks. Therefore, being able to detect and mitigate scanning is extremely important for any network.

KYE Attack. In SDN, an attacker can infer information regarding the type of defense mechanisms used to mitigate scanning and, depending on the detection mechanism employed, the detection threshold for scans. In order to infer such information, an attacker simply needs to send scanning probes from a spoofed address IP_A, varying the characteristics of the scan (i.e., increasing scanning rate, different duration of the scan, various success/failed connection ratios). During the probing, the attacker monitors the rules pushed on the flow table in response. As long as the scanning is not detected, the rules installed simply instruct the switch to forward the traffic coming from IP_A towards different exit ports, based on the destination address. When the scanning rate becomes high enough or the scanning activity lasted long enough for the attack to be detected [23], the controller will install rules implementing an appropriate defense measure against scanning.

Detection and Defense Mechanism Inference. Depending on the defense measure used by the network, different types of rules will be installed, for instance: traffic filtering [17], rate limiting [23,29], honeypot redirection [27], or whitehole network approaches [4,5,26]. All these defense mechanisms require the installation of very specific rules, which differ from the normal rules installed when no attack is detected (see Sect. 4.2). Consequently, by recognizing this change in the type of rules installed, the attacker can learn that the network scanning was detected. Moreover, the rules required by these mechanisms are easily identifiable and, just by looking at what rule is installed, the attacker can infer the defense mechanism used by the network (see Sect. 4.2). Finally, for some defense mechanisms that are activated on-demand by the controller, the attacker can also infer the traffic features that trigger detection by the network. For instance, if we consider TRW-CB [24], which is one of the most frequently used anomaly detection algorithms [7] and is already implemented in SDN [23,27], the attacker can learn the ratio between successful/unsuccessful connections used as detection criteria through repeated probing. Once the attacker discovers the detection threshold, he is then able to carry out the network scan undetected in a second phase, by alternating unsuccessful scanning with successful connections.

Implementation. In Sect. 5.1 we report on the implementation of this instance of the KYE attack. We show that, for realistic detection and defense mechanisms, an attacker is able to learn both the scanning traffic features that trigger detection, and the defense mechanism applied in response.

Denial of Service. DDoS attacks are one of the most widespread type of attacks due to their simplicity and effectiveness. As a consequence, most organizations adopt one or more DDoS detection and mitigation system. In the context of SDN, DDoS detection schemes tend to employ lightweight mechanisms, such s threshold and entropy-based systems [12,17] to avoid overloading the controller. Other more complex and computationally expensive approaches exist, like [10], where the authors employ machine learning techniques to detect possible DoS attacks. An attacker can perform a KYE attack to learn if a DoS detection mechanism exists, what defense measure is applied by the network and potentially even the detection criteria employed.

KYE Attack. The KYE Attack for DoS detection is very similar to the one used for network scanning; in the probing phase, the attacker starts a DoS with a low attack rate, simulating a behaviour that is as close as possible to that of a legit client, then gradually increases the profile of the attack. Throughout the attack, the attacker monitors the rules installed by the controller on the entry switch, looking for a change in the rules pushed. Indeed, under normal circumstances the controller will simply instruct the switch to route the traffic towards the destination host. However, when the DoS attack is detected, the controller pushes different rules based on the defense mechanism employed by the network, allowing the attacker to learn that the DoS was detected.

Detection and Defense Mechanisms Inference. Defense mechanisms against DoS, like traffic redirection [22], rate limiting [23,29] or traffic filtering [17], require very specific rules that an attacker can easily distinguish from normal routing rules (see Sect. 4.2). Therefore, as soon as these security rules are installed on the entry switch, the attacker will know that the DoS was detected. By analyzing the specific rules installed, he can also infer the defense mechanism applied (see Sect. 4.2). Additionally, when the attack is detected, the attacker can try to infer the detection criteria used by the network. Indeed, for certain type of detection mechanisms such as threshold [12] or entropy-based [17], it is possible to find a good approximation of when exactly an attack is detected. In order to learn these detection thresholds, an attacker can repeat the probing phase several times varying the characteristics of the attack. Upon detection, the attacker will log such characteristics, like duration, attack rate and number of packets sent from each IP address, for instance. After obtaining a sufficiently large sample, the attacker can look for correlations between the characteristics of the detected attacks to learn approximately what values trigger the detection. Even in case of more complex detection systems based on machine learning [10], the attacker can still obtain knowledge about the traffic features used for detection. Indeed, previous work on the area of machine learning shows that it is possible to infer meaningful information about the training set of a classifier [8], which in our case would reveal information about which flows are considered malicious or benign.

Access Control. Access control mechanisms, like firewalls, are the first and most basic defense mechanism used by networks to enforce security policies. Through its centralized view of the network and distributed enforcement of rules, SDN provides the optimal functionality to implement a consistent distributed firewall in the network [15,18,30]. Given that such access control systems are the first defense mechanism that an attacker needs to bypass before attacking a network, learning the exact configuration of such devices would provide a huge advantage in preparing an attack. While this would be extremely challenging in classical networks, due to the fact that access control rules are relegated only to specific security devices, this task is considerably simpler in SDN.

KYE Attack. By performing a KYE attack, the attacker can infer all the access control policies he is interested in by simply probing the entry switch. In its most basic form, the attacker will send a probe packet to test any given access control policy. For instance, the attacker can try to connect to a protected service using a set of different IPs, in order to understand which subnets are allowed to access that service. For each of these probes the controller will push either a forwarding rule, to forward the packets to their destination, or a *drop* rule if the access is not allowed [3]. By repeating the probing for all interesting services and using different source IP addresses, the attacker can map which addresses (or address ranges) are allowed towards/from a certain critical service.

Defense Mechanism Inference. For access control enforcement, the policy that is most used in general is to drop unauthorized traffic flows [3]. If such defense mechanism is in place, the attacker is able to recognize it immediately just by reading the new rule installed (see Sect. 4.2). SDN also allows for more complex defense mechanisms to enforce access control, like traffic redirection towards a honeypot/IDS for instance [22,27]. As we discuss in Sect. 4.2, the attacker can easily identify even this more complex mechanisms just through observation of the entry switch flow table.

Implementation. In Sect. 5.2 we report on the implementation of this instance of the KYE attack. We show that, given an access control mechanism, an attacker is able to learn the complete access control matrix enforced by the controller.

4.2 Correlating Flow Rules and Network Policies

Through the KYE attack, an attacker can infer the exact network-level defense mechanism employed against specific attacks. In this section, we present a non-exhaustive set of defense policies [11] that are used in relation to our examples in Sect. 4.1. Furthermore, we explain how an attacker can correlate a sequence of rules obtained during the probing phase to the network policy they implement.

Traffic Filtering. One of the most basic network-level defense mechanisms is traffic filtering. A traffic filtering policy can be employed to mitigate a large range of attacks, including scanning and DoS attacks [4,17]. In SDN, traffic filtering is implemented simply by installing a *drop* rule matching the offending network flows on the switches. An attacker monitoring the flow table of a switch can easily detect the application of such defense mechanism. Indeed, before the policy is applied, the control plane will push on the switch normal rules, instructing the switch to forward the inbound traffic based on the destination address. When the attack is detected and the filtering is applied, the control plane will install only a single drop rule for the all the traffic coming from the attacker's IP address.

Rate Limiting. Rate limiting is a simple, yet effective defense mechanism to mitigate a wide variety of attacks like scanning and DoS [23,29]. The most basic rate limiters, the ones assigning a maximum bandwidth to a given aggregate of network flows, are immediately recognizable for an attacker since they are directly defined in the rule matching the aggregate network flows [1]. More complex rate limiting approaches like those implemented in [23,29] limit the rate of new network flows by delaying the installation of rules. In particular, [29] introduces the notion of working set: for each given host, its working set is defined as the set of recently contacted hosts. Whenever a host creates a new network flow addressed at a host outside its working set, the controller will withhold the installation of the corresponding rule on the switch for a certain time. After this waiting time expires, the controller instructs the switch to forward the network flow without installing a rule. Only when the switch receives a positive reply from the destination host, the controller will install a new rule on the switch. An attacker can infer the presence of this defense mechanism by constantly probing the flow table of the switch after creating a new network flow. If rate limiting is in use, the attacker will notice that, even for extremely distant hosts, he will receive a response as soon as the rule is installed in the switch. Conversely, when no such technique is used, there will be a delay between the installation of the rule on the switch, which would happen as soon as the packet from the attacker reaches the switch, and the moment the reply is received. Therefore, by monitoring the delay in receiving a response after a rule is installed, the attacker can infer the use of this defense mechanism.

Whitehole Network. Another defense mechanism proposed in the literature is SYN proxy [4,26]. SYN proxy techniques aim at countering the SDN-specific control plane saturation attack [4,26]. Additionally, SYN proxy implements a whitehole network [26] at the switch level, providing mitigation also against network scans. When such countermeasures are employed, the scenario is slightly different since these are pro-active techniques that are always active, rather than triggered by the installation of a rule. Even in this case though, the attacker can infer the existence and the exact type of the defense mechanism employed by the network. Indeed when SYN proxy techniques are used, the attacker will receive a response SYN-ACK packet without a rule being installed on the switch [26]. Additionally, the attacker will always receive a response SYN-ACK packet to each and every of his probes, even if directed to himself. This behaviour exposes the use of proxy techniques at the data plane level to the attacker, who can attack the switches through vulnerabilities of the proxy approach [4].

Traffic Redirection. Traffic redirection is a popular defense mechanism since it provides many opportunities to defend a system [22,27]. For instance, a defender can opportunistically route malicious traffic towards a honeypot, allowing it to isolate the attacker and to study his behaviour [27]. In SDN these defense mechanisms are easy to detect for an attacker. Indeed, by monitoring how the control plane updates rule entries for some given network flows, the attacker can infer if his attack traffic is diverted towards a security middlebox/honeypot, nullifying the effect of the countermeasure. In order to do so, an attacker first generates a new legit network flow towards a given destination D_1 which is routed through a port P_i on the entry switch. The attacker then repeats this step with different destinations, until for a given destination D_n the controller pushes a rule instructing the switch to output the matching flow on a port $P_j <> P_i$. As a second step, the attacker generates probing traffic with a high profile (e.g., high scanning or DoS rate) towards destinations D_1 and D_n for a length of time, observing the rules installed in response. If traffic redirection techniques are in place, the control plane will install on the switch a new rule diverting the attack traffic towards the remote middlebox/honeypot. Therefore, all the attack traffic will be routed through the same output port on the switch. Since in the first phase the attacker selected the destinations D_1 and D_n such that packets towards them would be outputted on different ports, if all attack packets towards those same destinations are tunneled through the same output port, then a redirection mechanism is present in the network.

5   KYE Implementations

In order to prove the feasibility and effectiveness of the KYE attack, we implemented two instances of the attack on a test network. In this section, we present the detailed implementation of our attacks, that were aimed at disclosing:

1. The presence of a scanning detection and defense mechanism in the network. If present, we also wanted to estimate the detection threshold.
2. The presence of a subnetwork access control mechanism. If present, we wanted to learn the subnetwork access control matrix.

Figure 2 depicts the setup used for the evaluation, which includes: the attacker h_0, a single OpenFlow switch s_1 connected to the controller c, and 100 legit hosts $h_1 - h_{100}$. Hosts $h_1 - h_{100}$ represent known web servers that always reply to connection requests. Hosts $h_1 - h_{100}$, if needed, may be used by the attacker to obtain different connection success ratios during probing, and are not necessarily part of the target network.

Controller *c*

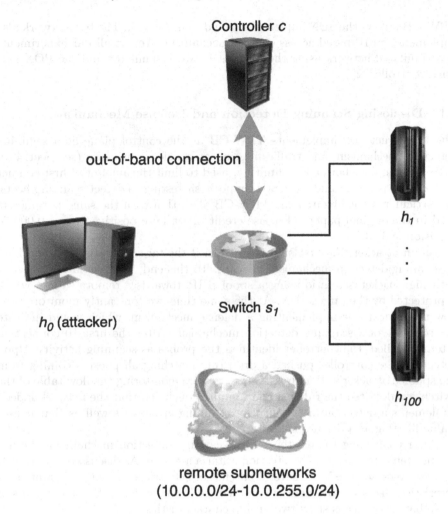

out-of-band connection

h_0 (attacker)

Switch s_1

h_1

h_{100}

remote subnetworks
(10.0.0.0/24-10.0.255.0/24)

Fig. 2. Experimental evaluation setup.

In order to simplify the simulation, in our experiments the target network is comprised only of the switch s_1 and the network controller c. Even though in our test network we deployed only a single controller and a single switch, our experiments do not lose generality. This is because the logic used by the controller is the same that would be used in a more complex network. Moreover, in general the controller pushes rules relative to a network flow on the first switch traversed by the flow. It is worth noting that it is not a requirement for the attacker to be directly connected to the OpenFlow switch, nor it is for hosts $h_1 - h_{100}$. This is just a simplification we adopted in order to run our simulation. In this test network, we implemented the TRW-CB scanning detection algorithm, which is one of the most used anomaly detection algorithms [7]. Our implementation of

TRW-CB follows the SDN implementation detailed in [23]. The test network also implements an IP-based access control mechanism. We ran all our experiments in a simulated network using the Mininet network simulator and the POX network controller [2].

5.1 Disclosing Scanning Detection and Defense Mechanisms

The target network implements TRW-CB at the control plane as a scanning detection mechanism, and traffic filtering as a defense measure (see Sect. 4.2). TRW-CB employs both credit limiting, used to limit the amount of first contact connections pending, and sequential hypothesis testing to detect scanning hosts. In particular, we configured the TRW-CB algorithm with the same parameters used in the original paper [24] (base credit of 10, false positive rate ≤ 0.00005, precision ≥ 0.99).

As an attacker, the first step is to learn if the target network has any kind of scanning detection mechanism in place. To this end, we first initiated a scan with high packet/sec ratio using a spoofed IP, towards a remote subnet which is protected by the target SDN. At the same time, we constantly monitored the flow table for a rule implementing a defense mechanism, which would indicate the presence of a scanning detection mechanism. After the first 10 connection attempts failed, the controller identified the probes as scanning activity. Upon detection, the controller pushed a drop rule matching all packets coming from the spoofed attacker's IP address. Since we were monitoring the flow table of the switch, we detected the rule installation and concluded that the network indeed implements a detection mechanism for scanning attacks, as well as that it uses traffic filtering as a defense measure.

After confirming the existence of a scanning detection mechanism, the following step is to learn which detection criteria are used. As discussed in Sect. 4.1, in order to do so we initiate several batches of network scans with different characteristics, like scan rate and successful/failed connections ratio. The results of these batches of scans show two visible characteristics:

1. The scanning activity is detected regardless of the scanning rate. This behaviour excludes rate-based scanning detection mechanisms.
2. For scan batches where connection requests were sent only towards h_1, h_{100} (which should all send back a response), we received replies only from some of them, as illustrated in Fig. 3.

The behaviour shown in Fig. 3 is consistent with rate limiting techniques, where connection requests sent at a rate above a certain threshold are dropped. To investigate this anomaly, we started a new scan towards h_1, h_{100} with slightly lower rate. The results are illustrated in Fig. 4. As we can see, connections are allowed in bursts: replies were received for the first 10 connections, then 39 requests were dropped, after which connection attempts 50 through 69 were successful, and then connections were dropped once again. Since the scanning rate was constant for all the 100 connection attempts, this behaviour excludes

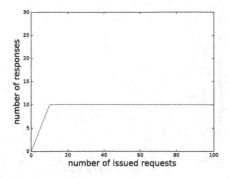

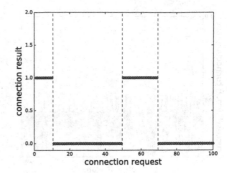

Fig. 3. Number of responses received vs. number of requests issued towards h_1, h_{100} at each batch.

Fig. 4. Connection result for each request of the batch sent towards a known host. 1 indicates a successful connection, 0 a failure (i.e., no response received).

a standard rate limiting technique. Indeed, from Fig. 4 we can see how a host is allowed to contact up to 10 new hosts (i.e., 10 starting credits), after which connections are blocked until pending replies are received. Upon receiving the replies, new credits are allocated to the host, whose connections are correctly forwarded once again. This pattern is consistent with the presence of a credit based rate limiting mechanism [24]. At this point, through the KYE attack, we learned that:

- The network is using a detection mechanism for scanning, which is not rate based.
- The network is using drop rules as a defense mechanism against scanning. Moreover, the network employs an additional preemptive defense measure in the form of credit based rate limiting. Each host is assigned a starting balance of 10 credits and for each successful connection the hosts receives 2 additional credits (the initial 10 successful connections allowed 20 more connections after replies were received).

In the final step of the KYE attack, we initiated several batches of scans, with varying successful/failed connection ratios and scan duration. Each scanning batch terminated either after all planned scans were preformed, or abruptly upon detection. Since we are only interested in the characteristics of the scanning attacks that are detected, we isolate detected batches from undetected ones. For the batches of scans that were detected, Fig. 5 shows the ratio of successful connections over the total number of connections issued and Fig. 6 shows the cumulative distribution function of the ratio of failed connections over total number of connections. As these two figures show, the scanning detection criteria employed by the network is clearly based on the ratio of successful and failed connections. Indeed, from Fig. 5 we see that network scans are never detected when the ratio of successful connection over the total number of issued connections is above ~ 0.45.

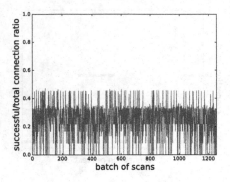
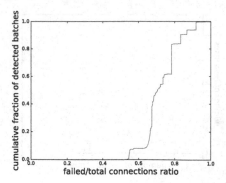

Fig. 5. Ratio of the number of successful connections over the number of total connections, for each batch of scans which resulted in detection.

Fig. 6. Empirical cumulative distribution function of the ratio of failed connections over total number of connections, for batches of scans which resulted in detection.

Conversely, from Fig. 6 we can see that network scans are detected when the ratio of failed connections over total number of issued connections is above ~ 0.55, and never detected when it is below that threshold.

5.2   Disclosing the Subnetwork Access Control Matrix

After learning the scanning detection criteria used by the network through a KYE attack, we show that we can also infer the complete access control matrix used by the network without being detected by the controller. In our test network, we configured the POX controller with a set of static access control policies, where access to a certain subnetwork is allowed only from a subset of all subnetworks. Whenever a connection request from an unauthorized address is received, the controller instructs the switch to drop the packet without installing any rule. If the connection request is from an authorized address, the controller installs a normal forwarding rule on the switch for subsequent packets. In this setting, we perform a KYE attack, sending scan probes from each subnetwork to every other. Since with the previous attack we inferred the detection criteria used by the network for scans, *we can now perform this network scan attack completely undetected.* The attack itself is very simple: at each scan probe, we spoof the source address to make it look like the source of the connection is part of a given subnetwork. We repeat the scan for each pair of source and destination remote subnetworks in the range $10.0.0.0\backslash24 - 10.0.255.0\backslash24$, while opening enough successful connections to remain below the detection threshold. After each scan, we read the flow table of the switch to detect which rule is installed. By monitoring the flow table, we see that no rules are installed when the source IP is not allowed to access the subnetwork, while a forwarding rule is installed when the access is authorized. Through this observation we are able to build

Table 1. Subnetwork access matrix for the target network, learned by the attacker through a KYE attack. Notation ✓: access allowed; notation ✗: access restricted.

	10.0.0.0/24	10.0.1.0/24	10.0.2.0/24	10.0.3.0/24	10.0.5.0/24
10.0.0.0/24	✓	✓	✗	✗	✗
10.0.1.0/24	✓	✓	✗	✗	✗
10.0.2.0/24	✗	✗	✓	✓	✗
10.0.3.0/24	✗	✗	✓	✓	✗
10.0.5.0/24	✗	✗	✗	✗	✓

the access control matrix illustrated in Table 1, which reflects exactly the access control rules that were set up at the network controller.

6   Related Work

SDN has become a popular research topic in recent years, especially in relation to security. In [21], Kreutz et al. discuss the effects of an attacker compromising a switch in the network, which can result in traffic injection attacks, man-in-the-middle attacks and traffic filtering. Similarly, in [6] the authors consider an attacker with full control over the switch and discuss several possible attacks like man-in-the-middle, state, and topology spoofing. However, in these works the attacker actively modifies the state of the switch, exposing him to detection by the controller through querying the state of the switch [9,20] or RTT analysis [6]. In [16], Klöti et al. prove that by analyzing the RTT for a specific network flow, an attacker is able to infer if a rule is already installed for that network flow. While the goal of this attack is to obtain some information on the state of a switch, the KYE attack allows to learn a much greater amount of information about the logic and policies of the network, such as attack detection threshold and defense mechanisms applied. More recently, Sonchack et al. [28] developed a timing attack aimed at disclosing sensitive information about the network. This attack shares the same goal of obtaining knowledge on the behaviour of the network with our attack, but differs in both how it is achieved and in the detail of information that can be gathered.

7   Conclusions

In this paper, we proposed a thorough analysis of the vulnerability introduced by the on-demand installation of rules in SDN. We presented the novel KYE attack, which allows an adversary to gather an extensive amount of information regarding the configuration of the network, ranging from security-related aspects to network engineering policies. We implemented the KYE attack and conducted a thorough evaluation, showing its feasibility and its efficacy against a popular scanning detection algorithm and against standard access control policies.

Acknowledgement. This work has been supported by the EU H2020 Programme under the SUNFISH project, grant agreement N.644666. Mauro Conti is supported by a Marie Curie Fellowship funded by the European Commission (agreement PCIG11-GA-2012-321980). This work is also partially supported by the EU TagItSmart! Project (agreement H2020-ICT30-2015-688061), the EU-India REACH Project (agreement ICI+/2014/342-896), and by the projects "Physical-Layer Security for Wireless Communication", and "Content Centric Networking: Security and Privacy Issues" funded by the University of Padua. This work is partially supported by the grant n. 2017-166478 (3696) from Cisco University Research Program Fund and Silicon Valley Community Foundation.

References

1. Openflow specification. https://www.opennetworking.org/images/stories/downloads/sdn-resources/onf-specifications/openflow/openflow-switch-v1.5.1.pdf. Accessed 03 2016
2. Pox network controller. https://github.com/noxrepo/pox. Accessed 05 2016
3. Al-Shaer, E.S., et al.: Modeling and management of firewall policies. IEEE Trans. Netw. Serv. Manage. **1**, 2–10 (2004)
4. Ambrosin, M., et al.: Lineswitch: efficiently managing switch flow in software-defined networking while effectively tackling DoS attacks. In: ACM Symposium on Information, Computer and Communications Security (2015)
5. Ambrosin, M., et al.: Lineswitch: tackling control plane saturation attacks in software-defined networking. In: IEEE/ACM Transactions on Networking (2016)
6. Antikainen, M., Aura, T., Särelä, M.: Spook in your network: attacking an SDN with a compromised openflow switch. In: Bernsmed, K., Fischer-Hübner, S. (eds.) NordSec 2014. LNCS, vol. 8788, pp. 229–244. Springer, Cham (2014). doi:10.1007/978-3-319-11599-3_14
7. Ashfaq, A.B., et al.: A comparative evaluation of anomaly detectors under portscan attacks. In: Symposium on Recent Advances in Intrusion Detection (2008)
8. Ateniese, G., et al.: Hacking smart machines with smarter ones: how to extract meaningful data from machine learning classifiers. Int. J. Secur. Netw. **10**, 137–150 (2015)
9. Benton, K., et al.: Openflow vulnerability assessment. In: ACM SIGCOMM Workshop on Hot Topics in Software Defined Networking (2013)
10. Braga, R., et al.: Lightweight DDoS flooding attack detection using NOX/OpenFlow. In: Conference on Local Computer Networks (2010)
11. Chung, C.J., et al.: Nice: network intrusion detection and countermeasure selection in virtual network systems. IEEE Trans. Dependable Secure Comput. **10**, 198–211 (2013)
12. Dhawan, M., et al.: Sphinx: detecting security attacks in software-defined networks. In: Network and Distributed System Security Symposium (2015)
13. Drutskoy, D., et al.: Scalable network virtualization in software-defined networks. IEEE Internet Comput. **17**, 20–27 (2013)
14. Ahmad, I., et al.: Security in software defined networks: a survey. IEEE Commun. Surv. Tutorials **17**, 2317–2346 (2015)
15. Suh, M., et al.: Building firewall over the software-defined network controller. In: International Conference on Advanced Communication Technology (2014)
16. Kloti, R., et al.: OpenFlow: a security analysis. In: IEEE International Conference on Network Protocols (2013)

17. Giotis, K., et al.: Combining OpenFlow and sFlow for an effective and scalable anomaly detection and mitigation mechanism on SDN environments. Comput. Netw. **62**, 122–136 (2016)
18. Hu, H., et al.: FLOWGUARD: building robust firewalls for software-defined networks. In: Workshop on Hot Topics in Software Defined Networking, HotSDN 2014 (2014)
19. Jain, S., et al.: B4: experience with a globally-deployed software defined WAN. In: SIGCOMM Computer Communication Review (2013)
20. Kamisiński, A., et al.: FlowMon: detecting malicious switches in software-defined networks. In: Automated Decision Making for Active Cyber Defense (2015)
21. Kreutz, D., et al.: Towards secure and dependable software-defined networks. In: ACM SIGCOMM Workshop on Hot Topics in Software Defined Networking (2013)
22. Mahimkar, A., et al.: Dfence: transparent network-based denial of service mitigation. In: USENIX Conference on Networked Systems Design and Implementation (2007)
23. Mehdi, S.A., Khalid, J., Khayam, S.A.: Revisiting traffic anomaly detection using software defined networking. In: Sommer, R., Balzarotti, D., Maier, G. (eds.) RAID 2011. LNCS, vol. 6961, pp. 161–180. Springer, Heidelberg (2011). doi:10.1007/978-3-642-23644-0_9
24. Schechter, S.E., Jung, J., Berger, A.W.: Fast detection of scanning worm infections. In: Jonsson, E., Valdes, A., Almgren, M. (eds.) RAID 2004. LNCS, vol. 3224, pp. 59–81. Springer, Heidelberg (2004). doi:10.1007/978-3-540-30143-1_4
25. Scott-Hayward, S., et al.: A survey of security in software defined networks. IEEE Commun. Surv. Tutorials (2016)
26. Shin, S., et al.: AVANT-GUARD: scalable and vigilant switch flow management in software-defined networks. In: ACM Conference on Computer and Communications Security (2013)
27. Shin, S., et al.: Fresco: modular composable security services for software-defined networks. In: Network and Distributed System Security Symposium (2013)
28. Sonchack, J., et al.: Timing-based reconnaissance and defense in software-defined networks. In: Annual Conference on Computer Security Applications (2016)
29. Twycross, J., et al.: Implementing and testing a virus throttle. In: USENIX Security Symposium (2003)
30. Wang, J., et al.: Towards a security-enhanced firewall application for openflow networks. In: Symposium on Cyberspace Safety and Security, CSS 2013 (2013)

SOOA: Exploring Special On-Off Attacks on Challenge-Based Collaborative Intrusion Detection Networks

Wenjuan Li[1], Weizhi Meng[2(✉)], and Lam-For Kwok[1]

[1] Department of Computer Science, City University of Hong Kong,
Kowloon Tong, Hong Kong
wenjuan.li@my.cityu.edu.hk
[2] Department of Applied Mathematics and Computer Science,
Technical University of Denmark, Kongens Lyngby, Denmark
weme@dtu.dk

Abstract. The development of collaborative intrusion detection networks (CIDNs) aims to enhance the performance of a single intrusion detection system (IDS), through communicating and collecting information from other IDS nodes. To defend CIDNs against insider attacks, trust-based mechanisms are crucial for evaluating the trustworthiness of a node. In the literature, challenge-based trust mechanisms are well established to identify malicious nodes by identifying the deviation between challenges and responses. However, such mechanisms rely on two major assumptions, which may result in a weak threat model and render CIDNs still vulnerable to advanced insider attacks in a practical deployment. In this paper, our motivation is to investigate the effect of On-Off attacks on challenge-based CIDNs. In particular, as a study, we explore a special On-Off attack (called *SOOA*), which can keep responding normally to one node while acting abnormally to another node. In the evaluation, we explore the attack performance under simulated CIDN environments. Experimental results indicate that our attack can interfere the effectiveness of trust computation for CIDN nodes.

Keywords: Intrusion Detection System · Collaborative network · On-off attacks · Challenge-based CIDN · Trust management

1 Introduction

Intrusion detection systems (IDSs) have been developed over decades to identify various network or system threats [15]. Based on the location, it can be classified as either *network-based (NIDS)* or *host-based (HIDS)*. In particular, HIDSs protect an end system or network application by auditing system events and look at the state of a computer system. NIDSs mainly monitor network traffic

---

W. Meng—The author was previously known as Yuxin Meng.

M.H.A. Au et al. (Eds.): GPC 2017, LNCS 10232, pp. 402–415, 2017.
DOI: 10.1007/978-3-319-57186-7_30

and identify attacks by sitting outside the firewall on the demilitarized zone (DMZ), or anywhere inside the private network [7].

Due to the increasing complexity of intrusions, many studies (e.g., [3,17]) have uncovered that a single or isolated IDS could be easily bypassed by advanced attacks, in which these attacks may cause potential damage if failed to detect timely (i.e., causing paralysis of the entire network). With the purpose of improving the detection capability of single IDSs, collaborative intrusion detection networks (CIDNs) have been developed that allow various IDS nodes to require and collect useful information from other nodes [17]. However, insider attacks are one big challenge for CIDNs, which can greatly degrade the network performance and security [3]. In this case, there is a strong need to design effective mechanisms to detect insider attacks in a collaborative environment.

To safeguard CIDNs against insider threats, designing trust-based mechanisms is one of the promising solutions. In the literature, challenge-based trust mechanisms (shortly *challenge mechanisms*) [6] have been developed, where testing nodes can send *challenges* to evaluate the trustworthiness of tested nodes. Under this mechanism, a challenge can contain a set of alarms requesting for severity. As the testing node extracts the alarms from its database, it knows the severity of the alert located in a challenge. Thus, it can compute its satisfaction level between the expected answer and the received feedback. A series of studies [4–6] have shown that such mechanism can prevent insider attacks, like collusion attacks, where malicious nodes collaborate to give false alarm rankings to reduce the effectiveness of alarm aggregation.

Motivation and Contributions. However, it is found that such challenge mechanism depends on two major assumptions [4,5]: (a) challenges are sent out in a way that makes them difficult to be distinguished from normal messages; and (b) malicious nodes always send feedback opposite to its truthful judgment. In practical deployment, we notice that malicious nodes may act more dynamic and complex. Consequently, these assumptions may be not realistic in practical scenarios and render CIDNs still vulnerable to *advanced* insider attacks. In this work, we aim to investigate the influence of a Special On-Off Attack, named *SOOA*, which can keep giving truthful responses to one node while providing untruthful answers to other nodes. Our contributions of this work can be summarized as below:

- We review existing challenge-based CIDNs and analyze the adopted assumptions. As a study, we design a special On-Off attack (named *SOOA*), which can keep responding normally to one node, but acting abnormally to another node. As a result, it may affect the trust computation for the target node, which would collect information from its partner nodes.
- In the evaluation, we explore the attack performance under a simulated CIDN environment, and the results demonstrate that our attack can greatly affect the trust computation and has a potential to compromise the robustness of CIDNs. In the end, we discuss some potential countermeasures to defend against such attack.

It is worth emphasizing that challenge mechanisms are an important way to protect CIDNs against common insider attacks. The major purpose of this work is to analyze its robustness on some advanced attacks. Our work aims to stimulate more attention in protecting CIDNs in real-world scenarios.

The remainder of this paper is organized as follows. Section 2 introduces the background of challenge-based CIDNs and analyzes the adopted assumptions. Section 3 describes our special On-Off attack ($SOOA$) and how it works in a real scenario. Section 4 explores the influence of $SOOA$ in a simulated CIDN and analyzes the collected results. Section 5 reviews related work. Finally, we conclude the work in Sect. 6.

2   Challenge-Based CIDNs

2.1   Background

To defend against insider attacks, various trust-based mechanisms have been proposed [1]. Among those, challenge-based trust mechanisms are one effective means to identify malicious nodes in CIDNs. Figure 1 describes the high-level architecture of a typical challenge-based CIDN.

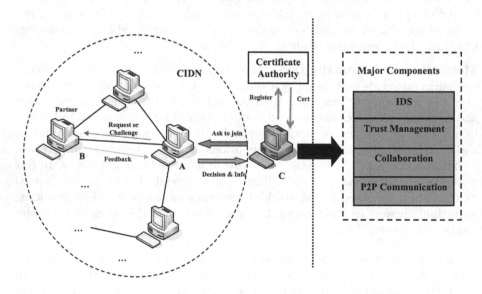

Fig. 1. The high-level architecture of a typical challenge-based CIDN.

In such CIDN, IDS nodes can be associated if they have a collaborative relationship. In particular, each IDS node can choose its partners or collaborators based on its own experience, and can maintain a list of their collaborated nodes, called *partner list* (or *acquaintance list*). Such list is customizable and stores information of other nodes (e.g., public keys and their trust values). If a new node wants to join the network, it has to firstly register to a trusted Certificate Authority (*CA*) and to obtain its unique proof of identity (e.g., a public key and a private key). As an example shown in Fig. 1, if node *C* wants to join the network, it needs to send an application to a network node, say node *A*. Then, node *A* makes a decision and sends back an initial *partner list*, if node *C* is accepted.

To enhance the performance of single IDS nodes, CIDNs allow IDS nodes to send messages and collect feedback to/from other nodes. There are two major types of messages during node interactions.

- *Challenges*. A challenge contains a set of IDS alarms asking for severity ranking. For instance, a testing node can send a challenge to other tested nodes and obtain their relevant feedback. As the testing node extracts the alarms from its own database, it can know the severity of the delivered alarms in advance. As a result, it can evaluate the tested nodes' trustworthiness (e.g., satisfaction level) through identifying the deviation between the expected and the received feedback.
- *Normal requests*. A normal request is used for alarm aggregation. For example, if a node wants to aggregate alarms, it can send a request to other IDS nodes, and those nodes should provide alarm ranking information as their feedback. It is worth noting that alarm aggregation is a very important feature for CIDNs, which aims to improve the detection performance. Moreover, alarm aggregation usually considers the feedback from only trusted nodes.

Major components. As shown in Fig. 1, an IDS node contains an *IDS component* and is composed of several major components, including *trust management component*, *collaboration component* and *P2P communication*. The details are discussed as below:

- *Trust management component*. This component is responsible for evaluating the trustworthiness of other nodes. Under the challenge mechanism, the trustworthiness of other nodes is mainly computed by comparing the expected answer with the received feedback. As discussed above, each node can send either *normal requests* or *challenges* for alert ranking (consultation). To protect challenges, it is worth noting that challenges should be sent out in a random manner and in a way that makes them difficult to be distinguished from a normal request for alarm ranking.
- *Collaboration component*. This component aims to help a node in evaluating the trustworthiness of others through delivering *normal requests* or *challenges*, and receiving the relevant *feedback*. If a tested node receives a request or challenge, this component will help send back its feedback. As shown in Fig. 1, if node *A* sends a *request/challenge* to node *B*, then node *B* will send back relevant feedback.
- *P2P communication*. This component is responsible for connecting with other IDS nodes and providing network organization, management and communication among various IDS nodes.

Robustness. A series of research studies (e.g., [4–6]) have shown that challenge-based trust mechanisms can protect CIDNs against common insider attacks including Sybil attack, newcomer attack and betrayal attack.

- *Sybil attack.* This attack indicates the situation when a malicious node creates a lot of fake identities [2]. The malicious node then can utilize these fake identities to gain larger influence on the process of alert aggregation. As shown in Fig. 1, as an IDS node should register itself to a *CA* and obtain a unique proof identity, this kind of attack can be mitigated.
- *Newcomer (re-entry) attack.* This attack indicates the situation when a malicious node registers as a new user aiming to erase its bad history. Challenge-based CIDNs can mitigate such attack by giving low initial trust values to all newcomers.
- *Betrayal attack.* This attack indicates the situation when a trusted node becomes a malicious one suddenly. Challenge mechanism employs a strategy: a high trust should be taken a long-time interaction and consistent good behavior to build, while only a few bad actions to ruin it. To achieve this, a forgetting factor is used to give more credits to recent behaviors.

On the whole, challenge-based CIDNs can enable collaborations among IDS nodes, as well as identify common insider attacks. However, in real-world deployment [8,9,11], we find that challenge-based trust mechanisms rely on two main assumptions, which may be vulnerable to some advanced insider attacks.

2.2   Assumption Analysis

As stated above, challenge-based trust mechanisms can defend against most common insider attacks. However, in real implementations [8,9], we notice that this mechanism depends heavily on two assumptions (or conditions).

- *Assumption-1.* Challenges are sent out in a random way and in a way that makes them difficult to be distinguished from normal messages.
- *Assumption-2.* Malicious nodes always send feedback opposite to its truthful judgment.

The first assumption indicates that an IDS node cannot distinguish a challenge from normal messages, ensuring that it has a small possibility for a malicious node to give manipulated feedback to challenges. However, this assumption still leaves a chance for attackers to figure out the challenges in practice. For example, Li *et al.* [11] identified that launching an advanced attack, called passive message fingerprint attack, can distinguish messages from challenges with a high probability.

The second assumption describes that malicious nodes always send feedback opposite to its truthful judgment, ensuring that the trust values of malicious nodes will decrease rapidly. For example, Fung *et al.* [6] adopted a *maximal harm model* where an adversary always chooses to report false feedback with the intention to bring the most negative impact to the request sender. However, in a practical scenario, this seems obviously not realistic. Even for a malicious node, it can still send truthful feedback and try to maintain its trust values.

Discussion. These two assumptions are reasonable in some cases, where attackers are naive and adopt a maximal harm model. Whilst in real scenarios, advanced attackers may perform much more dynamic behaviors to compromise a CIDN node (i.e., a strategy which is different from maximal harm model). For instance, a malicious node can respond truthful feedback to certain nodes and compromise the trust computation of another node. Overall, we find that these assumptions may result in a weak threat model in real-world applications and leave CIDNs still vulnerable to advanced attacks.

3   On-Off Attack

As discussed above, challenge-based CIDNs may be vulnerable to some advanced attacks in practice, due to the adopted assumptions. In this section, we introduce On-Off attacks and study a special On-Off attack (called $SOOA$), which can keep responding normally to one node while acting abnormally to another node. It is worth noting that we accept the first assumption, but assume that a malicious node can choose whether to send a malicious feedback or not.

On-Off Attacks. Generally, an On-Off attack [14] indicates the situation that an attacker behaves well and badly alternatively, which can compromise the network if they remain as trusted nodes. The typical attack has two states: *on-state*, when the associated action is effectively happening, and *off-state*, when the associated action is not happening. By behaving as a good node and as a bad node alternatively, this attack may cause the scheme to consider the behavior of a bad node as a temporary error. A high ratio of *off-state* in relation to *on-state* is a more effective attack, while a low ratio might make it more easy for a trust management scheme to detect the malicious behavior.

SOOA. As a study, we consider a special On-Off attack ($SOOA$) for challenge-based CIDNs, where a malicious node can keep sending truthful responses to one node, but sending malicious responses to another. This attack has a potential to affect the effectiveness of trust computation for a third node (target node). Here, we accept that a challenge is sent in a random manner and cannot be distinguished from normal messages, so that all malicious nodes are not able to identify a challenge. Figure 2 describes an example of $SOOA$: suppose node D is malicious and node A is the attack target, node B and node C are partner nodes for node A. Two attacking scenarios can be described as below.

– **Scenario 1: node D is not partner node for node A.** In this scenario, node D chooses to send truthful response to node C while send untruthful (or malicious) response to node B. Figure 2 shows that node A can communicate and collect data with/from its partner nodes; thus, node A may receive different (or opposite) reports on node D. This scenario often occurs for a hierarchical network structure, where a central server needs to collect information and judge the trustworthiness of each node.

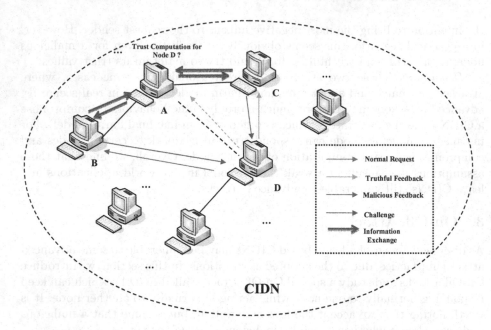

Fig. 2. An example of a special On-Off attack (SOOA) on challenge-based CIDNs.

– **Scenario 2: node D is a partner node for node A.** In this scenario, node D can response truthfully to node A, if they are partner nodes. In CIDNs, node A can judge the trustworthiness of node D through both its own trust computation and the judgement from other nodes. As a result, our special attack may maintain the trust values of node D above the threshold as for node A.

On the whole, our attack $SOOA$ can choose to give truthful feedback to several nodes, while respond untruthful feedback to others. As a result, it may affect the trust computation of certain nodes and maintain its trust values above the threshold. In this work, we mainly focus on *Scenario 2*, since a CIDN node usually aggregates alarms from its partner nodes.

4   Evaluation

In this section, we conduct a study to evaluate the attack performance in a simulated CIDN environment, where malicious node is a partner node for target node. Next, we introduce CIDN settings (i.e., how to compute trust values and satisfaction levels) and discuss experimental results.

4.1   CIDN Settings

There are 15 nodes in the simulated CIDN environment, which are randomly distributed in a 5×5 grid region. We use Snort [16] as IDS plugin that can be

Table 1. Simulation parameters in the experiment.

Parameters	Value	Description
λ	0.9	Forgetting factor
ε_l	10/day	Low request frequency
ε_h	20/day	High request frequency
r	0.8	Trust threshold
T_s	0.5	Trust value for new comers
m	10	Lower limit of received feedback
d	0.3	Severity of punishment

implemented in a node. Each IDS node can connect to other nodes and establish an initial *partner list* based on the distance. The initial trust values of all nodes in the *partner list* are set to $T_s = 0.5$ based on [5].

To evaluate the trustworthiness of partner nodes, each IDS node can send out challenges randomly to its partners with an average rate of ε. There are two levels of request frequency: ε_l and ε_h. For a highly trusted or highly untrusted node, the request frequency is low, since it should be very confident about the decision of their feedback. On the other hand, the request frequency should be high for other nodes whose trust values are close to threshold. To facilitate comparisons, all the settings can be referred to [5,9]. It is worth emphasizing that we set low request frequency to 10 per day, which is more strict than the frequency in [5]. The detailed parameters are summarized in Table 1.

Node expertise. Three expertise levels are employed for an IDS node as low (0.1), medium (0.5) and high (0.95). The expertise of an IDS can be represented using a beta function described as below:

$$f(p'|\alpha, \beta) = \frac{1}{B(\alpha, \beta)} p'^{\alpha-1}(1 - p')^{\beta-1}$$

$$B(\alpha, \beta) = \int_0^1 t^{\alpha-1}(1 - t)^{\beta-1}dt \tag{1}$$

where $p'(\in [0, 1])$ is the probability of intrusion examined by the IDS. $f(p'|\alpha, \beta)$ means the probability that a node with expertise level l responses with a value of p' to an intrusion examination of difficulty level $d(\in [0, 1])$. A higher value of l means a higher probability of correctly identifying an intrusion while a higher value of d means that an intrusion is more difficult to detect. In particular, α and β can be defined as [5]:

$$\alpha = 1 + \frac{l(1-d)}{d(1-l)}r$$

$$\beta = 1 + \frac{l(1-d)}{d(1-l)}(1-r) \tag{2}$$

where $r \in \{0, 1\}$ is the expected result of detection. For a fixed difficulty level, the node with higher level of expertise can achieve higher probability of correctly detecting an intrusion. For example, a node with expertise level of 1 can accurately identify an intrusion with guarantee if the difficulty level is 0.

Node Trust Evaluation. To evaluate the trustworthiness of a target node, a testing node can send a *challenge* to the tested node through a random generation process. The testing node then can compute a score to reflect its satisfaction level. Based on [4], we can evaluate the trustworthiness of a node i according to node j as follows:

$$T_i^j = (w_s \frac{\sum_{k=0}^{n} F_k^{j,i} \lambda^{tk}}{\sum_{k=0}^{n} \lambda^{tk}} - T_s)(1 - x)^d + T_s \qquad (3)$$

where $F_k^{j,i} \in [0,1]$ is the score of the received feedback k and n is the total number of feedback. λ is a *forgetting factor* that assigns less weight to older feedback response. w_s is a *significant weight* depending on the total number of received feedback, if there is only a few feedback under a certain minimum m, then $w_s = \frac{\sum_{k=0}^{n} \lambda^{tk}}{m}$, otherwise $w_s = 1$. x is the percentage of "don't know" answers during a period (e.g., from $t0$ to tn). d is a positive incentive parameter to control the severity of punishment to "don't know" replies. More details about equation derivation can be referred to [4,5].

Satisfaction Evaluation. Suppose there are two factors: an expected feedback ($e \in [0,1]$) and an actual received feedback ($r \in [0,1]$). Then, a function F ($\in [0,1]$) can be used to reflect the satisfaction by measuring the difference between the received answer and the expected answer as below [5]:

$$F = 1 - (\frac{e - r}{max(c_1 e, 1 - e)})^{c_2} \quad e > r \qquad (4)$$

$$F = 1 - (\frac{c_1(r - e)}{max(c_1 e, 1 - e)})^{c_2} \quad e \le r \qquad (5)$$

where c_1 controls the degree of penalty for wrong estimates and c_2 controls satisfaction sensitivity. A larger c_2 means more sensitive. In this work, we set $c_1 = 1.5$ and $c_2 = 1$ based on the simulation in [5].

4.2 Experiment

In this simulation, we conduct an experiment to explore the effect of $SOOA$ on challenge-based CIDNs. As shown in Fig. 2, suppose node A has seven partner nodes and node D is a partner node of node A. In this scenario, node D chooses to send truthful response to several partner nodes of node A, while send untruthful (or malicious) response to the rest partner nodes. The results are depicted in Figs. 3 and 4.

Figure 3 depicts the convergence of trust values for different expert nodes: low ($I = 0.1$), medium ($I = 0.5$) and high ($I = 0.95$). The results are in line with the

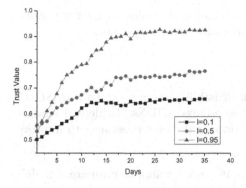
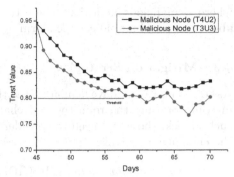

Fig. 3. Convergence of trust values of IDS nodes regarding three expertise levels.

Fig. 4. Trust values of malicious node (say node D) calculated by target node (say node A) under *SOOA*.

results observed in [4,5]: that is, nodes with higher expertise can achieve bigger trust values. The trust values of all nodes became stable after around 16 days in the simulated network.

As a study, we randomly selected one expert node ($I = 0.95$) as malicious one (say node D), which conducted our special attack from Day 45. The trust computation of target node (say node A) is shown in Fig. 4. We test two conditions: (1) node D sent truthful feedback to four partner nodes of node A while sent untruthful feedback to the remaining two partner nodes (T4U2); (2) node D responded truthful feedback to three partner nodes while sent untruthful feedback to the remaining three partner nodes (T3U3). It is worth noting that node D always sends truthful feedback to node A. The main observations are described as below:

- *T4U2*. In this condition, the trust value of node D computed by node A could gradually decrease closer to the threshold during the first ten days, because two partner nodes could report malicious actions of node D to node A. Afterwards, the trust value was maintained in the range from 0.81 to 0.82 at most cases, as there are four partner nodes reported that node D is normal. As the trust value is higher than the threshold 0.8, node D still has an impact on node A and its alarm aggregation.
- *T3U3*. In this condition, node D sent truthful feedback to three partner nodes of node A, but sent malicious feedback to the other three partner nodes. It is found that the trust value of node D computed by node A could keep decreasing during the first 15 days, where maintained around the threshold. As node D always sends truthful feedback to node A, its trust value may below or above the threshold crossly.

As compared to the results in [4,5], it is found that our attack can greatly degrade the effectiveness and robustness of challenge-based CIDNs, where a malicious node has a non-trivial chance to maintain its trust value above threshold and affect the alarm aggregation for a target node.

4.3 Mitigation Strategies

As stated above, we have demonstrated the feasibility of our special attack *SOOA* in compromising the robustness of challenge-based CIDNs. To defend against such attack, there is a need to consider additional countermeasures to improve the challenge mechanisms.

- *Impact of malicious actions.* In CIDNs, if a node wants to evaluate a node's trustworthiness, it can collect information from other trusted nodes. However, malicious nodes may conduct On-Off attack to leverage its trust value, whilst behave maliciously. To defend against such attack, one potential solution is to punish more on malicious actions, if detected by a node.
- *Additional measurement.* In challenge-based CIDNs, the trustworthiness of a node is mainly determined by challenges, whereas it may still leave a chance for attackers. To further increase the robustness of CIDNs, additional measures can be used to compute the trust values of a node, like packet-level trust [13].

Overall, our study validates that advanced attacks are able to compromise challenge-based CIDNs in real scenarios. To defend against these advanced threats, more advanced threat models should be considered in designing practical trust mechanisms for CIDNs.

5 Related Work

Collaborative intrusion detection networks (CIDNs) were developed to enhance the performance of single IDSs, which have less information about the deployed environment. The improvement can be achieved through requesting and collecting useful information from other IDS nodes. However, such collaborations may be vulnerable to insider attacks. To protect CIDNs against insider threats, designing robust trust-based mechanisms is one of the promising solutions.

Trust aware mechanism. Duma *et al.* [3] proposed a P2P-based overlay for intrusion detection (Overlay IDS) that used a trust-aware engine for correlating alerts and an adaptive scheme for managing trust. The trust-aware correlation engine is capable of filtering out warnings sent by untrusted or low quality peers and the adaptive trust management scheme uses past experiences of peers to predict their trustworthiness. Meng *et al.* [13] proposed a trust-based mechanism using Bayesian inference to identify insider attacks for medical smartphone networks. The evaluation validated the effectiveness of the proposed approach in real scenarios.

Challenge-based trust mechanism. To protect CIDNs, Fung *et al.* [6] proposed challenge-based mechanism, in which the trustworthiness of a node depends on the received answers to the challenges. Firstly they proposed a HIDS collaboration framework [4], where each HIDS could evaluate the trustworthiness of others based on its own experience by means of a forgetting factor. The forgetting factor aimed to give more emphasis on the recent experience of the peer. Then, they improved the built trust management model by using a Dirichlet-based model to measure the level of trustworthiness among IDS nodes according to their mutual experience [5]. This model had strong scalability properties and was robust against common insider threats. The experimental results proved that the new model could improve robustness and efficiency.

As challenge-based CIDNs can provide many benefits, Li *et al.* [8] aimed to improve the performance of challenge-based CIDNs and identified that different IDS nodes may have different levels of sensitivity in detecting different types of intrusions. Then, they proposed a notion of *intrusion sensitivity*, which measures the detection sensitivity of an IDS in detecting different kinds of intrusions. For instance, if a signature-based IDS node has a larger set of signatures (or rules) in detecting DoS attacks, then it should be considered as more powerful in detecting this kind of attacks than other nodes (which have relatively fewer related signatures). An intrusion sensitivity-based trust management model [9,12] was then developed for CIDNs through automating the allocation of intrusion sensitivity by using machine learning techniques in practice. A study was also conducted to investigate the effect of *intrusion sensitivity* on defending against pollution attacks, in which a group of malicious peers cooperate together by providing false alert rankings [10]. The above experimental results demonstrated that *intrusion sensitivity* can help decrease the trust values of malicious nodes more quickly, through emphasizing the impact of expert nodes.

Advanced attack. As challenge mechanisms can defend against common attacks well, research has been conducted on advanced attack. Li *et al.* [11] designed a kind of collusion attack, called *passive message fingerprint attack* (PMFA), which can collect messages and identify normal requests in a passive way. The experimental results indicated that such attack could enable malicious nodes to send malicious responses to normal requests while maintain their trust values. In this work, we design a special case of On-Off attacks and study its influence on the performance of challenge mechanisms.

6   Conclusion

Challenge-based CIDNs are developed allowing a single IDS node to collect useful information from other nodes. However, in real-world applications, we identify that such mechanisms may be still vulnerable to advanced insider attacks. In this paper, we focus on On-Off attacks and design a special On-Off attack (called *SOOA*), which can keep responding normally to one node while acting abnormally to another node. In the evaluation, we explore the attack performance under a simulated CIDN environment. Experimental results indicate that our attack can greatly interfere the effectiveness of trust computation for target nodes and has a potential to threaten the robustness of challenge-based CIDNs.

Our work aims to stimulate more research in designing robust CIDN frameworks in real-world scenarios. Future work includes exploring how to enhance existing framework to against advanced insider attacks.

References

1. Cho, J.-H., Chan, K., Adali, S.: A survey on trust modeling. ACM Comput. Surv. 48(2), Article 28, 40 p, October 2015
2. Douceur, J.R.: The sybil attack. In: Druschel, P., Kaashoek, F., Rowstron, A. (eds.) IPTPS 2002. LNCS, vol. 2429, pp. 251–260. Springer, Heidelberg (2002). doi:10. 1007/3-540-45748-8_24
3. Duma, C., Karresand, M., Shahmehri, N., Caronni, G.: A trust-aware, P2P-based overlay for intrusion detection. In: DEXA Workshop, pp. 692–697 (2006)
4. Fung, C.J., Baysal, O., Zhang, J., Aib, I., Boutaba, R.: Trust management for host-based collaborative intrusion detection. In: Turck, F., Kellerer, W., Kormentzas, G. (eds.) DSOM 2008. LNCS, vol. 5273, pp. 109–122. Springer, Heidelberg (2008). doi:10.1007/978-3-540-87353-2_9
5. Fung, C.J., Zhang, J., Aib, I., Boutaba, R.: Robust and scalable trust management for collaborative intrusion detection. In: Proceedings of the 11th IFIP/IEEE International Conference on Symposium on Integrated Network Management (IM), pp. 33–40 (2009)
6. Fung, C.J., Boutaba, R.: Design and management of collaborative intrusion detection networks. In: Proceedings of the 2013 IFIP/IEEE International Symposium on Integrated Network Management (IM), pp. 955–961 (2013)
7. Gong, F.: Next generation intrusion detection systems (IDS). McAfee Network Security Technologies Group (2003)
8. Li, W., Meng, Y., Kwok, L.-F.: Enhancing trust evaluation using intrusion sensitivity in collaborative intrusion detection networks: feasibility and challenges. In: Proceedings of the 9th International Conference on Computational Intelligence and Security (CIS), pp. 518–522. IEEE (2013)
9. Li, W., Meng, W., Kwok, L.-F.: Design of intrusion sensitivity-based trust management model for collaborative intrusion detection networks. In: Zhou, J., Gal-Oz, N., Zhang, J., Gudes, E. (eds.) IFIPTM 2014. IAICT, vol. 430, pp. 61–76. Springer, Heidelberg (2014). doi:10.1007/978-3-662-43813-8_5
10. Li, W., Meng, W.: Enhancing collaborative intrusion detection networks using intrusion sensitivity in detecting pollution attacks. Inf. Comput. Secur. 24(3), 265–276 (2016). Emerald
11. Li, W., Meng, Y., Kwok, L.-F., Ip, H.H.S.: PMFA: toward passive message fingerprint attacks on challenge-based collaborative intrusion detection networks. In: Chen, J., Piuri, V., Su, C., Yung, M. (eds.) NSS 2016. LNCS, vol. 9955, pp. 433–449. Springer, Cham (2016). doi:10.1007/978-3-319-46298-1_28
12. Li, W., Meng, Y., Kwok, L.-F., Ip, H.H.S.: Enhancing collaborative intrusion detection networks against insider attacks using supervised intrusion sensitivity-based trust management model. J. Netw. Comput. Appl. 77, 135–145 (2017). Elsevier
13. Meng, Y., Li, W., Xiang, Y., Choo, K.-K.R.: A bayesian inference-based detection mechanism to defend medical smartphone networks against insider attacks. J. Netw. Comput. Appl. 78, 162–169 (2017)
14. Perrone, L.P., Nelson, S.C.: A study of on-off attack models for wireless ad hoc networks. In: Proceedings of the 2006 Workshop on Operator-Assisted Community Networks, pp. 1–10 (2006)

15. Scarfone, K., Mell, P.: NIST Special Publication 800–94, Guide to Intrusion Detection and Prevention Systems (IDPS) (2007)
16. Snort: An an open source network intrusion prevention and detection system (IDS/IPS). http://www.snort.org/
17. Wu, Y.-S., Foo, B., Mei, Y., Bagchi, S.: Collaborative intrusion detection system (CIDS): a framework for accurate and efficient IDS. In: Proceedings of the 2003 Annual Computer Security Applications Conference (ACSAC), pp. 234–244 (2003)

Assessment of Security Threats via Network Topology Analysis: An Initial Investigation

Marcello Trovati[1(✉)], Win Thomas[2], Quanbin Sun[1],
and Georgios Kontonatsios[1]

[1] Department of Computer Science, Edge Hill University, Ormskirk, UK
Marcello.Trovati@edgehill.ac.uk
[2] Department of Computer Science, Gloucestershire University, Cheltenham, UK

Abstract. Computer networks have increasingly been the focus of cyber attack, such as botnets, which have a variety of serious cybersecurity implications. As a consequence, understanding their behaviour is an important step towards the mitigation of such threat. In this paper, we propose a novel method based on network topology to assess the spreading and potential security impact of botnets. Our main motivation is to provide a toolbox to classify and analyse the security threats posed by botnets based on their dynamical and statistical behaviour. This would potentially lead to a better understanding and prediction of cybersecurity issues related to computer networks. Our initial validation shows the potential of our method providing relevant and accurate results.

Keywords: Botnets · Cybersecurity · Network theory

1 Introduction

Security threats have been steadily increasing due to the emergence of new technology and methodologies, which has led to an expanding research effort to detect and minimise such threats [1,2]. More specifically, *botnets* due to their unique structure based on distributed communication command patterns across networks, are widely regarded as a serious security issue. In fact, they can successfully carry out surveillance attacks, perform DDoS extortion, general spam, as well as phishing. Furthermore, some of them utilise structured overlay networks, whose lack of centralisation enhance the ability of a botnet to evade detection whilst retaining a good level of robustness with respect to a churn process, where single machines are frequently cleansed [6]. It is estimated that their use has led to malicious activity resulting in a loss of millions of dollars per year [5].

In this paper, we introduce a novel method to assess security threats, based on the dynamical properties associated with networks generated by computer communication. In fact, their topology can provide an insight into specific features exhibited by botnets across computer networks. How connections change,

© Springer International Publishing AG 2017
M.H.A. Au et al. (Eds.): GPC 2017, LNCS 10232, pp. 416–425, 2017.
DOI: 10.1007/978-3-319-57186-7_31

Table 1. A selection of network connection flows

Time	Source	Destination	Protocol	Length
161.077519	PcsCompu_b5:b7:19	Broadcast	ARP	60
162.079007	PcsCompu_b5:b7:19	Broadcast	ARP	60
162.079013	PcsCompu_b5:b7:19	Broadcast	ARP	60
162.765245	147.32.84.165	147.32.84.255	NBNS	110
162.765253	147.32.84.165	147.32.84.255	NBNS	110
166.206344	147.32.80.9	147.32.84.165	DNS	503
166.207297	147.32.84.165	74.125.232.195	TCP	62
166.207308	147.32.84.165	74.125.232.195	TCP	62
166.215343	74.125.232.195	147.32.84.165	TCP	62
166.21559	147.32.84.165	74.125.232.195	TCP	60

their types and length of communication can provide a deeper and more efficient approach to security threat detection and prediction.

To achieve this, we consider five main parameters: *time, source, destination, protocol*, and *length*. Table 1 depicts a small example of these parameters of the connection flows.

The main motivation is to provide a set of tools to assess the behaviour of host-to-host communication to allow an agile, real-time assessment. In contrast to the current state of the art approaches, which tend to focus on the different parameters based on whether or not they are present in the collected data, we are aiming to exploit the topology of the network and the probabilistic information related to botnets behaviour. In fact, a dynamical investigation of such networks, can lead to the assessment of the likelihood of the maliciousness of computer communications.

The paper is structured as follows. In Sects. 2 and 3 we provide a description of existing technology and theories, and in Sect. 4 we detail our approach. In Sect. 5 we discuss the validation process and finally, Sect. 6 concludes our work and prompts to future research directions.

2   Related Work

In [3], the authors propose a detection method for botnets from large datasets of Netflow data, based on a variety of cloud computing paradigms especially MapReduce for detecting densely interconnected hosts which are potential botnet members.

BotGrep [5] is a tool to identify peer-to-peer communication structures based on the information about communicating pairs of nodes. This type of P2P detection is defined as a (communication) network, which exploits the spatial relationships in communication traffic. Furthermore, the authors argue that subnetworks with different topological patterns can be partitioned by using random walks, whilst comparing the relative mixing rates of the P2P subnetwork structure and the rest of the communication network. However, such approach is computationally expensive due to the typical size of such networks.

In [4], an approach based on a Markov chain model in introduced. In particular, botnet infection is modelled to identify behaviour that is likely to be associated with attacks, with a prediction rate over 98%. Another example of the utilisation of Markov chain for intrusion detection system is described in [8], where it is trained on a sequence of audit events. However, these types of approaches allow attack identification but they have limited intrusion prediction. In [9], the authors assess the set of bot lifecycle stages using Markov chains to identify the occurrence of infection. Similar to the previous approach, there is a focus on the identification of infection rather than on any predictive capability.

3   Network Theory

Networks have been extensively used to successfully model many complex systems, and their applications span across a variety of multidisciplinary research fields, ranging from mathematics and computer science, to biology, and the social sciences [12,13].

Networks are defined by a *node set* $V = \{v_i\}_{i=1}^n$, and the *edge set* $e_{v_i, v_j} \in E$, so that if v_a and $v_b \in V$ are connected, then $e_{v_a, v_j} \in E$ [2]. Note that in this paper, we do not allow self-loops, or in other words, $e_{v_i, v_i} \notin E$.

Scale-free networks, in particular, appear in a numerous contexts, such as the World Wide Web links, biological and social networks [2]. The main property of scale-free networks is based on their node degree distribution, which follows a power law. More specifically, for large values of k, the fraction p_k of nodes in the network having degree k, is modelled as

$$p_k \approx k^{-\gamma} \tag{1}$$

where γ has been empirically shown to be typically in the range $2 < \gamma < 3$ [2].

From Eq. 1, it follows that a relatively small number of hubs occur, which define the topological properties of the corresponding networks, as well as the way information spreads across them [15].

An important property of such networks is related to the creation of new nodes over time, which are likely to be connected to existing nodes that are already well connected. Since the connectivity of nodes follows a distribution which is not purely random, the dynamical properties of such networks and their general topological properties can lead to predictive capabilities [13].

4   Description of the Method

In this section we introduce the model whose objective is to understand, assess and predict the type and severity of security threats. As discussed above, the dynamical properties of networks can provide a useful insight into the system they model. In this paper, we will focus on the following properties:

- The topology of the network, or in other words, the level of connectedness between nodes measured by joining paths, and
- Their dynamical properties.

Loosely speaking, we are interested in the properties exhibited by the single threats and how they change over a specific amount of time.

As defined in Sect. 3, let $G = G(V, E)$ be a directed network where V is the node set and E is the arc set. The former contains the nodes, and the latter contains the arcs, or directed edges corresponding to requests from the source node to the target node. Let $\deg_{in}^{t}(v_i)$ and $\deg_{out}^{t}(v_i)$ be the in and out degrees of the node v_i at a given time t, that is the number of connection into and out of it, respectively. We then define the *maliciousness* of a node v_i at the time t, as

$$P_M^t(v_i)_{in} = \frac{|\deg_{in}^{M,t}(v_i)|}{|\deg_{in}^{t}(v_i)|} \tag{2}$$

or

$$P_M^t(v_i)_{out} = \frac{|\deg_{out}^{M,t}(v_i)|}{|\deg_{in}^{t}(v_i)|}, \tag{3}$$

where $|\deg_{in}^{M,t}(v_i)|$ and $|\deg_{out}^{M,t}(v_i)|$ are the number of malicious connections into or out of v_i, at a given time t.

For a time t and an arc $e_{v_i,v_j} \in E$, define its *weight* as

$$w_t(v_i, v_j) = f_t(r, p), \tag{4}$$

where $f_t(r, p)$ is a function of the *length of time* of a request r and the *number of request protocols* p from v_i and v_j. In this paper, we define

$$f_t(r, p) = \frac{1}{2}(w_r^t + w_p^t), \tag{5}$$

where w_r^t and w_p^t are the length of the time and the number of protocols of different requests, respectively.

We then define the probability of a malicious request at the time t from v_j to v_i as

$$P_M^t(v_i, v_j) = \frac{1}{3}(P_M^t(v_i)_{in} + P_M^t(v_j)_{out} + w_t(v_i, v_j)). \tag{6}$$

In order to consider the dynamics of this model, we assume that new requests arise according to time snapshots $t = 1, \ldots, T$. Let

$$\delta_T(v_i, v_j) = P_M^t(v_i, v_j) - P_M^{t-1}(v_i, v_j) \tag{7}$$

and define

$$\Delta_T(v_i, v_j) = \frac{1}{T-1} \sum_{t=2}^{T} \delta_T(v_i, v_j). \tag{8}$$

Finally, let the *probability of maliciousness* as

$$\tilde{P}_M^T(v_i, v_j) = \min\{\max\{\Delta_T(v_i, v_j), 0\}, 1\}. \tag{9}$$

Note the above equation can be extended to assess the (average) probability of malicious attacks from a set of nodes $\tilde{V}$ on a specific node as

$$\tilde{P}_M^T(v_i) = \frac{1}{|\tilde{V}|} \sum_{\tilde{v} \in \tilde{V}} \tilde{P}_M(v_i, \tilde{v}) \tag{10}$$

for $e_{v_i, \tilde{v}} \in E$ and $\tilde{v}$ is a node in $\tilde{V}$.

Algorithms 1 and 2 show the implementation of the above approach.

Algorithm 1. Evaluation of $\tilde{P}_M^T(v_i, v_j)$

1: Let $t = 0$
2: Determine $P_M^{t=0}(v_i, v_j)$
3: **for** $t = 1, \ldots T$ **do**
4:    Find $\Delta_T(v_i, v_j)$ and $\tilde{P}_M^T(v_i, v_j)$
5: **end for**
6: **return** $\tilde{P}_M^T(v_i, v_j)$

Algorithm 2. Evaluation of malicious attacks on node v_i

1: Let $t = 0$
2: **for** $\tilde{v} \in V \setminus v_i$ **do**
3:    Determine $P_M^{t=0}(v_i, \tilde{v})$
4:    **for** $t = 1, \ldots T$ **do**
5:       Find $\Delta_t(v_i, \tilde{v})$ and $\tilde{P}_M^T(v_i, \tilde{v})$
6:    **end for**
7: **end for**
8: **return** $\tilde{P}_M^T(v_i, \tilde{v})$

As discussed in Sect. 3, if the network G follows a scale-free structure, new arcs are likely to be added to highly connected nodes. As a consequence, Eqs. 2 and 3 can be modified to incorporate this property. Recall that the fraction of nodes p_k with degree k is

$$p_k \approx k^{-\gamma}.$$

For a scale-free network G, we then assume that

$$P_M^t(v_i, v_j) = \frac{1}{2}(\deg(v_i)^{-\gamma} + w_t(v_i, v_j)). \tag{11}$$

Note that in this case, we are considering the overall degree of the destination node v_i, rather than distinguishing between the in and out degree values of the source and destination nodes. Although we are providing fewer parameters in the model above, compared to Eq. 6, the initial validation appears to support the claim that (11) indeed provides good modelling capabilities.

The dynamics described by Eq. 9 can be used to provide some level of prediction of the number of malicious attacks. In this paper, we assume that the trend of $\tilde{P}_M^T(v_i, v_j)$ can give an insight into a "near future" behaviour of the communications from v_j to v_i. In particular, we shall assume that $\tilde{P}_M^T(v_i, v_j) \approx \tilde{P}_M^{T+1}(v_i, v_j)$, or in other words, they exhibit a similar trend. We acknowledge this is a simplistic approach as it does not consider potential variations that could occur. However, our initial validation seems again to support the above. In future research, we are aiming to fully investigate and extend the predictive properties of our approach by fully analysing the topology of a large set of communication networks.

5   Results

In this section, we will discuss the validation process, which was based on the publicly available datasets offered by the Malware Capture Facility Project [11]. More specifically, we used the CTU-MALWARE-CAPTURE-BOTNET-42 dataset, which contains relevant data generated by a Neris botnet. It used an HTTP based C&C channel, and all the actions performed by the botnet were communicated via C&C channels containing specific "click-fraud" spam based on advertisement services.

This was subsequently preprocessed via WireShark [10] to capture all the parameters relevant to our approach.

A directed network $G = G(V, E)$ was defined, where the node-set V contains the source and destination IPs mutually linked by a request. I particular, we had

- Number of nodes: 4247
- Number of arcs: 6588
- Average in and out degree: 1.5512

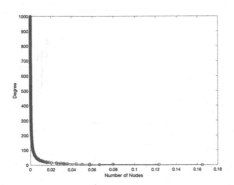

Fig. 1. The degree distribution of the network G.

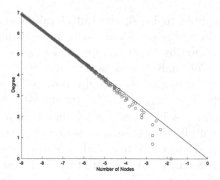

Fig. 2. The log node degree distribution of the network G depicted in Fig. 1, which is compared with a (theoretical) scale-free network with $\gamma = 1.9$. As it can be clearly seen, this is a good approximation of the node degree distribution of G.

Figures 1 and 2 show the degree distribution of the network G, which indicates the existence of few highly connected hubs. Note that this behaviour is similar to scale-free networks, as described by Eq. 1. In [14], a method to topologically reduce complex networks is discussed. When such method is applied to the network G, a value of $\gamma = 1.9$ is determined. As discussed in Sect. 3, for many complex systems γ is usually within the range $2 < \gamma < 3$, suggesting that the dataset used for the validation exhibits properties similar to many other systems from across various contexts. As discussed above, we are aiming to widen our investigation to a large set of malware botnet datasets to fully assess whether such behaviour can be indeed generalised.

In order to evaluate our approach, we trained the parameters of Eq. 5 on approximately 2000 malicious requests. First of all, we noticed that over 95% of the malicious requests had a TCP protocol, and among them we detected two main clusters for time length values in the interval $[0, 70]$ and $[950, 1400]$, as depicted in Fig. 3.

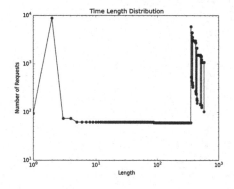

Fig. 3. The distribution of the time length requests.

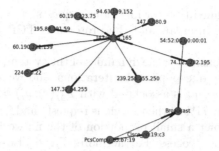

Fig. 4. A sub-network generated by the dataset described in Sect. 5.

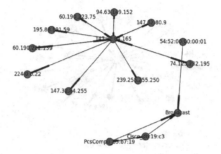

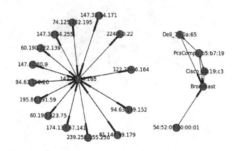

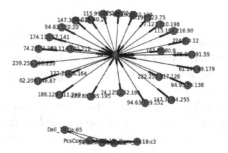

Fig. 5. A selection of the sub-networks generated by some time iterations on the dataset described in Sect. 5.

Therefore, we assumed that for malicious requests, $w_t = w_p = 0.6$ if the time length is within those intervals and the protocol is TCP, and $w_t = w_p = 0.2$ otherwise.

We subsequently considered the dynamics of the system, by analysing batches of approximately 300 requests per time iterations, and we assumed that a malicious request from v_j to v_i is associated with $\tilde{P}_M^T(v_i, v_j) > 0.7$. The analysis of the data produced that 71% of the malicious requests had indeed a $\tilde{P}_M(v_i) > 0.7$. Figures 4, 5 and 6 depict a small proportion of the network created in the first three iterations on the process. Furthermore, Fig. 6 also shows the malicious requests, which are depicted in red.

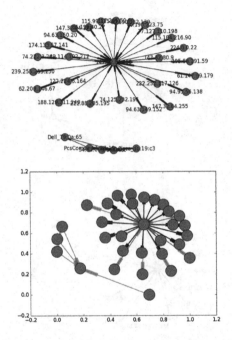

Fig. 6. The sub-networks generated by the fourth iteration, where the second figure highlights the malicious connections (Color figure online).

We subsequently evaluated the model defined by Eq. 11. In this case, $\tilde{P}_M(v_i, v_j) > 0.7$ for approximately 61% of the malicious requests. This decrease in accuracy was indeed expected due to the more general scope of the model, as discussed above.

Finally, we evaluated the level of prediction associated with our model, and we considered approximately 200 pairs of nodes exchanging request. Approximately 59% of the malicious requests exhibited the same trend $\tilde{P}_M^T(v_i, v_j) \approx \tilde{P}_M^{T+1}(v_i, v_j)$, and we noted this was particularly the case for larger values of T, as expected.

6   Conclusion

In this paper, we have discussed a method to assess and predict the malicious connection requests in terms of bonets. As indicated by the validation shows, this approach shows potential in providing a robust method to detect and predict malicious request activity. However, this is still at its infancy and in future research we are aiming to extend our investigation to consider more parameters and create a more comprehensive model. In particular, a full investigation of networks generated by such requests will require a deeper understanding of the topological properties of such networks to ensure a more comprehensive and accurate analysis, which will provide a robust, accurate and computationally effective approach.

References

1. Wang, W., Daniels, T.E.: A graph based approach toward network forensics analysis. ACM Trans. Inf. Syst. Secur. **12**(1), 1–33 (2008)
2. Liao, N., Tian, S., Wang, T.: Network forensics based on fuzzy logic and expert system. Comput. Commun. **32**(17), 1881–1892 (2009)
3. Francois, J., Wang, S., Bronzi, W., State, R., Engel, T.: BotCloud: detecting botnets using mapreduce. In: IEEE International Workshop on Information Forensics and Security, WIFS, Foz do Iguacu, Brazil, November 2011
4. Abaid, Z., Sarkar, D., Ali Kaafar, M., Jha, S.: The early bird gets the Botnet: a markov chain based early warning system for Botnet attacks. In: 41st Conference on Local Computer Networks (LCN). IEEE (2016)
5. Nagaraja, S., Mittal, P., Hong, C., Caesar, M., Borisov, N.: BotGrep: finding P2P bots with structured graph analysis. In: Proceedings of the 19th USENIX Conference on Security (2010)
6. Stover, S., Dittrich, D., Hernandez, J., Dietrich, S.: Analysis of the storm, nugache trojans: P2P is here. Login **32**(6), 1–8 (2007)
7. Loguinov, D., Kumar, A., Rai, V., Ganesh, S.: Graph-theoretic analysis of structured peer-to-peer systems: routing distances and fault resilience. In: Proceedings of ACM SIGCOMM, August 2003
8. Ye, N., et al.: A markov chain model of temporal behaviour for anomaly detection. In: Proceedings of the 2000 IEEE Systems, Man, and Cybernetics Information Assurance and Security Workshop, West Point, NY, vol. 166, p. 169 (2000)
9. Kidmose, E.: Botnet detection using hidden markov models. Master's thesis. Aalborg University, Denmark (2014)
10. https://www.wireshark.org, (Accessed 10 Feb 2017)
11. Malware Capture Facility Project, http://mcfp.weebly.com/, (Accessed 10 Feb 2017)
12. Palmieri, F.: Percolation-based routing in the internet. J. Syst. Softw. **85**(11), 2559–2573 (2012)
13. Trovati, M., Bessis, N.: An influence assessment method based on co-occurrence for topologically reduced big data sets. Soft Comput. **20**(5), 2021–2030 (2015)
14. Trovati, M.: Reduced topologically real-world networks: a big-data approach. Int. J. Distrib. Syst. Technol. (IJDST) **6**(2), 45–62 (2015)
15. Ebel, H., Mielsch, L.I., Bornholdt, S.: Scale-free topology of e-mail networks. Phys. Rev. E **66**, 035103 (2002)

You Surf so Strange Today: Anomaly Detection in Web Services via HMM and CTMC

Maddalena Favaretto, Riccardo Spolaor$^{(\boxtimes)}$, Mauro Conti, and Marco Ferrante

Department of Mathematics "Tullio Levi Civita", University of Padua, Padua, Italy
mfavaretto@studenti.unipd.it, {rspolaor,conti,ferrante}@math.unipd.it

Abstract. In recent years, with the increasing number of attacks against user privacy in web services, researchers put a significant effort on realizing more and more sophisticated Intrusion Detection Systems in order to identify potentially malicious activities. Among such systems, Anomaly Detection Systems rely on a baseline given by a normal behavior and consider every deviation from such behavior as an intrusion.

In this paper, we propose a novel Anomaly Detection System to detect intrusions in users' private areas in on-line web services. Such services usually record logs of user activity from different points: access, actions in a session and system responses. We design an ad-hoc mathematical model for each of these logs to build a profile for a normal behavior. In particular, we model users' accesses through a Hidden Markov Model (HMM) and Users' activity with a Continuous Time Markov Chain (CTMC). We propose a novel Anomaly Detection System algorithm that takes into consideration the deviation from the above Markov Processes. Finally, we evaluate our proposal with a thorough set of experiments, which results confirm the feasibility and effectiveness of our solution.

1 Introduction

The spread of Internet brought also a rapid increase of web services. On such services, users can access information and perform activities through a web browser, such as manage their money, send messages, store photos. The private nature of contents involved by such web services arouses interest of companies, that invest a huge amount of money to obtain such information. Unfortunately, private information are also target of attackers, that aim to obtain it exploiting network protocols and operating systems vulnerabilities. A useful tool to stop attacks are firewalls. However, the only use of firewalls most of the times is not enough. One of the weakness of firewalls is that they can only stop attacks from outside the network, but not the ones from the inside. Therefore, in order to cope with these attacks, researchers did put effort in Intrusion Detection Systems (IDSs), that are popular mechanisms to identify and stop intrusions.

We can categorize Intrusion Detection Systems into two main categories:

1. *Anomaly Detection Systems* (ADSs) identify as anomalous all behaviors different from a baseline behavior (called *normal*). Such systems consider anomalous behaviors as potential intrusions;

© Springer International Publishing AG 2017
M.H.A. Au et al. (Eds.): GPC 2017, LNCS 10232, pp. 426–440, 2017.
DOI: 10.1007/978-3-319-57186-7_32

2. *Misuse Detection Systems* (MDSs) are based on the match between known usage patterns and the sets of rules of known attacks. If the system detects a match, the observed sequence may be an attempt of intrusion.

Since ADSs rely on a baseline defined by a normal behavior and label as anomalous all deviations from that baseline, such systems may detect even unknown attacks. Conversely, MDSs are based on signatures, that are rules and features of known attacks. For this reason, MDSs are not able to detect novel attacks and even variants of well known attacks. However, MDSs have high detection rates only dealing with known attacks. On the other hand, ADSs may have a higher false alarm rate and a lower detection rate. ADSs classify behavioral patterns as normal or anomalous according to a baseline model. Some patterns may be reported as anomalous because the definition of normality is thorough. It is worth to noticing that in some cases anomalies may not be generated by intruders, but also by a system itself (e.g., malfunctioning).

An Anomaly Detection System is based on following concepts:

- Normal behavior is standard and generally it is easy to model;
- Intrusions deviate from normal behavior, therefore they may be identified as anomalies;
- the difference of anomalies from normal behavior may be quantitatively expressed.

The strengths of ADSs are the capability to detect also unknown attacks. Unfortunately, ADSs have also weaknesses:

- Normal activities may be detected as anomalous, due to an imperfect definition of normality, increasing the false alarm rate;
- They are not able to detect or to stop an intrusion which fits the normality model;
- In the case in which the normality model is trained incrementally, a hacker could perform an attrition action, injecting gradually its malicious behavior with the final purpose of hinder the model and being accepted as a normal behavior.

In Anomaly Detection Systems, normal and anomalous states are generally determined through empirical thresholds. Such thresholds are a trade-off between a high detection rate and a low false alarm rate. When calibrating empirical thresholds, the aim is both keeping the false alarm rate low and keeping the detection rate high.

Contributions. In this paper, we contribute to the state of the art by proposing a modular ADS, based on Hidden Markov Models (HMM) and Continuous Time Markov Chains (CTMC). Different logs register uses' activity at different levels of surfing. Therefore, each module of our system focus on a different point of recording of logs in a web service. In particular, we design a module that describe users' accesses to the reserved area via HMMs. While CTMCs are used to model the user' behavior in a session. Despite HMM have been used in ADS, we are the first to apply at the same time HMM and CTMC to model users' normal behavior and detect deviations. It is worth to notice that HMM was never employed to model a sequence of accesses to a reserved area. Moreover, we propose a new algorithm to detect anomalies which uses Continuous Time Markov Chain.

Organization. The paper is organized as follows. In Sect. 2, we survey the work that employed Markow models in Anomaly Detection. In Sect. 3, we introduce the mathematical definition of Hidden Markov Models and Continuous Time Markov Chains; Sect. 4 describes the core of the proposed algorithm; In Sect. 5, we describe the procedure used to test the proposed algorithm and we discuss the obtained results. Finally, we draw some conclusion in Sect. 6.

2   Related Work

In this section, we survey the state of the art reporting the important applications of HMM in IDS and ADS with different goals.

Behavioral Distance Measure. In [5] a HMM was used to compute the behavioral distance measure of two processes. Behavioral distance measure is a measure of the deviation of processes behavior respect to normality. Deviation in processes behavior may be due to an intrusion. The same process with the same input data runs on two different operating systems, or programs not equal but with similar running functionalities. In particular, there are different conditions in which the process is not vulnerable to the same attacks in the two cases. The increase of behavioral distance measure points out a successful attack. States set is $S = \{s_0, s_1, \ldots s_N, s_{N+1}\}$ where s_0 is an initial state and s_{N+1} is the final state generating the sequence of couples of output symbols, where output symbols are couples of system calls. In this model, the focus is on the set of states itself, rather than the probability of two sequences of system calls: a high probability means that similarity between processes is high. Therefore, if the probability of the two processes is higher than an empirical threshold, the system calls sequence will be considered as normal, otherwise as anomalous. The pros of this approach consists in a good in detecting attacks that imitates a normal behavior (i.e., mimic attacks). The cons is that the all users' requests have to be executed multiple times, thus this algorithm have a high computational cost.

SSH Brute Force Attacks. SSH brute-force attacks are hacker attacks executed stealing weak passwords. These attacks are characterized by periods of activity alternating with periods of inactivity. In particular at the beginning the hacker simply logs in and logs out, then he modifies the password into a more secure one and finally tries to get more privileges. In [14], HMMs are used to model flows in order to detect eventual SSH brute force attacks. Hidden states are periods of activity or inactivity, with a final state representing the end of the attack. Output symbols are vectors of created flows, transferred packets and bytes per second. HMM is used to simulate SSH brute force attacks. Obtained results show that HMMs are good in simulating such attacks. Therefore simulated attacks are employed to analyze statistical properties. Attacks are detected comparing statistical properties of real data sets with those of simulated attacks.

Investigating HMM capabilities in Anomaly Detection. In [7], Joshi et al. deal with the most classic way to employ HMMs in Anomaly Detection. The model is estimated according to an initial set of training data. In the recognition phase the estimated HMM is employed to detect anomalies: a sequence of outputs is classified as normal if it well fits the trained model. This means that the observed sequence has a sufficiently high probability, compared to a fixed empirical threshold.

More recently, Ariu et al. in [1] proved the capabilities of HMM proposing an ADS that relies on the analysis of HTTP payloads. Unfortunately, their proposal is not effective on our domain, since network traffic of reserved areas is encrypted (i.e., HTTPS).

Application of HMM to detect multi-stage network attacks. Multi-stage network attacks are network attacks occurring in stage over time. They are made of the following phases: reconnaissance, penetration, attack and exploitation. They are difficult to be detected because they are take an extended period of time and there is not a clear sequence of consecutive actions characterizing them. In [11], HMMs are employed to model the sequence of observed outputs and to detect anomalous sequences. In particular observable outputs may be bytes transferred, source host address and target host address. Data employed in parameters estimation are pre-filtered in order to have samples of normal and anomalous behaviour separately. Then the model is used for Anomaly Detection. This algorithm may be very efficient, the main cons is that there are not many cases of multi-stage network attacks, therefore estimation is not accurate.

System approach to Intrusion Detection using HMM. When a sequence of outputs has to be classified as normal or anomalous according to a HMM, generally it is normal if its probability is greater than a fixed threshold, otherwise anomalous. However it may happen that in an intrusion we observe a sequence of outputs having probability greater than the threshold. Indeed the threshold is empirically established according to the attitude towards risk. To avoid this situation, in [8], the outputs, that may be represented by CPU activity, or network activity, interrupt activity, IO utilization, memory activity, file access activity, system process activity, system calls activity, are modeled by a HMM. In particular, hidden states are possible different levels of alerting: normal, hostile intrusion attempt, friendly intrusion attempt, intrusion in progress, intrusion successful. According to the observed sequence of outputs, the most globally likely hidden sequence is determined and this provides an index of the level of intrusion.

Efficient HMM training scheme for Anomaly Intrusion Detection of Server Application based on system calls. The work in [6] proposes a new algorithm to estimate HMM. The main reason is that Hidden Markov Models are efficient in detecting anomalies, however it may be useful to re-estimate them over time, having more training sequence, while the training algorithm is computationally expensive. This paper propose an algorithm for parameter estimation, in which the training sequence is divided into more training sequences. Each of them is used to estimate a HMM, finally all single estimated models are merged into a unique HMM through a weighted sum.

Hidden semi-Markov Models for Anomaly detection. According to [15], a weakness of HMM is that the permanence time in a hidden state has exponential distribution, according to Markov Chains properties. However this distribution may not be correct. Therefore, a first generalization is assuming that a single hidden state may produce not only an output, but a sequence of outputs. Such a model is called Hidden semi-Markov Model. It has been employed in anomaly detection. In particular in this paper, hidden states may be *normality* or *anomaly*, while observable outputs are observable features, characterizing users' activity.

3   Background Knowledge

As the basis of our work, we consider two probabilistic models: HMM and CTMC. Both the models are themselves based on the notion of Markov Chain. Interested readers could find a more detailed description of Markov Chains in [10].

Markov Chain - Markov Chains are stochastic processes $(X_t)_{t\in\mathbb{N}}$ with values in a discrete set S, such that X_{t+1} depends only on X_t and not on the whole past of the process. S is called the *state space*. Markov chains are completely described by their initial A square matrix P is a *stochastic matrix* if $(p_{ij}|j \in S)$ is a probability distribution $\forall i \in S$. A discrete stochastic process $(X_t)_{t\in\mathbb{N}}$ is a *Markov Chain* with initial distribution λ and transition probability matrix P if two conditions are satisfied: (i) X_0 has distribution λ; (ii) $\forall i \in S$ conditional on $X_t = i$, X_{t+1} has distribution $(p_{ij}|j \in S)$ and is independent on $X_0, \ldots, X_{t-1}$.

We may prove that a stochastic process $(X_t)_{t=1,\ldots,T}$ is $Markov(\lambda, P)$ if and only if $\forall\, s_0, s_1, \ldots s_{T-1}, s_T \in S$, $\mathbb{P}(X_0 = s_0, X_1 = s_1, \ldots, X_{T-1} = s_{T-1}, X_T = s_T) = \lambda_{s_0} p_{s_0 s_1} \ldots p_{s_{T-1} s_T}$. The following *Markov Property*, strengthens the concept of independence from the past of the process: if $(X_t)_{t\in\mathbb{N}}$ is $Markov(\lambda, P)$, conditional on $X_\tau = s$, $s \in S$, $(X_{\tau+t})_{t\in\mathbb{N}}$ is $Markov(\delta_i, P)$ and is independent on $X_0, X_1, \ldots X_{\tau-1}$. Recall that $\delta_s = (\delta_{ss'}|s' \in S)$: $\delta_{ss'}$ is equal to 1 if $s' = s$ and 0 otherwise.

Given a Markov Chain $(X_t)_{t\in\mathbb{N}}$ with states set S, let $s, s' \in S$, s *leads to* s' if $\mathbb{P}(X_t = s', \exists t \geq 0|X_0 = s) > 0$. s *communicates* with s' if s leads to s' and s' leads to s. The *hitting time* of A is the random variable H^A: $H^A : \Omega \longrightarrow \mathbb{N} \cup \{+\infty\}$, $H^A(\omega) = \inf_{t\geq 0}\{X_t(\omega) \in A\}$, where $\inf \emptyset = +\infty$. The probability $(X_t)_{t\in\mathbb{N}}$ hits A leaving from state $s \in S$ is $h_s^A = \mathbb{P}(X_t \in A, \exists t \geq 0|X_0 = s) = \mathbb{P}(H^A < +\infty)$.

We denote $(h_s^A, s \in S)$ as h^A. If A is a closed class, the hitting probability is also called *absorption probability*. h^A is the minimal non negative solution of the linear system where $h_s^A = 1$ if $s \in A$, and $h_s^A = \sum_{s' \in S} p_{ss'} h_{s'}^A$ if $s \in S \setminus A$. We are interested in the expected hitting time of a subset $A \subset S$ leaving from state $s \in S$ that is $k_s^A = \mathbb{E}[h_s^A] = \sum_{t < +\infty} t \mathbb{P}(H_s^A = t) + \infty \mathbb{P}(H_s^A)$. We will use notation $k^A = (k_s^A, s \in S)$. k^A is the minimal non negative solution of the linear system where $k_s^A = 0$ if $s \in A$, and $k_s^A = 1 + \sum_{s' \notin A} p_{ss'} k_{s'}^A$ if $s \in S \setminus A$.

Continuous Time Markov Chain - Considering the previous definition of Markov Chains, let S be a countable set, a *Q-matrix* on S is a matrix $Q = (q_{ij})_{i,j \in S} \in \mathbb{R}^{|S| \times |S|}$ such that the following conditions are satisfied: (i) $0 \leq -q_{ii} < +\infty$ $\forall i \in S$; (ii) $q_{ij} \geq 0$ $\forall i, j \in S$, $i \neq j$; (iii) $\sum_{j \in S} q_{ij} = 0$ $\forall i \in S$. Although we have not defined Continuous Time Markov Chains yet, q_{ij} (out of the diagonal) is an indicator of the rate of transitions from state i to state j, while $1/q_i = 1/ - q_{ii} = 1/\sum_{j \in S, j \neq i} q_{ij}$ is the expected time spent in state i between two consecutive transitions.

A matrix Q is a Q-matrix if and only if $P(t) = e^{tQ}$ is a stochastic matrix $\forall t \geq 0$. Let S be a countable set, a *continuous time random process* is a family of random variables: $(X_t)_{t \geq 0} = \{X_t : \Omega \to S, t \geq 0\}$. The process may jump from a state to any other at arbitrary instants. Moreover it may jump from a state to another infinite times in a time interval of width 0 (in other words the process may jump instantly). To avoid this situation, we require the process to be right continuous. *Holding times* are the time of permanence in a state and so they are defined as the differences between two consecutive jump times. We denote holding times with $H_1, H_2, \ldots, H_n, \ldots$. For $n \in \mathbb{N}^*$ (where $\mathbb{N}^* = \mathbb{N} \setminus \{0\}$).

The distribution of the process $(X_t)_{t \geq 0}$ is completely determined by the distribution of the holding times and transition probabilities of the jump process. Let $(X_t)_{t \geq 0}$ be a stochastic process assuming values in the countable set S, $(X_t)_{t \geq 0}$ is a *Continuous Time Markov Chain* (CTMC) if $\forall 0 \leq t_1 < \cdots < t_n < t < s$ $\mathbb{P}(X_{t+s} = s_{t+s}|X_t = s_t, X_{t_n} = s_{t_n}, \ldots, X_{t_1} = s_{t_1}) = \mathbb{P}(X_{t+s} = s_{t+s}|X_t = s_t)$. The relation between Q-matrices and CTMCs is $q_{ij} = \lim_{h \to 0} \mathbb{P}(X_h = j|X_0 = i)/h$ and the transition probability matrix is $P = (p_{ij})_{i,j=1,\ldots,N}$, where $p_{ij} = q_{ij}/q_i = -q_{ij}/q_{ii}$ $\forall i, j = 1, \ldots, N$, $i \neq j$, and $p_{ii} = 0$ $\forall i = 1, \ldots, N$.

Moreover, $P_t = e^{tQ}$ $\forall t \geq 0$. where $(P_t)_{i,j=1,\ldots,N} = (p_{ij}(t))_{i,j=1,\ldots,N}$. Let π denote the initial distribution of the CTMC, then $\forall t \geq 0$: $\mathbb{P}(X_t = j) = \mathbb{P}(X_t = j, \bigcup_{i=1}^N \{X_0 = i\}) = \sum_{i=1}^N \mathbb{P}(X_t = j, X_0 = i) =$ and $\sum_{i=1}^N \mathbb{P}(X_t = j|X_0 = i) \mathbb{P}(X_0 = i) = \sum_{i=1}^N p_{ij}(t) \pi_i$. Let $(X_t)_{t \geq 0}$ be a CTMC with states set S, and $A \subset S$, the hitting time of subset A is the random variable $D^A : \Omega \longrightarrow [0, +\infty[\omega \longmapsto D^A(\omega) = \inf\{t \geq 0\{X_t(\omega) \in A\}$ Note that if H^A is the hitting time of the subset A for the jump process, then $\{D^A < +\infty\} = \{H^A < +\infty\}$ and $D^A = J_{H^A}$. The probability that the CTMC hits A leaving from i is $h_i^A = \mathbb{P}(D^A < +\infty|X_0 = i) = \mathbb{P}(H^A < +\infty|X_0 = i)$. h^A is the minimal non negative solution of the following linear system where $h_i^A = 1$ if $i \in A$, and $\sum_{j \in S} q_{ij} h_j^A = 0$ if $i \in S \setminus A$. The expected hitting time is denoted ad $k_i^A = E_i[D^A] = E[D^A|X_0 = i]$. The vector of expected hitting times

k^A is the minimal non negative solution of the linear system $k_i^A = 0$ if $i \in A$, and $-\sum_{j \in S} q_{ij} k_j^A = 1$ if $i \in S \setminus A$. Continuous Time Markov Models are calibrated according to the *Maximum Likelihood Criterion*. We assume to observe a particular realization, $y_1, t_1, y_2, t_2, \ldots y_{k-1}, t_{k-1}, y_k$, of the CTMC to be estimated, called training sequence. Then we compute the Q-matrix maximizing the likelihood of the training sequence. However, Markov Chains may not be reliable to represent reality of many applications, because real phenomena to be modeled are not simple. In particular, Continuous Time Markov Chain have a low number of parameters and this is good for parameters estimation, however it does not allow to model real complex processes. A first generalization of MC and CTMC is supposing that the Markov Chain is not observable but every state transition produces an observable output. This model is called Hidden Markov Model.

Hidden Markov Model - A HMM is made of a double embedded process: (i) the underlying, hidden Markov Chain, whose evolution is described by an initial distribution and a probability transition matrix; (ii) the process of the observed outputs produced by the sequence of hidden states. The generation of observable symbols is described by the observation matrix containing for every state the probability of generating each output. A Hidden Markov Model is particularly suitable to represent time series generating a sequence of observations with a huge amount of data. To completely describe a HMM we need the following elements: (i) Initial distribution π; (ii) Transition probability matrix $P = (p_{ij})_{i,j=1,\ldots,N}$; (iii) Observation symbol probability distribution B where $b_{ik} = b_i(k) = \mathbb{P}(O_t = v_k | X_t = s_i)$ is the probability of observing symbol v_k if the hidden state is s_i. B is a stochastic matrix. Some questions have to be solved before applying HMMs. The first problem is the efficient computation of the probability of a sequence of outputs. The second problem is inferring the sequence of hidden states generating a sequence of observations. Finally given a sequence of observations, we would like to estimate the parameters of the model in order to reliably describe real processes.

The algorithm solving the problem of the efficient computation of a given observation sequence probability is the *Forward-backward algorithm*. It is a recursive algorithm, based on the recursive computation of the forward variable, that is $\alpha_t(i) = \mathbb{P}(O_1, \ldots, O_t, X_t = s_i)$, where $O_1, \ldots O_t$ is the given sequence of observation. By the total law probability, $\mathbb{P}(O_1, \ldots O_t) = \sum_{i=1}^{N} \alpha_t(i)$. Since the following recursive relation is true: $\alpha_1(i) = \pi_i$, $\alpha_t(j) = [\sum_{i=1}^{N} \alpha_{t-1}(i) p_{ij}] b_j(O_t)$, $\forall t > 1, i, j \in S$ we may efficiently compute an observation sequence probability.

This issue concerns the discovering of the unknown part of the model: we would like to determine the most likely states sequence producing an observed output in a given HMM. The hidden sequence, optimal according to the chosen criterion is selected as the most likely sequence producing the observed data. The *Viterbi algorithm* usually employed to solve the second problem maximizes the probability of the whole states sequence given the observation sequence. The Viterbi algorithm solves a maximization problem in an efficient way by decomposing it in a sequence of recursive and easier maximizations.

We define $\delta_t(i) = \max_{X_1,\ldots,X_{t-1}} \mathbb{P}(X_1 \ldots X_{t-1}, X_t = s_i, O_1 \ldots O_t | \lambda)$ and exploit the following recursive relation: $\delta_{t+1}(j) = \max_{X_1,\ldots,X_t} \mathbb{P}(X_1 \ldots X_t, X_{t+1} = s_i, O_1 \ldots O_t O_{t+1} | \lambda) =$, and $\max_{j=1,\ldots,N}[\max_{i=1,\ldots,N} \delta_t(i)p_{ij}]b_j(O_{t+1})$.

Parameters estimation is fundamental such that HMM may represent real situations. If parameters are not correctly estimated, the model will not correctly describe reality. Given a sequence of observations, the procedure of parameters estimation is called *training*, while the observations sequence used to train the model is called *training sequence*. Parameters are estimated in order to maximize the probability of observing the training sequence. The problem of parameters estimation may be formulated as an optimization problem: we aim at determine the parameters with the constraints just described in order to maximize the likelihood of the training sequence. There is no analytical way to solve this optimization problem, so we use an optimization algorithm. The most widely used algorithm for this specific problem is the Baum-Welch algorithm, which is a particular case of the Expectation Maximization algorithm (for the Expectation Maximization algorithm see [2,3]). It is a statistical inference method for parameters estimation. In particular, in the case of HMM the Baum-Welch algorithm the maximization of the observation sequence probability. Paper [12] is the first and most important one containing a formal description of HMM (with integration [13] for the proofs of the scaled Baum-Welch algorithm, that is the Baum-Welch algorithm in which parameters are multiplied by an apposite constant in order to deal with greater quantities and maintain precision, without changing the output). While papers [9,17] describe a more sophisticated version of Hidden Markov Models in continuous time. This generalization may be useful to describe a sequence of accesses to a reserved area, however the computational cost is high.

4   Our Framework

The goal of our research is to design and implement an ADS that is able to detect intrusions in a reserved area of an on-line service. In the logs used for training our model, we assume that users always behaved normally and that no intruder tried to force the system. We also refer to such logs as *past* or *normal behaviour*. In practice, we employ such past behaviours in order to define a model of normal behaviour and to evaluated future accesses. If future accesses are quantitatively similar to past behaviour, our framework will report that the user is normally behaving, otherwise it will report an anomaly, e.g., an intruder may have entered the system. In particular, the algorithm is based on two basic elements:

- The normality model, describing authorized users' behavior;
- An anomaly rate, that is a quantity characterizing the model and may considerably and quantitatively vary if user's behavior does not fit the normality model.

Our framework performs such analysis by applying two probability models based on Markov Chains: Continuous Time Markov Chains and Hidden Markov Models.

Subsequently, we compare the anomaly rate with a threshold to state if a behavior is normal or anomalous. Such threshold is empirically determined, according to past observed behavior, excluding anomalous ones or assuming all past users were authorized to enter the reserved area. In what follow, we enter into the details of our framework. In Sect. 4.1, we describe the problem related to the domain of restricted areas that are the focus of our research. Then, we illustrate our proposal to solve the above mentioned problem in Sect. 4.2.

4.1 Description of the Problem

Reserved areas in on-line services usually involve three kinds of logs:

1. Access logs deal with the features of the access or a user to the service. (e.g., time, IP address, browser, device);
2. Session logs deal with user activity in the session. On such logs, it is possible to rebuild the sequence of visited pages and the amount of time spent in each page by the user;
3. Response logs are produced by the system and describing system response to each request by the user (e.g., information retrieval, queries on the database).

Given the different nature of such logs, we build three separate models. The parameters of each model are calibrated according to previous sessions. When a new session is recorded we separately analyze the access, the time spent on each web page, the sequence of visited pages and system response, according to the models estimated using previous sessions. Indeed, we design each model to give a score S for a new session, such that $S \geq 0$ means normality, while $S < 0$ means anomaly. Finally, we apply an algorithm that takes into account the weighted sum of the scores. If the output score of this algorithm is positive, we consider the whole session as normal. We establish the weight of each model empirically, according three factors: (i) the reliability of the logs considered by the model, (ii) the importance of the element analyzed by the model, and (iii) the interval in which the corresponding score may take value.

4.2 Our Proposal

In this section, we describe how we employ *HMM* and *CTMC* to first model a normal behaviour and then to state if a recorded access is normal or anomalous.

Access model - The access model take as input an access log, which contains the timing of access of an user. To describe this model that describe the sequence of accesses to the reserved area, we employ a HMM. In this model, we consider an individual access to the reserved area (along with its features) as an observable symbol. Since it may be possible that a reserved area is shared among more than one user (with the same username and password), the model have to associate a physical person to a hidden state of the Markov Chain. Assuming all past accesses are normal or excluding eventual intrusions, we estimate models parameters (e.g. the initial distribution π, the probability stochastic matrix P and the probability observation matrix B). We will apply the Baum-Welch algorithm to previously observed sessions.

After the training phase we will employ the model to detect anomalies. When we observe a new access we will compute the probability of the sequence of accesses of length n and ending with the last observed access. Call $\bar{P}$ the probability of the last n accesses. If $\bar{p} \geq p$, where p is a fixed threshold, the sequence of n accesses is normal, otherwise anomalous. In other words, if a sequence of accesses has a sufficiently high probability it is normal, otherwise anomalous. To state if probability is high we compare it with a threshold. Such threshold is empirically determined according to: (i) the attitude toward risk; (ii) previously observed probabilities of accesses we may consider normal. Note that it is important every sequence of accesses has fixed length n because as n increases, the probability of accesses sequence decreases, so it may not be compared with a constant threshold.

Session model - Continuous Time Markov Chains are Markov Chains remaining in every state for a random strictly positive time. Since CTMCs has not memory by definition, holding time in every state is exponentially distributed, because the exponential distribution is the only one with the *no memory* property. A CTMC is completely described by the initial distribution π and a Q-matrix Q which is a combination of the probability transition matrix describing transitions between states and the exponential parameters of exponential holding times. The sequence of states visited by the stochastic process is said *jump process*. In this model, every session is represented by a realization of the CTMC: there is a state for every page of the reserved area, therefore the jump process is the sequence of pages visited by the user, while holding times are the time spent by the user in every page. The model is trained according to the maximum likelihood criterion using past sessions. At this time we are ready to detect eventual anomalies.

Dealing with anomalies in holding times, for every page of the reserved area we may compute an acceptance range $[l, M]$ such that if the holding time falls in the interval it is considered normal, otherwise anomalous. Let $\mathbb{P}$ be the probability measure defined on $\mathbb{R}^+$ by the probability density function of the exponential density for a certain page. Let $\mu = \mathbb{P}(X \leq \mu) = \mathbb{P}(X \geq \mu) = 1/2$, where X is the holding time. The interval $[l, M]$ is characterized by $l < \mu < U$, $\mathbb{P}(]l, M[) = \mathbb{P}(]M, U[) = p/2$, where p is an empirical threshold: it is the probability of classify a holding time as normal (Fig. 1).

Dealing with the sequence of visited states, we compute the probability of the observed jump process $Y_1 \ldots Y_T$ and classify it s normal if $\mathbb{P}((Y_1 \ldots Y_T)) \geq p_T$, where p_T is an empirical threshold depending on the length T of the jump process. It may be computed according to two different points of view:

- We aim to classify as normal a fixed percentage of the whole set of T-length sequences. So we generate N T-length jump processes, according to a uniform probability matrix and compute their probability according to the Q-matrix. Finally we compute p such that the rate between normal generated sequences and all the generated sequences will be p.

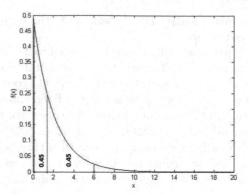

Fig. 1. The graph shows the probability density function of $X \sim Exp(\lambda)$, where $\lambda = 0.5$, the red points in the x axis define the acceptance interval. They are respectively l and M. $\mathbb{P}(X \in [l, M]) = 0.9$, $\mathbb{P}(X \in [\mu - l, \mu]) = 0.45$ and $\mathbb{P}(X \in [\mu, M]) = 0.45$. The lower border is $l = 0.1026$ and the upper one $M = 5.9915$.(Color figure online)

- We compute the threshold basing only on normal jump processes. According to the estimated Q-matrix, we generate n normal T-length jump processes, compute their probability and put them in ascending order. Then $p = c\tilde{p}$, where c is an empirical parameter and $\tilde{p}$ is the minimum probability among the computed ones.

System response model - We evaluate system response to users' requests through a stochastic matrix P, where $(P)_{ij}$ is the probability procedure j is active after request i. We estimate P according to the maximum likelihood criterion and the couple of request i and corresponding procedure j is considered anomalous if p_{ij} is lower than a fixed and empirical threshold.

5   Experimental Results

We implemented the algorithms discussed in this paper in Matlab. In particular, we exploited all available functions dealing with HMMs for the training phase and to compute probabilities. Similarly, we implemented the algorithms based on CTMC and the stochastic matrix. We tested our algorithms on a simulated dataset built to reflect real users' normal behaviour. In particular, we defined the parameters of normal behavior and used them to produce a training sample and then estimated the defined parameters using this sample. We then produced a testing sample using the defined parameters. Finally, we defined parameters describing anomalous behavior and generated a sample of anomalous behavior and we tested the algorithm. Unfortunately, due to high sensibility for the data involving the restricted area of a web service (especially data about user activity), none of the companies we contacted could give us such data. For this reason, we were not able to test our proposal on real data. Thus, the main opened question

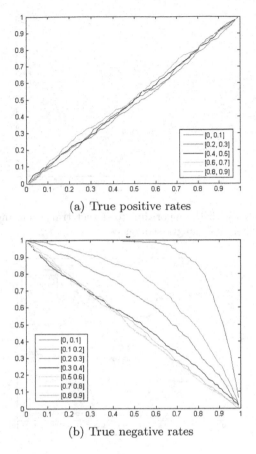

(a) True positive rates

(b) True negative rates

Fig. 2. True positive and true negative rates for different *anomalous* Q-matrices. Each anomalous Q-matrix has been produced randomly, with the constraint that the expected holding time of every state is the expected holding time of normal behavior multiplied for a constant. The constant belongs to the interval in legend.

is if the employed models well fit real data and the efficiency of the algorithm depends on this.

5.1 Performance of Our Proposal

HMMs have already been employed in Anomaly Detection to detect intrusion and it is known they well perform in the way we applied them. The main difference is the set of hidden states. Generally, in ADS hidden states concerned procedures, while in our proposal hidden states are people. Therefore, the performance of the model depends on the fitness of the model itself to represent a sequence of accesses to the reserved area.

The capability of our algorithm in detecting anomalous holding times depends on following elements: (i) the mean time spent by users in every page;

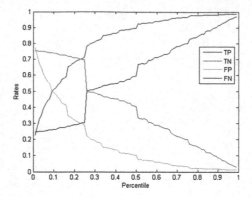

Fig. 3. Obtained rates with the algorithm to detect transition anomalies based on a random sample of different T-length sequences.

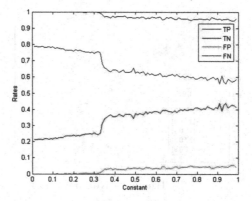

Fig. 4. Detection rates, x axis contains the constant used to determine the threshold together with the minimum probability of simulated sequences.

(ii) the entity of the mean holding time; (iii) the difference between the intruder's holding time in a state and authorized user's mean holding time. The algorithm to detect anomalous holding times is based on the idea that only holding time in a central neighborhood of the median may be considered normal. The measure of such interval depends on the attitude towards risk. As greater is the measure of the acceptance interval, as greater is the probability to classify every holding time as normal.

The algorithm to detect anomalous sequences of visited pages is more efficient in the detection using the method based only on normal sequences to calibrate the threshold p.

Figures 2, 3 and 4 summarize the results of our analysis as thresholds vary. In these graphs, we use the following notation:

- *true positive* (TP) are normal instances classified as normal;
- *true negative* (TN) are intrusions classified as anomalous;

- *false positive* (FP) are intrusions classified as normal;
- *false negative* (FN) are normal instances classified as anomalous.

The performance of an ADS is evaluated through these values: as greater the TP and TN are and as lower the FP and FN are, better the ADS performs.

To carry out these tests we have defined a priory the parameters of the model describing the authorized user's behavior and the parameters describing the intruder's behavior. We simulated many instances of normal behavior, estimated normal model parameters and finally we tested if the algorithm was able to distinguish instances produced by the normal and the intruder model.

5.2 Comparison with Other Similar Methods

Hidden Markov Models and Continuous Time Markov Chains are commonly used in Anomaly Detection, however there are not available examples of how to apply them in literature. This paper contains a first example of how Models based on Markov Chains may be used in Anomaly Detection to study authorized users normal behavior to distinguish intrusions as anomalies.

6 Conclusion

In this paper, we propose an example of application of HMM and CTMC to model users' behavior for Anomaly Detection. The proposed algorithms aim to detect the access by intruders in a reserved area. The main contribution of our work consists of two new elements that characterize our ADS framework. The first contribution is the HMM application focused on users' behaviour, rather than unobservable procedures. The second contribution is the design and implementation of algorithms to detect anomalies that rely on both in holding times and the jump process of a specific realization of a Continuous Time Markov Chain, according to a Q-matrix describing normal behavior.

As a future work, we intend to test our algorithms on actual logs of restricted areas. Such logs will not be synthetic but performed by real users. We also aim to investigate the different user behaviour according to the device used to access restricted areas (e.g., laptops, smartphones). Moreover, we intend to investigate an additional source of logs that consists in the flows of encrypted network traffic. An analysis on this additional source is promising to be used in an ADS, since researchers showed that it is possible to able to infer private informations such as the application installed [16] and even the actions performed by a user [4]. Finally, we intend to study possible improvements of our models, in order to find automatically the optimal fit on such scenarios.

Acknowledgment. Mauro Conti is supported by a Marie Curie Fellowship funded by the European Commission (agreement PCIG11-GA-2012-321980). This work is also partially supported by the EU TagItSmart! Project (agreement H2020-ICT30-2015-688061), the EU-India REACH Project (agreement ICI+/2014/342-896), "Physical-Layer Security for Wireless Communication", and "Content Centric Networking:

Security and Privacy Issues" funded by the University of Padua. This work is partially supported by the grant no. 2017-166478 (3696) from Cisco University Research Program Fund and Silicon Valley Community Foundation.

References

1. Ariu, D., Giacinto, G.: HMMPayl: an application of HMM to the analysis of the HTTP payload. In: WAPA (2010)
2. Bilmes, J.A. et al.: A gentle tutorial of the EM algorithm and its application to parameter estimation for gaussian mixture and hidden markov models. International Computer Science Institute (1998)
3. Chen, Y., Gupta, M.R.: EM demystified: an expectation-maximization tutorial. In: Electrical Engineering, Citeseer (2010)
4. Conti, M., Mancini, L.V., Spolaor, R., Verde, N.V.: Analyzing android encrypted network traffic to identify user actions. In: IEEE TIFS (2016)
5. Gao, D., Reiter, M.K., Song, D.: Behavioral distance measurement using hidden markov models. In: Zamboni, D., Kruegel, C. (eds.) RAID 2006. LNCS, vol. 4219, pp. 19–40. Springer, Heidelberg (2006). doi:10.1007/11856214_2
6. Hoang, X., Hu, J.: An efficient hidden markov model training scheme for anomaly intrusion detection of server applications based on system calls. In: Proceedings of IEEE ICON (2004)
7. Joshi, S.S., Phoha, V.V.: Investigating hidden markov models capabilities in anomaly detection. In: Proceedings of ACM SE (2005)
8. Khanna, R., Liu, H.: System approach to intrusion detection using hidden markov model. In: Proceedings of ACM IWCMC (2006)
9. Liu, Y.-Y., Li, S., Li, F., Song, L., Rehg, J.M.: Efficient learning of continuous-time hidden markov models for disease progression. In: Advances in Neural Information Processing Systems (2015)
10. Norris, J.R.: Markov Chains, vol. 2. Cambridge University Press, Cambridge (1998)
11. Ourston, D., Matzner, S., Stump, W., Hopkins, B.: Applications of hidden markov models to detecting multi-stage network attacks. In Proceedings of IEEE HICSS (2003)
12. Rabiner, L.R.: A tutorial on hidden markov models and selected applications in speech recognition. In: Proceedings of the IEEE (1989)
13. Rahimi, A.: An erratum for "a tutorial on hidden markov models and selected applications in speech recognition" (2000). On-line article
14. Sperotto, A., Sadre, R., Boer, P.-T., Pras, A.: Hidden markov model modeling of SSH brute-force attacks. In: Bartolini, C., Gaspary, L.P. (eds.) DSOM 2009. LNCS, vol. 5841, pp. 164–176. Springer, Heidelberg (2009). doi:10.1007/978-3-642-04989-7_13
15. Tan, X., Xi, H.: Hidden semi-markov model for anomaly detection. Appl. Math. Comput. **205**, 562–567 (2008)
16. Taylor, V.F., Spolaor, R., Conti, M., Martinovic, I.: AppScanner: automatic fingerprinting of smartphone apps from encrypted network traffic. In: Proceedings of IEEE EuroS&P (2016)
17. Zraiaa, M.: Hidden markov models: a continuous-time version of the Baum-Welch algorithm. Imperial College London (2010)

Parallel and Distributed Computing

CDLP: A Core Distributing Policy Based on Logic Partitioning

Alin Zhong, Shun Ren$^{(\boxtimes)}$, and Shouzhi Xu

College of Computer and Information Technology, China Three Gorges University,
Yichang 443002, China
535844264@qq.com

Abstract. With multi-core processors being increasingly employed by servers in cloud/data centers, how to take advantage of multi-core has been a key issue to improve the system performance. Data reuse in shared cache is an attractive approach to exploit multi-core, and therefore researchers present a number of solutions from different levels such as compiler and operating system. However, because of the lack of cooperation in two-level scheduling framework in virtualized system, the scheduling and distributing policy employed by VCPU (Virtual CPU) scheduler often counteract the endeavor of the guest operating in pursuing data reuse. Aiming the problem, we present CDLP: a novel dynamic core distributing policy based on logic partitioning, and we present a set of algorithms including core distribution, load balancing, core redistribution, core reclaiming. In order to verify the effectiveness and correctness of CDLP, we implement a prototype based on Xen platform, the experimental results demonstrate that CDLP can effectively realize data reuse and fully utilize processing resource.

Keywords: Multi-core · Data reuse · Distributing policy · Logic partitioning

1 Introduction

Currently, multi-core processors and virtualization platforms have been increasingly employed by cloud/data centers. The one of the features of multi-core processors is that multiple cores share the last cache. Implementing data reuse in shared cache can effectively reduce inter-core cache misses and improve the performance of multithreaded applications. To this end, researchers present varieties of methods for data reuse based scheduling policy in operating system. PDF [1, 2] is a typical scheduling algorithm towards data reuse. In PDF algorithm, a task is modeled as a DAG (Directed Acyclic Graph), and the sequential execution of the task is modeled as the depth-first scheduling of DAG, which will be realized based on parallelization when there are multiple processors. Blelloch et al. [1] and Chen et al. [3] empirically prove that the parallel depth-first scheduling can effectively achieve data reuse. Tam et al. [4] present a sharing-aware scheduling mechanism for multiprocessor to eliminate non-uniform data access, aiming to achieve data sharing in cache. Pericas et al. [5] propose a coarse-grained approach to the reuse distance method operating at the kernel level. Their work can generate reuse plots for parallel runs considerably larger than current approaches.

© Springer International Publishing AG 2017
M.H.A. Au et al. (Eds.): GPC 2017, LNCS 10232, pp. 443–459, 2017.
DOI: 10.1007/978-3-319-57186-7_33

Zhang W et al. [6] propose a cache matching algorithm which captures data locality both within threads and across multiple threads. The algorithm uses a small buffer to store parts of the incoming request sequences, then interleaves these into a single sequence that has a high cache hit rate. The algorithm can achieve high cache hit rate. However, their work only caters to traditional computer systems. In virtualized systems, because of the lack of cooperation in two-level scheduling framework, it is difficult to set the definite mapping between VCPUs and threads, and therefore the approaches for data reuse towards traditional computer system can't be apply to the virtualized system. Jin et al. [7] present a cache contention-aware virtual machine placement approach. They reduce cache contention by designating mapping sequence of VCPU to PCPU according the feather of applications running in virtual machines, but they carry out processor distributing based on the granularity of a virtual machine, lack of flexibility. Kim et al. [8] present a virtual machine scheduling policy towards the minimum of access conflict on LLC (Last Level Cache). They select the virtual machine with the maximum rate of cache accessing and the virtual machine with the minimum rate of cache accessing as a group and place them on cores sharing cache, and do the rest in the same manner until all virtual machines are placed. Their work can effective improve the performance of virtual machines, but their target is to reduce cache conflict instead of pursuing data reuse. Rao et al. [9] present an algorithm of VCPU random migration to improve the performance of multithreading applications. The difference with our work is that they aim the NUMA system.

In this paper, we present CDLP: a novel dynamic core distributing policy based on logic partitioning, which focus on data reuse. Our target is to improve the performance of the virtualized system based on multi-core processor. The main contributions of this paper are as follows:

- We present a novel dynamic core distributing policy based on logic partitioning, which aims to achieve data reused in shared cache.
- We devise a set of algorithms including core allocating, load balancing, core re-allocating, core reclaiming.
- We implement a prototype based on Xen [10] platform to verify the effectiveness and correctness of CDLP.

The remainder of the paper is structured as follows. Section 2 describes background. Section 3 elaborates CDLP. Section 4 describes the implementation of CDLP. The policy is evaluated in Sect. 5, and finally we conclude.

2   Background

In this section, we first describe the two-level scheduling framework in virtualized system, and then we give a description about the inter-core cache misses.

2.1 The Two-Level Framework in Virtualized System

Currently, virtualized systems are popular because of their merits of full utilization of physical resource and easy management. Virtualized systems are often divided three layers: hardware, VMM (Virtual Machine Monitor) and virtual machine. Hardware provides resource including processors, memory and I/O devices, VMM is responsible to allocate, monitor and reclaim hardware, and virtual machine provides an isolating execution environments for applications. The architecture of the virtualized system eliminates the coupling between operating system and hardware. Multiple virtual machines with different or same operating systems called guest OSs can share hardware by time-multiplexing or space partitioning. Every virtual machine has its own virtual hardware such as VCPUs, virtual memory and virtual I/O devices. VMM can distribute PCPUs (Physical CPUs) to virtual machine to support arbitrary policy.

It is easy to see that VMM and guest OS are two scheduling bodies locating different layers by observing partition of structures and functions of virtualized systems. As shown in Fig. 1, VMM scheduler, namely the first level scheduling, is responsible to schedule VCPUs onto PCPUs, while guest OS scheduler, namely the second level scheduling, is responsible for scheduling application threads or processes onto VCPUs,. The policies and mechanisms employed by two scheduling bodies are independent to each other.

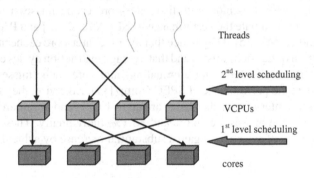

Fig. 1. Two-level scheduling framework.

The two-level scheduling framework enhances the flexibility of the system. VCPUs can be mapped to PCPUs by the means of both one to one and one-to-many. The VMM scheduler can employ agile policies in response to varying load condition. However, the two-level framework causes that the guest OS scheduler can't be aware of the structures and the functions of underlying hardware, and therefore makes it difficult that guest OS full exploits hardware efficiency through reasonably thread scheduling. Moreover, the VMM scheduler can't understand the characters of workloads running in virtual machines, increasing the difficulty of resource scheduling and distributing.

2.2 The Inter-core Cache Misses

The inter-core cache misses are incurred by the accessing conflict of multiple threads running in different cores. As shown in Table 1, (T_1, T_2, T_3, T_4) is a timing sequence that $core_1$ and $core_2$ access shared cache. For simplicity, here we assume that the shared cache has only one cache line. When the access series occurs shown in the first column in Table 1, a series of cache events in the last column will happen accordingly.

Table 1. Inter-core cache misses

Timing sequence	$Core_1$	$Core_2$	Cache event
T_1	Accessing location x		Compulsory cache misses, data in x is brought into the shared cache
T_2		Accessing location x	Data reuse
T_3		Accessing location y	Inter-core cache misses, data in y replaces cache line
T_4	Accessing location x		Inter-core cache misses, data in x replaces cache line

From the Table 1, we can see that data reuse occurs in T_2 while cache misses occur in T_3 and T_4. In order to demonstrate that inter-core cache misses isn't negligible, Kandemir et al. [11] evaluate the performance of SPLASH-2 [12] and PARSEC [13] in SIMICS [14] and GEMS [15]. They notice that average inter-core cache misses account for 61% proportion of L2 cache misses and that average instruction cycles can be reduced 33% if existing an ideal solution for eliminating inter-core cache misses. Srikantaiah et al. [16] evaluate the performance of SPEC Comp [17]. Likewise, they find that in all of L2 cache misses, inter-core cache misses are up to 40.3%, and intra-core cache misses and compulsory cache misses are 24.6% and 35.1%, individually. These results show that the performance of system will gain a substantial increase by achieving data reuse.

3 CDLP

This section first describes the method of logic portioning, and then elaborates CPLD and algorithms.

3.1 Logic Partitioning

The idea of logic partitioning is described as follows. Cores in system are divided to multiple BGs (Basic Groups). A BG is a collection of cores that share the same cache. Cores are mainly distributed to virtual machines in units of BGs. The VCPUs in virtual machines are mapped to cores by set associativity, which is determined by the distributing policy. A VCPU can only be scheduled to the BG with mapping relationship. Figure 2 shows how to partition BGs. Four cores are divided two BGs, which are mapped to the virtual machine VM_0 and VM_1 respectively. Logic partitioning is referred to opposed to global sharing. Global sharing is a mainstream pattern employed by virtualized platforms (e.g. Xen) nowadays.

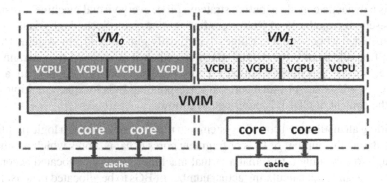

Fig. 2. Logic partitioning.

Figure 3 demonstrates the structure of the global sharing. In global sharing, all VCPUs are mapped cores by the means of full associativity, which is that a core can be distributed an arbitrary VCPU. Global sharing both facilitates load balancing and supports work-conserving scheduling that improves utilization of physical resources. However, global sharing can hurt the performance of cache.

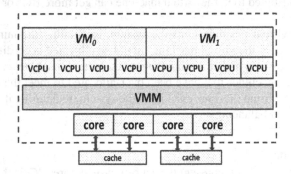

Fig. 3. Globally sharing.

Logic partitioning enable VCPUs in the same virtual machine be mapped to the cores shared the same cache, and therefore is favor of data reuse. In a general way, that VCPUs in a machine are mapped to the same BG is ideal. However, because of some reasons such as load balancing, cores in a virtual machine can be allocated across multiple BGs, and the effect of CDLP can be reduced.

3.2 Policy

3.2.1 Basic Idea

CDLP is a dynamic core distributing strategy. First, every virtual machine is distributed cores based on granularity of BGs according to its weight. Second, physical cores will be redistributed when virtual machines dynamically join or exit from system. Third, the BG can't be allocated other virtual machines when it is mapped to a certain virtual machine. Virtual machines multiplex cores in space-sharing. At last, in a virtual machine, VCPUs share physical cores in corresponding BGs by space-multiplexing. In detail, the content of CDLP is described as follows.

- Dividing all unallocated cores in system into multiple BGs through logic partitioning.
- Calculating the number of BGs or fragment cores (That is, cores which number isn't enough to constitute a BG) that a virtual machine should be allocated according to its weight, and then calculating actual number of BGs to be allocated in consideration of the maximum parallelism degree of the virtual machine (in virtual machine, the maximum parallelism degree is the number of its VCPUs), at last distributing BGs or fragment cores for every virtual machine.
- After distributing according to calculation, carrying out load balancing if there are free BGs or fragment cores in system. when load balancing, that a virtual machine whether or not gets BGs or fragment cores depends on its maximum parallelism degree. If its maximum parallelism degree is greater than the number of cores that have been distributed to it, the virtual machine can get more BGs or fragment cores, and vice versa.
- When a new virtual machine joins the system, calculating the number of BGs or fragment cores that the virtual machine should be allocated according to its weight. If free cores are enough, distributing them to the virtual machine, or else reclaiming cores of virtual machines that have been over-allocated to meet the new machine.
- When a certain virtual machine exits from the system, reclaiming its cores, and then carrying out load balancing again.

3.2.2 Algorithms

Let $C = \left\{ C_1, C_2, \ldots, C_{|C|} \right\}$ represent the set of physical cores. $|C|$ is the number of the cores. Assuming the number of cores of a BG is k, because the number of cores in each BG is equal, the number of BGs in system is $|C|/k$, and the set G of BGs can be represent as $\{G_1, G_2, \ldots, G_{|C|/k}\}$. Set a flag variable t_g for each BG, and initial value of t_g is set to 0. The variable t_g can be assigned to 0, 1 and 2, denoting cores of a BG unallocated, part-allocated, and full-allocated, individually. Let $V = \left\{ V_1, V_2, \ldots, V_{|V|} \right\}$ denote the set of virtual machines in system, and V is empty in initial state. $|V|$ represents the number of virtual machines. Let $\omega(V_i)$ denotes the weight of the ith virtual machine, which obeys the constraint $\sum_{i=1}^{|V|} \omega(V_i) = 1$, and Let $\Gamma(V_i)$ represent the number of VCPUs in virtual machine V_i. Essentially, $\Gamma(V_i)$ is the maximum parallelism degree of V_i. Let V_{lb} represent the queue of load balancing, and its value is empty in initial state. A virtual machine will enter V_{lb} when its number of cores allocated is less than its maximum parallelism degree. Let $PLB = \{PLB_1, PLB_2, \ldots, PLB_{|PLB|}\}$ denote the collection of cores allocated due to load balancing. The number of elements in PLB is $|PLB|$. Let $GLB = \{GLB_1, GLB_2, \ldots, GLB_{|GLB|}\}$ represent the collection of BGs allocated due to load balancing, and the number of elements in GLB is $|GLB|$. Let $GF(V_i) = \{GF(V_i)_1, GF(V_i)_2, \ldots, GF(V_i)_{|GF(Vi)|}\}$ represent the set of BGs allocated for V_i. $|GF(V_i)|$ denotes the number of elements in $GF(V_i)$. t_s is a flag variable for each element in $GF(V_i)$, which can be assigned to 0 or 1, denoting that the BG whether is monopolized by a virtual machine or is shared by multiple virtual machines, respectively. A global variable G_{free} is set to represent the number of unallocated BGs.

The initial core distributing algorithm is shown in Algorithm 1. The algorithm carries out initial core distribution for each machine according to their weight. If there are free cores in system, the algorithm will call load balancing process shown in Algorithm 2.

Algorithm 1. The initial core distributing algorithm.

1: $m=|C|/k$; $G_{free}=m$; $V_{lb}=\Phi$;/* m, the number of BGs in system. Φ, empty set. */
2: $\zeta(V_i)= | m \times \omega(V_i) |$; /*$\zeta(V_i)$, the number of BGs of V_i according to its weight.*/
3: **if** $\lfloor \Gamma(V_i)/k \rfloor <= \zeta(V_i)$ **then** $\psi(V_i)= \lfloor \Gamma(V_i)/k \rfloor$; /*$\psi(V_i)$, the actual number of BGs to be allocated V_i.*/
4:   $n_{cp}(V_i)= \Gamma(V_i)- \psi(V_i)\times k$; /* $n_{cp}(V_i)$, the number of cores that isn't enough to constitute a BG.*/
5: **else** $\psi(V_i)= \zeta(V_i)$; $n_{cp}(V_i)= \omega(V_i)\times m \times k - \psi(V_i)\times k$; **end if**
6: assign $\psi(V_i)$ BGs to V_i form G, and these BGs enter $GF(V_i)$, and set t_s to 2; $G_{free}= G_{free}-\psi(V_i)$;
7: **if** $n_{cp}(V_i) \neq 0$ **then** select a BG (assumed to be G_l) whose value of t_g is 0 from G, select $n_{cp}(V_i)$ cores from G_l to assign to V_i, and set t_g of G_l to 1;
8:   make G_l join $GF(V_i)$; $n_f(G_l)=k- n_{cp}(V_i)$; $G_{free}= G_{free}-1$; **end if** /* $n_f(G_l)$, the number of the rest of cores of G_l.*/
9: $\Psi(V_i)=\psi(V_i)\times k+ n_{cp}(V_i)$; /*$\Psi(V_i)$, the number of cores assigned V_i.*/
10: **if** $\Gamma(V_i) > \Psi(V_i)$ **then** V_i enter V_{lb} ; **end if**
11: $n=|P|-\psi(V_i)\times k - n_{cp}(V_i)$; **if** $n>0$ && $V_{lb} \neq \Phi$ **then** $n=$ load_balance(n); **end if** /*n, the number of the rest of cores in system. call load balancing

---

Algorithm 2 assigns free cores to virtual machines in V_{lb} according to the policy of FCFM (First-Come-First-Meet). In the course of assigning, the unallocated cores of BGs whose value of t_g is 1are selected in priority in order to reduce fragments. The virtual machine can't be distributed more cores when its number of cores is greater than $\Gamma(V_i)$.

Algorithm 2. Load balancing algorithm($load\_balance(n)$)

1: $flag=1$; /*flag variable.*/
2: **for each** V_i in V_{lb} **do**
3:   **while** $n>0$ && $flag==1$
4:     **if** there is a BG (assuming to be G_h)whose value of t_g is 1 in G, **then** G_h enter GLB;
5:       **if** G_h doesn't belong to $GF(V_i)$ **then** G_h enter $GF(V_i)$; **end if**
6:       **while** $n_f(G_h)>0$ distribute a free core to V_i from G_h and make it enter PLB; $\Psi(V_i)$++; $n_f(G_h)$--; $n=n-1$;/* $\Psi(V_i)$,the number of cores of V_i.*/
7:       **if** $n_f(G_h)==0$ **then** set t_g of G_h to 2; **end if**
8:       **if** $\Gamma(V_i)== \Psi(V_i)$ **then**$flag=0$; V_i exits from V_{lb}; **break; end if**
9:     **end while**
10:    **else** select a BG (assumed to be G_h) whose value of t_g is 0 from G;
11:      make G_h join $GF(V_i)$ and GLB; set t_g of G_h to 1; $G_{free}= G_{free}-1$;
12:      **while** $n_f(G_h)>0$ distribute a free core to V_i from G_h and make it enter PLB; $\Psi(V_i)$++; $n_f(G_h)$--; $n=n-1$;
13:      **if** $n_f(G_h)==0$ **then** set t_g of G to 2; **end if**
14:      **if** $\Gamma(V_i)== \Psi(V_i)$ **then** $flag=0$; V_i exits from V_{lb}; **break; end if**
15:    **end while**
16:   **end if**
17:   **end while**
18: **end for**
19: **return**(n);

The Algorithm 3 demonstrates the core redistributing algorithms when a new virtual machine joins the system. The algorithm sets a constraint that every virtual machine at least monopolizes a BG, and otherwise the system is considered to be overloaded.

Algorithm 3. Core redistributing algorithm when a new virtual machine enters system

1: $num_V=|V|$; num_V ++; /* num_V: the number of running virtual machines in system.*/
2: if $num_V>m$ then error(); end if /*the system overloads, fail to start virtual machine.*/
3: $\zeta(V_\Phi)=\lceil m \times \alpha(V_\Phi) \rceil$;
4: if $\lceil |\Gamma(V_\Phi) / k| \le \zeta(V_\Phi)$ then$\psi(V_\Phi)=\lceil |\Gamma(V_\Phi) / k| \rceil$; $n_{cp}(V_\Phi)=\Gamma(V_\Phi)-\psi(V_\Phi)\times k$; else $\psi(V_\Phi)=\zeta(V_\Phi)$; $n_{cp}(V_\Phi)=\omega(V_\Phi)\times m\times k-\psi(V_\Phi)\times k$; end if
5: if $\psi(V_\Phi) \le G_{free}$ && $(\psi(V_\Phi)\times k+n_{cp}(V_\Phi)) \le n$ then /* n, the number of the rest of cores in system. */
6:     assign $\psi(V_\Phi)$ BGs whose value of t_g to V_i, and make them enter $GF(V_\Phi)$, and set their t_g to 2; $G_{free}=G_{free}-\psi(V_\Phi)$;
7:     if $n_{cp}(V_\Phi)\ne 0$ then
8:         if exist a BG whose value of $t_g=1$ && the number of free cores of theBG$\ge n_{cp}(V_\Phi)$ then
9:             assign $n_{cp}(V_\Phi)$ cores in the BG to V_Φ, BG enter $GF(V_\Phi)$, set t_g to 2 if the number of free cores of the BG; set the t_c to 1;
10:             else if exist a BG whose $t_g=0$ then assign $n_{cp}(V_\Phi)$ cores to V_Φ from BGs whose $t_g=0$; the BG enter $GF(V_\Phi)$, set t_g to 1; $G_{free}=G_{free}-1$;
11:             else assign $n_{cp}(V_\Phi)$ cores to V_Φ from BGs whose $t_g=1$ && the sum of the number of their free cores $\ge n_{cp}(V_\Phi)$; BGs enter $GF(V_\Phi)$;
12:                 if the number of free cores of a BG is 0, set the value of t_g of the BG to 2; set the value of t_c of these BGs to 1;
13:         end if
14:         $n=n-\psi(V_\Phi)\times k-n_{cp}(V_\Phi)$);
15:     else $n=$ reclaim_$V_{lb}(n)$; /* reclaim cores.*/
16:         if $\psi(V_\Phi) \le G_{free}$ && $(\psi(V_\Phi)\times k+n_{cp}(V_\Phi)) \le n$ then repeat 9~14; else $n=$ reclaim_V(n); repeat 9~14; end if
17: end if
18: make V_Φ enter V;
19: for each VM V_i in V do $\Psi(V_i)=\psi(V_i)\times k+n_{cp}(V_i)$; if $\Gamma(V_i)> \Psi(V_i)$ then make V_i enter V_{lb}; end if end for
20: if $n>0$ && $V_{lb}\ne \Phi$ then $n=$ load_balance(n); end if

---

At first, the number of cores assigned the new virtual machine is calculated according to its weight. If free BGs are enough to allocate, the new virtual machine is distributed cores directly, or else the Algorithm 4 is called to reclaim cores used to load balancing to meet the new virtual machine. If the free cores isn't still enough to distribute, the Algorithm 5 is called to further reclaim cores. After distributing, the Algorithm 2 is called to carry out load balancing again.

Algorithm 4. Core reclaiming algorithm1 ($reclaim\_V_{lb}(n)$)

1: /* Core reclaiming algorithm1 used to reclaim cores due to load balancing.*/
2: for each P_i in PLB do
3:     $T_\theta=$ GetSystemTime(); /*get the system time*/
4:     if VCPU running in P_i is in *safe status* || (GetSystemTime()$-T_s) \ge \theta$ then/*θ is a time upper limit, its value is relative to scheduling time slice.*/
5:         make P_i free and remove it from PLB; $n_f(G_k)$++; $n=n+1$; else continue; end if /*G_k, the BG containing P_i */
6: end for
7: for each G_i in GLB do if $n_f(G_i)==k$ then $t_g=0$; G_{free}++; else $t_g=1$; end if remove G_i from GLB; end for
8: return(n);

Algorithm 5. Core reclaiming algorithm 2 （$recalim\_V(n)$）

1: $\Im=\Phi$; $nc=0$; $flag=1$;
2: **for** each V_i in V **do**
3:     $\Delta Ч(V_i)=\min(\Gamma(V_i), |C|\times \omega(V_i)) - \min(\Gamma(V_i), |C|\times (\omega(V_i)-\Delta\omega))$; /*$\Delta Ч(V_i)$, $\Delta\omega$, D-value of the number of cores and
4:     $\Delta\psi(V_i)=\lfloor \Delta n(V_i) / k \rfloor$; $\Delta n_{cp}(V_i)=\mathrm{mod}(\Delta n(V_i), k)$;/*$\Delta n_{cp}(V_i)$, the number of cores that isn't enough to constitute a BG.*/
5:     **if** $\Delta\psi(V_i)\neq 0$ **then**
6:         remove $\Delta\psi(V_i)$ BGs whose $t_s=0$ and $t_g=2$ from $GF(V_i)$; set t_g to 0 and enter cores in these BGS into $\Im$; $G_{free}=G_{free}+\Delta\psi(V_i)$; **end if**
7:     **if** $\Delta n_{cp}(V_i)\neq 0$ **then**
8:         **while** (exist a BG (assumed to be G_j) whose $t_s=1 \parallel t_s=0$&& $t_g=1$ in $GF(V_i)$ && $flag=1$
9:             **if** $n_{cp}(V_i)\leqslant$the number of cores assigned to V_i from G_j **then** select $\Delta n_{cp}(V_i)$ cores assigned to V_i from G_j to enter $\Im$; $n=n+$
10:                **if** (the number of cores assigned to V_i from G_j-$\Delta n_{cp}(V_i)$) $==$ 0 **then** remove G_j from $GF(V_i)$;
11:                    **if** $t_s==1$ **then** $t_s=0$; **else** $t_g=0$; G_{free}++; **end if**
12:                **else if** $t_g==2$ **then** $t_g=1$; **end if**
13:                **break**;
14:             **else**
15:                **for** each core assigned V_i in G_j **do**
16:                    **if** $nc<\Delta n_{cp}(V_i)$ **then** the core enter $\Im$; $nc=nc+$; n++; $nG_j(V_i)$--;
17:                        **if** $nG_j(V_i)==0$ **then** remove G_j from $GF(V_i)$; **if** $t_s==1$ **then** $t_s=0$; **else** $t_g=0$; G_{free}++; **end if end if**
20:                    **else** $flag=0$; **break**; **end if**
21:                **end for**
22:         **end while**
23:         **if** $nc<\Delta n_{cp}(V_i)$ **then** select a BG whose $t_s=0$ and t_g $=2$ from $GF(V_i)$, and from the BG select $\Delta n_{cp}(V_i)$-nc cores,
24:             and make them into $\Im$, and assign t_g to1; $n=n+\Delta n_{cp}(V_i)$-nc; **end if**
25:     **end if**
26: **end for**
27: **while** $\Im\neq\Phi$
28:     **for** each P_i in $\Im$ **do** $T_0=$ $GetSystemTime()$;
29:         **if** VCPU running in P_i is in safe status $\parallel$ （$GetSystemTime()$-T0） $\geqslant 0$ **then** make P_i free and remove it from $\Im$; **else**
30:         **end if**
31:     **end for**
32: **end while**
33: **return**(n);

As shown in Algorithms 4 and 5, the cores or BGs on which VCPUs with low worth run are always reclaimed in priority. We identify the worth of a VCPU by observing whether the VCPU is holding the spin-lock or not. When it isn't holding the spin-lock, the worth of the VCPU is low, and vice versa. A VCPU holding the spin-lock is consider unsafe. The parameter θ is a time upper limit whose value depends on scheduling the length of scheduling time slice. A core will be compulsively reclaimed when its accumulated time from the moment of first check is greater than θ though the VCPU running on the core is at the unsafe status.

When a virtual machine exits from the system due to the end of its life cycle or when all VCPUs running on a virtual machine are blocked, the redistribution of cores should be carried on again by the Algorithm 6.

Algorithm 6. Core redistributing algorithm when a new virtual machine exits from system

---

1: **for** each $GF(V_z)_i$ in $GF(V_z)$ **do**
2:     **if** $t_s==0$ **then**
3:         **for** each P_i in $GF(V_z)_i$ **do** make P_i free and remove it from V_z; $n=n+1$; **end for**
7:         $t_g=0$; G_{free}++;
9:     **else**
10:        **for** each P_i in $GF(V_z)_i$ **do if** P_i is the core assigned V_z **then** make P_i free and remove it from V_z; $n=n+1$; **end if end for**
16:        **if** $t_g==2$ **then** $t_g=1$; **end if**
19:        $t_s=0$;
20:     **end if**
21: **call** load_balance(n);

4   The Implementation of CDLP

In order to verify the correctness or effectiveness of CDLP, we implement a prototype. This section first describes the architecture of the prototype, and then introduce the design of the allocator.

4.1   The Architecture of the Prototype System

The prototype is build based on Xen3.4.0. Xen is a mainstream open source virtualized platform, developed by University of Cambridge. Xen mainly aims to X86 architecture. Compared with KVM [18], Xen has its own scheduler and memory management module. We select Xen because Xen has good stability and provides abundant APIs that can be conveniently revoked and encapsulated by scripting language and library. There are two possible approaches to implement our prototype: kernel functions and process. The core component of the prototype is the allocator. We implement the allocator by user processes. Ease of implementation and availability of debugging tools are our primary motivation in this way as opposed to kernel functions. Figure 4 shows the architecture of the prototype.

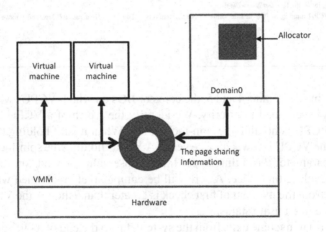

Fig. 4. The architecture of allocator

In Xen, *Domain0* is a privilege virtual machine responsible to manage other virtual machines (*DomainU*). *Domain0*, VMM and *DomainU* communicate with each other through the page sharing information [19], which provides CPU information including the status, time, event channel of VCPU and information of holding spin-lock of VCPUs. The allocator is located at *Domain0* and runs in user mode. The tasks of the allocator is to allocator cores for virtual machines according to CDLP. The VCPU scheduling is still carried out by Xen Credit scheduler [20].

4.2 The Design of the Allocator

The allocator runs in *Domain0* in the form of daemon process. We employ Python and libvirt [21] to implement allocator. Libvirt provides a abundant API library for virtual machine management, which supports multiple virtualized platform such as Xen and KVM.

The structure of the allocator is shown in Fig. 5. The allocator consists of five components: the algorithm module, the interface for getting the number of VCPUs, the interface for reading core information, the interface for setting VCPU and the interface for reading spin-lock information. The algorithm module, as the core of allocator, is responsible to carry out the logic of Algorithms 1–6. The information required by Algorithms 1–6 is provided by other four components. The interface for reading the number of VCPUs gets the number of VCPUs of each virtual machine to determine their maximum parallelism degree. The interface for reading core information gets the system information, including the number of cores sharing the same cache and the total number of cores in system, for partitioning cores into BGs and determining the number of BGs. The interface for setting VCPUs is called by the algorithm module to carry out core distributing or reclaiming. The interface for reading spin-lock information obtains information of holding spin-lock of VCPUs from the page sharing information to identify safe or unsafe state of VCPUs.

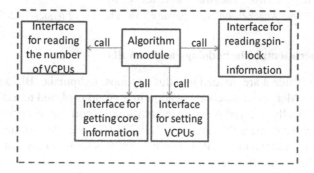

Fig. 5. The structure of the allocator

5 Performance Evaluation

In this section, we evaluate the performance of CDLP. We employ the rate of cache misses and running time of applications as the key metric.

5.1 Experimental Environments and Benchmarks

We conduct our performance evaluation in the machine with two Intel Xeon E5310 quad-core processors and employ Xen3.4.0 as the virtualized platform. The guest OS is Red Hat Enterprise Linux 5. Table 2 demonstrates the detail of hardware. We employ Xenprof [22] to get the rate of cache misses and command time built in Linux to get application running time. We select PARSEC, SPLASH-2, Hash Join [23] and Mergesort [24] as our benchmark. The detail of benchmarks is shown in Table 3.

Table 2. Machine configuration

CPU	L1	L2	Memory
Xeon E5310 1.6 GHz	32 K Dcache + 32 k ICache	2 × 4 MB, sharing L2 per two cores	8 GB, sharing bus

Table 3. Benchmarks

Applications	Description
LU	The size of input matrix is 4 k × 4 k,the size of block is 16, the number of threads can be indicate by command line parameters
pmake	Parallel compiling, employing −j to indicate the number of threads. The number of instruction to be compiled is 15,000
Blackscholes	The input data set is *native,* the maximum number of threads is indicated by −n
Bodytrack	The input data set is *native,* the maximum number of threads is indicated by −n
Hash Join	The size of input table is not more than 100 MB
Mergesort	The number of threads is the number of array couple that carry out merge sorting in parallelism. The size of work-set is 2 M
Apache	Select Apachebench to simulate client. The size of request is 200000

5.2 The Experimental Methodology and Results

Applications in Table 3 are divided into three groups: LU/pmake, Blackscholes/Bodytrack, Hash Join/Mergesort. Each application in a group is placed to a different virtual machine, individually. According to logic partitioning, cores in system can be divided into four BGs. We call these BGs BG0, BG1, BG2, BG3. In order to eliminate the effect of Domain0, we fix Domain0 in BG3. The value of θ is set to 30 ms that is equal to the size of scheduling time slice in Xen.

5.2.1 Performance

We configure virtual machines VM_0 and VM_1 with two VCPUs, 512 M memory, respectively, and assign the value of their weight to 256. The value of weight of Domain0 is set to 512. We run every application five times and get their average. The number of parallel threads of all applications is set to 8.

Figure 6 shows cache misses of LU/pmake, Blackscholes/Bodytrack, Hash Join/Mergesort in CDLP and Xen. We find that the rate of cache misses of three groups of applications are reduced 30.1%, 52.7% and 24.5% in CDLP, respectively, relative to the default policy of Xen. The reason that CDLP has a better cache performance gain is that CDLP distributes each application with different cache working set to different BGs to run, which reduces the inter-core cache misses. Figure 7 demonstrates the running time of applications in CDLP and Xen. Compared with Xen, the performance of applications has a 5%–30% increase in CDLP. When CDLP is employed, threads in the same applications are assigned to one or multiple BGs. Because cores in the same BGs share the same cache, and threads in the same application have overlapping cache working set, data reuse can be effectively implemented. We notice that LU and Blackscholes have less performance raise than others (only 5% and 8.57%, individually). The reason is that, for LU, the decrease of cache misses isn't enough to significantly improve its performance because of its small cache work set, and for Blackscholes, its performance raise is concealed due to its tiny calculation for data sharing.

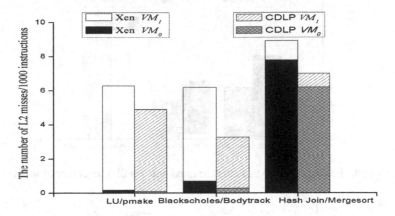

Fig. 6. L2 misses in CDLP and Xen

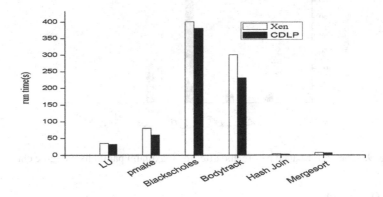

Fig. 7. The performance of applications in CDLP and Xen

5.2.2 Load Balancing

In order to verify the effectiveness of Algorithm 2 for load balancing, we modify the maximum parallelism degree of virtual machines. The number of VCPUs in VM_1 is changed from 2 to 4, while the one of VCPUs in VM_0 keeps invariable. As shown in Fig. 8, in CDLP, the number of L2 misses of pmake, Bodytrack and Mergesort running in VM_1 are reduce by 39.1%, 36.1% and 34.6%, respectively, and that the L2 misses are almost invariable for LU, Blackscholes and Hash Join in VM0. Likewise, the perform-ance of pmake, Bodytrack and Mergesort are raised by 73%, 85% and 88%, individually, as shown in Fig. 9. The reason is that when the maximum parallelism degree of VM1 changes from 2 to 4, CDLP assigns two BGs to VM1 by load balancing although the number of BGs assigned to it should be 1 according its weight, which shows that CDLP has good ability of load balancing.

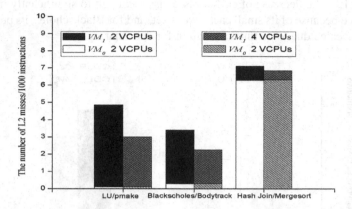

Fig. 8. L2 misses before and after the maximum parallelism degree changes

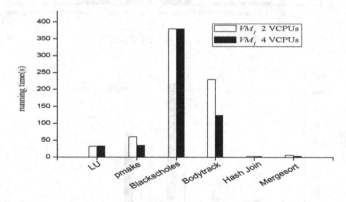

Fig. 9. The performance before and after the maximum parallelism degree changes.

5.2.3   Overhead

The overhead of core redistribution includes the time finding a assignable core and the time activating a VCPU to run in the core, depending on whether the core to be assigned is unallocated or allocated. We compare the overhead between CDLP and Xen by experimentation. We design following two scenarios:

- Scenario 1. The numbers of VCPUs of VM_0 and VM_1 are assigned to 4 and 5, respectively, and the weight both are 256. The weight of $Domain0$ is 512. We first start VM_0 and run applications (Apache and Bodytrace, individually) with 4 parallel processes or threads. After 30 s, we start VM_1 to run Blackscholes with 5 threads. Before VM_1 starts, VM_0 can be assigned 2 BGs, and therefore there is a free BGs (total 4 BGs in system, one of them is assigned to *Domain0*). When VM_1 starts, the number of BGs assigned to VM_1 is 1, which can be calculated according the weight of VM_1. So We can assign the BG to VM_1 without preempting cores from VM_0.

- Scenario 2. Relative to scenario 1, We only change the value of weight of VM_1 to 1280. We conduct the same experiments with scenario 1. When VM_1 starts, according to its weight, VM_1 should be assigned 2.5 BGs. Because there is only one free BG, in order to meet VM_1, some cores must be preempted from VM_0.

We insert tracking codes into the kernel and the allocator to get the core distributing time in CDLP and Xen.

From Table 4, we can find that in scenario 1, the overhead of CDLP is almost close to the one of Xen, and in scenario 2, the overhead of CDLP is more large than Xen. The reason resulting the difference is that in scenario 2 CDLP must spend time to find assignable cores duo to lack of free cores by call the Algorithms 4 and 5. Further, we can find that the overhead running Apache is more large than Bodytrace, and this is because that Apache is an I/O-intensive workloads whose frequency of holding lock is high, and therefore the probability of being unsafe status is high accordingly.

Table 4. The overhead of core distribution for VM_1

Policy	Scenario 1		Scenario 2	
	Appache	Bodytrace	Appache	Bodytrace
CDLP	2.20 ms	2.19 ms	40.7 ms	8.1 ms
Xen	2.15 ms	2.14 ms	3.95 ms	3.93 ms

Fortunately, although the overhead of CDLP is more large than Xen, this only increase the time of virtual machine starting, and doesn't hurt the performance of virtual machines.

6 Conclusion

Data reuse in shared cache for multithreading applications can effectively improve the performance of multithreading applications. However, because of the lack of cooperation in two-level scheduling framework in virtualized system, the scheduling and distributing policy employed by VCPU scheduler often counteract the endeavor of the guest operating for data reuse. We present CDLP: a novel dynamic core distributing policy based on logic partitioning, and we present a set of algorithms including core initially allocating, load balancing, core re-allocating and core reclaiming. In order to verify the effectiveness and correctness of CDLP, we implement a prototype base on Xen platform, the experimental results demonstrate that, compared with Xen, the rate of cache misses of three groups of applications are reduced 30.1%, 52.7% and 24.5%, and the performance of applications has a 5%–30% increase, respectively. However, CDLP can incur more overhead in the stage of virtual machine starting with I/O-intensive applications than Xen. In addition, we implement our prototype based on user processes instead of kernel functions that maybe better for performance. We will address these problems in the future work.

Acknowledgements. This work was supported by the National Key Research and Development Program of China under Grant 2016YFB0800403, the Natural Science Foundation of China (61174177), the Open Foundation of Hubei Engineering Research Center of Construction Quality Testing Equipment (2016KTE06), and BRCAST-KFKT2014001.

References

1. Blelloch, G.E., Gibbons, P.B.: Effectively sharing a cache among threads. In: Gibbons, P.B., Adler, M. (eds.) Proceedings of the Sixteenth Annual ACM Symposium on Parallelism in Algorithms and Architectures (SPAA 2004), Barcelona, Spain, 27–30 June 2004, pp. 235–244. ACM Press, New York (2004)
2. Blelloch, G.E., Gibbons, P.B., Matias, Y.: Provably efficient scheduling for languages with fine-grained parallelism. J. ACM **46**(2), 281–321 (1999)
3. Chen, S., Gibbons, P.B., Kozuch, M., et al.: Scheduling threads for constructive cache sharing on CMPs. In: Scheideler, C. (ed.) Proceedings of the 19th Annual ACM Symposium on Parallelism in Algorithms and Architectures (SPAA 2007), San Diego, CA, USA, 09–11 June 2007, pp. 105–115. ACM Press, New York (2007)
4. Tam, D., Azimi, R.,Stumm, M.: Thread clustering: sharing-aware scheduling on SMP-CMP-SMT multiprocessors. In: Ferreira, P., Gross, T.R., Veiga, L. (eds.) Proceedings of the 2nd ACM SIGOPS/EuroSys European Conference on Computer Systems (EuroSys 2007), Lisbon, Portugal, 21–23 March 2007, pp. 47–58. ACM Press, New York (2007)
5. Pericas, M., Taura, K., Matsuoka, S.: Scalable analysis of multicore data reuse and sharing. In: Proceedings of the 28th ACM International Conference on Supercomputing (ICS 2014), Muenchen, Germany, 10–13 June 2014, pp. 353–362. ACM Press, New York (2014)
6. Zhang, W., Liu, F., Fan, R.: Cache matching: thread scheduling to maximize data reuse. In: Proceedings of the High Performance Computing Symposium (HPC 2014), Tampa, FL, USA, 13–16 April 2014, no. 7. ACM Press, New York (2014)
7. Jin, H., Qin, H., Wu, S., et al.: CCAP: a cache contention-aware virtual machine placement approach for HPC cloud. Int. J. Parallel Program. (2013). ISSN 1573-7630
8. Kim, S., Eom, H., Yeom, H.Y.: Virtual machine scheduling for multicores considering effects of shared on-chip last level cache interference. In: Culler, D., Shirazi, B. (eds.) Proceedings of the 3rd International Green Computing Conference (IGCC 2012), San Jose, CA, USA, 04–08 June 2012, pp. 1–6. IEEE Computer Society, Washington (2012)
9. Rao, J., Wang, K., Zhou, X., et al.: Optimizing virtual machine scheduling in NUMA multicore systems. In: Zhang, L. (ed.) IEEE Proceedings of the 19th International Symposium on High Performance Computer Architecture (HPCA 2013), Shenzhen, China, 23–27 February 2013, pp. 206–317. IEEE Computer Society, Washington (2013)
10. Barham, P., Dragovic, B., Fraser, K., et al.: Xen and the art of virtualization. In: Scott, M.L., Peterson, L.L. (eds.) Proceedings of the 19th ACM Symposium on Operating Systems Principles (SOSP 2003), Bolton Landing, NY, USA, 19–22 October 2003, pp. 164–177. ACM Press, New York (2003)
11. Kandemir, M., Prashanth, S., Hari Krishna, S.: Optimizing shared cache behavior of chip multiprocessors. In: Albonesi, D.H., Martonosi, M., August, D.I., et al. (eds.) Proceedings of the 42nd Annual IEEE/ACM International Symposium on Microarchitecture (MICRO 2009), New York, 12–16 December 2009, pp. 505–516. ACM Press, New York (2009)

12. Woo, S.C., Ohara, M., Torrie, E., et al.: The SPLASH-2 programs: characterization and methodological considerations. In: Patterson, D.A. (ed.) Proceedings of the 22nd Annual International Symposium on Computer Architecture (ISCA 1995), S. Margherita Ligure, Italy, 22–24 June 1995, pp. 24–36. ACM Press, New York (1995)
13. Bienia, C., Kumar, S., Singh, J.P., et al.: The PARSEC benchmark suite: characterization and architectural implications. In: Moshovos, A., Tarditi, D., Olukotun, K. (eds.) Proceedings of the 17th International Conference on Parallel Architectures and Compilation Techniques (PACT 2008), Toronto, Canada, 25–29 October 2008, pp. 72–81. ACM Press, New York (2008)
14. Magnusson, P.S., Christensson, M., Eskilson, J., et al.: Simics: a full system simulation platform. J. Comput. 35(2), 50–58 (2002)
15. Martin, M., Sorin, D., Beckmann, B., et al.: Multifacet's general execution-driven multiprocessor simulator (gems) toolset. Comput. Architect. News 33(4), 92–99 (2005)
16. Srikantaiah, S., Kandemir, M., Jane, I.M.: Adaptive set pinning: managing shared caches in chip multiprocessors. In: Eggers, S.J., Larus, J.R. (eds.) Proceedings of the 13th International Conference on Architectural Support for Programming Languages and Operating Systems (ASPLOS 2008), Seattle, Washington, USA, 1–5 March 2008, pp. 135–144. ACM Press, New York (2008)
17. Aslot, V., Domeika, M.J., Eigenmann, R., et al.: SPECcomp: a new benchmark suite for measuring parallel computer performance. In: Eigenmann, R., Voss, M. (eds.) Proceedings of the International Workshop on OpenMP Applications and Tools: OpenMP Shared Memory Parallel Programming, pp. 1–10. Springer, London (2001)
18. Raghavendra, K.T.: Virtual CPU scheduling techniques for kernel based virtual machine (KVM). In: Diamond, S. (ed.) The Second IEEE International Conference on Cloud Computing in Emerging Markets (CCEM 2013), Bangalore, India, 16–18 October 2013, pp. 1–6. IEEE Computer Society Press, Washington (2013)
19. Zhong, A., Jin, H., Wu, S., et al.: Optimizing Xen hypervisor by using lock-aware scheduling. In: Proceedings of the Second International Conference on Cloud and Green Computing (CGC 2012), Xiangtan, China, 1–3 Novemenber 2012, pp. 31–38. IEEE Computer Society Press, Washington (2012)
20. Credit Based Scheduler. http://wiki.xensource.com/xenwiki/Creditscheduler
21. Libvirt. http://libvirt.org/
22. Menon, A., Santos, J.R., Turner, Y.: Diagnosing performance overheads in the Xen virtual machine environment. In: Hind, M. (ed.) Proceedings of the 1st ACM/USENIX International Conference on Virtual Execution Environments (VEE 2005), Chicago, Illinois, USA, 11–12 June 2005, pp. 13–23. ACM Press, New York (2005)
23. Chen, S., Ailamaki, A., Gibbons, P.B., et al.: Inspector joins. In: Böhm, K., Jensen, C.S., Haas, L.M., et al. (eds.) Proceedings of the 31st International Conference on Very Large Data Bases (VLDB 2005), Trondheim, Norway, 30 August–2 September 2005, pp. 817–828. ACM Press, New York (2005)
24. Mergesort. https://en.wikipedia.org/wiki/Merge_sort

A Profit-Maximum Resource Allocation Approach for Mapreduce in Data Centers

Xiaolu Zhang, Weidong Li, Xi Liu, and Xuejie Zhang$^{(\boxtimes)}$

School of Information Science and Engineering,
Yunnan University, Kunming, China
{zxl,weidong,xjzhang}@ynu.edu.cn, lxghost@126.com

Abstract. Resource allocation for Mapreduce data processing poses difficult challenges to system administrators in data centers. The extreme scale of Mapreduce applications require an efficiently profitable resource allocation algorithm that minimizes the energy consumption cost while maintaining the highest level of performance. In this paper, we propose a profit-maximum model that minimizes the cost of energy consumption and makespan. By adopting a minimum-weight b-matching rounding algorithm (MBRA) to find an integer solution, then assign map/reduce tasks to individual slots to build a complete resource allocation. Finally, we perform experiments on real workload to evaluate the profit-maximum model and analyze the performance of our proposed algorithm. The results show that MBRA is able to find a near-optimal integer solution that maximizes the profit per unit time in a lower runtime, and it is up to $30\% \sim 70\%$ in profit that is better than the current heuristic scheduling algorithm and the rounding algorithm.

Keywords: Profit · Energy consumption · Makespan · b-matching · Mapreduce

1 Introduction

With the growing demand for big data processing, the evolution of cloud computing technologies is towards more profit-effective and energy-saving solutions. Recently, the most popular approach for big data processing is using Mapreduce and its open-source implementation called Hadoop. Mapreduce framework can simplify the complexity of big data processing, which allows a programmer to define his/her data processing as a map function and a reduce function executed in a parallel manner deployed on Hadoop cluster in data centers without building and managing large installations of hardware and software platforms. Due to its efficiency and easiness, it has been widely employed by many companies, such as Facebook, Amazon, Twitter, Yahoo!, and applied in diverse areas, including data mining, machine learning, web indexing, social networks, and so on.

We observe that the existing cloud techniques for Mapreduce framework primarily focus on improving Mapreduce performances, such as reducing the maximum completion time (makespan) [1, 2] and the total completion time [3], load balancing [4] and increasing system throughput [5]. As the increase in computational capability of

© Springer International Publishing AG 2017
M.H.A. Au et al. (Eds.): GPC 2017, LNCS 10232, pp. 460–474, 2017.
DOI: 10.1007/978-3-319-57186-7_34

Mapreduce systems, they also result in a significant increase in energy consumption to support electrical infrastructures like computer servers, cooling equipment and substation power transformers [6]. The high energy cost of running Mapreduce systems has lead researchers to find efficient solutions that reduce the required energy consumption to process tasks. For example, an energy-aware scheduling method [7] was used to minimize the energy consumption. This paper considered both energy consumption and performance when processing a Mapreduce job, which schedules map and reduce tasks to individual slots without exceeding the deadline time. However, the goals of users to finish their workload quickly and accurately often conflict with the goals of service providers to consume less energy. Minimizing energy consumption and increasing performance is desirable for Mapreduce systems, and a set of efficient algorithms have been proposed that help system administrators quickly gain insight into trade-offs space between energy and performance. Tarplee et al. [8] found a novel algorithm to construct a near-Pareto profit maximizing scheduling that trades off between energy and performance. This algorithm combined the minimum energy consumption with the minimum makespan into a single profit per unit time objective. Our research is closely related to this work. We consider a profit per unit time model and offer a near-optimal integer resource allocation solution in a lower runtime that aim to minimize the electricity cost for energy consumption and makespan time when processing a Mapreduce job in order to maximize the profit for service providers. In summary, our contributions are as follows:

- We propose a profit-maximum model that minimizes the cost of energy consumption and makespan. We consider the characteristics of Mapreduce tasks, the energy consumption of a job, Service-Level Agreement (SLA) and the parameter for makespan, price of electricity, and service payment.
- We present a minimum-weight b-matching rounding algorithm (MBRA) to find a near-optimal resource allocation. This algorithm first inverts the profit-maximum model into a Linear Program (LP) problem, then rounds the LP's optimal solution to a near-optimal integer solution based on the bipartite graph b-matching algorithm.
- We perform simulation experiments on small and large jobs to evaluate the accuracy and efficiency of the proposed profit-maximum model and compare the performance of MBRA with energy-aware heuristic scheduling algorithm and energy-aware profit maximizing scheduling algorithm. Moreover, extensive simulations are performed to study the impact of the slot configuration on the efficiency of MBRA.

The remainder of this paper is organized as follows. We discuss the related works in Sect. 2. Section 3 first defines our profit-maximum model. Section 4 introduces a minimum-weight b-matching rounding algorithm to generate a near-optimal integer solution and analyzes the algorithm performance. In Sect. 5, we simulate our algorithm on real workload and analyze the results. Finally, Sect. 6 summarizes our conclusions and the future work for this research.

2 Related Work

There is a large amount of research works that focus on the optimization for Makespan. Moseley et al. [1] modeled Mapreduce task scheduling as the classical two-stage flow shop problem (FFS) and introduced a dynamic polynomial time approximation scheme (PTAS) algorithm if there is a fixed number of job-types for minimizing the makespan when all Mapreduce jobs arrive at the same time. Tang et al. [2] proposed a job ordering algorithm and a map/reduce slot configuration optimization algorithm based on Johnson's Rule to minimize makespan and total completion time for an offline workload. Zhu et al. [3] designed an approximation algorithm for preemptive and non-preemptive reduce tasks on the makespan minimization and the total complete time minimization. Ren et al. [9] proposed a job-scheduling algorithm that extends job priorities to guarantee rapid responses for small jobs to optimize the completion time of small Mapreduce jobs. Verma et al. [10] proposed a job scheduler that minimizes the makespan for Mapreduce production jobs with no dependencies by utilizing the characteristics and properties of the jobs in given workload.

There has been an increasing interest in researching the energy-efficiency solutions for Mapreduce systems to minimize the energy consumption. Song et al. [11] studied the characteristics of Mapreduce policies and presented an idea that a good data placement can optimize the energy consumption. Lin et al. [12] proposed a SLA-aware size-scaling framework for heterogeneous Mapreduce clusters by designing a hybrid data layout and a runtime estimation method to turn off nodes to minimize the energy consumption. Maheshwari et al. [13] proposed an algorithm that dynamically reconfigures Mapreduce framework by scaling up and down the number of nodes based on the cluster utilization. Lin et al. [14] studied four combination scenarios of the energy consumption and performance of a Mapreduce job, locally-stored and distributively-stored policy, and the delay assignment and non-delay assignment policy, but there was no specific task-scheduling operation to increase the energy efficiency.

Recent efforts have been made in regards to optimizing the energy cost of the resource allocation and task scheduling for service providers. Tian and Chen [15] proposed a cost function to solve the optimal amount of resource in order to minimize the cost within a deadline time or minimize the time under certain budget. Palanisamy et al. [16] presented a new Mapreduce cloud service model, called Cura, designed to implement a globally efficient resource allocation scheme that reduces the resource usage cost. Young et al. [17] studied an energy-constrained dynamic resource allocation problem that tries to finish the maximum number of tasks within the energy budget of the system. Tarplee et al. [8] proposed a profit maximizing scheduling algorithm that trades off between energy consumption and makespan in heterogeneous computing systems. In our previous study [18], we designed a task-type-based algorithm for the energy-aware profit maximizing scheduling problem, and proved that the worst-case performance ratio is close to 2.

From the above studies, we note that the proposing algorithms and cost models optimize the resource allocation and task scheduling for performance and energy metrics. However, their works limit most one metric and few works capture the cost model for Mapreduce systems. On the other hand, the optimal allocation or scheduling is known to be a NP-hard problem [19] and has high computational cost especially when the number of tasks is more than one thousand. Furthermore, due to the similar workload, tasks belonging to one task type often exhibit high degree of similarity in energy and performance properties. Therefore, we first design a profit per unit time model based on the task type in Mapreduce systems, and combine the two metrics to optimize the profit for service providers.

3   Mathematical Model

A Mapreduce job consists of a M set of map task types and a R set of reduce type tasks, which are executed on a A set of map slots and a B set of reduce slots. Let MT_i be the number of map tasks of type i and RT_i be the number of reduce tasks of type i. Let x_{ij} be the number of map tasks of type i assigned to a map slot j, $j \in A$, and y_{ij} be the number of reduce tasks of type i assigned to a reduce slot j, $j \in B$. Let EEC be a matrix with entries e_{ij}s, where e_{ij} is the estimated energy consumption for a task of type $i \in \{M, R\}$ executed on a slot $j \in \{A, B\}$. Similarly let EPT be a matrix with entries p_{ij}s, where p_{ij} is the estimated processing time of a task of type $i \in \{M, R\}$ executed on a slot $j \in \{A, B\}$.

Considering a profit model of a Mapreduce system, the revenue is the service money that the user pays for the data processing under the makespan and the cost to the provider is composed of makespan time cost and energy consumption cost. Let p be the price the user pays, c_1 be the cost per unit of time, c_2 be the cost per unit of energy, and MS be the makespan time which is defined as the maximum completion time of all tasks. Thus, the maximum profit per unit time problem is formulated as the following nonlinear integer program (NLIP).

$$
\begin{cases}
\max \dfrac{p - c_1 MS - c_2 \left(\sum\limits_{j \in A} \sum\limits_{i \in M} e_{ij} x_{ij} + \sum\limits_{j \in B} \sum\limits_{i \in R} e_{ij} y_{ij} \right)}{MS} \\
\sum\limits_{j \in A} x_{ij} = MT_i, \ \forall i \in M \\
\sum\limits_{j \in B} y_{ij} = RT_i, \ \forall i \in R \\
\sum\limits_{i \in M} p_{ij} x_{ij} + \sum\limits_{i \in R} p_{ij'} y_{ij'} \le MS, \forall j \in A, \forall j' \in B \\
x_{ij} \in Z^+ \cup \{0\}, \ \forall i \in M, \forall j \in A \\
y_{ij} \in Z^+ \cup \{0\}, \ \forall i \in R, \forall j \in B
\end{cases}
\tag{1}
$$

The objective of Eq. (1) seeks to maximize the profit per unit time for service providers, and the objective function P is defined as

$$P(MS, x_{ij}, y_{ij}) = \frac{p - c_1 MS - c_2(\sum_{j \in A} \sum_{i \in M} e_{ij} x_{ij} + \sum_{j \in B} \sum_{i \in R} e_{ij} y_{ij})}{MS}, \tag{2}$$

where x_{ij} and y_{ij} are the primary decision variables, MS is an auxiliary decision variable to control the completion time. The first constraint ensures that all of map tasks of a single type are assigned to a map slot for execution. The second constraint ensures that all of reduce tasks of a single type are assigned to a reduce slot for execution. The third constraint ensures that processing time of the job does not exceed its makespan. The last two constraints represent the positive integer requirements for the decision variables. In next section, we will employ the LP solution from this section and propose a minimum-weight b-matching rounding algorithm to build a feasible allocation efficiently.

4   MBRA Method

4.1   Optimal Solution to the Relaxation of NLIP

Note that Eq. (1) is a nonlinear integer program, which can not be solved optimally in polynomial time. Thus, we use a parameter substitution and decision variables substitution to convert the objective and constraints of Eq. (1) into a linear program (LP). The substitutions are

$$d \leftarrow \frac{1}{MS} \text{ and } \alpha_{ij} \leftarrow \frac{x_{ij}}{MS}, \forall i \in M, \forall j \in A, \beta_{ij} \leftarrow \frac{y_{ij}}{MS}, \forall i \in R, \forall j \in B.$$

The variables α_{ij} and β_{ij} can be interpreted as the average number of tasks of type i on a slot j per unit time and d is the number of sets per unit time. Thus, the profit per unit time becomes $pd - c_1 MS - c_2(\sum \sum_{j \in A, i \in M} e_{ij} \alpha_{ij} + \sum \sum_{j \in B, i \in R} e_{ij} \beta_{ij})$ and the new linear optimization problem is given by (3), where the four constraints in (1) are converted to constraints in (3).

In this paper, we solve this LP (3) by a simplex method in polynomial time and obtain the optimal solution $(\tilde{d}, \tilde{\alpha}_{ij}, \tilde{\beta}_{ij})$. Apparently, the solution $(\dot{d}, \dot{\alpha}_{ij}, \dot{\beta}_{ij})$ of LP (3) is a feasible solution responded to the optimal solution $(\dot{MS}, \dot{x}_{ij}, \dot{y}_{ij})$ of NLIP (1). Therefore, the objective function value of $(\tilde{d}, \tilde{\alpha}_{ij}, \tilde{\beta}_{ij})$ is no less than OPT, where OPT denotes the optimal objective function value $P(\dot{MS}, \dot{x}_{ij}, \dot{y}_{ij})$. This conclusion is given by the following lemma.

Lemma 1. The objective function value of the optimal fraction solution $(\tilde{d}, \tilde{\alpha}_{ij}, \tilde{\beta}_{ij})$ is $P(\tilde{d}, \tilde{\alpha}_{ij}, \tilde{\beta}_{ij})$, and $P(\tilde{d}, \tilde{\alpha}_{ij}, \tilde{\beta}_{ij}) \geq OPT$.

$$\begin{cases} \max pd - c_1 - c_2(\sum_{j \in A} \sum_{i \in M} e_{ij}\alpha_{ij} + \sum_{j \in B} \sum_{i \in R} e_{ij}\beta_{ij}) \\ \sum_{j \in A} \alpha_{ij} = d \cdot MT_i, \ \forall i \in M \\ \sum_{j \in B} \beta_{ij} = d \cdot RT_i, \ \forall i \in R \\ \sum_{i \in M} p_{ij}\alpha_{ij} + \sum_{i \in R} p_{ij'}\beta_{ij'} \le 1, \forall j \in A, \forall j' \in B \\ \alpha_{ij} \ge 0, \ \forall i \in M, \ \forall j \in A \\ \beta_{ij} \ge 0, \ \forall i \in R, \ \forall j \in B \\ d \ge 0 \end{cases} \tag{3}$$

4.2 Minimum-Weight B-Matching Rounding Algorithm

The fraction solution $(\tilde{d}, \tilde{\alpha}_{ij}, \tilde{\beta}_{ij})$ can be converted to the optimal solution of the relaxation of NLIP (1) according to the following Eq. (4).

$$\begin{cases} \widetilde{MS} = \frac{1}{\tilde{d}} \\ \tilde{x}_{ij} = \widetilde{MS}\, \tilde{\alpha}_{ij}, \forall i \in M, \forall j \in A \\ \tilde{y}_{ij} = \widetilde{MS}\, \tilde{\beta}_{ij}, \forall i \in R, \forall j \in B \end{cases} \tag{4}$$

A feasible way is found to calculate the integer solution as $x_{ij} = \lfloor \tilde{x}_{ij} \rfloor$ and $y_{ij} = \lfloor \tilde{y}_{ij} \rfloor$, and for unassigned tasks, they are assigned by a greedy allocation algorithm. However, in this way, this design results in the increase of energy consumption and makespan, in turn, which will perform a worse profit per unit time. Therefore, in our approach, we adopt a minimum-weight b-matching rounding algorithm by modifying the Shmoys & Tardos's rounding method in [20], which is to find a minimum-weight matching of auxiliary bipartite graphs, to convert an infeasible relaxation solution $(\widetilde{MS}, \tilde{x}_{ij}, \tilde{y}_{ij})$ of NLIP (1) into a feasible solution $(\widehat{MS}, \hat{x}_{ij}, \hat{y}_{ij})$.

We first construct two weighted bipartite graphs $B(\tilde{x}_{ij})$ and $B(\tilde{y}_{ij})$ based on the method applied in [20]. For a given solution $\tilde{x}_{ij}$, let x_{ij}^f be the fraction part of $\tilde{x}_{ij}$ and k_j be the sum of fraction parts.

$$x_{ij}^f = \tilde{x}_{ij} - \lfloor \tilde{x}_{ij} \rfloor, \forall i \in M, \forall j \in A \tag{5}$$

$$k_j = \sum_{i=1}^{n_1} x_{ij}^f, \forall j \in A \tag{6}$$

In the design of $B(\tilde{x}_{ij}) = (U, V, E, w)$, $U = \{u_1, u_2, \cdots, u_{n1}\}$ denotes the set of map task types, and $V = \{v_{js} | \forall j \in A, s = 1, 2, \cdots, k_j\}$ denotes the set of map slots, where the k_j nodes $\{v_{js} : s = 1, 2, \cdots, k_j\}$ correspond to map slot $j, j \in A$, and $n_1 = |M|$.

As in [20], edges of the graph $B(\tilde{x}_{ij})$ will respond to map type-map slot pairs (i,j) such that $x_{ij}^f > 0$. The E set of $B(\tilde{x}_{ij})$ is constructed in the following way. To construct the edges incident to the map task-type nodes corresponding to slot j, we sort the map task types in order of non-increasing estimated processing time. For simplicity of notation, we assume that $p_{1j} \geq p_{2j} \geq \cdots \geq p_{n_1 j}, \forall j \in A$.

If $\sum_{i=1}^{n_1} x_{ij}^f \leq 1$, then $k_j = 1$, which means there is only one node $v_{j1} \in V$ corresponding to map slot j. In this case, for each $x_{ij}^f > 0$, we contain $(u_i, v_{j1}) \in E$. Otherwise, finding the minimum index i_1 such that $\sum_{i=1}^{i_1} x_{ij}^f \geq 1$. Let E contain those edges, $(u_i, v_{j1}) \in E$, $i = 1, \cdots, i_1$, for each $x_{ij}^f > 0$. For each $s = 2, \cdots, k_j - 1$, we find the minimum index i_s, such that $\sum_{i=1}^{i_s} x_{ij}^f \geq s$. Let E contain those edges, $(u_i, v_{js}) \in E$, $i = i_{s-1} + 1, \cdots, i_s$, for each $x_{ij}^f > 0$. If $\sum_{i=1}^{i_s} x_{ij}^f > s$, $s = 1, 2, \cdots, k_j - 1$, we set $(u_{i_s}, v_{j,s+1}) \in E$. In the end, we include $(u_i, v_{jk_j}) \in E$, $i = i_{s+1} + 1, \cdots, n_1$, for each $x_{ij}^f > 0$.

The weight of each edge $(u_i, v_{js}) \in E$ is defined as $w(u_i, v_{js}) = p_{ij} \cdot e_{ij}$. The capacity of each task-type node $u_i \in U$ is defined as $b_i = \sum_{j \in A} x_{ij}^f$, where b_i is an integer since $\sum_{j \in A} x_{ij}^f = \sum_{j \in A} (\tilde{x}_{ij} - \lfloor \tilde{x}_{ij} \rfloor) = \sum_{j \in A} (\tilde{x}_{ij}) - \sum_{j \in A} (\lfloor \tilde{x}_{ij} \rfloor)$ is an integer value.

Next, We modify the minimum-weight matching method in [20], and adopt the minimum-weight b-matching method in [21] that obtains a BM, that means, each edge in BM matches b_i times of the task-type node u_i, to find an approximate integer solution $\hat{x}_{ij}$, as indicated by Eq. (7). With this solution, we assign a task of type $i, i \in M$ to the slot $j, j \in A$ according to each edge $(u_i, v_{js}) \in BM$.

$$\hat{x}_{ij} = \lfloor \tilde{x}_{ij} \rfloor + |\{(u_i, v_{js})|s = 1, 2, \cdots, k_j\} \cap BM|, \forall i \in M, \forall j \in A \qquad (7)$$

The above algorithm can be applied to construct a bipartite graph $B(\tilde{y}_{ij})$ and find an approximate integer solution $\hat{y}_{ij}$ for the reduce task assignment.

$$\hat{y}_{ij} = \lfloor \tilde{y}_{ij} \rfloor + |\{(u_i, v_{js})|s = 1, 2, \cdots, k_j\} \cap BM|, \forall i \in R, \forall j \in B \qquad (8)$$

Thus, the MBRA method to construct the allocation $(\hat{x}_{ij}, \hat{y}_{ij})$ from the optimal solution $(\tilde{x}_{ij}, \tilde{y}_{ij})$ of the relaxation of NLIP (1) is summarized as follows.

ALGORITHM MBRA

Step 1.   Construct the bipartite graphs $B(\tilde{x}_{ij})$ and $B(\tilde{y}_{ij})$ with weights on their edges based on the solution $(\tilde{x}_{ij}, \tilde{y}_{ij})$.

Step 2.   Find a minimum-weight b-matching BM that exactly matches all task-type nodes in $B(\tilde{x}_{ij})$ and $B(\tilde{y}_{ij})$.

Step 3.   Obtain the final integer solution from Eqs. (7) and (8).

Step 4.   Assign a task of type i to the slot j, for every i, j, according to the solution $(\hat{x}_{ij}, \hat{y}_{ij})$.

4.3   Performance Analysis

As we know, the LP (3) can be solved in polynomial time to obtain the solution $(\tilde{x}_{ij}, \tilde{y}_{ij})$. Furthermore, because there exists $N = n_1 + n_2 + |A||B|$ constraints in NLIP (1) at most and based on the property of Linear Program, the number of positive variables $(\tilde{x}_{ij}, \tilde{y}_{ij})$ is no more than N, where n_2 is the number of reduce task types, $n_2 = |M|$. Since the construction of the bipartite graphs $B(\tilde{x}_{ij})$ (or $B(\tilde{y}_{ij})$) and the fact that there are one or two corresponding edges in E for each $x_{ij}^f > 0$ (or $y_{ij}^f > 0$), there are at most $2N$ edges in E. Therefore, we conclude that our proposed MBRA can be run in polynomial time $O(N)$ depending on the number of task types and slots, and because $B(\tilde{x}_{ij})$ (or $B(\tilde{y}_{ij})$) is a sparse graph, the total runtime of the algorithm is strongly dominated by solving the LP (3), which is very desirable for extremely large-scale problems. An extension of experiments and analysis of the computation scalability of this result is available in Sect. 5.

Lemma 2. For any $j, j', j \in A, j' \in B$, we can find

$$\sum_{i \in M} p_{ij} \hat{x}_{ij} \leq \sum_{i \in M} p_{ij} \tilde{x}_{ij} + \max_{i \in M, j \in A} p_{ij},$$

$$\sum_{i \in R} p_{ij} \hat{y}_{ij} \leq \sum_{i \in R} p_{ij} \tilde{y}_{ij} + \max_{i \in M, j' \in B} p_{ij},$$

$$\sum_{j \in A} \sum_{i \in M} e_{ij} \hat{x}_{ij} \leq \sum_{j \in A} \sum_{i \in M} e_{ij} \tilde{x}_{ij},$$

$$\sum_{j \in B} \sum_{i \in R} e_{ij} \hat{y}_{ij} \leq \sum_{j \in B} \sum_{i \in R} e_{ij} \tilde{y}_{ij}.$$

Comparing the objective function values of $(\tilde{x}_{ij}, \tilde{y}_{ij})$ and $(\hat{x}_{ij}, \hat{y}_{ij})$, we obtain the following theorem.

Theorem 1

$$P(\hat{MS}, \hat{x}_{ij}, \hat{y}_{ij}) \geq \frac{P(\tilde{MS}, \tilde{x}_{ij}, \tilde{y}_{ij})}{1 + \frac{\max_{i \in M, j \in A} p_{ij} + \max_{i \in R, j \in B} p_{ij}}{\tilde{MS}}} \geq OPT$$

Proof. Recall the definition of P, we have

$$P(\overset{\wedge}{MS}, \hat{x}_{ij}, \hat{y}_{ij}) = \frac{p - c_1 \overset{\wedge}{MS} - c_2(\sum\limits_{j \in A} \sum\limits_{i \in M} e_{ij}\hat{x}_{ij} + \sum\limits_{j \in B} \sum\limits_{i \in R} e_{ij}\hat{y}_{ij})}{\overset{\wedge}{MS}}$$

$$= \hat{d}\,[p - \frac{c_1}{\hat{d}} - c_2(\sum\limits_{j \in A} \sum\limits_{i \in M} e_{ij}\hat{x}_{ij} + \sum\limits_{j \in B} \sum\limits_{i \in R} e_{ij}\hat{y}_{ij})]$$

Following the latter two inequalities in Lemma 2, we can obtain

$$\hat{d}[p - \frac{c_1}{\hat{d}} - c_2(\sum\limits_{j \in A} \sum\limits_{i \in M} e_{ij}\hat{x}_{ij} + \sum\limits_{j \in B} \sum\limits_{i \in R} e_{ij}\hat{y}_{ij})] \geq \hat{d}[p - \frac{c_1}{\hat{d}}$$

$$- c_2(\sum\limits_{j \in A} \sum\limits_{i \in M} e_{ij}\tilde{x}_{ij} + \sum\limits_{j \in B} \sum\limits_{i \in R} e_{ij}\tilde{y}_{ij})]$$

$$\approx \frac{\hat{d}}{\tilde{d}} \cdot P(\tilde{MS}, \tilde{x}_{ij}, \tilde{y}_{ij})$$

By the former two inequalities in Lemma 2 and the third constraint from NLIP (1), we can obtain

$$\frac{\tilde{MS}}{\overset{\wedge}{MS}} \geq \frac{1}{1 + \frac{\max_{i \in M, j \in A} p_{ij} + \max_{i \in R, j \in B} p_{ij}}{\tilde{MS}}}.$$

Therefore, we have

$$P(\overset{\wedge}{MS}, \hat{x}_{ij}, \hat{y}_{ij}) \geq \frac{P(\tilde{MS}, \tilde{x}_{ij}, \tilde{y}_{ij})}{1 + \frac{\max_{i \in M, j \in A} p_{ij} + \max_{i \in R, j \in B} p_{ij}}{\tilde{MS}}}. \tag{9}$$

Observe that there exists $\max_{i \in M, j \in A} p_{ij} \ll \tilde{MS}$ and $\max_{i \in R, j \in B} p_{ij} \ll \tilde{MS}$ when processing a large-scale Mapreduce job. Based on Lemma 1, Eq. (9) can be approximately expressed as $P(\overset{\wedge}{MS}, \hat{x}_{ij}, \hat{y}_{ij}) \geq OPT$. This theorem implies that our proposed algorithm can obtain an expected near-optimal solution.

5 Experimental Results

5.1 Experimental Setup

In this section, we perform simulation experiments to evaluate the accuracy and efficiency of the profit-maximum model our proposed in the aspects of profit per unit time, scalability and system performance. Moreover, due to varied slot demands for map and reduce tasks, we also testify the impact of the map/reduce slot configuration on the profit per unit time of MBRA. In our experiments, *EEC* and *EPT* matrices are needed to evaluate the algorithm. We gather these matrices obtained by running the Terasort benchmark on a Hadoop cluster composed of 4 Intel nodes, a total of 80 GB of memory, 64 processors, 4 TB of storage and 1 Gbps network speed from the literature [7]. These datasets allow us to model a heterogeneous Mapreduce system with different task types and slots. To perform experiments, the price and the cost of energy and time are given. Without loss of generality, we assume that $c_1 = 0.5$ and $c_2 = 1$ for all the experiments. As in [8], let E_{min} be the lower bound on the minimum energy consumed when ignoring makespan, and $p = \gamma E_{min}$, where $\gamma = p/E_{min}$ is a parameter that will be used to affect the price. When γ is large enough, the focus is to minimize the makespan. Therefore, experiments are conducted by increasing $\gamma \in [1.0, 1.5]$ to study the proposed algorithm.

To well reflect the efficiency, we compare MBRA with energy-aware Mapreduce scheduling algorithm [7] (EMSA) and Tarplee's rounding algorithm [8] (TRA). EMSA is an effective heuristic algorithm for minimizing the energy consumption in a heterogeneous Mapreduce system within a reasonable runtime. EMSA is run with a deadline constraint and assign map and reduce tasks to specific slots by assign-large and assign-small heuristic algorithms. In our experiments, we divide the tasks into different task types to schedule in order for our comparison. TRA is found in [8] which converts a non-linear profit maximization problem to an equivalent linear programming problem, and uses a rounding method and a local assignment to construct an integer allocation.

All simulated experiments are performed on an Intel Xeon 3.06 GHz E5 processor with 15.9 GB of RAM and 2 TB of storage. All algorithms are written in C# and Matlab is used to solve the LP problem.

5.2   Analysis of Results

Profit and Performance
We first evaluate the total energy consumption and the makespan of processing a small Mapreduce job consisting of 200 map and reduce tasks where map task types and reduce task types are 12 and 8 executed on 50 map slots and 50 reduce slots respectively. We vary the parameter γ from the set {1.0, 1.1, 1.2, 1.3, 1.4, 1.5}. Figures 1 and 2 plot the energy consumption and makespan of running MBRA, EMSA and TRA and the maximum profit per unit time under six different γs. The lines represent the trade-off space between energy consumption and makespan. Notice that EMSA consumes the most energy and makespan for the same workload, and MBRA saves more energy and makespan than TRA. The energy consumption and makespan of EMSA change little because the map/reduce task scheduling is not influenced by the parameter γ. In addition, as the total of energy consumption of MBRA or TRA increases, the γ increases, while the makespan decreases. For $\gamma = 1.0$, the maximum profit per unit time solution minimizes energy consumption alone while $\gamma = 1.5$ forces makespan to be minimized. The points where $\gamma = 1.1$ are roughly in the knee of the curves, where minimizing energy consumption and makespan simultaneously, which will find the maximum profit per unit time. In our simulations, the experiment results show that the

curves of energy consumption and makespan generated by MBRA, EMSA and TRA are unchanged after $\gamma = 1.5$. It means that minimizing makespan is the primary focus, which is more difficult than minimizing energy consumption.

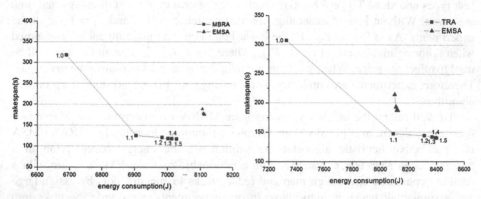

Fig. 1. The total energy consumption and makespan of MBRA and EMSA under different rs

Fig. 2. The total energy consumption and makespan of TRA and EMSA under different rs

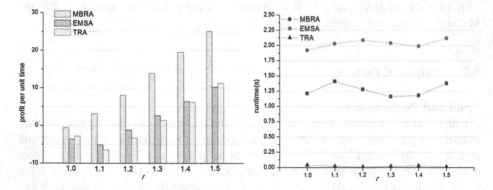

Fig. 3. The maximum profit per unit time of MBRA, EMSA and TRA under different rs

Fig. 4. The average runtime of MBRA, EMSA and TRA under different rs

Figure 3 shows the maximum profit per unit time produced by MBRA, EMSA and TRA with above workload and parameters. The maximum profit per unit time of MBRA is better than that of EMSA and TRA when γ is varied from 1.0 to 1.5. Especially, when $\gamma < 1.1$, EMSA and TRA methods produce negative objectives (or loss) while MBRA can produce an optimal solution. The loss might be caused by the increasing cost of energy consumption and makespan. Therefore, the system administrators will find the desirable allocation and resource price that achieve a positive profit ($\gamma \geq 1.1$). Figure 4 shows the average runtime of MBRA, EMSA and TRA under different parameter γ s. Obviously, there is a significant runtime reduction for the MBRA when comparing a heuristic EMSA that takes a longer time to find an optimal solution while TRA adopts a simple rounding method.

In addition, we use different workload to evaluate the scalability of MBRA. In this experiment, the number of tasks per map/reduce task type varies from 5 to 35, and the total number of tasks varies from 50 to 600. Figure 5 presents the maximum profit per unit time results of MBRA and TRA methods with different numbers of tasks executed on fixed map slots and reduce slots when $\gamma = 1.1$. The profit per unit time increases as the number of tasks increases, and comparing with TRA, the MBRA can produce a quality solution within a reasonable runtime. For example, to find the maximum profit per unit time solution for 100 tasks it takes 1.41 s, and 500 tasks it takes 4 s. Furthermore, the runtime is roughly linear in the number of tasks and extremely fast in all cases.

From all the above results, we conclude that MBRA obtains Mapreduce resource allocation for small and large jobs that produces better quality maximum profit per unit time with significantly lower energy consumption and makespan than the heuristic algorithm (EMSA) and the simple rounding algorithm (TRA), and requires less runtime than EMSA, making it the suitable candidate for processing Mapreduce jobs profitably for service providers in data centers.

Map/reduce slot configuration

To validate the impact of the slot configuration on the proposed MBRA method, we present two classes of experiments, small-scale and large-scale. In the small-scale experiments, we obtain the maximum profit per unit time under different map/reduce slot configurations by running a small Mapreduce job consists of 120 map tasks and 80 reduce tasks on a total of 100 map/reduce slots for all parameter γ s. For large-scale experiments, we obtain the maximum profit per unit time with the workload consists of 400 map tasks and 100 reduce tasks executed on a total of 100 slots.

Figure 6 presents the maximum profit per unit time of the small-scale job obtained by MBRA method for all parameter γ s under different map/reduce slot configurations. The curves show that the maximum profit per unit time with different parameter γ s are similar under different map/reduce slot configurations. It can be noted that the map/reduce slot configuration (70/30) is the optimal configuration that produces the maximum profit per unit time for all parameter γ s. Furthermore, the difference of the maximum profit per unit time between the worst-case map/reduce slot configuration (e.g., 50/50) and the optimal configuration (e.g., 70/30) is up to 174% when $\gamma = 1.2$.

Figure 7 presents the average runtime of the small-scale job under different γ s and map/reduce slot configurations. The results show that MBRA run with the map/reduce slot configuration (70/30) finds the allocation in less amount of runtime than other slot configurations. Moreover, we can witness that, the average runtime of MBRA becomes almost twice when we increase 1.3 times for map slots while decreases 3 times for reduce slots (map/reduce slot configuration 90/10).

We analyze the results of the large-scale job with the influence of the map/reduce slot configuration. Figure 8 presents the maximum profit per unit time for all parameter γ s under different map/reduce slot configurations. The curves show that the optimal configuration (60/40) generates the maximum profit per unit time for all γ s.

In large-scale experiments, the maximum average runtime of MBRA under the map/reduce slot configuration (60/40) is 3.485 s when $\gamma = 1.0$.

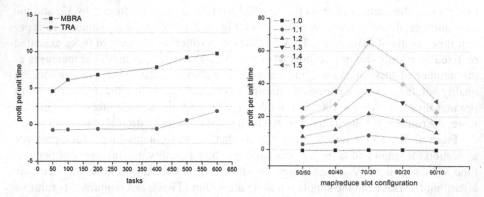

Fig. 5. The maximum profit per unit time of MBRA and TRA under different number of tasks

Fig. 6. The maximum profit per unit time of MBRA under different slot configurations and rs

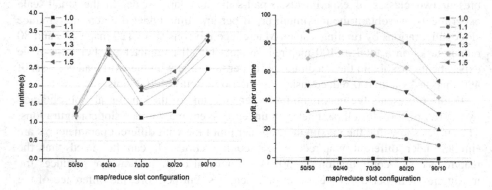

Fig. 7. The average runtime of MBRA under different slot configurations and rs

Fig. 8. The maximum profit per unit time of MBRA under different slot configurations and rs

In summary, the above results validate that finding an appropriate map/reduce slot configuration and an allocation to assign small- and large-scale map/reduce tasks to slots under a given total size of slots can optimize profit for service providers. Such optimization in maximum profit per unit time will be a great incentive to incorporate a slot configuration optimization algorithm to reduce the cost of energy consumption and makespan.

6 Conclusion

In this paper, we propose a novel economic model to maximize profit for processing a Mapreduce job in data centers. Our research takes energy consumption cost and makespan time cost into account and incorporates the concept of profit per unit time into the maximization model. We then present a minimum-weight b-matching rounding algorithm which rounds the optimal fraction solution to an approximate integer solution for the Mapreduce resource allocation problem. Furthermore, we prove that this algorithm can obtain a near-optimal solution theoretically. Finally, using real workload and via a large of simulations, we validate the effectiveness of our proposed profit-maximum model and analyze the performance of the minimum-weight b-matching rounding algorithm for small and large jobs.

The results in this paper can be extended in several directions. First, given the practical situation, the profit model can be designed to consider multiple Mapreduce jobs. Second, the profit model can be generalized to include idle energy consumption cost. Finally, the obtained economic model in this paper can be further extended to a pricing model of balancing providers and users in data centers.

Acknowledgments. This paper was supported by the National Natural Science Foundation of China (Nos. 61170222, 61662088, 11301466), the Natural Science Foundation of Yunnan Province of China (No. 2014FB114), and the Scientific Research Foundation of the Educational Department of Yunnan Province (No. 2015J0007).

References

1. Moseley, B., Dasgupta, A., Kumar, R., Sarlos, T.: On scheduling in map-reduce and flow-shops. In: Proceedings of the 23rd Annual ACM Symposium on Parallelism in Algorithms and Architectures, pp. 289–298 (2011)
2. Tang, S., Lee, B.S., He, B.: Dynamic job ordering and slot configurations for mapreduce workloads. IEEE Trans. Serv. Comput. **9**(1), 4–17 (2016)
3. Zhu, Y., Jiang, Y., Wu, W., Ding, L.: Minimizing makespan and total completion time in mapreduce-like systems. In: Proceedings of the 33rd Annual IEEE International Conference on Computer Communications (INFOCOM 2014), pp. 2166–2174 (2014)
4. Kolb, L., Thor, A., Rahm, E.: Load balancing for mapreduce-based entity resolution. In: Proceedings of the 28th IEEE International Conference on Data Engineering, pp. 618–629 (2012)
5. Wang, W., Zhu, K., Ying, L., Tan, J., Zhang, L.: MapTask scheduling in mapreduce with data locality: throughput and heavy-traffic optimality. IEEE/ACM Trans. Netw. **24**(1), 190–203 (2016)
6. Wang, X., Wang, Y., Zhu, H.: Energy-efficient task scheduling model based on MapReduce for cloud computing using genetic algorithm. J. Comput. **7**(12), 2962–2970 (2012)
7. Mashayekhy, L., Nejad, M.M., Grosu, D., Zhang, Q., Shi, W.: Energy-aware scheduling of mapreduce jobs for big data applications. IEEE Trans. Parallel Distrib. Syst. **26**(10), 2720–2733 (2015)

8. Tarplee, K.M., Maciejewski, A.A., Siegel, H.J.: Energy-aware profit maximizing scheduling algorithm for heterogeneous computing systems. In: Proceedings of the 14th IEEE/ACM International Symposium on Cluster, Cloud and Grid Computing (CCGrid 2014), pp. 595–603 (2014)

9. Ren, Z.J., Wan, J., Shi, W.S., Xu, X.H., Zhou, M.: Workload analysis, implications, and optimization on a production hadoop cluster: a case study on taobao. IEEE Trans. Serv. Comput. **7**(2), 307–321 (2014)

10. Verma, A., Cherkasova, L., Campbell, R.H.: Two sides of a coin: optimizing the schedule of mapreduce jobs to minimize their makespan and improve cluster performance. In: Proceedings of the 20th International Symposium on Modeling, Analysis and Simulation of Computer and Telecommunication Systems, pp. 11–18 (2012)

11. Song, J., Wang, Z., Li, T.T., Yu, G.: Energy consumption optimization data placement algorithm for mapreduce system. J. softw. **26**(8), 2091–2110 (2015)

12. Lin, B., Li, S.S., Liao, X.K., Meng, L.B., Liu, X.D., Huang, H.: Seadown: SLA-aware size-scaling power management in heterogeneous mapreduce cluster. J. Comput. **36**(5), 977–987 (2013)

13. Maheshwari, N., Nanduri, R., Varma, V.: Dynamic energy efficient data placement and cluster reconfiguration algorithm for mapreduce framework. Future Gener. Comput. Syst. **28**(1), 119–127 (2012)

14. Lin, J.C., Leu, F.Y., Chen, Y.: Impact of mapreduce policies on job completion reliability and job energy consumption. IEEE Trans. Parallel Distrib. Syst. **26**(5), 1364–1378 (2015)

15. Tian, F., Chen, K.: Towards optimal resource provisioning for running mapreduce programs in public clouds. In: Proceedings of 2011 IEEE International Conference on Cloud Computing (CLOUD 2011), pp. 155–162 (2011)

16. Palanisamy, B., Singh, A., Liu, L.: Cost-effective resource provisioning for mapreduce in a cloud. IEEE Trans. Parallel Distrb. Syst. **26**(5), 1265–1279 (2015)

17. Young, B.D., Apodaca, J., Briceño, L.D., Smith, J., Pasricha, S., Maciejewski, A.A., Siegel, H.J., Khemka, B., Bahirat, S., Ramirez, A., Zou, Y.: Deadline and energy constrained dynamic resource allocation in a heterogeneous computing environment. J. Supercomput. **63**(2), 326–347 (2013)

18. Li, W.D., Liu, X., Zhang, X.J., Cai, X.B.: A Task-type-based algorithm for the energy-aware profit maximizing scheduling problem in heterogeneous computing systems. In: Proceedings of the 15th IEEE/ACM International Symposium on Cluster, Cloud and Grid Computing (CCGrid 2015), pp. 1107–1110 (2015)

19. Jansen, K., Porkolab, L.: Improved approximation schemes for scheduling unrelated parallel machines. Math. Oper. Res. **26**(2), 324–338 (2001)

20. Shmoys, D.B., Tardos, É.: An approximation algorithm for the generalized assignment problem. Math. Prog. **62**(1–3), 461–474 (1993)

21. Huang, B.C., Jebara, T.: Fast b-matching via sufficient selection belief propagation. In: Proceedings of AISTATS, pp. 361–369 (2011)

An Efficient Implementation of the Algorithm by Lukáš et al. on Hadoop

Giuseppe Cattaneo[1], Umberto Ferraro Petrillo[2], Michele Nappi[1],
Fabio Narducci[1], and Gianluca Roscigno[1(✉)]

[1] Dipartimento di Informatica, Università degli Studi di Salerno,
84084 Fisciano, SA, Italy
{cattaneo,mnappi,fnarducci,giroscigno}@unisa.it
[2] Dipartimento di Scienze Statistiche,
Università di Roma "La Sapienza", 00185 Roma, Italy
umberto.ferraro@uniroma1.it

Abstract. Apache Hadoop offers the possibility of coding full-fledged distributed applications with very low programming efforts. However, the resulting implementations may suffer from some performance bottlenecks that nullify the potential of a distributed system. An engineering methodology based on the implementation of smart optimizations driven by a careful profiling activity may lead to a much better experimental performance as shown in this paper.

In particular, we take as a case study the algorithm by Lukáš *et al.* used to solve the Source Camera Identification problem (i.e., recognizing the camera used for acquiring a given digital image). A first implementation has been obtained, with little effort, using the default facilities available with Hadoop. A deep profiling allowed us to pinpoint some serious performance issues affecting the initial steps of the algorithm and related to a bad usage of the cluster resources. Optimizations were then developed and their effects were measured by accurate experimentation. The improved implementation is able to optimize the usage of the underlying cluster resources as well as of the Hadoop framework, thus resulting in a much better performance than the original naive implementation.

Keywords: Distributed computing · Hadoop · Source Camera Identification

1 Introduction

Current technologies provide decision-makers with the ability to collect a huge amount of data, i.e., Big Data, that requires the development of tools and methodologies with a high scalability degree. *Digital Image Forensics* area is one of the application fields where the problem of analyzing Big Data is arising [4,6,13,16]. Efficient solutions are usually available in the scientific literature. However, with the growth of digital photography, there is a need to assess how

© Springer International Publishing AG 2017
M.H.A. Au et al. (Eds.): GPC 2017, LNCS 10232, pp. 475–489, 2017.
DOI: 10.1007/978-3-319-57186-7_35

these solutions scale and/or how their performance can be optimized on distributed systems. Nowadays, paradigms and technologies, such as *MapReduce* [9] and Apache Hadoop [20], allow us to develop in a relatively simple way and without dealing with some of the most intricate aspects of distributed programming, such as inter-process data communication.

In this paper, which is a prosecution of the work has been presented in [7], we have engineered a Hadoop-based implementation of the Lukáš *et al.* algorithm [16] to solve the problem of *Source Camera Identification* (SCI). This consists in recognizing the camera used for acquiring a given digital image. The first implementation has been developed in a straightforward way with the help of the standard facilities available with Hadoop. The resulting distributed code exhibited shorter execution times than the original one when executed on a cluster of computers, although its performance was quite below expectations. A closer investigation revealed the existence of several performance issues due to the inability of this implementation to take full advantage of the underlying cluster resources. Therefore, we developed an engineering methodology aiming at pinpointing the causes behind the performance issues we observed and at solving them through the introduction of some theoretical and practical optimizations. The resulting implementations succeed in delivering a performance much better than the original distributed implementation.

The rest of the paper is organized as follows. Section 2 describes the *MapReduce* paradigm, with an emphasis on Apache Hadoop. Section 3 presents the case study, that is, the algorithm by Lukáš *et al.*. Section 4 presents the first attempt of porting the algorithm by Lukáš *et al.* on a Hadoop cluster and Sect. 5 shows the preliminary experimental results. In Sect. 6 we focus on some serious performance issues exhibited by our distributed implementation, and we propose and analyze further optimizations. Finally, in Sect. 7 we draw some conclusions and future directions of our work.

2   Apache Hadoop

In the recent years, several different architectural and technological solutions have been proposed for processing big amounts of data. An increasingly popular computing paradigm is *MapReduce* [9]. Within this paradigm, the computation takes a set of input <*key, value*> pairs, and produces a set of output <*key, value*> pairs. The user expresses the computation as two functions: *map* and *reduce*. The map function takes an input pair and produces a set of intermediate <*key, value*> pairs. The *MapReduce* framework groups together all the intermediate *values* associated with a same intermediate *key* and passes them to the reduce function. The reduce function accepts an intermediate *key* and the set of values for that *key*. Then it merges together these values to form a possibly smaller set of values. Typically zero or one output pair is produced per reduce function. Map and reduce functions are executed, as tasks, on the different computers of a distributed system.

Differently from traditional paradigms, such as explicit parallel constructs based on message-passing, the *MapReduce* allows for *implicit parallelism*.

Namely, all the operations related to the exchange of data between the nodes involved in a computation are modelled according to a file-based approach and are transparently accomplished by the underlying middleware. Activities like data distribution, data replication, synchronization, scheduling, fault tolerance, redundant execution, data local computation, load balancing and efficient use of the network and disks, are in charge of the *MapReduce* framework. In this way, the programmer is focused only on defining the behavior of the map and reduce functions, and on deciding how data will feed the corresponding map and reduce steps. In general, no specific skills in parallel and distributed systems are required. The *MapReduce* paradigm has been first successfully adopted by Google for creating scalable, fault tolerance and massively-parallel programs that process large amounts of data using large commodity clusters. However, *MapReduce* has now gained a wider audience and it is used in several fields like satellite data processing, bioinformatics and machine learning (see, e.g., [2, 8, 10, 15, 17]).

Apache Hadoop [20] is currently the most popular framework supporting the *MapReduce* paradigm. It is a Java based open source grid computing environment useful for reliable, scalable and distributed computing. From an architectural viewpoint, Hadoop is mainly composed of a data processing framework plus the *Hadoop Distributed File System* (HDFS) [19]. The data processing framework organizes a computation as a sequence of user-defined *MapReduce* operations on datasets of $<key, value>$ pairs. These operations are executed as tasks on the nodes of a cluster. The HDFS is a distributed file system optimized to run on commodity hardware and able to provide fault tolerance through replication of data. Some Hadoop features used for source camera identification are available in our previous contribution [7].

3   The Case Study: Lukáš *et al.* Algorithm

The Source Camera Identification (SCI) problem concerns the identification of the digital camera used for capturing a given input digital image. A common identification strategy consists in analyzing the *noise* in a digital image to find clues about the digital sensor that originated it. *Pixel Non-Uniformity* noise (PNU) is a deterministic noise resulting from the different sensitivity of the pixel detectors to light. This difference is due to the inhomogeneity of the wafers of silicon and the imperfections derived from the manufacturing process of the sensor. Thanks to its deterministic and systematic nature, the PNU noise is the ideal candidate for providing a sort of fingerprint of digital cameras. Lukáš *et al.* in [16] were pioneers in demonstrating the feasibility of using the PNU noise for solving the SCI problem. The authors observed that PNU was successful in identifying the source camera used to take the considered picture, even distinguishing between cameras of the same brand and model.

The problem of performing Source Camera Identification on large datasets has not received much attention in the scientific literature. One of the few contributions in this area is presented in [13]. Here the authors tested over one million images spanning 6, 896 individual cameras covering 150 models. Another relevant contribution is presented in [14] where the authors describe a fast searching algorithm based on the usage of a collection of *fingerprint digests*. They performed their experimentation on a database of 2,000 iPhones, proving the feasibility of the approach proposed.

In our work we exploited the original version of the SCI algorithm by Lukáš *et al.* [16] applied to color images in the RGB space. Let I be the RGB image under scrutiny and $CamSet = \{C_1, C_2, \ldots, C_n\}$ the set of candidate origin cameras for I. The algorithm operates in four steps:

- **Step I: Calculating Reference Patterns.** It computes the *Reference Pattern* RP_C, that is, the sensor fingerprint, for each camera C belonging to $CamSet$. The approach proposed by Lukáš *et al.* consists in estimating RP_C by extracting the *Residual Noises* (*RN*s) from a set of pictures taken by using C and, then, combining these noises together, as an approximation of the PNU noise. The residual noise of an image I can be defined as $RN_I = I - F(I)$, where $F(I)$ is a filter function that returns the noise-free variant of I. The operation described above is applied pixel-by-pixel (for each color channel) and is iterated over a group of images with the same spatial resolution, here named *enrollment* images, taken by using C. This returns a group of residual noises, including both a random noise component and the PNU noise estimation of C. The sum of the residual noises is then averaged to obtain a tight approximation of the camera C fingerprint, i.e., RP_C.

- **Step II: Calculating Correlation Indices.** A set of calibration and testing images using each of the cameras belonging to $CamSet$ is introduced. The *Pearson's correlation* between the fingerprint of each camera C and the residual noise of each image T taken from the calibration/testing set is computed (the higher the values, the higher the probability that an image T has been taken by using a camera C). Cropping or resizing operations are performed in case the resolution of T does not match the resolution of the images used for determining RP_C.

- **Step III: Identification System Calibration.** The identification is based on the definition of a set of three acceptance thresholds (one for each color channel) to be associated to each of the cameras under scrutiny. If the correlation between the residual noise of I and the Reference Pattern of a camera C, on each color channel, exceeds the corresponding acceptance threshold, then C is assumed to be the camera that originated I. The thresholds are chosen so to minimize the *False Rejection Rate* (FRR) for calibration images taken by using C, given an upper bound on the *False Acceptance Rate* (FAR) for calibration images taken by using a camera different than C (Neyman-Pearson approach). The correlations of the testing images are then used to validate the identification system by comparing them to the acceptance thresholds.

- **Step IV: Performing Source Camera Identification.** It concerns the identification of the camera that captured I. Here the algorithm first extracts the residual noise from I, RN_I, then correlates it with the Reference Patterns of all the input cameras using the system calibrated in the third step. If the correlation exceeds the decision threshold of a certain camera, on each of the color channels, a match is found.

4   A Naive Implementation of the Lukáš *et al.* Algorithm on Hadoop

We developed in Java a *MapReduce* based implementation of the Lukáš *et al.* algorithm[1]. It was split in four different modules, each corresponding to the four processing steps of the Lukáš *et al.* algorithm. A preliminary image loading activity on the HDFS is also performed. This task was accomplished by copying and keeping the images as separate files.

In the following, we describe in details these four modules.

Step I: Calculating Reference Patterns. The aim of this step is to calculate the Reference Pattern of a camera C, by analyzing a set of enrollment images with the same spatial resolution and taken by using C. In the map phase, each processing node receives a set of images, extracts their corresponding residual noises and outputs them. In the reduce phase, the processing function (one for each camera C) uses the set of residual noises of C produced in the previous tasks and combines them, thus generating the RP_C. This operation is repeated for each input camera. During this step, the input *key* is derived from the image meta-data and *value* stores the URL of the image on HDFS. When a map function is activated, it receives this record, loads the corresponding image in memory from HDFS and, finally, extracts the RN from the image. As an output, this function produces a new <*key, value*> pair, where *key* is the *camera id* and *value* is the URL of RN directly saved on HDFS. During the reduce phase, a function receives a tuple in the <*key, values*> format, where *key* is the identifier of a camera, e.g., C, and *values* is a set of the URLs to RNs (saved on HDFS) for that camera, as calculated during the map tasks. All the RNs of the same camera are summed and then averaged to form the Reference Pattern for C. As an output, the function generates a new <*key, value*> pair, where *key* is the identifier of C, and *value* is RP_C.

Step II: Calculating Correlation Indices. During this step, the algorithm extracts the RN of each calibration/testing image and correlates it with the RPs of all the input cameras. In the map phase, each processing node receives a list of input images to be correlated as <*key, value*> records, where *key* is derived from the image meta-data and *value* stores the image URL on HDFS. For each URL, the corresponding image is (possibly) transferred to the slave node, and the RN is extracted and correlated with the RPs of all the input cameras calculated in the previous step. For each correlation, a map function generates a new pair, where *key* is the string *"Correlation"* and *value* consists of: the *image id*, the *camera id* used for shotting the image, the RP *id*, a value indicating the correlation preprocessing *type*, plus the three correlation indices (one for each color channel). Since each slave has to load the RP of all the input cameras, we used the Hadoop `DistributedCache` mechanism to make each node transfer to its local file system a copy of these files, before starting the Hadoop job. In this step, no reduce task is required.

---

[1] A copy of the source code of our implementation is available upon request.

Step III: Identification System Calibration. In this step a set of three acceptance thresholds (one for each color channel) is calculated for each of the input cameras. The thresholds are determined using the Neyman-Pearson approach and exploiting the correlation values of the calibration images computed in the previous step. The correlation values of a set of testing images, calculated during Step II, are then used to validate the identification system by comparing them to the aforementioned thresholds. Since this step is computationally cheap, it is run directly on the master node, without using any form of parallelization.

Step IV: Performing Source Camera Identification. The aim of this step is to establish which camera has been used for capturing an image I. The input of the Hadoop job is the directory where the RPs have been stored. The output is the id of the camera recognized as the originating camera for the input image. For each input RP, a new map function is invoked. This function uses a copy of I for extracting its residual noise and for calculating its correlation with the input RP. Then, the job returns a file containing the list of the correlation values needed to perform the recognition phase using the thresholds computed in the previous step. Finally, the predicted *camera id* is returned.

5   Experimental Analysis

In this section we discuss the results of a preliminary experimental analysis we have conducted. We compared the performance of our Hadoop-based implementation of the Lukáš *et al.* algorithm with its non-distributed counterpart. The discussion also includes a description of the experimental settings and the datasets used in our analysis.

5.1   Experimental Settings

All the experiments were conducted on a homogeneous cluster of 33 PCs equipped with 4 GB of RAM, an *Intel Celeron G530* dual-core processor, *Windows 7* host operating system and a 100 Mbps Ethernet card. In this environment, we installed on each computer a virtual machine running the *Ubuntu 12.10 64-bit* guest operating system, and equipped with 3, 100 MB of RAM and 2 CPUs. Our cluster included 32 slave nodes and a master node, and the Hadoop version was 1.0.4. On each slave node, at most one map or reduce task was run. In addition, on each slave node, we set the properties that allow the framework to wait the end of all map tasks, before starting the reduce tasks, due to memory limits. According to our preliminary results, the HDFS replication factor was set to 2 and the HDFS block size was set to 64 MB.

The dataset used in our experiments is the same presented in [7]. It consists of 5160 JPEG images, shot using 20 different Nikon D90 digital cameras. This model has a CMOS image sensor and maximum image size of 4288×2848 pixels. 258 JPEG images were taken for each camera at the maximum resolution and with a very low JPEG compression. The images were organized in 130 enrollment images, 64 calibration images and 64 testing images for each camera. Enrollment images were taken from a *ISO Noise Chart 15739* [18], instead, calibration and testing images portray different types of scenes. The overall dataset is about 20 GB large, and about 40% of that size is due to enrollment images.

5.2   Preliminary Experimental Results

We developed Hadoop-based variants of the original Lukáš *et al.* algorithm. The first variant, here denoted HSCI, is the vanilla implementation of the algorithm described in Sect. 4. We focus on Step I and Step II only, because they are, by far, the most computationally expensive. In HSCI all the image files to be processed are initially loaded on HDFS. The files containing the RNs and the RPs obtained during the execution of the algorithm are also loaded on HDFS, as soon as they become available. As a consequence, map and reduce tasks take as an input (or provide as an output) a URL pointing at them.

We made a preliminary and coarse comparison between the performance of HSCI and the implementation running as a stand-alone (non-parallel) application, here named SCI, by measuring the overall execution time of the different steps of the algorithm in both settings. The results, available in Table 1, show that, when processing the second step of the algorithm, HSCI exhibits approximately a 16× speed up. On the contrary, the performance gain on the first step of the algorithm is almost negligible. Such a result is due to the reduce phase of this step. Each reduce task, in fact, has to collect from HDFS all the RNs generated during the map phase (in our experiments, 130 RNs for each RP file to generate, with the average size of a RN file of approximately 140 MB). This activity puts a heavy burden on the running time of the first step, as implemented by HSCI.

Table 1. Execution times, in minutes, of different preliminary distributed variants of the Lukáš *et al.* algorithm on a Hadoop cluster of 32 slave nodes, compared to the sequential counterpart, i.e., SCI, run on a single node.

Variant	Step I	Step II
SCI	888	5,257
HSCI	750	334
HSCI_Seq	290	304

In order to investigate the poor performance of HSCI during the first step of the Lukáš *et al.* algorithm, we analyzed the CPU and the network usage of slave nodes when running this step. The obtained results report that the CPU is mostly unused. Conversely, the network activity dominates both the map and reduce phases: the map phase, because of the time required to download from HDFS the input images and to write on HDFS the resulting RN files; the reduce phase, because of the time required to collect all the RN files produced in the map phase. A possible explanation for such long times is related to the problems of managing a very large number of small files [21].

A more efficient solution would be to fully exploit data local computation by further reducing the number of files to be processed and by placing the data on the slave nodes running the tasks in charge to process them. The solution we found consists in maintaining only two very large files containing all the image files. They have been coded as Hadoop `SequenceFile` objects and are: `EnrSeq`, used for storing a set of enrollment images, and `TTSeq`, used for storing a set of calibration and testing images. In both files, the images are ordered according to their originating *camera id*. Then, we used the input split capability available with sequence files for partitioning these two files among the different computing nodes, with the aim of promoting data local execution. Notice that the residual noises calculated during the first step of the algorithm are still written as separate files on HDFS as they become available, while the images are no longer directly downloaded from HDFS as individual files. In this case, in the sequence file input, the *key* of each pair is the meta-data of an image, while the *value* of that pair stores a binary copy of that image. The experimental performance of this implementation, labeled as `HSCI_Seq`, when running the first step of the Lukáš *et al.* algorithm, is much better than `HSCI` variant, with an execution time that is approximately 2.6× faster than `HSCI`. Also the second step of the algorithm seems to take advantage of this solution, as it is slightly faster than the `HSCI` solution.

6 Advanced Experimental Analysis

As already discussed in Sect. 5, a preliminary round of experimentations led us to develop a Hadoop-based variant of the Lukáš *et al.* algorithm, named `HSCI_Seq`, whose performance met enough our expectations. The same experiments revealed that the performance of this algorithm in a distributed setting is strongly influenced by the network activity required to load and/or to save files (RNs) on the underlying distributed file system.

In this section, we further analyze these phenomena. The results of a thorough profiling activity aimed at charactering the behavior of the `HSCI_Seq` implementation will be presented, in order to improve our understanding about the way an algorithm, such as the one by Lukáš *et al.*, performs when adapted to run on the Hadoop framework. We also assess the possibility of achieving further performance improvements.

6.1 Profiling `HSCI_Seq` Implementation

We recall from the previous section that the input dataset for our tests contains two sequence files: `EnrSeq` and `TTSeq`. During Step I, the processing of the `EnrSeq` file requires the creation of 130 map tasks, i.e., one for each HDFS block of input file, where the size of `EnrSeq` is about 8 GB and the HDFS block size is set to 64 MB. The average amount of data exchanged between map and reduce tasks is approximately 355 GB (without considering tasks and data replicas). In our experimental analysis of HSCI_Seq, the framework ran, in the average, 141 map tasks: 130 completed successfully and the remaining 11 killed by the framework. The existence of these additional tasks is due to the Hadoop speculative execution. In the reduce phase, we set the number of reduce tasks to 20, that is the number of RPs to be calculated. In our profiling experiment, 29 reduce tasks were launched by the Hadoop framework, with only 20 completing their execution and the other ones being killed by the framework. Our result shows that about 75% of the running time of HSCI_Seq during Step I is spent in the reduce phase. On one side, we suppose that this overhead is due to the time consumed by each reduce function to retrieve the corresponding RN files to sum from the HDFS, i.e., 130 RNs for each RP to be calculated. On the other side, we expect that this second phase would have lasted lesser as it performed simple computational operations such as multiple sums of matrices.

In order to clarify this behavior, we traced the start and the end execution time of each task, both map and reduce phase, in our experiment. In Fig. 1, we show an overview of the map and reduce tasks used by Hadoop when running the Step I of the HSCI_Seq algorithm. In some cases, the Hadoop framework may decide to issue a same task a second time (e.g., for recovering a task that has been assigned to a free slave node, without being completed). These cases are highlighted in the figure by coloring black the tasks that are killed when their twin tasks complete their executions. As it can be seen in the figure, the overall time spent by each slave node for processing map tasks is almost the same. In the reduce phase, we observe that some reduce tasks end as soon as they start or are killed immediately. That can be explained by the fact that these tasks have not been assigned a RP to be calculated. In fact, the overall number of slave nodes completing a reduce task and computing at least one RP is 12 against a total number of 20 RPs. This unbalanced assignment is due to the standard hash function used by the Hadoop partitioner service for the distribution of the keys (in our case, the id of the cameras) to be processed in the reduce tasks.

We further analyzed the behavior of tasks of Step I by profiling the CPU usage and the network activity. In Fig. 2 we report, for example, the CPU activity of *slave1*. During the first 60 min, spent on processing map tasks, a single core of the node was used almost at its maximum. Notice that, in our case, it is not possible to run two distinct map tasks on the same node because the amount of memory in it would not be enough. Instead, the second significant activity, i.e., that related to the execution of a reduce task covering about 65 min, featured a 10% average CPU usage. This seems to confirm that, during the reduce phase, the CPU of the involved slave nodes is nearly unused, as this phase is dominated by the network activity related to the retrieval from HDFS of the RN files to sum. This observation is also supported by the analysis of the incoming network throughput for *slave1* node during Step I, as illustrated in Fig. 3. The figure shows that there is an intense network activity for *slave1* along all the map phase and the reduce phase.

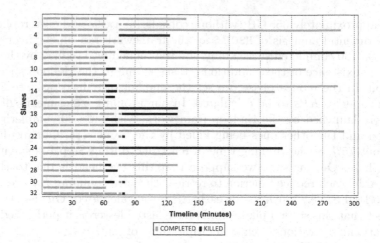

Fig. 1. HSCI_Seq implementation - An overview of map and reduce tasks launched during Step I. Reduce tasks start only after the termination of all map tasks.

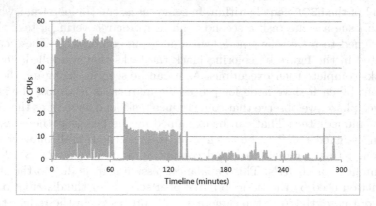

Fig. 2. CPU usage of *slave1*, in percentage, when running Step I of HSCI_Seq.

During Step II, at least 194 map tasks are created using the testing and calibration images available in the TTSeq file. In this experiment, the framework ran 210 map tasks: 194 completed successfully and the remaining 16 killed by the framework. Of all these tasks, 187 were data local map tasks. We recall that the Step II of the HSCI_Seq does not make use of the reduce phase, thus its execution time is approximately equal to the execution time of the map phase. An in-depth analysis of the map tasks revealed that they are characterized by an intense I/O activity, needed to load the Reference Patterns. However, these tasks also feature a very intense CPU activity, due to the work required to perform the correlations on big input files, as shown in Fig. 4 (the average CPU usage stays around 40%). That indicates, on one hand, that the CPU does not suffer much from delays due to I/O activity, and, on the other hand, that there is a margin

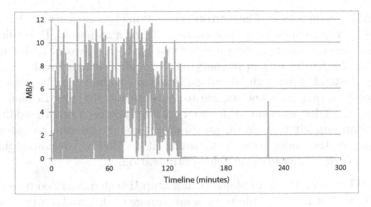

Fig. 3. Incoming network throughput of *slave1*, in MB/s, when running Step I of HSCI_Seq.

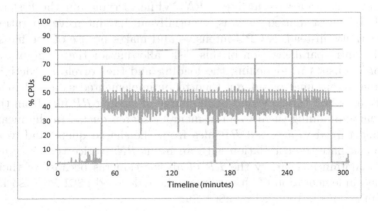

Fig. 4. CPU usage of *slave1*, in percentage, when running Step II of HSCI_Seq.

for optimization by taking advantage of the second core of the CPU, actually unused. As already stated above, in fact, the available memory in each node is likely to be insufficient to run two tasks at the same time. In addition, Fig. 4 shows that the CPU of *slave1* remains unused while waiting for the framework to copy the *RP*s from HDFS to the local file system.

6.2 Further Optimizations and Results

Following the profiling activity we pinpointed two issues affecting the performance of HSCI_Seq and we developed some practical optimizations to solve them.

Excessive network traffic. The excessive network traffic arising in Step I is mostly due to the transfer of a large number of *RN*s from map tasks to reduce tasks. Consequently, we required each map task to aggregate all the *RN*s generated for a same camera into one *RN* file, before sending it to the corresponding reduce task. The aggregation is done by summing all the RN files produced by a same node for a same camera during a map task. To facilitate this operation, the enrollment images are ordered by the *camera id* and the partial sum of the RN files is kept in memory by the node, without involving any I/O operation. Instead of using the standard Hadoop Combiner, we implemented an ad-hoc solution that does not require to store all the RN files in memory, but just their sum (this solution is denoted *in-map aggregation*). In addition, we used Hadoop implicit mechanism for directly passing this sum as *value* to the pair output by the node, rather than saving it on HDFS. We named HSCI_Sum the variant of HSCI_Seq featuring this optimization.

Poor CPU usage. The map phase during Step II is characterized by an intense CPU activity, but it is not able to take advantage of the availability of an additional CPU core. The standard behavior of the map task during Step II requires the loading from the local file system of a camera RP, followed by the calculation of its correlation with an input RN. While carrying out the first activity, the CPU is almost unused, as it is essentially an I/O-intensive operation. The second activity, instead, is CPU-intensive and makes no use of the file system. A possible intra-parallelization of this task, allowing for the usage of a second CPU core, consists in modelling the loading and the correlation activities on the producer-consumer paradigm, then to be implemented as a multi-threaded application. A first thread would be in charge of loading RP files from the local file system and adding them to an in-memory shared queue. In the meanwhile, the second thread would load RP files from the shared queue and would use them to calculate the correlation with an input RN. Notice that it is not possible to maintain in memory the RP of all the cameras because of their large size. The implementation of this strategy, here denoted HSCI_PC, also includes the optimizations introduced by HSCI_Sum.

Table 2. Execution times, in minutes, of the different steps of the variants of the Lukáš *et al.* algorithm on a Hadoop cluster of 32 slave nodes. For a comparison, see Table 1.

Variant	Step I	Step II
HSCI_Seq	290	304
HSCI_Sum	49	276
HSCI_PC	50	236

After developing the optimizations presented above, we performed another round of experiments in order to compare the optimized implementations to HSCI. The results, available in Table 2, report a significant performance improvement on HSCI_Seq. The first optimized code we consider is HSCI_Sum. This algorithm differs from HSCI_Seq in the way RNs are transmitted from map tasks to reduce tasks. Namely, it implements an aggregation strategy that drastically reduces the amounts of data exchanged between map and reduce tasks.

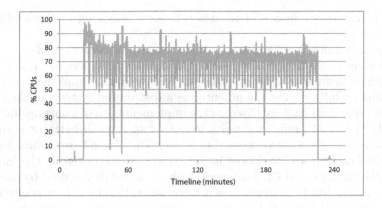

Fig. 5. CPU usage of *slave1*, in percentage, when running Step II of HSCI_PC.

For instance, in our experiments, the amount of data exchanged during Step I by HSCI_Sum is about 6% of that exchanged by HSCI_Seq in the same phase. This led to a consistent performance improvement in our experiments, since the Step I of HSCI_Sum required 49 min, in the average, to be accomplished against the 290 min required for the same step by HSCI_Seq. It is interesting to note that smaller amounts of data to exchange not only imply faster communications but could also result in a much smaller number of tasks being replicated and re-run by the Hadoop framework, thanks to shorter network congestions. In addition, the reduce phase takes just a few minutes.

HSCI_PC implementation uses the producer-consumer paradigm to evaluate correlations during the map phase of Step II, by means of a multi-threaded architecture. This approach brought a consistent performance gain compared to HSCI_Seq and HSCI_Sum, as the overall execution time of Step II dropped from 304 (HSCI_Seq) and 276 (HSCI_Sum) to 236 min (HSCI_PC). The result also includes a consistent increasing in the CPU usage, exhibited by HSCI_PC when processing the map phase of Step II and shown in Fig. 5 (for a comparison see Fig. 4).

7 Conclusion

In this paper, we discussed the engineering of an efficient Hadoop-based implementation of the Lukáš *et al.* algorithm, in order to solving the Source Camera Identification problem. We were able to quickly obtain a running distributed implementation for this algorithm, by leveraging the standard facilities available with the Hadoop framework. The vanilla distributed implementation exhibited a very poor performance. This motivated us to perform a thorough profiling activity which led, first, to pinpoint several performance issues and, then, to develop several both theoretical and practical optimizations, thus achieving a much better performance than the vanilla distributed implementation. In addition, other optimizations should be considered, for example, developing a custom partitioner in Step I to obtain a good balancing of the workload in reduce phase.

Software frameworks like Hadoop are attractive because they offer the possibility of coding full-fledged distributed applications with very low efforts. However, such an easiness of use implies a cost, as the resulting implementations may not be able to fully exploit the potential of a distributed system. In these cases, an engineering methodology based on the implementation of smart optimizations driven by a careful profiling activity may lead to a much better experimental performance, as demonstrated in this paper. To this end, we notice that the application pattern we considered in our paper, characterized by the interleaving of I/O-intensive and CPU-intensive tasks, is not only required by the Lukáš et al. algorithm but is an instance of a more general problem that is often found also in other application fields. As a consequence of this, the optimizations we developed in our case study are likely to improve in a systematic way the performance of Hadoop-based implementation of other algorithms as well. Along this line, an interesting future direction for our work would be the formalization of this methodology and its experimentation with other case studies, such as [1,3,5,11,12].

References

1. Bayram, S., Sencar, H.T., Memon, N., Avcibas, I.: Source camera identification based on CFA interpolation. In: IEEE International Conference on Image Processing (ICIP), vol. 3, pp. 69–72. IEEE (2005)
2. Cattaneo, G., Ferraro Petrillo, U., Giancarlo, R., Roscigno, G.: An effective extension of the applicability of alignment-free biological sequence comparison algorithms with Hadoop. J. Supercomput., 1–17 (2016). http://dx.doi.org/10.1007/s11227-016-1835-3
3. Cattaneo, G., Ferraro Petrillo, U., Roscigno, G., Fusco, C.: A PNU-based technique to detect forged regions in digital images. In: Battiato, S., Blanc-Talon, J., Gallo, G., Philips, W., Popescu, D., Scheunders, P. (eds.) ACIVS 2015. LNCS, vol. 9386, pp. 486–498. Springer, Cham (2015). doi:10.1007/978-3-319-25903-1_42
4. Cattaneo, G., Roscigno, G.: A possible pitfall in the experimental analysis of tampering detection algorithms. In: 17th International Conference on Network-Based Information Systems (NBiS), pp. 279–286, September 2014
5. Cattaneo, G., Roscigno, G., Bruno, A.: Using PNU-based techniques to detect alien frames in videos. In: Blanc-Talon, J., Distante, C., Philips, W., Popescu, D., Scheunders, P. (eds.) ACIVS 2016. LNCS, vol. 10016, pp. 735–746. Springer, Cham (2016). doi:10.1007/978-3-319-48680-2_64
6. Cattaneo, G., Roscigno, G., Ferraro Petrillo, U.: Experimental evaluation of an algorithm for the detection of tampered JPEG images. In: Linawati, M.M.S., Neuhold, E.J., Tjoa, A.M., You, I. (eds.) CT-EurAsia 2014. LNCS, vol. 8407, pp. 643–652. Springer, Heidelberg (2014). doi:10.1007/978-3-642-55032-4_66
7. Cattaneo, G., Roscigno, G., Ferraro Petrillo, U.: A scalable approach to source camera identification over Hadoop. In: IEEE 28th International Conference on Advanced Information Networking and Applications (AINA), pp. 366–373. IEEE (2014)

8. Choi, J., Choi, C., Ko, B., Choi, D., Kim, P.: Detecting web based DDoS attack using MapReduce operations in cloud computing environment. J. Internet Serv. Inf. Secur. (JISIS) **3**(3/4), 28–37 (2013)
9. Dean, J., Ghemawat, S.: MapReduce: simplified data processing on large clusters. Commun. ACM **51**(1), 107–113 (2008)
10. Ferraro Petrillo, U., Roscigno, G., Cattaneo, G., Giancarlo, R.: FASTdoop: a versatile and efficient library for the input of FASTA and FASTQ files for MapReduce Hadoop bioinformatics applications. Bioinformatics (2017). https://dx.doi.org/10.1093/bioinformatics/btx010
11. Fridrich, J., Lukáš, J., Goljan, M.: Detecting digital image forgeries using sensor pattern noise. In: SPIE, Electronic Imaging, Security, Steganography, and Watermarking of Multimedia Contents VIII, vol. 6072, pp. 1–11 (2006)
12. Gloe, T.: Feature-based forensic camera model identification. In: Shi, Y.Q., Katzenbeisser, S. (eds.) Transactions on Data Hiding and Multimedia Security VIII. LNCS, vol. 7228, pp. 42–62. Springer, Heidelberg (2012). doi:10.1007/978-3-642-31971-6_3
13. Goljan, M., Fridrich, J., Filler, T.: Large scale test of sensor fingerprint camera identification. In: IS&T/SPIE, Electronic Imaging, Security and Forensics of Multimedia Contents XI, vol. 7254, pp. 1–12. International Society for Optics and Photonics (2009)
14. Goljan, M., Fridrich, J., Filler, T.: Managing a large database of camera fingerprints. In: SPIE Conference on Media Forensics and Security, vol. 7541, pp. 1–12. International Society for Optics and Photonics (2010)
15. Golpayegani, N., Halem, M.: Cloud computing for satellite data processing on high end compute clusters. In: IEEE International Conference on Cloud Computing, pp. 88–92. IEEE (2009)
16. Lukáš, J., Fridrich, J., Goljan, M.: Digital camera identification from sensor pattern noise. IEEE Trans. Inf. Forensics Secur. **1**, 205–214 (2006)
17. McKenna, A., Hanna, M., Banks, E., Sivachenko, A., Cibulskis, K., Kernytsky, A., Garimella, K., Altshuler, D., Gabriel, S., Daly, M., et al.: The genome analysis toolkit: a MapReduce framework for analyzing next-generation DNA sequencing data. Genome Res. **20**(9), 1297–1303 (2010)
18. Precision Optical Imaging: ISO Noise Chart 15739 (2011). http://www.precisionopticalimaging.com/products/products.asp?type=15739
19. Shvachko, K., Kuang, H., Radia, S., Chansler, R.: The Hadoop distributed file system. In: IEEE 26th Symposium on Mass Storage Systems and Technologies (MSST), pp. 1–10. IEEE (2010)
20. The Apache Software Foundation: Apache Hadoop (2016). http://hadoop.apache.org/
21. White, T.: The small files problem. Cloudera (2009). http://www.cloudera.com/blog/2009/02/the-small-files-problem/

Integration of Data Distribution Service and Raspberry Pi

Marisol García-Valls[1](✉), Javier Ampuero-Calleja[1], and Luis Lino Ferreira[2]

[1] Universidad Carlos III de Madrid, Leganés, Spain
{mvalls,jampuero}@it.uc3m.es
[2] Polytechnic Institute of Porto, Porto, Portugal
llf@isep.ipp.pt

Abstract. Embedded computers such as Raspberry Pi are gaining market as they offer considerable computation power on a flexible platform that can run different operating systems and user level libraries. There are a number of contributions on building middleware for connecting devices based on embedded computers in various ways; however, the temporal behavior of these systems has not been sufficiently covered, despite the fact that this is essential to validate the system design, operation, and timeliness that is needed in domains such as cyber-physical systems (CPS). This paper analyzes the temporal behavior of the connection among embedded computers and servers in the context of time sensitive deployments where some nodes can be virtualized offering mixed criticality execution platforms. We provide a scheme for using the Data Distribution Service standard to connect embedded computers based on Raspberry Pi and servers to analyze the temporal response stability.

Keywords: Data Distribution Service · DDS · Raspberry Pi · Sensors · Embedded computer · Communication performance · Middleware · Mixed criticality systems

1 Introduction

Emerging application domains are envisioning complex interactions among *highly heterogeneous devices* over (also) heterogeneous communication links. Among the miriad of different devices, *embedded computers* are gaining a tremendous popularity as they offer a considerable computation power on a flexible platform capable of running different operating systems.

In some domains such as cyber-physical systems [21], these interactions must adhere to strict *time requirements*. Providing low-level programming of real-time network protocols is the traditional approach to guarantee the fulfillment of time deadlines as it can isolate the network effects on the operation of a system. Nevertheless, this is an approach that would impede meeting essential requirements such as *flexibility* in system design and development. For example, the addition of a new node in such a system would imply the recalculation of the static network schedule. This is not anymore possible in highly dynamic systems

© Springer International Publishing AG 2017
M.H.A. Au et al. (Eds.): GPC 2017, LNCS 10232, pp. 490–504, 2017.
DOI: 10.1007/978-3-319-57186-7_36

such as cyber-physical domains. As an example, let us think of a remote video surveillance system performing object tracking. This involves the activation and shut down of different devices over time (e.g. mobile nodes, IP cameras, etc.), depending on the movement and trajectory of the tracked object.

In such scenarios, solutions are needed that are based on the usage of *communication middleware* to provide *flexible interactions* while preserving certain ranges of *temporal guarantees* that suit the requirements of the specific application domain. Nevertheless, using distribution middleware has been neglected in areas such as critical systems, especially for those parts of higher criticality levels. This is due to the fact that, traditionally, middleware employs a set of libraries that make use of fairly sophisticated programming techniques rather oriented to provide an easy-to-use programming environment, of high development productivity, with reliable, fast, and efficient communication for mainstream (i.e., general purpose) systems. It mostly focuses on providing a friendly and productive environment than to providing strict temporal guarantees.

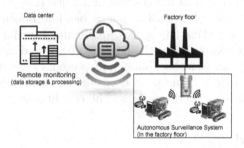

Fig. 1. Overall cyber-physical systems with interaction among powerful servers and autonomous low power embedded computers

Providing a flexible infrastructure that, at the same time, preserves timely operation is a complex problem especially in the presence of autonomous and mobile nodes. The target domain is exemplified in Fig. 1 that shows a large system distributed partly in a factory floor and partly in the cloud. The factory floor part contains a number of subsystems being one of them an autonomous surveillance system made of a number of autonomous mobile devices, equiped with different sensors. These nodes capture video data about their assigned area and transmit them to a server that is in charge of a first processing of the video and its further transmission to the cloud.

Over the last decade, a number of contributions on middleware design have appeared to provide enhanced functionality to distributed systems, but they focus mainly on enlarging the functional dimension of these systems. Also, a number of improvements to the networking protocols have appeared for augmenting bandwidth and improving reliability. To the best of our knowledge, there is no contribution that focuses on studying the interaction between heterogeneous nodes in a time-sensitive environment; nor on exploring the possibilities of using de facto middleware standards such as DDS (Data Distribution Service for real-time systems) for communication of nodes with heterogeneous computation power; this comprises servers (used for heavy processing and data transmission) and embedded computers (used for environment monitoring such as video capture, and readings of valuable data as temperature, humidity, movement, etc.).

This paper analyzes the temporal behavior of the DDS-based interaction between high computation power nodes and ARM-based embedded computers; precisely it focuses on Raspberry Pi devices as the embedded computers, given their high interest as they have gained large market share in both industry and academic worlds. This paper presents a flexible library to communication Raspberry Pi and servers using different underlying communication software (e.g., bare UDP and IP sockets; or data distribution middleware to exploit their quality of service parameters for timeliness and reliability). Our target system integrates heterogeneous nodes (ranging from individual sensors and/or embedded nodes that can be static or autonomously moving in an e.g. surveillance area) and base servers (that interact with the sensors and with other servers).

The paper is structured as follows. Section 2 describes background containing selected related work. Section 3 provides baseline information on the middleware technologies. Section 4 proposes an architecture for integrating Raspberry Pi embedded computers with servers (virtualized and non-virtualized) using DDS as communication backbone, and presents a flexible communication library. Section 5 provides experimental results of the usage of the library in heterogeneous conditions. Section 6 draws the conclusions.

2   Background

Embedded computers are used in a large number of application domains, as they facilitate the development of lower cost solutions that are, in turn, more energy efficient as compared to the usage of high end processors. The computation power of the processors that they use (e.g., ARM family processors) is considerable, supporting the use of comodity operating systems (such as Linux) and user level libraries (such as communication middleware) that aid the development of powerful applications. Middleware employs a set of libraries that make use of fairly sophisticated programming techniques oriented to provide an easy-to-use programming environment with reliable, fast, and efficient communication for general purpose systems. The main focus in on programmability and not on offering strict temporal guarantees. Then, technologies such as the following have been discarded for the most time-sensitive parts of critical systems: Corba [24], Java RMI [29], web services [22], Ice [30], JMS [4], REST, AMQP [20], RabbitMQ [25], Storm [2], River [1], or JBoss [18], among others. DDS [23], the most popular publish/subscribe data-centric standard, offers *quality of service* (QoS) *policies* that allow the designer to fine tune the communication among the endpoints (publishers and subscribers), but it does not guarantee any upper bound on the temporal behavior of the interactions and/or communication times.

The appearance of the cyber-physical systems paradigm envisions large scale systems composed by large numbers of heterogeneous subsystems and nodes across heterogeneous networks. This idea meets the Internet of Things [7]; where protocols for integration of devices need be designed [8]; and where security and reliability must be addressed [6]. Such complex scenarios require more productive design and development means where communication middleware can play a major role. Middleware for cyber-physical systems will have to meet the requirements exposed in [10] including model-based design, on-line reconfiguration and verification functionality to support system evolution at the pace dictated by changing environment conditions; and performance analysis such as [17] need be done for different domains. Some experiments for on-line reconfigurations using verification have been presented in [3,12]. In this area, a number of contributions to the design and implementation of real-time middleware have been proposed, but the great majority only provide partial solutions to very specific and limited problems of communication predictability. For instance, [11], a real-time middleware for distributed real-time applications, supports dynamic service-based reconfiguration; [14] presents a design of a real-time middleware that fine tunes specific internal parameters (such as thread pool size); [15] presents a distributed architecture based on a central manager that supports a dynamic number of clients connected to specific servers through the remote management of its thread pool; and [13] provides a middleware that is aware of the multicore processor architecture to prioritize selected client requests, improving service times of priority client requests.

Embedded computers are a key enabler for the realization of the cyber-physical systems vision. But these require to comply with some level of temporal guarantees. To the best of our knowledge, there is no contribution on the analysis of performance experienced by embedded computers such as Raspberry Pi based systems for building autonomous systems capable of communicating with servers (that can be virtualized providing a mixed criticality platform) through flexible standard-based paradigms such as the Data Distribution Service.

3   Overview of Technologies

Large systems such as those involving IoT and cyber-physical deployments present common characteristics although they have different requirements for temporal guarantees [9]. The following are some of their common characteristics:

- device heterogeneity in what concerns hardware and software characteristics (including the heterogeneous network links);
- devices with heterogeneous resources: some nodes can be sensors with limited computation power and autonomy; embedded computers with moderate but sufficient capacity; and servers with high end hardware and full fledged software;
- dynamic structure and interactions: the set of participant nodes, environment conditions, and requirements may vary over time;
- large scale: nodes, subsystems, and entities can be progressively integrated into larger subsystems;

– event handling complexity: a large number of events can be produced, of different types, and of varying nature (carrying their own information);
– intelligence and distributed management: autonomous decisions are taken considering the overall system conditions and those of its constituent parts.

Execution platforms. The heterogeneous nature of devices impacts the overall operation timeliness. On the high end, there is the presence of powerful many core servers with high performance in data processing and communication. On a lower end, there are embedded computers capable of playing the role of autonomous nodes with low power consumption and considerable computation power. These are typically connected to sensors that are at the lowest end of computation capacity given their restrictions on continued power supply and battery. Raspberry Pi is among the most popular choices in a number of domains. It is a powerful and low-cost platform with good hardware expansion capabilities such as different ports, a GPIO –or General Purpose Input/Output–, pins, etc. and a range of connectivity possibilities such as Ethernet or WiFi. One of the advantages of Raspberry Pi is low cost that has its origins on its initial educational focus. It has been demonstrated on a number of prototype applications such as health services [19], biometrics [27], control [26], or video systems [28], among others.

Middleware connectivity problem space. The problem of connecting distributed and remote systems (devices, sensors, components, micro controllers, servers, desktops, etc.) is handled with communication middleware for a number of domains and, especially, for those that fall in the category of best effort. Following, some technologies are described with respect to their interaction models, resource efficiency, and level of fine tuning of their quality of service parameters: *Java Messaging Service (JMS)* supports publish-subscribe messaging among multiple nodes. It has two application level routing options: point to point and publish-subscribe, typically over a centralized implementation. It is restricted to Java language and part of the Java Platform Enterprise Edition (Java EE) [5]. *MQTT* is a wire protocol that is message-centric allowing to transfer telemetry-style data provided as messages for application domains requiring low latency. *REST* is an application programming interface (API) for web applications that operate in client-server mode, having a simple interface with a reduced number of operations over resources. A resource is any coherent and meaningful addressable concept that is represented by a document that captures the state of the resource. *AMPQ* [20] (Advanced Messaging Protocol Queue) is an interoperability protocol emerged in the financial sector to avoid proprietary and non-interoperable connectivity. Interoperability is achieved by controling the behavior of the messaging provider and the client, i.e., it is a wire protocol. It provides message-oriented communication and flow control.

Data Distribution Service standard. The Data Distribution Service (DDS) is an OMG standard that provides a publish-subscribe (P/S), i.e., a decoupled and data-centric interaction model among remote components. It was designed for connectivity of large scale systems with heterogeneous devices requiring decoupled interoperation. The goal of DDS is to meet the requirements of real-time distributed applications for which a variety of quality of service (QoS) policies are specified. It is, nevertheless, limited by the actual available implementations and the support from the underlying networking level.

DDS relies on the concept of a *global data space* where entities exchange messages based on their type and content. Such entities are *remote nodes* or *remote processes*, although it is also possible to communicate from within the same local machine. Entities can take two roles; they can be *publishers* or *subscribers* of a given data type. Types are based on the concept of *topics* that are constructions supporting the actual data exchange. Topics are identified by a unique name, a data type and a set of QoS policies; also, they can use *keys* that enable the existance of different instances of a topic so that the receiving entities can differentiate the data source. Applications organize the communicating entities into *domains*. Essentially, a domain defines an application range where communication among related entities (an application) can be established. A domain becomes alive when a *participant* is created. A participant is an entity that owns a set of resources such as memory and transport. If an application has different transport needs, then two participants can be created. A participant may contain the following child entities: *publishers, subscribers, data writers, data readers*, and *topics*. Publishers and subscribers are an abstraction that manage the communication part, whereas the data writers and data readers are the abstractions that actually inject and retrieve the data.

4 Integration Architecture

4.1 Target System

The target scenario is presented in Fig. 2. It is particularized for a smart factory system composed of a number of nodes interacting to perform different functions towards a global goal of monitoring the operation of the factory floor that is divided into different cells. In this scenario, timely monitoring of the operation is performed to obtain useful on-line feedback to later adjust the operation in real-time and maximize the operation benefit.

For achieving such a timely supervision and actuation process, the following actors are present:

– *Autonomous monitoring nodes* based on *embedded computers (EC)* that perform surveillance activities over their corresponding cell collecting monitored data through a number of sensors. ECs collect data from the physical system and area that they monitor. Data are sent to servers for further processing and cross-processing.
– *Base servers (BS)* or cell processing nodes that are computers acting as base stations for collecting the data monitored by ECs. They also perform initial checks on the monitored data. One of the BS, has the role of a gateway node that connects the cell to the outside.
– *Data center (DC)* is a system in the factory for smart data processing. The factory also has a private data center for additional and heavy processing of monitored data; also, it is used for execution of other functions such as ERP

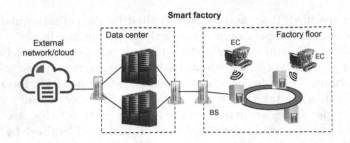

Fig. 2. Target system exemplified on a smart factory scenario

(Enterprise Resource Planning). The factory is also connected to an external cloud where specialized (possibly outsourced) processing can be carried out.

Temporal overheads have to be controlled to guarantee the timely operation on the factory processes. For this, an analysis of possible bottlenecks must be performed. One of the most important communication links to check is the interaction between the embedded computers and the base servers: BS-EC link.

The overall operation and communication process of ECs and BSs must be timely in order to perform real-time monitoring of the system status, decision, and actuation. The overall process comprises the following activities:

- raw data collection from the production cells;
- data pre-processing at cell level;
- transmission of raw data and pre-processed data to data center;
- deep processing of data at the data center; and
- transmission of actuation parameters to the cell actors.

As ECs are autonomous, they can move about their allowed surveillance zone (i.e. their cells) to monitor the status of the system. Then, ECs will use wireless or wired connection, depending on their mobility degree. Once ECs collect data, they send it to the BS to perform additional processing and computation to control the actuation over the physical processes.

4.2   Architecture Overview: Sotware Stack for BS-EC Links

The interaction between BS and EC uses middleware as part of a mixed criticality architecture that enables to consolidate BS usage to run applications or functions with different criticality levels in an isolated way. Figure 3 presents the software stack for the involved nodes. The software stack within each node type (BS or EC) follows the lines indicated below:

- *Mixed criticality system* principles. Different applications can coexist without interfering in their execution in the BS, that will be able to simultaneously run a number of functionalities such as the control of the physical process (e.g. a conveyor belt) and the interaction with an embedded computer.

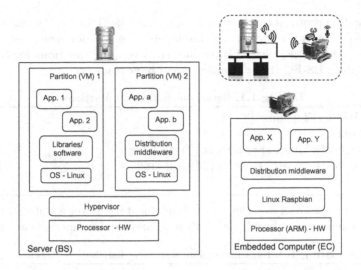

Fig. 3. Software stack for BS-EC link in a mixed criticality environment

- *Partitioned system.* Partitioning is a technique followed in real-time systems to achieve temporal and spatial isolation across applications over the same physical machine. BS are partitioned systems because they run different partitions or virtual machines (VMs) as part of the software stack. Figure 3 shows the partitions (i.e., virtual machines), the distribution middleware and layers of the BS software stack. It has a hypervisor or a virtual machine monitor that supports ARINC 653 scheduling for ensuring non-interference across the execution of partitions. Partitions have the notion of full execution isolation, whereas the mainstream related term is virtual machines. For this, a BS can run additional functions for performing the intensive data pre-processing in parallel with running the software for communication with ECs, without affecting the interaction time with ECs. A simple model for scheduling partitions using DDS in a distributed context is given in [16]. For each partition, the guest operating system performs the scheduling and management of the execution of the application functions inside that partition.
- *Decoupled distributed software.* The BS runs distribution middleware (precisely, Data Distribution Service) for decoupled communication with ECs. ECs require to send data to BSs and also BSs can send information and/or operation commands to BS. The effect of possible network delays is protected by accounting for the communication times on the execution time assigned to the communicating partitions.

4.3   Programming the Communication

A library is provided for supporting the communication among BS and EC. The library provides flexible interaction across the nodes as the underlying communication protocol can be modified, (e.g., basic IP or UDP sockets or Data Distribution Service) by means of a simple interface. The following code provides the main class BSEC_Flexcom listing only the two main functions for communication between BS-EC (bsec_transmit and bsec_receive).

Listing 1.1. Basic communication functions

```
class  BSEC_Flexcom {
  public :
    ret_code  bsec_transmit ( Data_Msg  *);
    ret_code  bsec_receive ( Data_Msg  *);
}
```

Listing 1.1 shows an overview of the implementation over a Data Distribution Service communication backbone. Both send and receive functions are sketched.

Listing 1.2. Implementation over data distribution system

```
struct  ADataType {   //  content    };
#pragma  keylist  ADataType  id
dds :: Topic<ADataType>  tsTopic (" ATopic ");

ret_code  bsec_transmit ( Data_Msg  *){
  dds :: Topic<ADataType>  tsTopic (" ATopic ");
  dds :: DataWriter<ADataType>  dw( tsTopic );
  ATopicType  ts  =  msg_content_fill ();
  dw . write ( ts );
  return  check_status ();
}

ret_code  receive ( Data_Msg  *){
  dds :: Topic<ADataType>  tsTopic (" ATopic ");
  dds :: DataReader<ADataType>  dr ( tsTopic );
  dds :: SampleInfoSeq  info ;
  ADataSeq  data ;
  dr . read ( data ,  info );
}
```

Listing 1.3. Setting of a periodic transmission with a reliable writer

```
<protocol>
 <rtps_reliable_writer >
  <disable_positive_acks_min_sample_keep_duration >
   <sec >DURATION_ZERO_SEC</sec >
   <nanosec >100000000</ nanosec >
  </disable_positive_acks_min_sample_keep_duration >
 </rtps_reliable_writer >
</protocol>
```

For the case of the implementation over DDS, it is possible to fine tune the communication by setting the appropriate values for the quality of service policies. This will adjust the communication performance as needed. Examples of fine tunning are disabling acknowledgement for sample delivery (see Listing 1.3 for setting to 100 ms).

5   Experimental Results

An experimental setting has been deployed to analyze the different relevant versions of the BS-EC link. BS hardware is based on Intel i7-4770 processor at 3.4 GHz, 8MB cache, with 8 GB DDR3 1600 RAM. BS runs a Linux Ubuntu 15.10 and kernel 4.2. The embedded processor is a Raspberry Pi with an ARM1176JZFS processor (i.e., ARM11 using an ARMv6-architecture core) with floating point unit, running at 700 Mhz, with 512 MB. A Netgear CG3300 router L2/L3 is used both for Ethernet (GigaE) and Wireless 802.11n, running a Raspian Whezzy operatinvg system, replacing the kernel to be 3.18.9-rt5-v7.

Experiments show the performance of the communication of Raspberry Pi ECs using DDS Connext 5.2.3 for communication to/from BS nodes. Measurements are performed over sequences of 1000 trials. Firstly, a control group over the bare machine server has been provided; then, the virtualized server has been configured to obtain the communication performance. Experiments also show different load conditions for both the server (PC) and the embedded computer (RPi). BSs are virtualized with Xen. The publisher node has a transmission period of 100 μs, for all scenarios.

Figure 4 shows the temporal behavior for the communication between server and embedded node for a scenario where the server is not virtualized (bare server) and it is progressively loaded. Experiments are conducted messages that are, both, smaller and larger than the MTU (maximum transmission unit). For different load conditions, the figure shows the communication cost for both directions:

- PC(P) - RPi (S): from the server to embedded computer; the base station acts as the publisher (P) and the embedded computer as the subscriber (S).
- RPI(P) - PC(S): from the embedded computer (publisher, P) to the base station (subscriber, S).

The maximum transmission time is similar for all load conditions, being the real maximum 104.8 μs for messages larger than MTU size and 5.1 ms for smaller ones. It is observed that the situation when the base station is the publisher and the embedded node is the subscriber outperforms the opposite situation; this is observed for, both, message sizes larger and smaller than the MTU. Times are overall stable as maximum and minimum cases are consistently around the average for practically all cases. The average times are consistently around the same value for both cases: 100 ms for messages smaller than MTU and 1.3 ms for messages larger than the MTU. Variations are minor with respect to the execution over a bare server. Worst cases for messages larger than MTU are consistently around the same value (4.8 ms), except for the near empty load scenario.

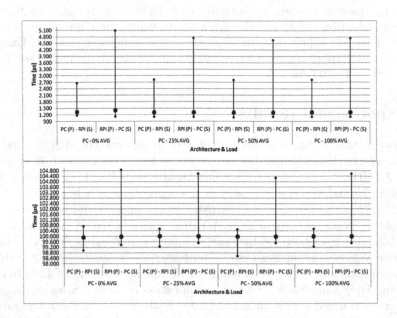

Fig. 4. Communication BS-EC for a progressively loaded bare BS. Top and bottom graphs show behavior for messages larger and smaller than MTU, respectively

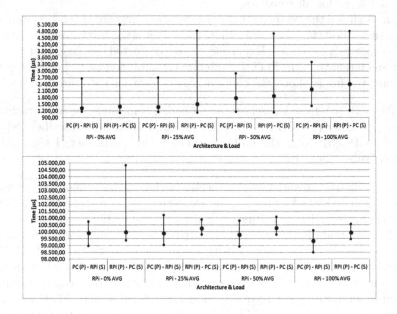

Fig. 5. Communication BS-EC for virtualized BS and progressively loaded EC

Figure 5 shows the communication time for the link BS-EC for a scenario where the embedded node is progressively loaded and the BS is not virtualized. Times are, overall, slightly less stable than in the previous case, ranging between 1.2 ms for messages smaller than MTU and 2.4 ms for the larger messages. Also, publisher BS and subscriber EC yield the best performance.

Figure 6 shows a virtualized BS that is progressively loaded. The average case ranges from 64.65 ms to 64.9 ms for messages larger than MTU; and from 1.23 μs to 1.05 μs for the smaller messages.

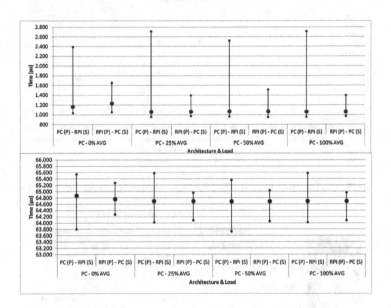

Fig. 6. Communication BS-EC for a virtualized BS that is progressively loaded

Figure 7 shows the temporal behavior for the communication when both nodes are progressively loaded simultaneously. In this case, worst case times increase, although the average times are constantly around 100 μs. The average case time experiments greater variation (between 1.1 ms and 2.2 ms) for the case of smaller message size. For messages larger than MTU, the time increases slightly as compared to the previous case, from 64.25 ms to 64.9 ms

Figure 8 presents a summary of the experiments comparing the above conditions to the scenarios over bare machine and for message sizes larger that the MTU. The *result* column indicates whether the BS is or not virtualized.

Overall, results show that the communication is stable both for bare machine and virtualized settings, for different load conditions and message sizes within the MTU limits and beyond. Worst case values are below 5% larger than the average cases. It is evidenced that Raspberry Pi communication using DDS shows stable behavior with dispersions that, for the largest case reach 438 μs.

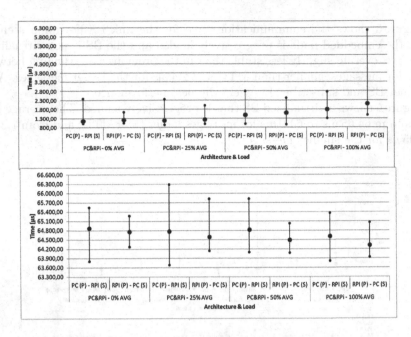

Fig. 7. Communication BS-EC for progressive loads at both nodes

		DATA LENGTH: 65 BYTES			
		Sockets UDP	Result	Middleware DDS	Result
0% LOAD	Virtualized	803,85 µs	Non-Virtualized	1199,01 µs	Virtualized
	Non-Virtualized	736,11 µs		1370,45 µs	
90-100% LOAD	Virtualized	1337,78 µs	Non-Virtualized	1738,2 µs	Virtualized
	Non-Virtualized	699,18 µs		1986,82 µs	

		DATA LENGTH: ≥ 63000 BYTES			
		Sockets UDP	Result	Middleware DDS	Result
0% LOAD	Virtualized	795,26 µs	Non-Virtualized	64814,39 µs	Virtualized
	Non-Virtualized	742,91 µs		99955,09 µs	
90-100% LOAD	Virtualized	1269,82 µs	Non-Virtualized	64554,63 µs	Virtualized
	Non-Virtualized	715,74 µs		99832,65 µs	

Fig. 8. Summarized analysis of P/S enabled communication for both bare and virtualized settings.

6   Conclusions

This paper analyzes the communication timeliness in the context of a distributed monitoring architecture based on autonomous embedded computers and servers that can support mixed criticality execution. Unlike in traditional cyber-physical systems requiring real-time behavior (that use the level 2 networking protocols to control access to the media and achieve predictable network schedules), our deployment uses a Data Distribution Service communication middleware over Internet Protocol that supports tuning some parameters of the communication. A number of contributions on the design of communication libraries for different domains have been provided; although, to the best of our knowledge, no analysis of the behavior of Raspberry Pi nodes in such a time-sensitive context as cyber-physical systems has been provided. We provide a flexible library that supports the usage of different underlying communication schemes, and we show its implementation for the Data Distribution Service. We provide an architecture for autonomous embedded computers on the analysis of the temporal behavior of the interoperation between embedded computer and servers in the context of a cyber-physical deployment. The analysis is performed for different load conditions at the end nodes and a different software stack at the BS (virtualized versus bare machine) and for sustained periodic interactions. Results show that the proposed design provides stable communication times, showing minor variations on the average transmission times for all load conditions. The heavy loaded scenarios show some performance improvements due to the Linux scheduler optimizations on the utilization of the cores at the BS side.

Acknowledgments. This work has been partly funded by the project REM4VSS (TIN2011-28339) and M2C2 (TIN2014-56158-C4-3-P) funded by the Spanish Ministry of Economy and Competitiveness.

References

1. Apache Software Foundation: Jini^{TM} network technologies specification. Apache River v2.2.0 (2013). https://river.apache.org/doc/spec-index.html
2. Apache Software Foundation: Storm 0.10.0 (2015). http://storm.apache.org
3. Bersani, M.M., García-Valls, M.: The cost of formal verification in adaptive CPS. An example of a virtualized server node. In: Proceedings of 17th IEEE High Assurance Systems Engineering Symposium (HASE), Orlando, Florida, January (2016)
4. Deakin, N.: JSR 343: Java^{TM} Message Service 2.0 (2013)
5. Deakin, N.: Java Message Service, version 2.0. Oracle (2013)
6. Esposito, C., Cotroneo, D., Russo, S.: On reliability in publish/subscribe services. Comput. Netw. **57**(5), 1318–1343 (2013)
7. Esposito, C., Castiglione, A., Palmieri, F., Ficco, M., Choo, K.K.R.: A publish/subscribe protocol for event-driven communications in the internet of things. In: Proceedings of DASC-PICom-DataCom-CyberSciTec, pp. 376–383 (2016)
8. Bormann, C., Casstellani, A.P., Shelby, Z.: CoAP: An application protocol for billions of tiny Internet nodes. IEEE Internet Comput. **16**(2), 62–67 (2012)
9. García-Valls, M., Cucinotta, T., Lu, C.: Challenges in real-time virtualization and predictable cloud computing. J. Syst. Architect. **60**(9), 736–740 (2014)
10. García-Valls, M., Baldoni, R.: Adaptive middleware design for CPS: Considerations on the OS, resource managers, and the network run-time. In: Proceedings of the 14th Workshop on Adaptive and Reflective Middleware (ARM). Co-located to ACM Middleware, Vancouver, Canada, December 2015
11. García-Valls, M., Fernández Villar, L., Rodríguez López, I.: iLAND: An enhanced middleware for real-time reconfiguration of service oriented distributed real-time systems. IEEE Trans. Industr. Inform. **9**(1), 228–236 (2013)

12. García-Valls, M., Perez-Palacin, D., Mirandola, R.: Time sensitive adaptation in CPS through run-time configuration generation and verification. In: Proceedings of the 38th IEEE Annual Computer Software and Applications Conference (COMP-SAC), pp. 332–337 (2014)
13. García-Valls, M., Calva-Urrego, C.: Improving service time with a multicore aware middleware. In: 32nd ACM/SIGApp Symposium on Applied Computing (SAC), Marrakech, Morocco (2017)
14. García-Valls, M., Calva-Urrego, C., de la Puente, J.A., Alonso, A.: Adjusting middleware knobs to assess scalability limits of distributed cyber-physical systems. Comput. Stand. Interfaces **57**, 95–103 (2017)
15. García-Valls, M.: A proposal for cost-effective server usage in CPS in the presence of dynamic client requests. In: Proceedings of 19th International Symposium on Real-Time Computing (ISORC), York, UK (2016)
16. García-Valls, M., Domínguez-Poblete, J., Touahria, I.E.: Using DDS in distributed partitioned systems. ACM Sigbed Review (2017)
17. García-Valls, M., Basanta-Val, P.: Analyzing point-to-point DDS communication over desktop virtualization software. Comput. Stand. Interfaces **49**, 11–21 (2017)
18. JBoss.: JBoss Messaging (2015). http://docs.jboss.org
19. Leccese, F., Cagnetti, M., Trinca, D.: A smart city application: A fully controlled street lighting isle based on raspberry-pi card, a zigbee sensor network and WiMAX. Sensors **14**, 24408–24424 (2014)
20. ISO/IEC Information Technology Task Force (ITTF): OASIS AMQP1.0 - Advanced Message Queuing Protocol (AMQP), v1.0 specification (ISO/IEC 19464: 2014) (2014)
21. Kim, K.D., Kumar, P.R.: Cyber physical systems: A perspective at the centennial. Proc. IEEE **100**(13), 1287–1308 (2012)
22. Oasis.: Web Services Reliable Messaging (WS-ReliableMessaging) 1.1 specification. Oasis standard (2016). http://docs.oasis-open.org/ws-rx/wsrm/200702/wsrm-1.1-spec-os-01.pdf
23. Object Management Group: A Data Distribution Service for Real-time Systems Version 1.2 (2007)
24. Object Management Group: Common Object Request Broker Architecture (CORBA) Specification, Version 3.1 Interfaces (2008)
25. Pivotal Software: RabbitMQ. AMQpp. 0-9-1 Model Explained (2016). http://www.rabbitmq.com/tutorials/amqp-concepts.html
26. Raguvaran, K., Thiyagarajan, J.: Raspberry PI based global industrial process monitoring through wireless communication. In: Proceedings of International Conference on Robotics, Automation, Control and Embedded Systems (RACE), Chennai (2015)
27. Shah, D., Haradi, V.: IoT based biometrics implementation on Raspberry Pi. In: Proceedings of the International Conference on Communication, Computing and Virtualization (ICCCV). Procedia Computer Science, Elsevier, pp. 328–336 (2016)
28. Senthilkumar, G., Gopalakrishnan, K., Kumar, V.S.: Embedded image capturing system using Raspberry Pi system. Int. J. Emerg. Trends Technol. Comput. Sci. **3**(2), 1–3 (2014)
29. Sun Microsystems: Java^{TM} Remote Method Invocation API (2016). http://docs.oracle.com/javase/7/docs/technotes/guides/rmi/
30. ZeroC Inc.: The Internet Communications Engine (2016). https://zeroc.com/downloads/ice/3.5/

Impact of Middleware Design
on the Communication Performance

Marisol García-Valls[1]([✉]), Daniel Garrido[2], and Manuel Díaz[2]

[1] Universidad Carlos III de Madrid, Leganés, Spain
`mvalls@it.uc3m.es`
[2] Universidad de Málaga, Málaga, Spain
`{dgarrido,mdr}@lcc.uma.es`

Abstract. The precise architectural approach of a communication middleware technology is of outmost importance in areas where a certain degree of control over the underlying platform is needed, e.g., for fine-grain management of temporal behavior or concurrency management. The design of the middleware libraries and, especially, the resulting execution environment that these provide affect the control level of the application code over the platform resources. In this paper, we describe and analyze the two main design approaches of communication middleware implementations, that offer two different execution environments to applications: *direct execution* and virtual machine *intermediation*. We exemplify this idea with a selected set of technologies that does not intend to be exhaustive, but simply representative of both possible middleware architectural design approaches. The goal is to show the impact of these architectures on the resulting communication performance, that we show as overhead, i.e., the percentage of time taken by both architectures with respect to a fixed remote operation with a fixed processing time.

Keywords: Middleware · Run time · Design · Communication · Performance · Programming model · Real-time

1 Introduction

Middleware technologies have been used extensively over the last decades as they significantly ease the programming effort of distributed systems. The rich functionality that middleware provides as off-the-shelf components also facilitates reuse of common functions across different designs that involve the communication among distributed processes.

The lack of certified implementations has been perceived as a risk factor in time-sentive application domains, confining middleware only to the less critical parts. The benefits of having an off-the-shelf certified communication bus based on middleware are of outmost importance in all domains to increase productivity, reliability, and to mature product versions. The abstraction of the underlying communication protocols, and networking details in general, their high level programming interface, and the relatively high location transparency

© Springer International Publishing AG 2017
M.H.A. Au et al. (Eds.): GPC 2017, LNCS 10232, pp. 505–519, 2017.
DOI: 10.1007/978-3-319-57186-7_37

of the application components are also a means to isolate possible failures and increase fault tolerance.

Given the lack of certified components, the reasons to decide on a specific technology to implement a distributed system have been based on the experiences in previous projects with respect to, e.g., performance, that is a top reason to decide on its future use. Among others, there are a number of reasons that impact the resulting performance of a middleware technology: its generated run-time environment, the level of control that the applications have over the platform resources, and the programming facilities.

This paper presents some of the important considerations over middleware that directly impact the functionality provided to applications: the *resulting execution environment*, and their associated *performance considerations*. The execution environment has a direct influence over the application's capacity to access the platform resources, and it also influences the provided performance. We also illustrate the programming ease for a selected set of middleware technologies for both architectures, and with the goal of showing their homogeneous programming model. The programming ease is extremely important in the sustainability and penetration of a technology.

This paper does not intend to be an exhaustive survey of all available technologies. The paper intends to select simply a representative set of both possible middleware architectures. As a result, some popular technologies such as DDS [13] or stream processors technologies [11] are not considered as they are additional possibilities for a particular middleware architecture, but not essential to this work. Studies of DDS performance have been conducted to analyze its architecture [10]; the behavior on mixed criticality partitioned/virtualized distributed systems [9], and over Internet protocols [2]. We analyze the impact measuring the communication overhead of both architectural designs.

The paper is structured as follows. Section 2 describes the background and related work. Section 3 presents the two broad run-time architectures and important considerations with respect to their programming models and the level of control that applications acquire over the platform resources. Section 4 presents a set of selected technology choices covering both types of run-time types; and eventually Sect. 5 provides an overview of their programming models and some comparison in their performance for selected technologies that cover both run-time types. Section 6 concludes the paper.

2 Background

For systems with real-time requirements, middleware has been typically seen as a source of unpredictable behavior. To adjust to the strict timeliness properties, their traditional approach has been to use specific communication standards that are highly reliable, tolerant to interference, and implement simple communication schemes. Examples in the avionics domain are the communication standard ARINC 429 and highly reliable buses such as MIL-STD1553; or CAN and TTP in factory automation and automotive.

More recently, Ethernet has gained penetration in the critical sectors as it is a commercial standard with a winning position across all technological markets, with relatively cheap and well proven equipment. Domains such as avionics have adopted this standard in, e.g., AFDX.

Only for the case of safety critical systems (e.g., avionics), the above low level communication schemes (centered around programming a specific network protocol/bus) have gained in the past over middleware technologies. The main reason has been the lack of certification of middleware components. Until recent days, there was practically no certified communication middleware, as it is now the case of some version of the DDS standard ([13]). Nevertheless, it has been used in either mainstream domains (e.g. video streaming) or non-critical parts of critical systems such as ground control stations.

The penetration of middleware in other sectors (such as video streaming [4], simulation [1], real-time cloud computing [3] or cyber-physical systems [7,17]) has matured the available technologies. New functionality has been introduced to support dynamic distributed systems (e.g. reconfiguration [16,17]). The level of control over the platform resources has been explored for resoure managers (e.g. [6] for single core processors, and recently exploiting the awareness of the underlying multicore technology [8]). Technologies such as CORBA [12], AMQP [5], RMI [14], Ice [15], WCF [21], or DDS [13], among others, are examples of these popular solutions to developing cross-domain distributed systems. Their suitability for a specific project has typically been decided ad-hoc, with light (though sometimes important) reasons such as the presence of engineers that know the technology or to the previous experience with a specific middleware.

The paper presents a selected number of middleware choices with respect to the above mentioned considerations. It does not intend to provide an exhaustive list but to survey a representative set; it leaves out some important technology such as DDS or Ada DSA as they have been analysed in previous work [10].

3   Run-Time Architecture Types

There are two main types of run-times that are created from the usage of specific middleware. The programming language can also influence the type of resulting run-time; e.g., languages such as Java and C#, require that the created applications run inside a virtual execution environment (a virtual machine). The virtual machine is typically an additional process in the platform that is scheduled by the operating system, therefore introducing execution overhead. The two main types of run-time architectures are (see Fig. 1(a), (b)):

- *Direct execution* (Fig. 1(a)); the middleware libraries are directly linked to the operating system code. Application code may use the operating system's system calls to access the platform resources; typically, the middleware includes wrappers to POSIX functions of the OS.
- *Gateway execution* (Fig. 1(b)); the middleware requires the installation of an additional software that, upon start up, generates a virtual machine where the application is executed. Applications' attempts to use the operating system

calls results in a call to the virtual machine, that acts as a gateway. The call is served by the operating system when the virtual machine process is scheduled for execution, resulting in applications having less control over the platform. Typically, these environments offer a specific set of functions that do not necessarily map to POSIX functions; they are typically less powerful.

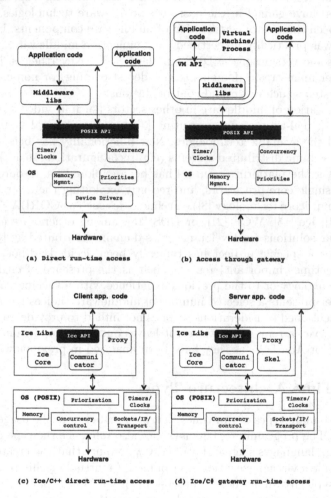

Fig. 1. Run-time architectures: (a) direct; (b) gateway. Ice example: (c) C++; (d) C#.

The differences between both run-time architectures are experienced by applications and the level of control that they have over:

– *Concurrency model*; some only offer threads inside the virtual machine process. Others offer the possibility of having multi-process and multi-threaded applications.

- *Concurrency control*; in some technologies the full POSIX API can be used for controling concurrency, whereas others are limited to the facilities offered by the programming language environment. This yields to different sets of synchronization constructs, or communication primitives (signals, etc.), among others.
- *Time measurement*; some environments offer timers, high resolution clocks for measuring processing time, elapsed wall clock time, etc., whereas gateway environments provide a few functions for coarse grain time measurements, as the scheduling boundaries of the virtual machine must be traversed.
- *Prioritized execution*; direct access environments allow to use the scheduler facilities to distinguish between, e.g. real-time and non real-time threads by using specific scheduling policies and setting the priority attributes of threads. Virtual machine run-times such as C# and Java allow thread priorization, that has effect only within the specific process boundaries.
- *Network protocols*; most middleware designs offer different types of transport such as TCP, UPD and also SSL. Direct access middleware can integrate with specific lower layer medium access protocols for, e.g., real-time networks. This will benefit network control at the cost of reduced portability and, most of the time, decreased performance.

The used programming language poses requirements on the execution platform. E.g. in Java, an execution time interpreter (a JVM) is needed, and the application code runs in the context of the JVM process. Application code can be multi-threaded inside this JVM process with the limitations of Java programming environment for issuing system calls to the platform. Also, for C#, a .NET Mono environment is needed as an additional process, similarly to Java domains.

Languages that force the appearance of a new execution environment, such as Java or C#, offer their own specific programming API that is sometimes limited in functionality such that it is not suited for applications requiring control over resources. Examples are low resolution clocks or local thread priorization, or lack of real-time scheduling policies, as opposed to POSIX.

POSIX environments provide finer control, as applications can use different types of clocks for fine grain time measurements. *Elapsed time* can be measured with CLOCK_REALTIME; and *processing time* can be measured with CLOCK_PROCESS_CPUTIME or CLOCK_THREAD_CPUTIME. Timers are associated to signals for indicating that a certain time has elapsed. Precise control over concurrent execution is possible with schedulers: SCHED_FIFO or SCHED_RR or other real-time policies can be used for setting a specific real-time scheduling policy; threads assigned to these schedulers become real-time threads, coexisting with other non real-time threads under the CFS scheduler.

In a C# environment, the above fine grain control is not possible as the virtual machine introduced by .NET Mono yields to the same effect as a Java virtual machine. For instance, measuring time with C# has to be done through the language constructs, e.g. `Chrono` class (which provides nanosecond resolution). Also, Java's time facilities are inadequate to programmers as they have typically not been thread safe (until JDK SE 8) and are coarse grain with poor control over elapsed time.

4   Specific Technologies

A number of middleware technologies are presented that exemplify both run-time architectures (direct and gateway). The presented set covers different communication standards and communication models. It is usual that most of these technologies are versatile and allow to be compiled to an executable that will run in a virtual machine or as a process over the operating system.

4.1   Ice

Ice is a versatile middleware, allowing the use of a broad range of programming languages (such as C++, Java, Python, C#, Visual Basic .Net, PHP, and Ruby). It can also execute over different operating systems (such as Linux, Solaris, Windows, or Mac OS, among others). It allows to build distributed applications following two communication models: object-oriented remote method invocations (Ice) and publish-subscribe (Ice Storm). It also supports synchronous and asynchronous invocations.

Ice design (see Fig. 1(a), (b)) was clearly influenced by CORBA; however, the API has been maintained quite simple and it is extremely easy to use, inspired in CORBA, but with the goal of avoiding the experienced mistakes of the latter. Its programming model is quite powerful as remote objets may implement different interfaces through a single object identify. It supports some level of dynamic behavior by sending proxies to clients, and activating servers on demand which favors performance when not needed.

The *Communicator* entity is the entrance point to all interactions. It dispatches requests to all facilities of Ice libraries. It controls the client-side and server-side thread pools. The *Adaptor* is a server-side entity that maps the requests to the server interface; also, it provides one or several end-points (communication ends) and binds itself to various servants. It supports the live cycle of objects ensuring that servants and remote objects are created without race conditions. The *Proxy* is an entity that is instantiated in the client that represents the remote object; it supports the remote invocations from clients as if they were local calls. The *Skeleton* is equivalent to the proxy but on the server side for translating incoming requests. The *Servant* is in charge of supporting the server-side operations to solve the requested invocations in a specific programming language.

Distributed applications can programmed in different languages; one end can use C++, so that the resulting execution environment will be direct access, and it is possible to use all the system calls of the operating system; the other end can be programmed in C#; in such a case, it is needed to integrate the libraries of Mono for .NET and a gateway run-time is created.

4.2   Corba

CORBA (Common Object Request Broker Architecture) is a standard from OMG. CORBA has all the features necessary to develop robust and efficient applications in different languages (e.g. C++, Java, Ada, etc.) or platforms.

It a number of implementations available, including open-source and commercial versions, from many different vendors. CORBA-based applications can mix languages or operating systems in a transparent way. The "magic" of CORBA is the use of interfaces as a kind of contracts where servers (e.g. C++ server) expose services which can be invoked by clients (e.g. Ada client). Later, the IDL CORBA compiler generates some glue code in both, server and client, to allow communication in a transparent way.

Figure 2(a) shows the basic execution flow between a client and a CORBA object in a general request `result = object.operation(args)`.

The first step for a client invocation is to obtain a reference of the target object. This reference can be obtained in different ways (e.g. Naming Service, factories, etc.). With this reference the client can perform the invocation on the target object. For this, the ORB (Object Request Broker) uses a stub class instance (automatically generated) representing the target object in the client space address. This proxy has the same interface as the remote object. So, the client application does not know anything about communications and uses the methods provided by the proxy, which have the same signature as the remote object. The stub is responsible for data packaging/unpackaging and the use of ORB operations to transmit the invocation to the ORB server.

In the server space address, the invocation is caught by the ORB, which locates the target object and uses a skeleton class to finally execute the request. If the operation has output arguments or a return value, the results are transmitted back to the client.

Standard CORBA is not well suitable for real-time systems. However, several CORBA extensions have enabled the reliability of the applications to be bettered. For instance, Real-time CORBA or RT-CORBA [18] is the CORBA extension for real-time systems. It included features for control processor resources, communication resources and memory resources in distributed real-time applications. Minimum CORBA [19] aims to use CORBA in embedded systems reducing the memory and code foot-print. Finally, FT CORBA or Fault Tolerance CORBA [20] is an OMG specification for building fault-tolerant distributed real-time and embedded applications.

4.3   Advanced Message Queueing Protocol

AMQP (Advanced Message Queuing Protocol) is a networking protocol based on messages independent from any platform to enable clients interoperability with messaging middleware servers called brokers. AMQP defines the network protocol and the server-side services through two items:

- *Messaging capabilities*; a set of these capabilities are call the *AMQ model*. The AMQ model consists of a set of components that route and store messages withing the broker service, plus a set of rules for wiring these components together.
- A *network wire-level protocol*, AMQP, that lets client applications talk to the server and interact with the AMQ model that it implements.

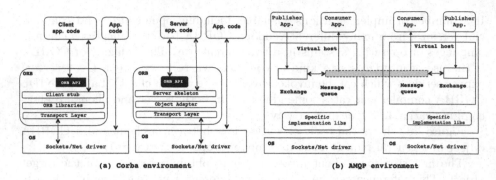

(a) Corba environment   (b) AMQP environment

Fig. 2. Run-time architectures for: (a) Corba; (b) AMQP.

The AMQ model is based on three entities (see Fig. 2(b)): *exchange* (that receive messages from publishers and route them to message queues based on arbitrary criteria as message properties or content); *message queue* (entities receiving messages and storing them until they can be safely consumed by clients); and *binding* that define the relationship between a message queue and an exchange and provide the message routing criteria.

AMQP wire protocol definition allows for all common messaging behaviors. It does not define a wire-level distinction between clients and brokers, the protocol is simetric. However, different implementations may have different capabilities.

AMQP is rather oriented to providing a simple message bus for integration of systems. The variety of realizations yields to both mentioned run-time architectures: direct (over C++ and POSIX compliant OS) and gateway (e.g. Java). For example, RabittMQ implementation may use either a C# Mono environment or a C++/POSIX environment.

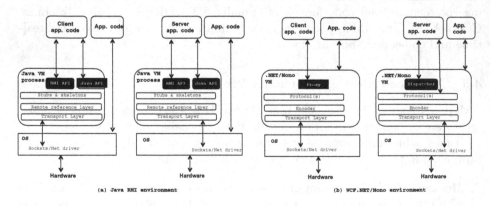

(a) Java RMI environment   (b) WCF.NET/Mono environment

Fig. 3. Architectures: (a) Java RMI; (b) WCF - Windows Communication Foundation.

4.4   Other Tecnologies

Java RMI. Java RMI (Remote Method Invocation) is a communication middleware for Java environments as shown in Fig. 3(a). Java RMI serves as the basis for a number of higher level communication facilities such as OSGi. It is an object-oriented middleware that executes in a Java virtual machine with the programming facilities of Java SDK class libraries. These comprise thread multi-programming, basic concurrency control constructions, or time measurement facilities with low resolution clocks. These course grain operations are not suited for applications requiring fine control over the platform resources.

WCF. Windows Communication Foundation (WCF) is the C#-based communication alternative [21]. WCF is based (and supports) on a previous idea, Web Services. However, WCF has several important advantages over Web services. It supports more protocols for transporting messages than WS, which only support sending messages using HTTP. WCF supports sending messages using HTTP, as well as TCP, named pipes, and MSMQ. More important, WCF can be extended to support additional transport protocols. Therefore, software developed using WCF can be adapted to work together with a wider variety of other software, thereby increasing the potential return on the investment.

5   Comparison and Results

In this section, the programming model of selected technologies is presented (Ice, Corba, Java RMI, and AMQP) to show the similarity in the programming concept. Later, results of practical selected execution cases are provided for both run-time architectures: direct and gateway. The selected evaluations are performed for Ice direct (Ice/C++), Ice with gateway execution (Ice/C#), AMQP gateway (RabittMQ implementation), and Corba (C++/TAO implementation).

5.1   Programming the Communication

Initially, the same Ice environment is shown for C# programming language. The syntax of Ice library functions is practically equivalent, except for the much simpler writting of the language.

Ice C# example for gateway execution.

```
public class Server {
 public static void Main(string []args){
  Ice.Communicator ic = null;
   ic = Ice.Util.initialize(ref args);
   Ice.ObjectAdapter adapter = ic.createObjectWithEndpoints(
    "AdapName", "tcp -p 10000");
   Ice.Object obj = new TimeServiceI();
   adapter.add(obj, ic.stringToIdentity("Servant"));
   adapter.activate();
   ic.waitForShutdown();    } }
```

The client side programming is also much simpler than the one of C++. It first acquires a `Communicator` class object, `ic` used for locating the remote object with `ic.stringToProxy("Servant:tcp -h 163.117.14x.xx -p 10000");`. Later, the invocation is straight forward: `rem.timeInt(i)`.

AMPQ# example gateway execution with RabittMQ, sever side.

```
var factory = new ConnectionFactory() {HostName = "163.117.14x.xx"};
var connection = factory.CreateConnection();
using(var channel = connection.CreateModel)) {
 channel.QueueDeclare(queue: "tx_queue", durable: false,
    exclusive: false, autoDelete: false, arguments: null);
 channel.BasicConsume(queue: "tx_queue", noAck = false,
    consumer: consumer);
 while (iteration_pending){
  consumer.Queue.Dequeue();
  var body = ae.Body;
  var props = ea.Properties;
  var replyProps = channel.CreateBasicProperties();
  replyProps.CorrelationId = props.CorrelationId;

  respBytes = Encoding.UTF8.GetBytes(resp = generateNumber());
  channel.BasicPublish(exchange: "", routingKey: props.ReplyTo,
    basicProperties: replyProps, body: respBytes);
  channel.BasicAck(deliveryTag: ea.DeliveryTag, multiple: false);  }
```

The client side in AMQP is elaborated in the same way, as there is no difference between server and client. Rather, both are simply end points of the communication using a message queue as either consumer or producer, depending on wether they are sending or receiving a messages.

Following, it is shown a Java RMI code of a distributed application for the same example of a time server. All the code (interfaces, and the communication endpoints code is in the Java language).

Java RMI gateway run-time: The remote object functions (TimeServiceI.java).

```
public interface TimeServiceI extends Remote{
 int timeInt(int i) throws RemoteException;
 float timeDouble(float i) throws RemoteException;    }
```

Java RMI gateway run-time: The server set up.

```
public class Server implements TimeServiceI{
    public int timeInt(int i){ ... }
    float timeDouble(float i){ ... }
    public static void main(String args[]){
    Server obj = new Server();
    TimeServiceI stub = (TimeService I)
    UnicastRemoteObject.exportObject(obj, 0);
    Registry registry = LocalRegistry.getRegistry();
    registry.bind("TheTimeService",stub);    }
}
```

Clients locate the remote object by checking the registry at the server side code residing at node host with `LocateRegistry.getRegistry(host)`. Later, a remote reference (stub) to the remote object is obtained with `TimeServiceI stub = (TimeServiceI) registry.lookup("TheTimeService")`. The remote invocations are simple, e.g. `stub.timeInt(i)`.

Below, the programming of a distributed application on a direct execution environment with Ice/C++ is shown. Initialy, the `TimeServiceI` interface is presented, and later an excerpt of the server side set up is provided.

Ice C++ example for a direct execution: The remote object functions (TimeServiceI.h).

```
class TimeServiceI : virtual public TimeService{
public:
  virtual ::Ice::Int TimeInt(::Ice::Int, const Ice::Current&);
  virtual ::Ice::Double TimeDouble(::Ice::Double,const Ice::Current&);};
```

Ice C++ example: Server set up.

```
Ice::CommunicatorPtr ic;
ic = Ice::initialize(arg, argv);
Ice::ObjectAdapterPtr adapter = ic->
   createObjectAdapterWithEndpoints("adapter", "udp -p 10000");
Ice::ObjectPTr object = new TimeServiceI;
adapter -> add(object, ic->stringToIdentity("TimeService"));
adapter -> activate();
ic -> waitForShutdown();
```

The above code shows the simplicity of distributed systems programming in Ice. The exemplified server provides two functions that return the server time to the invoking client. The client interactions needs first to first instantiate an Ice communicator object `Ice:CommunicatorPtr ic;` used for locating the remote object `ic->StringToProxy("TimeService:udp -h 163.117.14x.xx -p 10000")`; that returns a remote object `rem`. The invocation of the client is straightforward, e.g., `rem->TimeInt(i)`.

CORBA Inteface example

```
interface IExample {
    short method(in short arg1,in float arg2);
};
```

In the above interface, a method with two input arguments and a short value returned is declared. The next step is to use the IDL CORBA compiler (TAO-IDL in our case) which generates stubs and skeletons for client and server. In order to use a remote object implementing this interface, a CORBA client must perform several initialization steps. It then declares an instance of a class representing the remote object (with the code `orb->string_to_object`), and the client application can subsequently use this instance with all the methods provided by the interface.

CORBA instance declaration and client invocation

```
CORBA::ORB_var orb = CORBA::ORB_init (argc, argv, "");
// Obtain reference
CORBA::Object_var object =orb->string_to_object("file://ior");
IExample_var server = IExample::_narrow (object.in ());
// Remote invocation
float res = server->method(5,3.15);
```

First, it initializes the ORB object. Then, a reference for the remote object implementing the IExample interface is obtained, and finally, an interface method (method) is invoked. It should be noticed that the client uses a class named IExample_var that is the stub class automatically generated by the IDL compiler.

The server side is more complex. The remote object is contained in another application which activates this object allowing remote invocations to be received. Additional factors have to be considered such as the object adapter (POA) and its interaction with skeleton and servant. As in the case of the client side, some initial steps are necessary in order to activate a CORBA object. These initial steps are carried out in the server application and cover aspects such as the ORB initialization, obtaining the object adapter or object activation. The following code shows some of these steps:

CORBA server initialization, adapter get, and object activation

```
// Initialize the ORB
CORBA::ORB_var orb = CORBA::ORB_init(argc, argv, "orb");
// Obtain a reference to the RootPOA
CORBA::Object_var poaobj = orb->resolve_initial_references("RootPOA");
// Create a Example object
IExample_i hello;
//Activate the Servant
PortableServer::ObjectId_var oid = poa->activate_object(&hello);
```

CORBA server: Class for implementing the IDL interface

```
CORBA::Short IExample_i::method(CORBA::Short arg1, CORBA::Short arg2) {
   CORBA::Short temp;
   temp = arg1+arg2; // Example code
   return temp;
}
```

5.2   Comparison

This section presents a performance comparison for a selected set that covers the different aspects considered in this contribution. The impact of the two different middleware architectures in the overall remote communication is exemplified with a selected set of technologies that does not intend to be exhaustive, but simply representative of both possible middleware architectures. Precisely, Ice

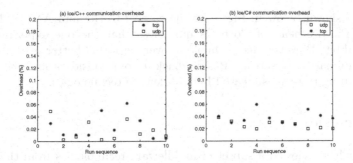

Fig. 4. Communication overhead for: (a) Ice/C++; (b) Ice/C#.

C++ and Corba are studied for the case of direct execution, and Ice C# and AMQP are studied for the case of virtual machine intermediation. The goal is to show the impact of these architectures in the resulting performance, that we show as overhead, i.e., the percentage of time taken by both architectures with respect to a fixed remote operation with a fixed processing time.

Experiments have been performed on an Ethernet network using normal transport protocols, TCP and UDP. Measurements are carried out at the client side, i.e., considering a whole round trip communication and an average processing time at the server of $1.9s$. The same setup is used for Ice/C#, Ice/C++, and AMQP Rabbit, made of a distributed system with two homogeneous nodes as end points of the communication. Both nodes are dual core Intel processors at 2.6 GHz, 1MG cache and 2GB RAM memory. The operating system is a Linux Ubuntu distribution v10.04 with kernel v2.6.32. The network is an Ethernet one and both nodes are in the same segment. The version of Ice is v3.1 [15]; the used version for AMQP Rabbit iv v3.6.0.

Following, it is shown the results of the execution of Ice, exemplified for two different transport protocols. As expected, UDP communication is more efficient, and so is Ice as there is no intermediation of a virtual machine execution (Fig. 4).

A different hardware set up has been used for Corba, that is based on Intel Core i7 at 2.0 GHz, 1GB RAM memory with a Cent OS 6.3 Linux distribution with kernel v2.6.32 and an Ethernet network. The version of TAO/C++ is 2.3.3.

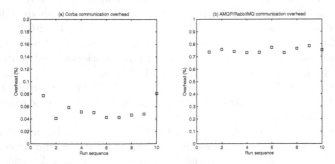

Fig. 5. Communication overhead for: (a) Corba; (b) AMQP with RabbitMQ.

Results are shown below in Fig. 5 for the case of Corba and AMQP. It can be seen that the overhead of Corba is quite less that the one experimented by AMQP Rabbit. However, Ice technology over performs better even in a much less powerful hardware setting. Results back up our considerations with respect to the resulting run-times created by middleware technologies.

6   Conclusion

This paper has reviewed a subset of middleware technologies from the point of view of their architectural design to identify its impact on performance; this is an interesting aspect for their selection as part of a software project. A few of the most common communication middleware have been selected that are representative of both design options. We have analyzed their execution run-time (i.e., gateway or direct) that provides different levels of control over platform resources. The programming models have been exemplified for different languages, e.g., Java, C#, and C++, and performance comparatives have been presented. Results show that gateway run-times have larger impact over the overall performance. The evolution of the technology also shows that performance has been improved across the years in the design of new technologies. For example, Ice (as a lighter weight Corba-inspired technology) shows better performance as compared to Corba over TAO. An interesting result is also that Ice direct run-time performs better compared to its gateway version.

Acknowledgements. This work has been partly funded by projects REM4VSS (TIN2011-28339) and M2C2 (TIN2014-56158-C4-3-P) granted by the Spanish Ministry of Economy and Competitiveness.

References

1. Díaz, M., Garrido, D., Troya, J.M.: Development of distributed real-time simulators based on CORBA. Simul. Model. Pract. Theor. **15**(6), 716–733 (2007)
2. Esposito, C., Russo, S., Di Crescenzo, D.: Performance assessment of OMG compliant data distribution middleware. In: Proceedings of IEEE International Symposium on Parallel and Distributed Processing, Miami, FL (2008)
3. García-Valls, M., Cucinotta, T., Lu, C.: Challenges in real-time virtualization and predictable cloud computing. J. Syst. Archit. **60**(2), 726–740 (2014)
4. García-Valls, M., Fernández-Villar, L., Rodríguez-López, I.: iLAND an enhanced middleware for real-time reconfiguration of service oriented distributed real-time systems. IEEE Trans. Ind. Inf. **9**(1), 228–236 (2013)
5. ISO/IEC Information Technology Task Force (ITTF). OASIS AMQP1.0 - Advanced Message Queuing Protocol (AMQP), v1.0 specification. ISO/IEC 19464:2014 (2014)
6. García-Valls, M., Alonso, A., Ruiz, J., Groba, A.: An architecture of a quality of service resource manager middleware for flexible embedded multimedia systems. In: Coen-Porisini, A., Hoek, A. (eds.) SEM 2002. LNCS, vol. 2596, pp. 36–55. Springer, Heidelberg (2003). doi:10.1007/3-540-38093-0_3

7. García Valls, M., Baldoni, R.: Adaptive middleware design for CPS: Considerations on the OS, resource managers, and the network run-time. In: Proceedings of 14th Workshop on Adaptive and Reflective Middleware (ARM@Middleware) (2015)
8. García-Valls, M., Calva-Urrego, C.: Improving service time with a multicore aware middleware. In: 32nd ACM/SIGAPP Symposium on Applied Computing (SAC), Marrakech, Morocco (2017)
9. García-Valls, M., Domínguez-Poblete, J., Touahria, I.E.: Using DDS in distributed partitioned systems. ACM Sigbed Rev. (2017, To appear)
10. García-Valls, M., Basanta-Val, P.: Analyzing point-to-point DDS communication over desktop virtualization software. Comput. Stand. Interf. **49**, 11–21 (2017)
11. Mattheis, S., Schuele, T., Raabe, A., Henties, T., Gleim, U.: Work stealing strategies for parallel stream processing in soft real-time systems. In: Herkersdorf, A., Römer, K., Brinkschulte, U. (eds.) ARCS 2012. LNCS, vol. 7179, pp. 172–183. Springer, Heidelberg (2012). doi:10.1007/978-3-642-28293-5_15
12. Object Management Group: The Common Object Request Broker. Architecture and Specification, Version 3.3 (2012). http://www.omg.org/spec/CORBA/3.3
13. Object Management Group: A Data Distribution Service for Real-time Systems Version 1.2. Real-Time Systems (2007)
14. Sun Microsystems: Java^{TM} Remote Method Invocation API (2016). http://docs.oracle.com/javase/7/docs/technotes/guides/rmi/
15. ZeroC Inc. The Internet Communications Engine (2016). https://zeroc.com/downloads/ice/3.5/
16. Zhang, Y., Guill, C., Lu, C.: Reconfigurable real-time middleware for distributed cyber-physical systems with aperiodic events. In: Proceedings of IEEE International Conference on Distributed Computing Systems (2008)
17. Zhang, Y., Guill, C., Lu, C.: Real-time performance and middleware for multiprocessor and multicore linux platforms. In: Proceedings of 15th IEEE International Conference on Embedded and Real-Time Computing Systems and Applications (RTCSA) (2009)
18. Object Management Group, Real-time CORBA Specification, OMG Document formal/02-08-02 ed (2002)
19. Object Management Group, Minimum CORBA Update, OMG Document realtime/2004-06-01 (2004)
20. Natarajan, B., Gokhale, A., Yajnik, S., Schmidt, D.C.: DOORS: towards high-performance fault tolerant CORBA. In: Proceedings of IEEE International Symposium on Distributed Objects and Applications, pp. 39–48 (2000)
21. McMurtry, C., Mercuri, M., Watling, N., Winkler, M.: Windows Communication Foundation Unleashed (WCF). Sams, Indianapolis (2007)

Ontologies and Smart Applications

Semantic Knowledge and Service Models for Energy-Aware Systems

Jarmo Kalaoja[✉]

VTT Technical Research Centre of Finland Ltd, Oulu, Finland
jarmo.kalaoja@vtt.fi

Abstract. The energy domain is affected by digitalization like any other domain. Interoperability between the energy-aware devices and grid, and even market actors, are opening a vast amount of use-cases and business models for smart energy services and possibilities to make the systems more efficient. Related standards in the energy domain and neighbouring domains are numerous and knowledge modelling needs to take this already grounded work into account. This research shows how energy-related information and concepts, from weather and energy market information to sensor data, are semantically described and how services using the semantic information can manifest themselves in the same semantic way to be used in a network of energy awareness-related services.

Keywords: Energy-aware · Knowledge model · Service model · Standards

1 Introduction

Meeting the challenges of environmental sustainability requires cross-industry co-operation and means for also consumers to impact their energy consumption in terms of amount and type of energy consumed. Unsustainable energy consumption results from a lack of sufficient means to control, monitor, estimate and adapt energy usage of customer systems versus the dynamic usage situations and environmental factors affecting both energy usage and its production. This task has proven difficult to current energy, automation and ICT systems, especially because energy consumption-related information is scattered in many standards and there is no convenient means to build solutions that require interworking and energy information exchange between the standards and related industries.

Smart grid is an infrastructure that enables the delivery of power from generation sources to end-users that can be monitored and managed in real time [1, 2]. Smart grids enable new energy products where a broad range of product and service providers, who have not worked together in the past, will be collaborating in future smart grid deployments. Besides electricity, smart grid concepts can be applied to a range of commodity infrastructures, including water, gas, electricity and hydrogen. A micro-grid is a small-scale power grid that can operate independently or in conjunction with an area's main electrical (smart) grid.

Our goal has been to take existing energy information-related standards and information standards used in different industrial sectors (e.g. CIM and BIM) as a starting

© Springer International Publishing AG 2017
M.H.A. Au et al. (Eds.): GPC 2017, LNCS 10232, pp. 523–537, 2017.
DOI: 10.1007/978-3-319-57186-7_38

point, and develop a new cross-industry knowledge model compatible with them. This enables advanced ICT-based solutions to share energy-aware software services in building and micro-grid environments working as a part of smart grids.

Another aspect that is required by the goal of energy awareness is to be able to step from traditional data models into the realm of knowledge models, i.e. to close the gap between data sources and their users by trying to document not only the structure, but the meaning behind data in a computer-understandable format. This is also the goal of semantic web technologies, and examples of successful adoption of those in the energy domain were also seen as a starting point for our work. While potentially providing directly reusable results, those also have given valuable insight into what best practices should be adopted, and what kind of problems in the domains of energy, environment and IOT should be addressed. Our main research questions are highlighted in Fig. 1:

1. How can we align information from various existing system-specific standard data models into semantic models provides easy access to knowledge related to energy awareness?
2. Can we provide a simple unifying knowledge model firmly based on the existing semantic technologies and best practices?
3. How can provide the knowledge as part of a service that can be shared by various stakeholders related to energy awareness?

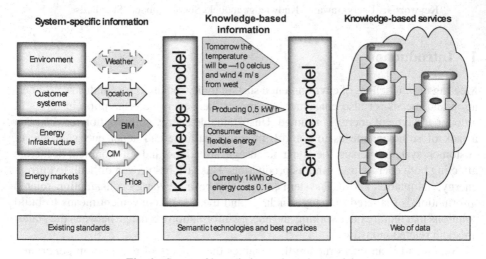

Fig. 1. Scope of knowledge and service models.

The remainder of the paper is structured as follows. Section 2 offers a justification for the relevance of this work by drawing upon the literature study. Section 3 describes the research focus and methodology adopted. Section 4 presents the requirements obtained from use-cases of energy-aware IS and the proposed knowledge and service models implementing those requirements.

2 Background

2.1 Energy Awareness-Related Standards

Standards on home and building management, management and automation of energy infrastructure and energy markets with balance settlement are considered especially important for the goal of energy awareness. Important developments in the field are Common Information Model (CIM)-based standards for both energy market and energy infrastructure data exchange, protocols for automated demand response mechanisms (such as OpenADR 2), detailed data of building structures and its energy characteristics as Building Information Models (BIM) [3–5]. However, a lot of work is still needed to align various approaches and adopt those in the practice while rapid development of new technologies, such as use of electric vehicles as part of a smart grid, brings new requirements and new standards for knowledge exchange. Figure 2 shows a snapshot of some of the most important standards related to energy awareness.

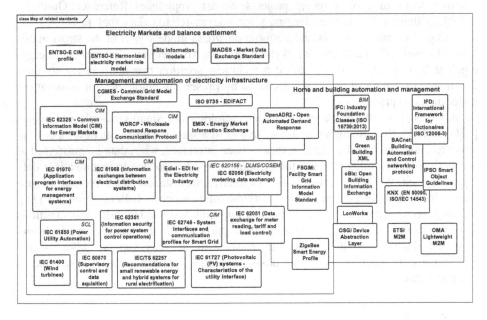

Fig. 2. A glossary of energy awareness-related standards.

2.2 Semantic Technologies for Smart Grid

Semantic technologies rely on use of the so-called semantic web stack with Resource Description Framework (RDF) as their common base [6]. RDF internally relies on a simple data model, the so called triple structure, and identification of resources or concepts with their URI:s. RDF is an abstract model that can be easily automatically converted between its various textual serializations such as Turtle, RDF/XML, or JSON-LD. Also, it can be accessed directly by implementations and stored into text files as such or into RDF stores providing them as databases that can be queried with SPARQL query language. It enables exposure of both the data and models the data relies on, on the web as so-called Linked Data or more generally Web of Data [7].

Semantic models often rely on specialized languages such as Web Ontology Language (OWL) that extends RDF with more complex types of associations between concepts and assertions enabling the formation of more complex ontologies capturing the domain knowledge. Ontology helps convey knowledge in a formal fashion, just like a programming language conveys mathematics in a formal fashion. While not implemented using semantic web technologies, IEC/CIM can be seen as the most complete and widely accepted ontology in the electric power industry and a combination of CIM and RDF could offer valuable flexibility in processing complex tasks [8]. A similar approach has been studied on the building domain by introduction of ifcOWL ontology with direct conversion of IFC/BIM models using EXPRESS data specification language schemas into OWL [9].

Work on the use of semantic technologies in the energy awareness field has been the research focus in various recent projects. Smart Appliances Reference Ontology (SAREF) defines a reference language for energy-related data that facilitates the matching of existing assets (standards/protocols/data models etc.) in the smart appliances domain [10]. The SESAME-S (Semantic SmArt Metering-Services for energy-efficient houses) [11] project studied a technical solution that actively assists end-consumers to make well-informed decisions by presenting ontologies for automation, meter data and pricing.

A thorough survey of use of semantic technologies in Smart Grid-related projects [12] concludes that although within the context of a single application, developers can strive to make the meaning clear in various user interfaces, when data is transferred to another context (another system), the meaning could be lost due to incompatible data representation. While open, royalty-free (semantic) web standards can provide a foundation for Smart Grid communication architecture, several challenges remain [13]. Heterogeneous participants need support for both low-level and high-level abstractions and a flexible schema incorporating some fixed parts while being easily expandable and adjustable. Furthermore there is need for privacy and security, support for large-scale complex event processing and continuous time-series data from sensors abstracted as event streams.

2.3   Semantic Services

Use of semantics in service models has promise to automate service architecture tasks either at runtime, i.e. helping the discovery, invocation, composition and invocation, or by decreasing complexity at development time by describing implicit domain knowledge and technical constraints in a formal way. Various approaches of semantic service models have been at least partially successful but still have only slowly been gaining popularity.

OWL-S [14] defines semantic service model language with three parts: service profile, process model and service grounding. The service profile is meant for human reading, providing applicability and provisioning information. The process model describes the inputs, outputs, pre-conditions and results helping clients to automatically interact with the service. The service grounding defines implementation details such as communication protocols, message formats and port numbers by mapping those to standards like WSDL. While its process model is powerful, but because of its complexity it also makes the language difficult to use in real applications.

Because of its simplicity, the so-called Representational State Transfer (REST), or RESTful approach, is gaining ground from traditional web services and also semantic approaches based on it have been proposed. Linked Data best-practices rules propose a common RESTful SPARQL endpoint for accessing all data resources based on use of URIs to name (identify) things that can be looked up (dereferenced) [7]. By adding descriptions of functionality this can be generalized as a (semantic) hypermedia API that functions similarly to a webpage, providing the user (man or machine) with guidance on what type of content they can retrieve, or what actions they can perform, as well as the appropriate links to do so. In SSWAP [15], services are identified by a URI and standard HTTP methods GET and POST are used to access the service descriptions and to invoke the services. Authentication and security relies on standard protocols such as SSL and HTTPS. The architecture of SSWAP is based on five basic concepts: Provider, Resource, Graph, Subject, and Object. The RESTdesc [16] service descriptions are described with N3 format that extends RDF with graphs as literals and variables starting with a question mark. Descriptions of how to use and manipulate resources can be retrieved from the resources themselves by use of HTTP "options" method, allowing a client to determine the options and/or requirements associated with a resource without implying a resource action. Hydra [17] is a lightweight vocabulary to create hypermedia-driven Web API enabling the creation of generic API clients and server that advertise valid state transitions to clients. A client can use the provided information to construct HTTP requests which modify the server's state so that a certain desired goal is achieved allowing clients to be decoupled from the server and adapt to changes more easily.

In SAREF [10] ontology, services represent functionality necessary to accomplish the task for which a device is designed. This idea is similar to the Web 2.0 service model [18] where the term capability denotes any functionality that results in a real-world effect. That functionality does not necessarily have to reside in a computer. SAREF ontology does not model the service API, allowing it to be used in combination with other vocabularies such as Hydra as technical service descriptions.

An interesting recent development in the IOT field is the concept of Digital Twin or Avatar which refers to a virtual companion of a physical asset such as a sensor or machine in cyberspace that can be used for various purposes. Digital Twins use data from Sensors installed on physical objects to represent their near real-time status, working condition or position.

3   Methodology

The Smart Grid Architecture Model (SGAM) [19, 20] framework and its methodology helps present clearly the design of smart grid use-cases in an architectural viewpoint allowing it to be both specific, but also neutral, regarding solution and technology. We argue that use of semantic technologies helps modelling both the knowledge related to both this information and functions on different domains and zones inside and between these interoperability layers. The goal of the use-case analysis phase is now to help understanding the interoperability requirements for knowledge-related functionalities and information that they both require and provide and model those with semantic technologies. Analysis of use-cases can be used as a tool to help focus on the most important domain information categories that must be modelled (Fig. 3).

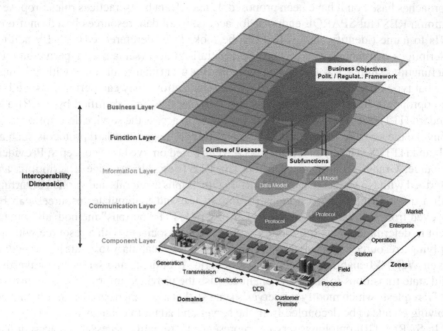

Fig. 3. SGAM reference architecture from [19].

We also argue that the usefulness of semantic knowledge in energy-aware systems can be improved by careful selection of well-known analysis and modelling patterns that support sharing the knowledge both within an application domain and between the domains. The patterns can be gathered from the state of the art on energy standards and projects that apply semantic technologies in the energy awareness domain.

3.1   Analysis of the Energy Awareness Interoperability Requirements

Use-case analysis tends to provide a large amount of detailed functional information. In order to help the authors of each use-case to focus on information interoperability it is essential to identify the stakeholders, algorithms, information items, and energy-related standards related to the use-case. This can be supported with excel-style templates added to a traditional use-case template. The concepts identified in templates can be exported as a comma-separated data format into UML tools where they can be re-arranged as one or more diagrams helping to modularize initial glossaries of required domain concepts.

The strength of UML tools in domain requirements analysis is that they support separate domain or stakeholder-specific diagrammatic views into the underlying model and the generation of an online version of the model on which domain experts can comment. Wiki-based sematic RDF editors could be used to provide a discussion and commenting forum for domain experts. Vocabularies can be refined in workshop-style VoCamp sessions. While not directly contributing to vocabularies, they provided some valuable ideas for implementation of the service model and knowledge models. The result is presented as an information model with a set of domain vocabularies and some upper-level vocabularies modelled with a platform-independent UML model.

3.2 Identification of Common Solution Patterns for Interoperability

In order to be useful, energy the domain ontologies should be based on a common semantic core that can be extended to sharing specific information between the domains. For example, we should be able to provide common data structures for both hourly weather data and historical energy consumption data in order to easily combine them and provide forecasts of future consumption. The weather and energy quantities, their units, and value formats used in data have to be modelled with common terms to ensure correct conversions. The links to real-world entities, processing steps and originators of information should be potentially traceable to ensure correctness of information. Information and knowledge should be able to be provided as services that can be consumed by various energy awareness-related stakeholders and supported by means to control functions of real-world devices.

3.3 Implementing the Semantic Model

In our opinion, a common weakness of traditional standardization efforts has been that while they focus on common data structures, even the core concepts that data represents are often defined only as human readable documentation that is not directly understandable by computer programs. A step forward are the CIM-based models that define their core domain concepts as UML profiles that can be adopted to various data exchange needs by modelling the exchanged data using the profile, and generating an implementation such as an XML schema from that. A problem is that specialized UML tools and interactive manual effort is needed during the implementation and original UML models are not directly exposed in a format that is readable for systems and applications. Automation of those tasks is possible but relies on model-driven toolchains, which has been difficult to adopt in practice in the energy domain. In the building domain, conceptually similar BIM models have been successful, potentially because of their use of specialized schema languages such as EXPRESS and construction domain-specific CAD toolchains.

While using UML at our initial analysis phase, we implement the knowledge model with semantic technologies based and OWL and RDF languages. Model-based tools for generating a semantic implementation from a platform-specific model, UML models are available but in practice they require use of a RDF UML profile and working procedures and deviation from assumed development workflow can cause problems in generation of correct implementations as RDF.

There are a number commercial and free-to-use sematic editors helping to work with abstract semantic models in an IDE-style environment with plug-ins to support task such as visualization of the model. In order to keep the model tools independent the use of textual Turtle language as the direct implementation language is becoming more popular. The main benefit of Turtle is that it supports easy definition of complex data graphs based on the ontology.

Implementation source code can be maintained online with Git-style version control tools to better support co-operative, open-source development and evolution of models supported with online visualizations and wiki support including examples for both developers and users.

4 Results

For our study an extensive set of almost 100 individual use-cases was proposed by both domain and ICT experts presenting various scenarios using the knowledge model. The general interoperability requirements and their solution patterns gathered from a background study and use-cases are summarized in the Table 1.

Table 1. Requirements and solution patterns identified.

Requirement	Solution patterns
Maintain domain-independent mapping between the data and real-world entities	Observations and measurements standard (feature of interest concept)
Describe underlying physical quantities and their units	Separating quantity, its unit and dimension as in QUDT and OM ontologies
Management, tailoring and transformation of (temporally, spatially, etc.) multidimensional data needed in use-cases	Data cubes and time-series of data as their slices
Modelling control information	Commands modelled in similar patterns as data
Maintaining end-to-end business model links in data	PROV (Provenance) data model
Modelling of functionality as services	Services and capabilities as proposed for Web 2.0

A set of 30 of the most important use-cases were analysed for the requirements they set to interoperability standards and information exchange between stakeholders with an Excel template. This analysis provided a list of initial knowledge activities with their input and output data requirements and associated stakeholders.

The concepts identified at this stage were modelled in detail with the UML tool and published online as a visual glossary allowing modularization of concepts into separate domains. Some of the vocabularies were later refined in workshop-style VoCamp sessions providing valuable ideas for concrete implementation of the service and core knowledge models.

The solution patterns and classifications of concepts into domain-specific modules were combined into a reference architecture for energy-aware systems. The architecture aims help modularization of knowledge into both domain-specific and domain-inde-pendent semantic modules with several abstraction levels of modelling support aspects. The initial division principle into modules is shown in Fig. 4 with the developed knowl-edge and service model modules highlighted. An ontology for time-series data was also developed, but it and the detailed domain vocabularies are out of the scope of this paper.

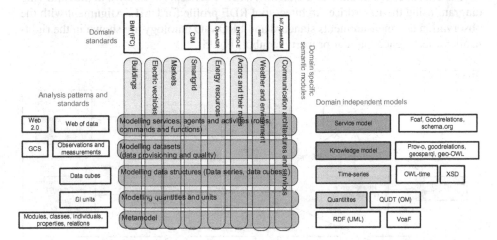

Fig. 4. Reference Architecture and the knowledge models for energy awareness.

The knowledge and service models comprise the core of our approach and are discussed in more detail in the following chapters. This core is supported by generic vocabulary for modelling complex data as time-series and a number of domain-specific vocabularies and quantities needed when modelling energy awareness knowledge. The domain-specific models are available online for open-source development and will be evolving independently. Note that one of those domain-specific slices is technical vocabularies for communication architectures. Several existing ontologies can poten-tially be reused directly or an energy awareness-specific subset defined and aligned with those.

As our UML model is platform independent, it does not support generation of (RDF or OWL) implementation directly. Unfortunately there were no existing tools to trans-form it into the UML RDF profile-based, platform-specific model that has generative tools. Manually doing the model transformation for a large model was also not feasible. A solution is to implement the vocabularies textually as OWL using Turtle language using the UML model as the specification, even if this breaks the reverse link from changes in the implementation to the original UML model, eventually making them inconsistent. For future work, these kind of model-driven tools could benefit the evolu-tion of domain-specific vocabularies supporting also their documentation.

4.1 Knowledge Model

The developed knowledge model supports a declarative definition of data bundles called evaluations that can be associated with real-world systems. The category of evaluation can be used for defining the intended role of data, such as historic data, forecast, plan, or (current state) observation of a system. The core concepts are shown in the following diagram using the Enterprise Architect tool RDF profile for UML. Alignment with the observation and measurements standard and PROV-O ontology are shown in the right-hand corner of each class or property symbol (Fig. 5).

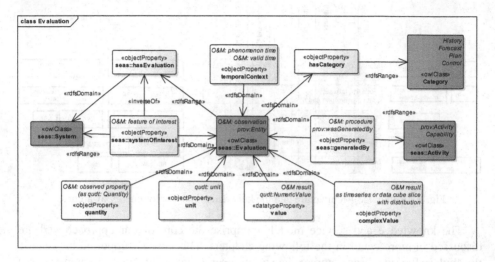

Fig. 5. Knowledge model.

Domain vocabularies link to a knowledge model through the *System* class. The *systemOfInterest* property between evaluation (data) and a system has the inverse relation *hasEvaluation*. Domain vocabularies are used to define the structure of systems. Examples of systems are a building and its rooms, various energy resources and energy contracts. This approach effectively allows the information to be modelled from two perspectives: as data is included as part of a system model or as individual droplets/bundles of information that can be sent and received by various stakeholders.

Using the *hasEvaluation* property, new qualitative data can be added to a system modelled with domain vocabulary. Instead of using a number of domain-specific property names it relies on describing the quantity, unit, data type or complex time-series structure using a common design pattern with provenance information.

Using the *systemOfInterest* (or featureOfInterest) property, for example, a single set of data contained in a message can be associated with a description linking it to the real world. As *systemOfInterest* is an object property it is possible either to provide a URI of an existing instance associated with the real world entity, or provide an instance defining the geospatial properties such as name, address, or coordinates.

Value and *complexValue* properties are defined as disjoint. At its simplest, an *Evaluation* contains only a single value such as area of a room expressed in square metres.

A *ComplexValue* provides an extension mechanism for the data model to include timeseries and data streams defined using external ontologies or other data structure standards used for environmental or energy information. The following code shows an example of temperature message data modelled with the knowledge model and a generic *TimeSeries* ontology in JSON-LD format:

```
{
    "@context": "http://example.com/weather.jsonld",
    "@type": "seas:Evaluation",
    "seas:category": "seas:Forecast"
    "seas:systemOfInterest": {"gn:name": "Helsinki"},
    "seas:temporalContext": {
        "seas:start": "2017-05-15T12:00:00+00:00",
        "seas:duration": "P2H"},
    "seas:quantity" : "seas:AirTemperature",
    "seas:unit": "seas:DegreeCelsius",
    "seas:complexValue": {
      "@type": "seas:TimeSeries",
      "seas:timeStep": "P1H",
        "seas:list":{"@list": [
        {"seas:value": 7.5},
        {"seas:value": 8.2}]}
    }
}
```

A directed RDF graph can be laid out as several JSON-LD serializations. Developers typically work with tree structures containing all the relevant information represented as objects. In the example the *seas:Evaluation* is used as a root object node but similarly the *System* i.e. *Helsinki* could be selected as the root and several *Evaluations* linked to it with *hasEvaluation* property. JSON-LD *Framing* allows developers to force a specific tree layout to a JSON-LD document. A *System* can also be purely digital concept. For example, a contract between energy customer and provider that can be modelled as a new system with energy prices on mutually exclusive temporal contexts (such as daytime/night-time or winter/summer) as its evaluations.

4.2 Service Model

The service model concentrates on describing how to the knowledge entities (modelled as evaluations with a knowledge model) are both used and generated by the services and how services link to agents and their roles in a specific domain. Orchestration and choreography of services and communication protocols are left out of the scope of the service model. With the SEAS service model new knowledge services are be defined by their capabilities, typically activities such as knowledge algorithms or functions actuating real-world devices. Activities can use semantic information as their inputs and may generate new semantic information as their outputs, or perform actuating functionality in the real world.

The service model allows maintaining the links between knowledge flowing and transformed in the end-to-end service architecture. Here it adopts two main analysis patterns: modelling of agents and their roles based on PROV-O, and modelling activities as processes that generate information based on observations & measurements patterns. The latter is generalized to cover also other types of activities such as forecasts and control or actuation (Fig. 6).

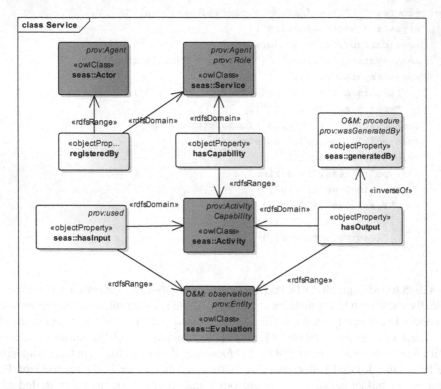

Fig. 6. Service model.

The service model uses a feature of OWL language called *punning* to allow definition of service descriptions as meta-class individuals of *Service* that define the meta-classes of its *Capabilities,* i.e. *Activities,* and their inputs and output as meta-classes modelled with *Evaluations* based on the knowledge model. This can be extended by providing domain-specific categorizations for activities and evaluations and more-specific OWL constraints that can be evaluated by reasoning.

For example, a weather forecasting service can be declared as having a capability in the category *Forecasting* by defining its input parameters as an evaluation with its *systemOfInterest* property linking it to the area for which a forecast is desired, with types of weather, quantities, units and a resulting data structure.

Following a simplified service description example in JSON-LD RDF format presents a description of a service that provides as its output the production forecast of a PV panel. As its input the service requires a weather forecast for the PV site and as its parameters information about PV and the properties of time-series to be provided as an output.

```
{
    "@context": "http://example.com/services.jsonld",
    "@id": "registry:PVForecastingService",
    "@type": "seas:Service",
    "seas":"hasCapability": {
      "@type": "seas:Activity",
      "seas:hasInput": [
        {
          "@type": "seas:Evaluation",
          "seas:category": {"@id": "seas:Forecast"},
          "seas:complexValue": {"@type": "seas:TimeSeries"},
          "seas:quantity":{"@id": "seas:Cloudiness"},
          "seas:systemOfInterest": {"@type": "gn:Feature"},
          "seas:unit": {"@id": "seas:Percent"}},
        {
          "@type": "seas:Evaluation",
          "seas:category": {"@id": "seas:Parameter"},
          "seas:systemOfInterest": {"@type": "seas:SolarPanel},
          "seas:temporalContext": {"@type": "seas:TemporalContext},
          "seas:complexValue": {"@type": "seas:TimeSeries"},
        }
      ],
      "seas:hasOutput": {
        "@type": "seas:Production",
        "seas:category": {"@id": "seas:Forecast"},
        "seas:complexValue": {"@type": "seas:TimeSeries"},
        "seas:quantity": {"@id": "seas:Energy"},
        "seas:systemOfInterest": {"@type": "seas:SolarPanel"},
        "seas:unit": {"@id": "seas:KiloWattHour"}
      }
    }
}
```

5   Conclusion

Based on an extensive set of use-cases and study of semantic and traditional standards related to energy-aware systems we propose, as part of a simplified reference architecture for energy awareness, two core ontologies: a knowledge model and a service model which can be extended with domain-specific vocabularies. Our knowledge model allows declarative presentation of data entities, i.e. evaluations that directly link to a real world entity corresponding to the "feature of interest" concept, in observations and measurements standards. The proposed semantic service model complements existing approaches for defining technical service interfaces, extending those with activities that use our declarative knowledge model as their inputs and outputs.

These models provided the basis of ontology design work of the energy awareness ICT infrastructure developed in the SEAS project. SEAS further developed open-source libraries that offer a familiar object API-type environment for engineers to work with the model. This reduces the computational requirements needed to process semantic data and reduces the need for prior knowledge of semantic technologies. Latest snapshot of developed ontologies are also available as open source[1] online in RDF/Turtle format.

References

1. IEC Smart Grid Standardization Roadmap; Edition 1.0, June 2010. http://www.iec.ch/zone/smartgrid/pdf/sg3_roadmap.pdf
2. Heiles, J. (ed.) SGEM Deliverable D1.3.1 Smart Grid Standardization Analysis Version 2.0, Nokia Siemens Networks, February 2012 (2012)
3. Koponen, P., Pykälä, M.-L., Peltonen, J., Ahonen, P.: Interfaces of consumption metering infrastructures with the energy consumers - review of standards. VTT Research Notes 2542 (2010)
4. EURELECTRIC: DSO Priorities for smart grid standardisation. A EURELECTRIC position paper, January 2013
5. Eastman, C., Teicholz, P., Sacks, R., Liston, K.: BIM Handbook: A Guide to Building Information Modeling for Owners, Managers, Designers, Engineers, and Contractors, 2nd edn. Wiley, New York (2011). ISBN 978-0-470-54137-1
6. Berners-Lee, T., Hendler, J., Lassila, O.: The semantic web. Sci. Am. **284**(5), 35–43 (2001)
7. Berners-Lee, T.: Linked data - design issues (2006). Accessed http://www.w3.org/DesignIssues/LinkedData.html
8. Gaha, M., Zinflou, A., Langheit, C., Bouffard, A., Viau, M., Vouligny, L.: An ontology-based reasoning approach for electric power utilities. In: Web Reasoning and Rule Systems, pp. 95–108 (2013)
9. Pauwelsa, P., Terkajb, W.: EXPRESS to OWL for construction industry: towards a recommendable and usable ifcOWL ontology. Autom. Constr. **63**, 100–133 (2016)
10. SmartM2M. Smart Appliances, Reference Ontology and oneM2M Mapping, ETSI TS 103 264 v1.1.1
11. Fensel, A., Tomic, S., Kumar, V., Stefanovic, M., Aleshin, S.V., Novikov, D.O.: SESAME-S: semantic smart home system for energy efficiency. Informatik-Spektrum **36**(1), 46–57 (2012)
12. Fang, X., Misra, S., Xue, G., Yang, D.: Smart grid—the new and improved power grid: a survey. Commun. Surv. Tutorials **14**(4), 944–980 (2012)
13. Wagner, A., Speiser, S., Harth, A.: Semantic web technologies for a smart energy grid: requirements and challenges. In: Patel-Schneider, F.P., Pan, Y., Hitzler, P., Mika, P., Zhang, L., Pan, J.Z., Glimm, B. (eds.) Proceedings of 9th International Semantic Web Conference (ISWC 2010) (2010)
14. W3C: OWL-S: Semantic Markup for Web Services (2004). https://www.w3.org/Submission/OWL-S/

---

[1] https://github.com/thesmartenergy/seas.

15. Gessler, D., Schiltz, G., May, G., Avraham, S., Town, C., Grant, D., Nelson, R.: SSWAP: a simple semantic web architecture and protocol for semantic web services. BMC Bioinform. **10**(1), 309 (2009)
16. Verborgh, R., Steiner, T., Van Deursen, D., Coppens, S., Mannens, E., Van de Walle, R., Vallés, J.: RESTdesc - a functionality-centered approach to semantic service description and composition. In: 9th Extended Semantic Web Conference (ESWC - 2012) (2014)
17. Dimou, A., Verborgh, R., Vander Sande, M., Mannens, E., Van de Walle, R.: Machine-interpretable dataset and service descriptions for heterogeneous data access and retrieval. In: Proceedings of the 11th International Conference on Semantic Systems, pp. 145–152 (2015)
18. Governor, J., Hinchcliffe, D., Nickull, D.: Web 2.0 architectures - what entrepreneurs and information architects need to know. O'Reilly Media/Adobe Developer Library (2009)
19. Dänekas, C., Neureiter, C., Rohjans, S., Uslar, M., Engel, D.: Towards a model-driven-architecture process for smart grid projects. In: Benghozi, P., Krob, D., Lonjon, A., Panetto, H. (eds.) Digital Enterprise Design & Management. AISC, vol. 261, pp. 47–58. Springer, Cham (2014)
20. Santodomingo, R., Uslar, M., Goring, A., Gottschalk, M., Nordstrom, L., Saleem, A., Chenine, M.: SGAM-based methodology to analyse Smart Grid solutions in DISCERN European research project. In: 2014 IEEE International Energy Conference (ENERGYCON), pp. 751–758 (2014)

Transferring Remote Ontologies to the Edge of Internet of Things Systems

Xiang Su[1(✉)], Pingjiang Li[1], Huber Flores[2], Jukka Riekki[1], Xiaoli Liu[3], Yuhong Li[4], and Christian Prehofer[5]

[1] Center for Ubiquitous Computing, University of Oulu, Oulu, Finland
xiang.su@ee.oulu.fi
[2] Department of Computer Science, University of Helsinki, Helsinki, Finland
[3] Biomimetics and Intelligent Systems Group, University of Oulu, Oulu, Finland
[4] State Key Laboratory of Networking and Switching Technology,
Beijing University of Posts and Telecommunications, Beijing, China
[5] fortiss, An-Institut Technische Universität München, Munich, Germany

Abstract. Edge computing paradigm allows computation to be moved from the central high powered Cloud or data center to the edge of the network. This paradigm often enables more efficient data processing near its source and sends only the data and knowledge that have value over the network. Our study focuses on performing semantic reasoning at the edge computing devices, which requires transferring ontologies to the edge devices. This paper presents different representations for transferring Web Ontology language (OWL) version 2 ontologies to the edge. We evaluate different representations in an experimental IoT system with edge nodes and compare lengths of different syntaxes and their computation effort of building models in Cloud and edge computing devices in terms of processing time.

Keywords: Internet of Things · Edge computing · OWL 2 · Ontology

1 Introduction

Internet of Things (IoT) systems not only gather a large quantity of data generated by things, but also focus on how data can be processed, visualized, and possibly acted upon. A new computing paradigm, edge computing, calls for performing data analytics and knowledge generation to occur at the periphery of the network. In the edge computing paradigm, sensors and connected devices transmit data to nearby edge computing devices, such as gateway devices that process or analyze the data, instead of delivering it to the Cloud or a remote data center. Major benefits of edge computing are improving time to action and reducing response time; conserving network resources and addressing battery life constraint; supporting security and privacy sensitive services and applications; and enabling scalable distributed data processing. In general, to enable the vision of edge computing in a typical IoT system, the information at edge computing devices is pushed from Cloud services and pulled from IoT devices [1,2].

© Springer International Publishing AG 2017
M.H.A. Au et al. (Eds.): GPC 2017, LNCS 10232, pp. 538–552, 2017.
DOI: 10.1007/978-3-319-57186-7_39

Compared with traditional base stations, just simply forwarding data traffic but do not actively processing the data, edge computing devices include more computing and storage capabilities. Hence, more advanced functions can be deployed on edge computing devices. For example, when the increment of the raw data is produced from the IoT devices but not all raw data is useful, edge computing devices process a considerable amount of the raw data, which saves bandwidth and reduces the latency. Moreover, the edge computing devices are close to end users, the response time will be predictable if the data is processed at edge computing devices [1].

We focus on utilising Semantic Web technologies in the edge computing devices of IoT systems. Semantic Web technologies give information well-defined meaning, better enabling computers and people to work in cooperation. One essential property is its universality powered by the "anything can link to anything" property of hypertext links. Semantic reasoning derives facts that are not explicitly expressed. To enable semantic reasoning functions, computers have to access structured collections of the information and sets of inference rules that they can use to conduct automated reasoning. Hence, Semantic Web community offers a set of languages that express data, knowledge, and rules for reasoning about the data. Knowledge is typically modeled with ontologies, which is a taxonomy defining the classes of objects and relations among them.

The components in IoT systems could reach a shared understanding by exchanging knowledge. This is especially important for edge computing devices in IoT systems, because they often share a part of an ontology from a comprehensive ontology on the Cloud or a server machine. In our earlier research, we studied how semantics could be embedded in the data generated by tiny IoT devices, and how the benefits of semantics could be utilized without sacrificing the efficiency of IoT in terms of energy consumption and reasoning latency [3,4]. In this paper, we focus on transferring ontologies to edge computing devices and developing knowledge models to perform semantic reasoning. We compare and evaluate different syntaxes for Web Ontology Language (OWL) version 2 [5] in an experimental IoT system with edge computing devices. We present a comparison of lengths of different syntaxes and their required computation effort of building models in Cloud and edge computing devices in terms of processing time. In our experiments, we demonstrate that by changing from a standard syntax to a lightweight syntax, it is possible to reduced 47.2% of data when we transfer the Semantic Sensor Network (SSN) ontology [6] ontology.

The remainder of this article is organized as follows. We present different syntaxes with examples in Sect. 2 and details of our experiment results in Sect. 3. We conclude the article with proposing future research directions in Sect. 4.

2   OWL 2 and Syntaxes for Transferring Ontologies

2.1   OWL 2

OWL 2 is a W3C standardized ontology language for the Semantic Web with formally defined meaning. Before the development and standardization of OWL and OWL 2, there were plenty of ontology languages, such as KL-ONE [7], F-logic [8], SHOE [9], DAML-ONT [10], OIL [11], and DAML+OIL [12]. These efforts finally lead to developing OWL, a comprehensive ontology language for the Semantic Web. OWL is a standard Semantic Web language based on Description Logic [13]. The main building blocks of OWL are concepts representing sets of objects, roles representing relationships between objects, and individuals representing specific objects. With OWL, complex concepts can be described through constructors that define the conditions on concept membership. OWL 2 is a revised extension of OWL, which is now commonly called OWL 1. OWL 2 extends OWL 1 with qualified cardinality restrictions and property chains. Moreover, OWL 2 provides support for defining properties to be reflexive, irreflexive, transitive, asymmetric, and to define disjoint pairs of properties. Three profiles, namely OWL 2 EL, OWL 2 QL, and OWL 2 RL, have been developed for balancing expressive power and reasoning efficiency, targeting different application scenarios. OWL 2 EL is suitable for applications utilizing ontologies to define very large numbers of classes and properties. OWL 2 QL can be tightly integrated with Relational Database Management Systems and can hence benefit from relational database technology. OWL 2 RL is suitable for applications that require scalable reasoning without sacrificing too much expressive power [14].

OWL 2 provides a rich collection of constructs for forming descriptions, and is compatible with existing Web standards. An OWL 2 ontology consists of a set of axioms which place constraints on sets of individuals and on the types of relationships between them. These axioms provide semantics by allowing systems to explicitly infer additional knowledge based on the data provided. OWL 2 provides a bidirectional mapping from the OWL Functional Syntax to Resource Description Framework (RDF) Graphs. This means that OWL can then be serialized into any RDF representations such as RDF/XML and Notation 3 (N3). Most current OWL tools utilize RDF/XML as the default syntax for serializing ontologies.

2.2   OWL 2 Syntaxes

An ontology can be developed with IRIs and a set of axioms. There are different languages for storing, sharing, and editing IRIs and axioms in OWL 2 ontologies. Among them, RDF/XML is the officially recommended exchange syntax by W3C, and others have been designed for particular purposes and applications. In this section, we compare different syntaxes for OWL in brief and we illustrates different syntaxes with an example in Appendix, which is a part of SSN ontology [6]. This small part of SSN ontology consists of simple concepts of *Input* class and *Output* classes and some relations of them, including *label, source, disjoint Class*, etc.

RDF/XML is the primary and widely supported syntax, as it is recommended by W3C. Because OWL supports a bidirectional mapping to RDF triples, it is convenient to be combined in RDF/XML. Other RDF based representations share this benefit, for example N3 and Turtle. However, RDF/XML is a verbose representation for OWL and can hence be difficult to read by human users.

For example, RDF/XML requires nesting and reification for complex class expressions, which results RDF verbose and difficult to read. Moreover, parsing RDF/XML requires two steps which means that much more memory is required for storing the ontology in memory. Turtle is more readable than RDF/XML and also widely supported. W3C selects Turtle as one of the syntaxes for OWL 2 and widely used tools and APIs such as Jena and the OWL API support Turtle.

OWL functional syntax is designed to be easier for OWL 2 specification purposes and to provide a foundation for the implementation of OWL 2 tools. Functional syntax is a simple text based syntax that is used as a bridge between the structural specification and concrete representations.

The design of RDF/XML makes it difficult to utilize off-the-shelf XML tools for tasks other than parsing and rendering it. Standard XML tools like XPath or XSLT do not work well with RDF/XML representations of ontologies [15]. Moreover, serializing OWL and OWL 2 requires resources, as OWL needs to be first mapped to RDF, and then RDF needs to be serialized to XML. To overcome these difficulties, OWL/XML is invented as a concrete syntax for a more regular and simpler XML syntax. The syntax is essentially derived directly from the Functional Syntax. However, OWL/XML suffers from verbose syntax and this often slows down parsing.

Manchester syntax [16] is designed for editing and presentation purposes. It provides for OWL ontologies a compact text based representation that is easy to read and write. The primary motivation for the design of the Manchester OWL syntax is to produce a syntax that can be used for editing class expressions. This effort has been extended so that it is possible to represent complete ontologies, and Manchester Syntax is now standardized by W3C. Different from above mentioned syntaxes, the Manchester syntax gathers together information about names in a frame-like manner. Manchester Syntax is cumbersome for representing some axioms in OWL, such as general class axioms.

Another recent effort is to serialize RDF in JSON format. The W3C RDF working group compares alternative JSON formats for RDF with examples. Based on this comparison, JSON-LD [17] is considered as the most promising format and becomes a W3C recommendation in early 2014. JSON-LD is designed to be completely compatible with JSON and it has a slightly better expressive power than the RDF model. This means that in practice it can be considered to be a JSON serialization for RDF. JSON-LD requires minimal effort from developers to transform normal JSON to JSON-LD. Only two keywords (@context and @id) need to be known for utilizing the basic features.

Entity Notation (EN) and Entity Notation Schema (EN Schema) [18] are lightweight knowledge representations for resource-constrained devices. Resource usage of CPU, memory, bandwidth, and energy for encoding and decoding these representations are considered at design time. EN is designed as a syntax of RDF and EN Schema extends the design for representing OWL 2 ontologies. Both EN and EN Schema have complete packet and short packet. The complete packet has a structure resembles the triple structure of RDF and OWL. The compact format can shorten the representation with templates and prefixes.

Attempto Controlled English [19] is a machine-oriented Controlled Natural Language (CNL), that is, a precisely defined subset of the English language, designed for writing unambiguous and precise specification texts for knowledge representation. Attempto Controlled English supports a bidirectional translation into and from OWL 2. Other representations with similar design goals are Sydney OWL syntax [20] and Ordnance Survey's Rabbit [21]. However, we are not aware of its compatibility with OWL 2. Schwitter et al. compared these three representations with examples [22]. However, we do not consider these languages suitable for transferring ontologies in IoT systems.

3   Experiments and Analysis

We present two experiments to evaluate different syntaxes of OWL 2 ontologies in a previous Section. We focus on (1) length comparison of different OWL 2 syntaxes and (2) computation effort of building a same Jena model in the Cloud and an edge computing device with different OWL 2 syntaxes in terms of processing time.

3.1   Length Comparision for OWL2 Syntaxes

Our first experiment is to evaluate different OWL 2 syntaxes with a set of seven ontologies, which are well known and widely utilized in pervasive computing, IoT, and other domains. These ontologies include COBRA-ONT [23], IoT-Lite ontology [24], Socially Interconnected Online Communities (SIOC) ontology [25], SSN ontology, and the Organization Ontology [26]. COBRA-ONT includes a collection of ontologies for describing vocabularies in an intelligent meeting room use case. We are testing with COBRA-ONT ontologies version 0.6 which contains ebiquity-geo, ebiquity-meetings and ebiquity-actions ontologies. The IoT-Lite ontology is a lightweight ontology to represent IoT resources, entities, and services. It is also a meta ontology that can be extended in different domains. The SSN ontology describes the sensors, observations and related concepts in pervasive environments. SIOC ontology is designed for describing online communities such as forums, blogs, mailing lists, and wikis. The Organization ontology is designed to enable publication of information on organizations and organizational structure including governmental organizations etc. It is designed as a generic, reusable core ontology that can be extended or specialized for use in particular situations. It is also a meta ontology that can be extended in different domains.

Figure 1 presents the comparison of the lengths of different syntaxes, including Functional syntax, EN Schema, Turtle, Manchester syntax, RDF/XML, JSON-LD, N-Triple, and OWL/XML (from left to right). Our experiment shows that sizes of different syntaxes vary for ontologies. Taking SSN ontology as an example, the length of EN Schema is about 36.6% of N-Triple and about 52.8% of RDF/XML. For IoT-Lite Ontology, the JSON-LD syntax is 5.2 times than the Manchester syntax. In ebiquity-meeting Ontology, the ratio is 2.3 which is

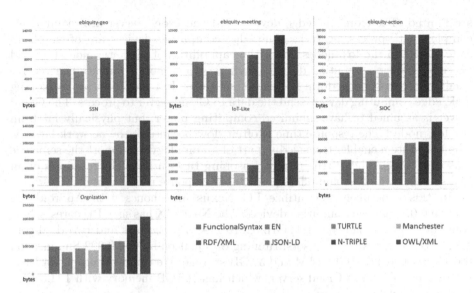

Fig. 1. Comparison of the lengths of different OWL 2 syntaxes.

the smallest among all the sets. The average ratio between the biggest format and the smallest one is 3.3 times.

In general, EN Schema, Turtle, and Manchester syntax are more compact than the other syntaxes. Especially, EN Schema is the most compact syntax for four ontologies, including COBRA-ONT ebiquity-meeting, SIOC, SSN, and the Organization Ontology. JSON-LD, N-Triple and OWL/XML appear to be the most verbose format. The RDF/XML is among the medium size. OWL/XML makes the biggest size ontologies in four out of eight ontologies. According to the results of this comparison, EN Schema, Turtle and Manchester syntax are considered to be optimized syntaxes when IoT system developers require to minimize the communication load for transferring ontologies. However, some syntaxes may have benefits of transferring certain structures in ontologies, for example, Turtle minimizes the lengths of representations of complex classes in most ontologies. Therefore, when certain structures are dominant in a ontology, it is often easier to select an optimized syntax.

3.2   Comparison of Building Ontology Models with OWL 2 Syntaxes

The second experiment focuses on building Jena models with different OWL syntaxes. The experiment is executed under a simulated IoT environment. Figure 2 presents a general architecture of the IoT system with edge nodes. The system consists of a IoT node layer, edge computing devices, and a Cloud server. The IoT node layer consists of end-point device such as sensors and single-chip devices. These devices are regraded as IoT nodes which can detect the environmental situation and generate real-time data. But the capacities of these device are limited. Therefore, the edge devices and the Cloud server are required for complex data processing tasks. The edge computing devices are often physically closed to the IoT nodes. With the capabilities of semantic modelling and processing, edge computing devices, such as smart mobile phones, can receive small ontologies and perform fast reasoning tasks. In regard of heavy reasoning task, edge computing devices send the data to Cloud server to process. The Cloud server is assumed to have unlimited computing power, but physically far from the IoT nodes. The response time is often slow because of the network latency. The IoT system enables transferring part of an ontology to support the semantic reasoning tasks. The distribution of reasoning tasks utilizes the resources of an IoT system to its best and offers predictable response time for users.

In this experiment, we utilize LG Nexus 5X phones with Android OS version 6.0.1 for edge computing devices. The Nexus 5X has six CPU cores, which consists of four Quad-core 1.44 GHz Cortex-A53 processors and two dual-core 1.82 GHz Cortex-A57 processors, running on Qualcomm MSM8992 Snapdragon 808 chip-set. It has 2 GB RAM and 32 GB storage. We utilize Amazon M4 Deca Extra Large Cloud as Cloud server, which has 160 GB memory with 124.5 EC2 Compute Units.

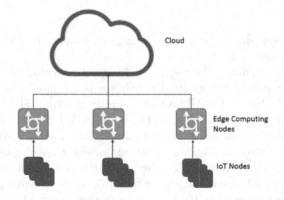

Fig. 2. A general architecture for IoT systems with edge computing nodes.

In our experiment, we evaluate the performance of different OWL 2 syntaxes by comparing the required time of building ontology models with Jena framework in an edge computing device. We again use the previously mentioned seven ontologies with different syntaxes and we include sample ontology in OWL 2 primer in this test. Figure 3 presents the Jena *OntModel* building time (in millisecond) among different ontologies with five selected syntaxes, including RDF/XML, JSON-LD, Turtle, EN Schema, and N-triple. EN Schema is not directly supported by Jena, so we add one step to transfer EN Schema to Turtle and the transferring time is around 20 ms. In the Jena framework, a RDF graph is built as a model and is implemented with the "Model" interface. The Jena framework includes object classes to represent graphs, resources, properties, and literals. The interfaces representing resources, properties, and literals are called

Resource, Property, and Literal respectively. For ontology, Jena use *OntModel*, which is an extension to the *InfModel* interface. Jena wraps an underlying model with this ontology interface, that presents a convenient syntax for accessing the language elements. We utilize OWL API to transfer syntaxes. To keep the minimum size of the ontology, all the transformed ontologies only contain the OWL axioms and annotation, while the comments are removed. We keep space characters as it is necessary for structure and separating elements.

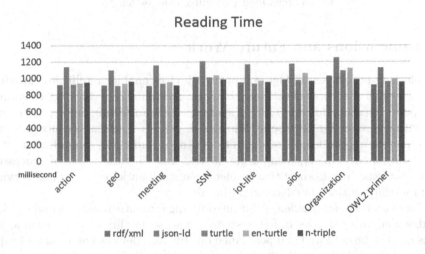

Fig. 3. Comparison of building ontology models with Jena framework with OWL2 syntaxes.

We find that for all ontologies, JSON-LD requires longer time than the other four syntaxes and the other four syntaxes consume comparable amount of time. RDF/XML, Turtle, and N-Triple appear to be the shortest format. In ebiquity-meeting Ontology, the JSON-LD format reading time is 27% longer than the shortest RDF/XML one. JSON-LD reading time is 23% longer than the smallest one for all the test cases in average.

Figure 4 presents the different *OntModel* building time on the Cloud with the increase of ontology size. The X-axis of Fig. 4 represents the size of the above mentioned ontologies. The Y-axis represents the modelling time on the Cloud (in millisecond). We notice a linear increment with the incremental size of ontologies. However, with larger amount of ontology data, Fig. 4 shows the processing time is increasing but considerably slower than the increasing of the data size. For example, the largest ontology is 23 times than the smallest one but the required modelling time is only 20% with Turtle syntax. From this experiment, we consider loading a large ontology, which often enables rich functions, but does not introduce too much modelling time for a Cloud server.

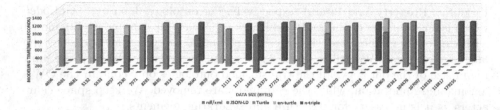

Fig. 4. Jena model building time by length.

4   Conclusions and Future Work

Transferring ontologies to edge computing devices enables intelligent functions for IoT systems, such as developing semantic models and performing reasoning. This paper presents different OWL 2 syntaxes for transferring ontologies to edge computing devices for developing knowledge models. Our main contribution is a comparison of the length of different syntaxes and their computation effort of building models in edge computing devices and Cloud in terms of processing time. Our experiments show that implementing semantic functions and services are practical solutions in edge computing devices.

However, there are challenges for introducing semantic functions and services in edge computing devices of IoT systems. First, scalability is a challenge as the tasks need to be deployed and performed on different devices based on real capabilities of these devices and communication networks. We need to minimize the overall cost in order to find an efficient deployment of tasks on to edge computing devices with different capabilities. Second, dynamic extensibility challenge of IoT systems should be addressed. When new IoT devices are sending data to edge nodes, how to balance the semantic functions with different edge computing devices to utilize their resources to their best? A flexible and extensible design is important to address this challenge. Third, data reliability and veracity challenges rise from the sensing and communication of data in IoT systems. Some solutions to handle unreliable conditions should be considered.

As future research, we will address these challenge of dynamic linking data from data sources to edge computing devices to achieve reasoning efficiency of whole IoT systems. Moreover, we will tackle the challenge of data veracity and variety to support intelligent decision making in IoT systems with edge computing devices.

Acknowledgments. The first author would like to thank Jorma Ollila Grant of Nokia foundation for funding this research.

Appendix

Example of SSN ontology with RDF/XML syntax:

```
<owl:Class rdf:about="http://purl.oclc.org/NET/ssnx/ssn#Input">
<rdfs:label>Input</rdfs:label>
<owl:disjointWith rdf:resource="http://purl.oclc.org/NET/
ssnx/ssn#Output"/>
<dc:source>http://marinemetadata.org/community/teams/ontdevices
</dc:source>
<rdfs:seeAlso>http://www.w3.org/2005/Incubator/ssn/wiki/SSN_Model#Process
</rdfs:seeAlso>
<rdfs:isDefinedBy>http://purl.oclc.org/NET/ssnx/ssn</rdfs:isDefinedBy>
<rdfs:comment>Any information that is provided to a process for its use.
</rdfs:comment>
</owl:Class>
<owl:Class rdf:about="http://purl.oclc.org/NET/ssnx/ssn#Output">
<rdfs:label>Output</rdfs:label>
<rdfs:comment>Any information that is reported from a process.
</rdfs:comment>
<dc:source>http://marinemetadata.org/community/teams/ontdevices
</dc:source>
<rdfs:isDefinedBy>http://purl.oclc.org/NET/ssnx/ssn</rdfs:isDefinedBy>
<rdfs:seeAlso>http://www.w3.org/2005/Incubator/ssn/wiki/SSN_Model#Process
</rdfs:seeAlso>
</owl:Class>
```

Example of SSN ontology with Turtle syntax:

```
<http://purl.oclc.org/NET/ssnx/ssn#Input>
  a owl:Class;
  rdfs:label "Input";
  owl:disjointWith <http://purl.oclc.org/NET/ssnx/ssn#Output>;
  dc11:source "http://marinemetadata.org/community/teams/ontdevices";
  rdfs:seeAlso "http://www.w3.org/2005/Incubator/ssn/wiki/
  SSN_Model#Process";
  rdfs:isDefinedBy "http://purl.oclc.org/NET/ssnx/ssn";
  rdfs:comment "Any information that is provided to a process for its
  use.".
<http://purl.oclc.org/NET/ssnx/ssn#Output>
  a owl:Class;
  rdfs:label "Output";
  rdfs:comment "Any information that is reported from a process.";
  dc11:source "http://marinemetadata.org/community/teams/ontdevices";
  rdfs:isDefinedBy "http://purl.oclc.org/NET/ssnx/ssn";
  rdfs:seeAlso "http://www.w3.org/2005/Incubator/ssn/wiki/
  SSN_Model#Process".
```

Example of SSN ontology with functional syntax:

```
Ontology:
AnnotationProperty: dc11:source
AnnotationProperty: rdfs:comment
AnnotationProperty: rdfs:isDefinedBy
```

```
AnnotationProperty: rdfs:label
AnnotationProperty: rdfs:seeAlso
Datatype: rdf:PlainLiteral

Class: <http://purl.oclc.org/NET/ssnx/ssn#Input>
Annotations:
  rdfs:isDefinedBy "http://purl.oclc.org/NET/ssnx/ssn",
rdfs:label "Input",
rdfs:seeAlso "http://www.w3.org/2005/Incubator/ssn/wiki/
SSN_Model#Process",
dc11:source "http://marinemetadata.org/community/teams/ontdevices",
rdfs:comment "Any information that is provided to a process
for its use."
DisjointWith: <http://purl.oclc.org/NET/ssnx/ssn#Output>
Class: <http://purl.oclc.org/NET/ssnx/ssn#Output>
Annotations:
  rdfs:isDefinedBy "http://purl.oclc.org/NET/ssnx/ssn",
rdfs:seeAlso "http://www.w3.org/2005/Incubator/ssn/
wiki/SSN_Model#Process",
dc11:source "http://marinemetadata.org/community/teams/ontdevices",
rdfs:comment "Any information that is reported from a process",
rdfs:label "Output".
DisjointWith: <http://purl.oclc.org/NET/ssnx/ssn#Input>
```

Example of SSN ontology with OWL/XML syntax:

```
<Ontology
<Declaration><Class IRI="http://purl.oclc.org/NET/ssnx/ssn#Output"/>
</Declaration>
<Declaration><Class IRI="http://purl.oclc.org/NET/ssnx/ssn#Input"/>
</Declaration>
<Declaration><AnnotationProperty abbreviatedIRI="dc11:source"/>
</Declaration>
<DisjointClasses>
<Class IRI="http://purl.oclc.org/NET/ssnx/ssn#Input"/>
<Class IRI="http://purl.oclc.org/NET/ssnx/ssn#Output"/>
</DisjointClasses>
<AnnotationAssertion>
<AnnotationProperty abbreviatedIRI="dc11:source"/>
<IRI>http://purl.oclc.org/NET/ssnx/ssn#Input</IRI>
<Literal datatypeIRI="http://www.w3.org/1999/02/22-rdf-syntax-ns#
PlainLiteral">
http://marinemetadata.org/community/teams/ontdevices</Literal>
</AnnotationAssertion>
<AnnotationAssertion>
<AnnotationProperty abbreviatedIRI="rdfs:comment"/>
<IRI>http://purl.oclc.org/NET/ssnx/ssn#Input</IRI>
<Literal datatypeIRI="http://www.w3.org/1999/02/22-rdf-syntax-ns#
PlainLiteral">
Any information that is provided to a process for its use.</Literal>
</AnnotationAssertion>
```

```
<AnnotationAssertion>
<AnnotationProperty abbreviatedIRI="rdfs:isDefinedBy"/>
<IRI>http://purl.oclc.org/NET/ssnx/ssn#Input</IRI>
<Literal datatypeIRI="http://www.w3.org/1999/02/22-rdf-syntax-ns#
PlainLiteral">
http://purl.oclc.org/NET/ssnx/ssn</Literal></AnnotationAssertion>
<AnnotationAssertion>
<AnnotationProperty abbreviatedIRI="rdfs:label"/>
<IRI>http://purl.oclc.org/NET/ssnx/ssn#Input</IRI>
<Literal datatypeIRI="http://www.w3.org/1999/02/22-rdf-syntax-ns#
PlainLiteral">Input</Literal></AnnotationAssertion>
<AnnotationAssertion>
<AnnotationProperty abbreviatedIRI="rdfs:seeAlso"/>
<IRI>http://purl.oclc.org/NET/ssnx/ssn#Input</IRI>
<Literal datatypeIRI="http://www.w3.org/1999/02/22-rdf-syntax-ns#
PlainLiteral">
http://www.w3.org/2005/Incubator/ssn/wiki/SSN_Model#Process</Literal>
</AnnotationAssertion>
<AnnotationAssertion>
<AnnotationProperty abbreviatedIRI="dc11:source"/>
<IRI>http://purl.oclc.org/NET/ssnx/ssn#Output</IRI>
<Literal datatypeIRI="http://www.w3.org/1999/02/22-rdf-syntax-ns#
PlainLiteral">
http://marinemetadata.org/community/teams/ontdevices</Literal>
</AnnotationAssertion>
<AnnotationAssertion>
<AnnotationProperty abbreviatedIRI="rdfs:comment"/>
<IRI>http://purl.oclc.org/NET/ssnx/ssn#Output</IRI>
<Literal datatypeIRI="http://www.w3.org/1999/02/22-rdf-syntax-ns#
PlainLiteral">
Any information that is reported from a process.</Literal>
</AnnotationAssertion>
<AnnotationAssertion>
<AnnotationProperty abbreviatedIRI="rdfs:isDefinedBy"/>
<IRI>http://purl.oclc.org/NET/ssnx/ssn#Output</IRI>
<Literal datatypeIRI="http://www.w3.org/1999/02/22-rdf-syntax-ns#
PlainLiteral">
http://purl.oclc.org/NET/ssnx/ssn</Literal></AnnotationAssertion>
<AnnotationAssertion>
<AnnotationProperty abbreviatedIRI="rdfs:label"/>
<IRI>http://purl.oclc.org/NET/ssnx/ssn#Output</IRI>
<Literal datatypeIRI="http://www.w3.org/1999/02/22-rdf-syntax-ns#
PlainLiteral">Output</Literal></AnnotationAssertion>
<AnnotationAssertion><AnnotationProperty abbreviatedIRI=rdfs:seeAlso"/>
<IRI>http://purl.oclc.org/NET/ssnx/ssn#Output</IRI>
<Literal datatypeIRI="http://www.w3.org/1999/02/22-rdf-syntax-ns#
PlainLiteral">
http://www.w3.org/2005/Incubator/ssn/wiki/SSN_Model#Process
</Literal></AnnotationAssertion>
</Ontology>
```

Example of SSN ontology with Manchester syntax:

```
Ontology:
AnnotationProperty: dc11:source
AnnotationProperty: rdfs:comment
AnnotationProperty: rdfs:isDefinedBy
AnnotationProperty: rdfs:label
AnnotationProperty: rdfs:seeAlso
Datatype: rdf:PlainLiteral
Class: <http://purl.oclc.org/NET/ssnx/ssn#Input>
Annotations:
  rdfs:isDefinedBy"http://purl.oclc.org/NET/ssnx/ssn",
  rdfs:label"Input",
  rdfs:seeAlso"http://www.w3.org/2005/Incubator/ssn/wiki/SSN_Model
  #Process",
  dc11:source"http://marinemetadata.org/community/teams/ontdevices",
  rdfs:comment"Any information that is provided to a process for its
  use."
DisjointWith: <http://purl.oclc.org/NET/ssnx/ssn#Output>
Class: <http://purl.oclc.org/NET/ssnx/ssn#Output>
Annotations:
  rdfs:isDefinedBy"http://purl.oclc.org/NET/ssnx/ssn",
  rdfs:seeAlso"http://www.w3.org/2005/Incubator/ssn/wiki/
  SSN_Model#Process",
  dc11:source"http://marinemetadata.org/community/teams/ontdevices",
  rdfs:comment"Any information that is reported from a process.",
  rdfs:label"Output"
DisjointWith:<http://purl.oclc.org/NET/ssnx/ssn#Input>
```

Example of SSN ontology with JSON-LD:

```
[{"@id":"http://purl.oclc.org/NET/ssnx/ssn#Input",
"@type":
  ["http://www.w3.org/2002/07/owl#Class"],
"http://www.w3.org/2000/01/rdf-schema#label":
  [{"@value":"Input"}],
"http://www.w3.org/2002/07/owl#disjointWith":
[{"@id":"http://purl.oclc.org/NET/ssnx/ssn#Output"}],
"http://purl.org/dc/elements/1.1/source":
[{"@value":"http://marinemetadata.org/community/teams/ontdevices"}],
"http://www.w3.org/2000/01/rdf-schema#seeAlso":
[{"@value":"http://www.w3.org/2005/Incubator/ssn/wiki/SSN_Model#
Process"}],
"http://www.w3.org/2000/01/rdf-schema#isDefinedBy":
[{"@value":"http://purl.oclc.org/NET/ssnx/ssn"}],
"http://www.w3.org/2000/01/rdf-schema#comment":
[{"@value":"Any information that is provided to a process for
its use."}]},
{"@id":"http://purl.oclc.org/NET/ssnx/ssn#Output",
"@type":["http://www.w3.org/2002/07/owl#Class"],
```

```
"http://www.w3.org/2000/01/rdf-schema#label":
[{"@value":"Output"}],
"http://www.w3.org/2000/01/rdf-schema#comment":
[{"@value":"Any information that is reported from a process."}],
"http://purl.org/dc/elements/1.1/source":
[{"@value":"http://marinemetadata.org/community/teams/ontdevices"}],
"http://www.w3.org/2000/01/rdf-schema#isDefinedBy":
[{"@value":"http://purl.oclc.org/NET/ssnx/ssn"}],
"http://www.w3.org/2000/01/rdf-schema#seeAlso":
[{"@value":"http://www.w3.org/2005/Incubator/ssn/wiki/SSN_Model#
Process"}]},
{"@id":"http://www.w3.org/2002/07/owl#Class"}]
```

Example of SSN ontology with EN Schema:

```
<owl:Class http://purl.oclc.org/NET/ssnx/ssn#Output
a owl:Class
rdfs:isDefinedBy http://purl.oclc.org/NET/ssnx/ssn
rdfs:seeAlso http://www.w3.org/2005/Incubator/ssn/wiki/SSN_Model#Process
rdfs:label"Output"
rdfs:comment"Any information that is reported from a process."
dc11:source http://marinemetadata.org/community/teams/ontdevices>
<owl:Class http://purl.oclc.org/NET/ssnx/ssn#Input
a owl:Class
rdfs:isDefinedBy http://purl.oclc.org/NET/ssnx/ssn
rdfs:seeAlso http://www.w3.org/2005/Incubator/ssn/wiki/SSN_Model#Process
rdfs:label"Input"
rdfs:comment"Any information that is provided to a process for its use."
owl:disjointWith http://purl.oclc.org/NET/ssnx/ssn#Output
dc11:source http://marinemetadata.org/community/teams/ontdevices>
```

References

1. Shi, W., Cao, J., Zhang, Q., Li, Y., Xu, L.: Edge computing: vision and challenges. IEEE Internet Things J. **3**(5), 637–646 (2016)
2. Su, X., Li, P., Li, Y., Flores, H., Riekki, J., Prehofer, P.: Towards semantic reasoning on the edge of IoT systems. In: Proceedings of the 6th International Conference on the Internet of Things, pp. 171–172, ACM Press, Stuttgart (2016)
3. Su, X., Riekki, J., Nurminen, J.K., Nieminen, J., Koskimies, M.: Adding semantics to internet of things. Concurrency Comput. Pract. Experience **27**(8), 1844–1860 (2015)
4. Maarala, A.I., Su, X., Jukka, R.: Semantic reasoning for advanced internet of things applications. IEEE Internet Things J. **2**(4), 1–13 (2016)
5. Hitzler, P., Krötzsch, M., Parsia, B., Patel-Schneider, P.F., Rudolph, S.: OWL 2 Web Ontology Language Primer, 2nd edn. https://www.w3.org/TR/owl2-primer/
6. Semantic sensor network ontology. http://purl.oclc.org/NET/ssnx/ssn
7. Woods, W.A., Schmolze, J.G.: The KL-ONE family. Comput. Math. Appl. **23**(2–5), 133–177 (1992)

8. Kifer, M., Lausen, G.: F-logic: a higher-order language for reasoning about objects, inheritance, and scheme. In: Proceedings of the 1989 ACM SIGMOD International Conference on Management of Data, pp. 134–146. ACM press, Portland (1989)
9. Heflin, J., Hendler, J., Luke, S.: SHOE : A Knowledge Representation Language for Internet Applications. Technical report CS-TR-4078, Department of Computer Science, University of Maryland (1999)
10. McGuinness, D.L., Fikes, R., Stein, L.A., Hendler, J.: DAML-ONT: an ontology language for the semantic web. In: Fensel, F., Hendler, J., Lieberman, H., Wahlster, W. (eds.) Spinning the Semantic Web: Bringing the World Wide Web to Its Full Potential. MIT Press, Cambridge (2002)
11. Fensel, D., van Harmelen, F., Horrocks, I., McGuinness, D.L., Patel-Schneider, P.F.: OIL: an ontology infrastructure for the semantic web. IEEE Intell. Syst. **16**(2), 38–45 (2001)
12. McGuinness, D.L., Fikes, R., Hendler, J., Stein, L.A.: DAML+OIL: an ontology language for the semantic web. IEEE Intell. Syst. **17**(5), 72–80 (2002)
13. Horrocks, I.: Reasoning with expressive description logics: theory and practice. In: Voronkov, A. (ed.) CADE 2002. LNCS (LNAI), vol. 2392, pp. 1–15. Springer, Heidelberg (2002). doi:10.1007/3-540-45620-1_1
14. Motik, B., Grau, B.C., Horrocks, I., Wu, Z., Fokoue, A., Lutz, C.: OWL 2 Web ontology language profiles, 2nd edn. http://www.w3.org/TR/owl2-profiles/
15. Yu, L.Y.: A Deveoper's Guide to the Semantic Web. Springer, Heidelberg (2014)
16. Horridge, M., Patel-Schneider, P.F.: OWL 2 Web Ontology Language Manchester Syntax, 2nd edn. https://www.w3.org/TR/owl2-manchester-syntax/
17. SON for Linking Data. http://json-ld.org/
18. Su, X.: Lightweight Data and Knowledge Exchange for Pervasive Environments. Acta Universitatis Ouluensis series C581 (2016)
19. Fuchs, N.E., Kaljurand, K., Kuhn, T.: Attempto controlled English for knowledge representation. In: Baroglio, C., Bonatti, P.A., Małuszyński, J., Marchiori, M., Polleres, A., Schaffert, S. (eds.) Reasoning Web, pp. 104–124. Springer, Heidelberg (2008)
20. Cregan, A., Schwitter, R., Meyer, T.: Sydney OWL syntax - towards a controlled natural language syntax for OWL 1.1. In: Proceedings of the OWLED 2007 Workshop on OWL: Experience and Directions, CEUR-WS, Innsbruck (2007)
21. Hart, G., Johnson, M., Dolbear, C.: Rabbit: developing a control natural language for authoring ontologies. In: Bechhofer, S., Hauswirth, M., Hoffmann, J., Koubarakis, M. (eds.) ESWC 2008. LNCS, vol. 5021, pp. 348–360. Springer, Heidelberg (2008). doi:10.1007/978-3-540-68234-9_27
22. Schwitter, R., Kaljurand, K., Cregan, A., Dolbear, C., Hart, G.: A comparison of three controlled natural languages for OWL 1.1. In: Proceedings of the 4th OWL Experiences and Directions Workshop, Washington, USA (2008)
23. Chen, H., Finin, T., Joshi, A.: An ontology for context-aware pervasive computing environments. Knowl. Eng. Rev. **18**(3), 197–207 (2003)
24. Bermudez-Edo, M., Barnaghi, P., Elsaleh, T.: IoT-lite Ontology. http://iot.ee.surrey.ac.uk/fiware/ontologies/iot-lite
25. Berrueta, D., Brickley, D., Decker, S., Fernández, S., Görn, C., Harth, A., Heath, T., Idehen, K., Kjernsmo, K., Miles, A., Passant, A., Polleres, A., Polo, L., Sintek, M.: SIOC Core Ontology Specification. https://www.w3.org/Submission/sioc-spec/
26. Reynolds, D.: The Organization Ontology. https://www.w3.org/TR/vocab-org/

A Mobile Context-Aware Information System to Support Tourism Events

Fabio Clarizia[1], Saverio Lemma[2(✉)], Marco Lombardi[2], and Francesco Pascale[3]

[1] DI, University of Salerno, Fisciano, Italy
fclarizia@unisa.it
[2] SIMASLab, University of Salerno, Fisciano, Italy
{slemma,malombardi}@unisa.it
[3] DIIn, University of Salerno, Fisciano, Italy
fpascale@unisa.it

Abstract. The experience of a touristic visit is a learning process very fascinating and interesting: the emotions can change according to the interests of the individuals, as well as of the physical, personal and social-cultural context. Applications for a mobile environment should take advantage of contextual information, such as position, to offer greater services to the user.

In this paper, it is introduced a Context Aware Approach for the tourism. This approach is based on a graphical formalism for the context representation, the Context Dimension Tree, which plays a fundamental role in tailoring the target application data according to the user information needs.

In particular, the proposed system is made available to the user as an adaptive mobile application, which allows a high degree of customization in recommending services and resources according to his/her current position and global profile. For example, the system can guide the tourist in the discovery of a town proposing him/her events mainly interesting for the user.

A case study applied to a Christmas event in Salerno, an Italian town, has been analyzed considering various users and an experimental campaign has been conducted, obtaining interesting results.

Keywords: Adaptive systems · Context-aware computing · e-Citizenship

1 Introduction

The Italian towns have a cultural heritage that often do not succeed in being completely enhanced. The natural, artistic and cultural resources present in the Italian towns, above all the smallest ones, many times remain hidden and are not enjoyed by the tourists. This problem typology becomes even more important when the tourist has few hours to visit a town: think, for instance, about some passengers of a cruise who in few hours have to visit an unknown place. The problem arises also for those people who, for work, live an experience in a town that they can visit in little time. Where eating? What seeing? How moving? These are the typical questions that such a user makes when he/she is in a station, an airport or a harbor. If in the big towns there are pre-constituted itineraries

© Springer International Publishing AG 2017
M.H.A. Au et al. (Eds.): GPC 2017, LNCS 10232, pp. 553–566, 2017.
DOI: 10.1007/978-3-319-57186-7_40

that can be easily made by the tourists, this is not always true in towns of little or medium dimension that, even if they have a sure interesting cultural heritage, often risk of not enhancing it completely.

On second thoughts, information necessary for the enhancement of the resources of a town are, in many cases, already present on the web: the social networks have much information about the resources present in a town. On the other hand, also the public institutions, usually, develop some contents in support of the cultural resources present in the territory, but not present in places not easily reachable by the tourists, above all the foreign ones. Moreover, often, there are also services that can be useful for a tourist who unlikely knows where finding them. Therefore, it is necessary to create a framework that can integrate contents and services to support a user inside a certain territorial context.

The adoption of Future Internet (FI) technology and of its most challenging components like the Internet of Things (IoT) and the Internet of Services (IoS), can constitute the basic building blocks to progress towards a unified ICT platform for a variety of applications within the large framework of smart cities projects [3, 14]. In addition, recent issues on participatory sensing, where every day mobile devices like cellular phones form interactive, participatory sensor networks enabling public and professional users to gather, analyze and share local knowledge [10, 20], seem to fit the smartness requirements of a city in which also people have to play an active role. Eventually, the cloud computing technologies provides a natural infrastructure to support smart services [12].

As previously said, one of the fields that can take great advantages from such technologies is tourism [25]. In this scenario, persons (citizens, tourists, etc.) and objects (cars, buildings, rooms, sculptures, etc.) equipped with appropriate devices (GPS, smartphone, video cameras, temperature/humidity sensors, etc.) constitute a particular social network in which all the mentioned entities can communicate [21].

Exchanged and produced data can be exploited by a set of applications in order to make the system "smart". From a more general point of view, the social network can be seen as composed of a set of Single Smart Spaces (S3) (indoor museums, archaeological sites, old town centers, etc.), each needing particular ICT infrastructure and service that transforms the physical spaces into useful smart environments. Here, one of the most challenging and interesting research problem is to model context awareness in a S3 and design context aware applications able to provide useful data and services depending on the current context occurrences [11, 13].

Context is not just a simple profile that describes the surroundings of data. Rather, context is better described as any piece of information that can be used to characterize the situation of an entity such as a person, a place, or any other relevant object/aspect in the interaction between a user and an application. In this paper, we try to give an answer to the problem of the context representation using the Context Dimension Tree formalism [4, 6].

On the basis of what has been previously described, this work will be organized in this way: in the following paragraph, we will describe the concept of context and how it can be declined in a modern way thanks to the use of new technologies. Then, we will introduce a context-based approach able to give, inside a Christmas event in a little town, services and contents useful for the user. Some experimental results will be presented in the last part of the paper.

2 Motivating Example

In this section, we describe a typical application in the tourist domain in order to better understand the main features of the proposed system. In particular, we consider a tourist that during her/his vacation in Campania desires to see Artist's Lights Christmas event in Salerno, a beautiful town located in the South of Italy.

Some of the features of context-aware systems are given below:

- contextual sensing: ability to sense context information and present it to the user;
- contextual adaptation: ability to execute or modify a service automatically at runtime based on the context;
- context resource discovery: ability to discover and use resources and services related to the current context;
- contextual augmentation: ability to supplement digital data with the user's context.

In particular, to be considered smart, the environment related to the Artist's Lights event should provide a set of smart services for:

- suggesting the visit of the most important Christmas lights;
- having information about the Christmas lights in Salerno;
- accessing to proper multimedia guides describing the Christmas lights that are in Salerno;
- recommending special visit paths (Il Mito, Il Sogno, Il Tempo, Il Natale);
- monitoring the weather condition;
- showing the timetable of the transport services located in Salerno;
- saving the visit in a multimedia album and sharing it with friends.

For improving their effectiveness, these services and contents have to be furnished to the user in the right context and at the right timing. Therefore, it is important the context awareness of the framework and the opportunity to use it by mobile devices [15]. Another important feature of the system is the ability to suggest resources that usually are not considered as mainstream.

In order to give the most suitable contents to the users, in this paper we introduce a context aware system able to tailor data and services depending on the context and the users' needs.

Data about resources and services are collected from a knowledge base built by a group of experts and collecting information from the various social networks.

In the next paragraphs, more details about context awareness and the application of the proposed approach in real context will be furnished.

3 Context Awareness

The term context has been defined by many researchers. One of the most cited definitions of context is the definition of Dey et al. [17] that defines context as "any information that can be used to characterize the situation of an entity. An entity is a person, place, or object that is considered relevant to the interaction between a user and an application, including the user and applications themselves."

We accept the definition of context provided by Dey et al. to be used in this research work, because this definition can be used to identify context from data in general.

The originators of the term context awareness are Schilit and Theimer who in 1994 introduced and defined Context-aware computing as "the ability of a mobile user's applications to discover and react to changes in the environment they are situated in" [26].

Pascoe et al. [24] describe context awareness as the ability of the computing devices to detect, sense, interpret and respond to aspects of a user's local environment and the computing devices them selves.

Dey and Abowd have refined these definitions into a more general definition what a context-aware system is. In this definition they use context in the definition of a context-aware system. Since context has already been defined and classified in the above it is logical to use these elements in the definition of context awareness: "A system is context-aware if it uses context to provide relevant information and/or services to the user, where relevancy depends on the user's task".

If we wanted to classify the context awareness categories, we could consider that presented in [7]:

1. Presentation of information and services to a user, is the systems ability to select appropriate information and services according to the current context and make these available to the user at the correct time.
2. Automatic execution of a service, is when the system automatically performs actions and updates the system according to events in the context.
3. Tagging of context to information for later retrieval, is applying information to the context so that the information may the retrieved later when the user enters the same context again.

Context-aware systems are changing over the years since its introduction, several existing context-aware systems were reviewed.

Based on the characteristics, existing context-aware systems are broadly classified into four categories, namely the first generation, second generation, third generation and fourth generation of context-aware systems [22].

Examples of first generation context-aware systems are tour guide, shopping assistant, phone call forwarding and location information providing.

The main focus during this generation is acquisition of location from the sources. This systems are named location based service systems.

The second generation context-aware systems initiated focusing on achieving more number of context-aware applications starting from homogenous devices to heterogenous devices.

Third generation of context-aware systems begins to focus on context knowledge sharing among the network. It concentrates on markup languages, for example Web Ontology Language (OWL).

Fourth generation of context-aware systems are working in ambient environment.

What are the mobile context-aware applications for?

In this section we will describe some systems and ideas behind the applications.

One of the very first attempts to make a context-aware system is the CyberGuide [1] which was created back in 1996. The CyberGuide was intended to work as a citywide guide system which could lead people to the sites which they wished to see and also provide a local mobile guide inside the different attractions around the city. Once inside a museum or a similar site the CyberGuide functions as a personal tour guide which leads the user around the exhibit and based on knowledge of the user's location provides information about the pieces of art in the vicinity.

SenSay [28] is one example of a context-aware system that attempts to adapt to dynamically-changing environmental and physiological states. The system relies on a sensor network that utilises a person's mobile phone as a primary source of context information, although the use of applications (e.g. calendars, task lists) and body-embedded sensors was also targeted.

AnonySense [27], a privacy-aware architecture for collaborative pervasive applications that use mobile sensing. Mobile sensor data is anonymized before its use by any of the applications.

SOCAM [19] is a service oriented ontology based context-aware middleware. It supports semantic representation and reasoning of context. It also divides context into upper and lower level ontologies such as interpreted context through physical world, and memory and battery status respectively. It allows adaptability by listening, detecting and invocating events for application services.

GeoNotes by Espinoza et al. is a system for abstracting location information for location-aware applications [18]. The system architecture is constructed to support shared information for mobile devices, exactly to leave notes atspecific places for other users to be read. A user creates notes and sticks it to certain places, where other users can read them. Notes can be targeted at a single user or a whole user group. Vice versa a specific user can create and apply filters to perceive only a subset of the notes associated to a certain place.

In the following paragraph, we will present an approach to the management of the context and the contextualization of its associated contents and services.

4   Contents and Services Contextualization

In order to make contextualized queries, it is necessary to define a model for the representation and management of the context itself, which allows filtering the resources obtained, on the basis of contextual parameters (user position, user profile, user friends, etc.): this operations are made through the Context Dimension Tree (CDT) [29].

Therefore, the result shows itself like a well-organized information that presents a general introduction about the place reached by the user, according to his/her interests and enriched with the experiences shared by similar users, and a list of the main suggested attractions about the near places visited by the friends.

In particular, CDT is used to be able to represent, in a graphic form, all possible contexts that you may have within an application. CDT plays a fundamental role in tailoring the information space according to the user's information needs, as well as an analysis of relevant features of context models. It is thus important to notice that this notion of context is strictly connected to the considered application and is not meant to model the general knowledge concerning one or more areas of interest, a situation where a data schema, or a domain-ontology may be better suited [5, 9, 16].

CDT is a tree composed of a triad <r; N; A> where r indicates its root, N is the set of nodes of which it is made of and A is the set of arcs joining these nodes.

A dimension node, which is graphically represented by the color black, is a node that describes a possible dimension of the application domain; a concept node, on the other hand, is depicted by the color white and represents one of the possible values that a dimension may assume. Each node is identified through its type and a label.

The children of the root node r are all dimension nodes, they are called top dimension and for each of them there may be a sub-tree. Leaf nodes, instead, must be concept nodes. A dimension node can have, as children, only concept nodes and, similarly, a concept node can have, as children, only dimension nodes. In addition to nodes, you can use other elements: the parameters, which may arise both from a dimension node (graphi-cally represented by a white square) and from a concept node (white triangle), submitting them to particular constraints. In fact, a concept node can have more than one parameter, while a dimension node can have only a parameter and only in case it has not already children nodes. The introduction of parameters is due to their usefulness in shaping the characteristics that can have an infinite or very high number of attributes. For example, a node representing Cost dimension risks having a high number of values that should be specified by as many concept children nodes. In a similar case, it is therefore preferred to use only one parameter, whose value will be specified in each case. Leaf nodes, in addition to concept nodes, can also be parameters. In general, each node has a parameter corresponding to a domain, dom(nP). For parameter nodes connected to concept nodes, the domain can be a set of key values from a relational database, while in case of param-eter nodes connected to dimension nodes, the domain is a set of possible concept nodes of dimension.

Therefore, CDT is used to systematically describe the user needs, and to capture the context the user is acting in. It plays a fundamental role in tailoring the target application data according to the user information needs. Once the possible contexts have been designed, each must be connected with the corresponding view definition. In this ways, when the context becomes current, the view is computed and delivered to the user [23].

In fact, through the CDT, it is possible, after analyzing the domain of application, to express the size characteristics and values they can take in a graphical way by, respec-tively, dimension nodes and concept nodes or parameters.

The assignment to a dimension of one of its possible values is a context element. The context element can be considered the main feature of the application, by which a context can be decomposed. The moment you make the formulation of the context, you must specify all the context elements that are part of it and that enable its creation.

Any context is expressible by an "and" combination of the context elements to which they are peculiar.

By definition, you can begin to understand how you will create views based on data relating to each context; in fact, they will be built starting from the portions of the database and then from the partial views, associated to the context element that takes part into context information.

The CDT elaboration is composed of methodologies and phases to obtain contextual resources. The methodology has been realized in order to manage the database and to carry out reductions of their content based on the context. The purpose is to help the designer in the definition of all contexts relevant to the considered application and, later, in the association to each context of the portion of the database containing the relevant data about the context.

The methodology consists of three main phases, which we will see in detail later: design phase of the CDT, definition phase of partial views and composition phase of global views [2].

1. Design phase of the Context Tree: in this phase, the CDT is designed to identify significant context elements for the considered application. In fact, it focuses on the definition of contexts and on the elements that compose them. These contexts must be identified and shaped, indicating particular elements that characterize each of them. As it has been said, it is available a special tool called CDT to make context design. Various CDT were made for specific environments in order to represent and manage a multitude of different contexts and in order to identify, represent, preserve and make available cultural points for each type of user.
2. Definition phase of partial views: after the definition of all the contexts and their context elements, in this step a different portion of the database is associated to each context element, containing the relevant data for it. In practice, the goal is to find the appropriate value for a given dimension, in order to obtain, by means of the values of all the dimensions, a valid query and specific to the context in which the user is located.
3. Composition phase of global views: this is the phase where you have the automatic generation of views associated with each context, which is made starting from partial views associated with context elements. After the creation of the global views of the contexts, the answers to questions that will be asked to the system will be developed from these views and, in particular, from the view associated with the context in which you are located when the query is performed.

In particular, once defined the values for each dimension, you can use all the information obtained in order to identify the right context and offer contextual resources for the user.

In Fig. 1, it is shown a general designed CDT, called Meta CDT, which is the starting point for the design of a specific CDT that can be exploited in contextual applications [15]. You may note six top dimensions, which correspond to the questions of the 5W1H method: Location (WHERE), Role (WHO), Time (WHEN), Situation (HOW), Interest (WHAT) and Utilization (WHY).

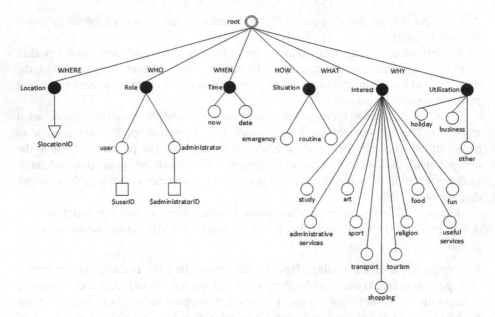

Fig. 1. Meta context dimension tree

In particular, there are two types of users and eleven categories of interests. In this case, as shown in Fig. 2, a partial view could be related to dimension "Role": once logged in, the application is able to recognize the user and to know more precisely whether he/she is, for example in tourist areas, a resident or a tourist. Thus, the value "tourist" of dimension "Role" is a partial view for the current context: using this knowledge, you can exclude certain resources, not suitable or useful to the tourist role.

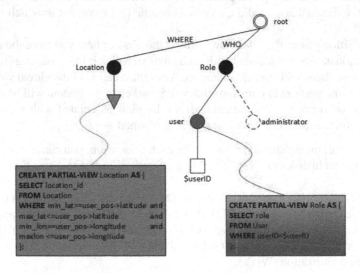

Fig. 2. Example of partial views

A context element is defined as an assignment d_name_i = value, where d_name_i indicates a possible size or undersize of CDT (it is the label of a dimension node), while value may represent the label of one of the concept nodes that are children of the considered dimension node or the value of a parameter referring to one of these concept nodes or the value of a parameter referring to the considered dimension node.

For example, these assignments are possible context elements:

```
Interest = "tourism", Location = $locationID (for exam-
ple, ID = 3), Role = $userID->role (for example, ID =
15), Utilization = "holiday".
```

A context is specified as: $^\wedge(d\_name_i$ = value): it is defined as an "and" among different context elements.

Several context elements, combined with each other by means of an "and", damage, therefore, the origin of a context [8].

For example, a possible framework that can be obtained from the previously seen CDT, through the context elements that we have listed, is:

```
C = [Location = $locationID (ID = 3)] ∧ [Role - $userID-
>role (ID = 15)] ∧ [Time = "now"] ∧ [Situation = "rou-
tine"] ∧ [Interest = "tourism"] ∧ [Utilization = "holi-
day"]
```

The context is defined as a user, interested in tourism, who uses the contextual app on vacation, in a called place.

5   A Context Aware App for Promoting Tourism Events

In this section, we will present a contextual app designed and implemented according to what was described previously. In particular, we have thought to apply the approach in the context of Artist's Lights Christmas event, that every year is held in Salerno (Regione Campania in Italy) and that involves hundreds of thousands of tourists.

From November to January, with light installations, some by local artists exclusively for Salerno, scattered through the main streets and in the most beautiful and attractive corners of the city center.

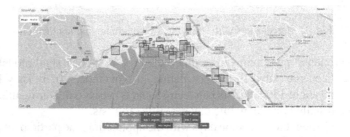

Fig. 3. Definition of the activation areas of services and contents

In this phase, we have collected the services and contents potentially useful for the citizens and situate them on the map defining the activation zones (Fig. 3).

Moreover, we have defined the different typologies of citizens (tourist and expert user) associating them to a previously established set of services and contents. Having the town a series of Christmas contents, we have developed services and contents in support of them too.

All information about places of worship and shops has been uploaded, for any building or area of potential.

The App has been developed with hybrid technologies (Ionic Framework and Apache Cordova) to allow an easier publication both in Android and Apple environment (Fig. 4).

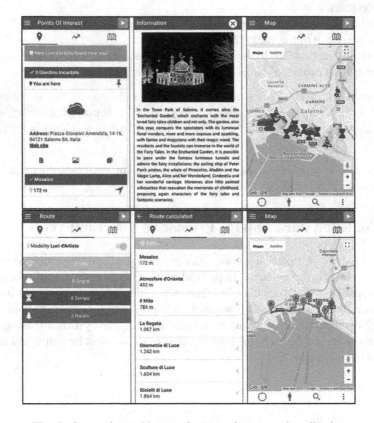

Fig. 4. Screenshots with some features of contextual application

The experimental phase aims to evaluate the proposed contextual model. Initially, the App has been presented to the population in November 2016. They have been involved overall about 1500 tourists between 18 and 60 years old. During this event, the app has been installed on the mobile devices of the tourists.

After having interacted for some days with the application, the participants have then answered on the basis of the Likert scale to fourteen statements, divided into four sections. To every question present in the section, five possible answers have been associated: I strongly agree – I agree – Undecided (Neither agree nor disagree) – I disagree- I strongly disagree.

The questionnaire in detail is the following:

- Section A: App – Context
  - A1. The App gives the user tailor-made contents and services in the right place.
  - A2. The App allows the user to know several item of the Artist's Lights.
  - A3. The App supplies services according to the interests selected in the user profile.
- Section B: App – Further aspects
  - B1. Information about each item of Artist's Lights is very useful.
  - B2. The contents, such as descriptions and images, are of high quality and represent one of the strong points of Artist's Lights
  - B3. The services associated to the items allow a higher immediacy than a classic research on the Internet.
- Section C: App – Functionality
  - C1. The plan itinerary service allows easily realizing an itinerary in the Artist's Lights according to the user's preferences.
  - C2. The explore surroundings service is very useful to know what there is nearby and eventually reach them.
  - C3. The functionality of QR code in inner environments can be well used.
- Section D: App – Future developments
  - D1. It would be interesting to have a higher integration with the main social networks.
  - D2. It would be interesting to insert the available time in the plan itinerary service.

Table 1 presents a synthesis of the answers of the participants to each declaration.

Table 1. Experimental results

Likert Scale	Strongly agree	Agree	Neither agree nor disagree	Disagree	Strongly disagree
A1	497	786	142	42	33
A2	741	568	92	63	36
A3	568	752	135	26	19
B1	515	762	90	75	58
B2	594	652	150	63	41
B3	654	701	120	17	8
C1	846	566	64	11	13
C2	627	713	79	46	35
C3	582	698	145	48	27
D1	657	689	87	38	29
D2	599	603	212	47	39

As shown in this table, of the 1500 participants who have interacted with the application, many agree and/or strongly agree that the system gives appropriate contextual information about the place, further aspects and functionality are very useful and future developments are interesting. Instead, only in few cases, the participants do not are particularly satisfied.

As can noticed from the Fig. 5, users show great appreciation for the app. In general, they appreciated the proposed contents and services.

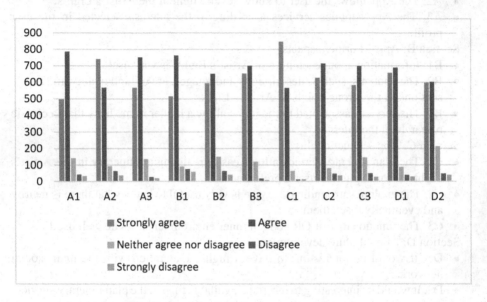

Fig. 5. Graphic analysis of experimental results

6   Conclusions

In this paper, it has been presented an approach able to offer personalized services and contents for the needs of the user according to the context where he/she is. In particular, it has been proposed the use of a Mobile Context-Aware App.

The app bases its contextual functioning on the adoption of the Context Dimension Tree that is able to shape the context and the actions to implement. It has been developed for the Artist's Lights Christmas event and the results have been satisfying.

The following activities have as purpose the application of the proposed methodology to more complex environments, for dimension and number of potential places to manage.

Acknowledgements.   The research reported in this paper has been supported by the Project Cultural Heritage Information System (CHIS) PON03PE_00099_1 CUP E66J140000 70007 – D46J1400000 0007 and the Databenc District.

References

1. Abowd, G.D., Atkenson, C.G., Hong, J., Long, S., Kooper, R., Pinkerton, M.: Cyberguide: a mobile context-aware tour guide. Wireless Netw. **3**(5), 421–433 (1997)
2. Annunziata, G., Colace, F., De Santo, M., Lemma, S., Lombardi, M.: ApPoggiomarino: a context aware app for e-citizenship. In: The 18th International Conference on Enterprise Information Systems (ICEIS) (2016)
3. Atzori, L., Iera, A., Morabito, G.: The internet of things: a survey. Comput. Netw. **54**(15), 2787–2805 (2010)
4. Bolchini, C., Curino, C., Schreiber, F.A., Tanca, L.: Context integration for mobile data tailoring. In: SEBD 2006, pp. 48–55 (2006)
5. Bolchini, C., Curino, C., Quintarelli, E., Schreiber, F.A., Tanca, L.: A survey of context models and a preliminary methodology for context driven data view definition. In: Technical report 4.1, ESTEEM Project (2006)
6. Bolchini, C., Curino, C., Quintarelli, E., Schreiber, F.A., Tanca, L.: Context information for knowledge reshaping. Int. J. Web Eng. Technol. **5**(1), 88–103 (2009)
7. Bisgaard, J.J., Heise, M., Steffenses, C.: How is Context and Context-awareness Defined and Applied? A Survey of Context-awareness. Aalborg University (2004)
8. Casillo, M., Cerullo, L., Colace, F., Lemma, S., Lombardi, M., Pietrosanto, A.: An adaptive context aware app for the tourism. In: Proceedings of the 3rd Multidisciplinary International Social Networks Conference on Social Informatics, Data Science, p. 26. ACM (2016)
9. Casillo, M., Colace, F., Lemma, S., Lombardi, M., Pietrosanto, A.: An ontological approach to digital storytelling. In: Proceedings of the 3rd Multidisciplinary International Social Networks Conference on Social Informatics, Data Science, p. 27. ACM (2016)
10. Colace, F., Foggia, P., Percannella, G.: A probabilistic framework for TV-news stories detection and classification. In: IEEE International Conference on Multimedia and Expo (ICME), no 1521680, pp. 1350–1353 (2005)
11. Colace, F., De Santo, M., Greco, L.: An adaptive product configurator based on slow intelligence approach. Int. J. Metadata Semant. Ontol. **9**(2), 128–137 (2014)
12. Colace, F., Greco, L., Lemma, S., Lombardi, M., Yung, D., Chang, S.K.: An adaptive contextual recommender system: a slow intelligence perspective. In: The Twenty-Seventh International Conference on Software Engineering and Knowledge Engineering (SEKE), pp. 64–71 (2015)
13. Colace, F., De Santo, M., Greco, L., Moscato, V., Picariello, A.: A collaborative user-centered framework for recommending items in online social networks. Comput. Hum. Behav. **51**, 694–704 (2015)
14. Colace, F., De Santo, M., Lemma, S., Lombardi, M., Rossi, A., Santoriello, A., Terribile, A., Vigorito, M.: How to describe cultural heritage resources in the web 2.0 Era? In: The Eleventh International Conference on Signal-Image Technology and Internet-Based Systems (SITIS), pp. 809–815 (2015)
15. Colace, F., Greco, L., Lemma, S., Lombardi, M., Amato, F., Moscato, V., Picariello, A.: Contextual aware computing and tourism: a case study. In: The Eleventh International Conference on Signal-Image Technology & Internet-Based Systems (SITIS), pp. 804–808 (2015)
16. Colace, F., De Santo, M., Greco, L., Napoletano, P.: Weighted word pairs for query expansion. Inf. Process. Manage. **51**(1), 179–193 (2015)
17. Abowd, G.D., Dey, A.K., Brown, P.J., Davies, N., Smith, M., Steggles, P.: Towards a better understanding of context and context-awareness. In: Gellersen, H.-W. (ed.) HUC 1999. LNCS, vol. 1707, pp. 304–307. Springer, Heidelberg (1999). doi:10.1007/3-540-48157-5_29

18. Espinoza, F., Persson, P., Sandin, A., Nyström, H., Cacciatore, E., Bylund, M.: *GeoNotes*: social and navigational aspects of location-based information systems. In: Abowd, G.D., Brumitt, B., Shafer, S. (eds.) UbiComp 2001. LNCS, vol. 2201, pp. 2–17. Springer, Heidelberg (2001). doi:10.1007/3-540-45427-6_2

19. Gu, T., Pung, H.K., Zhang, D.Q.: A service oriented middleware for building context aware services. J. Netw. Comput. Appl. **28**(1), 1–18 (2005)

20. Hernández-Muñoz, J.M., Vercher, J.B., Muñoz, L., Galache, J.A., Presser, M., Hernández Gómez, L.A., Pettersson, J.: Smart cities at the forefront of the future internet. In: Domingue, J., et al. (eds.) FIA 2011. LNCS, vol. 6656, pp. 447–462. Springer, Heidelberg (2011). doi: 10.1007/978-3-642-20898-0_32

21. Komninos, N., Schaffers, H., Pallot, M.: Developing a policy roadmap for smart cities and the future internet. In: eChallenges e-2011 Conference Proceedings, pp. 286–306 (2011)

22. Meena, K., Sivakumar, R.: Human-Computer Interaction (2014)

23. Parent, C., Schewe, K.-D., Storey, V.C., Thalheim, B. (eds.): ER 2007. LNCS, vol. 4801. Springer, Heidelberg (2007). doi:10.1007/978-3-540-75563-0

24. Pascoe, J., Ryan, N., Morse, D.: Using while moving: HCI issues in fieldwork (2000)

25. Schaffers, H., Komninos, N., Pallot, M., Trousse, B., Nilsson, M., Oliveira, A.: Smart cities and the future internet: towards cooperation frameworks for open innovation. In: Domingue, J., et al. (eds.) FIA 2011. LNCS, vol. 6656, pp. 431–446. Springer, Heidelberg (2011). doi:10.1007/978-3-642-20898-0_31

26. Schilit, B., Theimer, M.: Disseminating Active Map Information to Mobile Hosts (1994)

27. Shin, M., Cornelius, C., Peebles, D., Kapadia, A., Kotz, D., Triandopoulos, N.: AnonySense: a system for anonymous opportunistic sensing. J. Pervasive Mobile Comput. (2010)

28. Siewiorek, D., Smailagic, A., Furukawa, J., Krause, A., Moraveji, N., Reiger, K., Shaffer, J., Wong, F.L.: Sensay: a context-aware mobile phone. In: Proceedings of the 7th IEEE International Symposium on Wearable Computers, ISWC 2003, Washington, DC, USA (2003)

29. Tanca, L., Bolchini, C., Curino, C., Schreiber, F.A.: Context integration for mobile data tailoring. In: Italian Symposium on Database Systems (SEBD), pp. 48–55 (2006)

An Ontological Digital Storytelling to Enrich Tourist Destinations and Attractions with a Mobile Tailored Story

Fabio Clarizia[1], Saverio Lemma[2(✉)], Marco Lombardi[2], and Francesco Pascale[3]

[1] DI, University of Salerno, Fisciano, SA, Italy
fclarizia@unisa.it
[2] SIMASLab, University of Salerno, Fisciano, SA, Italy
{slemma,malomabrdi}@unisa.it
[3] DIIn, University of Salerno, Fisciano, SA, Italy
fpascale@unisa.it

Abstract. Storytelling has evolved over the years: its ability to enchant, transform and persuade makes it a formidable mean, malleable and customizable, but not easy to use. The use of new technologies allowing it to reach a far greater level of effectiveness: the audience can join in the storytelling process, thus impacting positively on engagement and facilitating the development of long lasting relationships.

Our contribution is a revisited digital storytelling approach to discovery cultural heritage and tourism. Some of the benefits which digital storytelling brings to the tourism industry are that it enriches tourist destinations and attractions, it preserves and explores local culture and it shows the authentic experience of cultural tourism. Furthermore, digital storytelling develops cross-cultural understanding.

In particular, we have chosen to employ an ontological model in order to realize a dynamic digital storytelling system, able to collect and elaborate social information and contents about the users giving them a personalized story based on the place they are visiting. The theoretical framework and experimental results are presented and described.

Keywords: Digital storytelling · Information retrieval · Pervasive systems

1 Introduction

Tourism is one of the most important ways to have revenue for economy of a Country: indeed, it has millions of persons, every years, all around the world, who travel into another country for a trip, different from the one where they live.

Starting from this consideration, the main aim is to improve the experience of the tourists giving the necessary tools for understanding the reality through a system that gives the correct information.

For a person who is in a place that doesn't know, is important that he can have all possible information, such as services and entertainment of the place, and he can able to orientate himself easily, knowing all of the cultural activity in that place [15].

© Springer International Publishing AG 2017
M.H.A. Au et al. (Eds.): GPC 2017, LNCS 10232, pp. 567–581, 2017.
DOI: 10.1007/978-3-319-57186-7_41

To do this, is necessary use a huge amount of data always available; understanding how is important for user, plays a critical role and is necessary filtering this data using user preference. The first problem is how we can access to the data to which the system will allow access.

Nowadays the problem is catch this data because current technologies do not allow collecting all possible information of each place on globe, however, there are many small services for the use of simple information, where for simple, means related to a specific category of data [11].

At this point, there is another difficulty, namely that of creating a system that is able to acquire information on the place where the user is located, and through all these services he can then processing and create an entirely new service.

Not all the information are used immediately but these require further processing to make them useful for our purposes [12].

The resulting system, finally, must allow a great interaction, especially in terms of content personalization.

The technique that is identified in a perfectly fitting with the requirements set out above is the Digital Storytelling, "the art of storytelling" in digital form.

The Digital Storytelling is characterized by the fact of giving to contents a paced and exciting narrative structure, but especially for the richness and variety of stimuli and content that allow to involve an extremely wide audience.

The term "digital storytelling" evoking "a story that integrates digital images, music and the author's voice in a short video or a multimedia presentation", that was proposed by Dana Atchley, founder with Joe Lambert of the Center for Digital Storytelling, who in the nineties, created a multimedia interactive system, presenting it in a theatrical performance.

The Digital Storytelling over the years has seen mainly two categories of uses: the first is based on a classical model, developed by the Center for Digital Storytelling, which provides an autobiographical narrative in digital format through an audio narration in the first person and characterized by a linear and closed structure, similar to that of traditional narrative. The other approach is characterized by a greater interactivity, which projects the public in the history allowing it to be an integral part and to be able to change the trend, all this with the aid of more media elements (images, texts, audio, video, music) without the use of an audio narration [9].

The objective of this work is to indicate an approach for the realization of a dynamic storytelling engine that can allow the dynamic supply of narrative contents, not necessarily predetermined and pertinent to the needs and the dynamic behaviors of the users. The adaptability to the context, the social networks and the mobile world represent the pivotal points, in order to give a technological solution to the digital storytelling, which combines, indeed, the adaptive, social and mobile approaches [10].

The adaptive approach inserts itself in order to enhance the idea of a narrative experience able to dynamically change in relation with the elements of the profile and the context [14]. For this purpose, it has been realized a model for the representation of all possible contexts in order to provide users of contextual resources [13]. The fundamental feature of the social component of our system is the sharing of the role of the author among many individuals, each of which, in turn, takes part into the creation of a portion or a segment of the story, but none of them can assume its paternity. Finally, we have chosen to create the system through a mobile application as it proves to be a perfect tool to have in real time all necessary information, facilitating the access to a series of information and conducting an educational role too.

In the following paragraph, we are going to analyze the main works concerning the digital storytelling. Later, we will describe a scenery as example and introduce the general architecture of the proposed model, presenting in detail each module. The paper ends with the description of a realized application and its experimentation.

2   Related Works

In this section, we are going to show several cases of use of the Digital Storytelling, in order to make the visitors' experience more interactive and engaging, proposing personalized stories using new technologies (geolocation, mobile applications, augmented reality, etc.).

In particular, the use of media and social media to share content and narrative artefacts has greatly transformed the way in which stories can be told and described ("collaborative" and "social" storytelling).

Unlike the traditional narrative in which the figure of the author and the reader are distinct and linked respectively to create the story or to suffer passively the story, in this case the reader can be the author in turn taking part in the narrative development. The concept of partnership implies "a many-hands" development of history.

With FaTe2 [2], for example, it is possible using other people's stories, compose stories collaboratively through a hypermedia space. Equipped with a web based multiuser and through the two or three dimensional virtual space, children aged 7 to 11 years old can "meet, chat, explore, play and perform storytelling activities in collaboration". The role of the boys then becomes: they are supported not only as spectators of history, but also as "storytellers". You can create characters, create dialogues in the form of comics, and edit an existing scene so changing history.

Wikinovel [1] is another case. This uses the wiki as a social means for facilitating a community of storytellers in the creation of collaborative stories. In addition to text-based social media, there are social multimedia-based media, such as Storybird, designed to facilitate students to create stories using text and images.

There are a very long sequence of "collaborative" and "social" storytelling that have specific teaching purposes and use of cultural heritage.

A prime example is given by [6], a research project funded by a partnership between the three German research institutes: the Computer Graphics Center (ZGDV eV), the Fraunhofer Institute for Computer Graphics (IGD Fh) and the European Media Laboratory (EML). The project aims to create an educational platform for the historical data. The prototype takes into account the "Thirty Years War" and what in this period happened in Heidelberg in Germany. The platform provides a variety of information about those, which were the cultural, historical, environmental, political and artistic aspects of the period considered (1618-1648). As the system is developed as an Augmented Reality (AR), the story of Geist takes place in the castle of Heidelberg.

Another example is Casting [7]: a software system that supports audio-based collaborative storytelling groups in the creation of non-linear stories. A client and a web portal constitute Casting. In particular, the client allows users to create a project team, add audio recordings, connect the audio recordings, select, and publish a linear story. The client users can retrieve the latest version of the story and synchronize their changes locally. The web portal, however, allows users to publish podcasts on the web and discuss, comment, rate and reuse audio-based stories.

What characterizes, however, the "mobile based" narratives (mobile storytelling) are the active persons who move around in physical locations by means of technological devices. In this context, the narrative can not be limited to only play a role of knowledge of the place or physical or virtual objects, but must also be articulated and be synchronized with the user movements [3]. In [4] Barbas et al. have asserted that "the biggest difference between this type of storytelling compared to traditional structures of the tale (oral, written, film and theater, hypertext, or ergodic literature) is related to the mixing of the individual imaginary and the collective imaginary with reality. The user experiences the story set in the real world and in real time. "; an example is the Project REXplorer, a real pervasive game that takes place throughout the city of Regensburg, transforming it into a huge museum. In this scenario, the games also require a new kind of storytelling that leaves free the player, but he can manage the execution of the game (the unfolding of the story): the decisions of the player are affecting the overall story of the game. In this way, the video games become a tool for the most effective learning of the traditional teaching methods [5].

3   Motivating Example

In this section, we want to describe a typical tourist example for better understanding the problem that we want to address and describe the main features of the implemented system.

Suppose a tourist who arrives for the first time at a port of a city and he/she has time available to visit the city. Upon arriving in a new place, the tourist has needed to know, in broad terms, the characteristics of the place and the reasons why this place is worthy of interest. In addition, a classic situation for a tourist is to plan of his/her activities and his/her own visits: not always a journey allows you to have the right time to completely visit a destination chosen and it is there that we are faced with the difficult of chose which attractions we can then actually visit.

The proposed system should allow the tourist to live in a complete manner the place that he/she is visiting through a real story of this place, starting from his/her story, going through the information of newspapers, finally to arrive at events the near future.

The system should not be limited to a simple list of data found on that place, but instead, has the task to present them in such a way that the user can be an active part to scrutinize the past, the present and the future.

- *Past*, the user can see a description of the places with the ability to investigate the events that have seen partecipe these places over the years, and all their history. Will be available, in appropriate category, with all the cultural attractiveness that the place offers, including details, opening hours to the public, visitor comments, etc. In addition, the application will display a history of visits that friends have done in that place.

- *Present*, the user can view the main points of interest such as restaurants, hotels or buildings used as cafe leisure and sports centers with the ability to "be accompanied" toward these places or display information such as ranking, phone number and prices. There will be a section dedicated to the weather conditions of the day with one description, temperature and ventilation. Will be available the information on the biggest news to keep informed about what is happening in the surrounding area. The system will allow you to search specific categories of activities according to their needs, such as banks, postal services, pharmacy, etc.
- *Future*, the user will have the ability to see events taking place nearby in the coming days, display the time, the date, and, in this case, "be accompanied" at the meeting point. In addition, it will be possible consulting the weather conditions for the next few days to allow better organization of plans.

4 System Architecture

In this section, we describe the architecture of the proposed system, which has the purpose to give the user a personalized tailor-made story, related to the place where he/she is.

The system architecture, shown in Fig. 1, is composed by three main blocks: a Teller Module, a Data Management Module and a Knowledge Base. It is made up of the Teller Module, divided into the search, elaboration and presentation submodules, which correspond respectively to three separate phases, which are fetch, decode and execute. The search submodule has the task of collecting the data online in order to give the elaboration submodule information on the basis of the user's current position (for example, Bing news, data from Wikipedia and users' comments on TripAdvisor and Google Places), the resources that are near him/her (e.g., a restaurant, a cinema) obtained from a general search on TripAdvisor and Google Places and information about user and his/her friends, obtained from his/her Facebook profile.

The elaboration submodule saves the data of the user and the resources received in the knowledge base, manages all received information and gives the presentation submodule data (description, news and weather forecast) about the town related to the user's current position, a list of recommended resources and places tagged by the user friends on Facebook.

Finally, the presentation module has the task of identifying and obtaining the contextual resources and proposing, as a well-structured story, all these personalized, adaptive and contextual information. The obtained final result is presented to the user through a mobile application.

The Knowledge Base is a special type of database for the management of knowledge and information: it is continuously updated by the results obtained through interaction with the application (user feedback), with elaboration submodule (which stores the data of the user and of the resources) and with the Data Management Module. The Knowledge Base is composed of two components: in particular, "Users", representing all users of

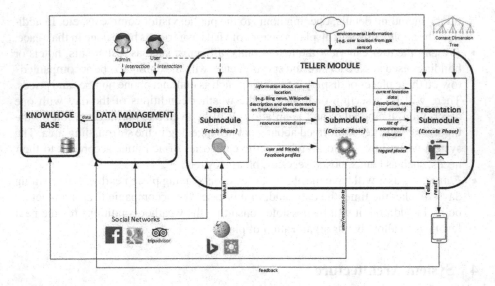

Fig. 1. System architecture

the application and "Resources", which forms all the points of interest; and finally the Data Management Module, used both by the administrators of the app and the users themselves. This module interacts with TripAdvisor, Facebook and Google API and deals with some important issues, including points of interest management, where the insertion can be done directly from map, manually or by search of interests.

In the following paragraph, all the submodules of the Teller Module will be analyzed in detail.

4.1 Teller Module

The Teller Module, consists of three sequential phases: fetch, where information of interest are collected; decode, which allows their interpretation and elaboration; execute, thanks to which the elaborated and personalized information is contextualized and finally proposed.

1. *Fetch phase*: The fetch phase is made up of three main operations: the acquisition of news about the current position, the search for resources and the acquisition of the profile and of the user's interests.

   As regards the first operation, initially it is gathered the position of the user through the GPS sensor of his/her mobile device: it is necessary to use a service of Reverse Geocoding, that is the process of translation of the geographical coordinates in a 'human-readable' address, made available by the Google Maps API.

   Then, to have the description of the locality based on the gathered position, information from Wikipedia has been chosen, in particular using the MediaWiki's RESTful web service API: an easy access to services, data and metadata through HTTP requests. Often, some coordinates of reference are associated to the pages of Wikipedia and our approach exploits this property: when you make a research of a page related to a village or a city, you obtain the nearest to the user's coordinates. The story to present is then enriched with news about the place, using Bing API, with weather information, through OpenWeatherMap and with the experiences lived by other users, using their comments on TripAdvisor and Google Places.

Then, it is made the research of the resources from two sources: TripAdvisor and Google Places. In the first case, model uses the map method of the TripAdvisor API, which allows looking for attractions (museums, sports structures, shops, etc.), hotels and restaurants through, respectively, the map attractions, map hotels and map restaurant methods. In case the user does not have a social account, he/she can get the main points of interest of the places where he/she is using the location-mapper method of the TripAdvisor API. In the second case, research is done from Google Places: our model uses nearby search and details methods of its API.

Finally, for the personalization of information, it is exploited the third operation of the fetch phase of our module, whose objective is to access the social data of the user to get, for example, his/her profile, likes, events and preferred places, friends. This happens using the Facebook API and the analysis of some principal methods, such as user likes, user friends, user events and tagged places.

2. *Decode phase*: The decode phase consists in the data elaboration: in particular, friendship calculation, likes matching and resources computing form it.

The friendship calculation is based on an algorithm of ours that considers the social interactions among the users and allows identifying a value of social friendship among friends on Facebook, used then to understand how much a friend of ours can influence us on the choice of a place or on the appreciation towards a category of interest.

The second operation consists in the management of information get from Facebook: the purpose is to identify, based on the likes that the user puts on the pages of the social network, of the categories of interest. This operation is extremely important because it allows identifying the user's tastes and preferences.

In particular, to determine the user's interests, as well as the categories to recommend, we consider his/her most recent likes on the pages of the Social Network: to any like it corresponds a specific subcategory of Facebook that our system associates to our category of interest; for example, to a like on a page related to an art gallery or a painter it will correspond an occurrence of the category Art & Culture. Then, the system makes a matching between the obtained categories of interest and the typologies of TripAdvisor and Google Places, in order to have the possibility to make specific researches of resources about these sources.

Finally, through the third operation of the decode phase, it is possible to calculate the index of approval towards the categories of interest and the index of recommendation towards the single obtained resources.

In order to model our system, we have chosen to use an ontological representation. On this subject, the W3C has defined a series of recommendations for the realization of the semantic web, among which an oriented and tagged graph model for the representation of the web resources (RDF), a specific language for the creation of ontologies (OWL), tools able to elaborate interference processes starting from an ontological model

(Reasoners), a tool of query for the information retrieval (SPARQL Protocol and Rdf Query Language).

Therefore, the base unit used to represent in a flexible way any kind of information is given by the so-called statement, that is, a triple like:

Subject – Predicate – Object

where the subject is a resource (identified in univocal way through a URI - Uniform Resource Identifier), the predicate is a feature and the object is another resource or a value.

On the basis of what has been said, it is possible to define a directed graph, shown in Fig. 2, in order to formulate a thorough and rigorous conceptual scheme in the field of the considered application domain.

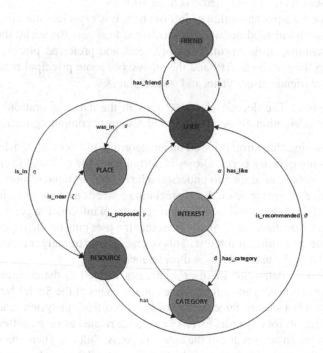

Fig. 2. Directed graph for the representation of the considered application domain

As it can be noticed from the figure, the graph is made of five nodes:

- *User* is a user of the system (e.g., instances of User: Alexander, Jack, George, …);
- *Interest* is a typology of interest that is associated to a LIKE of the user (instances of Interest: school, university, pizza, night club, …);
- *Category* represents a set of interests (e.g., culture, restaurant, nightlife, …);
- *Place* is any place, represented by a couple of geographical coordinates, to which TAGs of the users are associated (Salerno, University of Salerno, …);

- **Resource** is any resource, with a specific category, which can be proposed to the user (the Greek Temples of Paestum, the restaurant 'Gusto Italiano', …). The nodes are connected through some arches that represent the predicates:
- **has_friend**: an user can have one or more friends;
- **has_like**: an user can be interested in one or more typologies of interest;
- **has_category**: to any typology of interest one or more categories are associated;
- **is_proposed**: the categories are proposed to the user;
- **was_in**: an user has been in a determined place;
- **is_near**: a place is near a resource;
- **is_in**: a user can be in a resource;
- **is_recommended**: the resources are recommended to the user.

Starting from the directed graph made up of concepts (nodes) and relations (arches), it has been then defined a system giving to any relation a value between 0 and 1 (weighted graph):

- α = **weight_ui** represents the number of LIKEs of a *user u* concerning a specific typology of *interest i* ($\alpha \geq 0$, $\alpha \in N$);
- β = **weight_ic** is the degree of correspondence between a typology of *interest i* and a *category c* ($0 \leq \beta \geq 1$);
- γ = **weight_cu** represents the degree of recommendation of a *category c* to a *user u* ($0 \leq \gamma \geq 1$);
- δ = **weight_uf** represents the degree of friendship between a *user u* and another *user f* ($0 \leq \delta \geq 1$);
- ε = **weight_up** is the number of TAGs of the *user u* in the *place p* ($\varepsilon \geq 0$, $\varepsilon \in N$);
- ζ = **weight_pr** is the degree of nearness of a *place p* to a *resource r* ($0 \leq \zeta \geq 1$, with $\zeta = 1$ if $p \equiv r$);
- η = **weight_ur** represents the proximity of a *user u* to a *resource r* ($0 \leq \eta \geq 1$, with $\eta = 1$ if u is in r);
- θ = **weight_ru** represents the degree of recommendation of a *POI r* to a *user u* ($0 \leq \theta \geq 1$).

Now, the attention is going to focus on the level of friendship, that is, on the weight of the relation between the two users.

On this subject, not all the friends influence in the same way, but it needs to consider a friendship index among the users: the more a user is friend with another, the more the interests of the friend will influence the satisfaction of a category for the same user.

In order to do this, first of all it is useful to be aware that friendship is not a necessarily reflexive relation, in fact, it is possible that the user A considers the user B as 'best friend' while the user B considers 'friend' the user A.

In particular, the weight of friendship between current user and a friend of his/hers can be calculated as the friendship obtained with the friend a divided by the total of the friendship with all the friends:

$$FS = \frac{F_a}{\sum_{a=1}^{M} F_a} \tag{1}$$

where a is the friend on Facebook and M the total number of the friends. The friendship with the friend a is calculated as:

$$F_a = \sum_{i=1}^{N} w_i f(x_{a,i})$$ (2)

where i is the time of interaction (1 = like, 2 = event, 3 = photo); N is the total number of typologies of interactions (N = 3); w (communication parameter) represents the weight associated to any typology of interaction, in particular:

$$\sum_{i=1}^{N} w_i = 1 \text{ and } wi = \{0.1 \text{ for } i = 1, 0.2 \text{ for } i = 2, 0.7 \text{ for } i = 3\}$$

finally, the function that calculates xa, i, which is the number of interactions of a certain type i with the friend a, is the following:

$$f(x_{a,i}) = 1 - \frac{1}{\log(1 + X_i)} * \log\left[1 + (X_i - x_{a,i})\right]$$ (3)

where Xi is the total number of interactions of a certain type with the friends. In practice, if x = 0 (null interaction with the friend a), it is obtained that f(x) = 0, otherwise x = X (highest interaction with the friend a), we have that f(x) = 1.

Finally, in this way, it has been possible to implement a reasoner able to calculate resources for the user, depending on the identified categories of interest.

The satisfaction index Icat of a category for a user represents his/her interest towards a specific category and it defined as follows:

$$I_{cat._{u,c}} = \sum_{h=1}^{n.interests_u} \alpha_{u,i_k} * \beta_{i_{k,c}}$$ (4)

$$\bar{I}_{cat._{u,c}} = \frac{I_{cat._{u,c}}}{\sum_{k=1}^{n.categories} I_{cat._{u,c_k}}}$$ (5)

$$I_{cat._{u/\bar{u},c}} = I_{cat._{u,c}} + \sum_{j=1}^{n.friends_u} \delta_{u,\bar{u}} * I_{cat._{\bar{u},c}}$$ (6)

$$\bar{I}_{cat._{u/\bar{u},c}} = \frac{I_{cat._{u/\bar{u},c}}}{\sum_{k=1}^{n.categories} I_{cat._{u/\bar{u},c_k}}}$$ (7)

Equations (4, 5, 6, 7) are calculated considering the number of likes of the user u and of his/her friends ū related to social pages associated to a typology of interests I and the correspondence index of this towards the same category c.

In particular, (1) considers the individual user, (2) corresponds to (1) normalized, (3) also considers the user's friends, finally, (4) represents the (3) normalized.

The recommendation index Ires of a resource represents the user's potential satisfaction towards a specific resource and it defined as follows:

$$I_{res._{u,r_c}} = \bar{I}_{cat._{u,c}} + \left(\eta_{u,r_c} * \frac{rat}{5} + \frac{\sum \zeta_{p_0,r_c} * \delta_{u,\bar{u}}}{n.tagged\ places} \right) \quad (8)$$

$$\bar{I}_{res._{u,r_c}} = (w_{cat.} * \bar{I}_{cat._{u,c}}) + w_{res.} * [\left(\eta_{u,r_c} * \frac{rat}{5} \right) + \frac{\sum \zeta_{p_0,r_c} * \delta_{u,\bar{u}}}{n.tagged\ places}] \quad (9)$$

Equations (8, 9) are defined through the normalized index of category, the proximity of the resources from the user, the rating rat of the resource and the nearness of the resource to the places tagged p by a user friend ū.

In particular, in (9) w_{cat} and w_{res} represent respectively the associated weights with the first and second addend.

Once obtained the categories of reference, the resources are matched and searched on TripAdvisor and Google Places.

The model described until now gives only a conceptual framework that is needed to describe resources that can be elaborated by a computer, but in order that this can really happen, it is necessary a syntax that allows us to formalize the model and the computer to read and elaborate it. The W3C defines the XML syntax as suitable for this purpose. This syntax, called "XML/RDF", allows representing the graph through a document written in XML.

In particular, to describe all the personal information of the users (collected and calculated following the proposed model), it is possible to use the standard Friend of a friend (FOAF). Therefore, the FOAF descriptions include the main personal data of the user, the geographical localization, his/her interests, the names and the contacts of the friends, etc.

3. *Fetch phase*: The third phase of the process, execute, is based on the contextualization of the resources and presentation of personalized information. In this last phase, in fact, there are two operations: Context Dimension Tree filtering and information presentation.

In fact, to can access the set of available statements, it is necessary to have a tool that allows interrogating this set: this tool is the query language SPARQL.

As discussed before, the aim is to realize an adaptive Storytelling. Therefore, in order to make contextualized queries, it is necessary to define a model for the representation and management of the context itself, which allows filtering the resources obtained in the decode phase, on the basis of contextual parameters: this operations are made through the Context Dimension Tree (CDT) [8]. It is a tree composed of a triad <r; N; A> where r indicates its root, N is the set of nodes of which it is made of and A is the set of arcs joining these nodes. CDT is used to be able to represent, in a graphic form, all possible contexts that you may have within an application.

Finally, on the basis of the obtained results, through the operation of information presentation, personalized resources will be proposed to the user, within the personalized story. Therefore, the result shows itself like a well-organized story that presents a general introduction about the place reached by the user, enriched with the experiences shared by other users, a list of the main suggested attractions and information about the near places visited by the friends.

5 An Adaptive Telling App

The system described so far is made available for user via a mobile application, which must behave like a modern travel guide. This application must allow the user to view information such as description of the place, the history, attractions to visit and see the events that will be held and the friends who visited the place, in a "social" view, filtering the information based on profile.

This application, therefore, allows the user to view the past, present and the future of location where he/she is, everything in terms of history, attractiveness, weather, news, visits of friends and events. As a tour guide that respects, the application must accompany the user in the place visited, which this translates in features a software into portability and access at anytime from anywhere.

It is possible to identify the three main modes of interaction listed below:

- *The visits*, a user who visits places will make partecipe his/her friends with his/her visit and, therefore, will alter the contents displayed on the mobile devices of these.
- *The navigation*, through the application interface, the user can choose to display information on points of interest, or go there, or delve into the history of these places.
- *The personalization*, the user will have the option to filter the content that will be displayed in the application according to him/her tastes and preferences. Customizing the display contents can be done in two ways: manual and automatic. The first is realized in a dedicated settings page: in this page the user can select from one hand the categories of points of interest that subsequently he/she will intend visualize during the navigation, on the other hand, he/she will be able to select the cuisine that he/she likes and will give greater visibility to the restaurants who practice. The second, which happens to be one of the characterizing features of the application, will completely "alone" to analyze and then select the user's preferences based on their profile. However, it will not be required to set the preferences automatically: the user will have a page that display the attractiveness recommended for him/her in which the amount of "tips" will be in proportion to the user to that category of points of interest.

The screenshots of the application are presented in Fig. 3.

Fig. 3. Screenshots of the application

6   Experimental Results

Now, we are going to present the conducted analysis, using the realized App, to understand the influence on the user experience of the proposed digital storytelling model.

The 200 participants, recruited by invitation, are above all students or university professors and do not know the subject of the study. All live in different towns, in Italy or abroad, are between 18 and 57 years old, are registered to Facebook and have an Android or Apple mobile device.

The experimental phase has the task of evaluating the total storytelling model. Initially, the App has been distributed and installed by all the participants, to whom it has been requested to log in with Facebook credentials. After having interacted for some days with the application, the participants have then answered on the basis of the Likert scale to seven statements: (1) the system gives right information about the narration of the place; (2) the system has included in my profile the categories I am mainly interested in; (3) it has proposed me points of interest I am mainly interested in; (4) the experience of friends and other users has been useful for me; (5) the calculation of the social friendship is reliable and truthful compared to my real relationships; (6) the system is immediate and user-friendly; (7) the narration has been exhaustive through a personalized guide. Table 1 presents a synthesis of the answers of the participants to each declaration.

Table 1. Experimental results

Answer	1	2	3	4	5	6	7
Strongly agree	89	68	58	71	51	80	63
Agree	67	82	92	77	84	63	75
Neither agree nor disagree	19	24	14	31	28	26	27
Disagree	14	19	25	15	20	19	20
Strongly disagree	11	7	11	6	17	12	15

As shown in this table, of the 200 participants who have interacted with the application, many agree and/or strongly agree that the system gives appropriate information about the place, supplies categories of interest and the resources depending on their preferences, calculates a level of reliable friendship and the final narration results complete and pertinent. Instead, only in few cases, the participants do not are particularly satisfied.

7   Conclusions

In the first part of this paper, it has been briefly described digital storytelling, its history and how it is implemented in some examples of related works. Then, it has been proceeded to describe digital storytelling as a practical tool for the tourism and the impact of digital storytelling in such different fields, as cultural heritage. Therefore, it has been depicted a practical example of the conception and development of an activity based on digital storytelling for tourism.

In particular, it has been introduced an original approach for an enhanced visit experience through a real case, developing a mobile application. This application, which must behave like a modern travel guide, allows the user to view the past, present and the future of location where he/she is, everything in terms of history, attractiveness, weather, news, visits of friends and events, filtering these information based on user profile and contextual data.

Finally, it has been described the experimental process used to introduce our participants to the world of digital storytelling and to evaluate our approach.

In conclusion, it can be stated that the experience of using our mobile application was well accepted by the majority of the experimental campaign participants who were in agreement with test statements. For future versions, it can be planned to enhance the set of items in the story and the range of options for the user, thus allowing for different perspectives on the story. In order to obtain a more detailed personalized story, it can be included other social factors as well as emotions for the generation of user profiles and story navigation.

References

1. Liu, C.C., Liu, K.P., Chen, W.H., Lin, C.P., Chen, G.D.: Collaborative storytelling experiences in social media: influence of peer assistance mechanisms. Comput. Educ. **57**(2), 1544–1556 (2011)
2. Garzotto, F., Forfori, M.: FaTe2: storytelling edutainment experiences in 2D and 3D collaborative spaces. In: Proceedings of the 2006 Conference on Interaction design and children. ACM, pp. 113–116 (2006)
3. Lombardo, V., Damiano, R.: Storytelling on mobile devices for cultural heritage. New Rev. Hypermedia Multimedia **18**(1–2), 11–35 (2012)
4. Barbas, H. Correia, N.: Documenting InStory–mobile storytelling in a cultural heritage environment. In: 1st European Workshop on Intelligent Technologies for Cultural Heritage Exploitation, 17th European Conference on Artificial Intelligence, Riva del Garda, Italy, pp. 1–5 (2006)
5. Champagnat, R., Delmas, G., Augeraud, M.: A storytelling model for educational games. In: Proceedings of the First International Workshop on Story-Telling and Educational Games (STEG 2008) (2008)
6. Braun, N.: Storytelling in collaborative augmented reality environments. In: Proceedings of the 11th International Conference in Central Europe on Computer Graphics, Visualization and Computer Vision (2003). Geist
7. Schumann, J., Buttler, T., Lukosch, S.: Supporting asynchronous workspace awareness by visualizing the story evolution in collaborative storytelling. In: Kolfschoten, G., Herrmann, T., Lukosch, S. (eds.) CRIWG 2010. LNCS, vol. 6257, pp. 218–232. Springer, Heidelberg (2010). doi:10.1007/978-3-642-15714-1_17
8. Tanca, L., Bolchini, C., Curino, C., Schreiber, F.A.: Context integration for mobile data tailoring. In: Italian Symposium on Database Systems (SEBD), pp. 48–55 (2006)
9. Colace, F., Foggia, P., Percannella, G.: A probabilistic framework for TV-news stories detection and classification. In: IEEE International Conference on Multimedia and Expo (ICME), pp. 1350–1353 (2005). art. no. 1521680

10. Colace, F., De Santo, M., Greco, L., Moscato, V., Picariello, A.: A collaborative user-centered framework for recommending items in Online Social Networks. Comput. Hum. Behav. **51**, 694–704 (2015)
11. Colace, F., De Santo, M., Greco, L.: An adaptive product configurator based on slow intelligence approach. Int. J. Metadata Semant. Ontol. **9**(2), 128–137 (2014)
12. Colace, F., De Santo, M., Greco, L., Napoletano, P.: Weighted word pairs for query expansion. Inf. Process. Manage. **51**(1), 179–193 (2015)
13. Chang, S.K., Yung, D., Colace, F., Greco, L., Lemma, S., Lombardi, M.: An adaptive contextual recommender system: a slow intelligence perspective. In: Proceedings of the International Conference on Software Engineering and Knowledge Engineering (SEKE), pp. 64–71 (2015)
14. Colace, F., Greco, L., Lemma, S., Lombardi, M., Amato, F., Moscato, V., Picariello, A.: Contextual aware computing and tourism: a case study. In: Proceedings of the 11th International Conference on Signal-Image Technology and Internet-Based Systems (SITIS), pp. 804–808 (2015). art. no. 7400655
15. Colace, F., De Santo, M., Lemma, S., Lombardi, M., Rossi, A., Santoriello, A., Terribile, A., Vigorito, M.: How to describe cultural heritage resources in the web 2.0 Era?. In: Proceedings of the 11th International Conference on Signal-Image Technology and Internet-Based Systems (SITIS), pp. 809–815 (2015). art. no. 7400656

Healthcare Support Systems

Design of a Secure Emergency Communication System Based on Cloud for Pregnancy

Guan-Chen Li[1], Chin-Ling Chen[2,3($\boxtimes$)], Feng Lin[1], Jungpil Shin[4], and Cheng Gu[5]

[1] School of Information and Communication Engineering,
Shenyang Aerospace University, Liaoning, China
Chinalgc18@gmail.com, linfeng@sau.edu.cn
[2] Department of Computer Science and Information Engineering,
Chaoyang University of Technology, Taichung, Taiwan (R.O.C.)
clc@mail.cuyt.edu.tw
[3] School of Information Engineering, Changchun University of Technology,
Changchun, 130600 Jilin, China
[4] Graduate School of Computer Science and Engineering, The University of Aizu,
Tsuruga, Ikki-Machi, Aizuwakamatsu, Fukushima 965-8580, Japan
jpshin@u-aizu.ac.jp
[5] College of Electronic and Communication Engineering,
Tianjin Normal University, Tianjing, China
925682951@qq.com

Abstract. Due to the high maternal mortality, it is particularly necessary to attend pregnant woman by emergency communication system as timely treatment to avoid maternal deaths. In this paper, we propose an emergency communication system based on cloud computing and mobile devices for a pregnant woman to have a more efficiently and timely treatment. Moreover, security is the utmost important issue. The proposed scheme integrates proxy authorization of the Schnorr's signature, symmetric encryption technology, a message authentication code, and RFC 2631 to protect the communication messages and the pregnant woman's privacy not been revealed or stolen.

Keywords: RFC 2631 · Schnorr's signature · Cloud · Emergency

1 Introduction

With the rapid development of technology, the recent developments of network communication and cloud computing technologies have become a motivating force for the most important innovations in our society. Cloud computing can increase the speed of a deployed application and increase advance, speed up the computational ability and increase the security via security protocol [1]. Using cloud computing can provide an emergency communication for pregnancy to reduce maternal mortality during pregnancy or childbirth to achieve eugenics.

© Springer International Publishing AG 2017
M.H.A. Au et al. (Eds.): GPC 2017, LNCS 10232, pp. 585–595, 2017.
DOI: 10.1007/978-3-319-57186-7_42

The World Health Organization (WHO) reported that about 830 women die of complications related to pregnancy or childbirth globally every day. By the end of 2015, about 303,000 women had died during the period of their pregnancy, at childbirth or after childbirth [2]. It is particularly important that all pregnant women should be concerted by skillful antenatal care as timely controlling.

In an environment of emergency communication systems for pregnancy, the fundamental characteristics are that authority can provide more secure and efficient system. At first, message confidentiality and integrity are the most important [3]. Otherwise, if data confidentiality is compromised, it would easily causes misperceptions or unexpected circumstances, especially in an emergency application [4]. Sailunaz et al. [5] proposed a Cloud based Medical system (CMED), that consisting of both healthcare center and a portable healthcare service with a Community Health Worker (CHW), but we found their scheme cannot defend the replay attack and achieve non-repudiation issue. Mould-Millman et al. [6] proposed an Emergency Medical Dispatch (EMD) systems are a crucial component of effective Emergency Medical Services (EMS) systems for public which can access to out-of-hospital emergency care resources. But they failed to propose a secure protocol to achieve an emergency communication.

In our proposed system, we use cloud as a trusted third party that stores the pregnancy's Electronic Medical Record (EMR). When the pregnant woman falls into a dangerous situation, she can inform an emergency service center to immediately take action to arrange an appropriate hospital. We also propose a proxy signature [7] application based on the Schnorr's signature [8] to make data sharing more effectively for the hospital to download pregnancy's EMR from cloud to prepare the first aid measures.

2   Preliminary

In this section, we also briefly review the Schnorr's signature [9]. The security issue has been examined in the Random Oracle Model [10] under the Discrete Logarithm assumption by Pointcheval and Stern [11]. Because the Schnorr's method is appropriate for cloud-based applications, we choose to set up this appliance in our scheme.

2.1   Review the Schnorr's Signature

Let p and q are two large prime numbers with $q|(p-1)$. Let g is an element of multiplicative subgroup of order q in $\mathbb{Z}_q^*$; $h(\cdot)$ is a collision resistant one-way hash function. Next, we assume that a signer holds a private key SK, and the public key is $PK = g^{-SK} \bmod p$. The signer wants to sign a message m and executes the following steps.

1.   The signing process are described as follows:
     a.   Choose a nonce value $N \in \mathbb{Z}_q^*$.
     b.   Compute $S = h(m, g^N) \bmod p$.
     c.   Compute $E = (SK \cdot S) + N) \bmod p$.
     d.   The valid signed message is (S, E).

2. Verification process:
   a. Compute $V = g^E \cdot PK^S$
   b. The validity of signature is verified by: $h(m, V) \overset{?}{=} S$.

3 Our Scheme

In our scheme, we propose an emergency communication system involving four parties (cloud, pregnant woman, emergency service center and hospital) for providing timely treatment to avoid maternal deaths when dealing with the emergency event of pregnancy cases. In that case the pregnant woman can be quickly treated.

3.1 The Architecture of a Secure and Effective Emergency System

1. Cloud (C): A trusted third party provided by the cloud server of department of health that stores the pregnancy's electronic medical record (EMR).
2. Pregnant woman (P): A pregnant woman sends a message to the emergency service center when having childbirth or being in danger via a mobile device.
3. Emergency Service Center (ESC): Once receiving the pregnant woman's emergency message, the emergency service center reports the message to request a suitable hospital to provide a first aid, and accepts the delegation from the pregnant woman to communicate with an appropriate hospital.
4. Hospital (H): After receiving an emergency message from ESC, the hospital simultaneously downloads the EMR from the cloud and appoints a doctor to prepare to make a diagnosis.

The processes of our scheme are described as follows:

Step 1: First, the pregnant woman, the hospital and Emergency Service Center (ESC) have to register to be a legal user of the cloud.
Step 2: The pregnant woman goes to hospital to have an examination and creates her EMR to store it in the cloud.
Step 3: Before giving birth or being in danger, the pregnant woman informs the emergency service center by the mobile device.
Step 4: Upon receiving the emergency message from the pregnant woman, the emergency service center immediately sends a message to a suitable hospital to prepare a timely treatment.
Step 5: Delegation from the pregnant woman, the cloud server takes the EMR out for the hospital staff to download it that can immediately start its preparations for the pregnant woman.

3.2 Construct Session Key Model

In this paper, we use the RFC 2631 protocol [12] to build the session keys. In our scheme, we use the session key in three situations. First, the pregnant woman constructs a session key K_{P-ESC} with the ESC to protect the message when sending the proxy authorization message to the ESC. Second, the ESC and cloud use the session key K_{C-ESC} to protect the proxy signature. Third, the cloud and the hospital use the session key K_{C-H} to protect the security of the transmission EMR (Fig. 1).

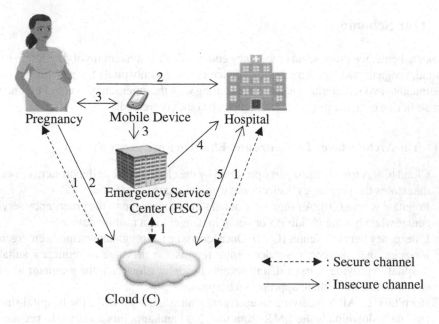

Fig. 1. The architecture of our scheme

The following notations are used throughout this study.

ID_X	X's identity
K_{ms}	the master private key of cloud
g	an element of order q in $\mathbb{Z}_q^*$
C_i	the ith cipher text
r_i	an ith random numbers
N_X	a nonce value generated by X
m_{cm}	the contact message
x	the proxy secret key
y	the proxy public key
m_E	the emergency message
T_i	the ith timestamp
$\oplus$	exclusive-or operation
$+$	addition operator
$h(\cdot)$	the one-way hash function
PW_P	the password of the pregnant woman
PK_X, SK_X	the public key and private key of X
K_{X-Y}	the session key between by X and Y

p, q:	two large prime number with $q \mid (p-1)$
$E_X(\cdot)$	symmetric encryption or algorithm
$D_X(\cdot)$	symmetric decryption algorithm
MAC_i	the ith message authentication code
$Time_i$	the ith finished time of diagnosis
Sig_X	the digital signature of X
m_V	the verification message
$Cert_P$	the certificate of the pregnant woman
$A \overset{?}{\leq} B$	determine if A is less or equal to B
$A \overset{?}{=} B$	determine whether A is equal to B

3.3 Registration Phase

In our scheme, the pregnant woman and ESC have to register with cloud to be a legal user using their identities.

Step 1: The pregnant woman offers the ID_P to the cloud to be a legal identity.

Step 2: When receiving the pregnant woman's identity ID_P, the cloud generates the master secret key K_{ms} and a nonce value $N_C \in \mathbb{Z}_q^*$, and then computes U, X, Y, Z as follows:

$$U = h(N_C, K_{ms}) \tag{1}$$

$$X = h(ID_P, h(PW_P)) \tag{2}$$

$$Y = U \oplus X \tag{3}$$

$$Z = (ID_P, h(PW_P)) \oplus U \tag{4}$$

$$Ep = ID_P + (EMR, Time_1) \tag{5}$$

The CS stores V, and sends the message $(Y, Z, h(.))$ to the pregnant woman's mobile device.

Step 3: The emergency service center sends the ID_{ESC} to cloud, the cloud computes the following parameters:

$$S_C = h(ID_{ESC}, g^{N_C}) \bmod p \tag{6}$$

$$E_C = ((SK_C \cdot S_C) + N_C) \bmod q \tag{7}$$

$$MAC_1 = h(ID_C, N_C, K_{ESC-C}) \tag{8}$$

Then CS stores the (ID_C, MAC_1) and sends the message (S_C, E_C, MAC_1) to the ESC.

Step 4: When acquiring the message, the ESC checks the validation as follows:

$$V = g^{E_c} \cdot PK^{S_c} \bmod p \tag{9}$$

$$h(ID_{ESC}, g^{N_c}) \overset{?}{=} h(ID_{ESC}, V) \tag{10}$$

3.4 Event Reporting and Delegation Phase

In this phase, the pregnant woman has to login the mobile device for the ESC to check the legality firstly. When the pregnant woman is in danger situation, she sends the emergency message to the ESC and delegates the ESC to communicate with cloud.

Step 1: The pregnant woman passes her own identity $ID_P{}'$ and password $PW_P{}'$ to login the mobile device for the mobile device to compute:

$$X' = h(ID'_P, h(PW'_P)) \tag{11}$$

$$U' = Y \oplus X' \tag{12}$$

$$Z' = X' \oplus U' \tag{13}$$

Then, the mobile device makes a comparison

$$Z \overset{?}{=} Z' \tag{14}$$

If the Eq. 14 is hold, it means the pregnant woman is the legal owner of the mobile device

Step 2: The pregnant woman generates a nonce $N_P \in \mathbb{Z}_q^*$ and uses the session key to encrypt a certificate $Cert_P$ and a contact address message m_{cm} (e.g. phone number of her family, home address et.), and then computes the following factors:

$$S_P = h(ID_P, Cert_P, g^{N_P}) \bmod p \tag{15}$$

$$E_P = (SK_P \cdot S_P) + N_P) \bmod q \tag{16}$$

$$C_1 = E_{K_{P-ESC}}(Cert_P, S_P, E_P, m_{cm}) \tag{17}$$

Afterward, the pregnant woman sends the message (C_1, ID_P) to the ESC.

Step 3: The ESC generates a random number r_1 and then generates a message authentication code MAC_2 as follows:

$$MAC_2 = h(ID_P, r_1, C_1, K_{P-ESC}) \tag{18}$$

The ESC sends the MAC_2 to the pregnant woman and stores MAC_2 in the database.

Step 4: Once the pregnant woman is time to childbirth, she sends the emergency message and the message authentication code MAC_2 to the ESC through the mobile device.

Step 5: After receiving the message (C_1, ID_P, MAC_2), the ESC uses the session key K_{P-ESC} to decrypt the message C_1

$$(Cert_P, S_P, E_P, m_{cm}, T_1) = D_{K_{P-C}}(C_1) \tag{19}$$

the ESC computes MAC_2'

$$MAC_2' = h(ID_P, r_1, C_1, K_{P-ESC}) \tag{20}$$

And then verifies the validity of $Cert_P$, and ID_P using S_P, E_P and MAC_2 as follows

$$MAC_2' \overset{?}{=} MAC_2 \tag{21}$$

$$V_P = g^{E_P} \cdot PK_P^{S_P} \bmod p \tag{22}$$

$$S_P \overset{?}{=} h(ID_P, Cert_P, V_P) \tag{23}$$

If the above Eqs. 21, and 23 are right, the ESC immediately reports the event to the hospital.

3.5 Verification and Diagnosing Phase

At this phase, the cloud verifies the ESC's identity via a proxy signature and sends the EMR to the hospital for a doctor to download via the authority from cloud. After diagnosing, doctor updates the latest EMR to a new EMR_{new}.

Step 1: The ESC generates a nonce $N_{ESC} \in \mathbb{Z}_q^*$ and computes the proxy secret key x to sign a verification message m_V as follows:

$$x = (E_P + E_C) \bmod q \tag{24}$$

$$m_V = (E_P, E_C, S_P, S_C, Cert_P, ID_{ESC}, ID_P, ID_H, m_{ca}) \tag{25}$$

$$S_{pro} = h(m_V, g^{N_{ESC}}) \bmod p \tag{26}$$

$$E_{pro} = (x \cdot S_{pro}) + N_C \bmod q \tag{27}$$

$$Sig_{m_V} = (S_{pro}, E_{pro}) \tag{28}$$

$$C_2 = E_{K_{C-ESC}}(m_V, Sig_{m_V}) \tag{29}$$

Afterwards, the ESC sends $(ID_{ESC}, C_2, MAC_1, ID_H)$ to the appointed hospital.

Step 2:   After receiving the message, the hospital uploads the message $(ID_{ESC}, C_2, MAC_1, ID_H)$ to the cloud.

Step 3:   When receiving the message, the cloud checks the message's validity by MAC_1 firstly:

$$MAC_1' = h(ID_C, N_C, K_{C-ESS}) \tag{30}$$

$$MAC_1' \overset{?}{=} MAC_1 \tag{31}$$

If the Eq. 31 is right, it means the identity of ESC is correct, and then the cloud can use the ID_{ESC} to find the corresponding session key K_{C-ESS} to decrypt message C_2 as follows:

$$(m_V, Sig_{mv}) = D_{K_{C-ESS}}(C_2) \tag{32}$$

After decrypting the message C_2, the cloud checks $Cert_P$ of the pregnant woman, verifies the correction of the proxy signature by proxy's public key y and checks the validation of the signature as follows:

$$V_P = g^{E_P} \cdot PK_P^{S_P} \bmod p \tag{33}$$

$$S_P \overset{?}{=} h(ID_P, Cert_P, V_P) \tag{34}$$

$$y = g^{-(E_P + E_C)} \bmod p \tag{35}$$

$$V_{pro} = g^{E_{Pro}} \cdot y^{S_{Pro}} \bmod p \tag{36}$$

$$S_{pro} \overset{?}{=} h(m_V, V_{pro}) \tag{37}$$

If Eqs. 34 and 37 are right, the cloud according to the m_V to search if there are the same identities (ID_P, ID_H) in the cloud database. If the identities are legal, the cloud sends the EMR, based on $E_P = ID_P + (EMR, Time_1)$ which is stored in cloud to the hospital, and uses the session key K_{H-C} to encrypt the EMR:

$$C_3 = E_{K_{H-C}}(Time_1, EMR, ID_P, T_1) \tag{38}$$

Then cloud sends the C_3, ID_P and timestamp T_1 to the hospital for a doctor to prepare a treatment for the pregnant woman.

Step 4:   When receiving the encrypt message C_3 at T_2, the doctor of the hospital verifies T_1 as follows:

$$T_2 - T_1 \overset{?}{\leq} \Delta T \tag{39}$$

If the verification Eq. 39 holds, the doctor decrypts the message as follows:

$$(Time_1, EMR, ID_P, T_1) = D_{K_{H-C}}(C_3) \tag{40}$$

4   Security Issues

In this section, we describe the security analysis of the proposed scheme. As the following descriptions, our scheme can withstand various possible attacks and conform to the security requirements.

1. Known attacks
a. *replay attack.*
   A replay attack is malevolently repeated a valid message when transmission. In our scheme, we employ the timestamp and use the nonces N_C and N_{ESC} to withstand the replay attack as follows:

$$MAC_1 = h(ID_C, N_C, K_{ESC-C}) \tag{8}$$

$$MAC_2 = h(ID_P, N_{ESC}, C_1, K_{P-ESC}) \tag{18}$$

$$T_2 - T_1 \overset{?}{\leq} \Delta T \tag{39}$$

Thus, our scheme can successfully withstand the replay attack.
b. *Defend man-in-the-middle attack.*
   This attack is a form which an attacker spies the message between each parties to control the entire communication. In our scheme, we use the session key K_{P-ESC}, K_{C-ESC}, and K_{C-H} to protect important messages as follows:

$$C_1 = E_{K_{P-ESC}}(Cert_P, S_P, E_P, m_{cm}) \tag{17}$$

$$C_2 = E_{K_{C-ESC}}(m_V, Sig_{mv}) \tag{29}$$

$$C_3 = E_{K_{H-C}}(Time_1, EMR, ID_P, T_1) \tag{38}$$

By the above equations, the attacker cannot intercept the important messages which are protected by the session key.
c. *Defend password guessing attack.*
   In our scheme, the security of the mobile device of the user is protected by the password. We assume the attacker knows the result of $X = h(ID_P, h(PW_P))$. Due to the password protected by the one-way hash function, it is impossible for him/her to guess the pregnant woman's password to complete the attack.
d. *Defend mobile device lost attacks.*
   In our scheme, if the pregnant woman's mobile device is lost and held by an attacker, based on the password guessing attack that the attacker cannot guess the password

to pass the password authentication, the pregnant woman need not to worry the illegal use of the mobile device.

2. Verifiability issue
   In our scheme, the cloud can confirm the identity of ESC from the delegation of the pregnant woman by proxy signature. In our protocol, the proxy signature as follows:

$$Sig_{m_v} = \left(S_{pro}, E_{pro}\right) \tag{28}$$

Cloud can verify the validity of S_{pro} by Eqs. 34, 35, 36 and 37. Thus, CS can confirm the delegation of the pregnant woman via a proxy signature.

3. Identifiability issue.
   Identifiability means that the receiver can identify the sender of message. Our scheme checks the session key of message authentication codes MAC_1 and MAC_2 to check the identity as follows:

$$MAC_1 = h(ID_C, N_C, K_{ESC-C}) \tag{8}$$

$$MAC_2 = h(ID_P, r_1, C_1, K_{P-ESC}) \tag{18}$$

4. Non-repudiation issue.
   Non-repudiation means that the application party provides correlated proof (e.g., a digital signature) for the other party to verify that cannot deny. In our scheme, we use a digital signature to solve the non-repudiation issue. From the above equations, our scheme can obtain the necessary evidence that our scheme can achieve the requirement of non-repudiation. We illustrate the non-repudiation proofs in Table 1.

Table 1. The non-repudiation proof of our scheme

Evidence	Evidence issuer	Evidence holder	Verification equation
(S_P, E_P)	Pregnant woman	ESC	$S_P \overset{?}{=} h(ID_P, Cert_P, V_P)$
$Sig_{m_v} = \left(S_{pro}, E_{pro}\right)$	ESC	Cloud	$S_{pro} \overset{?}{=} h(m_V, V_{pro})$

5. Integrity issue.
   Due to the encryption by the session key of transmitted messages between sender and receiver integrity is necessary, the attacker has to obtain the session key to decrypt and obtain the messages as only the cipher text can be intercepted. The proposed scheme uses the message authentication code (MAC) Eqs. 8 and 18 to ensure the messages' integrity.

5 Conclusions

The proposed scheme can provide emergency response and a communication system for calling help for pregnant women. In our scheme we based on cloud computing to ensure that a pregnant woman can rapidly receive the first aid, and the hospital can accord the identity of the pregnant woman via the proxy signature from ESC. The proposed scheme can achieve security requirements. It can defend against some known attacks such as replay attack, man-in-the-middle attack, password guessing attack and mobile device lost attack; it can also guarantee verifiability, identifiability, non-repudiation and integrity via integration of the symmetric encryption technology, Schnorr's signature, message authentication coding and RFC 2631.

Acknowledgements. This research was supported by the Ministry of Science and Technology, Taiwan, R.O.C., under contract number MOST 105-2221-E-324-007, MOST 105-2622-E-212-008 -CC2 and MOST103-2632-E-324-001-MY3.

References

1. Chen, C.L., Yang, T.T., Chiang, M.-L., Shih, T.F.: A privacy authentication scheme based on cloud for medical environment. J. MS **38**(11), 143 (2014)
2. Website of WHO. http://www.who.int/mediacentre/factsheets/fs348/en/
3. Platania, M., Obenshain, D., Tantillo, T., Amir, Y., Suri, N.: On choosing server-or client-side solutions for BFT. ACM Comput. Surv. **48**(4), 61 (2016)
4. Mavletova, A.: Data quality in PC and mobile web surveys. SSCR **31**(6), 725–743 (2013)
5. Sailunaz, K., Alhussein, M., Shahiduzzaman, M., Anowar, F., Mamun, K.A.A.: CMED: Cloud based medical system framework for rural health monitoring in developing countries. CEE **53**, 469–481 (2016)
6. Mould-Millman, N.K., de Vries, S., Stein, C., Kafwamfwa, M., Dixon, J., Yancey, A., Laba, B., Overton, J., McDaniel, R., Wallis, L.A.: Developing emergency medical dispatch systems in Africa–recommendations of the african federation for emergency medicine/international academies of emergency dispatch working group. Afr. J. EM **5**(3), 141–147 (2015)
7. Mambo, M., Usuda, K., Okamoto, E.: Proxy signatures: Delegation of the power to sign messages. IEICE **79**(9), 1338–1354 (1996)
8. Schnorr, C.-P.: Efficient signature generation by smart cards. J. Cryptology **4**(3), 161–174 (1991)
9. Chen, C.L., Chen, Y.Y., Lee, C.-C., Wu, C.-H.: Design and analysis of a secure and effective emergency system for mountaineering events. J. Supercomputing **70**(1), 54–74 (2014)
10. Bellare, M., Rogaway, P.: Random oracles are practical: A paradigm for designing efficient protocols. In: 1st ACM Conference on Computer and Communications Security, pp. 62–73. ACM, Fairfax (1993)
11. Pointcheval, D., Stern, J.: Security proofs for signature schemes. In: Maurer, U. (ed.) EUROCRYPT 1996. LNCS, vol. 1070, pp. 387–398. Springer, Heidelberg (1996). doi: 10.1007/3-540-68339-9_33
12. Rescorla, E.: Diffie-Hellman key agreement method (1999). https://www.ietf.org/rfc/rfc2631.txt

A Trust Application in Participatory Sensing: Elder Reintegration

Alexandra Mihaita (Mocanu)[1]([⊠]), Ciprian Dobre[1], Florin Pop[1],
Bogdan Mocanu[1], Valentin Cristea[1], and Christian Esposito[2]

[1] University Politehnica Bucharest, Bucharest, Romania
{alexandra.mihaita,bogdan.mocanu}@hpc.pub.ro,
{ciprian.dobre,florin.pop,valentin.cristea}@cs.pub.ro
[2] University of Salerno, Fisciano, Italy
esposito@unisa.it

Abstract. Whatever traveling abroad or within their's own cities, everyone aims at optimizing their route in terms of time, distance or even sightseeing. But, finding the best path in a crowded city is very challenging in terms of continuous changing traffic conditions, road maintenance state and user needs. Most people are busy with daily-basis activities, but elders tend to walk more and, therefore, they develop expertise on the traffic state and/or the presence of works going on the roads. Our driving ides is to take advantage of the knowledge that elderly can gather. For example, a tourist can go sightseeing in a new city by using an elder's advice. When decisions are based on information collected from other individual, trust management is a key problem. Also in our case, we must deal with the problem of the freshness of the elder's information and the trustworthiness of their knowledge. Our work presents a solution for this issue by proposing a new trust management in participatory sensing for path optimization using cloud based services.

Keywords: Participatory sensing · Trust management · Elder reintegration · Smart city

1 Introduction

In the current era of the information society, the pervasiveness of the ICT and the availability of reliable and powerful Internet access everywhere allows people to always be reachable by everyone, despite the respective physical distance among two individuals. Such pervasiveness of the Internet access is also able to provide the possibility of gather information about everything from multiple data sources. Internet has become the largest means to collect data about any possible subject, and or to receive opinions about the quality of a particular service so as to influence our decisions. For a concrete example, if we want to have dinner in a given restaurant, most of us use Internet to access the review of such a restaurant so as to find out if it is a good one or not. The key problem related to such an overwhelming availability of opinions, and their open nature

© Springer International Publishing AG 2017
M.H.A. Au et al. (Eds.): GPC 2017, LNCS 10232, pp. 596–610, 2017.
DOI: 10.1007/978-3-319-57186-7_43

(i.e., any one can insert an opinion without any sort of control), is represented by discerning among them and being able to detect false or altered information.

A representative example of data gathering from the Internet consists in traveling abroad in a foreign city with no previous knowledge about that city. Of course, it is common practice to look for information on the Internet about that most visited sightseeing places, the best restaurants and so on. Today, this means searching such information through a web engine, finding the web sites offering what we are looking for, and finding a lot of best top 5 attractions/restaurants/hotels, some having nothing in common with the others. The ranking among such places is not based on evident quality, but on qualitative opinions reported by the previous attendees, each with their personal opinions, preferences and attitudes. In fact, when it comes to making a choice regarding which one is better, everybody looks at different things. Those different things lead to users disagreeing with the authors' opinion. Moreover, certain of these opinions are based on a sporadic and fast attendance to the places of interest, where the experienced service may not have been satisfying due to some temporary conditions. Last, most of people should like to have a personalized route within a city interconnecting all the places of interest by using the shortest, the most scenographic or cheap route.

A way to have timely, more reliable opinions about a city and its place of interest is to ask to locals rather than occasional visitors. In fact, locals may hold all the up-dated information about routes and road conditions because they go through an experience of this on a daily basis. The driving idea of the work presented in this paper consists in designing a participatory sensing application for optimizing paths in terms of time, distance or sightseeing using local information based on user trust. The paper discusses the ability to use tips from locals regarding sightseeing or other objectives, information that prevalently comes from elders. As in any application aiming at aggregating opinions from humans, these kind of opinions may be affected by uncertainty and/or alterations. Therefore, there is a problem on how dealing with them without compromising the effectiveness of the overall application.

A community in which users volunteer in sharing pieces of information in order to transform into a body of knowledge represents an example of the so-called participatory sensing. Such a term was introduced in 2006 by a seminar work [3] as a future perspective and evolution of the ICT application within the society; however, such a term is no more a future opportunity provided by ICT, but a concrete reality used by billions of people nowadays. Such a large mass of opinions from multiple virtual individuals that can act collaboratively, selfishly or maliciously is meaningless if not being properly disciplined so as to detect and remove improper and incorrect opinions and promoting a truth-saying behavior.

Trust management is a key technique to protect ICT solutions from internal attacks, and is a valuable solutions for the mentioned problem. It consists in determining a trustworthiness degree of an opinion provider, such as an elder, and assessing the trustiness of the provided opinions. Our work provides a new approach for trust management by monitoring not only what a user says, but also its knowledge in saying that.

The paper is structured in 6 sections as following: in Sect. 2 multiple trust management systems are presented. Section 3 describes in details the trust management with its problems and proposed solutions. Further on, in Sect. 4 presents the proposed approach for trust management in a participatory system. Experimental results regarding the proposed approach are presented in Sect. 5. The final Sect. 6 presents the main conclusions of the proposed approach.

2   Related Work

As stated in the introduction, participatory sensing represents a community where user volunteer pieces of information in order to transform into a body of knowledge. A short related work of existing participatory sensing application is further presented. Also, issues like user privacy and trust management in different participatory sensing applications emphasize current trends and working problems.

Authors in reference [3] have captured since the beginning, in 2006, the main issues that the participatory sensing has: user privacy and trust computing. The proposed architecture is said to be beneficial in public health, urban planning and cultural identity and creative expressions, but has been tested with good results in the cultural identity and creative expressions domain.

Authors in reference [7] have used participatory sensing for measuring environmental impact. Their project is called PEIR - Personal Environmental Impact Report. User GPS data and cell tower is collected and sent to a private repository from where scientific models aggregate data. Along with data about GPS and cell tower connection, data about radio signal strength and battery information are collected and then uniquely identified by user International Mobile Equipment Identity (IMEI). The main applications of this project are carbon impact measurement, sensitive site impact, smog exposure and fast food exposure. This approach has not taken into account the possibility of having users that send false data into the system and their influence on metrics.

The authors of [8] presented GreenGPS a fuel efficient end-to-end navigation service that is based on participatory sensing. The proposed solution showed reduction of fuel consumption through a mobile application connected to the car chip. The experiments ran over 22 cars with different drivers with a total of 3200 miles of data. The analyzed data shows that taking the fastest route helps saving fuel with almost double the percentage obtained when taking the shortest route. One of the most important conclusion drained from the tests has been that data cleaning is important and that without that step, the information is altered. The privacy aspect of the GreenGPS is at the early stage of Discussions. The authors state that massive GPS data can be anonymized by splitting the road onto segments and aggregating the data without specifying from who it is.

The authors of paper [10] presented CATrust, a regression-based trust management model for a Internet ad-hock networks such: Internet of Things or peer to peer. The proposed model is based on a new mechanism based on recommendation filtering that is able to screen out dishonest recommendations, eave though the environment is hostile. This paper, evaluated resilience, accuracy and coverage properties through simulation and demonstrates that fact the CATrust model outperforms the existing approaches in missing good services and missing bad services probabilities.

In paper [1], is presented an interesting three-tier participatory sensing framework for pollution monitoring in the urban region of Bangladesh. The authors of the paper also proposed an Android application entitled My City, My Environment.

The authors of paper [2], proposed a recruitment participatory sensing framework based on social participation. Their trust approach is based on the social relationships between individuals, therefore they exploit the multi-hop friend relations in order to provide the most trustworthy path in the system. This framework was evaluated against simulation, and demonstrated the efficiency in terms of selecting a large number of participants with high trust in comparison with one-hop architecture approaches.

A good survey in mobile participation sensing is presented in paper [5]. The authors, analyzed several sensing models used in participatory sensing applications with respect to user privacy and information disclosure. Also in this paper are presented several countermeasures that can be applied in participatory sensing systems.

In book chapter [9], the authors presented a good overview Participatory Sensing Networks (PSN), by focusing on challenges and opportunities of such networks. The main focus of the authors is to show the fact that PSNs like Instagram, Waze and Foursquare can create valuable sensing information for the dynamics of an urban area through social behavior of the users.

The authors of paper [6], presented a new framework for crowd sensing named Social Network Assisted Trustworthiness Assurance (SONATA). Their approach is based on the vote trustworthiness in social network architectures. The malicious users are detected by adopting the Sybil detection scheme. The experimental results showed the fact that the SONATA framework improves the crowd sensing when less than 7% of the users are malicious.

Despite the approaches priorly presented in the papers cited above, we present a trust management approach for participatory sensing having elder reintegration as main key feature.

3   Case Study: Elder Reintegration

When talking about elder reintegration as a particular case study for trust in participatory sensing several aspects must be cleared: why participatory sensing, why is trust important in these applications and further more, why elder reintegration.

Participatory sensing applications represent a community in which user choose to gather and share data from their sensors for aggregation. Unlike opportunistic networks, the users are aware of the active application and sharing sensors data is done, not when the conditions fit, but when the users allow it.

The opportunistic approach has the disadvantage of incontrollable sharing data while the participatory sensing application has the disadvantage of many user interrupts. In order to better address the everyday user's needs a mixture of these two model of application has been proposed: users decide when and where they share data without the application having to constantly check for user agreement.

Communities with large number of users are very heterogeneous. Even though sensor data does not vary as much as their user's opinion, data correction must be made. But in order to do that, one must know how to correct the data. Taking into account the majority is not the best solution: say for example a group of friends want to go to the mountains side. They want their path to be the fastest so they can all alter the sensor data showing that path as being congested. Another user that goes to the mountain side says it is a clear path. The majority can therefore alter not only the data but also the reputation of the one user. Choosing the majority can lead to honest users not wanting to share data anymore. So in order to prevent such a behavior, an application must find an objective way to analyze users and their data. The proposed approach in this paper tries to resolve not only the majority problem but also problems with expired information. Expired means that an user can state something without actually having knowledge of it or having old data on the subject that does not apply anymore. The lack of knowledge is not an evidence of intentional bad behavior, only of lack of knowledge.

The last but not least important issue is that of the focus of the paper: elder reintegration. Today, everybody is busy and on the run until they retire. Then, they begin, all of the sudden, to have more time to spare going for a walk or visiting what they like: museums, theaters or other cultural objectives. To this respect, they increase their knowledge regarding clear paths and what is worth seeing in their city. Therefore, it can be stated that their added value to a simple GPS application is that they can give advice on paths or what is worth seeing in a new place personalized on what a quester's asks for.

Now to corroborate all the data, the proposed approach tries to solve trust management issues in participatory sensing applications based on human experience: elder reintegration. The current approach takes into account the elders's recommendations for tourists regarding fastest paths, shortest path or the one with most touristic objectives.

The main components of the architecture are the users of the system, the initial generated information formed by a set of predefined touristic objectives and maps and the user knowledge about those objectives. The system is based on request from some users and responses from others. These represent actual recommendations based on the comparison between the users profiles and between the prior two categories: known information and the certain one.

The proposed architecture takes into account two types of users: the givers and the receivers. The givers are the elders which choose to share their knowledge about city status: fastest paths, shortest paths and moreover, the most relevant sightseeing in an area of interest. The receivers are the visitors that need assistance when it comes to choosing what is worth seeing in a foreign city. The receivers need the information that the givers are willing to share while the givers meet others with similar interests based on their profile and are slowly reintegrated in modern society. A user can be either a receiver or a giver, but not both.

Elder Reintegration has a peer-to-peer architecture where users communicate via request and responses. The peer activity is made through dedicated mobile application TERI - Trust Elder ReIntegration. The system is based on the premises that the receiver has a smartphone with enabled GPS which is active during sightseeing. Each giver's GPS monitors computes how much does the user follow a suggested path and, at the end of the path or when the application is closed, it sends back to the giver the resulted percentage. The givers complete challenges and make recommendations via smartphone or tablet.

Each recommendation given by an elder to a tourist can be time, distance or sightseeing oriented. Based on this orientation, the profile of the giver and the profile of the receiver the recommendation is asserted a score. The higher the score, the higher the compatibility between the giver and the receiver in accordance to the orientation of the request.

The exchange of information is divided in 4 phases: initializing, learning, recommendation and adjustment phase. Each phase is important for the correction of the data and the trust computation of the user. The stages represent the actual flow of information that a user brings to the application: first a user must declare what it knows and what its interests are. Then, the system finds out how much does the user really know about its interests. After creating a profile of the residents of a city, they can begin to suggest paths to visitors. The final phase is that of correcting the recommendation. Each of these phases is further described in details.

Each user of the system has a trust with values between 0 and 1 where 0 means untruthful and 1 means total trust. Each feedback represents a score that the receiver shares about the quality of the recommendation of the giver and is between 0 and 10 where 0 represents bad recommendation and 10 represents a good, liked one. When entering the system, each user receives a value representing its initial trust which is further explained in the next chapter. Also, each giver stores a list of the receivers with which it has been in contact along with their percentage of availability to follow the suggested path whereas each receiver stores the list of all the givers with which it has been in contact along with their resulted trust. This way, each user can compute the trust of the others but not its own. Also, by not knowing if the other user gave a good or bad score, one can not alter the associated trust value without influencing its own trust.

The main advantage of the proposed approach is the ability to make suggestions for tourists not only in terms of fastest or shortest path but also for sightseeing along with a new trust management approach. The mobile application brings high mobility at the user side.

4   Trust Management

In order to determine as fairly as possible the trust of a user in a system, the trust is broken into several perspective: it monitors how much does the user trust what it knows, how much does the system trust the user says it knows and how much do the other users trust what he knew. These perspective correspond to different phases of the system and are presented next.

In the initialization phase, each user has to complete a user profile stating where he lives, what cities does he know and at what degree, the time spent in each city and preferably the neighborhoods which are most familiar. These information create an initial level of trust of the user in terms of credibility. These informations help create the initial trust of the givers and the main interest of the receivers for later suggestions (Fig. 1).

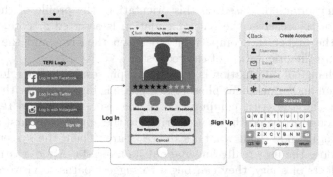

Fig. 1. Registration form

In the learning phase, each giver has to fill out a set of challenges where at first they state their interests and afterwards are tested regarding their knowledge in those areas. Categories of interests may be museums, theaters, hospitals, restaurants, florists etc. The second degree of trust has to be influential enough to reflect the user knowledge but without eliminating the importance of feedback. The challenges represent a virtual map of the city where they have to set as many touristic objectives in their area of interest as possible and afterward to respond to a set of choosing the best path to a place. The number of recognized objectives of the total number known by the system in that area of interest determines an second degree of trust of the giver. The deviation of the path suggested by the giver to the path suggested by a GPS application can determine the degree of knowledge in terms of fast traveling. This also represents a part of the second degree of trust of the giver. The receiver must also complete a set of challenged regarding their interests and the complete a set of challenges regarding those interests. This phase contributes to the computation of the score of a recommendation. The resulted trust after phase one and two represents initial trust (TI) represented by formula 1. The percentages of each element in the formula of trust computing have been determined stochastically.

$$TI = \beta \times TInitialize + (1 - \beta) \times TLearning, \; where \quad \beta = 0.1 \qquad (1)$$

After the learning phase starts the actual communication phase. At this point, the system accepts request from receivers and responses from elders. The system also accepts an emergency profile where it gives a user basic information about hospitals or public transport stations (Fig. 2).

Fig. 2. Learning challenges

The recommendation and feedback phases work hand in hand, in the sense that for each recommendation a feedback is to be made. But, the given feedback must also take into consideration the profile of the receiver. What fault does a giver have when a receiver refuses to use his recommendations and later give him a bad feedback. Since, each recommendation means following a path and the GPS of the receiver is necessary, it can also be used for comparison between the suggested path and the path taken. Based on the degree of similarity the feedback can have a bigger or smaller importance on the final result. If a total compliance of the suggested path means 100% valid opinion from the receiver (feedback vale), then 50% compliance of it should have only half the importance of the feedback. Considering the fact that trust has a value between 0 and 1 while feedback (F) has a value between 0 and 10, a division by 10 must be made in order to remain in stated interval of trust. More explicitly, considering feedback (F) a value between 0 and 10 representing the receiver satisfaction toward a suggested path and an obedience percentage (OP), a value between 0 and 1, representing the degree with which the receiver has followed the suggested path, the formula for trust communication between two users is stated in formula 7.

$$TrustFeedbackper Request/Response = 0.1 \times OP \times F \qquad (2)$$

The trust computation of the users has to reflect as best possible their knowledge so it has to be best divided between the system phases. For example, if the initial phase has a percentage higher that the learning phase, users that have lived for longer period of time in a place with lower knowledge would have greater score that a user with actual knowledge but has not lived there for as long. Also, a balance between the trust the system gives the user and the trust computed via the feedback received must be made. For example, if the feedback percentage is small, a giver with high level of trust can then send bad recommendations because it does not affect the general result. On the other hand, a user with good system trust that meets bad receivers could be destroyed if the percentage of feedback is too high. Therefore, the initial and learning phases must counter balance the feedback phase. Generically, a user's trust is composed of 55% initial trust (TI), which is gathered in the first and second phases, and 45% the trust from the other N number of users feedback (TF). The computation of the trust of other users feedback can be seen in formula 4.

$$TF = \frac{\sum_{I=1}^{n} 0.1 \times OP_{IR} \times F_{RI}}{|G|} \tag{3}$$

where $|G|$ is the cardinal of the list of givers that have previously had contact with. This formula can be rewritten as follows:

$$TF = 0.1 \times \frac{\sum_{I=1}^{|G|} OP_{IR} \times F_{RI}}{|G|} \tag{4}$$

The proposed approach for trust computation of a user therefore depends on what he think he knows (5.5 %), on what the system knows he knows (49,5%) and on the trust given by the other users (45%), summing it up in formula 5:

$$TotalTrust = \alpha \times TI + (1 - \alpha) \times TF, where \quad \alpha = 0.55 \tag{5}$$

The percentages of the trust levels after each phase in the formula 5 have been stochastically chosen based on the assumption that malicious majority must not influence decisively the total trust of a good user.

For example, a network is formed by X number of givers and Y number of receivers. The communication between a giver - G and a receiver - R can be done with previous knowledge of one another or for the first time. Whether they have previous knowledge about each other or if they have no previous knowledge of one another, the communication is made based on a set of pairs of request and responses as follows:

1. the receiver R formulates a request for visiting a city/neighborhood stating its orientation (fastest, shortest or sightseeing), its initial trust and the list of givers with which has previously spoken and their associated trust (Giver11,.., Giver1N).
2. the giver G sees the request and checks if it has knowledge about the city/neighborhood

3. the giver G contacts the list provided by the receiver R regarding the other givers (Giver11,.., Giver1N) with which the receiver has spoken
4. the givers (Giver11,..., Giver1N) send the associated obedience of the receiver R to the giver G
5. the giver - G computes the trust of the receiver R as a harmonic mean of the trust and percentages of the receiver (TR) as follows:

$$TR = \alpha \times TI + (1 - \alpha) \times 0.1 \times \frac{\sum_{I=1}^{|G|} OP_{IR} \times F_{RI}}{|G|} \tag{6}$$

where α is 0.55 and $|G|$ is the cardinal of the list of givers with which the receiver has been in contact.
6. the giver G decides whether to make a recommendation or not to the receiver R based on the resulted trust of the receiver R
7. the giver G which makes a recommendation send its list of previous contacted receivers (Receiver21,.., Receiver2M) and their associated obedience percentages
8. the receiver R computes the trust value of the giver G (TG)

$$TG = \alpha \times TI + (1 - \alpha) \times 0.1 \times \frac{\sum_{I=1}^{|R|} OP_{GI} \times F_{IG}}{|R|} \tag{7}$$

where α is 0.55 and $|R|$ is the cardinal of the list of receivers with which the giver has been in contact.
9. the receiver R chooses whether to accept the recommendation or not
10. if chose, at the end of the path, the receiver R send the path followed and the giver computes the obedience percentage
11. the receiver R adds to its list the feedback of the giver G
12. the giver G adds to its list the obedience percentage of the receiver.

5 Experimental Results

For the purpose of testing the computational approach for trust in participatory sensing a sample of 12 users was taken into consideration and mathematically modeled. Of these users, 7 have been considered givers and 5 have been considered receivers. For each of these users an initial trust value has been appointed and several random generated routes have been put in place in order to compute the user feedback trust.

The initial trust of a user is comprised of the trust after the first phase (user registering in the system) and the trust after the second phase (learning what the user actually knows). To this respect, the registration phase contains multiple questions at which the users has to respond: what cities does he know and how long has he lived there, what neighborhoods does he know in each of those cities, what kind of interests does he have (opera, theater, football, walking in the park etc.) and the places where he likes doing that, how often does he go outside and for how long. For this experiment each user can complete the survey with only

Table 1. Table of user trust after the first phase.

User no.	TI after first phase	TT after first phase
User1	0.2	0.011
User2	0.8	0.044
User3	0.5	0.027
User4	0.3	0.016
User5	0.9	0.049
User6	0.3	0.016
User7	0.7	0.038
User8	0.9	0.049
User9	1.0	0.055
User10	0.1	0.005
User11	0.6	0.033
User12	0.8	0.044

one value therefore the importance of each question is the same and statistically represents 0.78% of the total trust of the user. Randomly generated, the trust after the first phase of each user can be seen in Table 1.

The trust value obtained after first phase is presented in Fig. 3.

The second phase named learning phase represents a set of challenges that the user has to complete. If on the first phase the users state what they know, on the second phase the system evaluates if they really know as much as they say they do. This phase is very important in order to distinguish between malicious users and good users that have outdated information. More generically, this phase determines how much the user really knows what he think he knows. On this phase, the information given in the first phase is verified through a map where users have to rightfully place objectives of their interest and find fastest/shortest path to a destination in an area they declared as known.

The second phase has also been mathematically modeled and user profiles have been randomly generated.

For the third and fourth phase, recommendations and feedback, random requests and responses have been made. These request and responses have been made in 3 iterative steps in order to determine how accurate does one user influence another.

Table 2 represents a pair of users: receiver and giver and their mutual notation. Closing the application by the receiver without sharing the path taken with the giver is reflected by a 0 in the obedience percentage. This strong negative value is used in order to discourage the users from getting information from the system without feedback. A value of -1 means that the user has not had any requests/responses and therefore the feedback is null. Similar pairs of requests and responses are generated for second and third iteration (see Tables 3 and 4).

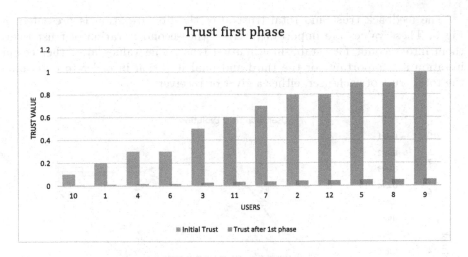

Fig. 3. Trust after first phase

Table 2. First iteration of request-responses.

Receiver	Giver	Feedback	Obedience percentage
User1	User8	7	0.67
User5	User12	9	0.89
User6	User2	5	0.49
User7	User8	10	0.33
User9	User10	4	0.70

Table 3. Second iteration of request-responses.

Receiver	Giver	Feedback	Obedience percentage
User1	User10	9	0.42
User5	User11	7	0.69
User6	User8	8	0.73
User9	User3	9	0.85

Table 4. Third iteration of request-responses.

Receiver	Giver	Feedback	Obedience percentage
User1	User4	8	0.76
User5	User11	7	0.92
User1	User2	9	0.34
User7	User3	5	0.84
User9	User12	5	0.68

The feedback trust and total trust after the first iteration is presented in Fig. 3. These values are important because the second iteration of trust takes them into account for establishing mutual trust. The values after the second iteration are important for the third and final iteration in order to determine the total trust of each user, either a giver or receiver.

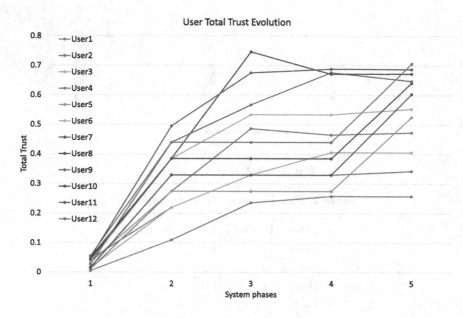

Fig. 4. Total trust evolution

An evolution of the total user trust after each stage is presented in Fig. 4. The system phases presented are: initialization in the system, learning in the system, first iteration of interactions, second iteration of interactions and third iteration of interactions. In this diagram it can be observed that the first phase introduces a weak starting point but it can not be eliminated because it is necessary for setting the challenges of phase two. As it can be seen in the diagram, phase two has a catalysis role for balancing the general user trust without letting it be strongly influenced by good or bad reviews. The next three phases represent iterations at with user interact and evaluate each other. The fact that the other user does not know the evaluation of the other helps maintaining a balance of trustfulnesses. This is done by the fact that a receiver does not know how much its grade influences the total trust of the iteration as neither does the giver.

6   Conclusions

In this paper we have presented a new type of application for path optimization using cloud based services in participatory sensing systems based on elder reintegration. The motivation behind this theme is that the pervasiveness of the ICT and the availability of reliable and powerful Internet access everywhere allows people to always be reachable by everyone, despite the respective physical distance among two individuals. Such pervasiveness of the Internet access is also able to provide the possibility of gather information about everything from multiple data sources. Internet has become the largest means to collect data about any possible subject, and or to receive opinions about the quality of a particular service so as to influence our decisions.

The driving idea of the work presented in this paper consists in designing a participatory sensing application for optimizing paths in terms of time, distance or sightseeing using local information based on user trust. The paper discusses the ability to use tips from locals regarding sightseeing or other objectives, information that prevalently comes from elders. The reason for this choice is quite simple, elders have great knowledge about the city where they have lived and can thus share that knowledge with people that might need it. As in any application aiming at aggregating opinions from humans, these kind of opinions may be affected by uncertainty and/or alterations. Therefore, there is a problem on how dealing with them without compromising the effectiveness of the overall application.

The paper has been structured in 6 sections as following: in Sect. 2 multiple trust management systems have been presented. Section 3 described in details the trust management with its problems and proposed solutions. Further on, in Sect. 4 was presented the proposed approach for trust management in a participatory system. Experimental results regarding the proposed approach were then discussed in Sect. 5. The final Sect. 6 presents the main conclusions of the proposed approach. An evolution of the total user trust after each stage is presented in Fig. 4 where it can be observed that the first phase introduces a weak starting point but it can not be eliminated because it is necessary for setting the challenges of phase two. The second phase is important for making a balanced general user trust. The third and fourth phases represent iterations at with user interact and evaluate each other giving mutual trust feedback.

In this paper, the trust management model for this type of application proposed was statistically evaluated. The fact that one user does not know the evaluation of the other user means that it is not determined to give good feedback to those who do not deserve it and opposite. The main diagram shows that the more the challenges the less impact the more the total trust of a user is equilibrated. This means that strong negative or positive feedback do not alter the total trust in a decisive manner.

Future work in trust applications for elder reintegration, we intend to validate the trust management model proposed through simulation and analyze its performances in case of abnormalities and malicious majority.

Acknowledgment. The research presented in this paper is supported by projects: *DataWay*: Real-time Data Processing Platform for Smart Cities: Making sense of Big Data - PN-II-RU-TE-2014-4-2731; *MobiWay*: Mobility Beyond Individualism: an Integrated Platform for Intelligent Transportation Systems of Tomorrow - PN-II-PT-PCCA-2013-4-0321.

References

1. Ahmed, A.A.N., Haque, H.F., Rahman, A., Ashraf, M.S., Saha, S., Shatabda, S.: A participatory sensing framework for environment pollution monitoring and management. arXiv preprint arXiv:1701.06429 (2017)
2. Amintoosi, H., Kanhere, S.S.: A trust-based recruitment framework for multi-hop social participatory sensing. In: 2013 IEEE International Conference on Distributed Computing in Sensor Systems (DCOSS), pp. 266–273. IEEE (2013)
3. Burke, J.A., Estrin, D., Hansen, M., Parker, A., Ramanathan, N., Reddy, S., Srivastava, M.B.: Participatory sensing. Center for Embedded Network Sensing (2006)
4. Carullo, G., Castiglione, A., Cattaneo, G., De Santis, A., Fiore, U., Palmieri, F.: Feeltrust: providing trustworthy communications in ubiquitous mobile environment. In: 2013 IEEE 27th International Conference on Advanced Information Networking and Applications (AINA), pp. 1113–1120. IEEE (2013)
5. Christin, D., Reinhardt, A., Kanhere, S.S., Hollick, M.: A survey on privacy in mobile participatory sensing applications. J. Syst. Softw. **84**(11), 1928–1946 (2011)
6. Kantarci, B., Carr, K.G., Pearsall, C.D.: Sonata: social network assisted trustworthiness assurance in smart city crowdsensing. Int. J. Distrib. Syst. Technol. (IJDST) **7**(1), 59–78 (2016)
7. Mun, M., Reddy, S., Shilton, K., Yau, N., Burke, J., Estrin, D., Hansen, M., Howard, E., West, R., Boda, P.: Peir, the personal environmental impact report, as a platform for participatory sensing systems research. In: Proceedings of the 7th International Conference on Mobile Systems, Applications, and Services, pp. 55–68. ACM (2009)
8. Saremi, F., Fatemieh, O., Ahmadi, H., Wang, H., Abdelzaher, T., Ganti, R., Liu, H., Hu, S., Li, S., Su, L.: Experiences with greengpsfuel-efficient navigation using participatory sensing. IEEE Trans. Mob. Comput. **15**(3), 672–689 (2016)
9. Silva, T.H., Celes, C.S.d.S., Neto, J.B.B., Mota, V.F., da Cunha, F.D., Ferreira, A.P., Ribeiro, A.I., de Melo, P.O.V., Almeida, J.M., Loureiro, A.A.: Users in the urban sensing process: challenges and research opportunities
10. Wang, Y., Chen, R., Cho, J.H., Swami, A., Lu, Y.C., Lu, C.T., Tsai, J.: Catrust: context-aware trust management for service-oriented ad hoc networks. IEEE Trans. Serv. Comput. (2016)

DABEHR: Decentralized Attribute-Based Electronic Health Record System with Constant-Size Storage Complexity

Ye Li[1], Kaitai Liang[2]($\boxtimes$), Chunhua Su[3], and Wei Wu[4]

[1] State Key Laboratory of Networking and Switching Technology,
Beijing University of Posts and Telecommunications, Beijing 100876, China
ye.li@se11.qmul.ac.uk
[2] School of Computing, Mathematics and Digital Technology,
Manchester Metropolitan University, Manchester, UK
k.liang@mmu.ac.uk
[3] Graduate School of Engineering, Osaka University, Suita, Japan
su@comm.eng.osaka-u.ac.jp
[4] Funjian Provincial Key Laboratory of Network Security and Cryptology,
School of Mathematics and Computer Science,
Fujian Normal University, Fuzhou, Fujian, China
weiwu81@gmail.com

Abstract. Under the trend of cloud computing, Internet users tend to outsource their electronic personal data to remote cloud to enjoy efficient data storage and processing services. In recent years, Electronic Health Record (EHR) system has been designed to provide cost-effective healthcare data management for patients, doctors, and other professional bodies. How to guarantee the security and privacy of personal health data while the record is stored, accessed and shared in open network that has gain widely attention in both academic and industrial communities. Attribute-Based Encryption (ABE), nowadays, is one of the promising techniques to secure personal health record. However, the access expressiveness, storage cost and privacy concern incurred by the usage of EHR systems still cannot be fully tackled by leveraging the existing ABE technologies. In this paper, we, for the first time, propose a novel decentralized key-policy ABE scheme for circuits. Based on the scheme, we build up an EHR system that allows access policy to be extreme expressive, and ciphertext to be maintained in constant level, so that doctors and other professionals can gain access to health record conveniently. Besides, our system supports white-box traceability so that malicious professionals (e.g., the one "selling" the access rights of health record) can be traced and identified. Furthermore, we present the formal security (in the selective-set model) and efficiency analysis for our system.

Keywords: Personal health record · Cloud computing · Attribute-based encryption · Decentralized · Constant-size ciphertext · Traceability

© Springer International Publishing AG 2017
M.H.A. Au et al. (Eds.): GPC 2017, LNCS 10232, pp. 611–626, 2017.
DOI: 10.1007/978-3-319-57186-7_44

1   Introduction

Cloud computing, emerging as an Internet application/service, has attracted many attentions over Internet users, scientific data centers and industries [2]. Cloud Security Alliance (CSA), however, points out that there unfortunately exist some unsolved security threats in cloud computing [32], in which information breaches and data loss are the top two on the threat list. One of the long-list advantages to use Attribute-Based Encryption (ABE) to protect the confidentiality of the data for cloud system [29,35] is that data encryptor has no need to store the public key(s) of data receiver(s). For instance, a data can be encrypted only under specified attributes (resp. access policy), so that it can be revealed by a system user as long as the secret key of the user satisfying certain access policy (resp. attributes). Nowadays, several ABE schemes supporting various features, such as outsourcing computing [10,16], hidden access structure and etc.

In recent years, EHR systems, with many advantages, such as providing effective data processing and management, have been widely used in national health services. The usage of EHR systems in open network, however, incurs some security and privacy concerns, e.g., the integrity and usability of health record. To design privacy-preserving EHR systems, many security scholars have increasingly shown their interests in using ABE. Ibraimi et al. [12] propose a piece of electronic health data sharing system on top of a Ciphertext Policy based ABE (CP-ABE) [4]. Akinyele et al. [1] design a secure and practical EHR system that allows mobile devices to generate and store self-protecting electronic health-care records, so that mobile users can still gain access to health data even if the server is off-line. Multi-authority ABE [5] is employed in [17] for the purpose of guaranteeing user privacy. Li et al. [17] construct a scheme to access EHR, which is stored in a semi-trusted cloud server, through a series of novel mechanisms for data access control using patient-centric framework. Liu et al. [26] implement a dynamic access policy EHR data sharing system. To allow PHR data to be shared securely, there are also some EHR systems, e.g., [31], that have been designed in the literature.

Although the aforementioned research works are built on top of ABE technique to propose secure EHR systems, there are several significant security and efficiency aspects that have not be tackled well. According to the features and potential security concerns of an EHR system, the following factors should be considered:

- Independence among authorities: for an EHR system, the management of user attributes is extreme crucial. User attributes should be possessed by multiple decentralized Attribute Authorities (AAs), where there exists no cooperation among the authorities. A centralized authority, here, is desirable no longer, because its attributes management may cost much and furthermore, once it is compromised or intruded by attackers, the whole system may encounter a huge security threat.
- Fine-grained access policy: a practical EHR system should provide fine-grained access policy for system users. Standing at the perspective of users' access

rights, the current access policy (supported by the existing EHR systems), such as threshold or access tree, may be not expressive enough. A more flexible and scalable access policy may be desirable.

– Traceability: an EHR system should provide a way for third party auditor to trace malicious insiders (e.g., doctors, other professionals) who intentionally leak the whole or partial decryption keys for beneficial purpose.

– Lightweight storage: the storage complexity of an EHR system may be linearly in the number of system users. The complexity may be expanded significantly while the system is deployed in city with large population. The ciphertext size of the existing Multi-Authority (MA)-ABE schemes is *almost* linearly growth with the size of attribute sets. That incurs huge storage stress to cloud server. Therefore, an EHR system with light storage complexity may be necessary as well.

Our Contributions. In this paper, we propose a key-policy decentralized ABE scheme with constant-size ciphertext for circuits to realize a secure EHR system. In our system, multiple attribute authorities can work independently without cooperation among each other and therefore Central Authority (CA) is unnecessary. We leverage circuits as access policy in the EHR system, for the first time, which is more expressive than other structures. Besides, our construction for circuits can achieve constant-size ciphertext that significantly reduces the storage overhead on the side of cloud server. Our scheme can support white-box traceability as well. We formally prove that the system is Chosen-Plantext (CPA) secure in the *selective-set* model. Through the comparison in terms of functionality, properties/features and efficiency with other existing research works, we can see that the system is the first of its type and only one that can realize decentralized ABE for circuits, but also possess lightweight storage cost and traceability, satisfying the practical and security requirements of EHR systems.

Organization of the Paper. The rest of the paper is organized as follows. Section 2 briefly describes some related works. Some preliminaries are introduced in Sect. 3. Section 4 describes the architecture of our cloud-based EHR system. Our system construction and the corresponding security and efficiency analysis are presented in Sects. 5 and 6, respectively. Finally, some conclusions are drawn in Sect. 7.

2   Related Work

ABE has been widely used as a data protection technology in cloud applications since 2003 for its special one-to-many data sharing mechanism. ABE was first introduced by Sahai and Waters [29], where a user can decrypt a give ciphertext if and only if his secret key description matches the prescribed description associated with the ciphertext. At the same time, Sahai and Waters left an interesting open problem - how to build a scheme where attributes may be from different authorities for practical scenario. Chase [5] gave the answer

614   Y. Li et al.

to the above problem by constructing a multi-authority ABE scheme, for the
first time. Afterwards, other ABE research works supporting various features,
such as [6,11,15,25,27], have been published in the literature. Jiang's [13,14]
schemes realize keyword search using centralized multi-authority ABE. Chase
and Chow [6] designed an improved multi-authority ABE scheme, where they
removed CA and leveraged the anonymous key issuing protocol to protect user
privacy. Nevertheless, multiple authorities have to cooperate with each other in
their paper. That contradicts to the design of multi-authority system. Lewko
and Waters [15] put forward a Decentralized ABE (DABE) scheme using Linear
Secret Sharing Scheme (LSSS) matrix, where each attribute authority (without
the help of CA) can independently generate secret keys for registered system
users. The aforementioned research works can used as secure building blocks in
many cloud computing applications.

To reduce storage complexity for cloud server, the propose of an ABE with
constant-size ciphertext [7] has created a new research direction for ABE. Later
on, an expressive Key-Policy (KP) based ABE scheme with constant-size ciphertexts was introduced in [3]. Wang et al. [33] put forward a constant-size ciphertexts KP-ABE, significantly improving computation efficiency. Li et al. [18]
designs a scheme to save storage cost using deduplication. These ABE schemes
may be potentially used to construct secure EHR sharing system. However, the
traceability to malicious insider should be achieved as well in an EHR system.
Traceable ABE [24] is designed for identifying malicious insiders from leaking
their decryption keys (fully/partially) for some special purposes (e.g. selling the
keys to black market). A scalable ABE scheme with white-box traceability was
introduced in [28]. [17] built EHR systems on top of special data access architectures. We note that there exist some cloud-based data sharing systems in the
literature, [19–23,34,36,37]. But their sharing techniques are quite different from
what we will discuss in this paper.

Here, we summarize two drawbacks of the aforementioned ABE schemes while
using them to construct EHR systems. The access structures are not expressive
enough to offer system users to enjoy flexible and efficient data access. Moreover,
the ciphertext size expands linearly with the number of attributes that may
increase storage complexity for EHR cloud server. To the best of our knowledge,
there is no attribute-based EHR systems that can achieve *all* the followings
simultaneously: independent decentralized authorities, expressiveness in access
policy, traceability, and light (constant) storage complexity. This paper is the
first to tackle the above open problem.

3 Preliminaries

3.1 Notations

The main notations are summarized in Table 1.

Table 1. Notations

U	A system user
GID	A global identifier
A_i	An authority i
I	The index set of authorities
S_i	The set of attributes that the A_i manages
S_C	The set of attributes that is associated with a ciphertext CT
S_U	The set of attributes that is available to the user U

3.2 Multilinear Maps

We describe the concept of the multilinear maps briefly, and refer readers to [8] for more details. Suppose a group generator $\mathcal{G}$, a security parameter λ and a positive integer n. Run $\mathcal{G}(1^\lambda, n)$, output a sequence of groups $\mathbb{G} = (\mathbb{G}_1, ..., \mathbb{G}_n)$. We set that g_i is a canonical p-order generator of $\mathbb{G}_i$ with $g = g_1$.

We say that a map $e_{i,j} : \mathbb{G}_i \times \mathbb{G}_j \longrightarrow \mathbb{G}_{i,j}$ is a multilinear map if it satisfies the following properties:

1. The groups from $\mathcal{G}$ are the same prime order.
2. If any $a, b \in \mathbb{Z}_p$ then $e_{i,j}(g_i^a, g_j^b) = g_{i+j}^{ab}$.
3. The map $e_{i,j}$ is non-degenerate: if $g_i \in \mathbb{G}_i$, $g_j \in \mathbb{G}_j$ then $e_{i,j} \in \mathbb{G}_{i+j}$.

Hereafter, we can simply denote $e(g_i^a, g_j^b) = g_{i+j}^{ab}$ for convenience.

The k-Multilinear decisional Diffie-Hellman(k-MDDH) extension assumption based on [9] is defined as follows.

k-MDDH Extension Assumption. The k-multilinear decisional Diffie-Hellman extension assumption states that given $g, g^s, g^{c_1}, g^{c_2}, ..., g^{c_n}$, it is hard to distinguish $T = g_n^{s \prod_{j \in [1,n]} c_j}$ from a random group element in $\mathbb{G}_n$ with negligible advantage, where $s, c_1, ..., c_n$ is chosen randomly from $\mathbb{Z}_p$.

3.3 Decentralized Attribute-Based Encryption for Circuits

Algorithms. A decentralized attribute-based encryption for circuits generally consists of the following six algorithms:

Global Setup$(\lambda, n, l) \rightarrow PP$. The setup algorithm takes as input the security parameter λ, the length n of input descriptors, a bound l on the circuit depth, and outputs public parameters PP.

Authority Setup$(PP) \rightarrow (SK_i, PK_i, f)$. Each authority runs the authority setup algorithm with PP as input to produce its own secret key and public key pair (SK_i, PK_i), and a description of a circuit f, In addition, it initializes an identity table T.

$Encrypt(M, PP, PK_i, x \in \{0,1\}^n) \rightarrow CT$. The encryption algorithm takes as input a message M, public parameters PP, the relevant attribute authorities' public keys PK_i, a bit string $x \in \{0,1\}^n$ representing the assignment of boolean variables. It outputs a ciphertext CT.

$KeyGen(SK_i, f, S_U, GID) \rightarrow SK$. The key generation algorithm takes in the authority's secret key SK_i, the description of a circuit f, the attributes set of user and the global identifier GID. It outputs the secret key SK, and next puts the tuple of GID into the identity table T.

$Decrypt(CT, SK) \rightarrow M$. The decryption algorithm takes in the ciphertext CT, secret key SK. It outputs the plaintext M if decryption succeeds, and terminate otherwise.

$Trace(SK, T) \rightarrow GID$ or $\emptyset$. The tracing algorithm takes as inputs a secret key SK and identity table T. It outputs the GID from the identity tables T implying SK is related to GID. Otherwise, the algorithm outputs $\emptyset$ implying SK can't be found in the table.

Security Model. We now define security model for decentralized ABE scheme for circuits on the basis of [5,6,9,25,30]. Our scheme can achieve CPA-secure under the selective-set model. It allows the adversary to query for any private keys as long as the queried keys cannot be used to decrypt the challenge ciphertext, in other words, the adversary can repeatedly ask for secret keys with different circuits, but should encrypt with the string x^* such that $f(x^*) = 0$. Some used notations are indicated in Table 1 and the formal security model is given as follows.

1. *Init.* The adversary $\mathcal{A}$ declares the challenge input x^* at the outset of the game. Here, we assume that *at least one authority* is uncorrupted.
   Global Setup. The challenger runs the *Global Setup* algorithm and sends public parameters to $\mathcal{A}$.
   Authority Setup. The simulator, $\mathcal{S}$, generates the authorities' public/secret keys, just as the challenger.
   - For corrupted authority: the simulator gives the public/secret keys to $\mathcal{A}$.
   - For honest authority: the simulator only gives the public keys to $\mathcal{A}$.
2. *Phase 1.* $\mathcal{A}$ can query secret keys for circuit descriptions f of its choice, where $f(x^*) = 0$. $\mathcal{S}$ returns $KeyGen(SK_i, f, S_U, GID)$.
3. *Challenge.* The adversary $\mathcal{A}$ submits two equal-length messages M_0, M_1. The simulator $\mathcal{S}$ flips a random coin $b \in \{0,1\}$ and returns the challenge ciphertext $CT^* = Encrypt(PP, x^*, M_b)$ to $\mathcal{A}$.
4. *Phase 2.* *Phase 1.* is repeated for additional f satisfying $f(x^*) = 0$.
5. *Guess.* The adversary outputs a guess b' of b.

4   The Architecture

The architecture of our key-policy decentralized AB-EHR system contains six entities, as shown in Fig. 1. A patient, owning his/her Personal Health Record

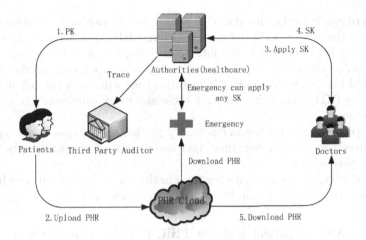

Fig. 1. Cloud-based decentralized AB-EHR system

(PHR), is allowed to encrypt the record in terms of different attributes and further upload the encryption to the cloud server. The ciphertext is only constant-size, i.e. the communication cost on the side of patient is constant. Each doctor (as well as health professional) is associated with a global identifier (GID). (Multiple) attribute authorities will check the GID to determine the privilege of access right and meanwhile, record the GID in a table for malicious behaviors tracing. Doctors or emergency professionals can decide the access policy to reveal a patient's PHR they need from the cloud server. The difference on the PHR retrieval between doctors and emergency professionals is that the latter can apply any decryption key from authorities. The third parity auditor (TPA) is used to trace malicious doctors or professionals (who sell the partial or whole decryption keys for profits) by GID. The multiple authorities (without the help of a central authority (CA)) can issue (access policy based) decryption keys to doctors or emergency professionals anytime.

4.1   The Workflow

The workflow and functionalities of our EHR system is shown in Fig. 1.

- **System Setup.** The initialization step includes two parts, one is the global setup and the other is authorities setup. Each authority outputs public key(s) to the corresponding PHR data owner(s), and keeps the secret key of the attribute authority secret. Meanwhile, each authority initializes an identity table used for traceability.
- **Encryption.** To prevent leaking the sensitive PHR data to public, an data owner firstly encrypts data using the public key according to doctor's and other healthcare professional's attributes, and next to upload the ciphertext to the EHR cloud server.

- **Decryption Key Generation.** A doctor (or a healthcare professional) has to obtain the decryption key before revealing PHR data. To do so, he sends the decryption key request to attribute authorities, in which the request consists of his global identifier and the access policy associated with which PHR data he would like to access to. Attribute authorities will check the privilege of the doctor by GID, record the GID in a table and eventually send the decryption key to him.
- **Decryption.** A doctor (or an emergency professional) can seek out a patient's PHR from the cloud server, download and next to decrypt the data by using the decryption key.
- **Traceability.** A malicious doctor (or a healthcare professional) can be traced and identified in the system by a third party auditor.

Use case. Alice, a patient with her PHR, plans to visit a local hospital to remedy her toothache tomorrow. She is allowed to firstly register on a cloud-based healthcare server, to encrypt her PHR (recorded by other clinic/health center) using the attributes $\{Dentistry, DoctorLevel, Date\}$, and to upload the encryption to the EHR cloud. Bob, a dentist of the hospital, may choose to gain access to Alice's PHR by using his decryption key, so that he can prepare the treatment for tomorrow in advance. To do so, he needs to request the decryption key with the $\{Dentistry \wedge Expert \wedge Tomorrow\}$ access policy using his GID from attribute authorities. The Attribute authorities will verify the GID. If the verification is valid, the authorities generate the key, send it to Bob, and further record Bob's GID. Using the key, Bob can read Alice's PHR. Note that only the required PHR (Alice's one) satisfying the access policy will be download form the cloud. For the emergency case, we assume that Cart is an emergency professional. When he rescues a patient who has hardly fever, he needs to know the pathogenesis of the patient. To read the PHR urgently, Cart can request the decryption key with access policy $\{Medicine \vee InfectiousDisease\}$ (from the attribute authorities), and next download and decrypt the data from the cloud server. It is significant for professionals to do so to save time in handling emergent patients.

5   Our EHR System

5.1   The Construction

- **Global Setup.** The setup algorithm takes as input a security parameter λ, the maximum depth l of a circuit, and the number n of boolean inputs. It runs $\mathcal{G}(1^\lambda, k = l + 1)$ and of groups $\mathbb{G} = (\mathbb{G}_1, ..., \mathbb{G}_k)$ of prime order p, with canonical generators $g_1, ..., g_k$. We let $g = g_1$ and h be the generators of $\mathbb{G}_{k-1}$. Suppose there are N authorities $A_1, A_2, ..., A_N$ in the system. A_i monitors a set of attributes $S_i = (s_{i,1}, s_{i,2}, ..., s_{i,n_i})$, for $i = 1, 2, ..., N$, $n_i \leq n$.
- **Authorities Setup.** The authority A_i chooses two random exponents $\alpha_i, \beta_i \in \mathbb{Z}_p$ and computes $X_i = g_k^{\alpha_i}, Y_i = g^{\beta_i}$. For each attribute $s_{ij} \in S_i$, A_i randomly

chooses $t_{ij} \in \mathbb{Z}_p$, and computes $T_{ij} = g^{t_{ij}}$. A_i publishes $PK_i = \{X_i, Y_i, T_{ij}\}$ as its public key, and keeps $SK_i = \{\alpha_i, \beta_i, t_{ij}\}$ as its secret, where $j = 1, 2, ..., n_i$. In addition, it initializes an identity table T.

- **Encryption.** The encryption algorithm inputs the public parameters, a descriptor input $x \in \{0,1\}^n$, a message bit of PHR $M \in \{0,1\}$ and a set of attributes S_C. This algorithm chooses a random value $s \in \mathbb{Z}_p$. If $M = 0$, it sets C_M to be a random group element in $\mathbb{G}_k$, otherwise it sets $C_M = \prod_{i \in I} g_k^{\alpha_i s}$, where $S_i \cap S_C$ is the set of s_{ij} such that $x_j = 1$ and I is the index set of authorities A_i satisfying $S_i \cap S_C \neq \emptyset$. The ciphertext is output and stored on the EHR cloud server as

$$CT = (C_1 = C_M, C_2 = g^s, C_3 = \prod_{i \in I} Y_i^s, C_{i,4} = \prod_{j \in S_i \cap S_C} T_{ij}^s)$$

- **Key Generation.** The key generation algorithm inputs the secret key of the attribute authority A_i, SK_i, and a description f of a circuit. Assume that a doctor (or a healthcare professional) has the global identifier $u \in \mathbb{Z}_p$ and a set of attributes S_U, a circuit has $n + q$ wires with n input wires, q gates and the wire $n + q$ designated as the output wire.

To create a key for a doctor (or a healthcare professional) u for attribute $s_{ij} \in S_i$, A_i first chooses $r_{i,1}, ..., r_{i,n+q} \in \mathbb{Z}_p$ and computes the key components $K_i = g_{k-1}^{\alpha_i + r_{i,n+q}} h^{u\beta_i}$ and $J_{ij} = h^{t_{ij}}$. The algorithm adds the tuple (K_i, u) into the identity table T.

A_i generates other key components for each wire w that depends on if w is an input wire, an OR gate, or an AND gate. The corresponding key components for each case will be generated as follows. We note that $r_{i,w}$ is associated with wire w.

- Input wire. If $w \in [1, n]$, it corresponds to the wth input. A_i randomly chooses $z_{i,w} \in \mathbb{Z}_p$, and the key components are $K_{i,1} = g^{r_{i,w}}$ and a set of $T_{ij}^{z_{i,w}}, j \in S_i \cap S_U$ $K_{i,2} = g^{-z_{i,w}}$.

- OR gate: If $w \in Gates$, $GateType(w) = OR$, and v is the depth of wire w, A_i randomly chooses $a_{i,w}, b_{i,w} \in \mathbb{Z}_p$. The key components are $K_{i,1} = g^{a_{i,w}}, K_{i,2} = g^{b_{i,w}}, K_{i,3} = g_v^{r_{i,w} - a_{i,w} r_{i,A(w)}}, K_{i,4} = g_v^{r_{i,w} - b_{i,w} r_{i,B(w)}}$, where $A(w)$ identifies w's first incoming wire and $B(w)$ identifies w's second incoming wire.

- AND gate:
  If $w \in Gates$, $GateType(w) = AND$, and v is the depth of wire w, A_i randomly chooses $a_{i,w}, b_{i,w} \in \mathbb{Z}_p$. The key components are $K_{i,1} = g^{a_{i,w}}, K_{i,2} = g^{b_{i,w}}, K_{i,3} = g_v^{r_{i,w} - a_{i,w} r_{i,A(w)} - b_{i,w} r_{i,B(w)}}$. The secret key SK consists of the description of f, K_i, J_{ij} and the key components for each wire w.

- **Decryption.** The decryption algorithm intakes the ciphertext CT, the secret key SK, and outputs the PHR. For the ciphertext with input x and a secret key corresponding with a circuit f, the decryptor can decrypt if $f(x) = 1$. To decrypt the ciphertext CT, the decryptor first checks whether the equation

$\prod_{j \in S_i \cap S_C} e(J_{ij}, (g^s)^u) = e(h^u, C_{i,4})$ holds. If it cannot pass the verification, it means that the keys are from malicious AA, and then stops the process, which can avoid the waste of network resource due to invalid secret keys; otherwise, the decryptor continues computing

$$D_{i,0} = e(K_i, g^s) = g_k^{\alpha_i s + r_{i,n+q} s} e(g^s, h^{u\beta_i})$$

Obviously, the latter part is easy to obtain by calculating $e(C_3, h^u)$. So we only need to compute $g_k^{r_{i,n+q} s}$.

We will assess the circuit from the bottom up. Under the case that w is at depth v, if $f_w(x) = 1$, the decryptor will compute $E_{i,w} = g_{v+1}^{r_{i,w} s}$. We also divide the wire w into three types, input wire, AND gate and OR gate, to discuss how to compute $E_{i,w}$ for all w where $f_w(x) = 1$.

- Input wire. If $w \in [1, n]$, it corresponds to the wth input. If $x_w = f_w(x) = 1$, the decryptor computes $E_{i,w} = e(g^{r_{i,w}} \prod_{j \in S_i \cap S_C} T_{ij}^{z_{i,w}}, g^s) e(K_{i,2}, C_{i,4}) = g_2^{r_{i,w} s}$.

- OR gate. The case is that $w \in Gates$, $GateType(w) = OR$, and v is the depth of wire w. Consider that $f_w(x) = 1$, if $f_{A(w)}(x) = 1$, the decryptor computes

$$E_{i,w} = e(E_{i,A(w)}, K_{i,1}) e(K_{i,3}, g^s) = g_{v+1}^{r_{i,w} s}$$

If $f_{A(w)}(x) = 0$, but $f_{B(w)}(x) = 1$, the $E_{i,w}$ can be computed similarly

$$E_{i,w} = e(E_{i,B(w)}, K_{i,2}) e(K_{i,4}, g^s) = g_{v+1}^{r_{i,w} s}$$

- AND gate. The case is that $w \in Gates$, $GateType(w) = AND$, and v is the depth of wire w. Consider that $f_w(x) = 1$, if $f_{A(w)}(x) = f_{B(w)}(x) = 1$, the decryptor computes

$$E_{i,w} = e(E_{i,A(w)}, K_{i,1}) e(E_{i,B(w)}, K_{i,2}) e(K_{i,3}, g^s) = g_{v+1}^{r_{i,w} s}$$

So, if $f(x) = f_{n+q}(x) = 1$, the decryptor can compute $E_{i,n+q} = g_k^{r_{i,n+q} s}$. Finally, the decryptor computes

$$\frac{\prod_{i \in I} D_{i,0}}{(\prod_{i \in I} E_{i,n+q}) e(C_3, h^u)} = \prod_{i \in I} g_k^{\alpha_i s}$$

If it equals C_M, output $M = 1$; otherwise output $M = 0$.

- **Traceability.** The tracing algorithm takes as inputs a secret key SK and the identity table T. The algorithm searches K_i in the identity table T. If K_i can be found in the table T, the algorithm outputs the corresponding u to identity a malicious doctor (or a healthcare professional). Otherwise, the algorithm outputs $\emptyset$.

Correctness. We present the correctness analysis for the above scheme. Since

$$D_i = \prod_{i \in I} D_{i,0} = \prod_{i \in I} e(K_i, g^s) = \prod_{i \in I} e(g_{k-1}^{\alpha_i + r_{i,n+q}} h^{u\beta_i}, g^s)$$

$$= \prod_{i \in I} g_k^{\alpha_i s + r_{i,n+q} s} \cdot \prod_{i \in I} e(g^s, h^{u\beta_i}),$$

$$E_i = \prod_{i \in I} E_{i,n+q} = \prod_{i \in I} g_k^{r_{i,n+q} s}, F_i = e(C_3, h^u) = e(\prod_{i \in I} g^{\beta_i s}, h^u) = \prod_{i \in I} e(g^s, h^{u\beta_i}),$$

we have,

$$C_M = \frac{D_i}{E_i \cdot F_i} = \frac{\prod_{i \in I} g_k^{\alpha_i s + r_{i,n+q} s} \cdot \prod_{i \in I} e(g^s, h^{u\beta_i})}{\prod_{i \in I} g_k^{r_{i,n+q} s} \cdot \prod_{i \in I} e(g^s, h^{u\beta_i})} = \prod_{i \in I} g_k^{\alpha_i s}.$$

6 System Analysis

6.1 Security Analysis

In this section, we prove that our proposed EHR system is CPA secure in the selective set model. The proof consists of two parts.

Theorem 1. *If there is an adversary $\mathcal{A}$ against the proposed EHR system with non-negligible advantage in the game defined in Sect. 3.3, there exists a simulator $\mathcal{S}$ that can break the k-MDDH extension assumption with a non-negligible advantage.*

Proof. Suppose there exists a probabilistic polynomial time adversary $\mathcal{A}$, who plays the security game as described in Sect. 3.3 and succeeds with non-negligible probability.

1. *Init.* We first let the challenger run the $\mathcal{G}(1^\lambda, k)$ and of groups $\mathbb{G} = (\mathbb{G}_1, ..., \mathbb{G}_k)$ and set a problem instance $g, g^s, g^{c_1}, g^{c_2}, ..., g^{c_k}, T$. T is either $g_k^{s \prod_{v \in [1,k]} c_v}$ or a random group element in $\mathbb{G}_k$. The adversary declares the challenge input $x^* \in \{0,1\}^n$. Suppose that the attributes set S^* is mapped to the input $x_j^* = 1$.
2. *Authority setup.* There should be at least one uncorrupted authority where the adversary cannot obtain the private key of authority.
   - Corrupted Authority-If the authority A_i is corrupted, $\mathcal{S}$ chooses random $\xi_i, b_i, y_{ij} \in \mathbb{Z}_p$ and sets: $X_i = g_k^{\xi_i}$, $Y_i = g^{b_i}$, $T_{ij} = g^{y_{ij}}$. $\mathcal{S}$ sends both (ξ_i, b_i, y_{ij}) and (X_i, Y_i, T_{ij}) to $\mathcal{A}$.
   - Honest Authority-If the authority A_i is uncorrupted, $\mathcal{S}$ chooses random $\xi_i, b_i, y_{ij} \in \mathbb{Z}_p$ and sets: $X_i = g_k^{\xi_i + \prod_{j \in [1,k]} c_j}$, $Y_i = g^{b_i}$, if $x_i^* = 1$, $T_{ij} = g^{y_{ij}}$, if $x_i^* = 0$, $T_{ij} = g^{y_{ij} + c_1}$. $\mathcal{S}$ sends (X_i, Y_i, T_{ij}) to $\mathcal{A}$.
3. *Phase 1.* The adversary $\mathcal{A}$ gives a circuit f where $f(x^*) = 0$. (1). If the authority A_i is corrupted, $\mathcal{A}$ can use (ξ_i, b_i, y_{ij}) to compute secret keys for decryption by itself. (2). If the authority A_i is uncorrupted, we still consider the gate w like the construction, where $depth(w) = v$. The value of $r_{i,w}$ relies on different cases of $f_w(x^*)$. If $f_w(x^*) = 1$, the simulator $\mathcal{S}$ takes $r_{i,w}$ as some known randomization value. If $f_w(x^*) = 0$, the simulator $\mathcal{S}$ takes $r_{i,w}$ as $-c_1...c_v$ plus some known randomization value. To the wire w, the key components generation is still divided into input wires, OR gate and AND gate.

- Input wire. Assume $w \in [1, n]$, then it corresponds to the wth input. If $f_w(x^*) = 1$, it chooses $r_{i,w}$ and $z_{i,w}$ at random from $\mathbb{Z}_p$. The key components are $K_{i,1} = g^{r_{i,w}}$ and a set of $T_{ij}^{z_{i,w}}$, $j \in S_i \cap S_U$ $K_{i,2} = g^{-z_{i,w}}$. If $f_w(x^*) = 0$, it sets $r_{i,w} = -c_1 c_2 + \eta_{i,w}$ and $z_{i,w} = c_2 + \theta_{i,w}$, where $\eta_{i,w}$ and $\theta_{i,w}$ are chosen at random from $\mathbb{Z}_p$. The key components are $K_{i,1} = g^{-c_2 c_1 + \eta_{i,w}}$ and a set of $T_{ij}^{c_2 + \theta_{i,w}}$, $j \in S_i \cap S_U$ $K_{i,2} = g^{-c_2 - \theta_{i,w}}$.

- OR gate. Assume $w \in Gates$, $GateType(w) = OR$, and $v = depth(w)$. If $f_w(x^*) = 1$, it chooses $a_{i,w}$, $b_{i,w}$ and $r_{i,w}$ at random from $\mathbb{Z}_p$. The key components are

$$K_{i,1} = g^{a_{i,w}}, K_{i,2} = g^{b_{i,w}}, K_{i,3} = g_v^{r_{i,w} - a_{i,w} r_{i,A(w)}}, K_{i,4} = g_v^{r_{i,w} - b_{i,w} r_{i,B(w)}}.$$

If $f_w(x^*) = 0$, it sets $a_{i,w} = c_{v+1} + \phi_{i,w}$, $b_{i,w} = c_{v+1} + \varphi_{i,w}$, and $r_{i,w} = -c_1 ... c_{v+1} + \eta_{i,w}$, where $\phi_{i,w}$, $\varphi_{i,w}$ and $\eta_{i,w}$ are chosen randomly from $\mathbb{Z}_p$. The key components are

$$K_{i,1} = g^{c_{v+1} + \phi_{i,w}}, K_{i,2} = g^{c_{v+1} + \varphi_{i,w}},$$
$$K_{i,3} = g_v^{\eta_{i,w} - c_{v+1} \eta_{i,A(w)} - \phi_{i,w}(-c_1 ... c_v + \eta_{i,A(w)})},$$
$$K_{i,4} = g_v^{\eta_{i,w} - c_{v+1} \eta_{i,B(w)} - \varphi_{i,w}(-c_1 ... c_v + \eta_{i,B(w)})}.$$

- AND gate. Assume $w \in Gates$, $GateType(w) = AND$, and $v = depth(w)$. If $f_w(x^*) = 1$, it chooses $a_{i,w}$, $b_{i,w}$ and $r_{i,w}$ at random from $\mathbb{Z}_p$. The key components are

$$K_{i,1} = g^{a_{i,w}}, K_{i,2} = g^{b_{i,w}}, K_{i,3} = g_v^{r_{i,w} - a_{i,w} r_{i,A(w)} - b_{i,w} r_{i,B(w)}}.$$

If $f_w(x^*) = 0$ and $f_{A(w)}(x^*) = 0$, it sets $a_{i,w} = c_{v+1} + \phi_{i,w}$, $b_{i,w} = \varphi_{i,w}$, and $r_{i,w} = -c_1 ... c_{v+1} + \eta_{i,w}$, where $\phi_{i,w}$, $\varphi_{i,w}$ and $\eta_{i,w}$ are chosen randomly from $\mathbb{Z}_p$. The key components are

$$K_{i,1} = g^{c_{v+1} + \phi_{i,w}}, K_{i,2} = g^{\varphi_{i,w}},$$
$$K_{i,3} = g_v^{\eta_{i,w} - c_{v+1} \eta_{i,A(w)} + \phi_{i,w} c_1 ... c_v - \phi_{i,w} \eta_{i,A(w)} - \varphi_{i,w} r_{i,B(w)}}.$$

So we have $r_{i,n+q} = -\prod_{v \in [1,k]} c_v + \eta_{i,n+q}$, $K_i = g_{k-1}^{\alpha_i + r_{i,n+q}} h^{u \beta_i} = g_{k-1}^{\xi_i + \eta_{i,n+q}} h^{u^* b_i}$ and $J_{ij} = h^{y_{ij} + c_1}$.

4. *Challenge.* Let I^* be the index set of attributes authorities, where $x_j^* = 1$. $\mathcal{S}$ creates the challenge ciphertext as $CT = (\prod_{i \in I^*} T \cdot g_k^{\xi_i s}, g^s, \prod_{i \in I^*}(g^s)^{b_i}, \prod_{j \in S^*}(g^s)^{y_{ij}})$. If $T = g_k^{s \prod_{v \in [1,k]} c_v}$, this is an encryption of 1; if T is a random group element in $\mathbb{G}_k$, it is an encryption of 0.

5. *Phase 2.* The repeated queries for additional circuit description under the same restrictions as *Phase 1*.

6. *Guess.* The adversary $\mathcal{A}$ will eventually output a guess M' of M. The simulator $\mathcal{S}$ guesses $T = g_k^{s \prod_{v \in [1,k]} c_v}$ is a tuple if $M' = 1$, otherwise T is a random group element in $\mathbb{G}_k$.

Theorem 2. *The proposed EHR system achieves collusion resistance.*

Proof. In our scheme, we tie a doctor's key components with different global identifiers u in K_i. If two doctors with different global identifiers u, u' attempt to collude by attributes j and k, they need to combine their keys to run the decryption algorithm. They can obtain the secret keys (K_i, J_{ij}), (K_i, J_{ik}) and other key components corresponding attribute j and k. In the decryption process, the term $e(g^s, h^{u\beta_i})$ of $D_{i,0}$ should be cancelled out as the valid decryption using C_3, so that the doctors can obtain $g_k^{\alpha_i s}$. Now, to the colluded doctor u and u', they can compute $e(\prod_{i \in I} g^{\beta_i s}, h^u)$ and $e(\prod_{i \in I} g^{\beta_i s}, h^{u'})$, but they cannot cancel out the term $e(g^s, h^{u\beta_i})$ of $D_{i,0}$ due to the difference between u and u', thus they cannot recover $\prod_{i \in I} g_k^{\alpha_i s}$. In other words, colluded doctors cannot successfully decrypt a target ciphertext here. Therefore, our proposed construction can hold against collusion attack.

6.2 Efficiency Analysis

In this section, we make the efficiency analysis for our EHR system in terms of the storage overhead, communication cost and computation complexity. Some notations are defined in Table 2.

Table 2. Complexity notations

$\lvert G \rvert$	The length of the element in $\mathbb{G}$
$\lvert G_T \rvert$	The length of the element in $\mathbb{G}_T$
$\lvert G_k \rvert$	The length of the element in $\mathbb{G}_k$
exp	The time of exponential operation
e	The time of bilinear pairing operation
m	The time of multilinear maps operation
$\lvert p \rvert$	The length of the element in $\mathbb{Z}_p$

Table 3. The comparison of ciphertext length, decryption time and key size

Scheme	Ciphertext size	Decryption time	Key size
Chase [5]	$(S_C + 1)\lvert G \rvert + \lvert G_T \rvert$	$S_C exp + (S_C + 1)e$	$\lvert G \rvert + S_C \lvert G \rvert$
Chase & Chow [6]	$(S_C + 1)\lvert G \rvert + \lvert G_T \rvert$	$I_C exp + (S_C + 1)e$	$\lvert G \rvert + S_C \lvert G \rvert$
Muller et al. [27]	$2I_C \lvert G \rvert + I_C \lvert G_T \rvert$	$2e$	$\lvert G \rvert + S_C(2\lvert G \rvert + \lvert G_T \rvert)$
Liu et al. [25]	$(2S_C + 1)\lvert G \rvert + \lvert G_T \rvert$	$(S_C + 1)exp + 2S_C e$	$(S_C + 1)\lvert G_{p_1 p_3} \rvert$
Lewko & Water [15]	$2S_C \lvert G \rvert + (S_C + 1)\lvert G_T \rvert$	$3S_C(e + exp)$	$S_C \lvert G \rvert$
Han et al. [11]	$(S_C + 2)\lvert G \rvert + \lvert G_T \rvert$	$S_C exp + (S_C + I_C + 1)e$	$(I_C + S_C)\lvert G \rvert$
Ours	$\lvert G_k \rvert + 3\lvert G \rvert$	$3I_C m + e$	$I_C \lvert G_k \rvert + (2I_C + S_C)\lvert G \rvert$

- **Storage Overhead.** We analyze the storage overhead of our systems on different aspects. In our proposal, the storage overhead of the attribute authority denotes as its secret key SK_i. The secret key SK contributes to a user's storage overhead. A PHR owner's storage overhead comes from the public keys of the authorities PK_i. The space usage of ciphertext CT is regarded as the storage overhead on the EHR cloud server. Therefore, in our proposal, the storage overhead of authority, healthcare professional, data owner and cloud server is $(2+S_A)|p|$, $I_C|G_k|+(2I_C+S_C)|G|$, $I_C|G_k|+(I_C+S_C)|G|$, $|G_k|+3|G|$, respectively.

- **Communication Cost.** Communication cost is mainly incurred by the keys and ciphertexts delivery in the system. Precisely speaking, the communication cost between attribute authorities and healthcare professional is the size of decryption key. The ciphertext size forms the communication cost not only between data owner and the cloud server but also between the cloud server and healthcare professional. Therefore, as shown in Table 3, the communication cost of delivering the decryption key from attribute authorities to healthcare professional, uploading ciphertext from data owner to the cloud server and downloading ciphertext from the cloud server to healthcare professional of our scheme is respectively $I_C|G_k| + (2I_C + S_C)|G|$, $|G_k| + 3|G|$, $|G_k| + 3|G|$.

- **Computation Complexity.** We make comparisons of ciphertext size, decryption time and secret key size with some related works in Table 3. From the perspective of light storage requirement in cloud-based EHR context, our scheme is the only one whose storage overhead is constant. In other words, the storage space of our system does not increase with the number of attributes and authorities. In this way, the cloud server can store much more data than other existing ABE schemes [5,6,11,15,25,27]. The communication cost between the cloud server and healthcare professional is significantly dropped. At the same time, our proposal needs much less decryption time than others [5,6,15,25], while [11,27] outperform ours in decryption. As to the key size, ours is a little longer than others, but we state that the healthcare professional can bear it.

To sum up, our scheme is the first of its type that can reduce the dependency of central authority, achieve expressive access structure (circuit), enjoy constant storage cost, and guarantee data confidentiality, achieving all needs in cloud-based EHR systems. Therefore, our scheme is more practical and scalable compared to others existing works.

7   Conclusion

In this paper, we constructed a secure and scalable cloud-based EHR system by leveraging decentralized ABE technique. The novel system allows users to use circuit to express fine-grained access policy, and furthermore keeps storage complexity constant on the side of cloud server. By security and efficiency analysis, we showed that our proposal is secure and scalable compared to other existing research works.

Acknowledgements. Wei Wu was supported by the National Natural Science Foundation of China under Grant 61472083 and Grant 61402110.

References

1. Akinyele, J., Pagano, M.: Securing electronic medical records using attribute-based encryption on mobile devices. In: SPSM, pp. 75–86 (2011)
2. Armbrust, M., Fox, A., Griffith, R.: A view of cloud computing. Commun. ACM **53**, 50–58 (2010)
3. Attrapadung, N., Libert, B., Panafieu, E.: Expressive key-policy attribute-based encryption with constant-size ciphertexts. In: PKC, pp. 90–108 (2011)
4. Bethencourt, J., Sahai, A., Waters, B.: Ciphertext-policy attribute-based encryption. In: S&P, pp. 321–334. IEEE (2007)
5. Chase, M.: Multi-authority attribute based encryption. In: Vadhan, S.P. (ed.) TCC 2007. LNCS, vol. 4392, pp. 515–534. Springer, Heidelberg (2007)
6. Chase, M., Chow, S.: Improving privacy and security in multi-authority attribute-based encryption. In: CCS, pp. 121–130 (2009)
7. Emura, K., Miyaji, A., Nomura, A., Omote, K., Soshi, M.: A ciphertext-policy attribute-based encryption scheme with constant ciphertext length. In: Bao, F., Li, H., Wang, G. (eds.) ISPEC 2009. LNCS, vol. 5451, pp. 13–23. Springer, Heidelberg (2009)
8. Garg, S., Gentry, C., Halevi, S.: Candidate multilinear maps from ideal lattices. In: Johansson, T., Nguyen, P.Q. (eds.) EUROCRYPT 2013. LNCS, vol. 7881, pp. 1–17. Springer, Heidelberg (2013)
9. Garg, S., Gentry, C., Halevi, S.: Attribute-Based Encryption for Circuits from Multilinear Maps. In: Crypto, pp. 479–499 (2013)
10. Green, M., Hohenberger, S., Waters, B.: Outsourcing the decryption of ABE ciphertexts. In: USENIX11, pp. 34–49 (2011)
11. Han, J., Susilo, W., Mu, Y.: Privacy-preserving decentralized key-policy attribute-based encryption. IEEE Trans. Parallel Distrib. Syst. **23**(11), 2150–2162 (2012)
12. Ibraimi, L., Asim, M., Petkovic, M.: Secure management of personal health records by applying attribute-based encryption. In: IEEE, pp. 71–74 (2009)
13. Jiang, P., Mu, Y., Guo, F., Wen, Q.: Secure-channel free keyword search with authorization in manager-centric databases. Comput. Secur. (2016). doi:10.1016/j.cose.2016.11.015
14. Jiang, P., Mu, Y., Guo, F., Wang, X., Lai, J.: Centralized keyword search on encrypted data for cloud applications. Secur. Commun. Netw. (2016). doi:10.1002/sec.1679
15. Lewko, A., Waters, B.: Decentralizing attribute-based encryption. In: Paterson, K.G. (ed.) EUROCRYPT 2011. LNCS, vol. 6632, pp. 568–588. Springer, Heidelberg (2011)
16. Li, J., Chen, X., Li, J., Jia, C., Ma, J., Lou, W.: Fine-grained access control system based on outsourced attribute-based encryption. In: Crampton, J., Jajodia, S., Mayes, K. (eds.) ESORICS 2013. LNCS, vol. 8134, pp. 592–609. Springer, Heidelberg (2013)
17. Li, M., Yu, S.: Scalable and secure sharing of personal health records in cloud computing using attribute-based encryption. IEEE Trans. Parallel Distrib. Syst. **24**(1), 131–143 (2013)
18. Li, J., Qin, C., Lee, P., Li, J.: Rekeying for encrypted deduplication In: DSN, pp. 618–629 (2016)

19. Liang, K., Huang, X., Guo, F., Liu, J.: Privacy-preserving and regular language search over encrypted cloud data. IEEE Trans. Inf. Forensics Secur. **11**(10), 2365–2376 (2016)
20. Liang, K., Su, C., Chen, J., Liu, J.: Efficient multi-function data sharing and searching mechanism for cloud-based encrypted data. In: AsiaCCS, pp. 83–94 (2016)
21. Liang, K., Fang, L., Susilo, W., Wong, D. A Ciphertext-Policy Attribute-Based Proxy Re-encryption with Chosen-Ciphertext Security. In: INCoS, pp. 552–559 (2013)
22. Liang, K., Au, M., Liu, K., Susilo, W., Wong, D., Yang, G., Phuong, T., Xie, Q.: A DFA-based functional proxy re-encryption scheme for secure public cloud data sharing. IEEE Trans. Inf. Forensics Secur. **9**(10), 1667–1680 (2014)
23. Liang, K., Susilo, W.: Searchable attribute-based mechanism with efficient data sharing for secure cloud storage. IEEE Trans. Inf. Forensics Secur. **10**(9), 1981–1992 (2015)
24. Liu, Z., Cao, Z.: White-box traceable ciphertext-policy attribute-based encryption supporting any monotone access structures. IEEE Trans. Inf. Forensics Secur. **8**(1), 76–88 (2013)
25. Liu, Z., Cao, Z., Huang, Q.: Fully secure multi-authority ciphertext-policy attribute-based encryption without random oracles. In: ESORICS, pp. 278–297 (2011)
26. Liu, X., Liu, Q.: Dynamic access policy in cloud-based Personal Health Record (PHR) systems. Inf. Sci. **379**, 62–81 (2017)
27. Muller, S., Katzenbeisser, S., Eckert, C.: On multi- authority ciphertext-policy attribute-based encryption. Bull. Korean Math. Soc. **46**(4), 803–819 (2009)
28. Ning, J., Dong, X., Cao, Z.: White-box traceable ciphertext-policy attribute-based encryption supporting flexible attributes. IEEE Trans. Inf. Forensics Secur. **10**(6), 1274–1288 (2015)
29. Sahai, A., Waters, B.: Fuzzy identity based encryption. In: Eurocrypt, pp. 457–473 (2005)
30. Sergey, G., Vinod, V., Hoeteck, W.: Attribute-based encryption for circuits. J. ACM **62**(6), 1–33 (2015)
31. Tamizharasi, G.S., Balamurugan, B., Manjula, R.: Attribute based encryption with fine-grained access provision in cloud computing. In: proceedings of the International Conference on Informatics and Analytics, Article No. 88 (2016)
32. The Cloud Security Alliance Top Threats Working Group. The Notorious Nine: Cloud Computing Top Threats in 2013 (2013). https://cloudsecurityalliance.org/research/top-threats
33. Wang, C., Luo, F.: An efficient key-policy attribute-based encryption scheme with constant ciphertext length. Math. Problems Eng. **2013**, 7 p. (2013). Article ID 810969
34. Wang, S., Liang, K., Liu, K., Chen, J., Yu, J., Xie, W.: Attribute-based data sharing scheme revisited in cloud computing. IEEE Trans. Inf. Forensics Secur. **11**(8), 1661–1673 (2016)
35. Waters, B.: Ciphertext-policy attribute-based encryption: an expressive, efficient, and provably secure realization. In: PKC, pp. 53–70 (2011)
36. Yang, Y., Liu, J., Liang, K., Choo, K., Zhou, J.: Extended proxy-assisted approach: achieving revocable fine-grained encryption of cloud data. In: ESORICS, pp. 146–166 (2015)
37. Zhang, P., Chen, Z., Liang, K., Wang, S., Wang, T.: A cloud-based access control scheme with user revocation and attribute update. In: ACISP, pp. 525–540 (2016)

Automatic Diagnosis Metabolic Syndrome via a $k-$Nearest Neighbour Classifier

Omar Behadada[1], Meryem Abi-Ayad[1],
Georgios Kontonatsios[2(✉)], and Marcello Trovati[2]

[1] Biomedical Engineering Laboratory, Faculty of Technology,
University of Tlemcen, Chetouane, Algeria
[2] Department of Computer Science, Edge Hill University, Ormskirk, UK
kontonag@edgehill.ac.uk

Abstract. In this paper, we investigate the automatic diagnosis of patients with metabolic syndrome, i.e., a common metabolic disorder and a risk factor for the development of cardiovascular diseases and type 2 diabetes. Specifically, we employ the k-Nearest neighbour (k-NN) classifier, a supervised machine learning algorithm to learn to discriminate between patients with metabolic syndrome and healthy individuals. To aid accurate identification of the metabolic syndrome we extract different physiological parameters (age, BMI, level of glucose in the blood etc.) that are subsequently used as features in the k-NN classifier. For evaluation, we compare the proposed k-NN algorithm against two baseline machine learning classifiers, namely Naïve Bayes and an artificial Neural Network. Cross-validation experiments on a manually curated dataset of 64 individuals demonstrate that the k-NN classifier improves upon the performance of the baseline methods and it can thus facilitate robust and automatic diagnosis of patients with metabolic syndrome. Finally, we perform feature analysis to determine potential significant correlations between different physiological parameters and the prevalence of the metabolic syndrome.

1 Introduction

The metabolic syndrome (MetS) is defined as the cluster of metabolic abnormalities (e.g., obesity, hypertension, glucose intolerance) that constitute high risk factors for the developments of cardiovascular diseases and type 2 diabetes mellitus [13]. Over the past decade, MetS has been rapidly increasing worldwide affecting both adults and children and thus pauses a major clinical and public health challenge [14,15].

MetS definition appeared for the first time about 25 years ago when this risk factors clustering and its association with insulin resistance suggested the existence of a unique pathophysiological condition [7]. In order to provide uniformity in the description of this phenomenon, different diagnostic criteria have been proposed for MetS. Firstly defined by The World Health Organisation in 1998 [8], many international agencies and organisations subsequently proposed various definitions, among which the most widely used are: the Third Report of the

© Springer International Publishing AG 2017
M.H.A. Au et al. (Eds.): GPC 2017, LNCS 10232, pp. 627–637, 2017.
DOI: 10.1007/978-3-319-57186-7_45

National Cholesterol Education Program Expert Panel on Detection, Evaluation and Treatment of High Blood Cholesterol in Adults (NCEP-ATPIII) (National Cholesterol Education Program 2002), the International Diabetes Federation (IDF) (International Diabetes Federation 2006), and the harmonising criteria of the International Diabetes Federation and American Heart Association/National Heart, Lung and Blood Institute (AHA/NHLBI) [9].

Whilst MetS pauses a major clinical and public health challenge, studies report that a large number of patients that meet the criteria of MetS remains largely undiagnosed. As an example, Helminen et al. [18], showed that the manual diagnosis of MetS by general practitioners in Finland achieves a sensitivity of 0.31 and a specificity of 0.73. Computer-aided techniques that employ machine learning methods to learn to identify patients with MetS can thus facilitate a more reliable diagnosis of the metabolic syndrome. Existing approaches for the automatic identification of MetS proposed different machine learning methods including Decision Trees [16], Artificial Neural Networks [19] and Tree Regression [20]. Worachartcheewan et al., [16] employed decision trees (i.e., J48 algorithm) to identify patients with metabolic syndrome among a Thai population. The results that they obtained showed that the proposed decision trees method achieved a robust performance. Moreover, the authors performed a feature analysis based on the branches of the trained decision trees to identify significant correlations between the different physiological parameters (used as features in the decision trees method) and the prevalence of metabolic syndrome. Ushida et al.,[19] used a fuzzy neural network, i.e., a specialised case of an artificial neural network, to discover associations between physiological factors and the metabolic syndrome. Theirs analysis demonstrated that there is a statistically significant correlation between the metabolic syndrome and an increased level of γ-glutamyltranspeptidase (γ-GTP) combined with an elevated white blood cell (WBC) count.

In this paper we propose k-Nearest Neighbour (k-NN) as classifier of metabolic Syndrome (MetS), in order to create a robust and accurate knowledge-based system, which provides a crucial insight into MetS diagnosis from a variety of information sources. We compare the k-NN classifier against Artificial Neural Networks and a Naïve Bayes classifier and we show that the proposed k-NN method obtains superior performance when compared to the baseline methods. Similarly to previous approaches, we perform a feature analysis based on the distribution of feature across positive (i.e., patients with MetS) and negative classes (i.e., healthy individuals) that reveal significant relationships between physiological parameters and the metabolic syndrome.

The remaining of the paper is structured as follows: in Sect. 2, data preparation and a feature analysis are discussed, and in Sect. 3 an overview of K−Nearest Neighbour (KNN) based classification is presented, which is subsequently investigated and assessed in Sect. 4. Finally, Sect. 5 concludes the paper and discusses future research directions.

2   Data Preparation

Table 1 summarises different characteristics of the dataset that we used in our experiments. A total of 50 metabolic syndrome patients were identified at EPSP-CHU Tlemcen (Algeria). All subjects received physical examination and anthropometric measure at diabetes centre (EPSP Tlemcen) and assessed by a questionnaire. Patients with cardiovascular, renal, hepatic or thyroid diseases were excluded from the study. The age of the patients is in the range of 40 to 69 (average age: 59.78 ± 9.7), Sexes repartition (24.49% Men and 74.51% Women). All subjects have metabolic syndrome according the International Diabetes Federation (IDF, 2005) definition. Patients' waist circumference was ≥94 cm (men) and ≥80 cm (women). A total of 14 volunteering patients in apparent good health were taken as control in the same range age as the patients, (19% Males and 45% Females) in the period between July 2015 and September 2015.

Table 1. Evaluation data

	Normal	MetS	Male	Female
Class	14	50	19	45
	21.88%	78.12%	29.69%	70.31%

2.1   Feature Selection

The descriptors utilised in the feature selection process are as follows

- Age: age of patients;
- ALAT: alanine amino transferase;
- BMI: body mass index;
- CHDL: Cholesterol high density lipoprotein;
- Creatinine: degradation product of creatinine phosphate in the muscle;
- CT: total cholesterol;
- CLDL: cholesterol low density lipoprotein;
- Glycaemia: level of glucose in the blood;
- Proteins: biological macromolecule formed of one or more polypeptide chains;
- Taille: height;
- TourDeTaille: waist circumference;
- Uree: An organic compound with the chemical formula $CO(NH_2)_2$;
- TGT: total triglyceride;
- ASAT: aspartate amino transferase, and finally
- Poids: weight.

2.2   Data Visualisation

Classifying two classes: Normal (Nor) and Metabolic Syndrome (MetS) with only one feature, namely Age ALAT, BMI, etc. is, in general, a complex task due to the lack of threshold for each class. Figures 1, 2, 3, 4, 5, 6 and 7 show the distribution of each feature across the two different classes. It can be observed that discriminating between healthy individuals (Nor) and patients with MetS using a single, isolated feature becomes a challenging task. Note that in Figs. 4, 5 and 6 it is possible to separate between Nor class and MetS, which is a promising aspect.

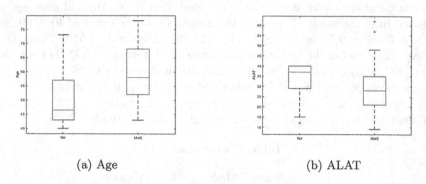

(a) Age   (b) ALAT

Fig. 1. The distribution of features Age and ALAT in different classes

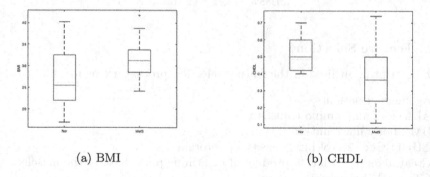

(a) BMI   (b) CHDL

Fig. 2. The distribution of features BMI and CHDL in different classes

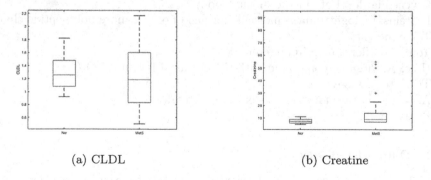

(a) CLDL   (b) Creatine

Fig. 3. The distribution of features CLDL and Creatine in different classes

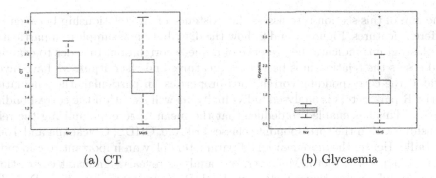

(a) CT   (b) Glycaemia

Fig. 4. The distribution of features CT and Glycaemia in different classes

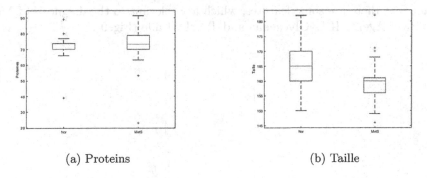

(a) Proteins   (b) Taille

Fig. 5. The distribution of features Proteins and Taille in different classes

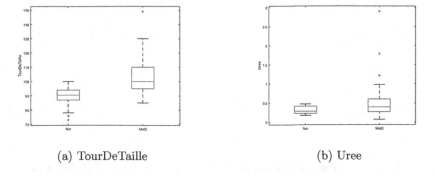

(a) TourDeTaille   (b) Uree

Fig. 6. The distribution of features TourDeTaille and Uree in different classes

2.3 Correlation Study

The aim of this section is to assess the existence of any relationship between the different features. Figures 7 and 8 show the distribution of samples. In particular, the histograms indicate the presence of a linear correlation. In order to evaluate and assess the relationships between all features and the output, we have investigated the corresponding correlations properties. In particular, the calculation of the R parameters is analysed individually, as well as within the corresponding classes. This has enabled to deduce that the mean feature maximising the relationships within the corresponding classes are Age, CHDL, Glycaemia and TourDeTaille. Hence, the aforementioned parameters play an important role in automatic diagnosis of MetS. Moreover, our analysis reveals significant correlations between different features: BMI/Age, BMI/Poids (weight), BMI/TourDeTaille, which can be justified by the fact that these parameters depend upon the body state.

We also found a strong relationship between CT/CLDL, which is expected since CT is the addition of CLDL and other component. In conclusion, we can claim that there are some features, which are relevant to the diagnosis of MetS like BMI, Age, CHDL, Glycaemia and TourDeTaille (Fig. 9).

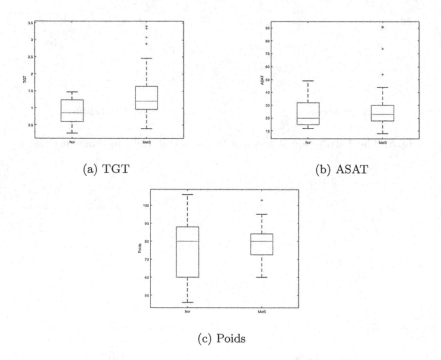

(a) TGT   (b) ASAT

(c) Poids

Fig. 7. The distribution of features TGT, ASAT and Poids in different classes

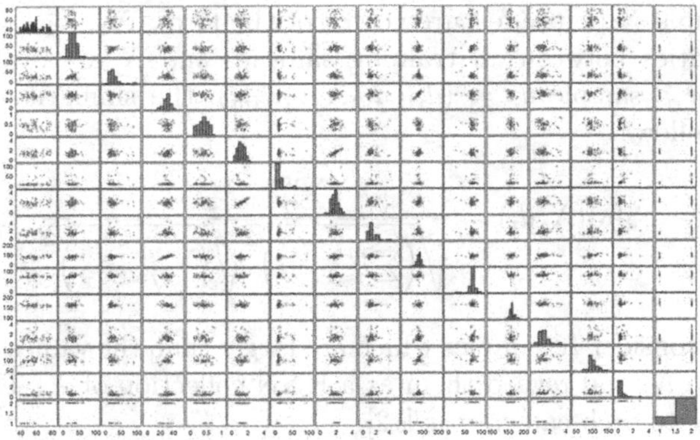

Fig. 8. A scatter plot of correlations between different features used for the automatic identification of the metabolic syndrome

	Age	ALAT	ASAT	BMI	CHDL	CLDL	Creatinine	CT	Glycemie	Poids	Proteines	Taille	TGT	TourDeTaille	Uree	Class
Age	1	-0.2355	-0.2357	0.3587	-0.0120	0.1006	0.1753	0.0962	0.1784	0.2059	0.0163	-0.3367	0.0004	0.2774	0.1191	0.4013
ALAT	-0.2355	1	0.4297	-0.034	-0.0579	0.1172	-0.0819	0.1138	-0.0495	0.1133	0.1375	0.2169	-0.1474	-0.0074	0.0909	-0.1426
ASAT	-0.2357	0.4297	1	-0.0004	0.0742	0.0691	0.0017	0.1152	-0.0527	0.1205	-0.1068	0.1218	0.0924	-0.0841	0.2758	0.0975
BMI	0.3587	-0.03447	-0.0004	1	-0.1780	0.1588	-0.0916	0.1475	0.1531	0.8854	0.0549	0.4504	0.0653	0.4427	0.0045	0.3651
CHDL	-0.0120	-0.0579	0.0742	-0.1780	1	0.1869	-0.0595	0.0289	-0.0925	-0.1898	0.0049	-0.0766	0.0910	-0.1342	0.0151	0.3422
CLDL	0.1006	0.1172	0.0691	0.1588	0.1869	1	-0.0571	0.8802	-0.2374	0.2258	0.0132	-0.0909	-0.0197	-0.0197	0.1215	0.1074
Creatinine	0.1753	-0.0819	0.0017	-0.0916	-0.0595	-0.0571	1	0.0478	0.3164	-0.0550	-0.4266	0.0537	0.2753	-0.0275	0.2527	0.2204
CT	0.0962	0.1138	0.1152	0.1475	0.0289	0.8802	0.0478	1	-0.1734	0.2455	0.0621	0.0868	0.0655	0.0267	0.1058	0.1376
Glycemie	0.1784	-0.0495	-0.0527	0.1531	-0.0925	-0.2374	0.3164	-0.1734	1	0.0431	0.06213	-0.1945	0.2402	0.0831	0.2623	0.4070
Poids	0.2059	0.1133	0.1205	0.8854	-0.1898	0.2258	-0.0550	0.2455	0.0431	1	0.0426	0.0434	0.0835	0.4235	0.0175	0.1798
Proteines	0.0163	0.1375	-0.1068	0.0549	0.0049	0.0132	-0.4266	0.0621	0.0426	0.0426	1	0.0247	-0.1570	0.0791	0.2126	0.1137
Taille	-0.3367	0.2169	0.1218	0.4504	-0.0766	-0.0909	0.0537	0.0868	-0.1945	0.0434	0.0247	1	-0.0413	-0.0413	0.0246	-0.2801
TGT	0.0004	-0.1474	0.0924	0.0653	0.0910	-0.0310	0.2753	0.0655	0.2402	0.0835	-0.1570	-0.0413	1	0.1969	0.0987	0.2791
TourDeTaille	0.2774	-0.0074	-0.0841	0.4427	-0.1342	-0.0197	-0.0275	0.0267	0.0831	0.4235	0.0791	-0.0413	0.1969	1	-0.07545	0.4561
Uree	0.1191	0.09099	0.2758	0.0045	0.0151	0.1215	0.2527	0.1058	0.2623	0.0175	0.2126	0.0246	0.0987	-0.07545	1	0.2055
Class	0.4013	-0.1426	0.0975	0.3651	-0.3422	0.1074	0.2204	0.1376	0.4070	0.1798	0.1137	-0.2801	0.2791	0.4561	0.2055	1

Fig. 9. Correlation coefficients

3 K-Nearest Neighbour (KNN)

k-NN is a non-parametric supervised machine learning algorithm [10] where classification rules are generated by the training samples without any additional data. Loosely speaking, the training phase is defined by vectors in a multidimensional feature space with a class label assigned to each of them. During the classification phase an unlabelled vector is automatically classified to a class category by identifying the most frequent label among the K nearest training samples. The best value of K depends on the data itself. In general, large values of K have an impact in the reduction of noise during the classification process. More specifically, as discussed in [11], the classification of a sample X via the k-NN algorithm includes the following steps:

- Consider $C_1, C_2, \ldots, C_j$ training categories so that, after feature reduction, they become an $m-$dimension feature vector;

- Let the sample X be the feature vector of the form $(X_1, X_2, \ldots X_m)$;
- The similarities between all training samples and X are evaluated. As an example, for a sample $d_i = (d_{i1}, d_{i2}, \ldots, d_{im})$, the similarity $\mathrm{SIM}(X, d_i)$ is defined as follows

$$\mathrm{SIM}(X, d_i) = \frac{\sum_{j=1}^{m} X_j d_{ij}}{\sqrt{\left(\sum_{j=1}^{m} X_j\right)^2} \sqrt{\left(\sum_{j=1}^{m} d_{ij}\right)^2}} \tag{1}$$

Subsequently, consider K samples which are larger than the values of $\mathrm{SIM}(X, d_i)$, for $i = 1, 2, \ldots, N$, and regard them as a KNN collection of X. The probability of X belonging to each category is [12]:

$$P(X, C_j) = \sum_d \mathrm{SIM}(X, d_i) y(d_i, C_j), \tag{2}$$

where $y(d_i, C_j)$ is a category attribute function, which satisfies

$$y(d_i, C_j) = \begin{cases} 1, & \text{if } d_i \in C_j \\ 0, & \text{if } d_i \notin C_j \end{cases} \tag{3}$$

The above equations allow to assign the sample X to be the category with the largest $P(X, C_j)$.

4   Results and Evaluation

In this paper, we have chosen a k-Nearest Neighbour approach, which was tested on the database described above, and the results are represented in Table 2 including a comparison with two baseline algorithms, namely artificial Neural Network (ANN) and Naïve Bayes classifier (NB). Evaluation metrics recorded in Table 2 are defined as follows:

- CorrectRate: Correctly Classified Samples/Classified Samples
- ErrorRate: Incorrectly Classified Samples/Classified Samples
- LastCorrectRate: the following equation applies only to samples considered the last time the classifier performance object was updated. This is Correctly Classified Samples/Classified Samples
- LastErrorRate: the following equation applies only to samples considered the last time the classifier performance object was updated, which is Incorrectly Classified Samples/Classified Samples
- InconclusiveRate: Nonclassified Samples/Total Number of Samples
- ClassifiedRate: Classified Samples/Total Number of Samples
- Sensitivity: Correctly Classified Positive Samples/True Positive Samples
- Specificity: Correctly Classified Negative Samples/True Negative Samples
- PositivePredictiveValue: Correctly Classified Positive Samples/Positive Classified Samples

Table 2. Performance (in terms of 14 evaluation metrics) achieved by the three machine learning models

Performance criteria	ANN	NB	k-NN
CorrectRate	0.97	0.66	1
ErrorRate	0.03	0.34	0
LastCorrectRate	0.97	0.66	1
LastErrorRate	0.03	0.34	0
InconclusiveRate	0	0	0
ClassifiedRate	1	1	1
Sensitivity	0.93	0.38	1
Specificity	0.98	0.94	1
PositivePredictiveValue	0.93	0.86	1
NegativePredictiveValue	0.98	0.6	1
PositiveLikelihood	46.43	6	0
NegativeLikelihood	0.07	0.7	0
Prevalence	0.22	0.5	0.22

- NegativePredictiveValue: Correctly Classified Negative Samples/Negative Classified Samples
- PositiveLikelihood: Sensitivity/(1 - Specificity)
- NegativeLikelihood: (1 - Sensitivity)/Specificity
- Prevalence: True Positive Samples/Total Number of Samples.

Experimental results demonstrate that the classification rate, the specificity and sensitivity achieved by the k-NN classifier is 100%, which is a clear indication that our proposed method is suitable to this type of data. The ANN model obtained a classification rate of 100%, however the sensitivity and specificity of the model were relatively lower of 93% and 98%, respectively. Regarding the NB baseline method, we note that the classification rate is also 100%, a specificity of 94% and a poor sensitivity performance of 38%.

We should also outline that our approach improves the criterion of transparency and interpretability of the process due to the simplicity of implementation of the algorithm. Furthermore, the readability of the results are also enhanced, which is an important aspect of the interpretation process carried out by cardiologists expert. Thus, our approach provides an advantage over other machine learning classification methods.

5   Conclusion

In this paper, we have presented an automatic classification approach for the diagnosis of patients with metabolic syndrome. The proposed classification method is based on the k-Nearest Neighbour algorithm which offers a number of advantages. Firstly, the models achieves a superior classification performance when compared to other supervised machine learning algorithms (i.e., Naïve Bayes and an artificial Neural Network). The contribution in the classification process is demonstrated by a sensitivity and specificity of 100%, which demonstrates a robust classification performance. Secondly, medical experts need automatic diagnostic support to facilitate and justify their decisions, which tends to lack in several techniques cited in the literature in particular neural networks. Our method offers physicians an explicit knowledge based on probability acquired from a medical database. Furthermore, our method offers more flexibility and transparency in the automatic diagnosis of the metabolic syndrome. In future research, we aim at investigating the integration of the approach presented in this paper with fuzzy partition rules [5], to provide an efficient and scalable tool in arrhythmia detection.

References

1. Li, J., Bioucas-Dias, J.M., Plaza, A.: Semisupervised hyperspectral image segmentation using multinomial logistic regression with active learning. IEEE Trans. Geosci. Remote Sens. **48**(11), 4085–4098 (2010)
2. Bohning, D.: Multinomial logistic regression algorithm. Ann. Inst. Stat. Math. **44**(1), 197–200 (1992)
3. Camps-Valls, G., Bruzzone, A.: Kernel-based methods for hyperspectral image classification. IEEE Trans. Geosci. Remote Sens. **43**(6), 1351–1362 (2005)
4. Behadada O., Trovati M., Chikh M.A. and Bessis N.: Big data-based extraction of fuzzy partition rules for heart arrhythmia detection: a semi-automated approach. Concurrency Comput.: Pract. Exp. (2015)
5. Biino, G., Concas, M.P., Cena, H., Parracciani, D., Vaccargiu, S., Cosso, M., Marras, F., D' Esposito, V., Beguinot, F., Pirastu, M.: Dissecting metabolic syndrome components: data from an epidemiologic survey in a genetic isolate. SpringerPlus **4**(1), 324 (2015)
6. Jaspinder, K.: A comprehensive review on metabolic syndrome. Cardiol. Res. Pract. **2014**, 943162 (2014). doi:10.1155/2014/943162
7. Meigs, J.B.: Invited commentary: insulin resistance syndrome? Syndrome X? Multiple metabolic syndrome? A syndrome at all? Factor analysis reveals patterns in the fabric of correlated metabolic risk factors. Am. J. Epidemiol. **152**, 908–912 (2000). doi:10.1093/aje/152.10.908
8. Alberti, K.G., Zimmet, P.Z.: Definition, diagnosis and classification of diabetes mellitus and its complications. Part 1: diagnosis and classification of diabetes mellitus provisional report of a WHO consultation. Diabet. Med. **15**, 539–553 (1998). doi:10.1002/(SICI)1096-9136(199807)15:7⟨539::AID-DIA668⟩3.0.CO;2-S
9. Alberti, K.G., Eckel, R.H., Grundy, S.M., Zimmet, P.Z., Cleeman, J.I., Donato, K., et al.: Harmonizing the metabolic syndrome: a joint interim statement of the international diabetes federation task force on epidemiology and prevention; national heart, lung, and blood institute; american heart association; world heart federation; international. Circulation **120**, 1640–1645 (2009). doi:10.1161/CIRCULATIONAHA.109.192644

10. Belur, V.D.: Nearest Neighbor (NN) Norms: NN Pattern Classification Techniques. Mc Graw-Hill Computer Science Series. IEEE Computer Society Press, Las Alamitos (1991)
11. Lihua, Y., Qi, D., Yanjun, G.: Study on KNN text categorization algorithm. Micro Comput. Inf. **21**, 269–271 (2006)
12. Suguna, N., Thanushkodi, K.: An improved k-nearest neighbor classification using genetic algorithm. Int. J. Comput. Sci. Issues **7**(2), 18–21 (2010)
13. Eckel, R.H., Grundy, S.M., Zimmet, P.Z.: The metabolic syndrome. Lancet **365**(9468), 1415–1428 (2005)
14. Heier, E.C., Meier, A., Julich-Haertel, H., Djudjaj, S., Rau, M., Tschernig, T., Geier, A., Boor, P., Lammert, F. and Lukacs-Kornek, V.: Murine CD103+ dendritic cells protect against steatosis progression towards steatohepatitis. Journal of Hepatology (2017)
15. Blachier, M., Leleu, H., Peck-Radosavljevic, M., Valla, D.C., Roudot-Thoraval, F.: The burden of liver disease in Europe: a review of available epidemiological data. J. Hepatol. **58**(3), 593–608 (2013)
16. Worachartcheewan, A., Nantasenamat, C., Isarankura-Na-Ayudhya, C., Pidetcha, P., Prachayasittikul, V.: Identification of metabolic syndrome using decision tree analysis. Diab. Res. Clin. Pract. **90**(1), e15–e18 (2010)
17. Makrilakis, K., Liatis, S., Grammatikou, S., Perrea, D., Stathi, C., Tsiligros, P., Katsilambros, N.: Validation of the finnish diabetes risk score (FINDRISC) questionnaire for screening for undiagnosed typpe 2 diabetes, dysglycaemia and the metabolic syndrome in Greece. Diab. Metab. **37**(2), 144–151 (2011). Vancouver
18. Helminen, E.E., Mntyselk, P., Nyknen, I., Kumpusalo, E.: Far from easy and accurate-detection of metabolic syndrome by general practitioners. BMC Fam. Pract. **10**(1), 76 (2009)
19. Ushida, Y., Kato, R., Niwa, K., Tanimura, D., Izawa, H., Yasui, K., Takase, T., Yoshida, Y., Kawase, M., Yoshida, T., Murohara, T.: Combinational risk factors of metabolic syndrome identified by fuzzy neural network analysis of health-check data. BMC Med. Inf. Decis. Making **12**(1), 80 (2012)
20. De Kroon, M.L., Renders, C.M., Kuipers, E.C., van Wouwe, J.P., Van Buuren, S., De Jonge, G.A., Hirasing, R.A.: Identifying metabolic syndrome without blood tests in young adults? The Terneuzen Birth Cohort. Eur. J. Public Health **18**(6), 656–660 (2008)

1st International Workshop on Digital Knowledge Ecosystems

Harnessing Mobile Pervasive Computing to Enhance Livelihood Processes: Farmer Response to a Mobile Agriculture Information System

L.N.C. De Silva[1(✉)], J.S. Goonetillake[1], G.N. Wikramanayake[1], and A. Ginige[2]

[1] The University of Colombo School of Computing, Colombo, Sri Lanka
{lnc,jsg,gnw}@ucsc.lk
[2] The University of Western Sydney, Sydney, Australia
A.Ginige@uws.edu.au

Abstract. Mobile technology is a remarkable milestone in the current advances in Information and Communication Technologies. It is pervasive and is evolving rapidly across nations. This mobile revolution had opened up new avenues and opportunities, to design innovative solutions to support livelihood activities of people in developing countries. Agriculture in Sri Lanka is a sector which had not been fully exploited to identify the potential of developing innovative solutions to support farming activities. Timely and relevant agriculture information is essential for farmers to make effective decisions which would in turn empower them. Providing the right information at the right time required for farming activities is a major challenge as this information is available in different places in different formats. We developed a mobile agriculture information system and deployed among thirty farmers due to the high mobile penetration reported among farmers in Sri Lanka. The deployed artefact was field tested to ensure its suitability to support their daily decision making process. The sample group strongly endorsed mobile artefact and mentioned the potential of harnessing the agriculture knowledge.

Keywords: Mobile agriculture information system · Agriculture knowledge · Mobile pervasive computing

1 Introduction

Information and Communication Technologies (ICT) refers to "technologies that provide access to information through telecommunications" [1]. Over the past decades ICT evolved rapidly providing the society with new potentials and capabilities [2–6]. The technologies evolved from mainframe single purpose computers to ultra-intelligent mobile devices. In order to keep in line with this technology evolution, front end and back end applications have also evolved at a rapid pace. In early 1970s most of the resources were assembled to a single host using multi core processors. With the introduction of the Web, computing has become ubiquitous and evolved from computer centric to network centric. The technology evolved further with the introduction of the

© Springer International Publishing AG 2017
M.H.A. Au et al. (Eds.): GPC 2017, LNCS 10232, pp. 641–655, 2017.
DOI: 10.1007/978-3-319-57186-7_46

second generation of Web (Web 2.0) and cloud computing [4, 7, 8] enabling towards human centric computing.

This has facilitated real-time communication among people using technologies such as instant messaging, voice over IP (VoIP) and video conferencing. With the above mentioned technologies, the people got the capability to collaborate online and share information among users through applications such as social networking. Hence the advances in ICT has enabled a "global village", in which people can communicate using various types of ICT applications irrespective of the distance or the location. According to Brahima Sanou the director of the ITU [2] "ICTs will play an even more significant role in the post 2015 development agenda and in achieving future sustainable development goals as the world moves faster and faster towards a digital society. Our mission is to connect everyone and to create a truly inclusive information society, for which we need comparable and high-quality data and statistics to measure progress." Mobile technology is a remarkable milestone in the current advances in ICT.

Mobile technology has grown rapidly over the past fifteen years [2, 3]. The low cost and mobility [6, 9] were the main driving forces behind the rapid growth in mobile subscribers. According to International Telecommunication Union (ITU), there would be more than seven (07) billion mobile cellular subscribers and three (03) billion individual users in the globe by the end of year 2015. This was equivalent to a penetration rate of 97% [3] of the world population. This was remarkably high whereas in the year 2000 it was reported to be only around 10%. More than half of these subscribers, which was around 66%, were reported to be from the developing countries. The mobile market evolved from basic feature phones to smart phone devices. Due to the extraordinary evolution of the mobiles, their prices were going down in the market at a rapid pace. As a result smart phones had become affordable in the developing markets. The average selling price of smart phones has come down by 30% in the Asian market compared to the price in year 2008. Such reductions in mobile phone prices have [10, 11] enabled even the poorest to own one. By the end of this decade, smart phone adaptation in the developed world was estimated to be around 80%, while that in the developing world would be around 63%. Thus, it is pervasive and is evolving rapidly across developing nations [12–15].

This has enabled myriad of opportunities due to accessibility of various services irrespective of the location. This evolution had impact significantly on the lives of the humans [6, 11, 12, 16]. Although the mobile growth is increasingly focused on developing countries [5], still the major emphasis is on developed nations and not many mobile applications have been designed for the people in developing countries [16–19]. The existing applications designed for the developed nations cannot provide the basic human needs of the people in developing countries. Thus, it is required to design innovative solutions to support livelihood activities of people in developing countries. This triggered the potential for identifying technology driven solutions to support livelihood activities of people in developing countries.

People in developing countries, working in sectors such as agriculture, fisheries and transportation face various issues related to their livelihood. One such major issue is their current inability to obtain a stable income. In turn this creates a drastic impact on their economy as well as of the country. In developing countries, the economy of the country is highly dependent on sectors such as agriculture [20, 21]. People engaged in these sectors need to secure their economy in order to contribute towards the country's economy. Economic security is very important for these people and for them it is a primary need.

In Sri Lanka, farmers cannot get a stable income due to issues such as over-production. Over-production of vegetables is only a symptom of a much deeper problem, where farmers do not get the right information at the right farming stage to make optimal decisions [22]. This lack of information creates an adverse impact on the decisions made by the farmers [23] and hence they face several issues in their livelihood. In this era information is a valuable resource for the mankind. Information updates and guides people on various aspects and enables better decision making in their daily activities. Advances in ICT in this regard could assist by providing timely information to address the issues due to lack of information. In turn this will enhance the flow of information to enable efficient decision making in their livelihood activities. The artefact mentioned in this paper aimed at providing a technology driven solution to address issues such as over-production.

In the domain of mobile applications, indeed, the characteristics of mobile devices (e.g., small size of display, power limitation, connectivity features) as well as the ever-changing user's context, makes usability requirements elicitation a further complex activity [24, 25]. Usability requirements derived from factors like the level of literacy of the intended users, their familiarity with mobile technology, their cultural background, and their religious beliefs may lead to the discovery of additional functional requirements [26].

Usability is a major concern of any interactive software solution [27]. According to ISO 9241-11 Ergonomics of Human System Interaction-Guidance on Usability (1998), the term usability is defined as "the extent to which a product can be used by specified users to achieve specified goals with effectiveness, efficiency and satisfaction in a specified context of use". Experts agreed that software "quality in use" is strongly influenced by the level of usability achieved. A systematic process to elicit, specify and test usability requirements is considered paramount to guarantee that the software product will be eventually deployed for its intended users [26]. IT artefacts improve the effectiveness and the efficiency of a business organization based on the extent to which the characteristics of that organization is met [28]. In real life scenarios there are instances where such artefacts have failed to reach the targeted users nor increase the performance of the business process [29–31]. For example, in Sri Lanka majority of ICT solutions designed for the farmers, neither could reach the farmers nor could improve the efficacy of the farming practices. In order to avoid such situations it is essential to identify the solutions that can actually reach the users in a domain to increase the performance.

Thus even though there have been very significant advances in mobile pervasive computing there are many instances; especially to support livelihood processes, where artefacts developed to harness these technologies failed to provide the intended benefits. We have successfully developed a mobile agriculture information system for farmers in Sri Lanka. This paper presents the approach that we used to develop the artefact and farmer response to this system. The remaining of the paper is structured as follows. Section 2 analyses the mobile agriculture information systems developed in other developing countries. Section 3 describes the methodology adapted in this study. Basic features of the mobile agriculture information artefact is explained in Sect. 4. Sections 5 and 6 explains the limited deployment of the mobile artefact and the final evaluation respectively. Finally, Sect. 7 concludes.

2   Literature Review

In literature, there are many mobile based agriculture information systems to assist farmers to carry out their agricultural activities. These can be clearly categorised into extension and knowledge systems, market information systems, procurement and trace-ability systems or inspection and certification systems [32]. AvaajOtalo (voice stoop) [33], eSagu agro-advisory solution developed by IIIT, a research institute in India [34], mKrishi [35] are few mobile based extension and knowledge systems in India. Market information systems in developing countries are especially targeted at providing market information [9, 32, 36]. The KACE [37] operated in Kenya, Esoko [38] and MFarm [39] provide market information to link farmers and buyers. Existing procurement and trace-ability systems were designed to reduce transportation cost which is the main contributor to the transactional cost spent by rural farmers in developing countries [32]. However, most of these applications in this category are yet another system that provide market information. In developing countries there are not that many applications to inspect the agriculture process and to manage certification except for few commercial tools such as Ecert [40] and RANDI [41].

In terms of services, these applications provide very few, similar kind of services to farmers. Most of these were limited only to extension and knowledge systems or market information systems. As a result these are only capable of providing a small subset of information required by the farmers. Many of the extension and knowledge systems such as mKrishi provide agriculture advice only through agriculture experts and they do not reuse the existing agriculture knowledge. Therefore, it requires large number of experts to resolve farmer issues, thus creating issues with respect to sustainability. Furthermore, none of these applications connect all major stakeholders as well as infor-mation in the system especially the situational knowledge. Therefore, they do not grow over time. Most of these emerged as small scale research base projects and were inactive at the end of the project due to lack of funds. Therefore, none of these applications are scalable. On the other end, most of these applications use basic voice or text inputs restricting the amount of services or information that can be presented through the application.

3   Research Methodology

The study is aimed at designing an innovative artefact based on mobile pervasive tech-nology with embedded utility. The Design Science Research (DSR) methodology [30] was selected in that regard as it looks at designing such innovative artifacts with increased performance. It is a problem solving paradigm which is capable of designing an innovative artefact to solve real world problems [28]. Artefacts are "innovations that define the ideas, practices, technical capabilities, products through which the analysis, design, implementation, and use of information systems can be effectively and efficiently accomplished" [28]. DSR is a matured growing field in IS [28, 42, 43] which is increasingly used in designing information systems [43]. DSR method is capable of making a significant impact on developing information systems as it seeks innovation and creativeness in designing the artefacts. DSR further conducts "applicable, yet rigorous research" [42] to design innovative artefacts. DSR can effectively guide the design of this innovative artefact by facilitating active participation of both researchers and end users. The research process captures the knowledge to guide the researchers to meet the desired outcomes [29]. The development of the artefact aims at achieving the utility of a solution to enhance both efficiency and effectiveness of the artefact.

In 2004, Hevner proposed a generic DSR framework for researchers conducting research on information systems design using this methodology [28]. Later in 2007 [44] it was presented as three cycles; Relevance, Design and Rigor [44]. The relevance cycle identify requirements from the contextual environment, input into the research activities and once developed the artefacts were introduced to the environment for field testing. The rigor cycle provides grounding knowledge to design the artefact and adds new knowledge back to the knowledge base. The design cycle operates within research activities of artefact construction and evaluation. Therefore, these three cycles operate within the contextual environment, design science research activities and knowledge base. Environment or the application domain is composed of people, organizational systems, technical systems, potential problems and opportunities. Design Science Research activities include building and designing of artefacts to meet the user requirements. The knowledgebase provides the fundamental knowledge using different modalities to ensure design rigor in DSR [44]. Scientific theories and methods, experience and expertise, meta-artefacts are to name a few fundamental knowledge sources referred in designing the artefact.

4   Mobile Agriculture Information Artefact

The previously mentioned cycles were used iteratively first to design and then to refine the artifact to increase usability [45, 46]. As usability was a major concern of any interactive software solution the following aspects were considered when designing the interfaces.

- Organisation of the functionalities in the Main Menu
- Navigation
- Use of Colours
- The user context and their social background

The designed interfaces were implemented and tested iteratively to ensure functional correctness. Basic functionalities provided through this system include *farmer registration, farmer log-in, crop selection, expense calculator, my offerings and input prices*. These are accessible via the landing page (Fig. 1(a)) of the application. It includes user registration, login, guest and password reset (password recovery) interfaces.

In addition to that it allows a user to select a language (Sinhala/Tamil/English). The following explains the important functionalities provided through this artefact.

Fig. 1. Crop selection interfaces in the deployed version of the mobile artefact

- **Farm registration:** First a farmer should register with the system. The registration process requires a user's National ID, phone number and name. The registration is verified by a SMS that is sent to the mobile phone number specified by the applicant farmer. The SMS contains a pin that the user must input in the form to complete the registration. A registered farmer can log in using the same pin. Once logged on to the system, the main screen will display the rest of the functionalities as shown in Fig. 1(b).
- **My information management:** The 'My Information' page allows a user to view and update their details such as name, mobile number, national ID, language and names of farms.
- **Crop selection:** Figure 1(c) to (h) illustrate the interfaces related to crop selection which is used to guide farmers through the process of selecting crops. The crop selection process is made up of various sub processes. First a farmer should register his farms. Next the farmer is presented a list of registered farms (Fig. 1(c)). In the context of this application, a farm represents some plot of land that a user has access to, for growing crops. A farm is covered by an area and it has geo-coordinates. Geo-coordinates of a farm were used to obtain an agro-ecological zone. The ontology knowledge base was subsequently queried to identify what crops will grow in that

agro-ecological zone. Once a farmer select a farm it will present the suitable crops that can be grown in his farm under the 'Crop List' tab as shown in Fig. 1(d). A Farmer then can select one or more crops to grow. Selected crops are marked with a ticked checkbox. After clicking the submit button a list will appear with all the varieties for the selected crops (Fig. 1(e)). Selecting a crop variety will display a pop-up containing some additional information about the variety. This has a button to add the crop to the shortlist (Fig. 1(f)). Pressing the 'Add to my crop plan' button will add the variety to the shortlist and will remove from the list of varieties being displayed. The shortlist tab will display all the crops which has been shortlisted (Fig. 1(g)). Clicking on an item in the list will display a pop-up (Fig. 1(h)) that led the user set/update the extent for the crop, as well as allowing the crop to be moved to the growing list and to calculate the expenses for the crop.

- **Expense calculation:** The expense calculator allows a user to generate an estimate of the costs to grow and harvest a crop. The process can begin in two ways. The first is by clicking on the 'Expense Calculator' item in the main menu. The other was via the Crop Selection process where a user decides to calculate the cost for a given crop in their shortlist.
- **Expense history viewing:** The expense history allows the user to view the expenses previously calculated for grown crops. The expenses are displayed in date order, with the newest one at the top.
- **My offerings management:** This was designed as a response to a farmer request in one of the field visits. This allows a farmer to indicate what he would like to sell including both goods (e.g. seeds & fertilizer) and services (e.g. labour). The interface shows a list of all offers made by the user (Fig. 2(a)). When making a new offer, the user has to choose the type of offer (Fig. 2(b)). Selecting one of these items will bring up a form where the user enters the required details. The required details will vary based on the offer (Fig. 2(c)).
- **Price viewing:** Farmers can view prices of products offered by suppliers by clicking on 'View Prices' on the main menu (Fig. 3(a)). A list of suppliers (commercial

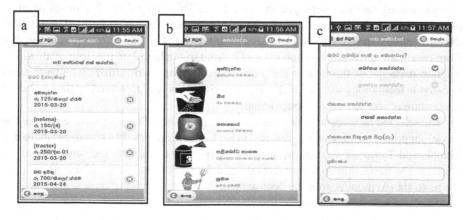

Fig. 2. My offers interfaces in the deployed version of the mobile artefact

suppliers for the time being) joined the system (Fig. 3(b)) will be displayed subsequently. Price details will be displayed in respect of each supplier (Fig. 3(c)). The product list displays the name, pack size and price of each product. Products are grouped into three main categories: seeds (Fig. 3(c)), fertilisers (Fig. 3(d)) and chemicals (Fig. 3(e)).

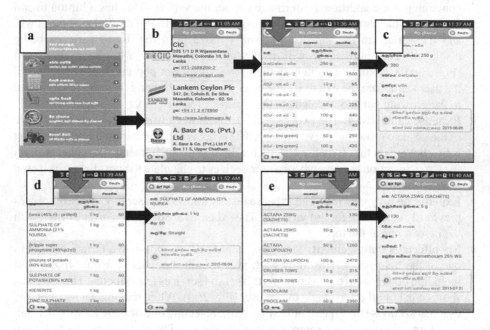

Fig. 3. View supplier functionality

5 Limited Deployment of the Mobile Artefact

The mobile artefact was deployed in April 2015. This was a fully functional research prototype. The infrastructure capacity could not support the whole farming population, thus the initial deployment was restricted to thirty (30) farmers. Farmers were selected from two main agro-zones; Dambulla and Polonnaruwa based on previous evaluations. Regular participants throughout the previous evaluations and farmers who were eager to earn the technology were given the first priority. This was approved by the respective agriculture officer to ensure farmer identity.

The selected farmers were provided a Samsung Galaxy Duos S3 mobile phone. The model supported all three languages used in Sri Lanka (supported 14 languages including Sinhala and Tamil). Two evaluations were carried out to validate the suitability of the artefact. The first evaluation was carried out during the deployment of the artefact and the next, six (6) months after the deployment.

6   Results and Evaluation

6.1   Pre-deployment Evaluation

The Pre-Deployment evaluation was done on the day of deployment. The deployed version of the mobile artefact and two questionnaires (Pre-questionnaire and Post-questionnaire) were used as research instruments. The pre-test questionnaire was given to identify their current practises in crop selection. This was done before introducing the mobile artefact. Next, the farmers were trained to use the mobile and the artefact. The post-questionnaire was given after farmers used the mobile artefact for around 30 min. This was done to get their first impression and to compare the increased crop knowledge of the artefact.

Based on the pre-questionnaire majority of farmers made their own initial decisions in crop selection for the coming season. This percentage was recorded to be around 97%. They made this decision few months prior harvesting the yield that was currently grown. The decision they made could be subjected to change for 30%, due to factors such as weather, irrigation, market price, seed quality, pest and diseases. A percentage around 28% changed their decision according to the advice received by seed sellers, market buyers, and agriculture field officers. Few farmers also changed their decision based on the advice received from neighbouring farmers.

A comparative study of the pre and post-questionnaire responses, was carried out to compare the increased crop knowledge of farmers after using the artefact for around 30 min. Based on the feedback it was found that farmers had realized that there were crops that can be grown in their farms which they had never thought of growing earlier. Farmers stated that their knowledge, regarding suitable crops and varieties that can be grown in their farms, increased in an average of 63%, after using the artefact. Similarly, knowledge increase on crop specific characteristics (such as colour, shape, size, weight, average yield, etc.) was reported to be around 64%.

Currently, it was observed that farmers grow only the known crop varieties to them. After using the artefact it was mentioned that some farmers had never thought of specific varieties that would provide a better yield and varieties that were less prone to diseases. A substantial percentage around 69% of farmers were willing to obtain information using the mobile artefact. Potential of using the mobile artefact to make decisions on crop selection was reported to be around 65%.

6.2   Post-deployment Evaluation

The post deployment evaluation was carried out in September 2015; six months after the deployment. This was done to validate the impact of the mobile artefact on farmers and their decision making. Usability aspects usefulness, ease of use, ease of learning and user satisfaction of the mobile artefact was also evaluated. The thirty (30) farmers were called for the evaluation and only 29 farmers participated. Among the twenty nine (29), three (3) farmers had never used the artefact ever since deployment due to connectivity issues. Responses were derived from only 26 farmers excluding those three (3) farmers.

The questionnaire comprised of two parts. Part A of the questionnaire gathered similar data as in the pre-questionnaire which was done during the deployment of the artefact. The responses received for part A was compared with responses received during the deployment. This was done to identify significant knowledge increase due to using the mobile artefact for six months. Based on the comparison results Fig. 4 was derived.

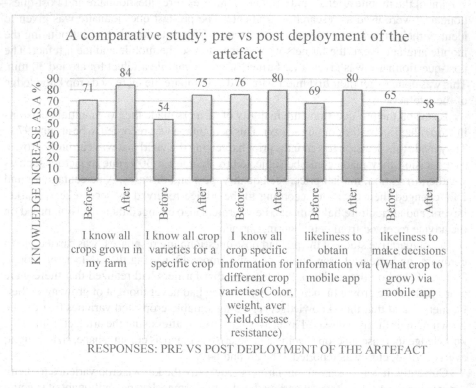

Fig. 4. Farmer responses

One farmer had grown a certain crop recommended by the artefact that he thought would not grow in his farm. The experiment was done in a small area and found that the crop can be grown successfully in his farm. The average knowledge increase on suitable crops that can be grown in one's farm, was reported to be around 84%. It was an increase of 13% with compared to the pre-deployment responses. A significant knowledge increase was reported on crop varieties with compared to pre-deployment and it was around 21% as shown in the Fig. 4. Farmers also stated that their current knowledge with respect to crop specific information such as colour, weight and average yield was increase around 80%. The knowledge increase was not that significant (4%) with compared to the two studies; Pre and Post deployment. On the same day of the deployment, the knowledge increase aforementioned was reported to be around 76%.

An average of 69% stated that they were willing to obtain information using the mobile artefact. After using the mobile artefact for six months this value reported an increase of 11%. The decision making capabilities were not influenced by using the mobile artefact and that had shown a decrease of 7%. One reason for this decrease was the limited amount of information presented via the deployed version of the mobile artefact. The deployed version of the mobile artefact could not populate fully with all crop specific information. Farmers also require time to get used to this artefact and should be willing to experiment on the recommendations.

The usability of the mobile artefact was measured in Part B of the questionnaire. It comprised of twenty six (26) questions based on a five (5) Likert scale. The questionnaire was sub divided into four parts to measure the usefulness (Q1–Q7), ease of use (Q8–Q15), ease of learning (Q16–Q21) and user satisfaction (Q22–Q24). The scales were varied from 1 to 5 based on the following Likert values.

- Strongly disagree to Strongly agree.
- Confusing to Very clear
- Difficult to Easy
- Inconsistent to Consistent

The following interpretations were done on the Likert scale values for ease of analysing the responses.

- Likert scale values 4 and 5 - "Accept"
- Likert scale value 3 - "Neither"
- Likert scale values 1 and 2 - "Reject"

The data analysis with respect to usefulness, ease of use, ease of learning and user satisfaction was illustrated in Fig. 5(A), (B), (C) and (D) respectively. The responses

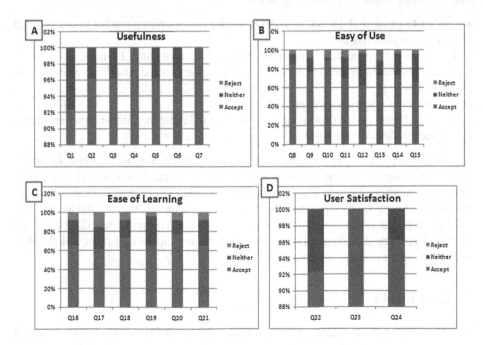

Fig. 5. User responses

were aggregated in each category to derive the overall utility of the mobile artefact (Fig. 6). The overall utility of the mobile artefact was very satisfactory.

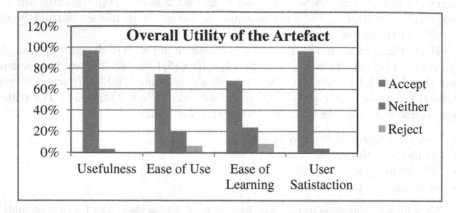

Fig. 6. Overall utility of the artefact

Farmers considered the mobile artefact to be important or beneficial particularly for younger farming generation in agriculture. They stated that this is an agricultural educational tool and this could act as a motivator to retain the next generation within the agriculture. They recognized the artefact as an enhanced global farm which will lead to social and economic development of farmers and in turn, the country. Farmers envisioned several benefits as mentioned below.

- Ability to create a stabilized market (Potential of controlling market prices through better crop planning).
- Economic and social development/livelihood enhancement of farmers.
- Ability for making better decisions on crop planning, thus controlling issues such as oversupply.
- Reduction of unnecessary expenses.
- Enhanced information flow to farmers, thereby reducing the information gap among farmers and other stakeholders in the agriculture sector.

Farmers requested more functionalities from the artefact. Farmers working in sectors such as floriculture and animal husbandry requested to expand the system to meet their needs. Few farmers mentioned that there could be situations where farmers will try to manipulate the market by inputting incorrect production levels. This is valid at this stage since proper data validations at the semantic level, was not supported via the mobile artefact. Reducing data manipulations using active participation of other stakeholders of the agriculture domain is a possibility [47].

7   Conclusion

Mobile technology is a remarkable milestone in the current advances in Information and Communication Technologies. It is pervasive and is evolving rapidly across nations.

This has enabled myriad of opportunities due to accessibility of information irrespective of the location. Even though there have been very significant advances in mobile pervasive computing there are many instances; especially to support livelihood processes, where artefacts developed to harness these technologies failing to bring about the intended benefits.

In this paper we have provided an example of harnessing the potential of mobile pervasive computing by using appropriate design approach to achieve optimal utility and validated it by conducting a pre and post deployment evaluation. The approach we took differs to what others have done as we were been able to identify a comprehensive set of information needs by following design science research methodology. This implementation evolution was basically achieved due to the characteristics of the design science research. Incremental participation and evolution of the mobile system are the main driving forces towards the success of our solution. Frequent interactions with users in a form that they can visualize the end artifact gave us more promising feedback for handling information processing and dissemination to address the information needs of the farming community.

Acknowledgement. Authors of this paper would like to acknowledge the farmers involved in this study and for their valuable inputs to make this a success. The support received from the Department of Agriculture and Agrarian Service Centres to facilitate the user study is also highly appreciated.

References

1. Christensson, P.: ICT Definition (2010). http://techterms.com. Cited 23 May 2015
2. Sanou, B.: ICT Facts and Figures. International Telecommunication Union (ITU) (2015)
3. International Telecommunication Union (ITU). ICT Facts and Figures (2015). http://www.itu.int/en/ITU-D/Statistics/Pages/default.aspx. Cited 2015
4. Evans, D.: How the Next Evolution of the Internet Is Changing Everything. The Internet of Things (2011)
5. GSM Associasion. The Mobile Economy 2016. GSMA (2016)
6. Standage, T.: Mobile Marvels. The Economist - A Special Report on Telecoms in Emerging Markets, London (2009)
7. Cormode, G., Krishnamurthy, B.: Key differences between web1.0 and web2.0. First Monday **13**(6) (2008)
8. Hoegg, R., et al.: Overview of business models for web 2.0 communities. In: Proceedings of GeNeMe 2006, pp. 23–37 (2006)
9. Qiang, C.Z., et al.: Mobile Applications for Agriculture and Rural Development (2011)
10. Hamblen, M.: Smartphone prices are dropping, and will continue to dip through '18. Computer World, 29 May 2014. Cited 20 July 2015
11. Froumentin, M., Boyera, S.: Mobile entrepreneurship in Africa. IT Prof. **13**(2), 60–62 (2011)
12. Aker, J.C., Mbiti, I.M.: Mobile phones and economic development in Africa. J. Econ. Perspect. **24**(3), 207–232 (2010)
13. Shankaraiah, N., Narayana Swamy, B.K.: Mobile communication as a viable tool for agriculture and rural development. In: M4D2012. Excel India Publishers, New Delhi (2012)
14. Naik, V.R., et al.: Mobile—A Catalyst in the Transfer of Agriculture Technology. In: M4D2012. Excel India Publishers, New Delhi (2012)

15. Minoru, E. (ed.): Next Generation Mobile Systems 3G and Beyond. Wiley, England (2005)
16. Gruber, H., Koutroumpis, P.: Mobile telecommunications and the impact on economic development. Econ. Policy **26**(67), 387–426 (2011)
17. Ginige, A.: Social Life Networks for the Middle of the Pyramid (2011). http://www.sln4mop.org//index.php/sln/articles/index/1/3. Cited 25 March 2012
18. Ginige, T., Ginige, A.: Towards Next Generation Mobile Applications for MOPS: Investigating Emerging Patterns to Derive Future Requirements (2011)
19. Jain, R.: The mobile web in developing countries. In: Position paper, W3C Workshop on the Mobile Web in Developing Countries, Bangalore, India (2006)
20. Ragan, C., Lipsey, R.: Challenges Facing the Developing Countries, in Economics. Pearson, Canada (2013)
21. Waverman, L., Meschi, M., Fuss, M.: The impact of telecoms on economic growth in developing countries. In: Sarin, A. (ed.) Africa: The Impact of Mobile Phones, pp. 10–23 (2005)
22. De Silva, L.N.C., et al.: Towards using ICT to enhance flow of information to aid farmer sustainability in Sri Lanka. In: 23rd Australasian Conference on Information Systems 2012, Geelong, Victoria, Australia, p. 10 (2012)
23. De Silva, L.N.C., et al.: A holistic mobile based information system to enhance farming activities in Sri Lanka. In: the IASTED International Conference on Engineering and Applied Science (EAS), Colombo, Sri Lanka (2012)
24. Hoober, S., Berkman, E.: Designing Mobile Interfaces. O' Reilly Media, Sebastopol (2011)
25. Ginige, A., et al.: Spatial data and mobile applications - general solutions for interface design. In: International Conference on Advanced Visual Interfaces (AVI 2012). ACM Press (2012)
26. ISO, ISO/IEC 25010:2011 Systems and software engineering, in Systems and software Quality Requirements and Evaluation (SQuaRE) – System and software quality models (2011)
27. Dix, A., et al.: Human Computer Interaction. Pearson Education Ltd., London (2004)
28. Hevner, A.R., et al.: Design science in information systems research. MIS Q. **28**(1), 75–105 (2004)
29. Hevner, A., Chatterjee, S.: Design science research in information systems. In: Design Research in Information Systems, pp. 9–22. Springer, USA (2010)
30. March, S.T., Storey, V.C.: Design science in the information systems discipline: an introduction to the special issue on design science research. MIS Q. **32**(4), 725–730 (2008)
31. Vaishnavi, V., Kuechler. W.: Design Science Research in Information Systems (2004). http://www.desrist.org/design-research-in-information-systems/. 23 October 2013
32. Parikh, T.S., Patel, N., Schwartzman, Y.: A Survey of Information Systems Reaching Small Producers in Global Agricultural Value Chains. In: International Conference on Information and Communication Technologies for Development (ICTD), Bangalore, India (2007)
33. Patel, N., et al.: Avaaj Otalo: a field study of an interactive voice forum for small farmers in rural India. In: Human Factors in Computing Systems, USA (2010)
34. Ratnam, B.V., Krishna Reddy, P., Reddy, G.S.: eSagu 1: An IT based personalized agricultural extension system prototype – analysis of 51 Farmers' case studies. Int. J. Educ. Dev. using Inf. Commun. Tech. (IJEDICT) **2**(1), 79–94 (2006)
35. Pande, A.K., Jagyasi, B.G., Jain, R.: mKRISHI: A Mobile Multimedia Agro Advisory System for Remote Rural Farmers
36. Magesa, M.M., Michael, K., Ko, J.: Agricultural market information services in developing countries: a review. Adv. Comput. Sci.: Int. J. (ACSIJ) **3**(3), 38–47 (2014)
37. Karugu, W.: Kenya Agricultural Commodity Exchange (KACE): Linking Small Scale Farmers to National and Regional Markets, New York (2010)
38. Esoko Networks. Esoko (2013). https://esoko.com/. Cited 3 October 2014

39. mFarm. mFarm (2013). http://mfarms.org/
40. Intact. Integrity Management Solutions, http://www.intact-systems.com/. Cited 06 June 2015
41. Schwartzman, Y., Parikh, T.S.: Using CAM-equipped mobile phones for procurement and quality control at a rural coffee cooperative. In: MobEAV: Mobile Web in the Developing World (2007)
42. Peffers, K., et al.: The design science research process: A model for producing and presenting information systems research. DESRIST (2006)
43. Hevner, A., Chatterjee, S.: Design science research in information systems. In: Design Research in Information Systems, pp. 9–21. Springer Science+Business Media (2010)
44. Hevner, A.R.: A three cycle view of design science research. Scand. J. Inf. Syst. 19(2), 87–92 (2007)
45. De Silva, L., et al.: Interplay of requirements engineering and human computer interaction approaches in the evolution of a mobile agriculture information system. In: Ebert, A., Humayoun, S.R., Seyff, N., Perini, A., Barbosa, Simone D.J. (eds.) UsARE 2012/2014. LNCS, vol. 9312, pp. 135–159. Springer, Cham (2016). doi:10.1007/978-3-319-45916-5_9
46. De Silva, L.N.C., et al.: Design science research based blended approach for usability driven requirements gathering and application development. In: Second International Workshop on Usability and Accessibility focused Requirements Engineering. IEEE Xplore, Karlskrona, Sweden (2014)
47. De Silva, L.N.C., et al.: Towards an agriculture information ecosystem. In: Australasian Conference on Information Systems (ACIS), Auckland, New Zealand (2014)

Social Computing: New Pervasive Computing Paradigm to Enhance Triple Bottom Line

Marie D. Fernando[✉], Athula Ginige, and Ana Hol

School of Computing, Engineering and Mathematics, Western Sydney University,
Penrith, NSW 2751, Australia
{Marie.Fernando,A.Ginige,A.Hol}@westernsydney.edu.au

Abstract. Recent technological advancements such as cloud computing, broadband connectivity, two-way communication enabled by web 2.0, and frontend devices as smartphones has enabled a new pervasive computing paradigm termed Social Computing. In this paper we have derived a Structural Model, Multistage Causal Model and an Overall Interaction and Information Flow Model to understand how Social Computing paradigm can enhance the triple bottom line. The key to success of new business models known as peer economies, sharing economies, market economies or knowledge economies is the ability to establish trust amongst online users as well as online users and the system. The trust is a characteristic that emerges within a user based on previous experience with other users and the system. Trust is also transitive. The Multistage Causal Model showed us a way to generate this trust via a series of interactions and exploiting the transitive property by aggregating the individual experiences. The structural model showed us the essential structural elements of a Social Computing application required to support the behaviour depicted by Multistage Causality Model. Overall Interaction and Information Flow Model showed us by providing information in a systematic way how user interactions can be facilitated and by captured user interactions further information can be generated towards building the trust. When user reaches a sufficient level of trust to offset perceived risks associated when dealing with a stranger, business transactions take place to enhance the triple bottom line. This deeper understanding will enable businesses to design a successful Social Computing application to fulfil a specific need.

Keywords: Social computing · New business models · Structural and behavioural models for social computing · Overall interaction and information flow model for social computing · Enhancing triple bottom line · Designing successful social computing applications

1 Introduction

Increasing availability of broadband connectivity either mobile or Wi-Fi, two way rich multimedia communication owing to Web 2.0, frontend devices with a large variety of sensors and backend cloud computing-a greener option [1] have formed an ubiquitously connected world today. Size of this connected population amounts to 51% of the global population [2]. We ascribe this ubiquitous connectivity as the enabler of this new

© Springer International Publishing AG 2017
M.H.A. Au et al. (Eds.): GPC 2017, LNCS 10232, pp. 656–671, 2017.
DOI: 10.1007/978-3-319-57186-7_47

pervasive computing paradigm termed Social Computing. Social Computing in a nutshell is a set of web and mobile based applications fulfilling societal and business needs to which we present an explanative definition in our previous work [3]. Two-way communication of these applications enabled age old community building practice online forming communities of scale that reached numbers as high as millions and billions [4]. Social interaction application Facebook founded in 2004 now has a user community of 1.79 billion [5]. This ability to build large communities has been success-fully exploited by some entrepreneurs to build successful new business models based on Social Computing paradigm. Epitomic example is accommodation sharing platform Airbnb founded in 2008 and has reached a user community of 80 million today [5].

These applications gathered user information and provided users with personalised information such as if the user booked an accommodation the application suggested details of available travel, transport, food, entertainment, sightseeing, etc. This made the application cater not only to a single business need but converting it in to micro or mini business ecosystem. Yet another new business model enabled by Social Computing was Social Life Networks [6] that enabled the members of a livelihood make informed deci-sions thus empowering livelihood members. More recent knowledge economy model is Knowledge Ecosystems [7–9], an example from Sri Lanka where a mobile based infor-mation system is being used for achieving sustainable agriculture production. In this system farmers were empowered with right information, on time, in right context such that farmers could take informed decisions as to what crops to grow.

While introducing these new business models Social Computing applications also transformed the existing traditional brick and mortar businesses. Most traditional busi-ness models successfully eTransformed in the pre and early millennium by adopting eBusiness models [10–13]. Specific example is Australia's almost two centuries old iconic department store David Jones Ltd. which eTransformed in 2003 and furthered their web presence by successfully adopting Social Computing in 2013. They launched their catalogue on a custom built business application and also became present in existing social applications such as Facebook, Twitter, Instagram, Pinterest and YouTube coupled with digital mirrors within their landmark stores which automatically posted photos to customers' social profiles. They claimed in their ASX report that by doing so they gained 711% sales increase within very first quarter [14].

On the whole this pervasive computing paradigm is impacting business profit outcomes by increasing revenue, social outcomes by empowering community members to share information and make informed decisions and green sustainability by intro-ducing environmentally sustainable practices through sharing properties, rides reducing energy consumption: thus enhancing triple bottom line (TBL). The triple bottom line (TBL) was first coined by Elkington [15] also known as three Ps: profit, people and planet, aiming to measure the financial, social and environmental performance of an organisation. Nevertheless from a very large number of Social Computing applications designed and developed today only 20% have become successful [16]. The observed widespread impact of successful social computing applications and also the reported high failure rate of applications motivated us to carry out an in-depth study to identify essential characteristics of a social computing application for it to be successful.

2   Related Literature on Phenomenon of Interest

The key to success of above new business models known as sharing economies, market economies or knowledge economies enabled by Social Computing was ability to establish trust amongst online users as well as online users and the system. Thus we first reviewed pertinent literature to this concept.

2.1   Definitions of Trust

Concept of trust has been investigated by scholars of many different domains and the unanimous agreement of all scholars was that it is hard to define what trust exactly is as it is a multidimensional, multidiscipline and multifaceted concept [17]. Thus we reviewed how different scholars perceived trust (Table 1).

Table 1. Scholarly definitions of trust

Author	Definition
Boon and Holmes (1991)	A state involving confident positive expectations about another's motives with respect to oneself in situations entailing risk
Gambetta (1990)	A particular level of the subjective probability with which an agent will perform a particular action
McKnight and Chervany (2000, 2003)	A cross-disciplinary concept: related to social structure, concerns personal trait, is a mechanism of economic choice and risk management. Definitions of trust can be classified based on the consideration of structural, disposition, attitude, feeling, expectancy, belief, intention, and behaviour
Corritore, Kracher, Wiedenbeck (2003)	On-line trust is an attitude of confident expectation in an online situation of risk that one's vulnerabilities will not be exploited

2.2   Characteristics of Trust

In spite of diversity amongst existing definitions of trust and literature being short of a precise one, its characteristics offered an inclusive insight into this concept [17].

(1) Trust is directed	(2) Trust is subjective
(3) Trust is context dependent	(4) Trust is measurable
(5) Trust depends on history	(6) Trust is dynamic
(7) Trust is conditionally transferable	(8) Trust can be a composite property

To further our understanding of how online trust functioned we reviewed the generic trust model presented by Yao-Hua Tan [18]. This generic model for trust in e-commerce consists two basic components, party trust and control trust: trust in the other party and trust in the control mechanisms that ensure the successful performance of the business transaction [18]. Authors propositioned that individuals engaged in business transactions if their level of trust exceeded their personal threshold.

Level of trust required is high when the value of the business transaction is high. Level of trust required is low if the individual is a risk seeker. In the centre of the Fig. 1 above is trustor's transaction trust. The determinants of the trustor's trust threshold as potential profit, the risk involved, and attitude toward risk or risk propensity (i.e., a risk-seeker, risk neutral or risk-averse) are in the lower half. The upper half of the figure shows the determinants of trust, such as the trustworthiness of the other party in the transaction and the reliability of the control mechanisms as procedures and protocols that monitor and control the successful performance of a transaction. E-transaction can be enabled either by lowering an actor's personal threshold or by raising the actor's trust level related to the transaction, rationalised the authors [18]. Though this model was developed in e-commerce era its generalisation harmonises with and gives insight to current day online trust building mechanism within Social Computing paradigm.

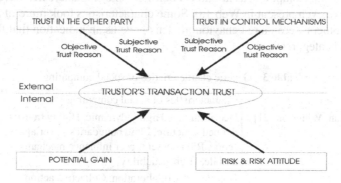

Fig. 1. Generic trust model adopted from Yao-Hua Tan [18]

Closely related literature to our phenomenon of interest was limited as this pervasive computing paradigm is considerably new. Early scholars reported survey results that there was a correlation between Facebook and enhancement in Communication and Collaboration Processes. But they failed to identify what this relationship was [19, 20]. Social Computing being an abstract concept, to uncover a relationship or observe emerging pattern formation between Social Computing and triple bottom line we looked at deconstructs of Social Computing such as definitions and characteristics.

2.3 Definitions of Social Computing

We reviewed how early scholars perceived Social Computing. Though we could not uncover a commonly agreed definition, by tabulating we discovered emerging key concepts as in Table 2.

Table 2. A summary of scholarly definitions of social computing

Scholarly author	Key concept in definition
(Liu et al. 2010)	Social context
(Parameswaran and Whinston 2007)	Social interaction, Aggregate knowledge
(Fu et al. 2009)	Collaboration, Focus on people
(Wang et al. 2007)	Social context
(Charron et al. 2006)	Power in individual, Power in communities

2.4 Characteristics of Social Computing

Having gained some understanding what Social Computing is through scholarly definitions we further probed into current literature in search for why this computing paradigm is highly adopted and how we can make further advantage from same. This investigation retorted to our why question to certain extent with listings of generic characteristics of Social Computing as in Table 3 below. Some characteristics were so generic that they were even present in Web 1.0. Some characteristics took more of a structural form while others were more behavioural. This gave us an indication that they needed a methodical categorization.

Table 3. Generic characteristics of social computing

Author	Characteristics of social computing
Parameswaran, Whinston [21]	Decentralized, Highly dynamic, Highly transient, loosely defined structure, Fluid boundaries - overlaps with customers scope, Rich content, peer influence mechanisms, Highly mobile, High scalability
Hassan [22]	Bottom-up, Collaboration, Collective action, Communication, Communities, Community interactions, Decentralized, Dynamic content, Dynamic information spaces, Easy to deploy and use, Flexible structure, Free content, Free-form structure, Hyperlinks and cross-references, Interactive, Mash-up, Online, Rich content, Scalable, Sharing, Social interactions
Huijboom et al. [23]	Empowerment, Transparency of users, Instant hype wave, (online communities are more) Inclusive, Community sense, In perpetual beta, Efficient allocation of resources, Long tail effect

Literature review strengthened the overall knowledge of key concepts arising from scholarly definitions, and some generic characteristics of it which indicated a need for a systematic categorization. But current scholarly literature has come short of a basis for the observed phenomena.

3 Developing a Causal Model to Understand Dynamics of New Business Models

The new business models built on Social Computing applications variously known as peer economy, sharing economy, market economy or knowledge economy are all based on exchanges among total strangers. For instance on accommodation sharing platform Airbnb a host opens up their home to a total stranger. On the other hand a traveling guest spends the night sharing accommodation at an individual premise owned by a lesser known total stranger or family. This business transaction has already taken place online before they physically met or exchanged premise keys through another mechanism. For any business transaction to take effect key is the trust: trust in the other party and trust in the control mechanisms that ensure the successful performance of the transaction as discussed under Fig. 1 above. Thus the key to success of these new business models is the mechanism to build trust. To uncover this multifaceted relationship as to how Social Computing is causing these new successful business models through trust building online and enhancing triple bottom line we carried out a deep causal analysis as below.

3.1 Methodology Based on Available Data

Despite current scholarly literature lacking an explanation to the "Phenomenon of Interest", the grey literature widely reported the societal and business transformations due to Social Computing. Thus we opted to analyse the available few scholarly scenarios in conjunction with well researched, up to date grey literature in reputed business magazines such as Economist, Harvard Business Review or Forbes, that reported the phenomenon. Author bias can be a concern when analysing secondary data. Scholars have postulated a Theory of Aggregation which articulates a random coefficient model that provided a natural approach to the problem of consistent aggregation. They demonstrated that least squares estimation in random coefficient model where data aggregated, was unbiased. They concluded that as the numbers in the aggregate N increase, the variance of the estimated parameters will tend to zero [24, 25]. Hence we analysed three or more publications per scenario by different authors aggregating different author perceptions enriching the data set diminishing the bias.

Among several available methodologies we reviewed content analysis enabled downsize large textual data sets into a manageable yet contextually rich amount of data such that emerging patterns can be observed. Content analysis theorist Quinlan [26] says that systematic reduction of data is achieved through condensation first and then categorization. Condensation is performed by manually or automatically coding the text and categorization is done by further grouping. Content analysis can take either a qualitative or a quantitative attempt, a more progressive form is qualitative approach which will examine in which context a certain relationship appeared within the text. Content analysis also can take an inductive approach for theory building and deductive approach for evaluation of existing theory. To investigate in which context this causality between Social Computing and triple bottom line exists, and to extract same as a new theory, we opted for qualitative inductive approach of content analysis as the optimal methodology.

To link the extracted individual causal relations in context to derive a reliable meaning we next used causal chain approach [27].

3.2 Open Coding

Open Coding helps condense large amount of textual data into a more adaptable yet contextually rich volume of data. This allows observation of any emerging patterns within the data. To begin open coding we did not have access to "Code References" or "Code Prescriptions" from the domain to guide us as Social Computing is fairly a new paradigm. Therefore we gathered scarcely available scholarly articles that reported supporting evidence of our phenomenon and open coded them such that we could use those codes as our "Code Reference" to open code our data set. We also had to decide what themes we would look for when scanning the large amount of text. Our phenomenon of interest is how Social Computing is enhancing triple bottom line hence Social Computing applications and triple bottom line necessarily became themes. Literature and our previous studies [3, 4, 28, 29] revealed Social Computing characteristics play a significant role within the phenomenon. Thus *(1) Social Computing Applications, (2) Social Computing Characteristics* and *(3) Triple Bottom Line* became themes we looked for when scanning the text for open coding. When we came across one of these themes in a sentence or a short paragraph in the text we highlighted that chunk of text and assigned a brief code in the format of "A caused B" where "A" is the cause that gave rise to the effect "B". Exemplar is in below Table 4 Parameswaran, Whinston [21] states "Popular blogs attract groups of users that engage in discussions" which we condensed into a textually meaningful code "Blogs caused Engagement" where "Blogs" are the cause and "Engagement" is the effect.

We derived a considerable number of codes from scholarly text which became our "Code Reference" for our data analysis. These codes from generic literature took a more generic form such as "Social Computing application" whereas grey literature that reported about a specific scenario on a specific application gave rise to more specific terms such as "Airbnb application". We have used abbreviations such as SCN for 'Social Computing networks', or substitutions such as "content sharing" (CS) for 'knowledge sharing' in keeping with the context of this paper and parent research. All these assimilations and guidelines for 'how to open code' were documented in an "Open Coding Procedure" such that this study can be replicated.

Table 4. Open codes extracted from scholarly text

Scholarly text [21, 30]	Causality	Cause	Effect
Due to broadband connectivity and powerful computers social computing has started growing phenomenally	Technology enabledSC (Social Computing)	Technology	SC
Popular blogs attract groups of users that engage in discussions	Blogs caused engagement	Blog	Engagement
Wikis are popularly used as knowledge sharing tools	Wikis caused content sharing (CS)	Wiki	CS
Key feature of social computing trends is the use of easy-to-use, mostly open-source computing tools	SC is easy to use	SC	Easy to use
Focus on processing at the client contributes to consequent scalability;	SC is scalable	SC	Scalability
Social computing take the information infrastructure to an environment for facilitating social interactions,	SC cause social interaction (SI)	SC	SI
Social computing networks find moderate use in placement and recruiting activities mainly by virtue of recommendations from peers.	SC gathered Aggregated Knowledge (AK)	SC	AK
Social computing networks find moderate use in placement and recruiting activities mainly by virtue of recommendations from peers	SC caused AK	SC	AK
	AK caused Recruiting	AK	Recruiting

3.3 Categorizing Codes

Open Coding helped condense the large amount of text into a long list of individual codes or causalities. In keeping with the content analysis theory we next categorized these individual codes that consisted of a cause and an effect. In other words we grouped these causes and effects as we perceived some of these causes and effects belonged to a more higher collective or generic group which we called 'Super Class' while others belonged to a more specific group which we called 'Sub Class'. One example from Table 4 above is that the effect in very first code "Social Computing" is more generic thus belongs to Super Class and cause in second code "Blog" is more specific thus belongs to Sub Class. Now there were six Super Classes beginning with primary antecedent of this phenomenon which is "Technology" that has given rise to Social Computing. Causality is a time series where something occurs first to give rise to another occurrence. Thus we used pure inductive reasoning to position these Super Classes in sequence in order of their occurrence and came up with Table 5 below.

Table 5. Categorization of open codes from scholarly text

#	Super class	Sub class
1	Technology	Broadband connectivity, powerful personal computers
2	Social Computing Applications	Blogs, Wikis
3	Application Characteristics	Content Sharing (CS), Social Interaction (SI), Aggregated Knowledge (AK)
4	Emergent Characteristics	Engagement, Easy to use
5	User Action	Recruiting
6	Triple Bottom Line	Scalability

3.4 Constructing Causal Chains

Within our "Code Reference" in Table 4 above we notice a certain pattern formation among last two codes: "SC caused AK" and "AK caused Recruiting". We recognise a link between the two. But to link we need a sequence of the causality. This is where immediate Sect. 3.3 above suffices with six sequential Super Classes which also contained Sub Classes. Thus we can link sequentially matching individual codes and develop long causal chains as below:

SC	→	AK		
		AK	→	Recruiting
SC	→	AK	→	Recruiting

One cause gave rise to an effect which became a cause to even higher effect. Some causal chains had more links while others had lesser number of links, hence to establish a generic pattern we needed a method.

3.5 Aligning Causal Chains

In Sect. 3.3 above, we categorized all codes (causes and effects) into six Super Classes in sequence of occurrence. We used same rule to align causal chains in sequence. Thus we listed six Super Classes horizontally in a table as in below Table 6 and aligned the causal chain underneath the relevant Super Class. Below are two causal chains derived from the same scenario: Facebook. While one causal chain took a shorter causal path of only 2 links the other took a longer causal path of 5 links, but systematic aligning illustrated they followed the same causal path. The short causal chain provided a valid causal inference between Social Computing and one bottom line yet the long causal chain

Table 6. Aligning causal chains

Techno-logy		SC App		ACH		ECH		UA		TBL
		Face-book	→	SI		————	——→			Community
Techno-logy	→	Face-book	→	SI	→	Belong-ingness	→	Sharing	→	Community

ACH=Application Characteristics, ECH=Emergent Characteristics, UA=User Actions. SI=Social Interaction

contributed a more explanative step by step causal inference between Social Computing and one bottom line. Thus the scope of this study became deriving longest possible causal chains for each scenario.

4   Multistage Causal Model and Structural Model

Our aim is to find out how Social Computing enabled enhancements to triple bottom line such that other businesses or even other domains can experience these benefits. As explained under Methodology section above, we analysed a large number of business scenarios and using NVivo11 extracted individual codes. The extracted codes from each scenario we imported into a code matrix such that pattern formation amongst codes is more visible. Then considering the six Super Classes we derived in Sect. 3.3 above we linked individual codes in sequence of occurrence and developed longest possible causal chains.

4.1   Multistage Causal Model for Social Computing and Triple Bottom Line

Close investigation of longest causal chains of all scenarios formed a common pattern which we abstracted as a Multistage Causal Model for Social Computing and triple bottom line as in Fig. 2 below.

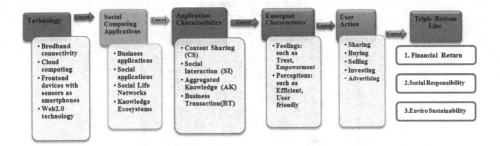

Fig. 2. Multistage causal model for social computing and triple bottom line

Thus we perceive that broadband connectivity, backend cloud computing, front end devices with sensors as smartphones and web 2.0 technologies have enabled Social Computing applications. These applications took the forms of business apps, social apps, social life networks or knowledge ecosystems. These applications comprised of 4 inherent dominant application characteristics (ACH) due to their functionality namely content sharing (CS), social interaction (SI), aggregated knowledge (AK) and Business Transaction (BT). Both SI and BT can be grouped as User Action (UA). The application characteristics CS and AK gave rise to emergent characteristics (ECH) within the user either a feeling such as connection, engagement, belongingness, self-esteem, trust, empowerment or a perception that the user attributed to the application such as easy to use, efficient, cost effective, or convenient. These emergent characteristics either a feeling or a perception triggered User Action (UA). Pertaining to basic psychology humans are motivated to act to fulfil a fundamental or secondary human needs [31]. It is these User Actions that fulfilled triple bottom line.

4.2 Structural Model for Social Computing

When the multistage causal analysis reached the categorisation stage it became clearly apparent that on the causal timeline the first half of causations were more structural and constructed the structure of Social Computing applications. The second half of causations was more behavioural and emerged within the user. The technology stack we identified as backend cloud computing, broadband connectivity mobile or Wi-Fi, front end devices with sensors as smart phones and two way communication enabled by web 2.0 enabled basic application functions. Basic functions included sign up, upload profile picture, status update, like, comment, share, tag, etc. supported with rich multimedia, access control and content personalisation.

Functionality of the application gave rise to application characteristics we identify as content sharing (CS), social interaction (SI), aggregated knowledge (AK) and business transaction (BT). These application characteristics act as cog wheels in tandem as graphically represented in Fig. 3 above one influencing the other and AK plays a dominant role as depicted. Application characteristics give rise to emergent characteristics within the user which are a feeling or a perception after using the application.

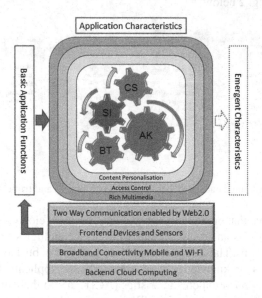

Fig. 3. Structural model for social computing. *CS: Content Sharing, SI: Social Interaction, AK: Aggregated Knowledge, BT: Business Transactions*

5   Overall Interaction and Information Flow Model for Social Computing

For business transactions to happen feeling of trust needs to emerge within users to off-set any perceived risks postulated trust theorists Yao-Hua Tan [18] and Yan, Holtmanns [17]. The trust emerges about a person or a thing based on past behaviours.

Thus a starting point for information flow is CS (Content Sharing) and encouraging users to interact socially using the shared content as in Fig. 4 below. SI (Social interaction) as opposed to BT(Business Transactions) needs a low level of trust.

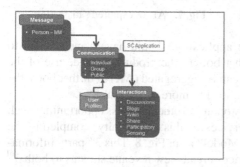
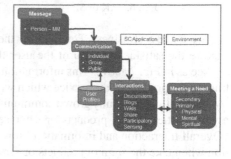

Fig. 4. CS leading to SI   **Fig. 5.** SI meeting some needs

Successful interaction will give rise to a feeling of belongingness thus meeting human needs and formation of a community as depicted in Fig. 5 above. The community theorists McMillan, Chavis [32] formulated in their "Theory of Community" four prime elements of a community: (1) Membership, (2) Influence, (3) Integration and Fulfilment of Needs and (4) Shared Emotional Connection. Thus it is apparent that forming into communities fulfil human needs. Membership gives a feeling that one has invested part of oneself to become a member and therefore a feeling of belongingness which is also an emergent characteristic (ECH) of Social Computing as per our analytical findings in Multistage Causal Model. Influence is a bidirectional concept where a member has influence over others and community has the ability to influence the member which happens through SI. Integration and fulfilment of needs can be better fulfilled within a community. Shared emotional connections are due to past experiences. Thus we perceive that community formation satisfies top 3 levels of human needs in Maslow's hierarchy of needs [31]: belongingness, self-esteem and self-actualisation. Communities also create a basis for communication.

Positive feedback in terms of comments and number of comments, "likes", "rank-ings", etc. give rise to a feeling of self-esteem if it refers to a person encouraging user to become an active member of the community and interact more. If these positive feedbacks, "likes" and rankings are about a product or a service it helps to build trust in that product or service. Here we can aggregate (AK) individual rankings and likes making use of the transitive property to increase the level of trust that will emerge within a user looking to buy a product or make use of a service. This can lead to a successful business transaction as illustrated in Fig. 6 below.

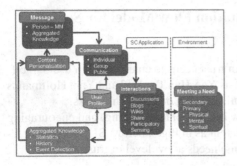 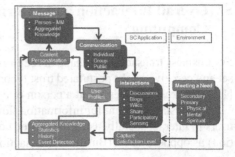

Fig. 6. AK of SI   **Fig. 7.** AK of captured satisfaction

After a BT (Business Transaction) the application should have a mechanism to capture the satisfaction level of the user that bought the product or made use of the service as in Fig. 7 above. This information can be aggregated (AK) to further boost the trust in the product or the service which will lead to more successful BTs.

Ability to successfully grow a community opens up other business opportunities such as 3rd parties to sell products or offer services to this community, completing the "Overall Interaction and Information Flow Model" as in Fig. 8. This 3rd party information when take the form of products or services create new revenue streams to both 3rd party users as well as application owners.

Thus by providing specific CS to the intended community will effect in necessary SI. Aggregation (AK) of SI will enable initial trust building for BT to take effect. When initial BT takes effect the aggregation (AK) of captured satisfaction level will further increase trust effecting in more and more BT. These business transactions (BT) can take

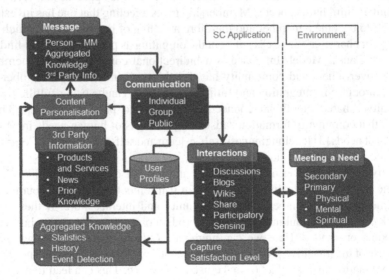

Fig. 8. Model for overall interaction and information flow patterns in social computing

the forms of enhancing the business profit, social responsibility or environmental sustainability thus enhancing TBL.

6 Discussion and Conclusion

On the whole a new set of business models diversely known as peer economies, sharing economies, market economies or knowledge economies enabled by Social Computing are emerging and growing fast. These new business models solely enabled by Social Computing are impacting business profit outcomes by increasing revenue, social outcomes by empowering community members to make informed decisions and green sustainability by introducing environmentally sustainable practices through sharing properties, rides reducing energy consumption: thus enhancing triple bottom line (TBL). Success of these business models is due to the ability to build online trust among members of a community to meet needs and wants. There are many applications which have been unsuccessful. We looked at the ways successful applications have been able to establish this online trust. We did so by conducting the causal analysis. During this causal analysis when we categorised the causes and effects into Super Classes and Sub Classes we uncovered four application characteristics (ACH) that are giving rise to different types of emergent characteristics (ECH). With these findings then we mapped out how the information will flow and people will interact with that information enabling us to generate aggregated knowledge (AK). This AK helped to build online trust. This trust enabled business transactions (BT). When the BT happens the nature of the BT empowers society by supplying an additional income, supplying information to make right decisions, or reducing pollution. These business models enable the communities to meet their needs and wants by sharing existing resources. It could be an exchange of space, a ride, a video, a book, tools or vehicles to name a few. All these exchanges will either have a monetary value, will empower the user or will have environmental value thus enhancing the TBL. Thus we conclude that the 3 models we are presenting in this paper will help to get a deeper understanding of the emerging pervasive Social Computing paradigm and design successful applications to enhance the triple bottom line.

References

1. Baliga, J., Ayre, R.W., Hinton, K., Tucker, R.S.: Green cloud computing: balancing energy in processing, storage, and transport. Proc. IEEE **99**(1), 149–167 (2011)
2. Kemp, S.: We are Social (2015). http://www.slideshare.net/wearesocialsg/digital-social-mobile-in-2015. Accessed 1 Oct 2015
3. Ginige, A., Fernando, M.D.: Towards a generic model for social computing and emergent characteristics. In: 2015 2nd Asia-Pacific World Congress on Computer Science and Engineering (APWC on CSE), pp. 1–10. IEEE (2015)
4. Fernando, M.D., Ginige, A., Hol, A.: Enhancing business outcomes through social computing. IADIS Int. J. WWW/Internet **14**(2), 91–108 (2016)
5. Statista: The Statistics Portal (2016). http://www.statista.com/. Accessed 15 Feb 2016

6. Ginige, A., Ginige, T., Richards, D.: Architecture for social life network to empower people at the middle of the pyramid. In: Mayr, H.C., Kop, C., Liddle, S., Ginige, A. (eds.) UNISCON 2012. LNBIP, vol. 137, pp. 108–119. Springer, Heidelberg (2013). doi: 10.1007/978-3-642-38370-0_10
7. Ginige, A.: Digital knowledge ecosystems: empowering users through context specific actionable information. Paper presented at the 10th Multi Conference on Computer Science and Information Systems 2016 Funchal, Madeira, Portugal (2016)
8. Ginige, A., Walisadeera, A., Ginige, T., Silva, L.D., Giovanni, P.D., Mathai, M., Goonetillake, J., Wikramanayake, G., Vitiello, G., Sebillo, M., Tortora, G., Richards, D., Jain, R.: Digital knowledge ecosystem for achieving sustainable agriculture production: a case study from Sri Lanka. Paper presented at the 3rd IEEE International Conference on Data Science and Advanced Analytics Montreal, Canada
9. Hol, A., Ginige, A., Lawson, R.: System level analysis of how businesses adjust to changing environment in the digital eco-system. In: 2007 Inaugural IEEE-IES Digital EcoSystems and Technologies Conference, pp. 153–158. IEEE (2007)
10. Ginige, A.: Re-engineering software development process for eBusiness application development. In: SEKE 2003, pp. 1–8 (2003)
11. Hol, A., Ginige, A.: Etransformation guide: an online system for SMEs. In: 2009 3rd IEEE International Conference on Digital Ecosystems and Technologies, pp. 133–138. IEEE (2009)
12. Hol, A.: Online system to guide etransforming SMEs. University of Western Sydney (2009)
13. Ginige, A.: Collaborating to win-creating an effective virtual organisation. In: International Workshop on Business and Information, pp. 26–27 (2004)
14. Reilly, C.: David Jones' strategy targets omnichannel, staffing and store renewal (2013). http://www.applianceretailer.com.au/2013/09/gpwdvqjiay/#.WJ3AK_JK-jY. Accessed 1 Feb 2014
15. Elkington, J.: Enter the triple bottom line. Triple Bottom Line: Does It All Add Up 11(12), 1–16 (2004)
16. Oppong, T.: Over 50 Startup Founders Reveal Why Their Startups Failed (2015). https://medium.com/@alltopstartups/free-ebook-0ver-50-startup-founders-reveal-why-their-start ups-failed-no-email-address-required-46b8e197bce2#.jp9i2k7bo
17. Yan, Z., Holtmanns, S.: Trust Modeling and Management: From Social Trust to Digital Trust, pp. 290–323. IGI Global (2008)
18. Yao-Hua Tan, W.T.: Toward a generic model of trust for electronic commerce. Int. J. Electron. Commer. 5(2), 61–74 (2000)
19. Ellison, N.B., Steinfield, C., Lampe, C.: The benefits of Facebook "friends:" social capital and college students' use of online social network sites. J. Comput. Mediated Commun. 12(4), 1143–1168 (2007)
20. Suwannatthachote, P., Tantrarungroj, P.: How facebook connects students' group work collaboration: a relationship between personal Facebook usage and group engagement. Creative Educ. 3(8), 15 (2013)
21. Parameswaran, M., Whinston, A.B.: Research issues in social computing. J. Assoc. Inf. Syst. 8(6), 22 (2007)
22. Hassan, H.A.: Corporate social computing taxonomy development. Paper presented at the Positive Design 2008, Monterrey, Mexico (2008)
23. Huijboom, N., van den Broek, T., Frissen, V., Kool, L., Kotterink, B., Meyerhoff Nielsen, M., Millard, J.: Key areas in the public sector impact of social computing. European Communities (2009)
24. Kuh, E.: An essay on aggregation theory and practice. In: Econometrics and Economic Theory, pp. 57–99. Springer, UK (1974)

25. Zellner, A.: On the aggregation problem: a new approach to a troublesome problem. In: Economic Models, Estimation and Risk Programming: Essays in Honor of Gerhard Tintner, pp. 365–374. Springer, Heidelberg (1969)
26. Quinlan, C.: Business research methods. South-Western Cengage Learning Andover (2011)
27. Joshi, A.: Reading the local context: a causal chain approach to social accountability. IDS Bull. **45**(5), 23–35 (2014)
28. Fernando, M.D., Ginige, A., Hol, A.: Impact of social computing on business outcomes. Paper presented at the 13th International Conference on Web Based Communities and Social Media (WBC 2016), Madeira, Portugal (2016)
29. Fernando, M.D., Ginige, A., Hol, A.: Structural and behavioural models for social computing applications. Paper presented at the 27th Australasian Conference of Information Systems, Wollongong, Australia (2016)
30. Parameswaran, M., Whinston, A.B.: Social computing: an overview. Commun. Assoc. Inf. Syst. **19**(1), 37 (2007)
31. Maslow, A.H.: A theory of human motivation. Psychol. Rev. **50**(4), 370–396 (1943). doi: 10.1037/h0054346
32. McMillan, D.W., Chavis, D.M.: Sense of community: a definition and theory. J. Community Psychol. **14**(1), 6–23 (1986)

Digital Knowledge Ecosystem for Empowering Users to Self-manage Diabetes Through Context Specific Actionable Information

Maneesh Mathai[1,2(✉)], Athula Ginige[1], Uma Srinivasan[2], and Federico Girosi[1,2]

[1] Western Sydney University, Sydney, Australia
{m.mathai,a.ginige,f.girosi}@westernsydney.edu.au
[2] CMCRC Health Market Quality Research Program, Sydney, Australia
umas@cmcrc.com

Abstract. Current high numbers of diabetes patients worldwide and the associated cost indicates current approaches to managing this chronic disease is not effective. The literature indicates the need to provide context specific actionable information to these patients to better manage diabetes which is not happening at present. Making use of wide spread digital connectivity now available due to rapid growth of mobile phone usage and concept of Digital Knowledge Ecosystem to enhance flow of information within a domain we applied scenario based design approach to develop a new scenario for better manage diabetes. The transformed scenario captures the current life situation such as exercise, food and emotional habit of the patient on a day to day basis using mobile application and sensor devices. This collected information is aggregated and provided to the care provider, allowing the care provider to understand which advice has been successfully followed and which of the advices need to be modified to suit the needs of the patient. The care provider can set up modified advice as protocols through the system. The protocols are then used by the system based on the context to generate the set of daily actions that the patient has to perform. We also developed the initial set of user interfaces to support the transformed scenario. Thus we have shown that conceptually now it is possible to have a new scenario to better manage diabetes overcoming deficiencies reported in literature of the current scenario.

Keywords: Actionable information · User empowerment · Mobile based information systems · Self-management of diabetes

1 Introduction

With an increase in ageing population worldwide and in Australia, there is growing interest in self-management interventions to address long-term chronic conditions such as diabetes. In 2015, the International Diabetes Federation's (IDF) Diabetes Atlas estimates that one in 11 adults has diabetes (415 million), one in two (46.5%) adults with diabetes is undiagnosed, 12% of global health expenditure is spent on diabetes (USD673 billion) [1]. Diabetes affects 1.7 million persons in Australia, and the latest estimate for costs of diabetes care is more than $14.6 billion [2]. Diabetes is the sixth cause of death

© Springer International Publishing AG 2017
M.H.A. Au et al. (Eds.): GPC 2017, LNCS 10232, pp. 672–684, 2017.
DOI: 10.1007/978-3-319-57186-7_48

in Australia. There are different types of diabetes; all types are complex and serious. The three main types of diabetes are type 1, type 2 and gestational diabetes. Of all diabetes in Australia, Type 1 and Type 2 diabetes account for 10% and 85% respectively [2]. In spite of the great strides that have been made in the treatment of diabetes in recent years, many patients do not achieve optimal outcomes and still experience devastating complications that result in a decreased length and quality of life with providers often struggling to give the recommended level of diabetes care within the constraints of a busy office setting [3]. Self-management can reduce up to 60% of type 2 diabetics.

Type 2 diabetes can initially be managed through lifestyle modifications which includes a healthy diet, regular exercise and monitoring blood glucose levels. The aim of diabetes management is to keep blood glucose levels as close to the target range between 4 to 6 mmol/L (fasting). This will help prevent both short-term and long-term complications [2]. At present, in Australia management of type 2 diabetes happen through primary health networks. Diabetes patients visit care providers who provide information on managing diabetes based on insulin levels, diet and exercise. Frequency of such visits can vary from a month to a year, typically being about 6 months. Literature shows that the dominant information provider is the general practitioners (GP), who typically has about 15 to 20 min to spend for each patient. The diabetic patient is provided with personalized advice and resources such as pamphlets, brochures or online web resources.

The information about diabetic management is given to the patient, but the patient has to translate the advice in a way that it suits with their day to day activities. They have to constantly make sure that they are following the guidelines till the next visit. Due to information requiring processing, understanding and not matching daily life style requirements, patient fail to manage their conditions. Timely information and education can enhance the ability of users to make informed choices about their health, lifestyle and modifiable disease risk factors. Due to unstructured and varied format, and lack of targeted delivery methods, information and knowledge does not often reach users when they need it most [4]. The information given to patient does not take into consideration the context of the patient and thus is not personalized to the needs of the patient. There is also very little feedback available during the interim period between visits to convert the advice into practice and to keep patients motivated.

With the increasing ubiquity of smart phones and its wide spread distribution, smart phones has the potential to become a tool for chronic disease management. In 2015, Australian smartphone penetration was 90%, 9% of Australians currently own a wearable device like a smart watch and another 30% plan to own one in the near future [5]. There has been a proliferation of mobile apps in the health and fitness area, which enables self-monitoring of individual's behaviors such as exercise, food and glucose. Wearable devices are capable of passively collecting information on heart rate, blood pressure and sleep. Dennison et al. [6] after carrying out a qualitative study on challenges for smart-phone applications in supporting health behavior change, states that users need features that are desirable and effective without requiring unacceptable levels of effort. With context-aware computing a mobile device's sensors and application can be used to obtain contextual information such as time, patient activity and location. Using this contextual information, now it is possible to develop mobile based information systems to deliver actionable information to empower users.

Such a mobile system has been developed for the agriculture domain to meet information needs of farmers and all other stakeholders [7–9, 14]. This system has now evolved into Digital Knowledge Ecosystem for Agribusiness and is getting widely adapted in many countries [7]. Digital Knowledge Ecosystem is the product of appropriate information sharing, management and knowledge inferencing software and associated hardware, ICT service providers, and users who are both information producers and consumers, or prosumers who dependent on one another for their information needs. Inspired by the success of the Digital Knowledge Ecosystem approach to empower farmers by providing context specific actionable information we decided to explore a similar approach to develop a mobile based information system to empower users to self-manage type 2 diabetes.

This paper is organised as follows. In the next section we review relevant literature. The review highlights the effectiveness of self-management in managing type 2 diabetes and the need to provide information in context. In Sect. 3 we explain the design methodology used; scenario based design and scenario transformation to understand and resolve the challenges in this research work. In Sect. 3, we also present the current and transformed scenario. In Sect. 4 we present the conclusions.

2   Review of Related Literature

To device a solution to current challenges in patient failing to manage their conditions we reviewed literature on self- Management and empowerment, information that is needed to manage diabetes and available technological solutions to deliver this information.

2.1   Self-management and Empowerment

Funnell and Anderson [3] maintain that the current health care system is poorly configured to effectively treat chronic diseases such as diabetes that require the development of a collaborative daily self-management plan as the current health care system is designed to deliver acute, symptom-driven care. Even though the self-management plans are made for individual patients, they usually fail to satisfy the patient's priorities, goals, resources, culture, and lifestyle. In order for the health provider to successfully empower the patient, the health provider must understand the past history of the patient, clarify the issues of the present and develop a plan for the future in collaboration with the patient [3]. The health provider must then periodically review the plans, check for deviations and suggest changes that can empower users to take remedial actions.

2.2 Information Needs of Diabetic Patients

The NDSS (National Diabetics Service Scheme), managed by Diabetes Australia, commissioned the 'best practice' report [4] to represent a process of systematic enquiry to describe and analyse consumer needs and identify a way forward to address the needs. NDSS created focus groups with a range of people with diabetes, and parents of children with diabetes. The aim of the focus groups created by NDSS was to identify the perceptions of a range of people with different types of diabetes, at different stages of the life cycle and with different sociocultural demographics. This helped NDSS to identify the needs for information and education and how to deliver information to address these needs for the diabetic community. Analysing the result of the focus groups, the NDSS report [4] found that the information must be relevant, timely and structured to meet the information needs of the patient. It should change in tandem with changes to the stage of the life cycle, different stages of the diabetes disease process, and the physical and psychological impact that comes with diabetics. The insights of this report highlights the need to make diabetic education effective by presenting the content in the context of the user helping the user to associate it with his daily activities. Timely information and education can enhance the ability of users to make informed choices about their health, lifestyle and modifiable disease risk factors. Due to unstructured and varied format, and lack of targeted delivery methods, information and knowledge does not often reach users when they need it most.

2.3 Diabetes Management with Mobile Health Technology

With 85% to 90% of diabetic patients having access to mobile technology, use of mobile health technologies is an innovative approach to help patients better manage their diabetes and related conditions [12].

The review by El-Gayar et al. [12] carried out a systematic assessment on a representation of currently available commercial applications and articles that were published in diabetic research area which was published during the period from January 1995 to August 2012. This review included all applications that supported any diabetes self-management task where the patient is the primary actor. The review used its evaluation method to filter out 71 applications and 16 articles for review, from 502 applications and 185 articles it initially selected. This review was aimed to determine whether diabetes applications have been helping patients with type 1 or type 2 diabetes self-manage their condition.

This review found that a total of 39% of the commercially available applications supported self-management tasks such as physical exercise, timely insulin dosage or medication, frequent blood glucose testing, and suitable diet. Out of 16 articles the review found that, 38% supported all four tasks. This review found that most of the decision support functionality relates only to insulin dosage suggestion and very few for lifestyle change, exercise, and diet. While clinical guidelines emphasize the role of self-management education as an integral part of diabetes care, the review found that only 18% had education component in the application with majority of applications providing general diabetes education. The review found that the information is often generic and is not personalized to the individual patient and only one application out of the entire application's reviewed provided personalized education. It was not clear from the review if behavioral science theory was used to design the applications and the review found no applications mentioning any specific detail of behavioral theory model in the application design.

The review of existing mobile application for diabetics [10, 12, 13] highlights the need for a systematic user centred design methodology to develop information systems that can improve the identified current deficiencies in the existing applications. It highlights the fact that due to lack of targeted personalized information, there is a mismatch between the information being provided to the patient and the information needed by the patient.

The review in this section highlights the effectiveness of self-management in managing type 2 diabetes and the need to provide information in context. The review brings attention to the analysis conducted by NDSS which emphasizes on the need for the information to be relevant, timely and structured to meet the needs of the patient. The review calls attention to the fact that user centred design methodology can be effective in designing information system to tackle the research challenge.

3 Transforming the Scenario

With scenario based design (SBD) [15] we can develop a rich understanding of current activities and work practices, and to use this understanding as a basis for activity transformation. In SBD, problem scenarios enumerate features of the current situation that are understood to have important consequences both positive and negative for the scenario actors. The problem scenarios are transformed and elaborated through several phases of iterative design.

3.1 Current Scenario

The goal of our research was to explore the challenges associated with enhancing the ability of users to make informed choices about their health, lifestyle and modifiable disease risk factors. For this, medical nutritional therapy is selected as an exploratory scenario as it is the key components of diabetes management that is managed through medical nutrition therapy (MNT), administered by a registered dietitian (RD) or nutrition professional [16].

The Nutrition Practice Guidelines for Type 2 Diabetes lay down the guidelines for the interaction a health care provider has with a patient on nutrition therapy. During the initial visit the health care provider understands the history of the patient by assessing the referral data, medical, lifestyle and psychosocial issues. The health care provider then carries out the intervention by suggesting nutrition prescription, education and goal setting. For the first, second and third follow up visit progress of short term goals are assessed, shortcomings identified and plans are modified accordingly. Then the ongoing follow up is planned once every 6–12 months and long term goals are planned along with plans for ongoing care. The flow of information in the current scenario is shown in Fig. 1.

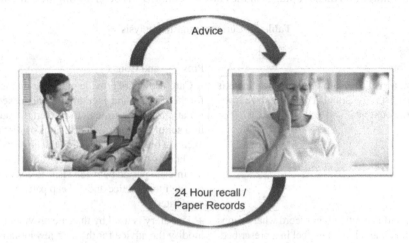

Fig. 1. Information flow pattern in the current scenario

During a visit to a care provider the patient is given a list of personalised advice to follow until the next visit. Care providers provide guideline on meals for the patients and encourage them to exercise. The patient needs to convert this advice into set of activities and decisions on diet and exercise on a daily basis until the next visit. Often some of these decisions will depend on what was done in the past few days. There is very little guidance available during this interim period between visits to convert the advice into practice and to keep patients motivated. Depending on their motivation level and competencies some patients might find additional information to complement their decision making. Some might record what actions were taken and how they feel in a prescribed diary that helps patients and care providers to track which activities were performed as well as what has worked and what has not. The diary is then used by the care provider to modify the advice for the next few months. If the patient has not systematically maintained the diary then care provider base their advice on what the patient can recollect during the visit about past activities, which may not create a holistic picture. This feedback now happens mostly when the patient visits the care provider, and there is not much feedback in between to keep the patient motivated. Flow of necessary information to the different stakeholders is quite weak in the current scenario.

Also in the current scenario, the care provider is not able to get the patient's precise emotional patterns, eating, and exercise habits. Patients are not receiving relevant timely information that is personalized to their needs and situations. The patents find it difficult to obtain information that matches their daily activities. The patients would also like to obtain constant feedback and reminders during the interim period between visits.

3.2   Current Scenario Analysis

The advantage and disadvantages of the current scenario has been highlighted in Table 1.

Table 1. Current scenario analysis

Claims	
Situation	Pros (+) and Cons (−)
During a visit to a care provider the patient is given a list of personalized advice to follow until the next visit	+ Care providers provide guideline on meals for the patients and encourage them to exercise − Patient finds it difficult to convert this advice into set of activities and decisions on diet and exercise on a daily basis until the next visit − There is very little guidance available during the interim period between visits to convert the advice into practice and to keep patients motivated
Motivated patients might record what actions were taken and how they feel in a prescribed diary	+ The diary is used by the care provider to modify the advice for the next few months − If the diary is not systematically maintained then care provider have to base their advice on what the patient can recollect during the visit about past activities
Care plans are created to manage and monitor the progress of the patient	+ Care provider can monitor progress to modify and suit the care plans to the needs of the patient − The monitoring happens during the visit, it is difficult for care provider to identify the fluctuations on a weekly or monthly basis − The care provider is not able to get the patient's precise emotional patterns, eating, and exercise habits

3.3   Deriving the Transformed Scenario

Based on the analysis of nutritional care process [11], the patient information needs has been identified. The patient needs to know what and how much to eat based on advice provided at the last visit to the care provider. The information provided needs to consider their food preferences, the type of meal (breakfast, lunch, tea, dinner), the patient's location (at home, restaurant, travelling), event (at home, a special function, party), the types of food and quantities eaten during the last few days. The patient needs information to change behaviour such as the irregularity in food consumption time, variation in size and content of food being consumed. The patient needs information on alternative options to change the most frequently consumed food that can cause blood sugar to increase. If the frequency of eating out is high, patient need information to motivate them to switch to home cooked meal or provide specific information that can help patient's select optimal restaurant meals. The patient needs to have information on their calorie, macro and micro nutrients intake on a day to day basis to manage their diet.

The patient also needs information on the amount of exercise that needs to be done each day (in terms of distance or time), its intensity, whether it is to be done in some outdoors suitable locations, the weather conditions and whether there is a social group or an event happening that the patient can join to do the exercise. The amount of exercise to be done will depend on the advice given, the exercise done in the last few days and the food that has been consumed.

The care provider would like to obtain information on the patient's profile which includes life style, social and psychological factors to provide effective advice. From the above analysis we identified a software application that can convert the advice provided to the user into smaller set of personalised information. The user can easily act on this information as it is tailored to user's information needs and is based on user's current situation. Since mobile device is one of the easily accessible device with wide variety of sensors built on to it, developing a mobile application seems to be the right direction.

The proposed system as shown in Fig. 2, captures the current life situation of the patient. It uses mobile applications to capture the exercise, food and emotional habit of the patient on a day to day basis. This information is aggregated and provided to the care provider and patient as summarized report, graphs and charts. The care provider is able to create customizable reports to get a holistic view of the health condition of the patient. This information will allow the care provider to understand which advice has been successfully followed and which of the advices need to be modified to suit the needs of the patient. The care provider can provide advice to the patient and set up the same advice as protocols through the system. The protocols are then used by the system based on the context to generate the set of daily actions that the patient has to perform.

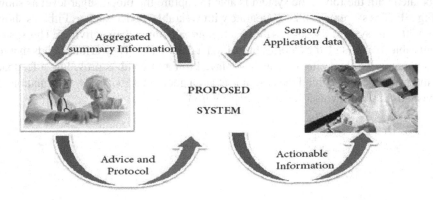

Fig. 2. Purposed scenario

With information becoming personalized to the need of the patient, patient can easily act on the provided information. The proposed system then aggregates the new information generated as a result of patient taking actions and matches it against protocols to provide insights to patients and care provider on the progress of converting advices into actions on a daily basis.

By aggregating information from individuals the system can also generate population statistics in near real time for decision makers and policy developers. They also can get rapid feedback on the effectiveness of these decisions and policies in managing chronic disease.

3.4   Initial Interface for Transformed Scenario

Based on the transformed scenario, we identified some core system functionalities. Based on the findings we developed the first set of mobile interfaces. These interfaces were developed to capture users profile such as demographics, precise emotional patterns, eating, and exercise habits.

Figure 3A, is the home screen, it highlights the total calories consumed, total calories burned and the last recorded blood sugar level for today. It also provides a summary for the last week, which include calories consumed, calories burned, lowest recorded sugar level and highest recorded sugar level. Figure 3B captures the different type of information associated with the patient such as life stage, disease stage, and demographics. Demographics include socio-economic status, education, gender, literacy, ethnicity, culture and food beliefs (vegetarian, non-vegetarian). These patient information allows the system to filter and provide relevant information for the patient.

Figure 3C is the food capture interface. The food is recorded by taking a picture and adding meta data to it. The metadata data include hunger level, mood level, location, date and time. The hunger level and mood level are important as it allows the system to track the emotional pattern of the user. The details of the food captured is added on to the system as shown in Fig. 3D. It allows the system to identify and calculate the calories associated with the food. The system is able to capture the blood sugar level as shown in Fig. 3E. The system is able to integrate with wearable device such as Fitbit as shown in Fig. 3F. The system also allows the user to manually input their activities. This system is thus able to calculate the calories burned on a daily basis. The various trends that has been captured by the system are also displayed to the user, thus providing a feedback for the user. The idea behind the design is to get a good idea about how information can be visualized and how user input can be captured.

Fig. 3. Interface for transformed scenario

4 Conclusion

It was found to better manage chronic condition such as diabetes, patients need context specific information at the right time to take informed decisions in their day to day activities. Review of related research highlighted the current deficiencies in the existing applications due to lack of targeted personalized information. There is a mismatch between the information being provided to the patient and the information needed by the patient. The personalized advice provided by the care provider has to be translated by the patient in a way that it suits with their day to day activities and constantly monitored to make sure that they are following the guidelines. To make this translation they need to search and combine advice given by care provider with other information such as calorific and nutritional values of different food items scattered in different locations making it difficult to find the right information at the right time. Due to available information requiring further processing, understanding and not matching daily life style requirements, patient fail to manage their conditions. Thus, the need to generate context based actionable information based on the advice given by care provider to aid patient with the decision making process is identified during this study.

Also, it was found a mobile based information system will be an effective way to aid patient in managing diabetes as most patients have access to a mobile and with context-aware computing mobile can provide personalized information that matches their information need. Thus, using scenario based design approach a transformed scenario was developed using a mobile based information system to provide context specific actionable information to overcome some of the major deficiencies in the current approach to manage diabetes.

The transformed scenario captures the current life situation such as exercise, food and emotional habit of the patient on a day to day basis using mobile application and sensor devices. This collected information is aggregated and provided to the care provider, allowing the care provider to understand which advice has been successfully followed and which of the advices need to be modified to suit the needs of the patient. The care provider can set up modified advice as protocols through the system. The protocols are then used by the system based on the context to generate the set of daily actions that the patient has to perform. The proposed system then aggregates the new information generated as a result of patient taking actions and matches it against protocols to provide insights to patients and care provider on the progress of converting advices into actions on a daily basis. We also developed the initial set of user interfaces to support the transformed scenario.

Further by aggregating information from individuals the system can also generate population statistics in near real time for decision makers and policy developers. They also can get rapid feedback on the effectiveness of these decisions and policies in managing chronic diseases making this an effective approach to create a Digital Knowledge Ecosystem connecting major stakeholders to enhance flow of information for managing chronic disease such as diabetes.

Acknowledgments. We wish to acknowledge the financial support and the data analytics platform provided by the Capital Markets Cooperative Research Centre under the Health Market Quality Program and our industry partner HAMBS Systems Ltd.

References

1. IDF: IDF Diabetes Atlas, 7 Edn. 26 Febraury 2015. http://www.diabetesatlas.org/
2. Diabetes Australia: What is diabetes? 18 November 2015. https://www.diabetes australia.com.au/what-is-diabetes
3. Funnell, M.M., Anderson, R.M.: Empowerment and self-management of diabetes. Clin. Diabetes **22**, 123–127 (2004)
4. Colagiuri, R., Goodall, S.: Information & Education for People with Diabetes: A Best Practice Strategy. Diabetes Australia, Canberra (2004)
5. Haptic Generation: Survey: Australian Smartphone and Tablet Usage, 18 November 2015. http://www.hapticgeneration.com.au/survey-tells-us-how-australians-use-smartphones-and-tablets/
6. Dennison, L., Morrison, L., Conway, G., Yardley, L.: Opportunities and challenges for smartphone applications in supporting health behavior change: qualitative study. J. Med. Internet Res. **15**, e86 (2013)
7. Ginige, A., Walisadeera, A.I., Ginige, T., Silva, L.D., Giovanni, P.D., Mathai, M., Goonetillake, J., Wikramanayake, G., Vitiello, G., Sebillo, M., Tortora, G., Richards, D., Jain, R.: Digital knowledge ecosystem for achieving sustainable agriculture production: a case study from Sri Lanka. In: 2016 IEEE International Conference on Data Science and Advanced Analytics (DSAA), pp. 602–611 (2016)
8. Ginige, A., De Silva, L., Ginige, T., Giovanni, P., Walisadeera, A.I., Mathai, M., Goonetillake, J., Wikramanayake, G., Vitiello, G., Sebillo, M.: Towards an agriculture knowledge ecosystem: a social life network for farmers in Sri lanka. In: 9th Conference of the Asian Federation for Information Technology in Agriculture (AFITA 2014): ICT's for future Economic and Sustainable Agricultural Systems, Perth, Australia, pp. 170–179 (2014)
9. Mathai, M., Ginige, A.: Task oriented context models for social life networks. In: Cordeiro, J., Sinderen, M. (eds.) ICSOFT 2013. CCIS, vol. 457, pp. 306–321. Springer, Heidelberg (2014). doi:10.1007/978-3-662-44920-2_19
10. Sieverdes, J.C., Treiber, F., Jenkins, C.: Improving diabetes management with mobile health technology. Am. J. Med. Sci. **345**(4), 289–295 (2013)
11. Lane-Carlson, M.: Nutrition Counseling Skills for the Nutrition Care Process, 4th edn. Elsevier, Amsterdam (2009)
12. El-Gayar, O., Timsina, P., Nawar, N., Eid, W.: Mobile applications for diabetes self-management: status and potential. J. Diabetes Sci. Technol. **7**, 247–262 (2013)
13. Sebillo, M., Tortora, G., Tucci, M., Vitiello, G., Ginige, A., Di Giovanni, P.: Combining personal diaries with territorial intelligence to empower diabetic patients. J. Vis. Lang. Comput. **29**, 1–14 (2015)
14. Giovanni, P.D., Romano, M., Sebillo, M., Tortora, G., Vitiello, G., Ginige, T., De Silva, L., Goonethilaka, J., Wikramanayake, G., Ginige, A.: User centered scenario based approach for developing mobile interfaces for social life networks. In: 2012 First International Workshop on Usability and Accessibility Focused Requirements Engineering (UsARE), pp. 18–24 (2012)

15. Rosson, M.B., Carroll, J.M.: Scenario based design. In: Human-computer Interaction, pp. 145–162. FL, Boca Raton (2009)
16. Morris, S.F., Wylie-Rosett, J.: Medical nutrition therapy: a key to diabetes management and prevention. Clin. Diabetes **28**, 12–18 (2010)

Human-Centered Design of a Personal Medication Assistant - Putting Polypharmacy Management into Patient's Hand!

Monica Sebillo$^{(\boxtimes)}$, Giuliana Vitiello, Danilo Cuciniello, and Serena Carrabs

Department of Computer Science, University of Salerno, Fisciano, Italy
{msebillo,gvitiello}@unisa.it

Abstract. Over the past years, the importance of home-care treatments have been emphasized by governments, promoting the adoption of self-care management models, which may have positive effects on patient's empowerment and on the overall healthcare system. In this context, polypharmacy management represents a major concern. A growing number of people are suffering from multiple chronic health conditions, which especially complicate the (self-) management of prescribed therapies, and puts a significant burden on patients' lives. To alleviate that burden, we have developed a mobile health application, Sedato, following a thorough usability engineering process. Usability principles and guidelines have been applied to design a mobile application, which helps patient assume drugs timely and safely. Besides a reliable notification system, a continuous monitoring activity is performed to keep record of patient's compliance to prescribed therapies. That information is shared in the context of a patient-centered digital health ecosystem, and is processed to produce knowledge relevant to the underlying territory.

Keywords: Selfcare management · Human-centered design · Digital knowledge ecosystem · Mobile health applications

1 Introduction

Over the past years, despite a growing number of chronic diseases, all over the world the application of spending review policies have strongly limited the resources available for healthcare. At the same time, the importance and the centrality of home care treatments have been emphasized by governments, promoting the adoption of healthcare models based on Self-Care-Management (SCM) and on Family-Coaching (FC), which could have positive effects on the overall healthcare system. Both SCM and FC support the goal of 'patient empowerment', the former allowing patients to play an active role in treating themselves, the latter relying on persons close to the patient (the so-called 'informal care givers'), who are directly in charge of managing his/her healthcare [8]. In the context of patient empowerment, a relevant issue is polypharmacy management. A growing number of people, especially elderly people, are suffering from multiple chronic health conditions, which especially complicate the (self-) management of prescribed therapies, and puts a significant burden on patients' lives. If a patient does

© Springer International Publishing AG 2017
M.H.A. Au et al. (Eds.): GPC 2017, LNCS 10232, pp. 685–699, 2017.
DOI: 10.1007/978-3-319-57186-7_49

not adhere correctly to the prescribed medication, he/she may encounter safety problems, including risk of toxicity or worse [1].

To alleviate that burden, we have developed a mobile health (m-health) application, which is the result of a thorough usability engineering process. The application, named Sedato, has been conceived as an assistive m-health application, which supports the patient (or his/her care giver) in the management of multiple medical prescriptions, embedded in a more general-purpose infrastructure connected to physicians and healthcare facilities, to gain patient empowerment.

Since the start of this project our challenge has been to create a product which chronic patients would be willing to use all life long. The problem domain analysis, resulting from a literature review and a contextual inquiry, revealed that the main reason why most existing systems failed lies in the poor interaction experience provided and in the low degree of user's engagement achieved [1]. We realized that was the challenge we had to address and that visual interaction could lead to a successful application.

Adequate usability principles and guidelines have been followed to design a mobile application, which helps patient assume drugs timely and safely, preventing missing doses or unwanted overdoses. Besides a reliable notification system, which also alerts patient when the available quantity of a given drug is about to finish, a continuous monitoring activity is also performed to keep record of patient's compliance to prescribed therapies, and to possibly share that information with the physician. That information is shared in the context of a patient-centered digital health ecosystem, and is processed to produce knowledge relevant to the underlying territory.

The paper is organized as follows. Section 2 explains the problem domain analysis and the derived requirements. Section 3 describes the new model of patient-centered digital health ecosystem as the underlying model of Sedato framework. In Sect. 4 the results of the design process are illustrated on the working prototype, which has been implemented for the Android platform. Related work and some final remarks are included in Sect. 5.

2   Problem Domain Analysis

An inquiry carried out with physicians and clinicians working in either public or private medical centers, in the metropolitan area of Salerno, allowed us to depict scenarios of established current practices in self-care management and to understand to what extent technological support is sought and later adopted by patients. We also wanted to identify the possible causes for the little adoption of existing mobile apps. Three categories of stakeholders were considered for our investigation, namely physicians, informal care givers/family members, and patients.

Initially, we interviewed 8 physicians. The first session of the interview aimed at understanding what strategies physicians usually adopt to improve patient's attitude towards complex medication therapies and the requested periodic checks. Physicians reported that, in case of polypharmacy, many patients, especially elderly people, need to be strongly encouraged for the intake of medications exactly at the prescribed times and with the indicated modalities and they are always recommended to undertake medical checks in agreement with their therapy calendar. They insist with patients on the impact of non-adherence on their health as well as on quality of their lives, but full adherence to the therapy is often missed. During the second session, we inquired physician on the use of mobile applications to support patients in therapy management tasks. We asked them to indicate what aspects of the therapy could be improved, if some light technological support was provided to the patient or to his/her care giver. Most physicians agreed that the regular intake of the prescribed medication could be better achieved through an alert system indicating doses and times. They also highlighted the need for a system able to monitor patient's adherence to a given medication plan and share that information with the physician, when needed.

Another relevant issue raised by physicians was the low level of support to interoperability among healthcare actors, in case of complex protocols for integrated cares (e.g., communication with/among different specialists and real-time access to patient's anamnesis for first aid interventions).

The 8 physicians also helped us select a group of 10 family members and 30 patients, who are suffering from multiple chronic health conditions and are subject to complex therapies and polypharmacy management. The group of patients was composed of 20 people aged over 60 and 10 people aged between 23 and 59. Family members represented elderly patients, whom they assist personally or paying some external care giver. We were able to conduct two focus groups with 22 and 18 participants each.

From patients' point of view, we perceived that their expectation from mobile technology as a means to improve quality of life is high. Independence in care management and safety were the major motivations coming out of the focus groups. Some participants, from the group aged under 60, also reported that they experienced the use of existing mobile applications for the management of diabetes care but no attention was given to their co-morbidities and the necessary polypharmacy management.

Since the initial phases of our analysis we kept in mind the claims coming out of the interviews with physicians and of the focus groups. The challenge was to conceive an m-health system which could improve care experience of patients/care givers while enhancing the overall adherence to complex therapies.

In summary, the main requirements were:

- easy setting and updates of medication plans,
- remind alerts for medication intake, with indication of doses,
- remind alerts when some medication stock is about to finish,
- easy arrangement of periodic/occasional medical checks, and
- easy information sharing with physicians, so as to improve physicians' decision making based on reliable historical data.

Considering the case of professional care givers or family members, who may need to assist more patients, a further requirement for the envisaged mobile application was

- to create and manage multiple patients' profiles.

The design activities that originated from the above requirements was aimed at exploiting the potentials of mobile technology to automate as much as possible in the self-care management activities of chronic patients, and to possibly transform the derived records of activities into useful information for physicians.

3   Promoting Patient-Centered Health Ecosystem

Handling the multidisciplinary complexity of data coming from a spatially enabled territory and supporting a fruitful information exchange which could empower the territory as well as its inhabitants, represent today major challenges for computer scientists [7]. The concept of digital knowledge ecosystem is being brought about as a possible solution, described as an open and shared environment with properties of scalability and sustainability, capable to realize services through the integration of four basic territory-oriented elements, namely *content, communities, practices and policy*, and *technology*. As a matter of fact, a digital knowledge ecosystem works as a collector of information derived from multiple sources, which can be processed to produce knowledge relevant to the underlying territory and support the exchange of know-how among local actors of different domains [3, 4, 6, 9]. The healthcare domain represents a field where such a territorial intelligence and information technology can be combined to strengthen the skills of a territory, to understand its phenomena, to interpret local dynamics involving patients, institutions and organizations [10]. The pervasiveness of mobile technology in people's lives has emphasized the role it plays in healthcare management and a new model of patient-centered digital health ecosystem has emerged, where mobile health (*m-health*) applications and services are used to collect data from patients and build new knowledge (Fig. 1) [5, 11–13].

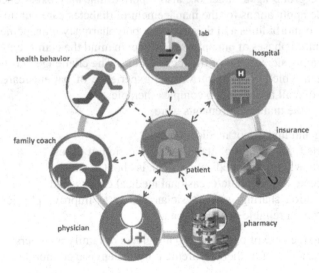

Fig. 1. A patient-centered health ecosystem vision

In the new model, mutual exchange of information and services among interested actors in a given territory could be strongly beneficial not only to the individual patient but also to the community he belongs to. Ultimately, the whole territory could contribute to the construction of a collective meaning, leverage collective knowledge, produce innovation in the healthcare management, and create cross-fertilization in terms of value added for different domains.

Preliminary results of such an approach have been experimented by developing a mobile-based information system, MyDDiary app, to address self-care management needs for diabetes patients [8].

MyDDiary was conceived as a solution to enable the user to keep track of his/her daily activities and healthcare actions, in a sort of personal diary, which can be shared with other stakeholders in possibly different domains. Figure 2(a) depicts MyDDiary Home interface, which offers the main functionality grouped by scope and context. Figure 2(b) shows the visual synthesis used for the 'Overview' function, which integrates three different parameters, namely the glycemic index, the calorie count and the percentage of fitness activity done in a given temporal range. Besides the hint that the patient himself/herself can obtain from such a view, this function allows different stakeholders to gain an immediate overview of the current health state of a diabetic user. As an example, the image could be automatically shared with the physician who could analyze it and make decisions about the trend of a specific treatment or detect alert situations.

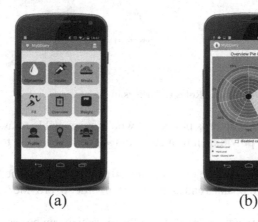

(a)   (b)

Fig. 2. (a) MyDDiary home interface. (b) The visual synthesis of user's activities.

The framework *Sedato* for medication personal assistance solutions we present in this paper evolved from a MyDDiary long term testing which gave us interesting feedback also concerning possible extensions satisfying requirements arisen from specific needs of a wider users community.

Figure 3 shows how the aforementioned model has been used to design *Sedato*, as resulting from our contextual inquiry described in Sect. 2. The schema is focused on the Web service of Sedato, which is responsible for receiving and sending data useful to the entire ecosystem. As a matter of fact, several actors could interact with it to consume and produce data. One of the main roles is represented by the patient, who provides data regarding s/he state of health, in order to obtain help and any feedback from the entire ecosystem. As an example, a diabetic patient needs information about the procedure for the treatment plans from a given Department of the Local Health Agency. On the other hand, the Health Department collects data from the approved plans to predict the supply of medicines in the future months to ensure an adequate level of healthcare in the territory. Such an ability to obtain aggregated information related to the territory in nearly real-time opens up the possibility for different companies, organizations and government agencies to enroll in this general-purpose infrastructure and adjust their processes as well as their services dynamically.

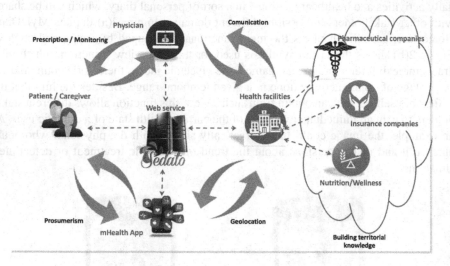

Fig. 3. Roles and actors in Sedato.

An additional important actor is physician, who is responsible to assist patients in the management of care, providing information and suggestions useful to improve their state of health.

The physician is also in charge of communicating with various medical facilities, such as pharmaceutical companies and nutritionists, in order to provide (or receive) data useful for the patient.

As part of this system, both the patient and the physician can be seen as:

- information providers, a useful enrichment of the ecosystem knowledge, and
- consumers, who use the expecially distributed technologies.

Such technologies underlie the so-called mHealth Applications, whose aim is to collect and distribute knowledge within a more general digital ecosystem, conceived also to promote territorial initiatives for a community care.

Finally, various kinds of statistics, ranging from the assumption of certain medications (useful to pharmaceutical companies) to epidemiological analysis on the nutritional needs of a patient, could be produced and shared with the interested stakeholders, new patterns can be discovered and additional facts built also by performing spatio-temporal analyses. The derived collective knowledge could be in turn convenient for the patient himself/herself when it is offered through, e.g., location based services. Figure 4 summarizes basic technologies used in *Sedato*.

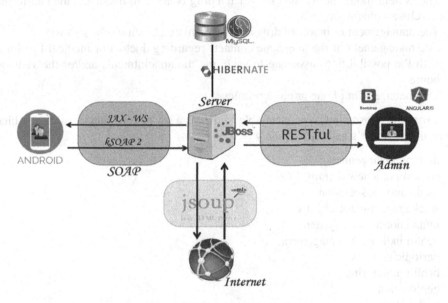

Fig. 4. Technologies in Sedato

Sedato is an Android based application, Java and JBoss have been used for the back end development, while the front-end has been realized by AngularJS and Bootstrap. Moreover, the middleware platform Hibernate guarantees the JBoss-MySQL connection and the RESTful communication is based on the JBoss-Admin connection. JBoss and Client interact via SOAP, in particular, the API JAX-WS for the Android-server communication and the kSOAP2 library for the reverse one. Finally, the parsing of data coming from the external source is based on the JSoup Java library.

4   Design for Usability – Visual Is the Key for Success

A scenario-based design process followed the analysis phase, focusing on activities, information representation and interaction threads. The project team strived to design usable interfaces which would especially support learnability and which would require the least cognitive effort by users, while providing a pleasant user experience and responding to their expectation with respect to self-care management support.

Claims derived from design scenarios included the following:

- For each patient profile, all functionalities should be equally accessible at any moment.
- When adding a new therapy, patient should be able to specify in a seamless way the medication list as well as times and doses for each medication.

- The management of a personal list of drugs, with the related stock quantities should be allowed.
- The system should notify the user when a drug is about to finish and the geo-locate the closest pharmacy.
- The management of intake of drugs using alarm clocks should be allowed.
- The management of the telephone contacts regarding doctors or medical facilities, with the possibility to associate to each one the appointments and/or the visits at home.
- The management of one or more profiles.

From the above claims we were able to derive a set of core functionalities, which may affect patient's daily life, namely

- therapy management
- creation of a new therapy
- medication association
- stockage automatic checks
- intake notification system
- health indicators management
- periodic updates
- health monitoring
- geolocation
- find a pharmacy
- find a hospital
- find a primary care/consulting physician

During the design process, we depicted a set of activity, information and interaction scenarios, which helped us identify appropriate metaphors for our target users, based on the activities they perform in the real world, the physical objects they manipulate to perform those activities and their behaviors. Table 1 provides an excerpt from the activity design phase.

Metaphors were also identified for the information and the interaction design phases, which would leverage users' familiarity with certain objects such as paper prescriptions, pills, phonebook, calendar, alarm clock, etc. The resulting design is illustrated in the following.

Before using the app, the user needs to register either as a caregiver or as a patient. In the former case, he is able to manage more patients, creating separate profiles which may exploit Sedato functionalities (see Fig. 5b). If the user is the patient himself, he may directly access all the app functionalities (see Fig. 5c).

Table 1. Excerpt from activity design tables.

Activity metaphors		
Activity	Metaphor	Design implications
Planning the therapy is like…	… scheduling a number of appointments with a friend	User may – set a number of alarms (with repetitions), and associate them with the therapy – make notes and write keywords for the scheduled activity – contact a physician for periodic check
Adding a drug is like …	… adding an item to the warehouse	User may – add a new medication, and – make stock updates

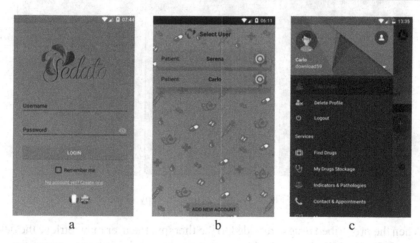

a   b   c

Fig. 5. The personal medication assistant Sedato (a) Login (b) Multi-patient management (only for caregivers) (c) Main navigation drawer with the possibility to modify patients' profiles.

Medication Therapy Management. After the physician has prescribed a new medication therapy, the user may record it creating a personalized therapy, where he specifies the name, the start date, the duration and the associated drugs. For each drug he selects the packaging, sets the daily doses and sets the alarms corresponding to the intake times over the 24 h (Fig. 6).

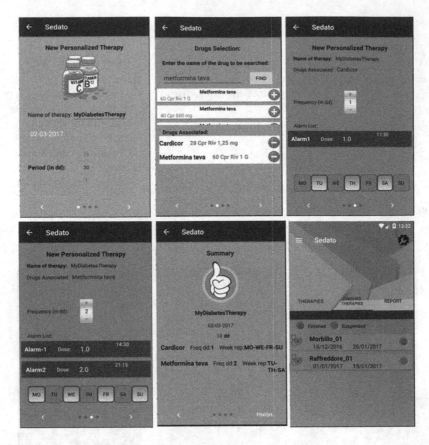

Fig. 6. Adding a new therapy

When the prescribed drugs are added to the therapy, the user may retrieve the details from an Italian public dataset (at http://www.torrinomedica.it/) and choose the right format and packaging. Once the therapy id started, the intake notification system is activated so as to alert the user at the right time and let him confirm or postpone the intake action. Those data are also used to monitor patient's adherence to the given therapy (Fig. 7).

Fig. 7. Intake notification and adherence monitoring.

Health Indicators Management. A set of health indicators, including blood pressure, glycemia, cholesterol, and triglycerides are periodically updated and transmitted to the primary physician to allow monitoring actions (Fig. 8).

Fig. 8. Intake notification and adherence monitoring.

Geolocation. The app also keeps track, for each drug, of the remaining amounts in the stocked packagings and notifies the user when the stockage is about to finish allowing him to locate the closest pharmacy (Fig. 9).

Fig. 9. Drugs shortage notification and pharmacy geolocation.

5   Related Work and Final Remarks

Several studies have demonstrated that poor adherence to drugs therapies can have a negative impact on both the potential clinical benefits of treatment and the cost-effectiveness of medicines. On the average, 50% patients fail to adhere to their prescribed regime and among the common causes are the difficulty to keep in mind drug names, doses and intake times, and the little perception of the beneficial effects of the prescribed treatment. This also generates additional costs for the healthcare system due to avoidable hospitalizations and to waste of resources (e.g., unused drugs), often funded by public healthcare systems. A notable amount of mobile apps have been developed to address the challenge to enhance adherence to medication plans. A recent study [2] reports on 160 apps available from different mobile platforms stores, which were evaluated and ranked against a set of desirable attributes, as described in Table 2.

As a result of the study, the authors report that most of the evaluated apps do not possess every desirable attribute but three commercial ones, MyMedSchedule [14], MyMeds [15], and MedSimple [16] do offer the widest range of features like medication databases, cloud data storage, and tools for health professionals to review data or "push" complex medical regimens to patients' mobile devices. In Table 3 we compare Sedato against the three best apps.

Table 2. The set of desirable attribute for an app which supports medication plan adherence [2].

Attribute	Description
Online data entry	Companion website(s) for data and medication regimen entry
Complex medication instructions	Capability to schedule medication instructions that are considered complex
Cloud data storage	Capability to back up and retrieve a medication regimen from a cloud storage system
Database of medications	A medication database is available allowing user to enter, search, and select medications using features such as autopopulation
Sync/export/print data	Capability to transmit, print, or export medication regimens and/or medication-taking behaviors for use by the patient or health care providers
Tracks missed and taken doses	Capability to remind patients to take their medication and to record taken and missed doses that could potentially be used to calculate adherence rates
Remote data entry by caregiver	Caregivers may remotely input and maintain the patient's medication regimen and "push" the regimen to the patient's device
Multiple platform app	Available on more than one platform
Free-only apps	Completely free (i.e., no fees for pro upgrades or charges to unlock additional features)
Generates reminders with no connectivity	Capability to generate medication reminders without the use of cellular (3G/4G/LTE) or wireless (Wi-Fi) connectivity
Multiple profile capable	Capability to generate medication reminders for multiple individuals on different medications (i.e., enabled family use)
Multilingual	Available in English plus any other language

The table shows that all the desired attributes characterize our app, except the multi-platform feature (Sedato is an Android app) and the cloud data storage. Although none of the existing apps was conceived as part of a digital knowledge ecosystem, the result of this comparison encouraged us to plan a longitudinal testing of Sedato with a group of people similar to those who took part in the initial inquiry. Apart from the 8 physicians, who will test the prescription and health monitoring functionalities in the ecosystem, the app will be given to patients to be deployed for a period of at least four months. The final goal of the user study will be to verify the extent to which Sedato can improve adherence and therapeutic outcomes in chronic conditions.

Table 3. Comparing Sedato to the three best apps resulting from a recent study.

	MyMedSchedule	MyMeds	MedSimple	Sedato
Online data entry	√	√	√	√
Complex medication instructions	√		√	√
Cloud data storage	√	√	√	√
Database of medications	√	√	√	√
Sync/export/print data	√		√	√
Tracking of missed and taken doses				√
Generates reminders with no connectivity		√	√	√
Multiple profile capable		√		√
Multilingual				√
Remote data entry by caregiver	√			√
Multiplatform app	√	√	√	
Cloud data storage	√	√	√	
Free-only app	√	√	√	√

References

1. Brown, M.T., Bussell, J.K.: Medication adherence: WHO cares? Mayo Clin. Proc. **86**(4), 304–314 (2011). doi:10.4065/mcp.2010.0575
2. Dayer, L., Heldenbrand, S., Anderson, P., Gubbins, P.O., Martin, B.C.: Smartphone medication adherence apps: potential benefits to patients and providers. J. Am. Pharm. Assoc. **53**(2), 172–181 (2014). doi:10.1331/JAPhA.2013.12202
3. Ginige, A., Walisadeera, A.I., Ginige, T., De Silva, L.N.C., Di Giovanni, P., Mathai, M., Goonetillake, J.S., Wikramanayake, G.N., Vitiello, G., Sebillo, M., Tortora, G., Richards, D., Jain, R.: Digital knowledge ecosystem for achieving sustainable agriculture production: a case study from Sri Lanka. In: DSAA 2016, pp. 602–611 (2016)
4. Ginige, A., Paolino, L., Romano, M., Sebillo, M., Tortora, G., Vitiello, G.: Information sharing among disaster responders - an interactive spreadsheet-based collaboration approach. Comput. Support. Coop. Work **23**(4–6), 547–583 (2014). ISSN: 0925-9724
5. Lui, L., Owgu, S.M.: A meta-analysis of mobile health and risk reduction in patients with diabetes mellitus: challenge and opportunity. J. Mob. Technol. Med. **1**(3), 17–24 (2012)
6. Romano, M., Onorati, T., Aedo, I., Díaz, P.: Designing mobile applications for emergency response: citizens acting as human sensors. Sensors **16**(3), 406 (2016)
7. Salvemini, M., Berardi, L., Sebillo, M., Vitiello, G., Farruggia, S., Murgante, B.: GI2NK geographic information: need to know towards a more demand-driven geospatial workforce education/training system. In: Gervasi, O., Murgante, B., Misra, S., Rocha, A.M.A.C., Torre, C., Taniar, D., Apduhan, B.O., Stankova, E., Wang, S. (eds.) ICCSA 2016. LNCS, vol. 9788, pp. 561–572. Springer, Cham (2016). doi:10.1007/978-3-319-42111-7_45
8. Sebillo, M., Tucci, M., Vitiello, G., Ginige, A., Di Giovanni, P.: Combining personal diaries with territorial intelligence to empower diabetic patients. J. Vis. Lang. Comput. **29**, 1–14 (2015). doi:10.1016/j.jvlc.2015.03.002. Elsevier
9. Sebillo, M., Tucci, M., Vitiello, G.: Visual synthesis of evolutionary emergency scenarios. In: Díaz, P., Bellamine Ben Saoud, N., Dugdale, J., Hanachi, C. (eds.) ISCRAM-med 2016. LNBIP, vol. 265, pp. 85–97. Springer, Cham (2016). doi:10.1007/978-3-319-47093-1_8

10. Sebillo, M., Vitiello, G., Paolino, L., Ginige, A.: Training emergency responders through augmented reality mobile interfaces. Multimedia Tools Appl. **75**, 9609–9622 (2016). doi:10.1007/s11042-015-2955-0. Springer Science

11. Serdaroglu, K., Uslu, G., Baydere, S.: Medication intake adherence with real time activity recognition on IoT. In: 2015 IEEE 11th International Conference on IEEE Wireless and Mobile Computing, Networking and Communications (WiMob), pp. 230–237 (2015)

12. Silva, B.M., Lopes, I.M., Marques, M.B., Rodrigues, J.J.P.C., Proença Jr., M.L.: A mobile health application for outpatients medication management. In: IEEE ICC 2013 - Selected Areas in Communications Symposium, pp. 4389–4393 (2013)

13. Zhu, Q., Liu, C., Holroyd, K.A.: From a traditional behavioral management program to an m-health app: lessons learned in developing m-health apps for existing health care programs. In: 2012 4th International Workshop on Software Engineering in Health Care (SEHC), pp. 69–72 (2012)

14. MyMedSchedule app. www.mymedschedule.com/

15. MyMeds app. https://www.my-meds.com

16. MedSimple app. https://www.medsimpleapp.com

A Digital Knowledge Ecosystem to Increase Participation in Emergency Warnings and Alerts Management

Paloma Díaz[✉], Teresa Onorati, and Ignacio Aedo

Interactive Systems DEI-Lab, Universidad Carlos III de Madrid, Madrid, Spain
{pdp,tonorati}@inf.uc3m.es, aedo@ia.uc3m.es

Abstract. Early warning contributes to reduce the damages when updated and reliable information is collected before a hazard happens, so that early response can be orchestrated. Integrating volunteers and citizens into data collection can help to get a better picture of the situation, since they are intelligent sensors equipped with mobile devices that can be used everywhere to collect and share information. In this paper we discuss the architecture of a digital knowledge ecosystem to support such participatory early warning process. This DKE deals with a complex knowledge coproduction problem by separating information according to its meaning, quality and reliability. The use of technological tools is aimed at supporting a self-organized, scalable and sustainable process. The different agents and interactions involved and some design requirements are drawn from a use case in the context of the Spanish early warning system.

Keywords: Emergency management · Citizen's participation · Technology acceptance models

1 Introduction

Digital Knowledge Ecosystems (DKE henceforth) have been defined in the literature as "distributed adaptive open socio-technical systems for knowledge sharing and management exhibiting properties of self-organization, scalability and sustainability" [1]. With the popularity of mobile computing and the capabilities offered by the web 2.0, Emergency Management (EM henceforth) can be characterized as an open socio-technical system where different people, including professional EM workers, politicians, decision makers and citizens, make use of technology to support a complex social problems related with critical events and disasters. Information and communication technologies can improve communication, coordination and collaboration in certain tasks involved in the four phases of the EM process, namely mitigation, preparedness, response, and recovery [2]. In such phases, the human agents involved would need to share information and coproduce knowledge about a changing and unstable situation. Crisis have been characterized as process not events, that evolve over time and have a social nature [3]. Each crisis or disaster is a new case, where existing knowledge, abilities and resources can be used but also where unpredictable events happen so predefined plans need to be adapted as the situation evolves [4, 5]. Hence, IT-supported EM can be considered as an example of digital knowledge ecosystem where different agents and communities

© Springer International Publishing AG 2017
M.H.A. Au et al. (Eds.): GPC 2017, LNCS 10232, pp. 700–711, 2017.
DOI: 10.1007/978-3-319-57186-7_50

interrelate using technology to reach the main goal of EM, which in the words of FEMA is to "reduce the vulnerability to hazards and cope with disasters" [6].

From the different phases of EM, mitigation is in charge of deciding how to act when a risk has been identified. At this stage, alerts and warnings tracking is a key activity which can be improved by integrating volunteers and citizen generated information [7–9] in a similar way as citizen science does [10]. Early warning is a key activity in EM that can considerably reduce the damages if updated and reliable information is collected before the hazard happens, so that early response can be orchestrated. EM is not just dealing with the effects of disasters and crisis when they happen, but it is also about reducing the vulnerability of communities by preparing them to react, reducing risks and vulnerabilities and strengthening the community resilience. A community is considered as resilient if it has developed a set of capacities as a group to recover effectively from disasters [11]. For that to be possible, communities of volunteers and other civic organizations need to be integrated in the process [5] to develop and strengthen their social capital and to acquire the knowledge and skills that will substantively empower them to contribute effectively to the process [12].

In this paper we explore how citizen generated information can be integrated in early warning systems. We will analyze the design requirements that have to be considered to empower both EM workers and decision makers and citizens in what has been identified as a coproduction system [13], that is a system where citizens and authorities can engage to provide a better service to the community. The goal is to deploy affordable technologies that can be accepted by all the agents involved in DKE. In the remaining of the paper we start by reviewing the theoretical basis of this work. In Sect. 3 we describe a design case to integrate citizens in early warning systems and we draw a number of design guidelines derived from this design experience in Sect. 4. Section 5 summarizes some conclusions and ongoing work.

2   Context and Related Works

This work analyzes how to deploy affordable technologies to improve real citizen participation in early warning activities. By affordable technologies we mean both economically affordable and cognitively and organizationally affordable. The goal is then to understand which kind of technologies will be accepted by organizations and end users, taking into account that end users include EM professional workers and decision makers, volunteers and other citizens engaged in the early warning process. Affordable technologies are required to support sustainable engagement. Early warning is a decision making activity characterized by the need to manage complex, chaotic and unpredictable situations [14] for which emergency workers often apply soft knowledge. Soft knowledge is the type of knowledge that can be transmitted but neither codified nor stored, such as skills, tacit knowledge, internalized experience or the cultural knowledge embedded in practice [15]. Since this kind of expertise cannot be externalized and coded, deploying intelligent systems to support their activity might become a challenge in terms of technology acceptance, and for that reason, the approach taken in this work is completely different. Technology will be used to provide decision makers with additional information generated by heterogeneous sources that will be presented in an interactive and interpretable way. In this way, technological interventions are devised as facilitators of situational awareness that support human agents in the decision making process. In the next paragraphs we review the literature that supports the approach followed to reach this goal, including the perspective of Technology Acceptance Models (TAM) and the participatory and co-productive approaches in EM.

2.1 TAM and the Design of Emergency Management Technologies

TAM proposals provide a theoretical underpinning to envision strategies that might be followed to develop affordable technologies that increase citizen participation in early warning systems. First introduced by Davis in 1989, TAM analyzed the impact of perceived usability and utility in acceptance [16]. More than a decade later it was extended by the authors to take into account the effect of social, cultural and organizational issues [17]. Similarly, Mathieson conducted studies driven by the fact that acceptance might not be volitional and demonstrated that the behavioral intention to use a technology is affected in many situations by external variables including the perceived resources available to use it [18]. Among such resources, Mathieson identifies control related issues, that is, the perception of controlling the system, user and system attributes and support from others. TAM evolved into the Unified Theory of Acceptance and Use of Technology (UTAUT) where factors such as performance expectancy, effort expectancy, social influence and facilitating conditions were considered as determinants factors to influence the use of a technology [19]. In [20] authors discuss how the lack of organizational and political support can negatively affect the adoption of an EM information system that had been positively evaluated as useful and usable. In this experience, the subjective impression of losing control over the process was a key factor to hinder the use of the system. In other TAM extension, Zhang et al. [21] studied the effect of personal emotions in the acceptance process and concluded that the perceived affective quality might influence the behavioral intention to use a technology. In terms of ICT technologies, this type of attribute can be aligned with the concept of *user engagement* that defines the quality of the interaction that motivates its use [22]. In this case, the personal impression of being more effective, for EM workers, and the feeling of being useful, for citizens and volunteers, could support a better acceptance level. In terms of ICT technologies, this type of attribute can be aligned with the concept of *user engagement* that defines the quality of the interaction that motivates and stimulates the use of the technology [22]. As a summary, to deploy technologies that will be used in working settings, the organizational perspective and goals have to be considered from the very beginning of the development. Similarly, the expectations, goals and needs of end users should also lead the design decisions to create useful and engaging experiences that guarantee the DKE sustainability.

2.2 Integrating Citizen Generated Information in Early Warning

The rational to integrate multiple sources of information in early warning systems is basically the same used in citizen science [10]. Citizens are intelligent sensors scattered through the affected areas who are equipped with mobile devices that can be used to capture and send information to decision makers [7]. The same than scientists realized that citizen crowds were a free source of labor and skills that could be exploited in their research [10], EM studies and real cases have demonstrated that citizens are the *first-first-responders* [23] and integrating them in EM is not an option but a key requirement to provide a more efficient and sustainable service [12, 13, 24].

The integration of official and non-official information sources, usually called back-channel communication [25], can provide better situational awareness to human agents. That is, integration of heterogeneous sources of information can be used to help decision makers to understand the situation and project its evolution so the best course of action can be decided in an informed way [26]. The use of spontaneously generated information on social networks as back-channel information has been proposed in the literature [8, 25, 27] though it raises some concerns from the point of view of EM workers and decisions makers as discussed in [16]. Though this option is quite convenient from the point of view of citizens who do not need to use an ad-hoc application to send information, the huge amount of data along with its lack of quality and pertinence decreases the acceptance of such approaches by EM workers and decision makers [16]. Mixed solutions like [28] combine spontaneously generated information and more curated data sent through domain specific applications.

Another key issue to consider is that citizens are not a homogeneous crowd of people sharing the same capabilities to capture and process relevant information. In [9] the integration of official volunteer groups in early warning activities is discussed. Prepared volunteers provide reliable information since they have specific skills to process the quality of data. However, less reliable and non-curated information sources can also be useful as far as they can be properly managed. Scalable and interpretable visualizations [29] can provide means to navigate through vast and heterogeneous crowd of back-channel informants. Citizen data need to be aggregated, filtered and reorganized in appropriate visualizations that support situational awareness.

3   Case Study: Early Warning as a Digital Knowledge Ecosystem

As discussed before, early warning digital systems can be considered as digital knowledge ecosystems (DKE) made up of different types of agents, humans and artificial, that interact to try to solve a complex and open problem. Early warning implies gathering information about potential risks to coproduce knowledge among different agents. The final goal is to support decisions makers in understanding the situation, project its potential evolution and decide how to react. Since risks and disaster are always unpredictable and plans need to be dynamically readjusted, the system has to be adaptive and flexible enough to accommodate different requirements. The DKE needs also to be sustainable, since the agents involved might vary from one event to the other. In this section we describe a case study that models a potential DKE to improve the early warning activities currently managed by the Spanish General Directorate of Emergencies and Civil Protection (DGPCE henceforth). The goal pursued is improved to take profit from digital technologies to integrate more informants in the process, including also citizens, in an efficient, scalable and sustainable way. The description of this case study is based on the previous experience of researchers on this kind of systems [9, 13, 27] and interviews carried out with stakeholders who work for the DGPCE. Early warning systems are often implemented as iterative cycles made up of four activities; collecting data and monitoring precursors, analyzing data to identify hazards, communicating hazards and starting early response activities [30]. In this paper we focus on the two first activities in which citizens take part in a DKE aimed at improving the situational awareness of decision makers. In both phases different agents with different roles who participate on an individual or collective way are involved as discussed in the next paragraphs and shown in Fig. 1.

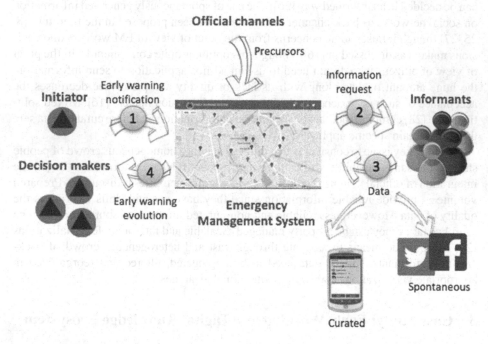

Fig. 1. The architecture of the early warning DKE (Color figure online)

Initiators are professional EM workers who generate early warnings that need to be monitored by the informants. In our scenario the initiator is always an operator in the EM agency who starts the process based on alerts issued by official or back-channel sources. The initiator determines who should receive the early warning notification, that is, which *informants* are involved, and the type of feedback that will be required to each of them. In this way, a more flexible process that avoids receiving useless information can be supported.

Informants provide data to support decision makers identifying whether a warning has to be issued to the affected population. Such data can be generated from official informants, like the "Instituto Geográfico Nacional" that supplies data about seismic activity, but also from back-channel informants, like volunteers and citizens that are in the potentially affected area and count on mobile devices to collect and send data. The quality and level of trust of the sources of information are different. Even back-channel informants are not a homogeneous crowd not at least from the perspective of professional EM. Some of them have a higher credibility based basically on their previous relationship with the EM agency. In our scenario, the REMER network is one of the more trusted back-channel informants. REMER is an official network of radio amateurs who collaborates with the DGPCE. Their members are volunteers but they are treated as permanent collaborators whose activity is determined by governmental authorities who already count on them in their protocols. The network has a hierarchical structure known and partly managed by the DGPCE, so their level of trust is even higher that the VOST volunteers. VOST (Virtual Operation Support Team) are groups of volunteers that help monitoring social networks to detect fake and relevant information as well as to provide researchers with information on the activity in social networks. It is non-governmental group spread around the world but since they are not under the umbrella of official EM agencies their credibility is lower than those of the REMER members. Finally, data received might be more curated and elaborated data collected through apps specifically designed to integrate citizens into the EM process, such as [27] for the response phase, or data spontaneous generated in social networks.

Decisions makers analyze the information available about the warning to decide whether the risk is evolving into a hazard that needs to be communicated to the population and the early response has to be activated or not. With that purpose they have to manage and prioritize the available data and apply their own knowledge about risks. As said before, we do not try to provide intelligent tools that automatically process this information; we rely upon the human analysts hard and soft knowledge to take such decisions. To facilitate a better situational awareness, data will be filtered, categorized, aggregated and prioritized using a knowledge modelling approach. The goal of knowledge modelling will be extracting information from data to be able to deploy a scalable, meaningful and useful representation that eases human analysis.

All these human agents can be provided with adequate technologies to make up a DKE able to deal with early warning in a more participatory and sustainable way. To be a DKE the resulting sociotechnical system need to be able to self-organize, scalable and sustainable [1]. Concerning the first attribute, self-organization is a key requirement in any EM process since they are always dynamic and the protocol always needs to be adapted to the specific hazard features or available resources [4]. This sociotechnical system becomes scalable as far as technologies facilitate decision makers to understand the situation, communicate with all the agents involved and coordinate the action. Finally, it will be sustainable if it is envisioned as a coproduction system where technology is exploited to provide a public service in which citizens and EM professionals engage in an effective way. As discussed in [13] for that to be possible the different capacities and skills of citizens need to be made explicit to EM workers using categories of participants visually distinguishable and accessible in the interface. Finally, it is important to keep in mind that each agent might use a different device depending on the task performed and on the context of use. For instance, mobile devices are used in the field to collect data but in the operation center desktop computers, big displays and tabletops might be used in the different stages of the process. For instance, big displays are usually employed to get a whole picture of the situation or to display complementary information. Tabletops are available in some control rooms to support collaborative decision making.

4   A Design Proposal for an Early Warning System DKE

In this section se describe how interactive technologies can be used to implement the DKE described in the previous section.

4.1   Creating Early Warnings in the DKE

To make *informants* aware of an early warning of a risk or hazard occurring nearby, the *initiators* can use the platform to send warnings and information about the current situation. As already explained, *informants* have different profiles so they receive different levels of details and they might be requested different types of feedback. The information provided to each *informant* is the one needed to perform the task assigned since superfluous data can provoke information overload [4].

In this case study, we have modeled the DKE as a responsive website that can be used from a mobile phone, a tablet or a desktop computer. From the interviews with the stakeholders, it turns out that generally citizens are reluctant to install on their phones a native application that probably will be used occasionally. For this reason, we propose as a scalable solution a responsive website that can be easily adapted to any screen size, platform and users' profile. Moreover, we also include the possibility to use different communication channels for sending the warnings, like emails, sms, social networks or even radio. In particular, we posit for giving to social networks a crucial role in the DKE considering that nowadays their usage for emergency communications is growing exponentially [25].

In Fig. 2, two different views of the reception of a warning are shown. In the desktop version (Fig. 2a), a new alert is represented as a red circle over the notification icon and a highlighted title and short description in the list of warnings. In the mobile devices, warnings are sent depending on the preferences of each user. Figure 2b shows an

a) Desktop view   b) Twitter message   c)Mobile view

Fig. 2.   Receiving warnings in the digital knowledge ecosystem. (Color figure online)

example of a flood warning sent as a Twitter direct message with a short description and a link to the main website where more details are available (Fig. 2c).

4.2   Monitoring Early Warnings in the DKE

Collecting updated information about what is currently going on can help decision makers in building a better understanding of the evolution of the early warning. As discussed before there are different types of *informants*. Official *informants* are part of the EM process and consequently they send accurate details. Back-channel *informants'* credibility depends on their profile. Citizens do not have technical knowledge for judging the situation in terms that can be useful for decision makers, whilst volunteers are usually prepared to provide quality information. Volunteer networks have also different experience in EM and a different relation with the official agencies. In our case, volunteers are separated into two trust levels: official (e.g. REMER) and spontaneous (e.g. VOST). Being able to quickly identify *informants* by their capabilities and reliability can help decision makers to better organize the notifications and make decisions about whether validation or more information is required.

The proposed EMS allows to send a new warning specifying on the map where the risk is located and then describing the details of the early warning. Once the notification has been sent, a colored mark is added on the map. The color depends on the reliability of the source (see Fig. 1): green for the official EM agencies, blue for the official volunteers, orange for the spontaneous volunteers and yellow for the general citizens. When the initiation is an official EM agency, the *initiator* decides which information has to be required and to whom, so the system adapts to evolving situations. If the first notification is started by a back-channel source, it has to be validated by the agency. Not all event notifications fire an early warning process. Early warning is a monitoring process that is started to check hazard precursors before an alert is issued [30]. About the form, Fig. 3a shows the desktop view for the most reliable informants where they are asked to specify the start and end date of the early warning, the severity level, the risk

a) Desktop view   b) Mobile view

Fig. 3.   Sending a warning in the digital knowledge ecosystem.

probability and a textual description. Moreover, they can attach a media content as a photo, video or audio recording. The last option automatically sends a notification to the involved *informants*. If citizens want to send information, they just choose the geographical position on the map and add a textual description or other media (see Fig. 3b for the mobile view).

Another interesting aspect of the DKE is the possibility to check for spontaneous sources of information (i.e. social networks) in a scalable way. When some exceptional circumstances occur, the volume of messages shared on social networks spread exponentially as demonstrated by events like the hurricane Sandy (October 2012) or the last terrorist attacks of Paris (November 2015). Authors have already proposed an automatic mechanism to semantically analyze the information flowing from these sources [31]. The result is a set of visualizations that decision makers can explore for adding the citizens' point of view to the general picture of the current risk. Here, we propose the integration of this semantic analysis for monitoring the social network activity (see Fig. 4).

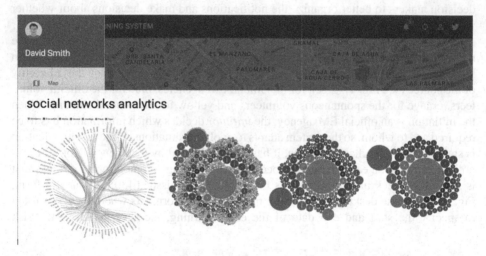

Fig. 4. Semantic visualizations of social network activities.

As a summary, Table 1 lists some requirements extracted from the descriptions of the DKE in Sects. 3 and 4. These requirements are not aimed at being an exhaustive list of the characteristics that have to be implemented in an early warning DKE, but summarize the experience gained through this work as well as in the literature. This approach has the properties of DKE, namely, self-organization, scalability and sustainability. The participants in each hazard are determined by the initiator and can be modified as the early warning process advances, so if the conditions change, the agents involve can change too. Also the information required per hazard are adaptable to the information needs of that specific case. The system is scalable since it offers mechanisms to sort out and filter information depending on the role. It is sustainable since it relies upon citizen capabilities to better support a complex knowledge problem but information can be even gathered from social networks. In this way, citizens can participate without being aware of it.

Table 1. Some design requirements for a DKE on emergency early warning

Multi-device platforms have to be implemented to support different tasks, performed in different contexts and by different users' profiles
Informants can have a different levels of reliability and trust, and these levels has to be made explicit in the information visualization so that decision makers can quickly identify relevant data
Warnings can be generated by the initiators or imported from external official sources, like the meteorological hazards institutes or the seismographic risks institutes
The system has to be scalable, sustainable and adaptive. EM workers need to be able to personalize all the components of the DKE (such as agents involved, preferred sources of information, type of feedback required, type of visualization of data) to cope with unexpected and variable situations
Interfaces have to be intuitive, easy to understand and easy to interact with. The information and interaction capabilities offered should avoid information overload. They have to be easy to remember since many users will not use them on a daily basis
If mobile apps are developed to collect authenticated and curated data, their design should minimize the storage space required in the user device. If not, users might remove the app as soon as the early warning process ends
Social networks can provide interesting data as far as data are organized, filtered and visualized in a meaningful and interpretable way
Different communication channels have to be offered for improving the citizen participation and to support different operation conditions in the network, including emails, sms, social network messages or radio transmissions

5 Conclusions

In this paper we have discussed how the emergencies early warning system can be envisioned as a digital knowledge ecosystem. The DKE is improved by integrating back-channel informants such as volunteers and citizens to acquire more updated data on the evolution of potential risks and hazards. Our approach is focused on establishing a right balance between improving the citizen participation in the EM and guaranteeing the reliability of collected information. For this reason, on the one hand we have to offer a scalable solution that anyone can use from different contexts, while on the other hand we have also to distinguish different trust and reliability levels so that decision makers are aware of the quality of the data before taking any decision.

Acknowledgement. This work is supported by the project PACE grant funded by the Spanish Ministry of Economy and Competitivity (TIN2016-77690-R).

References

1. Briscoe, G.: Complex adaptive digital ecosystems. In: Proceedings of the International Conference on Management of Emergent Digital EcoSystems, pp. 39–46. ACM (2010)
2. Petak, W.J.: Emergency management: a challenge for public administration. Publ. Adm. Rev. **45**, 3–7 (1985)
3. Oliver-Smith, A., Hoffman, S.M.: Theorizing disasters: nature, power and culture. In: Oliver-Smith, A. (ed.) Catastrophe and Culture: The Anthropology of Disaster. School of American Research Press, Santa Fe (2002)
4. Turoff, M., Chumer, M., Van de Walle, B., Yao, X.: The design of a dynamic emergency response management information system (Dermis). J. Inf. Technol. Theory Appl. (JITTA) **5**(4), 1–36 (2004)
5. Waugh, W.L., Streib, G.: Collaboration and leadership for effective emergency management. Public Adm. Rev. **66**(s1), 131–140 (2006)
6. Principles of Emergency Management. FEMA, Washington DC (2007)
7. Goodchild, M.F.: Citizens as sensors: the world of volunteered geography. GeoJournal **69**(4), 211–221 (2007)
8. Palen, L., Anderson, K.M., Mark, G., Martin, J., Sicker, D., Palmer, M., Grunwald, D.: A vision for technology-mediated support for public participation & assistance in mass emergencies & disasters. In: Proceedings of the 2010 ACM-BCS Visions of Computer Science Conference, p. 8. British Computer Society (2010)
9. Díez, D., Díaz, P., Aedo, I.: virtual communities of practice: design directions for technology-mediated collaboration in the early warning activity. In: Proceedings of 7th International Conference on Information Systems for Crisis Response and Management (ISCRAM 2010) (2010)
10. Silvertown, J.: A new dawn for citizen science. Trends Ecol. Evol. **24**(9), 467–471 (2009)
11. Norris, F.H., Stevens, S.P., Pfefferbaum, B., Wyche, K.F., Pfefferbaum, R.L.: Community resilience as a metaphor, theory, set of capacities, and strategy for disaster readiness. Am. J. Commun. Psychol. **41**(1–2), 127–150 (2008)
12. Dynes, R.R.: Social capital dealing with community emergencies. Homel. Secur. Aff. **2**, 1–26 (2006)
13. Díaz, P., Carroll, J.M., Aedo, I.: Coproduction as an approach to technology-mediated citizen participation in emergency management. Future Internet **8**(3), 41 (2016)
14. French, S., Niculae, C.: Believe in the model: mishandle the emergency. J. Homel. Secur. Emerg. Manag. **2**(1), Article No. 1 (2005)
15. Hildreth, P.M., Kimble, C.: The duality of knowledge. Inf. Res. **8**(1), 1–18 (2002)
16. Davis, F.D.: Perceived usefulness, perceived ease of use, and user acceptance of information technology. MIS Q. **13**, 319–340 (1989)
17. Venkatesh, V., Davis, F.D.: A theoretical extension of the technology acceptance model: four longitudinal field studies. Manag. Sci. **46**(2), 186–204 (2000)
18. Mathieson, K., Peacock, E., Chin, W.W.: Extending the technology acceptance model: the influence of perceived user resources. SIGMIS Database **32**(3), 86–112 (2001)
19. Venkatesh, V., Morris, M.G., Davis, G.B., Davis, F.D.: User acceptance of information technology: toward a unified view. MIS Q. **27**(3), 425–478 (2003)
20. Aedo, I., Díaz, P., Carroll, J.M., Convertino, G., Rosson, M.B.: End-user oriented strategies to facilitate multi-organizational adoption of emergency management information systems. Inf. Process. Manag. **46**(1), 11–21 (2010)

21. Zhang, P., Li, N., Sun, H.: Affective quality and cognitive absorption: extending technology acceptance research. In: Proceedings of the 39th Annual Hawaii International Conference on System Sciences, HICSS 2006, vol. 8, p. 207a. IEEE (2006)
22. O'Brien, H.L., Toms, E.G.: What is user engagement? A conceptual framework for defining user engagement with technology. J. Am. Soc. Inf. Sci. Technol. **59**(6), 938–955 (2008)
23. Stallings, R.A., Quarantelli, E.L.: Emergent citizen groups and emergency management. Public Adm. Rev. **45**, 93–100 (1985)
24. Ginige, A., Paolino, L., Romano, M., Sebillo, M., Tortora, G., Vitiello, G.: Information sharing among disaster responders-an interactive spreadsheet-based collaboration approach. Comput. Support. Coop. Work **23**(4–6), 547–583 (2014)
25. Sutton, J., Palen, L., Shklovski, I.: Backchannels on the front lines: emergent use of social media in the 2007 Southern California fire. In: Proceedings of Information Systems for Crisis Response and Management Conference (ISCRAM), Washington DC (2008)
26. Endsley, M.R.: Design and evaluation for situation awareness enhancement. In: Proceedings of the Human Factors and Ergonomics Society Annual Meeting, vol. 32(2), pp. 97–101. SAGE Publications (1988)
27. Malizia, A., Bellucci, A., Diaz, P., Aedo, I., Levialdi, S.: eStorys: a visual storyboard system supporting back-channel communication for emergencies. J. Vis. Lang. Comput. **22**(2), 150–169 (2011)
28. Diaz, P., Onorati, T., Olmo Pueblas, S.: Analyzing and visualizing emergency information in a multi device environment. In: Díaz, P., Bellamine Ben Saoud, N., Dugdale, J., Hanachi, C. (eds.) ISCRAM-med 2016. LNBIP, vol. 265, pp. 181–194. Springer, Cham (2016). doi: 10.1007/978-3-319-47093-1_16
29. Keim, D.A., Mansmann, F., Schneidewind, J., Ziegler, H.: Challenges in visual data analysis. In: Tenth International Conference on Information Visualization, (IV 2006), pp. 2–7 (2006)
30. de León, J.C.V., Bogardi, J., Dannenmann, S., Basher, R.: Early warning systems in the context of disaster risk management. Entwicklung Ländlicher Raum **2**, 23–25 (2006)
31. Onorati, T., Díaz, P.: Giving meaning to tweets in emergency situations: a semantic approach for filtering and visualizing social data. SpringerPlus **5**(1), 1782 (2016)

An Intelligent Framework for Predicting State War Engagement from Territorial Data

Giovanni Acampora[1], Genoveffa Tortora[2], and Autilia Vitiello[2(✉)]

[1] Department of Physics "Ettore Pancini",
University of Naples Federico II, 80126 Naples, Italy
giovanni.acampora@unina.it
[2] Department of Computer Science, University of Salerno, 84084 Fisciano, Italy
{tortora,avitiello}@unisa.it

Abstract. Involvement of a state in a war is one of the risks that have a relevant impact on society. Effective prediction of the possibility that a state is going to engage in a war is an important decision support tool for avoiding international crisis and safeguarding social well-being. The paper presents the proposal of an intelligent framework aimed to predict the engagement of a state in a war by using national territorial data captured in a digital knowledge ecosystem composed of local business companies and corporations' information systems. As shown by preliminary results, the proposed framework is feasible to achieve the designed goal.

Keywords: State war engagement · Intelligent framework · Territorial data

1 Introduction

The consequences of a war are extensive and long-lasting. Although their war experiences are different, both military personnel and civilians suffer in times of war. Often women and children are those most affected suffering the most unspeakable atrocities. In addition, armed conflict have important indirect negative consequences also on infrastructure, public health provision, and social order [1]. Hence, every effort must be made to avoid the onset of armed conflicts. Effective prediction of the possibility that a state is going to engage in a war could be a good support tool for avoiding international crisis and safeguarding social well-being. In the literature, some decision tools have been proposed to predict militarized disputes [2,3]. However, these tools are aimed at mainly understanding intuitive causal interpretation of interstate interactions rather than developing a tool to be used in real scenarios. Indeed, no architectures are proposed for them. Moreover, they are based on a dyadic vision of militarized conflicts. In this vision, disputes are predicted starting from a combination of the parameters of the two states in conflict. However, although dyadic vision is consolidated by conflict dynamics researchers, it could make unfeasible the implementation of decision tools in real scenarios.

M.H.A. Au et al. (Eds.): GPC 2017, LNCS 10232, pp. 712–721, 2017.
DOI: 10.1007/978-3-319-57186-7_51

Starting from these considerations, this paper presents the proposal of an intelligent framework for predicting the engagement of a state in a war by considering national territorial data rather than dyadic states' parameters. In more detail, the proposed framework is composed of three layers: the bottom layer is aimed at learning a model able to predict the possible engagement in a war of a state; the middle layer is devoted to execute the learned prediction model for each state; the top layer is aimed at graphically representing the results to make them usable for users. In particular, the proposed framework uses as prediction models the well-known neural networks. The learning of the neural networks is based on historical territorial data, whereas, their execution exploits territorial data characterizing the states at the moment of the execution. These current territorial data will be obtained by combining estimates by international organisations and information captured in a local digital knowledge ecosystem.

Some preliminary experiments have been carried out where the prediction model for one of the most relevant state in the world, the United States of America (USA), has been tested by using territorial data belonging to the well-known Correlates of War project[1]. The results of these preliminary experiments show the feasibility of the proposed intelligent framework.

The remaining of the paper is organized as follows. Section 2 discusses the territorial data used to learn the prediction model. Section 3 is the core of the paper since it discusses the designed intelligent framework. Section 4 describes the preliminary experiments and results. In Sect. 5, conclusions and future works are drawn.

2 Modeling State War Engagement Through Territorial Data

As defined in [4], Militarised Interstate Disputes (MID) refers to the threat of using military force between sovereign states in an explicit way. In other words, MID is a state that results from interactions between two states which can be either in peace or in conflict [5]. Typically, these interactions are expressed in the form of dyadic attributes which are two states parameters considered to influence the probability of military conflict [6]. In the literature, some approaches [2,3] based on computational intelligence techniques have been applied to predict militarized conflicts between states starting from dyadic variables. However, in real scenarios, it is difficult to estimate state parameters belonging to the present time, and above all, dyadic attributes between two states.

For this reason, in this work, the attention is moved from dyadic vision to national vision. Therefore, the proposed framework is aimed at predicting the engagement of a state in a war rather than the conflict between two states. In our national vision, the engagement of a state in a war is based only on state parameters representing territorial data. In detail, in order to predict the engagement of a state in a war, eight variables are used. The first six variables, named *total*

---

[1] http://www.correlatesofwar.org/.

population, urban population, military personnel, military expenditures, primary energy consumption, and *iron and steel production,* represent the national material capabilities; the last two variables, named *imports* and *exports,* represent the national trade. In detail, the *total population* is the size of a states civilian population in a year; the *urban population* is the size of a states urban population in a year; the *military personnel* is the size of a states military personnel in a year; the *military expenditures* is the states total military budget in a year; the *primary energy consumption* is a states consumption of energy (metric ton coal equivalent) in a year; and the *iron and steel production* reflects a states production of pig iron and steel in a year; the *imports* and *exports* are the total imports and total exports of a state in a year in US millions of dollars.

In the next section, a detailed description of the proposed framework and how it is able to predict the engagement of a state in a war by using the aforementioned territorial data is given.

3   The Proposed Framework

This paper presents the proposal of an intelligent framework aimed at predicting the propensity of states to engage in a war and, as a consequence, the onset of international crisis. The framework is based on a combination of territorial data and machine learning techniques such as Neural Networks (NNs). Figure 1 shows the overall architecture of the proposed framework. In detail, it is composed of three layers: the bottom layer is aimed at learning a model for each world state able to predict the possible engagement in a war of the corresponding state; the middle layer is devoted to execute the learned prediction model by using current territorial data for each state; the top layer is aimed at graphically representing the results produced by the middle layer. Hereafter, more details about the framework layers are given.

3.1   Learning Layer

The learning layer is devoted to generate a prediction model for each state aimed at predicting the engagement in a war of the corresponding state starting from historical territorial data. Therefore, this layer is composed of a collection of supervised learning algorithms, each one of them is devoted to train a prediction model for a state. In this work, the supervised learning algorithm chosen for all states is the scaled conjugate gradient algorithm [7]. The learned prediction model is represented by a neural network and it will be denoted as a *State Neural Network* (SNN).

From an implementative point of view, an SNN is a neural network characterized by eight neurons in the input layer, an output layer with a single node and an hidden layer composed of twenty neurons. The number of neurons in the hidden layer is a design choice, whereas, the size of the input and output layers is tied to the number of independent and dependent variables of the training data, respectively. In detail, the independent variables represent the eight

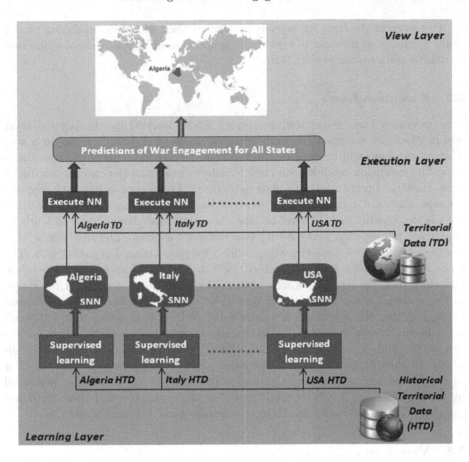

Fig. 1. Architecture of the proposed framework. For sake of space, only three states, Algeria, Italy and USA, are reported. In addition, the prediction of the war engagement for Algeria is only an example.

aspects relevant for modeling the engagement of a state in a war described in Sect. 2. The dependent variable, instead, can assume two values: 1 to indicate the engagement of a state in a war, 0 otherwise. The general scheme of an SNN is reported in Fig. 2.

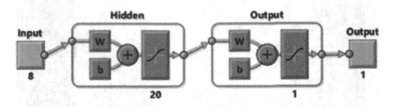

Fig. 2. The general scheme of the State Neural Networks (SNNs)

The work of the learning layer is performed once. However, updating phases could be designed in order to repeat the generation of SNNs by considering new territorial data obtained over time.

3.2   Execution Layer

The execution layer is devoted to run all SNNs learned by the bottom layer and produce the information about the propensity of states to engage in a war. This information will be used by the top layer to provide a graphical user interface. The execution modules run the SNNs by considering the current territorial data. Historical territorial data used to learn SNNs are relatively easy to recover because they are related to past years. Instead, obtaining current territorial data is not equally easy. Therefore, the execution layer is expected to work by exploiting information provided by two different sources. The first one is represented by the periodic estimates provided by international organisations. The second source, instead, is represented by a local digital knowledge ecosystem including business companies willing to provide information on their activities. In this context, for instance, the independent variable *exports* can be calculated by aggregating the information provided by all local companies that sell products abroad. At the same way, the independent variable *iron and steel production* can be calculated by summarizing the information provided by all local steelworks. In this digital knowledge ecosystem, local companies will work together to create and aggregate knowledge and will benefit of the knowledge produced by themselves since it will be used to predict the engagement of their state in a war: an information useful for them to organize their business strategies.

3.3   View Layer

The view layer is devoted to graphically report the results produced by the middle layer to users. The produced Graphical User Interface (GUI) will be pleasant and intuitive. It will allow to display the planisphere and highlight on it which states are going to engage in a war. The view layer can be implemented also on mobile devices in order to make more effective the fruition of the results

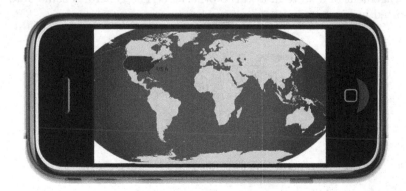

Fig. 3. A mobile GUI of the view layer

obtained by the middle layer (see Fig. 3). In this case, the development of GUI will deserve special attention, in order to face mobile device limitations, such as less screen dimension.

4 Preliminary Experiments and Results

In this section, let us discuss a set of preliminary experiments performed to study the feasibility of the proposed framework. In order to achieve this aim, the effectiveness of the prediction model represented by neural networks is analysed. In detail, the performance of the SNN for one of the most important states in the world, the United States of America (USA), are studied and discussed. The territorial data used to learn the USA SNN and to study its performance in predicting the engagement of USA in a war are extracted by well-known datasets belonging to the Correlates of War (COW) project. The performance evaluation will be carried out by using a set of metrics typically used to assess the quality of classification models since SNN is a classification model. In order to point out the benefits of the exploitation of SNNs, a comparative study is conducted between SNN and a set of popular classification models such as Linear Discriminant Analysis (LDA), Naive Bayes (NB) classifier, Support Vector Machine (SVM) and 1-Nearest Neighbor (1-NN). Hereafter, more details about the experimental configuration, the used evaluation metrics and the comparative study are given.

4.1 Experimental Session Configuration

All experiments involve a dataset composed of information extracted from data belonging to the Correlates of War (COW) project. This project aimed at facilitating the collection, dissemination, and use of accurate and reliable quantitative data in international relations. In particular, three datasets belonging to the COW data collection are used:

- National Material Capabilities[2] (v4.0), that contains annual values for total population, urban population, iron and steel production, energy consumption, military personnel, and military expenditure of all state members, currently from 1816 to 2012;
- National (Monadic) Trade[3] (v4.0), that contains information on individual states import and export levels in current U.S. dollars for the period 1870-2014;
- Inter-state War data set[4] (v4.0), that contains wars that take place between or among recognized states, denoted as inter-state wars, from 1816 to 2007.

The generated dataset (downloadable at http://old.di.unisa.it/dottorandi/avitiello/resources/DatasetWarEngagement.zip) contains a row for each year

---

[2] http://www.correlatesofwar.org/data-sets/national-material-capabilities.
[3] http://www.correlatesofwar.org/data-sets/bilateral-trade.
[4] http://www.correlatesofwar.org/data-sets/COW-war.

from 1870 to 2007. In turn, each row contains eight values representing the iron and steel production, the military expenditure, the military personnel, the energy consumption, the total population, the urban population, the total imports and the total exports for USA followed by 0 or 1 to indicate if the relative year has been a peace or war year, respectively.

Once generated the dataset, the experiments have followed a hold-out approach. In detail, the generated dataset has been randomly divided into two parts: the first one containing the 75% of the data has been used for the training phase, whereas, the remaining part has been used as testing data. The ratio 75–25 has been chosen being a common ratio in data mining.

Table 1 shows the parameters used for running each one of the compared approaches. These parameters represent the best settings experimentally. All compared classification models have been implemented in Matlab™.

Table 1. Settings of the compared classification models

Approach name	Setting
1-NN	$Distance = $ Euclidean
LDA	-
NB	$Distribution = $ Normal
SVM	$kernel = $ Polynomial, $order = 3$
SNN	$Maximum\ number\ of\ epochs = 5000$, $Minimum\ performance$ $gradient = 1e\text{-}12$

During the experiments, SNN has shown a non-deterministic behavior. Therefore, in this comparison, the reported results are related to the most frequent behavior carried out on 50 independent training phases. It is worth noting that this behavior has been shown in 16 out of 50 (32%) training phases, whereas, only in 11 out of 50 (22%), our approach has shown behaviours worse than the most frequent one. Hence, in 23 out of 50 (46%) training phases, our approach has shown behaviours better than that reported.

4.2 Evaluation Metrics

The comparison among the considered classification models is based on a set of performance metrics typically used in data mining. In detail, the correctness of a binary classification can be evaluated by computing the value *true positives* representing the number of correctly recognized positive class examples, the value *true negatives* representing the number of correctly recognized examples that do not belong to the positive class, the value *false positives* representing the number of examples that were incorrectly assigned to the positive class and the value *false negatives* representing the number of examples that were not recognized as positive class examples. These values are typically arranged in a so-called *confusion matrix* (see Fig. 4a). Starting from confusion matrix values, it is possible to compute the following set of metrics: *Accuracy, Precision, Recall* and *Fscore*. Formally,

$$Accuracy = \frac{tp + tn}{(tp + tn + fp + fn)} \tag{1}$$

$$Precision = \frac{tp}{(tp + fp)} \tag{2}$$

$$Recall = \frac{tp}{(tp + fn)} \tag{3}$$

$$Fscore = \frac{2 \cdot Precision \cdot Recall}{Precision + Recall} \tag{4}$$

where tp are the true positives, fp are the false positives, fn are the false negatives and tn are the true negatives. In our context, the positive class corresponds to the class representing the engagement of a state in a war. Together with these typical metrics, a common way to summarize the performance of a classification model is to graph a so-called Receiver Operating Characteristic (ROC) curve. This is generated by plotting the True Positive Rate (TPR) against the False Positive Rate (FPR) when varying the threshold for assigning observations to a given class. Formally,

$$TPR = \frac{tp}{(tp + fn)} \tag{5}$$

$$FPR = \frac{fp}{(fp + tn)} \tag{6}$$

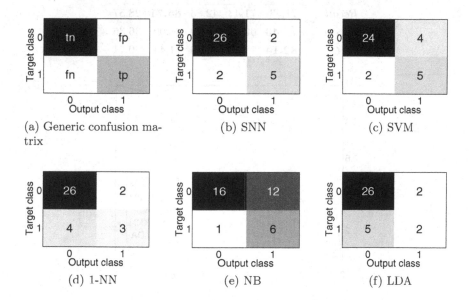

(a) Generic confusion matrix

(b) SNN

(c) SVM

(d) 1-NN

(e) NB

(f) LDA

Fig. 4. Confusion matrices for all compared classification models

where tp are the true positives, fp are the false positives, fn are the false negatives and tn are the true negatives. Usually, in order to quantify the performance summarized by a ROC curve, the Area Under the Curve (AUC) is computed. The higher the AUC value, the higher is the quality of the classification model. Therefore, together with the aforementioned evaluation metrics, also AUC values for all compared approaches are considered to assess their performance.

4.3   Comparative Study Results

Table 2 shows the results of all compared classification models in terms of the considered evaluation metrics. For the sake of completeness, Fig. 4b–f show the confusion matrices for all compared classification models and Fig. 5 shows the ROC curves.

By analysing Table 2, it is possible to point out that SNN is characterized by the best values for all evaluation metrics except for *Recall* where it is the second best performer after NB. However, NB achieves this high performance in *Recall* at the expense of the value of *Precision* that is the lowest. Therefore, even if SNN is the second performer in *Recall*, it is characterized by the best trade-off between *Precision* and *Recall* reflected by the best value of *Fscore*. Starting from

Table 2. Results (in percentage) for all compared classification approaches.

Metric	SNN	SVM	1-NN	NB	LDA
Accuracy	**88.57**	82.86	82.86	62.86	80.00
Precision	**71.43**	55.56	60.00	33.33	50.00
Recall	71.43	71.43	42.86	**85.71**	28.57
Fscore	**71.43**	62.50	50.00	48.00	36.36
AUC	**82.14**	78.57	67.86	71.43	60.71

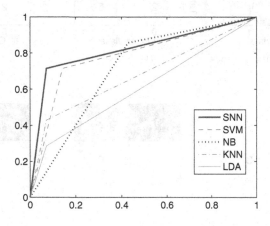

Fig. 5. Roc curves for all compared algorithms

these results, it is possible to state that SNN is the best performer to predict the engagement of a state in a war. Besides, its good performance allows to highlight the effectiveness of the proposed framework.

5 Conclusions and Future Works

This paper presents a proposal for an intelligent framework aimed at predicting the engagement of a state in a war starting from national territorial data. As shown by preliminary results, the proposed framework is feasible and character- ized by good performance with respect to well-known approaches. In the future, the behavior of the proposed approach will be tested by considering historical data of other world states in order to investigate its performance in all con- texts (for example, states smaller or more peaceful or, vice versa, more warlike than USA). Besides, a confirmation of expectations test involving a large num- ber of users will be performed in order to test the user satisfaction in using the developed GUI.

References

1. Plmper, T., Neumayer, E.: The unequal burden of war: the effect of armed conflict on the gender gap in life expectancy. Int. Organ. **60**(3), 723 (2016)
2. Tettey, T., Marwala, T.: Controlling interstate conflict using neuro-fuzzy modeling and genetic algorithms. In: 2006 International Conference on Intelligent Engineering Systems, pp. 30–34 (2006)
3. Tettey, T., Marwala, T.: Conflict modelling and knowledge extraction using com- putational intelligence methods. In: 11th International Conference on Intelligent Engineering Systems, pp. 161–166 (2007)
4. Gochman, C., Maoz, Z.: Militarized interstate disputes 1816–1976. J. Conflict Res- olut. **28**(4), 585–615 (1984)
5. Habtemariam, E., Marwala, T., Lagazio, M.: Artificial intelligence for conflict man- agement. In: 2005 IEEE International Joint Conference on Neural Networks, pp. 2583–2588 (2005)
6. Beck, N., King, G., Zeng, L.: Improving quantitative studies of international conflict: a conjecture. Am. Polit. Sci. Rev. **94**(1), 21–33 (2000)
7. Mller, M.F.: A scaled conjugate gradient algorithm for fast supervised learning. Neural Netw. **6**(4), 525–533 (1993)

1st Workshop on Cloud Security Modeling, Monitoring and Management (CS3M)

BYODCert: Toward a Cross-Organizational BYOD Paradigm

Alessio Merlo[(✉)]

DIBRIS, University of Genoa, Viale Francesco Causa, 13, 16145 Genoa, Italy
`alessio@dibris.unige.it`

Abstract. We introduce a novel architectural solution (BYODCert) for managing the Bring Your Own Device paradigm at a cross-organizational level by exploiting mobile device certifications. BYODCert acts as a trusted third party allowing organizations to verify the compliance of their employees' personal devices against BYOD security policies. BYO-DCert is implemented as a cloud service that can be adopted by organizations as an external and on-demand BYOD solution.

Keywords: Bring Your Own Device · App analysis · Android security · Public-key certification

1 Introduction

The *Bring Your Own Device* (BYOD) is a paradigm that pushes the adoption of personal devices inside organizations, with the aim to reduce the costs of the corporate ICT infrastructure. However, the adoption of personal devices in corporate environments has strong security implications. For instance, the device may carry malware that could harm the corporate ICT infrastructure or silently steal reserved data [1]. In this respect, reliable BYOD solutions must allow supporting the definition and enforcement of corporate security policies on devices joining the organization and, at the same time, grant the personal usage of the device (i.e., they should not be invasive in the mobile OS and should allow users to select and install applications from public stores).

Some proposals have been put forward in the last years to allow single organizations to support BYOD on mobile devices. However, such solutions are basically proprietary, OS-specific and support coarse-grained security policies. Furthermore, they are unable to cooperate, limiting the validity of the BYOD policies and their enforcement within the boundary of the single organization only. This ecosystem does not support a *cross-organizational* adoption of BYOD to enable an effective mobility of devices as well as the sharing of BYOD policies and analysis results among organizations.

To overcome such limitation, we present the BYODCert project. BYOD-Cert provides a new approach to BYOD, able to manage the same paradigm at a *cross-organizational level*. In detail, BYODCert is a service for *device certification*, allowing to publicly certify the compliance of an employee's personal

© Springer International Publishing AG 2017
M.H.A. Au et al. (Eds.): GPC 2017, LNCS 10232, pp. 725–735, 2017.
DOI: 10.1007/978-3-319-57186-7_52

device against BYOD security policies, independently from the organization the employee belongs to. BYODCert is implemented as a cloud service and its current implementation deals with Android-based devices.

BYODCert supports the following features:

1. **Definition of fine-grained BYOD policies** in a common, expressive policy specification language (i.e., ConSpec [2]) tailored to the policy specification needs of actual BYOD stakeholders (e.g. government agencies, companies, public-service corporations, ...).
2. **Automatic extraction of a device configuration**. Model extraction techniques are adopted to automatically build sound and complete models of the applications installed on a mobile device.
3. **Compliance verification**. Static analysis and model checking techniques are applied to verify the compliance of each extracted configuration w.r.t a BYOD policy.
4. **Customization of non-compliant devices** (where possible) by means of application instrumentation and monitoring techniques.
5. **Issuance and deployment of reliable signed certificates** stating the compliance of the device configuration against (a set of) BYOD policies.
6. **Support to policy-compliant installation of applications**, i.e., for each application the employee aims to install, BYODCert verifies whether its installation on the current device configuration leads to violate some acquired certifications.
7. **Verification of the correctness and the validity of a certificate** w.r.t. the actual device configuration. A set of proper security protocols allows BYODCert to reliably acquire the current device configuration and verify its compliance with the installed certificates.

BYODCert acts as a trusted third party among organizations. Organizations and personal devices register to BYODCert. Organizations write down and store their policies on BYODCert, while employees query BYODCert to verify the compliance of their device w.r.t. the policy of the organization they aim to join. In case, BYODCert issues and stores a signed certificate into the device. Then, the device shows the certificate to the organization that can accept the device or query BYODCert for verifying the current device configuration w.r.t. corresponding certificate.

Structure of the Paper. Section 2 discusses some related work, while Sect. 3 points out the motivations at the basis of BYODCert. Section 4 presents the general architecture of BYODCert, while Sect. 5 discusses some conclusions and future work.

2   Related Work

The diffusion of BYOD on mobile is jeopardized by malware and vulnerable applications. For such reasons, some stakeholders (e.g., IBM [3], Blackberry [4],

AppThority [5], Huawei [6], ...) offer proprietary solutions. Their proposals almost entirely rely on isolated, trusted environments in which all and only the applications selected by the BYOD administrator can run. However, with no security analysis, there is no reason for including or not a certain application among the trusted ones. Moreover, in this way it is not clear what kind of guarantees are actually provided.

Recent theoretical and technical developments have enabled a number of new methods for enforcing security policies on mobile applications. Most of them rely on formal policy specification frameworks like ConSpec [2] and the μ-calculus [7]. Policies can be either verified statically or monitored at runtime. Static verification is amenable as it prevents dangerous applications from being executed. However, it is not always feasible (mostly due to computational complexity) and requires a suitable abstract model of the application. Models can be directly extracted from the mobile code by means of reverse engineering methods. Common techniques for static verification include model checking [8] and symbolic execution [9]. Instead, runtime monitoring (e.g., [10]) consists of a controller which follows the execution of an application and checks the operations it performs. The main limitation of this approach is the continuous computational overhead paid for the security controls that can impact the battery duration of mobile devices [11].

A promising trade-off consists in the composition of static and dynamic techniques. For instance, the Security-by-Contract framework [12] uses a static analysis step for validating the mobile applications. If the step fails, the runtime monitoring is applied. However, this approach hardly copes with the current application distribution model, based on the idea of marketplace. Currently, a single proposal have been put forward for assessing BYOD security directly at application level, i.e., the BYODroid framework [13]. Such framework allows enforcing BYOD policy directly on applications through model checking. The viability of the approach has been empirically proven in [14], while the limitation of applying model checking for evaluating the compliance of BYOD policy on actual mobile devices is discussed in [15]. In a nutshell, evaluating the compliance of a set of applications (i.e., those installed on a personal device) with a security policy requires to compose a high number of application models, thereby resulting in too many states to explore through model checking. For this reason, in its original implementation BYODroid was able to successfully verify device configurations up to 12 applications. However, the recent adoption of new techniques has allowed BYODroid to verify up to 23 applications [16]. The main limitation of BYODroid is that its efficacy is limited to a single organization only, i.e., each organization should implement and maintain its BYODroid deployment, and there is no possibility to share policies nor analysis results among organizations.

BYODCert leverages the verification techniques at the basis of BYODroid to create a single, shared and cloud-based solution for BYOD.

3 Motivating Scenario

As previously discussed, the BYOD paradigm is based on the idea of allowing employees to use their personal devices within organizations, as a work tool. The adoption of BYOD has strong security constraints, since the personal device is not guaranteed to protect corporate data and resources from leakage and misuse. To this aim, the available solutions allow organizations to adopt some (often pre-defined) BYOD policies and enforce them on the employees personal devices. As remarked, most of such solutions are proprietary, heterogeneous and work only within the boundary of the single organization. Therefore, the current BYOD ecosystem is made of independent per-organization BYOD solutions, which are isolated and unrelated. For instance, let us consider the use case depicted in Fig. 1.

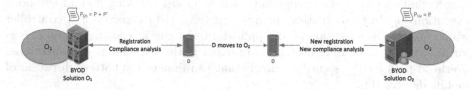

Fig. 1. Mobility of devices in a BYOD scenario.

An employee working for organization O_1 moves to organization O_2 (e.g., because O_2 is a commercial partner or a customer of O_1). Let us also suppose that O_1 and O_2 adopt two different BYOD solutions for policy verification and enforcement and that O_1 uses the policy $P_{O_1} = P + P$, i.e., a policy obtained from the composition of two sub-policies (e.g., dealing with different security aspects). Before joining O_1, the device D was validated against P_{O_1}. Next, the employee requires to join O_2 with the same personal device. The policy applied by O_2 is $P_{O_2} = P$ (i.e., one of the sub-policies of P_{O_1}). Although complying with P_{O_1} implies that also P_{O_2} is respected, if O_1 and O_2 use different BYOD solutions, the device must be verified again from scratch, before being allowed to join O_2. Things get even worse when dealing with incompatible BYOD solutions and mobile operating systems; for instance, imagine an organization adopting an Apple-based BYOD solution that has to deal with a personal device mounting a Blackberry OS: in this case, no analysis can be performed and the personal device cannot be admitted, independently from its actual compliance with the BYOD policy of the organization. All in all, previous use case indicates that current BYOD ecosystem suffers from three major limitations:

1. BYOD solutions do not cooperate, leading to impossible or replicated and potentially error-prone analyses in case of employees' mobility;
2. each organization has to adopt (i.e., purchase) and manage its own BYOD solution, resulting in increased costs for the ICT infrastructure; small organizations may not have financial means to adopt a permanent BYOD solution.

3. there is no solution allowing to share formalized policies and analysis results among entities, in order to support cooperation among BYOD stakeholders (e.g. corporations, SME, government agencies, . . .).

To overcome these limitations, BYODCert implements an open-source cross-organizational trusted third party solution. BYODCert acts as a policy-compliance attestation service in a Security-as-a-Service (SECaaS) fashion. In detail, BYODCert:

1. *supports single organizations in the definition and formalization of BYOD policies.* BYODCert adopts an easy-to-use, rich and fine-grained policy specification language allowing organization to freely and independently define their own BYOD policies. BYODCert also implements a policy repository allowing the organization for publishing and sharing their policies.
2. *automatically extracts models of the runtime behavior of applications installed on personal devices.* BYODCert adopts proper model extraction techniques to build complete models of each personal device configuration (i.e., set of installed applications) in terms of their runtime behavior. BYODCert keeps track of changes in the configuration of personal devices (i.e., installation/removal of applications) by properly updating the corresponding model.
3. *automatically enforces BYOD policies on personal devices.* BYODCertautomatically assesses whether the model of a personal device complies with the BYOD policy. Furthermore, in case of non-compliant devices, BYOD-Cert provides detailed information about the potential vulnerabilities and non-compliant applications. Also, BYODCert supports recovery strategies such as *application sanitization* or applications to be removed/updated.
4. *sanitizes (when possible) suspicious applications.* In case of a policy violation, BYODCert sanitizes the dangerous applications, limiting their execution within the boundary of a *policy monitor.* Application sanitization slightly impacts on the runtime behavior of the system (i.e., it requires the installation of a runtime monitor [17]) in order to be transparent (as far as possible) to the device owner.
5. *preserves policy-compliant device usages/modifications.* Employees may install or remove applications from their personal devices, thus leading to modifications in its configuration. In this case, they can query BYODCert for checking whether the installation of a specific application could impact the list of policies the device is currently compliant with. Then, BYODCert analyzes the compliance of the application w.r.t. the current device configuration and the BYOD policy, thereby providing a feedback to the employee. BYO-DCert also considers sanitizing the requested application to prevent non-compliant configurations.
6. *issues and deploys signed certificates into personal devices.* Certificates states the compliance of a device configuration against a given set of BYOD policies. The certificate is deployed on the personal device and can be shown to organizations when applying for joining. An organization verifies the certificate of a

personal device, checking whether the device complies with its own policy. In case, the organization can directly allow the device to join or require further checks to BYODCert directly.

Figure 2 shows how BYODCert deals with the use case described in Fig. 1. By means of the previous features, single organizations do not need to implement and maintain local BYOD solutions, and the cross-organizational BYOD interoperability is supported.

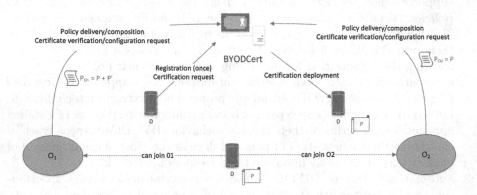

Fig. 2. The BYODCert workflow.

4   Architecture of BYODCert

BYODCert aims at enhancing current BYOD solutions in several ways. In particular, BYODCert:

1. supports the definition of fine-grained and formally defined security policies;
2. provides strong mathematical guarantees on the compliance of sets of applications against a BYOD policy;
3. frees the BYOD administrator from the burden to take security-critical decision on both personal devices and applications;
4. provides an unique, external and trusted solution, implemented in the cloud as Security-as-a-Service (SECaaS) that can be sold in a pay-as-you-go fashion, i.e., organizations pays according to the number of certifications they require and they do not have to deploy and maintain their own BYOD solution.

Albeit mathematical methods can be used to rigorously assess the security of mobile code, they cannot be directly applied to modern, complex application distribution paradigms as the one based on application marketplaces (Apple Store, Samsung Store, Google Play, ...) adopted by all mobile operating systems. Hence, at the basis of BYODCert lies an integrated framework that properly composes the formal techniques. The integration (i) produces new workflows for real world scenarios and (ii) preserves (or even extend) the overall

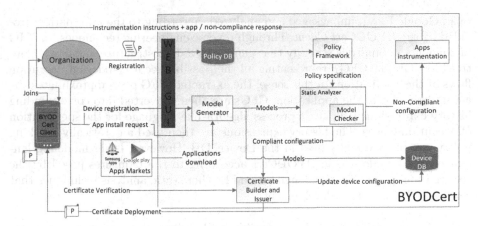

Fig. 3. The BYODCert architecture.

formal guarantees. In this respect, BYODCert implements an architecture able to support all the declared features (i.e. model extraction, analysis, enforcement, instrumentation and certification). At a high abstraction level, the architecture of BYODCert is depicted in the Fig. 3.

To implement the expected workflow, BYODCert relies on several components. We discuss here the single components, pointing out their final aims, as well as the approaches we adopted for their definition and implementation.

Web GUI. BYODCert implements a Web GUI aimed at supporting organizations in composing/managing their own policies in ConSpec, allowing to share the same policies publicly or privately. To this aim, BYODCert adopts a proper set of cryptographic schemes based on Broadcast Encryption to allow a safe and controlled policy sharing, following the Cooperative Access Control model proposed in [18]. Furthermore, it allows IT administrators to keep track of personal devices actually joining their organizations. Policies are stored in a Policy DB. The same GUI allows for registering the end-users and related personal devices, supporting each end-user when requiring new certifications and checking their certificates and personal device configurations.

Policy DB and Device DB. The Policy and the Device DBs store the submitted policies and the registered personal device configurations. The former stores all submitted policies and their modifications, thereby granting backtracking (to some extent). The latter keeps track of personal device configurations, their modifications (in terms of installed/removed applications) and the issued certificates (both valid and revoked).

Model Generator (MG). It produces behavioral models representing the execution flows of applications. Multi-application models can be obtained through composition. Application packages are retrieved directly from the standard stores (e.g., Google Play), unpackaged and analyzed, according to the information provided by the *BYODCert Client*. Through reverse engineering techniques, the MG implements an analysis strategy that generates a data structure, namely a Control Flow Graph (CFG), representing all the possible security-relevant execution flows of the application. In this sense, the extracted CFG over-approximates the actual behavior of the application. CFGs are then converted into corresponding history expressions [19], i.e., a process algebra-like language for the specification of execution traces. The history expressions are then used for statically checking policy compliance and stored in the Device DB. However, other modeling languages can be adopted in BYODCert according to the requisites posed by the selected policy specification language and further static analysis techniques that can be added in future development.

Policy Framework (PF). It is responsible for handling the security policies contained in the Policy DB. When policies are required for the security analyses, e.g., for static analysis, the PF retrieves them. Policies will be converted into equivalent specifications in a format accepted by the destination component, namely the Static Analyzer. For instance, policies requested by a static analyzer running the SPIN model checker [20] are translated into Promela, which is the SPIN input language.

Static Analyzer (SA). It executes the formal analysis algorithms (i.e., model checking) for detecting potential policy-violations. Given a set of application models (i.e., the device configuration) provided by the MG and the specification of the policy provided by the PF, the formal analysis checks whether the set of applications violates the policy. In case, it returns back a violating trace, used for instrumentation. Several model checkers can be adopted as alternative to SPIN, like e.g., [21]. Different analysis techniques can lead to better performances and effectiveness trade off. However, model checking per se cannot deal with arbitrary large models due to performance decay related to the well-known state explosion problem. A mitigation have been obtained by properly applying partial model checking (PMC) [22]. PMC consists in partially evaluating a security policy against part of a model. In our context, this case applies whenever a new application is installed on a device. By memorizing the configuration changes and the PMC results (in the Device DB), redundant static analyses can be avoided with clear advantages. An application to PMC applied to Android applications can be found in [15].

Applications Instrumentation (AI) and Runtime Monitoring (RM). Policy-violating applications can be sanitized by enforcing the security policy on their executions. Code instrumentation and runtime monitoring techniques are applied. Briefly, instrumentation consists in injecting security checks within the application code in order to intercept every possible security-relevant operation. At runtime, intercepted operations are interrupted and an alert is sent to a *security monitor* which controls the security policy and decides whether to allow or not the action.

The choice will depend on the organization the personal device is currently joining, in order to achieve a policy-driven application monitoring. In detail, if the device has currently joined an organization and the operation would violate the corresponding policy, the operation is not permitted. Otherwise (e.g., the operation does not violate the policy of the actual organization or the end-user is using its device outside organization for personal use) the operation may be permitted. In this way, the personal usage of the device outside the working hours is granted. Finally, the monitoring solution takes into account resource and performance constraints of mobile devices (i.e., the monitoring does not affect the usability of the device).

Certificate Issuer (CI). It generates a certificate stating the compliance of a device w.r.t. one or more policies. Certificates can be verified by the organization and, possibly, revoked automatically (e.g., if a device installs some dangerous software or non-instrumentable applications) by BYODCert. Proper signature schemes and protocols allow BYODCert to (1) securely store/remove certificates into/from personal devices, and (2) interact with the BYODCert client in order to reliably retrieve information on the device configuration. Since most of the security of the certification process relies on these protocols, the same protocols have been extensively evaluated through the Scyther tool [23], a state-of-the-art approach to security protocol analysis. The Scyther tool have formally proven the compliance of BYODCert protocols w.r.t. a set of desired security properties (e.g., remote attestation and authentication). Certifications, as well as the corresponding device configuration models, are stored into the Device DB.

BYODCert Client. The BYODCert client acts as an application installer. When registering to BYODCert, the personal device is redirected to the BYODCert client installation page. Installing the BYODCert client is the only necessary condition. The BYODCert client installation carries out some preliminary tasks including (i) the deactivation of all the native application installers/store clients (e.g., Google Play) and (ii) the acquisition of the initial configuration of the device (i.e., the set of installed applications). The extracted device configuration is sent to the BYODCert service and stored in the Device DB. After installing the BYODCert client, the device can only obtain new applications through it. From the end-user's perspective, the installation process does not change significantly. As a matter of fact, the BYODCert client looks like and behaves as a standard store client and handles all the operations related to the application management, e.g., applications searching, installation and removal. Moreover, the BYODCert client provides extra information about the security state of the device and how its certification could change after installing a given application. Furthermore, the BYODCert client keeps track of the organization the personal device is actually joining, consequently notifying BYODCert to support policy driven application monitoring.

5 Conclusion and Future Work

This paper has introduced the motivation at the basis of the BYODCert project, as well as the architecture of the actual deployment in the cloud. In this paper, we did not detail the specification of the protocols, schemes and tools adopted in the various components composing the BYODCert architecture, since the development of some parts is still in progress and under evaluation.

As a future extension of this work, complete detail on the specification of BYODCert will be provided, as well as an experimental assessment on actual BYOD scenarios and cloud different architectures [24].

References

1. Mazurczyk, W., Caviglione, L.: Steganography in modern smartphones, mitigation techniques. IEEE Commun. Surv. Tutor. **17**(1), 334–357 (2015). Firstquarter
2. Aktug, I., Naliuka, K.: Conspec: a formal language for policy specification. Sci. Comput. Program. **74**(1), 2–12 (2008)
3. Ibm byod solution. http://www.ibm.com/mobile/bring-your-own-device/. Accessed 7 Mar 2017
4. Blackberry byod solution. http://us.blackberry.com/bring-your-own-device. Accessed 7 Mar 2017
5. Appthority. https://www.appthority.com. Accessed 7 Mar 2017
6. Huawei byod solution. http://enterprise.huawei.com/topic/byod_en/. Accessed 7 Mar 2017
7. Kozen, D.: Results on the propositional-calculus. Theor. Comput. Sci. **27**(3), 333–354 (1983)
8. Clarke, E.M., Emerson, E.A., Sistla, A.P.: Automatic verification of finite-state concurrent systems using temporal logic specifications. ACM Trans. Program. Lang. Syst. **8**(2), 244–263 (1986)
9. King, J.C.: Symbolic execution and program testing. Commun. ACM **19**(7), 385–394 (1976)
10. Desmet, L., Joosen, W., Massacci, F., Naliuka, K., Philippaerts, P., Piessens, F., Vanoverberghe, D.: The s3ms.net run time monitor. Electron. Notes Theor. Comput. Sci. **253**(5), 153–159 (2009)
11. Merlo, A., Migliardi, M., Caviglione, L.: A survey on energy-aware security mechanisms. Pervasive Mob. Comput. **24**, 77–90 (2015). Cited by 7
12. Bielova, N., Dragoni, N., Massacci, F., Naliuka, K., Siahaan, I.: Matching in security-by-contract for mobile code. J. Log. Algebr. Program. **78**(5), 340–358 (2009). The 1st Workshop on Formal Languages and Analysis of Contract-Oriented Software (FLACOS07)
13. Armando, A., Costa, G., Merlo, A.: Bring your own device, securely. In: Proceedings of the 28th Annual ACM Symposium on Applied Computing, SAC 2013, pp. 1852–1858. ACM, New York (2013)
14. Armando, A., Costa, G., Verderame, L., Merlo, A.: Securing the bring your own device paradigm. Computer **47**(6), 48–56 (2014)
15. Armando, A., Costa, G., Merlo, A., Verderame, L.: Enabling BYOD through secure meta-market. In: Proceedings of the ACM Conference on Security and Privacy in Wireless and Mobile Networks, WiSec 2014, pp. 219–230. ACM, New York (2014)

16. Costa, G., Merlo, A., Verderame, L., Armando, A.: Automatic security verification of mobile app configurations. Future Gener. Comput. Syst. (2016). http://dx.doi.org/10.1016/j.future.2016.06.014
17. Falcone, Y., Currea, S., Jaber, M.: Runtime verification and enforcement for android applications with RV-Droid. In: Qadeer, S., Tasiran, S. (eds.) RV 2012. LNCS, vol. 7687, pp. 88–95. Springer, Heidelberg (2013). doi:10.1007/978-3-642-35632-2_11
18. Merlo, A.: Secure cooperative access control on grid. Future Gener. Comput. Syst. **29**(2), 497–508 (2013). Special section: recent advances in e-Science
19. Bartoletti, M., Degano, P., Ferrari, G.L.: History-based access control with local policies. In: Sassone, V. (ed.) FoSSaCS 2005. LNCS, vol. 3441, pp. 316–332. Springer, Heidelberg (2005). doi:10.1007/978-3-540-31982-5_20
20. Holzmann, G.: Spin Model Checker, the: Primer and Reference Manual, 1st edn. Addison-Wesley Professional, Boston (2003)
21. Cranen, S., Groote, J.F., Keiren, J.J.A., Stappers, F.P.M., de Vink, E.P., Wesselink, W., Willemse, T.A.C.: An overview of the mCRL2 toolset and its recent advances. In: Piterman, N., Smolka, S.A. (eds.) TACAS 2013. LNCS, vol. 7795, pp. 199–213. Springer, Heidelberg (2013). doi:10.1007/978-3-642-36742-7_15
22. Andersen, H.R.: Partial model checking. In: Proceedings of Tenth Annual IEEE Symposium on Logic in Computer Science, pp. 398–407, June 1995
23. Cremers, C.J.F.: The Scyther Tool: verification, falsification, and analysis of security protocols. In: Gupta, A., Malik, S. (eds.) CAV 2008. LNCS, vol. 5123, pp. 414–418. Springer, Heidelberg (2008). doi:10.1007/978-3-540-70545-1_38
24. Caviglione, L.: Can satellites face trends? the case of web 2.0. In: International Workshop on Satellite and Space Communications, pp. 446–450, September 2009

Security-Centric Evaluation Framework
for IT Services

Smrati Gupta[1]([⊠]), Jaume Ferrarons-Llagostera[1], Jacek Dominiak[1],
Victor Muntés-Mulero[1], Peter Matthews[1], and Erkuden Rios[2]

[1] CA Strategic Research, CA Technologies, 08940 Cornellà de Llobregat, Spain
{smrati.gupta,jaume.ferrarons-llagostera,jacek.dominiak,
victor.muntes-mulero,peter.matthews}@ca.com
[2] Tecnalia, Parque Tecnolóogico Bizkaia Edif. 700, 48160 Derio, Spain
erkuden.rios@tecnalia.com

Abstract. Tremendous growth and adoption of cloud based services within IT enterprises has generated important requirements for security provisioning. Users need to evaluate the security characteristics of different providers and their offered services. This generates an additional requirement for methods to compare cloud service providers on the basis of their capabilities to meet security requirements. This paper proposes a novel framework to assess and compare cloud services on the basis of their security offerings, leveraging existing best practices and standards to develop new relevant metrics. We provide comparison yardsticks related to security to evaluate cloud services such that the security robustness of cloud services can be computed using easy to evaluate deconstructed metrics. This paper provides a framework that can be leveraged to provide security enhancement plans both for users and providers.

Keywords: Cloud computing best practices · Certifications · Security controls

1   Introduction and Problem Statement

The dependency of all domains of IT on cloud computing and cloud services has exponentially increased in the last decade and will continue to grow. The cloud environment naturally provides a high level of availability, resilience and flexibility for services compared to in-house deployments. However, cloud environment can lead to serious exposure of components or entire applications to insecure environments. This can be perceived as a reduction of control for the user over data or services. In contrast, the cloud service providers get partial or full access leading to the possibility of serious security breaches. As cloud environments diversify to multiple architectures like federation or multi-cloud [1], the exposure of the data and resources deployed in cloud environment further expands to multiple providers [2]. Hence, security and privacy provisioning in the cloud

© Springer International Publishing AG 2017
M.H.A. Au et al. (Eds.): GPC 2017, LNCS 10232, pp. 736–747, 2017.
DOI: 10.1007/978-3-319-57186-7_53

environment has paramount importance in order to embed security into cloud service based applications at design time improving security at a lower cost.

Different cloud service providers offer security safeguards to satisfy various customer requirements. Cloud Security Alliance [3] has classified these safeguards that protect the customer data from security threats in different domains of security arena namely *government domains* or *operational domains*:

- *Government domains* include organizational security provisioning features such as: legal discovery, compliance and audit, portability and interoperability among services, information life-cycle management and governance, and enterprise risk management.
- *Operational domains* include provisioning in applied domains like: data center operations, incident response, notification and remediation, application security, encryption and key management, identity and access management and visualization.

There are a myriad of possible features that are to be provided by different cloud services to ensure security of applications. An end user, whether an individual developer or enterprise programmer, would find it difficult to compare the security levels offered by different providers. Lack of standardization in service descriptions does not ease up the task. There have been a number of attempts to develop a standard approach to service metrics description. The most notable is described by the US based National Institute of Standards and Technology in their document "Cloud Computing Service Metrics Description" [4]. This represents the first attempt to codify a description of a cloud service and the associated metrics. The document does not consider the derivation of a value for a particular measurement result but the cloud service metric model.

Furthermore, there are multiple best practices that attempt to provide baselines to show security provisioning in different domains. Cloud Control Matrix (CCM) by Cloud Security Alliance (CSA) [3] and Motion Picture Association of America (MPAA) [5] are examples of these. Cloud service providers use certifications to provide a standard assertion of their level of security provisioning. Certificates like ISO [6], COBIT [7], HIPAA [8], FERPA [9], FEdRAMP [10], Jericho Forum [11] etc. are granted on the basis of third party audits and assurance of satisfaction of standard and comparable security requirements. The marketplace is therefore populated with multiple certificates and best practices. Providers may or may not secure all of them. This exacerbates the difficulty of performing a comparative analysis among cloud services in the security domain.

There exist certain security frameworks that are able to encompass the different best practices and certificates and other methods to compare the security level of cloud providers. However, there is also a need to quantify such a comparative analysis among the cloud services in the newly emerging domains of multi-cloud and federated cloud services [1]. An independent understanding of certification is insufficient to admit comparative analysis when the number of vendors and claimed certifications are growing.

In order to solve these problems, we present a novel framework of comparison of cloud services on the basis of their level of security provisioning to users.

It provides a set of metrics that rely on different certificates and best practices available in the cloud computing marketplace. We propose the construction of such metrics so that it is possible to form a yardstick methodology to compare the cloud services in the arena of security. The current state-of-the-art lacks metrics to compare the services in security domain and this paper addresses such a gap.

The rest of the paper is organized as follows: Sect. 2 explains state-of-the-art and problem statement. In Sect. 3, we propose the metrics that measure the security provisioning of the different providers. Section 4 illustrates the effectiveness of our metrics using experimental analysis. Section 5 presents the conclusions and future work.

2   Related Work

The aim of our work is to provide numerical indicators to compare security provisions of the cloud providers to its users in different domains. Depending on the application requirements, the demand for security provisioning may be highly varied and conditional.

The problem of measuring the security level of cloud services has been studied in the past in literature. For example, authors of [12] build a system that applies the Analytic Hierarchical Process (AHP) to support the decision asking the application owner to rate the relevancy of each security aspect per component of the system. In [13] the authors use a cloud security taxonomy to score cloud services; the quality of each element in the taxonomy is extracted from online user reviews and comments. In [14], the authors use tree structures to deal with the complexity and compositional challenges of cloud services' SLAs. However, in these works, there is absence of concrete metrics that may be reproducible, and analysis relies on user perspectives.

Going a step farther, there have been reasonable efforts in order to design metrics that may evaluate cloud services based on non-security aspects as well. For example, SMI cloud in [15] provides a framework is presented for comparing Cloud services based on web data, and it recognizes that due to the lack of information for the security KPI they assigned a random number to the cloud services. Security domain is not examined in great detail. Another work in [16] presents a framework using fully quantitative and iterative convergence approach, that enables stakeholders to comparatively assess the relative robustness of different cloud vendor offerings and approaches in a defensible manner. It allows for security threat analysis and impact definition for Cloud platforms. We depart from this approach by using the threat measurement frameworks present in the literature like [17] along with cloud service providers database from [3] thereby moving the focus on evaluation of metrics assigning a absolute value for providers in security domains.

In addition, our previous work [18] compares cloud services on the basis of their ability to seamlessly function in a multi-cloud environment. It is proposed to score services on the basis of complex characteristics as ease of migration and interoperability levels. However, the area of security is not evaluated in this work.

Due to the complexity of computing metrics to measure security and the absence of enough information from cloud services to measure these metrics, it is necessary to develop security measurement metrics in the cloud service arena based on well accepted security frameworks. Security frameworks are voluntary guidance systems, meaning that they provide methods to evaluate cloud environment that are based on standards, guidelines and best practices to help organizations better evaluate their systems and assess security risks and management techniques. Key frameworks in the domain of cloud security are NIST Cloud Computing Security Reference Architecture [19] (NIST-RA) and Cloud Control Matrix (CCM) form the Cloud Security Alliance (CSA) [3]:

1. NIST-RA is a guide for planning and implementation teams to learn about the implications of different cloud computing deployment models to understanding the security risks involved in cloud computing.
2. CCM is specifically designed to provide fundamental security principles to guide cloud vendors and to assist prospective cloud customers in assessing the overall security risk of a cloud provider [20].

The existence of critical analysis based information in these frameworks forms a concrete basis to evaluate cloud services. However, there is a gap to quantify this information and measure it in a replicable manner. In the next section, we address this gap and propose metrics based on these frameworks to measure security level of cloud services.

3 Proposed Metrics for Measurement of Security Provisioning

In order to evaluate cloud services on the basis of their security provisioning, we design metrics that can assign measurable values to the services based on the information procured from the above mentioned security frameworks. For simplicity, we will use the CCM framework. However, our work can be easily extended to leverage the NIST framework.

The Cloud Security Alliance (CSA) [3] has a Cloud Control Matrix (CCM) [20] working group that designed and proposed a detailed questionnaire for providing security control transparency called the Cloud Control Matrix (CCM) [20] questionnaire or it's computable friendly equivalent Consensus Assessment Initiative Questionnaire (CAIQ) [21]. This questionnaire provides means for assessing the capabilities and competencies of cloud providers in terms of different attributes (e.g., compliance, information security, governance) [22]. CCM questionnaire as well as CAIQ forms are organised in specific security domains (e.g., Compliance (CO), Data Governance (DG), etc.) that are aligned with the CSA guidelines [20] for moving IT resources to the cloud. Each of the domains, in this paper referred to as control group, consists of several controls that resemble specific requirements to comply with the corresponding domain. There are, in total, 98 controls under 11 domains in the CAIQ and CCM framework, each of it identified by an unique control ID. Each of those controls has one or more questions that are designed to query about cloud providers capabilities and competencies regarding different attributes (e.g., audit planning, security policies, risk assessments) [22].

We propose to use this classification to design metrics that evaluate the cloud providers based on structured criteria. Furthermore, we propose extrapolation of metrics presented in [18] to security centric features of cloud environment exploiting the CCM framework. Let us define the notations that we use in rest of this paper:

Notations

- cp_x: Cloud provider x.
- $ncid$: Number of CCM Control IDs taken into account.
- $nthreats$: Number of threats taken into account.
- cg: Control Group: Aggregation of Control IDs in a specific security domain (This is same as Control domain in CCM and Control family in NIST).
- $threats(cp_x)$: Threats related to cloud provider x.
- $cgroups(cp_x)$: Control groups covered by cloud provider x.

A threat is defined as "a potential for violation of security, which exists when there is a circumstance, capability, action, or event that could breach security and cause harm" [23]. Threats are realised by exploiting vulnerabilities in the IT system. The relationship between vulnerabilities-threat and risk and using it is cloud service selection has been explained in [24]. The threats that the application components face may be mitigated using certain security provisions from the cloud service providers. These security provisions may be evaluated using the independent audits and thereby obtaining certifications. CSA provides a database that illustrates what security provisions are given by the providers based on how they answer the CAIQ questionnaire. These security provisions are organized and characterised on the basis of different Control Domains and Control IDs. The authors in [17] have presented an extensive threat catalogue and have mapped these threats to the CCM or NIST control IDs that mitigate (partially or completely) them.

For clarity, we propose the classification of our metrics into two categories based on coverage and quality.

Coverage. The security controls provided by CCM cover multiple dimensions of security provisions that may be offered by the providers. An important criteria to evaluate the security provisioning is the measurement of the number of the security features they provide. Coverage metrics estimate the numerical quantity of the security features that a provider can support. This may be measured in multiple dimensions as explained below:

1. CID Coverage: CID coverage represents the capacity of the provider to provide the control IDs (CIDs) out of those that are possible to be provided. This metric measures the percentage of CCM control IDs that the cloud provider is complying with. It is measured as:

$$\text{CID}_{cover}(cp_x) = \frac{\text{CID}(cp_x)}{ncid}$$

where $\text{CID}(cp_x)$ computes the number of control IDs in CCM for the provider cp_x and $ncid$ is the total number of control IDs. Higher the value of coverage CID, higher is the number of security provisions given by the provider among the provisions under consideration. Note that designing an accurate $ncid$ vector for a given application is crucial for a fitting comparison among different providers for different CID coverages they provide. This metric can help to evaluate the capacity of cloud providers to assure security in multiple ways defined by the CIDs.

2. Control Group Coverage: Control group coverage is a metric that measures the capacity of the provider to provide the security provisioning that covers multiple security domains through the control groups. Control group coverage measures the percentage of CCM control groups for which the cloud provider has at least one CCM Control ID available. It is expressed as the percentage of control groups covered by the cloud provider out of the total number of control groups.

$$\text{CGroup}_{cover}(cp_x) = \frac{\text{CGroups}(cp_x)}{ncgroups}$$

This means, it indicates the capacity of a provider to maximize the variety of security features offered. This metric evaluates the provider based on the number of domains of security aspects covered by the provider. Note the contrast with CID coverage that evaluates the providers on the basis of the number of security provisions without accounting for the domain.

Quality. The metrics under this category identify the quality of the coverage of security offered by a provider. More precisely, these metrics estimate the security quality of the cloud providers not only in terms of number of security provisions covered, but rather the variety and capabilities of cloud providers to address threats.

A threat may be mitigated by number of control IDs, and a control ID may mitigate multiple threats. However, it is assumed here that for complete mitigation of threat, all control IDs mapped in [17] are needed. It is consequently also assumed that all the control IDs have same level of impact in mitigating a threat. Note that this assumption may be modified by attaching different weights to different control IDs, but we leave it as a future work. Furthermore, the implementation of controls may not always mitigate the threats due to high-level description of the controls. Therefore there is a certain degree of error possibility attached to the controls that are abstractly defined. We ignore this error in our analysis. Let us denote t_y as the number of control IDs protecting from threat y. Also, we denote $t_{x,y}$ to the number of controls provided by provider x to protect against threat y. We now define the following metrics:

1. Threat Mitigation Coverage: This metric represents the capacity of a provider to provide the control IDs needed to mitigate relevant security threats that an application faces. It is evaluated as the ratio of the controls given by the provider that are needed to mitigate the threats to all the total controls that mitigate the threat based on [17].

$$threat_q(cp_x) = \frac{1}{|threats(cp_x)|} \sum_{y \in threats(cp_x)} \frac{t_{x,y}}{t_y}$$

A higher value of this metric represents a higher guarantee of mitigation of a particular threat that it faces.

2. Control Group Quality Coverage: Similar to previous metric, we define the control group quality coverage for a cloud provider. This metric represents the ratio of control groups that a cloud provider provides to cover each threat, over all the groups that are needed to mitigate the threat. It is defined as:

$$cgroup_q(cp_x) = \frac{1}{|cgroups(cp_x)|} \sum_{y \in cgroups(cp_x)} \frac{cg_{x,y}}{cg_y}$$

Consequently a higher value of this metric indicates a higher protection by the cloud provider to different variety of threats. A possible refined version of this metric may be Weighted Control Group Quality Coverage which would measure a weighted coverage with respect to the criticality of control groups. This will give an indication of the best minimum coverage. The criticality of controls in NIST is identified by the security control prioritization codes, while there is no prioritization in CCM. Nevertheless, the usability of such a metric should also be studied when application requirements prioritization does not match the control group prioritization of the standard.

A straightforward extension for these qualitative metrics can be based on user preferences for certain security requirements. For example, some kinds of threats or control groups could have greater impact to the application and a higher relevance should be assigned to them. For this reason, we present a final set of metrics based on Entropy.

Entropy. As before, the entropy metrics of each cloud provider has been computed based on the number of CCM control IDs a provider has per Threat and per Control Group respectively.

1. Threat protection index: This metric represents the probability of a cloud provider cp_x to protect from a threat t. It is defined as the ratio of CIDs that cloud provider cp_x provides to mitigate threat t over the total number of possible CID to mitigate t. More formally, it can be formulated as:

$$p_t(cp_x) = \frac{\text{CID}(cp_x) \cap \text{CID}(t)}{\text{CID}(t)}$$

Using this definition we define the threat entropy, similar to what is information entropy, as:

$$H_t(cp_x) = - \sum_{t \in threats} p_t(cp_x) \log p_t(cp_x)$$

The threat entropy of a cloud provider informs us about whether the security measures are mainly oriented to tackle a few threats or to mitigate (even if it is only partially) a wider range of aspects.

2. Control Group Protection index: This metric represents the probability of cloud provider cp_x to cover a specific control group cg. It is defined as the ratio of CIDs that the cloud provider cp_x provides that intersect with control group cg over the total number of possible CID that belong to cg.:

$$p_{cg}(cp_x) = \frac{\text{CID}(cp_x) \cap \text{CID}(cg)}{\text{CID}(cg)}$$

Hence, it shows the coverage of control IDs in each control group by a provider. In parallel we define the control group entropy as:

$$H_{cg}(cp_x) = - \sum_{cg \in cgroups} p_{cg}(cp_x) \log p_{cg}(cp_x)$$

This metric gives an intuition about the capacity of a cloud provider to provide security provisions that tackle similar type of security controls (belonging to the same group) or cover a wide range of provisions.

4 Experiments

In this section, we analyze the proposed metrics using real data to determine its accuracy in terms of providing intuition and comparative analysis across different providers. We use the data provided by the public database of cloud providers given by Cloud Security Alliance working group on Cloud Control Matrix [3, 20] through the Consensus Assessments Initiative Questionnaire (CAIQ) v.3.0.1. CAIQ offers a set of questions a cloud consumer and cloud auditor may wish to ask of a cloud provider. It provides a series of "yes/no" control assertion questions which can then be tailored to suit each unique cloud customers evident requirements. Using the sample data procured through this questionnaire, we have evaluated the values of our metrics.

4.1 Threat Coverage Analysis

We evaluated the CID coverage $CID_{cover}(cp_x)$, Threat Mitigation Coverage $threat_q(cp_x)$ and threat entropy $H_t(cp_x)$ for different providers. Figure 1 shows a plot with these three metrics for selected cloud providers. The metric CID coverage gives a direct indication of the number of control IDs supported by a

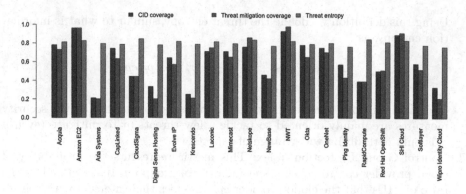

Fig. 1. CID coverage, threat mitigation coverage and threat entropy

provider. On an average, a higher CID coverage, can give a high threat mitigation coverage, however there may be providers that offer high CID coverage
but low threat mitigation (eg. Ping Identity, Caplinked). This is because, there
may be multiple control IDs in a particular control group that may address a
certain threat, but it does not guarantee mitigation of the variety of threats. On
the other hand, the threat entropy metric gives interesting information about
the capacity of a provider to give a good balance between the quality of threat
mitigation and quantity of control IDs. A low value of threat mitigation coverage and CID coverage may still provide high entropy (eg. Cloudsigma, Wipro
Identity Cloud). Therefore, it is critical to design the metrics based on the set
of control IDs that is relevant to the application.

4.2   Control Group Coverage Analysis

We made a similar experimental study to understand the comparative analysis
among the providers based on the control group coverage they provide. Figure 2
shows the control group coverage, quality and entropy. As hypothesised, a high
value of coverage almost never gives a high control group quality value. However,
it may give a high entropy (eg. Aria Systems, Krescendo). A high control group
coverage does provide a high distribution of provisioning in different domains and
hence it may be seen that it is reflected in high level of control group entropy.
Therefore, an analysis of control group quality may indicate the quality of the
particular control group provisioning and it may be a good metric to characterize
the requirement of a single application. However the requirements such as a
general robustness in terms of quality distribution of security provisioning across
different domains for one or multiple applications, may be better reflected by
characterization of cloud services using metrics such as Control group coverage
or Control group entropy.

Overall, depending on the requirement of the application, the cloud service
providers may be evaluated and compared on different metrics.

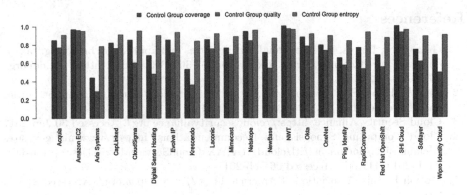

Fig. 2. Control group coverage, quality and entropy

5   Conclusions and Future Work

This paper provides a first attempt to score the cloud services on the basis of security provisions. The metrics use computable basis to make a numerical evaluation that may be fed into more complex systems like decision support systems for cloud service selection, graphical methods to assess cloud service provisioning in dynamic environments etc. As the cloud environments become more and more complex, the market faces the need to develop advanced decision support systems for cloud service selection. Consequently, the need to evaluate cloud services using a reproducible scale is critical. The evaluation should be not only taking into account the distinct domains like security but also the capacity of cloud services to inter-operate with other services thereby supporting multi-cloud environments. Furthermore, in this paper, we have made the assumption of controls being able to mitigate the threat partially or completely. However, this assumption may not always be true. Hence an interesting future work would be development of a framework that allows for a concrete basis to map security controls and threat mitigation and indicative of partial mitigation of threats as well. This would be critical in capturing the weighted metrics definition from Sect. 3. The contributions of this paper pave the way to develop complete systems that may help users to select the cloud services meeting their requirements. Such systems also need to address several other challenges like data gathering to make informed recommendations, inclusion of complex domains like financial repercussion of selecting certain services and so on. Such challenges form interesting challenges for future research work in the arena.

Acknowledgment. This work is partially supported by Secretaria de Universitats i Recerca of Generalitat de Catalunya (2014DI031) and conducted as a part of the MUSA project (Grant Agreement 644429) funded by the European Commission within call H2020-ICT-2014-1.

References

1. Grozev, N., Buyya, R.: Inter-cloud architectures and application brokering: taxonomy and survey. Softw. Pract. Exper. **44**(3), 369–390 (2014). http://dx.doi.org/10.1002/spe.2168
2. Ali, M., Khan, S.U., Vasilakos, A.V.: Security in cloud computing: opportunities and challenges. Inf. Sci. **305**, 357–383 (2015)
3. Cloud Security Alliance. https://cloudsecurityalliance.org/. Accessed 30 Jan 2017
4. Cloud Computing Synopsis and Recommendations. https://www.nist.gov/sites/default/files/documents/itl/cloud/RATAX-CloudServiceMetricsDescription-DRAFT-20141111.pdf. Accessed 06 Feb 2017
5. Motion Picture Association of America. http://www.mpaa.org/. Accessed 31 Jan 2017
6. International Organization for Standardization. http://www.iso.org. Accessed 31 Jan 2017
7. Control Objectives for Information and Related Technologies. http://www.isaca.org/cobit/pages/default.aspx. Accessed 31 Jan 2017
8. Health Insurance Portability and Accountability Act of 1996. https://www.hhs.gov/hipaa/. Accessed 31 Jan 2017
9. Family Educational Rights and Privacy Act. https://ed.gov/policy/gen/guid/fpco/ferpa/index.html. Accessed 31 Jan 2017
10. Federal Risk and Authorization Management Program. https://www.fedramp.gov/. Accessed 31 Jan 2017
11. Jericho Forum. https://collaboration.opengroup.org/jericho/index.htm. Accessed 31 Jan 2017
12. Na, S.-H., Huh, E.-N.: A methodology of assessing security risk of cloud computing in user perspective for security-service-level agreements. In: 2014 Fourth International Conference on Innovative Computing Technology (INTECH), pp. 87–92, August 2014
13. Shaikh, R., Sasikumar, M.: Trust model for measuring security strength of cloud computing service. Procedia Comput. Sci. **45**, 380–389 (2015)
14. Luna Garcia, J., Langenberg, R., Suri, N.: Benchmarking cloud security level agreements using quantitative policy trees. In: Proceedings of the ACM Workshop on Cloud Computing Security Workshop, pp. 103–112. ACM (2012)
15. Garg, S.K., Versteeg, S., Buyya, R.: SMICloud: a framework for comparing and ranking cloud services. In: 2011 Fourth IEEE International Conference on Utility and Cloud Computing, pp. 210–218, December 2011
16. Saripalli, P., Walters, B.: QUIRC: a quantitative impact and risk assessment framework for cloud security. In: 2010 IEEE 3rd International Conference on Cloud Computing (CLOUD), pp. 280–288. IEEE, July 2010. http://dx.doi.org/10.1109/cloud.2010.22
17. Casola, V., Benedictis, A.D., Rak, M., Rios, E.: Security-by-design in clouds: a security-SLA driven methodology to build secure cloud applications. Procedia Comput. Sci. **97**, 53–62 (2016). 2nd International Conference on Cloud Forward: From Distributed to Complete Computing. http://www.sciencedirect.com/science/article/pii/S1877050916320968
18. Ferrarons-Llagostera, J., Gupta, S., Munts-Mulero, V., Larriba-Pey, J.-L., Matthews, P.: Scoring cloud services through digital ecosystem community analysis. In: Proceedings of the EC-Web 2016: 17th International Conference on Electronic Commerce and Web Technologies (2016)

19. NIST Cloud Computing Security Reference Architecture. http://collaborate.nist. gov/twiki-cloud-computing/pub/CloudComputing/CloudSecurity/NIST_Security _Reference-_Architecture_2013.05.15_v1.0.pdf. Accessed 06 Feb 2017
20. Cloud Controls Matrix. https://cloudsecurityalliance.org/group/cloud-controls-matrix/. Accessed 30 Jan 2017
21. Consensus Assessments Initiative. https://cloudsecurityalliance.org/research-/ initiatives/consensus-assessments-initiative/. Accessed 17 Feb 2017
22. Habib, S.M., Ries, S., Mühlhäuser, M., Varikkattu, P.: Towards a trust management system for cloud computing marketplaces: using CAIQ as a trust information source. Secur. Commun. Netw. **7**(11), 2185–2200 (2014)
23. Shirey, R.: Internet security glossary, version 2 (rfc4949). https://www.ietf.org/ rfc/rfc2828.txt (2007). Accessed 06 Feb 2017
24. Gupta, S., Muntes-Mulero, V., Matthews, P., Dominiak, J., Omerovic, A., Aranda, J., Seycek, S.: Risk-driven framework for decision support in cloud service selection. In: 2015 15th IEEE/ACM International Symposium on Cluster, Cloud and Grid Computing, pp. 545–554, May 2015

Multi-cloud Applications Security Monitoring

Pamela Carvallo[1,2(✉)], Ana R. Cavalli[1,2], Wissam Mallouli[2],
and Erkuden Rios[3]

[1] SAMOVAR, Télécom SudParis, CNRS, Université Paris-Saclay, Évry, France
[2] Montimage, Paris, France
{pamela.carvallo,ana.cavalli,wissam.mallouli}@montimage.com
[3] Tecnalia, Derio, Spain
erkuden.rios@tecnalia.com

Abstract. The issue of data security and privacy in multi-cloud based environments requires different solutions for implementing and enforcing security policies. In these environments, many security aspects must be faced, such as security-by-design, risk management, data privacy and isolation, and vulnerability scans. Moreover, it also becomes necessary to have a system that interrelates and operates all security controls which are configured and executed independently on each component of the application (service) being secured and monitored. In addition, thanks to the large diffusion of cloud computing systems, new attacks are emerging, so threat detection systems play a key role in the security schemes, identifying possible attacks. These systems handle an enormous volume of information as they detect unknown malicious activities by monitoring different events from different points of observation, as well as adapting to new attack strategies and considering techniques to detect malicious behaviors and react accordingly.

To target this issue, we propose in the context of the MUSA EU Horizon 2020 project [1], a security assurance platform that allows monitoring the multi-cloud application deployed in different Cloud Server Providers (CSPs). It detects potential deviations from security Server Level Agreements (A formal, negotiated document that defines in quantitative and qualitative terms the service being offered to a Cloud Service Client (CSC). For more information see [8,17].) (SLAs) and triggers countermeasures to enforce security during application runtime.

Keywords: Cloud computing · Security monitoring · Service Level Agreement · Detection

1 Introduction

In this section we present the main challenges for monitoring of multi-cloud environments and the related work on threat detection systems. We also present in this section the paper organization.

M.H.A. Au et al. (Eds.): GPC 2017, LNCS 10232, pp. 748–758, 2017.
DOI: 10.1007/978-3-319-57186-7_54

1.1 Monitoring Challenges in Multi-cloud Environments

Monitoring is a solution that is required to control the correct operation of the whole system running in a multi-cloud environment. According to the taxonomy proposed by [12,13], the term multi-cloud denotes situations were a consumer (human or service) uses multiple independent clouds, unlike Cloud Federations that are achieved when a set of cloud providers voluntarily interconnect their infrastructures to allow sharing of resources among them. A few concrete multi-cloud solutions exist, addressed in research projects like MUSA, OPTIMIS, mOSAIC, MODAClouds, PaaSAge, Cloud4SOA [6,11]. It is out of the scope of this paper to offer a complete survey of such activities. We suggest the interested reader the following works: [5,13,19].

Malfunctioning or even minor problems in a Virtual Machine (VM) could introduce vulnerabilities and instability to other VMs, as well as the integrity of the host machine. In this paper, the monitoring function is needed to be able to precisely understand what is going on in the network, system and application levels, with a twofold objective. First, it is necessary for improving the security in the communications and services offered by the multi-cloud virtual environments. Second, from the administration and managements point of view, it will help ensure the environments health and guarantee that the system functions as expected and respects its security SLA.

Existing monitoring solutions to assess security can still be used in virtualized network environments. Nevertheless, they need to be adapted and correctly controlled since they were meant mostly for physical and not virtual systems and boundaries, and do not allow fine-grained analysis adapted to the needs of CSCs and virtualized networks. The lack of visibility and controls on internal virtual networks, and the heterogeneity of devices used make some performance assessment applications ineffective. On one hand, the impact of virtualization on these technologies needs to be assessed. For instance, Quality of Service (QoS) monitoring applications need to be able to monitor virtual connections. On the other hand, these technologies need to cope with ever-changing contexts and trade-offs between the monitoring costs and the benefits involved.

Tools such as Ceilometer [2], a monitoring solution for OpenStack, provide efficient collection of metering data in terms of CPU and network costs. However, it is focused on creating a unique contact point for billing systems to acquire all of the measurements they need, and it is not oriented to perform any action to try to improve the metrics that it monitors. StackTach [4] is another example oriented to billing issues that monitors performance and audits the OpenStacks Nova component. Similarly, but not specifically oriented to billing Collectd [9] gathers system performance statistics and provides mechanisms to store the collected values. A recent project from OPNFV named Doctor [3], focuses on the creation of a fault management and maintenance framework for high availability of network services on top of virtualized infrastructures. All the mentioned solutions do not consider their monitoring functionality to tackle security issues.

In terms of security, OpenStack provides a security guide [14] providing best practices determined by cloud operators when deploying their OpenStack solutions. Some tools go deeper in order to guarantee certain security aspects in OpenStack, for instance: Bandit [16] provides a framework for performing security analysis of Python source code while Consul [10] is a monitoring tool oriented to service discovery that also performs health checking to prevent routing requests to unhealthy hosts.

1.2 Related Work on Threat Detection Systems

Intrusion Detection Systems (IDS) in cloud-based environments usually correspond to a hardware device or software application that monitors activity (e.g. network, host, user) for malicious policy violations. Zbakh et al. evaluated in [18] several IDS architectures through proposed multi-criteria decision technique, according to the above introduced requirement together with few others such as:

- Performance
- Availability
- Scalability
- Secure and encrypted communication channels
- Transparency with respect to end-users
- Information Security Policies as input to the architecture
- Accuracy, including the number of false positives (FP), false negatives (FN)
- Detection methods used

According to such literature, IDS architectures may vary if they are distributed, centralized, agent-based or collaborative [18]. Patel et al. [15] provided an extended systematic-based study of intrusion detection systems, presenting a classification with regards to response time, alarm management, detection method, data collection type, among others. In general, these systems are designed with the following modules: data collection (Sect. 2.3) and preparation (Sect. 3.1) are performed through a sensor or existing database which works as an input for the data analysis and detection (Sect. 3.2). The latter engine corresponds to the module of the algorithms implemented to detect suspicious activities and known attack patterns.

In the context of this paper, we consider the monitoring of multi-cloud based application where each application component can be deployed in a different cloud service provider. This architecture brings more challenges to be able to fulfill an end-to-end security monitoring of the application execution and communication at runtime. To our knowledge, no security monitoring solution has been designed for such multi-cloud distributed systems. The main contribution of this paper is the design and development of a security assurance platform that provides an answer to these challenges.

1.3 Paper Organization

The paper is organized as follows. In Sect. 2, we present an overview of the multi-cloud security assurance platform, which is part of the approach developed in the MUSA project. The platform is composed by several modules that are described in detail. Section 3 presents the workflow implemented in this platform. Section 4 summarizes and gives some elements for discussion of the presented work. Finally, Sect. 5 gives the conclusion of this work.

2   The MUSA Security Assurance Platform SaaS

2.1   The MUSA Framework

The main goal of MUSA is to support the security-intelligent life-cycle management of distributed applications over heterogeneous cloud resources, through a security framework that includes: (a) security-by-design mechanisms to allow application self-protection at runtime, and (b) methods and tools for the integrated security assurance in both the engineering and operation of multi-cloud applications. MUSA overall concept is depicted in the figure below.

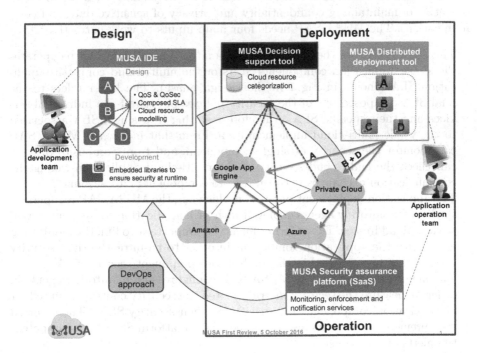

Fig. 1. MUSA overall concept

MUSA framework combines (1) a preventive security approach, promoting security-by-design practices in the development and embedding security mechanisms in the application, and (2) a reactive security approach, monitoring application runtime to mitigate security incidents, so multi-cloud application providers can be informed and react to them without losing end-user trust in the multi-cloud application. An integrated coordination of all phases in the application life-cycle management is needed in order to ensure the preventive oriented security to be embedded and aligned with reactive security measures.

MUSA focuses security from with reactive approach, where we designed and implemented a security assurance platform deployed as a service. This service is available following this link http://assurance-platform.musa-project.eu/ and a demonstration of the tool is available on YouTube following this link: https://www.youtube.com/watch?v=zc6p-0H9yFo.

2.2   The MUSA Security Assurance Platform Overview

The MUSA Security Assurance Platform (MUSA SAP) fits the operation phase of the MUSA framework and it is devoted to continuously monitor and analyze multi-cloud application security with the possibility of activating automatic reactions (based on security enforcement libraries) and sending notifications (alerts and violation information) in case of detecting security issues with the ultimate objective of maintaining confidentiality and privacy of sensitive data and communications. The MUSA SAP needs four main inputs to work correctly:

- The Security SLA of the application to monitor: The MUSA SAP recuperates the single application components SLAs or the multi-cloud composite application SLA (shown in Fig. 1 in the Design phase). The latter refers to the final SLA composed out of the security policies of each of the individual services and their specific SLAs, therefore resulting in a single SLA associated to the whole multi-cloud implementation. From that input, the MUSA SAP can monitor the security of single components and from composite SLA, it can check the end-to-end security of the multi-cloud application taking the communication exchanges between remote components into account.
- The application deployment plan: From this plan, the MUSA SAP recuperates the list of monitoring agents deployed with each application component as well as their IP addresses. This information is very important to link the monitoring agent with the application component in order to monitor the right security metrics that are specified in the application component security SLA.
- The monitoring agents: The MUSA SAP configures the monitoring agents in order to measure the security metrics related the security controls required for an application component (and specified in their security SLA). The reported measurements and events are correlated in the platform SaaS to detect potential alerts or violations.
- The enforcement agents: The MUSA SAP activates enforcement agents in case of security issue detection with the ultimate objective of maintaining confidentiality and privacy of sensitive data and communications.

2.3   MUSA SAP Monitoring Agents

To be able to deeply analyze security, the MUSA SAP relies on different agents to be installed in different VMs or containers where application components are deployed. These agents collect data coming from network, system and application internals and send them to the monitoring platform MUSA SAP. Among these agents, we have:

Network Monitoring Agent. This is a monitoring solution that combines a set of functionalities presented in the following list:
- Data capture, filtering and storage;
- Events extraction and statistics collection; and
- Traffic analysis and reporting providing, network, application, flow and user level visibility.

Through its real-time and historical data gathering, the network monitoring agent facilitates network performance monitoring and operation troubleshooting. With its advanced rules engine, the monitoring agent can correlate network events in order to detect performance, operational, and security incidents.

System Monitoring Agent. The System agent monitors system resources which may be the cause of server performance degradation and spots performance bottlenecks early on. The System agent relies on Linux `top` command which is used frequently by many system administrators to monitor Linux performance and it is available under many Linux/Unix like operating systems. The top command used to display all the running and active real-time processes in an ordered list and updates it regularly. It displays CPU usage, Memory usage, Swap Memory, Cache Size, Buffer Size, Process PID, User, Commands, among others. It also shows high memory and CPU utilization of all running processes.

Application Monitoring Agent. The role of the Application agent is to deliver information about the internal state of the multi-cloud application component to the MUSA SAP during its operation. It continuously checks and monitors application health. It notifies the MUSA SAP about measurements of execution details and other internal conditions of the application component. The application monitoring agent is a Java library built of two parts. The first part is an aspect to be weaved into the application code via point-cuts in order to send application-internal tracing information to the MUSA security assurance platform for analysis. It is composed of a set of functions that can be weaved in strategic application points to capture relevant internal data. The second part connects the aspect with the notification tool via a connector library and it provides a simple interface to send log data to the MUSA SAP in a secure way. In other words, the application monitoring agent is responsible for extracting the information from the application environment, and the connector is responsible for transferring it.

2.4   MUSA SAP Enforcement Agents

Prevention, monitoring, detection, and mitigation generally illustrate the defense life-cycle. Prevention involves the implementation of a set of defenses, practices, and configurations prior to any kind of attack, with the aim of reducing the impact of such attack. These issues could be addressed by network security, data protection, virtualization and isolation of resources. Traditionally, well-known countermeasures have focused on dealing with threats through a variety of methods devised around questions such as where is the attack detected? How is the attack detected? What is the response mechanism? Where to apply the response mechanism? Where is the control (decision) center from which filtering rules are taken? Previous studies have assessed the analysis of such mechanisms, for instance, Carlin et al. [7] studied vulnerabilities and countermeasures and proposed a flow chart showing the exiting DDoS cloud protection systems and comparing the implementation of different features in the proposed systems. Other methods utilized are profiling based techniques, in order to discriminate the mis-usability from users (e.g. trying to gain privileges); IDS, pattern matching in the search for specific confidential words trying to be breached, or queries in databases monitoring. The MUSA SAP integrates a set of security enforcement agents that can be easily deployed when a security breach is detected. As an example, a high availability framework to ensure application availability even under charge.

3   The MUSA SAP Workflow

The MUSA workflow is illustrated in Fig. 2 and it's composed of four main modules followed by the gathering of data from different monitoring agents. More details about these steps are provided in the next subsections.

3.1   Preprocessing the Data

This module has a particular challenge, which is extracting the right information from the collected data collected by different monitoring agents and from different CSPs, in order to build the correct usage profiles. This unit is meant to be dynamic, where features are analyzed in regard of time-based contextual information. This has the advantage of decreasing the usage of resources for the analysis of large amounts of data, therefore increasing the performance of the framework and reasoning detection. Also following this direction, it is relevant at the moment of keeping a non-redundant dataset. Additionally, in real cloud environments, periodic reports may be subject to loss or high latency, due to the applications elasticity or VM-related features (e.g. restarting a VM, rolling back.). Hence, it is relevant to be able to be resilient to the lack of all types of log information at all times and be able to construct the *possible* missing pieces by studying the whole picture of what type of features are being received and how to treat them to build the best profile of the database status.

3.2   Detecting Threats and Anomalies

The Threat Analyzer module consists in two sub-modules: Rule-based inspector and a Behavior profiler, as shown in Fig. 2.

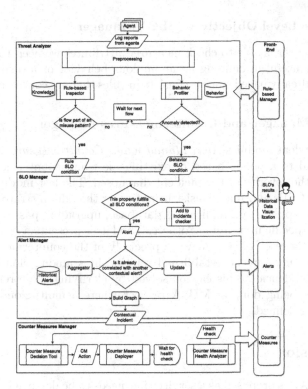

Fig. 2. The MUSA SAP workflow

The first resides in an engine that receives information events from the pre-possessing module, regarding users accessing to the sensitive data and they are checked against these permission rules. Additionally to this policy control, some of the attributes obtained from the agents, are inspected for specific pattern-matching detection.

The second module also receives the preprocessed data and comprehends two functions: the online-learning and the anomalies detection.

Most of the literature related to anomaly detection, establishes a separated two-stage process where systems are trained with *normal* data for second-stage comparison with new incoming information. This idea lacks of dynamism, as cloud behavior may vary in mid-long term, and is highly dependent of the nature of the training data. Therefore, we propose a self-learning module which is able to feed and update itself dynamically from new data flows. This system will discriminate if it is appropriate to self-feed itself or not, lowering the possibility of training the engine with *malicious activity* as *normal*.

The model uses a semi-supervised learning, given the fact that new input data has no a priori labeling and needs to be classified on the basis of their statistical properties only. The supervised component comprehends a smaller labeled dataset created in a lab environment, which learns from known attacks.

3.3 Service Level Objectives (SLO) Manager

The SLO Manager is able to check measured attributes we need to assert which objectives are useful in defining an anomalous behavior or a disrespected rule. The latter is already paved since it consists in rules that are continuously checked.

3.4 Alert Manager and Countermeasures Manager

The correspondent modules *Alert Manager* and *Countermeasure Manager* from Fig. 2, respond to a policy based of existing alert and countermeasure mechanisms, given the severity of the incident diagnosed. The last module is intended to advise the CSPs and may consist in notifying the administrator rolling back the composite application, replicating database, upgrading passwords complexity, disabling specific user, among others. The latter presents a crucial challenge because sometimes CSPs are unaware precisely of the countermeasures to consider, because there are no established relationships among cloud components and their dependencies. This can be solved by clarifying these relationships as it is currently being done in MUSA project where a multi-cloud composition model is being defined.

4 Discussion

The MUSA SAP is proposed as a service that needs to be deployed in the suitable CSP (or CSPs since we can divide the platform into independent components or microservices), offering security controls according to the application needs (including security requirements).

Starting from this statement, the MUSA framework can be applied in the design, SLA generation, CSP selection and deployment phases in order to better select the CSP that fulfills its requirements (including robustness against attacks). Moreover, the MUSA SAP is able to enforce the security by executing the necessary countermeasures to repel security issues or to mitigate their undesired effects.

Its real-time data collection and analysis, together with its virtualized nature, makes the MUSA SAP a strong prototype ready to be used in industrial environments. It offers multi-cloud application developers a cloud-based integrated tool to perform real-time, SLA-based, end-to-end security monitoring and enforcement. With the definition of personalized security SLAs, the automatic deployment of the monitoring probes, together with the virtualized operation, the multi-cloud application developers just need to specify their security requirements and the MUSA SAP will do the rest: monitoring heterogeneous sources (network, application, containers, etc.), analyzing the collected information in real-time, enforcing the security, and offering detailed visual reports to keep CSCs aware of their systems health.

5 Conclusion

In this paper, we have presented a security assurance platform for multi-cloud applications. This platform includes techniques to perform the monitoring of these applications that are deployed over heterogeneous cloud resources. This platform is also based on the concept of security SLA in order to detect potential deviations of security rules and trigger countermeasures to protect applications against attacks. The proposed framework presents several advantages: providing preventive security based on the use of security-by-design practices in the applications' development. It also guarantees applications protection by countermeasures techniques to mitigate security incidents and providing applications with reaction mechanisms. The MUSA SAP is being evaluated in the context of two industrial case studies: one related to *smart cities* and the other related to the transport industry. The preliminary results are positives and will be a subject of complementary publication.

Acknowledgment. The project leading to this paper has received funding from the European Unions Horizon 2020 research and innovation program under grant agreement No. 644429.

References

1. MUSA Project. http://www.musa-project.eu/. Accessed Jan 2017
2. Openstack ceilometer. http://docs.openstack.org/developer/ceilometer/. Accessed Jan 2017
3. OPNFV Doctor. http://wiki.opnfv.org/doctor. Accessed Jan 2017
4. Stacktach. http://stacktach.readthedocs.org/en/latest/index.html. Accessed Jan 2017
5. Lifecycle management of service-based applications on multi-clouds: a research roadmap (2013)
6. Multi-Cloud: expectations and current approaches (2013)
7. Carlin, A., Hammoudeh, M., Aldabbas, O.: Intrusion detection and countermeasure of virtual cloud systems - state of the art and current challenges. Int. J. Adv. Comput. Sci. Appl. **6**(6), 1–15 (2015)
8. Casola, V., Benedictis, A.D., Rak, M., Rios, E.: Security-by-design in clouds: a security-sla driven methodology to build secure cloud applications. Procedia Comput. Sci. **97**, 53–62 (2016). http://www.sciencedirect.com/science/article/pii/S1877050916320968, 2nd International Conference on Cloud Forward: From Distributed to Complete Computing
9. Collectd. http://collectd.org/. Accessed Jan 2017
10. Consul. https://www.consul.io/. Accessed Jan 2017
11. Ferry, N., Rossini, A., Chauvel, F., Morin, B.: Towards model-driven provisioning, deployment, monitoring, and adaptation of multi-cloud systems. In: 2013 IEEE Sixth International Conference on Cloud Computing (2013)
12. Global Inter-cloud Technology Forum: Use Cases and Functional Requirements for Inter-Cloud Computing. Technical report (2010)
13. Grozev, N., Buyya, R.: Inter-cloud architectures and application brokering: taxonomy and survey. Softw. - Pract. Exp. **44**(3), 369–390 (2012)

14. Guide, O.S.: http://docs.openstack.org/sec/. Accessed January 2017
15. Patel, A., Taghavi, M., Bakhtiyari, K., Celestino Júnior, J.: An intrusion detection and prevention system in cloud computing: a systematic review. J. Netw. Comput. Appl. **36**(1), 25–41 (2013)
16. Project, B.: http://wiki.openstack.org/wiki/Security/Projects/Bandit. Accessed Jan 2017
17. Rios, E., Mallouli, W., Rak, M., Casola, V., Ortiz, A.M.: SLA-driven monitoring of multi-cloud application components using the MUSA framework. In: ICDCS Workshops (2016)
18. Zbakh, M., Elmahdi, K., Cherkaoui, R., Enniari, S.: A multi-criteria analysis of intrusion detection architectures in cloud environments. In: 2015 International Conference on Cloud Technologies and Applications (CloudTech), pp. 1–9. IEEE (2015)
19. Zeginis, C., Kritikos, K., Garefalakis, P., Konsolaki, K., Magoutis, K., Plexousakis, D.: Towards cross-layer monitoring of multi-cloud service-based applications. In: Lau, K.-K., Lamersdorf, W., Pimentel, E. (eds.) ESOCC 2013. LNCS, vol. 8135, pp. 188–195. Springer, Heidelberg (2013). doi:10.1007/978-3-642-40651-5_16

Secure microGRID in Cloud:
The CoSSMic Case Study

Massimiliano Rak$^{(\boxtimes)}$ and Salvatore Venticinque

Department of Industrial and Information Engineering,
Università della Campania Luigi Vanvitelli, Via Roma 29,
81031 Aversa, CE, Italy
{massimiliano.rak,salvatore.venticinque}@unicampania.it

Abstract. Smart grids is now part of a wider smart energy concepts
that includes not only the provisioning of intelligences to the power grid
by an ICT solution, but also management of smart buildings, the monitoring and analysis of user's information, user's devices, environmental
parameters and others. In these kind of Internet of Things (IoT) systems
it needs to protect information based value across all the layers providing
security and resilience. In this paper we present a security assessment of
software architecture deployed in the Cloud to provide data management
for these kind of services in the CoSSMic project.

Keywords: Cloud security · Per-service SLA · Security Service Level
Agreement

1 Introduction

Moving applications to Cloud, for monitoring and controlling critical systems
is a hot topic in the research and technological context nowadays. Above all it
is due to the fact that many safety and security issues arises when technologies, originally developed to run in closed local area networks, are moved to the
Internet. Smart Grids is an example of critical application where user's information, configuration parameters and control of infrastructure must be protected to
assure safety and privacy, also enforcing right permissions according to defined
policies and authorization profiles.

With development of Internet of Thing applications, more and more devices,
which were not conceived to be integrated in such a critical system, are connected to the Grid in user's households and to the Internet by any kinds of
ICT technologies. CoSSMic (Collaborating Solar powered Smart Micro-grids) is
an European project that has developed a peer to peer platform for connecting
to the Smart Grid many kinds of off-the shelf devices in order to optimize the
utilization of green energy. The research activities did not focused on security
issues and developed the trials connecting peers by an isolated virtual private
network. The gap between a demonstrator to a production environment cannot
neglect security problems and the ways they affect safety. Moreover such issues
increase when the deployment model move from a local network to the Cloud.

© Springer International Publishing AG 2017
M.H.A. Au et al. (Eds.): GPC 2017, LNCS 10232, pp. 759–772, 2017.
DOI: 10.1007/978-3-319-57186-7_55

In this paper we introduce motivation and approaches to secure IoT in Cloud. Starting fro a practical example, focused on Smart Grid applications, we aims at illustrating how application of a security assessment procedure may help in identifying the main security issues on a complex and distributed architecture, and in helping application developers to prioritize the security enforcement activities.

As a consequence, we have analyzed and assessed the security granted by the CoSSMic platform components and analyzed the interaction between sensor nodes and the software service responsible for collecting and processing sensor data. The final result is the definition of the security policy granted by the overall platform, according to the chosen deployment. The reminder of this paper is organized as follows: next Section (Sect. 2) presents security issues of IoT and big data applications in Cloud. In Sect. 3 we introduce the CoSSMic project and the technological stack for data management in Sect. 4. Our approach to model security of Cloud application is described in Sect. 5 and Sect. 6 presents the application of such methodology to the CoSSMic case study. Finally discussion and conclusion are provided.

2   Secure IoT in Cloud

Smart Grid represents an application domain that belongs to a more general class of business problems where utilities companies have rolled out smart meters and analytics to extract information for monitoring, analyzing and improving their business. Meters could measure the consumption of water, gas, and electricity at regular intervals of one hour or less, generating huge volumes of interval data that needs to be analyzed. In particular smart grids include sophisticated sensors that monitor voltage, current, frequency, and other important operating characteristics. They have to incorporate and manage centralized and distributed power generation, intermittent sources of renewable energy enabling multi-directional power flow from many different Prosumers, and integrating real-time pricing and load management data. To gain operating efficiency, the company must monitor the data delivered by the sensor.

Smart grids is now part of a wider smart energy concepts that includes not only the provisioning of intelligences to the power grid by an ICT solution, but also management of smart buildings, the monitoring and analysis of user's information, user's devices, environmental parameters and others [1].

Unfortunately fragmentation of the smart grid is observed both across layers and within the same layers, because of different reasons which range from interoperability to security. In the current technological scenario more and more micro-grids are growing, which are all connected to the power grid.

Even if micro-smart grids were originally isolated from the smart grid, now the integration process has started and more and more data are collected and must be stored, aggregated and processed. For this reason the smart energy is already now a big data problem.

A big data solution can analyze power generation (supply) and power consumption (demand) data using smart meters.

However many issues, which affected different layer of the smart grid archi-tectures changes and become more relevant in Cloud and Big Data domain. It needs to protect information based value across all the layers providing *security* and *resilience*.

In these kind of Internet of Things (IoT) systems it needs to prevent system breaches that compromises of privacy and safety. Effective prevention requires the definition and enforcement of security policies at many layers. Actions range from physical hardening of sensors to firewall installation and configuration. Con-tinuous monitoring and assessment of the system security are necessary because working condition can dynamically change, new vulnerabilities may be discov-ered, degradation and obsolescence of techniques and technology may affect the security level.

Data flow from sensor to applications according to the value loop shown in Fig. 1. Hence security and resilience mechanism must be designed and imple-mented in each layer to provide specific protection of information-based value depicted in Fig. 1b).

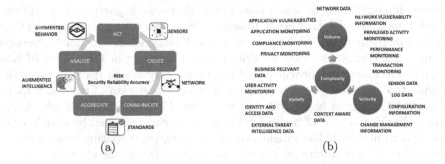

(a)   (b)

Fig. 1. .

Moving to Cloud data and computation introduce additional security issues. With reference to Fig. 1 here we focus on the security issues arising during the communication and aggregation phase, but also during the control phase when applications use actuators to controls consuming or producing devices. In this case relevant risks deal with privacy of sensor data, but also with modification of configuration and execution of unprivileged action commands.

The challenge is to make sure not to cross the fine line between collecting and using (big) data and ensuring citizens' rights of privacy.

It needs high levels of security policies and mechanisms to protect this data against unauthorized use and malicious attacks. In addition, smart applications integrated together across agencies also require high security since the data will move over various types of networks, some of which may be pen or unsecure. What makes such an issue more complex is that most big data technologies today, including Cassandra and Hadoop, suffer from a lack of sufficient security. Using cloud computing for these kind of systems raises security and network issues caused by the fact that the storage in the cloud is shared among several users. This makes it more vulnerable to attacks.

Cloud services collecting data will not have control on faulty sensors, wrongly calibrated, or beyond their lifetime, which produce wrong data. The challenge may also extend to the outputs of analysing existing data (given the possibility of errors) and reporting the results for use by others, who may not be aware of such issues.

3   The Case Study: CoSSMic

CoSSMic (Collaborating Smart Solar-powered Micro-grids - FP7-SMART-CITIES-2013) is an ICT European project that investigates regulatory, organizational and technical challenges about the transition from centralized power network to distributed Smart Solar powered Micro Grids operating in deregulated energy markets, where users can negotiate and exchange energy to achieve an individual and a global benefit. It aims at supporting the interaction among the common users, who belong to a new category of distributed prosumers (producers and consumers), according to innovative negotiation models that allow to achieve different kinds of agreement. CoSSMic research partners are Stiftelsen Sintef, International Solar Energy Research Center Konstanz, University of Campania "Luigi Vanvitelli" (SUN), Norges Teknisk-Naturvitenskapelige Universitet, Sunny Solartechnik, Boukje.com Consulting, University of Oslo. City of Konstanz in Germany and province of Caserta in Italy are project partners that provide trial sites for experimental activities and validation of results. SUN has developed the agents based software platform. The University of Oslo defined some behavior patterns of micro-intelligent networks, governed by selfish agents that seek to maximize the satisfaction of its users, participating in a market by mechanisms that will improve the overall performance of the electricity grid.

In CoSSMic a micro-grid is typically confined in a smart home or an office building, and embeds local generation and storage of solar power, and a number of power consuming devices. In addition electric vehicles will connect and disconnect dynamically, thus representing a dynamically varying storage capacity. In Fig. 2 an overview of the CoSSMic scenario is shown.

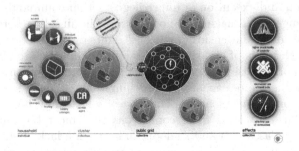

Fig. 2. CoSSMic reference scenario

CoSSMic users configure and plan their appliances setting constraints and preferences such as earliest, latest start time and priorities. They supervise the execution of their plan and to get useful information about their cost, energy consumption, production and exchange with the community. An example of constraint could require that electric water heater not switch on between 8.00 and 10.00 in the morning. An example of goal can be the preservation of the battery life, or the maximization of consumption of energy produced by the solar panels, before consuming the remaining power from GenCos.

The Multi Agent System (MAS) described in [2,3] allows for the deployment of agents of consumers and producers that will participate in the energy distribution. Software agents exploit the flexibility of users' plan, the weather forecast information, profile of devices consumption and energy availability from other smart-grids to find the optimal schedule in order to maximize the self consumption of the neighborhood.

The CoSSMic platform will run on embedded computer systems that will be provided to end users as a black box, to be plugged into the power network and connected to Internet. The Platform will be installed in every household and will join a community of other instances within the neighborhood. Instances of the platform communicate by a P2P overlay to negotiate the energy exchange.

User's information and sensor data are collected by a content management system (CMS) that expose a REST-full interface to application and a web Graphical Interface (GUI) to humans. Each platform instance will communicate with other households those information which are necessary for the energy negotiation. Examples of private information are the detailed data about production and consumption of devices, the constraints and goals set by the user, the effective schedule of appliances. An example of constraint could require that electric water heater not switch on between 8.00 and 10.00 in the morning. Data are communicated from sensor to the (CMS).

An example of goal can be the preservation of the battery life, or the maximization of consumption of energy produced by the solar panels, before consuming the remaining power from GenCos. The Multi Agent System (MAS) described in [2,3] allows for the deployment of consumers and producers agents that will participate in the energy distribution. They also use by the CMS API device drivers to send real time commands to electric devices in the smart house. For example, through device drivers, agents can switch on or switch off devices, when it does not violates any constraints, in order to save energy.

Design and development of an ICT infrastructure that support such a P2P overlay and allows for communication an information sharing is a critical activities that deals with the kind of data and with the CoSSMic application pattern.

The main configuration of CoSSMic platform, which has been implemented in the trials, is *All In Home* (Fig. 3). It means that all software resides on a home gateway and the agents use the network just to negotiate energy. In this configuration, the entire system resides inside the home. Everything is managed by a home gateway that encapsulates the functions of device management, information system and Multi-Agent System (MAS). The various devices in the home, using special driver, connect to the home gateway. Users use the web GUI, hosted at the home gateway in order to control and manage the system. Cloud services are only used by agents to exchange info about energy. The computation for the optimization is performed at each home, and the energy exchange occurs within the neighborhood.

The CoSSMic platform runs on embedded computer systems that have been provided to final users as a black box, to be plugged into the power network and connected to Internet. The Platform is installed in every household and joins a community of other instances within the neighborhood by an XMPP account. Instances of the platform communicate by a server-to-server XMPP overlay. In this case user's information will be bounded to the private network of each household and will be forwarded outside only with the user's agreement and for debugging purpose. Each platform instance will communicate with other households only for the energy negotiation.

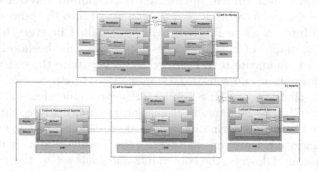

Fig. 3. CoSSMic reference scenario

The opposite foreseen deployment choice is *All In Cloud*. In this case, all data and services are in Cloud. This configuration requires that there is always access to the network and less assurance of privacy. The home gateway only forwards the information about devices to MAS and mediator, that is in the Cloud, and receive control actions. The optimization and energy exchange are still performed at the neighborhood level, but computation runs remotely. Cloud services can better process the huge, persistent flows of data generated by smart grids, so this deployment choice offers the advantages of a robust platform that can quickly respond to growing demand across a wide range of applications, as well as provide performance greater than current dedicated hardware installations. Moreover, it can quickly respond to unpredictable application behavior and network traffic in order to support such dynamic, always-on applications.

The utilization of a cloud platform, which supports critical requirements, as well as avoids dedicated IT investments, can bring a significant money saving [4,5]. On the other had, data security and privacy remain one of the biggest obstacles to migration Smart Grid applications in cloud [4]. In particular, scalable access to information on energy assets need to be balanced with data privacy and security (using identified data), which must not affect the performance of such mission-critical applications. With cloud deployment communication between user's devices and CMS, but also between sensors/actuators and the CMS is the main issue. Authentication and authorization mechanisms, and privacy introduce new vulnerabilities which were not relevant in a private network. Not only attack from malicious users must be prevented, but also the sharing of same resources, in terms of both storage and services by different users must be carefully managed.

4   CoSSMic Technologies

The technological stack implementing the CoSSMic CMS is shown in Fig. 4. The CoSSMic CMS is based on Emoncms[1] version 8, a powerful open-source web-app for processing, logging and visualising energy, temperature and other environmental data. It is a configurable framework with many modules that can be combined in different ways. It includes five core modules: input, feed, visualizations, dashboard, and user. The input module preprocesses meter input before it is inserted in the database, e.g., for creating histogram data. The feed module provides functionality for inserting, storing and retrieving time stamped data in the database. The visualizations module can analyze large data sets and generates graphics in different formats. The dashboard module includes the dashboard builder and viewer. The user module handles user actions and data, including authentication and sessions. The mediator provides uniform access to monitoring information to the agents based CoSSMic scheduler and to the users by a GUI. The communication protocol used both by users and application is http, which has been the protocol used by the project in private local network. It means that the communication between clients devices and the CMS do not use any kind of cryptography to preserve privacy. Two different mechanisms are provided. Users submit username and password. The MD5 has of user's password are store in a mysql database together with a salt and every user is identified by an integer identifier for authorization purpose. For each user's profile Emoncms creates a couple of API-keys. These must be used by applications that want

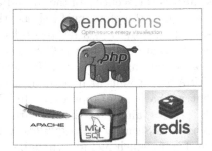

Fig. 4. CoSSMic CMS technological stack.

---

[1] http://www.emoncms.org.

to access the REST-Full Application Programming Interface of Emoncms. The two different keys are for reading and for writing information. The API key for writing own also reading privileges. Both the keys are stored into the mysql database as plain text.

Apache hosts the Emoncms application and the php is the execution engine. Mysql allows for storing configuration data, but time series of monitoring information are saved in binary files. Redis is a key-value store that is accessed by php-api for in memory cache and fast retrieval of frequently used information, whose persistence is granted anyway.

5   Securing (IoT) Cloud Applications

The goal of this paper is to state the level of security of an IT application, according to the terminology proposed by Bishop [6]: **security requirements** dictates what actions are allowed and which are forbidden, while the **security policy**, are specific statement of what is and is not allowed and to conclude **security mechanisms** are the technical solutions adopted to implement the security policy.

We express the security policy of the application using standard security controls that, according to NIST [7], i.e. standard safeguard or countermeasure able to meet a set of defined security requirements. Security controls are organized in families, each of them addressing a different security domain, moving from access control (AC) to identification and authentication (IA), to media (MP) and physical environment (PE) protection. Security controls include even organizative aspects, like personnel training and planning.

According to such terminology, in order to assess the security granted by the CoSSMiC IoT application, we aims at identify the security policy, expressed as a list of standard security controls, that the application is able to grant according to the specific design choices made in the application. The problem is made more complex by the distributed nature of the IoT applications and by their inherent flexibility: it is very easy, from functional point of view to add or remove smart devices from the architecture, even at runtime, but each of them (in particular due to their *smartness*) affects the security of the overall architecture.

In this paper we have skipped the problem of IoT security requirements specification, such a process will be subject of a future works, aiming at comparing the security policy offered at state of art by the CoSSMiC platform.

According to such considerations, we adapted the development process proposed in the project MUSA[2], that aims at developing secure cloud application. It is worth noticing that we have note applied the full MUSA life cycle, but only an extraction of the process, aiming at the evaluation of the security policy (that in MUSA are reported as Security Service Level Agreement), resulting in the process illustrated in Fig. 5, which includes the following actions:

---

[2] www.musa-project.eu.

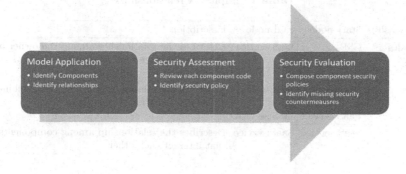

Fig. 5. The security evaluation process

1. Model the overall IoT application in terms of its components and the relationship that exists among them;
2. assess the security policy for each of them;
3. evaluate the overall application composing the security policy in order to generate the policy of the complete application.

It is worth noticing that this paper focuses on the first two steps, while the latest is described in a companion paper, due to the complexity of the process. For the interested reader we suggest the following readings about the MUSA project results [8,9].

5.1 The Modeling Technique

IoT Applications are described using a graph-based model, i.e. in terms of nodes that can be of different types (*node types*) and edges that represent the links among the nodes. The model we adopted, here described in a simplified version and born in the context of cloud application is named MACM (multicloud application composition model) and it includes the following node types:

CSP that represent a provider owner of the infrastructure that offers the physical environment where the application will be deployed and executed, depicted in yellow

IaaS:service that represents the specific (eventually virtual) machine where the application components are executed, depicted in blue;

PaaS:service represents a typical application server that is able to host other software modules and enable their execution.

SaaS:service a node type that represents a software component, typically a commercial-off-the-shelf (COTS) product, that will be deployed and executed on the machines, depicted in green.

The relationships used in this (simplified) version of the model are illustrated in Table 1.

Table 1. graphSLA relationships

Relationship	Start node	End node	Description
Provides	CSP	IaaS:service	Describes the relationship among the owner of the infrastructure and the machine it offers to execute the IoT application components
Hosts	IaaS:service or PaaS:service	PaaS:service or IaaS:service	Describes the relationship among the machines and the application components
Uses	SaaS:service	SaaS:service	Describes the relationship among components that interact each other

5.2 Security Policy Self-assessment

The main goal of the self-assess is to perform a detailed security review of the application components, identifying which are the security controls implemented in each of the specific components of the application. The most well known approach for conducting an in-depth security analysis of a product is Common Criteria[3]. It is used in particular in the banking sector to evaluate the software and hardware security of smart cards used in payment systems. Common criteria evaluations are typically long and expensive, and hardly applicable in the context of a security-by-design approach and for a in-development security analysis.

An interesting alternative, typically used in the context of web application development is the Application Security Verification Standard (ASVS 2.0) proposed by OWASP (http://www.owasp.org). The work of OWASP is well recognized in the community, and in fact the very first control of CSA's CCM (AIS-01) explicitly mentions this approach as an example of best practices for secure cloud application development. As further evidence of the value in adopting this strategy, the latest version of ASVS 2.0 was released in 2014 and is currently used as a certifiable standard for the evaluation of web applications. The ASVS 2.0 is presented as a security checklist which asks a series of questions against which you can assess your security features. It is possible create a custom security assessment checklist by taking the ASVS 2.0 as a foundation and removing any security check that relates more to client side security and/or HTML/Javascript considerations, focusing solely on server side requirements.

In order to drive a time-limited self-assessment that helps in stating the security policy for each component, we tested a simple approach: we associated the ASVS questions to NIST security controls, in order to identify which controls can be considered correctly implemented (and at what level) when an ASVS question is positively answered. In addition to ASVS control we reported a set of specific questions extracted by the security controls definition in the NIST framework. The result of such an activity is a database of *questions*, linked to each security control and to specific service types (as an example we make ASVS questions for web applications like EMONCMS, while for other kind of components, e.g. databases, we rely on other sources and/or custom questions derived from the security controls definition).

---

[3] http://www.commoncriteriaportal.org/.

6   A Security Model for CoSSMic

The CoSSMic application described in Sect. 3 was modeled, according to our modeling technique, as illustrated in Fig. 6. The application relies on three main commercial-off-the-shelf software components: the web server (Apache), redis (a Key-value store used to optimize the memory usage) and a database (MySQL). The web server hosts the PHP module that, acting as an application server, hosts in turn EMONCMS, the core of the CoSSMic application. The smart devices interact with the system using dedicated applications (*Device Drivers*) that interact with EMONCMS in a bidirectional way: EMONCMS send them commands in order to apply a reconfiguration, and independently each device driver sends data to EMONCMS for monitoring purposes.

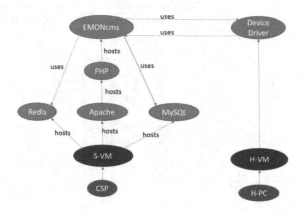

Fig. 6. The deployment model for the CoSSMic application in the *AllInCloud* scenario

According to the *AllInCloud* deployment scenario, that we have analyzed in this paper, a shared machine (*S-VM*), provided by a public or private CSP, hosts the core of the architecture, while each of the software components are hosted on a virtual machine (*H-VM*) hosted in a home PC (*H-PC*), which acts as the base station to control the architecture.

6.1   Components Self Assessment and Overall Evaluation

According to the self-assessment process proposed above, we invited software developers to reply to questions and, as a result, to identify which are the correctly implemented security controls. Even if simplified respect to the common criteria, such security review result still to be a time-expensive process, but organizing the process by security domain (i.e. focusing each time on single security control family) resulted in a limited and acceptable effort to be conducted at any stage of the software development.

Table 2 summarize the result of the self-assessment for some of the security controls in the secure communication NIST family (i.e. all controls whose name starts with SC). The first column of the table reports the security controls, while each of the other columns reports the result of the assessment for each of the CoSSMic components. In order to help table readability we subdivided the column in (i) *Infrastructure*, which contains the column related to the infrastructure components like PCs and virtual machines, (ii) *COTS*, associated to the standard software components used in the project and (iii) to the components customized in the context of the CoSSMic project. It is wort noticing that assessment of standard COTS software and Infrastructure components can be easily reused in different contexts.

Table 2. Security SLA of the CSP and SLA templates of the nodes

Control	Infrastructure				COTS components				CoSSMic software		CoSSMic
	CSP	H-PC	S-VM	H-VM	MySQL	Redis	Apache	PHP	E-CMS	Driver	
SC-1	1	1	1	1	1	0	1	1	1	1	1
SC-2	1	1	1	1	1	0	1	1	1	0	0
SC-2(1)	1	1	1	1	1	0	1	1	1	0	0
SC-3	1	1	1	1	1	0	1	1	0	0	0
SC-3(1)	1	0	0	0	0	0	1	1	0	0	0
SC-3(2)	1	1	1	1	1	0	0	0	0	0	0
SC-3(3)	1	0	0	0	0	0	0	0	0	0	0
SC-3(4)	1	0	0	0	1	0	0	0	0	0	0
SC-3(5)	1	0	0	0	0	0	0	0	0	0	0
SC-4	1	1	1	1	1	0	1	1	0	1	0

For simplicity's sake we reported in the table only few of the controls of the SC (Secure Communication) family. The last column of Table 2 contains the result of the composition process (described in a paper under publication), which describe the result in terms of security of the overall CoSSMic application.

It is worth noticing that the application is mainly considered insecure and unprotected in terms of secure communications (which is expected from a project prototype). The most interesting results rely on the identification of the motivation for such security weakness that enable us to give a priority to the actions needed to enforce security into the overall application.

It is interesting to note that the Infrastructure side cover many of the security controls, even if some advanced features (control enhancements) are not implemented. The public CSP offers all the correct countermeasures in terms of secure communications, but the virtual image adopted (Ubuntu 16.04) has some limits: a possible action is adoption of a secured linux distribution as selinux[4]. It is worth noticing that adoption of such an image needs a non-trivial effort in configuration. Further analysis illustrate that this action, even if recommended, can be post-poned and has very low priority, due to the limits of the other application components.

---

[4] https://www.nsa.gov/what-we-do/research/selinux/.

The *Redis* component looks to be one of the most unsecure pieces of the architecture, but the result of composition analysis (and feedback from the composer tool) outlines that *Redis* operates only locally and it becomes unsecure only if hosted over virtual machines different from the component that uses it. EMONCMS and Sensor Drivers are the most unsecure components: the first one has a very limited documentation (which affect the security) and enable communication even without a secure the channel. In fact all Drivers uses HTTP (not HTTPS) to communicate. The feedback offered by our tools offers even hints about the configuration to be adopted. AS an example a HSTS configuration is suggested for the Apache layer, in order to force the adoption of only secured (HTTPS) channels for the hosted applications.

7 Conclusions

In this paper we have illustrated a security assessment technique for a IoT application, that aims at identifying security issues from the very early design stages. The proposed approach rely on a detailed modeling of the application using a graph-based model born in the cloud context and named MACM (Multicloud Application Composition Model) and a self-assessment security review based on questionnaires, that enable to identify the security policy granted by the overall application, in terms of standard security controls.

According to such preliminary analysis we were able to identify the main security issues at design time of the IoT application, helping to make design choice and give priority to security enforcement activities.

The promising results of this preliminary analysis outline that with an acceptable effort it is possible to identify design choice that will simplify the introduction of security features in further developments. According to the experience done we aims at improving the approach in the future, extending the set of questions and controls supported and, mainly, introducing a risk analysis process before starting the security assessment in order to make a preliminary selection of the controls to be evaluated according to the concrete application security requirements.

Acknowledgment. This research is partially supported by the grant H2020-ICT-07-2014-644429 (MUSA). The authors would like to thank Luigi Montella, whose work during the master degree thesis was partially reused in this paper.

References

1. Amato, A., Aversa, R., Di Martino, B., Scialdone, M., Venticinque, S., Hallsteinsen, S., Horn, G.: Software agents for collaborating smart solar-powered micro-grids. In: Caporarello, L., Di Martino, B., Martinez, M. (eds.) Smart Organizations and Smart Artifacts. LNISO, vol. 7, pp. 125–133. Springer, Cham (2014). doi:10.1007/978-3-319-07040-7_14

2. Amato, A., Di Martino, B., Scialdone, M., Venticinque, S., Hallsteinsen, S., Jiang, S.: A distributed system for smart energy negotiation. In: Fortino, G., Di Fatta, G., Li, W., Ochoa, S., Cuzzocrea, A., Pathan, M. (eds.) IDCS 2014. LNCS, vol. 8729, pp. 422–434. Springer, Cham (2014). doi:10.1007/978-3-319-11692-1_36
3. Amato, A., Di Martino, B., Scialdone, M., Venticinque, S.: Multi-agent negotiation of decentralized energy production in smart micro-grid. In: Camacho, D., Braubach, L., Venticinque, S., Badica, C. (eds.) Intelligent Distributed Computing VIII. SCI, vol. 570, pp. 155–160. Springer, Cham (2015). doi:10.1007/978-3-319-10422-5_17
4. Simmhan, Y., Giakkoupis, M., Cao, B., Prasanna, V.K.: On using cloud platforms in a software architecture for smart energy grids. In: International Conference on Cloud Computing Technology and Science (CloudCom). IEEE, December 2010. (poster [CORE C])
5. Wang, W.Y.C., Rashid, A., Chuang, H.-M.: Toward the trend of cloud computing. J. Electron. Commer. Res. **12**(4), 238–242 (2011)
6. Bishop, M.: What is computer security? IEEE Secur. Priv. **99**, 67–69 (2003)
7. N.I.O. Standards and Technology: NIST Special Publication 800-53 Information Security. CreateSpace, Paramount (2011)
8. Afolaranmi, S.O., Moctezuma, L.E.G., Rak, M., Casola, V., Rios, E., Lastra, J.L.M.: Methodology to obtain the security controls in multi-cloud applications. In: CLOSER 2016 - Proceedings of the 6th International Conference on Cloud Computing and Services Science, vol. 1, pp. 327–332. SCITEPRESS (2016). http://www.scitepress.org/DigitalLibrary/HomePage.aspx
9. Casola, V., De Benedictis, A., Rak, M., Rios, E.: Security-by-design in clouds: a security-SLA driven methodology to build secure cloud applications. Procedia Comput. Sci. **97**, 53–62 (2016). www.scopus.com

Towards Model-Based Security Assessment
of Cloud Applications

Valentina Casola, Alessandra De Benedictis$^{(\boxtimes)}$, and Roberto Nardone

Department of Electrical Engineering and Information Technology,
Università di Napoli Federico II, Naples, Italy
{casolav,alessandra.debenedictis,roberto.nardone}@unina.it

Abstract. Security issues are still posing limitations to the full exploitation of the potential of the cloud computing paradigm, and cloud developers are more and more required to take security into account from the very beginning of the development process. Unfortunately, the application of classical security best practices may be not enough due to the involvement of cloud services provided by third-parties and out of the control of the developer. In this paper, to overcome this issue, we introduce and discuss a model-based process for the security assessment of cloud applications. In particular, we suggest a complete process that can be executed within the lifecycle of a cloud application, from the requirement elicitation up to the validation (both static and dynamic through the generation and execution of suitable test cases) of the final deployment against security requirements. In this work, we sketch the process main phases and illustrate the high-level modelling languages that have been defined to describe an application at different levels of abstraction and to formalize both security requirements of applications and security features offered by existing cloud services. A running example involving the assessment of a simple yet realistic cloud application is used throughout the paper to better illustrate the proposal and to demonstrate its feasibility and effectiveness.

Keywords: Model-based security assessment · Secure cloud applications · Cloud security

1   Introduction and Motivation

Virtualization, scalability and flexibility features have enabled the widespread adoption of the cloud computing paradigm by both enterprises and individual users. However, security issues related to the protection of sensitive data stored in and passing through cloud infrastructures, and in general to the management of the security vulnerabilities that may arise when outsourcing to the cloud part or all of an enterprise's IT business, are still posing limitations to the full exploitation of the potential of cloud computing.

When developing security-critical cloud-based applications, developers should take security into account from the very beginning. This primarily

© Springer International Publishing AG 2017
M.H.A. Au et al. (Eds.): GPC 2017, LNCS 10232, pp. 773–785, 2017.
DOI: 10.1007/978-3-319-57186-7_56

requires to clearly identify the security requirements of the application, which may need the intervention of a security expert. With requirements in mind, the developer can apply best practice guidelines to implement the software pieces under his/her control in order to put in place the needed security controls. Indeed, this may be not enough, since the actual level of security of the application strongly depends on the cloud services used for its implementation and deployment.

Recently, several initiatives have been carried out in both the industrial and the academic world aimed at analyzing the main cloud security challenges and risks, and at identifying a set of guidelines to provide secure cloud services. In June 2016, the Cloud Security Alliance (CSA) has released the last version of their Cloud Control Matrix [5], a framework of cloud-oriented security controls strictly related to other relevant existing standards such as the ISO 27001/27002 [9,10] and the NIST Security Control Framework [14]. Based on the CCM controls, the CSA has prepared a questionnaire (Consensus Assessments Initiative Questionnaire [6]) that has been submitted to the main Cloud Service Providers (CSPs) for a self-assessment of the level of security they currently offer. It is worth noticing that, although this is the only information publicly available at the state of art about CSPs' security, it does not provide any guarantee regarding the security features of acquired services, while it can only be used as a starting point for a security assessment process to be conducted by the developer before the application release.

Among the different possible techniques, model-based approaches guarantee the possibility to assess the correct fulfillment of security-related requirements before the deployment of a cloud application. This would also prevent possible vulnerabilities due to misconfigurations of the acquired cloud services or to incomplete security requirements.

In this paper, we want to promote the usage of model-based approaches to assess the security of cloud applications and, with respect to the existing literature, we suggest a complete process that can be executed within the lifecycle of a cloud application, starting from the requirement elicitation and ending with the static validation of the final deployment plan against security requirements. In addition, our process devises a further step of test case generation that, based on specified requirements, suggests the execution of proper security tests aimed to validate the concrete system with respect to their correct implementation [2]. Such a process can be implemented in a general framework that would support the developer during the design, the implementation and the deployment of a cloud application.

The introduced process strongly relies on the adoption of specific high-level modeling languages, each defined with respect to a process phase. These languages enable the description of the cloud application at different levels of abstraction, from the functional/behavioral level up to the cloud deployment level, and allow to formalize both security requirements of applications and security features offered by existing cloud services. The main difference of the proposed approach with respect to the existing literature, is in the description of the cloud applications through few and well-defined concepts. In fact, the developer is not required to be a security expert, but he/she has only to identify the security requirements and the security controls he/she want to implement. The proposed process will guide him/her in the selection of suitable cloud services to map the application functionalities and will provide him/her with a formal validation of the obtained deployment plan. Moreover, since the final outcome of the proposed approach is the generation of proper security tests to run on the cloud application, the security validation does not cover only the produced models but it is conducted on the deployed system.

The paper is structured as follows. Section 2 illustrates an overview of the proposed security assessment process and presents a case study application that will be used as a running example to help the reader better understand the process phases. Section 3 discusses in detail each phase of the proposed process by also providing concrete examples. Section 4 discusses some related work on model-based security assessment. Finally, Sect. 5 draws our conclusions and sketches future directions.

2   Model-Based Security Assessment Process Overview

In this section, the proposed model-based security assessment process is sketched. As anticipated in Sect. 1, it is part of a more general framework including tools and techniques able to support a cloud developer in all the phases of an application design and development. The security assessment process is depicted in the upper box in Fig. 1, while the lower box represents the actual application development process, which is carried out in parallel and produces the software artifacts for the implementation of the application by also taking care of the acquisition and configuration of the cloud resources needed for their execution.

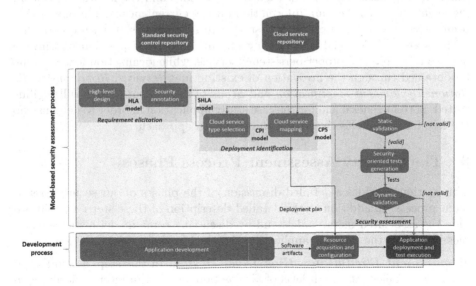

Fig. 1. Model-based security assessment process

As shown in the figure, the security assessment process consists of three main phases, namely (i) *Requirement elicitation*, (ii) *Deployment identification* and (iii) *Security assessment*, which in turn include a set of sub-phases that will be described in detail in the next section. In the first phase, the functional and security requirements of the application are specified through proper high-level architectural models. In the second phase, the developer identifies the cloud resources to use for the implementation and deployment of the application. The result of this phase is an enhanced model of the application that takes into account the deployment aspects. In the third phase, the selected deployment is validated to verify that (security) requirements set in the first phase have been correctly met. Validation is carried out in two steps: first, a static validation is performed based on the models produced in the previous phases; then, if the static validation succeeds, a dynamic validation based on the execution of suitable security-oriented tests follows. As shown in the figure, based on the feedback obtained by the static validation phase, some of the above phases and respective sub-phases may be re-iterated with the purpose of removing existing flaws and obtaining a cloud application that formally satisfies the requirements. The feedback coming from the dynamic validation phase, instead, may be used to refine the application development phase by updating the generated software artifacts or the deployment/configuration parameters.

Running Example. The running example, used in the following to describe in detail the entire process, is represented by a cloud-based application that allows people to localize their friends on a map and to communicate with them via instant messaging to organize events and meetings. As a general requirement, the application is meant to offer a web-based interface to users, by which they can create and manage a personal account, set and manage connections with other (friend) accounts, register their own positions and the location of upcoming events on a map, obtain information on the current position of one of their friend accounts or of an event, and start a messaging session with one of their friend accounts. Personal accounts, events and associated position information have to be stored in a proper persistence service, while localization features must be obtained through the invocation of existing map services. *Requirement elicitation*, *Deployment identification* and *Security assessment* phases will be illustrated, both in general and for the case study application in order to demonstrate the feasibility and effectiveness of the proposed approach.

3   The Security Assessment Process Phases

This section provides a detailed discussion of the phases of our security assessment process. In addition to the detailed description of these steps, we will provide the associated meta-models and by discussing some model instance examples related to the example application sketched in the previous section.

Requirement Elicitation - High-Level Design. In this step, a cloud application is modeled, at a high-level of abstraction, as a set of interconnected components. The *high-level architecture* (HLA) model of the application obtained as a result of this phase has to be compliant with the meta-model shown in Fig. 2, where the two entities `Component` and `Link` are considered.

For what concerns the case study application, we assume that the components identified by the developer are the following: (1) *web application*, by which the users interact with the system, asking for the localization and messaging functionalities; (2) *database* devoted to storing the users' profiles, friendship relations, messages and all other data; (3) *map service* offering earth maps used by the application to localize friends. The HLA model of the case study application is shown in Fig. 3. In this model, the three components are depicted as three ovals, while the communication links are represented by dotted arrows. As shown, communication links are present between the *web application* and the *database* and between the *web application* and the *map service*.

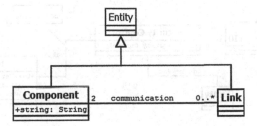

Fig. 2. High-level architectural meta-model

Fig. 3. Case study high-level architectural model

Requirement Elicitation - Security Annotation. In the second step of the process, the HLA model is annotated with the security requirements. In our process, the developer, possibly aided by a security expert, specifies the security requirements of each application component in terms of the *security controls* that the component must implement. Needed security controls may be either known at the beginning of the development process or derived through a different procedure. In [4] for example, the Authors discuss the application of a risk assessment procedure to get security requirements of an application.

Security controls are stored in the **standard security control repository** (see Fig. 1), which includes, for each control, the set of associated *metrics* (if any). A metric is a parameter that can be used as a requirement in the configuration of the implementation of a control: e.g., the developer may require that the NIST *SC-8* control - *Transmission confidentiality and integrity* - be implemented through the set-up of the SSL `protocol` based on an RSA `cryptosystem` with `key-length` equal to 1024. Parameters `protocol`, `cryptosystem` and `key-length` are the metrics associated with control SC-8. Note that a metric may be associated with more than one control, and a control may have no associated metrics. When annotating a component or a link, the developer must specify the needed control IDs and, for each control (when applicable), the required conditions over associated metrics. A metric condition is expressed by the triple: `<metric_ID, qualifier, V>`, where `qualifier` is a relational operator and `V` is a value or a range of values.

The Security annotation phase has the *Security-annotated High-Level Architecture* (SHLA) model as output. The associated meta-model is reported in Fig. 4. Note that security controls and metrics can be associated to generic entities, namely to components and links.

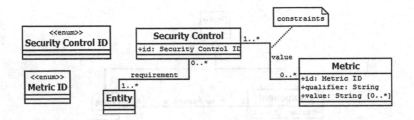

Fig. 4. Security-annotated high-level architectural meta-model

The SHLA model of the chosen case study is depicted in Fig. 5. In this application, both the *web application* component and the *database* component must implement the security control *AC-2: Account Management*: the needed policies to assign account managers, to establish conditions for a group and role membership and so on must be ensured by both this components. In addition, the *web application* component must guarantee the following controls:

- *AC-2(5): inactivity logout*, with an inactivity logout time lower or equal than 180 s;
- *AC-2(7): role-based schemes*;
- *AC-7: unsuccessful logon attempts*, with a maximum of 3 consecutive unsuccessful access attempts and a lock time period of 15 min.

The *database* component must guarantee the security control *AC-2(5): inactivity logout*, with an inactivity logout time lower or equal than 10 s. In addition, it has also to offer the control *CP-6: alternate storage site* that requires the presence of an alternate storage site. Specifically, the developers needs 2 replicas, properly located in North America, South America or Asia but not in Europe (since the main server is located there). She/he has to annotate this information by using the metrics *allowed regions* and *denied regions*, that can be used within the context of the control *CP-6*.

Finally, the control *SC-8: transmission confidentiality and integrity* must be guaranteed on the communication link between the *web application* component and the *database* component. The developer specifies that the adopted protocol must be SSL using a cryptosystem implemented through the RSA algorithm with a key length of 256 bits. No security requirement is set both for the *map service* and for its communication link with the *web application* component.

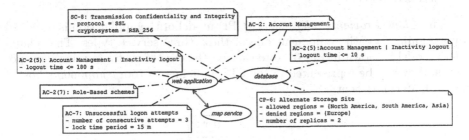

Fig. 5. Case study - security-annotated high-level architectural model

Deployment Identification - Cloud Service Type Selection. The HLA model is abstract and does not contain any information about the actual implementation of components and their use of cloud resources; the developer has now to identify the cloud service types to assign to each application component. In the *cloud service type section* step, the developer assigns to each component a cloud service type, which will be used in the next step for the actual mapping onto existing cloud services.

Due to the strongly heterogeneous current cloud landscape, classifying cloud application components is not an easy task. Nevertheless, from a high-level point of view, it is possible to identify a few general categories of components based on their deployment model. In this discussion, we consider three main types of components:

- *SaaS components*: they consist in pre-built pieces of software offering specific functionalities through a web interface according to the Software-as-a-Service paradigm (e.g., an online support service like Zendesk or a map service like Google Maps). These components are not under the control of the developer, who is solely responsible for their invocation.
- *Custom-on-IaaS components*: they represent pieces of software developed/ configured ad-hoc that need cloud-based resources for their execution. The resources considered here are basically virtual machines (VMs), of a specific *size* (current providers offer several types of VMs based on the number of CPU cores and on the RAM and HD capacity) and running a specific operating system. An example of custom-on-IaaS component is a web application component: the software is completely developed ad-hoc but it needs a web server hosted by a virtual machine to be executed. Another example may be a custom database component: even in this case, the database is completely managed by the developer who is also responsible for the installation and configuration of the underlying DBMS, which runs on a virtual machine.

– *IaaS component*: they represent servers, storage, network and operating systems delivered as-a-service. A typical IaaS component is a virtual machine. One different example of IaaS component is a storage-as-a-service component like Amazon S3, which offers a web-based interface to access and manage buckets of objects.

The *Cloud Provider-Independent* (CPI) model of the application is obtained by assigning to each component one of these three service types. The related meta-model is shown in Fig. 6. Note that, in the case of custom-on-IaaS components, they will be represented in the CPI model as custom components hosted by an IaaS component.

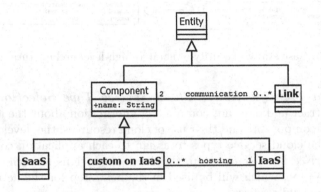

Fig. 6. Cloud provider-independent meta-model

The CPI model of the considered case study is shown in Fig. 7. As formalized by this model, the developer requires that the *map service* and the *database* component be offered as a SaaS and an IaaS component, respectively. The *web application* is instead developed as a custom-on-IaaS component running on a virtual machine (IaaS).

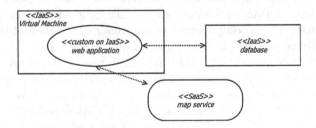

Fig. 7. Case study - cloud provider-independent model

Cloud Service Mapping. In the *cloud service mapping* step, the developer obtains (either manually or by an automated process) the *Cloud Provider-Specific* (CPS) model of the application, which identifies the concrete cloud resources that must be acquired by the developer to deploy the application

components. We assume that a set of available cloud services of the SaaS and
IaaS type is initially known, among which the developer can select the services
to assign to logical components. For what regards custom-on-IaaS components,
their mapping onto cloud services involves the sole IaaS infrastructure (i.e., the
virtual machines) used for their deployment and execution.

Available cloud services are stored in the **cloud service repository** in form
of suitable models that include also the provided security features, in the same
format used for annotating the high-level component in the SHLA model (i.e.,
controls and respective metric conditions). When a specific service is selected in
the CPS model to map a logical component, the set of security controls that have
been declared for the service is used to annotate the corresponding component,
as shown in the meta-model of Fig. 8.

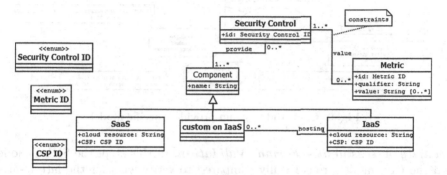

Fig. 8. Cloud provider-specific meta-model

Note that, in the case of custom-on-IaaS components, the developer commits
to taking care personally of the implementation of the security controls identified
in the SHLA model, since the component is under his/her control. Associated
security controls are then simply included in the CPS model to annotate the
custom component.

Note that, as shown in Fig. 1, in addition to the CPS model, the *cloud service
mapping* phase produces the *deployment plan*, which can be directly used to configure and deploy the application artifacts developed in the parallel development
phase.

In order to better explain the generation of the CPS model, let us consider
the case study application, whose CPS model is depicted in Fig. 9. As shown,
the *map service* is obtained by the *GoogleMaps* service offered by Google; no
additional annotation is needed since no security control has been requested for
this component. The *database* component is implemented through the *AmazonS3*
service offered by the Amazon CSP. With respect to the requested security controls, the annotations over this model highlight that the logout time for the
control *AC-2(5)* offered by *AmazonS3* is 20 s, while the alternate storage sites
are North America and Asia. Regarding the communication link with the web
application, this component offers from its side the possibility of communicating through the SSL protocol with the required cryptosystem. Regarding the

web application component, it has been classified as a custom-on-IaaS component, therefore the developer has committed to taking care of the implementation of the security controls that have been requested for the component in the security-annotation step, namely *AC-2(7)*, *AC-7* and *SC-8* (web application side). The security control *AC-2* must be guaranteed at both *web application* and *virtual machine* levels: both these components are linked with the related annotation. The selected IaaS container of the *web application* component is the *AmazonEC2-T1.micro* instance offered by Amazon.

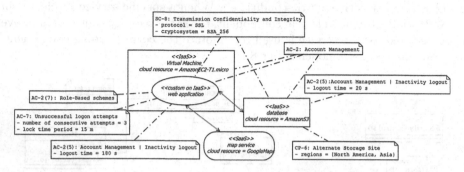

Fig. 9. Case study - cloud provider-specific model

Security Assessment - Formal Validation. In this step, the SHLA model and the CPS model are statically compared to verify whether the latter satisfies the requirements identified by the former. In particular, the controls and respective metrics declared for the cloud services selected in the CPS model are compared with those used to annotate the high-level architectural model during the Requirement elicitation phase. As shown in Fig. 1, based on the validation feedback, some of the steps of the process may be reiterated. For instance, it may be needed to update the CPI or CPS model in order to meet the requirements, since specified service types or service instances do not allow to obtain the desired security features. In other cases, if some requirements cannot be met with any of the available services, the developer may want to relax or change them in order to obtain a compromise solution.

In our case study, an inconsistency can be found in the inactivity logout time offered by the *database* component: the requirement reported in the SHLA model asked for a maximum of 10 s, while the actual IaaS service selected for its implementation implements a logout time of 20 s. This inconsistency shall be highlighted to the developer that can choose either to change the deployment plan (by selecting a different configuration of a different plan) or to continue the deployment of the cloud application by updating the requirement.

Security Assessment - Security Test Generation and Execution. If the formal validation succeeds, the dynamic validation takes place, which is carried out by means of the generation and execution of proper security tests on the running application, aimed at identifying possible flaws in the actual configuration and deployment of the application. This phase is particularly needed in presence of custom-on-IaaS components, which are developed ad-hoc with the "agreement" that they should implement the security controls (and related metrics) identified in the Security annotation step.

For example, if considering our case study, the *web application* component must ensure some specific controls that are left to the developer, who may introduce bugs in his/her software artifacts. Analogously, some errors may be raised in the deployment of the real application leading to a different configuration with respect to the modeled one. Hence, the dynamic validation steps is in charge for generating specific test cases able to stress the controls reported in the CPS model. For instance, suitable test cases may be created to check for the measurement of the logout time, or to perform known and standard penetration tests in the communication between the *web application* component and the *database* component, with the aim at assessing the correct instantiation of the SSL protocol.

Test feedback is then used to refine the development phase, in order to update the generated artifacts if needed or to change the configuration and deployment parameters.

4   Related Work

Model-based security assessment of IT infrastructures has a long story, and several approaches and solutions can be found in the literature [15]. Proposed approaches are based on combinatorial formalisms (e.g., Attack Trees [12], Bayesian Networks [13]), state-based formalisms (e.g., Markov Models, Stochastic Petri Nets), model checking (e.g., automatic attack graphs generation [1]), or on a combination of different methods and formalisms [3]. A recent trend in model-based approaches for security assessment devises the representation of the system under analysis through high-level specification languages. In fact, some existing modeling languages such as *UMLSec* [11], *cloudML* [8], *SecAM* [16], and others, allow the developer to represent the system under analysis through concepts that are familiar to him/her. From these high-level models, different evaluations can be conducted also transforming these specifications into formal models [7]. In details, *UMLSec* allows to annotate security-related information within UML diagrams in a system specification; *cloudML* allows instead to model the provisioning and deployment of a multi-cloud application at two levels of abstraction (independent and dependent from the cloud provider); *SecAM* is a UML profile allowing for attack/resilience, cryptography, security mechanisms, and access control issues to be expressed within UML models.

Compared to existing ones, our approach allows to describe a cloud application through more simple concepts that enable to model the application high-level security requirements without the need for strong security expertise. Moreover, the model-based assessment process is integrated within a more complex process aimed at guiding a developer through all the design, development and deployment phases.

5   Conclusions and Future Work

In this paper, we introduced a model-based approach for the security assessment of cloud applications, meant to support a developer in all the phases from the requirement elicitation to the identification of the application deployment configuration. We defined specific high-level modeling languages to model the application at different levels of abstraction across the main phases of the process and provided a running example to demonstrate their usage step-by-step. We introduced a two-step validation process, consisting in a static validation based on a proper model comparison, followed by a dynamic validation based on the generation and execution of security-oriented test cases.

The paper represents a work in progress, therefore we only sketched the process phases and gave an overview of the needed techniques and tools. Next steps include the (i) specification of the security models of existing cloud services, the (ii) definition of the technique to use for the static validation, the (iii) identification of suitable threat models, referred to application component types and to their possible deployments, to be used to generate the test cases.

Acknowledgment. This research is partially supported by the project MUSA (Grant Agreement no. 644429) funded by the European Commission within call H2020-ICT-2014-1.

References

1. Ammann, P., Wijesekera, D., Kaushik, S.: Scalable, graph-based network vulnerability analysis. In: Proceedings of the 9th ACM Conference on Computer and Communications Security, pp. 217–224. ACM (2002)
2. Benerecetti, M., De Guglielmo, R., Gentile, U., Marrone, S., Mazzocca, N., Nardone, R., Peron, A., Velardi, L., Vittorini, V.: Dynamic state machines for modelling railway control systems. Sci. Comput. Program. **133**, 116–153 (2017)
3. Bijani, S., Robertson, D.: A review of attacks and security approaches in open multi-agent systems. Artif. Intell. Rev. **42**(4), 607–636 (2014)
4. Casola, V., De Benedictis, A., Rak, M., Rios, E.: Security-by-design in clouds: a security-SLA driven methodology to build secure cloud applications. Procedia Comput. Sci. **97**, 53–62 (2016). 2nd International Conference on Cloud Forward: From Distributed to Complete Computing
5. Cloud Security Alliance. Cloud Control Matrix v3.0.1, June 2016. https://cloudsecurityalliance.org/download/cloud-controls-matrix-v3-0-1/
6. Cloud Security Alliance. Consensus Assessments Initiative Questionnaire v3.0.1, May 2016. https://cloudsecurityalliance.org/download/consensus-assessments-initiative-questionnaire-v3-0-1/
7. Drago, A., Marrone, S., Mazzocca, N., Nardone, R., Tedesco, A., Vittorini, V.: A model-driven approach for vulnerability evaluation of modern physical protection systems. Softw. Syst. Model., 1–34 (2016). doi:10.1007/s10270-016-0572-7
8. Ferry, N., Song, H., Rossini, A., Chauvel, F., Solberg, A.: CloudMF: applying MDE to tame the complexity of managing multi-cloud applications. In: IEEE/ACM 7th International Conference on Utility and Cloud Computing (UCC), pp. 269–277. IEEE (2014)

9. International Organization for Standardization. ISO/IEC 27001: Information technology Security techniques Information security management systems Requirements (2013)
10. International Organization for Standardization: ISO/IEC 27002:2013 Information Technology. Security Techniques, Code of Practice for Information Security Management (2013)
11. Jürjens, J.: UMLsec: extending UML for secure systems development. In: Jézéquel, J.-M., Hussmann, H., Cook, S. (eds.) UML 2002. LNCS, vol. 2460, pp. 412–425. Springer, Heidelberg (2002). doi:10.1007/3-540-45800-X_32
12. Kotenko, I., Stepashkin, M.: Attack graph based evaluation of network security. In: Leitold, H., Markatos, E.P. (eds.) CMS 2006. LNCS, vol. 4237, pp. 216–227. Springer, Heidelberg (2006). doi:10.1007/11909033_20
13. Liu, Y., Man, H.: Network vulnerability assessment using Bayesian networks. In: Defense and Security, pp. 61–71. International Society for Optics and Photonics (2005)
14. National Institute of Standards Technology. NIST SP-800-53: Recommended Security Controls for Federal Information Systems (2013)
15. Nicol, D.M., Sanders, W.H., Trivedi, K.S.: Model-based evaluation: from dependability to security. IEEE Trans. Dependable Secure Comput. 1(1), 48–65 (2004)
16. Rodríguez, R.J., Merseguer, J., Bernardi, S.: Modelling security of critical infrastructures: a survivability assessment. Comput. J. 58(10), 2313–2327 (2015)

Security Assurance of (Multi-)Cloud Application with Security SLA Composition

Massimiliano Rak$^{(\boxtimes)}$

Department of Industrial and Information Engineering,
Universitá della Campania Luigi Vanvitelli, via Roma 29, 81031 Aversa, CE, Italy
massimiliano.rak@unicampania.it

Abstract. Despite the diffusion of the cloud computing paradigm, cloud security is still considered one of the main inhibitors for the adoption of cloud-based solution. Security Service Level Agreements (Security SLAs), i.e. agreements among providers and customers that states the level of security granted on the services delivered, adopted to enable a Cloud Service Provider (CSP) to declare its security policy and a way to measure them from cloud service customer (CSC) point of view. Security SLAs, however, not completely solve the security issue in cloud when we have complex supply chains. This paper proposes a technique to automatically generate Security SLA, relying on CSP declaration and on the services, composing the application. Security SLAs and cloud applications are modeled, enabling automatic reasoning over the security offerings and the evaluation of the security policy over an orchestration of cloud services.

Keywords: Cloud security · Service Level Agreement · SecSLA · Security SLA · Security policy · Policy composition

1 Introduction

Cloud security is still considered one of the main inhibitors for the adoption of cloud-based solution in many environments. The perception of limited security is given by the loss of control that a cloud service customer (CSC) over the cloud services: What exactly are the security measures adopted by the cloud service provider (CSP)? How to verify the effective enforcement of the security policies declared by CSPs?

Security Service Level Agreements (Security SLAs), i.e. agreements among providers and customers that state the level of security granted on the services delivered, are considered nowadays the main way to address this issue: CSPs declares their security policies and a set of Service Level Objectives (SLOs) in terms of thresholds on well defined security metrics.

Even if at state of art CSPs still do not offer Security SLAs, EU Projects like SPECS [1] and SLA Ready [2] proposed models to represent in a standard way

© Springer International Publishing AG 2017
M.H.A. Au et al. (Eds.): GPC 2017, LNCS 10232, pp. 786–799, 2017.
DOI: 10.1007/978-3-319-57186-7_57

the security policies and to measure and quantify such security features. More-over, tools like the CSA STAR registry[1] and Cloud 28+[2], collects the infor-mation needed to evaluate a CSP security policy according to their security self-assessment declarations.

Security SLAs, however, do not completely solve the security issue for a cloud application: in most of the cases Security SLAs focuses on the security policy that a CSP is able to implement, but not what is granted on a specific service (as well outlined in [3] with the concept of *per-service SLA*). As a simple example consider an SLA offered by a CSP (like Amazon or Google), that states the adoption of certain security policy. Even if this offer some assurance, little can be said about the level of security of the specific virtual machine that a CSC acquires: security policies address the provider internal security organization, not the security of the VMs operating system, as an example.

This is exacerbated in the case of complex supply chains. Consider for exam-ple a CSC that acquires a software-as-a-service from a CSP which, in turn, acquires its infrastructure in cloud from another CSP: what exactly can be granted to the final end user?

Assuming that a (multi-)cloud application is an application made of multiple components deployed over resources acquired in the cloud, the above described problems can be simply synthesized in the evaluation of the Security SLA that such cloud application is able to respect, taking into account the composing services.

This paper proposes a technique to address such problem, using security SLAs as a basis to represent the security associated to each component of a (multi-)cloud application. The proposed technique derives the security SLA that can be granted by each service and component, knowing how they are relatively connected and the starting security SLA of the CSP. It is worth noticing that this paper focuses on the evaluation of the security policy granted, while we will address in future works the composition problems related to the quantitative verification of the Security SLA, i.e. the composition of SLOs.

The paper is organized as follows: next Sect. 2 briefly introduce the security SLA model and the related concepts. Section 3 describes the (simplified) model adopted to represent the cloud application and exploit the cloud application characteristics that affect the security policy. Section 4 illustrates the composi-tion technique used to derive the composite SLA and shows an example of the technique. The paper ends with a Sect. 5 that states the related work and Sect. 6 on conclusions and future work.

2   The Security SLA Model

The term security is generic and hides a large number of different requirements. As Bishop outlines [4] security requirements dictate that some actions (and system states) be allowed and others disallowed, instead a security policy is a

---

[1] https://cloudsecurityalliance.org/star/#_registry.

[2] http://www.cloud28plus.com/.

specific statement of what is and is not allowed and it defines the system's security. Security SLAs, are a recent results produced by projects like SPECS and SLA-Ready, which enable to express security policy associated to each cloud service. In the following we adopt the SPECS Security SLA model, described in detail in [5]. It is based on the WS-Agreement standard [6], which has been extended with provider-specific information and security-related concepts.

In particular, in such model, the security policy are specified in terms of the set of enforced standard security controls. According to NIST [7], security controls are *safeguard or countermeasure prescribed for an information system or an organization designed to protect the confidentiality, integrity, and availability of its information and to meet a set of defined security requirements*. The NIST control framework, similarly to ISO 27001, lists more than 900 security controls, assigning to each of them a name and a unique identifier and illustrating a detailed description that states how to correctly implement it and verify its correct implementation.

Security controls are organized in families, each of them addressing a different security domain, moving from access control (AC) to identification and authentication (IA), to media (MP) and physical environment (PE) protection. Security controls include even organizative aspects, like personnel training and planning.

In practice, the set of controls declared in a Security SLA express the security policy adopted by a provider (possibly related to a specific service) and can be used to concretely evaluate the security requirements that the provider is able to fulfill. Moreover, the proposed model expresses the Service Level Objectives (i.e. the security levels that the cloud services grants) in terms of the (security) metrics associated to such controls that can be used to monitor their correct implementation.

A security SLA built accordingly to the SPECS security SLA model can be synthetically represented using a graph-based model (named **graphSLA** model), which enables an automatic reasoning over the security policies.

The graphSLA model is defined in terms of (i) node types, which are characterized by a name and that may have specific properties, and (ii) edges, which are characterized by a name and that link only predefined node types. In graphical representations, each node type will be represented in different colors. The model assigns a property `name` to each node, which is used as logic identifier. As an example the name of a `ControlFamily` node type will be the acronym of the Control family it represents.

Table 1 summarize the different node types of the SPECS *graphSLA* model. The table has a row for each node type while columns report the type name, a description of the node type and the color used to represent it graphically.

Table 2, instead, summarizes the relationships we use in the *graphSLA* representation of the SLA. The table reports the start and end node for each relationship and a brief description that summarizes the meaning of the relationship.

Figure 1 illustrates an example of graph-based representation (please note that some links and nodes are hidden for simplicity's sake).

Table 1. The graph SLA node types

Node type	Description	Colour
Service	It represents the target service of the security SLA (i.e. the service that implements the declared security policy)	Green
SLA	It is the root node for a security SLA	Red
ControlFamily	It represent a NIST control family that have at least one security control declared as implemented in the security policy	Purple
Control	It represents a security control declared in the security policy associated to the SLA	Light red
SecurityMetric	This node represents a security metric used to verify a security control	Yellow
SLO	The node representing the Service level objective. The node has a property which is a string representation of the expression that must be respected	Blue

It is worth noticing that the SPECS Security SLA representation in WS-agreement and in graphSLA are semantically equivalent and it is always possible to move from one to the other. We developed a set of tools that enable such translations, which are publicly available on our code repositories (http://bitbucket.org/cerict/).

A SPECS Security SLA contains more information than the security policy associated to the target service (i.e. the service granted by the SLA), as an example it contains the security metrics definition and the SLOs that uses such metrics. In this paper we will focus only on the security policy granted by a Security SLA, which can be easily extracted, cutting out of the graph all the

Table 2. graphSLA relationships

Relationship	Start node	End node	Description
SecurityFamilyIn	Control family	SLA	Outlines that an SLA grants control of the ControlFamily
SecurityControlIn	Control	Control family	The security control of the family is implemented
SLOIn	SLO	SLA	The SLA grants the SLO
MeasureWith	SLO	Security metric	The SLo uses the security metric to define the objective
MetricMappedTo	Security metric	Control	The security metric gives an evidence about the implementation of the control

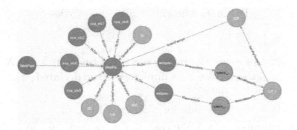

Fig. 1. An example of security SLA represented as a graph SLA (Color figure online)

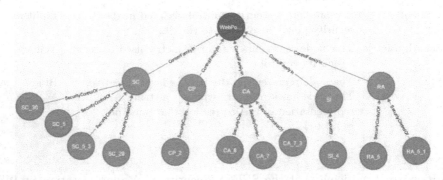

Fig. 2. An example of security policy represented as a graph SLA (Color figure online)

nodes and edges which are not used for policy representation. The result, as illustrated in Fig. 2, is a three-level tree where the first level (root) is the SLA node, the second level contains the control families and the third level the specific security controls. It is worth noticing that the tree representation assumes that controls are independent of one another, i.e. they can be independently verified.

3   (Multi-)Cloud Application and SLA Composition

The goal of this paper is to identify the Security SLA of a *cloud application*, a term we use to describe a collection of cooperating software components (simply *components*, in what follows) offered as-a-service. A component can be directly offered as-a-service by a CSP, or by deploying a suitable software artifact over a cloud service of infrastructure capability type (i.e., over a virtual machine). We will use the locution *cloud application deployment* to identify the mapping of components to resources that leads to a running cloud application by acquiring pre-deployed components provided by a CSP, and/or by deploying custom components over a set of leased virtual machines. As an example, let us consider an application made up of a web application W (i.e., a software that offers an HTTP interface) which uses a mySQL database DB. According to the above-defined terminology, W and DB are cloud application components. As shown in Fig. 3, a possible cloud application deployment can involve a single virtual

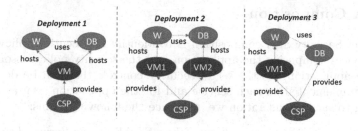

Fig. 3. Deployment examples (Color figure online)

machine that executes both W and DB; an alternative deployment requires two virtual machines, hosting W and DB, respectively; a third alternative can rely on a virtual machine hosting W, while the DB is offered directly by the CSP (in this case, the number and location of the VM(s) used for running the database service are usually unknown).

Application described as above can be described using a graph-based model, named **multicloud application composition model (MACM)**, (here described in a simplified version) that adopts the following node types:

IaaS:service a node type that represents a service of Infrastructure-as-a-service capability type, depicted in red
SaaS:service a node type that represents a service of Software-as-a-service capability type, depicted in blue
CSP a node type that represents a Cloud service Provider, depicted in green.

The relationships used in this (simplified) version of the model are illustrated in Table 3. Note that deployments illustrated in Fig. 3 are compliant with such a model. Moreover, each different deployment may result in different security policies that depend on both the policy of each component and the way in which they are inter-connected (i.e. the relationship of the **macm** model).

Table 3. graphSLA relationships

Relationship	Start node	End node	Description
Provides	CSP	Service	Describes what are the services offered directly by a CSP. It is worth noticing that they can be of any capability type
Hosts	IaaS	Service	Describes the relationship among an IaaS or PaaS service and the service which is executed on top of them
Uses	Service	SaaS	Describes the relationship among a services S and a SaaS service when S uses the software-as-a-service functionalities

4   SLA Composition

The goal of Security SLA composition is to identify the security policy of each of the services composing the application and the security policy associated to the whole application, i.e. the set of security controls that can be declared as correctly implemented on each service and for the application seen as a whole. According to such consideration we introduce the following terms:

Definition 1. *Given a service S we define SLAT(S), or Service Level Agreement Template, the document that describe the security policy S implements according to its internal configuration and not taking into account the effect of deployments.*

SLA templates are typically the result of security reviews and static declaration made trough process like certification or manual audit. It is out of the scope of this paper to illustrate such processes, for which we invite the reader to check the results of MUSA project (http://www.musa-project.eu).

Definition 2. *Given a service S we define SLA(S) the SLA that the service is able to grant taking into account the effect of deployments.*

As illustrated in Fig. 4, the security composition process translates each SLAT associated to the services to a SLA. It is worth noticing that the CSP always exposes an SLA, which is the starting point of our composition rules and does not vary, independently of the involved components (the CSP offer always the same grants). Moreover, MACM is able to assign the responsibility of the SLAs and, in case of violation, identify who is responsible in case of complex deployment schemes; description of this feature is out of the scope of this paper.

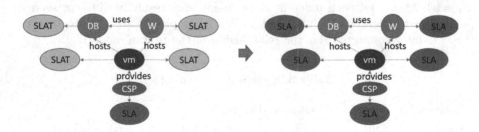

Fig. 4. The SLA composition process

The main assumption we make is that each security control is independent of the others and can be independently verified. According to such consideration, the SLA composition process takes place for each control of the standard framework. As an example, two completely independent processes will be carried out to verify control AC-2 (that states the rules adopted to manage accounts in the access control) and to verify control AC-3 (that verifies the authorization enforcement mechanisms).

4.1   Notation and Evaluation of SLA Terms

We will use the following notation: N indicate the set of all the nodes in the graph of cardinality n, $N_i \in N$ denotes one single node. Moreover, SCs indicates the set of all the controls and $c_j \in SCs$ a single security control, a family of controls like AC, will be represented as a set with the ID of the family, as an example AC is the Access Control Family.

We use the notation $\text{SLA}(c_j, N_i)$ to indicate the boolean variable that assumes value 1 if the service associated to node N_i declares the security control c_j in its policy, 0 otherwise. Similarly $\text{SLAT}(c_j, N_i)$ is the boolean variable associate to the SLA templates. Moreover, we denote $\text{SLA}(c_j, \text{app})$ the boolean variable that assumes value 1 if the application declares the security control c_j in its policy, 0 otherwise.

According to the definition of the security controls, a (multi-)cloud application has a security control declared in its policy if and only if all the services composing the application declare such control in their SLA, as expressed in Eq. 1.

$$\text{SLA}(c_j, \text{app}) = \bigwedge_1^n \text{SLA}(c_j, N_i) \tag{1}$$

It is worth noticing that the SLA of the overall application depends on the SLA of the components that, in turn, depends on their SLA templates and on the SLAs of components with which they are in relationship with. As a summary, the correct implementation of a security control over a node (i.e. a service) depends on:

- the declaration of the service itself in the SLAT of the service, that we will denote as $\text{SLAT}(c_j, N) = 1$;
- if the node has a relationship with another node, the security control implementation depends on the implementation of the control on the other node.

In order to well clarify the above concepts, let's consider the case of the web application previously illustrated in Fig. 3. If DB implements an access control system applying all the controls of the NIST family AC, but the hosting vm(s) does not have any access control (as an example enabling access to everyone) the service DB cannot declare that it correctly implements access control security controls. Such concept can be expressed, according to the proposed formalism as follows:

$$\forall c_j \in AC$$

$$\text{SLA}(c_j, \text{DB}) = \text{SLAT}(c_j, \text{DB}) \wedge \text{SLA}(c_j, \text{vm}) \tag{2}$$

Moreover, each relationship affects the security controls in different ways, as an example let's consider the case of access control for the web application W and the database DB. If DB (and the underlying vm implements correctly access control procedures, it is not relevant if W implements them or not for the

SLA of the DB itself. On the other side, if the DB does not offer any access control and the application W implements such controls, the application W still cannot declare the AC controls in its SLA, because the data stored in the DB will be not protected. As a consequence we can declare that:

$$\forall c_j \in AC$$
$$\mathrm{SLA}(c_j, W) = \mathrm{SLAT}(c_j, W) \wedge \mathrm{SLA}(c_j, vm) \wedge \mathrm{SLA}(c_j, DB) \quad (3)$$

4.2 SLA Composition Technique

SLA Composition technique relies on the considerations done above, in fact for each node N_i of MACM we can build a rule in the form of Eq. 4, taking into account all the relationship in which the node is involved and the role the node have in them.

$$\forall N_i \in N$$
$$\mathrm{SLA}(c_j, N_i) = f(\mathrm{SLAT}(c_j, N_i), \mathrm{SLA}(c_j, N_j)_{j=1..n}) \quad (4)$$

In order to write such rules, we analyzed one by one all the NIST security controls[3], summarizing the functions to involve in a set of dedicated tables, as the ones illustrated in Table 4 evaluating how each relationship affects each security control[4]. The goal of the table is to outline how each relationship affects the security control for the specific node. Note that for simplicity's sake we are reporting a table summarizing a full family of controls, but we use a per-control, set of tables in our composition tools.

Table 4. The rules for the AC family

Relationship	Node role	Rule to apply
Provides	Target	$\mathrm{SLA}(S) \wedge \mathrm{SLAT}(T) \wedge X$
Hosts	Source	$1 \wedge \mathrm{SLAT}(T) \wedge X$
Hosts	Target	$\mathrm{SLA}(S) \wedge X$
Uses	Source	$\mathrm{SLA}(T) \wedge X$
Uses	Target	$1 \wedge X$

The simple procedure adopted to create the function using the proposed table is:

- set the function to $F = X$;
- for each relationship, according to the role of the node in the relationship (i.e. source or target), substitute X with the rule proposed in the table.

---

[3] The process is in course and we have analyzed about 300 of them.

[4] Note that only some of the MACM relationships are reported in this paper.

– if all relationship where analyzed remove the last X.

According to such consideration we can build up a system of boolean equations for each security control c_j, in the variables $SLA(c_j, N_i)i = 1...n$. Each node N_i contribute to the system with an equation that summarize all the relationships in which it is involved. Moreover we have a variable $SLA(c_j, N_i)$ for each node N_i in the graph. We introduce accordingly the following definitions:

Definition 3. *The MACM model is SLA-compatible for the Security Control c_j if the equation system has at least a solution.*

Definition 4. *The MACM model is SLA-valid for the Security Control c_j if the equation system has only one solution.*

Due to space motivation, we will analyze the condition needed to grant a *SLA-valid* model and its implications in a future work. In case the system in not *SLA-valid for the Security Control c_j* the control c_j will be set to 0 to all nodes (i.e. the control is not correctly implemented).

The above approach enable us to evaluate $SLA(c_j, N_i)$ for all the controls and all the nodes and, applying Eq. 1, to evaluate even $SLA(c_j, app)$.

4.3 An Example of Composition

In order to fully illustrate the above example we will show how to apply the process for the simple application according to the application in Fig. 4. This example was built taking into account a real (and much more complex) application deployed over a public CSP (maintained anonymous in this paper) and using a common Ubuntu 16.4 linux distribution as a base image for the virtual machine vm. Table 5 summarizes in the first four column the information available for the composition: in the first column a 1 indicate that the security control is available in the offerings from the CSP, similarly a 1 in the second, third and fourth column means that the SLA Template of VM, DB or W respectively contains the control in the row.

Please note that for this simple example we used only few security controls of the AC family, whose composition rules are already exposed in Table 4.

Applying the composition technique, for each security control (a row in the table) we proceed with an independent composition process. Accordingly for each of the nodes in the MACM (VM, DB and W) we generate an equation, taking into account all the relationship for which each node is involved in. Applying the procedure described previously the result is the system 5. The fifth, sixth and seventh columns in Table 5 illustrate the results of solving the system 5 using the first four column as parameters (in all the cases the application demonstrated to be *SLA-valid*). The Last column in the table contains 1 if the overall application has the security control in its SLA, applying the Eq. 1.

$$\begin{cases} SLA(c_j, vm) = SLA(c_j, CSP) \wedge SLAT(c_j, vm) \\ SLA(c_j, DB) = SLA(c_j, CSP) \wedge SLAT(c_j, DB) \wedge SLA(c_j, vm) \\ SLA(c_j, W) = SLA(c_j, CSP) \wedge SLAT(c_j, W) \wedge SLA(c_j, vm) \wedge SLA(c_j, DB) \end{cases} \quad (5)$$

Table 5. Security SLA of the CSP and SLA templates of the nodes

Control	Input data				Output data			App
	SLA CSP	SLAT vm	SLAT DB	SLAT W	SLA vm	SLA DB	SLA W	
AC-1	1	1	1	1	1	1	1	1
AC-2	1	1	1	1	1	1	1	1
AC-2(1)	1	1	1	1	1	1	1	1
AC-2(2)	1	0	0	1	0	0	0	0
AC-2(4)	1	1	0	1	1	0	0	0
AC-2(5)	1	0	0	1	0	0	0	0
AC-2(9)	1	1	1	0	1	1	0	0
AC-3	1	1	1	1	1	1	1	1
AC-3(1)	1	1	1	1	1	1	1	1
AC-3(2)	0	0	0	0	0	0	0	0
AC-3(5)	1	1	1	0	1	1	0	0
AC-3(6)	1	0	1	0	0	0	0	0
AC-3(9)	1	1	1	1	1	1	1	1
AC-3(10)	1	1	1	0	1	1	0	0
AC-4	1	1	1	1	1	1	1	1

5   Related Work

Composition of Service Level Agreements is a topic that arised and growed up with the spread diffusion of SLA in SOA and GRID architectures, interesting proposal can be found in [8–11]. These papers have the same goals of this paper, but focuses on SLA that addresses typical performance requirements, which hardly can be reused in security contextes.

The first paper, [8], proposes a technique based on ontologies to compose SLA from different providers. SLAs are represented according two a twp-layer model: upper layer focuses on description of the SLA context (providers, Initiators) and service description, while the lower layer on the metrics details. Service orchestration is modeled as a workflow, the paper focuses on performance metrics (e.g. Response Time) and on reliability ones (e.g. MTTR).

[9] proposes a tool (CASCO) that aims at supporting the creation of SLA for a service based on service composition. It relies on WS Agreement [6] and aims at proposing a user-friendly approach to write down the rules, taking into consideration the services used. It gives no details about the correctness and effective usability of the SLA, but only on the usability of the tool.

[10,11] suggests the idea of provider and service level SLAs, the main assumption is that each service publishes its own SLAs. Their approach focuses on searching services according to requirements using information extracted from SLA.

Regarding security policies, instead [12] and its extended version [13], proposes a general purpose framework for policy composition in SOA architectures.

Policies are expressed in WS-policy and includes access control and data protection policies. It uses a logic-based approach for policy composition and uses prolog to evaluate policy composition.

[14] explores the concept of defeasible policy composition, wherein policies are represented in defeasible logic and composition is based on rules for nonmonotonic inference. The paper addresses policy composition in the context of SOA and uses WS-policy as a language fo policy representation, which are made of SAML assertions. The paper offers a mathematical model to derive the assertions starting from the policy of composed services.

The Aniketos project, [15], proposes a framework in which applications are described in terms of workflow, using a dedicated language (BPMN). The Aniketos platform enable to compose services adopting set of predefined composition plans and it is able to derive the security policy and the respect of security requirements of the orchestrating application using different XML languages (described in [16]) respectively for policy and policy composition description.

The main limit of security composition approaches is the difference among abstract representation of security in policies and the concrete system behaviour. [17] proposes a language for describing security policy in SOA applications. The goal is to specify security attributes in order to identify possible security flaws. The proposed language enable representation of abstract and concrete policies being the first ones linked to requirements and the second one (concrete policies) related to the implementation in terms of mechanisms. The language supports automatic generation of concrete policies from abstract ones. The paper lack in the description of the final implementation, as an example in demonstrating how the policy can be used to configure a firewall, which is declared as one of the possible objectives. The proposed technique is interesting, but, in our opinion relies it is hardly applicable in real contexts, except for specific security domains (like the configuration of the firewall proposed in the paper).

In practice the main limits of the security policy composition techniques is the security assurance problem. Such a problem can be addressed in a similar way, as outlined in [18] that focuses on security assurance, defined as to be the objective confidence that an entity meets its security requirements. The paper model the aggregation problem as the process of aggregation n-tuples, which represent specific security attributes, into a single value.

The approach proposed on this paper, as illustrated above, relies on the usage of standard security controls for the policy declarations, which are commonly used in certification processes and are proven to be effective. The resulting policies are more high level, but offer clear specification of the security level offered to customers. The main drawback of our approach is due to the difficulties of applying the rules to controls described in natural language. The results of projects like SPECS [1], that offered a way to represent formally and automatically reason over such models enable finally to use the controls in an automated way, as illustrated in this paper.

6 Conclusions and Future Works

In this paper we proposed a composition technique that enable to evaluate the security policy, expressed in terms of standard security controls and used to declare a security SLA, of an application made of orchestrated cloud services. The technique relies on graph-based models that synthesize the main features of the SLAs and of the distributed application. The paper has illustrated a technique to produce the composed security SLA, using information available in the context of the MUSA project, whose tools enable to concretely deploy the application and monitor the security SLA. The results proposed in this paper will be improved in future works on this topic, as outlined in the paper: a extended version of this paper will explore the properties of the equations used to derive the SLAs, in order to show that the problem has always a solution. Moreover the quantitative aspects of the SLA will be addressed, showing how to compose, similarly, the service level objectives. An additional work will focus on completing the analysis of the NIST framework, in order to cover all the security controls, and proposing a technique to compose policies declared using different security control frameworks. Last but no least, we aims at removing the security control independence assumption, in order to enable more complex policy representations.

Acknowledgment. This research is partially supported by the grant H2020-ICT-07-2014-644429 (MUSA). The author would like to thank Marco Toscano, whose work during the master degree thesis was partially reused in this paper.

References

1. Casola, V., De Benedictis, A., Rak, M., Villano, U.: Preliminary design of a platform-as-a-service to provide security in cloud. In: CLOSER - Proceedings of the 4th International Conference on Cloud Computing and Services Science, Barcelona, Spain, 3–5 April, pp. 752–757 (2014)
2. SLA Ready Consortium: The SLA ready project web site (2015). http://www.sla-ready.eu/
3. Casola, V., De Benedictis, A., Modic, J., Rak, M., Villano, U.: Per-service security SLA: a new model for security management in clouds. In: 2016 IEEE 25th International Conference on Enabling Technologies: Infrastructure for Collaborative Enterprises (WETICE), pp. 83–88, June 2016
4. Bishop, D.M.: What is computer security? IEEE Secur. Priv. **1**, 67–69 (2003). University of California
5. Casola, V., De Benedictis, A., Rak, M., Modic, J., Erascu, M.: Automatically enforcing security SLAs in the cloud. IEEE Trans. Serv. Comput. (2016, preprints)
6. Andreieux, A.: Web services agreement specification (2007). https://www.ogf.org/documents/GFD.107.pdf
7. NIST: SP 800-53 Rev 4: recommended security and privacy controls for federal information systems and organizations. National Institute of Standards and Technology, Technical report (2013). http://nvlpubs.nist.gov/nistpubs/SpecialPublications/NIST.SP.800-53r4.pdf

8. Liu, H., Bu, F., Cai, H.: SLA-based service composition model with semantic support. In: IEEE Asia-Pacific Services Computing Conference (2012)
9. Zappatore, M., Longo, A., Bochicchio, M.A.: SLA composition in service networks. In: Proceedings of the 30th Annual ACM Symposium on Applied Computing - SAC 2015, pp. 1219–1224. ACM Press, New York (2015). http://dl.acm.org/citation. cfm?doid=2695664.2699490
10. Bennani, N., Guegan, C., Musicante, M., Solar, G.: SLA-guided data integration on cloud environments. In: IEEE International Conference on Cloud Computing, CLOUD, pp. 934–935 (2014). http://www. scopus.com/inward/record.url?eid=2-s2.0-84919799134&partnerID=40& md5=ca5042e7d0fe0b96389d1cc764acd78c
11. Bennani, N., Ghedira-Guegan, C., Vargas-Solar, G., Musicante, M.A.: Towards a secure database integration using SLA in a multi-cloud context. Constraint no. 2 (2015)
12. Satoh, F., Tokuda, T.: Security policy composition for composite services. In: 2008 Eighth International Conference on Web Engineering, pp. 86–97. IEEE, July 2008. http://ieeexplore.ieee.org/document/4577872/
13. Satoh, F., Tokuda, T.: Security policy composition for composite web services. IEEE Trans. Serv. Comput. 4(4), 314–327 (2011). http://ieeexplore.ieee.org/document/5560635/
14. Lee, A.J., Boyer, J.P., Olson, L.E., Gunter, C.A.: Defeasible security policy composition for web services. In: Proceedings of the Fourth ACM Workshop on Formal Methods in Security - FMSE 2006, pp. 45–54 (2006). http://portal.acm.org/ citation.cfm?doid=1180337.1180342
15. Errico, M.D., Malmignati, F., Andreotti, G.F.: A platform for secure and trustworthy service composition, pp. 67–72 (2014)
16. Zhou, B., Llewellyn-Jones, D., Shi, Q., Asim, M., Merabti, M., Lamb, D.: A compose language-based framework for secure service composition. In: 2012 International Conference on Cyber Security, SocialInformatics, pp. 195–202. IEEE, December 2012. http://ieeexplore.ieee.org/lpdocs/epic03/wrapper.htm? arnumber=6542544ieeexplore.ieee.org/document/6542544/
17. Dell'Amico, M., Serme, G., Idrees, M.S., de Olivera, A.S., Roudier, Y.: HiPoLDS: a security policy language for distributed systems. In: Askoxylakis, I., Pöhls, H.C., Posegga, J. (eds.) WISTP 2012. LNCS, vol. 7322, pp. 97–112. Springer, Heidelberg (2012). doi:10.1007/978-3-642-30955-7_10
18. Pham, N., Riguidel, M.: Security assurance aggregation for IT infrastructures. In: ICSNC, pp. 37–39 (2007)

Security Issues in Cloud Computing

Parnian Najafi Borazjani[✉]

FireEye, Milpitas, CA, USA
Parnian.najafi@fireeye.com

Abstract. Cloud computing is a mixture of resources and services that are offered through the internet. Despite flexibility, efficiency, and lower costs, security worries and privacy issues make users skeptical of using cloud computing. In this paper, we discuss the most current security threats to cloud computing and how malicious users find a way to abuse cloud computing resources. Our work has helped security professionals and researchers understand real-life examples and trends surrounding security threats to cloud computing and how to mitigate them.

Keywords: Cloud security · Cloud computing · APT · DDOS · Data breach · Secured API · Account hijacking

1 Introduction

Cloud computing, which is becoming more ubiquitous, represents the next generation of distributed computing systems. Gartner has predicted that, by 2020, corporate no-cloud policies will be rare. Cloud computing is a mixture of hardware and software computing resources that are provided on demand via the internet. These resources can be datacenters, applications, storage, etc. Cloud computing allows organizations to focus on their core businesses rather than managing the computer infrastructure. There are different service models that can be used in the cloud.

This survey paper provides a comprehensive study of security issues in cloud computing and their respective solutions from an industry perspective. Analysis of the security issues discussed would open some issues for further research. The rest of the paper is organized as follows. Section 2 elaborates a general view of cloud computing concepts such as various cloud service models and cloud deployment models. Section 3 discusses the related work and contributions of other researchers. Section 4 discusses threats to cloud computing. Finally, Sect. 5 concludes the survey.

2 Background

Cloud computing adoption continues to grow around the world. However, security and privacy concerns affect the growth rate in different countries. Cloud computing service types and deployment types used by businesses are highly dependent on the characteristics of the required services. Cloud computing is classified based on two separate

© Springer International Publishing AG 2017
M.H.A. Au et al. (Eds.): GPC 2017, LNCS 10232, pp. 800–811, 2017.
DOI: 10.1007/978-3-319-57186-7_58

models: cloud service models and cloud deployment models. Cloud computing deployment models distinguish the size, access type, and ownership of the cloud resources. On the other hand, cloud service models merely define the types of computing services that are provided by the cloud provider. In the latter categorization, service-oriented architecture is used, which advocates the concept of "everything as a service".

2.1 Cloud Service Models

Software-as-a-Services (SaaS). In the Software-as-a-service (SaaS) model, users can remotely access and use software on demand from the internet. They do not have to install the software locally and can access the resources using their browsers. One instance of the service can allow many end users to use a specific service. In the SaaS model, users are not responsible for software installation or maintenance, as that is accommodated on Platform-as-a-Service (PaaS), Infrastructure-as-a-Service (IaaS), or directly on the cloud infrastructure's physical layer [1].

Platform-as-a-Service (PaaS). Platform-as-a-Service (PaaS) provides users with an application development environment, which can be an operating system, database, programming language execution environment, or web server. In the PaaS model, users do not have to install these platforms on their systems, as it can run on the IaaS (discussed below) or the cloud's physical layer [1].

Infrastructure as a service (IaaS). Those using infrastructure, such as hardware, storage, or servers, that can pay for the resources can run and deploy any software and operating system necessary [1] (Fig. 1).

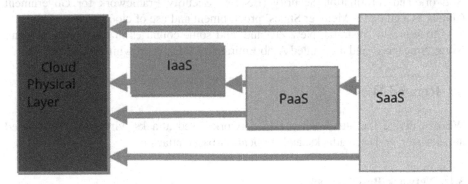

Fig. 1. Cloud computing layers [1]

2.2 Cloud Deployment Models

There are different cloud deployment models, such as public clouds, private clouds, and hybrid clouds, all of which are discussed below.

Public Cloud. The public cloud's infrastructure is hosted on the cloud provider's premises. Cloud users do not have control over the cloud infrastructure or the data hosted by the cloud provider. The infrastructure is shared between users of the same cloud, which is called co-tenant architecture.

Private Cloud. A private cloud may be built within individual organizations and dedicates resources to that single organization. A private cloud usually uses software that facilitates the cloud functionality, such as the VMware vCloud Director [2] and Open-Stack [3]. This solution is usually more expensive than the public cloud, but provides a more secure solution.

Hybrid Cloud. Organizations often have sensitive data or critical applications they want to keep in-house while, at the same time, wanting scalable services for their account. In such cases, organizations use a composition of private and public cloud infrastructures. In this way, companies can use public clouds for high-load tasks and private clouds for sensitive information.

2.3 Cloud Use Around the World

The U.S. Government has adopted a cloud-first policy for federal agencies, and the private sector has also started to adopt cloud use [4]. Many organizations have started to use special cloud-based solutions geared to the federal government.

The European Union (EU) is taking steps to move the government and public administrations to the cloud. The delayed start can be attributed to regulations and standards surrounding data sharing and privacy. The EU is using European Union Agency for Network and Information Security (ENISA) Security Framework for Government Clouds as a guide for Member States' procurement and use of cloud services [5].

Cloud use in Australia, New Zealand, and some countries in Asia, such as Hong Kong, Singapore, and the United Arab Emirates (UAE), is growing rapidly [6].

3   Related Work

We can divide the attack surface to network-based attacks, virtual machine-based attacks, storage-based attacks, and application-based attacks.

3.1 Network-Based Attacks

Cloud services depend on network connections from clients to the cloud platform. Attackers using DoS/DDOS attacks may affect the quality and availability of cloud services. These type of attacks result in temporary or permanent loss of cloud services. Riquet et al. discussed the cloud computing vulnerability to distributed attacks in detail and showed how firewalls and intrusion detection systems fail to recognize these large-scale coordinated attacks [7].

3.2 Virtual Machine-Based Attacks

Attackers may use side-channel attacks to extract the cryptographic keys, resource use, and other private data from another virtual machine that is located on the same physical machine [8, 9].

3.3 Storage-Based Attacks

A growing number of cloud services and applications take advantage of data stored on cloud computing resources. This would create a myriad of security concerns ranging from location of data, availability, integrity, sanitization, reliability, data loss and leakage, and metadata protection [10]. Private data stored on cloud storage devices may be stolen by attackers or malicious insiders [11].

3.4 Application-Based Attacks

Attackers may use malicious code injection at the application level by exploiting vulnerabilities in insecure interfaces. Moreover, attackers may embed malicious code in the files that are communicated over the network [12]. Web services and protocols may be subject to message header manipulation attacks [13].

4   Cloud Security Threats

In this section, we address the most common and novel threats to cloud computing.

4.1 Data Breaches

There is a vast amount of data stored in the cloud, making it an attractive target. If sensitive data is stored in the cloud and not properly secured, the damage could be quite severe. Different types of data, ranging from financial data and health information to trade secrets and intellectual property, are stored in the cloud, and a breach of such information could result in different fines, lawsuits, and criminal charges. In addition, a significant breach will result in additional costs related to necessary investigations and customer notifications. A breach may even damage the brand or result in the loss of business. While cloud providers are responsible for providing security controls, customers are responsible for protecting their own data. For instance, cloud providers would offer the means to encrypt the data at rest on the client and server side, but customers are responsible for incorporating them. Moreover, organizations should ensure they are using multi-factor authentication and integrating user permissions in their systems. This will help contain victimized users from excessive sharing in the event of compromise.

- Cloud-based password manager "LastPass" has experienced two data breaches. In June 2015, LastPass [14] announced that attackers had accessed email addresses, server per user salts, authentication hashes, and password reminders. In 2011,

LastPass [15] announced that it may have been breached, which may have resulted in customers' emails and password hashes being compromised.

4.2 Broken Authentication

Most of the data breaches happen due to weak passwords, sloppy authentication, or poor certificate and key management. Identity management is the key to ensuring that appropriate permissions are given to the appropriate people. In some cases, credential and cryptographic keys are stored in plain text on public-facing repositories. It is vitally important to protect keys and to use proper public key infrastructure. Appropriate key management should be in place since not only because key maintenance is imperative, but also because key revocation is important to consider. Multi-factor authentication should also be considered. The Anthem breach that exposed more than 80 million customers' data was due to stolen user credentials. Anthem did not have multi-factor authentication in place, which affected multiple brands used by Anthem [16]. Some companies leave their credential or private keys hardcoded in the source codes that are uploaded to publicly accessible repositories such as GitHub. This helps malicious users break authentication to access the accounts illegally.

• To find private keys, attackers use scripts that are used by attackers and security professionals alike. For instance, TruffleHog [17] can locate private keys as it checks the content of Github to find text blobs larger than 20 characters, and then evaluates the Shannon entropy for a hexadecimal character set and base64 character set to find high entropy strings that can be private keys.

4.3 Account Hijacking

In account hijacking attacks, attackers compromise cloud services accounts to access the data. In this attack, cloud users, not the cloud provider's systems, are typically targeted using social engineering, different methods of credential theft, and malware. Account hijacking enables attackers to modify data, plant malware, manipulate transactions, or launch other attacks from affected accounts.

• In June 2015, the Hawkeye malware [18] surfaced. This malware harvested credentials for a variety of companies and unspecified cloud services.
• Dyre malware campaigns targeted salesforce.com account credentials [19].
• Gameover Zeus [20] and Neverquest malware targeted Amazon Elastic Compute Cloud (EC2) [21].
• Actors traded compromised Dropbox accounts on underground communication channels [22].

4.4 Hacked APIs and Interfaces

Organizations use APIs to connect to cloud services and applications, making them the most exposed part of the system. Therefore, any problems in APIs and interfaces may expose the inner systems. Common attack vectors for API are parameter attacks, identity attacks, and man-in-the-middle (MiTM) attacks.

Parameter attacks exploit data such as URL, HTTP header, query parameters, and the http request content that is sent to the API (e.g., SQL injection). Identity attacks can exploit vulnerabilities in authentication, authorization, and sessions. MiTM attacks can alter the data in flight, replay requests, or reveal confidential data when unsigned or unencrypted data is passed.

Solutions such as IP address restriction can help secure the APIs. Organizations may deny or accept requests from some users originating from particular IP addresses. Monitoring use patterns and access locations can help identify denial-of-service (DoS) attacks. Heavy nested data structures and enormous messages can also be signs of a DoS attack. An API key is sometimes used in place of personal identifiers. In such cases, if the API key is not properly secured, the personal identifier can be determined, so the API key should not be treated as an authoritative credential. The use of unencrypted API keys is another issue; if the key is being intercepted by attackers, they can reuse it. In this way, the receiver cannot determine the legitimacy of the source. To detect malicious content, APIs should decode the attachments and submit them to an anti-virus scanner before being transferred to its destination. Another important issue is using SSL/TLS in the API to protect it from MiTM attacks. Correct configuration of SSL/TLS is important to ensure that it is not vulnerable to downgrade attacks.

Since the APIs provide the documentation for connection and use, and database mapping is obvious, it is easier to determine whether an API is vulnerable to a SQL injection attack. The best way to mitigate this vulnerability is to sanitize the inputs and evaluate the data that enters the organization against the schema of legitimate inputs.

- A notable data breach due to an insecure API included the U.S. Internal Revenue Service (IRS) having 300,000 IRS records exposed due to a vulnerability in the API [23].

4.5 System Vulnerability Exploitation

Attacks targeting system vulnerabilities in cloud infrastructure can be more devastating. Resources on the cloud may be shared between several organizations or different parts of organizations. Therefore, the vulnerabilities may pose a bigger problem in the cloud computing environment. Regular vulnerability scanning and proper change control processes that facilitate prompt patch management can prove beneficial in limiting damage. Below is an example of a widespread vulnerability that adversely affected cloud services.

- In January 2015, the widely reported "FREAK" vulnerability affected more than 600 cloud services. It is unknown how widely the vulnerability was exploited [24].

4.6 Malicious Insider

Malicious insider attacks involve employees affiliated with cloud service providers abusing their privilege access to perform malicious activity. Attacks can range from data theft and data manipulation to destroying the entire infrastructure. Limiting user access, logging and monitoring system changes, and proper use of encryption can minimize insider threats.

- A developer at AWS mistakenly deleted some instructional data for the provider's Elastic Load Balancing (ELB) service, which resulted in some customers' web assets being inaccessible for almost 24 h. It was an unintentional incident, but illustrates the damage a malicious employee can cause [25].

4.7 Data Loss

Criminals are increasingly using ransomware to target businesses rather than individuals. Since the impact on businesses is greater, there is a higher probability they will make the payment. Malicious hackers or malware are known to permanently delete cloud data, which is done for several reasons ranging from covering their tracks to harming the business. To avoid this situation, cloud providers should distribute the data across multiple regions. Back-up best practices should be used in addition to a daily online data backup; it is also critical to maintain offsite storage. If back-up workstations are connected to the network, ransomware can also lock data on the back-up drives. If cloud users are encrypting the data they save on the cloud, they should ensure they use proper key management. If they lose the key, they will also lose the data.

4.8 Liability Due to Inadequate Due Diligence

It is essential to perform due diligence to understand all risks associated with using the cloud environment as well as the legal and compliance responsibilities that accompany cloud use. Responsibilities regarding incident response procedures, encryption compliance requirements, and security standards should be clearly determined. Data ownership and availability are other issues that should be considered.

- In March 2013, researchers discovered that several companies using cloud storage on the Amazon's Simple Storage Service (S3) set their buckets as public, exposing billions of pieces of customer data to the public. Although there were no indications that a breach occurred, sensitive data such as email addresses, passwords, and documents could have been accessed. This public bucket is not a vulnerability of S3, as the capability to create access control lists (ACLs) is present. In this case, bucket owners misconfigured it and exposed sensitive data [26].

4.9 Abuse of Cloud Service Technology

Cloud platforms provide attackers with complete anonymity and an extensive range of hacking capabilities at little or no cost. Many cloud providers offer their services for free for a limited period to attract more customers. Attackers use these marketing specials to sign up using fake credentials and launch their attacks using the vast capabilities provided by the cloud. The same person may use another fake identity as soon as the old one is burned or the trial period is over.

Hackers may also use cloud services to scale their computing capabilities. In 2015, Imperva revealed a man-in-the-cloud (MiTC) attack [27]. Using this method, attackers can authenticate to the cloud-based storage by stealing a token (created when the cloud syncing service, which is usually encrypted, is used on a user's computer for the first time). As a result, hackers do not need to know targeted users' credentials. Attackers can then access users' files, steal their information, or even add malware to their cloud storage.

The auto sync technology in cloud services may allow malicious software installed on one of the machines to spread to other machines and networks. These sync mechanisms encapsulate the files in cloud storage traffic, which results in the malicious files easily passing through the firewall. This issue clearly depicts the trade-off between usability and security.

APT29 used Hammertoss [28], which communicates with compromised web servers or online storage repositories such as Github to download contents that usually use steganography to conceal encrypted commands. The malware later uploads captured victim data to cloud storage services when the instruction contains the username and password for cloud storage in the code.

The backdoor LOWBALL uses the legitimate cloud-storage service as command and control (C&C) server and communicates over TCP port 443. The Dropbox API uses a hard-coded bearer access token, and the malware can download, upload, and execute files. In one case, a threat group monitored the Dropbox account to see the responses from compromised computers and placed a file that contained the commands to be executed on the target computer. The results were later uploaded to the Dropbox account [29].

In some cases, cloud providers are used to distribute breached data. For instance, in 2012, Turkish hacking group Redhack [30] used Dropbox to release the identities and photos of hundreds of foreign diplomats in Turkey.

Attackers may add or modify an executable file in users' virtual storage to infect other users in the network with malicious code. They may change the file to match a specific user's activity or modify documents to contain executable malicious code such as ActiveX and macros, and then re-upload them to the cloud.

Cloud security providers may have their brands abused, and cloud services may host malware or be exploited to serve as a launching pad for malware. For example, we have noted that the Dridex malware campaign hosted malicious files on Dropbox [31]. Moreover, a malicious email campaign incorporated Office356 in the "from" address to enhance its perceived legitimacy. We have seen several instances in which cloud services were used as the C&C server.

In general, cloud services can be used to conduct nefarious activities such as launching distributed denial-of-service (DDoS) attacks, hosting malware or phishing infrastructure, automating vulnerability searching, conducting network reconnaissance, deceiving intrusion protection system (IPS) for remote port scanning, and conducting a variety of other attacks ranging from client-side attacks to cracking passwords.

Below are some real-life examples of these abuses:

- Some malware families such as Neverquest [32] and Gameover Zeus [13] include AWS among their keywords for credential collection [14].

- In 2014, compromised EC2 credentials were used for destructive activity against CodeSpaces [33] following an extortive DDoS attack that resulted in its end of service.

4.10 Distributed Denial-of-Service

DDoS attacks against cloud providers are usually conducted to extort money from customers or the provider and can also make the asset unavailable. These attacks can financially impact targeted companies, as they will be required to spend more on resources to combat attacks. DDoS attacks can not only affect the availability of the services in the short run, they may also affect their availability in the long term. In many cases, companies using cloud services that are being adversely affected by DDoS attacks must invest in additional anti-DDoS resources to withstand or mitigate those attacks.

- The Dyn DDoS attack [34] was big enough to break the internet. Cloud providers that relied on DNS service from Dyn were affected [35, 36].
- In May 2015, cloud provider HotSchedules, which hosts services for the restaurant industry, was reportedly hit by a 45-h DDoS attack, with traffic ranging from 10–15 Gbps. The attack was unusual in that it was not accompanied by a demand for money, making attackers' motives unclear [37].

4.11 Shared Threats

Since cloud security providers use shared infrastructure and applications, a vulnerability in either one affects all who are using the cloud. For example, if a vulnerability is found at the hypervisor level, all hosts on that hypervisor may be affected. Therefore, it is extremely important to ensure that host- and network-based intrusion detection systems are used. Moreover, it is important to segment the network on the cloud, even when the same tenant is using the whole cloud; cloud providers do not want the infection or attack to spread due to a lack of security measures. It is also important to ensure that these resources are properly patched and use strong authentication methods (perhaps multi-factor authentication). Sharing resources may result in leaked information if resources are not properly isolated. We have seen side-channel attacks being used on the VM to extract private keys. Moreover, researchers have found instances of Java VM sandbox escape.

4.12 Phishing

In 2016, cloud storage ranked among the most phished industry, and researchers have stated that there is a strong possibility that cloud storage services will be the most targeted industry in 2017. Phishing attacks targeting cloud service providers are mostly impacting two companies - Google (Google Drive/Docs) and Dropbox [38]. Researchers have found that phishing attacks targeting SaaS companies have tripled in 2016 as compared to 2015. Moreover, phishing attacks have increasingly affected cloud storage sites such as Adobe (adobeID) and DocuSign. In addition, targeting of Webmail and online services doubled from 2013 to 2016 [38]. Researchers have found that the major vulnerability in cloud storage services and SaaS is due to reusing email usernames and passwords as account credentials on cloud services [38]. Basically, email addresses are replaced as unique usernames, and some users may use the same password as their email password. Therefore, attackers can easily harvest username and password pairs via phishing attacks.

Attackers are targeting sites with massive user bases to harvest email address and password pairs. In addition, cloud domains are being used to host phishing content (a U.S.-based cloud services provider was subject to a phishing campaign in Aug/September 2016).

4.13   Espionage Activity on Cloud Providers

Cloud service providers are sometimes targeted due to their use of cutting-edge technology, but they also possess proprietary IPs and work with the government, making them perfect targets for commercial cyber espionage. For example, in late 2014, APT1 [39] targeted and stole data from a company that provided innovative cloud-based services and solutions to the federal government.

5   Conclusion

Some businesses mistakenly believe that cloud providers are addressing all these security needs, but providers and users have a mutual obligation to protect their assets. This paper presents a comprehensive industry focused survey on cloud security issues and the best-known counter measures available to cloud providers. Companies should identify entry points by scanning public-facing websites, gather information about those sites, and scan internal networks for vulnerabilities. It is also important to educate cloud users about spear-phishing and social engineering techniques that are commonly used to gain a foothold in or infect the network.

References

1. Almorsy, M., Grundy, J., Müller, I.: An analysis of the cloud computing security problem (2016). arXiv preprint arXiv:1609.01107
2. VMware vCloud Director. https://www.vmware.com/products/vcloud-director.html
3. OpenStack. https://www.openstack.org/software/
4. OMB announces 'cloud first' policy for agencies, Federal News Radio, 23 November 2010, and Jeffrey Zients, "Driving IT Reform: An Update," Office of Management and Budget, 19 November 2010. http://www.federalnewsradio.com/?nid=249&sid=2129860
5. ENISA. https://www.enisa.europa.eu/publications/security-framework-for-govenmental-clouds
6. Cloud usage in APAC. http://www.asiacloudcomputing.org/images/documents/cri2016_acca.pdf
7. Riquet, D., Grimaud, G., Hauspie, M.: Large-scale coordinated attacks: Impact on the cloud security. In: 2012 Sixth International Conference on Innovative Mobile and Internet Services in Ubiquitous Computing, Palermo, pp. 558–563 (2012). doi:10.1109/IMIS.2012.76, http://ieeexplore.ieee.org/stamp/stamp.jsp?tp=&arnumber=6296915&isnumber=6296822

8. Zhang, Y., Juels, A., Reiter, M.K., Ristenpart, T.: Cross-VM side channels and their use to extract private keys. In: Proceedings of the 2012 ACM Conference on Computer and Communications Security, pp. 305–316. ACM, 16 October 2012
9. Tandon, S., Srushti, S.B., Agrawal, V.: Cache-based side-channel attack on aes in cloud computing environment. Int. J. Eng. Res. Technol. **3**(10), 1080–1084 (2014)
10. Hussein, N.H., Khalid, A., Khanfar, K.: A Survey of Cryptography Cloud Storage Techniques (2016)
11. Cloud Security Alliance: Secaas Implementation Guidance, Category 7: Security Information and Event Management, pp. 1–33 (2012)
12. Mazurczyk, W., Szczypiorski, K.: Is cloud computing steganography-proof? In: 2011 Third International Conference on Multimedia Information Networking and Security (MINES), pp. 441–442 (2011). http://dx.doi.org/10.1109/MINES.2011.95
13. Gruschka, N., Iacono, L.: Vulnerable cloud: Soap message security validation revisited. In: 2009 IEEE International Conference on Web Services, ICWS 2009, pp. 625–631 (2009). http://dx.doi.org/10.1109/ICWS.2009.70
14. Lastpass breach (2015). https://krebsonsecurity.com/2015/06/password-manager-lastpass-warns-of-breach/
15. Lastpass breach (2011). https://www.cnet.com/news/lastpass-ceo-reveals-details-on-security-breach/
16. Anthem Hack. https://blog.digicert.com/anthem-hack-preventable/
17. TruffleHog. https://github.com/dxa4481/truffleHog
18. Hawkeye Malware. http://www.trendmicro.es/media/wp/piercing-hawkeye-whitepaper-en.pdf
19. Dyre Malware campaigns targeting salesforce. https://help.salesforce.com/articleView?id=Security-Alert-Dyre-Malware&type=1
20. Gameover Zeus. https://aws.amazon.com/security/security-bulletins/zeus-botnet-controller/
21. Neverquest. https://www.secureworks.com/research/banking-botnets-the-battle-continues
22. Dropbox Breach. http://fortune.com/2016/08/26/heres-why-dropbox-is-urging-users-to-reset-their-passwords/
23. Insecure API case in IRS. http://www.forbes.com/sites/kurtmarko/2015/05/27/irs-hack_fido-leadership/#31e162d62df0
24. FREAK vulnerability. https://www.scmagazine.com/more-than-600-cloud-services-still-vulnerable-to-freak-data-shows/article/536548/
25. Amazon ELB Service Event. https://aws.amazon.com/message/680587/
26. Misconfiguration consequences in Amazon S3 buckets. https://community.rapid7.com/community/infosec/blog/2013/03/27/1951-open-s3-buckets
27. Man-In-The-Cloud-Attack. https://www.imperva.com/docs/HII_Man_In_The_Cloud_Attacks.pdf
28. Hammertoss. https://www2.fireeye.com/rs/848-DID-242/images/rpt-apt29-hammertoss.pdf
29. LOWBALL. https://www.fireeye.com/blog/threat-research/2015/11/china-based-threat.html
30. RedHack. http://thehackernews.com/2016/10/turkey-redhack.html
31. Evolution of Dridex. https://www.fireeye.com/blog/threat-research/2015/06/evolution_of_dridex.html
32. Neverquest. https://www2.fireeye.com/rs/848-DID-242/images/rpt-fin6.pdf
33. CodeSpaces. https://arstechnica.com/security/2014/06/aws-console-breach-leads-to-demise-of-service-with-proven-backup-plan/
34. Dyn DDoS Attack. http://dyn.com/blog/dyn-statement-on-10212016-ddos-attack/
35. Dyn DDos Attack Effect on Amazon Web Services. http://www.ciodive.com/news/how-amazon-responded-to-the-dyn-ddos-attack/429050/

36. Dyn DDoS Attack Exposes. http://www.infoworld.com/article/3134023/security/dyn-ddos-attack-exposes-soft-underbelly-of-the-cloud.html
37. Hotschedules DDOS. https://www.hotschedules.com/news/inside-a-vicious-ddos-attack/
38. Phishing in the cloud. https://pages.phishlabs.com/rs/130-BFB-942/images/2017%20PhishLabs%20Phishing%20and%20Threat%20Intelligence%20Report.pdf
39. APT1. https://www.fireeye.com/content/dam/fireeye-www/services/pdfs/mandiant-apt1-report.pdf

Erratum to: An Orchestrated Security Platform for Internet of Robots

Mehrnoosh Monshizadeh, Vikramajeet Khatri ⓘ,
Raimo Kantola, and Zheng Yan

Erratum to:
Chapter "An Orchestrated Security Platform for Internet
of Robots" in: M.H.A. Au et al. (Eds.):
Green, Pervasive, and Cloud Computing, **LNCS 10232,**
https://doi.org/10.1007/978-3-319-57186-7_23

The original version of this chapter unfortunately contained a mistake.
The ORCID identifier for the second author, Vikramajeet Khatri, was missing.
His ORCID is: 0000-0002-3386-8952.

The updated online version of this chapter can be found at
https://doi.org/10.1007/978-3-319-57186-7_23

Author Index

Printed in the United States
By Bookmasters